A SELECTION OF LEGAL MAXIMS,

CLASSIFIED AND ILLUSTRATED.

By HERBERT BROOM, LL.D.,

OF THE INNER TEMPLE, BARRISTER-AT-LAW; READER IN COMMON LAW TO THE INNS OF COURT.

Maxims are the condensed Good Sense of Nations.—SIR J. MACKINTOSH.

Juris Præcepta sunt hæc; honeste vivere, alterum non lædere, suum cuique tribuere.—I. 1. 1. 3.

EIGHTH AMERICAN,
FROM THE FIFTH LONDON EDITION,

WITH REFERENCES TO AMERICAN CASES.

THE LAWBOOK EXCHANGE, LTD.
Clark, New Jersey

ISBN-13: 9781584770527 (hardcover)
ISBN-13: 9781616190743 (paperback)

Lawbook Exchange edition 2010

The irregular pagination is reproduced as it was found in the original work. The quality of this reprint is equivalent to the quality of the original work.

THE LAWBOOK EXCHANGE, LTD.
33 Terminal Avenue
Clark, New Jersey 07066-1321

Please see our website for a selection of our other publications and fine facsimile reprints of classic works of legal history:
www.lawbookexchange.com

Library of Congress Cataloging-in-Publication Data

Broom, Herbert, 1815-1882.
A selection of legal maxims, classified and illustrated / by Herbert Broom. –8th American from the 5th London ed.
p. cm.
Previously published: Philadelphia : T. & J.W. Johnson & Co., 1882.
Includes bibliographical references and index
ISBN 1-58477-052-X (cloth : alk. paper)
1. Legal maxims—Great Britain. I. Title.

KD315 .B76 2000
340—dc21 99-049329

Printed in the United States of America on acid-free paper

A

SELECTION

OF

LEGAL MAXIMS,

CLASSIFIED AND ILLUSTRATED.

By HERBERT BROOM, LL.D.,

OF THE INNER TEMPLE, BARRISTER-AT-LAW; READER IN COMMON LAW TO THE INNS OF COURT.

Maxims are the condensed Good Sense of Nations.—SIR J. MACKINTOSH.

Juris Præcepta sunt hæc; honeste vivere, alterum non lædere, suum cuique tribuere.—I. 1. 1. 3.

EIGHTH AMERICAN,
FROM THE FIFTH LONDON EDITION,

WITH REFERENCES TO AMERICAN CASES.

PHILADELPHIA:

T. & J. W. JOHNSON & CO.,

LAW BOOKSELLERS, PUBLISHERS AND IMPORTERS,

535 CHESTNUT STREET.

1882.

PRESS OF

HENRY B. ASHMEAD,

1102 and 1104 Sansom St.

PREFACE TO THE FIFTH LONDON EDITION.

In this Edition the text has been carefully revised, and redundant or obsolete matter has been expunged, its place having been supplied by illustrations of Legal Maxims, extracted from the most recent reported cases.

The increasing favor shown by professional and non-professional readers for this work has stimulated my endeavors to render it more worthy of their confidence.

H. B.

The Temple,
April 28, 1870.

PREFACE TO THE FOURTH EDITION.

IN this Edition the very numerous cases illustrative of Legal Maxims reported since the last issue of the work have been inserted; the text has been carefully revised; and it is hoped that this Book of Principles may, in its amended form, prove useful to the Practitioner and the Student.

H. B.

THE TEMPLE,
March 30, 1864.

PREFACE TO THE THIRD EDITION.

In again preparing this work for the press I have specially endeavored to preserve its elementary character, remembering that it was not designed to exhibit minute details, but as a repertory of Legal Principles.

The last Edition of these Selections of Maxims has now been carefully revised, cases accumulated during ten years have been sifted and examined, and every effort has faithfully been made to render the book, in its present form, accurate and useful.

In regard to subjects of interest or importance to the Student, here but incidentally touched upon, occasional references have been given to my "Commentaries on the Common Law"—designed as a companion to, and therefore printed uniformly with, the present volume.

The indulgence of the learned reader must be once more solicited, to pardon errors or omissions which, notwithstanding anxious and repeated perusal of the proofs, may have escaped detection.

H. B.

The Temple,
June 11, 1858.

PREFACE TO THE SECOND EDITION.

THE reasonableness of the hope which I formerly ventured to express, as to the utility of a work upon Elementary Legal Principles, has, I think, been established, as well by the rapid sale of the first edition of this treatise, as by the very flattering communications respecting it which have been made to me by some of the most distinguished members of that profession for which it was designed. Thus kindly encouraged, I have endeavored to avail myself of the opportunity for improvement which the preparation of a new edition affords, by making a careful revision of the entire work, by the insertion of many important Maxims which had been previously unnoticed, and by the addition of much new matter illustrative of those originally commented upon or cited. During the interval which has elapsed since the first appearance of this work, I have, moreover, devoted myself to a perusal of various treatises upon our own law, which I had not formerly, from lack of time or opportunity, consulted; to the examination of an extensive series of American Reports, and also to a review of such portions of and commentaries upon the Roman Law as seemed most likely to disclose the true sources from which very many of our ordinary rules and maxims have been ultimately derived. I trust that a very slight comparison of the present with the former edition of this work will suffice to show that the time thus employed with a view to its improvement has not been unprofitably spent; but that much new matter has been collected and inserted, which may reasonably be expected to prove alike serviceable to the practitioner and the student.

Besides the additions just alluded to, I may observe, that the order of arrangement formerly adopted has been on the present occasion in some respects departed from. For instance, that portion of the work which related to property and its attributes has now been subdivided into three sections, which treat respectively of its acquisition, enjoyment and transfer: a mode of considering this subject which has been adopted for the sake of simplicity, and with a view to showing in what manner the most familiar and elementary maxims of our Law may be applied to the exposition and illustration of its most difficult and comprehensive branches. Further, it may be well to mention, that, in the alphabetical list of maxims which precedes the text, I have now inserted not only such as are actually cited in the body of the work, but such also, from amongst those with which I have become acquainted, as seem to be susceptible of useful practical application, or to possess any real value. The list, therefore, which has thus been compiled, with no inconsiderable labor, from various sources, and to which some few notes have been appended, will, I trust, be found to render this volume more complete, as a treatise upon Legal Maxims, than it formerly was; and will, moreover, appear, on examination, to possess some peculiar claims to the attention of the reader.

It only remains for me further to observe, that, in preparing this volume for the press, I have anxiously kept before me the twofold object with a view to which it was originally planned. On the one hand, I have endeavored to increase its usefulness to the practitioner by adding references to very many important and, for the most part, recent decisions illustrative of those principles of law to the application of which his attention must necessarily be most frequently directed; whilst, on the other hand, I have been mindful of preserving to this work its strictly elementary character, so that it may prove no less useful than formerly to the student as a compendium of legal principles, or as introductory to a systematic course of reading upon any of the various branches of our Common Law.

In conclusion, I can truly say, that, whatever amount of time and labor may have been bestowed upon the preparation of this work, I shall esteem myself amply compensated if it be found instrumental in extending knowledge with regard to a science which yields to none either in direct practical importance or in loftiness of aim—if it be found to have facilitated the study of a system of jurisprudence which, though doubtless susceptible of improvement, presents, probably, the most perfect development of that science which the ingenuity and wisdom of man have hitherto devised.

HERBERT BROOM.

THE TEMPLE,
March 16, 1848.

PREFACE TO THE FIRST EDITION.

In the Legal Science, perhaps more frequently than in any other, reference must be made to first principles. Indeed, a very limited acquaintance with the earlier Reports will show the importance which was attached to the acknowledged Maxims of the Law, in periods when civilization and refinement had made comparatively little progress. In the ruder ages, without doubt, the great majority of questions respecting the rights, remedies and liabilities of private individuals were determined by an immediate reference to such Maxims, many of which obtained in the Roman Law, and are so manifestly founded in reason, public convenience and necessity, as to find a place in the code of every civilized nation. In more modern times, the increase of commerce, and of national and social intercourse, has occasioned a corresponding increase in the sources of litigation, and has introduced many subtleties and nice distinctions, both in legal reasoning and in the application of legal principles, which were formerly unknown. This change, however, so far from diminishing the value of simple fundamental rules, has rendered an accurate acquaintance with them the more necessary, in order that they may be either directly applied, or qualified, or limited, according to the exigencies of the particular case, and the novelty of the circumstances which present themselves. If, then, it be true, that a knowledge of first principles is at least as essential in Law as in other sciences, certainly in none is a knowledge of those principles, unaccompanied by a sufficient investigation of their bearing and practical application, more likely to lead into grievous error.

In the present work I have endeavored, not only to point out the most important Legal Maxims, but also to explain and illustrate their meaning; to show the various exceptions to the rules which they enunciate, and the qualifications which must be borne in mind when they are applied. I have devoted considerable time, and much labor, to consulting the Reports, both ancient and modern, as also the standard treatises on leading branches of the Law, in order to ascertain what Maxims are of most practical importance, and most frequently cited, commented on and applied. I have likewise repeatedly referred to the various collections of maxims which have heretofore been published, and have freely availed myself of such portions of them as seemed to possess any value or interest at the present day. I venture, therefore, to hope, that very few Maxims have been omitted which ought to have found place in a work like that now submitted to the profession. In illustrating each rule, those cases have in general been preferred as examples in which the particular Maxim has either been cited, or directly stated to apply. It has, however, been necessary to refer to many other instances in which no such specific reference has been made, but which seem clearly to fall within the principle of the rule; and whenever this has been done, sufficient authorities have, it is hoped, been appended, to enable the reader, without very laborious research, to decide for himself whether the application suggested has been correctly made, or not.

In arranging the Maxims which have been selected as above mentioned, the system of classification has, after due reflection, been adopted: first, because this arrangement appeared better calculated to render the work, to some extent, interesting as a treatise, exhibiting briefly the most important Rules of Law, and not merely useful as a book of casual reference; and, secondly, because by this method alone can the intimate connection which exists between Maxims appertaining to the same class be directly brought under notice and appreciated. It was thought better, therefore, to incur the risk of occasional false or defective classification, than to pursue the easier course of alphabetical arrangement. An Alphabetical List has, however, been appended, so that immediate reference may be made to any required Maxim. The plan actually adopted may be thus stated:—I have, in the first two chapters, very briefly treated of Maxims which relate to Constitutional Principles, and the mode in which the Laws are administered. These, on account of their comprehensive character, have been placed first in order, and have been briefly considered, because they are so very generally known and so easily comprehended. After these are placed certain Maxims which are rather deductions of reason than rules of

Law, and consequently admit of illustration only. Chapter IV. comprises a few principles which may be considered as fundamental, and not referable exclusively to any of the subjects subsequently noticed, and which follow thus: Maxims relating to Property, Marriage and Descent; the Interpretation of Written Instruments in general; Contracts; and Evidence. Of these latter subjects, the Construction of Written Instruments, and the Admissibility of evidence to explain them, as also those Maxims which embody the Law of Contracts, have been thought the most practically important, and have therefore been noticed at the greatest length. The vast extent of these subjects has undoubtedly rendered the work of selection and compression one of considerable labor; and it is feared that many useful applications of the Maxims selected have been omitted, and that some errors have escaped detection. It must be remarked, however, that, even had the bulk of this volume been materially increased, many important branches of Law to which the Maxims apply must necessarily have been dismissed with very slight notice; and it is believed that the reader will not expect to find, in a work on Legal Maxims, subjects considered in detail, of which each presents sufficient materials for a separate treatise.

One question which may naturally suggest itself remains to be answered: For what class of readers is a work like the present intended? I would reply, that it is intended not only for the use of students purposing to practice at the bar, or as attorneys, but also for the occasional reference of the practicing barrister, who may be desirous of applying a Legal Maxim to the case before him, and who will therefore search for similar, or, at all events, analogous cases, in which the same principle has been held applicable and decisive. The frequency with which Maxims are not only referred to by the Bench, but cited and relied upon by Counsel in their arguments; the importance which has, in many decided cases, been attached to them; the caution which is always exercised in applying, and the subtlety and ingenuity which have been displayed in distinguishing between them, seem to afford reasonable grounds for hoping, that the mere selection of Maxims here given may prove useful to the profession, and that the examples adduced, and the authorities referred to by way of illustration, qualification or exception, may, in some limited degree, add to their utility.

In conclusion, I have to express my acknowledgments to several professional friends of practical experience, ability and learning, for many valuable suggestions which have been made, and much useful information which has been communicated, during the preparation of this work, and of which I have very gladly availed myself. For such defects and errors as will, doubtless, notwithstanding careful revision, be apparent to the reader, it must be observed that I alone am responsible. It is believed, however, that the Professional Public will be inclined to view with some leniency this attempt to treat, more methodically than has hitherto been done, a subject of acknowledged importance, and one which is surrounded with considerable difficulty.

HERBERT BROOM.

THE TEMPLE,
January 30, 1845.

CONTENTS.

The pages referred to are those enclosed in brackets [ ].

CHAPTER I.

SEC. I.—RULES FOUNDED ON PUBLIC POLICY.

SEC. II.—RULES OF LEGISLATIVE POLICY.

CHAPTER II.

MAXIMS RELATING TO THE CROWN.

CHAPTER III.

SEC. I.—THE JUDICIAL OFFICE.

Sec. II.—The Mode of Administering Justice.

CHAPTER IV.

Rules of Logic.

CHAPTER V.

Fundamental Legal Principles.

CHAPTER VI.

Acquisition, Enjoyment and Transfer of Property.

Sec. I.—The Mode of Acquiring Property.

Sec. II.—Property—its Rights and Liabilities.

Sec. III.—The Transfer of Property.

CHAPTER VII.

Rules relating to Marriage and Descent.

CHAPTER VIII.

The Interpretation of Deeds and Written Instruments.

CHAPTER IX.

The Law of Contracts.

CHAPTER X.

Maxims applicable to the Law of Evidence.

ALPHABETICAL LIST OF LEGAL MAXIMS.

*** Throughout this List, Wingate's Maxims are indicated by the letter (W). Lofft's Reports (Ed. 1790), to which is appended a very copious Collection of Maxims, are signified by the letter (L). The Grounds and Rudiments of Law (Ed. 1751), by the letter (G); and Halkerston's Maxims (Ed. 1823), by the letter (H); the reference in the last instance only being to the number of the page, in the others to that of the Maxim. Of the above Collections, as also of those by Noy (9th Ed.) and Branch (5th Ed.), use has, in preparing the following List, been freely made. Some few Maxims from the Civil Law have also been inserted, the Digest being referred to by the letter (D), as in the body of the Work.

The figures at the end of the line without the Parenthesis denote the pages of this Treatise where the Maxim is commented upon or cited.

PAGE

A COMMUNI observantiâ non est recedendum (W. 203).

A verbis legis non est recedendum 622

Ab abusu ad usum non valet consequentia.(a) .

Absoluta sententia expositore non in diget (2 Inst. 533).

Abundans cautela non nocet (11 Rep. 6).

Accessorium non ducit, sed sequitur, suum principale . 491, 492, 493

Accessorium non trahit principale 496

Accessorius sequitur naturam sui principalis 497

Accusator post rationabile tempus non est audiendus, nisi se bene de omissione excusaverit (Moor 817).

Acta exteriora indicant interiora secreta 301

Actio non datur non damnificato (Jenk. Cent. 69).

Actio personalis moritur cum personâ . 904, 905, 909, 915, 916, n.

Actio quælibet it suâ viâ (Jenk. Cent. 77).

Actionum genera maxime sunt servanda (L. 460).

Actore non probante absolvitur reus (Hob. 103).

(a) In Stockdale v. Hansard, 9 Ad. & E. 116 (36 E. C. L. R.), Lord Denman, C. J., observes that the above maxims cannot apply "where an abuse is directly charged and offered to be proved."

PAGE

Actor sequitur forum rei (Branch M. 4).

Actori incumbit onus probandi (Hob. 103).

Actus curiæ neminem gravabit . 122

Actus Dei nemini facit injurium . 230

Actus Dei nemini nocet . . 241

Actus incæptus cujus perfectio pendet ex voluntate partium revocari potest, si autem pendet ex voluntate testiæ personæ vel ex contingenti revocari non potest (b) (Bac. Max. reg. 20).

Actus judiciarius coram non judice irritus habetur, de ministeriali autem a quocunque provenit ratum esto (L. 458).

Actus legis nemini facit injuriam 127, 409

Actus legis nemini est damnosus . 126

Actus legitimi non recipiunt modum (Hob. 153).

Actus non facit reum nisi mens sit rea . 306, 316, 324, 367, 807, n.

(b) The law, observes Lord Bacon, makes this difference, that, if the parties have put it in the power of a third person, or of a contingency, to give a perfection to their act, then they have put it out of their own reach and liberty to revoke it; but where the completion of their act or contract depends upon the mutual consent of the original parties only, it may be rescinded by express agreement. So, in judicial acts, the rule of the civil law holds, *sententia interlocutoria revocari potest*, that is, an order may be revoked, but a judgment cannot.—Bac. M. reg. 20.

(*a*) See Kippen *v.* Darley, 3 Macq. Sc. App. Cas. 203.

(*b*) See the Note to Mostyn *v.* Fabrigas, 1 Smith L. C., 6th ed., 651; Story Confl. Laws, tit. "*Contracts.*"

(*c*) Arg. A.-G. *v.* Cholmley, 2 Eden 313.

(*d*) "Every exception that can be accounted for is so much a confirmation of the rule, that it has become a maxim, *exceptio probat regulam*," per

Lord Kenyon, C. J., 3 T. R. 722. See also Id. 38; 4 T. R. 793; 1 East 647, n ; per Lord Campbell, C. J., 4 E. & B. 832 (82 E. C. L. R.); arg. Lyndon *v.* Standbridge, 2 H. & N. 48.

(*a*) This maxim may properly be applied in those cases only where a witness speaks to a fact with reference to which he cannot be presumed liable to mistake; see, per Story, J., The Santissima Trinidad, 7 Wheaton (U. S.) R. 338, 339.

(*b*) Cited E. of Derby *v.* Bury Impt. Coms., L. R. 4 Ex. 226; Kidston *v.* Empire Ins. Co., L. R. 1 C. P. 546; arg. Thames Conservators *v.* Hall, L. R. 3 C. P. 419.

(*c*) In the various treatises upon the law of evidence will be found remarks as to the weight which should be attached to the confession of a party. Respecting the above maxim, Lord Stowell has observed, that, "What is taken *pro confesso* is taken as indubitable truth. The plea of guilty by the party accused shuts out all further inquiry. *Habemus confitentem reum* is demonstration, *unless indirect motives can be assigned to it.*" Mortimer *v.* Mortimer, 2 Hagg. 315.

(*a*) See this maxim under a somewhat different form, *post*, p. 465.

(*a*) See (*ex. gr.*) Neves *v.* Burrage, 14 Q. B. 504, 511, 512 (68 E. C. L. R.).

(*b*) "The law," says Lord Bacon, "giveth that favor to lawful acts, that, although they be executed by several authorities, yet the whole act is good;" if, therefore, tenant for life and remainderman join in granting a rent, "this is one solid rent out of both their estates, and no double rent, or rent by confirmation;" Bac. Max reg 24; and if tenant for life and reversioner join in a lease for life reserving rent, this shall enure to the tenant for life only during his life, and afterwards to the reversioner. See 1 Crabb Real Prop. 179.

(*c*) Cited arg. Hodgson *v.* Beauchesne, 12 Moo. P. C. C. 308; Lloyd *v.* Guibert, L. R. 1 Q. B. 115.

(*d*) A principal is civilly liable for those acts only which are strictly within the scope of the agent's authority, *post*, p. 843. But if a man incite another to do an unlawful act, he shall not, in the language of Lord Bacon, "excuse himself by circumstances not pursued;" as if he command his servant to rob I. D. on Shooter's Hill, and he doth it on Gad's Hill; or to kill him by poison, and he doth it by violence: Bac. Max. Reg. 16, cited Parkes *v.* Prescott, L. R. 4 Ex. 169, 182.

(*a*) Cited per Bovill, C. J., Fletcher *v.* Alexander, L. R. 3 C. P. 381.

(*b*) Applied to a patent, arg. Re Newall and Elliott, 4 C. B. N. S. 290 (93 E. C. L. R.).

(a) See A.-G. v. Hitchcock, 1 Exch. 91, 92, 102.

(b) Cited White v. Trustees of British Museum, 6 Bing. 319 (19 E. C. L. R.); Ilott v. Genge, 3 Curt. 175.

(c) Cited 2 Bla. Com., 21st ed., 162; Co. Litt. 3 a; arg. 1 M. & S. 172; per Buller, J., 3 T. R. 664. See, per Knight-Bruce, L. J., Boyse v. Rossborough, 3 De G., M. & G. 846.

(*a*) Cited per Parke, B., Morgan *v.* Thomas, 8 Exch. 304.

(*b*) See Louisville R. C. *v.* Litson, 2 Howard (U. S.) R. 523.

(*a*) See Briggs *v.* Oliver, 4 H. & C. 403; Longmore *v.* Great Western R. C., 19 C. B. N. S. 185 (115 E. C. L. R.); Shepherd *v.* Bristol and Exeter R. C., L. R. 3 Ex. 189, 192; Scott *v.* London & St. Katherine's Dock Co., 3 H. & C. 596; Downes *v.* Ship, L. R. 3 H. L. 354.
(*b*) Cited per Lord Wensleydale, Baird *v.* Fortune, 4 Macq. Sc. App. Cas. 151.

(*c*) See Ditcher *v.* Denison, 11 Moo. P. C. C. 343.
(*d*) See Reg. *v.* Millis, 10 Cl. & Fin. 534 (cited *post*), where this maxim was applied; A.-G. *v.* Dean, &c., of Windsor, 8 H. L. Cas. 392; Baker *v.* Lee, Id. 512; Beamish *v.* Beamish, 9 H. L. Cas. 274, 338; per Lord Campbell, C. J., Dansey *v.* Richardson, 3 E. & B. 723.
(*e*) See 1 Bla. Com., 21st ed., 484.
(*f*) See Kidston *v.* Empire Ins. Co., L. R. 1 C. P. 546; Earl of Kintore *v.* Lord Inverury, 4 Macq. Sc. App. Cas. 522.
(*g*) See 4 Bla. Com., 21st ed., 363; Horwood *v.* Smith, 2 T. R. 753.

(*a*) See as to this maxim, Goddard's Case, 2 Rep. 4; per Bayley, J., Styles *v.* Wardle, 4 B. & C. 911 (10 E. C. L. R.); per Patteson, J., Browne *v.* Burton, 17 L. J. Q. B. 50; citing Clayton's Case, 5 Rep. 1, and recognizing Steele *v.* Mart, 4 B. & C. 272, 279; Tupper *v.* Foulkes, 6 C. B. N. S. 797 (99 E. C. L. R.). See, also, Shaw *v.* Kay, 1 Exch. 412; per Jervis, C. J., Davis *v.* Jones, 17 C. B. 634 (84 E. C. L. R.); Cumberlege *v.* Lawson, 1 C. B. N. S. 709, 720 (87 E. C. L. R.); Xenos *v.* Wickham, 14 C. B. N. S. 435 (108 E. C. L. R.); s. c., 13 Id. 385, L. R. 2 H. L. 296; Kidner *v.* Keith, 15 C. B. N. S. 35 (109 E. C. L. R.).

(*b*) 3 Bla. Com., 21st ed., 309; cited per Tindal, C. J., 1 Bing. N. C. 522 (27 E. C. L. R.). This maxim is taken from the Roman law, see C. 3. 1. 13. § 6.

TABLE OF CASES.

The pages referred to are those enclosed between brackets [ ].

B.

C.

E.

F.

H.

K.

U.

V.

W.

Y.

Z.

LEGAL MAXIMS.

CHAPTER I.

§ I.—RULES FOUNDED ON PUBLIC POLICY.

THE Maxims contained in this section are of such universal application, and result so directly and manifestly from motives of public policy or simple principles on which our social relations depend, that it has been thought better to place them first in this collection,—as being, in some measure, introductory to more precise and technical rules which embody the elementary doctrines of English law, and are continually recurring to the notice of practitioners in our courts of justice.

SALUS POPULI SUPREMA LEX.

(Bacon, Max., reg. 12.)

That regard be had to the public welfare, is the highest law.

There is an implied assent on the part of every member of society, that his own individual welfare shall, in cases of necessity, yield to that of the community; and that his property, liberty, and life shall, under certain circumstances, be placed in jeopardy or even sacrificed for the *public good.[1] "There are," says Buller, J.,[2] "many cases in which individuals sustain an injury for which [*2]

[1] *Alibi diximus res subditorum sub eminenti dominio esse civitatis, ita ut civitas, aut qui civitatis vice fungitur, iis rebus uti, easque etiam perdere et alienare possit, non tantum ex summâ necessitate, quæ privatis quoque jus aliquod in aliena concedit, sed ob publicam utilitatem, cui privatas cedere illi ipsi voluisse censendi sunt qui in civilem cœtum coierunt.* Grotius de Jure Belli et Pac., Bk. 3, c. 20, s. 7, § 1.—*Le Talut du peuple est la suprême loi.* Mont. Esp. des Lois, L. XXVII. Ch. 23. *In casu extremæ necessitatis omnia sunt communia.* 1 Hale, P. C. 54.

[2] Per Buller, J., Plate Glass Co. *v.* Meredith, 4 T. R. 797; Noy, Max., 9th ed., 36; Dyer 60 b.; 12 Rep. 12, 13.

the law gives no action; as, where private houses are pulled down, or bulwarks raised on private property, for the preservation and defence of the kingdom against the king's enemies." Commentators on the civil law, indeed, have said,[1] that, in such cases, those who suffer have a right to resort to the public for satisfaction; but no one ever thought that our own common law gave an action against the individual who pulled down the house or raised the bulwark.[2] On the same principle, viz., that a man may justify committing a private injury for the public good, the pulling down of a house when necessary, in order to arrest the progress of a fire, is permitted by the law.[3]

Likewise, in less stringent emergencies the maxim is, that a private mischief shall be endured, rather than a public inconvenience;[4] and, therefore, if a highway be out of repair and impassable, a passenger may lawfully go over the adjoining land, since it is for [*3] the public good *that there should be, at all times, free passage along thoroughfares for subjects of the realm.[5] And in American courts it has been held,[6] that if a traveller in a highway by unexpected and unforeseen occurrences, such as a sudden flood or heavy drifts of snow, is so obstructed that he cannot reach his destination without passing over the adjacent lands, he is privileged so to do. "To hold a party guilty of a trespass for passing over another's land, under the pressure of such a necessity, would be pushing individual rights of property to an unreasonable extent, and giving them a protection beyond that which finds a sanction in the rules of law. The temporary and unavoidable use of private property under the circumstances supposed must be regarded as one of those incidental burdens to which all property in a civilized

[1] See Puff. de Jure Nat. Bk. 8, c. 5, s. 7; Grotius de Jure Bell. et Pac., Bk. 3, c. 20, s. 7, § 2.

[2] Per Buller, J., 4 T. R. 797.

[3] Noy, Max., 9th ed., 36; 12 Rep. 12; Dyer 36 b.; Plowd. 322; Finch's Law 39; Russell *v.* Mayor of New York, 2 Denio (U. S.) R. 461, 474.

[4] Absor *v.* French, 2 Show. 28; Dawes *v.* Hawkins, 8 C. B. N. S. 848, 856, 859 (98 E. C. L. R.); per Pollock, C. B., A. G. *v.* Briant, 15 M. & W. 185.

[5] Per Lord Mansfield, C. J., Taylor *v.* Whitehead, Dougl. 749; per Lord Ellenborough, C. J., Bullard *v.* Harrison, 4 M. & S. 393; Dawes *v.* Hawkins, 8 C. B. N. S. 848 (98 E. C. L. R.); Robertson *v.* Gantlett, 16 M. & W. 296 (*a*). Secus of a private right of way. *Ib.*

[6] Campbell *v.* Race, 7 Cushing (U. S.) R. 408.

community is subject." "Highways," says Lord Mansfield, C. J., in Taylor *v.* Whitehead,[1] "are for the public service, and if the usual track is impassable, it is for the general good that people should be entitled to pass in another line."

In the instances above put, an interference with private property is obviously dictated and justified *summâ necessitate*, by the immediate urgency of the occasion, and a due regard to the public safety or convenience. The general maxim under consideration, however, likewise applies to cases of more ordinary occurrence, in which the legislature *ob publicam utilitatem*, disturbs the possession or restricts the enjoyment of the property of individuals; *very stringent provisions being sometimes enacted "for purposes of general public good, involving great restrictions upon particular classes of men."[2] [*4]

"The great end," it has been observed,[3] "for which men entered into society was to secure their property. That right is preserved sacred and incommunicable[4] in all instances where it has not been taken away or abridged by some public law for the good of the whole. The cases where this right of property is set aside by positive law are various. Distresses, executions, forfeitures, taxes, &c., are all of this description, wherein every man, by common consent, gives up that right for the sake of justice and the general good."

It is, however, a rule of law which has been designated as a "legal axiom," requiring no authority to be cited in support of it, that "no pecuniary burden can be imposed upon the subjects of this country, by whatever name it may be called, whether tax, due, rate,[5] or toll, except upon clear and distinct legal authority, established by those who seek to impose the burden."[6]

[1] 2 Dougl. 745, 749.

[2] Per Alderson, B., A. G. *v.* Lockwood, 9 M. & W. 401.

[3] Per Lord Camden, Entick *v.* Carrington, 19 How. St. Tr. 1066.

[4] *i. e.*, not to be made the common right or property of more than one—Johnson, Dict., by Todd, ad verb.

[5] As to sewerage rates, see Judgm., Taylor *v.* Loft, 8 Exch. 278.

[6] Per Wilde, C. J., Gosling *v.* Veley, 12 Q. B. 407 (64 E. C. L. R.). "The law of England is most careful to protect the subject from the imposition of any tax, except it be founded upon and supported by clear and distinct lawful authority." Per Martin, B., Gosling *v.* Veley, 4 H. L. Cas. 727. Per Lord Truro, Id. 781. "The law requires clear demonstration that a tax is lawfully imposed." Judgm., Burder *v.* Veley, 12 A. & E. 247 (40 E. C. L. R.). "It

[*5] In the familiar instance, likewise, of an Act of Parliament *for promoting some specific object or undertaking of public utility, as a turnpike, navigation, canal, railway, or paving Act, the legislature will not scruple to interfere with private property, and will even compel the owner of land to alienate his possessions on receiving a reasonable price and compensation[1] for so doing; but such an arbitrary exercise of power[2] is indulged with caution; the true principle applicable to all such cases being, that the private interest of the individual is never to be sacrificed to a greater extent than is necessary to secure a public object of adequate importance.[3] The courts, therefore, will not so construe an Act of Parliament as to deprive persons of their estates and transfer them to other parties without compensation, in the absence of any manifest or obvious reason of policy for thus doing, unless they are so fettered by the express words of the statute[4] as to be unable to extricate themselves, for they will not suppose that the legislature had such an intention.[5]

is a well-settled rule of law that every charge upon the subject must be imposed by clear and unambiguous language." Per Bayley, J., Denn *v.* Diamond, 4 B. & C. 245 (10 E. C. L. R.); per Bramwell, B., A. G. *v.* Lord Middleton, 3 H. & N. 138.

[1] In the case of an action brought to obtain compensation by a person whose land has been taken possession of by the crown or by any private individual, the items recoverable will be:—1. The value of the land; 2. The consequential injury; 3. The expense to which the complainant has been put in maintaining his action. Per Pollock, C. B., Re Laws, 1 Exch. 447.

As to the items recoverable in respect of depreciation of property under the Lands Clauses Act, 1845, see Duke of Buccleuch *v.* Metrop. Board of Works, L. R. 3 Ex. 306.

[2] See per Lord Eldon, C., 1 My. & K. 162. Judgm., Tawney *v.* Lynn and Ely R. C., 16 L. J. (Chan.) 282; Webb *v.* Manchester and Leeds R. C., 4 My. & Cr. 116.

[3] See judgm., Simpson *v.* Lord Howdon, 1 Keen 598, 599; Lister *v.* Lobley, 7 A. & E. 124 (34 E. C. L. R.).

[4] "The word 'statute' has several meanings. It may mean (*ut supra*) what is popularly called an Act of Parliament or a code, such as the Stat. of Westminster I., or all the Acts passed in one session, which was the original meaning of the word." Per Lord Campbell, C. J., Reg. *v.* Bakewell, 7 E. & B. 851 (90 E. C. L. R.).

[5] See per Lord Abinger, C. B., Stracey *v.* Nelson, 12 M. & W. 540, 541; per Alderson, B., Doe d. Hutchinson *v.* Manchester and Rosendale R. C., 14 M. & W. 694; Anon., Lofft 442; R. *v.* Croke, Cowp. 29; Clarence R. C. *v.* Great North of England R. C., 4 Q. B. 46 (45 E. C. L. R.).

[*6] *And "where an Act of Parliament is susceptible of two constructions, one of which will have the effect of destroying the property of large numbers of the community and the other will not," the court will "assume that the legislature intended the former to be applied to it."[1] Also, as judicially observed, where large powers are entrusted to a company to carry their works through a great extent of country without the consent of the owners and occupiers of land through which they are to pass, it is reasonable and just, that any injury to property which can be shown to arise from the prosecution of those works should be fairly compensated to the party sustaining it,[2] and likewise it is required that the authority given should be strictly pursued and executed.[3]

In accordance with the maxim under notice, it was held, that, where the commissioners appointed by a paving Act occasioned damage to an individual, without any excess of jurisdiction on their part, neither the commissioners nor the paviors acting under them were liable to an action, the statute under which the commissioners acted not giving them power to award satisfaction to the individuals who happened to suffer; and it was observed, that some individuals suffer an inconvenience under all such Acts of Parliament, but the interests of individuals must give way *to the accommodation [*7] of the public[4]—*privatum incommodum publico bono pensatur.*[5] And "where authority is given by the legislature to do an act,

[1] Per Erle, C. J., The Vestry of Chelsea app., King resp., 17 C. B. N. S. 629 (112 E. C. L. R.).

[2] Judgm., Reg. *v.* Eastern Counties R. C., 2 Q. B. 359 (42 E. C. L. R.); Blakemore *v.* Glamorganshire Canal Company, 1 Mylne & K. 162, and 2 Cr. M. & R. 133, 141; York and North Midland R. C. *v.* Reg., 1 E. & B. 858 (72 E. C. L. R.); s. c. (in Q. B.), Id. 178, 203–4, 228, 246; Great Western R. C. *v.* Reg., Id. 874, 253; Reg. *v.* Lancashire and Yorkshire R. C., 1 E. & B. 228 (72 E. C. L. R.).

[3] See Taylor *v.* Clemson, 2 Q. B. 978, 1031 (42 E. C. L. R.); s. c., 11 Cl. & F. 610; per Lord Mansfield, C. J., R. *v.* Croke, 1 Cowp. 26; Ostler *v.* Cooke, 13 Q. B. 143 (66 E. C. L. R.).

[4] Plate Glass Company *v.* Meredith, 4 T. R. 794, and Boulton *v.* Crowther, 2 B. & C. 703 (9 E. C. L. R.); cited per Williams, J., Pilgrim *v.* Southampton and Dorchester R. C., 7 C. B. 228 (62 E. C. L. R.); Wilson *v.* Mayor of New York, 1 Denio (U. S.) R. 595, 598; see Sutton *v.* Clarke, 6 Taunt. 29 (1 E. C. L. R.); cited 10 C. B. N. S. 777, 779 (100 E. C. L. R.); Alston *v.* Scales, 9 Bing. 3 (23 E. C. L. R.).

[5] Jenk. Cent. 85.

parties injured by the doing of it have no legal remedy, but should appeal to the legislature."[1]

Cases concerning the liability of trustees or commissioners appointed for carrying out or taking charge of public works will be noticed under the maxim *respondeat superior*.[2] Here, however, may conveniently be stated two propositions having reference to the context. 1st. Persons clothed with such official character, though acting gratuitously, will clearly be liable for negligence or breach of duty; and 2dly, if trustees acting gratuitously in the performance of a statutory public duty have by their servants the means of knowing of the existence of a nuisance on the trust property, and are negligently ignorant of and omit to remove it, they will be responsible for damage caused thereby to a third person.[3]

We shall hereafter have occasion to consider minutely the general principles applicable for interpreting statutes passed with a view to the carrying out of undertakings calculated to interfere with private property. [*8] We may, *however, observe, in connection with our present subject, that the extraordinary powers with which railway and other similar companies are invested by the legislature, are given to them "in consideration of a benefit which, notwithstanding all other sacrifices, is, on the whole, hoped to be obtained by the public;" and that, since the public interest is to protect the rights of all individuals, and to save them from liabilities beyond those which the powers given by such Acts necessarily occasion, they must always be carefully looked to, and must not be extended further than the legislature has provided, or than is necessarily and properly required for the purposes which it has sanctioned.[4] It is, moreover, important to notice the distinction which exists between public and private Acts of Parliament, with

[1] See per Wilde, C. J., 7 C. B. 226 (62 E. C. L. R.); Mayor of Liverpool *v.* Chorley Waterworks Company, 2 De G., M. & G. 852, 860.

[2] *Post*, Chap. IX.

[3] Mersey Docks Trustees *v.* Gibbs; Same *v.* Penhallow, L. R. 1 H. L. 93, where the cases are collected; Coe *v.* Wise, L. R. 1 Q. B. 711; Ohrby *v.* Ryde Commissioners, 5 B. & S. 743, 750 (117 E. C. L. R.); following Hartnall *v.* Ryde Commissioners, 4 B. & S. 361 (116 E. C. L. R.); Collins *v.* Middle Level Commissioners, L. R. 4 C. P. 279. See Hyams *v.* Webster, L. R. 2 Q. B. 264; Southampton and Itchin Bridge Company *v.* Southampton Board of Health, 8 E. & B. 801 (92 E. C. L. R.).

[4] Per Lord Langdale, M. R., Colman *v.* Eastern Counties R. C., 10 Beav. 14.

reference to the obligations which they impose. "Where an Act of Parliament, in express terms, or by necessary implication, empowers an individual or individuals to take or interfere with the property or rights of another, and, upon a sound construction of the Act, it appears to the court that such was the intention of the legislature—in such cases it may well be the duty of the court, whose province it is to declare and not to make the law, to give effect to the decrees of the legislature so expressed. But, where an Act of Parliament merely enables an individual or individuals to treat with property of his or their own, for their own benefit, and does not, in terms or by necessary implication, empower him or them to take or interfere with the property or rights of others, questions of a very different character arise;" and here the distinction above mentioned becomes material, for public Acts bind all the *queen's subjects; but of private Acts of Parliament, [*9] meaning thereby not merely private estate Acts, but local and personal,[1] as opposed to general public Acts, "it is said, that they do not bind strangers, unless by express words or necessary implication the intention of the legislature to affect the rights of strangers is apparent in the Act; and whether an Act is public or private does not depend upon any technical considerations (such as having a clause or declaration that the Act shall be deemed a public Act), but upon the nature and substance of the case."[2]

On the other hand, where a statute authorizes the stopping up and diverting of a highway, and thus interferes with the rights of the public with a view to promoting the convenience of an individual, such provisions as the Act contains framed for ensuring compensation to the public must receive a liberal construction. "The rights of the public and the convenience of the individual constantly come into opposition;" in such cases "there may be sometimes vexatious opposition on the one hand, but there may be also on the other very earnest pursuit of individual advantage, regardless of the rights and convenience of the public. Full effect, therefore, ought to be given to provisions by which, while due concession

[1] See Cock *v.* Gent, 12 M. & W. 234; Shepherd *v.* Sharp, 1 H. & N. 115; Dwarris on Statutes, 2d ed., 463.

[2] Per Wigram, V.-C., Dawson *v.* Paver, 5 Hare 434 (citing Barrington's Case, 8 Rep. 138 a, and Lucy *v.* Levington, 1 Ventr. 175).

is made to the individual, proper protection is also afforded to the public."[1]

From the principle under consideration, and from the very nature [*10] of the social compact on which municipal law *is theoretically founded, and under which every man, when he enters into society, gives up a part of his natural freedom, result those laws which, in certain cases, authorize the infliction of penalties, the privation of liberty, and even the destruction of life, with a view to the future prevention of crime, and to insuring the safety and well-being of the public; penal laws, however, should evidently be restrained within the narrowest limits which may be deemed by the legislature compatible with the above objects, and should be interpreted by the judges, and administered by the executive, in a mild and liberal spirit. A maxim is, indeed, laid down by Lord Bacon, which might at first appear inconsistent with these remarks; for he observes, that the law will dispense with what he designates as the "*placita juris*," "rather than crimes and wrongs should be unpunished, *quia salus populi suprema lex*," and "*salus populi*, is contained in the repressing offences by punishment," and, therefore, *receditur a placitis juris potius quam injuriæ et delicta maneant impunita*.[2] This maxim must, at the present day, be understood to apply to those cases only in which the judges are invested with a discretionary power to permit such amendments to be made, *ex. gr.*, in an indictment, as may prevent justice from being defeated by mere verbal inaccuracies, or by a non-observance of certain legal technicalities;[3] and a distinction must, therefore, still be remarked between the "*placita*" and the "*regulæ*" *juris*, inasmuch as the law will rather suffer a particular offence to escape without punishment, than permit a violation of its fixed and positive rules.[4]

[1] Reg. *v.* Newmarket R. C., 15 Q. B. 702, 713 (69 E. C. L. R.).

[2] Bac. Max., reg. 12.

[3] See 14 & 15 Vict. c. 100, ss. 1, 24.

[4] Bac. Max., reg. 12. The doctrine of our law as to avoiding contracts on the ground that they are opposed to public policy, will hereafter be considered.

*NECESSITAS INDUCIT PRIVILEGIUM QUOAD JURA PRIVATA. [*11]

(Bacon, Max., reg. 5.)

With respect to private rights, necessity privileges a person acting under its influence.

As a general rule, the law charges no man with default where the act done is compulsory, and not voluntary, and where there is not a consent and election on his part; and, therefore, if either there be an impossibility for a man to do otherwise, or so great a perturbation of the judgment and reason as in presumption of law man's nature cannot overcome, such necessity carries a privilege in itself.[1]

Necessity, as contemplated in the above rule, may be considered under three different heads:—1. Necessity of self-preservation; 2. Of obedience; 3. Necessity resulting from the act of God or of a stranger.[2]

1. Where two persons, being shipwrecked, have got on the same plank, but, finding it not able to save them both, one of them thrusts the other from it, and he is drowned; this homicide is excusable through unavoidable necessity, and upon the great universal principle of self-preservation, which prompts every man to save his own life in preference to that of another, where one of them must inevitably perish.[3] So, if a ferryman overload his boat with merchandise, a passenger may, in case of necessity, throw overboard the goods to save his own life and the lives of his fellow-passengers.[4] For the same reason, where one man attacks another, and the latter, without *fighting, flies, and, after retreating as far as he [*12] safely can, until no other means of escape remain to him, then turns round and kills his assailant, this homicide is excusable as being committed in self-defence; the distinction between this kind of homicide and manslaughter being, that here the slayer could not otherwise escape although he would,—in manslaughter he would not escape if he could.[5] The same rule extends to the principal civil and natural relations of life; therefore, master and servant,

[1] Bac. Max., reg. 5, cited arg. 1 T. R. 32; Jenk. Cent. 280.

[2] Bac. Max., reg. 5; Noy, Max., 9th ed., 32.

[3] Bac. Max., reg. 5.

[4] Mouse's Case, 12 Rep. 63.

[5] Arch. Cr. Pl., 16th ed., 586.

parent and child, husband and wife, killing an assailant in the necessary defence of each other respectively, are excused, the act of the relation assisting being construed the same as the act of the party himself.[1]

It should, however, be observed, that, as the excuse of self-defence is founded on necessity, it can in no case extend beyond the actual continuance of that necessity by which alone it is warranted; for, if a person assaulted does not fall upon the aggressor till the affray is over, or until the latter is running away, this is revenge, and not defence. There is another instance of necessity to be mentioned,—where a man, being in extreme want of food or clothing, steals either, in order to relieve his present necessities. In this case the law of England admits no such excuse as that above considered; but the crown has a power to soften the law, and to extend mercy in a case of peculiar hardship.[2]

2. Obedience to existing laws is a sufficient extenuation of guilt before a civil tribunal.[3] As, where the proper officer executes a [*13] criminal in strict conformity with his *sentence, or where an officer of justice, or other person acting in his aid, in the legal exercise of a particular duty, kills a person who resists or prevents him from executing it.[4] And where a known felony is attempted upon any one, not only the party assaulted may repel force by force, but his servant attending him, or any other person present, may interpose to prevent the mischief, and, if death ensue, the party so interposing will be justified.[5] So, in executing process, a sheriff, it has been observed, acts as a ministerial officer in pursuance of the command he receives in the king's name from a court of justice, which command he is bound to obey. He is not a volunteer, acting from his own free will or for his own benefit, but imperatively commanded to execute the king's writ. He is the servant of the law, and the agent of an overruling necessity; and if the service of the law be a reasonable service, he is (in accordance

[1] Fost. Disc. Hom. 274.

[2] 4 Com. by Broom & Hadley 30, 31.

[3] Ejus vero nulla culpa est cui parere necesse sit. D. 50, 17, 169.

[4] 4 Com. by Broom & Hadley 211, 212.

[5] Fost. Disc. Hom. 274.

with the above maxim) justly entitled to expect indemnity,[1] so long as he acts with diligence, caution, and pure good faith; and, it should be remembered, he is not at liberty to accept or reject the office at his pleasure, but must serve if commanded by the crown.[2] "The law has always held the sheriff strictly, and with much jealousy, to the performance of his duty in the execution of writs—both from the danger there is of fraud and collusion with defendants, and also because it is a disgrace to the crown and the administration of justice, if the king's writs remain unexecuted."[3] In *this [*14] case, therefore, the rule of law usually applies,—*necessitas quod cogit defendit.*[4] Although instances do occur where the sheriff is placed in a situation of difficulty because he is the mere officer of the court, and the court are bound to see that suitors obtain the fruits of decisions in their favor.[5]

In the private relations of society, the same principle is likewise, in some cases, applicable; as, where obedience proceeds from the matrimonial subjection of the wife to the husband, from which the law presumes coercion, and which, in many cases, excuses the wife from the consequences of criminal misconduct. Thus, if a larceny be committed by a feme covert in the presence of her husband, the law presumes that she acted under his immediate coercion, and excuses her from punishment.[6] The presumption, however, may be rebutted by evidence; and if it appear that the wife was principally instrumental in the commission of the crime, acting voluntarily, and not by constraint of her husband, although he was present and concurred, she will be guilty and liable to punishment;[7] and if in the

[1] For instance, by Interpleader, as to which see per Maule, J., 3 C. B. 341, 342 (54 E. C. L. R.). Per Rolfe, B., 15 M. & W. 197. Per Alderson, B., 14 Id. 801.

[2] Per Vaughan, B., Garland *v.* Carlisle (in error), 2 Cr. & M. 77; s. c., 4 Cl. & F. 701.

[3] Judgm., Howden *v.* Standish, 6 C. B. 520 (60 E. C. L. R.). As to the sheriff's duty in respect of executing criminals capitally convicted, see R. *v.* Antrobus, 2 A. & E. 788 (29 E. C. L. R.).

[4] 1 Hale, P. C. 54.

[5] See particularly Stockdale *v.* Hansard, 11 A. & E. 253 (39 E. C. L. R.); Christopherson *v.* Burton, 3 Exch. 160; per Jervis, C. J., Gregory *v.* Cotterell, 5 E. & B. 584 (85 E. C. L. R.); Hooper *v.* Lane, 6 H. L. Cas. 443.

[6] 1 Hale, P. C. 45; 1 Hawk., c. 1, s. 9.

[7] 1 Hale, P. C. 516.

absence of her husband she commit a like offence, even by his order or procurement, her coverture will be no excuse.

But the relation which exists between parent and child, or master and servant, will not excuse or extenuate the commission of any crime, of whatever denomination; for the command to commit a crime is void in law, [*15] *and can protect neither the commander nor the instrument.[1]

3. In criminal cases, idiots and lunatics are not chargeable for their own acts, if committed when in a state of incapacity, it being a rule of our law, that *furiosus solo furore punitur*,—a madman is only punished by his madness;[2] the reason of this rule obviously being, that, where there exists an incapacity or a defect of understanding, inasmuch as there can be no consent of the will, so the act done cannot be culpable.[3] Every man is, however, *presumed* to be sane, and to possess a sufficient degree of reason to be responsible for his actions, until the contrary has been satisfactorily proved; and in order to establish a defence on the ground of insanity, it must be clearly shown that, at the time of the committing of the act, the party accused was laboring under such a defect of reason, from disease of the mind, as not to know the nature and quality of the act he was doing, or if he did know what he was doing, that he did not know he was doing what was wrong. "If," said the majority of the judges, in answer to the questions proposed to them, some years since, by the House of Lords, relative to insane criminals, "the accused was conscious that the act was one which he ought not to do, and if that act was, at the same time, contrary to the law of the land, he is punishable; and the usual course, therefore, has been to leave the question to the jury, whether the party accused had a sufficient degree of reason to know that he was doing an act that was wrong; and this [*16] *course we think is correct; accompanied with such observations and explanations as the circumstances of each particular case may require."[4]

Where the party charged with an offence was, at the time of its

[1] 1 Hale, P. C. 44, 516.

[2] Co. Litt. 247 b.

[3] As to the tests of mental disease, see Smith *v.* Tebbitt, L. R. 1 P. & D. 398.

[4] M'Naghten's Case, 10 Cl. & F. 200; Reg. *v.* Higginson, 1 Car. & K. 129 (47 E. C. L. R.).

commission, under the influence of insane delusion, the application of the general rule above laid down is, in practice, often attended with considerable difficulty, and the rule itself will require to be modified according to the peculiar nature of the delusion and the infinite diversity of facts which present themselves in evidence. The following rules and illustrations, mentioned by the learned judges, will be found to throw considerable light upon this difficult and interesting subject:—1st. Where an individual labors under an insane delusion, in respect of some particular subject or person, and knew, at the time of committing the alleged crime, that he was acting contrary to law, he will be punishable according to the nature of the crime committed. And, 2dly, where such delusion is as to existing facts, and the individual laboring under it is not in other respects insane, he must be considered in the same situation as to responsibility as if the facts with respect to which the delusion existed were real. For instance, if a man, under the influence of his delusion, supposes another to be in the act of attempting to take away his life, and he kills that man, as he supposes, in self-defence, he would be exempt from punishment; whereas, if his delusion was that the deceased had inflicted a serious injury upon his character and fortune, and he killed him in revenge for such supposed injury, he would be liable to punishment.[1]

[*17] *The immunity from punishment which our law, through motives of humanity and justice, allows to persons mentally affected, is not extended to him who commits a felony, or other offence, whilst in a state of drunkenness; he shall not be excused, because his incapacity arose from his own default, but is answerable equally as if he had been, when the act was done, in the full possession of his faculties,[2] a principle of law which is embodied in the familiar adage, *qui peccat ebrius luat sobrius*.[3] As for a drunkard, says Sir E. Coke,[4] who is *voluntarius dæmon*, he hath no privilege thereby, but what hurt or ill soever he doeth, his drunkenness doth aggravate it, *omne crimen ebrietas et incendit et detegit*. But,

[1] 10 Cl. & F. 211.

[2] Bac. Max., reg. 5 *ad finem*. As to the *civil* liability which may be incurred by one intoxicated see Gore *v.* Gibson, 13 M. & W. 623; Hamilton *v.* Grainger, 5 H. & N. 40.

although drunkenness is clearly no excuse for the commission of any crime, yet proof of the fact of drunkenness may be very material, as tending to show the *intention* with which the particular act charged as an offence was committed, and whether the act done was accidental or designed.[1]

In accordance with the principle—*necessitas inducit privilegium*—the law excuses the commission of an act *primâ facie* criminal, if such act be done involuntarily, and under circumstances which show that the individual doing it was not really a free agent. Thus, if A., by force, take the hand of B., in which is a weapon, and therewith kill C., A. is guilty of murder, but B. is excused; though if merely a moral force be used, as threats, duress of imprisonment, [*18] or even an assault to the peril of his *life, in order to compel him to kill C., this is no legal excuse.[2]

It must be observed, however, that necessity privileges only *quoad jura privata*, and that if the act to be done be against the commonwealth, necessity does not excuse—*privilegium contra rempublicam non valet*;[3] and hence protection is not allowed in the case of a wife, if the crime be *malum in se*, and prohibited by the law of nature, or if it be heinous in its character or dangerous in its consequences; if a married woman, for instance, be guilty of treason, murder, or offences of the like description, in company with and by coercion of her husband, she is punishable equally as if she were sole.[4] So, if a man be violently assaulted, and has no other possible means of escaping death than by killing an innocent person, this fear and force shall not acquit him of murder, for he ought rather to die himself, than escape by the murder of an innocent man.[5]

Lastly, cases do, although rarely, occur, in which an individual may be required to sacrifice his own life for the good of the community, and in which, consequently, the necessity of self-preservation, which excuses *quoad jura privata*, is overruled by that higher necessity which regard to the public welfare imposes, and in such cases, therefore, the maxim applies *necessitas publica major est quàm*

[1] Broom's Com., 4th ed., 887, 888, where cases bearing upon the subject above adverted to are collected.

[2] 1 Hale, P. C. 434; 1 East, P. C. 225.

[3] Bac. Max., reg. 5; Noy, Max., 9th ed., 34; arg. 4 St. Tr. 1169.

[4] 4 Com. by Broom & Hadley 28. [5] *Id.* 30.

privata. Death, it has been observed, is the last and farthest point of particular necessity, and the law imposes it upon every subject, that he prefer the urgent service of his king and country to the safety of his life.[1]

---

*SUMMA RATIO EST QUÆ PRO RELIGIONE FACIT. [*19]

(Co. Lit. 341 *a.*)

That rule of conduct is to be deemed binding which religion dictates.

The maxim above cited from the commentaries of Sir E. Coke is, in truth, derived from the Digest; where Papinian, after remarking that certain religious observances were favored by the Roman law, gives as a reason *summan esse rationem quæ pro religione facit.*[2]

The doctrine, thus expressed, and recognized by our own law, must be understood in a somewhat qualified sense, and should be cautiously applied, for, whilst on the one hand "there are many social duties which are not enforced, and many wicked deeds which are not punished by human laws,"[3] so, on the other, an act springing from very laudable motives may expose to punishment.[4]

It may, however, safely be affirmed that, if ever the laws of God and man are at variance, the former are to be obeyed in derogation of the latter; that the law of God is, under all circumstances, superior in obligation to that of man; and that, consequently, if any general custom were opposed to the divine law, or if any statute were passed directly contrary thereto,—as if it were enacted generally, that no one should give alms to any object in ever so necessitous a condition,—such a custom, or such an Act, would be void.[5]

It may further be observed, that, upon these two foundations, the law of Nature and the law of Revelation, *depend all human laws; that is to say, no human laws can be suffered to contradict these. For instance, in the case of murder: this is expressly forbidden by the divine, and demonstrably by the natural [*20]

1 Bac. Max., reg. 5; Noy, Max., 9th ed., 34. In connection with the subject above considered, see the maxim "*Lex non cogit impossibilia,*" *post.*

2 Dig. 11. 7. 43.

3 Per Cur. 1 Denio (U. S.) R. 206.

4 See, for instance, Reg. *v.* Sharpe, Dearsl. & B. 160.

5 Doct. & Stud., 18th ed., 15, 16; Noy, Max., 9th ed., 2; Finch's Law 75, 76.

law, and if any human law should allow or enjoin us to commit it, we are bound to transgress that human law, or else we must offend both the natural and the divine.[1] "Neither are positive laws, even in matters seemingly indifferent, any further binding than they are agreeable with the laws of God and nature."[2]

It cannot, however, be doubted that obedience to the laws of our country, provided such laws are not opposed to the law of God, is a moral duty; and, therefore, although disobedience is justifiable in the one case supposed of a contradiction between divine and human laws, yet this is not so, either where the human law affirms the divine in a matter not indifferent in itself,—as where it forbids theft,—or where the human law commands or prohibits in a matter purely indifferent; and in both these cases it becomes a moral duty on the part of the subject to obey.[3]

Not only would the general maxim which we have been considering apply, if a conflict should arise between the law of the land and the law of God, but it likewise holds true with reference to foreign laws, wheresoever such laws are deemed by our courts inconsistent with the divine; for although it is well known that courts of justice in this country will recognize foreign laws and institutions, and will administer the *lex loci* in determining as to the validity of contracts, and in adjudicating upon the rights and liabilities of litigating parties, yet, inasmuch as the [*21] *proceedings in our courts are founded upon the law of England, and since that law is in part founded upon the law of nature and the revealed law of God, it follows, that, if the right sought to be enforced is inconsistent with either of these, the English municipal courts cannot recognize it; and it may, therefore, be laid down generally, that what is called international comity, or the *comitas inter communitates*, cannot prevail here in any case where its observance would tend to violate the law of this country, the law of nature, or the law of God.[4]

[1] 1 Com. by Broom & Hadley 35.

[2] Treat. Eq. 2.

[3] Plowd. 268, 269.

[4] See per Best, J., Forbes *v.* Cochrane, 2 B. & C. 471 (9 E. C. L. R.).

Other illustrations of the maxim commented upon *supra* will doubtless suggest themselves to the reader; thus, property consecrated to divine uses cannot be taken in execution by temporal hands—the glebe or churchyard cannot be taken under an elegit. Judgm., Parry *v.* Jones, 1 C. B. N. S. 345 (87 E. C. L. R.).

DIES DOMINICUS NON EST JURIDICUS.

(Noy, Max. 2.)

Sunday is not a day for judicial or legal proceedings.

The Sabbath-day is not *dies juridicus*, for that day ought to be consecrated to divine service.[1] The keeping one day in seven holy as a time of relaxation and refreshment, as well as for public worship, is, indeed, admirable service to a state, considered merely as a civil institution; and it is the duty of the legislature to remove, as much as possible, impediments to the due observance of the Lord's day.[2] The Houses of Parliament indeed may, in case of necessity, sit on a Sunday;[3] *but the judges cannot do so, [*22] that day being exempt from all legal business by the common law;[4] an affidavit purporting to be sworn on a Sunday might be rejected;[5] and where an installment of money under a judge's order becomes due on a Sunday, it will be payable on the following day.[6]

So, by stat. 29 Car. 2, c. 7, s. 6, service of a writ of summons or other process[7] on a Sunday is void, and no subsequent act of the defendant will be deemed a waiver of this irregularity;[8] and, by the same section, no arrest can be made upon a Sunday, except for

[1] Co. Litt. 135, a; Wing. Max. 5 (p. 7); Finch's Law 7; arg. Winsor *v.* Reg., 6 B. & S. 143, 164 (118 E. C. L. R.). Query whether a verdict in a criminal case can be taken and recorded on a Sunday? Id.

[2] See the preamble of stat. 3 & 4 Will. 4, c. 31.

[3] Per Sir Geo. Grey, Feb. 19, 1866, Hans. Parl. Deb. 3d series, vol. 181, p. 763.

[4] Per Patteson, J., 3 D. & L. 330; per Erle, C. J., Mumford *v.* Hitchcocks, 14 C. B. N. S. 369 (108 E. C. L. R.); Fish *v.* Broket, Plowd. 265; s. c., Dyer 181, b; Noy, Max., 9th ed., 2; Mackalley's Case, 11 Rep. 65, a; 3 & 4 Will. 4, c. 42, s. 43.

[5] Doe d. Williamson *v.* Roe, 3 D. & L. 328.

[6] Morris *v.* Barrett, 7 C. B. N. S. 139 (97 E. C. L. R.).

[7] But transmission of notice of chargeability of a pauper and order and grounds of removal by the ordinary post would not be void under the above statute, though made on a Sunday; Reg. *v.* Inhabitants of Leominster, 2 B. & S. 391 (110 E. C. L. R.).

[8] Taylor *v.* Phillips, 3 East 155; M'Ileham *v.* Smith, 8 T. R. 86. And a writ tested or returnable on a Sunday would be void. Chit. Arch. Pr., 11th ed., 157, 187.

treason, felony, breach of the peace, or, generally, for some indictable offençe,[1] or after a negligent escape.[2] So, service of the declaration in ejectment, or of a rule of court, must not be made on that day; nor can an attachment be put in force, or an execution be executed then.[3] [*23] *Bail may, it seems, take their principal on Sunday.[4] It has been held, also, that when the 20th of July, which is the last day for service of notice of claim under the Registration Act, 6 & 7 Vict. c. 18, s. 4, happens to fall on a Sunday, service at the dwelling-house of the overseer upon that day is good service, for such delivery is no violation of any known rule of law, the overseer who receives the notice not being called upon to perform any duty which can interfere with the most scrupulous observance of the Lord's day.[5]

If the day fixed for the commencement of term happens to be a Sunday, it must, for the purpose of computation, and in the absence of any express statutory provisions, be considered as the first day of the term, although, as the courts do not sit, no judicial act can be done, or be supposed to be done, till the following Monday.[6] Where, however, the last day of term falls on a Sunday, it is enacted by 1 Will. 4, c. 3, s. 3, that the Monday next following shall be deemed and taken to be the last day of term.

Again, the stat. 29 Car. 2, c. 7, s. 1, enacts, that no tradesman,

[1] Rawlins *v.* Ellis, 16 M. & W. 172. Re Eggington, 2 E. & B. 717 (75 E. C. L. R.). See Samuel *v.* Buller, 1 Exch. 439, where service of a warrant of detainer on Sunday was held not to be void. In Percival *v.* Stamp, 9 Exch. 167, 171, Parke, B., observes that, "if an arrest be made on a Sunday or in a way not authorized by law, the sheriff cannot afterwards make that valid by detaining the party under a legal writ, but must first give him an opportunity of going at large, and then execute the legal writ. But that is not so with regard to an execution against goods."

[2] Moore's Case, 2 Lord Raym. 1028.

[3] Chit. Arch. Pr., 11th ed., 163, 1709; Rowberry *v.* Morgan, 9 Exch. 730; followed in Peacock, app., Reg. resp., 4 C. B. N. S. 264, 267 (93 E. C. L. R.); distinguished per Erle, C. J., Hughes *v.* Griffiths, 13 C. B. N. S. 334 (106 E. C. L. R.). Morrison *v.* Manley, 1 Dowl. N. S., 773; Kenworthy *v.* Peppiatt, 4 B. & Ald. 288 (6 E. C. L. R.).

[4] Chit. Arch. Pr., 11th ed., 868.

[5] Rawlins *v.* Overseers of West Derby, 2 C. B. 72, 82 (52 E. C. L. R.); see Reg. *v.* Inhabitants of Leominster, 2 B. & S. 391, 400 (110 E. C. L. R.).

[6] Chit. Arch. Pr., 11th ed., 157. As to reckoning Sunday in the time limited for certain proceedings under stat. 2 Will. 4, c. 39, s. 11, Id. 159.

artificer, workman, laborer, or other person whatsoever,[1] shall do or exercise any worldly labor, business, or work of his ordinary calling on Sunday (works of necessity and charity only excepted), and that *every person of the age of fourteen years offending in the premises shall forfeit the sum of 5*s*.[2] The effect of which enactment is, that if a man, in the exercise of his ordinary calling,[3] make a contract on a Sunday, that contract will be void, so as to prevent a party who was privy to what made it illegal from suing upon it in a court of law, but not so as to defeat a claim made upon it by an innocent party.[4] A horse-dealer, for instance, cannot maintain an action upon a contract for the sale and warranty of a horse made by him upon a Sunday;[5] though, if the contract be not completed on the Sunday, it will not be affected by the statute.[6] [*24]

In a case before the House of Lords, it appeared, that an apprentice to a barber in Scotland, who was bound by his indentures "not to absent himself from his master's business on holiday or week-day, late hours or early, without leave, went away on Sundays without leave, and without shaving his master's customers:—*Held* by the Lords (reversing the interlocutors of the Court of Session), that the apprentice could not be lawfully required to attend his master's shop on Sunday, for the purpose of shaving his customers, and that that work, and all other sorts of handicraft, were illegal *in England as well as in Scotland, not being works of necessity, mercy, or charity.[7] [*25]

Where, in an action of assumpsit for breach of the warranty of a

[1] A farmer is not within the statute, Reg. *v.* Cleworth, 4 B. & S. 927 (116 E. C. L. R.).

[2] Exceptions to the above general rule are in certain cases allowed by statute, see R. *v.* Younger, 5 T. R. 449; Reg. *v.* Whiteley, 3 H. & N. 143.

[3] See R. *v.* Inhabs. of Whitnash, 7 B. & C. 596 (14 E. C. L. R.); Smith *v.* Sparrow, 4 Bing. 84 (13 E. C. L. R.); Peate *v.* Dicken, 1 Cr., M. & R. 422; Scarfe *v.* Morgan, 4 M. & W. 270.

[4] Judgm., Fennell *v.* Ridler, 5 B. & C. 408 (11 E. C. L. R.), explaining Lord Mansfield's remarks in Drury *v.* De la Fontaine, 1 Taunt. 135.

[5] Fennell *v.* Ridler, 5 B. & C. 406 (11 E. C. L. R.).

[6] Bloxsome *v.* Williams, 3 B. & C. 232 (10 E. C. L. R.); Smith *v.* Sparrow, 4 Bing. 84 (13 E. C. L. R.). See also Williams *v.* Paul, 6 Bing. 653 (19 E. C. L. R.), (observed upon in Simpson *v.* Nicholls, 3 M. & W. 240); Beaumont *v.* Brengeri, 5 C. B. 301 (57 E. C. L. R.); Norton *v.* Powell, 4 M. & Gr. 42 (43 E. C. L. R.).

[7] Phillips *v.* Innes, 4 Cl. & Fin. 234.

horse, the defendant alone was in the exercise of his ordinary calling, and it appeared that the plaintiff did not know what his calling was, so that, in fact, defendant was the only person who had violated the statute:—The court held that it would be against justice to allow the defendant to take advantage of his own wrong, so as to defeat the rights of the plaintiff, who was innocent.[1] And for the like reason, in an action by the endorsee against the acceptor of a bill of exchange which was drawn on a Sunday, it was held that the plaintiff might recover, there being no evidence that it had been accepted on that day; but the court said, that, if it had been accepted on a Sunday, and such acceptance had been made in the ordinary calling of the defendant, and if the plaintiff was acquainted with this circumstance when he took the bill, he would be precluded from recovering on it, though the defendant would not be permitted to set up his own illegal act as a defence to an action at the suit of an innocent holder.[2] A bill of exchange falling due on a Sunday is payable on the preceding day.

A person, however, can commit but one offence on the same day by exercising his ordinary calling in violation of the statute of Charles; and if a justice of the peace convict him in more than one penalty for the same day, it is an excess of jurisdiction.[3]

[*26] *In addition to the class of cases decided under the statute just cited, we may refer to one of a somewhat different description, in which, however, the principle of public policy which dictated that statute was discussed. In the case alluded to, a question arose as to the validity of a by-law, by which the navigation of a certain canal was ordered to be closed on every Sunday throughout the year (works of necessity only excepted). In support of this by-law was urged the reasonableness of the restriction sought to be imposed thereby, and its conformity in spirit and tendency with those enactments by which Sunday trading is prohibited; the court, however, held, that the navigation company had no power, under their Act, to make the by-law in question, their power being confined to the making of laws for the government and orderly use of the navigation, but not extending to the regulation of moral or

[1] Bloxsome *v.* Williams, 3 B. & C. 232 (10 E. C. L. R.); cited 5 B. & C. 408, 409 (11 E. C. L. R.).

[2] Begbie *v.* Levi, 1 Cr. & J. 180.

[3] Crepps *v.* Durden, Cowp. 640; cited 4 E. & B. 422 (82 E. C. L. R.).

religious conduct, which must be left to the general law of the land, and to the laws of God.[1] A railway company is bound to deliver up luggage deposited at the luggage and cloak office on Sunday as on other days, unless protected by special condition printed on the receipt ticket.[2]

---

§ II.—Rules of Legislative Policy.

In this section are comprised certain maxims relating to the operation of statutes, and developing elementary principles, which the legislature of every civilized country must, for the most part, observe in its enactments. These *maxims are three in [*27] number: 1st, that a later shall repeal an earlier and conflicting statute; 2dly, that laws shall not have a retrospective operation; and, 3dly, that enactments should be framed with a view to ordinary rather than extraordinary occurrences. We shall hereafter have occasion to consider the rules applicable to the construction of statutes, and may, for the present, confine our attention to the maxims of legislative policy just enumerated.

Leges posteriores priores contrarias abrogant.

(1 Rep. 25 b.)

When the provisions of a later statute are opposed to those of an earlier, the earlier statute is considered as repealed.

The legislature, which possesses the supreme power in the state, possesses, as incidental to that power, the right of changing, modifying, and abrogating the existing laws. To assert that any one Parliament can bind a subsequent Parliament by its ordinances, would in fact be to contradict the above plain proposition; if, therefore, an Act of Parliament contains a clause, "that it shall not be lawful for the king, by authority of Parliament, during the space of seven years, to repeal and determine the same Act," such a clause, which is technically termed "*clausula derogatoria*," will be simply void, and the Act may, nevertheless, be repealed within seven years,[1] for *non impedit clausula derogatoria quo minus ab eâdem potestate res dissolvantur a quibus constituentur.*[2] And again, *perpetua lex est nullam legem humanam ac positivam perpetuam esse, et clausula quæ abrogationem excludit ab initio non valet.*[2] The principle thus [*28] set *forth seems to be of universal application, and it will be remembered that, as regards our own Parliament, an Act may now be altered, amended or repealed in the same session in which it is passed, "any law or usage to the contrary notwithstanding."[3]

It is then an elementary and necessary rule, that a prior statute shall give place to a later—*Lex posterior derogat priori.*[4] *Non est novum ut priores legés ad posteriores trahantur,*[5] provided the intention of the legislature to repeal the previous statute be expressed in clear and unambiguous language, and be not merely left to be inferred from the subsequent statute.[6] For a more ancient statute will not be repealed by a more modern one, unless the latter expressly negative the former, or unless the provisions of the two statutes are manifestly repugnant, in which latter case the earlier enactment will be impliedly modified or repealed:[7] implied repeals, moreover, are not favored by the law, since they carry with them a tacit reproach, that the legislature has ignorantly, and without knowing it, made one Act repugnant to and inconsistent with another:[8] and the repeal itself casts a reflection upon the wisdom of former Parliaments.[9]

[*29] *"The rule," says Lord Hardwicke, "touching the repeal of laws, is *leges posteriores priores contrarias abrogant;* but

[1] Bac. Max., reg. 19.

[2] Id.

[3] 13 & 14 Vict. c. 21, s. 1.

[4] See Mackeld. Civ. L. 6.

[5] D. 1. 3. 26. *Constitutiones tempore posteriores potiores sunt his quæ ipsas præcesserunt.* D. 1. 4. 4. A rule of court may be overridden by a statute; see Harris *v.* Robinson, 2 C. B. 908 (52 E. C. L. R.).

[6] See Phipson *v.* Harvett, 1 Cr., M. & R. 473; judgm., Reg. *v.* St. Edmund's, Salisbury, 2 Q. B. 84 (42 E. C. L. R.).

[7] Gr. & Rud. of Law 190; arg. Reg. *v.* Mayor of London, 13 Q. B. 1 (66 E. C. L. R.); 19 Vin. Abr. 525, "Statutes," (E. 6), pl. 132. See per Lord Kenyon, C. J., Williams *v.* Pritchard, 4 T. R. 2, 4; Albert *v.* Pritchard, L. R. 1 C. P. 210; Rix *v.* Borton, 12 A. & E. 470 (40 E. C. L. R.); Dakins *v.* Seaman, 9 M. & W. 777.

[8] Vin. Abr. "Statutes" (E. 6), 132, cited arg. Phipson & Harvett, 1 Cr., M. & R. 481.

[9] Dwarr. Stats., 2d ed., 533.

subsequent Acts of Parliament, in the affirmative, giving new penalties, and instituting new methods of proceeding, do not [*necessarily*][1] repeal former methods and penalties of proceeding, ordained by preceding Acts of Parliament, without negative words."[2] Nor does an affirmative statute giving a new right of itself of necessity destroy a previously existing right, unless the intention of the legislature be apparent that the two rights should not exist together.[3] In order to repeal an existing enactment, a statute must have either express words of repeal,[4] or must be contrary to, or inconsistent with, the provisions of the law said to be repealed, or at least mention must be made of that law, showing an intention of the framers of the later Act of Parliament to repeal the former.[5] But "the law will not allow the *exposition to revoke or alter by construction of general words any particular statute, where the words may have their proper operation without it."[6] [*30]

[1] Michell *v.* Brown, 1 E. & E. 267, 274 (102 E. C. L. R.), where Lord Campbell, C. J., observes, "If a later statute again describes an offence created by a former statute, and affixes a different punishment to it, varying the procedure, &c., giving an appeal where there was no appeal before, we think that the prosecutor must proceed for the offence under the later statute. If the later statute expressly altered the quality of the offence, as by making it a misdemeanor instead of a felony, or a felony instead of a misdemeanor, the offence could not be proceeded for under the earlier statute, and the same consequence seems to follow from altering the procedure and the punishment." See Evans *v.* Rees, 9 C. B. N. S. 391 (99 E. C. L. R.).

[2] Middleton *v.* Crofts, 2 Atk. 674, cited Wynn *v.* Davis, 1 Curt. 79. Vin. Abr. "Statutes" (E. 6), pl. 132, cited arg. Macdougall *v.* Paterson, 11 C. B. 767 (73 E C. L. R.).

[3] O'Flaherty *v.* M'Dowell, 6 H. L. Cas. 142, 157.

[4] "It is a rule of law that one *private* Act of Parliament cannot repeal another, except by express enactment." Per Turner, L. J., Trustees of Birkenhead Docks *v.* Birkenhead Dock Co., 33 L. J. Ch. 457 ; s. c., 4 De G., M. & G. 732; Purnell app., Wolverhampton New Waterworks Co., resp., 10 C. B. N. S. 597, 591 (100 E. C. L. R.).

[5] Per Sir H. Jenner, 1 Curt. 80. See also the cases cited; arg. Reg. *v.* Mayor of London, 13 Q. B. 1 (66 E. C. L. R.) ; Bramston *v.* Mayor, &c., of Colchester, 6 E. & B. 246 (88 E. C. L. R.); Parry *v.* Croydon Commercial Gas and Coke Co., 11 C. B. N. S. 579 (103 E. C. L. R.) ; Great Central Gas Co. *v.* Clarke, 11 C. B. N. S. 814, 835, 841 (103 E. C. L. R.) ; s. c., 13 Id. 838 ; Daw *v.* Metropolitan Board of Works, 12 C. B. N. S. 161 (104 E. C. L. R.) ; Michell *v.* Brown, 1 E. & E. 267 (102 E. C. L. R.).

[6] Lyn *v.* Wyn, O. Bridgm. Judgments 122, 127 ; cited per Smith, J., Conservators of the Thames *v.* Hall, L. R. 3 C. P. 421.

Where, then, both Acts are merely affirmative, and the substance such that both may stand together, the later does not repeal the former, but they shall both have concurrent efficacy.[1] For instance, if, by a former law, an offence be indictable at the quarter sessions, and the later law makes the same offence indictable at the assizes; here the jurisdiction of the sessions is not taken away, but both have concurrent jurisdiction, and the offender may be prosecuted at either, unless the new statute subjoins express negative words,—as that the offence shall be indictable at the assizes, and not elsewhere.[2] So, the general rule of law and construction undoubtedly is, that, where an Act of Parliament does not create a duty or offence, but only adds a remedy in respect of a duty or offence which existed before, it is to be construed as cumulative; this rule must, however, in each particular case, be applied with due attention to the language of the Act of Parliament in question.[3] If, for example, a crime be created [*31] *by statute, with a given penalty, and be afterwards repeated in a subsequent enactment with a lesser penalty attached to it, the new Act would, in effect, operate to repeal the former penalty; for though there may no doubt be two remedies in respect of the same matter, yet they must be of different kinds.[4]

It has long been established, that, when an Act of Parliament is repealed, it must be considered (except as to transactions past and closed) as if it had never existed.[5] An indictment, however, for a

[1] Dr. Foster's Case, 11 Rep. 62, 63; Stuart *v.* Jones, 1 E. & B. 22 (72 E. C. L. R.); arg. Ashton *v.* Poynter, 1 Cr., M. & R. 739; R. *v.* Aslett. 1 B. & P., N. R. 7; Langton *v.* Hughes, 1 M. & S. 597; Com. Dig. "Parliament" (R. 9).

[2] 1 Com. by Broom & Hadley 93. See also the arguments in Reg. *v.* St. Edmund's, Salisbury, 2 Q. B. 72 (42 E. C. L. R.); Reg. *v* Justices of Suffolk, Id. 85. And see Reg. *v.* Deane, 2 Q. B. 96 (42 E. C. L. R.).

[3] Judgm., Richards *v.* Dyke, 3 Q. B. 268 (43 E. C. L. R.); Michell *v.* Brown, 1 E. & E. 267 (102 E. C. L. R.); Dwarr. Stats., 2d ed., 530, 532. See Thibault *v.* Gibson, 12 M. & W. 88.

[4] Henderson *v.* Sherborne, 2 M. & W. 239; cited and approved in Robinson *v.* Emerson, 4 H. & C. 355, per Lord Abinger, C. B., A. G. *v.* Lockwood, 9 M. & W. 391; R. *v.* Davis, Leach C. C. 271. See also Wrightup *v.* Greenacre, 10 Q. B. 1 (59 E. C. L. R.), recognizing Pilkington *v.* Cooke, 16 M. & W. 615.

[5] Per Lord Tenterden, C. J., Surtees *v.* Ellison, 9 B. & C. 752 (17 E. C. L. R.); Dean *v.* Mallard, 15 C. B. N. S. 19, 25 (109 E. C. L. R.); per Lord Campbell, C. J., Reg. *v.* Inhabs. of Denton, 18 Q. B. 770 (83 E. C. L. R.); Taylor *v.* Vansittart, 4 E. & B. 910 (82 E. C. L. R.); per Parke, B., Simpson *v.* Ready, 11 M. & W. 346.

conspiracy to violate the provisions of a statute will lie after the repeal of such statute for an offence committed before the repeal.[1] By Act of Parliament the liability to repair certain highways in a parish was taken from the parish and cast upon certain townships in which the highways respectively were, a form of indictment being given by the Act against such townships for non-repair, which would have been insufficient at common law. One of the townships was indicted under the Act which before trial was repealed without any reference to depending prosecutions:—the Court of Queen's Bench arrested a judgment given against the township on such indictment.[2]

There is, moreover, a difference to be remarked between *temporary* statutes and statutes which have been repealed; *for, [*32] although the latter (except so far as they relate to transactions already completed under them) become as if they had never existed, yet, with respect to the former, the extent of the restrictions imposed, and the duration of the provisions, are matters of construction.[3]

Formerly, when a statute which repealed another was itself subsequently repealed, the first statute was—if nothing inconsistent with such an intention appeared[4]—thereby revived, without any formal words for that purpose;[5] though where a contract for insuring tickets in the lottery was void by statute when made, such contract was held not to be set up again by a repeal of the statute between the time of contracting and the commencement of the suit.[6] And it is now expressly enacted that "where any Act repealing in whole or in part any former Act, is itself repealed, such last repeal shall not revive the Act or provisions before repealed," unless words be added, reviving them.[7] Also, wherever "any Act shall be made repealing in whole or in part any former Act, and substituting some provision or provisions instead of the provision or provisions repealed, such provision or provisions so repealed shall

[1] Reg. *v.* Thompson, 16 Q. B. 832 (71 E. C. L. R.).

[2] Reg. *v.* Inhabs. of Denton, 18 Q. B. 761 (83 E. C. L. R.). See Foster *v.* Pritchard, 2 H. & N. 151.

[3] Per Parke, B., Stevenson *v.* Oliver, 8 M. & W. 241.

[4] Hellawell *v.* Eastwood, 6 Exch. 295.

[5] The Bishops' Case, 12 Rep. 7. See 2 Inst. 685.

[6] Jaques *v.* Withy, 1 H. Bla. 65, cited per Coleridge, J., Hitchcock *v.* Way, 6 A. & E. 946 (33 E. C. L. R.).

[7] 13 & 14 Vict. c. 21, s. 5.

remain in force until the substituted provision or provisions shall come into operation by force of the last made Act."[1]

Prior to the stat. 33 Geo. 3, c. 13, it was not possible to know [*33] the precise day on which an Act of Parliament *received the royal assent, and all Acts passed in the same session of Parliament were considered to have received the royal assent on the same day, and were referred to the first day of the session; but, by the above statute, it is provided that a certain parliamentary officer, styled "the clerk of the Parliaments," shall indorse, on every Act of Parliament, "the day, month, and year, when the same shall have passed and shall have received the royal assent, and such indorsement shall be taken to be a part of such Act, and to be the date of its commencement, where no other commencement shall be therein provided." When, therefore, two Acts, passed in the same session of Parliament, are repugnant or contradictory to each other, that Act which last received the royal assent will prevail, and will have the effect of repealing wholly, or *pro tanto*, the previous statute.[2] The same principle, moreover, applies where the proviso of the Act is directly repugnant to the purview of it; for in this case the proviso shall stand, and be held to be a repeal of the purview, as it speaks the last intention of the makers.[3]

Not merely does an old statute give place to a new one, but, where the common law and the statute differ, the common law gives place to the statute,[4] if expressed in negative terms.[5] And, in like manner, an ancient custom may be abrogated and destroyed by the express provisions of a statute; or where inconsistent with and [*34] repugnant to its positive language.[6] But "the law *and customs of England cannot be changed without an Act of

[1] 13 & 14 Vict. c 21, s. 6. See Levi *v.* Sanderson, L. R. 4 Q. B. 330; Mirfin *v.* Attwood, Id.; Mount *v.* Taylor, L. R. 3 C. P. 645; Butcher *v.* Henderson, L. R. 3 Q. B. 335.

[2] R. *v.* Justices of Middlesex, 2 B. & Ad. 818 (22 E. C. L. R.); Paget *v.* Foley, 2 Bing. N. C. 691 (29 E. C. L. R.).

[3] A. G. *v.* Chelsea Waterworks Co., Fitzgib. 195, cited 2 B. & Ad. 826 (22 E. C. L. R.).

[4] Co. Litt. 115, b; Paget *v.* Foley, 2 Bing. N. C. 679 (29 E. C. L. R.); per Lord Ellenborough, C. J., R. *v.* Aslett, 1 N. R. 7; Dresser *v.* Bosanquet, 4 B. & S. 460, 486 (116 E. C. L. R.).

[5] Bac. Abr., 7th ed., "Statute" (G).

[6] Merchant Tailors' Co. *v.* Truscott, 11 Exch. 855; Salters' Co. *v.* Jay, 3 Q. B. 109 (43 E. C. L. R.); Huxham *v.* Wheeler, 3 H. & C. 75.

Parliament, for this, that the law and custom of England is the inheritance of the subject, which he cannot be deprived of without his assent in Parliament."[1]

Statutes, however, "are not presumed to make any alteration in the common law, further or otherwise than the Act does expressly declare; therefore, in all general matters the law presumes the Act did not intend to make any alteration, for if Parliament had had that design they would have expressed it in the Act."[2]

NOVA CONSTITUTIO FUTURIS FORMAM IMPONERE DEBET, NON PRÆTERITIS.

(2 Inst. 292.)

A legislative enactment ought to be prospective, not retrospective, in its operation.

Every statute which takes away or impairs a vested right acquired under existing laws, or creates a new obligation, imposes a new duty, or attaches a new disability, in respect of transactions or considerations already past, must be deemed retrospective[3] in its operation, and opposed to sound principles of jurisprudence.[4] In the Roman law we find it laid down generally that *nemo potest mutare consilium suum in alterius injuriam;*[5] *and this [*35] maxim has by the civilians[6] been specifically applied as a restriction upon the law-giver, who was thus forbidden to change his mind to the prejudice of a vested right; and that this interpretation of the rule is at all events in strict conformity with the spirit of the civil law appears clearly by a reference to the Code, where the principle, which we here propose to consider, is thus stated: *Leges et constitutiones futuris certum est dare formam negotiis, non ad facta præterita revocari; nisi nominatim et de præ-*

[1] 12 Rep. 29.

[2] Per Trevor, C. J., 11 Mod. 150. See 26 & 27 Vict. c. 125, s. 1.

[3] Per Story, J., 2 Gallis. (U. S.) R. 139. In the judgment of Kent, C. J., Dash *v.* Van Kleeck, 7 Johns. (U. S.) R. 503 *et seq.*, the rule as to *nova constitutio* is fully considered, and various cases and authorities upon this subject are reviewed.

[4] Instances of retrospective legislation are given in the arg., the Wiltes Peerage, L. R. 4 H. L. 146.

[5] D. 50, 17, 75.

[6] Taylor, Elem. Civ. Law, 168.

terito tempore et adhuc pendentibus negotis cautum sit.[1] Laws should be construed as prospective, not as retrospective unless they are expressly made applicable to past transactions, and to such as are still pending.[2] And parties must *primâ facie* be taken to contract with reference to the existing law only, unless there be enough to show that they contracted with reference to possible alterations in the law.[3]

Though a distinction must be noticed between new enactments which affect vested rights and those which merely affect the procedure in courts of justice. When a new enactment deals with rights of action, unless it is so expressed in the Act, an existing right of action is not taken away. But where the enactment deals with procedure only, unless the contrary is expressed, the enactment applies to all actions whether commenced before or after the passing of the Act.[4]

[*36] *It is, however, in general true, that a statute shall not be so construed as to operate retrospectively, or to take away a vested right, unless it contain either an enumeration of the cases in which it is to have such an operation, or words which can have no meaning unless such a construction is adopted.[5]

On various occasions it has, in accordance with the above doctrine, been laid down, that, where the law is altered by a statute pending an action, the law, as it existed when the action was commenced, must decide the rights of the parties in the suit, unless the legislature express a clear intention to vary the relation of litigant parties to each other.[6] The Statute of Frauds (29 Car. 2, c. 3) was passed in 1676, and by sect. 4 provides, that, from and after

[1] Cod. 1, 14, 7. [2] See 15 Mass. (U. S.) R. 454.

[3] Per Parke, B., Vansittart *v.* Taylor, 4 E. & B. 912 (82 E. C. L. R.); Mayor of Berwick *v.* Oswald, 3 E. & B. 653 (77 E. C. L. R.); s. c. 1 E. & B. 295; 5 H. L. Cas. 856; with which compare Mayor of Dartmouth *v.* Silly, 7 E. & B. 97 (77 E. C. L. R.); Pybus *v.* Gibb, 6 E. & B. 902 (88 E. C. L. R.).

[4] Wright *v.* Hale, 6 H. & N. 227, 230, 232; followed in Kimbray *v.* Draper, L. R. 3 Q. B. 160.

[5] 7 Bac. Abr., 7th ed., "Statute" (C), p. 439. See Latless *v.* Holmes, 4 T. R. 660; cited Whitaker *v.* Wisbey, 12 C. B. 52 (74 E. C. L. R.); Doe d. Johnson *v.* Liversedge, 11 M. & W. 517; Dash *v.* Van Kleeck, 7 Johnson (U. S.) R. 477.

[6] Hitchcock *v.* Way, 6 A. & E. 943, 951 (33 E. C. L. R.); Paddon *v.* Bartlett, 3 A. & E. 895, 896 (30 E. C. L. R.); per Lord Abinger, C. B., Chappell *v.* Purday, 12 M. & W. 305, 306.

the 14th June, 1677, no action shall be brought whereby to charge any person upon any agreement made upon consideration of marriage, &c., unless the agreement upon which such action shall be brought, or some memorandum thereof, shall be in writing, and signed by the party or some other person thereunto by him lawfully authorized; and the question was, whether a promise of marriage made before the new Act, but to be performed after, would sustain an action without note in writing. The court were of opinion that the action lay, notwithstanding the statute, which it was agreed did not extend to promises made before the 24th of June; and judgment was given for the plaintiff.[1]

[*37] *Moon *v.* Durden[2] may be cited as a leading decision in reference to the application of the above maxim. The 8 & 9 Vict. c. 109, s. 18, which received the royal assent on the 8th August, 1845, enacts that "all contracts and agreements by way of gaming or wagering shall be null and void; and that no suit shall be brought or *maintained* in any court of law or equity for recovering any sum of money or valuable thing alleged to be won upon any wager, or which shall have been deposited in the hands of any person to abide the event upon which any wager shall have been made;" this section was held not to defeat an action for a wager which had been commenced before the passing of the Act. In the case just cited, Parke, B., observes that the language of the clause above set out, if taken in its ordinary sense, "applies to all contracts both past and future, and to all actions both present and future on any wager whether past or future." But it is, as Lord Coke says, "a rule and law of Parliament, that regularly *nova constitutio futuris formam imponere debet non præteritis.* This rule, which is in effect that enactments in a statute are generally to be construed to be prospective, and intended to regulate the future conduct of persons, is deeply founded in good sense and strict justice, and has been acted upon in many cases.[3] * * * But this

[1] Gilmore *v.* Shuter, Jones R. 108; s. c., 2 Lev. 227.

[2] 2 Exch. 22, recognized in Pettamberdass *v.* Thackoorseydass, 7 Moore P. C. C. 239; arg. James *v.* Isaacs, 12 C. B. 795 (74 E. C. L. R.); Pinhorn *v.* Sauster, 8 Exch. 138, 142; Hobson *v.* Neale, Id. 131; Vansittart *v.* Taylor, 4 E. & B. 910 (82 E. C. L. R.); Langton *v.* Haynes, 1 H. & N. 366; Reg. *v.* Inhabs. of Madeley, 15 Q. B. 43 (69 E. C. L. R.); Harris *v.* Lawrence, 1 Exch. 697; Parker *v.* Crouch, Id. 699. See also A. G. *v.* Sillem, 10 H. L. Cas. 704.

[3] Citing Gilmore *v.* Shuter, T. Jones 108; s. c., 2 Shaw 16; Edmonds *v.* Lawley, 6 M. & W. 285; Moore *v.* Phillips, 7 M. & W. 536.

rule, which is one of construction only, will certainly yield to the intention of the [*38] *legislature; and the question in this and every other similar case is, whether that intention has been sufficiently expressed." In this case Rolfe, B., also remarks that the principle as to *nova constitutio* "is one of such obvious convenience and justice that it must always be adhered to in the construction of statutes, unless in cases where there is something on the face of the enactment putting it beyond doubt that the legislature meant it to operate retrospectively."[1] To a like effect, in Marsh *v.* Higgin,[2] Wilde, C. J., says that "sometimes, no doubt, the legislature finds it expedient to give a retrospective operation to an Act to a considerable extent; but then care is always taken to express that intention in clear and unambiguous language." And by a like rule of construction have the courts been guided in construing the first[3] and fourteenth[4] sections of "The Mercantile Law Amendment Act, 1856."

Where a patent originally void was amended under 5 & 6 Will. 4, c. 83,[5] by filing a disclaimer of part of the invention, the above Act was held not to have a [*39] *retrospective operation, so as to make a party liable for an infringement of the patent prior to the time of entering such disclaimer. "The rule," observed Parke, B., "by which we are to be guided in construing Acts of Parliament, is to look at the precise words, and to construe them in their ordinary sense, unless it would lead to any absurdity or

[1] Bearing upon the above subject, see Smallcombe *v.* Olivier, 13 M. & W. 77, 87; A. G. *v.* Bristol Waterworks Co., 10 Exch. 884; Elliott *v.* Bishop, Id. 927; Boodle *v.* Davis, 8 Exch. 351; Waugh *v.* Middleton, Id. 352; Larpent *v.* Bibby, 5 H. L. Cas. 481; A. G. *v.* Marquis of Hertford, 3 Exch. 670, 687, 688; Reg. *v.* Inhabs. of St. Mary, Whitechapel, 12 Q. B. 120 (64 E. C. L. R.); Leary *v.* Patrick, 15 Q. B. 266, 271 (69 E. C. L. R.); Mackenzie *v.* Sligo and Shannon R. C., 18 Q. B. 862 (83 E. C. L. R.); per Williams, J., Upton *v.* Townend, 17 C. B. 50 (84 E. C. L. R.). And see the cases cited by counsel, arg. 12 Q. B. 109, 131 (64 E. C. L. R.); Reg. *v.* Inhabs. of Christchurch, Id. 149.

[2] 9 C. B. 551, 567 (67 E. C. L. R.), and cases there cited. There is no rule of law which prohibits a retrospective rate; from the language of the Act under which it is laid must be gathered the intention of the legislature: Harrison *v.* Stickney, 2 H. L. Cas. 108, 125.

[3] Williams *v.* Smith, 4 H. & N. 559; s. c., 2 Id. 443.

[4] Jackson *v.* Woolley, 8 E. & B. 778, 784 (92 E. C. L. R.).

[5] As to which see Ralston *v.* Smith, 11 H. L. Cas. 223.

manifest injustice, and, if it should, so to vary and modify them as to avoid that which it certainly could not have been the intention of the legislature should be done. Now, if the construction contended for was to be considered as the right construction, it would lead to the manifest injustice of a party who might have put himself to great expense in the making of machines or engines, the subject of the grant of a patent, on the faith of that patent being void, being made a wrong-doer by relation: that is an effect the law will not give to any Act of Parliament, unless the words are manifest and plain."[1] "Those whose duty it is to administer the law," observed Erle, C. J., in a recent case,[2] "very properly guard against giving to an Act of Parliament a retrospective operation, unless the intention of the legislature that it should be so construed is expressed in clear, plain, and unambiguous language; because it manifestly shocks one's sense of justice that an act legal at the time of doing it should be made unlawful by some new enactment. Modern legislation has almost *entirely removed that blemish from [*40] the law; and wherever it is possible to put upon an Act of Parliament a construction not retrospective, the courts will always adopt that construction."

Where, indeed, the words of a statute are manifest and plain, the court will give effect to them, notwithstanding any particular hardship, inconvenience or detriment, which may be thereby occasioned. For instance, by letters patent granted to the plaintiff, it was amongst other things provided that if he should not particularly describe and ascertain the nature of his invention, and in what manner the same was to be performed, by an instrument in writing under his hand and seal, and cause the same to be enrolled in her majesty's High Court of Chancery within four calendar months next and immediately after the date of the said letters patent, then the said letters patent should become void. By an Act of Parliament, 4 & 5 Vict. c. 1, subsequently obtained, which

[1] Perry *v.* Skinner, 2 M. & W. 471, 476. As to which see, however, per Jervis, C. J., Reg. *v.* Mill, 10 C. B. 389, 391 (70 E. C. L. R.); per Parke, B., Wallington *v.* Dale, 7 Exch. 907. See also Stocker *v.* Warner, 1 C. B. 148, 167 (50 E. C. L. R.); Russell *v.* Ledsam, 14 M. & W. 574; s. c., 16 Id. 633; 1 H. L. Cas. 687. As to the general principle illustrated in the text, see further: Doe d. Evans *v.* Pye, 5 Q. B. 767, 772 (48 E. C. L. R.); Thompson *v.* Lack, 3 C. B. 540 (54 E. C. L. R.), and cases cited *ante*.

[2] Midland R. C. app., Pye resp., 10 C. B. N. S. 191 (100 E. C. L. R.).

recited that letters patent had been granted to the plaintiff; that the specification was enrolled within six months, instead of being enrolled within four months after the date thereof, as required by the letters patent; that such non-enrollment had arisen from inadvertence and misinformation; and that it was expedient that the patent should be rendered valid to the extent thereinafter mentioned: it was enacted, that the letters patent should, during the remainder of the term, be considered, deemed, and taken to be as valid and effectual to all intents and purposes as if the specification thereunder so enrolled by the plaintiff within six months after the date thereof had been enrolled within four months. In case for infringement of the patent by the defendant, who had himself obtained letters patent for a *bonâ fide* improvement upon [*41] *the plaintiff's invention prior to the passage of the said Act of Parliament, and at a time when the plaintiff's patent had ceased to have any validity by reason of its non-enrollment: it was held, that the Act of Parliament in question operated as a complete confirmation of the plaintiff's patent, although such a construction imposed upon the defendant the hardship of having his patent destroyed by an *ex post facto* law.[1]

The preceding may perhaps be considered as a strong, but is by no means a solitary, instance[2] of a statute being held to have a retrospective operation. Thus, the plaintiff sued in Hilary Term, 1829, for a debt which had accrued due more than six years previously: it was held that the statute 9 Geo. 4, c. 14, which came into operation on the 1st January, 1829, precluded him from recovering on an oral promise to pay the debt made by defendant in February, 1828.[3] In this case the action was brought *after* the statute had begun to operate; but the same principle was applied where the action was brought *before*, though not tried till *after*, the

[1] Stead *v.* Carey, 1 C. B. 496 (50 E. C. L. R.). See further as to retrospective statutes per Dr. Lushington, The Ironsides, Lush. Adm. R. 465.

[2] See, as to stat. 2 & 3 Vict. c. 37, s. 1, Hodgkinson *v.* Wyatt, 4 Q. B. 749 (45 E. C. L. R.); as to stat. 6 & 7 Vict. c. 73, s. 37, Brooks *v.* Bockett, 9 Q. B. 847 (58 E. C. L. R.); as to stat. 20 & 21 Vict. c. 85, s. 21, Midland R. C. app., Pye resp., 10 C. B. N. S. 179 (100 E. C. L. R.); as to stat. 21 & 22 Vict. c. 90, Wright *v.* Greenroyd, 1 B. & S. 758, 762 (101 E. C. L. R.).

[3] Towler *v.* Chatterton, 6 Bing. 258 (19 E. C. L. R.), recognized in Reg. *v.* Leeds and Bradford R. C., 18 Q. B. 343 (83 E. C. L. R.). See also Bradshaw *v.* Tasker, 2 My. & K. 221; Fourdrin *v.* Gowdey, 3 My. & K. 383.

statute came in force.[1] There are, moreover, several authorities for extending remedial enactments to inchoate transactions,[2] yet these appear to have turned on the peculiar wording of particular *Acts, which seemed to the court to compel them to give the law an *ex post facto* operation.[3] We may also, in connection with this part of the subject, observe that, where an Act of Parliament is passed to correct an error by omission in a former statute of the same session, it relates back to the time when the first Act passed, and the two must be taken together as if they were one and the same Act, and the first must be read as containing in itself in words the amendments supplied by the last.[4] [*42]

The injustice and impolicy of *ex post facto*[5] or retrospective legislation are yet more apparent with reference to criminal laws[6] than to such as regard property or contracts; and, with reference to the operation of a new criminal law, the maxim of Paulus,[7] adopted by Lord Bacon, applies, *nunquam crescit ex post facto præteriti delicti æstimatio*, the law does not allow a later fact, a circumstance or matter subsequent, to extend or amplify an offence; it construes neither penal laws nor penal facts by intendment, but considers the offence in degree as it stood at the time when it was committed.[8]

---

*AD EA QUÆ FREQUENTIUS ACCIDUNT JURA ADAPTANTUR. [*43]

(2 Inst. 137.)

The laws are adapted to those cases which most frequently occur.

Laws ought to be, and usually are, framed with a view to such cases as are of frequent rather than such as are of rare or acci-

[1] Kirkhaugh *v.* Herbert, and an anonymous case, cited 6 Bing. 265 (19 E. C. L. R.).

[2] See the cases cited, arg. 6 A. & E. 946 (33 E. C. L. R.), and *supra*.

[3] Judgm., 6 A. & E. 951 (33 E. C. L. R.). See Burn *v.* Carvalho, 1 A. & E. 895 (28 E. C. L. R.).

[4] 2 Dwarr. Stats. 685.

[5] As to the meaning and derivation of this expression, see note, 2 Peters (U. S.) R. 683.

[6] "There can," moreover, "be no doubt that every so-called Indemnity Act involves a manifest violation of justice, inasmuch as it deprives those who have suffered wrongs of their vested right to the redress which the law would otherwise afford them, and gives immunity to those who have inflicted those wrongs." Judgm., Phillips *v.* Eyre, L. R. 4 Q. B. 242.

[7] D. 50. 17. 138. § 1.

[8] Bac. Max., reg. 8.

dental occurrence, or, in the language of the civil law, *jus constitui oportet in his quæ ut plurimum accidunt non quæ ex inopinato;*[1] for, *neque leges neque senatus-consulta ita scribi possunt ut omnes casus qui quandoque inciderint comprehendantur, sed sufficit ea quæ plerumque accidunt contineri*,[2] laws cannot be so worded as to include every case which may arise, but it is sufficient if they apply to those things which most frequently happen. Public Acts, it may likewise be observed, are seldom made for one particular person, or limited to one single case; but they are made for the common good, and prescribe such rules of conduct as it is useful to observe in the ordinary occurrences of life.[3]

A few illustrations of the maxim above cited will suffice:

Where a private Act of Parliament, intituled "An Act to enable the N. Union Society for Insurance against Loss by Fire to sue in the name of their Secretary, and to be sued in the names of their Directors, Treasurers and [*44] *Secretary," enacted that all actions and suits might be commenced in the name of the secretary, as nominal plaintiff: it was held that this Act did not enable the secretary to petition, on behalf of the society, for a commission of bankruptcy against their debtor; for the expression "to sue," generally speaking, means to bring actions, and *ad ea quæ frequentius accidunt jura adaptantur.*[4]

Again, where the construction of the stat. 11 Geo. 2, c. 19, which gives a remedy to a landlord whose tenant has fraudulently removed goods from the demised premises, unless they have been *bonâ fide* sold to one not privy to the fraud, was under consideration: and it was urged that the landlord was not empowered by the statute to enter the close of a third person, or to break his locks, for the purpose of seizing the goods, unless he was a party to, or

[1] D. 1. 3. 3. See Lord Camden's judgment in Entick *v.* Carrington, 19 How. St. Tr. 1061. Sir R. Atkyns observes, that "laws are fitted *ad ea quæ frequentius accidunt*, and not for rare and extraordinary events and accidents." See his "Enquiry into the Power of dispensing with Penal Statutes," cited 11 St. Tr. 1208. "The rule is *ad ea quæ frequentius accidunt leges adaptantur*," per Bramwell, B., 9 H. L. Cas. 52; per Willes, J., 10 H. L. Cas. 429.

[2] D. 1. 3. 10.

[3] See Wood's Treatise of Laws 121.

[4] Guthrie *v.* Fisk, 3 B. & C. 178 (10 E. C. L. R.). Arg. A. G. *v.* Jackson, Cr. & J. 108; Wing. Max. 716. *Argumentum à communiter accidentibus in jure frequens est*, Gothofred, ad D. 44. 2. 6.

at least cognizant of, their fraudulent removal; and further, that the breaking open of his gates without a previous request to open them was unjustifiable: the court held that neither of these conditions need be observed as necessary to the exercise of the right given by the statute, "for, generally, goods fraudulently removed are not secreted in a man's close or house without his privity or consent. The legislature may be presumed to have had this[1] in their contemplation: *ad ea quæ frequentius accidunt jura adaptantur.*"

In Miller *v.* Salomons,[2] speaking of the statute law, Parke, B., thus paraphrases the above maxim:—"If, *in the vast majority of [*45] possible cases—in all of ordinary occurrence—the law is in no degree inconsistent or unreasonable, construed according to its plain words, it seems to me to be an untenable proposition, and unsupported by authority, to say that the construction may be varied in every case, because there is one possible but highly improbable one in which the law would operate with great severity, and against our own notions of justice. The utmost that can be reasonably contended is, that it should be varied in that particular case, so as to obviate that injustice—no further."

The principle under consideration holds as well in reference to the unwritten as to the statute law. Thus, in Hawtayne *v.* Bourne,[3] Parke, B., in reference to the authority of an agent to raise money in cases of necessity by pledging the credit of his principal, observes that no such power exists, except in the case "of the master of a ship, and of the acceptor of a bill of exchange, for the honor of the drawer. The latter derives its existence from the law of merchants; and in the former case, the law, which generally provides for ordinary events, and not for cases which are of rare occurrence, considers how likely and frequent are accidents at sea, when it may be necessary in order to have the vessel repaired, or to provide the means of continuing the voyage, to pledge the credit of her owners; and therefore it is that the law invests the master with power to raise money, and by an instrument of hypothecation to pledge the ship itself, if necessary."

[1] Williams *v.* Roberts, 7 Exch. 618, 628; see Thomas *v.* Watkins, Id. 630.

[2] 7 Exch. 549; s. c., 8 Id. 778.

It is then true, that, "when the words of a law extend not to an [*46] inconvenience rarely happening, but do to those *which often happen, it is good reason not to strain the words further than they reach, by saying it is *casus omissus*, and that the law intended *quæ frequentius accidunt.*" "But," on the other hand, "it is no reason, when the words of a law do enough extend to an inconvenience seldom happening, that they should not extend to it as well as if it happened more frequently, because it happens but seldom."[1] Where, however, a *casus omissus* does really occur in a statute, either through the inadvertence of the legislature,[2] or on the principle *quod semel aut bis existit prætereunt legislatores*,[3] the rule is, that the particular case thus left unprovided for must be disposed of according to the law as it existed prior to such statute —*Casus omissus et oblivioni datus dispositioni communis juris relinquitur;*[4] "a *casus omissus*," observes Buller, J.,[5] "can in no case be supplied by a court of law, for that would be to make laws."

[1] Vaugh. R. 373; Fenton *v.* Hampton, 11 Moore, P. C. C. 365; with which acc. Doyle *v.* Falconer, L. R. 1 P. C. 328.

[2] Reg. *v.* Inhabs. of Denton, 5 B. & S. 821, 828 (117 E. C. L. R.); Cobb *v.* Mid Wales R. C., L. R. 1 Q. B. 348, 349.

[3] D. 1. 3. 6.

[4] 5 Rep. 38. See Robinson *v.* Cotterell, 11 Exch. 476.

[5] Jones *v.* Smart, 1 T. R. 52; per Lord Abinger, C. B., Lane *v.* Bennett, 1 M. & W. 73; arg. Shepherd *v.* Hills, 11 Exch. 64.

*CHAPTER II. [*47]

MAXIMS RELATING TO THE CROWN.

THE principal attributes of the crown are sovereignty or pre-eminence, perfection, and perpetuity; and these attributes are attached to the wearer of the crown by the constitution, and may be said to form his constitutional character and royal dignity. On the other hand, the principal duty of the sovereign is to govern his people according to law; and this is not only consonant to the principles of nature, of liberty, of reason, and of society, but has always been esteemed an express part of the common law of England, even when prerogative was at the highest. In the pages immediately following are collected some of the more important technical rules, embodying the above general attributes of the crown, with remarks as to their meaning and qualifications.[1]

REX NON DEBET ESSE SUB HOMINE, SED SUB DEO ET SUB LEGE, QUIA LEX FACIT REGEM.

(Bract. Lib. i. fo. 5.)

The king is under no man, yet he is in subjection to God and to the law, for the law makes the king.

The head of the state is regarded by our law in a two-fold character—as an individual liable like any other to *the accidents of mortality and its frailties; also as a corporation sole,[2] endowed with certain peculiar attributes, the recognition [*48]

[1] See further, on the subject of this chapter, Mr. Allen's Treatise on the Royal Prerogative, ed. 1849, and Mr. Chitty's Treatise on the Prerogative of the Crown, particularly chaps. i., ii., xv., xvi.; 1 Com. by Broom & Hadley, chap. vii.; Fortescue de Laud. Leg. Ang., by Amos, chap. ix.; Finch's Law 81; Plowd. Com., chap. xi.; Bracton, chap. viii.

[2] Mr. Allen, however, observes, at page 6 of his Treatise on the Royal Prerogative, that "there is something higher, more mysterious, and more remote from reality in the conception which the law of England forms of the king than enters into the notion of a corporation sole."

whereof leads to important consequences. Politically, the sovereign is regarded in this latter character, and is invested with various functions, which the individual, as such, could not discharge. "The person of the king," it has been said,[1] "is by law made up of two bodies: a natural body, subject to infancy, infirmity, sickness, and death; and a political body, perfect, powerful, and perpetual." These two bodies are inseparably united together, so that they may be distinguished, but cannot be divided. More often, however, the sovereign would seem to be regarded by our law in his political than in his individual and natural capacity, and the attributes of his former are blended with those of his latter character. As conservator of the public peace, the crown in any criminal proceeding represents the community at large, prosecutes for the offence committed against the public, and can alone exercise the prerogative of pardoning. As the fountain of justice, no court can have compulsory jurisdiction over the sovereign; an action for a personal wrong, [*49] therefore, will not lie against the king;[2] for which rule, *indeed, another more technical reason has been assigned—that the king cannot by his writ command himself to appear *coram judice*. As the dispenser of law and equity, the king is present in all his courts; whence it is that he cannot be nonsuit in an action, nor does he appear by attorney.[3]

The *Case of Prohibitions*[4] shows, however, that the king is not above the law, for he cannot in person assume to decide any case, civil or criminal, but must do so by his judges; the law being "the golden met-wand and measure to try the causes of the subjects, and which protected his majesty in safety and peace,"—the king being thus, in truth, *sub Deo et lege*. This case shows also that an action will not lie against the crown for a personal tort, for it is there laid down that "the king cannot arrest a man for suspicion of treason or felony, as others of his lieges may; the reason given being

[1] Bagshaw, Rights of the Crown of England, 29; Plowd. 212 a, 217 a, 238; Allen, Royal Pre. 26; Bac. Abr. Prerogative (E. 2).

[2] *Post.* As to proceedings by or against foreign potentates in our courts, see Wadsworth *v.* Queen of Spain, and De Haber *v.* Queen of Portugal, 17 Q. B. 171 (79 E. C. L. R.); Duke of Brunswick *v.* King of Hanover, 2 H. L. Cas. 1; Munden *v.* Duke of Brunswick, 10 Q. B. 656 (59 E. C. L. R.).

[3] 1 Com. by Broom & Hadley, 323; Finch's Law, by Pickering, 82.

[4] Prohibitions del Roy, 12 Rep. 63; Plowd. 241, 553.

that if a wrong be thus done to an individual, the party grieved cannot have remedy against the king. But although in these and other respects, presently to be noticed, the king is greatly favored by the law, being exempted from the operation of various rules applicable to the subject, he is on the whole, and essentially, beneath not superior to it, theoretically in some respects above, but practically bound and directed by its ordinances.[1]

---

*Rex nunquam moritur. [*50

(Branch, Max., 5th ed. 197.)

The king never dies.

The law ascribes to the king, in his political capacity, an absolute immortality; and, immediately upon the decease of the reigning prince in his natural capacity, the kingly dignity and the prerogatives and politic capacities of the supreme magistrate, by act of law, without any interregnum or interval, vest at once in his successor, who is, *eo instante*, king, to all intents and purposes; and this is in accordance with the maxim of our constitution, *In Angliâ non est interregnum.*[2]

"It is true," says Lord Lyndhurst,[3] "that *the king never dies*, the demise is immediately followed by the succession, there is no interval; the sovereign always exists, the person only is changed."

So tender, indeed, is the law of supposing even a possibility of the death of the sovereign, that his natural dissolution is generally called his demise—*demissio regis vel coronæ*—an expression which signifies merely a transfer of property; and when we speak of the demise of the crown, we mean only that, in consequence of the disunion of the king's natural body from his body politic,[4] the kingdom is transferred or demised to his successor; and so the royal dig-

[1] See the Debate in the House of Lords on Life Peerages, Hansard, vol. 140, pp. 263, &c. In Howard *v.* Gosset, 10 Q. B. 386 (59 E. C. L. R.), Coleridge, J., observes that "the law is supreme over the House of Commons *as over the crown itself;" et vide post*, p. 53.

[2] Jenk. Cent. 205. See Cooper's Account of Public Records, vol. 2, 323, 324. Allen, Royal Prerog. 44.

[3] Visc. Canterbury *v.* A. G., 1 Phill. 322.

[4] *Ante*, p. 48.

nity remains perpetual. It has, doubtless, usually been thought prudent, when the sovereign has been of tender years, at the period of the devolution upon him of the royal dignity, to appoint a protector, guardian, or regent, to discharge the functions of royalty for a limited time; but the very necessity of such extraordinary [*51] *provision is sufficient to demonstrate the truth of that maxim of the common law, that in the king is no minority,[1] for he has no legal guardian; and the appointment of a regency must, therefore, be regarded merely as a provision made by the legislature, in order to meet a special and temporary emergency.[2]

It seems that the Duchy of Cornwall vests in the king's eldest son and heir apparent at the instant of his birth, without gift or creation, and as if minority could no more be predicated of him than of the sovereign himself.[3]

The throne then goes by descent, not by succession, and if lands be given to the king and his "heirs," this word "heirs" will be held to include the "successors" to the crown, although on the demise of the sovereign, according to the course of descent recognized at the common law, the land might have gone in some other channel. Hence, if the king die without issue male, but leaving two daughters, lands held to him and his heirs will go to his eldest daughter as succeeding to the crown; whereas, in the case of a subject, lands whereof he was seised would pass to his daughters, in default of male issue, as coparceners.[4] Similarly, if real estate be given to the king and his heirs, and afterwards the reigning dynasty be changed, and another family be placed upon the throne, the land in question would go to the successor, and then descend in the new line.[5] And a grant of land to the king forever creates in him an estate [*52] of perpetual inheritance,[6] *whereas the like words would but give an estate for life to any of his subjects.

In regard also to personal property, the crown is differently circumstanced from an individual or from a corporation sole; for,

[1] Bac. Abr. Prerogative (A.).

[2] 1 Com. by Broom & Hadley, 295; 1 Plowd. 177, 234. And see the stat. 3 & 4 Vict. c. 52.

[3] Per Lord Brougham, C., Coop. R. 125.

[4] Grant on Corporations 627. See also the stat. 25 & 26 Vict. c. 37, relating to the private estates of the sovereign.

[5] Grant, Corp. 627.

[6] 2 Com. by Broom & Hadley, 216.

according to the ordinary rule, such property will not, in the case of a corporation sole, go to the successor—in the king's case, by our common law, it does so.[1] And it may be worthy of remark, that the maxim, "the king never dies," founded manifestly in notions of expediency, and in the apprehension of danger which would result from an interregnum, does not hold in regard to other corporations sole. A parson, for instance, albeit clothed with the same rights and reputed to be the same person as his predecessor, is not deemed by our law to be continuously in possession of his office, nor is it deemed essential to the preservation of his official privileges and immunities that one incumbent should, without any interval of time or interruption, follow another. Such a corporation sole may, during an interval of time, cease to be visibly *in esse*, whereas the king never dies,—his throne and office are never vacant.

Rex non potest peccare.

(2 Rolle, R. 304.)

The king can do no wrong.

It is an ancient and fundamental principle of the English constitution, that the king can do no wrong.[2] But this maxim must not be understood to mean that the king is above the laws, in the unconfined sense of those words, and that everything he does is of course just *and lawful. Its true meaning is, First, that the sovereign, individually and personally, and in his natural capacity, is independent of and is not amenable to any other earthly power or jurisdiction; and that whatever may be amiss in the condition of public affairs is not to be imputed to the king, so as to render him answerable for it personally to his people. Secondly, the above maxim means, that the prerogative of the crown extends not to do any injury, because, being created for the benefit of the people, it cannot be exerted to their prejudice, and it is therefore a fundamental general rule, that the king cannot sanction any act forbidden by law; so that, in this point of view, he is under, and not above, the laws, and is bound by them equally with his sub-

[*53]

[1] Grant, Corp. 626.

[2] Jenk. Cent. 9, 308.

jects.[1] If, then, the sovereign personally command an unlawful act to be done, the offence of the instrument is not thereby indemnified; for though the king is not himself under the coercive power of the law, yet in many cases his commands are under the directive power of the law, which makes the act itself invalid if unlawful, and so renders the instrument of execution thereof obnoxious to punishment.[2] As in affairs of state the ministers of the crown are held responsible for advice tendered to it, or even for measures which might possibly be known to emanate directly from the sovereign, so may the agents of the sovereign be civilly or criminally answerable for lawless acts done—if that may be imagined—by his command.

The king, moreover, is not only incapable of doing wrong, but even of thinking wrong. Whenever, therefore, it happens that, by misinformation or inadvertence, [*54] *the crown has been induced to invade the private rights of any of its subjects,—as by granting any franchise or privilege to a subject contrary to reason, or in any way prejudicial to the commonwealth or a private person,—the law will not suppose the king to have meant either an unwise or an injurious action, for *eadem mens præsumitur regis quæ est juris et quæ esse debet præsertim in dubiis*,[3] but declares that the king was deceived in his grant; and thereupon such grant becomes void upon the supposition of fraud and deception either by or upon those agents whom the crown has thought proper to employ.[4] In like manner, also, the king's grants are void whenever they tend to prejudice the course of public justice.[5] And, in brief, to use the words of a learned judge,[6] the crown cannot, in derogation of the right of the public, unduly limit and fetter the exercise of the prerogative which is vested in the crown for the public good. The crown cannot dispense with anything in which the subject has an interest,[7] nor make a grant in violation of the common law of the

[1] Chitt. Pre. Cr. 5; Jenk. Cent. 203. See Fortescue, de Laud. Leg. Ang. (by Amos) 28.

[2] 1 Hale, P. C. 43, 44, 127. Per Coleridge, J., Howard *v.* Gosset, 10 Q. B. 386 (59 E. C. L. R.).

[3] Hobart 154.

[4] Gledstanes *v.* The Earl of Sandwich, 5 Scott N. R. 719; R. *v.* Kempe, 1 Lord Raym. 49, cited Id. 720; Finch's Law 101; Vigers *v.* Dean, &c., of St. Paul's, 14 Q. B. 909 (68 E. C. L. R.).

[5] Chitt. Pre. Cr. 385. [6] See per Platt, B., 2 E. & B. 884 (75 E. C. L. R.).

[7] Thomas *v.* Waters, Hardr. 443, 448.

land,[1] or injurious to vested rights.[2] In this manner it is, that, while the sovereign himself is, in a personal sense, incapable of doing wrong, yet his acts may in themselves be contrary to law, and, on that account, be avoided or set aside by the law.

It must further be observed, that even where the king's grant purports to be made *de gratiâ speciali, certâ scientiâ, et mero motu*, the grant will, nevertheless, be *void, if it appears to the court that the king was deceived in the purpose and intent thereof; and this agrees with a text of the civil law, which says, that the above clause *non valet in his in quibus præsumitur principem esse ignorantem;* therefore, if the king grant such an estate as by law he could not grant, forasmuch as the king was deceived in the law, his grant will be void.[3] Thus the crown cannot by grant of lands and tenements create in them a new estate of inheritance, or give them a new descendible quality,[4] and the power of the crown is alike restricted as regards the grant of a peerage or honor.[5] [*55]

It does not seem, however, that the above doctrine can be extended to invalidate an act of the legislature, on the ground that it was obtained by a *suggestio falsi*, or *suppressio veri.* It would indeed be something new, as forcibly observed by Cresswell, J.,[6] to impeach an Act of Parliament by a plea stating that it was obtained by fraud.

In connection with this part of our subject, it is worthy of remark, that the power which the crown possesses of calling back its grants, when made under mistake, is not like any right possessed by individuals; for, when it has been deceived, the grant may be recalled notwithstanding any derivative title depending upon it, and those who have deceived it must bear the consequences.[7]

The doctrine just stated applies also in the case of a patent which has in some way improvidently emanated *from the crown. Thus, in Morgan *v.* Seward,[8] Parke, B., observed as follows: [*56]

[1] 2 Roll. Abr. 164.

[2] R. *v.* Butler, 3 Lev. 220; cited per Parke, B., 2 E. & B. 894 (75 E. C. L. R.).

[3] Case of Alton Woods, 1 Rep. 53.

[4] Per Lord Chelmsford, The Wiltes Peerage, L. R. 4 H. L. 152.

[5] The Wiltes Peerage, L. R. 4 H. L. 126.

[6] Stead *v.* Carey, 1 C. B. 516 (50 E. C. L. R.); per Tindal, C. J., Id. 522.

[7] Judgm., Cumming *v.* Forrester, 2 Jac. & W. 342.

[8] 2 M. & W. 544, cited arg. Nickels *v.* Ross, 8 C. B. 710 (65 E. C. L. R.); Beard *v.* Egerton, Id. 207; Croll *v.* Edge, 9 C. B. 486 (67 E. C. L. R.). See Reg. *v.* Betts, 15 Q. B. 540, 547 (69 E. C. L. R.).

"That a false suggestion of the grantee avoids an ordinary grant of lands or tenements from the crown, is a maxim of the common law, and such a grant is void, not against the crown merely, but in a suit against a third person.[1] It is on the same principle that a patent for two or more inventions, where one is not new, is void altogether, as was held in Hill *v.* Thompson,[2] and Brunton *v.* Hawkes;[3] for although the statute[4] invalidates a patent for want of novelty, and consequently by force of the statute the patent would be void, so far as related to that which was old; yet the principle on which the patent has been held to be void altogether is, that the consideration for the grant is the novelty of all, and the consideration failing, or, in other words, the crown being deceived in its grant,[5] the patent is void, and no action maintainable upon it."

The rule upon the subject now touched upon has been yet more fully laid down,[6] as follows:—"If the king has been deceived by any false suggestion as to what he grants or the consideration for his grant; if he appears to have been ignorant or misinformed as to his interest in the subject matter of his grant; if the language of [*57] his grant be so general, that you cannot in reason apply it to *all that might literally fall under it; or if it be couched in terms so uncertain that you cannot tell how to apply it with that precision which grants from one so especially representing the public interest ought in reason to have; or if the grant reasonably construed would work a wrong, or something contrary to law; in these and such like cases the grant will be either wholly void or restrained, according to circumstances; and equally so, whether the technical words, *ex certâ scientiâ et mero motu*, be used or not. But this is held upon the very same principle of construction on which a grant from a subject is construed, viz., the duty of effectuating the intention of the grantor." To hold the grants valid or unrestrained in the cases just put, would be, as is said, *in deceptione domini regis*, and not *secundum intentionem*.

[1] Citing Trevell *v.* Carteret, 3 Lev. 135; Alcock *v.* Cook, 5 Bing. 340 (15 E. C. L. R.).

[2] 8 Taunt. 375 (4 E. C. L. R.).

[3] 4 B. & Ald. 542 (6 E. C. L. R.).

[4] 21 Jac. 1, c. 3.

[5] "The crown is deceived if it grants a patent for an invention which is not new," per Pollock, C. B., Hills *v.* London Gas Light Co., 5 H. & N. 340.

[6] Reg. *v.* Eastern Archipelago Co., 1 E. & B. 310, 337, 338 (72 E. C. L. R.): s. c., 2 E. & B. 856 (75 E. C. L. R.); The Wiltes Peerage, L. R. 4 H. L. 126.

On the principle enunciated by the maxim under consideration, no suit or action can be brought for a personal wrong against the sovereign; as to any cause of complaint which a subject may happen to have against the sovereign in respect of some personal injury of a private nature, but distinct from a mere claim of property, the sovereign is not personally chargeable. The law will, in such a case, presume that subject cannot have sustained any such personal wrong from the crown, because it feels itself incapable of furnishing any adequate remedy,—and want of right and want of remedy are the same thing in law.[1]

In connection with the context the following case deserves attention. The personal estate of an intestate who leaves no next of kin belonged at common law absolutely *to the crown. It is [*58] now paid into the treasury, and forms part of the public revenue.[2] In The Attorney-General v. Köhler[3] a question arose,—could money which had erroneously been paid to the solicitor to the treasury, as nominee of one sovereign, in virtue of the above prerogative, be recovered from the solicitor to the treasury for the time being under a succeeding sovereign?—and in delivering his opinion adversely to the claimant, Lord Cranworth observed as follows:—"It is very difficult to say on what ground her majesty or her majesty's treasurer can be considered as under any obligation to refund, or rather pay the money. It never came to her majesty's hands. The crown is a corporation sole, and has perpetual continuance. Can a succeeding sovereign, upon the principle that 'the king never dies,'[4] be held responsible for money paid over in error to and spent by a predecessor, which that predecessor might lawfully have disposed of for his own use, supposing it to have rightfully come to his hands? Does the successor for such a purpose represent his predecessor? These are questions difficult of solution. Let me put a case between subjects, nearly analogous to the present, in which the sovereign is concerned. Suppose a bishop lord of a manor, and that on the death of the copyholder he claims a heriot, alleging such to be the custom of his manor; and suppose that the

[1] Chitt. Pre. Cr. 339, 340; Jenk. Cent. 78; Viscount Canterbury v. A. G., 1 Phill. 306; Buron v. Denman, 2 Exch. 167, 189; Feather v. Reg, 6 B. & S. 257 (118 E. C. L. R.); Doe d. Leigh v. Roe, 8 M. & W. 579; *ante*, p. 48.

[2] See stat. 15 & 16 Vict. c. 3. [3] 9 H. L. Cas. 654.

[4] *Ante*, p. 50.

heir of the copyholder, relying on the assurance of the bishop, that the heriot was due by the custom of the manor, accordingly pays to the bishop a sum of money by way of composition for the heriot; the bishop dies, and then it is discovered that no heriot was payable to the bishop in respect of the copyhold *held of him; but that it was in fact payable to the lord of an adjoining manor, who thereupon recovered it against the copyhold heir. It could not be pretended that the copyholder would have any right against the bishop's successor. His right would be against the executor of the bishop to whom the payment had been made, on an erroneous allegation by him that there was a custom in his manor entitling him to it. On the same principle, reasoning by analogy from the case as it would have stood between subject and subject, the right of the present respondents would be a right against the executors either of King George III. or King George IV., it is immaterial to consider which, certainly not against Queen Victoria."[1] Under circumstances such as were here disclosed no redress could be enforced against the crown or its officers, though perhaps the treasury might, with the aid of Parliament, if needful, discharge the claim put forward.

[*59]

With respect to injuries to the rights of property, these can scarcely be committed by the crown, except through the medium of its agents, and by misinformation or inadvertency, and the law has furnished the subject with a decent and respectful mode of terminating the invasion of his rights, by informing the king of the true state of the matter in dispute, viz., by Petition of Right;[2] a remedy which is open to the subject where his land, goods or money "have found their way into the possession *of the crown, and the purpose of the petition is to obtain restitution or, if restitution cannot be given, compensation in money; or where the claim arises out of a contract as for goods supplied to the crown or to the public service."[3]

[*60]

[1] 9 H. L. Cas. 671–2.

[2] The procedure in which has been amended by stat. 23 & 24 Vict. c. 34. See per Jervis, C. J., Eastern Archipelago Co. *v.* Reg., 2 E. & B. 914 (75 E. C. L. R.); De Bode *v.* Reg., 3 H. L. Cas. 449. As to the jurisdiction of a court of equity, and the rules by which it will be guided, when the proceedings are against the crown, see per Lord Brougham, C., Clayton *v.* A. G., Coop. R. 120.

[3] Feather *v.* Reg., 6 B. & S. 294 (118 E. C. L. R.), following Tobin *v.* Reg.,

If, for instance, a legacy is claimed under the will of a deceased sovereign, it seems that the only course to be pursued by the claimant, for the recovery of such legacy, is by Petition of Right to the grace and favor of the reigning sovereign. "Is there any reason," said Lord Langdale, in a modern case,[1] "why a Petition of Right might not have been presented? I am far from thinking that it is competent to the king, or rather to his responsible advisers, torefuse capriciously to put into a due course of investigation any proper question raised on a Petition of Right. The form of the application being, as it is said, to the grace and favor of the king, affords no foundation for any such suggestion."

In another remarkable case,[2] the petitioner by Petition of Right claimed compensation from the crown for damage alleged to have been done in the preceding reign to some property of the petitioner, while speaker of the House of Commons, by the fire which, in the year 1834, destroyed the two Houses of Parliament; and the question consequently arose, whether, assuming that the parties whose negligence caused the fire were the servants of the *crown (it being contended that they were the servants of the Commissioners of Woods and Forests), the sovereign was responsible for the consequences of their negligence. The argument, with reference to this point, turned chiefly upon the meaning of the legal maxim—that *the king can do no wrong;* and the Lord Chancellor, in deciding against the petitioner, intimated an opinion, that since the sovereign is clearly not liable for the consequences of his own personal negligence, he cannot be made answerable for the acts of his servants. "If it be said," continued Lord Lyndhurst, "that the master is answerable for the negligence of his servant, because it may be considered to have arisen from his own misconduct or negligence in selecting or retaining a careless servant, that principle cannot apply to the sovereign, to whom negligence or misconduct cannot be imputed, and for which, if they occur in fact, the law affords no remedy."

[*61]

16 C. B. N. S. 310 (111 E. C. L. R.); Churchward *v.* Reg., 6 B. & S. 807 (118 E. C. L. R.).

[1] Ryves *v.* Duke of Wellington, 9 Beav. 579, 600. In his Treatise on the Exchequer Practice (2d ed. p. 84), Mr. Serjeant Manning suggests that the prayer of the petition, although to the grace and favor of the king, seems to be within the words and spirit of Magna Charta—*nulli negabimus justitiam.*

[2] Viscount Canterbury *v.* A. G., 1 Phill. 306.

"The maxim that the king can do no wrong applies," it has been said, "to personal as well as to political wrongs; and not only to wrongs done personally by the sovereign, if such a thing can be supposed to be possible, but to injuries done by a subject by the authority of the sovereign. For from the maxim that the king cannot do wrong it follows, as a necessary consequence, that the king cannot authorize wrong. For to authorize a wrong to be done is to do a wrong, inasmuch as the wrongful act when done becomes in law the act of him who directed or authorized it to be done. It follows that a Petition of Right which complains of a tortious act done by the crown, or by a public servant by the authority of the crown, discloses no matter of complaint which can entitle the petitioner to redress. As in the eye of the law no such wrong can be done, so [*62] in law no right to redress can arise, *and the petition therefore which rests on such a foundation falls at once to the ground."[1] The authority of the crown would however afford no defence to an action brought for an illegal act committed by an officer of the crown.[2]

The ordinary maxim, *respondeat superior*,[3] has then no application to the crown, for the crown cannot, in contemplation of law, command a wrongful act to be done. It may be stated moreover, as a rule of the common law, that the crown cannot be prejudiced by the *laches* or acts of omission of any of its officers. Of which rule an apt illustration presents itself in Reg. *v.* Renton.[4] There a person had been taken into custody under a writ of extent, issued at suit of the crown, for certain penalties incurred by a violation of the excise laws; whilst in custody he was, by order of the Commissioners of Excise, and without a *habeas corpus ad testificandum* having first been obtained, removed from prison, with a view to his giving evidence touching matters connected with the writ of extent; and it was contended that this removal out of legal custody operated in law as an escape, so that the defendant's liability was in fact discharged. The Court of Exchequer held that the escape having been permitted by the *laches* of the Commissioners could not so operate as to prejudice the crown, for "the crown cannot be prejudiced by the misconduct or negligence of any of its officers, whether

[1] Judgm., Feather *v.* Reg., 6 B. & S. 395–6 (118 E. C. L. R.).

[2] Id., *post.*

[3] *Post*, Chap. IX.

[4] 2 Exch. 216.

with respect to the rights of property, or the right to the custody of the debtor, till the debt is paid."[1]

Further, if it be asked, what remedy is afforded to the *subject for such public oppressions, or acts of tyranny, as have [*63] not, in fact, been instigated by bad advisers, but have proceeded from the personal delinquency of the monarch himself,—the answer is, that there is no legal remedy, and that to such cases, so far as the ordinary course of law is concerned, the maxim must be applied that the sovereign can do no wrong.[2] And lastly, if a subject, when appearing as suitor in a court of justice, has aught to complain of, it is against the judge that his remedy (if any) must be taken—not against the crown: the court indeed, even at the behest of the king, can neither deny nor delay to do justice.[3]

NON POTEST REX GRATIAM FACERE CUM INJURIA ET DAMNO ALIORUM.

(3 Inst. 236.)

The king cannot confer a favor on one subject which occasions injury and loss to others.

It is an ancient and constant rule of law,[4] that the king's grants are invalid when they destroy or derogate from rights, privileges, or immunities previously vested in another subject: the crown, for example, cannot enable *a subject to erect a market or fair [*64] so near that of another person as to affect his interests

[1] Per Pollock, C. B., 2 Exch. 220. [2] Bla. Com., by Stewart, 256.

[3] The stat. 20 Ed. 3, c. 1, contains these remarkable words: "We have commanded all our justices that they shall from henceforth do equal law and execution of right to all our subjects, rich and poor, without having regard to any person, and without omitting to do right for any letters or commandment which may come to them *from us*, or from any other or by any other cause." Thus does our law, holding that the "king can do no wrong," in some cases incapacitate him from doing it by express and positive ordinances.

[4] 3 Inst. 236; Vaugh. R. 338. The maxim commented on *supra* was cited per Talfourd, J., in the Eastern Archipelago Co. *v.* Reg., 2 E. & B. 874 (75 E. C. L. R.). A similar doctrine prevailed in the civil law. See Cod. 7. 38. 2.

therein.[1] Nor can the king grant the same thing in possession to one, which he or his progenitors have granted to another.[2] If the king's grant reciting that A. holds the manor of Blackacre for life, grants it to B. for life; in this case the law implies that the second grant is to take effect after the determination of the first.[3] And if the king, being tenant for life of certain land, grant it to one and his heirs, the grant is void, for the king has taken upon himself to grant a greater estate than he lawfully could grant.[4]

On the same principle, the crown cannot *at common law*[5] pardon an offence against a penal statute after information brought, for thereby the informer has acquired a private property in his part of the penalty. Nor can the king pardon a private nuisance while it remains unredressed, or so as to prevent an abatement of it, though afterwards he may remit the fine; and the reason is that, though the prosecution is vested in the crown, to avoid multiplicity of suits, [*65] yet (during its continuance) this *offence savors more of the nature of a private injury to each individual in the neighborhood, than of a public wrong.[6] So, if the king grant lands, forfeited to him upon a conviction for treason, to a third person, he cannot afterwards, by his grant, devest the property so granted in favor of the original owner.

[1] Chitt. Pre. Cr. 119, 132, 386; Earl of Rutland's Case, 8 Rep. 57; Alcock *v.* Cooke, 5 Bing. 340 (15 E. C. L. R.); Gledstanes *v.* Earl of Sandwich, 5 Scott N. R. 689, 719. Re Islington Market Bill, 3 Cl. & F. 513. See Mayor of Exeter *v.* Warren, 5 Q. B. 773 (48 E. C. L. R.).

[2] Per Cresswell, J., 1 C. B. 523 (50 E. C. L. R.); arg. R. *v.* Amery, 2 T. R. 565; Chitt. Pre. Cr. 125. But the grant of a mere license or authority from the crown, or a grant during the king's will, is determined by the demise of the crown. (Id. 400.) See n. 1, *supra.*

[3] Earl of Rutland's Case, 8 Rep. 56 b.

[4] Case of Alton Woods, 1 Rep. 44 a.

[5] By stat. 22 Vict. c. 32, the crown is empowered "to remit, in whole or in part, any sum of money which, under any Act now in force, or hereafter to be passed, may be imposed as a penalty or forfeiture on a convicted offender, although such money may be, in whole or in part, payable to some party other than the crown."

[6] Vaugh. R. 333.

NULLUM TEMPUS OCCURRIT REGI.

(2 Inst. 273.)

Lapse of time does not bar the right of the crown.

In pursuance of the principle, already considered, of the sovereign's incapability of doing wrong, the law also determines that in the crown there can be no negligence or laches; and, therefore, it was formerly held, that no delay in resorting to his remedy would bar the king's right; for the time and attention of the sovereign must be supposed to be occupied by the cares of government, nor is there any reason that he should suffer by the negligence of his officers, or by their fraudulent collusion with the adverse party;[1] and although, as we shall hereafter see, the maxim *vigilantibus et non dormientibus jura subveniunt* is a rule for the subject, yet *nullum tempus occurrit regi* is, in general, the king's plea.[2] From this doctrine it followed, not only that the civil claims of the crown sustained no prejudice by lapse of time, but that criminal prosecutions for felonies or misdemeanors might be commenced at any distance of time from the commission of the offence; and this is, to some extent, still law, though it has been qualified by the *legislature in modern times; for by stat. 9 Geo. 3, c. 16, in suits relating to landed property, the lapse of sixty years and adverse possession for that period operate as a bar even against the prerogative, in derogation of the above maxim,[3] that is, provided the acts relied upon as showing adverse possession are acts of ownership done in the assertion of a right, and not mere acts of trespass not acquiesced in on the part of the crown.[4] Again, the Statute of Limitations, 21 Jac. 1, c. 16, s. 3, does not bind the king;[5] but, by 32 Geo. 3, c. 58, the crown is barred, in informa-

[*66]

[1] Godb. 295; Hobart 347; Bac. Abr., 7th ed., "*Prerogative*" (E. 6); *ante*, p. 62.

[2] Hobart 347.

[3] See Doe d. Watt *v.* Morris, 2 Scott 276; Goodtitle *v.* Baldwin, 11 East 488.

[4] Doe d. William IV. *v.* Roberts, 13 M. & W. 520. "The crown certainly may dedicate a road to the public, and be bound by long acquiescence in public user:" per Lord Denman, C. J., Reg. *v.* East Mark, 11 Q. B. 822-3 (63 E. C. L. R.).

[5] Judgm., Lambert *v.* Taylor, 4 B. & C. 151, 152 (10 E. C. L. R.); Bac. Abr., 7th ed., "*Prerogative*" (E. 5).

tions for usurping corporate offices or franchises, by the lapse of six years;[1] and by stat. 7 Will. 3, c. 3, an indictment for treason (except for an attempt to assassinate the king) must be found within three years after the commission of the act of treason.[2] And under the 11 & 12 Vict. c. 12,[3] a period of limitation is prescribed within which to prosecute for the offences mentioned in the Act.

An important instance of the application of the doctrine, *nullum tempus occurrit regi*, presents itself where church preferment lapses to the crown. Lapse is a species of forfeiture, whereby the right of presentation to a church accrues to the ordinary, by neglect of the patron to present,—to the metropolitan, by neglect of the ordinary,—[*67] *and to the crown, by neglect of the metropolitan: the term in which the title to present by lapse accrues from one of the above parties to the other is six calendar months, after the expiration of which period the right becomes forfeited by the person neglecting to exercise it. But no right of lapse can accrue when the original presentation is in the crown; and in pursuance of the above maxim, if the right of presentation lapses to the crown, prerogative intervenes, and, in this case, the patron shall never recover his right till the crown has presented; and if, during the delay of the crown, the patron himself presents, and his clerk is instituted, the crown, by presenting another, may turn out the patron's clerk, or, after induction, may remove him by *quare impedit;*[4] though if neither of these courses is adopted, and the patron's clerk dies incumbent, or is canonically deprived, the right of presentation is lost to the crown.[5]

Again, if a bill of exchange be seized under an extent before it has become due, the neglect of the officer of the crown to give notice of dishonor, or to make presentment of the bill, will not discharge the drawer or indorsers; and this likewise results from the

[1] See Bac. Abr., 7th ed., "*Prerogative*" (E. 6), 467, and stat. 7 Will. 4 & 1 Vict. c. 78, s. 23; R. *v.* Harris, 11 A. & E. 518 (39 E. C. L. R.).

[2] See also stat. 5 & 6 Vict. c. 51, s. 1.

[3] S. 4. See further, as to the period of limitation in criminal procedure, Arch. Cr. Pl., 16th ed. 68.

[4] 6 Rep. 50.

[5] 2 Com. by Broom & Hadley, 450, 452; cited arg. Storie *v.* Bishop of Winchester, 9 C. B. 90 (67 E. C. L. R.); and 17 C. B. 653 (84 E. C. L. R.); Baskerville's Case, 7 Rep. 111; Bac. Abr., 7th ed., "*Prerogative*" (E. 6); Hobart 166; Finch's Law 90.

general principle above stated, that laches cannot be imputed to the crown.[1]

To high constitutional questions involving the prerogative, the maxim under our notice must doubtless be applied with much caution, for it would be dangerous and *absurd to hold that a power [*68] which has once been exercised by the crown—no matter at how remote soever an epoch—has necessarily remained inherent in it, and we might vainly attempt to argue in support of so general a proposition. During the discussion in the House of Lords on life peerages, it was said that although the rights and powers of the crown do not suffer from lapse of time, nevertheless one of the main principles on which our constitution rests is the long-continued usage of Parliament, and that to go back for several centuries in order to select a few instances in which the crown has performed a particular act by virtue of its prerogative before the constitution was formed or brought into a regular shape—to rely on such precedents, and to make them the foundation of a change in the composition of either House of Parliament, would be grossly to violate the principles and spirit of our constitution.[2] But although the most zealous advocate of the prerogative could not by precedents, gathered only from remote ages, shape successfully a sound constitutional theory touching the powers and privileges of the crown, it would be far from correct to affirm that its rights can fall into desuetude, or, by mere non-user, become abrogated. *Ex. gr.*: Assuming that the right of veto upon a bill which has passed through Parliament has not been exercised for a century and a half, none could deny that such a right is still vested in the crown.[3]

---

*Quando Jus Domini Regis et Subditi Concurrunt, Jus Regis præferri debet. [*69]

(9 Rep. 129.)

Where the title of the king and the title of a subject concur, the king's title shall be preferred.[4]

In the above case, *detur digniori* is the rule,[5] and accordingly, if a chattel be devised to the king and another jointly, the king shall

[1] West on Extents 28, 30.

[2] Hansard, vol. 140, p. 263 *et seq.*

[3] 3 Id. p. 284.

[4] Co. Litt. 30, b.

[5] 2 Ventr. 268.

have it, there being this peculiar quality inherent in the prerogative that the king cannot have a joint property with any person in one entire chattel, or such a property as is not capable of division or separation; where the titles of the king and of a subject concur, the king shall have the whole. The peculiarity of this doctrine of our law, so favorable to the prerogative, may justify the giving a few illustrations of its operations:—1st. As regards chattels real: if the king either by grant or contract become joint tenant of such a chattel with another person, he will *ipso facto* become entitled to the whole in severalty. 2d. As regards chattels personal: if a horse be given to a king and a private person, the king shall have the sole property therein; if a bond be made to the king and a subject, the king shall have the whole penalty; if two persons possess a horse jointly, or have a joint debt owing them on bond, and one of them assigns his part to the king, the king shall have the horse or debt; for our law holds it not consistent with the dignity of the crown to be partner with a subject, and where the king's title and that of a subject concur or are in conflict, the king's title is to be preferred.[1] By applying this maxim to one [*70] possible state of facts, a rather curious *result is arrived at: if there be two joint tenants of a chattel, one of whom is guilty of felony, this felonious act works a forfeiture of one undivided moiety of the chattel in question to the crown, and the crown being thus in joint possession with a subject, takes the whole.[2]

Further, the king's debt shall, in suing out execution, be preferred to that of every other creditor who had not obtained judgment before the king commenced his suit.[3]

The king's judgment formerly affected all land which the king's debtor had at or after the time of contracting his debt;[4] but now no debts or liabilities to the crown incurred after November 1, 1865, affect land as to a *bonâ fide* purchaser for valuable consideration, or a mortgage, whether with or without notice, unless registration of the writ or process of execution has, previously to the conveyance or mortgage, been executed.[5]

[1] 2 Com. by Broom & Hadley 603, 604.

[2] See Hales *v.* Petit, Plowd. 253.

[3] Stat. 33 Hen. 8, c. 39, s. 74; see also 32 & 33 Vict. c. 46.

[4] 13 Eliz. c. 4.

[5] 28 & 29 Vict. c. 104, s. 4. See further as to former legislation on the above subject, Williams, Real Prop., 8th ed. 85–87.

Again, the rule of law is, that, where the sheriff seizes under a fi. fa., and, after seizure, but before sale,[1] under such writ, a writ of extent is sued out and delivered to the sheriff, the crown is entitled to the priority, and the sheriff must sell under the extent, and satisfy the crown's debt, before he sells under the fi. fa. Nor does it make any difference whether the extent is in chief or in aid, *i. e.*, whether it is directly against the king's debtor, or brought to recover a debt due from some third party to such debtor; it having been the practice in very ancient times, that, if the king's debtor was unable to satisfy the king's debt out of his own *chattels, the king would betake himself to any third person who [*71] was indebted to the king's debtor,[2] and would recover of such third person what he owed to the king's debtor, in order to get payment of the debt due from the latter to the crown.[3] And the same principle was held to apply where goods in the hands of the sheriff, under a fi. fa., and before sale, were seized by the officers of the customs under a warrant to levy a penalty incurred by the defendant for an offence against the revenue laws; the court observing, that there was no sound distinction between a warrant issued to recover a debt to the crown and an extent.[4]

In Reg. *v.* Edwards,[5] decided under the former bankrupt law, the facts were as under:—An official assignee having been appointed to a bankrupt's estate, later on the day of his appointment an extent issued at the suit of the crown against the bankrupt for a crown debt, and the question was which should have priority; the court decided that where the title of the crown and the subject accrue on the same day, the king's title shall be preferred. The seizure under the extent, therefore, was upheld, and the title of the official assignee was ignored. The decision in Reg. *v.* Edwards may however be supported on a principle other than that just stated, viz., that "whether between the crown and a subject, or between subject and subject, judicial proceedings are to be considered as having

[1] See R. *v.* Sloper, 6 Price 114.

[2] See R. *v.* Larking, 8 Price 683.

[3] Giles *v.* Grover, 9 Bing. 128, 191 (23 E. C. L. R.), recognizing R. *v.* Cotton, Parker R. 112. See A. G. *v.* Trueman, 11 M. & W. 694; A. G. *v.* Walmsley, 12 M. & W. 179; Reg. *v.* Austin, 10 M. & W. 693.

[4] Grove *v.* Aldridge, 9 Bing. 428 (23 E. C. L. R.).

[5] 9 Exch. 32, 628.

taken place at the earliest period of the day on which they are done."[1]

[*72] *In connection with the maxim before us we may add, that the king is not bound by a sale in market overt, but may seize to his own use a chattel which has passed into the hands of a *bonâ fide* purchaser for value.[2]

ROY N'EST LIE PER ASCUN STATUTE, SI IL NE SOIT EXPRESSEMENT NOSME.

(Jenk. Cent. 307.)

The king is not bound by any statute, if he be not expressly named to be so bound.[3]

The king is not bound by any statute, if he be not expressly named therein, unless there be equivalent words, or unless the prerogative be included by necessary implication; for it is inferred, *primâ facie*, that the law made by the crown, with the assent of the Lords and Commons, is made for subjects, and not for the crown.[4] Thus in considering the question, What is the occupation of real property which is liable to be rated under the stat. 43 Eliz. c. 2, s. 1? it has been observed[5] that "the only occupier of property exempt from the operation of the Act is the king, because he is not named in the statute, and the direct and immediate servants of the crown, whose occupation is the occupation of the crown itself, also come within the exemption. . . . . No exemption is thereby [*73] given to charity or to public purposes beyond *that which is strictly involved in the position that the crown is not bound by the Act." So the provisions in the C. L. Proc. Act, 1852, relating to the abolition of writs of error (ss. 148–158), have been held not

[1] Wright *v.* Mills, 4 H. & N. 491; Judgm. 9 Exch. 631. See Evans *v.* Jones, 3 H. & C. 423.

[2] 2 Inst. 713.

[3] Jenk. Cent. 307; Wing. Max. 1.

[4] Per Alderson, B., A. G. *v.* Donaldson, 10 M. & W. 123, 124, citing Willion *v.* Berkley, Plowd. 236; De Bode *v.* Reg., 13 Q. B. 373, 5, 8 (66 E. C. L. R.). Per Lord Cottenham, C., Ledsam *v.* Russell, 1 H. L. Cas. 697; Doe *v.* Archbishop of York, 14 Q. B. 81, 95 (68 E. C. L. R.).

[5] Per Lord Westbury, C., Mersey Docks *v.* Cameron, Jones *v.* Mersey Docks, 11 H. L. Cas. 501, 503; Reg. *v.* McCann, L. R. 3 Q. B. 141, 145, 146.

to apply to judgments of outlawry in civil suits, for as soon as judgment of outlawry has been given, the crown becomes interested.[1] So the prerogative of the crown to remove into the Court of Exchequer a cause which touches its revenue, is unaffected by the County Courts Act.[2] Nor does the Lands Clauses Consolidation Act (8 & 9 Vict. c. 18) affect the interests of the crown.[3] Neither is the prerogative of the crown to plead and demur without leave to a Petition of Right under 23 & 24 Vict. c. 34 affected by that statute.[4]

The rule above stated seems, however, to apply only where the property or peculiar privileges of the crown are affected; and this distinction is laid down, that where the king has any prerogative, estate, right, title, or interest, he shall not be barred of them by the general words of an Act, if he be not named therein.[5] Yet, if a statute be intended to give a remedy against a wrong, the king, though not named, shall be bound by it;[6] and the king is impliedly bound by statutes passed for the public good, the preservation of public rights, and the suppression of public wrongs, the relief and maintenance *of the poor, the general advancement of learning, religion, and justice, or for the prevention of fraud;[7] [*74] and, though not named, he is bound by the general words of statutes which tend to perform the will of the founder or donor;[8] and the king may likewise take the benefit of any particular Act, though he be not especially named therein.[9]

[1] Arding v. Holmer, 1 H. & N. 85. [2] Mountjoy v. Wood, 1 H. & N. 53.

[3] Re Cuckfield Burial Board, 19 Beav. 153. See also Reg. v. Beadle, 7 E. & B. 492 (90 E. C. L. R.).

[4] Tobin v. Reg., 14 C. B. N. S. 505 (108 E. C. L. R.); s. c., 16 Id. 310; Feather v. Reg., 6 B. & S. 293.

[5] Magdalen College Case, 11 Rep. 74 b, cited Bac. Abr. "*Prerogative*" (E. 5); Com. Dig. "*Parliament*" R. 8. See the qualifications of this proposition laid down in Dwarr. Stats., 2d ed., 523 *et seq.*

[6] Willion v. Berkley, Plowd. 239, 244. See the authorities cited arg. R. v. Wright, 1 A. & E. 436 *et seq.* (28 E. C. L. R.).

[7] Magdalen College Case, 11 Rep. 70 b, 72; Chit. Pre. Crown 382.

[8] Vin. Abr., "*Statutes*" (E. 10), pl. 11; 5 Rep. 146; Willion v. Berkley, Plowd. 236.

[9] Judgm., R. v. Wright, 1 A. & E. 447 (28 E. C. L. R.). In A. G. v. Radloff, 10 Exch. 94, Pollock, C. B., observes, that "the crown is not bound with reference to matters affecting its property or person, but is bound with respect to the practice in the administration of justice."

But, as above stated, Acts of Parliament which would divest the king of any of his prerogatives do not, in general, extend to or bind the king, unless there be express words to that effect: therefore, the Statutes of Limitation and Set-off are irrelevant in the case of the king, nor does the Statute of Frauds relate to him,[1] nor does a local Act imposing tolls and duties affect the crown.[2] Also, by mere indifferent statutes, directing that certain matters shall be performed as therein pointed out, the king is not, in many instances, prevented from adopting a different course in pursuance of his prerogative.[3]

In fine, the modern doctrine bearing on the subject before us is said[4] to be that by general words in an Act of Parliament, the king may be precluded of such inferior claims as might belong indifferently to him or to a [*75] *subject (as the title to an advowson or a landed estate), but not stripped of any part of his ancient prerogative, nor of those rights which are incommunicable and appropriate to him as essential to his regal capacity.

NEMO PATRIAM IN QUA NATUS EST EXUERE NEC LIGEANTIÆ DEBITUM EJURARE POSSIT.

(Co. Lit. 129 a.)

A man cannot abjure his native country nor the allegiance which he owes to his sovereign.

Of the above maxim we shall here very briefly state the significance at common law,—important modifications of its operation being projected by the legislature.

"The law of England, and of almost all civilized countries, ascribes to each individual at his birth two distinct legal states or conditions; one by virtue of which he becomes the subject of some

[1] Chit. Pre. Crown 366, 383; R. *v.* Copland, Hughes 204, 230; Vin. Abr. "*Statutes*" (E. 10).

[2] Mayor, &c., of Weymouth *v.* Nugent, 6 B. & S. 22, 35 (118 E. C. L. R.).

[3] Chit. Pre. Crown 383, 384.

[4] Dwarr. Stats., 2d ed., 523–4. See also Mayor, &c., of London *v.* A. G., 1 H. L. Cas. 440. As to the mode of construing grants from the crown, see the maxim "*Verba chartarum fortius accipiuntur contra proferentem*," *post*, Chap. VIII.

particular country, binding him by the tie of natural allegiance, and which may be called his political *status;* another by virtue of which he has ascribed to him the character of a citizen of some particular country, and, as such, is possessed of certain municipal rights, and subject to certain obligations, which latter character is the civil *status* or condition of the individual, and may be quite different from his political *status.* The political *status* may depend on different laws in different countries, whereas the civil *status* is governed universally by one single principle, namely, that of domicile, which is the criterion established by law for the purpose of determining civil *status;* for it is on this basis that the personal rights of the party, that is to say, the law which determines his majority or *minority, his marriage, succession, testacy, or intestacy, must depend."[1] [*76]

Allegiance is defined, by Sir E. Coke, to be "a true and faithful obedience of the subject due to his sovereign."[2] And in the words of the late Mr. Justice Story, "Allegiance is nothing more than the tie or duty of obedience of a subject to the sovereign under whose protection he is; and allegiance by birth is that which arises from being born within the dominions and under the protection of a particular sovereign. Two things usually occur to create citizenship: first, birth, locally within the dominions of the sovereign; secondly, birth, within the protection and obedience, or, in other words, within the legiance of the sovereign. That is, the party must be born within a place where the sovereign is, at the time, in full possession and exercise of his power, and the party must also, at his birth, derive protection from, and consequently owe obedience or allegiance to, the sovereign as such *de facto.* There are some exceptions, which are founded upon peculiar reasons, and which indeed illustrate and confirm the general doctrine."[3]

Allegiance is the tie which binds the subject to the crown, in

[1] Per Lord Westbury, Udny *v.* Udny, L. R. 1 Sc. App. 457. See Moorhouse *v.* Lord, 10 H. L. Cas. 272; Shaw *v.* Gould, L. R. 3 H. L. 55.

[2] Calvin's Case, 7 Rep. 5; s. c., Broom's Const. L. 4, and note thereto, Id. 26, *et seq.*, where the cases which concern allegiance at common law, and the operation of the statutes hitherto passed affecting it, are considered. And see the stat. 21 & 22 Vict. c. 93 (and as to Ireland the stat. 31 & 32 Vict. c. 20), which enables a person to establish, under the circumstances specified in and as provided by the Act, his right to be deemed a natural-born subject.

[3] 3 Peters (U. S.) R. 155.

return for that protection which the crown affords to the subject, and is distinguished by our customary law into two sorts or species, [*77] the one natural, *the other local. Natural allegiance is such as is due from all men born within the dominions of the crown, immediately upon their birth; and to this species of allegiance it is that the above maxim is applicable.[1] It cannot be forfeited, cancelled or altered by any change of time, place, or circumstance, nor by anything but the united concurrence of the legislature. The natural-born subject of one prince cannot, by any act of his own, not even by swearing allegiance to another, put off or discharge his natural allegiance to the former,[2] *origine propriâ neminem posse voluntate suâ eximi manifestum est;*[3] for this natural allegiance was intrinsic and primitive, and antecedent to the other, and cannot be divested without the concurrent act of that prince to whom it was first due.[4] Hence, although a British subject may, in certain cases, forfeit his rights as such by adhering to a foreign power, he yet remains at common law always liable to his duties; and if, in the course of such employment, he violates the laws of his native country, he will be exposed to punishment when he comes within reach of her tribunals.

The tie of natural allegiance may, however, be severed with the concurrence of the legislature—for instance, upon the recognition of the United States of America, as free, sovereign, and independent states, it was decided that the natural-born subjects of the English crown adhering to the United States ceased to be subjects of the crown of England, and became aliens and incapable of inheriting lands in England.[5]

[*78] *We shall merely add, that local allegiance is such as is due from an alien or stranger born whilst he continues

[1] Foster, Cr. Law 184.

[2] Vide per Jervis, C. J., Barrick *v.* Buba, 16 C. B. 493 (81 E. C. L. R.); citing Albretcht *v.* Sussman, 2 Ves. & B. 323.

[3] Cod. 10. 38. 4.

[4] See Foster, Cr. Law 184; Hale, P. C. 68; Judgm., Wilson *v.* Marryat, 8 T. R. 45; S. C., affirmed in error, 1 B. & P. 430.

[5] Doe d. Thomas *v.* Acklam, 2 B. & C. 779 (9 E. C. L. R.); Doe d. Stansbury *v.* Arkwright, 5 C. & P. 575 (24 E. C. L. R.). In Blight's Lessee *v.* Rochester, 7 Wheaton (U. S.) R. 535, it was held, that British subjects born before the Revolution are equally incapable with those born after of inheriting or transmitting the inheritance of lands in the United States.

within the dominion and protection of the crown; but it is merely of a temporary nature, and ceases the instant such stranger transfers himself from one kingdom to another. For, as the prince affords his protection to an alien only during his residence in this realm, the allegiance of an alien is confined, in point of time, to the duration of such his residence, and, in point of locality, the dominions of the British empire;[1] the rule being, that *protectio trahit subjectionem et subjectio protectionem*[2]—a maxim which extends not only to those who are born within the king's dominions, but also to foreigners who live within them, even though their sovereign is at war with this country, for they equally enjoy the protection of the crown.

Upon the maxims concerning allegiance and protection above noticed, innovations have been announced by the government as contemplated, which, when fully developed and carried out by international arrangements, will restrict within comparatively narrow limits their operation.

[1] Chit. Pre. Crown 16. See Wolff *v.* Oxholm, 6 M. & S. 92; R. *v.* Johnson, 6 East 583.

[2] Calvin's Case, 7 Rep. 5; Craw *v.* Ramsay, Vaughan, R. 279; Co. Litt. 65 a.

[*79] *CHAPTER III.

§ I.—The Judicial Office.

The maxims contained in this section exhibit briefly the more important of those duties which attach to persons filling judicial offices, and discharging the functions which appertain thereto. It would have been inconsistent with the plan and limits of this volume to treat of such duties at greater length, and would not, it is believed, have materially added to its utility.[1]

Boni Judicis est ampliare Jurisdictionem.

(Chanc. Prec. 329.)

It is the duty of a judge, when requisite, to amplify the limits of his jurisdiction.

This maxim, as above worded and literally rendered, might lead the student into error. Lord Mansfield once suggested that for the word *jurisdictionem*, *justitiam* should be substituted,[2] and in reference to it Sir R. Atkyns[3] remarked as follows:—"It is indeed commonly [*80] *said *boni judicis est ampliare jurisdictionem*. But I take that to be better advice which was given by the Lord Chancellor Bacon to Mr. Justice Hutton upon the swearing him one of the judges of the Court of Common Pleas,—that he would take care to contain the jurisdiction of the court within the ancient mere-stones without removing the mark."[4]

[1] As to the authority of, and necessity of adhering to, judicial decisions, see Ram's Treatise on the Science of Legal Judgment, chaps. iii., v., and xiv.

[2] "The true text is, *boni judicis est ampliare justitiam*, not *jurisdictionem*, as it has been often cited;" per Lord Mansfield, C. J., 1 Burr. 304.

[3] Arg. R. *v.* Williams, 13 St. Tr. 1430; Et vide per Cresswell, J., Dart *v.* Dart, 32 L. J. P. M. & A. 125.

[4] Bacon's Works, by Montague, vol. vii., p. 271. As on the one hand a judge cannot extend his jurisdiction, so on the other hand, "the superior courts at Westminster, and the judges, are not at liberty to decline a jurisdiction imposed upon them by Act of Parliament." Judgm., Furber *v.* Sturney, 3 H. & N. 531.

The true maxim of English law accordingly is "to amplify its remedies, and, *without usurping jurisdiction*, to apply its rules, to the advancement of substantial justice;"[1] the principle therefore upon which our courts of law act is to enforce the performance of contracts not injurious to society, and to administer justice to a party who can make that justice appear, by enlarging the legal remedy, if necessary, in order to attain the justice of the case; for the common law of the land is the birthright of the subject, and *bonus judex secundum æquum et bonum judicat, et æquitatem stricto juri præfert.*[2] "I commend the judge," observes Lord Hobart, "who seems fine and ingenious, so it tend to right and equity; and I condemn them who, either out of pleasure to show a subtle wit, will destroy, or out of incuriousness or negligence will not labor to support, the act of the party by the art or act of the law."[3]

[*81] *The action for money had and received may be mentioned as peculiarly illustrative of the principle above set forth; for the foundation of this action is, that the plaintiff is in conscience entitled to the money sought to be recovered; and it has been observed, that this kind of equitable action to recover back money which ought not in justice be kept is very beneficial, and, therefore, much encouraged. It lies only for money which, *ex æquo et bono*, the defendant ought to refund.[4] "The ground," observed Tindal, C. J., in Edwards *v.* Bates,[5] "upon which an action of this description is maintainable, is that the money received by the defendants is money which, *ex æquo et bono*, ought to be paid over to the plaintiff. Such is the principle upon which the action has

[1] Per Lord Abinger, C. B., Russell *v.* Smyth, 9 M. & W. 818; cited arg. Kelsall *v.* Marshall, 1 C. B. N. S. 255 (87 E. C. L. R.); see also per Lord Mansfield, C. J., 4 Burr. 2239.

[2] Per Buller, J., 4 T. R. 344. See Ashmole *v.* Wainwright, 2 Q. B. 837 (42 E. C. L. R.).

[3] Hobart 125. "I do exceedingly commend the judges that are curious and almost subtile * * to invent reasons and means to make acts according to the just intent of the parties, and to avoid wrong and injury which by rigid rules might be wrought out of the act." Per Lord Hobart, Id. 277. Cited per Turner, V. C., Squire *v.* Ford, 9 Hare 57.

[4] Per Lord Mansfield, C. J., Moses *v.* Macfarlane, 2 Burr. 1012; Litt *v.* Martindale, 18 C. B. 314 (86 E. C. L. R.); per Pollock, C. B., Aikin *v.* Short, 1 H. & N. 214; Holt *v.* Ely, 1 E. & B. 795 (72 E. C. L. R.); Somes *v.* British Empire Shipping Co., 8 H. L. Cas. 338.

[5] 8 Scott N. R. 414; s. c., 7 M. & Gr. 590 (49 E. C. L. R.).

rested from the time of Lord Mansfield. When money has been received without consideration, or upon a consideration that has failed, the recipient holds it *ex æquo et bono* for the plaintiff."[1]

The power of directing an amendment of the record, which a [*82] judge at Nisi Prius in certain cases possesses,[2] *may likewise be instanced as one which is confided to him by the legislature, in order that it may be applied "to the advancement of substantial justice."

The general maxim under consideration is also applicable with reference to the jurisdiction of a judge at chambers, and to the important and arduous duties which are there discharged by him.[3]

The proceeding by application to a judge at chambers has indeed been devised and adopted by the courts, under the sanction of the legislature, for the purpose of preventing the delay, expense and inconvenience which must ensue if applications to the courts were in all cases, and under all circumstances, indispensably necessary. A judge at chambers is usually described as acting under the delegated authority of the court, and his jurisdiction is different from that of a judge sitting at Nisi Prius; in the former case the judge has a wider field for the exercise of his discretion, and in some instances has a supreme jurisdiction, which is not subject to the review of the court in banc.[4]

In a modern case, where it was held that a judge at chambers has jurisdiction to fix the amount of costs to be paid as the condition of making an order, the maxim to which we have here directed attention was expressly applied. "As to the power of the judge to tax costs," remarked Vaughan, J., "if he is willing to do it, and

[1] See Martin *v.* Andrews, 7 E. & B. 1 (90 E. C. L. R.); Garton *v.* Bristol and Exeter R. C., 1 B. & S. 112 (101 E. C. L. R.); Baxendale *v.* Great Western R. C., 14 C. B. N. S. 1 (108 E. C. L. R.); s. c., affirmed 16 C. B. N. S. 137 (111 E. C. L. R.); Roberts *v.* Aulton, 2 H. & N. 432; Barnes *v.* Braithwaite, Id. 569.

[2] See 15 & 16 Vict. c. 76, s. 222; Blake *v.* Done, 7 H. & N. 465; Clay *v.* Oxford, L. R. 2 Ex. 54; Vanderbyl *v.* M'Kenna, L. R. 2 C. P. 252; Garrard *v.* Guibilei, 11 C. B. N. S. 616 (103 E. C. L. R.); 17 & 18 Vict. c. 125, s. 96; 3 & 4 Will. 4, c. 42, s. 23, in reference to which latter statute see per Rolfe, B., Cooke *v.* Stratford, 13 M. & W. 387.

[3] Much business at judges' chambers is now transacted by the Masters in pursuance of stat. 30 & 31 Vict. c. 68.

[4] Bagley, Ch. Pr. 1, 2, 4; Broom's Com., 4th ed., 55 *et seq.* Per Lord Ellenborough, C. J., Alner *v.* George, 1 Camp. 393.

can save expense, it is clear that what the officer of the court may do, the judge may do, and *boni judicis est ampliare jurisdictionem*, i. e. *justitiam*."[1]

*Again, in construing an Act of Parliament, it is a settled rule of construction, that cases out of the letter of a statute, yet within the same mischief or cause of the making thereof, shall be within the remedy thereby provided;[2] and, accordingly, it is laid down, that for the sure and true interpretation of all statutes (be they penal or beneficial, restrictive or enlarging of the common law), four things must be considered: 1st, what was the common law before the making of the Act; 2dly, what was the mischief for which the common law did not provide; 3dly, what remedy has been appointed by the legislature for such mischief; and 4thly, the true reason of the remedy: and then the duty of the judges is to put such a construction upon the statute, as shall suppress the mischief, and advance the remedy—to suppress subtle inventions and evasions for continuing the mischief *pro privato commodo*, and to add force and life to the cure and remedy, according to the true intent of the makers of the Act *pro bono publico*.[3] [*83]

In expounding remedial laws, then, the courts will extend the remedy so far as the words will admit.[4] Where, however, a case occurs which was not foreseen by the legislature, it is the duty of the judge to declare it *casus omissus;* or where the intention, if entertained, is not expressed, to say of the legislature, *quod voluit non dixit;* or where the case, though within the mischief, is *not clearly within the meaning, or where the words fall short of the intent, or go beyond it,—in every such case it is held the duty of the judge, in a land jealous of its liberties, to give effect to the expressed sense or words of the law in the order in which they are found in the Act, and according to their fair and [*84]

[1] Collins *v.* Aron, 4 Bing. N. C. 233, 235 (33 E. C. L. R.). See Clement *v.* Weaver, 4 Scott N. R. 229, and cases cited Id. 231, n. (44).

[2] Co. Litt. 24 b; Jenk. Cent. 58, 60, 226.

[3] Heydon's Case, 3 Rep. 7; cited A. G. *v.* Walker, 3 Exch. 258; Miller *v.* Salomons, 7 Exch. 522; per Parke, B., Id. 552; per Coleridge, J., In the matter of Gedge, 9 Jurist 470; Judgm., Jackson *v.* Burnham, 8 Exch. 179, 180; 11 Rep. 61 b.

See, generally, as to the interpretation of statutes, *post*, Chap. VIII.

[4] Per Lord Kenyon, C. J., Turtle *v.* Hartwell, 6 T. R. 429.

ordinary import and understanding;[1] for it must be remembered, that the judges are appointed to administer, not to make, the law, and that the jurisdiction with which they are entrusted has been defined and marked out by the common law or Acts of Parliament.[2] It is, moreover, a principle consonant to the spirit of our constitution, and which may be traced as pervading the whole body of our jurisprudence, that *optima est lex quæ minimum relinquit arbitrio judicis, optimus judex qui minimum sibi*[3]—that system of law is best which confides as little as possible to the discretion[4] of the judge—that judge the best who relies as little as possible on his own opinion.

Further, be it remembered, that "there is no court in England which is entrusted with the power of administering justice without restraint. That restraint has been imposed from the earliest times. And, although instances are constantly occurring where the courts [*85] might profitably *be employed in doing simple justice between the parties, unrestrained by precedent, or by any technical rule, the law has wisely considered it inconvenient to confer such power upon those whose duty it is to preside in courts of justice. The proceedings of all courts must take a defined course, and be administered according to a certain uniform system of law, which, in the general result, is more satisfactory than if a more arbitrary jurisdiction was given to them. Such restrictions have prevailed in all civilized countries; and it is, probably, more advantageous that it should be so, though at the expense of some occasional injustice. The only court in this country which is not so fettered is the supreme court of the legislature;"[5] for "certain it is," says Lord Coke, "that *Curia Parliamenti suis propriis legibus subsisit.*"[6]

[1] 2 Dwarr. Stats., 2d ed., 704. [2] R. *v.* Almon, Wilmot's Notes, 256.

[3] Bac. Aphorisms 46. See per Wilmot, C. J., Collins *v.* Blantern, 2 Wilson 341; per Buller, J., Master *v.* Miller, 4 T. R. 344, affirmed in error, 2 H. Bla. 141; Co. Litt. 24 b; per Tindal, C. J., 6 Scott N. R. 180; 5 H. L. Cas. 785, 958.

[4] *Discretio est discernere per legem quid sit justum*, 4 Inst. 41, cited per Tindal, C. J., 6 Q. B. 700 (51 E. C. L. R.). See Rooke's Case, 5 Rep. 99, 100; 1 W. Bla. 152; 1 Burr. 570; 3 Bulstr. 128. "Discretion, when applied to a court of justice, means *sound* discretion *guided by law*. It must be governed by rule, not by humor: it must not be arbitrary, vague, and fanciful, but legal and regular." Per Lord Mansfield, C. J., R. *v.* Wilkes, 2 Burr. 25, 39.

[5] Per Maule, J., Freeman *v.* Tranah, 12 C. B. 413, 414 (74 E. C. L. R.).

[6] 4 Inst. 50.

DE FIDE ET OFFICIO JUDICIS NON RECIPITUR QUÆSTIO, SED DE SCIENTIA SIVE SIT ERROR JURIS SIVE FACTI.

(Bac. Max., reg. 17.)

The bona fides and honesty of purpose of a judge cannot be questioned, but his decision may be impugned for error either of law or of fact.

The law, says Lord Bacon, has so much respect for the certainty of judgments, and the credit and authority of judges, that it will not permit any error to be assigned which impeaches them in their trust and office, and in willful abuse of the same, but only in ignorance and mistaking either of the law or of the case and matter in fact;[1] *and, therefore, it cannot be assigned for error, that a judge did that which he ought not to do, as that he entered a verdict for the defendant where the jury gave it for the plaintiff.[2] [*86] It is, moreover, a general rule of great antiquity, that no action will lie against a judge of record for any act done by him in the exercise of his judicial functions, provided such act, though done mistakenly, were within the scope of his jurisdiction.[3] "The rule that a judicial officer cannot be sued for an adjudication according to the best of his judgment upon a matter within his jurisdiction, and also the rule that a matter of fact so adjudicated by him cannot be put in issue in an action against him, have been uniformly maintained."[4]

"The doctrine," says Mr. Chancellor Kent,[5] "which holds a judge exempt from a civil suit or indictment for any act done or omitted to be done by him sitting as judge, has a deep root in the common law. It is to be found in the earliest judicial records, and it has

[1] Bac. Max., reg. 17; Bushell's Case, Vaugh. R. 138, 139; 12 Rep. 25.

[2] Bac. Max., reg. 17; per Holt, C. J., Groenvelt *v.* Burwell, 1 Lord Raym. 468; s. c., 1 Salk. 397; 12 Rep. 24, 25.

[3] Smith *v.* Boucher, Cas. Temp. Hardw. 69; Calder *v.* Halket, 3 Moo., P. C. C. 28, with which compare Gahan *v.* Lafitte, 8 Moo. P. C. C. 382; Scott *v.* Stansfeld, L. R. 3 C. P. 220; Taaffe *v.* Downes, Id. 36 n. (a); Houlden *v.* Smith, 14 Q. B. 841 (68 E. C. L. R.); Judgm., Mostyn *v.* Fabrigas, Cowp. 161; Phillips *v.* Eyre, L. R. 4 Q. B. 225, 229 (45 E. C. L. R.); Pease *v.* Chaytor, 1 B. & S. 658 (101 E. C. L. R.); Hamilton *v.* Anderson, Macq. Sc. App. Cas. 363.

[4] Judgm., Kemp *v.* Neville, 10 C. B. N. S. 549 (100 E. C. L. R.); s. c., Broom's Const. L. 734, and note thereto, Id. 762 *et seq.*, where the cases are collected; per Erle, C. J., Wildes *v.* Russell, L. R. 1 C. P. 730.

[5] Yates *v.* Lansing, 5 Johnson (U. S.) R. 291; s. c. (in error), 9 Id. 396.

been steadily maintained by an undisturbed current of decisions in the English courts, amidst every change of policy, and through [*87] every revolution of their government. A *short view of the cases will teach us to admire the wisdom of our forefathers, and to revere a principle on which rests the independence of the administration of justice."

This freedom from action and question at the suit of an individual, it has likewise been observed, is given by our law to the judges, not so much for their own sake as for the sake of the public, and for the advancement of justice, that, being free from actions, they may be free in thought and independent in judgment, as all who are to administer justice ought to be; and it is not to be supposed beforehand, that those who are selected for the administration of justice will make an ill use of the authority vested in them. Even inferior justices cannot be called in question for an error in judgment, so long as they act within the bounds of their jurisdiction. In the imperfection of human nature, it is better that an individual should occasionally suffer a wrong, than that the general course of justice should be impeded and fettered by constant and perpetual restraints and apprehensions on the part of those who are to administer it. Corruption is quite another matter; so also are neglect of duty and misconduct. For these there is, and always will be, some due course of punishment by public prosecution.[1]

[*88] An action, then, does not lie against a judge, civil[2] *or ecclesiastical,[3] acting judicially in a matter within the scope of his jurisdiction.[4] Nor can a suit be maintained against persons

[1] Judgm., Garnett *v.* Ferrand, 6 B. & C. 625, 626 (13 E. C. L. R.); Thomas *v.* Churton, 2 B. & S. 475 (110 E. C. L. R.); Vaugh. R. 383. See R. *v.* Johnson, 6 East 583, s. c., 7 East 65, in which case one of the judges of the Court of Common Pleas in Ireland was convicted of a libel. As to the principles which guide the Court of Queen's Bench in interfering by criminal information in the case of justice, see Reg. *v.* Badger, 4 Q. B. 468, 474 (45 E. C. L. R.). The judges are not liable to removal, except upon address of both houses of Parliament; see stats. 13 Will. 3, c. 2, and 1 Geo. 3, c. 23.

[2] Dicas *v.* Lord Brougham, 6 C. & P. 249 (25 E. C. L. R.); Kemp *v.* Neville, 10 C. B. N. S. 523 (100 E. C. L. R.) (where the action was brought against the Vice-Chancellor of the University of Cambridge); Tinsley *v.* Nassau, Mo. & Mal. 52 (22 E. C. L. R.); Johnstone *v.* Sutton, 1 T. R. 513; per Holt, C. J., 1 Lord Raym. 468; Garnett *v.* Ferrand, 6 B. & C. 611 (14 E. C. L. R.).

[3] Ackerley *v.* Parkinson, 3 M. & S. 411, 425; Beaurain *v.* Scott, 3 Camp. 388.

[4] Ib. See Wingate *v.* Waite, 6 M. & W. 739, 746; Hamilton *v.* Anderson, 3 Macq. Sc. App. Cas. 363.

so acting with a more limited authority, as the steward of a court baron,[1] or commissioners of a court of request;[2] and, as already intimated, magistrates, acting in discharge of their duty, and within the bounds of their jurisdiction, are irresponsible even where the circumstances under which they are called upon to act would not have supported the complaint, provided that such circumstances were not disclosed to them at the time of their adjudication.[3]

"If," as judicially remarked, "a magistrate commit a party charged before him in a case where he has no jurisdiction, he is liable to an action of trespass.[4] But if the charge be of an offence over which, if the offence charged be true in fact, the magistrate has jurisdiction, the magistrate's jurisdiction cannot be made to depend upon the truth or falsehood of the facts, or upon the evidence being sufficient or insufficient to establish the *corpus delicti* brought under investigation."[5]

*And where the authority is given to justices by statute, [*89] and they appear to have acted within the jurisdiction so given, and to have done all that the particular statute requires them to do, in order to originate their jurisdiction, their conviction, drawn up in due form, and remaining in force, is a protection and conclusive evidence for them in any action which may be brought against them for the act so done.[6] That is to say, "in an action

[1] Holroyd *v.* Breare, 2 B. & Ald. 473. See Judgm., Bradley *v.* Carr, 3 Scott N. R. 521, 528.

[2] Carratt *v.* Morley, 1 Q. B. 18 (41 E. C. L. R.); Andrews *v.* Marris, Id. 3, and cases there cited. See Morris *v.* Parkinson, 1 Cr., M. & R. 163.

[3] Pike *v.* Carter, 3 Bing. 78 (11 E. C. L. R.); Lowther *v.* Earl of Radnor, 8 East 113; Brown *v.* Copley, 8 Scott N. R. 350; Pitcher *v.* King, 9 A. & E. 288 (36 E. C. L. R.); 2 Roll. Abr. 552, pl. 10.

[4] See, for instance, Newbould *v.* Coltman, 6 Exch. 189; Pedley *v.* Davis, 10 C. B. N. S. 492 (100 E. C. L. R.).

[5] Per Tindal, C. J., Cave *v.* Mountain, 1 M. & Gr. 257, 261 (39 E. C. L. R.); recognized Reg. *v.* Bolton, 1 Q. B. 66, 75 (41 E. C. L. R.); Reg. *v.* Grant, 14 Q. B. 43 (68 E. C. L. R.). See Reg. *v.* Inhabs. of Hickling, 7 Q. B. 880 (53 E. C. L. R.); following Brittain *v.* Kinnaird, 1 B. & B. 432; Ayrton *v.* Abbott, 14 Q. B. 1, 23 (68 E. C. L. R.).

[6] Per Abbott, C. J., Basten *v.* Carew, 5 B. & C. 652, 653; s. c., 5 D. & R. 558 (16 E. C. L. R.); Baylis *v.* Strickland, 1 Scott N. R. 540; Fernley *v.* Worthington, 1 Scott N. R. 432; Painter *v.* Liverpool Gas Co., 3 A. & E. 433 (30 E. C. L. R.); Webb *v.* Bachelour, Ventr. 273; Tarry *v.* Newman, 15 M. & W. 645; Stamp *v.* Sweetland, 8 Q. B. 13 (55 E. C. L. R.). See also Hazeldine *v.* Grove, 3 Q. B. 997, 1006 (43 E. C. L. R.).

brought against a magistrate, a subsisting conviction—good upon the face of it, in a case to which his jurisdiction extends, being produced at the trial, is a bar to the action, provided that the conviction was not made maliciously and without reasonable and probable cause, and provided also that the execution has been regular, although the magistrate may have formed an erroneous judgment upon the facts; for that is properly the subject of appeal."[1] Ample protection, it will be remembered, is, by a recent enactment, the provisions of which cannot here be set out, extended to justices of the peace.[2]

Having thus briefly stated the general rule applicable with respect to the right of action against persons invested with judicial functions, we may remark that there is one very extensive class of cases [*90] which may, on *a cursory observation, appear to fall within its operation, but which is, in fact, governed by a different although not less important principle. We refer to cases in which the performance of some public duty is imposed by law upon an individual who, by neglecting or refusing to perform it, causes an injury to some other party; here, as a general rule, the injury occasioned by the breach of duty, without proof of *mala fides*, lays the foundation of an action for recovery of damages, by way of compensation to the party injured.[3] This principle, moreover, applies where persons required to perform ministerial acts are at the same time invested with the judicial character; and, in accordance therewith, in the celebrated Auchterarder Case,[4] the members of the presbytery were held liable, collectively and individually, to make compensation in damages, for refusing to take the presentee to a church on trial, as they were bound to do, according to the law of Scotland. The legislature, observed Lord Brougham in the case referred to, can, of course, do no wrong, and its branches are

[1] Paley, Conv., 4th ed., 388.

[2] 11 & 12 Vict. c. 44, as to which see Paley, Conv., 4th ed., 399 *et seq.*; Sommerville *v.* Mirehouse, 1 B. & S. 652 (101 E. C. L. R.); Pease *v.* Chaytor, Id. 658; Pedley *v.* Davis, 10 C. B. N. S. 492 (100 E. C. L. R.); Gelen *v.* Hall, 2 H. & N. 379.

[3] See Barry *v.* Arnaud, 10 A. & E. 646 (37 E. C. L. R.); cited Mayor of Lichfield *v.* Simpson, 8 Q. B. 65 (55 E. C. L. R.). Per Lord Brougham, M'Kenna *v.* Pape, 1 H. L. Cas. 7; Steel *v.* Shomberg, 4 E. & B. 620 (82 E. C. L. R.); Scott *v.* Mayor of Manchester, 2 H. & N. 204.

[4] Ferguson *v.* Earl of Kinnoul, 9 Cl. & Fin. 251.

equally placed beyond all control of the law. So, "the courts of justice, that is the superior courts, courts of general jurisdiction, are not answerable, either as bodies or by their individual members, for acts done within the limits of their jurisdiction. Even inferior courts, provided the law has clothed them with judicial functions, are not answerable for errors in judgment; and where they may not act as judges, but only have a discretion confided to them, an erroneous exercise of that *discretion, however plain the miscarriage may be, and however injurious its consequences, they shall not answer for. This follows from the very nature of the thing. It is implied in the nature of judicial authority, and in the nature of discretion where there is no such judicial authority. But where the law neither confers judicial power nor any discretion at all, but requires certain things to be done, every body, whatever be its name, and whatever other functions of a judicial or of a discretionary nature it may have, is bound to obey; and, with the exception of the legislature and its branches, every body is liable for the consequences of disobedience; that is, its members are liable, through whose failure or contumacy the disobedience has arisen, and the consequent injury to the party interested in the duty being performed."[1] [*91]

But although the honesty and integrity of a judge acting in his judicial capacity cannot be questioned,[2] abundant means are afforded for obtaining redress, if any error be committed by him, arising either from ignorance of law or from a misconception of his judicial duties. If such an error be committed by him whilst sitting at Nisi Prius, the court in banc will, on motion,[3] interfere to rectify it, either by granting a new trial, by directing a nonsuit, or that the verdict be entered *non obstante veredicto*, or by arresting the judgment, if the cause of action be defectively set forth on the record. Where the alleged error consists in a misdirection by the *judge, a bill of exceptions may be tendered to his directions.[4] [*92]

[1] Per Lord Brougham, 9 Cl. & Fin. 289, 290, whose judgment has throughout an especial reference to the subject of judicial liability.

[2] As to libellous strictures upon the conduct of public functionaries, see Gathercole *v.* Mial, 15 M. & W. 319, 332, 338.

[3] As to the right of appeal where the rule is refused or discharged, see C. L. Proc. Act, 1854, sects. 34–42.

[4] See Roe d. Lord Trimlestown *v.* Kemmis, 9 Cl. & Fin. 749; C. L. Proc. Act, 1852, s. 157.

With respect to the mode of proceeding in a civil case where error in law or in fact[1] has occurred, reference should more particularly be made to those portions of the Common Law Procedure Act, 1852, below specified.[2]

Where error has occurred in a criminal proceeding, it is set right by the Court for the consideration of Crown Cases Reserved, or by writ of error, which may be brought when the Attorney-General's fiat has been obtained for it.[3]

With respect to an award, which, when made in pursuance of a submission to arbitration in the usual manner, is equivalent to a judicial decision upon the points at issue between the parties, the general rule is, that, if an arbitrator makes a mistake, which is not apparent on the face of his award, the party injured has no redress, nor will the court review the arbitrator's decision as to the facts, or allow the merits of the case to be gone into. If no corruption be shown, the court will decline to interfere.[4]

[*93] *QUI JUSSU JUDICIS ALIQUOD FECERIT NON VIDETUR DOLO MALO FECISSE, QUIA PARERE NECESSE EST.

(10 Rep. 76.)

Where a person does an act by command of one exercising judicial authority, the law will not suppose that he acted from any wrongful or improper motive, because it was his bounden duty to obey.[5]

Where a court has jurisdiction of the cause, and proceeds *inverso ordine*, or erroneously, then the party who sues, or the officer or

[1] Error does not lie to the Exchequer Chamber or House of Lords on a judgment pronounced upon allegations of error in fact merely: Irwin *v.* Grey, L. R. 2 H. L. 20; s. c., L. R. 1 C. P. 171.

[2] Sect. 146 *et seq.*

[3] Ex parte Newton, 4 E. & B. 869 (82 E. C. L. R.); Re Newton, 16 C. B. 97 (81 E. C. L. R.); Reg. *v.* Stokes, 1 Dem. C. C. 307. See further as to this, *post*, p. 110, n. 3.

[4] See per Pollock, C. B., Hagger *v.* Baker, 14 M. & W. 10. See Re Hopper, L. R. 2 Q. B. 367; Phillips *v.* Evans, 12 M. & W. 309; Fuller *v.* Fenwick, 3 C. B. 704 (54 E. C. L. R.); Hutchinson *v.* Shepperton, 13 Q. B. 955 (66 E. C. L. R.); Russell, Arbitr., 3d ed., 656.

[5] This maxim is derived from the Roman law, see D. 50. 17. 167, § 1.

minister of the court who executes according to its tenor[1] the precept or process of the court, will not be liable to an action.[2] But when the court has not jurisdiction of the cause, then the whole proceeding is *coram non judice*,[3] and actions will lie against the above-mentioned parties without any regard to the precept or process; and in this case it is not necessary to obey one who is not judge of the cause, any more than it is to obey a mere stranger, for the rule is, *judicium à non suo judice datum nullius est momenti.*[4]

Accordingly, in Gosset *v.* Howard,[5] it was held that *the [*94] warrant of the speaker of the House of Commons, having issued in a matter over which the House had jurisdiction, was to be construed on the same principle as a mandate or writ issuing out of a superior court acting according to the course of common law, and that it afforded a valid defence to an action for assault and false imprisonment brought against the serjeant-at-arms, who acted in obedience to such warrant.

In the last-mentioned case it is observable that the matter in respect of which the warrant issued was admitted to be within the jurisdiction of the House, and it is peculiarly necessary to notice this, because, in the previous case of Stockdale *v.* Hansard,[6] it was held to be no defence in law to an action for publishing a libel, that the defamatory matter was part of a document which was, by order of the House of Commons, laid before the House, and thereupon became part of the proceedings of the House, and which was after-

[1] See Munday *v.* Stubbs, 10 C. B. 432 (70 E. C. L. R.).

[2] See Prentice *v.* Harrison, 4 Q. B. 852 (45 E. C. L. R.); Brown *v.* Jones, 15 M. & W. 191; Judgm., Ex parte Story, 8 Exch. 201.

[3] See Tinniswood *v.* Pattison, 3 C. B. 243 (54 E. C. L. R.); *Factum a judice quod ad officium ejus non pertinet ratum non est:* D. 50. 17. 170.

[4] Marshalsea Case, 10 Rep. 70; Taylor *v.* Clemson, 2 Q. B. 1014, 1015 (42 E. C. L. R.); s. c., 11 Cl. & F. 610; cited Ostler *v.* Cooke, 13 Q. B. 143, 162 (66 E. C. L. R.); Morrell *v.* Martin, 4 Scott N. R. 313, 314; Jones *v.* Chapman, 14 M. & W. 124; Baylis *v.* Strickland, 1 Scott N. R. 540; Marshall *v.* Lamb, 5 Q. B. 115 (48 E. C. L. R.); Watson *v.* Bodell, 14 M. & W. 57; Thomas *v.* Hudson, Id. 353; Van Sandau *v.* Turner, 6 Q. B. 773 (51 E. C. L. R.); Lloyd *v.* Harrison, 6 B. & S. 36 (118 E. C. L. R.).

[5] 10 Q. B. 411 (59 E. C. L. R.), reversing the judgment in the court below. See Ex parte Fernandez, 10 C. B. N. S. 3 (100 E. C. L. R.); s. c., 6 H. & N. 717.

[6] 9 A. & E. 1 (36 E. C. L. R.); s. c., Broom's Const. L. 870, and note thereto, Id. 966, *et seq.*

wards, by order of the House, printed and published by the defendant. The decision in this case resulted from the opinion entertained by the court being adverse to the existence of the privilege under which the defendant sought to justify the alleged wrongful act, and, in consequence of this decision, the stat. 3 & 4 Vict. c. 9 was passed, which enacts, that all proceedings, whether by action or criminal prosecution, similar to the above, shall be stayed by bringing before the court or judge a certificate, under the hand of the Chancellor or of the speaker of the House of Commons, to the effect, that the publication in question is by order of either House [*95] of *Parliament, together with an affidavit verifying such certificate.[1]

A reference to Andrews v. Marris[2] may serve further to illustrate the above general and important doctrine:—The commissioners of a court of request ordered a debt claimed by the plaintiff to be paid by certain installments, "or execution to issue." The clerk of the court, on default of payment, and on application made to him by the plaintiff, issued a precept for execution without the further intervention of the court. It was held that the commissioners were required, when acting on such default, to execute judicial powers, which could not be delegated; and, therefore, that the clerk who made such precept was liable in trespass for its execution, though the proceeding was conformable to the practice of the court, inasmuch as the court could not institute such a practice; but it was further held that the serjeant who executed the precept, and who was the ministerial officer[3] of the commissioners bound to execute

[1] Entick v. Carrington, 19 Howell St. Tr. 1030, is the leading case in regard to the power of arresting the person, and seizing papers, under a Secretary of State's warrant. See Leach v. Money, Wilkes v. Wood, and Entick v. Carrington, Broom's Const. L. 525, 548, 558, and note thereto, Id. 613, *et seq.*; Foster v. Dodd, L. R. 3 Q. B. 67.

[2] Andrews v. Marris, 1 Q. B. 3, 16, 17 (41 E. C. L. R.), recognized in Carratt v. Morley, Id. 29; and distinguished in Dews v. Riley, 11 C. B. 434, 444 (73 E. C. L. R.); Levy v. Moylan, 10 C. B. 189 (70 E. C. L. R.). As to the liability of the party at whose suit execution issued, or of his attorney, see Carratt v. Morley, *supra;* Coomer v. Latham, 16 M. & W. 713; Ewart v. Jones, 14 M. & W. 774; Green v. Elgie, 5 Q. B. 99 (48 E. C. L. R.); Kinning v. Buchanan, 8 C. B. 271 (65 E. C. L. R.); Abley v. Dale, 11 C. B. 378, 379 (73 E. C. L. R.); *post*, p. 124, n. 4.

[3] As regards the liability of ministerial officers, an important distinction to be observed is between cases in which there has been an adjudication and

their warrants, having no means whatever of ascertaining whether they issued upon valid judgments, or were otherwise *sustainable or not, was well defended by it, because the subject-matter of the suit was within the general jurisdiction of the commissioners, and the warrant appeared to have been regularly issued. The court observed that his situation was exactly analogous to that of the sheriff in respect of process from a superior court; and that it is the well-known distinction between the cases of the party and of the sheriff or his officer, that the former, to justify his taking body or goods under process, must show the judgment in pleading as well as the writ, but for the latter it is enough to show the writ only.[1] [*96]

The case of a justification at common law by a constable under the warrant of a justice of the peace offers another illustration of the rule now under consideration; for if the warrant issued by the justice of the peace, in the shape in which it is given to the officer, is such that the party may lawfully resist it,[2] or, if taken on it, will be released on habeas corpus, it is a warrant which, in that shape, the magistrate had no jurisdiction to issue, which, therefore, the officer need not have obeyed, and which, at common law, on the principle above laid down, will not protect him against an action at suit of the party injured.[3] Where the cause is expressed but imperfectly, the officer may not be expected to judge as to the sufficiency of the statement; and, therefore, if the subject-matter be within the jurisdiction of the magistrate, he may be bound to execute it, and, as a consequence, be entitled to protection; *but where no cause is expressed, there is no question as to the want of jurisdiction.[4] [*97]

"A rule," observes Lord Denman, C. J., delivering judgment in Reg. *v.* Inhabitants of Stainforth,[5] "has been often recognized in respect of proceedings by magistrates requiring all the facts to be

those in which there has been an order only, see Foster *v.* Dodd, L. R. 3 Q. B. 67, 76.

[1] See Cotes *v.* Michill, 3 Lev. 20; Moravia *v.* Sloper, Willes 30, 34.

[2] Reg. *v.* Tooley, 2 Lord Raym. 1296, 1302.

[3] As to the legality of an arrest under a warrant which is not in possession of the constable, see Galliard, app., Laxton, resp., 2 B. & S. 363 (110 E. C. L. R.).

[4] Per Coleridge, J., 10 Q. B. 390 (59 E. C. L. R.). See in illustration of the remarks, *supra*, Clark *v.* Woods, 2 Exch. 395, and cases there cited.

[5] 11 Q. B. 75 (63 E. C. L. R.). See also Reg. *v.* Inhabs. of Totness, Id. 80.

stated which are necessary to show that a tribunal has been lawfully constituted, and has jurisdiction. There is good reason for the rule where a special authority is exercised which is out of the ordinary course of common law, and is confined to a limited locality, as in case either of warrants or arrest, commitment, or distress, or of convictions, or orders by local magistrates where the duty of promptly enforcing the instrument is cast on officers of the law, and the duty of unhesitating submission on those who are to obey. It is requisite that the instrument so to be enforced and obeyed should show on inspection all of the essentials from which such duties arise."

A plea of justification by a constable acting under the warrant of a justice will accordingly by the common law be bad if it does not show that the justice had jurisdiction over the subject-matter upon which the warrant is granted.

By stat. 24 Geo. 2, c. 44, s. 6, it is enacted, that no action shall be brought against any constable, head-borough, or other officer, or against any person or persons acting by his order or in his aid, for any thing done in obedience to any warrant under the hand or seal of any justice of the peace, until demand shall have been made [*98] of the perusal and copy of such warrant, and the same *refused or neglected for the space of six days after such demand: that in case, after such demand and compliance therewith, any action shall be brought against such constable, &c., for any such cause as aforesaid, without making the justice or justices who signed or sealed the said warrant defendant or defendants, then, on producing or proving such warrant at the trial, the jury shall give their verdict for the defendant or defendants, notwithstanding any defect of jurisdiction in such justice or justices; and if such action be brought against the justice and constable jointly, then, on proof of such warrant, the jury shall find for such constable, notwithstanding such defect of jurisdiction as aforesaid; and this statute applies as well where the justice has acted without jurisdiction, as where the warrant which he has granted is improper.[1]

It should be observed, however, that the officer must show that he acted in obedience to the warrant,[2] and can only justify that

[1] Per Lord Eldon, C. J., Price *v.* Messenger, 2 B. & P. 158; Atkins *v.* Kilby, 11 A. & E. 777 (39 E. C. L. R.).

[2] See Hoye *v.* Bush, 3 Scott N. R. 86.

which he *lawfully* did under it;[1] and where the justice cannot be liable, the officer is not entitled to the protection of the statute; for the Act was intended to make the justice liable instead of the officer; where, therefore, the officer makes such a mistake as will not make the justice liable, the officer cannot be excused.

Besides the statute 24 Geo. 2, c. 44, above mentioned, there are other enactments, which, on grounds of public policy, specially extend protection to persons who act *bonâ fide*, though mistakenly, in pursuance of their provisions; and as throwing light upon their practical *operation, attention may specially be directed to [*99] Hughes *v.* Buckland,[2] which was an action of trespass against the defendants, being servants of A. B., for apprehending the plaintiff, whilst fishing in the night-time near the mouth of a river in which A. B. had a several fishery; at the trial, much evidence was given to show that A. B.'s fishery included the place where the plaintiff was apprehended; the jury, however, defined the limits of the fishery so as to exclude that place by a few yards, but they also found that A. B. and the defendants "*bonâ fide* and reasonably" believed that the fishery extended over that spot: it was held, that the defendants were entitled to the protection of the stat. 7 & 8 Geo. 4, c. 29, s. 75, which is framed for the protection "of persons acting in the execution" of that Act, and doing anything in pursuance thereof. "The object of the clause in question," observed Pollock, C. B., in the course of his judgment, "was to give protection to all parties who honestly pursued the statute. Now, every act consists of *time*, *place*, and *circumstance*. With regard to *circumstance*, it is admitted, that, if one magistrate acts where two are required, or imposes twelve months' imprisonment where he ought only to impose six, he is protected if he has a general jurisdiction over the subject matter, or has reason to think he has. With respect to *time*, the case of Cann *v.* Clipperton[3] shows that a party may be protected although he arrests another after the time when the statute authorizes the arrest. *Place* is another ingredient; and I am unable to distinguish the present case from that of a magistrate who is protected, although he acts out of his jurisdiction. A party is protected if he acts *bonâ fide*, and in

[1] Peppercorn *v.* Hoffman, 9 M. & W. 618, 628.

[2] 15 M. & W. 346.

[3] 10 A. & E. 188 (37 E. C. L. R.).

[*100] reasonable *belief that he is pursuing the Act of Parliament."[1] And the proper question for the jury in a case such as referred to will be this:—"Did the defendant honestly believe in the existence of those facts which, if they had existed, would have afforded a justification under the statute?"—the belief of the defendant resting upon some reasonable grounds.[2]

Lastly, we may observe, that, when considered with reference to foreign communities, the jurisdiction of every court, whether *in personam* or *in rem,* must, so far as regards the compelling obedience to its decrees,[3] necessarily be bounded by the limits of the kingdom in which it is established, and unless, by virtue of international treaties,[4] such jurisdiction has been extended, it clearly cannot enforce process beyond those natural limits, according to the maxim, *Extra territorium jus dicenti impune non paretur.*[5]

[*101] *"Municipal law may," however, "provide that judgments and decrees may be lawfully pronounced against

[1] "A thing is considered to be done in pursuance of a statute, when the person who does it is acting honestly and *bonâ fide*, either under the powers which the Act confers, or in discharge of the duties which it imposes." Per Parke, B., Jowle *v.* Taylor, 7 Exch. 61; Downing *v.* Capel, L. R. 2 C. P. 461; Poulsum *v.* Thirst, Id. 449; Whatman *v.* Pearson, L. R. 3 C. P. 422.

[2] Per Williams, J., Roberts *v.* Orchard, 2 H. & C. 774, as explained in Leete *v.* Hart, L. R. 3 C. P. 322, 324, 325; Heath *v.* Brewer, 15 C. B. N. S. 803 (109 E. C. L. R.).

"The calendar month required by the statute 5 & 6 Vict. c. 97, s. 4, begins at midnight of the day on which the notice was given; and generally it ends at midnight of the day with the corresponding number of the next ensuing month in the calendar:" per Blackburn, J., Freeman *v.* Read, 4 B. & S. 185, 186 (116 E. C. L. R.).

[3] See per Lord Cranworth, C., Hope *v.* Hope, 4 De G., M. & G. 345–6.

[4] See In re Tivnan, 5 B. & S. 645 (117 E. C. L. R.).

[5] D. 2, 1, 20; Story, Confl. Laws, § 539; arg. Canadian Prisoners' Case (rep. by Fry), p. 48; Reg. *v.* Lewis, Dearsl. & B. 182; Reg. *v.* Anderson, L. R. 1 C. C. 161.

"It is a conceded principle that the laws of a state have no force *proprio vigore* beyond its territorial limits. But the laws of one state are frequently permitted, by the courtesy of another, to operate in the latter for the promotion of justice, when neither that state nrr its citizens will suffer any inconvenience from the application of the foreign law. This courtesy or comity is established, not only from motives of respect for the laws and institutions of foreign countries, but from considerations of mutual utility and advantage." Per Ruggles, C. J., Hoyt *v.* Thompson, 1 Selden (U. S.) R. 340.

As illustrating the maxim, *supra*, see Re Mansergh, 1 B. & S. 400 (101 E. C. L. R.).

natural-born subjects when absent abroad, and may also enact that they may be required to appear in the courts of their native country even whilst resident in the dominions of a foreign sovereign. If a statutory jurisdiction be thus conferred, courts of justice, in the exercise of it, may lawfully cite and on non-appearance give judgment in civil cases against natural-born subjects whilst they are absent beyond seas in a foreign land. This jurisdiction depends on the statute or written law of the country. Where it is not expressly given, it cannot be lawfully assumed. If such a law does not exist the general maxim applies, *Extra territorium jus dicenti impune non paretur.*[1]

Even Parliament has no power, save in respect of matters of procedure, to legislate for foreigners out of the dominions and beyond the jurisdiction of the British crown.[2] "It is clear," observed Parke, B., in Jefferys *v.* Boosey,[3] "that the legislature has no power over any persons except its own subjects, that is, persons natural-born subjects or residents or whilst they are within the *limits of the kingdom. The legislature can impose no duties except on them; and when legislating for the benefit of persons, must *primâ facie* be considered to mean the benefit of those who owe obedience to our laws, and whose interests the legislature is under a correlative obligation to protect." [*102]

AD QUÆSTIONEM FACTI NON RESPONDENT JUDICES, AD QUÆSTIONEM LEGIS NON RESPONDENT JURATORES.

(8 Rep. 308.)

It is the office of the judge to instruct the jury in points of law—of the jury to decide on matters of fact.[4]

The object in view on the trial of a cause is to find out, by due examination, the truth of the point in issue between the parties, in

[1] Per Lord Westbury, C., Cookney *v.* Anderson, 32 L. J. Ch. 427, 428. Further, "where it is well settled by the comity of nations that any question of private rights falls to be decided by the law of a particular country, it would seem reasonable that the courts of that country should receive jurisdiction, and the power of citing absent parties, though residing in a foreign land." Id. ibid.

[2] Lopez *v.* Burslem, 4 Moore P. C. C. 300, 305.

[3] 4 H. L. Cas. 815, 926.

[4] Co. Litt. 295 b; 9 Rep. 13; Bishop of Meath *v.* Marquis of Winchester, 3

order that judgment may thereupon be given, and therefore the facts of the case must, in the first instance, be ascertained (usually through the intervention of a jury),[1] for *ex facto jus oritur*—the law arises out of the fact.[2] If the fact be perverted or misrepresented the law which arises thence will unavoidably be unjust or partial; and, in order to prevent this, it is necessary to set right the fact and establish the truth contended for, by appealing to some mode of probation or trial which the law of the country has ordained for a criterion of truth and falsehood.[3]

[*103] *Where, then, the question at issue between the litigating parties is one of fact merely, *quæstio facti*, such issue must be determined by the jury; but if, as frequently happens, it is *quæstio juris*, this may either be decided by the judge at Nisi Prius, or may be raised and argued before the court in banc on demurrer, special verdict or special case, or in an appellate court, or a court of error.

A few instances must suffice to show the application of the above rule. Thus, there are two requisites to the validity of a deed: 1st, that it is sufficient in law, on which the court shall decide; 2dly, that certain matters of fact, as sealing and delivery, be duly proved, on which it is the province of the jury to determine;[4] and, where interlineations or erasures are apparent on the face of a deed, it is now the practice to leave it to the jury to decide whether the rasing or interlining was before the delivery.[5]

Again, it is the duty of the court to construe all written instruments,[6] as soon as the true meaning of the words in which they are

Bing. N. C. 217 (32 E. C. L. R.); s. c., 4 Cl. & Fin. 557; Bushnell's Case, Vaugh. R. 149; per Lord Westbury, Fernie *v.* Young, L. R. 1 H. L. 78.

[1] As to the province of the jury in ancient times, see Sir F. Palgrave's Essay on the Original Authority of the King's Council, p. 53.

[2] See for instance Caterall *v.* Hindle, L. R. 2 C. P. 368.

[3] 2 Inst. 49.

[4] Co. Litt. 255, a; Altham's Case, 8 Rep. 308; Dr. Leyfield's Case, 10 Rep. 92, cited Jenkin *v.* Peace, 6 M. & W. 728.

[5] Co. Litt. 225, b. See Doe d. Fryer *v.* Coombs, 3 Q. B. 687 (43 E. C. L. R.); Alsager *v.* Close, 10 M. & W. 576. And see the maxim, *ubi eadem ratio ibi idem jus* (*post*, Chap. IV.), where additional cases on this subject are cited.

[6] "The construction of a specification, like other written documents, is for the court. If the terms used require explanation, as being terms of art or of

couched, and the surrounding circumstances, if any, have been ascertained as facts by the jury;[1] and it is the duty of the jury to take the *construction from the court either absolutely, if there be no words to be construed or explained,[2] as words of art or phrases used in commerce, and no surrounding circumstances to be ascertained,—or conditionally, when those words or circumstances are necessarily referred to them.[3] Unless this were so, there would be no certainty in the law, for a misconstruction by the court is the proper subject, by means of a bill of exceptions, of redress in a court of error, but a misconstruction by the jury cannot be set right at all effectually.[4] Accordingly the construction of a doubtful document given in evidence to defeat the Statute of Limitations is for the court, and not for the jury; but if it be explained by extrinsic facts, from which the intention of the parties may be collected, they are for the consideration of the jury.[5] It may indeed be laid down generally, that although it is the province of the court to construe a written instrument, yet where its effect depends not merely on the construction and meaning of the instru-

[*104]

scientific use, explanatory evidence must be given, and with its aid the court proceeds to the office of construction:" per Lord Chelmsford, C., Simpson v. Holliday, L. R. 1 H. L. 320.

[1] Even where a written instrument has been lost, and parol evidence of its contents has been received, its construction is for the court: Berwick v. Horsfall, 4 C. B. N. S. 450 (93 E. C. L. R.).

[2] See Elliott v. The South Devon R. C., 2 Exch. 725.

[3] "Parcel or no parcel" is a question of fact for the jury, but the judge should tell the jury what is the proper construction of any documents which may have to be considered in deciding that question: Eyle v. Richards, L. R. 1 H. L. 222.

[4] Judgm., Neilson v. Harford, 8 M. & W. 823. Per Erskine, J., Shore v. Wilson, 5 Scott N. R. 988; Cheveley v. Fuller, 13 C. B. 122 (76 E. C. L. R.). See per Maule, J., Doe d. Strickland v. Strickland, 8 C. B. 743, 744 (65 E. C. L. R.); Booth v. Kennard, 2 H. & N. 84; Bovill v. Pimm, 11 Exch. 718; Lindsay v. Janson, 4 H. & N. 699, 704; Parker v. Ibbetson, 4 C. B. N. S. 346 (93 E. C. L. R.).

[5] Morrell v. Frith, 3 M. & W. 402; Doe d. Curzon v. Edmunds, 6 M. & W. 295. See Worthington v. Grimsditch, 7 Q. B. 479 (53 E. C. L. R.); Rackham v. Marriott, 2 H. & N. 196; s. c., 1 Id. 605; Sidwell v. Mason, 2 H. & N. 306; Godwin v. Culling, 4 Id. 373; Cornforth v. Smithard, 5 H. & N. 13; Buckmaster v. Russell, 10 C. B. N. S. 745 (100 E. C. L. R.); Holmes v. Mackrell, 3 C. B. N. S. 789 (99 E. C. L. R.); Cockrill v. Sparkes, 1 H. & C. 699; Francis v. Hawkesley, 1 E. & E. 1052 (102 E. C. L. R.).

[*105] ment, but upon collateral facts and *extrinsic circumstances, the inferences to be drawn from them are to be left to the jury.[1] And where a contract is made out partly by written documents and partly by parol evidence, the whole must be submitted to the jury so that they may determine what was the real contract, if any, between the parties.[2]

Again, in an action for indicting maliciously and without probable cause, the question of probable cause is a mixed proposition of law and fact: whether the circumstances alleged to show it probable or not probable are true and existed, is a matter of fact; but whether, supposing them true, they amount to a probable cause, is a question of law.[3] It therefore falls within the legitimate province of the jury to investigate the truth of the facts offered in evidence, and the justness of the inferences to be drawn from such facts; whilst, at the same time, they receive the law from the judge, viz., that according as they find the facts[4] proved or not proved, and the inferences warranted or not, there was reasonable and probable [*106] ground for the prosecution, or the reverse; and this *rule holds, however complicated and numerous the facts may be.[5]

[1] Etting *v.* U. S. Bank, 11 Wheaton (U. S.) R. 59.

As to the office of the jury in interpreting an ambiguous contract, see Smith *v.* Thompson, 8 C. B. 44 (65 E. C. L. R.), cited *post*, Chap. VIII.

[2] Bolckow *v.* Seymour, 17 C. B. N. S. 107 (84 E. C. L. R.); Rogers *v.* Hadley, 2 H. & C. 227.

[3] Johnstone *v.* Sutton (in error), 1 T. R. 545, 547; per Maule, J., 9 C. B. 152 (67 E. C. L. R.); per Alderson, B., Hinton *v.* Heather, 14 M. & W. 134; per Coleridge, J., Haddrick *v.* Heslop, 12 Q. B. 275 (64 E. C. L. R.); per Pollock, C. B., Heslop *v.* Chapman, 23 L. J. Q. B. 52; Gibbons *v.* Alison, 3 C. B. 181 (54 E. C. L. R.); Blackford *v.* Cod, 2 B. & Ad. 179 (22 E. C. L. R.); Reynolds *v.* Kennedy, 1 Wils. 232; James *v.* Phelps, 11 A. & E. 483 (39 E. C. L. R.); Broughton *v.* Jackson, 18 Q. B. 378 (83 E. C. L. R.).

See further as to the action for malicious prosecution, Basébé *v.* Matthews, L. R. 2 C. P. 684.

[4] Among the facts to be ascertained is the belief, or absence of belief, by defendant, that he had reasonable and probable cause: Turner *v.* Ambler, 10 Q. B. 252, 260 (59 E. C. L. R.); James *v.* Phelps, 11 A. & E. 483 (39 E. C. L. R.); Delegal *v.* Highley, 3 Bing. N. C. 950 (32 E. C. L. R.).

[5] Panton *v.* Williams, 2 Q. B. 169, 194 (42 E. C. L. R.), (which is the leading case upon this subject, see per Williams, J., West *v.* Baxendale, 9 C. B. 149 (67 E. C. L. R.), cited argument, Peck *v.* Boyes, 7 Scott N. R. 441); Michell *v.* Williams, 11 M. & W. 205; per Bramwell, B., Hailes *v.* Marks, 7 H. & N. 63. In an action of slander, it will be for the jury to say whether

In cases of libel also, it has been the course for a long time for the judge first to give a legal definition of the offence, and then to leave it to the jury to say, whether the facts necessary to constitute that offence are proved to their satisfaction; and this course is adopted, whether the libel is the subject of a criminal prosecution or of a civil action; and although the judge *may*, as a matter of advice to them in deciding that question, give his own opinion as to the nature of the publication, yet he is not bound to do so as a matter of law.[1]

Again, the *amount* of costs is a matter wholly within the province of the court to determine in those cases where a party is entitled to them, but the *right* to costs is given by the statute law. Now, where the *amount* merely depends on a fact which it is necessary to notice on the record,—as, for instance, where a successful plaintiff or defendant is entitled to double costs,—the court may award them on the taxation; but where the right to *any* costs is in question, and depends upon a fact the determination of which is not by the statute law vested in the court, and which must be stated on the record to justify *the award of costs contrary to the usual course, the fact, if the opposite party insists upon it, ought to be tried by a jury.[2] [*107]

We have seen that it is for the jury, not for the judge, to determine what was the contract between the parties, where it is evidenced partly by written instruments, partly by matters of fact.[3] And we may add that the rules by which an English court ought to be governed, in construing a foreign contract, have been thus stated[4]—Where a written contract is made in a foreign country, and in a foreign language, the court, in order to interpret it, must obtain 1st, a translation of the instrument; 2dly, an explanation of the terms of art, if it contains any; 3dly, evidence of any foreign

the words were spoken with the meaning assigned to them in the innuendo: Hemmings *v.* Gasson, E., B. & E. 346 (96 E. C. L. R.). See Bushell's Case, Vaugh. R. 147; Ewart *v.* Jones, 14 M. & W. 774.

[1] Parmiter *v.* Coupland, 6 M. & W. 105. See also Padmore *v.* Lawrence, 11 A. & E. 380 (39 E. C. L. R.); Alexander *v.* North-Eastern R. C., 6 B. & S. 340 (118 E. C. L. R.); Stace *v.* Griffith, L. R. 2 P. C. 420, and cases collected in Broom's Com., 4th ed., 758.

[2] Judgm., Watson *v.* Quilter, 11 M. & W. 767.

[3] *Ante*, p. 105.

[4] Per Lord Cranworth, Di Sora *v.* Phillips, 10 H. L. Cas. 633.

law applicable to the case; and 4thly, evidence of any peculiar rules of construction, if any such rules exist, by the foreign law. With this assistance the court must interpret the contract itself on ordinary principles of construction.

The maxim under consideration may be further illustrated by the ordinary case of an action for the price of goods supplied to the defendant's wife. Here the real question is, whether the wife was or was not authorized by the husband to order the goods in question, and it is in general for the jury to say whether the wife had any such authority, and whether the plaintiff, who supplied the goods, must not have known that the wife was exceeding the authority given her in pledging the husband's credit.[1] So, in an action [*108] against an attorney for negligence, *the question of negligence is one of fact for the jury;[2] and, although whether there is any evidence is a question for the judge,[3] yet whether the evidence is sufficient is a question for the jury;[4] and very many

[1] Per Parke, B., Lane *v.* Ironmonger, 13 M. & W. 370. See the cases upon this subject, collected, Broom's Com., 4th ed., pp. 597 *et seq.*

[2] Hunter *v.* Caldwell, 10 Q. B. 69 (59 E. C. L. R.); Chapman *v.* Van Toll, 8 E. & B. 396 (92 E. C. L. R.); Cox *v.* Leech, 1 C. B. N. S. 617 (87 E. C. L. R.); Long *v.* Orsi, 18 C. B. 610 (86 E. C. L. R.); Purves *v.* Landell, 12 Cl. & F. 91; and cases cited, Broom's Com., 4th ed., 88, 672.

[3] See per Pollock, C. B., Hodges *v.* Ancrum, 11 Exch. 216.

[4] Per Buller, J., Carpenters' Co. *v.* Hayward, Dougl. 375. It is also for the jury and not for the court to determine the amount of damages occasioned by a tort, and the court will not interfere unless they are grossly disproportioned to the injury sustained, or unless the verdict were obtained by means of perjury, or there were fraud or misconduct on the part of the plaintiff, such as to deprive the defendant of a fair opportunity of laying his case before the jury, or unless it clearly appear that the jury acted under prejudice or misconception of the evidence. See Smith *v.* Woodfine, 1 C. B. N. S. 660, 667 (87 E. C. L. R.); Berry *v.* Da Costa, L. R. 1 C. P. 331; Creed *v.* Fisher, 9 Exch. 472; Thompson *v.* Gordon, 15 M. & W. 610; Williams *v.* Currie, 1 C. B. 841 (50 E. C. L. R.); Armytage *v.* Haley, 4 Q. B. 917 (45 E. C. L. R.); Lowe *v.* Steele, 15 M. & W. 380; Strutt *v.* Farlar, 16 M. & W. 249; Howard *v.* Barnard, 11 C. B. 653 (73 E. C. L. R.); Highmore *v.* Earl of Harrington, 3 C. B. N. S. 142 (91 E. C. L. R.).

The court will not grant a new trial in an action for slander on the ground that the damages are low, unless there has been some mistake in point of law on the part of the judge who presided, or in the calculation of figures by the jury. See per Byles, J., Forsdike *v.* Stone, L. R. 3 C. P. 612; Rendall *v.* Hayward, 5 Bing. N. C. 424 (35 E. C. L. R.); Kelly *v.* Sherlock, L. R. 1 Q. B. 686.

other instances will readily suggest themselves to the reader, in which the same comprehensive and fundamental principle is equally applicable.

But although the general principle is as above laid down, there are many exceptions to it.[1] Thus, questions of reasonableness—reasonable cause, reasonable time, and the like—are, strictly speaking, matters of fact, even where it falls within the province of the judge or the court to decide them.[2]

*So, where a question arises as to the admissibility of evidence, the facts upon which its admissibility depends are [*109] to be determined by the judge, and not by the jury. If the opposite course were adopted, it would be equivalent to leaving it to the jury to say whether a particular thing were evidence or not.[3] And the question whether a document comes from the proper custody or whether it is properly stamped must be decided by the judge, for the jury are not sworn to try any such issues.[4]

There are also certain statutes which give to the court in particular cases cognizance of certain facts; and there is another and distinct class of cases in which the court, having a discretionary power over its own process, is called upon to depart from the usual course, upon the suggestion of some matter which renders such departure expedient or essential for the purposes of justice; as where a venue is to be changed because an impartial trial cannot be had, or where the sheriff is a party.[5]

If at the close of the plaintiff's case there is no evidence upon which the jury could reasonably and properly find a verdict for

[1] Judgm., Watson *v.* Quilter, 11 M. & W. 767.

[2] See per Lord Abinger, C. B., Startup *v.* Macdonald, 7 Scott N. R. 280; Co. Litt. 566; Burton *v.* Griffiths, 11 M. & W. 817; Graham *v.* Van Diemen's Land Co., 11 Exch. 101; per Crompton, J., Great Western R. C. *v.* Crouch, 3 H. & F. 189; Hogg *v.* Ward, Id. 417; Goodwyn *v.* Cheveley, 4 H. & N. 631; Brighty *v.* Norton, 3 B. & S. 305 (113 E. C. L. R.); Massey *v.* Sladen, L. R. 4 Ex. 13; Vestry of Shoreditch *v.* Hughes, 17 C. B. N. S. 137 (112 E. C. L. R.).

[3] Per Alderson, B., Bartlett *v.* Smith, 11 M. & W. 486; Boyle *v.* Wiseman, 11 Exch. 360.

[4] Per Pollock, C. B., Heslop *v.* Chapman, 23 L. J. Q. B. 52; Siordet *v.* Kuczynski, 17 C. B. 251 (84 E. C. L. R.); per Pollock, C. B., Sharples *v.* Rickard, 2 H. & N. 57; Tattersall *v.* Fearnly, 17 C. B. 368. See 17 & 18 Vict. c. 125, § 31.

[5] See some instances mentioned, Judg., 11 M. & W. 768.

him, the judge ought to direct a non-suit. Formerly, if there were a *scintilla* of evidence in support of a case, the judge was held [*110] bound to leave it to the *jury. "But a course of recent decisions (most of which are referred to in Ryder *v.* Wombwell)[1] has established a more reasonable rule, viz., that in every case, before the evidence is left to the jury, there is a preliminary question for the judge, not whether there is literally no evidence, but whether there is any upon which a jury can properly proceed to find a verdict for the party producing it, upon whom the *onus* of proof is imposed."[2]

It remains to add, that where the judge misconceives his duty, and presents the question at issue to the jury in too limited and restrained a manner, and where, consequently, that which ought to have been put to them for the exercise of their judgment upon it as a matter of fact or of inference, is rather left to them as matter of law, to which they feel bound to defer, the court in banco will in its discretion remedy the possible effect of such misdirection by granting a new trial.

So, likewise, in a penal action, the court will grant a new trial when they are satisfied that the verdict is in contravention of law, whether the error has arisen from the misdirection of the judge or from a misapprehension of the law by the jury, or from a desire on their part to take the exposition of the law into their own hands.[3]

[*111] *And we may observe, in conclusion, that the court in banco always shows its anxiety to correct any miscarriage which may have been occasioned by an infraction of either branch

[1] L. R. 4 Exch. 32.

[2] Judgm., Giblin *v.* McMullen, L. R. 2 P. C. 355. As to the province of the judge and jury, and the evidence where the action is brought—for goods, alleged to be necessaries, supplied to an infant, see Ryder *v.* Wombwell, *supra* —for damages alleged to have been caused by negligence, see Giblin *v.* McMullen, *supra;* Heugh *v.* London and North-Western R. C., L. R. 5 Exch. 51; Welfare *v.* London and Brighton R. C., L. R. 4 Q. B. 693; Daniel *v.* Metropolitan R. C., L. R. 3 C. P. 591; Crafter *v.* Metropolitan R. C., L. R. 1 C. P. 300; Smith *v.* London and South-Western R. C., L. R. 5 C. P. 98—for slander where there is some evidence of actual or express malice, see Jackson *v.* Hopperton, 16 C. B. N. S. 829 (111 E. C. L. R.); and cases there cited.

[3] See A.-G. *v.* Rogers, 11 M. & W. 670, cited in A.-G. *v.* Sillem, 2 H. & C. 469.

A new trial cannot be had in a case of felony: Reg. *v.* Bertrand, L. R. 1 P. C. 520; Reg. *v.* Murphy, 2 Id. 35.

of the maxim, *ad quæstionem legis respondent judices, ad quæstionem facti respondent juratores*, acting in accordance with the principle[1] emphatically laid down by Lord Hardwicke in these words: "It is of the greatest consequence to the law of England and to the subject that these powers of the judge and jury be kept distinct, that the judge determine the law, and the jury the fact; and if ever they come to be confounded it will prove the confusion and destruction of the law of England."[2]

IN PRÆSENTIA MAJORIS CESSAT POTENTIA MINORIS.

(Jenk. Cent. 214.)

In presence of the major the power of the minor ceases.

This maxim is usually[3] cited with special reference to the transcendent nature of the powers vested in the Court of Queen's Bench, and therefore, although akin to one subsequently noticed,[4] may properly be included in this section.

The high court just named keeps all inferior jurisdictions within the bounds of their authority and corrects *irregularities in their proceedings. [*112] It commands magistrates and others to do what their duty requires in every case where there is no other specific remedy. It protects the liberty of the subject by speedy and summary interposition. It takes cognizance both of criminal and civil causes; the former in what is called the crown side, or crown office; the latter in the plea side of the court.[5] To it also error lies from some inferior criminal courts.

To this supremacy of the Court of Queen's Bench may be attributed the fact, that on its coming into any county the power and authority of other criminal tribunals therein situate are *pro tempore* suspended;[6] *in præsentiâ majoris cessat potestas minoris.*[7]

[1] Upon which, however, much innovation has been made, advantageously for the community, by recent legislation: see the C. L. Proc. Act, 1854, sects. 3–17, *et seq.*, and various provisions of the County Court Acts.

[2] R. *v.* Poole, Cas. tem. Hardw. 28.

[3] See 10 Rep. 73, b; Lord Sanchar's Case, 9 Rep. 118, b; 2 Inst. 166.

[4] See the maxim, *Omne majus continet in se minus, post*, Chap. IV.

[5] 3 Com. by Broom & Hadley 119; per Erle, J., Reg. *v.* Gillyard, 12 Q. B. 530 (64 E. C. L. R.).

[6] 4 Inst. 73. See stat. 25 Geo. 3, c. 18, § 1.

[7] Per Coleridge, J., 13 Q. B. 740 (66 E. C. L. R.).

It has been held,[1] however, that the authority of a court of quarter sessions, whether for a county or a borough, is not in law either determined or suspended by the coming of the judges into the county under their commission of assize, oyer and terminer, and general gaol delivery, though "it would be highly inconvenient and improper, generally speaking, for the magistrates of a county to hold their sessions concurrently with the assizes, even in a different part of the county."

---

§ II. The Mode of Administering Justice.

Having in the last section considered some maxims relating peculiarly to the judicial office, the reader is here [*113] *presented with a few which have been selected in order to show the mode in which justice is administered in our courts, and which relate rather to the rules of practice than to the legal principles observed there.

Audi alteram Partem.

No man should be condemned unheard.

It has long been a received rule,[2] that no one is to be condemned, punished, or deprived of his property in any judicial proceeding, unless he has had an opportunity of being heard;[3] in the words of the moralist and poet—

[1] Smith *v.* Reg., 13 Q. B. 738, 744 (66 E. C. L. R.).

[2] In Re Brook, 16 C. B. N. S. 416 (111 E. C. L. R.), Erle, C. J., says, "It is an indispensable requirement of justice that the party who has to decide shall hear both sides, giving each an opportunity of hearing what is urged against him."

[3] Per Parke, B., Re Hammersmith Rent-charge, 4 Exch. 97; per Lord Campbell, C. J., Reg. *v.* Archbishop of Canterbury, 1 E. & E. 559 (102 E. C. L. R.); per Lord Kenyon, C. J., Harper *v.* Carr, 7 T. R. 275, and in R. *v.* Benn, 6 Id. 198; per Bayley, B., Capel *v.* Child, 2 Cr. & J. 558 (see Daniel *v.* Morton, 16 Q. B. 198 (71 E. C. L. R.)); Bagg's Case, 11 Rep. 93, b; R. *v.* Chancellor, &c., of the University of Cambridge, 1 Str. 557; R. *v.* Gaskin, 8 T. R. 209; Reg. *v.* Saddlers' Co., 10 H. L. Cas. 404.

Quicunque aliquid statuerit, parte inauditâ alterâ,
Æquum licet statuerit, haud æquus fuerit.[1]

A writ of sequestration, therefore, cannot properly issue from the Consistory Court of the diocese to a vicar, who has disobeyed a monition from his bishop, without notice previously given to the incumbent, to show cause why it should not issue; for the sequestration is a proceeding partly *in pœnam*, and no proposition is more clearly established than that "a man cannot incur the *loss [*114] of liberty or property for an offence by a judicial proceeding until he has had a fair opportunity of answering the charge against him, unless, indeed, the legislature has expressly or impliedly given an authority to act without that necessary preliminary."[2]

An award made in violation of the above principle may be set aside.[3]

No person should be punished for contempt of court, which is a criminal offence, unless the specific offence charged against him be distinctly stated, and an opportunity of answering it be given to him.[4] "The laws of God and man," says Fortescue, J., in Dr. Bentley's Case,[5] "both give the party an opportunity to make his defence, if he has any." And immemorial custom cannot avail in contravention of this principle.[6]

In conformity also with the elementary principle under consideration, when a complaint has been made, or an information exhibited before a justice of the peace, the accused person has due notice

[1] Seneca Trag. Medea, cited 6 Rep. 52, a; 11 Rep. 99, a; per Parke, B., 4 Exch. 97; 14 C. B. 165 (78 E. C. L. R.).

[2] Bonaker *v.* Evans, 16 Q. B. 162, 171 (71 E. C. L. R.), followed, but distinguished in Bartlett *v.* Kirkwood, 2 E. & B. 771 (75 E. C. L. R.). See Daniel *v.* Morton, 16 Q. B. 198 (71 E. C. L. R.); Ex parte Hopwood, 15 Q. B. 121 (69 E. C. L. R.); Ex parte Story, 8 Exch. 195; 12 C. B. 767, 775 (74 E. C. L. R.); Reynolds *v.* Fenton, 3 C. B. 187 (54 E. C. L. R.); Meeus *v.* Thellusson, 8 Exch. 638; Ferguson *v.* Mahon, 11 A. & E. 179 (39 E. C. L. R.).

[3] Thornburn *v.* Barnes, L. R. 2 C. P. 384, 401; Re Brook, 16 C. B. N. S. 403 (111 E. C. L. R.).

[4] In re Pollard, L. R. 2 P. C. 106, 120.

[5] R. *v.* Chancellor, &c., of Cambridge, 1 Str. 557; per Maule, J., Abley *v.* Dale, 10 C. B. 71 (70 E. C. L. R.); per Lord Campbell, C. J., Ex parte Ramshay, 18 Q. B. 190 (83 E. C. L. R.); per Byles, J., 14 C. B. N. S. 194 (108 E. C. L. R.).

[6] Williams *v.* Lord Bagot, 3 B. & C. 772 (10 E. C. L. R.).

given him, by summons or otherwise, of the accusation against him, in order that he may have an opportunity of answering it.[1]

[*115] A statute establishing a gas-light company enacted that *if any person should refuse or neglect, for a period of ten days after demand, to pay any rent due from him to the company for the supply of gas, such rent should be recovered by the company or their clerk by warrant of a justice of the peace and execution thereunder. A warrant issued by a justice under this Act, without previously summoning and hearing the party to be distrained upon, was held to be illegal, though a summons and hearing were not in terms required by the Act; for the warrant is in the nature of an execution; without a summons the party charged has no opportunity of going to the justice, and a man shall not "suffer in person or in purse without an opportunity of being heard."[2]

The Metropolis Local Management Act, 1855 (18 & 19 Vict. c. 120), s. 76, empowers the vestry or district board to alter or demolish a house where the builder has neglected to give notice of his intention to build seven days before proceeding to lay or dig the foundation. Held, that this enactment does not empower the board to demolish such building without first giving the party guilty of the omission an opportunity of being heard,[3] for "a tribunal which is by law invested with power to affect the property of one of her majesty's subjects, is bound to give such subject an opportunity of being heard before it proceeds," and "that rule is of universal application and founded upon the plainest principles of justice."[4]

[*116] Doubtless the rule just stated universally prevails, *unless where by force of the express wording of a statute an exception is engrafted on it. For instance: By the Tithe Commutation Act (6 & 7 Will. 4, c. 71), s. 82, when the half-yearly payment of rent-charge on land shall be in arrear and unpaid for

[1] Paley, Conv., 4th ed., 67, 93, where many cases illustrating the text are collected. See Bessell *v.* Wilson, 1 E. & B. 489 (72 E. C. L. R.).

[2] Painter *v.* Liverpool Oil Gaslight Co., 3 A. & E. 433 (30 E. C. L. R.); Hammond *v.* Bendyshe, 13 Q. B. 869 (66 E. C. L. R.); Reg. *v.* Totnes Union, 7 Q. B. 690 (53 E. C. L. R.); Bessell *v.* Wilson, 1 E. & B. 489 (72 E. C. L. R.); Gibbs *v.* Steadman, 8 B. & C. 528 (15 E. C. L. R.).

[3] Cooper *v.* Wandsworth Board of Works, 14 C. B. N. S. 180 (108 E. C. L. R.), cited per Byles, J., Re Brook, 16 C. B. N. S. 419 (111 E. C. L. R.).

[4] Per Willes, J., 14 C. B. N. S. 190 (108 E. C. L. R.).

the space of forty days, and there shall be no sufficient distress upon the premises liable to the payment thereof, a judge of one of the superior courts is empowered, upon an affidavit of the fact, to order a writ to issue to the sheriff requiring him to summon a jury to assess the arrears of the rent-charge remaining unpaid, and to return the inquisition thereupon taken as directed in the Act: it was held, that such order could be made upon an *ex parte* application to the judge.[1]

NEMO DEBET ESSE JUDEX IN PROPRIA SUA CAUSA.

(12 Rep. 113.)

No man can be judge in his own cause.

It is a fundamental rule in the administration of justice, that a person cannot be judge in a cause wherein he is interested:[2] *nemo sibi esse judex vel suis jus dicere debet;*[3] and, therefore, in the reign of James I., it was solemnly adjudged that the king cannot take any cause, whether civil or criminal, out of any of his courts, and give judgment upon it himself; but it must be determined and adjudged in some court of justice according to the law and custom of England; and in the case referred to, "the judges informed the king that no king, after the conquest, *assumed to himself [*117] to give any judgment in any case whatsoever which concerned the administration of justice; but these were solely determined in the courts of justice,"[4] and *Rex non debet esse sub homine sed sub Deo et lege.*[5]

It is, then, a rule, observed in practice, and of the application of which instances not unfrequently occur, and where a judge is inter-

[1] Re Hammersmith Rent-charge, 4 Exch. 87, citing Re Camberwell Rent-charge, 4 Q. B. 151 (45 E. C. L. R.).

[2] Per Cur. 2 Stra. 1173; Roll. Abr., *Judges*, Pl. 11; 4 H. L. Cas. 96, 240.

[3] C. 3, 5, 1.

[4] Prohibitions del Roy, 12 Rep. 63 (cited Bridgman *v.* Holt, 2 Show. P. Ca. 126); 4 Inst. 71. In Gorham *v.* Bishop of Exeter, 15 Q. B. 52 (69 E. C. L. R.); s. c., 10 C. B. 102 (70 E. C. L. R.); 5 Exch. 630; an argument based on the maxim above exemplified was vainly urged. See also Ex parte Medwin, 1 E. & B. 609 (72 E. C. L. R.); R. *v.* Hoseason, 14 East 606.

[5] Fleta, fo. 2, c. 5; *ante*, p. 47.

ested in the result of a cause he cannot, either personally or by deputy, sit in judgment upon it.[1] If, for instance, a plea allege a prescriptive right vested in the lord of the manor to seize cattle damage feasant, and to detain the distress until fine paid for the damages, at the lord's will, this prescription will be void, and the plea consequently bad; "because it is against reason, if wrong be done any man, that he thereof should be his own judge;[2] and it is a maxim of law, that *aliquis non debet esse judex in propriâ causâ, quia non potest esse judex et pars;*[3] *nemo potest esse simul actor et judex;*[4] no man can be at once judge and suitor.

A leading case in illustration of this maxim is Dimes *v.* The Proprietors of the Grand Junction Canal,[5] [*118] *where the facts were as under:—the canal company filed a bill in equity against a landowner in a matter touching their interest as copyholders in certain land. The suit was heard before the Vice-Chancellor, who granted the relief sought by the company, and the Lord Chancellor—who was a shareholder in the company, this fact being unknown to the defendant in the suit—affirmed the order of the Vice-Chancellor. It was held on appeal to the House of Lords, that the decree of the Lord Chancellor was under the circumstances voidable and ought to be reversed. Lord Campbell, C. J., observing: "It is of the last importance that the maxim that 'no man is to be a judge in his own cause' should be held sacred. And that is not to be confined to a cause in which he is a party, but applies to a cause in which he has an interest. * * * * We have again and again set aside proceedings in inferior tribunals, because an individual, who had an interest in a cause, took a part in the decision. And it will have a most salutary effect on these tribunals when it is

[1] Brooks *v.* Earl of Rivers, Hardw. 503; Earl of Derby's Case, 12 Rep. 114; per Holt, C. J., Anon., 1 Salk. 396; Worsley *v.* South Devon R. C., 16 Q. B. 539 (71 E. C. L. R.).

[2] Litt. § 212.

[3] Co. Litt. 141, a.

[4] See Reg. *v.* Great Western R. C., 13 Q. B. 327 (66 E. C. L. R.); Reg. *v.* Dean, &c., of Rochester, 17 Q. B. 1 (79 E. C. L. R.); followed in Reg. *v.* Rand, L. R. 1 Q. B. 230, 233; Re Ollerton, 15 C. B. 796 (80 E. C. L. R.); Re Chandler, 1 C. B. N. S. 323 (87 E. C. L. R.).

[5] 3 H. L. Cas. 759; as to which see London and North-Western R. C. *v.* Lindsay, 3 Macq. Sc. App. Cas. 114; Re Dimes, 14 Q. B. 554 (68 E. C. L. R.); Ellis *v.* Hopper, 3 H. & N. 766; Williams *v.* Great Western R. C., Id. 869; Lancaster and Carlisle R. C. *v.* Heaton, 8 E. & B. 952 (92 E. C. L. R.).

known that this high court of last resort, in a case in which the Lord Chancellor of England had an interest, considered that his decree was on that account a decree not according to law, and should be set aside. This will be a lesson to all inferior tribunals to take care, not only that in their decrees they are not influenced by their personal interest, but to avoid the appearance of laboring under such an influence."

The opinion delivered by the judges to the House in the case just cited[1] shows, however, that the decision of a judge made in a cause in which he has an interest is, *in a case of necessity, unimpeachable, *ex. gr.*, if an action were brought [*119] against all the judges of the Court of Common Pleas in a matter over which they had exclusive jurisdiction.[2] Nor does the principle under consideration apply to avoid the award of a referee to whom, though necessarily interested in the result, parties have contracted to submit their differences,[3] though ordinarily it is "contrary to reason that an arbitrator or umpire should be sole and uncontrolled judge in his own cause."[4]

Conformable to the general rule was a decision in the following case:—Upon an appeal to the Quarter Sessions of the borough of Cambridge, by a water company against an assessment to the poor-rate, the deputy recorder of the borough presiding, the rate was reduced and costs given to the appellants; at the time of hearing the appeal the deputy recorder was a shareholder in the company, and although he had in fact sold his shares he had not completed the transfer of them; he was held incompetent to try the appeal.[5]

In like manner, proceedings had before commissioners under a statute which forbade persons to act in that capacity when interested, have been adjudged void.[6]

Neither can a justice of the peace, who is interested[7] *in a [*120] matter pending before the Court of Quarter Sessions, take

[1] 3 H. L. Cas. 787; citing Year Book, 8 Hen. 6, 19; 2 Roll. Abr. 93.

[2] Per Lord Cranworth, C., Ranger *v.* Great Western R. C., 5 H. L. Cas. 88. See Ex parte Menhennet, L. R. 5 C. P. 16.

[3] Ranger *v.* Great Western R. C., 5 H. L. Cas. 72.

[4] Per Parke, B., Re Coombs, 4 Exch. 841. Russell, Arbitr., 2d ed. 375.

[5] Reg. *v.* Recorder of Cambridge, 8 E. & B. 637 (92 E. C. L. R.).

[6] Reg. *v.* Aberdare Canal Co., 14 Q. B. 854 (68 E. C. L. R.).

[7] "There is no doubt that any direct pecuniary interest, however small, in

any part in the proceedings, unless indeed all parties know that he is interested, and consent, either tacitly or expressly, to his presence and interference.[1] In such a case, it has been recently held that the presence of one interested magistrate will render the court improperly constituted, and vitiate the proceedings; it being no answer to the objection, that there was a majority in favor of the decision, without reckoning the vote of the interested party.[2] And, on the same principle, where a bill was preferred before the grand jury at the assizes against a parish for non-repair of a road, the liability to repair which was denied by the parish, the Court of Queen's Bench granted a criminal information against the parish, on the ground that two members of the grand jury were large landed proprietors therein, took part in the proceedings on the bill, and put questions to the witnesses examined before them; one of them, moreover, having stated to the foreman that the road in question was useless, and the bill having been thrown out by the grand jury;[3] for, "It is very important that no magistrate who is interested in the case before the court should interfere while it is being heard in any way that may [*121] create a suspicion that *the decision is influenced by his presence or interference."[4]

The mere presence on the bench, however, of an interested magistrate during part of the hearing of an appeal, will not be deemed sufficient ground for setting aside an order of sessions made on such hearing, if it be expressly shown that he took no part in the hear-

the subject of inquiry, does disqualify a person from acting as a judge in the matter." Per Blackburn, J., Reg. *v.* Rand, L. R. 1 Q. B. 232.

See further as to the interest which will or will not disqualify, Wildes *v.* Russell, L. R. 1 C. P. 722; Reg. *v.* Manchester, Sheffield, and Lincolnshire R. C., L. R. 2 Q. B. 336, 339.

[1] Reg. *v.* The Cheltenham Commissioners, 1 Q. B. 467 (41 E. C. L. R.); Wakefield Board of Health *v.* West Riding, &c., R. C., 6 B. & S. 794 (118 E. C. L. R.); Reg. *v.* Justices of West Riding, Id. 802. "Nothing is better settled than this, that a party aware of the objection of interest cannot take the chance of a decision in his favor, and afterwards raise the objection." Per Cockburn, C. J., 6 B. & S. 802 (118 E. C. L. R.).

[2] Reg. *v.* Justices of Hertfordshire, 6 Q. B. 753 (51 E. C. L. R.). See Re Underwood and Bedford and Cambridge R. C., 11 C. B. N. S. 442 (103 E. C. L. R.).

[3] Reg. *v.* Upton St. Leonard's, 10 Q. B. 827 (59 E. C. L. R.). See Esdaile *v.* Lund, 12 M. & W. 734.

[4] Per Wightman, J., Reg. *v.* Justices of Suffolk, 18 Q. B. 416, 421 (83 E. C. L. R.). See Reg. *v.* Justices of Surrey, 21 L. J. M. C. 195.

ing, came into court for a different purpose, and did not in any way influence the decision.[1]

It has been laid down[2] that "even an Act of Parliament made against natural equity, as to make a man a judge in his own case, is void in itself; for *jura naturæ sunt immutabilia*, and they are *leges legum*." But although it is contrary to the general rule of law, not only in this country but in every other, to make a person judge in his own cause, "the legislature can, and no doubt in a proper case would, depart from that general rule," and an intention to do so being clearly expressed, the courts would give effect to their enactment.[3] And if a particular relation is created by statute between A. and B., and a duty is imposed upon A. to investigate and decide charges preferred against B., the maxim *nemo sibi esse judex vel suis jus dicere debet* would not apply.[4]

Lastly, "There is no ground whatever for saying that the governor of a colony cannot give his official consent to a legislative measure in which he may be individually interested. It might as well be asserted that the sovereign *of these realms could not give assent to a bill in Parliament in which the sovereign was personally concerned."[5] [*122]

ACTUS CURIÆ NEMINEM GRAVABIT.

(Jenk. Cent. 118.)

An act of the court shall prejudice no man.

The above maxim "is founded upon justice and good sense; and affords a safe and certain guide for the administration of the law."[6] In virtue of it where a case stands over for argument from term to term on account of the multiplicity of business in the court, or for judgment from the intricacy of the question, the party ought not to be prejudiced by that delay, but should be allowed to enter up his

[1] Reg. *v.* Justices of London, 18 Q. B. 421 (*c*) (83 E. C. L. R.).
[2] Day *v.* Savadge, Hob. 85, 87, cited arg. 5 Exch. 671.
[3] Per Blackburn, J., Mersey Docks Trustees *v.* Gibbs, L. R. 1 H. L. 110.
[4] Wildes *v.* Russell, L. R. 1 C. P. 722, 747.
[5] Judgm., Phillips *v.* Eyre, L. R. 4 Q. B. 244.
[6] Per Cresswell, J., 12 C. B. 415 (74 E. C. L. R.).

judgments retrospectively to meet the justice of the case;[1] and, therefore, if one party to an action die during a *curia advisari vult*, judgment may be entered *nunc pro tunc*, for the delay is the act of the court, and therefore neither party should suffer for it.[2]

In a case involving issues both of law and fact, the issues of fact were tried in the month of August, 1843, a verdict was found for the plaintiff, and a rule for a new trial was discharged in Trinity Term, 1844; in the same term the demurrers were set down in the special paper, but did not come on for argument until May, 1845, when judgment was given upon them for the plaintiff. The [*123] *plaintiff having died in March, 1845, the court made absolute a rule to enter judgment as of Trinity Term, 1844.[3] It being in accordance with the principles of the common law, irrespective of the stat. 17 Car. 2, c. 8, that, wherever, in such cases as the above, the delay is the act of the court, and not that of the party, the judgment may be entered *nunc pro tunc*, unless, indeed, it can be shown that the other party would be prejudiced by entering the judgment as prayed, which would, no doubt, be a sufficient ground to justify the court in refusing to interfere.[4]

Where, however, the delay is not attributable to the act of the court, the maxim *supra* does not apply.[5]

Again, a peremptory undertaking to proceed to trial is not an undertaking to try at all events: and where the plaintiff having peremptorily undertaken to try at a particular sittings, gave notice of trial, and entered the cause as a special jury cause, on the last day, and there being only two days' sittings, it was made a remanet; the court held that the plaintiff was not in default, so as to

[1] Per Garrow, B., 1 Y. & J. 372.

[2] Cumber *v.* Wane, 1 Stra. 425; Moor *v.* Roberts, 3 C. B. N. S. 844 (91 E. C. L. R.); per Tindal, C. J., Harrison *v.* Heathorn, 6 Scott N. R. 797; Toulmin *v.* Anderson, 1 Taunt. 384; Jenk. Cent. 180. See Lanman *v.* Lord Audley, 2 M. & W. 535.

[3] Miles *v.* Bough, 3 D. & L. 105, recognizing Lawrence *v.* Hodgson, 1 Yo. & J. 368, and Brydges *v.* Smith, 8 Bing. 29 (21 E. C. L. R.); Miles *v.* Williams, 9 Q. B. 47.

[4] Miles *v.* Bough, *supra*, and cases there cited; Vaughan *v.* Wilson, 4 B. N. C. 116 (13 E. C. L. R.); Green *v.* Cobden, 4 Scott 486; Evans *v.* Rees, 12 A. & E. 167 (40 E. C. L. R.).

[5] Freeman *v.* Tranah, 12 C. B. 406 (74 E. C. L. R.); recognized in Heathcote *v.* Wing, 11 Exch. 358; Fishmongers' Co. *v.* Robertson, 3 C. B. 970 (54 E. C. L. R.).

entitle the defendant to judgment as in case of a nonsuit, for not proceeding to trial pursuant to the undertaking.[1]

And if the plaintiff is under a peremptory undertaking to try at a particular sittings, and when the cause comes on to be tried, applies to the judge and obtains leave to *postpone it, and it [*124] is thereupon postponed, the defendant will not be entitled to make absolute the rule for judgment as in case of a nonsuit, for the non-trial of the cause arose from the act of the judge, not by the neglect of the plaintiff.[2] Where, however, a plaintiff under a peremptory undertaking to try at the first sitting in term, duly gave notice of trial, and passed the record but two days before the sitting day, obtained a rule for a special jury, and in consequence thereof the cause was passed over and made a remanet, the plaintiff was held to have broken his undertaking;[3] in this case the plaintiff's own act effectually prevented the trial from taking place, as he had undertaken that it should do.

The preceding examples will probably be sufficient to illustrate the general doctrine, which is equally founded on common sense and on authority, that the act of a court of law shall prejudice no man;[4]

[1] Lumley *v.* Dubourg, 14 M. & W. 295; Rizzi *v.* Foletti, 5 C. B. 852 (57 E. C. L. R.); Rogers *v.* Vandercombe, 1 B. C. R. 183.

[2] Jackson *v.* Carrington, 4 Exch. 41. See Bennett *v.* Peninsular and Oriental Steam Boat Co., 16 C. B. 29 (81 E. C. L. R.).

[3] Levy *v.* Moylan, 10 C. B. 657 (70 E. C. L. R.).

[4] In connection with this rule may be noticed the following cases:—If an individual prefers a complaint to a magistrate and procures a warrant to be granted upon which the accused is taken into custody, the complainant in such case is not liable in trespass for the imprisonment, even though the magistrate had no jurisdiction: Brown *v.* Chapman, 6 C. B. 365, 376 (60 E. C. L. R.). See further on this subject Broom's Com., 4th ed., 730. One who mistakenly prefers a charge against another before a magistrate will not be liable in trespass for a remand judicially ordered by him: Lock *v.* Ashton, 12 Q. B. 871 (64 E. C. L. R.). See also Freegard *v.* Barnes, 7 Exch. 827. Nor is an execution creditor liable to the person whose goods have been wrongfully taken in execution for damage sustained by him in consequence of their sale under an interpleader order: Walker *v.* Olding, 1 H. & C. 621. The above and similar cases seem properly referable to the rule, *Nullus videtur dolo facere qui jure suo utitur*, D. 50. 17. 55.

A defendant who is taken in execution under a *ca. sa.* issued on a judgment for less than £20, without the order of the judge who tried the cause, may maintain an action of trespass against the plaintiff and his attorney: Brooks *v.* Hodgkinson, 4 H. & N. 712. See Gilding *v.* Eyre, 10 C. B. N. S. 592 (100 E. C. L. R.); Huffer *v.* Allen, L. R. 2 Ex. 15.

[*125] and in conformity *with this doctrine it has been observed, that, as long as there remains a necessity, in any stage of the proceedings in an action, for an appeal to the authority of the court, or any occasion to call upon it to exercise its jurisdiction, the court has, even if there has been some express arrangement between the parties, an undoubted right, and is, moreover, bound to interfere, if it perceives that its own process or jurisdiction is about to be used for purposes which are not consistent with justice.[1]

Cases do, however, occur, in which injury is caused by the act of a legal tribunal, as by the laches or mistake of its officer; and where, notwithstanding the maxim as to *actus curiæ*, the injured party is altogether without redress.[2]

Lastly, it is the duty of a judge to try the causes set down for trial before him, and yet, if he refused to hold his court, although there might be a complaint in Parliament respecting his conduct, no action would lie against him.[3] So, in the case of a petition to the crown to establish a peerage, if, in consequence of the absence of peers, a committee for privileges could not be held, the claimant, although necessarily put to great expense, and perhaps exposed to the loss of his peerage by death of witnesses, would be wholly without redress.[4] In the above, and other similar cases, a wrong might [*126] be inflicted *by a judicial tribunal, for which the law could supply no remedy.

ACTUS LEGIS NEMINI EST DAMNOSUS.

(2 Inst. 287.)

An act in law shall prejudice no man.[5]

Thus, the general principle is, that if a man marry his debtor, the debt is thereby extinguished;[6] but still a case may be so cir-

[1] Wade *v.* Simeon, 13 M. & W. 647; Thomas *v.* Harding, 3 C. B. N. S. 254 (91 E. C. L. R.); Sherborn *v.* Lord Huntingtower, 13 C. B. N. S. 742 (106 E. C. L. R.); Burns *v.* Chapman, 5 C. B. N. S. 481, 492 (94 E. C. L. R.).

[2] See Grace *v.* Clinch, 4 Q. B. 606 (45 E. C. L. R.); Leech *v.* Lamb, 11 Exch. 437; In re Llanbeblig and Llandyfrydog, 15 L. J., M. C., 92. In Winn *v.* Nicholson, 7 C. B. 824 (62 E. C. L. R.), however, Coltman, J., remarks that, "no doubt the court will correct the mistake of its own officer." See Wilkes *v.* Perks, 5 M. & Gr. 376 (44 E. C. L. R.); Hazer *v.* Wade, 1 B. & S. 728 (101 E. C. L. R.); Morgan *v.* Morris, 3 Macq. Sc. App. Cas. 323.

[3] *Ante*, p. 85, *et seq.*

[4] Arg. 9 Cl. & F. 276.

[5] 6 Rep. 68.

[6] 1 Inst. 264, b.

cumstanced as not to come within that rule; for instance, a bond conditioned for the payment of money after the obligor's death, made to a woman in contemplation of the obligor's marrying her, and intended for her benefit if she should survive, is not released by the marriage, but an action will lie at her suit against the executor; and this results from the principle that the law will not work a wrong, for the bond was given for the purpose of making provision for the wife in the event of her surviving the obligor, and it would be iniquitous to set it aside on account of the marriage, since it was for that very event that the bond was meant to provide.[1]

So, where an authority given by law has been abused, the law places the party so abusing it in the same situation as if he had, in the first instance, acted wholly without authority;[2] and this, it has been observed,[3] is a *salutary and just principle, founded [*127] on the maxim, that the law wrongs no man: *actus legis nemini facit injuriam.*

In Fictione Juris semper Æquitas existit.

(11 Rep. 51.)

A legal fiction is always consistent with equity.

According to a commentator on the Roman law, *Fictio nihil aliud est quam legis adversus veritatem in re posibili ex justâ causâ dispositio;*[4] and *fictio juris* is defined to be a legal assumption that a thing is true which is either not true, or which is as probably false as true;[5] the rule on this subject being, that the court will

[1] Milbourn *v.* Ewart, 5 T. R. 381, 385; Cage *v.* Acton, 1 Lord Raym. 515; Fitzgerald *v.* Fitzgerald, L. R. 2 P. C. 83; Smith *v.* Stafford, Hobart 216. See another instance of rule, Calland *v.* Troward, 2 H. Bla. 324, 334; and see Nadin *v.* Battie, 5 East 147; 1 Prest. Abs. of Tit. 346.

[2] 6 Bac. Ab. 559, Trespass (B.); Six Carpenters' Case, 8 Rep. 290, cited under the maxim *acta exteriora indicant interiora secreta, post,* Chap. V.

[3] Arg. 11 Johnson (U. S.) R. 380.

[4] Gothofred. ad D. 22, 3, s. 3. See Spence, Chan. Jurisd. 213, 214. Law. Mag. and Rev., vol. 3, pt. 1, p. 60.

[5] Bell's Dict. and Dig. of Scotch Law 427; Finch's Law 66.

The doctrine that "money to be laid out in land is to be treated as land,"

not endure that a mere form or fiction of law, introduced for the sake of justice, should work a wrong contrary to the real truth and substance of the thing.[1] "It is a certain rule," says Lord Mansfield, C. J.,[2] "that a fiction of law shall never be contradicted so as [*128] to defeat the end *for which it was invented, but for every other purpose it may be contradicted." Its proper operation is to prevent a mischief or remedy an inconvenience which might result from applying some general rule of law. Hence, we read that if a man disseises me, and during the disseisin cuts down the trees or grass, or the corn growing upon the land, and afterwards I re-enter, I shall have an action of trespass against him, for after my regress the law as to the disseisor and his servants supposes the freehold always to have continued in me; but if my disseisor makes a feoffment in fee, gift in tail, or lease for life or years, and afterwards I re-enter, I shall not have trespass against those who came in by title; for this fiction of the law, that the freehold always continued in me, is moulded to meet the ends of justice, and shall not, therefore, have relation to make him who comes in by title a wrongdoer, but in this case I shall recover all the mesne profits against my disseisor.[3] It has been held also in a modern case,[4] that although the customary heir of a copyhold tenement cannot maintain trespass without entry, there is after entry a relation back to the time of accruing of the legal right to enter, so as to support an action for trespasses committed prior to such entry; this relation being "created by law for the purpose of preventing wrong from being dispunishable upon the same principle

long established in courts of equity, "is in truth a mere fiction." Vide per Kelley, C. B., in Re De Lancey, L. R. 4 Ex. 358; s. c., affirmed, 5 Id. 102. So the doctrine, that a deed executing a power refers back to the instrument creating the power, so that the appointee takes under him who created the power, and not under him who executes it, is a fiction of law; and so it was considered in Bartlett *v.* Ramsden, 1 Keb. 570. See also per Lord Hardwicke, C., Duke of Marlborough *v.* Lord Godolphin, 2 Ves. sen. 78, who explains the above proposition; Clere's Case, 6 Rep. 17.

[1] Per Lord Mansfield, C. J., Johnston *v.* Smith, 2 Burr. 962. See 10 Rep. 40; Id. 89.

[2] Mostyn *v.* Fabrigas, Cowp. 177; per Bramwell, B., A.-G. *v.* Kent, 1 H. & C. 28.

[3] Liford's Case, 11 Rep. 51; Hobart 98, cited per Coleridge, J., Garland *v.* Carlisle, 4 Cl. & Fin. 710.

[4] Barnett *v.* Earl of Guilford, 11 Exch. 19, 33.

on which the law has given it to other cases."[1] By fiction of law, all judgments were formerly[2] supposed to be recovered in term and to relate *to the first day of the term, but in practice judgments were frequently signed in vacation; and it was held [*129] that, where the purposes of justice required that the true time when the judgment was obtained should be made apparent, a party might show it by averment in pleading; and it was observed generally, that, wherever a fiction of law works injustice, and the facts, which by fiction are supposed to exist, are inconsistent with the real facts, a court of law ought to look to the real facts.[3]

It has, indeed, been affirmed as a broad general principle, that "the truth is always to prevail against fiction," and hence, although for some purposes the whole assizes are to be considered as one legal day, "the court is bound, if required for the purpose of doing substantial justice, to take notice that such legal day consists of several natural days, or even of a fraction of a day." Evidence may therefore be adduced to show that an assignment of his goods by a felon *bonâ fide* made for a good consideration after the commission day of the assizes, was in truth made before the day on which he was tried and convicted, and, on proof of such fact, the property will be held to have passed by the assignment.[4]

Still less will a legal fiction be raised so as to operate to the detriment of any person, as in destruction of a lawful vested estate, for *fictio legis inique operatur *alicui damnum vel injuriam.*[5] [*130] The law does not love that rights should be destroyed, but, on the contrary, for the supporting of them invents notions and fictions.[6] And the maxim *in fictione juris subsistit æquitas* is often

[1] Some of which are specified in the judgment in Barnett *v.* Earl of Guilford, *supra.*

[2] But now, by R. G., H. T., 1855, Reg. 56, "all judgments, whether interlocutory or final, shall be entered of record of the day of the month and year, whether in term or vacation, when signed, and shall not have relation to any other day, but it shall be competent for the court or a judge to order a judgment to be entered *nunc pro tunc.*"

[3] Lyttleton *v.* Cross, 3 B. & C. 317, 325 (10 E. C. L. R.).

[4] Whitaker *v.* Wisbey, 12 C. B. 44, 58, 59 (74 E. C. L. R.). See Reg. *v.* Edwards and Wright *v.* Mills, cited *ante*, p. 71, and the maxim *de minimis non curat lex, post.*

[5] 36 Rep. 3; per Cur., Waring *v.* Dewbury, Gilb. Eq. R. 223.

[6] Per Gould, J., Cage *v.* Acton, 1 Lord Raym. 516, 517.

applied by our courts for the attainment of substantial justice, and to prevent the failure of right.[1] "Fictions of law," as observed by Lord Mansfield, "hold only in respect of the ends and purposes for which they were invented. When they are urged to an intent and purpose not within the reason and policy of the fiction, the other party may show the truth."[2]

EXECUTIO JURIS NON HABET INJURIAM.

(2 Inst. 482.)

The law will not in its executive capacity work a wrong.

It was a rule of the Roman, as it is of our own, law, that if an action be brought in a court which has jurisdiction, upon insufficient grounds or against the wrong party, no injury is thereby done for which an action can be maintained—*Is qui jure publico utitur non videtur injuriæ faciendæ causâ hoc facere, juris enim executio non habet injuriam;*[3] and *Nullus videtur dolo facere qui suo jure utitur,*[4] he is not to be esteemed a wrongdoer who merely avails himself of his legal rights. On the other hand, if an individual, [*131] under color of the *law, does an illegal act, or if he abuses the process of the court to make it an instrument of oppression or extortion, this is a fraud upon the law, by the commission of which liability will be incurred.[5]

In a leading case,[6] illustrative of this latter proposition, the facts were as follows: A *ca. sa.* having been sued out against the Countess of Rutland, and the officers entrusted with the execution of the sheriff's warrant being apprehensive of a rescue, the plaintiff was advised to enter a feigned action in London, according to custom, against the said countess, to arrest her thereupon, and then take her body in execution on the *ca. sa.* In pursuance of this advice, the countess was arrested and taken to the Compter, "and at the

[1] Low *v.* Little, 17 Johnson (U. S.) R. 348.

[2] Morris *v.* Pugh, 3 Burr. 1243.

[3] D. 47, 10, 13, s. 1; Hobart 266.

[4] D. 50, 17, 55. See examples of this rule, *ante*, p. 124.

[5] See per Pollock, C. B., Smith *v.* Monteith, 13 M. & W. 439. "The court has a general superintending power to prevent its process from being used for the purpose of oppression and injustice." Per Jervis, C. J., Webb *v.* Adkins, 14 C. B. 407 (78 E. C. L. R.). See Alleyne *v.* Reg., 5 E. & B. 399 (85 E. C. L. R.); M'Gregor *v.* Barrett, 6 C. B. 262 (60 E. C. L. R.); *ante*, p. 126.

[6] Countess of Rutland's Case, 6 Rep. 53.

door thereof the sheriff came, and carried the countess to his house, where she remained seven or eight days, till she paid the debt." It was, however, held, that the said arrest was not made by force of the writ of execution, and was, therefore, illegal; "and the entering of such feigned action was utterly condemned by the whole court, for, by color of law and justice, they, by such feigned means, do against law and justice, and so make law and justice the author and cause of wrong and injustice."

Again, in Hooper *v.* Lane[1] it was held in accordance with the spirit of the maxim under our notice, that if the sheriff having in his hands two writs of *ca. sa.*, the one valid and the other invalid, arrests on the latter only, he *cannot afterwards justify the [*132] arrest under the valid writ. Nor can the sheriff, whilst a person is unlawfully in his custody by virtue of an arrest on an invalid writ, arrest that person on a good writ: "to allow the sheriff to make such an arrest while the party is unlawfully confined by him, would be to permit him to profit by his own wrong,[2] and therefore cannot be tolerated."[3]

We shall hereafter[4] have occasion to consider the general doctrine respecting the right to recover money paid under compulsion. We may, however, take this opportunity of observing that, where such compulsion consists in an illegal restraint of liberty, a contract entered into by reason thereof will be void; if, for instance, a man is under duress of imprisonment, or if, the imprisonment being lawful, he is subjected to undue and illegal force and privation, and in order to obtain his liberty, or to avoid such illegal hardship, he enters into a contract, he may allege this duress in avoidance of the contract so entered into; but an imprisonment is not deemed sufficient duress to avoid a contract obtained through the medium of its coercion, if the party was in proper custody under the regular process of a court of competent jurisdiction; and this distinction results from the above rule of law, *executio juris non habet injuriam.*[5]

[1] 6 H. L. Cas. 433. [2] *Post*, Chap. V.

[3] Per Lord Cranworth, 6 H. L. Cas. 551.

[4] See the maxim, *Volenti non fit injuria*, *post*, Chap. V.

[5] 2 Inst. 482; Stepney *v.* Lloyd, Cro. Eliz. 646; Anon., 1 Lev. 68; Waterer *v.* Freeman, Hobart 266; R. *v.* Southerton, 6 East 140; Anon., Aleyn R. 92; 2 Roll. R. 301.

Further, although, as elsewhere stated, an action will not lie to [*133] recover damages for the inconvenience *occasioned to a party who has been sued by another without reasonable or sufficient cause,[1] yet, if the proceedings in the action were against A., and a writ of execution is issued by mistake against the goods of B., trespass will clearly lie, at suit of the latter, against the execution creditor,[2] or against his attorney, who issued execution;[3] and where an attorney deliberately directs the execution of a warrant, he, by so doing, takes upon himself the chance of all consequences, and will be liable in trespass if it prove bad.[4] In cases similar to the above, however, the maxim as to *executio juris* is not in truth strictly applicable, because the proceedings actually taken are *not* sanctioned by the law, and therefore the party taking them, although acting under the color of legal process, is not protected.

CURSUS CURIÆ EST LEX CURIÆ.

(3 Bulst. 53.)

The practice of the court is the law of the court.[5]

[*134] "Every court is the guardian of its own records and *master of its own practice;"[6] and where a practice has existed

[1] Per Rolfe, B., 11 M. & W. 756; and cases cited under the maxim, *Ubi jus ibi remedium*, *post*, Chap. V.

[2] Jarmain *v.* Hooper, 7 Scott N. R. 663; Walley *v.* M'Connell, 13 Q. B. 903 (66 E. C. L. R.); see Riseley *v.* Ryle, 11 M. & W. 16; Collett *v.* Foster, 2 H. & N. 356; Churchill *v.* Siggers, 3 E. & B. 929 (79 E. C. L. R.); Roret *v.* Lewis, 5 D. & L. 371; Dimmack *v.* Bowley, 2 C. B. N. S. 542.

[3] Davies *v.* Jenkins, 11 M. & W. 745; Rowles *v.* Senior, 8 Q. B. 677 (55 E. C. L. R.), and cases there cited.

[4] Green *v.* Elgie, 5 Q. B. 99 (48 E. C. L. R.).

[5] "It was a common expression of the late Chief Justice Tindal, that the course of the court is the practice of the court;" per Cresswell, J., Freeman *v.* Tranah, 12 C. B. 414 (74 E. C. L. R.).

"The power of each court over its own process is unlimited; it is a power incident to all courts, inferior as well as superior; were it not so, the court would be obliged to sit still and see its own process abused for the purpose of injustice." Per Alderson, B., Cocker *v.* Tempest, 7 M. & W. 502, cited, per Willes, J., Stammers *v.* Hughes, 18 C. B. 535 (86 E. C. L. R.).

[6] Per Tindal, C. J., Scales *v.* Cheese, 12 M. & W. 687; Gregory *v.* Duke of

it is convenient (unless in cases of extreme urgency and necessity)[1] to adhere to it, because it is the practice, even though no reason can be assigned for it;[2] for an inveterate practice in the law generally stands upon principles that are founded in justice and convenience.[3] Hence, if any necessary proceeding in an action be informal, or be not done within the time limited for it, or in the manner prescribed in the practice of the court, it may often be set aside for irregularity, for *via trita via tuta;*[4] and the courts of law will not sanction a speculative novelty without the warrant of any principle, precedent or authority.[5]

It has been remarked, moreover, that there is a material distinction between those things which are required to be done by the common or statute law of the land, and things required to be done by the rules and practice of the court. Anything required to be done by the law of the land must be noticed by a court of error, but a court of error does not notice the practice of another court.[6] Moreover, "where, by an Act of Parliament, power is *given [*135] to a single judge to decide a matter, his decision is not absolutely final; but the court adopt the same rule as where he acts in the exercise of his ordinary jurisdiction; and though the legislature says that he shall have power finally to determine a matter, that does not mean that the practice of the court shall be departed from."[7]

In a court of equity, as in a court of law, the maxim, *cursus curiæ est lex curiæ*, is frequently recognized and applied. The

Brunswick, 2 H. L. Cas. 415; Mellish *v.* Richardson, 1 Cl. & Fin. 221, cited Newton *v.* Boodle, 6 C. B. 529 (60 E. C. L. R.); per Alderson, B., Ex parte Story, 8 Exch. 199; Jackson *v.* Galloway, 1 C. B. 280 (50 E. C. L. R.); Reg. *v.* Justices of Denbighshire, 15 L. J. Q. B., 335; per Lord Wynford, Ferrier *v.* Howden, 4 Cl. & Fin. 32. But see Fleming *v.* Dunlop, 7 Cl. & Fin. 43.

[1] See, for instance, Finney *v.* Beesley, 17 Q. B. 86 (79 E. C. L. R.).

[2] Per Lord Ellenborough, C. J., Bovill *v.* Wood, 2 M. & S. 25; 15 East 226; per Lord Campbell, C. J., Edwards *v.* Martyn, 21 L. J. Q. B. 88; s. c., 17 Q. B. 693 (79 E. C. L. R.).

[3] Per Lord Eldon, C., Buck 279. See per Lord Abinger, C. B., Jacobs *v.* Layborn, 11 M. & W. 690.

[4] Wood *v.* Hurd, 3 B. N. C. 45 (32 E. C. L. R.); 10 Rep. 142.

[5] See Judgm., Ex parte Overseers of Tollerton, 3 Q. B. 799 (43 E. C. L. R.).

[6] Per Holroyd, J., Sandon *v.* Proctor, 7 B. & C. 806, cited arg. Bradley *v.* Warburg, 11 M. & W. 455.

[7] Per Rolfe, B., Shortridge *v.* Young, 12 M. & W. 7.

court will however, as several times remarked,[1] adapt its practice and course of proceeding to the existing state of society, and not, by too strict an adherence to forms and rules established under different circumstances, decline to administer justice and to enforce rights for which there is no remedy elsewhere.

Lastly, even where the course of practice in criminal law has been unfavorable to parties accused, and contrary to the principles of justice and humanity, it has been held that such practice constituted the law, and could not be altered without the authority of Parliament.[2]

CONSENSUS TOLLIT ERRORUM.

(2 Inst. 123.)

The acquiescence of a party who might take advantage of an error obviates its effect.

In accordance with this rule, if the venue in an action is laid in the [*136] wrong place, and this is done *per assensum *partium*, with the consent of both parties, and so entered of record, it shall stand;[3] and where, by consent of both plaintiff and defendant, the venue was laid in London, it was held, that no objection could afterwards be taken to the venue, notwithstanding it ought, under a particular Act of Parliament, to have been laid in Surrey, for *per Curiam—Consensus tollit errorem.*[4] Consent cannot, however (unless by the express words of a statute), give jurisdiction,[5] for a mere nullity cannot be waived.

On the maxim under consideration depends also the important doctrine of waiver, that is, the passing by of a thing;[6] a doctrine

[1] Per Lord Cottenham, C., Wallworth *v.* Holt, 4 My. & Cr. 635; Taylor *v.* Salmon, Id. 141–2; Mare *v.* Malachy, 1 My. & Cr. 559.

[2] Per Maule, J., 8 Scott N. R. 599, 600.

[3] Fineux *v.* Hovenden, Cro. Eliz. 664; Co. Litt. 126, a, and Mr. Hargrave's note (1); 5 Rep. 37; Dyer 367. See Crow *v.* Edwards, Hob. 5.

[4] Furnival *v.* Stringer, 1 B. N. C. 68.

[5] See Andrews *v.* Elliott, 6 E. & B. 338 (88 E. C. L. R.) (recognized in Tyerman *v.* Smith, Id. 719, 724), which illustrates the above maxim; Lawrence *v.* Wilcock, 11 A. & E. 941 (39 E. C. L. R.); Vansittart *v.* Taylor, 4 E. & B. 910, 912 (82 E. C. L. R.).

[6] Toml. Law. Dict., tit. *Waiver*. See Earl of Darnley *v.* London, Chatham and Dover R. C., L. R. 2 H. L. 43; Ramsden *v.* Dyson, L. R. 1 H. L. 129, cited *post*.

which is of very general application both in the science of pleading and in those practical proceedings which are to be observed in the progress of a cause from the first issuing of process to the ultimate signing of judgment and execution.

With reference to pleading, however, the rule that an error will be cured by the consent or wavier of the opposite party must be taken with considerable limitation; for, although faults in pleading are in some cases aided by pleading over, it frequently happens that a party who has pleaded over, without demurring, may nevertheless afterwards avail himself of an insufficiency in the pleading of his adversary; and the reason is, that, although the effect of a demurrer is to admit the truth of all matters of *fact sufficiently pleaded on the other side, yet, by pleading, a party [*137] does not admit the sufficiency in the law of the facts adversely alleged;[1] for, when judgment is to be given, whether the issue be in law or fact, and whether the cause have proceeded to issue or not, the court is in general bound to examine the whole record, and adjudge according to the legal right as it may on the whole appear; so that if, after pleading over, a demurrer arise at some subsequent stage, the court will take into consideration retrospectively the sufficiency in law of matters to which an answer in fact has been given; and hence it follows, that advantage may often be taken by either party of a legal insufficiency in the pleading on the other side, either by motion in arrest of judgment, or motion for judgment *non obstante veredicto*, or on error, according to the circumstances of the case.[2]

These remarks are confined, however, to defects in matter of *substance;* for, with respect to objections of mere *form*, it is laid down that, if a man pleads over, he shall never take advantage of any slip committed in the pleading of the other side.[3]

When applied to the proceedings in an action, waiver may be defined to be the doing something after an irregularity committed, and with a knowledge of such irregularity, where the irregularity might have been corrected before the act was done; and it is essential to distinguish a proceeding which is merely irregular from one which is completely defective and void. In the latter case the pro-

[1] Steph. Pl., 6th ed., 136. See Brooke *v.* Brooke, Sid. 184.
[2] Steph. Pl., 6th ed., 112, 139, 140.
[3] Per Holt, C. J., Anon., 2 Salk. 519.

ceeding is a nullity, which cannot be waived by any laches or subsequent proceedings of the opposite party.

[*138] *Where, however, an irregularity has been committed, and where the opposite party knows of the irregularity, it is a fixed rule, observed as well by courts of equity as of common law, that he should come in the first instance to avail himself of it, and not allow the other party to proceed to incur expense. "It is not reasonable afterwards to allow the party to complain of that irregularity, of which, if he had availed himself in the first instance, all that expense would have been rendered unnecessary;"[1] and, therefore, if a party, after any such irregularity has taken place, consents to a proceeding which, by insisting on the irregularity, he might have prevented, he waives all exceptions to the irregularity. This is a doctrine long established and well known. *Consensus tollit errorem* is a maxim of the common law, and the dictate of common sense.[2]

It may appear in some measure superfluous to add, that the consent which cures error in legal proceedings may be implied as well as expressed: for instance—where, at the trial of a cause, a proposal was made by the judge in the presence of the counsel on both sides, who made no objection, that the jury should assess the damages contingently, with leave to the plaintiff to move to enter a verdict for the amount found by the jury, it was held that both parties were bound by the proposal, and that the plaintiff's counsel was not therefore at liberty to move for a new trial on the ground of misdirection,[3] for *qui tacet consentire videtur*,[4] the silence of counsel implied their [*139] *assent to the course adopted by the judge, and "a man who does not speak when he ought shall not be heard when he desires to speak."[5]

[1] Per Lord Lyndhurst, C., St. Victor *v.* Devereux, 14 L. J. Chan. 246.

[2] See 7 Johnson (U. S.) R. 611.

[3] Morrish *v.* Murrey, 13 M. & W. 52; Booth *v.* Clive, 10 C. B. 827 (70 E. C. L. R.); Hughes *v.* Great Western R. C., 14 C. B. 637 (78 E. C. L. R.). See also Harrison *v.* Wright, 13 M. & W. 816.

[4] Jenk. Cent. 32. See judgment, Gosling *v.* Veley, 7 Q. B. 455 (53 E. C. L. R.); Houldsworth *v.* Evans, L. R. 3 H. L. 263.

[5] 2 Comstock (U. S.) R. 281. See Martin *v.* Great Northern R. C., 16 C. B. 179, 196–7 (81 E. C. L. R.); Perry *v.* Davis, 3 C. B. N. S. 769; Beaudry *v.* Mayor, &c., of Montreal, 11 Moo. P. C. C. 399.

"If a client be present in court and stand by and see his solicitor enter into

Communis Error facit Jus.

(4 Inst. 240.)

Common error sometimes passes current as law.

The law so favors the public good, that it will in some cases permit a common error to pass for right;[1] as an instance of which may be mentioned the case of common recoveries, which were fictitious proceedings introduced by a kind of *pia fraus* to elude the statute *de Donis*, and which were at length allowed by the courts to be a bar to an estate tail, so that these recoveries, however clandestinely introduced, became by long use and acquiescence a most common assurance of lands, and were looked upon as the legal mode of conveyance whereby tenant in tail might dispose of his lands and tenements.[2]

*However, the above maxim, although well known and therefore here inserted, must be received and applied with very great caution. [*140]

"It has been sometimes said," observed Lord Ellenborough, "*communis error facit jus;* but I say, *communis opinio* is evidence of what the law is—not where it is an opinion merely speculative and theoretical, floating in the minds of persons; but where it has been made the groundwork and substratum of practice."[3] So it was remarked by another learned and distinguished judge,[4] that he hoped never to hear this rule insisted upon, because it would be to

terms of an agreement, and make no objection whatever to it, he is not at liberty afterwards to repudiate it." Per Sir J. Romilly, M. R., Swinfen *v.* Swinfen, 24 Beav. 559. See Chambers *v.* Mason, 5 C. B. N. S. 59 (94 E. C. L. R.); Prestwich *v.* Poley, 18 C. B. N. S. 806.

[1] Noy, Max., 9th ed., p. 37; 4 Inst. 240; per Blackburn, J., Reg. *v.* Justices of Sussex, 2 B. & S. 680 (110 E. C. L. R.), and in Jones *v.* Tapling, 12 C. B. N. S. 846-7 (104 E. C. L. R.); s. c., 11 H. L. Cas. 290; Waltham *v.* Sparkes, 1 Lord Raym. 42. See also the remarks of Lord Brougham in Phipps *v.* Ackers, 9 Cl. & Fin. 598 (referring to Cadell *v.* Palmer, 10 Bing. 140 (25 E. C. L. R.)), and in the Earl of Waterford's Peerage claim, 6 Cl. & Fin. 172; also in Devaynes *v.* Noble, 2 Russ. & My. 506; Janvrin *v.* De la Mare, 14 Moo. P. C. C. 334.

[2] Noy, Max., 9th ed., pp. 37, 38; Plowd. 33 b.

[3] Isherwood *v.* Oldknow, 3 M. & S. 396, 397; per Vaughan, B., Garland *v.* Carlisle, 2 Cr. & M. 95; Co. Litt. 186, a.

[4] Mr. Justice Foster, cited per Lord Kenyon, C. J., R. *v.* Eriswell, 3 T. R. 725; arg. Smith *v.* Edge, 6 T. R. 563.

set up a misconception of the law in destruction of the law; and in another case, it was observed that "even *communis error*, and a long course of local irregularity, have been found to afford no protection to one *qui spondet peritiam artis.*[1] Some useful and stringent remarks on the practical application and value of the above maxim were made also by Lord Denman, C. J., delivering judgment in the House of Lords, in a well-known case, involving important legal and constitutional doctrines; in the course of this judgment, which is well worthy of careful perusal, his lordship took occasion to remark, that a large portion of the *legal opinion* which has passed current for law falls within the description of "law taken for granted;" and that "when, in the pursuit of truth, we are obliged to investigate the grounds of the law, it is plain, and has often been proved by recent experience, that the mere statement [*141] and re-statement *of a doctrine—the mere repetition of the *cantilena* of lawyers—cannot make it law, unless it can be traced to some competent authority, and if it be irreconcilable to some clear legal principle."[2]

The foregoing remarks may be thus exemplified:—A general understanding has prevailed, founded on the practice of a long series of years, that if patented inventions were used in any of the departments of the public service, the patentees would be remunerated by the ministers or officers of the crown administering such departments, as though the use had been by private individuals. In numerous instances payments had been made to patentees for the use of patented inventions in the public service, and even the legal advisers of the crown appeared also to have considered the right as well settled. There was, further, little doubt that on the faith of the understanding and practice many inventors had, at great expense of time and money, perfected and matured inventions, in the expectation of deriving a portion of their reward from the adoption of their inventions in the public service. It was, nevertheless, held that the language of the patent should be interpreted according to the legal effect of its terms, irrespective of the practice.[3]

[1] 6 Cl. & Fin. 199.

[2] Lord Denman's judgment in O'Connell *v.* Reg., edited by Mr. Leahy, p. 28. See also the allusions to Hutton *v.* Balme, and Reg. *v.* Millis, Id., pp. 13, 24. Et vide per Pollock, C. B., 2 H. & N. 139.

[3] Feather *v.* Reg., 6 B. & S. 289–292 (118 E. C. L. R.).

*De minimis non curat Lex. [*142]

(Cro. Eliz. 353.)

The law does not concern itself about trifles.

Courts of justice do not in general take trifling and immaterial matters into account;[1] and they will not, for instance, take notice of the fraction of a day, except in those cases where there are conflicting rights, for the determination of which it is necessary that they should do so.[2]

A familiar instance of the application of this maxim occurs likewise in the rule observed by the courts at Westminster, that new trials shall not be granted, at the instance either of plaintiff or defendant, on the ground of the verdict being against evidence, where the damages are less than 20*l.*[3]

"In ordinary," as remarked by Lord Kenyon, C. J.,[4] "where the damages are small, and the question too inconsiderable to be retried, the court have frequently refused to send the case back to another jury. But, *wherever a mistake of the judge has [*143] crept in and swayed the opinion of the jury, I do not recollect a single case in which the court have ever refused to grant a new trial."

A superior court also will stay proceedings in an action of debt

[1] Bell, Dict. and Dig. of Scotch Law 284; per Sir W. Scott, 2 Dods. Adm. R. 163; Graham *v.* Berry, 3 Moo. P. C. C. N. S. 223.

[2] Judgm., 14 M. & W. 582; per Holt, C. J., 2 Lord Raym. 1095; Reg. *v.* St. Mary, Warwick, 1 E. & B. 816 (72 E. C. L. R.); Wright *v.* Mills, 4 H. & N. 488, 493, 494; Evans *v.* Jones, 3 H. & C. 423; Page *v.* More, 15 Q. B. 684–6 (69 E. C. L. R.); Boosey *v.* Purday, 4 Exch. 145 (which illustrates the above proposition in connection with the law of copyright).

[3] Branson *v.* Didsbury, 12 A. & E. 631 (40 E. C. L. R.); Manton *v.* Bales, 1 C. B. 444; Macrow *v.* Hull, 1 Burr. 11; Burton *v.* Thompson, 2 Burr. 664; Apps *v.* Day, 14 C. B. 112 (78 E. C. L. R.); Hawkins *v.* Alder, 18 C. B. 640 (86 E. C. L. R.); see Allum *v.* Boultbee, 9 Exch. 738, 743; per Maule, J., 11 C. B. 653 (73 E. C. L. R.).

[4] Wilson *v.* Rastall, 4 T. R. 753. See Vaughan *v.* Wyatt, 6 M. & W. 496, 497; per Parke, B., Twig *v.* Potts, 1 Cr., M. & R. 93; Lee *v.* Evans, 12 C. B. N. S. 368 (104 E. C. L. R.); Mostyn *v.* Coles, 7 H. & N. 872, 876. In Haine *v.* Davey, 4 A. & E. 892 (31 E. C. L. R.), a new trial was granted for misdirection, though the amount in question was less than 1*l.* See Poole *v.* Whitcombe, 12 C. B. N. S. 770 (104 E. C. L. R.).

brought there, if it appear that the sum sought to be recovered is under 40*s*.[1]

In further illustration of the maxim *de minimis non curat lex*, we may observe that there are some injuries of so small and little consideration in the law that no action will lie for them;[2] for instance, in respect to payment of tithe, the principle which may be extracted from the case appears to be, that for small quantities of corn, involuntarily left in the process of raking, tithe shall not be payable, unless there be any particular fraud or intention to deprive the parson of his full right. Where, however, a farmer pursued such a mode of harvesting barley, that a considerable quantity of rakings was left scattered after the barley was bound into sheaves, the court held, that tithe was payable in respect of these rakings, although no actual fraud was imputed to the farmer, and although he and his servants were careful to leave as little rakings as possible in that mode of harvesting the crop.[3]

[*144] *It may be observed, however, that for an injury to real property incorporeal in action may be supported, however small the damage, and therefore a commoner may maintain an action on the case for an injury done to the common, though his proportion of the damage be found to amount only to a farthing;[4] and generally the superior courts of law have jurisdiction to hear and determine all suits, without any reference to the magnitude of the amount claimed or demanded, or to the extent of the injury complained of, subject, however, to the power of the judge to certify under stat. 43 Eliz. c. 6, where the damages recovered are less than 40*s*., and thereby deprive the plaintiff of his costs; and subject likewise to the provisions as to costs and jurisdiction contained in the County Court and some other Acts.

[1] Kennard *v.* Jones, 4 T. R. 495; Wellington *v.* Arters, 5 T. R. 64; Stutton *v.* Bament, 3 Exch. 831, 834. See Nurdin *v.* Fairbanks, 5 Exch. 738.

[2] See per Powys, J., Ashby *v.* White, 2 Lord Raym. 944, answered by Holt, C. J., Id. 953; Whitcher *v.* Hall, 5 B. & C. 269, 277 (11 E. C. L. R.); 2 Bla. Com., 21st ed., 262, where the rule respecting land gained by alluvion is referred to the maxim treated of in the text. The maxim "would apply only with respect to gradual accretions not appreciable except after the lapse of time," per Pollock, C. B., 2 H. & N. 138; and in Ford *v.* Lacey, 7 Id. 155.

[3] Glanville *v.* Stacey, 6 B. & C. 543 (13 E. C. L. R.).

[4] Pindar *v.* Wadsworth, 2 East 154. See 22 Vin. Abr. "*Waste*" (N.); Harrop *v.* Hirst, L. R. 4 Ex. 43, and other cases cited *post*, Chap. V.

The law having reference to the rights of a riparian proprietor to apply to his own use the running water, as stated by Mr. Chancellor Kent, in his commentaries,[1] and recognized by our courts,[2] illustrates how the maxim under notice may be applied. Every proprietor of land on the banks of a river has naturally an equal right to the use of the water flowing in the stream adjacent to his land, as it was wont to run without diminution or alteration. No proprietor has a right to use the water *to the prejudice of other proprietors above or below him, unless he has a prior right to divert it, or a title to some exclusive enjoyment. [*145] Streams of water, however, are intended for the use and comfort of man, and it would be unreasonable and contrary to the universal sense of mankind to debar every riparian proprietor from the application of the water to domestic, agricultural and manufacturing purposes, provided the use of it be made without causing material injury or annoyance to his neighbor below him. There will, no doubt, inevitably be, in the exercise of a perfect right to the use of the water, some evaporation and decrease of it, and some variations in the weight and velocity of the current; but *de minimis non curat lex;* and a right of action by the proprietor below would not necessarily flow from such consequences, but would depend upon the nature and extent of the complaint or injury, and the manner of using the water. All that the law requires of the party, by or over whose land the stream passes, is that he should use the water in a reasonable manner, and so as not to destroy or render useless, or materially diminish or affect the application of the water, by the proprietors above or below on the stream.

"The same law," it has been observed, "will be found to be applicable to the corresponding rights to air and light. These also are bestowed by Providence for the common benefit of man, and so long as the reasonable use by one man of this common property

[1] 7th ed. vol. 3, pp. 537–539.

[2] Judgm., Embrey *v.* Owen, 6 Exch. 369–371; Dickenson *v.* Grand Junction Canal Co., 7 Exch. 282; Sampson *v.* Hoddinott, 1 C. B. N. S. 590 (87 E. C. L. R.); s. c. affirmed, 3 Id. 591; Miner *v.* Gilmour, 12 Moo. P. C. C. 131 (where the rights of a riparian proprietor, as regards the use of water running by his land, are explained and defined); Nuttall *v.* Bracewell, 4 H. & C. 714; Rochdale Canal Co. *v.* King, 14 Q. B. 122, 136 (68 E. C. L. R.); Wood *v.* Waud, 3 Exch. 748. See Medway Navigation Co. *v.* Earl of Romney, 9 C. B. N. S. 575 (99 E. C. L. R.).

does not do actual and perceptible damage to the right of another to the similar use of it, no action will lie. A man cannot occupy a dwelling and consume fuel in it for domestic purposes, without its in some degree impairing the natural purity of the air; he cannot [*146] erect a building or *plant a tree near the house of another without in some degree diminishing the quantity of light he enjoys; but such small interruptions give no right of action; for they are necessary incidents to the common enjoyment by all.[1]

Nor only in cases analogous to those above mentioned, but in others of a different description, viz., where trifling irregularities or even infractions of the strict letter of the law are brought under the notice of the court, the maxim *de minimis non curat lex* is of frequent practical application.[2] It has, for instance, been applied to support a rate, in the assessment of which there were some comparatively trifling omissions of established forms.[3] So, with reference to proceedings for an infringement of the revenue laws,[4] Sir W. Scott observed—"The court is not bound to a strictness at once harsh and pedantic in the application of statutes. The law permits the qualification implied in the ancient maxim *de minimis non curat lex.*[5] Where there are irregularities of very slight consequence, it does not intend that the infliction of penalties should be inflexibly severe. If the deviation were a mere trifle, which, if [*147] continued in *practice, would weigh little or nothing on the public interest, it might properly be overlooked."

Lastly, in an indictment against several for a misdemeanor all are principals, because the law does not descend to distinguish different shades of guilt in this class of offences.

[1] Judgm., 6 Exch. 372–3.

[2] See in connection with criminal liability for a nuisance, Reg. *v.* Charlesworth, 16 Q. B. 1012 (71 E. C. L. R.); Reg. *v.* Betts, Id. 1022; Reg. *v.* Russell, 3 E. & B. 942 (77 E. C. L. R.).

[3] White *v.* Beard, 2 Curt. 493. But where the amount of a poor-rate at so much in the pound on the assessable value of premises involves the fraction of a farthing, a demand by the overseer of the whole farthing is excessive and illegal. Morton, app., Brammer, resp., 8 C. B. N. S. 791, 798 (98 E. C. L. R.), citing Baxter *v.* Faulam, 1 Wils. 129.

[4] The Reward, 2 Dods. Adm. R. 269, 270.

[5] This maxim may likewise be applied as follows:—"When we say that there is no evidence to go to a jury, we do not mean that there is literally none, but that there is none which ought reasonably to satisfy a jury that the fact sought to be proved is established." Per Maule, J., Jewell *v.* Parr, 13 C. B. 916 (76 E. C. L. R.); *ante*, pp. 109, 110.

Omnis Innovatio plus Novitate perturbat quam Utilitate prodest.

(2 Bulstr. 338.)

Every innovation occasions more harm and derangement of order by its novelty, than benefit by its abstract utility.

It has been an ancient observation in the laws of England, that, whenever a standing rule of law, of which the reason, perhaps, could not be remembered or discerned, has been wantonly broken in upon by statutes or new resolutions, the wisdom of the rule has in the end appeared from the inconveniences that have followed the innovation;[1] and the judges and sages of the law have therefore always suppressed new and subtle inventions in derogation of the common law.[2]

It is, then, an established rule to abide by former precedents, *stare decisis*, where the same points come again in litigation, as well to keep the scale of justice even and steady, and not liable to waver with every new judge's opinion, as also because, the law in that case *being solemnly declared and determined, what before was uncertain, and perhaps indifferent, is now become a permanent rule, which it is not in the breast of any subsequent judge to alter or swerve from according to his private sentiments; he being sworn to determine, not according to his own private judgment,[3] but according to the known laws and customs of the land,—not delegated to pronounce a new law, but to maintain and expound the old one[4]—*jus dicere et non jus dare.*[5]

[*148]

[1] 1 Com. by Broom & Hadley 60. See Ram's Science of Legal Judgment 112, *et seq.*

Lord Bacon tells us in his Essay on Innovations, that, "as the births of living creatures at first are ill-shapen, so are all innovations which are the births of time."

[2] Co. Litt. 282 b, 379 b; per Grose, J., 1 M. & S. 394.

[3] See per Lord Camden, 19 Howell's St. Tr. 1071; per Williams, J., 4 Cl. & Fin. 729; per Best, C. J., Newton *v.* Cowie, 4 Bing. 241 (13 E. C. L. R.); per Alderson, B., 4 Exch. 806.

[4] Per Lord Kenyon, C. J., 5 T. R. 682; 6 Id. 605; and 8 Id. 239; per Grose, J., 13 East 321; 9 Johnson (U. S.) R. 428; per Lord Hardwicke, C., Ellis *v.* Smith, 2 Ves. jun. 16.

[5] 7 T. R. 696; 1 B. & B. 563 (5 E. C. L. R.); Ram's Science of Legal Judgment, p. 2; arg. 10 Johnson (U. S.) R. 566. "My duty," says Alderson, B., in Miller *v.* Salomons, 7 Exch. 543, "is plain. It is to expound and not to make the law—to decide on it as I find it, not as I may wish it to be;" per Coltman, J., 4 C. B. 560–1 (56 E. C. L. R.).

And here we may observe the important distinction which exists between the legislative and the judicial functions. To legislate, *jus facere* or *jus dare*, is to exercise the will in establishing a rule of action. To administer the law, *jus dicere*, is to exercise the judgment in expounding and applying that rule according to legal principles. "The province of the legislature is not to construe but to enact, and their opinion not expressed in the form of law as a declaratory provision would be, is not binding on courts whose duty is to expound the statutes they have enacted,"[1] for the maxim of the Roman law, *ejus est interpretari cujus est condere*,[2] does not under our constitution hold.

Our common-law system, as remarked by a learned judge, consists in the applying to new combinations of [*149] *circumstances, those rules of law which we derive from legal principles and judicial precedents;[3] and for the sake of attaining uniformity, consistency and certainty, we must apply those rules where they are not plainly unreasonable and inconvenient to all cases which arise, and we are not at liberty to reject them, and to abandon all analogy to them, in those to which they have not yet been judicially applied, because we think that the rules are not as convenient and reasonable as we ourselves could have devised. "It appears to me to be of great importance to keep this principle of decision steadily in view, not merely for the determination of the particular case, but for the interests of law as a science."[4]

Accordingly where a rule has become settled law, it is to be followed, although some possible inconvenience may grow from a strict observance of it, or although a satisfactory reason for it is wanted, or although the principle and the policy of the rule may be questioned.[5] If, as has been observed, there is a general

[1] Judgm., 14 M. & W. 589.

[2] See Tayl. Civ. L., 4th ed., 96.

[3] As to the value of precedents: Palgr. Orig. Auth. King's Council, 9, 10. "An unnecessary departure from precedents, whether it spring from the love of change, or be the result of negligence or ignorance on the part of the pleader, ought not to be encouraged. It can only lead to useless litigation, delay and expense." See per Cur., Austin *v.* Holmes, 3 Denio (U. S.) R. 244.

[4] Per Parke, J., Mirehouse *v.* Rennell, 1 Cl. & Fin. 546. "When the law has become settled, no speculative reasoning upon its origin, policy or expediency should prevail against it." 3 Denio (U. S.) R. 50.

[5] Per Tindal, C. J., Mirehouse *v.* Rennell, 8 Bing. 557 (21 E. C. L. R.). See the authorities cited, Ram's Science of Legal Judgment 33–35.

hardship affecting a general class of cases, it is a consideration for the legislature, not for a court of justice. If there is a particular hardship from the particular circumstances of the case, nothing can be more dangerous or mischievous than upon those particular circumstances to deviate from a general *rule of [*150] law;[1] "hard cases," it has repeatedly been said, are apt to "make bad law,"[2] and *misera est servitus ubi jes est vagum aut incertum*[3]—obedience to law becomes a hardship when that law is unsettled or doubtful; which maxim applies with peculiar force to questions respecting real property; as, for instance, to family settlements, by which provision is made for unborn generations; "and if, by the means of new lights occurring to new judges, all that which was supposed to be law by the wisdom of our ancestors is to be swept away at a time when the particular limitations are to take effect, mischievous indeed will be the consequence to the public."[4]

So, likewise, with respect to matters which do not affect existing rights or properties to any great degree, but tend principally to influence the *future* transactions of mankind, it is generally more important that the rule of law should be settled, than that it should be theoretically correct.[5]

The above remarks as to the necessity of observing established principles apply to rules acted upon in courts of equity, as well as in the tribunals of common law, it *being a maxim that— [*151] *jus respicit æquitatem*,[6] the law pays regard to equity.

[1] Per Lord Loughborough, 2 Ves. jun. 426, 427; per Tindal, C. J., Doe d. Clarke *v.* Ludlam, 7 Bing. 180 (20 E. C. L. R.); per Pollock, C. B., Reg. *v.* Woodrow, 15 M. & W. 412; per Wilde, C. J., Kepp *v.* Wiggett, 16 L. J. C. P. 237; s. c., 6 C. B. 280 (60 E. C. L. R.).

[2] See 4 Cl. & Fin. 378; per Coleridge, J., 4 H. L. Cas. 611. "It is necessary that courts of justice should act on general rules, without regard to the hardship which in particular cases may result from their application." Judgm., 4 Exch. 718. See also Judgm., 3 Exch. 278.

[3] 4 Inst. 246; Shepherd *v.* Shepherd, 5 T. R. 51 n. (*a*); 2 Dwarr. Stats. 786; Bac. *Aphorisms*, vol. 7, p. 148; arg. 9 Johnson (U. S.) R. 427, and 11 Peters (U. S.) R. 286.

[4] Per Lord Kenyon, C. J., Doe *v.* Allen, 8 T. R. 504. See per Ashhurst, J., 7 T. R. 420.

[5] See per Lord Cottenham, C., Lozon *v.* Pryse, 4 My. & Cr. 617, 618.

[6] Co. Litt. 24 b. A court of law will also, in some cases, notice equitable rights: see per Parke, B., 12 M. & W. 445, and in 16 L. J. Exch. 163. "I

For, where a rule of property is settled in a court of equity, and is not repugnant to any legal principle, rule or determination, there is a propriety in adopting it at law, since it would be absurd and injurious to the community that different rules should prevail in different courts on the same subject.[1] And it was observed by Lord Eldon, while speaking of the practice of conveyancers in a case concerning a lease under a power, that courts of law should inquire of decisions in courts of equity, not for points founded on determinations merely equitable, but for legal judgments proceeding upon legal grounds, such as those courts of equity have for a long series of years been in the daily habit of pronouncing as the foundation of their decisions and decrees.[2]

The judicial rule—*stare decisis*[3]—does, however, admit of exceptions, where the former determination is most evidently contrary to reason—much more, if it be clearly contrary to the divine law. But, even in such cases, subsequent judges do not pretend to make [*152] a new *law, but to vindicate the old one from misrepresentation. For if it be found that the former decision is manifestly absurd or unjust, it is declared, not that such a sentence was *bad law*, but that it was *not law;* that is, that it is not the established custom of the realm, as has been erroneously determined.[4]

We may appropriately conclude these remarks with observing, that, whilst on the one hand innovation on settled law is to be avoided, yet, "the mere lateness of time at which a principle has become established is not a strong argument against its soundness, if nothing has been previously decided inconsistent with it, and it

have no doubt," observes Lord Campbell, C. J., in Sims *v.* Marryat, 17 Q. B. 292 (79 E. C. L. R.), that the judges of a common law court take judicial notice, not only of the doctrines of equity, but of those of every branch of English law when they incidentally come before them."

[1] Farr *v.* Newman, 4 T. R. 636.

[2] Smith *v.* Doe, 7 Price 590; s. c., 2 B. & B. 599. So in Ralston *v.* Hamilton, 4 Macq. Sc. App. Cas. 405, Lord Westbury, C., observes, "The rules which govern the transmission of property are the creatures of positive law, and when once established and recognized, their justice or injustice in the abstract is of less importance to the community than that the rules themselves shall be constant and invariable."

[3] As to which, see Gifford *v.* Livingston, 2 Denio (U. S.) R. 392–3.

[4] 1 Com. by Broom & Hadley 60.

be in itself consistent with legal analogies."[1] Nay, it is even true that "a froward retention of custom is as turbulent a thing as an innovation; and they that reverence too much old times are but a scorn to the new."[2]

[1] Judgm., Gosling *v.* Veley, 7 Q. B. 441 (53 E. C. L. R.); per Lord Denman, C. J., 10 Q. B. 950.

[2] Bacon's Essays, "Of Innovations."

[*153]

*CHAPTER IV.

RULES OF LOGIC.

THE maxims immediately following have been placed together, and entitled "Rules of Logic," because they result from a very simple process of reasoning. Some of them, indeed, may be considered as axioms, the truth of which is self-evident, and consequently admit of illustration only. A few examples have in each case been given, showing how the particular rule has been held to apply, and other instances of a like nature will readily suggest themselves to the reader.[1]

UBI EADEM RATIO IBI IDEM JUS.

(Co. Litt. 10 a.)

Like reason doth make like law.[2]

The law consists, not in particular instances and precedents, but in the reason of the law;[3] for reason is the life of the law—nay, the common law itself is nothing else but reason; which is to be understood of an artificial perfection of reason, acquired by long study, observation and experience, and not of every man's natural reason.[4]

[*154] *The following instances will serve to show in what manner the above maxim may be practically applied:—

When any deed, as a bond, is altered in a point *material*[5] by the obligee, or by a stranger without his privity, the deed thereby be-

[1] The title of this division of the subject has been adopted from Noy's Maxims, 9th ed., p. 5.

[2] Co. Litt. 10 a.

[3] Ashby *v.* White, 2 Lord Raym. 957: the judgment of Lord Holt in this celebrated case well illustrates the position in the text.

[4] Co. Litt. 97 b.

[5] *Secus,* if the alteration be in a point immaterial, Aldous *v.* Cornwell, L. R. 3 Q. B. 573, where the action was on a promissory note. See Andrews *v.* Lawrence, 19 C. B. N. S. 768 (99 E. C. L. R.).

comes void;[1] for the law will not permit a man to take the chance of committing a fraud, and when that fraud is detected, of recovering on the instrument as it was originally made. In such a case the law intervenes, and says, that the deed thus altered no longer continues the same deed, and that no person can maintain an action upon it; and this principle of the law is calculated to prevent fraud and to deter men from tampering with written securities.[2] The broad principle thus recognized has been likewise established in regard to bills of exchange and promissory notes;[3] on all such instruments a duty arises analogous to the duty arising on deeds, and a "party who has the custody of an instrument made for his benefit is bound to preserve it in its original state." The law having been long settled as to deeds, was held to be also applicable to those mercantile *instruments, which, though not under seal, yet possess properties, the existence of which, in the case of deeds, was, it must be presumed, the foundation of the rule above stated,—*ubi eadem est ratio eadem est lex;* and therefore, in the case below cited, it was held that an *unauthorized*[4] alteration in the date of a bill of exchange after acceptance, whereby the payment would be accelerated, even when made by a stranger, avoids the instrument, and that no action can be afterwards brought upon it by an innocent holder for a valuable consideration.[5] By a yet more recent decision, the

[*155]

[1] Pigot's Case, 11 Rep. 26 b, cited Davidson *v.* Cooper, 11 M. & W. 799; s. c., in error, 13 Id. 343. Whelpdale's Case, 5 Rep. 119 a; per Lord Denman, C. J., Harden *v.* Clifton, 1 Q. B. 524 (41 E. C. L. R.); Agricultural Cattle Insurance Co. *v.* Fitzgerald, 16 Q. B. 432 (71 E C. L. R.); Doe d. Tatum *v.* Catomore, 16 Q. B. 745; Keane *v.* Smallbone, 17 C. B. 179 (79 E. C. L. R.); arg. Bamberger *v.* Commercial Credit Mutual Ass. Soc., 15 C. B. 676, 692 (80 E. C. L. R.). See Gollan *v.* Gollan, 4 Macq. Sc. App. Cas. 585.

[2] Master *v.* Miller, 4 T. R. 320; s. c., affirmed in error, 2 H. Bla. 140. Gardner *v.* Walsh, 5 E. & B. 83 (85 E. C. L. R.) (overruling Catton *v.* Simpson, 8 A. & E. 136 (35 E. C. L. R.)); Burchfield *v.* Moore, 3 E. & B. 683 (77 E. C. L. R.); Saul *v.* Jones, 1 E. & E. 63 (72 E. C. L. R.); Warrington *v.* Early, 2 E. & B. 763 (75 E. C. L. R.). See Green *v.* Attenborough, 3 H. & C. 468; West *v.* Steward, 14 M. & W. 46; Fazakerley *v.* M'Knight, 6 E. & B. 795 (88 E. C. L. R.); Hamelin *v.* Bruck, 9 Q. B. 306 (58 E. C. L. R.).

[3] Master *v.* Miller, 4 T. R. 320.

[4] See Tarleton *v.* Shingler, 7 C. B. 812 (62 E. C. L. R.); 4 Scott N. R. 732, n. (29).

[5] Master *v.* Miller, *supra;* Hirschfeld *v.* Smith, L. R. 1 C. P. 340; Lord Falmouth *v.* Roberts, 9 M. & W. 471; Judgm., Davidson *v.* Cooper, 11 M. &

same doctrine was extended to the case of bought and sold notes; and it was held, that a vendor, who, after the bought and sold notes had been exchanged, prevailed on a broker, without the consent of the vendee, to add a term to the bought note, for his (the vendor's) benefit, thereby lost all title to recover against the vendee.[1] And the Court of Exchequer have since held that the same principle applies to a guarantee, and that it is a good ground of defence, that the instrument has, whilst in the plaintiff's hands, received a material alteration,[2] from some person to the defendant unknown, and without his knowledge or consent.[3]

[*156] *So, the insertion of material words in the margin of a charter-party by the broker, but without the knowledge of the owner, has in a recent case[4] been held to vitiate it. "It is, no doubt," observed Martin, B., delivering the judgment, "apparently a hardship that, where what was the original charter-party is perfectly clear and indisputable, and where the alteration or addition was made without any fraudulent intention, and by a person not a party to the contract, a perfectly innocent man should thereby be deprived of a beneficial contract; but, on the other hand, it must be borne in mind, that, to permit any tampering with written documents, would strike at the root of all property, and that it is of the most essential importance to the public interest that no alteration whatever should be made in written contracts, but that they should continue to be and remain in exactly[5] the same state and condition as when signed and executed, without addition, alteration, rasure, or obliteration."[6]

W. 800; s. c., in error, 13 M. & W. 343; Mason *v.* Bradley, 11 M. & W. 590; Parry *v.* Nicholson, 13 M. & W. 778; Gould *v.* Coombs, 1 C. B. 543 (87 E. C. L. R.); Bradley *v.* Bardsley, 14 M. & W. 372; Crotty *v.* Hodges, 5 Scott N. R. 221; Bell *v.* Gardiner, 4 Scott N. R. 621; Baker *v.* Jubber, 1 Id. 26. See Harrison *v.* Cotgreave, 4 C. B. 562 (93 E. C. L. R.).

[1] Powell *v.* Divett, 15 East 29; Mollet *v.* Wackerbarth, 5 C. B. 181 (94 E. C. L. R.).

[2] See Sanderson *v.* Symonds, 1 B. & B. 426 (5 E. C. L. R.).

[3] Davidson *v.* Cooper, 11 M. & W. 778, 800; s. c., 13 M. & W. 343; Parry *v.* Nicholson, 13 M. & W. 778; Mason *v.* Bradley, 11 M. & W. 590; Hemming *v.* Trenery, 9 A. & E. 926 (36 E. C. L. R.); Calvert *v.* Baker, 4 M. & W. 407.

[4] Crookewit *v.* Fletcher, 1 H. & N. 893.

[5] An immaterial alteration, however, does not avoid the instrument, *ante*, p. 154, n. 5.

[6] Judgm., 1 H. & N. 912–13, recognizing Davidson *v.* Cooper, *supra*. As to

We may add, in connection with the subject here touched upon, that, inasmuch as a deed cannot be altered, after it is executed, without fraud or wrong, and the presumption is against fraud or wrong, interlineations or erasures apparent on the face of a deed will be presumed to have been made before its execution; but, as a testator may alter his will after execution without fraud or wrong, the presumption is, that an alteration[1] appearing on its *face, [*157] was in the absence of evidence to the contrary, made subsequent to its execution.[2]

There are, however, some things for which, as Lord Coke observes, no reason can be given,[3] and with reference to which the words of the civil law hold true—*non omnium quæ à majoribus constituta sunt ratio reddi potest;*[4] and therefore, we are compelled to admit, that in the legal science, *qui rationem in omnibus quærunt rationem subvertunt.*[5] It is, indeed, sometimes dangerous to stretch the invention to find out legal reasons for what is undoubted law;[6] and this observation applies peculiarly to the mode of construing an Act of Parliament, in order to ascertain and carry out the intention of the legislature: in so doing, the judges will bend and conform their legal reason to the words of the Act, and will rather construe them literally than strain their meaning beyond the obvious intention of Parliament.[7] The spirit of the maxim prefixed to these remarks, here, however, manifestly prevails; for, as we read in the Digest,[8] *non possunt omnes articuli singillatim aut legibus aut senatûs-consultis comprehendi: sed cum in aliquâ causâ sententia eorum manifesta est, is, qui jurisdictioni præest, ad similia procedere atque*

the effect of an erasure in an affidavit, see Re Bingle, 15 C. B. 449 (80 E. C. L. R.). As to altering a record, see Suker *v.* Neale, 1 Exch. 468.

[1] There is, however, a "marked distinction" between an alteration and an interlineation. In the goods of Cadge, L. R. 1 P. & D. 543.

[2] Doe d. Tatum *v.* Catomore, 16 Q. B. 745; Doe d. Shallcross *v.* Palmer, Id. 747; In the goods of Hardy, 30 L. J. P. M. & A. 143.

[3] Hix *v.* Gardiner, 2 Bulstr. 196; cited arg. Leuckhart *v.* Cooper, 3 Bing. N. C. 104 (32 E. C. L. R.).

[4] D. 1, 3, 20.

[5] 2 Rep. 75, a.

[6] Per Alderson, B., Ellis *v.* Griffith, 16 M. & W. 110.

[7] T. Raym. 355, 356; per Lord Brougham, C., Leith *v.* Irvine, 1 My. & K. 289. As to the mode of construing Acts of Parliament, see further, *post*, Chap. VIII.

[8] D. 1, 3, 12, and 13.

ita jus dicere debet. Nam, ut ait Pedius, quotiens lege aliquid unum vel alterum introductum est, bona occasio est, cœtera, quæ [*158] **tendunt ad eamden utilitatem, vel interpretatione, vel certè jurisdictione suppleri.*

Further, although it is laid down that the law is the perfection of reason, and that it always intends to conform thereto, and that what is not reason is not law, yet this must not be understood to mean that the particular reasons of every rule in the law can at the present day be always precisely assigned: it is sufficient if there be nothing in it flatly contradictory to reason, and then the law will presume that the rule in question is well founded, *multa in jure communi*, as Lord Coke observes, *contra rationem disputandi, pro communi utilitate introducta sunt*[1]—many things have been introduced into the common law, with a view to the public good, which are inconsistent with sound reason. *Quod verò contra rationem juris receptum est, non est producendum ad consequentias.*[2]

The maxim cited from Lord Coke is peculiarly applicable when the reasonableness of an alleged custom has to be considered: in such a case, it does not follow, from there being at this time no apparent reason for such custom, that there never was.[3] If, however, it be in tendency contrary to the public good, or injurious or prejudicial to the many, and beneficial only to some particular person, such custom is and must be repugnant to the law of reason, for it could not have had a reasonable commencement.[4]

[*159] *Again—A clerk who has held preferment in one bishopric is not, on being presented to a living in another bishopric, bound, as a condition precedent to his examination on the question of fitness, to produce letters testimonial and commendatory from his former bishop—if such a rule existed a door would thus be opened to very arbitrary and capricious proceedings, rendering the title of the clerk and the right of the patron dependent on the will of the prior bishop—such a conclusion would be at variance

[1] Co. Litt. 70 b. *Multa autem jure civili contra rationem disputandi pro utilitate communi recepta esse innumerabilibus rebus probari potest:* D. 9, 2, 51, § 2.

[2] D. 1, 3, 14.

[3] Arg. Tyson *v.* Smith, in error, 9 A. & E. 406, 416.

[4] Judgm., 9 A. & E. 421, 422 (36 E. C. L. R.). See further as to the reasonableness and validity of a custom, *post*, Chap. X.

with reason, and therefore repugnant to what is called "the policy of the law."[1]

We may conclude these remarks with calling to mind the well-known saying: *lex plus laudatur quando ratione probatur*[2]—then is the law most worthy of approval, when it is consonant to reason; and with Lord Coke we may hold it to be generally true, "that the law is unknown to him that knoweth not the reason thereof, and that the known certainty of the law is the safety of all."[3]

CESSANTE RATIONE LEGIS CESSAT IPSA LEX.

(Co. Litt. 70 b.)

Reason is the soul of the law, and when the reason of any particular law ceases, so does the law itself.[4]

For instance, a member of Parliament is privileged from arrest during the session, in order that he may *discharge his public duties, and the trust reposed in him; but the reason [*160] of this privilege ceases at a certain time after the termination of the parliamentary session, because the public has then no longer an immediate interest in the personal freedom of the individuals composing the representative body, and *cessante causâ cessat effectus.*[5]

Again, where trees are excepted out of a demise, the soil itself is not excepted, but sufficient nutriment out of the land is reserved to sustain the vegetative life of the trees, for, without that, the trees which are excepted cannot subsist; but if, in such a case, the lessor fells the trees, or by the lessee's license grubs them up, then, according to the above rule, the lessee shall have the soil.[6] The

[1] Bishop of Exeter *v.* Marshall, L. R. 3 H. L. 17, 54.

[2] 1 Inst. Epil., cited per Lord Kenyon, C. J., Porter *v.* Bradley, 3 T. R. 146; and Dalmer *v.* Barnard, 7 Id. 252; arg. Doe d. Cadogan *v.* Ewart, 7 A. & E. 657 (34 E. C. L. R.).

[3] 1 Inst. Epil. "Certainty is the mother of repose, and therefore the common law aims at certainty:" per Lord Hardwicke, C., 1 Dick. 245.

[4] 7 Rep. 69; per Willes, C. J., Davis *v.* Powell, Willes 46, cited arg. 8 C. B. 786 (65 E. C. L. R.).

[5] See arg. Cas. temp. Hardw. 32; Gowdy *v.* Duncombe, 1 Exch. 430.

[6] Liford's Case, 11 Rep. 49, cited Hewitt *v.* Isham, 7 Exch. 79, and *post*, Chap. VI., s. 3.

same principle applies where a right exists of common *pur cause de vicinage:* a right depending upon a general custom and usage, which appears to have originated, not in any actual contract, but in a tacit acquiescence of all parties for their mutual benefit. This right does not, indeed, enable its possessor to put his cattle at once on the neighboring waste, but only on the waste which is in the manor where his own lands are situated; and it seems that the right of common vicinage should merely be considered as an excuse for the trespass caused by the straying of the cattle, which excuse the law allows by reason of the ancient usage, and in order to avoid multiplicity of suits which might arise where there is no separation or inclosure of adjacent commons.[1]

[*161] *But the parties possessing the respective rights of common may, if they so please, inclose against each other, and, after having done so, the right of common *pur cause de vicinage* can no longer be pleaded as an excuse to an action of trespass if the cattle stray, for *cessante ratione legis cessat lex.*[2]

A further illustration may be taken from the law of principal and agent, in which it is an established rule,[3] that where a contract not under seal for the sale of goods is made by an agent in his own name for an undisclosed principal, and on which therefore either the agent or the principal may sue, the defendant as against the latter is entitled to be placed in the same situation at the time of the disclosure of the real principal, as if the agent dealing in his own name had been in reality the principal: and this rule is to prevent the hardship under which a purchaser would labor, if, after having been induced by peculiar considerations,—such, for instance, as the consciousness of possessing a set-off,—to deal with one man, he could be turned over and made liable to another, to whom those considerations would not apply, and with whom he would not willingly have contracted. Where, however, the party contracting either knew, had the means of knowing, or must, from the circum-

[1] Jones *v.* Robin, 10 Q. B. 581, 620 (59 E. C. L. R.). See also Clarke *v.* Tinker, Id. 604; Prichard *v.* Powell, Id. 589.

[2] 4 Rep. 38; Co. Litt. 122 a; Finch's Law 8; per Powell, J., Broomfield *v.* Kirber, 11 Mod. 72; Gullett *v.* Lopes, 13 East 348; Judgm., Wells *v.* Pearcy, 1 Bing. N. C. 556, 566 (27 E. C. L. R.); Heath *v.* Elliott, 4 Bing. N. C. 388 (33 E. C. L. R.).

[3] Sims *v.* Bond, 5 B. & Ad. 393 (27 E. C. L. R.).

stances of the case, be presumed to have known, that he was dealing not with a principal but with an agent, the reason of the above rule ceases, and there the right of set-off cannot be maintained.[1]

*As regards the consent of parents to the marriage of [*162] their minor children, the Judge Ordinary recently observed[2] that "any analogy which existed between marriages by banns and marriages by notice to the registrar has been effaced—the attempt at securing that consent in marriages of the latter class by publicity relinquished—and the procurement of actual consent substituted in the same manner as had always been used in marriages by license. There is no reason, therefore, why those decisions which have hitherto only been applied to marriages by banns, and which have their foundation in the necessity for securing that publicity through which it is the object of banns to reach the parents' consent, should be applied to marriages in which that consent is otherwise attained and secured, *cessante ratione cessat et lex.*"

The law, proceeding on principles of public policy, has wisely said, that, where a case amounts to felony, the party injured shall not at once recover against the felon in a civil action; and this rule has been laid down and acted upon in order to secure the punishment of offenders; after the trial, however, and after the prisoner has been either acquitted or convicted, the case no longer falls within the reason on which the rule is founded, and then an action for the civil injury resulting from the wrongful act is maintainable.[3]

The science of pleading, also, will be found to present many apt illustrations of the axiom under consideration; **ex. gr.*, [*163] the general rule respecting the allegation of title in pleading is, that it is not necessary to allege title more precisely than is sufficient to show a liability in the party charged, or to defeat his present claim; and, except so far as these objects may require, a party is not compellable to show the precise estate which his adversary holds, even in a case where, if the same person were pleading

[1] Broom's Com., 4th ed., 539.

[2] Holmes *v.* Simmons, L. R. 1 P. & D. 528.

[3] Stone *v.* Marsh, 6 B. & C. 557, 564 (13 E. C. L. R.); Wellock *v.* Constantine, 2 H. & C. 146; per Buller, J., 4 T. R. 332. See White *v.* Spettigue, 13 M. & W. 603; Lee *v.* Bayes, 18 C. B. 599 (86 E. C. L. R.). See another instance of the application of this maxim, per Lord Ellenborough, C. J., Richards *v.* Heather, 1 B. & Ald. 33.

his own title, such precise allegation would be necessary; and the reason of this difference is, that a party must be presumed to be ignorant of his adversary's title, though he is bound to know his own.[1]

DE NON APPARENTIBUS ET NON EXISTENTIBUS EADEM EST RATIO.

(5 Rep. 6.)

Where the court cannot take judicial notice of a fact, it is the same as if the fact had not existed.[2]

The above "old and well-established maxim in legal proceedings," which "is founded on principles of justice as well as of law,"[3] applies where reliance is placed by a party on deeds or writings which are not produced in court, and the loss of which cannot be accounted for or supplied in the manner which the law has prescribed, in which case they are to be treated precisely as if non-existent.[4] So, on error brought for error in law, the court will not look out of the record;[5] and on a special verdict they will [*164] neither assume a fact not stated *therein, nor draw inferences of facts necessary for the determination of the case from other statements contained therein.[6]

In reading an affidavit also, the court will look solely at the facts deposed to, and will not presume the existence of additional facts or circumstances in order to support the allegations contained in it. To the above, therefore, and similar cases, occurring not only in civil but also in criminal proceedings, the maxim *quod non apparet non est*[7]—that which does not appear must be taken in law as if it were not[8]—is emphatically applicable.[9]

[1] See Judgm., Heap *v.* Livingston, 11 M. & W. 900.

[2] See per Buller, J., R. *v.* Bishop of Chester, 1 T. R. 404, "That which does not appear will not be presumed to exist," arg. 5 C. B. 53; per Cockburn, C. J., Reg. *v.* Overseers of Walcot, 2 B. & S. 560 (110 E. C. L. R.).

[3] See 12 Howard (U. S.) R. 253.

[4] Bell's Dict. of Scotch Law 287.

[5] Steph. Plead., 6th ed., 113.

[6] Tancred *v.* Christy, 12 M. & W. 316; Caudrey's Case, 5 Rep. 5; *ante*, p. 103.

[7] 2 Inst. 479; Jenk. Cent. 207.

[8] Vaugh. R. 169.

[9] The matter of an indictment ought to be full, express, and certain, and to import all the truth which is necessary by law: 4 Rep. 44, 47.

In an action by two commissioners of taxes[1] on a bond against the surety of a tax-collector, appointed under the provisions of the stat. 43 Geo. 3, c. 99, it appeared that the Act contained a proviso that no such bond should be put in suit against the surety for any deficiency, other than what should remain unsatisfied after sale of the lands, tenements, &c., of such collector, in pursuance of the powers given to the commissioners by the Act; it further appeared that, at the time when the said bond was put in suit, the obligor had lands, &c., within the jurisdiction of the plaintiffs, but of which they had no notice or knowledge: it was held, that seizure and sale of lands and other property of the collector, of the existence of which the commissioners had no notice or knowledge, was not a condition precedent to their right to proceed against the surety; this conclusion resulting, as was *observed, from the plain and sound principle contained in the above maxim.[2] [*165]

So, where a notice of dishonor of a bill of exchange describes the bill generally as "Your draft on A. B.," the court held, on motion for a nonsuit, that, if there were other bills or drafts to which the notice could refer, it was for the defendant to show such to be the fact; and as he had not done so, that the above maxim must be held to apply; for, inasmuch as it did not appear that there were other bills or notes, the court could not presume that there were any.[3]

Again, the increase *per alluvionem* is described to be when the sea, by casting up sand and earth by degrees, increases the land, and shuts itself within its previous limits.[4] In general, the land thus gained belongs to the crown, as having been a part of the very *fundus maris;* but if such alluvion be formed so imperceptibly and insensibly, that it cannot by any means be ascertained that the sea ever was there—*idem est non esse et non apparere*, and the land thus formed belongs as a perquisite to the owner of the land adjacent.[5]

[1] Gwynne *v.* Burnell, 6 Bing. N. C. 453 (37 E. C. L. R.); s. c., 1 Scott N. R. 711; 7 Cl. & Fin. 572.

[2] Per Vaughan, J., 6 Bing. N. C. 539 (37 E. C. L. R.); s. c., 1 Scott N. R. 798. See arg. Mather *v.* Thomas, 10 Bing. 47.

[3] Shelton *v.* Braithwaite, 7 M. & W. 436; Bromage *v.* Vaughan, 9 Q. B. 608 (58 E. C. L. R.); Mellersh *v.* Rippen, 7 Exch. 578.

[4] See Gifford *v.* Lord Yarborough, 5 Bing. 163 (15 E. C. L. R.).

[5] Hale, De Jure Maris, pt. 1, c. 4, p. 14; R. *v.* Lord Yarborough, 3 B. & C.

Lastly, it has been suggested[1] "that there is a distinction between process of superior and inferior courts; in the former, *omnia præsumuntur ritè esse acta*,[2] in [*166] *the latter the rule *de non apparentibus et non existentibus eadem est ratio* applies."

NON POTEST ADDUCI EXCEPTIO EJUSDEM REI CUJUS PETITUR DISSOLUTIO.

(Bac. Max., reg. 2.)

A matter, the validity of which is at issue in legal proceedings, cannot be set up as a bar thereto.

The above maxim, which is in strict accordance with logical reasoning, may be thus more generally expressed: where the legality of some proceeding is the subject matter in dispute between two parties, he who maintains its legality, and seeks to take advantage of it, cannot rely upon the proceeding itself as a bar to the adverse party; for otherwise the person aggrieved would be clearly without redress. "It were impertinent and contrary in itself," says Lord Bacon, "for the law to allow of a plea in bar of such matter as is to be defeated by the same suit, for it is included; and otherwise a man could never arrive at the end and effect of his suit."[3]

A few instances will be sufficient to show the application of this rule. Thus, if a man be attainted and executed, and the heir bring error upon the attainder, it would be bad to plead corruption of blood by the same attainder; for otherwise the heir would be without remedy ever to reverse the attainder.[4] In like manner, although a person attainted cannot be permitted to sue for any civil

97, 106 (10 E. C. L. R.); s. c., 1 Dow N. S. 178. This right has also been referred to the principle, *de minimis non curat lex*, arg. 3 B. & C. 99 (10 E. C. L. R.).

[1] Arg. Kinning *v.* Buchanan, 8 C. B. 286 (65 E. C. L. R.); *ante*, p. 96.

[2] *Post*, Chap. X.

[3] Bac. Max., reg. 2. Pusey *v.* Desbouvrie, 3 P. Wms. 317.

[4] Bac. Max., reg. 2. See 4 Bla. Com., 21st ed., 392; Loukes *v.* Holbeach, 4 Bing. 420, 423 (13 E. C. L. R.), cited and commented on, Byrne *v.* Manning, 2 Dowl. N. S. 403.

right in a court of law, yet he may take proceedings, *and will be heard for the purpose of reversing his attainder.[1] [*167]

On the same principle, in a court of equity, although a party in contempt is not generally entitled to take any proceeding in the cause, he will nevertheless be heard if his object be to get rid of the order or other proceeding which placed him in contempt, and he is also entitled to be heard for the purpose of resisting or setting aside for irregularity any proceedings subsequent to his contempt.[2] And where a man does not appear on a vicious proceeding, he is not to be held to have waived that very objection which is a legitimate cause of his non-appearance.[3]

Where the judge of an inferior court had illegally compelled a plaintiff who appeared to be nonsuited, and upon a bill of exceptions being brought, the nonsuit was entered on the record, the defendant was not allowed to contend that the entry on record precluded the plaintiff from showing that he had refused to consent to the nonsuit, for that would have been setting up as a defence the thing itself, which was the subject of complaint,—a course prohibited by the above maxim.[4] So, where a writ of error is brought, the judgment or opinion of the court below cannot, with propriety, be cited as an authority on the argument, because such judgment and opinion are *then under review.[5] The courts at Westminster, it has been said,[6] rightly abstain from over-ruling [*168] cases which have been long established, because if they did so, they would only disturb without finally settling the law. But when an appeal from any of their judgments is made to the House of Lords, however they may be warranted by previous authorities, the very

[1] See 1 Taunt. 84, 93.

The same principle applies in the case of proceedings to reverse outlawry: Jenk. Cent. 106; Finch's Law 46; Matthews *v.* Gibson, 8 East 527; Craig *v.* Levy, 1 Exch. 570.

[2] Per Lord Cottenham, C., Chuck *v.* Cremer, 1 Coop. 205; King *v.* Bryant, 3 My. & Cr. 191. See 1 Daniell's Ch. Pr. 3d ed., 354 *et seq.*

[3] Per Knight Bruce, V.-C., 15 L. J. (Bankruptcy) 7.

[4] Strother *v.* Hutchinson, 4 Bing. N. C. 83, 90; cited arg. Penny *v.* Slade, 5 Bing. N. C. 327 (35 E. C. L. R.); commented on and distinguished in Corsar *v.* Reed, 17 Q. B. 540 (79 E. C. L. R.).

[5] See per Alexander, C. B., R. *v.* Westwood, 7 Bing. 83 (20 E. C. L. R.); per North, C. J., Barnardiston *v.* Soane, 6 St. Tr. 1094. See also, in further illustration of the above maxim, Masters *v.* Lewis, 1 Lord Raym. 57.

[6] Per Lord Chelmsford, 11 H. L. Cas. 510, *et vide* opinion of judges, Id. 477.

object of the appeal being to bring those authorities under review for final determination, the House cannot upon the principle of *stare decisis*[1] refuse to examine the foundation upon which they rest.

The principal maxim seems also to apply, when the matter of the plea is not to be avoided in the same but in a different suit: and therefore, if a writ of error be brought to reverse an outlawry in any action, outlawry in another action shall not bar the plaintiff in error; for otherwise, if the outlawry was erroneous, it could never be reversed;[2] the general rule, however, being that an outlaw cannot enforce any proceeding for his own benefit.[3]

[*169] *ALLEGANS CONTRARIA NON EST AUDIENDUS.

(Jenk. Cent. 16.)

He is not to be heard who alleges things contradictory to each other.

The above, which is obviously an elementary rule of logic, and is not unfrequently applied in our courts of justice, will receive occasional illustration in the course of this work.[4] We may for the present observe that it expresses, in technical language, the trite saying of Lord Kenyon, that a man shall not be permitted to "blow hot and cold" with reference to the same transaction, or insist, at different times, on the truth of each of two conflicting allegations, according to the promptings of his private interest.[5]

[1] *Ante*, p. 147.

[2] Jenk. Cent. 37; Gilb. For. Rom. 54. See Bac. Max., reg. 2.

[3] Per Parke, B., Reg. *v.* Lowe, 8 Exch. 698. See Re Pyne, 5 C. B. 407 (57 E. C. L. R.); Davis *v.* Trevanion, 2 D. & L. 743; Walker *v.* Thelluson, 1 Dowl. N. S. 578.

[4] See particularly cases bearing upon the doctrine of *estoppel in pais*, which are collected under the maxim, *Nullus commodum capere potest de injuriâ suâ propriâ*, *post*, Chap. V.

[5] See Wood *v.* Dwarris, 11 Exch. 493; Andrews *v.* Elliott, 5 E. & B. 502 (85 E. C. L. R.); Tyerman *v.* Smith, 6 E. & B. 719 (88 E. C. L. R.); Morgan *v.* Couchman, 14 C. B. 100 (78 E. C. L. R.); Humblestone *v.* Welham, 5 C. B. 195 (57 E. C. L. R.); Williams *v.* Thomas, 4 Exch. 479; Taylor *v.* Best, 14 C. & B. 487 (78 E. C. L. R.); Reg. *v.* Evans, 3 E. & B. 363 (77 E. C. L. R.); Williams *v.* Lewis, 7 E. & B. 929 (90 E. C. L. R.); General Steam Navigation Co. *v.* Slipper, 11 C. B. N. S. 493 (103 E. C. L. R.); Elkin *v.* Baker, Id. 526, 543;

In Cave *v.* Mills,[1] the maxim under notice was by the majority of the Court of Exchequer held applicable. There the plaintiff was surveyor to the trustees of certain turnpike roads; as such surveyor it was his duty to make all contracts, and to pay the amounts due for labor and *materials required for the repair of the roads, he being authorized to draw on the treasurer to a certain amount. His expenditure, however, was not strictly limited to that amount, and in the yearly accounts presented by him to the trustees a balance was generally claimed as due to him, and was carried to the next year's account. Accounts were thus rendered by the plaintiff for three consecutive years showing certain balances due to himself. These accounts were audited, examined, and allowed by the trustees at their annual meeting, and a statement based on them of the revenue and expenditure of the trust was published as required by stat. 3 Geo. 4, c. 126, s. 78. The trustees, moreover, believing the accounts to be correct, paid off with moneys in hand a portion of their mortgage debt. The plaintiff afterwards claimed a larger sum in respect of payments which had in fact been made by him, and which he ought to have brought into the accounts of the above years, but had knowingly omitted. It was held that the plaintiff was estopped from recovering the sums thus omitted, for "a man shall not be allowed to blow hot and cold—to affirm at one time and deny at another—making a claim on those whom he has deluded to their disadvantage, and founding that claim on the very matters of the delusion. Such a principle has its basis in common sense and common justice, and whether it is called 'estoppel,' or by any other name, it is one which courts of law have in modern times most usefully adopted."

[*170]

So where a vendor has recognized the right of his vendee to dispose of goods remaining in the actual possession of the vendor, he cannot defeat the right of a person claiming under the vendee on

Green *v.* Sichel, 7 C. B. N. S. 747 (97 E. C. L. R.); Pearson *v.* Dawson, E., P. & E. 448 (96 E. C. L. R.); Haines *v.* East India Co., 11 Moo. P. C. C. 39; Smith *v.* Hodson, 4 T. R. 211, 217; Brewer *v.* Sparrow, 7 B. & C. 310 (14 E. C. L. R.); Lythgoe *v.* Vernon, 4 H. & N. 180.

A man is not entitled to stand by and allow proceedings to go on against him to judgment, and then to ask the court to interfere on his behalf on the ground that his name was misspelt. Judgm., Churchill *v.* Churchill, L. R. 1 P. & D. 486.

[1] 7 H. & N. 913. See Van Hasselt *v.* Sack, 13 Moo. P. C. C. 185.

the ground that no property passed to the latter by reason of the [*171] want of *a specific appropriation of the goods.[1] Nor can an individual who has procured an act to be done sue as one of several co-plaintiffs for the doing of that very act.[2] Where a party accepts costs under a judge's order, which, but for such order, would not at that time be payable, he cannot afterwards object that the order was made without jurisdiction.[3] And if A. agrees with C. to pay him so much per ton for manufacturing and selling a substance invented and patented by B., it is not competent to A., having used the invention by B.'s permission, to plead in answer to an action for moneys due in respect of such use that the patent was void and the license given superfluous.[4] A person cannot act under an agreement and at the same time repudiate it.[5]

Again, "where a person is charged as a member of a partnership, not because he is a member, but because he has represented himself as such, the law proceeds on the principle, that if a person so con duct himself as to lead another to imagine that he fills a particular situation, it would be unjust to enable him to turn round and say that he did not fill that situation. If, therefore, he appears to the world—or, as the common and more correct expression is, if he [*172] appears to the party who is seeking to *charge him—to be a partner, and has represented himself as such, he is not allowed afterwards to say that that representation was incorrect, and that he was not a partner."[6] So a person cannot in the same transaction buy in the character of principal, and at the same time charge the seller for commission as his agent.[7] And a person acting professedly as agent for another may be estopped from saying that

[1] Woodley *v.* Coventry, 2 H. & C. 164.

[2] Brandon *v.* Scott, 7 E. & B. 234 (90 E. C. L. R.).

[3] Tinkler *v.* Hilder, 4 Exch. 187. See Wilcox *v.* Odden, 15 C. B. N. S. 837 (109 E. C. L. R.); Freeman, app., Read, resp., 9 C. B. N. S. 301 (99 E. C. L. R.).

A party who attends before an arbitrator under protest, cross-examines his adversary's witnesses and calls witnesses on his own behalf, does not thereby preclude himself from afterwards objecting that the arbitrator was proceeding without authority: Ringland *v.* Lowndes, 18 C. B. N. S. 514 (114 E. C. L. R.).

[4] Lawes *v.* Purser, 6 E. & B. 930 (88 E. C. L. R.). See Harrup *v.* Bailey, 6 E. & B. 218, cited under the maxim, *volenti non fit injuria*, *post*, Chap. V.

[5] Crossley *v.* Dixon, 10 H. L. Cas. 293, 310.

[6] Per Rolfe, B., Ness *v.* Angas, 3 Exch. 813.

[7] Salomons *v.* Pender, 3 H. & C. 639.

he was not such agent.[1] Also it seems a true proposition that "where parties have agreed to act upon an assumed state of facts, their rights between themselves depend on the conventional state of facts, and not on the truth,"[2] and it is not competent to either party afterwards to deny the truth of such statement.[3]

So, where rent accruing due subsequently to the expiration of a notice to quit is paid by the tenant and accepted by the landlord, that is an act of the parties which evidences an intention that the tenancy should be considered as still subsisting. So, if there be a distress, the distrainor affirms by a solemn act that a tenancy subsists; and it is not competent to him afterwards to deny it.[4]

In like manner, the maxim under consideration applies, in many cases, to prevent the assertion of titles inconsistent with each other, and which cannot contemporaneously take effect.[5] And it is laid down that "a person *who has a power of appointment, if he chooses to create an estate or a charge upon his estate, by a voluntary act, cannot afterwards use the power for the purpose of defeating that voluntary act;" and if a bond be given to the crown under the stat. 33 Hen. 8, c. 39, binding all lands over which he has at the time of executing the bond a disposing power, the giving such bond is to be deemed a voluntary act on the part of the obligor, so that he cannot, by afterwards exercising the power, defeat the right of the crown.[6]

[*173]

The maxim also applies in cases of estoppel,[7] and whenever the

[1] Rogers *v.* Hadley, 2 H. & C. 227. [2] Blackb. Contr. Sale 163.

[3] M'Cance *v.* London and North-Western R. C., 3 H. & C. 343.

[4] Per Maule, J., Blyth *v.* Dennett, 13 C. B. 181; per Crompton, J., Ward *v.* Day, 4 B. & S. 353 (116 E. C. L. R.); s. c., affirmed in error, 5 B. & S. 359 (117 E. C. L. R.); and see per Lord Brougham, C., Clayton *v.* A.-G., 1 Coop. (Rep. temp. Cottenham) 124.

[5] 1 Swanst. 427, note.

[6] Reg. *v.* Ellis, 4 Exch. 652, 661; s. c., affirmed in error, 6 Exch. 921.

[7] Some of which are considered, *post*, Chap. V. For instance, the owner of land cannot treat the occupier as tenant and trespasser at one and the same time.

As to the estoppel on acceptor of bill of exchange, Ashpitel *v.* Bryan, 5 B. & S. 723 (117 E. C. L. R.); Morris *v.* Bethell, L. R. 5 C. P. 47; Phillips *v.* Im Thurn, L. R. 1 C. P. 463, 18 C. B. N. S. 694 (114 E. C. L. R.).

The reason why in the case of a partnership a party is bound by an acceptance which is not his own, but that of his co-partner, is founded on the law of estoppel in pais; having consented to the exercise by another of an appar-

equitable doctrine of election is called into requisition, to prevent a person from repudiating the onerous, whilst he accepts the beneficial, conditions attaching to the subject-matter of the legacy [*174] or devise.[1] So, *if a stranger begins to build on land, supposing it to be his own, and the real owner, perceiving his mistake, abstains from setting him right, and leaves him to persevere in his error, a court of equity will not afterwards assist the real owner asserting his title to the land.[2]

Lastly, where a witness in a court of justice makes contradictory statements relative to the same transaction, the rule applicable in determining the degree of credibility to which he may be entitled obviously is, *allegans contraria non est audiendus.*[3]

OMNE MAJUS CONTINET IN SE MINUS.

(5 Rep. 115.)

The greater contains the less.[4]

On this principle, if a man tender more than he ought to pay, it is good; and the other party ought to accept so much of the sum

ent authority to accept bills so as to bind him (even though such authority had been fraudulently exercised) as against a person who has taken the bill *bonâ fide* and without notice of the fraud, the acceptor is estopped from denying the acceptance, per Willes, J., 18 C. B. N. S. 432–3 (114 E. C. L. R.).

The estoppel against a bailee from disputing the title of his bailor, and setting up a *jus tertii*, ceases when the bailment on which the estoppel is founded is determined by what is equivalent to an eviction by title paramount: Biddle *v.* Bond, 6 B. & S. 225 (118 E. C. L. R.). A mere wrongdoer may be estopped from setting up a *jus tertii:* Bourne *v.* Fosbrooke, 18 C. B. N. S. 515 (114 E. C. L. R.).

See also in further illustration of the above maxim, Doe d. Hudson *v.* Leeds and Bradford R. C., 16 Q. B. 796 (71 E. C. L. R.).

[1] As instances of this doctrine, see Talbot *v.* Earl of Radnor, 3 My. & K. 252; Messenger *v.* Andrews, 4 Russ. 478. On the same ground rests the Scotch doctrine of "approbate and reprobate," as to which see Kerr *v.* Wauchope, 1 Bligh 121.

[2] Ramsden *v.* Dyson, L. R. 1 H. L. 129, 141, 168.

[3] See 17 & 18 Vict. c. 125, s. 22; 28 & 29 Vict. c. 18, s. 3.

[4] Finch Law 21; D. 50. 17. 113. 110, pr.

tendered as is due to him.[1] But a tender by a debtor of a bank-note of a larger amount than the sum due, and out of which he requires change, is not a good tender, for the creditor may be unable to take what is due and return the difference;[2] though if the creditor knows the amount due to him, and is offered *a larger sum, and, without any objection on the ground of change, makes quite a collateral objection, that will be a good tender.[3] [*175] Where, however, a party has separate demands for unequal sums against several persons, an offer of one sum for the debts of all, not distinguishing the claims against each, is not a valid tender, and will not support a plea by one of the debtors, that *his* debt was tendered.[4]

The above maxim admits, moreover, of familiar and obvious illustration in the power which tenant in fee-simple possesses over the estate held in fee; for he may either grant to another the whole of such estate, or charge it in any manner he thinks fit, or he may create out of it any less estate or interest; and to the estate or interest thus granted he may annex such conditions, provided they be not repugnant to the rules of law, as he pleases.[5] In like manner, a man having a power may do less than such power enables him to do; he may, for instance, lease for fourteen years,

[1] 3d Resolution in Wade's Case, 5 Rep. 115; cited arg. Rivers *v.* Griffiths, 5 B. & Ald. 631 (7 E. C. L. R.), and recognized Dean *v.* James, 4 B. & Ad. 546 (24 E. C. L. R.); Astley *v.* Reynolds, 2 Stra. 916; Wing. Max., p. 208.

A demand of a larger sum than is due may be good as a demand of the lesser sum: Carr *v.* Martinson, 1 E. & E. 456 (102 E. C. L. R.).

See, as another instance of the maxim, *supra*, Rylands *v.* Kreitman, 19 C. B. N. S. 351 (99 E. C. L. R.).

[2] Betterbee *v.* Davis, 3 Camp. 70, cited 4 B. & Ad. 548 (24 E. C. L. R.); Robinson *v.* Cook, 6 Taunt. 336 (1 E. C. L. R.); Blow *v.* Russell, 1 C. & P. 365 (12 E. C. L. R.).

[3] Per Lord Abinger, C. B., Bevans *v.* Rees, 5 M. & W. 308; Black *v.* Smith, Peake N. P. C. 88; Saunders *v.* Graham, Gow R. 121 (5 E. C. L. R.); Douglas *v.* Patrick, 3 T. R. 683. See Hardingham *v.* Allen, 5 C. B. 793 (57 E. C. L. R.); Ex parte Danks, 2 De G., M. & G. 936.

[4] Strong *v.* Harvey, 3 Bing. 304 (11 E. C. L. R.). See also Douglas *v.* Patrick, *supra*. Tender of part of an entire debt is a bad tender: Dixon *v.* Clark, 5 C. B. 365 (57 E. C. L. R.); Searles *v.* Sadgrave, 5 E. & B. 539 (85 E. C. L. R.). Nor is a tender qualified or clogged with a condition good: Finch *v.* Miller, 5 C. B. 428 (57 E. C. L. R.); Bowen *v.* Owen, 11 Q. B. 130 (63 E. C. L. R.).

[5] 1 Prest. Abstr. Tit. 316, 377.

under a power to lease for twenty-one years;[1] or, if he have a license or authority to do any number of acts for his own benefit, he may do some of them and need not do all.[2] In these [*176] *cases, the rule of the civil law applies—*Non debet cui plus licet quod minus est non licere;*[3] or, as it is usually found expressed in our books, *cui licet quod majus non debet quod minus est non licere*[4]—he who has authority to do the more important act shall not be debarred from doing that of less importance; a doctrine founded on common sense, and of very general importance and application, not only with reference to the law of real property, but to that likewise of principal and agent, as we shall hereafter see. On this principle, moreover, if there be a custom within any manor that copyhold lands may be granted in fee-simple, by the same custom they are grantable to one and the heirs of his body for life, for years, or in tail.[5] So, if there be a custom that copyhold lands may be granted for life, by the same custom they may be granted *durante viduitate*, but not *è converso*, because an estate during widowhood is less than an estate for life.[6]

The doctrine of merger may also be specified in illustration of the maxim now before us, for "when a less estate and a greater estate, limited subsequent to it, coincide and meet in one and the same person without any intermediate estate, the less is immediately annihilated; or in the law phraseology is said to be merged, that is, sunk or drowned in the greater; or to express the same thing in other words, the greater estate is accelerated so as to become at once an estate in possession."[7]

[*177] *Further, it is laid down as generally true, that, where more is done than ought to be done, that portion for which there was authority shall stand, and the act shall be void *quoad* the

[1] Isherwood *v.* Oldknow, 3 M. & S. 382. See an instance of syllogistic reasoning founded on the above maxim: Johnstone *v.* Sutton, in error, 1 T. R. 519.

[2] Per Lord Ellenborough, C. J., Isherwood *v.* Oldknow, 3 M. & S. 392.

[3] D. 50. 17. 21.

[4] 4 Rep. 23; also *majus dignum trahit ad se minus dignum;* Co. Litt. 355 b; 2 Inst. 307; Noy, Max., 9th ed., p. 26; Finch Law 22.

[5] 4 Rep. 23; Wing. Max., p. 206.

[6] Co. Copyholder, s. 33; Noy, Max., 9th ed., p. 25. See another example, 9 Rep. 48.

[7] 2 Com. by Broom & Hadley, 326, 327.

excess only,[1] *quando plus fit quam fieri debet, videtur etiam illud fieri quod faciendum est:*[2] as in the instance of a power above referred to, if a man do more than he is authorized to do under the power, it shall be good to the extent of his power. Thus, if he have power to lease for ten years, and he lease for twenty years, the lease for the twenty years shall in equity be good for ten years of the twenty.[3]

So, if the grantor of land is entitled to certain shares only of the land granted; and if the grant import to pass more shares than the grantor has, it will nevertheless pass those shares of which he is the owner.[4] Where also there is a custom that a man shall not devise any greater estate than for life, a devise in fee will be a good devise for life, if the devisee will claim it as such.[5]

Lastly, in criminal law, the principle above exemplified sometimes applies, *ex. gr.*, on an indictment charging a misdemeanor the jury may find the prisoner guilty of any lesser misdemeanor which is necessarily included in the offence as charged.[6]

---

*QUOD AB INITIO NON VALET IN TRACTU TEMPORIS NON CONVALESCIT. [*178]

(Noy, Max., 9th ed., p. 16.)

That which was originally void, does not by lapse of time become valid.

The above rule is one of very general importance in practice, in pleading, and in the application of legal principles to the occurrences of life.[7] And, accordingly, in that part of the Digest entitled "*De Regulis Juris*," we find it laid down in these words—*Quod initio vitiosum est non potest tractu temporis convalescere.*[8]

[1] Noy, Max., 9th ed., p. 25.
[2] 5 Rep. 115.
[3] See Bartlett *v.* Rendle, 3 M. & S. 99; Doe d. Williams *v.* Matthews, 5 B. & Ad. 298 (27 E. C. L. R.).
[4] 3 Prest. Abstr. Tit. 35.
[5] Gr. & Rud. of Law, p. 242.
[6] Reg. *v.* Taylor, L. R. 1 C. C. 194, 196. See Reg. *v.* Hodgkiss, Id. 212.
[7] See instances of the application of this rule in the case of marriage with a deceased wife's sister, Fenton *v.* Livingstone, 3 Macq. Sc. App. Cas. 497, 555; of the surrender of a copyhold, Doe d. Tofield *v.* Tofield, 11 East 246; of a parish certificate, R. *v.* Upton Gray, 10 B. & C. 807 (21 E. C. L. R.); R. *v.* Whitchurch, 7 B. & C. 573 (14 E. C. L. R.); of an order of removal, R. *v.* Chilverscoton, 8 T. R. 178.
[8] D. 50, 17, 29, 210.

Instances in which the above rule applies will be found to occur in various parts of this work, particularly in that which treats of the law of contracts. The following cases have here been selected, in order to give a general view of its application in different and distinct branches of the law.

If a bishop makes a lease of lands for four lives, which is contrary to the stat. 13 Eliz. c. 10, s. 3, and one of the lives falls in, and then the bishop dies, yet this lease will not bind his successor, for those things which have a bad beginning cannot be brought to a good end.[1] So, if a man seised of lands in fee make a lease for twenty-one years, rendering rent to begin presently, and the same day he makes a lease to another for the like term, the [*179] *second lease is void; and if the first lessee surrender his term to the lessor, or commit any act of forfeiture of his lease, the second lessee shall not have his term, because the lessor at the making of the second lease had nothing in him but the reversion.[2]

Again, in the case of a lease for years, there is a distinction between a clause by which, on a breach of covenant, the lease is made absolutely void, and a clause which merely gives the lessor power to re-enter. In the former case, if the lessor make a legal demand of the rent, and the lessee neglect or refuse to pay, or if the lessee be guilty of any breach of the condition of re-entry, the lease is *void* and absolutely determined, and cannot be set up again by acceptance of rent due after the breach of the condition, or by any other act; but if, on the other hand, the clause be, that for non-payment of the rent it shall be lawful for the lessor to re-enter, the lease is only *voidable*, and may be affirmed by acceptance of rent accrued afterwards, or other act, provided the lessor had notice of the breach of condition at the time; and it is undoubted law, that, though an acceptance of rent or other act of waiver may make a voidable lease good, it cannot make valid a deed,[3] or a lease which was void *ab initio*.[4]

Where a remainder is limited to A., the son of B., he having no

[1] Noy, Max., 9th ed., p. 16. See Doe d. Brammall *v.* Collinge, 7 C. B. 939 (62 E. C. L. R.); Doe d. Pennington *v.* Taniere, 12 Q. B. 998 (64 E. C. L. R.).

[2] Smith *v.* Stapleton, Plowd. 432; Noy, Max., 9th ed., p. 16.

[3] See De Montmorency *v.* Devereaux, 7 Cl. & Fin. 188.

[4] Doe d. Bryan *v.* Banks, 4 B. & Ald. 401 (6 E. C. L. R.); Co. Litt. 215 a; Jones *v.* Carter, 15 M. & W. 719.

such son, and afterwards a son is born to him, whose name is A., during the continuance of the particular estate, he will not take by this remainder.[1]

*So, where uses are raised by a deed which is itself void, as in the instance of the conveyance of a freehold *in futuro*, the uses mentioned in the deed cannot arise.[2] When the estate to which a warranty is annexed is defeated, the warranty is also defeated;[3] and when a spiritual corporation to which a church is appropriate is dissolved, the church is disappropriated.[4] [*180]

In the ordinary case, also, of a will void by reason of its not being duly attested according to the provisions of the statute, or on account of the coverture of the testatrix at the time of making the will, all the dispositions and limitations of property contained therein are also necessarily void, nor can the original defect in the instrument be cured by lapse of time.[5]

In the above and similar cases, accordingly, the maxim applies, *debile fundamentum fallit opus*[6]—where the foundation fails all goes to the ground.

So, where a living becomes vacant by resignation or canonical deprivation, or if a clerk presented be refused for insufficiency, these being matters of which the bishop alone is presumed to be cognizant, the law requires him to give notice thereof to the patron;[7] otherwise he can take no advantage by way of lapse; neither in this case shall any lapse accrue to the metropolitan or to the crown, for the first step or beginning fails—*quod non habet principium* **non habet finem*[8]—it being universally true, that neither the archbishop nor the crown shall ever present by lapse, but where the immediate ordinary might have collated by lapse within six months, and has exceeded his time.[9] [*181]

1 Noy, Max., 9th ed., p. 17; 2 Com. by Broom & Hadley 320–1.

2 Arg. Goodtitle *v.* Gibbs, 5 B. & C. 714 (10 E. C. L. R.).

3 Litt. s. 741, and Butler's note (1); Co. Litt. 389 a; but this may with more propriety be referred to the maxim, *sublato principali tollitur adjunctum.* Ib.

4 Noy, Max., 9th ed., p. 20.

5 Gr. & Rud. of Law and Equity, p. 289; Noy, Max., 9th ed., p. 15.

6 Noy, Max., 9th ed., p. 20; per Blackburn, J., Mersey Docks Trustees *v.* Gibbs, L. R. 1 H. L. 116.

7 See Bishop of Exeter *v.* Marshall, L. R. 3 H. L. 17.

8 Wing. Max., p. 79; Co. Litt. 345 a.

9 2 Com. by Broom & Hadley 452; Co. Litt. 345 a.

In connection with the practice of our courts, also, the above maxim admits of many important applications; when, for instance, any proceeding taken by one of the adverse parties is altogether unwarranted, and different from that which, if any, ought to have been taken, then the proceeding is a nullity, and cannot be waived by any act of the party against whom it has been taken. So it is clear, that pleading over cannot supply a defect in matter of substance,[1] although in some cases an imperfection in the pleading will be aided or cured by verdict; and, with respect to this latter proposition, the rule is thus laid down, that, where a matter is so essentially necessary to be proved, that had it not been in evidence, the jury could not have given such a verdict as that recorded, there the want of stating that matter in express terms in a declaration, provided it contains terms sufficiently general to comprehend it in fair and reasonable intendment, will be cured by the verdict; and where a general allegation must, in fair construction, so far require to be restricted that no judge and no jury could have properly treated it in an unrestrained sense, it may reasonably be presumed after verdict that it was so restrained at the trial.[2]

In every case, however, where an objection to the sufficiency [*182] *of the cause of action apparent on the record is sustained after verdict, the effect will be as fatal as if the objection had been taken at an earlier stage of the proceedings, in accordance with the obvious principle under consideration—*debile fundamentum fallit opus*.[3]

Notwithstanding the very general application of the maxim which we have above briefly considered, some few cases do occur where an act done contrary to the express direction or established practice of the law will not be found to invalidate the subsequent proceedings, and where, consequently, *quod fieri non debet factum valet*.[4]

[1] *Ante*, p. 136–7.

[2] Jackson *v.* Pesked, 1 M. & S. 234; 1 Wms. Saund. 228 (1).

[3] Finch's Law 14, 36; Wing. Max. 113, 114. See, also, the judgment, Davies dem., Lowndes ten., 8 Scott N. R. 567, where the above maxim is cited and applied.

[4] Gloss. in l. 5, Cod. 1. 14. *Pro infectis*: D. 1. 14, 3. Wood Inst. 25; 5 Rep. 38. This maxim holds true likewise in certain cases, some of which are hereafter noticed, relating to contracts. Under the stat. 7 Geo. 2, c. 8, it was held, that an executory contract to transfer stock which the party was not

The Banwen Iron Company *v.* Barnett[1] seems to *fall within the class of cases to which the maxim just cited applies. There a certificate of complete registration had been granted by the Registrar of Joint Stock Companies, pursuant to the stat. 7 & 8 Vict. c. 110, s. 7; although the deed of settlement omitted some of the provisions required to be inserted therein: and it was held that a shareholder could not, in answer to an action brought against him for calls, object that the certificate had been granted upon the production of an insufficient deed. [*183]

Conformably to the principle on which the foregoing case was decided, the maxim *quod fieri non debet factum valet* will in general be found strictly to apply wherever a form has been omitted which ought to have been observed, but of which the omission is *ex post facto* immaterial.[2] It frequently happens, indeed, that a particular act is directed to be done by one clause of a statute, and that the omission of such act is, by a separate clause, declared immaterial with reference to the validity of proceedings subsequent thereto.

possessed of might be void and illegal, and yet that the actual transfer of the stock by such party, or on his procurement, might be legal; and that the apparent difficulty (which, in fact, arose from applying the principle *quod ab initio non valet tractu temporis non convalescit*) disappeared on reference to the provisions of the Act, which were framed with a view to secure in every case an actual transfer of all stock bargained to be sold, and within the mischief contemplated by which Act the above case does not consequently fall: M'Callan *v.* Mortimer, in error, 9 M. & W. 636, 640; s. c., 7 M. & W. 20; 6 M. & W. 58. The maxim cited in the text may sometimes apply to an order of justices of the peace: Reg. *v.* Lord Newborough, L. R. 4 Q. B. 585, 587.

It may apply also in a criminal proceeding; thus, "It is very doubtful whether a judge has power to adjourn a case after a jury have retired to consider the verdict, and it is also a doubtful question whether the having refreshment would not have vitiated their verdict; though, perhaps, the maxim *quod fieri non debet factum valet* might have applied, and the refreshment having been ordered by the judge might not be illegal." Per Blackburn, J., Winsor *v.* Reg., 6 B. & S. 183 (118 E. C. L. R.).

[1] 8 C. B. 406, 433 (65 E. C. L. R.). See Pilbrow *v.* Pilbrow's Atmospheric R. C., 5 C. B. 440 (57 E. C. L. R.).

[2] Per Lord Brougham, 6 Cl. & Fin. 708; arg. 9 Wheaton (U. S.) R. 478. "There is a known distinction between circumstances which are of the *essence* of a thing required to be done by an Act of Parliament, and clauses *merely directory*." Per Lord Mansfield, C. J., R. *v.* Loxdale, 1 Burr. 447, adopted per Tindal, C. J., Southampton Dock Co. *v.* Richards, 1 Scott 239, and cited arg. 7 Id. 695.

In all such cases, it is true that what ought not to have been done is valid when done. Thus, residence in the parish before proclamation is directed by the stat. 26 Geo. 2, c. 33, "For the better preventing of Clandestine Marriages," as a requisite preliminary to the celebration of a marriage by banns; but if this direction, although very material for carrying out the object of that Act, be [*184] not complied with, *the marriage will nevertheless be valid under the 10th section, for here the legislature has expressly declared, that non-observance of this statutory direction shall, after the marriage has been solemnized, be immaterial.[1] The applicability of this maxim, in regard to the validity of a marriage irregularly solemnized, was also discussed in Beamish *v.* Beamish, which will hereafter more conveniently be noticed.[2]

Lastly, it is said, that "void things" may nevertheless be "good to some purpose;"[3] as if A., by indenture, let B. an acre of land in which A. has nothing, and A. purchase it afterwards, this will be a good lease;[4] and the reason is, that what, in the first instance, was a lease by estoppel only,[5] becomes subsequently a lease in interest, and the relation of landlord and tenant will then exist as perfectly as if the lessor had been actually seised of the land at the time when the lease was made.[6]

[1] See per Lord Brougham, 6 Cl. & Fin. 708 *et seq.*

[2] 5 Irish C. L. Rep. 136; s. c., 6 Id. 142; 9 H. L. Cas. 374.

[3] Finch's Law 62.

[4] Noy, Max., 9th ed., p. 17, and authorities cited, Id. n. (*a*).

[5] See Cuthbertson *v.* Irving, 4 H. & N. 742, 754; s. c., 6 Id. 135; Duke *v.* Ashby, 7 Id. 600.

[6] Blake *v.* Foster, 8 T. R. 487; Stokes *v.* Russell, 3 T. R. 678; per Alderson, B., 6 M. & W. 662; Webb *v.* Austin, 8 Scott N. R. 419; Pargeter *v.* Harris, 7 Q. B. 708 (53 E. C. L. R.); Co. Litt. 47 b., 1 Platt on Leases 53, 54; Bac. Abr. *Leases* (*o*).

ARGUMENTUM AB INCONVENIENTI PLURIMUM VALET IN LEGE.

(Co. Litt. 66 a.)

An argument drawn from inconvenience is forcible in law.[1]

In doubtful cases arguments drawn from inconvenience are *of great weight.[2] Thus, arguments of inconvenience are sometimes of great value upon the question of intention. [*185] If there be in any deed or instrument equivocal expressions, and great inconvenience must necessarily follow from one construction, it is strong to show that such construction is not according to the true intention of the grantor; but where there is no equivocal expression in the instrument, and the words used admit only of one meaning, arguments of inconvenience prove only want of foresight in the grantor. But because he wanted foresight, courts of justice cannot make a new instrument for him: they must act upon the instrument as it is made;[3] and generally, if there be any doubts what is the law, judges solve such doubts by considering what will be the good or bad effects of their decision; but if the law is clear, inconveniences afford no argument of weight with the judge: the legislature only can remedy them.[4] And again, "where the law is known and clear, though it be inequitable and inconvenient, the judges must determine as the law is, without regarding the unequitableness or inconvenience. These defects, if they happen in the law, can only be remedied by Parliament; therefore we find many statutes repealed and laws abrogated by Parliament as inconvenient, which, before such repeal or abrogation, were, in the courts of law, to be strictly observed. But *where the law is doubtful and not clear, the judges ought to interpret the law to be [*186]

[1] Co. Litt. 97, 152 b. As to the argument *ab inconvenienti*, see per Sir W. Scott, 1 Dods. 402; per Lord Brougham, 6 Cl. & Fin. 671; 1 Mer. 420.

The argument *ab inconvenienti* was applied in Sheppard *v.* Phillimore, L. R. 2 P. C. 450, 460.

[2] Per Heath, J., 1 H. Bla. 61; per Dallas, C. J., 7 Taunt. 527 (2 E. C. L. R.); 8 Id. 762 (4 E. C. L. R.); per Holroyd, J., 3 B. & C. 131 (10 E. C. L. R.); Judgm., Doe *v.* Acklam, 2 B. & C. 798 (11 E. C. L. R.).

[3] Per Sir J. Leach, V.-C., A.-G. *v.* Duke of Marlborough, 3 Madd. 540; per Burrough, J., Deane *v.* Clayton, 7 Taunt. 496 (2 E. C. L. R.); per Best, C. J., Fletcher *v.* Lord Sondes, 3 Bing. 590 (11 E. C. L. R.).

[4] Per Lord Northington, C., Pike *v.* Hoare, 2 Eden 184; per Abbott, C. J., 3 B. & C. 471 (10 E. C. L. R.).

as is most consonant to equity and least inconvenient."[1] And hence, the doctrine, that *nihil quod est inconveniens est licitum*,[2] which is frequently advanced by Sir E. Coke, must certainly be received with some qualifications, and must be understood to mean, that against the introduction or establishing of a particular rule or precedent inconvenience is a forcible argument.[3]

This argument *ab inconvenienti*, moreover, is, under many circumstances, valid to this extent, that the law will sooner suffer a private mischief than a public inconvenience—a principle which we have already had occasion to consider in its general application. It is better to suffer a mischief which is peculiar to one, than an inconvenience which may prejudice many.[4]

Lastly, in construing an Act of Parliament, the same rule applies. If the words used by the legislature, in framing any particular clause, have a necessary meaning, it will be the duty of the court to construe the clause accordingly, whatever may be the inconvenience of such a course.[5] Where a statute is imperative no reasoning *ab inconvenienti* should prevail. But, unless it is very clear that violence would be done to the language of the Act by adopting any other construction, any great inconvenience which might result from that suggested may certainly afford fair ground [*187] for supposing that it could *not be what was contemplated by the legislature, and will warrant the court in looking for some other interpretation.[6]

[1] Vaugh. R. 37, 38.

[2] Co. Litt. 66 a; cited per Pollock, C. B., 4 H. L. Cas. 145, and per Lord Truro, Id. 195.

[3] Ram, Science of Legal Judgment 57.

[4] Co. Litt. 97 b, 152 b; Hobart 224; *ante*, pp. 1, 5.

[5] Per Erle, J., Wansey, app., Perkins, resp., 8 Sc. N. R. 969; per Parke, J., Mirehouse *v.* Rennell, 1 Cl. & Fin. 546.

[6] Judgm., Doe d. Governors of Bristol Hospital *v.* Norton, 11 M. & W. 928; Judgm., Turner *v.* Sheffield R. C., 10 M. & W. 434.

Lord Bacon, it will be remembered, tells us in his Essays ("Of Judicature," *ad. fin.*), that "Judges ought, above all, to remember the conclusion of the Roman Twelve Tables, *salus populi suprema lex;* and to know that laws, except they be in order to that end, are but things captious, and oracles not well inspired." See also per Pollock, C. B., 4 H. L. Cas. 152.

NIMIA SUBTILITAS IN JURE REPROBATUR, ET TALIS CERTITUDO CERTITUDINEM CONFUNDIT.

(4 Rep. 5.)

The law does not allow of a captious and strained intendment, for such nice pretence of certainty confounds true and legal certainty.[1]

A pleading is not objectionable as ambiguous or obscure if it be certain to a common intent, that is, if it be clear enough, according to reasonable intendment or construction, though not worded with absolute precision.[2]

It is said, however, that all pleadings in estoppel, and also the plea of alien enemy, must be certain in every particular, which seems to amount to this, that they must meet and remove by anticipation every possible answer of the adversary, for they are regarded unfavorably by the courts, as having the effect of excluding the truth.[3]

And here we may observe another maxim of law *intimately connected with that under consideration, viz.: [*188] *apices juris non sunt jura*[4]—it is an excellent and profitable law which disallows curious and nice exceptions, tending to the overthrow or delay of justice.[5] True it is, however, that, by the ingenuity of special pleaders, the courts are sometimes placed in a difficulty[6] in coming to a correct conclusion in the administration of justice; and where such is the case, they can only dispose of the matter in the way which seems to them to be most in accordance

[1] Wing. Max. p. 26.

[2] Steph. Plead., 6th ed., 312. See Hammond *v.* Dod, Cro. Car. 6; Harlow *v.* Wright, Cro. Car. 105.

[3] Steph. Plead., 6th ed., 273. See Casseres *v.* Bell, 8 T. R. 166; Le Bret *v.* Papillon, 4 East 502; recognized Allen *v.* Hopkins, 13 M. & W. 101; Alcinous *v.* Nygren, 4 E. & B. 217 (82 E. C. L. R.); Shepeler *v.* Durant, 23 L. J. C. P. 140.

[4] 10 Rep. 126.

[5] Co. Litt. 304, b; Wing. Max. p. 19. See Yonge *v.* Fisher, 5 Scott N. R. 893; per Eyre, C. J., Jones *v.* Chune, 1 B. & P. 364; cited per Cresswell, J., Wilson *v.* Nisbett, 4 Scott N. R. 778; Newton *v.* Rowe, 7 Id. 545. A grant from the crown under the great seal shall not, *propter apices juris*, be made void and of no effect. (Earl of Rutland's Case, 8 Rep. 112; cited arg. R. *v.* Mayor of Dover, 1 Cr., M. & R. 732.) See also Richardson *v.* Barnes, 4 Exch. 128.

[6] See Vander Donck *v.* Thellusson, 8 C. B. 821 (65 E. C. L. R.).

with the established rules of pleading. Whoever really understands the important objects of pleading will always appreciate it as a most valuable mode of furthering the administration of justice, though some cases are calculated to create in the minds of persons unacquainted with the science but a mean opinion of its value.[1]

"The object of having certain recognized forms of pleadings is to prevent the time of the court from being occupied with vain and useless speculations as to the meaning of ambiguous terms;"[2] and, therefore, as remarked by Sir E. Coke, "the order of good pleading is to be observed, which, being inverted, great prejudice may grow to the party tending to the subversion of law—*Ordine placitandi servato servatur et jus.*"[3]

[*189] However, in some cases, the court may be bound to *pronounce upon *apices juris*, and in doing so it has no pleasure in disappointing the expectations of parties suing; but the certainty of the law is of infinitely more importance than any consideration of individual inconvenience.[4]

[1] Per Lord Abinger, C. B., Fraser *v.* Welsh, 8 M. & W. 634.

[2] Per Pollock, C. B., Williams *v.* Jarman, 13 M. & W. 133.

[3] Co. Litt. 303, a.

[4] Per Lord Ellenborough, C. J., Bell *v.* Janson, 1 M. & S. 204; and in Robertson *v.* Hamilton, 14 East 532; Judgm., Galloway *v.* Jackson, 3 Scott N. R. 773. In Brancker *v.* Molyneux, 4 Scott N. R. 767, and in Yonge *v.* Fisher, 5 Id. 896, an objection is described as being *inter extremos apices juris.*

*CHAPTER V. [*190]

FUNDAMENTAL LEGAL PRINCIPLES.

MANY of the principles set forth and illustrated in this chapter are of such general application that they may be considered as exhibiting the very grounds or foundations on which the legal science rests. To these established rules and maxims the remark of Sir W. Blackstone (Com. 21st ed., vol. i., p. 68) is peculiarly applicable:—Their authority "rests entirely upon general reception and usage, and the only method of proving that this or that maxim is a rule of the common law, is by showing that it hath been always the custom to observe it." It would, indeed, be highly interesting and useful to trace from a remote period, and through successive ages, the gradual development of these principles, to observe their primitive and more obvious meaning, and to show in what manner and under what circumstances they have been applied by the "living oracles" of the law to meet the increasing exigencies of society, and those complicated facts which are the result of commerce, civilization and refinement. Such an inquiry would, however, be too extensive to be compatible with the plan of this work; our object, therefore, in the following pages, is limited to exhibiting a series of the elementary and fundamental rules of law, accompanied by a few observations, when necessary, with occasional references to the civil law, and a sufficient *number of cases to exemplify the meaning and qualifications of the maxims cited. [*191]

These will be found to comprise the following important principles: that where there is a right there is a remedy, and if there be no remedy by action, the law will in some cases give one in another way—that the law looks not at the remote, but at the immediate cause of damage—that the act of God shall not, by the instrumentality of the law, work an injury—that damages shall not in general be recovered for the non-performance of that which was impossible to be done—that ignorance of the law does not, although ignorance of facts does, afford an excuse—that a party shall not convert that which was done by himself, or with his assent, into a wrong—that a man shall not take advantage of his own tortious act—that the abuse of an authority given by law shall, in some cases, have a retrospective operation in regard to the liability of the party abusing it—that the intention, not the act, is regarded by the law—and that a man shall not be twice vexed in respect of the same cause of action.

UBI JUS IBI REMEDIUM.

(See 1 T. R. 512.)

There is no wrong without a remedy.[1]

Jus, in the sense in which it is here used, signifies "the legal authority to do or to demand something."[2]

Remedium may be defined to be the right of action, or the means given by law for the recovery of a right, and, according to the above elementary maxim, whenever the [*192] *law gives anything, it gives a remedy for the same: *lex semper dabit remedium.*[3] If a man has a right, he must, it has been observed in a celebrated case, have a means to vindicate and maintain it, and a remedy if he is injured in the exercise and enjoyment of it; and, indeed, it is a vain thing to imagine a right without a remedy, for want of right and want of remedy are reciprocal.[4]

It appears, then, that *remedium*, although sometimes used as synonymous with *actio*, has, in the maxim which we now propose to consider, a more extended signification than the word "action" in its modern sense. An "action" is, in fact, one peculiar mode pointed out by the law for enforcing a remedy, or for prosecuting

[1] Johnstone *v.* Sutton (in error), 1 T. R. 512; Co. Litt. 197, b. See also Lord Camden's judgment in Entick *v.* Carrington, 19 How. St. Trials 1066.

[2] Mackeld. Civ. Law 6.

[3] Jacob, Law Dict., title "*Remedy;*" Bac. Abr., "*Actions in General*" (B). The reader is referred for general information as to the nature of legal rights and remedies to Broom's Com., 4th ed., Bk. i., chap. 3. "Upon principle, wherever the common law imposes a duty, and no other remedy can be shown to exist, or only one which has become obsolete or inoperative, the Court of Queen's Bench will interfere by mandamus." Judgm., 12 A. & E. 266. See also Gosling *v.* Veley, 7 Q. B. 451 (53 E. C. L. R.).

[4] Per Holt, C. J., Ashby *v.* White, 2 Lord Raym. 953; per Willes, C. J., Winsmore *v.* Greenbank, Willes 577; Vaugh. R. 47, 253.

a claim or demand, in a court of justice—*action n'est auter chose que loyall demande de son droit*[1]—an action is merely the legitimate mode of enforcing a right, whereas *remedium* must here be understood to signify rather the right of action, or *jus persequendi in judicio quod sibi debetur*,[2] which is in terms the definition of the word *actio* in the Roman law.[3]

The maxim *ubi jus ibi remedium* has been considered so valuable, that it gave occasion to the first invention of that form of action called an action on the case; for the *Statute of Westminster 2 (13 Edw. 1, c. 24), which is only in affirmance of [*193] the common law on this subject, and was passed to quicken the diligence of the clerks in the Chancery, who were too much attached to ancient precedents, enacts, that, "whensoever from thenceforth a writ shall be found in the Chancery, and in a like case, falling under the same right and requiring like remedy, no precedent of a writ can be produced, the clerks in Chancery shall agree in forming a new one; and if they cannot agree, it shall be adjourned till the next Parliament, where a writ shall be framed by consent of the learned in the law, lest it happen for the future that the court of our lord the king be deficient in doing justice to the suitors."

The principle adopted by courts of law accordingly is, that the novelty of the particular complaint alleged in an action on the case is no objection, provided that an injury cognizable by law be shown to have been inflicted on the plaintiff;[4] in which case, although there be no precedent, the common law will judge according to the law of nature and the public good.[5]

It is, however, important to observe this distinction, that, where cases are new in principle, it is necessary to have recourse to legislative interposition in order to remedy the grievance; but where the case is only new in the instance, and the sole question is upon the application of a principle recognized in the law to such new case, it will be just as competent to courts of justice to apply the

[1] Co. Litt. 285, a. [2] I. 4. 6. pr.

[3] See Phillimore, Introd. to Rom. L. 61.

[4] Per Pratt, C. J., Chapman *v.* Pickersgill, 2 Wils. 146; Novello *v.* Sudlow, 12 C. B. 177, 190 (74 E. C. L. R.); *et vide* per Coleridge, J., Gosling *v.* Veley, 4 H. L. Cas. 768; Catchpole *v.* Ambergate, &c., R. C., 1 E. & B. 111 (72 E. C. L. R.).

[5] Jenk. Cent. 117.

principle to any case that may arise two centuries hence as it was two centuries ago.[1]

[*194] *In accordance with the spirit of the maxim, *ubi jus ibi remedium*, it was held, in a case usually cited to illustrate it, that a man who has a right to vote at an election for members of Parliament, may maintain an action against the returning officer for *maliciously*[2] refusing to admit his vote, though his right was never determined in Parliament, and though the persons for whom he offered to vote were elected;[3] and in answer to the argument, that there was no precedent for such an action, and that establishing such a precedent would lead to a multiplicity of actions, Lord Holt observed, that, if men will multiply injuries, actions must be multiplied too, for every man that is injured ought to have his recompense.[4]

It is true, therefore, that, in trespass and for torts generally, new actions may be brought as often as new injuries and wrongs are repeated.[5] And every statute made against an injury, mischief or grievance, impliedly gives a remedy, for the party injured may, if no remedy be expressly given, have an action upon the statute; [*195] and if a penalty be given by statute, but no action for the *recovery thereof be named, an action of debt will lie for the penalty.[6] So, where a statute requires an act to be done for the benefit of another, or forbids the doing of an act which may be

[1] Per Ashhurst, J., Pasley *v.* Freeman, 3 T. R. 63; per Park, J., 7 Taunt. 515 (2 E. C. L. R.); Fletcher *v.* Lord Sondes, 3 Bing. 550 (11 E. C. L. R.).

[2] Proof of malice is essential to the maintenance of such an action. Tozer *v.* Child, 7 E. & B. 377 (90 E. C. L. R.); s. c., 6 Id. 289, citing Lord Holt's judgment in Ashby *v.* White (ed. 1837).

Where damage is occasioned by a wrongful act, *i. e.*, an act which the law esteems an injury, malice is *not* a necessary ingredient in the right of action. Judgm., Rogers *v.* Dutt, 13 Moo. P. C. C. 236.

[3] Ashby *v.* White, 2 Ld. Raym. 338; cited Stockdale *v.* Hansard, 9 A. & E. 135 (36 E. C. L. R.), and in Rochdale Canal Co. *v.* King, 14 Q. B. 122, 138 (68 E. C. L. R.). In connection with Ashby *v.* White, see also Pryce *v.* Belcher, 3 C. B. 58 (54 E. C. L. R.); s. c., 4 Id. 866 (where the maxim above illustrated was much considered), and Tozer *v.* Child, *supra; et vide* Jenkins *v.* Waldron, 11 Johns. (U. S.) R. 120.

[4] 2 Ld. Raym. 955; Millar *v.* Taylor, 4 Burr. 2344.

[5] Hambleton *v.* Veere, 2 Wms. Saund. 171, b (1); cited per Lord Denman, C. J., Hodsoll *v.* Stallebrass, 11 A. & E. 306 (39 E. C. L. R.).

[6] 2 Dwarr. Stats. 677.

to his injury, though no action be given in express terms by the statute for the omission or commission, the general rule of law is, that the party injured shall have an action;[1] for "where a statute gives a right, there, although in express terms it has not given a remedy, the remedy which by law is properly applicable to that right follows as an incident."[2] And, in like manner, when a person has an important public duty to perform, he is bound to perform that duty, and if he neglects or refuses so to do, and an individual in consequence sustains injury, that may lay the foundation for an action to recover damages by way of compensation for the injury that he has so sustained.[3]

There is, however, a class of cases from which it is important to distinguish those above referred to, in which a damage is sustained by the plaintiff, but a damage not occasioned by any thing which the law esteems an injury. This kind of damage is termed in law *damnum absque injuriâ*,[4] and for it no action can be maintained.[5] *For instance, if a person build a house on the edge of his land, and the proprietor of the adjoining land, after twenty [*196]

[1] Ashby *v.* White, *supra*, cited arg. 9 Cl. & Fin. 274; Hilcoat *v.* Archbishop of Canterbury, 10 C. B. 327 (70 E. C. L. R.); Caledonian R. C. *v.* Cort, 3 Macq. Sc. App. Cas. 833.

[2] See per Maule, J., Braithwaite *v.* Skinner, 5 M. & W. 327; citing per Holt, C. J., Ewer *v.* Jones, Salk. 415; s. c., 2 Ld. Raym. 937; per Willes, J., Wolverhampton New Waterworks Co. *v.* Hawkesford, 6 C. B. N. S. 356 (95 E. C. L. R.).

[3] Per Lord Lyndhurst, C., 9 Cl. & Fin. 279; citing Sutton *v.* Johnstone, 1 T. R. 493; Bartlett *v.* Crozier, 15 Johns (U. S.) R. 254, 255.

[4] As to distinction between *damnum* and *injuria*, see Hall *v.* Mayor of Bristol, L. R. 2 C. P. 322; Smith *v.* Thackerah, L. R. 1 C. P. 564.

[5] Broom's Com., 4th ed., 75 *et seq.*; Cooke *v.* Waring, 2 H. & C. 332.

"In this country we do not recognize the absolute right of a person to a particular name to the extent of entitling him to prevent the assumption of that name by a stranger. The right to the exclusive use of a name in connection with a trade or business is familiar to our law; and any person using that name after a relative right of this description has been acquired by another, is considered to have been guilty of a fraud, or at least of an invasion of another's right, and renders himself liable to an action, or he may be restrained from the use of the name by injunction. But the mere assumption of a name which is the patronymic of a family by a stranger who had never before been called by that name, whatever cause of annoyance it may be to the family, is a grievance for which our law affords no redress." Per Sir R. Phillimore, Du Boulay *v.* Du Boulay, L. R. 2 C. P. 441–2.

years have elapsed, dig so near that it falls down, an action on the case will lie, because the plaintiff has by twenty years' use acquired a presumptive right to the support, and to infringe that right is an injury.[1] But, if the owner of land adjoining a newly-built house dig in a similar manner, and produce similar results, in this case, though there is damage, yet, as there is no right to the support, no injury is in legal contemplation committed by withdrawing it, and consequently no action will be maintainable, unless the weight of the house did not contribute to the subsidence.[2] The cases [*197] *infra*[3] are worthy of *perusal, with reference not merely to the proposition just stated, but to the right of the surface-owner under various and dissimilar circumstances to the support of the subjacent strata.

Further, it often happens, in the ordinary proceedings of life, that a man may *lawfully* use his own property so as to cause damage to his neighbor, which is not *injuriosum*;[4] or he may, whilst pursuing the reasonable exercise of an established right,[5] casually

[1] Stansell *v.* Jollard, Selw. N. P., 10th ed., 435; Hide *v.* Thornborough, 2 Car. & K. 250 (61 E. C. L. R.); Dodd *v.* Holme, 1 A. & E. 493 (28 E. C. L. R.); Backhouse *v.* Bonomi, 9 H. L. Cas. 503; s. c., E., B. & E. 422 (96 E. C. L. R.), which is the leading case illustrative of the proposition stated in the text: Smith *v.* Thackerah, L. R. 1 C. P. 564.

[2] Brown *v.* Robins, 4 H. & N. 186; Stroyan *v.* Knowles, 6 H. & N. 454.

[3] Wyatt *v.* Harrison, 3 B. & Ad. 876 (23 E. C. L. R.); Gayford *v.* Nicholls, 9 Exch. 702; Hilton *v.* Whitehead, 12 Q. B. 734 (64 E. C. L. R.); Rowbotham *v.* Wilson, 8 H. L. Cas. 348, cited Murchie *v.* Black, 19 C. B. N. S. 208 (99 E. C. L. R.); Humphries *v.* Brogden, 12 Q. B. 739 (64 E. C. L. R.); as to which see Solomon *v.* Vintners' Co., 4 H. & N. 598–9, cited per Wood, V.-C., Hunt *v.* Peake, 29 L. J. Chanc. 785; North-Eastern R. C. *v.* Elliot, 10 H. L. Cas. 333; Allaway *v.* Wagstaff, 4 H. & N. 681; Rogers *v.* Taylor, 2 H. & N. 828, 834; Brown *v.* Robins, 4 H. & N. 186; Smart *v.* Morton, 5 E. & B. 30 (85 E. C. L. R.); Richards *v.* Rose, 9 Exch. 218; Smith *v.* Kendrick, 7 C. B. 515 (62 E. C. L. R.); Haines *v.* Roberts, 6 E. & B. 625, 643 (88 E. C. L. R.); Fletcher *v.* Great Western R. C., 4 H. & N. 242; approved in Great Western R. C. *v.* Bennett, L. R. 2 H. L. 27; Judgm., Keyse *v.* Powell, 2 E. & B. 144 (75 E. C. L. R.); Caledonian R. C. *v.* Sprot, 2 Macq. Sc. App. Cas. 449; Richards *v.* Harper, L. R. 1 Ex. 199; Popplewell *v.* Hodkinson, L. R. 4 Ex. 248.

[4] Rogers *v.* Dutt, 13 Moo. P. C. C. 209, 237, 241, well illustrates the above proposition.

[5] The Eleanor, 2 Wheaton (U. S.) R. 358; Panton *v.* Holland, 17 Johns. (U. S.) R. 100.

cause an injury, which the law will regard as a misfortune merely, and for which the party from whose act it proceeds will be liable neither at law nor in the forum of conscience.

In cases of this nature a loss or damage is indeed sustained by the plaintiff, but it results from an act done by another free and responsible being, which is neither unjust nor illegal.[1] Thus, the establishment of a rival school, which draws away the scholars from a school previously established, is illustrative of such a loss.[2] So, a man may lawfully build a wall on his own ground in such a manner as to obstruct the lights of his neighbor, who may not have acquired a right to them by grant or adverse user. He may obstruct the prospect from his neighbor's *house.[3] He may build [*198] a mill near the mill of his neighbor, to the grievous damage of the latter by loss of custom.[4] He may, by digging in his own land, intercept or drain off the water collected from underground springs in his neighbor's well. In these and similar cases, the inconvenience caused to his neighbor falls within the description of *damnum absque injuriâ*, which cannot become the ground of an action.[5] And although it may seem to be a hardship upon the party injured to be without a remedy, by that consideration courts of justice ought not to be influenced. Hard cases, it has been already observed, are apt to introduce bad law.[6]

[1] See Kennett and Avon Navigation Co. *v.* Witherington, 18 Q. B. 531 (83 E. C. L. R.); Laing *v.* Whaley, 3 H. & N. 675, 901; s. c., 2 Id. 476; with which compare Hodgkinson *v.* Ennor, 4 B. & S. 229 (116 E. C. L. R.).

[2] Bell, Dict. and Dig. of Scotch Law 252; Bac. Abr., "*Action in General*" (B).

[3] See Re Penny, 6 E. & B. 660, 671 (90 E. C. L. R.).

[4] As to liability for obstructing the current of air to a windmill, see Webb *v.* Bird, 10 C. B. N. S. 268 (100 E. C. L. R.).

[5] Acton *v.* Blundell, 12 M. & W. 341, 354; cited Judgm., Dickinson *v.* Grand Junction Canal Co., 7 Exch. 300; s. c., 15 Beav. 260; and in Smith *v.* Kenrick, 7 C. B. 566 (62 E. C. L. R.), and commented on per Coleridge, J., diss., Chasemore *v.* Richards, 2 H. & N. 190 *et seq.*; s. c., 7 H. L. Cas. 349; Baird *v.* Williamson, 15 C. B. N. S. 376 (109 E. C. L. R.); per Bramwell, B., Ibbottson *v.* Peat, 3 H. & C. 647, 650; per Pollock, C. B., Dudden *v.* Guardians of Clutton Union, 1 H. & N. 630. See Rawstron *v.* Taylor, 11 Exch. 369; Broadbent *v.* Ramsbotham, Id. 602; Beeston *v.* Weate, 5 E. & B. 986 (85 E. C. L. R.); Wardle *v.* Brocklehurst, 1 E. & E. 1058 (102 E. C. L. R.).

[6] *Ante*, p. 150. Per Lord St. Leonards, 7 H. L. Cas. 93; per Lord Campbell, Id. 628; per Rolfe, B., 10 M. & W. 116. In Walker *v.* Hatton, 10 M. &

Again, where process is served by mistake on a wrong person, and all the proceedings in the action are taken against him, the defendant so wrongfully sued will undoubtedly have a good defence to the action, and will consequently recover his costs; but if it be asked what further remedy he has for the inconvenience and trouble he has been put to, the answer is, that, in point of law, if the proceedings have been adopted purely through mistake, [*199] *though injury may have resulted to him, it is *damnum absque injuriâ*, and no action will lie. Indeed, every defendant against whom an action is unnecessarily brought, experiences some injury or inconvenience beyond what the costs will compensate him for.[1]

It has been held too that an action does not lie against a man for a statement made by him in the course of a judicial proceeding, even though it be alleged to have been made "falsely and maliciously, and without any reasonable and probable cause."[2]

Again, if the legislature directs or authorizes the doing of a particular thing, the doing of it cannot be wrongful; though, if damage thence results, it may be just and proper that compensation should be made for it. No action lies, however, for what is *damnum sine injuriâ*; the remedy, if any, being to apply for compensation under the provision of the statute legalizing what would otherwise be a wrong. And this is so whether the thing be authorized for a public purpose or for private profit. For example, no action will lie against a railway company for erecting a line of railway authorized by its Acts, so long as the directors pursue the authority given them, any more than it would lie against the trustees of a turnpike

W. 259, Gurney, B., says, "The plaintiff may have been extremely ill-used, but I think he has no remedy."

[1] Per Rolfe, B., Davies *v.* Jenkins, 11 M. & W. 755, 756; Cotterell *v.* Jones, 11 C. B. 713 (73 E. C. L. R.); Hobart 266; Ewart *v.* Jones, 14 M. & W. 774; Yearsley *v.* Heane, Id. 322; recognized judgm., Phillips *v.* Naylor, 3 H. & N. 25; s. c., 4 Id. 565; Daniels *v.* Fielding, 16 M. & W. 200; De Medina *v.* Grove, 10 Q. B. 152, 172 (59 E. C. L. R.); Churchill *v.* Siggers, 3 E. & B. 929 (77 E. C. L. R.); Farley *v.* Danks, 4 E. & B. 493 (82 E. C. L. R.); Fivaz *v.* Nicholls, 2 C. B. 501 (52 E. C. L. R.); Collett *v.* Foster, 2 H. & N. 356; Jennings *v.* Florence, 2 C. B. N. S. 467 (89 E. C. L. R.). See further, judgm., Wren *v.* Weild, L. R. 4 Q. B. 735.

[2] Revis *v.* Smith, 18 C. B. 126, 143 (86 E. C. L. R.); acc. Henderson *v.* Broomhead, 4 H. & N. 569. The class of cases *supra* is adverted to by Cockburn, C. J., diss. in Dawkins *v.* Lord Paulet, L. R. 5 Q. B. 107. See Blagrave *v.* Bristol Waterworks Co., 1 H. & N. 369.

road for *making their road under their Acts; though the one road is made for the profit of the shareholders in the company and the other is not. In either case the act is not wrongful, because it is authorized by the legislature.[1] [*200]

"The rule," accordingly, "is well established that for any act done which is injurious to property, but which an Act of Parliament has authorized to be done, though the consequence of the act is *damnum* to the owner, it ceases to be *injuriâ;* and the loss would fall upon him, as no damages could be recovered in an action." To prevent that injustice, the legislature sometimes says that in lieu of an action the party affected shall have compensation in the manner provided by the Act. Where, however, the particular Act of Parliament does not authorize the wrong, and consequently the action is not taken away, the case is not one for compensation, but the remedy is by action.[2]

In most of the cases to which we have just been adverting, the party aggrieved has no remedy, because no right has, in contemplation of law, been invaded. Every injury, however, to a legal right necessarily imports a damage in the nature of it, though there be no pecuniary loss.[3] Thus, where a prisoner is in execution on final process, the creditor has a right to the body of his debtor, every hour till the debt is paid; and an escape of the debtor, for ever so short a time, is necessarily a damage to him, *and the action for an escape lies.[4] In like manner, if a banker has re- [*201]

[1] Per Blackburn, J., Mersey Docks Trustees *v.* Gibbs, L. R. 1 H. L. 112.

[2] Per Blackburn, J., Reg. *v.* Darlington Board of Health, 5 B. & S. 526 (117 E. C. L. R.); s. c., affirmed in error, 6 B. & S. 562; Cracknell *v.* Mayor, &c., of Thetford, L. R. 4 C. P. 629; Coe *v.* Wise, L. R. 1 Q. B. 711; Hammersmith and City R. C. *v.* Brand, L. R. 4 H. L. 171; Broadbent *v.* Imperial Gas Co., 7 H. L. Cas. 600; and cases cited *ante*, p. 5, n. 5.

[3] Per Lord Holt, C. J., Ashby *v.* White, 2 Lord Raym. 955.

[4] Williams *v.* Mostyn, 4 M. & W. 153, recognized in Wylie *v.* Birch, 4 Q. B. 566, 577 (45 E. C. L. R.), and Clifton *v.* Hooper, 6 Q. B. 468; Lloyd *v.* Harrison, 6 B. & S. 36 (118 E. C. L. R.); s. c., affirmed in error, L. R. 1 Q. B. 502. See Macrae *v.* Clarke, L. R. 1 C. P. 403; Arden *v.* Goodacre, 11 C. B. 367, 371 (73 E. C. L. R.); Hemming *v.* Hole, 7 C. B. N. S. 487 (97 E. C. L. R.).

The reasoning in the text has no application to the case of not levying on goods, to support an action for which actual damage must be shown: Hobson *v.* Thelluson, L. R. 2 Q. B. 642, 651.

An action lies at suit of the tenant against his landlord for an excessive distress without proof of actual damage: Chandler *v.* Doulton, 3 H. & C. 553.

ceived sufficient funds from his customer, he is bound to honor his check; and if he make default in doing so, he will be liable, although no actual damage has been sustained by the customer in consequence of such default,[1] and an attorney who compromises a suit contrary to instructions from his client will be liable without proof of special damage.[2]

From the preceding examples it will be inferred, that an injury to a right may consist either in a *misfeasance* or a *nonfeasance;* and it may not be improper here to remark, that there is in fact a large class of cases, in which the foundation of the action lies in a privity of contract between the parties, but in which, nevertheless, the remedy for the breach or non-performance is indifferently [*202] *either assumpsit or case. Such are actions against attorneys, surgeons, and other professional men, for want of competent skill or proper care in the service they undertake to render. Actions, also, against common carriers, against shipowners on bills of lading, or against bailees of different descriptions, may often be brought in tort or contract, at the election of the plaintiff. Nor is it true that this election is only given where the plaintiff sues for a *misfeasance* and not for a *nonfeasance*, for the action of case upon tort very frequently occurs where there is a simple non-performance of the particular contract, as in the ordinary instance of case against shipowners for not safely and securely delivering goods according to the bill of lading; the principle in all such cases being, that the contract creates a duty, and the neglect to perform that duty, or the nonfeasance, is a ground of action upon tort.[3] So that, "where

[1] Marzetti *v.* Williams, 1 B. & Ad. 415, recognized 6 Q. B. 475 (51 E. C. L. R.); Rolin *v.* Steward, 14 C. B. 595 (78 E. C. L. R.); Warwick *v.* Rogers, 6 Scott N. R. 1; Gray *v.* Johnston, L. R. 3 H. L. 1, 14, where Lord Westbury says, "A banker is bound to honor an order of his customer with respect to the money belonging to that customer which is in the hands of the banker; and it is impossible for the banker to set up a *jus tertii* against the order of the customer, or to refuse to honor his draft, on any other ground than some sufficient one resulting from an act of the customer himself."

As to the duty of a banker towards his customer, see also Hardy *v.* Veasey, L. R. 3 Ex. 107; Prehn *v.* Royal Bank of Liverpool, L. R. 5 Ex. 92.

[2] Fray *v.* Voules, 1 E. & E. 839, 848, 849 (102 E. C. L. R.), recognizing Marzetti *v.* Williams, *supra;* see Butler *v.* Knight, L. R. 2 Ex. 109.

[3] Judgm., Boorman *v.* Brown, 3 Q. B. 525, 526 (43 E. C. L. R.); s. c., affirmed 11 Cl. & Fin. 1; Farrant *v.* Barnes, 11 C. B. N. S. 553 (103 E. C. L. R.)

there is an employment, which employment itself creates a duty, an action on the case will lie for a breach of that duty, although it may consist in doing something contrary to an agreement made in the course of such employment by the party upon whom the duty is cast."[1]

"An action," however, "will not lie at the suit of A. for the breach by B. of a duty which B. owes to C."[2] Nor *will [*203] an action for a mandamus lie under the C. L. Proc. Act, 1854, s. 68, to compel the fulfillment of a duty arising merely from a personal contract,[3] or where there is any other remedy.[4]

Having stated it as generally true, that, when a right has been invaded, an action for damages will lie,[5] although no damage has been actually sustained, we may observe, that the principle on which many such cases proceed, is, that it is material to the establishment and preservation of the right itself, that its invasion should not pass with impunity; and in these cases, therefore, *nominal* damages only are usually awarded, because the recovery of such damages sufficiently vindicates the plaintiff's right; as, for instance, in trespass *qua. cl. fr.*, which is maintainable for an entry on the land of another, though there be no real damage, because repeated acts of going over the land might be used as evidence of a title to do so, and thereby the right of the plaintiff might be injured; or, in an action by a commoner for an injury done to his common, in which

(following Brass *v.* Maitland, 6 E. and B. 470 (88 E. C. L. R.), and cases there cited). Preston *v.* Norfolk R. C., 2 H. & N. 735, 752; per Lord Abinger, C. B., Winterbottom *v.* Wright, 10 M. & W. 115; Marzetti *v.* Williams, 1 B. & Ad. 415, 426.

[1] Per Jervis, C. J., Courtenay *v.* Earle, 10 C. B. 83 (70 E. C. L. R.); citing Boorman *v.* Brown, *supra*. See Howard *v.* Shepherd, 9 C. B. 297, 322.

[2] Per Willes, J., Barker *v.* Midland R. C., 18 C. B. 59 (86 E. C. L. R.), referring to Winterbottom *v.* Wright, 10 M. & W. 109.

[3] Benson *v.* Paull, 6 E. & B. 273, distinguished in Norris *v.* Irish Land Company, 8 E. & B. 512, 526 (92 E. C. L. R.).

[4] Bush *v.* Beavan, 1 H. & C. 500, 514; per Mellor, J., Burland *v.* Hull Board of Health, 3 B. & S. 279 (113 E. C. L. R.).

An action for a mandamus may, however, lie even when no actual damage has been sustained: Fotherby *v.* Metropolitan R. C., L. R. 2 C. P. 188.

[5] This proposition is more fully stated and illustrated in Broom's Com., 4th ed., pp. 652 *et seq.* See Blofeld *v.* Payne, 4 B. & Ad. 410 (24 E. C. L. R.); Rogers *v.* Nowill, 5 C. B. 109 (57 E. C. L. R.); Wells *v.* Watling, 2 W. Bla. 1333; Pindar *v.* Wadsworth, 2 East 154; *ante*, p. 200.

action evidence need not be given of the exercise of the right of common by the plaintiff.[1]

[*204] *It is not, indeed, by any means true, as a general proposition, that the actual injury offers, in an action *ex delicto*, the proper measure of damages to be given; for instance, my neighbor may take from under my house coal, which I have no means of getting at, and yet I may recover the value, notwithstanding I have sustained no real injury;[2] and other cases might readily be instanced showing that such an action may be maintainable without evidence being adduced of pecuniary loss or *damnum* to the plaintiff.[3]

The maxim, however, *ubi jus ibi remedium*, though generally, is not universally true, and various cases occur to which it does not apply, or at least in which the remedy cannot be in the shape of a civil action to recover damages. Some of these are cases in which the act done is a grievance to the entire community, no one of whom is injured by it more than another. In such cases, the mode of punishing the wrongdoer is usually by indictment only;[4] although if any person has suffered a particular damage beyond that suffered by the public, he may maintain an action in respect thereof; [*205] thus, if A. *dig a trench across the highway, this is the subject of an indictment; but if B. fall into it and sustain

[1] Per Taunton, J., 1 B. & Ad. 426 (20 E. C. L. R.); Wells *v.* Watland, 2 W. Bla. 1233; 1 Wms. Saunds. 346 a, note; cited per Martin, B., and Kelly, C. B., Harrop *v.* Hirst, L. R. 4 Ex. 43, 45, 47, which shows the test to be whether the act complained of would if repeated operate in derogation of the right of another; if so, an action will lie at the suit of the person whose right may be affected, without proof of individual or specific damage.

[2] See per Maule, J., Clow *v.* Brogden, 2 Scott N. R. 315, 316; per Lord Denman, C. J., Taylor *v.* Henniker, 12 A. & E. 488, 492 (40 E. C. L. R.); which case is overruled by Tancred *v.* Leyland (in error), 16 Q. B. 669 (71 E. C. L. R.). Pontifex *v.* Bignold, 3 Scott N. R. 390.

[3] Embrey *v.* Owen, 6 Exch. 653; Dickinson *v.* Grand Junction Canal Company, 7 Exch. 282; Northam *v.* Hurley, 1 E. & B. 665 (72 E. C. L. R.), recognized in Whitehead *v.* Parks, 2 H. & N. 870; Rolin *v.* Steward, 14 C. B. 595 (78 E. C. L. R.); Matthews *v.* Discount Corp., L. R. 4 C. P. 228. In reference to the question whether substantial damage must be proved, the wording of a statute *may* be material; *ex. gr.*, see Rogers *v.* Parker, 18 C. B. 112 (74 E. C. L. R.); Medway Navigation Company *v.* Earl of Romney, 9 C. B. N. S. 575 (99 E. C. L. R.).

[4] Co. Litt. 56 a; per Channell, B., Harrop *v.* Hirst, L. R. 4 Ex. 47. See Reg. *v.* Train, 2 B. & S. 640 (110 E. C. L. R.).

a damage, then the particular damage thus sustained will support an action.[1]

Where, for instance, the crown, by letters-patent, granted to a corporation the borough or town of L., together with the pier or quay belonging thereto, and it appeared from the whole instrument that the things granted were, in fact, the consideration for repairing certain buildings and erections, the court held that the corporation, by accepting the letters-patent, bound themselves to do the repairs; and that this obligation being one which concerned the public, an indictment would lie, in case of non-repair, against the mayor and burgesses for their general default, and an action on the case for a direct and particular damage sustained in consequence by an individual.[2] So, in the ordinary case of a nuisance arising from the act or default of a person bound to repair a *ratione tenuræ*, an indictment may be sustained for the general injury to the public, and an action on the case for a special and particular injury to an individual.[3] It is indeed an important rule, that *the law gives no private remedy for anything but a [*206] private wrong, and that, therefore, no action lies for a public or common nuisance; and the reason of this is, that the damage being common to all the subjects of the crown, no one individual can ascertain his particular proportion of it, or, if he could, it would be extremely hard if every subject in the kingdom were allowed to harass the offender with separate actions.[4] So "where a statute prohibits the doing of a particular act affecting the public,

[1] Per Holt, C. J., 2 Lord Raym. 955; Winterbottom *v.* Lord Derby, L. R. 2 Ex. 316; arg. Davidson *v.* Wilson, 11 Q. B. 895 (63 E. C. L. R.); Simmons *v.* Lillystone, 8 Exch. 431; Hart *v.* Bassett, T. Jones 156; Chichester *v.* Lethbridge, Willes 73; Rose *v.* Miles, 4 M. & S. 101; Rose *v.* Groves, 6 Scott N. R. 645, and cases there cited; Kearns *v.* Cordwainers' Co., 6 C. B. N. S. 388, 401 (95 E. C. L. R.); Dobson *v.* Blackmore, 9 Q. B. 991 (58 E. C. L. R.).

[2] Mayor, &c., of Lyme Regis *v.* Henley (in error), 3 B. & Ad. 77 (23 E. C. L. R.); s. c., 2 Cl. & Fin. 331; Nicholl *v.* Allen, 1 B. & S. 916, 934, 936 (101 E. C. L. R.). See R. *v.* Ward, 4 A. & E. 384 (31 E. C. L. R.).

[3] 3 B. & Ad. 93 (23 E. C. L. R.), citing Year Book, 12 Hen. 7, fol. 18; Co. Litt. 56 a; Rose *v.* Groves, 6 Scott N. R. 645, and the cases there cited. See also, as to the liability to repair, Russell *v.* Men of Devon, 2 T. R. 667, 671, cited judgm., M'Kinnon *v.* Penson, 8 Exch. 327; s. c., affirmed in error, 9 Exch. 609; Young *v.* Davis, 2 H. & C. 197, affirming s. c., 7 H. & N. 760. As to the rights to abate a nuisance, *post*, Chap. VI. § 2.

[4] Co. Litt. 56 a; 1 Chit. Gen. Pr. Law 10.

no person has a right of action against another merely because he has done the prohibited act. It is incumbent on the party complaining to allege and prove that the doing of the act prohibited has caused him some special damage, some peculiar injury beyond that which he may be supposed to sustain in common with the rest of the queen's subjects by an infringement of the law. But where the act prohibited is obviously prohibited for the protection of a particular party, there it is not necessary to allege special damage."[1]

Again, where the damage resulting from the act of another is too remote,[2] or in other words, flows not naturally, legally, and with sufficient directness from the *alleged injury, the plaintiff will [*207] not be entitled to recover;[3] for instance, the temporary obstruction of a highway, which prevented the free passage of persons along it, and so incidentally interrupted the resort to the complainant's public house, is not, by reason of remoteness, the subject of an action at common law as an individual injury sustained by the plaintiff distinguishing his case from that of the rest of the public; and such interruption of persons who would have resorted to the plaintiff's house but for the obstruction of the highway, is a consequential injury too remote to be within the provisions of the 16th section of the Railway Clauses Consolidation Act (8 & 9 Vict. c. 20), entitling "parties interested" to compensation.[4]

[1] Judgm., Chamberlaine *v.* The Chester and Birkenhead R. C., 1 Exch. 876-7.

[2] Com. Dig., "*Action upon the case for Defamation*" (F. 21). See Fitzjohn *v.* Mackinder, 9 C. B. N. S. 505; s. c., 8 Id. 78; Barber *v.* Lesiter, 7 Id. 175; Steward *v.* Gromett, Id. 191; Walker *v.* Goe, 4 H. & N. 350; 3 Id. 395; Assop *v.* Yates, 2 H. & N. 768; Hoey *v.* Felton, 11 C. B. N. S. 142 (103 E. C. L. R.); Collins *v.* Cave, 6 H. & N. 131; s. c., 4 Id. 225; Allsop *v.* Allsop, 5 H. & N. 534, approved in Lynch *v.* Knight, 9 H. L. Cas. 577, 592; Martinez *v.* Gerber, 3 Scott N. R. 386; Dawson *v.* The Sheriffs of London, 2 Ventr. 84, 89; Everett *v.* London Assurance, 19 C. B. N. S. 126 (115 E. C. L. R.); Burrows *v.* March Gas Co., L. R. 5 Exch. 67.

[3] Per Patteson, J., Kelley *v.* Partington, 5 B. & Ad. 651 (27 E. C. L. R.); Bac. Abr., "*Actions in General*" (B.); Haddon *v.* Lott, 15 C. B. 411 (80 E. C. L. R.); Butler *v.* Kent, 19 Johns. (U. S.) R. 223. See also Boyle *v.* Brandon, 13 M. & W. 738, and cases cited under the maxim, *In jure non remota causa sed proxima spectatur*, *post*, p. 216.

[4] Ricket *v.* Metropolitan R. C., L. R. 2 H. L. 175, 188, 196; Cameron *v.* Charing Cross R. C., 19 C. B. N. S. 764 (99 E. C. L. R.); Herring *v.* Metro-

In an action for slander, the special damage must be the legal and natural consequence of the words spoken, otherwise it will not sustain the declaration. It is not sufficient to prove a mere wrongful act of a third person induced by the slander, as, that he dismissed the plaintiff from his employ before the end of the term for which they had contracted; for this is an illegal act, which the law will not presume to be a natural result of the words spoken.[1] So, where the plaintiff, being director *of certain musical [*208] performances, brought an action on the case against the defendant, for publishing a libel on a public singer, engaged by the plaintiff, alleging that she was thereby debarred from performing in public through the apprehension of being ill received, so that the plaintiff lost the profits which would have otherwise accrued to him as such director, it was held that the damage was too remote, and the action not maintainable.[2]

The above test, for determining whether any particular damage is too remote or not, although probably the most accurate which can be given, must, nevertheless, be applied with much caution; for an action is sometimes maintainable where the damage does not, at first sight, appear to flow, either naturally or directly, from the alleged wrongful act; *ex. gr.*, case was held to lie against the defendant for not repairing his fences, *per quod* the plaintiff's horses escaped into the defendant's close, and were there killed by the falling of a haystack; the court being of opinion that the damage was not too remote.[3] And even in trespass, a person who sets in motion a dangerous thing, which occasions mischief, will be liable, if the circumstances show such mischief to have resulted from a continuation of the original force applied to the moving body by

politan Board of Works, Id. 510; Reg. *v.* Vaughan, L. R. 4 Q. B. 190; Reg. *v.* Metropolitan Board of Works, Id. 358; Hammersmith and City R. C. *v.* Brand, L. R. 4 H. L. 171; Beckett *v.* Midland R. C., L. R. 3 C. P. 82; Eagle *v.* Charing Cross R. C., L. R. 2 C. P. 638.

[1] Vicars *v.* Wilcocks, 8 East 1; observed upon in Lynch *v.* Knight, 9 H. L. Cas. 577, 590, 600. See Knight *v.* Gibbs, 1 A. & E. 43 (28 E. C. L. R.); Ward *v.* Weeks, 4 M. & P. 706.

[2] Ashley *v.* Harrison, 1 Esp. 48; Lumley *v.* Gye, 2 E. & B. 216 (75 E. C. L. R.), may be considered a leading case upon the above subject.

[3] Powell *v.* Salisbury, 2 Yo. & J. 391; Lee *v.* Riley, 18 C. B. N. S. 722 (114 E. C. L. R.); Wanstall *v.* Pooley, 6 H. L. Cas. 910, note. See also Tarner *v.* Walker, L. R. 2 Q. B. 301, 1 Q. B. 641.

the defendant, or if he can be considered, in legal language, as the *causa causans*.[1]

[*209] *There are also cases in which, on grounds of public policy, an action may not lie,[2] *ex. gr.*, an action on the case for a malicious prosecution, though the act complained of be admitted to be malicious; as, at the suit of a subordinate against his commanding officer for libellous statements contained in an official report,[3] or for an act done in the course of discipline and under the powers legally incident to his situation, notwithstanding that the perversion of his authority is made the ground of the action;[4] and the principle of all such cases is, that the law will rather suffer a private mischief than a public inconvenience.[5] Again, the matter litigated may be *alieni fori*;[6] thus no action at law lies to recover damages from an executor for not paying a general legacy,[7] nor by a *cestui que trust* against a trustee for breach of trust,[8] nor for disturbance of a pew in the body of the church, unless attached to a house.[9] In these [*210] *cases there are remedies, but not by actions in the courts of common law;[10] and, although it is

[1] Scott *v.* Shepherd, 2 W. Bla. 892; s. c., 3 Wils. 403; Collins *v.* Middle Level Commissioners, L. R. 4 C. P. 279, 287. Per Lord Ellenborough, C. J., Leame *v.* Bray, 3 East 596; Gilbertson *v.* Richardson, 5 C. B. 502 (57 E. C. L. R.); Wormes *v.* Storey, 11 Exch. 427; Guille *v.* Swan, 19 Johns. (U. S.) R. 381; Vanderburgh *v.* Truax, 4 Denio (U. S.) R. 464; Piggot *v.* Eastern Counties R. C., 3 C. B. 229 (54 E. C. L. R.) (which was case for damage caused by a spark from an engine); per Martin, B., Blyth *v.* Birmingham Waterworks Co., 11 Exch. 783. See the maxim, *Sic utere tuo ut alienum non lædas, post,* Chap. VI., § 2.

[2] See per North, C. J., Barnardiston *v.* Soame, 6 St. Tr. 1099; Henderson *v.* Broomhead, cited *ante*, p. 199; Swinfen *v.* Lord Chelmsford, 5 H. & N. 890 (see Chambers *v.* Mason, 5 C. B. N. S. 59 (94 E. C. L. R.)); Kennedy *v.* Broun, 13 C. B. N. S. 677 (106 E. C. L. R.).

[3] Dawkins *v.* Lord Paulet, L. R. 5 Q. B. 94.

[4] Johnstone *v.* Sutton (in error), 1 T. R. 510, 548.

[5] Johnstone *v.* Sutton (in error), 1 T. R. 510, 548; Dawkins *v.* Lord Paulet, L. R. 5 Q. B. 94. An action does not lie against a man for maliciously doing his duty, Id. 114; Dawkins *v.* Lord Rokeby, 4 F. & F. 841. See Hodgkinson *v.* Fernie, 3 C. B. N. S. 139 (91 E. C. L. R.).

[6] See per North, C. J., 6 St. Tr. 1098.

[7] 2 Wms. Exors., 6th ed., 1783; Barlow *v.* Browne, 16 M. & W. 126.

[8] 7 Chitt. Pl., 7th ed., 3.

[9] Mainwaring *v.* Giles, 5 B. & Ald. 356 (7 E. C. L. R.).

[10] *Quære*, whether an action at law lies against a clergyman for refusing to perform the marriage ceremony? Davis *v.* Black, 1 Q. B. 900 (41 E. C. L. R.); cited 1 Roberts, R. 183.

ordinarily true that "every wrong has its remedy," it is equally true that "the remedy must be appropriately pursued."[1] We have, moreover, already seen that, from motives of public policy, the sovereign is not personally answerable for negligence or misconduct; and if such misconduct occurs in fact, the law affords no remedy. We may add, that a mandamus, the object of which writ is to enforce a clear legal right where there is no other means of doing it, will not lie to the crown, or its servants strictly as such, to compel the payment of money alleged to be due from the crown.[2]

Lastly, where the act of another, though productive of injury to an individual, amounts to a felony, the private remedy is (except where the stat. 9 & 10 Vict. c. 93,[3] s. 1, applies)[4] suspended[5] until justice shall have been satisfied; for public policy requires that offenders against the law shall be brought to justice; and, therefore, *it is a rule of the law of England, that a man shall not be allowed to make a felony the foundation of a civil action, [*211] nor to waive the felony and go for damages;[6] and where, at the trial of an action, the case is found to involve a charge of felony against the defendant, which has not been prosecuted, the judge may properly direct a verdict to be entered for him.[7] For a mere

[1] Per Maule, J., Lewis *v.* Clifton, 14 C. B. 255 (78 E. C. L. R.). See Stevens *v.* Jeacocke, 11 Q. B. 731 (63 E. C. L. R.), cited arg. 1 H. & N. 382; Marshall *v.* Nicholls, 18 Q. B. 882 (83 E. C. L. R.); Boyce *v.* Higgins, 14 C. B. 1 (78 E. C. L. R.); Hollis *v.* Marshall, 2 H. & N. 755, 765; Glynn *v.* Thomas, 11 Exch. 870 (where a grievous wrong had been done, yet the law gave no remedy, *vide* per Erle, J., Loring *v.* Warburton, E. B. & E. 508 (96 E. C. L. R.)); Watkins *v.* Great Northern R. C., 16 Q. B. 961 (71 E. C. L. R.); Kennet and Avon Navigation Co. *v.* Witherington, 18 Q. B. 531 (83 E. C. L. R.); Gwyn *v.* Hardwicke, 1 H. & N. 49; Couch *v.* Steel, 3 E. & B. 402 (77 E. C. L. R.); Reeves *v.* White, 17 Q. B. 995 (79 E. C. L. R.).

[2] *Ante*, p. 57; Viscount Canterbury *v.* A.-G., 1 Phill. 306; In re Baron de Bode, 6 Dowl. P. C. 776.

[3] Amended by 27 & 28 Vict. c. 95.

[4] See Pym *v.* Great Northern R. C., 2 B. & S. 759 (110 E. C. L. R.); s. c., 4 Id. 396; Dalton *v.* South-Eastern R. C., 4 C. B. N. S. 396 (93 E. C. L. R.).

[5] *Ante*, p. 162. As to the restitution of stolen property, see stat. 24 & 25 Vict. c. 96, s. 100.

[6] Judgm., Stone *v.* Marsh, 6 B. & C. 564 (13 E. C. L. R.); Crosby *v.* Leng, 12 East 409; Williams *v.* Bayley, L. R. 1 H. L. 200; per Rolfe, B., 13 M. & W. 608. See also, per Sir W. Scott, The Hercules, 2 Dods. 375, 376; 1 H. Bla. 588; Higgins *v.* Butcher, Yelv. 89; Chowne *v.* Baylis, 31 L. J. Chanc. 757.

[7] Wellock *v.* Constantine, 2 H. & C. 146.

misdemeanor, however, such as an assault, battery, or libel, the right of action is subject to no such impediment as just mentioned; and even where a felony has been committed, it seems that the rule of public policy above set forth applies only to proceedings between the plaintiff and the felon himself, or, at the most, the felon and those with whom he must be sued, and does not apply where an action is brought against a third party, who is innocent of the felonious transaction.[1] Moreover, it is clear that the liability to an action cannot of itself furnish any answer to an indictment for fraud.[2]

[*212] *QUOD REMEDIO DESTITUITUR IPSA RE VALET SI CULPA ABSIT.

(Bac. Max., reg. 9.)

That which is without remedy avails of itself, if there be no fault in the party seeking to enforce it.

There are certain extra-judicial remedies as well for real as personal injuries, which are furnished or permitted by the law, where the parties are so peculiarly circumstanced as to make it impossible to apply for redress in the usual and ordinary methods.

"The benignity of the law is such," observes Lord Bacon, "that when, to preserve the principles and grounds of law, it deprives a man of his remedy without his own fault, it will rather put him in a better degree and condition than in a worse; for if it disable him to pursue his action, or to make his claim, sometimes it will give him the thing itself by operation of law without any act of his own; sometimes it will give him a more beneficial remedy."[3]

On this principle depended the doctrine of remitter, which, prior to the abolition of real actions, was applicable where one who had

[1] White *v.* Spettigue, 13 M. & W. 603, 606; Lee *v.* Bayes, 18 C. B. 599 (86 E. C. L. R.); Stone *v.* Marsh, 6 B. & C. 551 (13 E. C. L. R.); Marsh *v.* Keating, 1 Bing. N. C. 198 (27 E. C. L. R.).

[2] Judgm., Reg. *v.* Kenrick, 5 Q. B. 64, 65 (48 E. C. L. R.); in connection with which case, see Reg. *v.* Abbott, 1 Den. C. C. 273; Reg. *v.* Eagleton, Dearsl. 376, 515; Reg. *v.* Burgon, Dearsl. & B. 11; Reg. *v.* Roebuck, Id. 24; Reg. *v.* Keighley, Id. 145; Reg. *v.* Sherwood, Id. 251; Reg. *v.* Bryan, Id. 265; Reg. *v.* Goss, Bell 208; Reg. *v.* Ragg, Id. 214; Reg. *v.* Lee, L. & C. 418.

[3] Bac. Max., reg. 9; 6 Rep. 68.

the true property, or *jus proprietatis*, in lands, but was out of possession, and had no right to enter without recovering possession by real action, had afterwards the freehold cast upon him by some subsequent and, of course, defective title, in which case he was remitted or sent back by operation of law to his ancient and more certain title, and the right of entry which he had gained by a bad title was held to be, *ipso facto*, annexed to his own inherent good one, so that his defeasible estate was utterly defeated and annulled by the instantaneous *act of law, without his participation or consent.[1] The reason of this was, because he who possessed the right would otherwise have been deprived of all remedy; for, as he himself was the person in possession of the freehold, there was no other person against whom he could bring an action to establish his prior right; and hence the law adjudged him to be in by remitter, that is, in the like condition as if he had lawfully recovered the land by suit.[2] There could, however, according to the above doctrine, be no remitter where issue in tail was barred by the fine of his ancestor, and the freehold was afterwards cast upon him; for he could not have recovered such estate by action, and, therefore, could not be remitted to it.[3] Neither will the law supply a title grounded upon matter of record; as if a man be entitled to a writ of error, and the land descend to him, he shall not be in by remitter.[4] And if land is expressly given to any person by Act of Parliament, neither he nor his heirs shall be remitted, for he shall have no other title than is given by the Act.[5]

[*213]

The following instance is that usually given in order to show the operation and explain the meaning of the doctrine of remitter. Suppose that A. disseises B., that is, turns him out of possession, and afterwards demises the land to B. (without deed) for a term of years, by which B. enters, this entry is a remitter to B., who is in of his former and better title.[6]

*In Doe d. Daniel *v.* Woodroffe, which went by writ of error before the Court of Exchequer Chamber and House

[*214]

[1] 3 Com. by Broom & Hadley 15–17. See this subject treated at length, Vin. Ab., "*Remitter*:" Shep. Touch., by Preston, 156, n. (82), 286.

[2] Finch's Law 19; 3 Com. by Broom & Hadley 16; Litt., s. 661.

[3] 3 Com. by Broom & Hadley 17. See also Bac. Max., vol. 4, p. 40.

[4] Bac. Max., reg. 9 *ad finem*.

[5] 1 Rep. 48.

[6] Finch's Law 61.

of Lords,[1] the law of remitter was much considered, and several important points were decided, which are here stated shortly, for the consideration of the reader. The facts of this case were as under:—

H. W. being tenant in tail in possession of certain lands, with the reversion to the heirs of her late husband, executed a deed-poll in 1735, which operated as a covenant to stand seised to the use of her only son, G. W., in fee. G. W. afterwards, and during the lifetime of his mother, suffered a recovery of the same lands to the use of himself in fee. He died in 1779, without issue, having by his will devised the lands to trustees and their heirs, in trust to pay an annuity to his nephew, and subject thereto to his great-nephew, W. B., for life, with certain remainders over. The trustees entered into and continued in possession until the death of the annuitant, in 1790, when they gave possession to W. B., who continued in possession of the rents and profits of the entirety up to the time of his death, in 1824; and did various acts, showing that he claimed and held under the will. Upon the facts thus shortly stated, the court decided, 1st, that the base fee created by the deed-poll did not, upon H. W.'s death, become merged in the reversion in fee in G. W.; as the estate tail still subsisted as an intermediate estate: 2dly, that G. W. was not remitted to his title under the estate tail, the recovery suffered by him having estopped him; 3dly, that W. B., although taking by the Statute of Uses, was capable of being [*215] remitted, as the *estate tail had not been discontinued; 4thly, that the acts done by W. B. did not amount to a disclaimer by him of the estate tail, as a party cannot waive an estate to which he would be remitted, where the remitter would enure to the benefit of others as well as himself; 5thly, that the right of entry first accrued on the death of G. W., in 1779, when there was first an available right of entry, and, consequently, that the entry by W. B. in 1790 was not too late; and, 6thly, it was held, reversing the judgment given in the court below, that the entry and remitter of W. B., in 1790, did not operate to remit A. W. (his coparcener) to the other moiety of the estate; the court observing, with reference to the last of the above points, that possession of

[1] 2 H. L. Cas. 811; s. c., 15 M. & W. 769; cited per Rolfe, B., Spottswood *v.* Barrow, 5 Exch. 113; and in Cowen *v.* Milbourn, L. R. 2 Ex. 235; and arg. Tarleton *v.* Liddell, 17 Q. B. 406 (79 E. C. L. R.).

land by one parcener cannot, since the passing of the statute 3 & 4 Will. 4, c. 27, be considered as the possession of a co-parcener, and, consequently, that the entry of one cannot have the effect of vesting the possession in the other.[1]

The principle embodied in the above maxim likewise applies in the case of *retainer*,[2] that is, where a creditor is made executor or administrator to his debtor. If a person indebted to another makes his creditor his executor, or if such creditor obtains letters of administration to his debtor, in these cases the law gives him a remedy for his debt, by allowing him to *retain* so much as will pay himself before any other creditor whose debts are of *equal* degree. This, be it observed, is a remedy by the mere act of law, and grounded upon this reason, that the executor cannot, without an evident absurdity, commence a suit *against himself[3] as representative of the deceased to recover that which is due to him in [*216] his own private capacity; but having the whole personal estate in his hands, so much as is sufficient to answer his own demand is, by operation of law, applied to that particular purpose:[4] and, in this case, the law, according to the observation of Lord Bacon above given, rather puts him in a better degree and condition than in a worse, because it enables him to obtain payment before any other creditor of equal degree has had time to commence an action. An executor *de son tort* is not, however, allowed to retain, for that would be contrary to another rule of law, which will be hereafter considered—that a man shall not take advantage of his own wrong.[5]

[1] Judgm., 15 M. & W. 769.

[2] Bac. Max., reg. 9; arg. Thomson *v.* Grant, 1 Rus. 540 (a). But the principle of retainer is by some writers referred to the maxim, *potior est conditio possidentis*. See 2 Wms. Exors., 5th ed., 937 (n); 2 Fonblan. Eq., 5th ed., 406 (m).

[3] A man cannot be at once *actor* and *reus* in a legal proceeding—*nemo agit in seipsum* (Jenk. Cent. 40). See in support and illustration of this rule, per Best, C. J., 4 Bing. 151 (13 E. C. L. R.); Faulkner *v.* Lowe, 2 Exch. 595 (the authority of which case is questioned per Williams, J., Aulton *v.* Atkins, 18 C. B. 253 (86 E. C. L. R.)); Rose *v.* Poulton, 2 B. & Ald. 822.

[4] 3 Com. by Broom & Hadley 11.

[5] Id. 12. See Thomson *v.* Harding, 2 E. & B. 630 (75 E. C. L. R.).

IN JURE NON REMOTA CAUSA SED PROXIMA SPECTATUR.

(Bac. Max., reg. 1.)

In law, the immediate, not the remote, cause of any event is regarded.

"It were infinite for the law to consider the causes of causes, and their impulsions one of another; therefore it contenteth itself with the immediate cause, and judgeth of acts by that, without looking to any further degree."[1] The above maxim thus explained, [*217] or rather paraphrased, *by Lord Bacon, although of general application,[2] is, in practice, usually cited with reference to that particular branch of the law which concerns marine[3] insurance; and we shall, therefore, in the first place, illustrate it by briefly adverting to some cases connected with that subject.

It is, then, a well-known and established rule, that in order to entitle the assured to recover upon his policy, the loss must be a direct and not too remote a consequence of the peril insured against; and that, if the proximate cause of the loss or injury sustained be not reducible to some one of the perils mentioned in the policy, the underwriter will not be liable.[4] If, for instance, a merchant vessel is taken in tow by a ship of war, and thus exposed to a tempestuous sea, the loss thence arising is properly ascribable to the perils of the sea.[5] And where a ship meets with sea damage, which checks

[1] Bac. Max., reg. 1; Babcock *v.* Montgomery County Mutual Insurance Co., 4 Comst. (U. S.) R. 326.

[2] As to remote damage and the liability of one who is the *causa causans*, *ante*, pp. 206, 208. See per Lord Mansfield, C. J., Wadham *v.* Marlow, 1 H. Bla. 439, note.

[3] In Marsden *v.* City and County Ass. Co., L. R. 1 C. P. 232, the same principle was applied to an insurance on plate glass in a shop front; in Everett *v.* London Ass., 19 C. B. N. S. 126 (115 E. C. L. R.), it was applied to an insurance against fire, the damage having been directly caused by an explosion of gunpowder; in Fitton *v.* Acc. Death Ins. Co., 17 C. B. N. S. 122 (112 E. C. L. R.), to an insurance against death by accident.

[4] Taylor *v.* Dunbar, L. R. 4 C. P. 206.

"The general rule is clear, that to constitute interest insurable against a peril, it must be an interest such that the peril would by its proximate effect cause damage to the assured." Judgm., Seagrave *v.* Union Mar. Ins. Co., L. R. 1 C. P. 320.

[5] Hagedorn *v.* Whitmore, 1 Stark. N. P. C. 157 (2 E. C. L. R.). See Grill *v.* General Iron Screw Collier Co., L. R. 3 C. P. 476; s. c., L. R. 1 C. P. 600.

her rate of sailing, so that she is taken by an enemy, from whom she would otherwise have escaped, the loss is to be ascribed to the capture, not to the sea damage.[1] So, *the underwriters [*218] are liable for a loss arising immediately from a peril of the sea, or from fire, but remotely from the negligence of the master and mariners;[2] and, where a ship, insured against the perils of the sea, was injured by the negligent loading of her cargo by the natives on the coast of Africa, and being pronounced unseaworthy was run ashore in order to prevent her from sinking and to save the cargo, the court held, that the rule *Causa proxima non remota spectatur* must be applied, and that the immediate cause of loss, viz., the stranding, was a peril of the sea.[3]

A policy of insurance contained the following clause: that "the assurers took no risk in port but sea risk." It appeared that the ship was driven from her moorings, and stranded within the port of Cadiz; and that while she lay on dry land, and above high-water mark, she was forcibly taken possession of and burnt by the French troops. It further appeared that the cargo was not injured by the stranding, and that no effort was made to unload the ship after she was stranded: it was held that the loss of the cargo must be attributed to the act of the French, which was a peril not insured against, and not to the stranding of the vessel, which was within the words of the policy; that, although the stranding of the vessel *led to her subsequent destruction by the enemy, yet [*219] the latter was the immediate cause of the loss, according to the maxim, *Causa proxima et non remota spectatur*.[4] So, where the ship, being delayed by the perils of the sea from pursuing her

[1] Judgm., Livie *v.* Janson, 12 East 653; citing Green *v.* Elmslie, Peake N. P. C. 212; Hahn *v.* Corbett, 2 Bing. 205 (9 E. C. L. R.).

[2] Walker *v.* Maitland, 5 B. & Ald. 171 (7 E. C. L. R.); Busk *v.* R. E. A. Co., 2 B. & Ald. 73; per Bayley, J., Bishop *v.* Pentland, 7 B. & C. 223 (14 E. C. L. R.); Phillips *v.* Nairne, 4 C. B. 343, 350–1 (56 E. C. L. R.). See Hodgson *v.* Malcolm, 2 N. R. 336; Judgm., Waters *v.* Louisville Insurance Co., 11 Peters (U. S.) R. 220, 222, 223; Columbine Insurance Co. *v.* Lawrence, 10 Peters (U. S.) R. 517; The Patapsco Insurance Co. *v.* Coulter, 3 Peters (U. S.) R. 222; General Mutual Insurance Co. *v.* Sherwood, 14 Howard (U. S.) R. 351.

[3] Redman *v.* Wilson, 14 M. & W. 476; Laurie *v.* Douglas, 15 Id. 746; Corcoran *v.* Gurney, 1 E. & B. 456 (72 E. C. L. R.).

[4] Patrick *v.* Commercial Insurance Co., 11 Johns. (U. S.) R. 14.

voyage, was obliged to put into port to repair, and in order to defray the expenses of such repairs, the master, having no other means of raising money, sold part of the goods, and applied the proceeds in payment of these expenses, the court held, that the underwriter was not answerable for this loss, for the damage was to be considered, according to the above rule, as not arising immediately from, although in a remote sense it might be said to have been brought about by, a peril of the sea.[1]

A policy of insurance on bags of coffee on a voyage from Rio to New Orleans and thence to New York, contained the following exception: "Warranted free from capture, seizure and detention, and all the consequences thereof, or of any attempt thereat, and *free from all consequences of hostilities*, &c." The insured ship, whilst on her voyage, ran ashore, and was eventually lost south of Cape Hatteras. It appeared in evidence that at Cape Hatteras, until the secession of the Southern States of America, a light had always been maintained, and that the light had for hostile purposes been extinguished by the Confederates whilst in possession of the adjacent country. If the light had been maintained the ship might have been saved. Whilst she was ashore near the land a portion [*220] of the *coffee was saved by certain officers acting on behalf of the Federal Government, and a further portion thereof might in like manner have been got ashore but for the interference of the Confederate troops, in consequence of which the entire residue of the cargo was wholly lost. The question upon the above facts arose—had the goods insured, or any, and if so, what portion of them, been lost by the perils of the sea, or by perils from which they were by the policy warranted free? The court unanimously held that the insurers were liable as for a partial loss in respect of the coffee which remained on board incapable of being saved—the proximate cause of the loss being a peril of the sea; but that as to so much of the coffee as was got ashore, and as to so much as would have been saved but for the interference of the troops, this was a loss by a consequence of

[1] Powell *v.* Gudgeon, 5 M. & S. 431, 436; recognized Sarquy *v.* Hobson, 4 Bing. 131 (13 E. C. L. R.); Gregson *v.* Gilbert, cited Park, Mar. Insur., 8th ed., 138. See also Bradlie *v.* Maryland Insurance Co., 12 Peters (U. S.) R. 404, 405.

hostilities within the warranty, so that in respect of it the insurers were not liable.[1]

"The maxim, *causa proxima non remota spectatur*," remarked Erle, C. J., in delivering his judgment in the above case, "is particularly applicable to insurance law. The loss must be immediately connected with the supposed cause of it. Now the relation of cause and effect is matter which cannot always be actually [accurately ?] ascertained; but if, in the ordinary course of events, a certain result usually follows from a given cause, the immediate relation of one to the other may be considered to be established. Was the putting out the light at Cape Hatteras so immediately connected with the loss *of this ship as to make the one the consequence of the other? Can it be said that the absence of the light would have been followed by the loss of the ship if the captain had not been out of his reckoning? It seems to me that these two events are too distantly connected with each other to stand in the relation of cause and effect. I will put an instance of what I conceive to be 'a consequence of hostilities,' within the meaning of this policy. Suppose there was a hostile attempt to seize the ship, and the master, in seeking to escape capture, ran ashore, and the ship was lost; there the loss would be a loss by the consequences of hostilities within the terms of this exception. Or, suppose the ship chased by a cruiser, and, to avoid seizure, she gets into a bay, where there is neither harbor nor anchorage, and in consequence of her inability to get out she is driven on shore by the wind, and lost; that again would be a loss resulting from an attempt at capture, and would be within the exception. But I will suppose a third case—the ship chased into a bay where she is unable to anchor or to make any harbor, and putting out again on a change of wind, but, in pursuing her voyage, encountering a storm, which but for the delay she would have escaped, and being overwhelmed and lost: there, although it may be said that the loss never would have occurred but for the hostile attempt at seizure,

[*221]

[1] Ionides *v.* Universal Marine Insurance Co., 14 C. B. N. S. 259 (108 E. C. L. R.); cited per Willes, J., Marsden *v.* City and County Ass. Co., L. R. 1 C. P. 240. Lloyd *v.* General Iron Screw Collier Co., 3 H. & C. 284; Sully *v.* Duranty, Id. 270.

Dent *v.* Smith, L. R. 4 Q. B. 414, is important in reference to the subject, *supra*.

and that the consequence of the attempt at seizure was the cause without which the loss would not have happened, yet the proximate cause of loss would be the perils of the sea, and not the attempt at seizure. Take another instance: the warranty extends to loss from all the consequences of hostilities. Assume that the vessel is about to enter a port having two channels, in one of which torpedoes are [*222] sunk in order to protect the port from hostile *aggression, and the master of the vessel, in ignorance of the fact, enters this channel, and his ship is blown up: in that case the proximate cause of the loss would clearly be the consequences of hostilities, and so within the exception. But, suppose the master being aware of the danger presented in the one channel, and in order to avoid it, attempts to make the port by the other, and by unskillful navigation runs aground and is lost—in my opinion that would not be a loss within the exception, not being a loss proximately connected with the consequences of hostilities, but a loss by a peril of the sea, and covered by the policy."

The preceding cases, conjointly with those below cited, in which the maxim before us has, under different states of facts, been applied,[1] will sufficiently establish the general proposition, that, in order to recover for a loss on a maritime policy, the loss must be shown to have been directly occasioned by some peril insured against;[2] but this rule, although generally and substantially true, must not be applied in all cases literally and without qualification.[3] Thus, where a loss by fire was one of the perils insured against, and the loss resulted from fire occasioned by the barratrous act of the master and crew, it was held, that the loss by fire so caused was not [*223] within the policy.[4] So, where salvage is decreed by a Court of *Admiralty, for services rendered to a vessel in

[1] Naylor *v.* Palmer, 8 Exch. 739; s. c. (affirmed in error), 10 Exch. 382, where the loss resulted from the piratical act of emigrant passengers; M'Swiney *v.* Royal Exchange Assurance Company, 14 Q. B. 634, 646 (68 E. C. L. R.); which is observed upon per Cur., Chope *v.* Reynolds, 5 C. B. N. S. 651, 652 (94 E. C. L. R.).

[2] See also, per Story, J., Smith *v.* Universal Insurance Company, 6 Wheaton (U. S.) R. 185; per Lord Alvanley, C. J., Hadkinson *v.* Robinson, 3 B. & P. 388; Phillips *v.* Nairne, 4 C. B. 343 (56 E. C. L. R.).

[3] See 14 Peters (U. S.) R. 108, 110, where several instances are given, showing how the rule must be modified.

[4] Per Story, J., Waters *v.* Louisville Insurance Company, 11 Peters (U. S.) R. 219, 220.

distress, the vessel having been long before dismasted, or otherwise injured or abandoned by her crew, in consequence of the perils of the sea, the salvage decreed might, at first sight, seem far removed from, and unconnected with, the original peril, and yet, in the law of insurance, it is constantly attributed to it as the direct and proximate cause; and the underwriters are held responsible for the loss incurred, although salvage be not specifically and in terms insured against.[1]

Again, it may, in general, be said, that everything which happens to a ship in the course of her voyage, by the immediate act of God, without the intervention of human agency, is a peril of the sea;[2] for instance, if the ship insured be driven against another by stress of weather, the injury which she thus sustains is admitted to be direct, and the insurers are liable for it; but if the collision causes the ship injured to do some damage to the other vessel, both vessels being in fault, a positive rule of the Court of Admiralty requires that the damage done to both ships be added together, and that the combined amount be equally divided between the owners of the two; and, in such a case, if the ship insured has done more damage than she has received, and is consequently obliged to pay the balance, this loss can neither be considered a necessary nor a proximate effect of the perils of the sea. It grows out of a provision of the law of nations, and cannot be charged upon the underwriters.[3]

[*224] *The maxim before us, however, is not to be applied in the class of cases above noticed, if it would contravene the fundamental rule of insurance law, that the assurers are not liable for a loss occasioned by the wrongful act of the assured, and the manifest intention of the parties.[4] Thus, where a vessel laden with hides and tobacco had, in the course of the voyage, shipped large quantities of sea-water, and at the termination of the voyage it was discovered that the sea-water had rendered the hides putrid, and that the putrefaction of the hides had imparted an ill flavor to the

[1] See 14 Peters (U. S.) R. 108, 110. [2] Park, Mar. Insur., 8th ed., 136.

[3] De Vaux *v.* Salvador, 4 A. & E. 420, 431 (31 E. C. L. R.) (cited 6 E. & B. 790 (88 E. C. L. R.)), the decision in which case is controverted, 14 Peters (U. S.) R. 111. See per Lord Campbell, C. J., Dowell *v.* General Steam Navigation Company, 5 E. & B. 195 (85 E. C. L. R.); per Sir W. Scott, 2 Dods. 85, and the maxim, *Sic utere tuo ut alienum non lædas—post*, Chap. VI., § 2.

[4] Judgm., 6 E. & B. 948, 949 (88 E. C. L. R.).

tobacco, and had thereby injured it, it was held that the damage thus occasioned to the tobacco was a loss by perils of the sea.[1]

But though the rule adverted to clearly holds in connection with insurance law, that "no man shall take advantage of his own wrong,"[2] the misconduct of the assured need not, in order to exempt the assurers from liability, be the direct and proximate cause—the *causa causans*—of the loss; if their misconduct was *causa sine quâ non*, the *efficient cause* of the loss, the assured will be disentitled to recover.[3] The question in any such case for solution must, therefore, be—"whether the loss was fortuitous, or whether it was induced or occasioned by, or proceeded from, the wrongful act or neglect of the assured.[4] This will not lead to the consideration of an [*225] *indefinite series of causes supposed to act upon each other.[5] Unless the proximate cause of the loss was put in motion by the wrongful act or neglect of the assured, so that the jury can clearly see that without this act or neglect the loss would not have happened, they cannot say the assured induced or occasioned the loss, and the underwriter would be held liable, the proximate cause being a peril for which, by the policy, he is liable."[6] If, therefore, ballast is thrown overboard by the negligent and improper, though not barratrous, act of the master and crew, whereby the ship becomes unseaworthy and is lost by perils of the sea, which otherwise she would have overcome, the underwriters will be liable.[7]

[1] Montoya *v.* London Assurance Company, 6 Exch. 451, cited judgm., 6 E. & B. 948 (88 E. C. L. R.).

[2] Thompson *v.* Hopper, 6 E. & B. 172, 191 (88 E. C. L. R.); Fawcus *v.* Sarsfield, Id. 192; Phillips *v.* Nairne, 4 C. B. 343 (56 E. C. L. R.).

[3] The above test is applied by Pollock, C. B., in Wilson *v.* Newport Dock Company, 4 H. & C. 235, in regard to the conduct of the insurers.

[4] Or even from over-prudence on his part: Philpott *v.* Swann, 11 C. B. N. S. 270 (103 E. C. L. R.).

[5] *Ante*, p. 216. See Alston *v.* Herring, 11 Exch. 822.

[6] Judgm., Thompson *v.* Hopper, 6 E. & B. 950, 952 (88 E. C. L. R.) (citing Bell *v.* Carstairs, 14 East 374, which is a leading case illustrating the qualification of Lord Bacon's maxim adverted to *supra*). The judgment in Thompson *v.* Hopper was reversed by the Exch. Ch., which differed from the Q. B. in regard to the mode of applying the maxim *supra*. See s. c., E. B. & E. 1038, 1045, 1051 (96 E. C. L. R.), cited Aubert & Gray, 3 B. & S. 171, 172 (113 E. C. L. R.).

[7] Sadler *v.* Dixon, 8 M. & W. 895, cited Wilton *v.* Atlantic Royal Mail Steam Company, 10 C. B. N. S. 465 (100 E. C. L. R.).

The remarks just made, as well as the general principle—that the law looks to the immediate, not to the remote, cause of damage, may be further illustrated by the following cases:—An action was brought against the defendants, as carriers by water, for damage done to the cargo by water escaping through the pipe of a steam-boiler, in consequence of the pipe having been cracked by frost; and the court held that the plaintiff was entitled to recover, because the damage resulted from the negligence of the captain in filling his boiler before the proper time had arrived for so doing, although it was urged in argument, that the above maxim applied, and [*226] *that the immediate cause of the damage was the act of God.[1]

Again,—the plaintiff put on board defendant's barge a quantity of lime, to be conveyed from the Medway to London; the master of the barge deviated unnecessarily from the usual course, and, during the deviation, a tempest wetted the lime, and the barge taking fire in consequence thereof, the whole was lost. It was held, that the defendant was liable, and that the cause of loss was sufficiently proximate to entitle plaintiff to recover under a declaration alleging the defendant's duty to carry the lime without unnecessary deviation, and averring a loss by unnecessary deviation; a duty being implied on the owner of a vessel, whether a general ship, or hired for the express purpose of a voyage, to proceed without unnecessary deviation in the usual course.[2]

The maxim as to remoteness has an important application in connection with the measure of damages:[3] the question which in practice most frequently presents itself, being—the particular item of damage properly referable to the cause of action alleged and proved

[1] Siordet *v.* Hall, 4 Bing. 607 (13 E. C. L. R.); *post*, p. 230.

[2] Davis *v.* Garrett, 6 Bing. 716 (19 E. C. L. R.).

[3] With respect to damages in general, it has been said that they are of three kinds: 1st, nominal damages, which occur in cases where the judge is bound to tell the jury only to give such; as, for instance, where the seller brings an action for the non-acceptance of goods, the price of which has risen since the contract was made; 2dly, general damages, which are such as the jury may give when the judge cannot point out any measure by which they are to be assessed except the opinion and judgment of a reasonable man; 3dly, special damages, which are given in respect of any consequences reasonably or probably arising from the breach complained of: per Martin, B., Prehn *v.* Royal Bank of Liverpool, L. R. 5 Ex. 99, 100.

by the complainant.[1] The general rule[2] for our guidance upon [*227] *this subject, where the action is founded in contract, as laid down by the Court of Exchequer in Hadley *v.* Baxendale,[3] and since recognized,[4] is as follows:—" Where two parties have made a contract which one of them has broken, the damages which the other party ought to receive in respect of such breach of contract should be such as may fairly and reasonably be considered either arising naturally, *i. e.*, according to the usual course of things, from such breach of contract itself, or such as may reasonably be supposed to have been in the contemplation[5] of both parties at the time they made the contract as the probable result of the breach of it."[6] Of this rule the former alternative clause may be sufficiently illustrated by cases already cited;[7] the latter is, in the

[1] Hodgson *v.* Sidney, 4 H. & C. 492.

[2] Which was much considered in Wilson *v.* Newport Dock Co., 4 H. & C. 232.

[3] 9 Exch. 341; Woodger *v.* Great Western R. C., L. R. 2 C. P. 318; Theobald *v.* Railway Passengers' Assurance Co., 10 Exch. 45; Hamlin *v.* Great Northern R. C., 1 H. & N. 408; Hales *v.* London and North-Western R. C., 4 B. & S. 66 (116 E. C. L. R.); Burton *v.* Pinkerton, L. R. 2 Ex. 340; Borries *v.* Hutchinson, 18 C. B. N. S. 445 (114 E. C. L. R.); Fletcher *v.* Tayleur, 17 C. B. 21 (84 E. C. L. R.). See Pounsett *v.* Fuller, 17 C. B. 660; Sikes *v.* Wild, 1 B. & S. 587 (101 E. C. L. R.); s. c., affirmed in error, 4 B. & S. 421 (116 E. C. L. R.).

[4] See Gee *v.* Lancashire and Yorkshire R. C., 6 H. & N. 211; Portman *v.* Middleton, 4 C. B. N. S. 322, 328 (93 E. C. L. R.); Randall *v.* Roper, E., B. & E. 84, 90 (96 E. C. L. R.); Spark *v.* Heslop, 1 E. & E. 563, 602 (102 E. C. L. R.); Collard *v.* South-Eastern R. C., 7 H. & N. 79, 86, following Smeed *v.* Foord, 1 E. & E. 602; Dingle *v.* Hare, 7 C. B. N. S. 145 (97 E. C. L. R.); Wilson *v.* Lancashire and Yorkshire R. C., 9 C. B. N. S. 632 (99 E. C. L. R.).

[5] Mere knowledge on the part of the contractor or bailee might not be sufficient—it must form part of the contract: British Columbia Saw-Mill Co. *v.* Nettleship, L. R. 3 C. P. 499, 508, which should be compared with Hadley *v.* Baxendale, *supra.*

[6] See Engell *v.* Fitch, L. R. 4 Q. B. 549, 668, where the rule *supra* was applied in an action against the vendor of realty for breach of contract: Cory *v.* Thames Ironworks Co., L. R. 3 Q. B. 181; Lock *v.* Fourze, 19 C. B. N. S. 96 (115 E. C. L. R.).

[7] *Supra*, n. 3. See also Lumley *v.* Gye, 2 E. & B. 216 (75 E. C. L. R.); Crouch *v.* Great Northern R. C., 11 Exch. 742; Randall *v.* Trimen, 18 C. B. 786; Hill *v.* Balls, 2 H. & N. 299, 305; Collen *v.* Wright, 8 E. & B. 647 (75 E. C. L. R.), affirming s. c., 7 Id. 301; Kelner *v.* Baxter, L. R. 2 C. P. 174;

*judgment specified, thus explained and exemplified by the court: "If the special circumstances under which the contract was actually made were communicated by the plaintiffs to the defendants and thus known to both parties, the damages resulting from the breach of such a contract which they would reasonably contemplate would be the amount of injury which would ordinarily follow from a breach of contract under these special circumstances, so known and communicated. But, on the other hand, if these special circumstances were wholly unknown to the party breaking the contract, he at the most could only be supposed to have had in his contemplation the amount of injury which would arise generally, and in the great multitude of cases not affected by any special circumstances, from such a breach of contract. For had the special circumstances been known, the parties might have specially provided for the breach of contract by special terms as to the damages in that case; and of this advantage it would be very unjust to deprive them."[1] The general doctrine as to remoteness of damage and the principle deducible from Hadley *v.* Baxendale apply in actions founded upon tort, as well as in actions *ex contractu.*[2] [*228]

The maxim, *In jure non remota causa sed proxima spectatur*, does not, however, apply to any transaction originally founded in fraud or covin; for the law will look to the corrupt beginning, and consider it as one entire act, according to the principle, *dolus circuitu* **non purgatur*[3]—fraud is not purged by circuity.[4] [*229]

Neither does the above maxim, according to Lord Bacon, ordi-

Spedding *v.* Nevell, L. R. 4 C. P. 212; Rolph *v.* Crouch, L. R. 3 Exch. 44; Richardson *v.* Dunn, 8 C. B. N. S. 655 (98 E. C. L. R.).

[1] See Great Western R. C. *v.* Redmayne, L. R. 1 C. P. 329, and cases there cited; Williams *v.* Reynolds, 6 B. & S. 495 (118 E. C. L. R.).

[2] See, for instance, Mullett *v.* Mason, L. R. 1 C. P. 559.

[3] "*Dolus* here means any wrongful act tending to the damage of another:" Judgm., 6 E. & B. 948 (88 E. C. L. R.). "There can be no *dolus* without a breach of the law:" per Willes, J. (citing the above maxim), Jeffries *v.* Alexander, 8 H. L. Cas. 637, and in Thompson *v.* Hopper, E., B. & E. 104; *et vide* per Bramwell, B., Id. 1045; per Williams, J., Id. 1054; Fitzjohn *v.* Mackinder, 9 C. B. N. S. 505, 514 (99 E. C. L. R.).

[4] Bac. Max., reg. 1; Noy, Max., 9th ed., p. 12; Tomlin's Law Dict., tit. *Fraud.*

narily hold in criminal cases, because in them the intention is matter of substance, and, therefore, the first motive, as showing the intention, must be principally regarded.[1] As, if A., of malice prepense, discharge a pistol at B., and miss him, whereupon he throws down his pistol and flies, and B. pursues A. to kill him, on which he turns and kills B. with a dagger; in this case, if the law considered the immediate cause of death, A. would be justified as having acted in his own defence; but, looking back, as the law does, to the remote cause, the offence will amount to murder, because committed in pursuance and execution of the first murderous intent.[2]

Nevertheless an indictment will sometimes fail to be sustainable on the ground of remoteness.[3] For instance, if the trustees of a road neglect to repair it in pursuance of powers vested in them by statute, and one passing along the road is accidentally killed by reason of the omission to repair, the trustees are not indictable [*230] *for manslaughter, for "not only must the neglect, to make the party guilty of it liable to the charge of felony, be personal, but the death must be the immediate result of that personal neglect."[4]

ACTUS DEI NEMINI FACIT INJURIAM.

(2 Bla. Com., 21st ed., 122.)

The act of God is so treated by the law as to affect no one injuriously.

The act of God signifies, in legal phraseology, any inevitable accident occurring without the intervention of man, and may,

[1] Bac. Max., vol. iv., p. 17. [2] Bac. Max., reg. 1.

[3] See Reg. *v.* Bennett, Bell C. C. 1, where fireworks kept by the prisoner in contravention of stat. 9 & 10 Will. 3, c. 7, s. 1, either accidentally or through the negligence of his servants exploded, and, setting fire to a neighboring house, caused a person's death. Held, that the illegal act of the prisoner in keeping the fireworks was too remotely connected with the death to support an indictment for manslaughter.

[4] Reg. *v.* Pocock, 17 Q. B. 34, 39 (79 E. C. L. R.); Reg. *v.* Hughes, Dearsl. & B. 248. See also Reg. *v.* Gardner, Dearsl. & B. 40, with which compare Reg. *v.* Martin, L. R. 1 C. C. 56.

indeed, be considered to mean something in opposition to the act of man, as storms, tempests, and lightning.[1] The above maxim may, therefore, be paraphrased and explained as follows: it would be unreasonable that those things which are inevitable by the act of God, which no industry can avoid, nor policy prevent, should be construed to the prejudice of any person in whom there has been no laches.[2]

Thus, if a sea-bank or wall, which the owners of particular lands are bound to repair, be destroyed by tempest, without any default in such owners, the commissioners of sewers may order a new wall to be erected at the expense of the whole level;[3] and the reason of this *is, that although, by the law, an individual be bound to keep the wall in repair, yet that which comes by the act of God, and is so inevitable that it can by no foresight or industry of him that is bound be prevented, shall not charge such party.[4] But there must be no default in the owner; for, where the owner of marsh lands was bound by the custom of the level to repair the sea-walls abutting on his own land, and by an extraordinary flood-tide the wall was damaged, the court refused to grant a mandamus to the commissioners of sewers to reimburse him the expense of the repairs, it appearing, by affidavit, that the wall had been previously presented for being in bad repair, and was out of repair at the time the accident happened.[5]

[*231]

In another more recent case, it was held, that a land-owner may be liable, by prescription, to repair sea-walls, although destroyed by extraordinary tempest; and, therefore, on presentment against such owner for suffering the walls to be out of repair, it ought not, in point of law, to be left as the sole question for the jury, whether the walls were in a condition to resist *ordinary* weather and tides; but it is a question to be determined on the evidence, whether the

[1] Per Lord Mansfield, C. J., Forward *v.* Pittard, 1 T. R. 33; Bell Dict. & Dig. of Scotch Law, p. 11; Trent Navigation *v.* Wood, 3 Esp. 131; Oakley *v.* Portsmouth and Ryde Steam Packet Co., 11 Exch. 618; Blyth *v.* Birmingham Waterworks Co., 11 Exch. 781.

[2] 1 Rep. 97.

[3] R. *v.* Somerset (Commissioners of Sewers), 8 T. R. 312; Wing. Max., p. 610.

[4] Keighley's Case, 10 Rep. 139; Reg. *v.* Bamber, 5 Q. B. 279 (48 E. C. L. R.).

[5] R. *v.* Essex (Commissioners of Sewers), 1 B. & C. 477 (8 E. C. L. R.).

proprietor was bound to provide against the effects of ordinary tempests only, or of extraordinary ones also.[1]

On the same principle, where part of land demised to a tenant is lost to him by any casualty, as the overflowing of the sea, this appears to be a case of eviction, in which the tenant may claim an apportionment of the rent, provided that the loss be total; for, if [*232] there be merely a *partial irruption of water, the exclusive right of fishing, which the lessee would thereupon have, would be such a preception of the profits of the land as to annul his claim to an apportionment.[2] Where, also, land is surrounded suddenly by the rage or violence of the sea, without any default of the tenant, or if the surface of a meadow be destroyed by the eruption of a moss, this is no waste (if the injury be repaired in a convenient time), but the act of God, that *vis major* for which the tenant is not responsible.[3]

With respect to the liability of either landlord or tenant, where premises under demise are destroyed by fire, the rule is, that, in the absence of any special contract between the parties, the landlord is never liable to rebuild, even if he has received the value from an insurance office;[4] neither is the tenant, since the stat. 6 Anne, c. 31, s. 6; but the latter is liable to the payment of rent until the tenancy is determined.[5]

In Izon *v.* Gorton,[6] the defendants were tenants from year to year to the plaintiff, of the upper floors of a warehouse, at a rent payable quarterly; the premises were destroyed by an accidental fire in the middle of a quarter, and were wholly untenantable until [*233] rebuilt about seven months after; and it was held that the relation of *landlord and tenant was not determined by

[1] Reg. *v.* Leigh, 10 A. & E. 398 (37 E. C. L. R.).

[2] 1 Roll. Abr. 236, l. 40; Bac. Abr., "*Rent*" (M. 2). See Dyer 56.

[3] Per Tindal, C. J., Simmons *v.* Norton, 7 Bing. 647, 648 (20 E. C. L. R.); Com. Dig., "*Waste*" (E. 5).

[4] Pindar *v.* Ainsley, cited per Buller, J.; Belfour *v.* Weston, 1 T. R. 312; Bayne *v.* Walker, 3 Dow. R. 233; Leeds *v.* Cheetham, 1 Sim. 146; with which acc. Lofft *v.* Dennis, 1 E. & E. 474, 481 (102 E. C. L. R.).

[5] Paradine *v.* Jane, Aleyn R. 27. As to the stat. 6 Anne, c. 31, see Lord Lyndhurst's judgment in Viscount Canterbury *v.* A.-G., 1 Phill. 306.

[6] 5 Bing. N. C. 591 (35 E. C. L. R.); recognized Surplice *v.* Farnsworth, 8 Scott N. R. 307. See Packer *v.* Gibbins, 1 Q. B. 421 (41 E. C. L. R.); Upton *v.* Townend, 17 C. B. 30 (84 E. C. L. R.).

the destruction of the premises, but that the defendants remained liable for the rent until the tenancy should be in the usual way put an end to, and that such rent was recoverable in *assumpsit* for use and occupation.

Where there is a general covenant by the lessee to repair and leave repaired at the end of the term, the lessee is clearly liable to rebuild in case of the destruction of the premises by accidental fire, or by any other unavoidable contingency, as lightning, or an extraordinary flood. And the principle on which this rule depends is, that if a party, by his own contract, creates a duty or a charge upon himself, he is bound to make it good, if he can, notwithstanding any accident by inevitable necessity; for, if he had chosen to guard against any loss of this kind, he should have introduced it into the contract by way of exception;[1] and, accordingly, an exception of accidents caused by fire and tempest is now usually introduced into leases, in order to protect the lessee.

Where the lessee covenants to pay rent, he is, in accordance with the above principles, bound to pay it whatever injury may happen to the demised premises;[2] *and a tenant from year to year, in order to free himself from liability in such a case, should give a regular notice to quit. [*234]

The principle under consideration is likewise applicable in other contracts than those between landlord and tenant.[3] Thus, where

[1] Paradine *v.* Jane, Aleyn R. 27; cited per Lord Ellenborough, C. J., 10 East 533, and Spence *v.* Chodwick, 10 Q. B. 517, 530 (59 E. C. L. R.); per Lord Campbell, C. J., Hall *v.* Wright, E., B. & E. 761 (96 E. C. L. R.); per Martin, B., Id. 789; Brown *v.* Royal Insur. Co., 1 E. & E. 853, 859 (102 E. C. L. R.); arg. Brecknock Co. *v.* Pritchard, 6 T. R. 751; recognized per Lord Kenyon, C. J., Id. 752; Finch Law 64.

"By the common law of England a person who expressly contracts absolutely to do a thing, not naturally impossible, is not excused for non-performance because of being prevented by the act of God." Judgm., Lloyd *v.* Guibert, L. R. 1 Q. B. 121, citing Paradine *v.* Jane, *supra*.

[2] In an action of debt for rent due under a lease, held, that the destruction of the premises by fire would not excuse the lessee from payment of the rent according to his covenant: Hallett *v.* Wylie, 3 Johnson (U. S.) R. 44.

[3] "The act of God is in some cases said to excuse the breach of a contract. This is, in fact, an inaccurate expression, because where it is an answer to a complaint of an alleged breach of contract, that the thing done or left undone was so by the act of God, what is meant is, that it was not within the contract." Judgm., Baily *v.* De Crespigny, L. R. 4 Q. B. 185; citing per Maule,

performance of a contract depends on the continued existence of a given person or thing, a condition may be implied that the impossibility arising from the perishing of the person or thing shall excuse the performance.[1]

"Where personal considerations," it has been said,[2] "are of the foundation of the contract, as in cases of principal and agent, and master and servant, the death of either party puts an end to the relation; and in respect of service after the death, the contract is dissolved, unless there be a stipulation, express or implied, to the contrary." To an action for breach of a covenant to serve contained in an apprenticeship deed, the defendant, the father of the apprentice, pleaded that the apprentice was prevented "by the act of God, to wit, by permanent illness happening and arising after the making of the indenture, from remaining with or serving" the plaintiff during the said term; and this plea was held good in excuse of performance, on the ground that, from the nature of the contract, it was necessarily to be implied that the continued [*235] *existence of the apprentice in a state to perform his part of it was contemplated by the contracting parties, and that, if prevented by the act of God, the performance was to be excused.[3]

Again, the plaintiffs contracted to erect certain machinery on the defendant's premises, at specific prices for particular portions, and

J., Canham *v.* Barry, 15 C. B. 619 (80 E. C. L. R.); and in Mayor of Berwick *v.* Oswald, 3 E. & B. 665 (77 E. C. L. R.); Shelley's Case, 1 Rep. 98 a; Brewster *v.* Kitchell, 1 Salk. 198.

[1] Judgm., Taylor *v.* Caldwell, 3 B. & S. 826 (113 E. C. L. R.).

[2] Per Willes, J., Farrow *v.* Wilson, L. R. 4 C. P. 744, 746.

[3] Boast *v.* Firth, L. R. 4 C. P. 1.

In Hall *v.* Wright, E., B. & E. 749 (96 E. C. L. R.), Crompton, J., observes, "Where a contract depends upon personal skill, and the act of God renders it impossible, as, for instance, in the case of a painter employed to paint a picture who is struck blind, it may be that the performance might be excused, and his death might also have the same effect."

And Pollock, C. B., remarks (Id. 793), "All contracts for personal services which can be performed only during the lifetime of the party contracting, are subject to the implied condition that he shall be alive to perform them, and should he die his executor is not liable to an action for the breach of contract occasioned by his death." See Stubbs *v.* Holywell R. C., L. R. 2 Ex. 311, 314.

Where incapacity to perform a contract is occasioned by the act of God, the contractor may be justified in determining the contract. See Judgm., Cuckson *v.* Stone, 1 E. & E. 257 (102 E. C. L. R.).

to keep it in repair for two years—the price to be paid upon the completion of the whole. After some portions of the work had been finished—other portions being in course of completion—the premises, with the machinery and materials thereon, were accidentally destroyed by fire: Held, that both parties were excused from further performance of the contract, but that the plaintiffs were not entitled to sue in respect of those portions of the work which had been completed, the *ratio decidendi* being thus expressed:—"The plaintiffs having contracted to do an entire work for a specific sum, can recover nothing unless the work be done, or it can be shown that it was the defendant's fault that the work was incomplete, or that there is something to justify the conclusion that the parties have entered into a fresh contract."[1]

*So if the condition of a bond was possible at the time of making it, and afterwards becomes impossible by the act [*236] of God, the obligor shall be excused;[2] and it is said that, if the condition be in the disjunctive, with liberty to the obligor to do either of two things at his election, and both are possible at the time of making the bond, and afterwards one of them becomes impossible by the act of God, the obligor shall not be bound to perform the other.[3]

A., upon the marriage of B., his daughter, covenanting with her husband, C., his executors, &c., by deed or will, to give, leave, and bequeath unto B. one eighth part or share (that being an equal share with his other children) of all the real and personal estate of which he should die seised or possessed. B. having died in the lifetime of A., and A. having by will devised and bequeathed his real and personal estate for the benefit of his widow and some surviving daughters, it was held that C. had not any right of action against the executors of A.[4]

1 Appleby *v.* Myers, L. R. 2 C. P. 651, 661.

2 Per Williams, J., 9 C. B. N. S. 747 (99 E. C. L. R.); Com. Dig., "*Condition,*" L. 12, D. 1; 2 Bla. Com., 21st ed., 340; Co. Litt. 206 a; Williams *v.* Hide, Palm R. 548. See Roll. Abr. 450, 451.

3 Com. Dig., "*Condition,*" D. 1; Laughter's Case, 5 Rep. 22; followed in Jones *v.* How, *infra;* Wing. Max., p. 610. See per Crompton, J., Exposito *v.* Bowden, 4 E. & B. 974, 975 (82 E. C. L. R.); s. c., 7 Id. 763; 1 B. & S. 194 (101 E. C. L. R.).

4 Jones *v.* How, 9 C. B. 1 (67 E. C. L. R.); cited arg. L. R. 2 C. P. 237. It is obvious, however, that a man may, for a good consideration, contract to do

Again, if a lessee covenants to leave a wood in as good a plight as the wood was in at the time of making the lease, and afterwards [*237] the trees are blown down by tempests, *he is discharged from his covenant.[1] Further, we read, that, where the law prescribes a means to perfect or settle any right or estate, if, by the act of God, which no industry can avoid, nor policy prevent, this means becomes impossible in any circumstance, no one who was to have been benefited, if the means had been with all circumstances executed, shall be prejudiced for not executing it in that which has thus become impracticable, unless he has been guilty of some laches, and has neglected something possible for him to perform.[2]

In a devise or conveyance of lands, on a condition annexed to the estate conveyed, which is possible at the time of making it, but afterwards becomes impossible by the act of God, there, if the condition is *precedent*, no estate vests at law or in equity, because the condition cannot be performed; but, if *subsequent*, the estate becomes absolute in the grantee, for the condition is not broken.[3] Thus, where a man enfeoffed another, on the condition subsequent of re-entry, if the feoffor should within a year go to Paris about the feoffee's affairs, but feoffor died before the year had elapsed, the estate was held to be absolute in the feoffee.[4] So, where a man devised his estate to his eldest daughter, on condition that she should marry his nephew on or before her attaining twenty-one years; but the nephew died young, and the daughter was never required, and never refused, to marry him, but, after his death, and before attaining twenty-one years, married; it was held, that the condition was unbroken, having become impossible by the act of God.[5]

that which he cannot be sure that he will be able to do (see per Maule, J., Canham *v.* Barry, 15 C. B. 619 (80 E. C. L. R.), and in Jones *v.* How, 9 C. B. 10 (67 E. C. L. R.), and which may by the *actus Dei* become impracticable, and yet be absolutely bound, *i. e.*, bound, on default, to compensate the contractee in damages.

[1] 1 Rep. 98.

[2] Shelley's Case, 1 Rep. 97 b.

[3] Com. Dig. "*Condition*," D. 1; Co. Litt. 206 a; and Mr. Butler's note (1); Id. 218 a, 219 a.

[4] Co. Litt. 206 a.

[5] Thomas *v.* Howell, 1 Salk. 170; Aislabie *v.* Rice, 8 Taunt. 459 (4 E. C. L. R.).

*By the custom of the realm, common carriers are bound to receive and carry the goods of the subject for a reasonable hire or reward, to take due care of them in their passage, to deliver them safely and within a reasonable time,[1] or in default thereof to make compensation to the owner for loss, damage, or delay, which happens while the goods are in their custody. Where, however, such loss, damage, or delay arises from the act of God, as storms, tempests, and the like, the maxim under consideration applies, and the loss must fall upon the owner, and not upon the carrier:[2] in this case, *res perit suo domino.*[3] For damage occasioned by accidental fire, resulting neither from the act of God nor of the king's enemies, a common carrier, being an insurer, is responsible.[4] But where an injury is sustained by a passenger, from an inevitable *accident*,[5] as, from the upsetting of the coach in consequence of the horses taking fright, the coach-owner is not liable, provided there were no negligence in the driver.[6] And the breach of a contract to convey a passenger from A. to B., if caused by *vis major*, would seem to be excusable.[7] [*238]

*Death is a dispensation of Providence which sometimes renders applicable the rule as to *actus Dei;* one familiar instance of such application occurs where rent is apportioned, under stat. 11 Geo. 2, c. 19, s. 15 (the provisions of which are extended [*239]

[1] Taylor *v.* Great Northern R. C., L. R. 1 C. P. 386.

[2] Amies *v.* Stevens, Stra. 128; Trent Navigation *v.* Wood, 3 Esp. 127; per Powell, J., Coggs *v.* Bernard, 2 Lord Raym. 910, 911; per Tindal, C. J., Ross *v.* Hill, 2 C. B. 890 (52 E. C. L. R.); Walker *v.* British Guarantee Society, 18 Q. B. 277, 287 (83 E. C. L. R.).

[3] As to this maxim, see Bell, Dict. and Dig. of Scotch Law 857; Appleby *v.* Myers, L. R. 2 C. P. 651, 659, 660; Bayne *v.* Walker, 3 Dow R. 233; Payne *v.* Meller, 6 Ves. 349; Bryant *v.* Busk, 4 Russ. 1; Logan *v.* Le Mesurier, 6 Moo. P. C. C. 116.

[4] Story on Bailments, 5th ed., s. 528; Collins *v.* Bristol and Exeter R. C., 1 H. & N. 517.

[5] As to the meaning of this word, see Fenwick *v.* Schmalz, L. R. 3 C. P. 313; Readhead *v.* Midland R. C., L. R. 4 Q. B. 379.

[6] Aston *v.* Heaven, 2 Esp. 533; per Parke, J., Crofts *v.* Waterhouse, 3 Bing. 321. See Sharp *v.* Grey, 9 Bing. 457; Perren *v.* Monmouthshire R. and Can. Co., 11 C. B. 855.

[7] Per Lord Campbell, C. J., Denton *v.* Great Northern R. C., 25 L. J. Q. B. 129; s. c., 5 E. & B. 860 (85 E. C. L. R.); Bridden *v.* Great Northern R. C., 28 L. J. Ex. 51; Great Western R. C. of Canada *v.* Braid, 1 Moo. P. C. C. 101, and cases there cited. See Kearon *v.* Pearson, 7 H. & N. 386.

by 4 & 5 Will. 4, c. 22), on the death of a lessor who has only a life estate, and who happens to die before or on the day on which rent is reserved or made payable. The right to emblements, also, is referable to the same principle; for those only are entitled to emblements who have an uncertain estate or interest in land, which it determined either by the act of God or of the law, between the period of sowing and the severance of the crop; and the object of the rule respecting emblements is to compensate for the labor and expense of tilling, sowing, and manuring the land to encourage husbandry and promote the public good, lest in the absence of some special protection, the ground should remain uncultivated.[1] Without entering minutely into this subject, the law respecting it (which will, however, be again adverted to)[2] may be thus stated: where the right to occupy land depends on the continuance of the life of the occupier or some other person, and is determined by the death of either after the land has been sown, but before the severance of the crop, the occupier, or his personal representatives, as the case may be, shall be entitled to one crop of that species only which ordinarily repays the labor by which it is produced within the [*240] year *within which that labor is bestowed, though the crop may, in extraordinary seasons, be delayed beyond that period.[3]

The following cases may also be noticed as applicable to the present subject, and as showing that death, which is the act of God, shall not be allowed to prejudice an innocent party if such a result can be avoided:—Lessor and lessee, in the presence of the lessor's attorney, signed an agreement that a lease should be prepared by lessor's attorney, and paid for by lessee. The lease was prepared accordingly, but the lessor, who had only a life estate in the property to be demised, died, and the lease consequently was never executed. It was held, that the lessor's attorney was entitled to recover from lessee the charge for drawing the lease, for it was known to all the parties that the proposed lessor had only a life estate; and the non-execution of the lease was owing to no fault of the attorney, who ought not, therefore, to remain unpaid.[4]

[1] Co. Litt. 55 a.

[2] See the maxim, *Quicquid plantatur solo solo cedit*—*post*, Chap. VI. § 2.

[3] Judgm., Graves *v.* Weld, 5 B. & Ad. 117, 118 (27 E. C. L. R.); citing Kingsbury *v.* Collins, 4 Bing. 202. See, also, Latham *v.* Atwood, Cro. Car. 515.

[4] Webb *v.* Rhodes, 3 Bing. N. C. 732 (32 E. C. L. R.).

For another illustration of the above maxim, see Morris *v.* Matthews, 2 Q.

The case of Reg. *v.* The Justices of Leicestershire,[1] where a peremptory mandamus was issued to Quarter Sessions to hear an appeal against a bastardy order of two justices, offers another apt illustration of the maxim now before us. There it appeared that the appellant, having entered into the proper recognizances, on the same day sent by post a written notice of his having done so in pursuance of the stat. 8 & 9 Vict. c. 10, s. 3, addressed to [*241] *the mother of the child; three days, however, before this notice was posted, the woman had died, and upon this state of facts the Sessions refused to hear the appeal, considering that the appellant had not complied with the requirements of the statute. But the Court of Queen's Bench held that as the duty of the appellant to give the notice in question was cast upon him by the law, not by his own voluntary contract, he was excused from performing that duty, inasmuch as it had become impossible by the act of God.[2]

The above general rule must, however, be applied with due caution:[3] *ex. gr.*, notice of appeal having been given from the decision of a revising barrister, a case was thereupon drawn up by the barrister, and approved and signed by the attorneys of the respective parties; the revising barrister shortly afterwards died, and the case approved and signed by the two attorneys was found amongst his papers, but was *not signed by him.* The Court of Common Pleas held, that, under the stat. 6 & 7 Vict. c. 18, s. 42, they had no jurisdiction to hear the appeal, and that the case did not fall within the operation of the general maxim under consideration.[4] And where, after the indictment—arraignment—the jury charged—and evidence given on a trial for a capital offence, one of the jurymen became incapable, through illness, of proceeding to verdict, the court of oyer and terminer discharged the jury, charged a fresh jury with the prisoner, and convicted him, although it was argued that *actus Dei nemini nocet,* and that the sudden illness *was a [*242] Godsend, of which the prisoner ought to have the benefit.[5]

B. 293 (42 E. C. L. R.). See also per Best, C. J., Tooth *v.* Bagwell, 3 Bing. 375 (11 E. C. L. R.).

[1] 15 Q. B. 88 (69 E. C. L. R.).

[2] See, also, in further illustration of the maxim as to *actus Dei*, Newton *v.* Boodle, 3 C. B. 795 (54 E. C. L. R.).

[3] Lord Raym. 433.

[4] Nettleton *v.* Burrell, 8 Scott N. R. 738, 740; cited per Maule, J., Pring *v.* Estcourt, 4 C. B. 72 (56 E. C. L. R.).

[5] R. *v.* Edwards, 4 Taunt. 309, 312.

Lastly, illness of a material witness is a sufficient ground to excuse a plaintiff in not proceeding to try, and so would be the death of one of two co-defendants, no suggestion of it having been made on the record, the trial being thus suspended by the act of God.[1]

LEX NON COGIT AD IMPOSSIBILIA.

(Co. Litt. 231, b.)

The law does not seek to compel a man to do that which he cannot possibly perform.

This maxim, or, as it is also expressed, *impotentia excusat legem*,[2] is intimately connected with that last considered, and must be understood in this qualified sense, that *impotentia* excuses when there is a necessary or invincible disability to perform the mandatory part of the law, or to forbear the prohibitory.[3]

The law itself and the administration of it, said Sir W. Scott, with reference to an alleged infraction of the revenue laws, must yield to that to which everything must bend—to necessity; the law, in its most positive and peremptory injunctions, is understood to disclaim, as it does in its general aphorisms, all intention of compelling to impossibilities, and the administration of laws must adopt that general exception in the consideration of all particular cases. "In the performance of that duty, it has three points to which its attention must be directed. In the first place, it must see that the [*243] nature of the *necessity pleaded be such as the law itself would respect, for there may be a necessity which it would not. A necessity created by a man's own act, with a fair previous knowledge of the consequences that would follow, and under circumstances which he had then a power of controlling, is of that nature. Secondly, that the party who was so placed used all practical endeavors to surmount the difficulties which already formed that necessity, and which on fair trial he found insurmountable. I do not mean all the endeavors which the wit of man, as it exists in the acutest understanding, might suggest, but such as may reasonably be expected from a fair degree of discretion and an ordinary

[1] Pell *v.* Linnell, L. R. 3 C. P. 441.
[2] Co. Litt. 29, a.
[3] Hobart 96.

knowledge of business. Thirdly, that all this shall appear by distinct and unsuspected testimony, for the positive injunctions of the law, if proved to be violated, can give way to nothing but the clearest proof of the necessity that compelled the violation."[1]

It is, then, a general rule which admits of ample practical illustration, that *impotentia excusat legem;* where the law creates a duty or charge, and the party is disabled to perform it, without any default in him, and has no remedy over, there the law will in general excuse him:[2] *ex. gr.*, if performance of the condition of a bond be rendered impracticable by an Act of Parliament the obligor will be discharged.[3]

The maxim under notice may, in the first place, be exemplified by reference to the law of mandamus:—

[*244] *A writ of mandamus issuing to a railway or other company, enjoining them to prosecute works in pursuance of statutory requirements, supposes the required act to be possible, and to be obligatory when the writ issues; and, in general, the writ suggests facts showing the obligation, and the possibility of fulfilling it;[4] though, where an obligation is shown to be incumbent on the company, onus lies upon those who contest the demand of fulfillment of proving that it is impossible;[5] if they succeed in doing so, the doctrine applies that "on mandamus, *nemo tenetur ad impossibilia.*"[6]

Again we find it laid down, that, "where H. covenants not to do an act or thing which was lawful to do, and an Act of Parliament comes after and compels him to do it, the statute repeals the cove-

[1] The Generous, 2 Dods. 323, 324.

[2] Paradine *v.* Jane, Aleyn 27; cited per Lawrence, J., 8 T. R. 267. See Evans *v.* Hutton, 5 Scott N. R. 670, and cases cited, Id. 681.

[3] Brown *v.* Mayor, &c., of London, 9 C. B. N. S. 726 (99 E. C. L. R.); s. c., 13 Id. 828.

[4] Reg. *v.* London and North-Western R. C., 16 Q. B. 864, 884 (71 E. C. L. R.); Reg. *v.* Ambergate, &c., R. C., 1 E. & B. 372, 381 (72 E. C. L. R.). See Reg. *v.* York and North Midland R. C., 1 E. & B. 178; s. c. (reversed in error), Id. 858; Reg. *v.* Great Western R. C., 1 E. & B. 253; s. c. (reversed in error), Id. 874; Reg. *v.* South-Eastern R. C., 4 H. L. Cas. 371; Reg. *v.* Lancashire and Yorkshire R. C., 1 E. & B. 228 (72 E. C. L. R.); s. c. (reversed in error), Id. 873 (a); Tapping on Mandamus 359.

[5] Reg. *v.* York, Newcastle and Berwick R. C., 16 Q. B. 886, 904 (71 E. C. L. R.); Reg. *v.* Great Western R. C., 1 E. & B. 774 (72 E. C. L. R.).

[6] Per Lord Campbell, C. J., Reg. *v.* Ambergate, &c., R. C., 1 E. & B. 380 (72 E. C. L. R.). See Reg. *v.* Coaks, 3 E. & B. 249 (77 E. C. L. R.).

nant. So, if H. covenants to do a thing which is lawful, and an Act of Parliament comes in and hinders him from doing it, the covenant is repealed. But, if a man covenants not to do a thing which then was unlawful, and an Act comes and makes it lawful to do it, such Act of Parliament does not repeal the covenant."[1] If, [*245] before the expiration of the *running days allowed by a charter-party for loading, the performance of his contract by the shipper becomes, by virtue of an Order in Council, illegal, he is discharged.[2]

A declaration in covenant set forth that the defendant demised by deed certain premises to the plaintiff for a term of years, the defendant covenanting that neither he nor his assigns would, during the term, permit any messuage, &c., to be built on a paddock fronting the demised premises. Breaches, 1st, that the defendant during the term permitted a railway station to be built on the paddock; 2dly, that the defendant assigned the paddock to a railway company, who erected the railway station on the paddock. To this declaration the defendant pleaded that after the making of the lease the railway company required to take the paddock under statutory powers then conferred on them—that the said company did for the purposes of their undertaking compulsorily purchase and take the paddock, and defendant assigned it to them in completion of their purchase, and that the company afterwards built upon such paddock the erections complained of, which were reasonably required for the purpose of their undertaking. Replication—that though the erections were reasonable, it was not necessary or compulsory for the company to build them. On demurrers to the above plea and replication, the defendant was, in virtue of the principal maxim, held entitled to judgment, having been discharged

[1] Brewster *v.* Kitchell, 1 Salk. 198; Davis *v.* Cary, 15 Q. B. 418 (69 E. C. L. R.); Wynn *v.* Shropshire Union R. and Can. Co., 5 Exch. 420, 440, 441; Doe d. Lord Anglesey *v.* Churchwardens of Rugeley, 6 Q. B. 107, 114 (51 E. C. L. R.). See also Doe d. Lord Grantley *v.* Butcher, Id. 115 (b).

[2] Reid *v.* Hoskins, 6 E. & B. 953 (88 E. C. L. R.); s. c., 5 Id. 729, 4 Id. 979; Avery *v.* Bowden, 6 E. & B. 953, 962; s. c., 5 Id. 714. See Exposito *v.* Bowden, 4 E. & B. 963 (82 E. C. L. R.); s. c., 7 Id. 763; 1 B. & S. 194 (101 E. C. L. R.); Pole *v.* Cetcovitch, 9 C. B. N. S. 430 (99 E. C. L. R.). Parties may by apt words bind themselves by a contract as to any future state of the law; per Maule, J., Mayor of Berwick *v.* Oswald, 3 E. & B. 665 (77 E. C. L. R.); s. c., 5 H. L. Cas. 856; Mayor of Dartmouth *v.* Silly, 7 E. & B. 97 (90 E. C. L. R.).

from his *covenant by the subsequent Act of Parliament, [*246] which put it out of his power to perform it. In thus deciding, the court made the following remarks, which are pertinent to our present subject:—

"There can be no doubt that a man may by an absolute contract bind himself to perform things which subsequently become impossible, or to pay damages for the non-performance, and this construction is to be put upon an unqualified undertaking, where the event which causes the impossibility was, or might have been, anticipated and guarded against in the contract, or where the impossibility arises from the act or default of the promissor. But where the event is of such a character that it cannot reasonably be supposed to have been in the contemplation of the contracting parties when the contract was made, they will not be held bound by general words which, though large enough to include, were not used with reference to the possibility of the particular contingency which afterwards happens." The plaintiff in the case above abstracted was accordingly held to be one of a numerous class of persons injured by the construction of a railway for whom compensation had not been provided by the legislature.[1]

If, however, as above stated, a person, by his own contract, absolutely engages to do an act, it is deemed to be his own fault and folly that he did not thereby *expressly* provide against contingencies, and exempt himself from responsibility in certain events; in such case therefore, that is, in the instance of an absolute and general contract, the performance is not excused by an inevitable accident or other contingency, although not *foreseen by, [*247] nor within the control of, the party.[2] And, if the condition of a bond be impossible at the time of making it, the condition alone is void, and the bond shall stand single and unconditional.[3]

[1] Baily *v.* De Crespigny, L. R. 4 Q. B. 180, 185, 189.

[2] Per Lawrence, J., Hadley *v.* Clarke, 8 T. R. 267; per Lord Ellenborough, C. J., Atkinson *v.* Ritchie, 13 East 533, 534; Marquis of Bute *v.* Thompson, 13 M. & W. 487; Hills *v.* Sughrue, 15 M. & W. 253, 262; Jervis *v.* Tomkinson, 1 H. & N. 195, 208; Spence *v.* Chodwick, 10 Q. B. 517, 528 (59 E. C. L. R.), (recognized Atkinson *v.* Ritchie, *supra*); Schilizzi *v.* Derry, 4 E. & B. 873 (82 E. C. L. R.); Hale *v.* Rawson, 4 C. B. N. S. 85 (93 E. C. L. R.); Adams *v.* Royal Mail Steam Packet Co., 5 C. B. N. S. 492 (94 E. C. L. R.).

[3] Co. Litt. 206, a; Sanders *v.* Coward, 15 M. & W. 48; Judgm., Duvergier *v.* Fellows, 5 Bing. 265 (15 E. C. L. R.). See also Dodd, Eng Lawy. 100.

When performance of the condition of a bond becomes impossible by the act of the obligor, such impossibility forms no answer to an action on the bond;[1] for "in case of a private contract, a man cannot use as a defence an impossibility brought upon himself."[2] But the performance of a condition shall be excused by the default of the obligee, as by his absence, when his presence was necessary for the performance,[3] or if he do any act which renders it impossible for the obligor to perform his engagement.[4] And, indeed, it may be laid down generally, as clear law, that, if there is an obligation defeasible on performance of a certain condition, and the performance of the condition becomes impossible by the act of the obligee, the obligor shall be excused from the performance of it.[5]

[*248] *It seems, however, that the performance of a condition precedent, on which a duty attaches, is not excused where the prevention arises from the act or conduct of a mere stranger. If a man, for instance, covenant that his son shall marry the covenantee's daughter, a refusal by her will not discharge the covenantor from making pecuniary satisfaction.[6] So, if A. covenant with C. to enfeoff B., A. is not released from his covenant by B.'s refusal to accept livery of seisin.[7]

Where an estate is conveyed on condition expressed in the grant, and such condition is impossible at the time of its creation, it is void; and if it be a condition subsequent, that is to be performed after the estate is vested, the estate shall become absolute in the tenant; as, if a feoffment be made to a man in fee-simple, on con-

[1] Judgm., Beswick *v.* Swindells, 3 A. & E. 883 (30 E. C. L. R.).

[2] Per Lord Campbell, C. J., Reg. *v.* Caledonian R. C., 16 Q. B. 28 (71 E. C. L. R.).

[3] Com. Dig., "*Condition*," L. 4, 5; cited, per Tindal, C. J., Bryant *v.* Beattie, 4 Bing. N. C. 263 (33 E. C. L. R.).

[4] Com. Dig., "*Condition*," L. 6; per Parke, B., Holme *v.* Guppy, 3 M. & W. 389; Thornhill *v.* Neats, 8 C. B. N. S. 831, 846 (98 E. C. L. R.); Russell *v.* Da Bandeira, 13 Id. 149, 203, 205. See Roberts *v.* Bury Commissioners, L. R. 4 C. P. 759.

[5] Judgm., Hayward *v.* Bennett, 3 C. B. 417, 418 (54 E. C. L. R.) (citing Co. Litt. 206, a); s. c., 5 C. B. 593.

[6] Perkins, s. 756.

[7] Co. Litt. 209, a; per Lord Kenyon, C. J., Cook *v.* Jennings, 7 T. R. 384, and in Blight *v.* Page, 3 B. & P. 296, n. See Lloyd *v.* Crispe, 5 Taunt. 249 (1 E. C. L. R.); Bac. Abr. "*Conditions*," Q. 4; cited, Thornton *v.* Jenyns, 1 Scott N. R. 66.

dition that, unless he goes to Rome in twenty-four hours, the estate shall determine; here the condition is void, and the estate made absolute in the feoffee;[1] but if such conduct be precedent, the grantee shall take nothing by the grant, for he has no estate until the condition be performed.[2]

Further, where the consideration for a promise is such that its performance is utterly and naturally impossible, such consideration is insufficient, for no benefit can, by *any implication, be conferred on the promissor,[3] and the law will not notice an act the completion of which is obviously ridiculous and impracticable. In this case, therefore, the maxim of the Roman law applies —*Impossibilium nulla obligatio est.*[4] Moreover, a promise is not binding if the consideration for making it be of such a nature that it was not in fact or law in the power of the promisee, from whom it moved, to complete such consideration, and to confer on the promissor the full benefit meant to be derived therefrom.[5] Thus if a man contract to pay a sum of money in consideration that another has contracted to do certain things, and it should turn out before anything is done under the contract, that the latter party was incapable of doing what he engaged to do, the contract is at an end; the party contracting to pay his money is under no obligation to pay for a less consideration than that for which he has stipulated.[6] But if a party by his contract lay a charge upon himself, he is bound to perform the stipulated act, or to pay damages for the non-completion,[7] unless the subject-matter of the contract were at the time manifestly and essentially impracticable; for the *improbability* of the performance does not render the promise void,

[*249]

[1] Co. Litt. 206 a; Com. Dig., "*Condition*," D. 1; 1 Fonbl. Eq., 5th ed., 212.

[2] Id. per Cockburn, C. J., Earl of Shrewsbury *v.* Scott, 6 C. B. N. S. 178 (95 E. C. L. R.). In regard to the distinction between conditions precedent and conditions subsequent, the leading case is Egerton *v.* Earl Brownlow, 4 H. L. Cas. 1. See Clavering *v.* Ellison, 7 H. L. Cas. 720.

[3] Chanter *v.* Leese, 4 M. & W. 295; per Holt, C. J., Courtenay *v.* Strong, 2 Lord Raym. 1219.

[4] D. 50. 17. 185; 1 Pothier, Oblig., pt. 1, c. 1, s. 4, § 3; 2 Story, Eq. Jurisp., 6th ed., 763.

[5] Harvey *v.* Gibbons, 2 Lev. 161; Nerot *v.* Wallace, 3 T. R. 17.

[6] Per Lord Abinger, C. B., 4 M. & W. 311.

[7] See Thornborow *v.* Whitacre, 2 Lord Raym. 1164; Pope *v.* Bavidge, 10 Exch. 73; Hale *v.* Rawson, 4 C. B. N. S. 85, 95 (93 E. C. L. R.).

because the contracting party is presumed to know whether the completion of the duty he undertakes be within his power; and therefore, an engagement upon a sufficient consideration for the performance of an act, even by a third person, is binding, [*250] *although the performance of such act depends entirely on the will of the latter.[1] Neither will the promissor be excused, if the performance of his promise be rendered impossible by the act of a third party;[2] although if an exercise of public authority render impossible the further performance of a contract which has been in part performed, the contract is, *ipso facto*, dissolved.[3]

However, if a party, by his own act, disables himself from fulfilling his contract, he thereby makes himself at once liable for a breach of it, and dispenses with the necessity of any request to perform it by the party with whom the contract has been made;[4] and this is in accordance with an important rule of law, and which we shall presently consider; viz., "that a man shall not take advantage of his own wrong."[5]

To a declaration for breach of promise of marriage, a plea that after the promise, and before breach, the defendant became afflicted with disease, which rendered him "incapable of marriage without great danger of his life, and therefore unfit for the married state," was recently held bad,[6] in accordance with the general rule that a

[1] 1 Pothier, Oblig., pt. 1, c. 1, s. 4, § 2; M'Neil *v.* Reid, 9 Bing. 68 (23 E. C. L. R.).

[2] Thurnell *v.* Balbirnie, 2 M. & W. 786; Brogden *v.* Marriott, 2 Bing. N. C. 473 (29 E. C. L. R.).

[3] Melville *v.* De Wolf, 4 E. & B. 844, 850 (82 E. C. L. R.); Esposito *v.* Bowden, Id. 963, 976.

[4] Lovelock *v.* Franklin, 8 Q. B. 371 (55 E. C. L. R.); Hochster *v.* De la Tour, 2 E. & B. 678 (15 E. C. L. R.); cited and distinguished in Churchward *v.* Reg., L. R. 1 Q. B. 208; per Williams, J., 3 C. B. N. S. 166 (91 E. C. L. R.); Danube, &c., R. C. *v.* Xenos, 13 C. B. N. S. 825 (106 E. C. L. R.); Lewis *v.* Clifton, 14 C. B. 245 (78 E. C. L. R.); arg. Reid *v.* Hoskins, 6 E. & B. 960–1 (88 E. C. L. R.), and 5 Id. 737, 4 Id. 982; Avery *v.* Bowden, 5 E. & B. 722 (85 E. C. L. R.); s. c., 6 Id. 953. See Jonassohn *v.* Young, 4 B. & S. 300 (116 E. C. L. R.).

[5] *Post*, p. 279.

[6] Hall *v.* Wright, E., B. & E. 746 (96 E. C. L. R.). See Beachey *v.* Brown, Id. 796; Baker *v.* Cartwright, 10 C. B. N. S. 124 (100 E. C. L. R.).

Quære, whether the decision in Reg. *v.* Millis, 10 Cl. & F. 534, applies to a marriage "of necessity entered into where the presence of a minister in holy

*man who has voluntarily contracted shall either perform his contract or pay damages for breach of it, the plea, moreover, not showing an impossibility of performance. [*251]

The following additional illustrations of the maxim before us may also be specified. Where documents are stated in the answer to a bill in equity to be in the possession of A., B., and C., the court will not order that A. shall produce them, and that, as observed by Lord Cottenham, for the best possible reason, viz., that he could not produce them.[1] So, to render a man tenant by the curtesy of land, it is necessary that the wife should have had actual seisin or possession of the land, and not merely a bare right to possess; and therefore a man cannot be tenant by the curtesy of a remainder or reversion.[2] There are, however, some incorporeal hereditaments of which a man may be tenant by the curtesy, though there have been no actual seisin of the wife; as in the case of an advowson in gross, where the church has not become void in the lifetime of the wife, which a man may hold by the curtesy, because it is impossible ever to have actual seisin of it, and *impotentia excusat legem.*[3]

The appellant having applied to justices to state a case under the stat. 20 & 21 Vict. c. 43, received the case from them on Good Friday, and transmitted it to the proper court on the following Wednesday. He was held to have sufficiently complied with the requirements of the second section of the Act, which directs that the case shall be *transmitted by the appellant within three days after he has received it; for the offices of the court having been closed from Friday till Wednesday it would have been impossible to have transmitted the case sooner.[4] [*252]

To several maxims in some measure connected with that above considered, it may, in conclusion, be proper briefly to advert. First, it is a rule, that *lex spectat naturæ ordinem*,[5] the law respects the order and course of nature, and will not force a man to demand

orders may have been impossible." Per Lord Cranworth, Beamish v. Beamish, 9 H. L. Cas. 348; per Lord Wensleydale, Id. 352.

[1] Murray v. Walter, 1 Cr. & Ph. 124. See Taylor v. Rundell, Id. 111.

[2] 2 Com. by Broom & Hadley 247. [3] Id. 248.

[4] Mayor v. Harding, L. R. 2 Q. B. 410, where Mellor, J., says, that where a statute requires a thing to be done within any particular time, such time may be circumscribed by the fact of its being impossible to comply with the statute on the last day of the period so fixed.

[5] Co. Litt. 197, b.

that which he cannot recover.[1] Thus, where the thing sued for by tenants in common is in its nature entire, as in a *quare impedit*, or in detinue for a chattel, they must of necessity join in the action, contrary to the rule which in other cases obtains, and according to which they must sue separately.[2] Secondly, it is a maxim of our legal authors, as well as a dictate of common sense, that the law will not itself attempt to do an act which would be vain, *lex nil frustra facit*, nor to enforce one which would be frivolous—*lex neminem cogit ad vana seu inutilia*,—the law will not, in the language of the old reports, enforce any one to do a thing which will be vain and fruitless.[3]

[*253] *IGNORANTIA FACTI EXCUSAT—IGNORANTIA JURIS NON EXCUSAT.

(Gr. and Rud. of Law 140, 141.)

Ignorance of fact excuses—ignorance of the law does not excuse.[4]

Ignorance may be either of law or of fact—for instance, if the heir is ignorant of the death of his ancestor, he is ignorant of a fact; but if, being aware of his death, and of his own relationship, he is nevertheless ignorant that certain rights have thereby become vested in himself, he is ignorant of the law.[5] Such is the example

[1] Litt., s. 129; Co. Litt. 197 b.

[2] Litt., s. 314; cited Marson *v.* Short, 2 Bing. N. C. 120 (29 E. C. L. R.); Co. Litt. 197 b.

"One tenant in common cannot be treated as a wrong-doer by another, except for some act which amounts to an ouster of his co-tenant, or to a destruction of the common property." Per Smith, J., Jacobs *v.* Seward, L. R. 4 C. P. 329, 330.

[3] Per Kent, C. J., 3 Johnson (U. S.) R. 598; 5 Rep. 21; Co. Litt. 127 b., cited, 2 Bing. N. C. 121; Wing. Max., p. 600; R. *v.* Bishop of London, 14 East 420 (a); per Willes, J., Bell *v.* Midland R. C., 10 C. B. N. S. 306 (100 E. C. L. R.).

[4] "It is said *ignorantia juris haud excusat*, but in that maxim the word *jus* is used in the sense of denoting general law, the ordinary law of the country." "When the word *jus* is used in the sense of denoting a private right, that maxim has no application." Per Lord Westbury, Cooper *v.* Phipps, L. R. 2 H. L. 170.

[5] D. 22. 6. 1. The doctrines of the Roman law upon the subject treated in the text are shortly stated in 1 Spence's Chan. Juris. 632–3.

given to illustrate the distinction between *ignorantia juris* and *ignorantia facti* in the Civil Law, where the general rule upon the subject is thus laid down: *Regula est, juris quidem ignorantiam cuique nocere, facti vero ignorantiam non nocere*[1]—ignorance of a material fact may excuse a party from the legal consequences of his conduct; but ignorance of the law, which every man is presumed to know, does not afford excuse—*ignorantia juris, quod quisque scire tenetur, neminem excusat.*[2] With respect to the "presumption of legal knowledge" here spoken of, we may observe, that, although ignorance of the law does not excuse persons, so as to exempt them from the consequences of their acts, as, for example, from *punishment for a criminal offence,[3] or damages for breach of contract, the law nevertheless takes [*254] notice that there may be a doubtful point of law, and that a person may be ignorant of the law, and it is quite evident that ignorance of the law does in reality exist.[4] It would, for instance, be contrary to common sense to assert, that every person is acquainted with the practice of the courts; although, in such case, there is a presumption of knowledge to this extent, that *ignorantia juris non excusat*, the rules of practice must be observed, and any deviation from them will entail consequences detrimental to the suitor.[5] It

[1] D. 22. 6. 9 pr.; Cod. 1. 18. 10. The same rule is likewise laid down in the Basilica, 2. 4. 9. See Irving's Civil Law, 4th ed., 74.

[2] 2 Rep. 3 b; 1 Plowd. 343; per Lord Campbell, 9 Cl. & F. 324; per Erle, C. J., Pooley *v.* Brown, 11 C. B. N. S. 575 (103 E. C. L. R.); Kitchen *v.* Hawkins, L. R. 2 C. P. 22.

[3] *Post*, p. 267.

[4] "The maxim is *ignorantia legis neminem excusat*, but there is no maxim which says that for all intents and purposes a person must be taken to know the legal consequences of his acts." Per Lush, J., L. R. 3 Q. B. 639.

In reference to the equitable doctrine of election, Lord Westbury, C., observes, that although "it is true as a general proposition that knowledge of the law must be imputed to every person," "it would be too much to impute knowledge of this rule of equity." Spread *v.* Morgan, 11 H. L. Cas. 602.

See also Noble *v.* Noble, L. R. 1 P. & D. 691, 693.

[5] See per Maule, J., Martindale *v.* Falkner, 2 C. B. 719, 720 (52 E. C. L. R.); cited per Blackburn, J., Reg. *v.* Mayor of Tewkesbury, L. R. 3 Q. B. 635; per Willes, J., Poole *v.* Whitcomb, 12 C. B. N. S. 775 (104 E. C. L. R.); per Lord Mansfield, C. J., Jones *v.* Randall, 1 Cowp. 40; per Coltman, J., Sargent *v.* Gannon, 7 C. B. 752 (62 E. C. L. R.); Edwards *v.* Ward, 4 C. B. 315 (56 E. C. L. R.). See also Newton *v.* Belcher, 12 Q. B. 921 (64 E. C. L. R.); Newton *v.* Liddiard, Id. 925.

is, therefore, in the above qualified sense alone that the saying, that "all men are presumed cognizant of the law,"[1] must be understood.

The following case, decided by the House of Lords, will illustrate the above general rule, and will likewise show that our courts must necessarily recognize the existence of doubtful points of law, since the adjustment of claims involving them is allowed to be a good consideration for a promise,[2] and to sustain an agreement between [*255] the *litigating parties:—The widow, brother, and sister, of an American who died in Italy, leaving considerable personal estate in the hands of trustees in Scotland, agreed, by advice of their law agent, to compromise their respective claims to the succession, by taking equal shares. The widow, after receiving her share, brought an action in Scotland to rescind the agreement, on the ground of having thereby sustained injury, through ignorance of her legal rights and the erroneous advice of the law agent; there was, however, no allegation of fraud against him or against the parties to the agreement. It was held, that, although the fair inference from the evidence was, that she was ignorant of her legal rights, and would not have entered into the agreement had she known them, yet as the extent of her ignorance and of the injury sustained was doubtful, and there was no proof of fraud or improper conduct on the part of the agent, she was bound by his acts, and affected by the knowledge which he was presumed to have of her rights, and was therefore not entitled to disturb the arrangement which had been effected.[3]

"If," remarked Lord Cotterham, C., in the above case, "it were necessary to show knowledge in the principal, and a distinct understanding of all the rights and interests affected by the complicated arrangements which are constantly taking place in families, very few, if any, could be supported."

It is, then, a true rule, if understood in the sense above assigned to it, that every man must be taken to be cognizant of the law; for otherwise, as observed by Lord Ellenborough, C. J., there is no

[1] Grounds and Rudiments of the Law 141.

[2] Per Maule, J., 2 C. B. 720 (52 E. C. L. R.). See Wade *v.* Simeon, 1 C. B. 610 (50 E. C. L. R.).

[3] Stewart *v.* Stewart, 6 Cl. & Fin. 911; Clifton *v.* Cockburn, 3 My. & K. 99; *vide* Cod. 1. 18. 2; Teede *v.* Johnson, 11 Exch. 840.

saying to what extent the *excuse of ignorance might not be carried; it would be urged in almost every case;[1] and, [*256] from this rule, coupled with that as to ignorance of fact, are derived the two following important propositions:—1st, that money paid with full knowledge of the facts, but through ignorance of the law, is not recoverable, if there be nothing unconscientious in the retaining of it; and, 2dly, that money paid in ignorance of the facts is recoverable, provided there have been no laches in the party paying it, and there was no ground to claim it in conscience.[2]

In a leading case on the first of the above rules, the facts were these—the captain of a king's ship brought home in her public treasure upon the public service, and treasure of individuals for his own emolument. He received freight for both, and paid over one-third of it, according to an established usage in the navy, to the admiral under whose command he sailed. Discovering, however, that the law did not compel captains to pay to admirals one-third of the freight, the captain brought an action for money had and received, to recover it back from the admiral's executrix; and it was held that he could not recover back the private freight, because the whole of that transaction was illegal; nor the public freight, because he had paid it with full knowledge of the facts, although in ignorance of the law, and because it was not against conscience for the executrix to retain it.[3]

*The following cases may also here be noticed:—A., tenant to B., received notice from C., a mortgagee of B.'s [*257] term, that the interest was in arrear, and requiring payment to her

[1] Bilbie *v.* Lumley, 2 East 469; Preface to Co. Litt.; Gomery *v.* Bond, 3 M. & S. 378.

[2] See note to Marriot *v.* Hampton, 2 Smith L. C., 6th ed., 376 *et seq.*; Wilkinson *v.* Johnston, 3 B. & C. 429 (10 E. C. L. R.); per Lord Mansfield, C. J., Bize *v.* Dickason, 1 T. R. 286, 287; Platt *v.* Bromage, 24 L. J. Ex. 63. See Lee *v.* Merrett, 8 Q. B. 820 (55 E. C. L. R.), observed upon in Gingell *v.* Purkins, 4 Exch. 723, recognizing Standish *v.* Ross, 3 Exch. 527.

[3] Brisbane *v.* Dacres, 5 Taunt. 143 (1 E. C. L. R.); per Lord Ellenborough, C. J., Bilbie *v.* Lumley, 2 East 470; Cumming *v.* Bedborough, 15 M. & W. 438; Branston *v.* Robins, 4 Bing. 11 (13 E. C. L. R.); Stevens *v.* Lynch, 12 East 38; per Lord Eldon, C., Bromley *v.* Holland, 7 Ves. jun. 23; Lowry *v.* Bourdieu, Dougl. 468; Gomery *v.* Bond, 3 M. & S. 378; Lothian *v.* Henderson, 3 B. & P. 420; Dew *v.* Parsons, 2 B. & Ald. 562 (22 E. C. L. R.). See arg. Gibson *v.* Bruce, 6 Scott N. R. 309; Smith *v.* Bromley, cited 2 Dougl. 696, and 6 Scott N. R. 318; Atkinson *v.* Denby, 6 H. & N. 778; s. c., 7 Id. 934.

(C.) of the rent then due. A., notwithstanding this notice, paid the rent to B., and was afterwards compelled, by distress, to pay the amount over again to C. Held, that the money having been paid to B. with full knowledge of the facts could not be recovered back.[1]

In an action for money paid to the defendant's use by drawer against acceptor of an accommodation bill, the plaintiff must show not merely that the money paid *pro tanto* discharges the liability of the acceptor to the holder of the bill, but also that it was paid at the request, express or implied, of the defendant—a mere voluntary payment by the plaintiff will not entitle him to recover.[2]

Where, however, there is *bona fides*, and money is paid with full knowledge of the facts, though there be no debt, still it cannot be recovered back;[3] as, where an underwriter having paid the loss, sought to recover the amount paid, on the ground that a material circumstance had been concealed; it appearing, however, that he knew of this at the time of the adjustment, it was held that he could not *recover.[4] And the same principle has been held to extend to an allowance on account, as being equivalent for this purpose to the payment of money.[5]

Secondly, when money paid by the plaintiff to the defendant under *bonâ fide* forgetfulness or ignorance[6] of facts, which disentitled the defendant to receive it, may be recovered back as money

[1] Higgs *v.* Scott, 7 C. B. 63 (62 E. C. L. R.). See Wilton *v.* Dunn, 17 Q. B. 294 (79 E. C. L. R.).

[2] Sleigh *v.* Sleigh, 5 Exch. 514.

[3] Per Patteson, J., Duke de Cadaval *v.* Collins, 4 A. & E. 866 (31 E. C. L. R.); Bloor *v.* Huston, 15 C. B. 266 (80 E. C. L. R.). See the maxim, *Volenti non fit injuria*—*post*, p. 268.

[4] Bilbie *v.* Lumley, 2 East 469; Gomery *v.* Bond, 3 M. & S. 378; Lothian *v.* Henderson, 3 B. & P. 420.

[5] Skyring *v.* Greenwood, 4 B. & C. 281 (10 E. C. L. R.); cited and recognized, Bate *v.* Lawrence, 8 Scott N. R. 131, in Reg. *v.* Lords of the Treasury, 16 Q. B. 362 (71 E. C. L. R.), and in Swan *v.* North British Australasian Co., 7 H. & N. 632; per Best, C. J., Bramston *v.* Robins, 4 Bing. 15 (13 E. C. L. R.); Holland *v.* Russell, 4 B. & S. 14 (116 E. C. L. R.); Cave *v.* Mills, 7 H. & N. 925, 926 (cited *ante*, p. 169). As to the question,—when may an account settled between parties be reopened on the ground of error? see M'Kellar *v.* Wallace, 8 Moore P. C. C. 378; Perry *v.* Attwood, 6 E. & B. 691 (88 E. C. L. R.).

[6] D. 12. 6. 1.

had and received.[1] The principle, it has been said,[2] upon which the action for money had and received to recover money paid by mistake is maintainable, is clear and simple—"No man should by law be deprived of his money which he has parted with under a mistake, and where it is against justice and conscience that the receiver should retain it. If A. pay money to B. supposing him to be the agent of C., to whom he owes the money, and B. be not the agent, it may be *recovered back again. If A. and B. are settling an account, and make a mistake in summing up the items— A. pays B. 100*l.* too much—he may recover it back again;" but the law is different where money is paid with full knowledge of the facts.[3] [*259]

Where, however, money is paid to another under the influence of a mistake, that is, upon the supposition that a specific fact is true, which would entitle the other to the money, but which fact is untrue, and the money would not have been paid if it had been known to the payer that the fact was untrue, an action will lie to recover it back, and it is against conscience to retain it,[4] though a demand may be necessary in those cases in which the party receiving may have been ignorant of the mistake. If, indeed, the money is intentionally paid, without reference to the truth or falsehood of the fact, the plaintiff, being a mere volunteer,[5] or if the plaintiff mean to waive

[1] Kelly *v.* Solari, 9 M. & W. 54 (cited and distinguished per Earle, C. J., Chambers *v.* Miller, 13 C. B. N. S. 133 (76 E. C. L. R.)); Lucas *v.* Worswick, 1 Moo. & Rob. 293; Strickland *v.* Turner, 7 Exch. 208; cited per Pollock, C. B., 8 Exch. 49; Mills *v.* Alderbury Union, 3 Exch. 590; Barber *v.* Brown, 1 C. B. N. S. 121 (87 E. C. L. R.).

"It seems from a long series of cases from Kelly *v.* Solari (*supra*) down to Dails *v.* Lloyd, 12 Q. B. 531 (64 E. C. L. R.), that where a party pays money under a mistake of fact he is entitled to recover it back, although he may at the time of the payment have had means of knowledge of which he has neglected to avail himself;" per Erle, C. J., Townsend *v.* Crowdy, 8 C. B. N. S. 493–4 (98 E. C. L. R.); Stewart *v.* London and North-Western R. C., 3 H. & C. 135.

[2] Per Kelly, C. B., Freeman *v.* Jeffries, L. R. 4 Ex. 197, 198.

[3] *Ante*, p. 257.

[4] See Milnes *v.* Duncan, 6 B. & C. 671 (13 E. C. L. R.); Bize *v.* Dickason, 1 T. R. 285; cited per Mansfield, C. J., Brisbane *v.* Dacres, 5 Taunt. 162 (1 E. C. L. R.); Harris *v.* Lloyd, 5 M. & W. 432. It is a good plea to an action on a promissory note that the note was obtained by a misrepresentation, whether of law or of fact: Southall *v.* Rigg, and Forman *v.* Wright, 11 C. B. 481, 492–3 (73 E. C. L. R.).

[5] See Aiken *v.* Short, 1 H. & N. 210. It is obvious that "if a person voluntarily pays money for another, he cannot sue the latter for it; in order to

all inquiry into the fact,[1] and that the person receiving shall have the money at all events whether it be true or false, the latter is certainly entitled to retain it; but if it is paid under the impression of a fact which is untrue, it may, generally speaking, be recovered back, however careless the party paying may have been in omitting [*260] to use *due diligence, or to inquire into the fact;[2] and, therefore, it does not seem to be a true position in point of law, that a person so paying is precluded from recovering by laches, in not availing himself of the means of knowledge in his power,[3] though, if there be evidence of means of knowledge, the jury will very readily infer actual knowledge.[4]

In an action on a marine policy of insurance, the question was, whether the captain of a vessel which sailed to a blockaded port knew of the blockade at a particular period; and it was observed by Lord Tenterden, C. J., that, if the possibility or even probability of actual knowledge should be considered as legal proof of the fact of actual knowledge, as a *presumptio juris et de jure*, the presumption might, in some cases, be contrary to the fact, and such a rule might work injustice; and that the question, as to the knowledge possessed by a person of a given fact, was for the decision and judgment of the jury. It was also remarked, in the same case, that the probability of actual knowledge upon consideration of time, place, the opportunities of testimony, and other circumstances, may in some instances be so strong and cogent as to cast the proof of ignorance on the other side in the opinion of the jury, and, in the absence of such proof of ignorance, to lead them to infer knowledge; but that such inference properly belongs to them.[5]

render him liable, it must be shown that there was a previous authority or an adoption of the payment;" per Martin, B., Wycombe Union *v.* Eton Union, 1 H. & N. 699.

[1] Per Willes, J., Townsend *v.* Crowdy, 8 C. B. N. S. 490 (98 E. C. L. R.).

[2] Per Parke, B., Kelly *v.* Solari, 9 M. & W. 58, 59, recognized Bell *v.* Gardiner, 4 Scott N. R. 621, 633, 634; per Ashhurst, J., Chatfield *v.* Paxton, cited 2 East 471, n. (*a*). See D. 22. 6. 9. § 2.

[3] Per Parke, B., 9 M. & W. 58, 59, controverting the dictum of Bayley, J., in Milnes *v.* Duncan, 6 B. & C. 671 (13 E. C. L. R.); Lucas *v.* Worswick, 1 Moo. & Rob. 293; Bell *v.* Gardiner, 4 Scott N. R. 621, 635. See per Dallas, C. J., Martin *v.* Morgan, 1 B. & B. 291 (5 E. C. L. R.).

[4] Per Coltman, J., 4 Scott N. R. 633.

[5] Harratt *v.* Wise, 9 B. & C. 712, 717 (17 E. C. L. R.).

*In ejectment by A., claiming title under a second mortgage, it was held that a tenant, who had paid rent to the [*261] lessor of the plaintiff under a mistake of the facts, although estopped from disputing A.'s title at the time of the demise, might nevertheless show in defence a prior mortgage to B., together with notice from, and payment of rent to B.; and that he was not precluded from this defence by having paid rent to A. under a mistake.[1]

Although a tenancy from year to year is ordinarily implied from the mere receipt of rent, this presumption may be rebutted by showing that it was received in ignorance of the death of a party upon whose life the premises were held.[2]

A policy of insurance was granted by the defendants on the life of A., at a certain premium, payable on the 13th of October in each year—with a condition that the policy should be void, *inter alia*, "if the premiums were not paid within thirty days after they should respectively become due, but that the policy might be revived within three calendar months on satisfactory proof of the health of the party on whose life the insurance was made," and payment of a certain fine. On the 13th of October, 1855, an annual premium became due, and on the 12th of November following A. died, the premium remaining unpaid, and the thirty days allowed by the condition having then expired. On the 14th of November the plaintiff for whose benefit the policy had been effected, sent the defendants a check for the premium, for which on the next day cash was obtained, and a receipt given as for *"the premium for the [*262] renewal of the policy to October 13, 1856, inclusive,"—both parties being ignorant that A. was then dead. The policy was held not to have been revived by the payment—the whole transaction, including such payment and receipt, having been "founded upon a mistake."[3]

Further, it has been stated,[4] as a general rule, that "in matters

[1] Doe d. Higginbotham *v.* Barton, 11 A. & E. 307 (39 E. C. L. R.). See also Watson *v.* Lane, 11 Exch. 769; Perrott *v.* Perrott, 14 East 422, which was a case as to the cancellation of a will.

[2] Doe d. Lord *v.* Crago, 6 C. B. 90 (60 E. C. L. R.).

[3] Pritchard *v.* Merchants' Life Assurance Co., 3 C. B. N. S. 622 (91 E. C. L. R.).

[4] Per Pollock, C. B., Emery *v.* Webster, 9 Exch. 242, 246, which well illustrates the proposition in the text.

connected with the administration of justice, where a mistake is discovered before any further step is taken, the court interferes to cure the mistake, taking care that the opposite party shall not be put to any expense in consequence of the application to amend the error." In some cases also, where at the time of applying to the court the applicant is ignorant of circumstances material to the subject matter of his motion, he may be permitted to open the proceedings afresh; for instance, under very peculiar circumstances the court reopened a rule for a criminal information, it appearing that the affidavits on which the rule had been discharged were false.[1]

In courts of equity, as well as of law, the twofold maxim under consideration is admitted to hold true; for on the one hand it is a general rule in accordance with the maxim of the civil law, *non videntur qui errant consentire*,[2] that equity will relieve where an act has been done, or contract made, under a mistake, or ignorance of a material fact;[3] and on the other hand, it is *laid down as a general proposition, that in courts of equity the ignorance of the law shall not affect agreements, nor excuse from the legal consequences of particular acts,[4] and this rule, as observed by Mr. J. Story, is fully borne out by the authorities.[5] For instance, a bill was filed to redeem an annuity, suggesting that it was part of the agreement that it should be redeemable, but that the clause for redemption was left out of the annuity deed, under the idea that, if inserted, the transaction would be usurious; the court refused relief, no case of fraud being established by the evidence.[6]

[*263]

[1] R. *v.* Eve, 5 A. & E. 780 (31 E. C. L. R.); Bodfield *v.* Padmore, Id. 785, n.

[2] D. 50. 17. 116, § 2.

[3] 1 Story, Eq. Jurisp., 6th ed., 165. See Scott *v.* Littledale, 8 E. & B. 815 (92 E. C. L. R.); Simmons *v.* Heseltine, 5 C. B. N. S. 554, 565 (94 E. C. L. R.).

If parties contract under a mutual mistake and misapprehension as to their relative and respective rights, the agreement thus made is liable to be set aside in equity as having proceeded upon a common mistake: Cooper *v.* Phibbs, L. R. 2 H. L. 149, 170.

[4] 1 Fonbl. Eq., 5th ed., 119, note.

[5] 1 Story, Eq. Jurisp., 6th ed., 128. The case of the Directors of the Midland Great Western R. C. *v.* Johnson, 6 H. L. Cas. 798, illustrates the text.

[6] Lord Irnham *v.* Child, 1 Brown C. C. 92; cited and distinguished per Lord Eldon, C., Marquis Townshend *v.* Stangroom, 6 Ves. jun. 332; per Lord

Where a deed of appointment was executed absolutely, without introducing a power of revocation, which was contained in the deed creating the power, and this omission was made through a mistake in law, and on the supposition that the deed of appointment, being a voluntary deed, was therefore revocable, relief was likewise refused by the court.[1] So, where two are jointly bound by a bond, and the obligee releases one, supposing, erroneously, that the other will remain bound, the obligee will not be relieved in equity upon the mere ground of his mistake of the law, for *ignorantia juris non excusat.*[2] Nor will a court of *equity direct payments, [*264] made under a mistaken construction of a doubtful clause in a settlement, to be refunded after many years of acquiescence by all parties, and after the death of one of the authors of the settlement, especially where subsequent family arrangements have proceeded on the footing of that construction.[3] It is, however, well settled that a court of equity will relieve against a mistake or ignorance of fact; and in several cases, which are sometimes cited as exceptions to the general rule as to *ignorantia juris*, it will be found that there was a mistake or misrepresentation of fact sufficient to justify a court of equity in interfering to give relief.[4] In a leading case,[5] illustrative of this remark, the testator, being a freeman of the city of London, left to his daughter a legacy of 10,000*l.*, upon condition that she should release her orphanage part, together with all her claim or right to his personal estate, by virtue of the custom[6] of the city of London or otherwise. Upon her father's death, his daughter accepted the legacy, and executed the release, and, before executing it, her brother informed her that she had it in her election either to have an account of her father's

Hardwicke, C., Pullen *v.* Ready, 2 Atk. 591; Mildmay *v.* Hungerford, 2 Vern. 243. See Judgm., Hunt *v.* Rousmaniere's Administrators, 1 Peters (U. S.) R. 1, 15; commenting on Lansdowne *v.* Lansdowne, 2 Jac. & W. 205.

[1] Worrall *v.* Jacob, 3 Meriv. 256, 271.

[2] Harman *v.* Cam, 4 Vin. Abr. 387, pl. 3; 1 Fonbl. Eq., 5th ed., 119, note.

[3] Clifton *v.* Cockburn, 3 My. & K. 76; A.-G. *v.* Mayor of Exeter, 3 Russ. 395.

[4] The reader is referred to 1 Story, Eq. Jurisp., 6th ed., Chap. V., where the cases are considered.

[5] Pusey *v.* Desbouvrie, 3 P. Wms. 315. See also M'Carthy *v.* Decaix, 2 R. & M. 614.

[6] See Pulling, Laws and Customs of London 180 *et seq.*

personal estate, or to claim her orphanage part. Upon a bill afterwards filed by the husband of the daughter in her right against the brother, who was executor under the will, Lord Talbot, C., expressed an opinion[1] that the release should be set aside, and the daughter [*265] be restored to her orphanage *share, which amounted to upwards of 40,000*l.* The decision thus expressed seems, in part, to have rested on the ground, that the daughter had not been informed of the actual amount to which she would be entitled under the custom, and did not appear to have known that she was entitled to have an account taken of the personal estate of her father, and that when she should be fully apprised of this, and not till then, she was to make her election; and it is a rule that a party is always entitled to a clear knowledge of the funds between which he is to elect before he is put to his election.[2] In like manner, it has been held, in a recent case, which is frequently cited with reference to this subject, that, where a person agrees to give up his claim to property in favor of another, such renunciation will not be supported if, at the time of making it, he was ignorant of his legal rights and of the value of the property renounced, especially if the party with whom he dealt possessed, and kept back from him, better information on the subject.[3]

Upon an examination, then, of the cases which have been relied upon as exceptions to the general rule[4] observed by courts of equity, some, as in the instances above mentioned, may be supported upon the ground that the circumstances disclosed an ignorance of fact as well as of law, and in others there will be found to have existed [*266] either actual misrepresentation, undue influence, *mental imbecility, or that sort of surprise which equity regards as a just foundation for relief. It is, indeed, laid down broadly that, if a party acting in ignorance of a plain and settled principle of law, is induced to give up a portion of his property to another, under the name of a compromise, a court of equity will grant re-

[1] The suit was compromised.

[2] 3 P. Wms. 321 (*x*).

[3] M'Carthy *v.* Decaix, 2 R. & M. 614; considered in Warrender *v.* Warrender, 2 Cl. & Fin. 488.

[4] Bearing upon the subject touched upon in the text, see per Sir J. Leach, Cockerill *v* Cholmeley, 1 Russ. & My. 418, 424, 425; s. c., affirmed 1 Cl. & F. 60; and see s. c., 3 Russ. 565, where the facts are set out at length; Marq. of Breadalbane *v.* Marq. of Chandos, 2 My. & Cr. 711; s. c., 4 Cl. & F. 43.

lief; and this proposition may be illustrated by the case of an heir-at-law, who, knowing that he is the eldest son, nevertheless agrees, through ignorance of the law, to divide undevised fee-simple estates of his ancestor with a younger brother, such an agreement being one which would be held invalid by a court of equity. Even in so simple a case, however, there may be important ingredients, independent of the mere ignorance of law, and this very ignorance may well give rise to a presumption of imposition, weakness or abuse of confidence, which will give a title to relief; at all events, in cases similar to the above, it seems clear that the mistake of law is not, *per se*, the foundation of relief; but is only the medium of proof by which some other ground of relief may be established, and on the whole it may be safely affirmed that a mere naked mistake of law, unattended by special circumstances, will furnish no ground for the interposition of a court of equity, and that the present disposition of such a court is rather to narrow than to enlarge the operation of exceptions to the above rule.[1]

In criminal cases the above maxim as to *ignorantia facti* applies when a man, intending to do a lawful act, does that which is unlawful. In this case there is not *that conjunction between the deed and the will which is necessary to form a criminal act; but, in order that he may stand excused, there must be an ignorance or mistake of fact, and not an error in point of law; as if a man, intending to kill a thief or housebreaker in his own house, and under circumstances which would justify him in so doing, by mistake kills one of his own family, this is no criminal action; but if a man thinks he has a right to kill a person excommunicated or outlawed wherever he meets him, and does so, this is willful murder. For a mistake in point of law, which every person of discretion not only may, but is bound and presumed to know, is, in criminal cases, no sort of defence.[2] *Ignorantia eorum quæ quis scire tenetur non excusat.*[3]

[*267]

[1] See 1 Story, Eq. Juris., 6th ed., 133, *et seq.*; per Lord Cottenham, C., Stewart *v.* Stewart, 6 Cl. & Fin. 964–971. See also Spence, Chanc. Juris. 633, *et seq.*

[2] 4 Com. by Broom & Hadley 26; Doct. and Stud., Dial. ii., c. 46. A plea of ignorance of the law was rejected in Lord Vaux's Case, 1 Bulstr. 197. See also Re Barronet, 1 E. & B. 1, 8 (72 E. C. L. R.).

[3] Hale, Pl. Cr. 42. "The law is administered upon the principle that every

Lastly, every man is presumed to be cognizant of the statute law of this realm, and to construe it aright; and if any individual should infringe it through ignorance, he must, nevertheless, abide by the consequences of his error. It will not be competent to him to aver, in a court of justice, that he has mistaken the law, this being a plea which no court of justice is at liberty to receive.[1] Where, however, the passing of a statute could not have been known to an accused at the time of doing an act thereby rendered criminal, the crown would probably [*268] *think fit, in case of conviction, to exercise its prerogative of mercy.[2]

VOLENTI NON FIT INJURIA.

(Wing. Max. 482.)

That to which a person assents is not esteemed in law an injury.

It is a general rule of the English law that no one can maintain an action for a wrong where he has consented to the act which occasions his loss;[3] and this principle has often been applied under states of facts showing that, though the defendant was in the wrong, the plaintiff's negligence had contributed to produce the damage consequential on the act complained of.[4] Cases such as now alluded to will hereafter be noticed in connection with the maxims *Sic utere tuo ut alienum non lædas*[5] and *Respondeat superior.*[6]

one must be taken conclusively to know it without proof that he does know it:" per Tindal, C. J., 10 Cl. & F. 210.

[1] Per Sir W. Scott, The Charlotta, 1 Dods. R. 392; per Lord Hardwicke, Middleton *v.* Croft, Stra. 1056; per Pollock, C. B., Cooper *v.* Simmons, 7 H. & N. 717; The Katherina, 30 L. J., P., M. & A. 21.

[2] R. *v.* Bailey, Russ. & Ry. 1; R. *v.* Esop, 7 C. & P. 456 (32 E. C. L. R.).

[3] Per Tindal, C. J., Gould *v.* Oliver, 4 B. N. C. 142 (33 E. C. L. R.); cited s. c., 2 Scott N. R. 257; per Lord Campbell, C. J., Haddon *v.* Ayers, 1 E. & E. 148 (102 E. C. L. R.); per Wood, V.-C., A.-G. *v.* College of Physicians, 30 L. J., Chanc. 769. See Bird *v.* Holbrook, 4 Bing. 628, 639, 640 (13 E. C. L. R.); Wootton *v.* Dawkins, 2 C. B. N. S. 367 (89 E. C. L. R.); Plowd. 501; D. 50. 17. 203.

[4] Per Curtis, J., Byam *v.* Bullard, 1 Curtis (U. S.) R. 101. Caswell *v.* Worth, 6 E. & B. 849 (85 E. C. L. R.), and Senior *v.* Ward, 1 E. & E. 385, 393 (102 E. C. L. R.), well illustrate the text. See also Holmes *v.* Clark, 6 H. & N. 349; Adams *v.* Lancashire and Yorkshire R. C., L. R. 4 C. P. 739.

[5] *Post*, Chap. VI., s. 2. [6] *Post*, Chap. IX.

In accordance with the rule *volenti non fit injuria*, in an action for criminal conversation, prior to the statute 20 & 21 Vict. c. 85, the law was clearly settled to be, that the husband's consent to his wife's adultery went in bar of his action: if the husband were guilty of negligence, or even of loose or improper conduct not amounting to a *consent, it only went in reduction of damages.[1] And it is observable that the claim for "damages from any person on the ground of his having committed adultery" with the wife of the petitioner, under s. 33[2] of the Act just cited, is to be "heard and tried on the same principles, in the same manner, and subject to the same or the like rules and regulations as actions for criminal conversation" were tried and decided in courts of common law before the passing of that enactment.[3] [*269]

The following cases, involving dissimilar states of facts, will be found further to illustrate the maxim under consideration:—Although the deck of a vessel is *primâ facie* an improper place for the stowage of a cargo, or any part of it, yet, when the loading on the deck has taken place with the consent of the merchant, it is obvious that no remedy against the shipowner or master for a wrongful loading of the goods on deck can exist.[4] So, if a person says, generally, "There are spring-guns in this wood," and if another then takes upon himself to go into the wood, knowing that he is in hazard of meeting with the injury which the guns are calculated to produce, he does so at his own peril, and must take the consequences of his own act.[5] Moreover, although, as will hereafter *appear, the maxim *Injuria non excusat injuriam* is of frequent applicability, "a wrong-doer cannot, any more than [*270]

[1] Per Buller, J., Duberley *v.* Gunning, 4 T. R. 657; per De Grey, C. J., Howard *v.* Burtonwood, cited 1 Selw. N. P., 10th ed., 8, n. (3); Id. 10, n. (6); per Alderson, J., Winter *v.* Henn, 4 C. & P. 498 (19 E. C. L. R.). As to the application and meaning of the maxim, *Volenti non fit injuria*, in the ecclesiastical courts, see per Sir J. Nicholl, Rogers *v.* Rogers, 3 Hagg. 57; cited, Phillips *v.* Phillips, 1 Robertson 158; per Sir W. Scott, Forster *v.* Forster, 1 Consist. R. 146; Stone *v.* Stone, 1 Robertson 99; Judgm., Cocksedge *v.* Cocksedge, Id. 92; 2 Curt. 213; Shelf. on Marriage and Div. 445, *et seq.*

[2] See also ss. 28–30.

[3] See Comyn *v.* Comyn, 32 L. J., P., M. & A. 210; 3 Com. by Broom & Hadley 411.

[4] Gould *v.* Oliver, 2 Scott N. R. 257, 264; s. c., 4 B. N. C. 134 (33 E. C. L. R.).

[5] Per Bayley, J., Ilott *v.* Wilkes, 3 B. & Ald. 311 (5 E. C. L. R.).

one who is not a wrong-doer, maintain an action, unless he has a right to complain of the act causing the injury, and complain thereof against the person he has made defendant in the action."[1] No man by his wrongful act can impose a duty on another,[2] nor can one who avails himself of a mere license to enter upon premises impose upon their owner a duty to have them in a safe condition.[3] So, if a man, passing in the dark along a footpath, should happen to fall into a pit, dug by the owner of the adjoining field, in such a case, the party digging the pit would be responsible for the damage sustained if the pit were dug across the road; but if it were only in an adjacent field, the case would be very different, for the falling into it would then be the act of the injured party himself.[4]

Again, if an action be brought for slander of title, the special damage laid being, that a third party was thereby deterred from purchasing the lands in question and the plaintiff was prevented from disposing of the same, the action will fail if it appear that, [*271] prior to the speaking of *the words, a valid contract of sale had been entered into; and that, subsequently thereto, such contract had been rescinded at request of the intended purchaser, but with the plaintiff's consent.[5]

By a local Act, a right of appeal was given to any person thinking himself aggrieved by the order of commissioners appointed under it; one who had been present at a meeting, and concurred in a resolution upon which the order appealed against was founded, was held disentitled to appeal against the order.[6]

[1] Degg *v.* Midland R. C., 1 H. & N. 773, 780, followed in Potter *v.* Faulkner, 1 B. & S. 800 (101 E. C. L. R.); Griffiths *v.* Gidlow, 3 H. & N. 648; Lygo *v.* Newbold, 9 Exch. 302; Skipp *v.* Eastern Counties R. C., 9 Exch. 223, 225; Great Northern R. C. *v.* Harrison, 10 Exch. 376; Pardington *v.* South Wales R. C., 1 H. & N. 392; Wise *v.* Great Western R. C., 1 H. & N. 63. And see Cleveland *v.* Spier, 16 C. B. N. S. 399 (111 E. C. L. R.).

[2] Judgm., 1 H. & N. 782.

[3] Gautret *v.* Egerton, L. R. 2 C. P. 371, with which compare Indermaur *v.* Dames, Id. 311, and cases cited *post*, Chap. VI., sect. 2.

[4] Judgm., Jordin *v.* Crump, 8 M. & W. 787, 788. See also Horne *v.* Widlake, Yelv. 141; cited and followed per Ruggles, C. J., Hamilton *v.* White, 1 Selden (U. S.) R. 12, 13. And see the cases hereafter cited in connection with Jordin *v.* Crump, *supra*, and Barnes *v.* Ward, 9 C. B. 392 (67 E. C. L. R.); with which *acc.* Hadley *v.* Taylor, L. R. 1 C. P. 53.

[5] Kendall *v.* Stone, 1 Selden (U. S.) R. 14.

[6] Harrup *v.* Bayley, 6 E. & B. 224 (88 E. C. L. R.).

In addition to the above and similar decisions, there is, as already intimated, an extensive class of cases illustrating the maxim *Volenti non fit injuria*, in which redress is sought for an injury which has resulted from the negligence of both plaintiff and defendant, and in many of which it has been held, that the former is precluded from recovering damages.[1]

Another important application of the maxim in question, is to cases in which money which has been voluntarily paid is sought to be recovered, on the ground that it was not, in fact, due.

The first rule which we shall notice in reference to cases of this description, is that where a man has actually paid what the law would not have compelled him to pay, but what in equity and conscience he ought to have paid, he cannot recover it back again in an action for money had and received. Thus, if a man pay a debt, which could have been barred by pleading the Statute of Limitations, or one contracted during infancy, which, in justice, *he ought to discharge, in these cases, though the law would not have compelled payment, yet, the money being paid, it will not oblige the payee to refund it.[2] [*272]

There is also a large class of cases in which it has been held, that money paid voluntarily cannot be recovered, although the original payment was not required by any equitable consideration; and these cases are very nearly allied in principle to those which have been considered in treating of a payment made in ignorance of the law.

Thus, an occupier of lands, during a course of twelve years, paid the property-tax to the collector, under stat. 46 Geo. 3, c. 65, and likewise the full rent as it became due to the landlord, without claiming, as he might have done, any deduction on account of the tax so paid; and it was held, that the occupier could not maintain an action for money had and received against the landlord, for any part of the tax so paid, on the ground that the payment being voluntary, could not, according to the principle above stated, be recovered.[3] So, where a tenant pays property-tax assessed on the prem-

[1] See remarks on the maxim *Sic utere tuo ut alienum non lædas*, *post*, Chap. VI. § 2.

[2] Per Lord Mansfield, C. J., Bize *v.* Dickason, 1 T. R. 286, 287; Farmer *v.* Arundel, 2 W. Bla. 824.

[3] Denby *v.* Moore, 1 B. & Ald. 123; cited, per Bayley, J., Stubbs *v.* Parsons,

ises, and omits to deduct it in his next payment of rent, he cannot afterwards recover the amount as money paid to the use of the landlord.[1]

[*273] The maxim under consideration holds, however, in those *cases only where the party has a freedom of exercising his will; and therefore, where a debtor from mere necessity, occasioned, for instance, by a wrongful detainer of goods, pays more than the creditor can in justice demand, he shall not be said to pay it willingly, and has a right to recover the surplus so paid.[2] So, likewise, may money paid to recover possession of goods wrongfully detained,[3] or under pressure of an extortionate demand, *colore officii*,[4] be recovered.

All the cases, indeed, upon this subject, show, that where a party is in, claiming under legal process, the owner of the goods contending that the possession is illegal and paying money to avert the evil and inconvenience of a sale, may recover it back in an action for money had and received, if the claim turn out to have been unfounded.

Where, on the contrary, money is voluntarily paid, with full knowledge of all the facts,[5] or where a party pays the money, *intending to give up his right*, he cannot afterwards bring an action for money had and received, though it is otherwise where, at the

3 B. & Ald. 518 (5 E. C. L. R.). See also Cartright *v.* Rowley, 2 Esp. 723; Fulham *v.* Down, 6 Esp. 26, note; Bull, N. P. 131; cited, 8 T. R. 576; Spragg *v.* Hammond, 2 B. & B. 59 (6 E. C. L. R.); per Dallas, C. J., Andrew *v.* Hancock, 1 B. & B. 43 (5 E. C. L. R.).

[1] Cumming *v.* Bedborough, 15 M. & W. 438; Franklin *v.* Carter, 1 C. B. 750 (50 E. C. L. R.). See Payne *v.* Burridge, 12 M. & W. 727; Sweet *v.* Seager, 2 C. B. N. S. 119 (89 E. C. L. R.), (distinguished in Tidswell *v.* Whitworth, L. R. 2 C. P. 326); Thompson *v.* Lapworth, L. R. 3 C. P. 149, 160.

[2] See per Lord Mansfield, C. J., Smith *v.* Bromley, cited Dougl. 696, and followed in Atkinson *v.* Denby, 6 H. & N. 778; s. c., 7 Id. 934; per Patteson, J., and Coleridge, J., Ashmore *v.* Wainwright, 2 Q. B. 845, 846 (42 E. C. L. R.), which case is commented on, Parker *v.* Bristol and Exeter R. C., 6 Exch. 704, 706.

[3] Oates *v.* Hudson, 6 Exch. 346. See Kearns *v.* Durell, 6 C. B. 596 (60 E. C. L. R.).

[4] Steele *v.* Williams, 8 Exch. 625; Traherne *v.* Gardner, 5 E. & B. 913 (85 E. C. L. R.); Re Combs, 4 Exch. 839, 841.

[5] Remfry *v.* Butler, E., B. & E. 887, 897 (96 E. C. L. R.), followed in Stray *v.* Russell, 1 E. & E. 905, 911 (102 E. C. L. R.); s. c., Id. 916; Chapman *v.* Shepherd, Whitehead *v.* Izod, L. R. 2 C. P. 228, 238; Barber *v.* Pott, 4 H. & N. 759.

time of paying the money, the party gives notice that he intends to resist the claim, and that he yields to it merely for the purpose of *relieving himself from the inconvenience of having his goods sold.[1] [*274]

In Close *v.* Phipps,[2] the attorney for a mortgagee, who had advertised a sale of the mortgaged property, under the power reserved to him, for non-payment of interest, having extorted from the administratrix of the mortgagor money exceeding the sum really due for principal, interest, and costs, under a threat that he would proceed with the sale unless his demands were complied with, it was held, that the administratrix might recover back the money so paid as money had and received to her use. "The interest of the plaintiff," observed Tindal, C. J., "to prevent the sale, by submitting to the demand, was so great, that it may well be said, the payment was made under what the law calls a species of duress."

The plaintiff having, in the month of August, pawned some goods with the defendant for 20*l.*, without making any agreement for interest, went in the October following to redeem them, when the defendant insisted on having 10*l.* as interest for the 20*l.* The plaintiff tendering him 20*l.*, and 4*l.* for interest, knowing the same to be more than the legal interest amounted to, the defendant still insisted on having 10*l.* as interest; whereupon the plaintiff, finding that he could not otherwise get his goods back, paid defendant the sum which he demanded, and brought an action for the surplus beyond the legal interest as money had and received to his use. The court held, that the action would well lie, for it was a payment by compulsion.[3]

*In connection with cases such as the foregoing, it may be well to add that "the compulsion of law which entitles a person paying the debt of another to recover against that other as for money paid, is not such a compulsion of law as would avoid a contract, like imprisonment." Restraint of goods, by reason of the non-payment of a debt due by one to another, is sufficient com- [*275]

[1] Per Tindal, C. J., Valpy *v.* Manley, 1 C. B. 602, 603 (50 E. C. L. R.).

[2] 8 Scott N. R. 381; recognizing Parker *v.* Great Western R. C., 7 M. & Gr. 253 (49 E. C. L. R.). See 1 C. B. 788, 798 (50 E. C. L. R.).

[3] Astley *v.* Reynolds, Stra. 915; Parker *v.* Bristol and Exeter R. C., 6 Exch. 702; Hills *v.* Street, 5 Bing. 37 (15 E. C. L. R.); Bosanquet *v.* Dashwood, Cas. temp. Talbot 38.

pulsion of the law to entitle a person who has paid the debt, in order to relieve his goods from such restraint, to sustain a claim for money paid.[1]

Where an action was brought to recover back money paid to the steward of a manor for producing, at a trial, some deeds and court-rolls, for which he had charged extravagantly, the objection was taken that the money had been voluntarily paid, and therefore could not be recovered back again; but, it appearing that the money was paid through necessity and the urgency of the case, it was held to be recoverable.[2] On the same principle, where a railway company, by a general arrangement with carriers, in consideration of such carriers loading, unloading, and weighing the goods forwarded by them, made a *deduction in their favor of [*276] 10*l.* per cent. from the charges made to the public at large for the carriage of goods, it was decided that the plaintiff, a carrier, who, although willing to perform the above duties, was excluded from participation in the said arrangement, was entitled to recover from the company the above percentage, as well as other sums improperly exacted from him by the company, such payments not having been made voluntarily, but in order to induce the company to do that which they were bound to do without them, and for the refusal to do which an action on the case[3] might have been maintained against them.[4]

[1] Judgm., Johnson *v.* Royal Mail Steam Packet Co., L. R. 3 C. P. 44, 45, where the following state of facts is put *per Cur.* "A. lends B. his horse for a limited period, which would imply that he must pay the expense of the horse's keep during the time he retains it. B. goes to an inn and runs up a bill which he does not pay, and the innkeeper detains the horse. In the meantime A. has sold the horse out-and-out for its full price to C., and C. is informed that the horse is at the inn; he proceeds there to take him away, but is told he cannot take him until he pays the bill, and he pays the bill accordingly and gets his horse. Can C., who in order to get his horse is obliged to pay the debt of another, sue that other in an action for money paid? We are clearly of opinion that he could."

[2] Anon. *v.* Pigot, cited 2 Esp. 723. See Traherne *v.* Gardner, 5 E. & B. 913 (85 E. C. L. R.).

[3] Pickford *v.* Grand Junction R. C., 10 M. & W. 399. See Kent *v.* Great Western R. C., 3 C. B. 714 (54 E. C. L. R.).

[4] Parker *v.* Great Western R. C., 7 M. & Gr. 253 (49 E. C. L. R.); cited per Williams, J., Kearns *v.* Durell, 6 C. B. 602 (60 E. C. L. R.), and per Cresswell, J., Devaux *v.* Connolly, 8 C. B. 657 (65 E. C. L. R.).

An action for money had and received lies to recover back money which has been obtained through compulsion, although it has been received by defendant acting for a principal and has been paid over by him, unless the money were paid to the agent expressly for the use of the principal.[1]

In another class of cases which necessarily fall under present consideration, it has been decided, that money may be recovered back if paid under compulsion of law, imposed upon defendant by the fraudulent practices of the plaintiff in the original proceedings, or if the payment be made under the compulsion of colorable legal process. For instance, plaintiff being a foreigner, ignorant of the English language, was arrested by the defendant for a fictitious debt of 10,000*l.* upon a writ, which *was afterwards [*277] set aside for irregularity. Plaintiff, in order to obtain his release, agreed in writing to pay 500*l.*, and to give bail for the remainder of the sum. The 500*l.* was to be as a payment in part of the writ, and both parties were to abide the event of the action, the agreement containing no provision for refunding the money if the action should fail. The 500*l.* was accordingly paid, and an action having been brought to recover it back, the jury found for the plaintiff, and that the defendant knew that he had no claim upon the plaintiff. The Court of Queen's Bench discharged a rule for a new trial or to enter a nonsuit, on the ground that the arrest, according to the finding of the jury, was fraudulent, and that the money was parted with under the arrest to get rid of the pressure:[2] it being a true position that, "if an undue advantage be taken of a person's situation, and money be obtained from him by compulsion, such money may be recovered in an action for money had and received."[3]

The authorities above cited will sufficiently establish the position,

[1] Snowden *v.* Davis, 1 Taunt. 359; Parker *v.* Bristol and Exeter R. C., 6 Exch. 702, 707.

[2] Duke de Cadaval *v.* Collins, 4 A. & E. 858 (31 E. C. L. R.). See Smith *v.* Monteith, 13 M. & W. 427; De Medina *v.* Grove, 10 Q. B. 152, 172 (59 E. C. L. R.).

[3] 1 Selw. N. P., 10th ed., 83; cited and adopted by Coleridge, J., 4 A. & E. 867 (31 E. C. L. R.); Pitt *v.* Combes, 2 A. & E. 459 (29 E. C. L. R.); per Gibbs, J., Brisbane *v.* Dacres, 5 Taunt. 156 (1 E. C. L. R.); Jendwine *v.* Slade, 2 Esp. 573; Follett *v.* Hoppe, 5 C. B. 226 (57 E. C. L. R.); Green *v.* Laurie, 1 Exch. 335.

that money paid under compulsion of fraudulent legal process, or of wrongful pressure exercised upon the party paying it, may, in general, be recovered back, as money had and received to his use; and it therefore only remains to add, that, *à fortiori*, money will be recoverable which is paid, and that the instrument may be avoided [*278] which is executed under threats of personal *violence, duress, or illegal restraint of liberty;[1] and this is in strict accordance with the maxims laid down by Lord Bacon: *Non videtur consensum retinuisse si quis ex præscripto minantis aliquid immutavit*,[2] and *corporalis injuria non recipit æstimationem de futuro*.[3]

Lastly, it is worthy of observation, that there are cases where an intentional wrong-doer will be, to a certain extent, protected by the law through motives of public policy. Thus, a horse with a rider on him cannot be distrained damage feasant, on the ground of the danger to the peace which might result if such a distress were levied; and, therefore, to a plain trespass, justifying the taking of a horse, cart, and other chattels, damage feasant, it is a good replication that the horse, cart, and chattels were, at the time of the distress, in the actual possession and under the personal care of, and then being used by, the plaintiff.[4]

[1] See De Mesnil *v.* Dakin, L. R. 3 Q. B. 18 (43 E. C. L. R.); Clark *v.* Woods, 2 Exch. 395; Skeate *v.* Beale, 11 A. & E. 983, 990 (39 E. C. L. R.); Wakefield *v.* Newbon, 6 Q. B. 276, 280 (51 E. C. L. R.). As to what may constitute duress, see per Lord Cranworth, C., Boyse *v.* Rossborough, 6 H. L. Cas. 45; Cumming *v.* Ince, 11 Q. B. 112 (63 E. C. L. R.); Powell *v.* Hoyland, 6 Exch. 67; Edward *v.* Trevellick, 4 E. & B. 59 (82 E. C. L. R.).

[2] Bac. Max., reg. 22; *post; Nil consensui tam contrarium est quàm vis atque metus*, D. 50. 17. 116.

[3] Bac. Max., reg. 6.

[4] Field *v.* Adames, 12 A. & E. 649 (40 E. C. L. R.), and cases there cited; Storey *v.* Robinson, 6 T. R. 138; Bunch *v.* Kennington, 1 Q. B. 679 (41 E. C. L. R.), where Lord Denman, C. J., observes, that "perhaps the replication in Field *v.* Adames was rather loose." See Gaylard *v.* Morris, 3 Exch. 695; Sunbolt *v.* Alford, 3 M. & W. 248.

*NULLUS COMMODUM CAPERE POTEST DE INJURIA SUA PROPRIA. [*279]

(Co. Litt. 148 b.)

No man should take advantage of his own wrong.

It is a maxim of law, recognized and established, that no man shall take advantage of his own wrong;[1] and this maxim, which is based on elementary principles, is fully recognized in courts of law and of equity, and, indeed, admits of illustration from every branch of legal procedure. The reasonableness and necessity of the rule being manifest, we shall proceed at once to show its practical application by reference to decided cases; and, in the first place, we may observe, that a man shall not take advantage of his own wrong to gain the favorable interpretation of the law[2]—*frustrâ legis auxilium quœrit qui in legem committit;*[3]—and, therefore, A. shall not have an action of trespass against B., who lawfully enters to abate a nuisance caused by A.'s wrongful act,[4] nor shall an executor, *de son tort*, obtain that assistance which the law affords to a rightful executor.[5] So if A., on whose goods a distress has been levied, by his *own misconduct prevent the distress from being [*280] realized, A. cannot complain of a second distress as unlawful.[6] So B., into whose field cattle have strayed through defect of fences, which he was bound to repair, cannot distrain such cattle damage feasant in another field, into which they have got by break-

[1] Per Lord Abinger, C. B., Findon *v.* Parker, 11 M. & W. 680; Daly *v.* Thompson, 10 M. & W. 309; Malins *v.* Freeman, 4 Bing. N. C. 395, 399 (33 E. C. L. R.); per Best, J., Doe d. Bryan *v.* Bancks, 4 B. & Ald. 409 (6 E. C. L. R.); Co. Litt. 146, b; Jenk. Cent. 209; 2 Inst. 713; D. 50. 17. 134, § 1.

"No man is allowed to take advantage of his own wrong; far less of his wrong intention which is not expressed;" per Willes, J., Rumsey *v.* North-Eastern R. C., 14 C. B. N. S. 653 (78 E. C. L. R.).

It "is contrary to all legal principle" that "the plaintiff can take advantage of his own wrong." Per Willes, J., Ames *v.* Waterlow, L. R. 5 C. P. 55.

See also Dean, &c., of Christ Church *v.* Duke of Buckingham, 17 C. B. N. S. 391 (112 E. C. L. R.).

[2] 1 Hale P. C. 482.

[3] 2 Hale P. C. 386.

[4] Dodd. 220, 221. See Perry *v.* Fitzhowe, 8 Q. B. 757 (55 E. C. L. R.), and analogous cases cited, *post*, Chap. VI. § 2, *ad fin.*

[5] See Carmichael *v.* Carmichael, 2 Phill. 101; Paull *v.* Simpson, 9 Q. B. 365 (58 E. C. L. R.); *ante*, p. 216.

[6] Lee *v.* Cooke, 3 H. & N. 203; s. c., 2 Id. 584.

ing through a hedge, which had been kept by him in good repair, because B.'s negligence was *causa sine quâ non* of the mischief.[1] So if a man be bound to appear on a certain day, and before that day the obligee put him in prison, the bond is void.[2]

Hyde *v.* Watts[3] is strikingly illustrative of the maxim, that a man shall not be permitted to take advantage of his own wrong. That was an action of debt for work and labor, to which the defendant pleaded a release under an indenture or trust deed for the benefit of such of his creditors as should execute the same. The replication set out the indenture *in hæc verba*, by which it appeared that the defendant covenanted, *inter alia*, to insure his life for 1500*l.*, and to continue the same so insured during a period of three years; and, in case of his neglect or refusal to effect or to keep on foot this insurance, the indenture was to be utterly void to all intents and purposes whatsoever:—breach, that the defendant did not insure his life, whereby the said indenture became utterly void. The material question in the above case was, whether the deed, in case of a neglect on the part of the defendant to effect or keep alive the policy for 1500*l.*, was absolutely void, and incapable of being confirmed as to *all* parties, or only [*281] *void as against the plaintiff, who was a party to the deed, if he should so elect; and the latter was held by the Court of Exchequer to be the true construction, by reason of the absurd consequences which would follow, if the defendant, against the consent of all other parties interested in the validity of the indenture, could avail himself of his own wrong, and thus absolve himself and the trustees from liability on their respective covenants.

In another case also illustrative of the subject before us, the defendants, who were merchants, employed a person licensed to act as agent at the Custom-house in London, under the stat. 3 & 4 Will. 4, c. 2, s. 144, to pay the duty on goods, and to procure their delivery from the warehouse for home consumption. The defendants, in fact, paid the amount of duty to the person thus employed by them; and, he having subsequently represented to them that he had duly paid the duty upon certain goods, they sent for and

[1] Singleton *v.* Williamson, 7 H. & N. 410.

[2] Noy, Max., 9th ed., p. 45; Arg. Williams *v.* Gray, 9 C. B. 737 (67 E. C. L. R.).

[3] 12 M. & W. 254, and cases cited, Id. 262, 263.

obtained such goods from the warehouseman upon presentation of the usual merchant's order. The duty, however, not having really been paid, the merchants were held liable to an information in respect of such non-payment, it not being competent to them to set up the default of their own agent by way of defeasance, and thus to take advantage of their own wrong.[1]

The following instance, familiar doubtless to the reader, may also serve further to illustrate the same general principle:—If tenant for life or years fell timber-trees, they will belong to the lessor; for the tenant cannot, by his own wrongful act, acquire a greater property in them than he would otherwise have had.[2] *Where the lessee is evicted from part of the lands demised, by title paramount, he will have to pay a ratable proportion for the remainder;[3] whereas, if he be evicted from part of the lands by his landlord, no apportionment, but a suspension of the whole rent, takes place, except in the case of the king; and there is no suspension, if the eviction has followed upon the lessee's own wrongful act, as for a forfeiture, but an apportionment only.[4] And it is a well-known rule that a lessor or grantor cannot dispute, with his lessee or grantee, his own title to the land which he has assumed to demise or convey.[5] Nor can a grantor derogate from his own grant.[6] [*282]

It is moreover a sound principle that he who prevents a thing being done shall not avail himself of the non-performance he has occasioned. Hence, in an action for breach of covenant in not insuring, the tenant may defend himself by showing that the landlord prevented him from insuring, by representing that he had himself insured, and that, in fact, the covenant had not been broken if such representation were true.[7] If a man make the feoffment in fee upon condition that the feoffee shall reinfeoff him before a certain

[1] A.-G. *v.* Ansted, 12 M. & W. 520, 529. See Reg. *v.* Dean, Id. 39.

[2] Wing. Max., p. 574.

[3] Smith *v.* Malings, Cro. Jac. 160. See The Mayor of Poole *v.* Whitt, 15 M. & W. 571; Selby *v.* Browne, 7 Q. B. 632 (53 E. C. L. R.).

[4] Walker's Case, 3 Rep. 22; Wing. Max., p. 569. See Boodle *v.* Campbell, 8 Scott N. R. 104.

[5] Judgm., Doe d. Levy *v.* Horne, 3 Q. B. 766 (43 E. C. L. R.); cited, per Alderson, B., 15 M. & W. 576.

[6] 2 Shepp. Touchst., by Preston, 286.

[7] See Judgm., Doe d. Mustin *v.* Gladwin, 6 Q. B. 963 (51 E. C. L. R.).

day, and before that day the feoffor disseise the feoffee, and hold him out by force until the day be past: in this case the estate of the feoffee is absolute, because the feoffor shall not take advantage [*283] of his own wrongful act, which occasioned the *non-performance of the condition.[1] And, generally, where the condition of a bond was possible at the time of making it, and afterwards becomes impossible by the act of the obligee himself, as in the case of imprisonment of the obligor above mentioned, the obligation shall be saved.[2] So, where, by the terms of a contract, a service to be performed by A. for B. is to be paid for in goods, A. cannot declare in debt for the value of the service, but must sue on the special contract. But if B., by his own act, render the delivery of the goods impossible, A. may sue in debt for the value of the service.[3] So where an agreement for the purchase of a medical practice, and the mode of making the stipulated payments for it, implied that the business was to be carried on by the purchaser for a certain period, he was held liable for breach of contract in having, by his willful default during such period, incapacitated himself from carrying on the business.[4]

An insurance company covenanted with A. for valuable consideration to appoint him their agent at G., together with B., and that if B. should be displaced from the agency, they would pay A. a certain sum; the company, having transferred their business to another company, and wound up their affairs and dissolved themselves, were held to have displaced A. within the meaning of the covenant.[5]

To an action of covenant against a master for not teaching his [*284] apprentice, it is a good plea that the *apprentice would not be taught, and by his own willful act prevented the master from teaching him, for "the cause of the apprentice not being taught is that he has made it impossible, and the master cannot be called on to perform an impossibility."[6]

[1] Co. Litt. 206, b.

[2] Com. Dig., "*Condition*" (D. 1). See Hayward *v.* Bennett, 3 C. B. 404 (54 E. C. L. R.); s. c., 5 Id. 593.

[3] Keys *v.* Harwood, 2 C. B. 905 (52 E. C. L. R.).

[4] M'Intyre *v.* Belcher, 14 C. B. N. S. 654 (78 E. C. L. R.).

[5] Stirling *v.* Maitland, 5 B. & S. 840, 853 (117 E. C. L. R.); citing Charnley *v.* Winstanley, 5 East 266.

[6] Raymond *v.* Minton, L. R. 1 Ex. 244, 246.

So if a man promises to marry a woman on a future day, and before that day marries another woman, he is instantly liable to an action for breach of promise of marriage.[1] If a man contracts to execute a lease on and from a future day for a certain term, and before that day executes a lease to another for the same term, he may be immediately sued for breaking the contract.[2] If a man contracts to sell and deliver specific goods on a future day, and before that day he sells and delivers them to another, he is immediately liable to an action at the suit of the person with whom he first contracted to sell and deliver them.[3] And, generally, "the man who wrongfully renounces a contract into which he has deliberately entered cannot justly complain if he is immediately sued for a compensation in damages by the man whom he has injured; and it seems reasonable to allow an option to the injured party either to sue immediately or to wait till the time when the act was to be done, still holding it as prospectively binding for the exercise of the option which may be advantageous to the innocent party, and cannot be prejudicial to the wrongdoer."[4] And so "where a *contract is for the performance of a thing on a given [*285] day it is competent to the party who is to perform it to declare before the day that he will not perform it, and then the other party has the option of treating that as a breach of the contract.[5]

"All the cases admit," says Lord Alvanley, in Touteng *v.* Hubbard,[6] "that where a party has been disabled from performing his

[1] Short *v.* Stone, 8 Q. B. 358 (55 E. C. L. R.). See Caines *v.* Smith, 15 M. & W. 189; Wild *v.* Harris, 7 C. B. 999 (62 E. C. L. R.).

[2] Ford *v.* Tiley, 6 B. & C. 325 (13 E. C. L. R.); Lovelock *v.* Franklyn, 8 Q. B. 371 (55 E. C. L. R.).

[3] Bowdell *v.* Parsons, 10 East 359.

[4] Hochster *v.* De la Tour, 2 E. & B. 678, 691 (75 E. C. L. R.); recognized Avery *v.* Bowden, 5 E. & B. 728 (85 E. C. L. R.); and cited Crookewit *v.* Fletcher, 1 H. & N. 915, and per Jervis, C. J., 6 E. & B. 961 (88 E. C. L. R.); Bartholomew *v.* Markwick, 15 C. B. N. S. 711, 716 (109 E. C. L. R.); per Maule, J., Lewis *v.* Clifton, 14 C. B. 253 (78 E. C. L. R.); Cort *v.* Ambergate, &c., R. C., 17 Q. B. 127 (79 E. C. L. R.); Emmens *v.* Elderton, 4 H. L. Cas. 624; s. c., 6 C. B. 160 (60 E. C. L. R.), 4 Id. 479; Barrick *v.* Buba, 2 C. B. N. S. 563 (52 E. C. L. R.). See Lewis *v.* Peachey, 1 H. & C. 518.

[5] Per Erle, C. J., Danube, &c., R. C. *v.* Xenos, 11 C. B. N. S. 175 (103 E. C. L. R.); s. c., 13 Id. 825.

[6] 3 B. & P. 302, adopted Esposito *v.* Bowden, 4 E. & B. 978 (82 E. C. L. R.);

contract by his own default, it is not competent to him to allege the circumstances by which he was prevented as an excuse for his omission;" and "if a man binds himself to do certain acts which he afterwards renders himself unable to perform, he thereby dispenses with the performance of conditions precedent to the act which he has so rendered himself unable to perform."[1]

Again, where a creditor refuses a tender sufficient in amount, and duly made, he cannot afterwards, for purposes of oppression or extortion, avail himself of such refusal; for although the debtor still remains liable to pay whenever required so to do, yet the tender operates in bar of any claim for damages and interest for not paying or for detaining the debt, and also of the costs of an action brought to recover the demand.[2]

According to the same principle, if articles of unequal value are [*286] mixed together, producing an article of a different *value from that of either separately, and, through the fault of the person mixing them, the other party cannot tell what was the original value of his property, he must have the whole.[3] "At law," remarks Lord Redesdale, in Bond *v.* Hopkins,[4] "fraud destroys rights: if I mix my corn with another's he takes all;[5] but if I induce another to mix his corn with mine, I cannot then insist on having the whole, the law in that case does not give me his corn." So, where the plaintiff, pretending title to hay standing in defendant's land, mixed some of his own with it, it was held that the defendant thereby became entitled to the hay.[6]

By the mixture of bales of cotton on board ship, and their becoming undistinguishable by reason of the action of the sea, and

s. c. (reversed in error), 7 Id. 763 (90 E. C. L. R.). See Reid *v.* Hoskins, 4 E. & B. 979; s. c., 5 Id. 729, 6 Id. 953; Avery *v.* Bowden, 5 E. & B. 714 (85 E. C. L. R.); s. c., 6 Id. 962 (88 E. C. L. R.). See Webster *v.* Newsome, 5 H. & N. 42.

[1] Judgm., 8 C. B. 762 (65 E. C. L. R.).

[2] *Vide* per Williams, J., Smith *v.* Manners, 5 C. B. N. S. 636 (94 E. C. L. R.).

[3] Per Lord Eldon, C., Lupton *v.* White, 15 Ves. 442. See Colwill *v.* Reeves, 2 Camp. N. P. C. 575; Warde *v.* Eyre, 2 Bulstr. 323.

[4] 1 Scho. & Lefr. 433.

[5] In Aldridge *v.* Johnson, 7 E. & B. 899 (90 E. C. L. R.), Lord Campbell, C. J., observes, "Where the owner of such articles as oil or wine mixes them with similar articles belonging to another, that is a wrongful act by the owner for which he is punished by losing his property."

[6] Popham 38, pl. 2.

without the fault of their respective owners, these parties become tenants in common of the cotton in proportion to their respective interests; but such a result would follow in those cases only where, after the adoption of all reasonable means and exertions to identify or separate the goods, it has been found impracticable to do so.[1]

In general, the act of the officer is, in point of law, the act of the sheriff, yet, where the officer is guilty of misconduct, and that misconduct is produced by the act of the execution creditor, it is not competent to the latter to say that the act of the officer, done in breach of his duty *to the sheriff, and induced by the execution creditor himself, is the act of the sheriff.[2] Also, [*287] if a man employs an attorney to defend an action in which he has no interest, and the attorney defends the action accordingly, it does not lie in the mouth of the person who employs him to say that he was guilty of maintenance in employing him.[3]

Again, where a party is sued by a wrong name, and suffers judgment to go against him, without attempting to rectify the mistake, he cannot afterwards, in an action against the sheriff for false imprisonment, complain of an execution issued against him by that name;[4] and, if a bond, or any other instrument, is executed under an assumed name, the obligor, or party executing it, is bound thereby in the same manner as if he had executed it in his true name.[5] So, "if a man, having an opportunity of seeing what he is served with, willfully abstains from looking at it, that is virtually personal service;"[6] and, where one of the litigating parties takes a step after having had notice that a rule has been obtained to set aside the proceedings, he does so in his own wrong, and the step taken subsequently to notice will be set aside.[7]

The foregoing examples have been selected in order to show in what manner the rule, which they will serve to illustrate, has been

[1] Spence *v.* Union Marine Ins. Co., L. R. 3 C. P. 427. See Webster *v.* Power, L. R. 2 P. C. 69.

[2] Per Bayley, J., Crowder *v.* Long, 8 B. & C. 603, 604 (15 E. C. L. R.).

[3] Per Lord Abinger, C. B., 11 M. & W. 681.

[4] Fisher *v.* Magnay, 6 Scott N. R. 588; Morgan *v.* Bridges, 1 B. & Ald. 647. See De Mesnil *v.* Dakin, L. R. 3 Q. B. 18; Kelly *v.* Lawrence, 3 H. & C. 1.

[5] 13 Peters (U. S.) R. 428. See Judgm., Truman *v.* Loder, 11 A. & E. 594, 595 (39 E. C. L. R.).

[6] Per Tindal, C. J., Emerson *v.* Brown, 8 Scott N. R. 222.

[7] Per Pollock, C. B., Tiling *v.* Hodgson, 13 M. & W. 638.

[*288] applied to promote the ends of justice, *in various and dissimilar circumstances. The maxim under review applies also with peculiar force to that very extensive class of cases in which fraud is alleged to have been committed by one of the parties to a transaction, and is relied upon as a defence by the other. Both courts of equity and courts of law have, it has been observed by Lord Mansfield, a concurrent jurisdiction to suppress and relieve against fraud, although the interposition of the former is often necessary for the better investigation of the truth, and in order to give more complete redress.[1] We do not, in this treatise, propose to consider in what manner a court of equity will deal with fraud, nor how, if fraud be proved, it will interfere to give relief: but we may state the principle which is by that court invariably acted upon to be, that the author of wrong, who has put a person in a position in which he had no right to put him, shall not take advantage of his own illegal act, or, in other words, shall not avail himself of his own wrong.[2] But, although it is peculiarly, and often exclusively,[3] the province of a court of equity to relieve against fraud, there are very many cases in which a court of law will adjudge void a transaction on the ground of fraud and covin, or will expressly refuse to sanction dishonest views and practices by enabling an individual to acquire through the medium of his deception any right or interest.

[*289] In a leading case on this subject,[4] the facts were, *that A. was indebted to B. in 400*l.*, and was indebted also to C. in 200*l.*; C. brought an action of debt against A., and, pending the writ, A., being possessed of goods and chattels of the value of 300*l.*, in secret made a general deed of gift of all his goods and chattels, real and personal, whatsoever, to B., in satisfaction of his

[1] Bright *v.* Enon, 1 Burr. 396.

[2] Per Lord Cottenham, C., Hawkins *v.* Hall, 4 My. & Cr. 281.

[3] See Doe d. Richards *v.* Lewis, 11 C. B. 1035 (73 E. C. L. R.).

[4] Twyne's Case, 3 Rep. 80 (with which compare Evans *v.* Jones, 3 H. & C. 423); Graham *v.* Furber, 14 C. B. 410, 418 (78 E. C. L. R.); Tarleton *v.* Liddell, 17 Q. B. 390 (79 E. C. L. R.); Fermor's Case (3 Rep. 77) is also a leading case to show that the courts will not sustain or sanction a fraudulent transaction. In that case it was held, that a fine fraudulently levied by lessee for years should not bar the lessor; and see the law on this subject stated per Tindal, C. J., in Davies *v.* Lowndes, 5 Bing. N. C. 172 (15 E. C. L. R.). See also Wood *v.* Dixie, 7 Q. B. 892 (53 E. C. L. R.).

debt, but nevertheless remained in possession of the said goods, some of which he sold; he also shore the sheep, and marked them with his own mark. Afterwards C. obtained judgment, and issued a *fi. fa.* against A., and the question arose, whether the above gift was, under the circumstances, fraudulent and of no effect, by virtue of the statute 13 Eliz. c. 5; and it was determined, for the following reasons, that the gift was fraudulent within the statute:—1st, this gift has the signs and marks of fraud, because it is general, without excepting the wearing-apparel, or other necessaries, of the party making it; and it is commonly said, that *dolosus versatur in generalibus*[1]—a person intending to deceive deals in general terms; a maxim, we may observe, which has been adopted from the civil law, and is frequently cited and applied in our courts;[2] 2dly, the donor continued in possession and used the goods as his own, and by reason thereof he traded and trafficked with others, and defrauded and deceived them;[3] 3dly, the gift was made in secret, and *dona* **clandestina sunt semper suspiciosa*[4]—clandestine gifts are always open to suspicion; 4thly, it was made pending the writ; 5thly, in this case there was a trust between the parties, for the donor possessed the goods and used them as his own, and fraud is always apparelled and clad with trust, and trust is the cover of fraud; and, 6thly, the deed states, that the gift was made honestly, truly, and *bonâ fide*, and *clausulæ inconsuetæ semper inducunt suspicionem*—unusual clauses always excite suspicion.

[*290]

In the foregoing case, it will be observed, that the principal transaction was invalidated on the ground of fraud, according to the principle, that a wrongful or fraudulent act shall not be allowed to conduce to the advantage of the party who committed it; *nul prendra advantage de son tort demesne.*[5] And this principle further

[1] Wing. Max. 636; 2 Rep. 34; 2 Bulstr. 226; 1 Roll. R. 157; Moor 321; Mace *v.* Cammel, Lofft 782.

[2] Presbytery of Auchterarder *v.* Earl of Kinnoul, 6 Cl. & Fin. 698, 699; Spicot's Case, 5 Rep. 58.

[3] Cited per Lord Mansfield, C. J., Worseley *v.* Demattos, 1 Burr. 482; Martindale *v.* Booth, 3 B. & Ad. 498 (23 E. C. L. R.). See this subject considered in the note to Twyne's Case, 1 Smith L. C., 6th ed., 1; arg. Wheeler *v.* Montefiore, 2 Q. B. 138 (42 E. C. L. R.).

[4] Noy, Max., 9th ed., p. 152; Latimer *v.* Batson, 4 B. & C. 652 (10 E. C. L. R.); per Lord Ellenborough, C. J., Leonard *v.* Baker, 1 M. & S. 253 (28 E. C. L. R.).

[5] 2 Inst. 713; Branch, Max., 5th ed., p. 141.

extends so as ofttimes to preclude a party to a fraud from setting it up as a defence,—a topic which will most conveniently be discussed in connection with the maxim, *In pari delicto potior est conditio possidentis* or *defendentis*.[1]

The doctrine of estoppel *in pais*, which has in many recent cases been applied, is obviously referable to the principle set forth in the maxim before us, and may be thus exemplified:—

In an action of trover, it appeared that the goods in question were seized while in the actual possession of a third party, under an execution against such third party, and sold to the defendant. [*291] It further appeared that no *claim had been made by the plaintiff after the seizure, and that the plaintiff had consulted with the execution creditor as to the disposal of the property, without mentioning his own claim, after he knew of the seizure, and of the intention to sell the goods; it was held, that a jury might properly infer, from the plaintiff's conduct, that he had authorized the sale, and had, in point of fact, ceased to be the owner; and Lord Denman, C. J., in delivering the judgment of the court, laid down the following principle, which will be found applicable to a large class of cases, and results directly from the maxim that *no man shall take advantage of his own wrong*. "The rule of law," said his lordship, "is clear, that, where one, by his words or conduct, *willfully* causes another to believe the existence of a certain state of things, and induces him to act on that belief, so as to alter his own previous position, the former is concluded from averring against the latter a different state of things as existing at the same time."[2] So, in Gregg *v.* Wells,[3] it was held, that the owner of goods, who stands by, and voluntarily allows another to treat them as his own, whereby a third person is induced to buy them *bonâ fide*, cannot recover them from the vendee. "A party," says the Lord Chief Justice, "who negligently or culpably stands by, and allows another to contract, on the faith and understanding of a fact

[1] *Post*, Chap. IX.

[2] Pickard *v.* Sears, 6 A. & E. 469 (33 E. C. L. R.), (cited per Lord Denman, C. J., Nickells *v.* Atherstone, 10 Q. B. 949 (59 E. C. L. R.)); with which compare Richards *v.* Johnston, 4 H. & N. 660. See Machu *v.* London and South-Western R. C., 2 Exch. 420; Foster *v.* Mentor Life Assurance Co., 3 E. & B. 48 (77 E. C. L. R.).

[3] 10 A. & E. 90, 98 (37 E. C. L. R.). See Doe d. Groves *v.* Groves, 10 Q. B. 486 (59 E. C. L. R.); Nickells *v.* Atherstone, Id. 944, 949.

which he can contradict, cannot afterwards dispute that fact in an *action against the person whom he has himself assisted [*292] in deceiving."

The principle thus stated by Lord Denman in Pickard *v.* Sears, and more broadly in Gregg *v.* Wells, was well explained by the Court of Exchequer in Freeman *v.* Coke,[1] the judgment in which case must now be considered to lay down the governing rule upon the subject.[2] By the term "*willfully*" above used, is to be understood "if not that the party represents that to be true which he knows to be untrue, at least that he *means* his representation to be acted upon, and that it is acted upon accordingly; and if, whatever a man's real intention may be, he so conducts himself that a reasonable man would take the representation to be true, and believe that it was meant that he should act upon it, and did act upon it as true, the party making the representation would be equally precluded from contesting its truth; and conduct by negligence or omission, where there is a duty cast upon a person by usage of trade or otherwise to disclose the truth, may often have the same effect. As, for instance, a retiring partner omitting to inform his customers of the fact in the usual mode, that the continuing partners were no longer authorized to act as his agents, is bound by all contracts made by them with third persons, on the faith of their being so authorized. * * * In truth, in most cases *to [*293] which the doctrine in Pickard *v.* Sears is to be applied, the representation is such as to amount to the contract or license of the party making it." [3]

[1] 2 Exch. 654, 663–4; In re Bahia and San Francisco R. C., L. R. 3 Q. B. 584, 594, 597; Swan *v.* North British Australasian Co., 2 H. & C. 175, 188, affirming s. c., 7 H. & N. 603; per Crompton, J., Howard *v.* Hudson, 2 E. & B. 13 (75 E. C. L. R.); Price *v.* Groom, Id. 542, 548; Waller *v.* Drakeford, 1 E. & B. 749 (72 E. C. L. R.). See Schuster *v.* M'Kellar, 26 L. J. Q. B. 281.

[2] Per Williams, J., Simpson *v.* Accidental Death Insurance Co., 2 C. B. N. S. 289 (89 E. C. L. R.); per Erle, C. J., White, app., Greenish, resp., 11 C. B. N. S. 229, 230 (103 E. C. L. R.); per Lord Chelmsford, C., Clarke *v.* Hart, 6 H. L. Cas. 655–6.

[3] *Vide* per Lord Chelmsford, C., 6 H. L. Cas. 656. See also in illustration of the text, Martyn *v.* Gray, 14 C. B. N. S. 824 (108 E. C. L. R.); Stephens *v.* Reynolds, 5 H. & N. 513; Gurney *v.* Evans, 3 Id. 122; Summers *v.* Solomon, 7 E. & B. 879 (90 E. C. L. R.); Ramazotti *v.* Bowring, 7 C. B. N. S. 857 (97 E. C. L. R.); Castellani *v.* Thompson, 13 C. B. N. S. 105, 121–2 (106 E. C. L. R.).

The rule as to estoppel *in pais*, by words or conduct, may, accordingly, be thus stated in two propositions: 1st, "If a man so conducts himself, whether intentionally or not, that a reasonable person would infer that a certain state of things exists, and acts on that inference, he shall be afterwards estopped from denying it;"[1] 2dly,[2] "If a man has willfully made a false assertion, calculated to lead others to act upon it, and they have done so to their prejudice, he is forbidden as against them to deny that assertion. * * * If he has led others into the belief of a certain state of facts by conduct of culpable neglect, calculated to have that result, and they have acted on that belief to their prejudice, he shall not be heard afterwards as against such persons to show that that state of facts did not exist. In short and popular language, a man is not permitted to charge the consequences of his own fault on others, and complain of that which he has himself brought about."[3]

The cases above noticed are evidently in principle identical with those in which it has been held, that a person who has expressly [*294] made a verbal representation, on *the faith of which another has acted, shall not afterwards be allowed to contradict his former statement, in order to profit by that conduct which it has induced.[4] "If there be one principle of law more clear than another, it is this, that where a person has made a deliberate statement with the view to induce another to act, and he has acted upon it, the former is not at liberty to deny the truth of the statement so made."[5] Whenever an attempt is made in the course of legal proceedings to violate this principle, the law replies in the words of a maxim which we have already cited,[6] *allegans contraria*

[1] Per Bramwell, B., Cornish *v.* Abington, 4 H. & N. 556.

[2] See the cases collected in Ex parte Swan, 7 C. B. N. S. 400 (97 E. C. L. R.) (particularly Bank of Ireland *v.* Trustees of Evans' Charities, 5 H. L. Cas. 389), and in n. 1, *supra.*

[3] Per Wilde, B., Swan *v.* North British Australasian Co., 7 H. & N. 633–4; s. c., affirmed 2 H. & C. 175.

[4] Trickett *v.* Tomlinson, 13 C. B. N. S. 663 (106 E. C. L. R.).

[5] Per Bramwell, B., M'Cann *v.* London and North-Western R. C., 7 H. & N. 490.

[6] *Ante*, p. 169. See also Cannam *v.* Farmer, 3 Exch. 698; Halifax *v.* Lyle, Id. 446; Money *v.* Jorden, 21 L. J. Chanc. 531; Fairhurst *v.* Liverpool Adelphi Loan Association, 9 Exch. 422; Standish *v.* Ross, 3 Exch. 527; Freeman *v.* Steggall, 14 Q. B. 202 (68 E. C. L. R.); Morgan *v.* Couchman, 14 C. B. 100 (78 E. C. L. R.); Dunstan *v.* Paterson, C. B. N. S. 495 (89 E. C. L. R.).

non est audiendus, and, by applying the doctrine of estoppel therein contained, prevents the unjust consequences which would otherwise ensue.[1] We may, therefore, lay it down as a general rule, applicable alike in law and equity, that a party shall not entitle himself to substantiate a claim, or to enforce a defence, by reason of acts or misrepresentations which proceeded from himself, or were adopted or acquiesced in by him after full knowledge of their nature and quality;[2] and further, that where misrepresentations have been made by one of two litigating parties, in his dealings with the other, a court of law will either decline to interfere, or will so *adjust the equities between the plaintiff and defendant, as to prevent an undue advantage from accruing to that party who is unfairly endeavoring to take advantage of his own wrong.[3] [*295]

If, therefore, the acceptor of a bill of exchange at the time of acceptance *knew* the payee to be a fictitious person, he shall not take advantage of his own fraud; but a *bonâ fide* holder may recover against him on the bill, and declare on it as payable to bearer;[4] and, generally, a person will not be allowed as plaintiff in a court of law to rescind his own act, on the ground that such act was a fraud on another person, whether the party seeking to do this has sued in his own name or jointly with such other person.[5]

[1] Price *v.* Carter, 7 Q. B. 838 (53 E. C. L. R.); Reg. *v.* Mayor of Sandwich, 10 Q. B. 563, 571 (59 E. C. L. R.); Banks *v.* Newton, 11 Q. B. 340 (63 E. C. L. R.); Petch *v.* Lyon, 9 Q. B. 147, and cases there cited; Braithwaite *v.* Gardiner, 8 Q. B. 473 (55 E. C. L. R.). See Dresser *v.* Bosanquet, 4 B. & S. 460, 486 (10 E. C. L. R.).

[2] Vigers *v.* Pike, 8 Cl. & Fin. 562.

[3] See Harrison *v.* Ruscoe, 15 M. & W. 231, where an unintentional misrepresentation was made in giving notice of the dishonor of a bill; Rayner *v.* Grote, Id. 359, where an agent represented himself as principal (citing Bickerton *v.* Burrell, 5 M. & S. 383); Humble *v.* Hunter, 12 Q. B. 310 (64 E. C. L. R.); Schmaltz *v.* Avery, 16 Q. B. 655 (71 E. C. L. R.); Cox *v.* Hubbard, 4 C. B. 317, 319 (56 E. C. L. R.); Cooke *v.* Wilson, 1 C. B. N. S. 153 (87 E. C. L. R.).

[4] Gibson *v.* Minet (in error), 1 H. Bla. 569.

[5] Per Lord Tenterden, C. J., Jones *v.* Yates, 9 B. & C. 538 (17 E. C. L. R.); Sparrow *v.* Chisman, Id. 241; Wallace *v.* Kelsall, 7 M. & W. 264; which cases are recognized; Gordon *v.* Ellis, 8 Scott N. R. 305; Brandon *v.* Scott, 7 E. & B. 234 (90 E. C. L. R.); Husband *v.* Davis, 10 C. B. 645 (70 E. C. L. R.). See Heilbut *v.* Nevill, L. R. 4 C. P. 354.

Allied to the preceding maxim is that cited by Lord Coke,[1] *Quod semel placuit in electionibus amplius displicere non potest:* it may be thus illustrated:—A policy insuring plaintiff's premises against fire was executed by defendants, reserving to themselves "the right of reinstatement in preference to the payment of claims." The premises having been damaged by fire, the defendants elected to reinstate them, but did not do so. To an action for not paying, compensating, and reinstating, the *defendants pleaded [*296] that they elected to reinstate, and were proceeding to do so, when the Commissioners of Sewers, under "The Metropolitan Building Act, 1855,"[2] caused the premises to be taken down as being in a dangerous condition, such dangerous condition not having been caused by damage from the fire. This plea was, on demurrer, held bad. "The case," observed Lord Campbell, C. J., "stands as if the policy had been simply to reinstate the premises in case of fire; because where a contract provides for an election, the party making the election is in the same position as if he had originally contracted to do the act which he elected to do." This being so, the defendants were bound by their election, and in the event of performance of their contract becoming impossible, or more expensive than had been anticipated, were liable to pay damages for non-performance.[3]

The maxim above cited from Lord Coke might admit of ample illustration from the relation of landlord and tenant, and rights incident thereto; *ex. gr.*, where a lease has been forfeited,[4] and the landlord can elect whether to enter or not; if either by word or by act he determine that the lease shall continue, and communicates his determination to the tenant, the election is completed, and the rule applies that "if a man once determines his election, it shall be determined forever;"[5] a rule which is a branch of the general law, that where a man has an election or option to enter into an estate vested in another, or to deprive another of some existing right, before the party having the option acts, he must [*297] elect, once for all, whether *he will do that act or not.[6]

[1] Co. Litt. 146 a.

[2] 18 & 19 Vict. c. 122.

[3] Brown *v.* Royal Insurance Co., 1 E. & E. 853 (102 E. C. L. R.).

[4] See note to Dumpor's Case, 1 Smith L. C., 6th ed., 36.

[5] Com. Dig., "*Election*" (C. 2).

[6] Per Blackburn, J., Ward *v.* Day, 4 B. & S. 356 (116 E. C. L. R.), which illustrates the text.

"In order," however, "that a person who is put to his election should be concluded by it, two things are necessary:—1st, a full knowledge of the nature of the inconsistent rights and of the necessity of electing between them; 2d, an intention to elect manifested, either expressly, or by acts which imply choice and acquiescence."[1]

Further, we may remark that the maxim which precludes a man from taking advantage of his own wrong is, in principle, very closely allied to the maxim, *Ex dolo malo non oritur actio*, which is likewise of very general application, and will be treated of more conveniently hereafter in the chapter upon Contracts. The latter maxim is, indeed, included in that above noticed; for it is clear, that, since a man cannot be permitted to take advantage of his own wrong, he will not be allowed to found any claim upon his own iniquity—*Nemo ex proprio dolo consequitur actionem*; and, as before observed, *frustra legis auxilium quærit in legem committit*.[2]

Nevertheless, the principal maxim under our notice, and likewise the kindred rule, *Fraus et dolus nemini patrocinari debent*,[3] are sometimes qualified in operation by the maxim, cited at a former page[4]—*Quod fieri non debet factum valet*.[5] "Fraud," as observed,[6] *"renders any transaction voidable at the election of the party defrauded; and if, when it is avoided, nothing has occurred to alter the position of affairs, the rights and remedies of the parties are the same as if it had been void from the beginning; but if any alteration has taken place, their rights and remedies are subject to the effect of that alteration." This may be illustrated by Reg. *v.* The Saddlers' Company,[7] where the facts were as under:—By the charter of the Saddlers' Company, the warden and assistants were empowered to elect assistants from the freemen, and to

[*298]

[1] Per Lord Chelmsford, Spread *v.* Morgan, 11 H. L. Cas. 615.

[2] The following cases also illustrate the maxim that a man shall not be permitted to take advantage of his own wrong or default; respecting the right to costs: Pope *v.* Fleming, 5 Exch. 249; the enrollment of memorial of an annuity: Molton *v.* Camroux, 4 Exch. 17; s. c., 2 Exch. 487; an action against the sheriff for an escape: Arden *v.* Goodacre, 11 C. B. 371, 377 (73 E. C. L. R.).

[3] 3 Rep. 78 b.

[4] *Ante*, p. 182.

[5] Cited per Martin, B., and Wilde, B., 6 H. & N. 787, 792.

[6] Per Blackburn, J., 10 H. L. Cas. 420–1; citing Clarke *v.* Dickson, E., B. & E. 148 (96 E. C. L. R.), and Feret *v.* Hill, 15 C. B. 207 (80 E. C. L. R.).

[7] 10 H. L. Cas. 404.

remove any for ill-conduct, or other reasonable cause, and to make such by-laws as should seem to them salutary and necessary for the good government of the body in general and its officers. A by-law was duly made in these terms, "that no person who has been a bankrupt or become otherwise insolvent shall hereafter be admitted a member of the court of assistants, unless it be proved to the satisfaction of the court that such person, after his bankruptcy or insolvency, has paid his creditors in full," &c. D. being otherwise qualified, but being in insolvent circumstances, and unable to pay his creditors twenty shillings in the pound, was elected an assistant, and after his election, of which he was not aware, but before his admission, he made to the agents of the wardens and assistants a statement, false to his own knowledge, that he was solvent; he was then admitted, and exercised the office of assistant. The by-law, as above stated, being adjudged good, it was further held, that the mere statement of a falsehood by D. did not nullify his election, [*299] and that D. could not be legally removed from his office by *the wardens and assistants of the company without being heard in his defence.[1]

In Hooper *v.* Lane,[2] cited at p. 131, which strikingly illustrates the rule that "no man shall take advantage of his own wrong," various instances are put by a learned judge,[3] exemplifying that the rule in question "only applies to the extent of undoing the advantage gained, where that can be done, and not to the extent of taking away a right previously possessed." The instances adduced are as under:—"If A. lends a horse to B., who uses it and puts it in his stable, and A. comes for it, and B. is away and the stable locked, and A. breaks it open and takes his horse, he is liable to an action for the trespass to the stable; and yet the horse could not be got back, and so A. would take advantage of his own wrong. So, though a man might be indicted at common law for a forcible entry, he could not be turned out if his title were good. So, if goods are bought on a promise of cash payment, the buyer, on non-payment, is subject to an action, but may avail himself of a set-off, and the goods cannot be gotten back. So, if I promise a man I

[1] See the maxim, *Audi alteram partem*, *ante*, p. 113.

[2] 6 H. L. Cas. 443; Ockford *v.* Freston, and Chapman *v.* Freston, 6 H. & N. 466, 472, 480, 481.

[3] Bramwell, B., 6 H. L. Cas. 461.

will sell him more goods on credit if he pays what he already owes, and he does so, and I refuse to sell, I may retain the money. So, if I force another from a fishing-ground at sea, and catch fish, the fish are mine."

The maxim, moreover, according to the opinion of the learned judge whose words have been above cited, "is never applicable where the right of a third party is to be affected. * * * Can one man by his wrongful act to another *deprive a third of [*300] his right against that other? * * A. obtains goods from B. under a contract of sale, procured by A. from B. by fraud. A. sells to C.; C. may retain the goods.[1] Surely A. might recover the price from C. at which he sold to him; yet he would in so doing take advantage of his own wrong. So, if my lessee covenants at the end of his term to deliver possession to me, and in order to do so forcibly evicts one to whom he had sub-let for a longer term, and I take possession without notice, surely I can keep it; at least, at the common law I could. So, if a sub-lessee at an excessive rent purposely omits to perform a covenant, the performance of which would be a performance of the lessee's covenant to his lessor, and by such non-performance the lessee's covenant is broken, and the first lessor enters and avoids the lease and evicts the sub-lessee, the sub-lessee may defend himself against a claim for rent by his lessor;[2] yet there he takes advantage of his own wrong, because of the right of the third person. So, if I sell goods, the property not to pass till payment or tender, and the vendee has a week in which to pay, and during that week I resell and deliver to a third person, no action is maintainable against me as for a detention or conversion, but only for non-delivery: yet there I take advantage of my own wrong, because the right of a third party has accrued."[3]

[1] White *v.* Garden, 10 C. B. 919 (70 E. C. L. R.).
[2] Logan *v.* Hall, 4 C. B. 598 (56 E. C. L. R.).
[3] Per Bramwell, B., 6 H. L. Cas. 461-2.

[*301] *ACTA EXTERIORA INDICANT INTERIORA SECRETA.

(8 Rep. 291.)

Acts indicate the intention.[1]

The law, in some cases, judges of a man's previous intentions by his subsequent acts; and, on this principle, it was decided in a well-known case, that if a man abuse an authority given him *by the law*, he becomes a trespasser *ab initio*,[2] but that, where he abuses an authority given him *by the party*, he shall not be a trespasser *ab initio*. The reason assigned for this distinction being, that, where a general authority or license is given by the law, the law judges by the subsequent act, *quo animo*, or to what intent, the original act was done; but when the party himself gives an authority or license to do anything, to enter upon land, he cannot for any subsequent cause convert that which was originally done under the sanction of his own authority or license into a trespass *ab initio;* and in this latter case, therefore, the subsequent acts only will amount to trespasses.[3]

For instance, the law gives authority to enter into a common inn or tavern; in like manner to the owner of the ground to distrain damage feasant;[4] and to the commoner to enter upon the land to see his cattle. But, if he who enters into the inn or tavern commits [*302] a trespass, *or if the owner who distrains a beast damage feasant works or kills the distress, or if the commoner cuts down a tree, in these and similar cases the law adjudges that the party entered for the specific purpose of committing the particular injury, and because the act which demonstrates the intention is a trespass, he shall be adjudged a trespasser *ab initio;*[5] or, in other

[1] The remarks in illustration of the maxim *Actus non facit reum nisi mens sit rea* (*post*, p. 306) should be read in connection with those which immediately follow.

[2] See North *v.* London and South-Western R. C., 14 C. B. N. S. 132 (108 E. C. L. R.).

[3] The Six Carpenters' Case, 8 Rep. 290; per Erle, J., Ambergate, &c., R. C. *v.* Midland R. C., 23 L. J., Q. B. 17, 20. See Jacobsohn *v.* Blake, 6 M. & Gr. 919 (46 E. C. L. R.); Peters *v.* Clarson, 7 M. & Gr. 548 (49 E. C. L. R.); Webster *v.* Watts, 11 Q. B. 311 (63 E. C. L. R.); Wing. Max., p. 108.

[4] See Layton *v.* Hurry, 8 Q. B. 811 (55 E. C. L. R.); Gulliver *v.* Cosens, 1 C. B. 788 (50 E. C. L. R.).

[5] 8 Rep. 291; Wing. Max., p. 109; Oxley *v.* Watts, 1 T. R. 12; Bagshaw *v.* Goward, Cro. Jac. 147; Aitkenhead *v.* Blades, 5 Taunt. 198 (1 E. C. L. R.).

words, the subsequent illegality shows the party to have contemplated an illegality all along, so that the whole becomes a trespass.[1] For the same reason, a custom to seize a heriot is an authority given by the law, and an abuse of it renders the party making a seizure a trespasser *ab initio;*[2] and if a sheriff continues in possession after the return day of the writ, this irregularity makes him a trespasser *ab initio.*[3]

One consequence of the above doctrine, as to the abuse of an authority given by law, was, that, if a party entering lawfully[4] to make a distress committed any subsequent abuse, he became a trespasser *ab initio;* and, as this was found to bear hard on landlords, it was enacted by stat. 11 Geo. 2, c. 19, s. 19,[5] that where any distress shall be made for any rent justly due, and any irregularity or unlawful act shall be afterwards done by the party distraining, *or his agent, the distress shall not be deemed unlawful, nor the distrainer a trespasser *ab initio*, but the [*303] party grieved may recover satisfaction for the damage in a special action of trespass, or on the case,[6] at the election of the plaintiff, and if he recover he shall have full costs. Where a landlord distrained for rent, amongst other things, goods which were not distrainable in law, he was held to be a trespasser *ab initio* as to those particular goods only.[7]

Also, by stat. 17 Geo. 2, c. 38, s. 8, where any distress shall be made for money justly due for the relief of the poor, the party distraining shall not be deemed a trespasser *ab initio*, on account of

[1] Per Littledale, J., Smith *v.* Egginton, 7 A. & E. 176 (34 E. C. L. R.); distinguished in Moone *v.* Rose, L. R. 4 Q. B. 486, 492 (45 E. C. L. R.). See Taylor *v.* Cole, 3 T. R. 292.

[2] Price *v.* Woodhouse, 1 Exch. 559.

[3] Aitkenhead *v.* Blades, 5 Taunt. 198 (1 E. C. L. R.). See Ash *v.* Dawnay, 8 Exch. 237; Percival *v.* Stamp, 8 Exch. 167; cited, *post.*

[4] Where the entry is effected in an unlawful manner, trespass of course lies. See Attack *v.* Bramwell, 3 B. & S. 520 (113 E. C. L. R.).

[5] See also stat. 2 W. & M. c. 5; Judgm., Thompson *v.* Wood, 4 Q. B. 498 (45 E. C. L. R.); Rodgers *v.* Parker, 18 C. B. 112 (86 E. C. L. R.).

[6] See Winterbourne *v.* Morgan, 11 East 395, 401; Etherton *v.* Popplewell, 1 East 139.

[7] Harvey *v.* Pocock, 11 M. & W. 740, with which compare Price *v.* Woodhouse, 1 Exch. 559. As to the effect of ratification by the landlord of the act of the bailiff, see Lewis *v.* Reed, 13 M. & W. 834, and cases cited, *post*, Chap. IX.

any act subsequently done by him; but the party grieved may recover satisfaction for the special damage in an action of trespass, or on the case, with full costs, unless tender of amends is made before action is brought.

With respect to the second proposition laid down in the Six Carpenters' Case, viz., that the abuse of authority or license given by the party will not make a person a trespasser *ab initio*, it should be observed, that such a license to do an act which *per se* would be a trespass, is in some cases implied by law. Thus, all the old authorities say that, where a party places upon his own close the goods of another, he, by so doing, gives to the owner of them an implied license to enter for the purpose of recaption.[1] If a man takes my goods, and carries them into *his own land, I may justify [*304] my entry into the said land to take my goods again, for they came there by his own act.[2] So, a man may sometimes justify an entry on his neighbor's land to retake his own property which has by accident been removed thither; as in the instance of fruit falling into the ground of another, or in that of a tree which is blown down, or, through decay, falls into the ground of a neighbor: in these cases, the owner of the fruit or of the tree may, by his plea, show the nature of the accident, and that he was not responsible for it, and thus justify the entry.[3] This distinction must, however, be remarked, that, if the fruit or tree had fallen in the particular direction in consequence of the owner's act or negligence, he could not justify the entry.[4]

Another case also occurs in which the law presumes a license. Thus, if A. wrongfully place goods in B.'s building, B. may lawfully go upon A.'s close adjoining the building, for the purpose of removing and depositing the goods there for A.'s use; that is to say, the law allows a person to enter into a plaintiff's own close, for the purpose of depositing there the plaintiff's own goods, which he had

[1] Per Parke, B., Patrick *v.* Colerick, 3 M. & W. 485; acc. Burridge *v.* Nicholetts, 6 H. & N. 383, 388, 392; 2 Roll. R. 565, pl. 54.

[2] Vin. Abr., "*Trespass*" (1) a; cited, 3 M. & W. 485, and arg. Williams *v.* Roberts, 7 Exch. 626. See Earl of Bristol *v.* Wilsmore, 1 B. & C. 514 (8 E. C. L. R.), which also illustrates the rule, that "fraud vitiates a contract:" *post*, Chap. IX.

[3] Per Tindal, C. J., Anthony *v.* Haney, 8 Bing. 192 (21 E. C. L. R.).

[4] Millen *v.* Hawery, Latch. 13; Vin. Abr., "*Trespass*," H. a 2, L. a; per Tindal, C. J., 8 Bing. 192 (21 E. C. L. R.).

wrongfully placed on the premises of the defendant.[1] So, also, if a man finds cattle trespassing on his own land he may chase them out, and is not bound to distrain them damage feasant.[2] And if a distrainor takes the distress *out of the place where it was originally [*305] impounded, and misuses it, the owner may retake his property without rendering himself liable for a rescue or pound-breach.[3]

Where, however, the goods are placed on the ground or premises of a third party, the common law is different; for, if individuals were allowed to use private force as a remedy for private injuries, the public peace would be endangered, and therefore, the right of recaption shall never be exerted where such exertion must occasion strife and bodily contention.[4] If, for instance, my horse is taken away, and I find him on a common, in a fair, or at a public inn, I may, it is said, lawfully seize him to my own use, but I cannot justify breaking open a private stable, or entering on the grounds of a third person to take him, unless he be feloniously stolen.[5] Nevertheless, if A. take chattels out of the actual possession of B., and against his will, B. might justify using force sufficient to defend his right, and retake the chattels;[6] and recaption is expressly permitted in any case falling within the provisions of stat. 11 Geo. 2, c. 19, s. 1.[7]

Lastly, it was resolved in the principal case, that a *mere [*306] *non-feasance* will not make a man a trespasser *ab initio*.[8]

[1] Vin. Abr., "*Trespass*," 516, pl. 17 (I. a); Roll. Abr. I. pl. 17, p. 566; cited, judgm., Rea *v.* Sheward, 2 M. & W. 426.

[2] Tyrringham's Case, 4 Rep. 38; cited 2 M. & W. 426.

[3] Smith *v.* Wright, 6 H. & N. 821.

[4] "The law of England appears to me, both in spirit and in principle, to prevent persons from redressing their grievances by their own act:" per Pollock, C. B., Hyde *v.* Graham, 1 H. & C. 598.

[5] 3 Com. by Broom & Hadley 4–5; per Parke, B., 3 M. & W. 485; per Tindal, C. J., and Park, J., 8 Bing. 192, 193; 2 Roll. R. 55, 56, 208; 6 M. & Gr. 1056 (a) (46 E. C. L. R.). As to entering on the land of another to search for goods stolen, see 2 Roll. R. 565, pl. 15; Webb *v.* Beavan, 7 Scott N. R. 936.

[6] Blades *v.* Higgs, 11 H. L. Cas. 621.

Secus if the property in the chattels had become vested in A.: Chambers *v.* Miller, 13 C. B. N. S. 125 (106 E. C. L. R.).

[7] See Williams *v.* Roberts, 7 Exch. 618.

[8] 8 Rep. 290; West *v.* Nibbs, 4 C. B. 172, 187 (56 E. C. L. R.). See Gard-

ACTUS NON FACIT REUM NISI MENS SIT REA.

(3 Inst. 107.)

The act itself does not make a man guilty unless his intention were so.

Having just seen that the law will, in some cases, imply the nature of a previous intention from a subsequent act, we purpose in the next place to consider the maxim, *Actus non facit reum nisi mens sit rea,* with reference mainly to penal statutes, to criminal law, and to civil proceedings for slander and libel; for although the principle involved in it applies in many other cases,[1] we shall defer for the present the consideration of its meaning when so applied, and restrict our remarks almost wholly in this place to an examination of the important doctrine of *criminal intention.*

"It is," says Lord Kenyon, C. J.,[2] "a principle of natural justice and of our law, that the intent and the act must both concur to constitute the crime;" "a man," as remarked by Erle, C. J.,[3] "cannot be said to be guilty of a delicit, unless to some extent his mind goes with the act," and the first observation which suggests itself in limitation of the principle thus enunciated is, that whenever [*307] *the law positively forbids a thing to be done, it becomes thereupon *ipso facto* illegal to do it willfully, or, in some cases, even ignorantly,[4] or, may be, to effect an ulterior laudable object,[5] and consequently the doing it may form the subject-matter of an indictment, information, or other penal proceeding, *simpliciter* and without the addition of any corrupt motive.[6] If there be an

ner *v.* Campbell, 15 Johnson (U. S.) R. 401; Jacobsohn *v.* Blake, 6 M. & Gr. 919 (46 E. C. L. R.).

[1] See the maxim, *Caveat emptor, post,* Chap. IX.

[2] 7 T. R. 514. Bowman *v.* Blyth, 7 E. & B. 26 (90 E. C. L. R.), offers a simple illustration of the above proposition.

Et vide Hearne *v.* Garton, 2 E. & E. 66, 74 (105 E. C. L. R.); Coward *v.* Baddeley, 4 H. & N. 478, 481.

[3] Buckmaster, app., Reynolds, resp., 13 C. B. N. S. 68 (106 E. C. L. R.).

[4] *Ante,* p. 267.

[5] Reg. *v.* Hicklin, L. R. 3 Q. B. 360, 372, where Cockburn, C. J., says, "I think the old sound and honest maxim, that you shall not do evil that good may come, is applicable in law as well as in morals."

[6] Per Ashhurst, J., R. *v.* Sainsbury, 4 T. R. 457; cited 2 A. & E. 612; R. *v.* Jones, Stra. 1146; per Lord Mansfield, C. J., R. *v.* Woodfall, 5 Burr. 2667; per Pollock, C. B., Hipkins *v.* Birmingham Gas Light Co., 5 H. & N. 84; per Martin, B., Id. 86. See Re Humphreys, 14 Q. B. 388 (68 E. C. L. R.); Reg.

infraction of the law the intention to break the law must be inferred, *ex. gr.*, where a man publishes a work manifestly obscene he must be taken to have had the intention which is implied from that act.[1]

So it has been held,[2] that a dealer in tobacco, having in his possession adulterated tobacco, although ignorant of the adulteration, is liable under the stat. 5 & 6 Vict. c. 93, s. 3, to the penalties therein mentioned, and this decision merely affirms the principle established in previous cases,[3] and shows that penalties may be incurred under a prohibitory statute, without any intention on the part of *the individual offending against the statute law, [*308] to infringe its provisions.[4]

In like manner, in an action against the defendant for penalties under the stat. 3 & 4 Will. 4, c. 15, s. 2, "for representing a pantomime of which the plaintiff was the author, without his license, at a place of dramatic entertainment," it was held unnecessary to prove that the defendant knew that the plaintiff was the author; inasmuch as he had infringed property of the plaintiff protected by the Act, he was, consequently, an offender within its terms.[5]

So, "public policy has, for the protection of the Bank of England against forgery, rendered it criminal to make paper bearing the same water-mark as Bank of England notes. The making of such paper is in itself an indifferent act; but inasmuch as it may afford facilities for forgery, the legislature has on that account prohibited the act."[6]

v. Thomas, L. & C. 313; Morden, app., Porter, resp., 7 C. B. N. S. 611 (97 E. C. L. R.).

[1] Reg. *v.* Hicklin, L. R. 3 Q. B. 360, 370, 373.

In A.-G. *v.* Sillem, 2 H. & C. 431, 535, where the question as to intent was much considered, Bramwell, B., observes, "I think it cannot properly be said that a man does an act with intent, unless he intends the act to bring about the thing intended, or unless the act is particularly fitted to do so."

[2] Reg. *v.* Woodrow, 15 M. & W. 404.

[3] A.-G. *v.* Lockwood, 9 M. & W. 378, 401; R. *v.* Marsh, 4 D. & Ry. 261.

[4] It may be requisite to determine whether an act, *ex. gr.* shooting a pigeon, was done unlawfully, so as to be brought within the words of a statute: Taylor *v.* Newman, 4 B. & S. 89 (116 E. C. L. R.), with which compare Hudson *v.* MacRae, Id. 585.

[5] Lee *v.* Simpson, 3 C. B. 871 (54 E. C. L. R.). See Russell *v.* Briant, 8 C. B. 836 (65 E. C. L. R.); Gambart *v.* Sumner, 5 H. & N. 5.

[6] Per Pollock, C. B., Atkyns *v.* Kinnier, 4 Exch. 782. See 24 & 25 Vict. c. 98, s. 14.

In general, however, the intention of the party at the time of committing an act charged as an offence is as necessary to be proved as any other fact laid in the indictment, though it may happen that the proof of intention consists in showing overt acts only, the reason in such cases being, that every man is *primâ facie* supposed to intend the necessary, or even probable or natural, consequences of his own act.[1] Thus, a prisoner was indicted *for [*309] setting fire to a mill, with intent to injure and defraud the occupiers; and it was held that, as such injury was a necessary consequence of setting fire to the mill, the *intent* to injure might be inferred.[2] So, in order to constitute the crime of murder, which is always stated in the indictment to be committed with malice aforethought, it is not necessary to show that the prisoner had any enmity to the deceased; nor would proof of absence of ill-will furnish the accused with any defence, when it is proved that the act of killing was intentional, and done without any justification or excusable cause.[3] And it is, as a general proposition, true, that if an act manifestly unlawful and dangerous be done deliberately, the mischievous intent will be presumed, unless the contrary be shown.[4]

It is also a rule, laid down by Lord Mansfield, and which has been said to comprise all the principles of previous decisions upon this subject,[5] that, so long as an act rests in bare intention, it is not punishable by our law; but when an act is done, the law judges not only of the act itself, but of the intent with which it was done; and if the act be coupled with an unlawful and malicious intent, though in itself the act would otherwise have been innocent,

[1] Per Lord Campbell, 9 Cl. & Fin. 321; per Littledale, J., R. *v.* Moore, 3 B. & Ad. 188 (23 E. C. L. R.), and in Reg. *v.* Lovett, 9 C. & P. 466 (38 E. C. L. R.); per Lord Ellenborough, C. J., Newton *v.* Chantler, 7 East 143, and in R. *v.* Dixon, 3 M. & S. 15 (30 E. C. L. R.); cited Reg. *v.* Hicklin, L. R. 3 Q. B. 375; R. *v.* Harvey, 2 B. & C. 261, 267 (9 E. C. L. R.); Wilkin *v.* Manning, 9 Exch. 575, 582; Pennell *v.* Reynolds, 11 C. B. N. S. 709 (103 E. C. L. R.), and cases there cited; Bell *v.* Simpson, 2 H. & N. 410. See Dearden *v.* Townsend, L. R. 1 Q. B. 10.

[2] R. *v.* Farrington, Russ. & Ry. 207; per Bayley, J., R. *v.* Harvey, 2 B. & C. 264 (9 E. C. L. R.).

[3] Per Best, J., 2 B. & C. 268.

[4] 1 East P. C. 231.

[5] Per Lawrence, J., R. *v.* Higgins, 2 East 21.

yet, the intent being criminal, the act likewise becomes criminal and punishable.[1]

*It is accordingly important to distinguish an *attempt*[2] [*310] from a bare *intention;* for the former a man may—and most justly, in many cases—be made answerable; for the latter he cannot be so. The "will is not to be taken for the deed," unless there be some external act which shows that progress has been made in the direction of it, or towards maturing and effecting it. If there be an attempt, if there be something tangible and ostensible of which the law can take hold, which can be alleged and proved—there is nothing offensive to our ideas of justice in declaring it to be criminal and punishable. Hence, an attempt to commit a felony is, in many cases, a misdemeanor; and the general rule is, that "an attempt to commit a misdemeanor is a misdemeanor, whether the offence is created by statute, or was an offence at common law.[3] Moreover, under various statutes, attempts to commit particular offences are indictable and punishable as therein specified, and the statute 14 & 15 Vict. c. 100, s. 9, enables a jury to convict of the attempt upon an indictment for commission of the substantive offence, wherever the evidence suffices to establish the one though not the other.[4]

Our law, moreover, will sometimes, with a view to determining the intention, couple together two acts which have been separated the one from the other by an appreciable interval of time, and ascribe to the latter of these acts that character and quality which undeniably attached and was ascribable to the earlier; and the doctrine of *relation is also occasionally brought into play [*311] with a view to determining the degree of guilt of an offender. Thus A. whilst engaged in the prosecution of some felonious act, undesignedly causes the death of B.; in strictness A. may be convicted of murder, the felonious purpose conjoined with the homicide being held to fill out the legal conception of that crime.[5] So,

[1] R. *v.* Scofield, cited 2 East P. C. 1028; Dugdale *v.* Reg., 1 E. & B. 435, 439 (72 E. C. L. R.).

[2] Which Dr. Johnson defines to be an "essay" or "endeavor" to do an act: Dict. *ad verb.* See Reg. *v.* M'Pherson, Dearsl. & B. 197; Reg. *v.* Collins, L. & C. 471; Reg. *v.* Cheeseman, Id. 140.

[3] Russ. Cr., 3d ed., vol. 1, p. 47.

[4] See Reg. *v.* Hapgood, L. R. 1 C. C. 221.

[5] Fost. Disc. Hom. 258, 259; Crim. L. Com., 1st Rep., 40, 41.

in Reg. *v.* Riley,[1] a felonious intent was held to relate back, and couple itself with a continuing act of trespass, so as, taken in connection with it, to constitute the crime of larceny.

The first part of the rule already adverted to[2]—that "so long as an act rests in bare intention it is not punishable"—agrees, we may observe, with that laid down by Ulpian:[3] *Cogitationis pœnam nemo patitur;* and by Montesquieu,[4] who says, *Les lois ne se chargent de punir que les actions extérieures;* and must evidently be recognized, unless where the worst form of tyranny prevails. In the case of treason, however, the old maxim, *Voluntas reputatur pro facto*[5]—the will is taken for the deed—is said to apply to its full extent; by which, however, we must understand, that if a treasonable design be entertained, and if any open or overt act be done towards effectuating such design, then the mere imagination of the heart is, in contemplation of law, as guilty as it would have been if carried into actual execution; even in this case, however, the mere treasonable intention, to wit, the compassing and imagining the death of the sovereign, although strictly charged in the indictment as the substantive treason, cannot be brought within legal [*312] *cognizance, unless accompanied by overt acts, which furnish the means and evidence whereby the intention may be made manifest.[6] For instance, although mere words spoken by an individual not relating to any treasonable act or design then in agitation do not amount to treason, since nothing can be more equivocal and ambiguous than words,[7] yet words of advice and persuasion, and all consultations for the furtherance of traitorous plans, are certainly overt acts of treason; and if the words be set down in writing, this writing, as arguing more deliberate intention, has been held to be an overt act of treason, on the principle that *scribere est agere;*[8] but even in this case the bare words are not the treason, but the deliberate act of writing them; the compassing and imagination, which is the purpose and intent of the heart, is manifested by the specific overt act.

[1] Dearsl. 149. [2] *Ante*, p. 309. [3] D. 48. 19. 18.
[4] Esp. des Lois, Bk. 12, c. 11. [5] 3 Inst. 5, 69.
[6] 1 East P. C. 58; stat. 7 & 8 Will. 3, c. 3, s. 8.
[7] 4 Bla. Com. by Stewart 80; 1 Hawk. P. C. by Curwood, p. 14, n. (6).
[8] 2 Roll. R. 89. As to the maxim, *supra*, see Algernon Sidney's Case, 9 How. St. Tr. 818; Fost. Disc. High. Tr. 198.

Likewise, with respect to misdemeanors, the rule is, that a bare criminal intent is not in itself indictable if merely expressed in words, gestures, or otherwise, without further proceeding to the crime to which it points.[1] The gist of the offence of conspiracy, however, "is the bare engagement and association to break the law, whether an act be done in pursuance thereof by the conspirators or not;"[2] and, provided the indictment *show either that the conspiring together was for an unlawful purpose [*313] or to effect a lawful purpose by unlawful means, this will be sufficient; and whether anything has been done in pursuance of it or not is immaterial, so far as regards the sufficiency of the indictment.[3]

The observations already made as to the meaning of the word "attempt," in connection with criminal law, may here generally be referred to: it is worthy also of remark, that in Reg. *v.* Eagleton,[4] the court, after observing that, although "the mere *intention* to commit a misdemeanor is not criminal, some *act* is required to make it so," add, "we do not think that *all* acts towards committing a misdemeanor are indictable. Acts remotely leading towards the commission of the offence are not to be considered as *attempts* to commit it, but acts immediately connected with it are:" the doctrine of "remoteness," already commented on,[5] has here, consequently, an important application.

[1] Dick. Quar. Sess., by Serjeant Talfourd, 5th ed., 286. See per Lord Abinger, C. B., R. *v.* Meredith, 8 C. & P. 590 (34 E. C. L. R.).

[2] Per Tindal, C. J., O'Connell *v.* Reg., 11 Cl. & F. 233; Judgm., R. *v.* Kenrick, 5 Q. B. 61 (48 E. C. L. R.).

"A conspiracy consists not merely in the intention of two or more, but in the agreement of two or more to do an unlawful act, or to do a lawful act by unlawful means. So long as such a design rests in intention only it is not indictable. When two agree to carry it into effect, the very plot is an act in itself, and the act of each of the parties, promise against promise, *actus contra actum*, capable of being enforced if lawful, punishable if for a criminal object or for the use of criminal means." Opinion of the judges in Mulcahy *v.* Reg., L. R. 3 H. L. 317.

[3] See further as to the offence of conspiracy, per Lord Denman, C. J., R. *v.* Seward, 1 A. & E. 713 (28 E. C. L. R.); per Bayley, J., R. *v.* Gill, 2 B. & Ald. 205; 9 Rep. 56, 57. See also King *v.* Reg., 7 Q. B. 782, 795 (53 E. C. L. R.); Lord Denman's judgm. in O'Connell *v.* Reg., by Leahy, p. 19; Gregory *v.* Duke of Brunswick, 6 M. & Gr. 205, 953 (46 E. C. L. R.); s. c., 3 C. B. 481 (54 E. C. L. R.), which was an action on the case for conspiracy.

[4] Dearsl. 515. See Reg. *v.* Roberts, Id. 539; Reg. *v.* Gardner, Dearsl. & B. 40, with which compare Reg. *v.* Martin, L. R. 1 C. C. 56.

[5] *Ante*, pp. 206, 216.

A point, moreover, analogous to that just noticed, and by no means free from difficulty, sometimes arises where a person is indicted for attempting to commit a particular offence; in this case, [*314] with a view to satisfying *ourselves whether or not he can be convicted of the attempt, we must consider whether, if he had succeeded in carrying out his object, he could have been convicted of the substantive offence[1]—whether there was such a beginning as would, if interrupted, have ended in the completion of the act.[2]

Having thus briefly noticed that, with some few peculiar exceptions, in order to constitute an offence punishable by law, a criminal intention must either be presumable, as when an unlawful act is done willfully, or must be proved to have existed from the surrounding circumstances of the case, it remains to add, that, since the guilt of offending against any law whatsoever necessarily supposes willful disobedience, such guilt can never justly be imputed to those who are either incapable of understanding the law or of conforming themselves to it; and, consequently, that persons laboring under a natural disability of distinguishing between good and evil, by reason of their immature years, or of mental imbecility, are not punishable by any criminal proceeding for an act done during the season of incapacity;[3] the maxims of our own, as of the civil law, upon this subject being, *In omnibus pœnalibus judiciis et œtati et imprudentiæ succurritur*,[4] and *Furiosi nulla voluntas est*.[5] With regard to acts in violation of the law, an allowance is made in respect of immaturity of years and judgment; and one who is devoid of reason is not punishable, because he can have no criminal intention.

[*315] *In two cases, which were actions upon policies of life insurance, the doctrine relative to criminal intention was much considered. In the first of these, a proviso in the policy declared that the same should be void, *inter alia*, in case the assured "should die by his own hands;" and the learned judge who pre-

[1] See Reg. *v.* Garrett, Dearsl. 232, in connection with which case see, now, stat. 24 & 25 Vict. c. 96, s. 89.

[2] Reg. *v.* Collins, L. & C. 471.

[3] Hawk. P. C. by Curwood, Bk. 1, c. 1; 4 Com. by Broom & Hadley, Chap. 2.

[4] D. 50. 17. 108.

[5] D. 50. 17. 5; D. 1. 18. 13, § 1.

sided at the trial of the cause left it to the jury to say whether, at the time of committing the act which immediately occasioned death, the deceased was so far deprived of his reason as to be incapable of judging between right and wrong; and this question was answered by the jury in the negative, a further question being, by assent of parties, reserved for the court, viz., whether the proviso included only *criminal* self-destruction. After argument in banco, three judges of the Court of Common Pleas held, in opposition to the opinion of the chief justice, that the words of the proviso above stated were large enough, according to their ordinary acceptation, to include all *intentional* acts of self-destruction, whether criminal or not, if the deceased was laboring under no delusion as to the physical consequences of the act which he was committing, and if the act itself was a voluntary and willful act; and they thought that the question "whether at the time he was capable of understanding and appreciating the moral nature and quality of his purpose," was not relevant to the inquiry, further than as it might help to illustrate the extent of his capacity to understand the physical character of the act itself.[1] In a subsequent case,[2] which came, by bill of exceptions, *before the Court of Exchequer Chamber, the proviso [*316] was that the policy should be void if the insured should "commit suicide, or die by duelling or the hands of justice;" and the majority of the court held that the word "suicide" must be interpreted in accordance with its ordinary meaning, and must be taken to include every act of self-destruction, provided it were the intentional act of the party, knowing at the time the probable consequences of what he was about to do. The above decisions are obviously of much importance with reference to the law of life insurance, and show in what manner and in what qualified sense the maxim, *Actus non facit reum nisi mens sit rea*, must be understood, when applied to this branch of law.

With regard to persons of immature years, the rule is, that no infant within the age of seven years can be guilty of felony,[3] or be

[1] Borradaile *v.* Hunter, 5 M. & Gr. 639 (57 E. C. L. R.); Dormay *v.* Borradaile, 5 C. B. 380 (57 E. C. L. R.).

[2] Clift *v.* Schwabe, 3 C. B. 437 (54 E. C. L. R.); Dufaur *v.* Professional Life Ass. Co., 25 Beav. 599. See Horn *v.* Anglo-Australian, &c., Ass. Co., 30 L. J., Ch., 511; Amicable Ass. Soc. *v.* Bolland, 2 Dow & C. 1.

[3] Marsh *v.* Loader, 14 C. B. N. S. 535 (108 E. C. L. R.).

punished for any capital offence; for within that age, an infant is, by presumption of law, *doli incapax*, and cannot be endowed with any discretion, and against this presumption no averment shall be received.[1] This legal incapacity, however, ceases when the infant attains the age of fourteen years, after which period his act becomes subject to the same rule of construction as that of any other person.[2]

Between the ages of seven and fourteen years an infant is deemed *primâ facie* to be *doli incapax;* but in this case the maxim applies *malitia supplet ætatem*[3]—malice (which is here used in its legal sense, and means the doing of a wrongful act intentionally, without [*317] just *cause or excuse,[4] supplies the want of mature years. Accordingly, at the age above-mentioned, the ordinary legal presumption may be rebutted by strong and pregnant evidence of mischievous discretion; for the capacity of doing ill or contracting guilt is not so much measured by years and days, as by the strength of the delinquent's understanding and judgment. In all such cases, however, the evidence of malice ought to be strong, and clear beyond all doubt and contradiction.[5] And two questions ought, moreover, to be left for the consideration of the jury: first, whether the accused committed the offence; and, secondly, whether at the time he had a guilty knowledge that he was doing wrong.[6] In the case of rape, we may add, it is a presumption of law, not

[1] 4 Com. by Broom & Hadley 18.

[2] Id.

[3] Dyer, 104 b.

[4] Arg., Mitchell *v.* Jenkins, 5 B. & Ad. 590 (27 E. C. L. R.). "Malice, in the legal acceptation of the word, is not confined to personal spite against individuals, but consists in a conscious violation of the law to the prejudice of another;" per Lord Campbell, 9 Cl. & Fin. 321. See also per Pollock, C. B., Sherwin *v.* Swindall, 12 M. & W. 787, 788; per Littledale, J., M'Pherson *v.* Daniels, 10 B. & C. 272 (21 E. C. L. R.); per Best, J., R. *v.* Harvey, 2 B. & C. 267, 268 (9 E. C. L. R.).

[5] 4 Com. by Broom & Hadley 19.

[6] R. *v.* Owen, 4 C. & P. 236 (19 E. C. L. R.).

An infant, or one *non compos*, is liable *civilly* for a tortious act, as a trespass; see Burnard, app., Haggis, resp., 14 C. B. N. S. 45 (108 E. C. L. R.); per Lord Kenyon, C. J., Jennings *v.* Rundall, 8 T. R. 337; Johnson *v.* Pye, 1 Lev. 169; Bartlett *v.* Wells, 1 B. & S. 836 (101 E. C. L. R.), with which *acc.* De Roo *v.* Foster, 12 C. B. N. S. 272 (104 E. C. L. R.); per *curiam*, Weaver *v.* Ward, Hobart 134; Bac. Max., reg. 7, *ad finem.*

admitting of proof to the contrary, that within the age of fourteen years this particular offence cannot, by reason of physical inability, be committed.[1]

A libel is "anything written or printed,[2] which, from *its [*318] terms, is calculated to injure the character of another, by bringing him into hatred, contempt, or ridicule, and which is published without lawful justification or excuse;"[3] and, again, "everything printed or written, which reflects on the character of another, and is published without lawful justification or excuse, is a libel, whatever the intention may have been."[4]

With respect to libel and slander, the rule, as deduced from an extensive class of cases, is that, where an occasion exists, which, if fairly acted upon, furnishes a legal protection to the party who makes the communication complained of, the *actual intention* of the party affords a boundary of legal liability. If he had that legitimate object in view which the occasion supplies, he is neither civilly nor criminally amenable; if, on the contrary, he used the occasion as a cloak for maliciousness, it can afford him no protection.[5] It must, moreover, be observed, that, as the honesty and integrity with which a communication of hurtful tendency is made cannot exempt from civil liability, unless it be coupled with an occasion recognized by the law, so responsibility may attach, if the mode or

[1] Reg. *v.* Philips, 8 C. & P. 736 (34 E. C. L. R.); Reg. *v.* Jordan, 9 C. & P. 118 (38 E. C. L. R.); Reg. *v.* Brimilow, Id. 366; R. *v.* Groombridge, 7 C. & P. 582 (32 E. C. L. R.). But an infant under fourteen years of age may be a principal in the second degree. (R. *v.* Eldershaw, 3 C. & P. 396 (14 E. C. L. R.)). As to the liability of an infant for misdemeanor, see 4 Com. by Broom & Hadley 17.

[2] The full definition of a libel, however, includes defamation of another by *signs;* see Du Bost *v.* Beresford, 2 Camp. N. P. C. 511.

[3] Per Parke, B., Gathercole *v.* Miall, 15 M. & W. 321; Digby *v.* Thompson, 4 B. & Ad. 821 (24 E. C. L. R.); Bloodworth *v.* Gray, 8 Scott N. R. 9; Pemberton *v.* Calls, 10 Q. B. 461 (59 E. C. L. R.).

[4] Per Parke, B., O'Brien *v.* Clement, 15 M. & W. 437; O'Brien *v.* Bryant, 15 M. & W. 168; Darby *v.* Ouseley, 1 H. & N. 1; Fray *v.* Fray, 17 C. B. N. S. 603 (112 E. C. L. R.); Cox *v.* Lee, L. R. 4 Ex. 284; Walker *v.* Brogden, 19 C. B. N. S. 65 (115 E. C. L. R.).

[5] 1 Stark. Sland. and Lib., 2d ed., Prel. Dis. p. lxxxvi. See per Parke, B., Parmiter *v.* Coupland, 6 M. & W. 108.

An action for libel will lie against a corporation aggregate: Whitfield *v.* South-Eastern R. C., E., B. & E. 115 (96 E. C. L. R.).

nature of the communication in any respect exceeds that which the legal occasion warrants.[1]

[*319] *The rule applicable for determining whether a particular communication is privileged, has been thus stated:—"A communication, made *bonâ fide* upon any subject-matter in which the party communicating has an *interest*, or in reference to which he has a *duty*, is privileged, if made to a person having a corresponding interest or duty, although it contain criminatory matter which, without this privilege, would be slanderous and actionable."[2]

If, for instance, a man received a letter informing him that his neighbor's house would be plundered or burnt on the night following by A. and B., which he himself believed, and had reason to believe, to be true, he would be justified in showing that letter to the owner of the house, though it should turn out to be a false accusation of A. and B.[3] So, if A. knew that B. was about to employ an agent, whom he (A.) suspected to be a man of unprincipled character, A. would be justified in communicating his knowledge to B., although he was in fact mistaken; but he would not be justified in doing so in the hearing of other persons who were not interested in the fact, for the occasion warrants a communication to B. only, and, as to [*320] the rest, it is mere excess, not warranted by the *occasion.[4] In like manner, a character of a servant *bonâ fide*

[1] See Spill *v.* Maule, L. R. 4 Ex. 232; Kelly *v.* Tinling, L. R. 1 Q. B. 699; Fryer *v.* Kinnersley, 15 C. B. N. S. 422 (109 E. C. L. R.).

[2] Judgm., Harrison *v.* Bush, 5 E. & B. 348 (85 E. C. L. R.); Whiteley *v.* Adams, 15 C. B. N. S. 392, 419, 421 (109 E. C. L. R.); Force *v.* Warren, Id. 806. The subject of privileged communications was much considered in Coxhead *v.* Richards, 2 C. B. 569 (52 E. C. L. R.); Blackham *v.* Pugh, Id. 611; Dawkins *v.* Lord Paulet, L. R. 5 Q. B. 94; Scott *v.* Stansfeld, L. R. 3 Ex. 220; Wason *v.* Walter, L. R. 4 Q. B. 73; Ex parte Wason, L. R. 4 Q. B. 573; Kelly *v.* Tinling, L. R. 1 Q. B. 699; Lawless *v.* Anglo-Egyptian Cotton Co., L. R. 4 Q. B. 262; Beatson *v.* Skene, 5 H. & N. 838. See Tighe *v.* Cooper, 7 E. & B. 639 (90 E. C. L. R.); Davison *v.* Duncan, 7 E. & B. 229; Lewis *v.* Levy, E., B. & E. 537 (96 E. C. L. R.).

[3] Per Tindal, C. J., 2 C. B. 596 (52 E. C. L. R.); Amann *v.* Damm, 8 C. B. N. S. 597 (98 E. C. L. R.).

[4] 1 Stark. Sland. and Lib., 2d ed., Prel. Dis. p. lxxxvii. See Padmore *v.* Lawrence, 11 A. & E. 380 (39 E. C. L. R.); Toogood *v.* Spyring, 1 Cr., M. & R. 181; followed by Coltman, J., 2 C. B. 599 (52 E. C. L. R.), and Cresswell, J., Id. 603; Kine *v.* Sewell, 3 M. & W. 297; Goslin *v.* Corry, 8 Scott N. R. 21.

given is a privileged communication,[1] and in giving it *bonâ fide* is to be presumed; and, even though the statement be untrue in fact, the master will be held justified by the occasion in making that statement, unless it can be shown to have proceeded from a malicious mind, one proof of which may be, that it is false to the knowledge of the party making it.[2] So, a comment upon a literary production, exposing its follies and errors, and holding up the author to ridicule, will not be deemed a libel, provided such comment does not exceed the limits of fair and candid criticism, by attacking the character of the writer unconnected with his publication; and a comment of this description, subject to the above proviso, every one has a right to publish, although the author may suffer a loss from it. But if a person, under the pretence of criticising a literary work, defames the private character of the author, and, instead of writing in the spirit and for the purpose of fair and candid discussion, travels into collateral matter, and introduces facts not stated in the work, accompanied by injurious comments upon them, such person is a libeller, and liable to an action.[3]

[*321] *In the case of an author, just supposed, or of an actor, whose performances are, by the acknowledged usages of society, held out to public criticism, and likewise in that of a minister of the crown, or of a judge, or any other public functionary, it seems clear that comments *bonâ fide* and honestly made upon the conduct of the individual thus before the public, are perfectly justifiable; and if an injury be sustained in consequence of such criticism, it is an injury for which the law affords no redress by damages. It may, indeed, not unfrequently be difficult to say how far the criticism in question applies to the *public* and how far to the *private* conduct of the individual, and yet this distinction is highly

[1] See Affleck *v.* Child, 9 B. & C. 403, 406 (17 E. C. L. R.), recognizing the rule laid down by Lord Mansfield, C. J., in Edmonson *v.* Stevenson, cited Bull. N. P. 8; Pattison *v.* Jones, 8 B. & C. 578 (15 E. C. L. R.).

[2] Judgm., Fountain *v.* Boodle, 3 Q. B. 11, 12 (43 E. C. L. R.); Somerville *v.* Hawkins, 10 C. B. 583 (70 E. C. L. R.); Taylor *v.* Hawkins, 16 Q. B. 308 (71 E. C. L. R.); Manby *v.* Witt, and Eastmead *v.* Witt, 18 C. B. 544 (86 E. C. L. R.).

[3] Carr *v.* Hood, 1 Camp. 355, n. (recognized, Green *v.* Chapman, 4 Bing. N. C. 92 (13 E. C. L. R.)); Campbell *v.* Spottiswoode, 3 B. & S. 769 (113 E. C. L. R.); Thompson *v.* Shakell, M. & M. 187 (22 E. C. L. R.); Soane *v.* Knight, Id. 74. See Paris *v.* Levy, 9 C. B. N. S. 342 (99 E. C. L. R.).

important, since much greater latitude is allowed to comments upon the former than upon the latter, and remarks perfectly unobjectionable in the one case might be unjustifiable and libellous in the other. Of course no general rule upon such a subject can be stated, nor can a difference of opinion amongst the highest authorities, in regard to a distinction so subtle, excite surprise.[1]

With respect to the evidence of intention in an action for libel, the rule is, that a mere wicked and mischievous intention cannot make matter libellous which does not come within the definition of a libel already given; but, if libellous matter be published under circumstances which do not constitute a legal justification, and injury ensue, the malicious intention to injure will be presumed, according to the principle stated at the commencement of these remarks, that every man must be presumed to intend the natural [*322] and ordinary consequences of his own *act.[2] In such case, however, the spirit and *quo animo* of the party publishing the libel are fit to be considered by the jury in estimating the amount of injury inflicted on the plaintiff.[3]

So, in ordinary actions for slander, malice in law may be inferred from the act of publishing the slanderous matter, such act itself being wrong and intentional, and without just cause or excuse; but in actions for slander *primâ facie* excusable, on account of the cause of publishing the slanderous matter, malice in fact must be

[1] See the opinions of the Court of Exchequer in Gathercole *v.* Maill, 15 M. & W. 319; James *v.* Brook, 9 Q. B. 7 (58 E. C. L. R.).

[2] Fisher *v.* Clement, 10 B. & C. 472 (21 E. C. L. R.); Haire *v.* Wilson, 9 B. & C. 643 (17 E. C. L. R.); Parmiter *v.* Coupland, 6 M. & W. 105, recognized Baylis *v.* Lawrence, 3 P. & D. 526; per Best, C. J., Levi *v.* Milne, 4 Bing. 199 (13 E. C. L. R.).

[3] 1 Stark. Sland. and Lib., 2d ed., Prel. Dis., p. cxxxviii., cxxxix.; 2 Id. 242, n. (b), 322, 323. See Pearson *v.* Lemaitre, 6 Scott N. R. 607; Wilson *v.* Robinson, 7 Q. B. 68 (53 E. C. L. R.); Barrett *v.* Long, 3 H. L. Cas. 395.

The following cases may be consulted with reference to pleas of justification of matter *primâ facie* libellous: Tighe *v.* Cooper, 7 E. & B. 639 (90 E. C. L. R.); Prior *v.* Willson, 1 C. B. N. S. 95 (87 E. C. L. R.); Tidman *v.* Ainslie, 10 Exch. 63. See Earl of Lucan *v.* Smith, 1 H. & N. 481. To an action for a libel published in a newspaper, it is no defence that the alleged libel consists of a true and accurate report of the proceedings at a public meeting held under a local Act for the improvement of a town: Davison *v.* Duncan, 7 E. & B. 229 (90 E. C. L. R.); *acc.* Popham *v.* Pickburn, 7 H. & N. 891.

proved;[1] and, in an action for slander of title, the plaintiff must give evidence both that the statement was false, and that it was malicious, and although want of probable cause may justify a jury in inferring malice, yet it is clear that the court will not draw such an inference from the fact, that defendant has put a wrong construction on a complicated Act of Parliament.[2]

*The respective functions of judge and jury at the trial of an action for libel or slander have been thus indicated.[3] [*323] "It is matter of law for the judge to determine whether the occasion of writing or speaking criminatory language which would otherwise be actionable repels the inference of malice, constituting what is called a privileged communication; and if at the close of the plaintiff's case there be no intrinsic or extrinsic evidence of malice," then, "it is the duty of the judge to direct a nonsuit or a verdict for the defendant, without leaving the question of malice to the jury, as a different course would be contrary to principle, and would deprive the honest transactions of business and of social intercourse of the protection which they ought to enjoy."

Connected with the subject of criminal intention above briefly discussed are two important rules relative thereto, which are laid down by Lord Bacon in his collection of maxims. The first is—*In criminalibus sufficit generalis malitia intentionis cum facto paris gradûs.* "All crimes," he remarks, "have their conception in a corrupt intent, and have their consummation and issuing in some particular fact, which, though it be not the fact at the which the intention of the malefactor levelled, yet the law giveth him no advantage of the error, if another particular ensue of as high a nature." Thus, if a poisoned apple be laid in a certain place, with a view to poison A., and B. comes by chance and eats it, this

[1] Padmore *v.* Lawrence, 11 A. & E. 380 (39 E. C. L. R.); Toogood *v.* Spyring, 1 Cr., M. & R. 181; Huntly *v.* Ward, 6 C. B. N. S. 514 (95 E. C. L. R.); Kine *v.* Sewell, 3 M. & W. 297; Griffiths *v.* Lewis, 7 Q. B. 61 (53 E. C. L. R.). See Coxhead *v.* Richards, and cases cited *ante.*

[2] Pater *v.* Baker, 3 C. B. 831 (54 E. C. L. R.), recognizing Pitt *v.* Donovan, 1 M. & S. 639; Brook *v.* Rawl, 4 Exch. 521; Judgm., Wren *v.* Wield, L. R. 4 Q. B. 734.

[3] Judgm., Cooke *v.* Wildes, 5 E. & B. 340 (85 E. C. L. R.), recognizing Somerville *v.* Hawkins, 10 C. B. 583 (70 E. C. L. R.); Taylor *v.* Hawkins, 16 Q. B. 308 (71 E. C. L. R.); and per Maule, J., Gilpin *v.* Fowler, 9 Exch. 615. See also Homer *v.* Taunton, 5 H. & N. 661; Croft *v.* Stevens, 7 H. & N. 570.

amounts nevertheless to murder, although the malicious intention of [*324] the *person who placed the apple was directed against A., and not against B.[1]

The second of Lord Bacon's rules above adverted to is as follows: *Excusat aut extenuat delictum in capitalibus quod non operatur idem in civilibus.* "In capital causes, *in favorem vitæ*, the law will not punish in so high a degree, except the malice of the will and intention appear; but in civil trespasses, and injuries that are of an inferior nature, the law doth rather consider the damage of the party wronged than the malice of him that was the wrongdoer.[2] For instance, the law makes a difference between killing a man upon malice aforethought, and upon present heat and provocation, *in maliciis voluntas spectatur non exitus;*[3] but, if I slander a man, and thereby damnify him in his name and credit, it is not material whether I do so upon sudden choler, or of set malice; but I shall be, in either case, answerable for damages.[4] For there is a distinction in this respect, which will be further illustrated hereafter, between answering *civiliter et criminaliter* for acts injurious to others: in the latter case, the maxim ordinarily applies, *actus non facit reum nisi mens sit rea;* but it is ofttimes otherwise in civil actions, where the intent may be immaterial if the act done were injurious to another;[5] of which rule a familiar instance occurs in the liability of a sheriff, who, by mistake, seizes the goods of the wrong party under a writ of *fi. fa.* So, an action for the in- [*325] fringement of a patent "is maintainable in *respect of what the defendant *does*, not of what he *intends;*"[6] the patentee is not the less prejudiced because the invasion of his right was unintentional.[7]

We may add that whilst, on the one hand, "an act which does not amount to a legal injury cannot be actionable because it is done

[1] Bac. Max., reg. 15; D. 47; 10, 18, § 3; Wood. Inst. 307; R. *v.* Oneby, 2 Ld. Raym. 1489; Reg. *v.* Smith, Dearsl. 559; Reg. *v.* Fretwell, L. & C. 443.

[2] Bac. Max., reg. 7.

[3] D. 48. 8. 14.

[4] Bac. Max., reg. 7.

[5] Per Lord Kenyon, C. J., 2 East 103, 104.

[6] Stead *v.* Anderson, 4 C. B. 806, 834 (56 E. C. L. R.); Lee *v.* Simpson, 3 C. B. 871 (54 E. C. L. R.), cited Judgm., Reade *v.* Conquest, 11 C. B. N. S. 492 (103 E. C. L. R.).

[7] Per Shadwell, V.-C. E., Heath *v.* Unwin, 15 Sim. 552; s. c. (in error), 5 H. L. Cas. 505.

with a bad intent,"[1] on the other hand, an act *primâ facie* lawful may be unlawful if done with an improper or lawless object: *ex. gr.*, "I take it to be clear law," says Erle, J., in Reg. *v.* Pratt,[2] "that if in fact a man be on land where the public have a right to pass and repass, not for the purpose of passing and repassing, but for other and different purposes, he is in law a trespasser."

One case, in which the principle *in favorem vitæ*, adverted to by Lord Bacon,[3] was considered, may here be noticed, since it involves a point of considerable importance, and has attracted much attention. It was decided by the House of Lords, on writ of error from the Court of Queen's Bench in Ireland, that the privilege of peremptory challenge on the part of the prisoner extends to all felonies, whether capital or not; and it was observed by Wightman, J. (delivering his opinion on a question proposed for the consideration of the judges, and commenting on the position, that the privilege referred to was allowed only *in favorem vitæ*, and did not extend to cases in which the punishment is not capital), that it would seem that the origin of the privilege in felony may *have been [*326] the capital punishment usually incident to the quality of crime; but that the privilege was, at all events, annexed to the quality of crime called felony, and continued so annexed in practice in England (at least down to the time when the question was raised), in all cases of felony, whether the punishment was capital or not.[4]

As a fitting conclusion to our remarks upon the subject of criminal intention, and the maxim of Lord Bacon, lastly above mentioned, we may observe, in the words of a distinguished judge, that, in criminal cases generally, and especially in cases of larceny, "the variety of circumstances is so great, and the complications thereof so mingled, that it is impossible to prescribe all the circumstances evidencing a felonious intent, or the contrary, but the same must be left to the due and attentive consideration of the judge and jury,

[1] Judgm., Stevenson *v.* Newnham, 13 C. B. 297 (76 E. C. L. R.); Dawkins *v.* Lord Paulet, L. R. 5 Q. B. 94, 114.

[2] 4 E. & B. 867 (82 E. C. L. R.), citing Dovaston *v.* Payne, 2 H. Bla. 527.

[3] *Ante*, p. 324.

[4] Gray *v.* Reg., 11 Cl. & Fin. 427; Mulcahy *v.* Reg., L. R. 3 H. L. 306. The right of peremptory challenge by the crown was much considered in Mansell *v.* Reg., 8 E. & B. 54 (92 E. C. L. R.).

wherein the best rule is, *in dubiis*, rather to incline to acquittal than conviction."[1]

Tutius semper est errare in acquietando quam in puniendo, ex parte misericordiæ, quam ex parte justitiæ.[2]

[*327] *NEMO DEBET BIS VEXARI PRO UNA ET EADEM CAUSA.

(5 Rep. 61.)

It is a rule of law that a man shall not be twice vexed for one and the same cause.[3]

According to the Roman law, as administered by the prætors, an action might be defended in any of the following modes:[4] 1. By a simple denial or traverse of the facts alleged as the ground of action; 2. By pleading new facts which constituted, *ipso jure*, a bar to the plaintiff's claim, although such claim might, in the first instance, have been well founded, as payment or a release; 3. By showing such facts as might induce the prætor, on equitable grounds, to declare certain defences admissible, the effect of which, if established, would be not, indeed, to destroy the action, *ipso jure*, but to render it ineffectual by means of the "exception" thus specially prescribed by the prætor for the consideration of the judge, to whose final decision the action might be referred. *Exceptio* is, therefore, defined to be, *quasi quædam exclusio quæ opponi actioni cujusque rei solet, ad elidendum id, quod in intentionem consentionemve deductum est*,[5] and, according to Paulus, *Exceptio est conditio quæ modo eximit reum damnatione, modo minuit condemnationem.*[6]

In the class of exceptions just adverted to was included the *exceptio rei judicatæ*, from which the plea of judgment recovered in our own law may be presumed to have derived its origin.[7] The *res*

[1] 1 Hale, P. C. 509; *Quod dubitas ne feceris*,—especially in cases of life: 1 Hale P. C. 300—if the matter *sub judice* be doubtful, the court cannot give judgment upon it: per Willes, J., Beckett *v.* Midland R. C., L. R. 1 C. P. 245.

[2] 2 Hale P. C. 290.

[3] 5 Rep. 61.

[4] Mackeld. Civ. Law 207.

[5] Brisson. (*ed curâ Heinec.*) ad verb. *Res.*

[6] D. 44. 1. 22. pr.

[7] See 1 Cl. & Fin. 435; Phillimore Rom. L. 43.

judicata was, in fact, a result of the definitive sentence, or decree of the judge, *and was binding upon, and in general unimpeachable by the litigating parties;[1] and this was expressed by the well-known Roman maxim, *Res judicata pro veritate accipitur*[2] which must, however, be understood to have applied only when the same question which had been once judicially decided was again raised between the same parties, the rule being *exceptionem rei judicatæ obstare quoties eadem quæstio inter easdem personas revocatur.*[3] The mode in which this particular exception was, in practice, made available under the Roman law may thus be illustrated. A. having purchased a chattel from B., who had, in fact, no title to it, on being sued by the rightful owner, obtains a judicial decision in his favor. A., however, subsequently loses the chattel, which comes into the hands of the true owner, against whom he, therefore, brings his action; and to a plea denying A.'s title may be successfully applied the *res judicata*, or prior judgment, between the same parties.[4] The *exceptiones*, then, which were unknown to the old Roman law, were originally introduced in order to mitigate its rigor by letting in defences which were not admissible or valid *stricti juris;* by long usage, however, these exceptions became established in such a manner as to be recognized by the *jus civile*, and ceasing to depend merely upon the will of the prætor, became in some measure compulsory upon him; there is, therefore, a wide distinction between the meaning of the word "*exceptio*," as used in the prætorian and in the civil law; and by modern writers an "exception" is often employed as synonymous with "defence," and is made to *include any matter which can be set up by the defendant in opposition to the plaintiff's claim.[5]

[*328]

[*329]

In our own law, the plea of judgment recovered at once suggests itself as analogous to the "*exceptio rei judicatæ*" above mentioned, and as directly founded on the general rule that "a man shall not be twice vexed for the same cause." "If," as remarked by Lord Kenyon, C. J., "an action be brought, and the merits of the ques-

[1] Brisson. ad verb. *Res.* Pothier, ad D. 42. 1. pr.

[2] D. 50. 17. 207.

[3] D. 44. 2. 3. Pothier, ad D. 44. 1. 1. pr.

[4] D. 44. 2. 24.

[5] Mackeld. Civ. Law 209, note. See further as to the *Exceptiones*, Phillimore Rom. L. 47, 53, *et seq.*

tion be discussed between the parties, and a final judgment[1] obtained by either, the parties are concluded, and cannot canvass the same question again in another action,[2] although, perhaps, some objection or argument might have been urged upon the first trial, which would have led to a different judgment." In such a case, the matter in dispute having passed *in rem judicatam*, the former decision is conclusive between the parties, if either attempts, by commencing another action, to reopen the question.[3]

[*330] *"After a recovery by process of law," says the same learned judge, "there must be an end of litigation; if it were otherwise there would be no security for any person,"[4] and great oppression might be done under the color and pretence of law.[5] To unravel the grounds and motives which may have led to the determination of a question once settled by the jurisdiction to which the law has referred it, would be extremely dangerous; it is better for the general administration of justice that an inconveni-

[1] A judgment or sentence "is a judicial determination of a cause agitated between real parties; upon which a real interest has been settled. In order to make a sentence, there must be a real interest, a real argument, a real prosecution, a real defence, a real decision. Of all these requisites, not one takes place in the case of a fraudulent and collusive suit. There is no judge; but a person invested with the ensigns of a judicial office is misemployed in listening to a fictitious cause proposed to him; there is no party litigating, there is no party defendant, no real interest brought into question." Per Wedderburn, S.-G., arg. in The Duchess of Kingston's Case, 20 Howell St. Tr. 478, 479; adopted per Lord Brougham, Earl of Bandon *v.* Becher, 3 Cla. & F. 510. See Doe d. Duntze *v.* Duntze, 6 C. B. 100 (60 E. C. L. R.); Finney *v.* Finney, L. R. 1 P. & D. 483; Conradi *v.* Conradi, Id. 514; 31 & 32 Vict. c. 54.

[2] Also, "The law will never compel a person to pay a sum of money a second time which he had paid once under the sanction of a court having competent jurisdiction." Judgm., Wood *v.* Dunn, L. R. 2 Q. B. 80, citing Allen *v.* Dundas, 3 T. R. 125.

[3] Per Lord Kenyon, C. J., Greathead *v.* Bromley, 7 T. R. 456; Huffer *v.* Allen, 4 H. & C. 634; s. c., L. R. 2 Ex. 15; Lord Bagot *v.* Williams, 3 B. & C. 325 (10 E. C. L. R.); Place *v.* Potts, 8 Exch. 705; s. c. (affirmed in error), 10 Exch. 370, 5 H. L. Cas. 383; Tommey *v.* White, 1 H. L. Cas. 160; s. c., 3 Id. 49; 4 Id. 313; Overton *v.* Harvey, 9 C. B. 324, 337 (67 E. C. L. R.).

[4] 7 T. R. 269; Co. Litt. 303 b.

"The reason why a matter once adjudicated upon is not permitted to be opened again is because it is expedient that there should be an end to litigation." Per Lush, J., Commings *v.* Heard, L. R. 4 Q. B. 673.

[5] 6 Rep. 9.

ence should sometimes fall upon an individual, than that the whole system of law should be overturned and endless uncertainty be introduced.[1]

The general rule, then, both at law and in equity, is to refuse a second trial where the propriety of the verdict in the former is not impeached as against law or evidence, though there be material evidence for the party against whom the verdict has passed which was not adduced, unless it be shown to have been discovered after the trial, or unless the verdict has been obtained by fraud or surprise.[2] If a mistake in practice or inadvertence furnished reasons for a new trial, it would encourage litigation and reward ignorance and carelessness at the *expense of the other party;[3] and therefore, our law in such cases wisely acts upon the maxim, [*331] *Interest reipublicæ ut sit finis litium*,[4]—it is for the public good that there be end to litigation; and if there be any one principle of law settled beyond all question it is this, that whensoever a cause of action, in the language of the law, *transit in rem judicatam*, and the judgment thereupon remains in full force and unreversed, the original cause of action is merged, and gone for ever.[5] A plea of *res judicata* must show either an actual merger or that the same point has already been decided between the same parties—that the plaintiff had an opportunity of recovering, and but for his own fault might have recovered in the original suit that which he seeks to recover in the second action.[6] "I apprehend," said a learned judge in a recent case, "that if the same matter or cause of action has already been finally adjudicated on between the parties by a court of competent jurisdiction, the plaintiff has lost

[1] Judgm., Reg. *v.* Justices of West Riding, 1 Q. B. 631 (41 E. C. L. R.); Schumann *v.* Weatherhead, 1 East 541; Vin. Abr. "*Judgment*" (M. a.).

[2] See 1 Ves. jun. 134; as to granting a new trial where the proceeding is quasi-criminal, see Reg. *v.* Russell, 3 E. & B. 942 (77 E. C. L. R.); *ante*, p. 110.

[3] See per Spencer, J., 1 Johnson (U. S.) R. 555.

[4] 6 Rep. 9; per Willes, J., Great Northern R. C. *v.* Mossop, 17 C. B. 140 (84 E. C. L. R.); judgm., Cammell *v.* Sewell, 3 H. & N. 647; per Sir J. Romilly, M. R., Ex parte Brotherhood, 31 L. J. Chanc. 865; per Lord Campbell, C., Beavan *v.* Mornington, 8 H. L. Cas. 540.

[5] 11 Peters (U. S.) R. 100, 101. See, also, 18 Johnson (U. S.) R. 463.

[6] Nelson *v.* Couch, 15 C. B. N. S. 99, 108, 109 (80 E. C. L. R.), and cases there cited.

his right to put it in suit, either before that or any other court. The conditions for the exclusion of jurisdiction on the ground of *res judicata*, are, that the same identical matter shall have come in question already in a court of competent jurisdiction, that the matter shall have been controverted, and that it shall have been finally decided."[1]

[*332] *In Marriot *v.* Hampton,[2] which is strikingly illustrative of the preceding remarks, the facts were as follows: A. sued B. for the price of goods sold, for which B. had before paid, and obtained a receipt. Not being able to find the receipt, and having no other proof of the payment, B. was obliged to submit to pay the money again; but having afterwards found the missing document,[3] he thereupon brought an action against A. for money had and received, to recover back the amount of the sum the payment of which had been thus wrongfully enforced. But Lord Kenyon was of opinion at the trial, that, after the money had been paid under legal process, it could not be recovered back again; and this opinion was fully confirmed by the court in banc.[4] The same principle has likewise been held to apply where the payment was made without knowledge, or reasonable means of knowledge, of the facts on which the original demand proceeded;[5] and it may be laid down as a general rule, that, where money has been paid by one party to the other after *bonâ fide* legal proceedings have been actually commenced, which money is afterwards discovered not to have been really due, the party who has paid will nevertheless be precluded from recovering it as money had and received to his use.[6]

[1] Per Willes, J., Langmead *v.* Maple, 18 C. B. N. S. 270 (114 E. C. L. R.).

[2] 7 T. R. 269. In accordance with the principle on which the decision in Marriot *v.* Hampton proceeded, "a man against whom damages have been recovered in an action of trespass cannot recover back the amount in an action for money had and received on proof that no trespass was in fact committed:" per Maule, J., Follett *v.* Hoppe, 5 C. B. 238. See Smith *v.* Monteith, 13 M. & W. 427.

[3] See D. 44. 2. 27.

[4] Marriot *v.* Hampton, *supra.*

[5] Hamlet *v.* Richardson, 9 Bing. 644, 645 (23 E. C. L. R.).

[6] Marriot *v.* Hampton, 7 T. R. 269; with which compare Canaan *v.* Reynolds, 5 E. & B. 301 (85 E. C. L. R.); per Patteson, J., Duke de Cadaval *v.* Collins, 4 A. & E. 866 (31 E. C. L. R.); Judgm., Wilson *v.* Ray, 10 A. & E. 88 (51 E. C. L. R.); Brown *v.* M'Kinally, 1 Esp. 279; per Holroyd, J., Milnes *v.* Duncan, 6 B. & C. 679 (13 E. C. L. R.); Moses *v.* Macfarlane, 2 Burr. 1009, must be considered as overruled; see per Eyre, C. J., Phillips *v.*

In accordance also with the same principle, *it has been [*333] held that *assumpsit* will not lie by the party against whom a *fi. fa.* has issued on a subsisting judgment to recover the sum levied under it, on the ground that such judgment was signed on a warrant of attorney, which was obtained by fraud or duress.[1] The principle above stated does not however apply where the original transaction was *res inter alios acta.*[2]

Having thus premised that a court of law will not, except under peculiar circumstances, reopen a question which has once been judicially decided between the parties,[3] we may remark that the maxim of the civil law already cited—*res judicata pro veritate accipitur*—is generally recognized and applied by our own.[4] [*334] "The *authorities," as observed by Lord Tenterden, C.

Hunter, 2 H. Bla. 414; per Heath, J., Brisbane *v.* Dacres, 5 Taunt. 160 (1 E. C. L. R.).

[1] De Medina *v.* Grove, 10 Q. B. 152, 168 (59 E. C. L. R.).

[2] Per Maule, J., Follett *v.* Hoppe, 5 C. B. 243 (57 E. C. L. R.); *post*, Chap. X.

[3] It must be taken as a positive rule, that when parties consent to withdraw a juror, no future action can be brought for the same cause; per Pollock, C. B., Gibbs *v.* Ralph, 14 M. & W. 805; per Lord Abinger, C. B., Harries *v.* Thomas, 2 M. & W. 37, 38.

[4] See per Knight Bruce, V.-C., 1 Y. & Coll. 588, 589; Preston *v.* Peeke, E., B. & E. 336 (96 E. C. L. R.); per Wightman, J., Mortimer *v.* South Wales R. C., 1 E. & E. 382–3 (102 E. C. L. R.); Notman *v.* Anchor Ass. Co., 6 C. B. N. S. 536 (95 E. C. L. R.); Kelly *v.* Morray, L. R. 1 C. P. 667; Williams *v.* Sidmouth R. and Harb. Co., L. R. 2 Ex. 284.

"The court is always at liberty to look at its own records and proceedings" (per Kelly, C. B., Craven *v.* Smith, L. R. 4 Ex. 149); and nothing can be assigned for error, in fact, which is inconsistent with the record (Irwin *v.* Grey, 19 C. B. N. S. 585 (115 E. C. L. R.)).

As to the efficacy of a judgment of the House of Lords, see A.-G. *v.* Dean, &c., of Windsor, 8 H. L. Cas. 369; Beamish *v.* Beamish, 9 Id. 274.

The resolution of a committee for privileges in favor of a claimant of a peerage agreed to by the House and communicated to the crown, followed by a writ of summons to the claimant by the title of the dignity claimed, establishes the right to that dignity (at all events from the date of the writ of summons), which can never afterwards be called in question. But a resolution of a committee for privileges is in no sense a judgment, and though admitted to be *primâ facie* valid and conclusive, does not establish a precedent which future committees are bound to follow. Wiltes Peerage, L. R. 4 H. L. 126, 147–8.

As to the finality of an award, see Hodgkinson *v.* Fernie, 3 C. B. N. S. 189 (91 E. C. L. R.); Commings *v.* Heard, L. R. 4 Q. B. 669.

J.,[1] "are clear, that a party cannot be received to aver as error in fact a matter contrary to the record," and "a record imports such absolute verity that no person against whom it is admissible shall be allowed to aver against it,"[2] and this principle is invariably acted upon by our courts.[3] It is necessary, however, in order to comprehend the full bearing and importance of the above rule, that we should consider more particularly in what manner, and between what parties, a judgment recovered may be rendered operative as a bar to legal proceedings; and upon this subject The Duchess of Kingston's Case[4] is usually cited as the leading authority. "From the variety of cases," there says Lord Chief Justice De Grey, "relative to judgment being given in evidence in civil suits, these two deductions seem to follow as generally true: First, that the judgment of a court of concurrent jurisdiction directly upon the point, is as a plea, a bar, or as evidence, conclusive, between the same parties, upon the same matter directly in question in another court. Secondly, that the judgment of a court of exclusive jurisdiction directly upon the point is, in like manner, conclusive upon the same matter, between the same parties,[5] coming [*335] incidentally in question in another *court for a different purpose. But neither the judgment of a concurrent or exclusive jurisdiction is evidence of any matter which came collaterally in question, though within their jurisdiction, nor of any matter incidentally cognizable, nor of any matter to be inferred by argument from the judgment."

In connection with the above passage, and with the subject now under consideration, we may observe, 1st, that although a judgment recovered, if for the same cause of action, and between parties substantially the same, will be admissible in evidence, yet, in order to render it *conclusive* as an estoppel, it must, *if the opportunity presents itself*,[6] be so pleaded.[7]

[1] Judgm., R. *v.* Carlile, 2 B. & Ad. 367 (22 E. C. L. R.).

[2] Ib.; 1 Inst. 260.

[3] Reed *v.* Jackson, 1 East 355.

[4] 20 Howell St. Tr. 538.

[5] Judgm., King *v.* Norman, 4 C. B. 898 (56 E. C. L. R.); Needham *v.* Bremner, L. R. 1 C. P. 583.

[6] See Whittaker *v.* Jackson, 2 H. & C. 926.

[7] Doe *v.* Huddart, 2 Cr., M. & R. 316; per Parke, B., Doe d. Strode *v.* Seaton, Id. 731; Doe *v.* Wright, 10 A. & E. 763 (37 E. C. L. R.). The proper requisites to a plea of judgment recovered are thus specified by Vinnius, lib. 4, tit.

In Todd *v.* Stewart,[1] the effect of a plea of judgment recovered for a less sum than that sued for in the action then before the court was much considered. That was an action of debt on simple contract for 400*l.*; the defendant pleaded as to 43*l.* 6*s.* 9*d.* payment, and as to the residue that plaintiffs impleaded defendants for the same in an action on promises, and recovered 314*l.* 8*s.* as well for their damages in the said action as for their costs. The replication alleged that the residue of the said causes of action, in the declaration mentioned, were not the causes of action in respect of which the judgment was *recovered; and on the issue thus raised the jury found for the defendants. It was held by the Court of Exchequer Chamber that the above plea was good after verdict, and that it amounted to an ordinary plea of judgment recovered. [*336]

2dly. We may remark, that a judgment recovered will be admissible as evidence, not only between the same parties, if suing in the same right,[2] but likewise between their privies, whether in blood, law, or estate;[3] and that a judgment will, moreover, be evidence between those who, although not nominally, are really and substantially the same parties.[4]

In the well-known case of King *v.* Hoare,[5] it was held, that a judgment *without* satisfaction recovered against one of two joint debtors may be pleaded in bar of an action against the other contracting party, and the court observed, that "If there be a breach of contract or wrong done, or any other cause of action, by one against another, and judgment be recovered in a court of record,

13, s. 5:—*Hæc autem exceptio* (*rei judicatæ*) *non aliter genti obstat quam si eadem quæstio inter easdem personas revocetur; itaque ita demum nocet si omnia sint eadem, idem corpus, eadem quantitas, idem jus, eadem causa petendi, eademque conditio personarum;* cited, arg. Ricardo *v.* Garcias, 12 Cl. & Fin. 368. See Nelson *v.* Couch, cited, *ante*, p. 331.

[1] 9 Q. B. 758, 767 (59 E. C. L. R.).

[2] Outram *v.* Morewood, 3 East 346, 365; Com. Dig. *Estoppel* (C.); 5 Rep. 32 b.

[3] Trevivan *v.* Lawrence, Salk. 276.

[4] Kinnersley *v.* Cope, 2 Dougl. 517, commented on, 3 East 366, and recognized in Simpson *v.* Pickering, 1 Cr., M. & R. 529; Strutt *v.* Bovingdon, 5 Esp. 56; Hancock *v.* Welsh, 1 Stark. N. P. C. 347 (2 E. C. L. R.).

[5] 13 M. & W. 494; Buckland *v.* Johnson, 15 C. B. 145 (80 E. C. L. R.). See Holmes *v.* Newlands, 5 Q. B. 634 (48 E. C. L. R.); Florence *v.* Jenings, 2 C. B. N. S. 454 (89 E. C. L. R.).

the judgment is a bar to the original cause of action, because it is thereby reduced to a certainty, and the object of the suit attained so far as it can be at that stage, and it would be useless and vexatious to subject the defendant to another suit for the purpose of obtaining the same result. Hence the legal maxim *Transit in rem judicatum*—the cause of action is changed into matter of [*337] *record, which is of a higher nature, and the inferior remedy is merged in the higher. This appears to be equally true where there is but *one cause of action*, whether it be against a single person or many. The judgment of a court of record changes the nature of that cause of action, and prevents its being the subject of another suit, and the cause of action being single, cannot afterwards be divided into two." The rule here laid down does not, however, apply in the case of a joint and several contract, for there the instrument sued on comprises the joint contract of all and the several contracts of each of the contracting parties, and gives different and distinct remedies to the person with whom the contract has been entered into.[1]

A judgment recovered *with* satisfaction against one of two or more joint and several debtors will be a bar to an action against another of them;[2] but otherwise, it would seem, if the judgment be not satisfied.[3]

3dly. We may observe, that a judgment recovered will be evidence whenever the cause of action is the same,[4] although the form of the second action be different from *that of the first;[5] [*338] and the record, when produced, must be such as to show

[1] Judgm., 13 M. & W. 504, 505, 507, citing Ward *v.* Johnson, 15 Mass. (U. S.) R. 148; per Jervis, C. J., Buckland *v.* Johnson, 15 C. B. 164 (80 E. C. L. R.); per Bayley, B., Lechmere *v.* Fletcher, 1 C. & M. 623; Higgens's Case, 6 Rep. 44 b, 46 a, cited per Jervis, C. J., Price *v.* Moulton, 10 C. B. 570 (70 E. C. L. R.); Dick *v.* Tolhausen, 4 H. & N. 695. See Henry *v.* Goldney, 15 M. & W. 494; Haigh *v.* Paris, 16 M. & W. 144.

[2] Per Parke, B., Morgan *v.* Price, 4 Exch. 619.

[3] King *v.* Hoare, 13 M. & W. 494, and cases there cited; per Popham, C. J., Broom *v.* Wooton, Yelv. 67; s. c., Cro. Jac. 73, as explained 13 M. & W. 505; Phillips *v.* Ward, 2 H. & C. 773.

[4] Per cur., Williams *v.* Thacker, 1 B & B. 514 (5 E. C. L. R.); cited, arg. Hopkins *v.* Freeman, 13 M. & W. 372; Guest *v.* Warren, 9 Exch. 379; per Beardsley, C. J., Dunckle *v.* Wiles, 5 Denio (U. S.) R. 303; Fetter *v.* Beal, 1 Lord Raym. 339, 692; cited, Sayer on Damages 89.

[5] See, per Buller, J., Foster *v.* Allanson, 2 T. R. 483; Pease *v.* Chaytor, 32 L. J., M. C. 121. *Bona fides non patitur ut bis idem exigatur;* D. 50. 17. 57.

on its face that the cause of action in the second case may be the same as that for which the judgment was recovered in the former action.[1] A recovery in trover will vest the property in the chattel sued for in the defendant, and will be a bar to an action of trespass for the same thing;[2] and "If two jointly convert goods, and one of them receive the proceeds, you cannot, after a recovery against one in trover, have an action against the other for the same conversion, on an action for money had and received to recover the value of the goods, for which a judgment has already passed in the former action."[3]

If, however, it be doubtful whether the second action is brought *pro eâdem causâ* it is a proper test to consider whether the same evidence would sustain both actions,[4] and what was the particular point or matter determined in the former action; for a judgment in each species of action is final only for its own purpose and object, and *quoad* the subject-matter adjudicated upon, and no further; for instance, a judgment for the plaintiff in trespass affirms a right of possession to be, as between *the plaintiff and defendant, [*339] in the plaintiff at the time of the trespass committed, but in a subsequent ejectment between the same parties, would not be conclusive with respect to the general right of property in the *locus in quo*.[5] Where, in an action for the stipulated price of a specific chattel, the defendant pleaded payment into court of a sum which the plaintiffs took out in satisfaction of the cause of action, it was held, that the defendant in that action was not thereby estopped from suing the plaintiffs for negligence in the construction of the chattel.[6]

[1] Per Crompton, J., Wadsworth *v.* Bentley, 23 L. J. Q. B. 3; Ricardo *v.* Garcias, 12 Cl. & F. 368, 387.

[2] Per Lord Hardwicke, C. J., Smith *v.* Gibson, Cas. temp. Hardw. 319; Buckland *v.* Johnson, 15 C. B. 145 (80 E. C. L. R.); Moor *v.* Watts, 1 Lord Raym. 614.

[3] Per Jervis, C. J., 15 C. B. 161 (80 E. C. L. R.); citing Cooper *v.* Shepherd, 3 C. B. 266; Adams *v.* Broughton, Andr. 18; Jenk. Cent. 4th cent. cas. 88.

[4] See Hadley *v.* Green, 2 Tyrw. 390; Wiat *v.* Essington, 2 Lord Raym. 1410; Clegg *v.* Dearden, 12 Q. B. 576 (64 E. C. L. R.) (with which compare Smith *v.* Kenrick, 7 C. B. 515 (62 E. C. L. R.)); per Lord Westbury, C., Hunter *v.* Stewart, 31 L. J. Chanc. 346, 350.

[5] See Judgm., 3 East 357.

[6] Rigge *v.* Burbidge, 15 M. & W. 589; recognizing Mondel *v.* Steele, 8 M. & W. 858.

Not merely is it true, moreover, that the facts actually decided by an issue in any suit cannot be again litigated between the same parties, and are evidence between them, and that conclusive, for the purpose of terminating litigation; but so likewise are the material facts alleged by one party, which are directly admitted by the opposite party, or indirectly admitted by taking a traverse on some other facts, provided that the traverse thus taken be found against the party making it.[1] "The statements," however, "of a party in a declaration or plea, though for the purposes of the cause he is bound by those that are material, and the evidence must be confined to them upon an issue, ought not, it should seem, to be treated as confessions of the truth of the facts stated.[2]

With respect to the action of ejectment, we may remark, that by [*340] the judgment therein the plaintiff *obtains possession of the lands recovered by the verdict, but does not acquire any title thereto, except such as he previously had; if, therefore, he had previously a freehold interest in them, he is in as a freeholder; if he had a chattel interest, he is in as a termor; and if he had no title at all, he is in as a trespasser, and will be liable to account for the profits to the legal owner.[3] Moreover, although a judgment in ejectment is admissible in evidence in another ejectment between the same parties,[4] yet it is not conclusive evidence, because a party may have a title to possession of land at one time, and not at another; nor can a judgment be pleaded in ejectment by way of estoppel, for the issue is made up in this action without pleadings; and hence there is a remarkable difference between ejectment and other actions with regard to the application of the maxim under consideration.[5] The courts of common law have, however, sometimes interfered to stay proceedings in ejectment,

[1] Boileau *v.* Rutlin, 2 Exch. 665, 681; recognized, per Parke, B., Buckmaster *v.* Meiklejohn, 8 Exch. 687. See Carter *v.* James, 13 M. & W. 137, and the remark upon that case, per Pollock, C. B., Hutt *v.* Morrell, 3 Exch. 241.

[2] Judgm., Boileau *v.* Rutlin, *supra.*

[3] Per Lord Mansfield, C. J., Taylor d. Atkyns *v.* Horde, 1 Burr. 114. The effect of a judgment in ejectment is, under the C. L. P. Act, 1852, s. 207, "the same as that of a judgment in the action of ejectment heretofore used."

[4] Doe d. Strode *v.* Seaton, 2 Cr., M. & R. 728.

[5] The order of a county court judge under the 19 & 20 Vict. c. 108, s. 50, is not analogous to a judgment in ejectment so as to entitle a landlord to maintain an action for mesne profits: Campbell *v.* Loader, 3 H. & C. 520.

either in order to compel payment of the costs in a former action,[1] or where such proceedings were manifestly vexatious and oppressive.[2]

*Upon the whole, it seems that we may fitly sum up these remarks upon the conclusiveness of a judgment of a court of competent authority, *quoad* the subject-matter in respect whereof such judgment is relied upon as a bar to future litigation, in the words of a learned judge, who, in a case below cited, thus expresses himself: "It is, I think, to be collected, that the rule against reagitating matter adjudicated is subject generally to this restriction—that, however essential the establishment of particular facts may be to the soundness of a judicial decision, however it may proceed on them as established, and however binding and conclusive the decision may, as to its immediate and direct object, be, those facts are not all necessarily established conclusively between the parties, and that either may again litigate them for any other purpose as to which they may come in question, provided the immediate subject of the decision be not attempted to be withdrawn from its operation, so as to defeat its direct object. This limitation to the rule appears to me, generally speaking, to be consistent with reason and convenience, and not opposed to authority."[3] [*341]

4thly. But although the judgment of a court of competent jurisdiction upon the same matter will, in general, be conclusive between the same parties, such a judgment may nevertheless be set aside on the ground of mistake,[4] or may be impeached on the ground of fraud;[5] for "fraud," in the language of De Grey,

[1] Doe d. Brayne *v.* Bather, 12 Q. B. 941 (64 E. C. L. R.); Morgan *v.* Nicholl, 3 H. & N. 215. See Prowse *v.* Loxdale, 32 L. J. Q. B. 227; Hoare *v.* Dickson, 7 C. B. 164 (62 E. C. L. R.); Stead *v.* Williams, 5 C. B. 528 (57 E. C. L. R.); Stilwell *v.* Clarke, 3 Exch. 264; Danvers *v.* Morgan, 17 C. B. 530 (84 E. C. L. R.).

[2] See Cobbett *v.* Warner, L. R. 2 Q. B. 108 (42 E. C. L. R.); Doe d. Pultney *v.* Freeman, cited 2 Sellon Pract. 144; Doe d. Henry *v.* Gustard, 5 Scott N. R. 818; Thrustout d. Park *v.* Troublesome, Andr. 297, recognized Haigh *v.* Paris, 16 M. & W. 144.

[3] Per Knight Bruce, V.-C., Barrs *v.* Jackson, 1 Yo. & Coll. 597–8; where, however, the rule was wrongly applied: see s. c., 1 Phill. 582.

[4] Cannan *v.* Reynolds, 5 E. & B. 301 (85 E. C. L. R.).

[5] "It may be conceded that if a judgment has been obtained by fraud, or is contrary to natural justice, it may be impeached in a collateral proceeding;" per Byles, J., Wildes *v.* Russell, L. R. 1 C. P. 745.

"There is no more stringent maxim than that no one shall be permitted to

[*342] *C. J.,[1] "is an extrinsic collateral act, which vitiates the most solemn proceedings of courts of justice." Lord Coke says[2] "it avoids all judicial acts, ecclesiastical or temporal." And in a modern case[3] before the House of Lords, it was observed, that the validity of a decree of a court of competent jurisdiction upon parties legally before it may be questioned, on the ground that "it was pronounced through fraud, contrivance, or covin of any description, or not in a real suit, or, if pronounced in a real and substantial suit, between parties who were really not in contest with each other."

In connection with the finality of judgment,[4] we may add that [*343] the practice is "inveterate and every-day *occurrence at chambers of setting aside judgments, whether regular or irregular, whether after execution executed or before, on terms."[5]

We have, in the preceding remarks, endeavored to point out the

aver against a record; but where fraud can be shown this maxim does not apply:" per Pollock, C. B., Rogers *v.* Hadley, 2 H. & C. 247.

[1] Duchess of Kingston's Case, *ante*, p. 334. See Ex parte White, 4 H. L. Cas. 313.

[2] Fermor's Case, 3 Rep. 78 a.

[3] Earl of Bandon *v.* Becher, 3 Cl. & Fin. 510; Meddowcroft *v.* Huguenin, 4 Moore, P. C. C. 386; Perry *v.* Meddowcroft, 10 Beav. 122; per Lord Eldon, C., Gore *v.* Stackpole, 1 Dow 18; Patrick *v.* Shedden, 2 E. & B. 14 (75 E. C. L. R.); Phillipson *v.* Earl of Egremont, 6 Q. B. 587, 604 (51 E. C. L. R.); Green *v.* Nixon, 27 L. J. Chanc. 819, 821; per Tindal, C. J., Fowler *v.* Rickerby, 2 M. & Gr. 777 (40 E. C. L. R.); Dodgson *v.* Scott, 2 Exch. 457; Bank of Australasia *v.* Nias, 16 Q. B. 717 (71 E. C. L. R.); Shattock *v.* Carden, 6 Exch. 725; Place *v.* Potts, 5 H. L. Cas. 383; Harris *v.* Willis, 15 C. B. 710 (80 E. C. L. R.). In Allen *v.* M'Pherson, 1 H. L. Cas. 191, it was held, that if probate of a will alleged to have been executed under undue influence and false representations be granted in the Ecclesiastical Court, the Court of Chancery has no jurisdiction in the matter.

[4] As to the finality of a judgment of the Consular Court at Constantinople, see Barber *v.* Lamb, 8 C. B. N. S. 95 (98 E. C. L. R.)—of the judgment of a foreign court, see Hobbs *v.* Henning, 17 C. B. N. S. 791 (112 E. C. L. R.); Scott *v.* Pilkington, 2 B. & S. 11 (110 E. C. L. R.); Brissac *v.* Rathbone, 6 H. & N. 301; Frayes *v.* Worms, 10 C. B. N. S. 149 (100 E. C. L. R.); Castrique *v.* Imrie, 8 C. B. N. S. 405 (98 E. C. L. R.); Cammell *v.* Sewell, 3 H. & N. 617, 646; s. c., 5 Id. 728; Sheehy *v.* Professional Life Ass. Co., 3 C. B. N. S. 597 (91 E. C. L. R.); Vanquelin *v.* Bovard, 15 C. B. N. S. 341 (109 E. C. L. R.).

[5] Per Coleridge, J., Cannan *v.* Reynolds, 5 E. & B. 307 (85 E. C. L. R.). See Webster *v.* Emery, 10 Exch. 901; s. c., 9 Exch. 242.

most direct application in civil proceedings of the rule that a man shall not be *bis vexatus*, which rule is in fact included in the general maxim, *Interest reipublicæ ut sit finis litium.* This latter maxim has, as may readily be supposed, a wide application; it in fact embraces the whole doctrine of estoppels, which is obviously founded in common sense and sound policy, since, if facts once solemnly affirmed to be true were to be again denied whenever the affirmant saw his opportunity, there would never be an end to litigation and confusion. To the same maxim may likewise be referred the principle of the limitation of actions, which we shall treat of hereafter,[1] the statutes of set-off, which were enacted to prevent the necessity of cross actions,[2] and the rule which forbids the circuity in legal proceedings—*circuitus est evitandus;*[3] in accordance with which a court of law will endeavor to prevent circuity and multiplicity of suits, where the circumstances of the litigant parties are such that, on changing their relative positions of plaintiff [*344] *and defendant, the recovery by each would be equal in amount.[4]

The rule just cited, which is intended to avoid "the scandal and absurdity"[5] of a circuity of action, is deserving of far more minute consideration than can here be given to it. According to this rule a defendant is entitled to set up a cross demand by way of defence, provided he can show that "the sum which he claims to be entitled to recover back is of necessity the identical sum which the plain-

[1] See maxim, *Vigilantibus et non dormientibus jura subveniunt; post,* Chap. IX.

[2] Judgm., Hill *v.* Smith, 12 M. & W. 631; per Pollock, C. B., Turner *v.* Berry, 5 Exch. 860; per Lord Campbell, C. J., Walker *v.* Clements, 15 Q. B. 1050 (69 E. C. L. R.). See Rees *v.* Watts, 11 Exch. 410; s. c., 9 Id. 696; Gingell *v.* Purkins, 4 Exch. 720; Luckie *v.* Bushby, 13 C. B. 864 (76 E. C. L. R.); Bell *v.* Carey, 8 C. B. 887 (65 E. C. L. R.).

"The courts are always astute to promote set-off in aid of justice and honesty;" per Byles, J., Alliance Bank *v.* Holford, 16 C. B. N. S. 463 (111 E. C. L. R.).

[3] 5 Rep. 31; Co. Litt. 348 a; 2 Saund. R. 150. See Wilders *v.* Stevens, 15 M. & W. 208; Milner *v.* Field, 5 Exch. 829.

[4] See Carr *v.* Stephens, 9 B. & C. 758 (17 E. C. L. R.); per Parke, B., Penny *v.* Innes, 1 Cr., M. & R. 442; arg. Hall *v.* Bainbridge, 5 Q. B. 242 (48 E. C. L. R.); Simpson *v.* Swan, 3 Camp. 291.

[5] Per Lord Denman, C. J., Walmesley *v.* Cooper, 11 A. & E. 221-2 (39 E. C. L. R.); per Jervis, C. J., 15 C. B. 62 (80 E. C. L. R.).

tiff is suing for,"[1] or where the damages would necessarily be the same.[2]

Plaintiff by agreement in writing agreed to serve defendant for the term of ten years in the capacity of a brewer, and in consideration thereof, and "of the due, full, and complete service" of plaintiff "as aforesaid," defendant agreed, *inter alia*, to pay plaintiff "the weekly sum of 2*l.* 10*s.* during the said term of ten years." Plaintiff entered into defendant's service under the agreement, but some years afterwards fell ill, and was unable to attend personally to business. In an action for wages alleged to have accrued during the period of plaintiff's illness, a plea was held good which averred [*345] that the plaintiff was not, *during any part of the time for and in respect of which such wages were claimed, "ready and willing, or able to render, and did not in fact, during any part of such time, render the agreed or any service." It was objected, indeed, on behalf of the plaintiff, that his breach of the contract declared upon could only be ground for a cross action, but the court held that, to avoid circuity, it might well be considered the action should be barred, so as to prevent an unjust advantage therein, and to put an end to litigation.[3]

Difficulty is sometimes felt in applying the rule as to circuity above exemplified. Thus, in assumpsit by payee against maker of two promissory notes for 200*l.* and 140*l.*, the defendant pleaded in bar that after the notes became due it was mutually agreed by plaintiff, defendant, and A., that A. should pay to plaintiff 25*l.* per annum by quarterly payments, and so long as A. so paid, the right of action on the notes should be suspended, and that A. had hitherto made the quarterly payments. This plea was held to

[1] Charles *v.* Altin, 15 C. B. 46, 62 (80 E. C. L. R.); Alston *v.* Herring, 11 Exch. 822, 831; Schloss *v.* Heriot, 14 C. B. N. S. 59 (108 E. C. L. R.); Thompson *v.* Gillespy, 5 E. & B. 209, 223 (85 E. C. L. R.); Bartlett *v.* Holmes, 13 C. B. 630, 638 (76 E. C. L. R.); Stimson *v.* Hall, 1 H. & N. 831; Atterbury *v.* Jarvie, 2 H. & N. 114; Bell *v.* Richards, 2 H. & N. 311; Owen *v.* Wilkinson, 5 C. B. N. S. 526 (94 E. C. L. R.); Pedder *v.* Mayor, &c., of Preston, 12 C. B. N. S. 535 (104 E. C. L. R.). See Beecham *v.* Smith, E., B. & E. 442 (96 E. C. L. R.); Minshull *v.* Oakes, 2 H. & N. 793.

[2] Speeding *v.* Young, 16 C. B. N. S. 824, 826–7 (111 E. C. L. R.), citing Alston *v.* Herring, 11 Exch. 822. See De Rosaz *v.* Anglo-Italian Bk., L. R. 4 Q. B. 462.

[3] Cuckson *v.* Stones, 1 E. & E. 248 (102 E. C. L. R.).

offer no answer to the action, inasmuch as if plaintiff were barred of his right to sue on the notes, such right would by law be extinguished altogether; which appeared not to be the intention of the agreement, and the defendant was therefore held entitled merely to his right of action on the agreement, if plaintiff had sued on the notes before default made in payment of the annuity.[1]

We may add that, as a general rule, "where two parties have judgments against each other, the court will, for the *purpose of avoiding uncertainty, vexation, and expense, order them to be set off against each other."[2] [*346]

The principle of law just now alluded to—"that the right to bring a personal action once existing, and by act of the party suspended for ever so short a time, is extinguished and discharged, and can never revive"—is very old and well established.[3] It is usually applied where persons have by their own acts placed themselves in circumstances incompatible with the application of the ordinary legal remedies.[4]

In accordance with the doctrine which forbids circuity, are the maxims, *Frustra petis quod statim alteri reddere cogeris*[5]—*Dolo facit qui petit quod redditurus est*,[6] which may be illustrated by the rule that one partner cannot at common law sue his co-partners in respect of a partnership debt,[7] and by cases already cited.[8]

Recurring to a consideration of the principal maxim, we may add to what has been above said concerning it, that where two or more actions are brought by the same plaintiff at the same time against the same defendant, for causes of action which might have been

[1] Ford *v.* Beech, 11 Q. B. 852 (63 E. C. L. R.); s. c., Id. 842; cited in Frazer *v.* Jordan, 8 E. & B. 309, 310 (92 E. C. L. R.); Gibbons *v.* Vouillin, 8 C. B. 483 (65 E. C. L. R.); Belshaw *v.* Bush, 11 C. B. 191 (73 E. C. L. R.), (as to which see Cook *v.* Lister, 13 C. B. N. S. 543 (106 E. C. L. R.)); Webb *v.* Spicer and Webb *v.* Salmon, 13 Q. B. 886, 894 (66 E. C. L. R.); Salmon *v.* Webb, 3 H. L. Cas. 510.

[2] Per Willes, J., Alliance Bank *v.* Holford, 16 C. B. N. S. 463 (111 E. C. L. R.).

[3] Judgm., 11 Q. B. 867 (63 E. C. L. R.), where cases are cited in support of the above propositions.

[4] Judg., 11 Q. B. 870 (63 E. C. L. R.).

[5] Jenk. Cent. 256.

[6] Phillimore Jurisp. 233.

[7] Story on Partnership 325. See Boulter *v.* Peplow, 9 C. B. 493 (67 E. C. L. R.); Sedgwick *v.* Daniell, 2 H. & N. 319; Broom's Pr. C. C., 2d ed., 99.

[8] *Ante*, p. 344, n. 1.

joined in the same suit, the court, or a judge at chambers, if they deem the proceedings oppressive, will in general compel the plaintiff to consolidate them, and to pay the costs of the application.[1] Where several actions are brought upon the same policy of insurance the court, or a judge, upon [*347] *application of the defendants, will grant a rule or order to stay the proceedings in all the actions but one, the defendants undertaking to be bound by the verdict in such action, and to pay the amount of their several subscriptions and costs, if the plaintiff should recover, together with such other terms as the court or judge may think proper to impose upon them.[2] And where many actions are oppressively and vexatiously brought by the same plaintiff, for the purpose of trying the same question, the court or a judge will interfere, either by staying the proceedings or giving time to plead in all the actions but one upon terms.[3]

An important application of the general principle now under notice occurs in criminal law, for there it is a well-established rule, that when a man has once been indicted for an offence, and acquitted, he cannot afterwards be indicted for the same offence, provided the first indictment were such that he could have been lawfully convicted upon it by proof of the facts contained in the second indictment; and if he be thus indicted a second time he may plead *autrefois acquit*, and it will be a good bar to the indictment;[4] and this

[1] Cecil *v.* Brigges, 2 T. R. 639; 2 Sellon Pract. 144; 2 Chitt. Arch. Pr., 11th ed., 1347.

[2] Doyle *v.* Anderson, 1 A. & E. 635 (28 E. C. L. R.). See Syers *v.* Pickersgill, 27 L. J. Exch. 5.

[3] 2 Chitt. Arch. Pr., 11th ed., 1348. See Frith *v.* Guppy, L. R. 2 C. P. 32; Sturges *v.* Lord Curzon, 1 H. & N. 17.

In the case of a bill of exchange every party to the instrument may be sued at the same time by the holder, for, by the custom of merchants, every such party is separately liable: per Pollock, C. B., 3 H. & C. 981. See Woodward *v.* Pell, L. R. 4 Q. B. 55.

Where the master of a ship signs a bill of lading in his own name and is sued upon it, and judgment is obtained against him, though not satisfied, the owner of the ship cannot be sued upon the same bill of lading: Priestly *v.* Fernie, 3 H. & C. 977.

[4] Reg. *v.* Bird, 2 Den. C. C. 94, 198–200, 214; Reg. *v.* Knight, L. & C. 378; R. *v.* Vandercomb, 2 East P. C. 519; cited, per Gurney, B., R. *v.* Birchenough, 1 Moo. Cr. Cas. 479. See Reg. *v.* Button, 11 Q. B. 929 (63 E. C. L. R.); Reg. *v.* Machen, 14 Q. B. 74 (68 E. C. L. R.); Reg. *v.* Gaunt, L. R. 2 Q. B.

plea is clearly founded *on the principle, that no man shall be placed in peril of legal penalties more than once upon the same accusation—*nemo debet bis puniri pro uno delicto.*[1] Which great fundamental maxim of our criminal law means that "a man shall not twice be put in peril after a verdict has been returned by the jury; that verdict being given on a good indictment, and one on which the prisoner could be legally convicted and sentenced. It does not, however, follow, if from any particular circumstance a trial has proved abortive, that then the case shall not be again submitted to the consideration of a jury, and determined as right and justice may require."[2]

[*348]

Thus an acquittal upon an indictment for murder may be pleaded in bar of another indictment for manslaughter; and an acquittal upon an indictment for burglary and larceny may be pleaded to an indictment for the larceny of the same goods; because in either of these cases the prisoner might, on the former trial, have been convicted of the offence charged against him in the second indictment;[3] the true test by which to decide whether a plea of *autrefois acquit* is a sufficient bar in any particular case being—whether the evidence necessary to support the second indictment would have been sufficient to procure a legal conviction upon the first.

On the principle that "a man should not twice be put in jeopardy for one and the same offence," a plea of **autrefois convict* will operate to bar a second indictment unless the judgment on the former has been reversed for error.[4] It may, however, be laid down generally, that where, "by reason of some defect in the record, either in the indictment, place, trial, process, or the like, the prisoner was not lawfully liable to suffer judgment for the offence charged on that proceeding," he cannot, after rever-

[*349]

466; Reg. *v.* Moah, Dearsl. 626. As to the meaning of the words "conviction" and "acquittal," see per Tindal, C. J., Burgess *v.* Boetefeur, 8 Scott N. R. 211, 212; Re Newton, 13 Q. B. 716 (66 E. C. L. R.).

[1] 4 Rep. 40, 43; 1 Chitt. Crim. Law 452; per Pollock, C. B., Re Baker, 2 H. & N. 248.

[2] Per Cockburn, C. J., Winsor *v.* Reg., L. R. 1 Q. B. 311; s. c., affirmed in error, Id. 390.

[3] 2 Hale P. C. 246. See also Helsham *v.* Blackwood, 11 C. B. 111 (73 E. C. L. R.).

[4] Reg. *v.* Drury, 18 L. J., M. C., 189. See Reg. *v.* Morris, cited *post*, p. 350.

sal of the judgment, properly be said to have been "in jeopardy" within the meaning of the maxim under consideration.[1] So where, on a trial for misdemeanor, the jury are improperly, and against the will of the defendant, discharged from giving a verdict after the trial has begun, this is not equivalent to an acquittal.[2]

The general rule, which obtains as well in purely civil as in criminal cases, being that "a man shall not be twice vexed in respect of the same matter," is subject to exceptions. For instance,—a man may at common law be compelled to make reparation in damages to the injured party, and be liable also to punishment for a breach of the public peace in consequence of the same act,[3] and may thus be said in common parlance to be twice punished for the same offence.[4] So, it has been held [*350] *that a conviction for an assault by justices at petty sessions, at the instance of the person assaulted, and imprisonment consequent thereon, do not bar an indictment for manslaughter against the defendant, should the person assaulted afterwards die from the effects of the assault, for "the form and the intention of the common law pleas of *autrefois convict* and *autrefois acquit* show that they apply only where there has been a former judicial decision on the same accusation in substance, and where the question in dispute has been already decided."[5] If there be a continuing breach by a workman of a contract to serve his master, the servant may, under the stat. 4 Geo. 4,

[1] Per Coleridge, J., Reg. *v.* Drury, *supra;* Reg. *v.* Green, Dearsl. & B. 113. See also Lord Denman's judgment, O'Connell *v.* Reg., by Mr. Leahy, pp. 19 *et seq.*, and p. 44; Reg. *v.* Gompertz, 9 Q. B. 824, 839 (58 E. C. L. R.).

[2] Reg. *v.* Charlesworth, 1 B. & S. 160 (101 E. C. L. R.); *et vide* per Cockburn, C. J., Id. 507, as to the maxim *supra.*

[3] See stat. 25 & 26 Vict. c. 88, ss. 11, 22.

[4] Per Grier, J., 14 Howard (U. S.) R. 20. See stat. 24 & 25 Vict. c. 100, ss. 44, 45 (as to which see Hartley *v.* Hindmarsh, L. R. 1 C. P. 533; Reg. *v.* Elrington, 1 B. & S. 688 (101 E. C. L. R.); Hancock *v.* Somes, 1 E. & E. 795 (102 E. C. L. R.); Costar *v.* Hetherington, Id. 802); Justice *v.* Gosling, 12 C. B. 39 (74 E. C. L. R.); R. *v.* Mahon, 4 A. & E. 575 (31 E. C. L. R.); Anon. Id. 576, n.

In Scott *v.* Lord Seymour, 1 H. & C. 219, an action was held maintainable here by a British subject against another British subject for an assault committed at Naples, although proceedings for the same assault were pending in a Neapolitan court. See Cox *v.* Mitchell, 7 C. B. N. S. 55 (97 E. C. L. R.) Phillips *v.* Eyre, L. R. 4 Q. B. 225.

[5] Reg. *v.* Morris, L. R. 1 C. C. 90, 94.

c. 34, s. 3, be convicted more than once of the offence thereby constituted.[1] In construing, however, a statute which gives a penalty to a common informer, the court will take care not to impose a heavier burthen than the legislature contemplated.[2] A party attached for contempt in not performing an award, and sentenced to imprisonment, on undergoing such imprisonment is not thereby exonerated from performance of the award.[3] Although the general rule is, that a landlord cannot distrain twice for the same rent, he may under special circumstances be justified in doing so.[4] A court of law will not stay an action on the ground that a suit in equity is pending in which the same *demand comes in question, unless the court of equity has stayed the action by injunction.[5] [*351]

In conclusion, we may further mention one remarkable exception which formerly existed to the principle above stated and illustrated. This occurred in the proceedings in case of appeal of death, which might be instituted against a supposed offender after trial and acquittal, and by which punishment for some heinous crime was demanded, on account of the particular injury suffered by an individual, rather than for the offence against the public;[6] but this method of prosecution having attracted the attention of the legislature in the celebrated case of Ashford *v.* Thornton,[7] was abolished by stat. 59 Geo. 3, c. 46.

[1] Unwin *v.* Clarke, L. R. 1 Q. B. 417. See also Allen *v.* Worthy, L. R. 5 Q. B. 163; Ex parte Short, Id. 174.

[2] Per Byles, J., Garrett *v.* Messenger, L. R. 2 C. P. 585.

[3] Reg. *v.* Hemsworth, 3 C. B. 745 (54 E. C. L. R.).

[4] Bagge *v.* Mawby, 8 Exch. 641, 649; Wollaston *v.* Stafford, 15 C. B. 278 (80 E. C. L. R.). See Lee *v.* Cooke, cited, *ante*, p. 280.

[5] Pearse *v.* Robins, 26 L. J. Ex. 183. See 15 & 16 Vict. c. 76, s. 226; Simpson *v.* Sadd, 16 C. B. 26 (81 E. C. L. R.); Phelps *v.* Prothero, Id. 370.

See also, as bearing on the subject touched upon *supra*, Ward *v.* Broomhead, 7 Exch. 726; Lievesley *v.* Gilmore, L. R. 1 C. P. 570; Hookpayton *v.* Bussell, 9 Exch. 279; Giles *v.* Hutt, 3 Exch. 18; Great Northern R. C. *v.* Kennedy, 4 Exch. 417; as to a second arrest *pro eâdem causâ*, see Masters *v.* Johnson, 8 Exch. 63; Hamilton *v.* Pitt, 7 Bing. 230 (20 E. C. L. R.); *et vide* Mellin *v.* Evans, 1 Cr. & J. 82, and Talbot *v.* Bulkeley, 16 M. & W. 196, where the maxim commented on in the text is cited and applied.

[6] 4 Com. by Broom & Hadley 420, n. (*g*); 1 Chit. Crim. Law 452.

[7] 1 B. & Ald. 405.

[*352] *CHAPTER VI.

Acquisition, Enjoyment and Transfer of Property.

In the present chapter are contained three sections, which treat respectively of the acquisition, enjoyment, and transfer of property. In connection with the first-mentioned of these subjects, one maxim only has been considered, which sets forth the general principle, that title is acquired by priority of occupation; a principle so extensively applicable, and embracing so wide a field of inquiry, that the following pages will be found to present to the reader little more than a mere outline of a course of investigation, which, if pursued in detail, would prove alike interesting and instructive. It is, indeed, only proper to observe *in limine*—since, from the titles which have been selected with a view to showing clearly the mode of treatment adopted, much more might reasonably be expected in the ensuing pages than has been attempted—that a succinct statement of the more important only of the rights, liabilities, and incidents annexed to property has here been offered; so that a perusal of the contents of this chapter may prove serviceable in recalling the attention of the *practitioner* to the application and illustration of principles with which he must necessarily have been previously familiar; and may, without wearying his attention, direct the *student* to sources of information whence may be derived more copious and accurate supplies of knowledge.

[*353] *§ I.—The Mode of Acquiring Property.

Qui prior est Tempore, potior est Jure.

(Co. Litt. 14 a.)

He has the better title who was first in point of time.

The title of the finder to unappropriated land or chattels must evidently depend either upon the law of nature, upon international law, or upon the laws of that particular community to which he belongs. According to the law of nature, there can be no doubt that priority of occupancy alone constitutes a valid title, *quod nullius est id ratione naturali occupanti conceditur;*[1] but this rule has been so much restricted by the advance of civilization, by international laws, and by the civil and exclusive ordinances of each separate state, that it has comparatively little practical application at the present day. It is, indeed, true, that an unappropriated tract of land, or a desert island, may legitimately be seized and reduced into possession by the first occupant, and, consequently, that the title to colonial possessions may, and in some cases does, in fact, depend upon priority of occupation. But within the limits of this country, and between subjects, it is apprehended that the maxim which we here propose to consider has no longer any direct application as regards the acquisition of title to reality by entry and occupation. It was, indeed, formerly held, that where a tenant *pur autre vie* died, living the *cestui que* **vie*, the party who first entered upon the land thus left untenanted became entitled to the residue of the estate therein; but the law upon this subject has been much modified by successive enactments, and such estate, if not devised, would, under the circumstances supposed, now vest in the personal representatives of the deceased.[2] It is, moreover, a general rule, that whenever the owner or person actually seised of land dies intestate and without heir, the law vests the ownership of such land either in the crown,[3] or in the subordinate lord of the fee by escheat;[4] and this is in accordance with the spirit of the ancient feudal doctrine expressed in the maxim, *Quod nullius est, est domini regis.*[5]

[*354]

On the maxim, *Prior tempore, potior jure*, may depend, however, the right of property in treasure trove, in wreck, derelicts,[6] waifs,

[1] D. 41. 1. 3; I. 2. 1. 12.

[2] See 2 Com. by Broom & Hadley 268–272.

[3] So, "there is no doubt that, by the law of the land, the crown is entitled to the undisposed of *personal estate* of any person who happens to die without next of kin:" 14 Sim. 18; Robson *v.* A.-G., 10 Cl. & Fin. 497; Dyke *v.* Walford, 5 Moore P. C. C. 434.

[4] 2 Com. by Broom & Hadley 397.

[5] Fleta, lib. 3; Bac. Abr., "*Prerogative*" (B).

[6] Goods are "'derelict' which have been voluntarily abandoned and given up as worthless, the mind of the owner being alive to the circumstances at the time:" per Tindal, C. J., Legge *v.* Boyd, 1 C. B. 112 (50 E. C. L. R.).

and estrays, which, being *bona vacantia*, belong by the law of nature to the first occupant or finder, but which have, in some cases, been annexed to the supreme power by the positive laws of the state.[1] "There are," moreover, "some few things which, notwithstanding the general introduction and continuance of property, must still unavoidably remain in common; being such that nothing but an usufructuary *property is capable of being had in them; and therefore they still belong to the first occupant during the time he holds possession of them, and no longer. Such (among others) are the elements of light, air and water, which a man may occupy by means of his windows, his garden, his mills, and other conveniences. Such, also, are the generality of those animals which are said to be *feræ naturæ*, or of a wild and untamable disposition: [2] which any man may seize upon, and keep for his own use or pleasure. All these things, so long as they remain in possession, every man has a right to enjoy without disturbance; but, if once they escape from his custody, or he voluntarily abandons the use of them, they return to the common stock, and any man else has an equal right to seize and enjoy them afterwards."[3]

[*355]

So, the finder of a chattel lying apparently without an owner may, by virtue of the maxim under notice, acquire a special property therein.[4]

[1] The reader is referred for information on these subjects to 2 Com. by Broom & Hadley, Chap. VIII.

[2] See Rigg *v.* Earl of Lonsdale, 1 H. & N. 923; s. c., 11 Exch. 654; followed in Blades *v.* Higgs, 12 C. B. N. S. 501 (104 E. C. L. R.); Morgan *v.* Earl of Abergavenny, 8 C. B. 768 (65 E. C. L. R.); Ford *v.* Tynte, 31 L. J. Chanc. 177; Hannam *v.* Mockett, 2 B. & C. 934 (9 E. C. L. R.); Ibottson *v.* Peat, 3 H. & C. 644.

[3] 2 Com. by Broom & Hadley 12; Wood Civ. L., 3d ed., 82; Holden *v.* Smallbrooke, Vaugh. 187. See Acton *v.* Blundell, 12 M. & W. 324, 333; Judgm., Embrey *v.* Owen, 6 Exch. 369, 372; Chasemore *v.* Richards, 2 H. & N. 168; s. c., 7 H. L. Cas. 349.

[4] Armory *v.* Delamirie, 1 Stra. 504 (cited White *v.* Mullett, 6 Exch. 7; and distinguished in Buckley *v.* Gross, 3 B. & S. 564 (113 E. C. L. R.)); Bridges *v.* Hawkesworth, 21 L. J. Q. B. 75. See also Wallar *v.* Drakeford, 1 E. & B. 749 (72 E. C. L. R.); Mortimer *v.* Cradock (C. P.), 7 Jur. 45; Merry *v.* Green, 7 M. & W. 623.

"There is no authority," however, "nor sound reason for saying that the goods of several persons which are accidentally mixed together thereby absolutely cease to be the property of their several owners, and become *bona*

In accordance with the maxim, *Qui prior est tempore*, [*356] **potior est jure*, the rule in descents is, that amongst males of equal degree the eldest shall inherit land in preference to the others, unless, indeed, there is a particular custom to the contrary; as in the case of gavelkind, by which land descends to all the males of equal degree together; or borough English, according to which the youngest son, and not the eldest, succeeds on the death of his father; or burgage tenure, which prevails in certain towns, and is characterized by special customs.[1] Where A. had three sons, B., C. and D., and D., the youngest, died, leaving a daughter E., and then A. purchased lands in borough English and died, it was held, in accordance with the custom, that the lands should go to E.[2] The right of primogeniture above mentioned does not, however, exist amongst females, and therefore, if a person dies possessed of land, leaving daughters only, they will take jointly as coparceners.[3]

Further, it is a general rule, that, where there are two conflicting titles, the elder shall be preferred, and of this one instance has already been noticed in considering the law of remitter; for, if a disseisor lets the land to a disseisee for years, or at will, and the latter enters, the law will say that he is in on his ancient and better title.[4] So, where there are conflicting rights as to real property, courts of equity will inquire, not which party was first in possession, but under what instrument he *was in posses- [*357] sion, and when his right is dated in point of time; or, if there be no instrument, they will ask when did the right arise—who had the prior right?[5] It forms, moreover, the general rule between encumbrancers and purchasers, that he whose assignment

vacantia." Judgm., Spence *v.* Union Marine Ins. Co., L. R. 3 C. P. 438; *ante*, p. 286.

[1] 2 Com. by Broom & Hadley 168, 170, 383. See Muggleton *v.* Barnett, 1 H. & N. 282; s. c., 2 Id. 653.

[2] Clements *v.* Scudamore, 2 Ld. Raym. 1024.

[3] 2 Com. by Broom & Hadley 356. In Godfrey *v.* Bullock, 1 Roll. 623, n. (3); cited 2 Ld. Raym. 1027; the custom was, that, in default of issue male, the eldest daughter should have the land.

[4] Noy, Max., 9th ed., p. 53; Co. Litt. 347 b; Wing. Max., p. 159; *ante*, p. 213.

[5] Argument of Sir E. Sugden in Cholmondeley *v.* Clinton, 2 Meriv. 239; Scott *v.* Scott, 4 H. L. Cas. 1065, 1082.

of an equitable interest in a fund is first in order of time, has, by virtue of that circumstance alone, the better right to call for the possession of the fund.[1] This rule prevails amongst mortgagees, who are considered purchasers *pro tanto;* and where, therefore, of three mortgages, the first is bought in by the owner of the third, such third mortgagee thereby acquires the legal title, and, having thus got the law on his side, with equal equity, will be permitted to tack the first and third mortgages together to the exclusion of the second;[2] and thus the priority of equitable titles may be changed by the diligence of one of the claimants in obtaining the legal estate to himself, or to a trustee, for the protection of his equitable interest.[3]

It will, however, be borne in mind that the doctrine of tacking only applies where the legal has been annexed to the equitable [*358] estate in the manner above indicated; *where, therefore, the legal estate is outstanding, the several encumbrancers will be paid off according to their actual priority in point of time, and in strict accordance with the maxim, *Prior tempore, potior jure.*[4] Indeed, it may be laid down as a general rule that, as between mere equitable claims, equity will give no preference, and mortgages, judgments, statutes and recognizances will be alike payable, according to their respective priority of date.[5] We may add, also, that a prior lien gives a prior claim, which is entitled to prior satisfaction out of the fund upon which it attaches, unless such lien either be intrinsically defective, or be displaced by some act of the party

[1] "Grantees and encumbrancers claiming in equity take and are ranked according to the dates of their securities, and the maxim applies *Qui prior est tempore, potior est in jure.* The first grantee is *potior*, that is *potentior*. He has a better and superior, because a prior equity:" per Lord Westbury, C., Phillips *v.* Phillips, 31 L. J. Chanc. 325.

[2] Willoughby *v.* Willoughby, 1 T. R. 773, 774; Robinson *v.* Davison, 1 Bro. C. C., 5th ed., 61; Brace *v.* Duchess of Marlborough, 2 P. Wms. 491; 1 My. & K. 297; 2 Sim. 257. See Hopkinson *v.* Rolt, 9 H. L. Cas. 514. "The doctrine of tacking is founded on an application of the equitable maxims—that *he who seeks equity shall do equity to the person from whom he requires it*—and *where equities are equal, the law shall prevail.*" Coote Mortg., 3d ed., 385.

[3] 3 Prest. Abs. Tit. 274, 275.

[4] Brace *v.* Duchess of Marlborough, 2 P. Wms. 491, 495; cited per Lord Hardwicke, C., Willoughby *v.* Willoughby, 1 T. R. 773.

[5] Coote Mortg., 3d ed., 410. See also 2 Com. by Broom & Hadley 310.

holding it, which may operate in a court of law or equity to postpone his right to that of a subsequent claimant.[1]

In the case of hypothecation bonds, however, the last executed must be first paid. "According to the rule of law applicable to instruments of this description," as observed by Lord Stowell, "that which is last in point of time must, in respect of payment, supersede and take precedence of the others."[2]

On the same principle, a mortgagee may recover in ejectment, without previously giving notice to quit, against a tenant who claims under a lease from the mortgagor, granted *after* the mortgage, and without the privity of the mortgagee; for the tenant stands exactly in the place of the mortgagor, and the possession of the [*359] *mortgagor cannot be considered as holding out a false appearance, since it is of the very nature of the transaction that the mortgagor should continue in possession; and whenever one of two innocent parties must be a loser, then the rule applies, *Qui prior est tempore, potior est jure.* If, in the instance just given, one party must suffer, it is he who has not used due diligence in looking into the title.[3]

It may, in pursuance of these remarks, be almost unnecessary to call to mind, that, in very many cases where a question arises as to the title to goods, it does, in fact, resolve itself into this consideration,—in whom did the title first become vested? Thus, it is a general rule of the law of England, that a man who has no authority to sell cannot, by making a sale, transfer the property to another;[4] that is to say, he cannot, in this manner, divest of his property the party previously entitled. To this rule there is, indeed, one exception, viz., the case of a sale of goods in market overt;[5] which, however, does not bind the crown.[6] The law relat-

[1] See Judgm., Rankin *v.* Scott, 12 Wheat. (U. S.) R. 179.

[2] 1 Dods. Adm. R. 2. The Betsey, 1 Dods. Adm. R. 289; The Rhadamanthe, Id. 201, 204.

[3] Keech *v.* Hall, Dougl. 21. See Judgm., Dearle *v.* Hall, 3 Russ. R. 20. As to the relation of mortgagor and mortgagee, see, further, Judgm., Trent *v.* Hunt, 9 Exch. 21, 22; followed in Snell *v.* Finch, 13 C. B. N. S. 651 (106 E. C. L. R.); Moss *v.* Gallimore, 1 Smith L. C., 6th ed., 561, and note thereto; Hickman *v.* Machin, 4 H. & N. 716, 722.

[4] Per Abbott, C. J., Dyer *v.* Pearson, 3 B. & C. 42 (10 E. C. L. R.).

[5] 3 B. & C. 42 (10 E. C. L. R.); Peer *v.* Humphrey, 2 A. & E. 495 (29 E. C. L. R.). See Scattergood *v.* Sylvester, 15 Q. B. 506 (69 E. C. L. R.).

[6] Chit. Pre. Cr. 195, 285.

ing to the sale of goods and to market overt will be again adverted to under the maxim, *Caveat emptor*, to which very comprehensive principle it is usually referred.[1]

We may further observe, that the respective rights of execution [*360] creditors *inter se*,[2] must often be determined *by applying the maxim as to priority under consideration. For instance, where two writs of execution against the same person are delivered to the sheriff, he is bound to execute that writ first which was first delivered to him;[3] unless, indeed, the first writ or the possession held under it were fraudulent, in which case the goods seized cannot be considered as in the custody of the law at the date of the delivery of the second writ, which latter, therefore, shall have priority; and where goods seized under a *fi. fa.* founded on a judgment fraudulent against creditors remain in the sheriff's hands, or are capable of being seized by him, he ought to sell, or seize and sell, such goods under a subsequent writ of *fi. fa.* founded on a *bonâ fide* debt.[4] Where, moreover, a party is in possession of goods apparently the property of a debtor, the sheriff who has a *fi. fa.* to execute is bound to inquire whether the party in possession is so *bonâ fide*, and, if he find that the possession is held under a fraudulent or an unregistered[5] bill of sale, he is bound to treat it as null and void, and levy under the writ.[6]

Further, by the stat. 29 Car. 2, c. 3, s. 16, it was enacted that "no writ of *fieri facias*, or other writ of execution, shall bind the property of the goods of the party against whom such writ of [*361] execution issued forth, but from the time that such writ shall be delivered to the *sheriff;" the operation of this

[1] *Post*, Chap. IX.

[2] See Anderson *v.* Radcliffe, E., B. & E. 806 (96 E. C. L. R.).

[3] Per Ashhurst, J., Hutchinson *v.* Johnston, 1 T. R. 131; Judgm., Drewe *v.* Lainson, 11 A. & E. 537 (39 E. C. L. R.); Jones *v.* Atherton, 7 Taunt. 56 (2 E. C. L. R.); 29 Car. 2, c. 3, s. 16. See Aldred *v.* Constable, 6 Q. B. 370 (51 E. C. L. R.); Atkinson Sher. L., 3d ed., 179.

[4] Christopherson *v.* Burton, 3 Exch. 160; Shattock *v.* Carden, 6 Exch. 725; Imray *v.* Magnay, 11 M. & W. 267; Drewe *v.* Lainson, 11 A. & E. 529 (39 E. C. L. R.).

[5] See Richard *v.* James, L. R. 2 Q. B. 285.

[6] Lovick *v.* Crowder, 8 B. & C. 135, 137 (15 E. C. L. R.); Warmoll *v.* Young, 5 B. & C. 660, 666 (11 E. C. L. R.). See also the cases cited, arg. 12 M. & W. 664.

clause being that if, after the writ was so delivered, the defendant made an assignment of the goods, except in market overt, the sheriff might take them in execution.[1] But now, by stat. 19 & 20 Vict. c. 97, s. 1, "no writ of *fieri facias* or other writ of execution, and no writ of attachment against the goods of a debtor, shall prejudice the title to such goods acquired by any person *bonâ fide* and for a valuable consideration before the actual seizure or attachment thereof by virtue of such writ;" provided such person had not, at the time when he acquired such title, notice that such or any other writ of execution or attachment had been delivered to and remained unexecuted in the hands of the sheriff.[2]

It has been held, that if a writ of *fi. fa.* be delivered to the sheriff, and notice be subsequently given to restrain execution, the writ cannot be considered as in the hands of the sheriff to be executed, within the meaning of the section of the statute just cited, and in this case, therefore, the sheriff will be bound to execute a subsequent writ of *fi. fa.*, which may be issued during such stay of execution, and before order given to proceed with the execution of the first-mentioned writ.[3]

We may, in the next place, observe, that the law *relative to patents and to copyright is altogether referable to the above maxim as to priority. [*362] With respect to patents, the general rule is, that the original inventor of a machine, who has first brought his invention into actual use, is entitled to priority as patentee, and that consequently a subsequent original inventor will be unable to avail himself of his invention; and this is evidently in accordance with the strict rule, *qui prior est tempore, potior est jure.*[4] If, therefore, several persons simultaneously discover the

[1] Per Lord Hardwicke, C., Lowthal *v.* Tonkins, 2 Eq. Cas. Abr. 381; cited 4 East 539. "That the general property in goods, even after seizure, remains in the debtor, is clear from this, that the debtor may after seizure, by payment, suspend the sale and stop the execution;" per Patteson, J., 9 Bing. 138 (23 E. C. L. R.); adopted per Alderson, B., Playfair *v.* Musgrove, 14 M. & W. 246. And see, further, as to the statute, *supra*, per Lord Ellenborough, C. J., 4 East 538; Briggs *v.* Sowry, 8 M. & W. 729, 739; Giles *v.* Grover, 9 Bing. 128 (23 E. C. L. R.).

[2] See per Mellor, J., Hobson *v.* Thelluson, L. R. 2 Q. B. 651.

[3] Hunt *v.* Hooper, 12 M. & W. 664; Sturgis *v.* Bishop of London, 7 E. & B. 542, 553 (90 E. C. L. R.). See Levi *v.* Abbott, 4 Exch. 588, 590.

[4] See 3 Wheaton (U. S.) R., App. 24.

same thing, the party first communicating it to the public under the protection of the patent becomes the legal inventor, and is entitled to the benefit of it.[1]

A person, however, to be entitled to a patent for an invention must be *the first and true inventor;*[2] so that, if there be any public user thereof by himself or others prior to the granting of the patent,[3] or if the invention has been previously made public in this country by a description contained in a work, whether written or printed, which has been publicly circulated, one who afterwards takes out a patent for it will not be considered as the true and first inventor within the meaning of the stat. 21 Jac. 1, c. 3, even though, in the latter case, he has not borrowed his invention from such publication.[4] Although, moreover, it is generally true that a [*363] new principle, *or *modus operandi*, carried into practical and useful effect by the use of new instruments, or by a new combination of old ones, is an original invention, for which a patent may be supported;[5] yet, if a person merely substitutes, for part of a patented invention, some well-known equivalent, whether chemical or mechanical, this, being in truth but a colorable variation, will amount to an infringement of the patent;[6] and where letters patent were granted for improvements in apparatus for the manufacture of certain chemical substances, and the jury found that the apparatus was not new, but that the patentee's mode of connecting the parts of that apparatus was new, the court, in an action for an alleged infringement of the patent, directed the verdict

[1] Per Abbott, C. J., Forsyth *v.* Riviere, Webs. Pat. Cas. 97, note; per Tindal, C. J., Cornish *v.* Keene, Id. 508.

[2] See Norman Pat., Chap. 8.

[3] The Househill Coal and Iron Co. *v.* Neilson, 9 Cl. & Fin. 788. See Brown *v.* Annandale, Webs. Pat. Cas. 433. And generally, in regard to the question, what is such prior user as will avoid a patent, see Norman Pat., Chap. 5.

[4] Stead *v.* Williams, 7 M. & Gr. 818 (49 E. C. L. R.). Stead *v.* Anderson, 4 C. B. 806 (56 E. C. L. R.). See Booth *v.* Kennard, 2 H. & N. 84.

[5] Boulton *v.* Bull, 2 H. Bla. 463; s. c., 8 T. R. 95; Hall's Case, Webs. Pat. Cas. 98; cited, per Lord Abinger, C. B., Losh *v.* Hague, Id. 207, 208; Holmes *v.* London and North-Western R. C., 12 C. B., 831, 851 (74 E. C. L. R.). See Tetley *v.* Easton, 2 C. B. N. S. 106 (89 E. C. L. R.); Patent Bottle Envelope Co. *v.* Seymer, 5 Id. 164.

[6] See Heath *v.* Unwin, 13 M. & W. 583; s. c., 12 C. B. 522 (74 E. C. L. R.); 5 H. L. Cas. 505. And see further on this subject, Newton *v.* Grand Junction R. C., 5 Exch. 331; Newton *v.* Vaucher, 6 Exch. 859.

to be entered for the defendant, upon an issue taken as to the novelty of the invention;[1] and "no sounder or more wholesome doctrine" in reference to this subject was ever established than that a patent cannot be had "for a well-known mechanical contrivance merely when it is applied in a manner or to a purpose which is not quite the same, but is analogous to the manner or the purpose in or to which it has been hitherto notoriously used."[2]

*"A copyright is the exclusive right of multiplying copies of an original work or composition, and consequently preventing others from so doing,"[3] the great object of the law of copyright being "to stimulate by means of the protection secured to literary labor, the composition and publication to the world of works of learning and utility;"[4] and the right of an author accordingly depends on the same principle as that of a patentee, viz., priority of invention or composition and publication. It was, indeed, at one time thought, that a foreigner resident abroad would by first publishing his work in Great Britain acquire a copyright therein;[5] but this interpretation of the repealed[6] stat. 8 Anne, c. 19, was declared by the highest tribunal to be erroneous in Jefferys *v.* Boosey;[7] and it is clear that a foreigner, whether resident here or not, cannot have an English copyright, if he has first published his work abroad, before any publication of it in this country.[8] But an [*364]

[1] Gamble *v.* Kurtz, 3 C. B. 425 (54 E. C. L. R.).

[2] Per Lord Westbury, C., Harwood *v.* Great North R. C., 11 H. L. Cas. 682.

In order to obtain an extension of the term of letters patent, the petitioner must establish, 1, that the invention is of considerable merit; 2, that it is of public utility; and 3, that there has been inadequate remuneration. In re McDougal's Patent, L. R. 2 P. C. 1; In re McInnes' Patent, Id. 54.

[3] Judgm., 14 M. & W. 316. See, generally, as to copyright, Millar *v.* Taylor, 4 Burr. 2303; Jefferys *v.* Boosey, 4 H. L. Cas. 815; s. c., 6 Exch. 580; Routledge *v.* Low, L. R. 3 H. L. 100; Sweet *v.* Benning, 16 C. B. 459 (81 E. C. L. R.).

The term of copyright in books is now fixed by stat. 5 & 6 Vict. c. 45. See also 10 & 11 Vict. c. 95.

As to copyright in works of art, see 25 & 26 Vict. c. 68; Gambart *v.* Ball, 14 C. B. N. S. 306 (108 E. C. L. R.); approved in Graves *v.* Ashford, L. R. 2 C. P. 410.

[4] Per Lord Cairns, C., L. R. 3 H. L. 108.

[5] See the cases cited, 4 H. L. Cas. 959, 960, 974.

[6] See 5 & 6 Vict. c. 45, s. 1.

[7] 4 H. L. Cas. 815, where the cases bearing on the above subject are collected.

[8] Chappell *v.* Purday, 14 M. & W. 303; Boucicault *v.* Delafield, 33 L. J.

alien friend, who, during his temporary residence in a British colony, publishes in the United Kingdom a book of which he is [*365] the author, is, under the *stat. 5 & 6 Vict. c. 45, entitled to the benefit of English copyright.[1]

Lastly, we may observe that the maxim under consideration may sometimes be applied in reference to the practice of the courts of law.[2]

---

§ II.—PROPERTY—ITS RIGHTS AND LIABILITIES.

In this section are contained remarks upon the legitimate mode of enjoying property, the limits and extent of that enjoyment, and the rights and liabilities attaching to it. The maxims commented upon, in connection with this subject, are four in number: that a man shall so use his own property as not to injure his neighbor—that the owner of the soil is entitled likewise to that which is above and underneath it—that what is annexed to the freehold becomes, in many cases, subject to the same rights of ownership—that "every man's house is his castle."

SIC UTERE TUO UT ALIENUM NON LÆDAS.

(9 Rep. 59.)

Enjoy your own property in such a manner as not to injure that of another person.[3]

A man must enjoy his own property in such a manner as not to [*366] invade the legal rights of his neighbor—*Expedit *reipublicæ ne suâ re quis male utatur.*[4] "Every man," observed

Chanc. 38. See Beard v. Egerton, 3 C. B. 97 (54 E. C. L. R.); 7 Vict. c. 12, s. 19; 15 & 16 Vict. c. 12.

[1] Routledge v. Low, L. R. 3 H. L. 100.

[2] See per Tindal, C. J., 3 Bing. N. C. 260 (32 E. C. L. R.).

[3] Such is the literal translation of the above maxim; its true legal meaning would rather be, "So use your own property as not to injure *the rights* of another." See arg. Jeffries v. Williams, 5 Exch. 797.

The maxim is cited, commented on, or applied, in Bonomi v. Backhouse, E., B. & E. 637, 639, 643 (96 E. C. L. R.); s. c., 9 H. L. Cas. 511 (in connection with which see Smith v. Thackerah, L. R. 1 C. P. 564); Chasemore v. Richards, 7 H. L. Cas. 388; per Pollock, C. B., Bagnall v. London and North-Western R. C., 7 H. & N. 440; In re Groucott v. Williams, 4 B. & S. 149, 155–6 (116 E. C. L. R.).

[4] I. 1. 8. 2.

Lord Truro,[1] "is restricted against using his property to the prejudice of others;" and, as further remarked by the same learned lord, "the principle embodied in the maxim, *Sic utere tuo ut alienum non lædas*, applies to the public in at least as full force as to individuals. There are other maxims equally expressive of the principle—*Nihil quod est inconveniens est licitum*,[2] and *Salus reipublicæ suprema lex*;"[3] to so large a class of cases, indeed, and under circumstances so dissimilar, is the rule before us capable of being applied, that we can here merely suggest some few leading illustrations of it, omitting references to many reported decisions which might be found, perhaps, equally well to exemplify its meaning.

In the first place, then, we must observe that the invasion of an established right will in general, *per se*, constitute an injury, for which damages are recoverable; for in all civil acts our law does not so much regard the intent of the actor as the loss and damage of the party suffering. In trespass *qu. cl. fr.*, the defendant pleaded, that he had land adjoining plaintiff's close, and upon it a hedge of thorns; that he cut the thorns, and that they, *ipso invito*, fell upon the plaintiff's land, and the defendant took them off as soon as he could, which was the *same trespass, &c. On demurrer, judgment was given for the plaintiff, on the ground that, though a man do a lawful thing, yet, if any damage thereby befalls another, he shall be answerable if he could have avoided it. Thus, if a man lop a tree, and the boughs fall upon another, *ipso invito*, yet an action lies; so, if a man shoot at a butt, and hurt another unawares, an action lies. A. has land through which a river runs to turn B.'s mill; A. lops the trees growing on the river side, and the loppings accidentally impede the progress of the stream, which hinders the mill from working: A. will be liable. So, if I am building my own house, and a piece of timber falls on my neighbor's house, and injures it, an action lies; or, if a man assault me, and I lift up my staff to defend myself, and in lifting it strike another, an action lies by that person, and yet I did a lawful thing; and the reason of all these cases is, because he that is damaged ought to be recompensed; but it is otherwise in criminal cases, for in them it is generally true, as we have seen in

[*367]

[1] Egerton *v.* Earl Brownlow, 4 H. L. Cas. 195.

[2] *Ante*, p. 186.

[3] *Ante*, p. 1.

the preceding chapter, that *actus non facit reum nisi mens sit rea*:[1] the intent and the act must concur to constitute the crime.[2]

Accordingly, in considering whether a defendant is liable to a plaintiff for damage which the latter may have sustained, the question in general is, not whether the defendant has acted with due care and caution, but [*368] *whether his acts have occasioned the damage; and this doctrine is founded on good sense. For when one person in managing his own affairs causes, however innocently, damage to another, it is obviously only just that he should be the party to suffer. He is bound *sic uti suo ut non lædat alienum*.[3]

In the next place it may be laid down, as a true proposition, that, although bare negligence unproductive of damage to another will not give a right of action, negligence causing damage will do so:[4] negligence being defined to be "the omission to do something which a reasonable man, guided upon those considerations which ordinarily regulate the conduct of human affairs, would do, or doing something which a prudent and reasonable man would not do;"[5] negligence, moreover, not being "absolute or intrinsic," but "always relative to some circumstances of time, place, or person."[6]

[1] See Lambert *v.* Bessey, T. Raym. 422; Weaver *v.* Ward, Hob. 134; per Blackstone, J., Scott *v.* Shepherd, 3 Wils. 403; per Lord Kenyon, C. J., Haycraft *v.* Creasy, 2 East 104; Turberville *v.* Stampe, 1 Ld. Raym. 264; cited Jones *v.* Festiniog R. C., L. R. 3 Q. B. 736; recognized, Vaughan *v.* Menlove, 3 Bing. N. C. 468 (32 E. C. L. R.); Piggot *v.* Eastern Counties R. C., 3 C. B. 229 (54 E. C. L. R.); Grocers' Co. *v.* Donne, 3 Bing. N. C. 34 (32 E. C. L. R.); Aldridge *v.* Great Western R. C., 4 Scott N. R. 156.

[2] Per Lord Kenyon, C. J., Fowler *v.* Padget, 7 T. R. 514; cited, 3 Inst. 54; Borradaile *v.* Hunter, 5 Scott N. R. 429, 430.

[3] Per Lord Cranworth, Rylands *v.* Fletcher, L. R. 3 H. L. 341, citing Lambert *v.* Bessey, *supra*, n. 1.

[4] See Broom's Com., 4th ed., 656; Whitehouse *v.* Birmingham Can. Co., 27 L. J. Ex. 25; Bayley *v.* Wolverhampton Waterworks Co., 6 H. & N. 241; Duckworth *v.* Johnson, 4 H. & N. 653.

[5] Per Alderson, B., Blyth *v.* Birmingham Waterworks Co., 11 Exch. 784.

Laches has been defined to be "a neglect to do something which by law a man is obliged to do;" per Lord Ellenborough, C. J., Sebag *v.* Abitbol, 4 M. & S. 462; adopted per Abbott, C. J., Turner *v.* Hayden, 4 B. & C. 2 (10 E. C. L. R.).

[6] Judgm., Degg *v.* Midland R. C., 1 H. & N. 781; approved in Potter *v.* Faulkner, 1 B. & S. 800 (101 E. C. L. R.). As to proof of negligence, *ante*, p. 110, n. 2; Assop *v.* Yates, 2 H. & N. 768; Perren *v.* Monmouthshire R.

*Having thus premised, the following instances will serve to show in what manner the maxim which we have placed at the head of these remarks is applied, to impose restrictions, first, upon the enjoyment of property,[1] and, secondly, upon the acts and conduct of each individual member of the community. In illustration of the first branch of the subject, we may observe, that, if a man builds a house so close to mine that his roof overhangs mine, and throws the water off upon it, this is a nuisance, for which an action will lie.[2] So, an action will lie, if, by an erection on his own land, he obstructs my ancient lights and windows; for a man has no right to erect a new edifice on his ground so as to prejudice what has long been enjoyed by another[3]—*ædificare in tuo proprio solo non licet quod alteri noceat.*[4] In like manner, if a man, by negligence and carelessness in pulling down his house, occasion damage to, or accelerate the fall of, his neighbor's, he will be clearly liable,[5] although the mere circumstance of juxtaposition does not, [*369]

C., 11 C. B. 855 (73 E. C. L. R.); Vose *v.* Lancashire and Yorkshire R. C., 2 H. & N. 728; Harris *v.* Anderson, 14 C. B. N. S. 499 (108 E. C. L. R.); Reeve *v.* Palmer, 5 C. B. N. S. 84 (94 E. C. L. R.); Manchester, &c., R. C., app., Fullerton, resp., 14 C. B. N. S. 54 (108 E. C. L. R.); Roberts *v.* Great Western R. C., 4 C. B. N. S. 506 (93 E. C. L. R.); North *v.* Smith, 10 C. B. N. S. 572 (100 E. C. L. R.); Manley *v.* St. Helen's Canal and R. C., 2 H. & N. 840; Willoughby *v.* Horridge, 12 C. B. 742 (74 E. C. L. R.); Templeman *v.* Haydon, Id. 507; Melville *v.* Doidge, 6 C. B. 450; Grote *v.* Chester and Holyhead R. C., 2 Exch. 251; Dansey *v.* Richardson, 3 E. & B. 144 (72 E. C. L. R.); Roberts *v.* Smith, 2 H. & N. 213; Cashill *v.* Wright, 6 E. & B. 891 (88 E. C. L. R.); Holder *v.* Soulby, 8 C. B. N. S. 254 (98 E. C. L. R.).

[1] See per Holt, C. J., Tenant *v.* Goldwin, 2 Ld. Raym. 1092–3, followed in Hodgkinson *v.* Ennor, 4 B. & S. 241 (116 E. C. L. R.).

[2] Penruddocke's Case, 5 Rep. 100; Fay *v.* Prentice, 1 C. B. 828 (50 E. C. L. R.).

[3] *Vide*, per Pollock, C. B., Bagnall *v.* London and North-Western R. C., 7 H. & N. 440; s. c., 1 H. & C. 544, which well illustrates the maxim commented on, *supra*. See Dodd *v.* Holme, 1 A. & E. 493 (28 E. C. L. R.); recognized, Bradbee *v.* Mayor, &c., of London, 5 Scott N. R. 120; Partridge *v.* Scott, 3 M. & W. 220; recognizing Wyatt *v.* Harrison, 3 B. & Ad. 871 (23 E. C. L. R.); Brown *v.* Windsor, 1 Cr. & J. 20.

[4] 3 Inst. 201.

[5] Bradbee *v.* Mayor, &c., of London, 5 Scott N. R. 120; per Lord Denman, C. J., Dodd *v.* Holme, 1 A. & E. 505 (28 E. C. L. R.). See Peyton *v.* Mayor, &c., of London, 9 B. & C. 725 (17 E. C. L. R.); Butler *v.* Hunter, 7 H. & N. 826, where the maxim *Respondeat superior* applied to exonerate the defendant from liability.

[*370] in the absence of any right of easement, render it *necessary for a person who pulls down his wall to give notice of his intention to the owner of an adjoining wall, nor is such person, if he be ignorant of the existence of the adjoining wall, bound to use extraordinary caution in pulling down his own.[1]

Neither is any "obligation towards a neighbor cast by law on the owner of a house, merely as such, to keep it repaired in a lasting and substantial manner: the only duty is to keep it in such a state that his neighbor may not be injured by its fall; the house may, therefore, be in a ruinous state, provided it be shored sufficiently, or the house may be demolished altogether."[2] Where, however, several houses belonging to the same owner are built together, so that each requires the support of the adjoining house, and the owner parts with one of these houses, the right to such support is not thereby lost.[3]

Where a person builds a house on his own land, which has been previously excavated to its extremity for mining purposes, it has been held that he does not thereby acquire a right to support for the house from the adjoining land of another; at least, such right will not be acquired until twenty years have elapsed since the house first stood on excavated land, and was in part supported by the adjoining land, in which case a *grant* from the owner of the adjoining land of such right to support may be inferred; and this case is an [*371] authority to show, that a man, by *building a house on the extremity of his own land, does not thereby acquire any right of easement for support, or otherwise, over the adjoining land of his neighbor. He has no right to load his own soil, so as to make it require the support of that of his neighbor, unless he has some grant to that effect.[4]

[1] Chadwick *v.* Trower, 6 Bing. N. C. 1; reversing s. c., 3 Bing. N. C. 334 (32 E. C. L. R.); cited 5 Scott N. R. 119; Grocers' Co. *v.* Donne, 3 Bing. N. C. 34 (37 E. C. L. R.); Davis *v.* London & Blackwall R. C., 2 Scott N. R. 74.
See further, as to the right to support by an adjacent house, Solomon *v.* Vintners' Co., 4 H. & N. 585, where the cases are collected.

[2] Judgm., Chauntler *v.* Robinson, 4 Exch. 170. As to the right of support for a sewer, see Metropolitan Board of Works *v.* Metropolitan R. C., L. R. 4 C. P. 192.

[3] Richards *v.* Rose, 9 Exch. 218.

[4] Partridge *v.* Scott, 3 M. & W. 220, 228; recognized, Acton *v.* Blundell, 12 M. & W. 352; Judgm., Gayford *v.* Nicholls, 9 Exch. 707, 708. See Jeffries *v.*

As between the owner of the surface of the land and the owner of the subjacent mineral strata, and as between the owners of adjoining mines, questions frequently arise involving a consideration of the maxim, *Sic utere tuo ut alienum non lædas*,[1] and needing an interpretation of it not too much infringing on the rights of ownership. In Humphreys *v.* Brogden,[2] the plaintiff, being the occupier of the surface of land, sued the defendant in case, for negligently and improperly, and without leaving any sufficient pillars and supports, and contrary to the custom of mining in that district, working the subjacent minerals, *per quod* the surface gave way. Issue being joined on a plea of not guilty to this declaration, it was proved at the trial that plaintiff was in occupation of the surface, which was not built upon, and defendant of the subjacent minerals, but there was no evidence showing how the occupation of the superior and inferior strata came into *different hands. The [*372] jury found that the defendant had worked the mines carefully and according to the custom, but without leaving sufficient support for the surface. And the Court of Q. B. held, that upon this finding the verdict should be entered for the plaintiff, because of common right the owner of the surface is entitled to support from the subjacent strata.

The *primâ facie* rights and obligations of parties so situated relatively to each other, as above supposed, may, however, be varied by the production of title deeds or other evidence.[3]

In Smith *v.* Kenrick,[4] the mutual obligations of the owners of

Williams, 5 Exch. 792, 800; followed in Bibby *v.* Carter, 4 H. & N. 153. As to the right of the owner of land to lateral support, see, also, Judgm., 12 Q. B. 743 (64 E. C. L. R.); Hunt *v.* Peake, cited *ante*, p. 196, n. 3.

[1] See In re Groucott *v.* Williams, 4 B. & S. 149 (116 E. C. L. R.).

[2] 12 Q. B. 739 (64 E. C. L. R.) (with which compare Hilton *v.* Whitehead, Id. 734); Haines *v.* Roberts, 7 E. & B. 625 (90 E. C. L. R.); s. c., 6 E. & B. 643 (88 E. C. L. R.); Rowbotham *v.* Wilson, 8 H. L. Cas. 348; s. c., 8 E. & B. 123 (92 E. C. L. R.), 6 Id. 593 (1 E. C. L. R.); Smart *v.* Morton, 5 E. & B. 30 (85 E. C. L. R.); Backhouse *v.* Bonomi, 9 H. L. Cas. 503; s. c., E., B. & E. 503 (96 E. C. L. R.); Smith *v.* Thackerah, L. R. 1 C. P. 564; Blackett *v.* Bradley, 1 B. & S. 940 (101 E. C. L. R.).

[3] Per Lord Campbell, C. J., in Humphries *v.* Brogden, and Smart *v.* Morton, *supra;* Rowbotham *v.* Wilson, *supra.*

See Solomon *v.* Vintners' Co., 4 H. & N. 599, 601.

There is no right, such as above considered, to the support of water: Popplewell *v.* Hodkinson, L. R. 4 Ex. 248.

[4] 7 C. B. 515, 564 (62 E. C. L. R.), with which compare Baird *v.* Williamson,

adjoining mines were much considered by the Court of C. P., who conclude as follows—that "it would seem to be the natural right of each of the owners of two adjoining coal mines—neither being subject to any servitude to the other—to work his own in the manner most convenient and beneficial to himself, although the natural consequence may be that some prejudice will accrue to the owner of the adjoining mine, so long as that does not arise from the negligent or malicious conduct of the party."

From the above and similar cases we may infer that much caution is needed in applying the maxim now under our notice—in determining how far it may, on a given state of facts, restrict the [*373] mode in which property may be *enjoyed or used; a principle here applicable under very dissimilar circumstances being, that "If a man brings or uses a thing of a dangerous nature on his own land, he must keep it in at his own peril, and is liable for the consequences if it escapes and does injury to his neighbor."[1] "The person," therefore, "whose grass or corn is eaten down by the escaping cattle of his neighbor, or whose mine is flooded by the water from his neighbor's reservoir,[2] or whose cellar is invaded by the filth of his neighbor's privy, or whose habitation is made unhealthy by the fumes and noisome vapors of his neighbor's alkali works,[3] is damnified without any fault of his own; and it seems but reasonable and just, that the neighbor who has brought something on his own property, which was not naturally there, harmless to others so long as it is confined to his own property, but which he knows will be mischievous if it gets on his neighbor's, should be obliged to make good the damage which ensues if he does not succeed in confining it to his own property."[4]

15 C. B. N. S. 376 (109 E. C. L. R.), which is distinguished from Smith *v.* Kenrick, *supra*, by Lord Cranworth, Rylands *v.* Fletcher, L. R. 3 H. L. 341–2.

[1] Jones *v.* Festiniog R. C., L. R. 3 Q. B. 736; Rylands *v.* Fletcher, L. R. 3 H. L. 330, 339, 340, where many cases illustrating the text are collected.

[2] "Suppose A. has a drain through the lands of B. and C., and C. stops up the inlet into his land from B.'s, and A. nevertheless, knowing this, pours water in the drain and damages B., A. is liable to B." Judgm., Harrison *v.* Great Northern R. C., 3 H. & C. 238; Collins *v.* Middle Level Commissioners, L. R. 4 C. P. 279.

[3] St. Helen's Smelting Co. *v.* Tipping, 11 H. L. Cas. 642.

[4] Judgm., Fletcher *v.* Rylands, L. R. 1 Ex. 280, adopted per Lord Cairns, C., in s. c., L. R. 3 H. L. 340.

Again, the rule of law which governs the enjoyment of a stream flowing in its natural course over the surface of land belonging to different proprietors is well established, and is illustrative of the maxim under notice. According to this rule, each proprietor of the land has a right to the *advantage of the stream flowing in its natural course over his land, and to use the same [*374] as he pleases for any purposes of his own, provided that they be not inconsistent with a similar right in the proprietor of the land above or below; so that neither can any proprietor above diminish the quantity or injure the quality of the water, which would otherwise naturally descend; nor can any proprietor below throw back the water without the license or the grant of the proprietor above.[1] Where, therefore, the owner of land applies the stream running through it to the use of a mill newly erected, or to any other purpose, he may, if the stream is diverted or obstructed by the proprietor of land above, recover against such proprietor for the consequential injury to the mill; and the same principle seems to apply where the obstruction or diversion has taken place prior to the erection of the mill, unless, indeed, the owner of land higher up the stream has acquired a right to any particular mode of using the water by prescription, that is, by user continued until the presumption of a grant has arisen.[2]

What has been just said applies generally to surface water, flowing naturally over land—between which and water so artificially flowing the distinction is important as regards the mode of applying our principal maxim, and was thus recently explained:—

*"The flow of a natural stream creates natural rights and liabilities between all the riparian proprietors along [*375] the whole of its course. Subject to reasonable use by himself, each proprietor is bound to allow the water to flow on without altering the quantity or quality. These natural rights and liabilities may

[1] Mason *v.* Hill, 5 B. & Ad. 1 (27 E. C. L. R.); Wright *v.* Howard, 1 Sim. & Stu. 190; cited Judgm., 12 M. & W. 349; cited Judgm., Embrey *v.* Owen, 6 Exch. 368–373; Chasemore *v.* Richards, 7 H. L. Cas. 349; Rawstron *v.* Taylor, 11 Exch. 369; Broadbent *v.* Ramsbotham, Id. 602. See, also, Whaley *v.* Laing, 3 H. & N. 675, 901; Hipkins *v.* Birmingham and Staffordshire Gas Light Co., 6 H. & N. 250; s. c., 5 Id. 74; Hodgkinson *v.* Ennor, cited *ante*, p. 369.

[2] Judgm., Mason *v.* Hill, 5 B. & Ad. 25 (27 E. C. L. R.), where the Roman law upon this subject is briefly considered.

be altered by grant or by user of an easement to alter the stream, as by diverting, or fouling, or penning back, or the like. If the stream flows at its source by the operation of nature, that is, if it is a natural stream, the rights and liabilities of the party owning the land at its source are the same as those of the proprietors in the course below. If the stream flows at its source by the operation of man, that is, if it is an artificial stream, the owner of the land at its source or the commencement of the flow is not subject to any rights or liabilities towards any other person, in respect of the water of that stream. The owner of such land may make himself liable to duties in respect of such water by grant or contract; but the party claiming a right to compel performance of those duties must give evidence of such right beyond the mere suffering by him of the servitude of receiving such water."[1]

Rights and liabilities in respect of artificial streams when first flowing on the surface are entirely distinct from rights and liabilities in respect to natural streams so flowing. The water in an artificial stream flowing in the land of the party by whom it is caused to flow is the property of that party, and is not subject to any rights or liabilities in respect of other persons. If the stream so brought to the surface is made to flow upon the land of a neighbor without [*376] his consent, it is a wrong, *for which the party causing it so to flow is liable. If there is a grant by the neighbor, the terms of the grant regulate the rights and liabilities of the parties thereto. If there is uninterrupted user of the land of the neighbor for receiving the flow as of right for twenty years, such user is evidence that the land from which the water is sent into the neighbor's land has become the dominant tenement having a right to the easement of so sending the water, and that the neighbor's land has become subject to the easement of receiving that water. But such user of the easement of sending on the water of an artificial stream is of itself alone no evidence that the land from which the water is sent has become subject to the servitude of being bound to send on the water to the land of the neighbor below. The enjoyment of the easement is of itself no evidence that the party enjoying it has become subject to the servitude of being bound to exercise the easement for the benefit of the neighbor.

[1] Judgm., Gaved *v.* Martyn, 19 C. B. N. S. 759, 760 (115 E. C. L. R.), and cases there cited. See Nuttall *v.* Bracewell, L. R. 2 Ex. 1.

* * * A party by the mere exercise of a right to make an artificial drain into his neighbor's land, either from mine or surface, does not raise any presumption that he is subject to any duty to continue his artificial drain by twenty years' user, although there may be additional circumstances by which that presumption could be raised, or the right proved. Also, if it be proved that the stream was originally intended to have a permanent flow, or if the party by whom or on whose behalf the artificial stream was caused to flow is shown to have abandoned permanently, without intention to resume the works by which the flow was caused, and given up all right to and control over the stream, such stream may become subject to the laws relating to natural streams."[1]

*With respect to water flowing in a subterraneous course, it has been held, that, in this, the owner of land through [*377] which it flows has no right or interest (at all events, in the absence of an uninterrupted user of the right for more than twenty years) which will enable him to maintain an action against a landowner, who, in carrying on mining operations in his own land in the usual manner, drains away the water from the land of the first-mentioned owner, and lays his well dry;[2] for, according to the principle already stated, if a man digs a well in his own land, so close to the soil of his neighbor as to require the support of a rib of clay or of stone in his neighbor's land to retain the water in the well, no action would lie against the owner of the adjacent land for digging away such clay or stone, which is his own property, and thereby letting out the water; and it would seem to make no difference as to the legal rights of the parties if the well stands some distance within the plaintiff's boundary, and the digging by the defendant, which occasions the water to flow from the well, is some distance within the defendant's boundary, which is, in substance, the very case above stated.[3]

The principle which the above instances have been selected to

[1] Judgm., Gaved *v.* Martyn, 19 C. B. N. S. 758, 759, 760 (115 E. C. L. R.), and cases there cited.

[2] Acton *v.* Blundell, 12 M. & W. 324; Chasemore *v.* Richards, 2 H. & N. 168 (where see, particularly in reference to the maxim *supra*, per Coleridge, J., *diss.*); s. c., 7 H. L. Cas. 349; South Shields Waterworks Co. *v.* Cookson, 15 L. J. Ex. 315.

[3] Judgm., 12 M. & W. 352, 353.

illustrate, likewise applies where various rights, which are at particular times unavoidably inconsistent with each other, are exercised concurrently by different individuals: as, in the case of a highway, where right of common of pasture and right of common of turbary may exist at the same time; or of the ocean, [*378] *which in time of peace is the common highway of all;[1] in that of a right of free passage along the street, which right may be sometimes interrupted by the exercise of other rights;[2] or in that of a port or navigable river,[3] which may be likewise subject at times to temporary obstruction. In these and similar cases, where such different co-existing rights happen to clash, the maxim, *Sic utere tuo ut alienum non lædas*, will, it has been observed, generally serve as a clue to the labyrinth.[4] And, further, the possible jarring of pre-existing rights can furnish no warrant for an innovation which seeks to create a new right to the prejudice of an old one; for there is no legal principle to justify such a proceeding.[5]

Not only, moreover, does the law give redress where a substantive injury to property is committed, but, on the same principle, the erection of anything offensive so near the house of another as to render it useless and unfit for habitation is actionable;[6] the

[1] Per Story, J., The Marianna Flora, 11 Wheaton (U. S.) R. 42.

[2] *Ante*, p. 207.

[3] See Mayor of Colchester *v.* Brooke, 7 Q. B. 339 (53 E. C. L. R.); Morant *v.* Chamberlin, 6 H. & N. 541; Dobson *v.* Blackmore, 9 Q. B. 991; Dimes *v.* Petley, 15 Q. B. 276 (69 E. C. L. R.); Reg. *v.* Betts, 15 Q. B. 1022. As to the liability of the owner of a vessel, anchor, or other thing, which having been sunk in a river obstructs the navigation, see Brown *v.* Mallett, 5 C. B. 599, recognized 2 H. & N. 854; Hancock *v.* York, &c., R. C., 10 C. B. 348 (70 E. C. L. R.); White *v.* Crisp, 10 Exch. 312; per Bovill, C. J., Vivian *v.* Mersey Docks Board, L. R. 5 C. P. 29; Bartlett *v.* Baker, 3 H. & C. 153.

As to the liability of a shipowner for negligently damaging a telegraphic cable, see Sub-marine Telegraph Co. *v.* Dickson, 15 C. B. N. S. 757 (109 E. C. L. R.).

See also Mersey Docks Trustees *v.* Gibbs, Same *v.* Penhallow, L. R. 1 H. L. 93; White *v.* Phillips, 15 C. B. N. S. 245 (109 E. C. L. R.).

[4] Judgm., R. *v.* Ward, 4 A. & E. 384 (31 E. C. L. R.); Judgm., 15 Johns. (U. S.) R. 218; Panton *v.* Holland, 17 Id. 100.

[5] Judgm., R. *v.* Ward, *supra*.

[6] Per Burrough, J., Deane *v.* Clayton, 7 Taunt. 497 (2 E. C. L. R.); Doe d. Bish *v.* Keeling, 1 M. & S. 95 (28 E. C. L. R.). See Simpson *v.* Savage, 1 C. B. N. S. 347 (87 E. C. L. R.); Mumford *v.* Oxford, Worcester and Wolverhampton R. C., 1 H. & N. 34.

action in such case being *founded on the infringement or violation of the rights and duties arising by reason of [*379] vicinage.[1] The doctrine upon this subject, as laid down by the Court of Exchequer Chamber,[2] and substantially adopted by the House of Lords,[3] being, "that whenever, taking all the circumstances into consideration, including the nature and extent of the plaintiff's enjoyment before the acts complained of, the annoyance is sufficiently great to amount to a nuisance according to the ordinary rule of law, an action will lie, whatever the locality may be;" but trifling inconveniences merely are not to be regarded,[4] for *lex non favet votis delicatorum.*[5] An action, however, does not lie if a man build a house whereby my prospect is interrupted,[6] or open a window whereby my privacy is disturbed; in which latter case, the only remedy is to build on the adjoining land opposite to the offensive window.[7] In these instances the general principle applies—*qui jure suo utitur neminem lædit.*[8]

In connection with the law concerning nuisances, the practitioner may have to decide between asserted rights which are in conflict with each other—the right to erect or maintain, and the right to abate a nuisance—in doing *so the following propositions, [*380] recently stated,[9] may guide him. 1. That a person may justify an interference with the property of another for the purpose of abating a nuisance, if that person is the wrongdoer, but only so

[1] Alston *v.* Grant, 3 E. & B. 128 (77 E. C. L. R.); judgm., 4 Exch. 256, 257.

[2] Bamford *v.* Turnley, 3 B. & S. 62, 77 (113 E. C. L. R.).

[3] St. Helen's Smelting Co. *v.* Tipping, 11 H. L. Cas. 642.

[4] Id. 644, 655.

[5] 9 Rep. 58 a.

See further as to what may constitute a nuisance, Reg. *v.* Bradford Nav. Co., 6 B. & S. 631 (118 E. C. L. R.); Cleveland *v.* Spier, 16 C. B. N. S. 399 (111 E. C. L. R.).

[6] Com. Dig., "*Action upon the Case for a Nuisance*" (C.): Aldred's Case, 9 Rep. 58. According to the Roman law it was forbidden to obstruct the prospect from a neighbor's house: see D. 8. 2. 3. & 15; Wood Civ. Law, 3d ed., 92, 93.

[7] Per Eyre, C. J., cited 3 Camp. 82; Jones *v.* Tapling, 11 H. L. Cas. 290; *post*, p. 383.

[8] *Vide* D. 50. 17. 151. & 155. § 1.

[9] Roberts *v.* Rose, 4 H. & C. 103, 105–6 (in error affirming s. c., 3 H. & N. 162). See further as to abating a nuisance, Drake *v.* Pywell, 4 H. & C. 78.

far as his interference is necessary to abate the nuisance. 2. That it is the duty of a person who enters upon the land of another in abating a nuisance, to do it in a way the least injurious to the owner of the land. 3. That where there is an alternative way of abating a nuisance, if one way would cause injury to the property of an innocent third party or to the public, that cannot be justified although the nuisance may be abated by interference with the property of the wrongdoer. Therefore, where the alternative way involves an interference with the property either of an innocent person or of the wrongdoer, the interference must be with the property of the wrongdoer.

By stat. 2 & 3 Will. 4, c. 71,[1] s. 2,[2] it is provided, that, where an easement, such as is therein mentioned, "shall have been actually enjoyed by any person claiming right thereto without interruption, for the full period of twenty years," such claim shall not be defeated or destroyed by showing only that such easement was first enjoyed at a time prior to such period of twenty years, though it may be defeated in any other way in which it might have been defeated prior to that statute.

[*381] In case for annoying plaintiff in the enjoyment of his *house, by causing offensive smells to arise near to, in and about it, defendant pleaded enjoyment as of right for twenty years of a mixen on defendant's land contiguous and near to plaintiff's house, whereby, during all that time, offensive smells necessarily and unavoidably arose from the said mixen; and, after verdict for the defendant, the Court of Queen's Bench held the plea bad, because it did not show a right to cause offensive smells in the plaintiff's premises, nor that any smells had, in fact, been used to pass beyond the limits of defendant's own land.[3]

Again, if the owner of adjacent land erects a building so near

[1] As to the applicability of this statute to easements or profits *à prendre* in gross, see Shuttleworth *v.* Le Fleming, 19 C. B. N. S. 687 (115 E. C. L. R.); Mounsey *v.* Ismay, 3 H. & C. 486.

[2] As to which see Staffordshire and Worcestershire Can. Nav. *v.* Birmingham Can. Nav., L. R. 1 H. L. 254; Gaved *v.* Martyn, 19 C. B. N. S. 372 (115 E. C. L. R.).

[3] Flight *v.* Thomas, 10 A. & E. 590 (37 E. C. L. R.). See also Holford *v.* Hankinson, 5 Q. B. 584 (48 E. C. L. R.); Arkwright *v.* Gell, 5 M. & W. 203; Beeston *v.* Weate, 5 E. & B. 986 (85 E. C. L. R.); Ward *v.* Robins, 15 M. & W. 237.

the house of the plaintiff as to prevent the air and light from entering and coming through the plaintiff's windows, an action will, in some cases, lie.[1] The law on this subject formerly was, that no action would lie, unless a right had been gained in the lights by prescription;[2] but it was subsequently held, that, upon evidence of an adverse enjoyment of lights for twenty years or upwards unexplained, a jury might be directed to presume a right by grant or otherwise, even though no lights had existed there before the commencement of the twenty years;[3] and although, formerly, if the period of enjoyment fell short of twenty years, a presumption in favor of the plaintiff's right might have been raised from other circumstances, it is now enacted by 2 & 3 Will. 4, c. 71, s. 6, that no presumption shall be *allowed or made in support of any claim upon proof of the exercise of the enjoyment of the [*382] right or matter claimed for less than twenty years; and by sect. 3 of the same statute, that, "when the access and use of light to and for any dwelling-house, workshop or other building, shall have been *actually enjoyed*[4] therewith for the full period of twenty years, *without interruption*,[5] the right thereto shall be deemed absolute and indefeasible, any local usage or custom to the contrary notwithstanding, unless it shall appear that the same was enjoyed by some consent or agreement expressly made or given for that purpose by deed or writing." And by sect. 4, it is further enacted, that "the period of twenty years shall be taken to be the period next before some suit or action wherein the claim shall have been brought into question; and no act or matter shall be deemed to be an interruption within the meaning of the statute, unless the same shall have been submitted to, or acquiesced in, for one year after the party interrupted shall have had notice thereof, and of the person making or authorizing the same to be made." The last section of this Act is applicable not only to obstructions preceded and followed by portions of the twenty years, but also to an obstruction ending with that period; and, therefore, a prescriptive title to the access and

[1] In regard to the right to enjoyment of light and air, see White v. Bass, 7 H. & N. 722; Frewen v. Philipps, 11 C. B. N. S. 449 (103 E. C. L. R.).

[2] See D. 8. 2. 9.

[3] 2 Selw. N. P., 12th ed., 1134.

[4] See Courtauld v. Legh, L. R. 4 Ex. 126.

[5] See Bennison v. Cartwright, 5 B. & S. 1 (117 E. C. L. R.); Plasterers' Co. v. Parish Clerks' Co., 6 Exch. 630.

use of light may be gained by an enjoyment for nineteen years and 330 days, followed by an obstruction for thirty-five days.[1]

It may be well to add that "where a person has wrongfully [*383] *obstructed another in the enjoyment of an easement, as for instance, by building a wall across a path over which there is a right of way, public or private, any person so unlawfully obstructed may remove the obstruction; and if any damage thereby arises to him who wrongfully set it up, he has no right to complain. His own wrongful act justified what would otherwise have been a trespass." But "every man may open any number of windows looking over his neighbor's land; and, on the other hand, the neighbor may, by building on his own land within twenty years after the opening of the window, obstruct the light which would otherwise reach it.[2]

To the instances already given, showing that, according to the maxim, *Sic utere tuo ut alienum non lædas*, a person is held liable at law for the consequences of his negligence, may be added the following:—It has been held, that an action lies against a party for so negligently constructing a hay-rick on the extremity of his land, that, in consequence of its spontaneous ignition, his neighbor's house was burnt down.[3] So, the owners of a canal, taking tolls for the navigation, are, by the common law, bound to use reasonable care in making the navigation secure, and will be responsible for the breach of such duty, upon a similar principle to that which [*384] makes a shopkeeper, who *invites*[4] the public to his shop, liable for *neglect in leaving a trap-door open without any

[1] Flight *v.* Thomas (in error), 11 A. & E. 688 (39 E. C. L. R.), affirmed 8 Cl. & Fin. 231. See Eaton *v.* Swansea Waterworks Co., 17 Q. B. 267 (79 E. C. L. R.).

[2] Per Lord Cranworth, Tapling *v.* Jones, 11 H. L. Cas. 311.

[3] Vaughan *v.* Menlove, 3 Bing. N. C. 468 (32 E. C. L. R.); Turberville *v.* Stampe, Ld. Raym. 264; s. c., 1 Salk. 13; Jones *v.* Festiniog R. C., L. R. 3 Q. B. 733 (43 E. C. L. R.). As to liability for fire, caused by negligence, see further, Filliter *v.* Phippard, 11 Q. B. 347 (63 E. C. L. R.); per Tindal, C. J., Ross *v.* Hill, 2 C. B. 899 (52 E. C. L. R.), and 3 C. B. 241 (54 E. C. L. R.); Smith *v.* Frampton, 1 Ld. Raym. 62; Visc. Canterbury *v.* A.-G., 1 Phil. 306; Smith *v.* London and South-Western R. C., L. R. 5 C. P. 98, and cases cited, *post*, p. 394, n. 2.

[4] See Nicholson *v.* Lancashire and Yorkshire R. C., 3 H. & C. 534; Holmes *v.* North-Eastern R. C., L. R. 4 Ex. 254; Lunt *v.* London and North-Western R. C., L. R. 1 Q. B. 277, 286.

protection, by which his customers suffer injury.[1] The trustees of docks will likewise be answerable for their negligence and breach of duty causing damage.[2]

Where, however, in cases involving an inquiry as to liability for negligence, the immediate and proximate cause of damage is the unskillfulness or negligence of the plaintiff himself, he clearly cannot recover.[3] Thus, some bricklayers, employed by the defendant, had laid several barrowfuls of lime rubbish before the defendant's door, and, whilst the plaintiff was passing in a one-horse chaise, the wind raised a cloud of dust from the lime rubbish, which frightened the horse, although usually very quiet; he, consequently, started on one side, and would have run against a wagon which was meeting them, but the plaintiff hastily pulled him round, and the horse then ran over a lime heap lying before another man's door; by the shock the shaft was broken, and the horse, being thus still more frightened, ran away, and, the chaise being upset, the plaintiff was thrown out and hurt: it was held, that, as the immediate and proximate cause of the injury was the unskillfulness of the driver, the action could not be maintained.[4]

In very many recent cases, of which some only can be cited here[5] without adequate analysis or discussion, the *doctrine of contributory negligence has been considered. The result [*385] of such cases seems to be that where the doctrine referred to is involved, the question for the jury will be as follows—"Whether the damage was occasioned entirely by the negligence or improper conduct of the defendant, or whether the plaintiff himself so far contributed to the misfortune by his own negligence or want of

[1] Parnaby *v.* Lancaster Canal Co., 11 A. & E. 223, 243 (39 E. C. L. R.); Birkett *v.* Whitehaven Junction R. C., 4 H. & N. 730; Chapman *v.* Rothwell, E., B. & E. 168 (96 E. C. L. R.); Bayley *v.* Wolverhampton Waterworks Co., 6 H. & N. 241; and cases cited, *post.*

[2] Mersey Docks Trustees *v.* Gibbs; Same *v.* Penhallow, L. R. 1 H. L. 93, and cases cited, *ante*, p. 7, n. 3.

[3] Schloss *v.* Heriot, 14 C. B. N. S. 59 (108 E. C. L. R.).

[4] Flower *v.* Adam, 2 Taunt. 314.

[5] Burrows *v.* March Gas, &c., Co., L. R. 5 Ex. 67; Fordham *v.* London, Brighton and South Coast R. C., L. R. 4 C. P. 619; Coleman *v.* South-Eastern R. C., 4 H. & C. 699; Adams *v.* Lancashire and Yorkshire R. C., L. R. 4 C. P. 739; Skelton *v.* London and North-Western R. C., L. R. 2 C. P. 631; Mangan *v.* Atterton, L. R. 1 Ex. 239; Hughes *v.* Macfie; Adams *v.* Same, 2 H. & C. 734.

ordinary and common care and caution, that, but for such negligence or want of ordinary care and caution on his part, the misfortune would not have happened. In the first case the plaintiff would be entitled to recover; in the latter not, as but for his own fault the misfortune would not have happened. Mere negligence or want of ordinary care or caution would not, however, disentitle him to recover unless it were such that but for that negligence or want of ordinary care and caution the misfortune could not have happened, nor if the defendant might by the exercise of care on his part have avoided the consequences of the neglect or carelessness of the plaintiff."[1] [*386] Ordinary *care, it has been observed, must mean that degree of care which may reasonably be expected from a person in the plaintiff's situation;[2] and in the absence of such ordinary care on the part of the plaintiff, the case will fall within and be governed by the general rule of the English law, and no one can maintain an action for a wrong where he has consented or has *directly*[3] and materially contributed to the act which occasions his loss.[4]

[1] Per Wightman, J., Tuff *v.* Warman, 5 C. B. N. S. 585 (94 E. C. L. R.); Wetherley *v.* Regent's Canal Co., 12 C. B. N. S. 2, 8 (104 E. C. L. R.); Ellis *v.* London and South-Western R. C., 2 H. & N. 424; Martin *v.* Great Northern R. C., 16 C. B. 179 (81 E. C. L. R.); Bridge *v.* Grand Junction R. C., 3 M. & W. 244; recognized in Davies *v.* Mann, 10 M. & W. 546; cited and explained per Lord Campbell, C. J., Dowell *v.* Steam Nav. Co., 5 E. & B. 195 (85 E. C. L. R.); Holden *v.* Liverpool New Gas & Coke Co., 3 C. B. 1 (54 E. C. L. R.); Caswell *v.* Worth, 5 E. & B. 849 (85 E. C. L. R.); Clayards *v.* Dethick, 12 Q. B. 439 (64 E. C. L. R.); cited per Blackburn, J., Wyatt *v.* Great Western R. C., 6 B. & S. 720 (118 E. C. L. R.); Wise *v.* Great Western R. C., 1 H. & N. 63; Marriott *v.* Stanley, 1 Scott N. R. 392; Goldthorp *v.* Hardmans, 13 M. & W. 377; Pardington *v.* South Wales R. C., 11 Exch. 392; Dakin *v.* Brown, 8 C. B. 92 (65 E. C. L. R.); Thorogood *v.* Bryan, 8 C. B. 115, as to which see per Williams, J., Tuff *v.* Warman, 2 C. B. N. S. 750 (89 E. C. L. R.); Waite *v.* North-Eastern R. C., E., B. & E. 719, 727 (96 E. C. L. R.); The Milan, 1 Lush. Adm. R. 388, 403.

[2] Judgm., 1 Q. B. 36 (41 E. C. L. R.).

"Though degrees of care are not definable, they are with some approach to certainty distinguishable" by a jury "led by a cautious and discriminating direction of the judge." Judgm., Giblin *v.* McMullen, L. R. 2 P. C. 337.

[3] Dowell *v.* Steam Nav. Co., 5 E. & B. 195 (85 E. C. L. R.); Dynan *v.* Leach, 26 L. J. Ex. 221; Clarke *v.* Holmes, 7 H. & N. 937; Senior *v.* Ward, 1 E. & E. 385 (102 E. C. L. R.); Williams *v.* Clough, 3 H. & N. 258. See also Burrows *v.* March Gas, &c., Co., L. R. 5 Ex. 67.

[4] See per Tindal, C. J., Gould *v.* Oliver, 2 Scott N. R. 257. See Smith *v.* Dobson, 3 Scott N. R. 336; Taylor *v.* Clay, 9 Q. B. 713 (58 E. C. L. R.).

In cases such as are now before us the rule as to remoteness would seem, however, to have a twofold applicability,—for, first, a plaintiff will not necessarily be disentitled to redress whose negligence was but *remotely* connected with the accident;[1] and secondly, it may well be doubted whether "a person who is guilty of negligence is responsible for all the consequences which may under any circumstances arise, and in respect of mischief which could by no possibility have been foreseen, and which no reasonable person would have anticipated."[2]

[*387] *It is not, however, true, as a general proposition, that misconduct, even willful and culpable misconduct, must necessarily exclude the plaintiff who is guilty of it from the right to sue; for not unfrequently the rule holds that *injuria non excusat injuriam;*[3] a trespasser, although liable to an action for the injury which he does, does not necessarily forfeit his right of action for an injury which he has sustained;[4] *ex. gr.*, by falling into a hole newly[5] excavated on defendant's premises, adjoining to a public way, and rendering it unsafe to persons lawfully using the way with ordinary care.[6] If the defendant has been guilty of a breach

[1] Tuff *v.* Warman, 2 C. B. N. S. 740 (89 E. C. L. R.); s. c., 5 Id. 573; Wetherley *v.* Regent's Canal Co., 12 C. B. N. S. 2, 7 (104 E. C. L. R.); Dowell *v.* Steam Nav. Co., 5 E. & B. 195 (85 E. C. L. R.); Morrison *v.* General Steam Nav. Co., 8 Exch. 733.

[2] Per Pollock, C. B., Greenland *v.* Chaplin, 5 Exch. 248; and in Rigby *v.* Hewitt, Id. 243.

[3] See Alston *v.* Herring, 11 Exch. 822; Dimes *v.* Petley, 15 Q. B. 276 (69 E. C. L. R.); Roberts *v.* Rose, L. R. 1 Ex. 82; Ellis *v.* London and South-Western R. C., 2 H. & N. 424; and analogous cases cited, *post.*

[4] See Judgm., Degg *v.* Midland R. C., 1 H. & N. 780.

[5] A highway may be dedicated to the public, and accepted by them, subject to the inconveniences and risks caused by an existing erection or excavation: Fisher *v.* Prowse, and Cooper *v.* Walker, 2 B. & S. 770 (110 E. C. L. R.); Robbins *v.* Jones, 33 L. J. C. P. 1, 6; s. c., 15 C. B. N. S. 121 (109 E. C. L. R.). See Mercer *v.* Woodgate, L. R. 5 Q. B. 26.

[6] Barnes *v.* Ward, 9 C. B. 392, 420 (67 E. C. L. R.); In re Williams *v.* Groucott, 4 B. & S. 149, 157 (116 E. C. L. R.); Binks *v.* South Yorkshire R. C., 3 B. & S. 244 (113 E. C. L. R.); Hounsell *v.* Smyth, 7 C. B. N. S. 731 (97 E. C. L. R.); Hardcastle *v.* South Yorkshire R. C., 4 H. & N. 67.

With Barnes *v.* Ward, *supra*, compare Stone *v.* Jackson, 16 C. B. 199 (81 E. C. L. R.); Holmes *v.* North-Eastern R. C., L. R. 4 Ex. 254; Indermaur *v.* Dames, L. R. 1 C. P. 274; and Cornwell *v.* Metropolitan Commissioners of Sewers, 10 Exch. 771, 774, where Alderson, B., says, "Suppose there is an

[*388] of duty—public or private[1]—*producing the damage complained of, he will in general, under circumstances such as here supposed, be responsible. Nor does this proposition, if rightly understood, conflict with the rule already stated,[2] that "no man by his wrongful act can impose a duty."[3]

In Bird *v.* Holbrook[4] the defendant for the protection of his property, some of which had been stolen, set a spring-gun, without notice, in a walled garden, at a distance from his house, and the plaintiff, who climbed over the wall in pursuit of a stray fowl, having been shot, and seriously injured, the defendant was held liable in damages.[5] It was, indeed, observed in a subsequent case, that this decision proceeded on the ground, that setting spring-guns without notice was, independently of the statute[6] then in force,[7] an unlawful act; but, it was likewise remarked that, although the correctness of such a position might perhaps be questioned, yet, if it were sound, the above ruling was correct,[8] and on the whole we may,

inclosed yard with several dangerous holes in it, and the owner allows the public to go through the yard, does that cast on him any obligation to fill up the holes? Under such circumstances *caveat viator*." See Corby *v.* Hill, 4 C. B. N. S. 556 (93 E. C. L. R.).

[1] See Collis *v.* Selden, L. R. 3 C. P. 495; Seymour *v.* Maddox, 16 Q. B. 326 (71 E. C. L. R.); Southcote *v.* Stanley, 1 H. & N. 247, which is explained per Williams, J., Corby *v.* Hill, 4 C. B. N. S. 565 (93 E. C. L. R.); and with which compare Chapman *v.* Rothwell, E., B. & E. 168, 170 (96 E. C. L. R.); Bolch *v.* Smith, 7 H. & N. 736; Wilkinson *v.* Fairie, 1 H. & C. 633; White *v.* Phillips, 15 C. B. N. S. 245 (109 E. C. L. R.); Brass *v.* Maitland, 6 E. & B. 470, 484 (88 E. C. L. R.); followed in Farrant *v.* Barnes, 11 C. B. N. S. 553; and Hutchinson *v.* Guion, 5 C. B. N. S. 149 (94 E. C. L. R.).

[2] *Ante*, p. 270.

[3] Judgm., 1 H. & N. 782; Dalton *v.* Denton, 1 C. B. N. S. 672 (87 E. C. L. R.).

[4] 4 Bing. 628, with which compare Wootton *v.* Dawkins, 2 C. B. N. S. 412 (89 E. C. L. R.). See also Judgm., Mayor of Colchester *v.* Brooke, 7 Q. B. 339 (53 E. C. L. R.), citing Davies *v.* Mann, *ante*, p. 385, n. 1.

[5] Bird *v.* Holbrook, 4 Bing. 628 (13 E. C. L. R.); cited 1 Q. B. 37 (41 E. C. L. R.), and in Judgm., 1 H. & N. 780; Ilott *v.* Wilkes, 3 B. & Ald. 304 (5 E. C. L. R.). See also arg., 1 Scott N. R. 393, 394.

[6] 7 & 8 Geo. 4, c. 18.

[7] See now statute 24 & 25 Vict. c. 100, s. 31.

[8] Judgm., Jordin *v.* Crump, 8 M. & W. 789, where the court agreed in opinion with Gibbs, C. J., in Deane *v.* Clayton, 7 Taunt. 489 (2 E. C. L. R.), which was an action for killing plaintiff's dog by a spike placed on defendant's land for the preservation of his game.

it seems, conclude, with reference to this subject, that although the law, in certain cases, forbids the setting of instruments capable of causing injury to man, where such injury will be a probable consequence of setting them, *yet with the exception of those cases, a man has a right to do what he pleases with his own land.[1] [*389]

As bearing to some extent upon the doctrine of contributory negligence, and the legal principles discussed in Bird *v.* Holbrook, the cases below cited,[2] which have reference to the liability of a railway company for damage sustained by cattle trespassing on their line or by persons crossing it, may further be consulted.

With respect to one important class of cases of frequent occurrence, falling directly within the general principle under review, viz., where damage is caused by collision between two vessels, it has been judicially observed in the Admiralty Court, that "there are four possibilities under which an accident of this sort may occur. In the first place, it may happen without blame being imputable to either party, as where the loss is occasioned by a storm, or any other *vis major*. In that case, the misfortune must be borne by the party on whom it happens to light, the other not being responsible to him in any degree. Secondly, a misfortune of this kind may arise where both parties are to blame, where there has been a want of due diligence or of skill on both sides. In such a case, the rule of law is, that the loss must be apportioned between them, as having been occasioned by the fault of both of *them. Thirdly, it may happen by the misconduct of the suffering party only, and then the rule is, that the sufferer must bear his own burthen. Lastly, it may have been the fault of the ship which ran the [*390]

[1] Judgm., 8 M. & W. 787.

[2] Fawcett *v.* York and North Midland R. C., 16 Q. B. 610 (71 E. C. L. R.); Ricketts *v.* East and West India Docks, &c., R. C., 12 C. B. 160 (74 E. C. L. R.); Manchester, Sheffield, and Lincolnshire R. C. *v.* Wallis, 14 C. B. 213 (78 E. C. L. R.); Midland R. C. *v.* Daykin, 17 C. B. 126 (84 E. C. L. R.); Bessant *v.* Great Western R. C., 8 C. B. N. S. 368 (98 E. C. L. R.); Marfell *v.* South Wales R. C., Id. 525; Ellis *v.* London and South-Western R. C., 2 H. & N. 424.

Stubley *v.* London and North-Western R. C., 4 H. & C. 83; Stapley *v.* London, Brighton, and South Coast R. C., Id. 93; Nicholson *v.* Lancashire and Yorkshire R. C., 3 H. & C. 534; Holmes *v.* North-Eastern R. C., L. R. 4 Ex. 254; Lunt *v.* London and North-Western R. C., L. R. 1 Q. B. 277, 286.

other down; and, in this case, the injured party would be entitled to an entire compensation from the other.[1]

Again with reference to restitution in a case of capture, Lord Stowell has observed: "The natural rule is, that, if a party be unjustly deprived of his property, he ought to be put, as nearly as possible, in the same state as he was before the deprivation took place; technically speaking, he is entitled to restitution, with costs and damages. This is the general rule upon the subject; but, like all other general rules, it must be subject to modification. If, for instance, any circumstances appear which show that the suffering party has himself furnished occasion for the capture,—if he has, by his own conduct, in some degree contributed to the loss,—then he is entitled to a somewhat less degree of compensation than what is technically called simple restitution."[2]

The law also, through regard to the safety of the community, [*391] *requires that persons having in their custody instruments of danger should keep them with the utmost care.[3] Where, therefore, defendant, being possessed of a loaded gun, sent a young girl to fetch it, with directions to take the priming out, which was accordingly done, and a damage accrued to the plaintiff's son in consequence of the girl's presenting the gun at him and drawing the trigger, when the gun went off; it was held, that the defendant was liable to damages in an action on the case.[4] "If," observed

[1] Judgm., The Woodrop-Sims, 2 Dods. Adm. R. 85; Hay *v.* Le Neve, 2 Shaw, Scotch App. Cas., 395; Judgm., De Vaux *v.* Salvador, 4 A. & E. 431 (31 E. C. L. R.); The Agra, L. R. 1 P. C. 501; Brown *v.* Wilkinson, 15 M. & W. 391; Dowell *v.* Steam Nav. Co., 5 E. & B. 195 (85 E. C. L. R.); Tuff *v.* Warman, cited *ante*, p. 385; Morrison *v.* General Steam Nav. Co., 8 Exch. 733; General Steam Nav. Co. *v.* Morrison, 13 C. B. 581 (76 E. C. L. R.).

The *onus probandi* lies on the party seeking to recover compensation: Morgan *v.* Sim, 11 Moo. P. C. C. 307.

See further as to the principles of law applicable in cases of collision, Bland *v.* Ross, 14 Moo. P. C. C. 210; The Milan, 1 Lush. Adm. R. 388.

As to exemption from liability under stat. 17 & 18 Vict. c. 104, s. 388, see General Steam Nav. Co. *v.* British and Colonial Steam Nav. Co., L. R. 4 Ex. 238; The Iona, L. R. 1 P. C. 426; The Velasquez, Id. 494.

[2] The Acteon, 2 Dods. Adm. R. 51, 52; The Ostsee, 9 Moo. P. C. C. 157.

[3] "The law of England, in its care for human life, requires consummate caution in the person who deals with dangerous weapons;" per Erle, C. J., Potter *v.* Faulkner, 1 B. & S. 805 (101 E. C. L. R.); Rylands *v.* Fletcher, L. R. 3 H. L. 330, cited *ante*, p. 373, also exemplifies the text.

[4] Dixon *v.* Bell, 5 M. & S. 198.

Lord Denman, delivering the judgment of the Court of Queen's Bench in another and more recent case, "I am guilty of negligence in leaving anything dangerous in a place where I know it to be extremely probable that some other person will unjustifiably set it in motion, to the injury of a third, and if that injury should be brought about, I presume that the sufferer might have redress by action against both or either of the two, but unquestionably against the first."[1] In the case referred to, the evidence showed that the defendant had negligently left his horse and cart unattended in the street; and the plaintiff, a child seven years old, having got upon the cart to play, another child incautiously led the horse on, whereby plaintiff was thrown down and hurt; and, in answer to the argument, that plaintiff could not recover, having, by his own act, *contributed to the accident, it was observed, that the [*392] plaintiff, although acting without prudence or thought, had shown these qualities in as great a degree as he could be expected to possess them, and that his misconduct, at all events, bore no proportion to that of the defendant.[2]

The rule of law applicable for determining the liability of one who lends, or allows to another the use of, a chattel which by reason of its defective condition causes damage to the latter, has been thus laid down:[3] "The duties of the borrower and lender are in some degree correlative. The lender must be taken to lend for the purpose of a beneficial use by the borrower; the borrower therefore is not responsible for reasonable wear and tear; but he is for negligence, for misuse, for gross want of skill in the use; above all, for anything which may be qualified as legal fraud. So, on the other hand, as the lender lends for beneficial use he must be responsible for defects in the chattel, with reference to the use for which he knows the loan is accepted, of which he is aware, and owing to which directly the borrower is injured."[4]

[1] Lynch *v.* Nurdin, 1 Q. B. 29, 35 (41 E. C. L. R.), with which compare Mangan *v.* Atterton, L. R. 1 Ex. 239; Lygo *v.* Newbold, 9 Exch. 302; Great Northern R. C. *v.* Harrison, 10 Exch. 376; Austin *v.* Great Western R. C., L. R. 2 Q. B. 442; Caswell *v.* Worth, 5 E. & B. 849 (85 E. C. L. R.).

[2] Lynch *v.* Nurdin, *supra.* See Waite *v.* North-Eastern R. C., E., B. & E. 719 (96 E. C. L. R.); Illidge *v.* Goodwin, 5 C. & P. 190 (24 E. C. L. R.).

[3] Blakemore *v.* Bristol and Exeter R. C., 8 E. & B. 1035, 1050–1 (92 E. C. L. R.); followed in McCarthy *v.* Young, 6 H. & N. 329, 336.

[4] Citing the maxim of the Roman law, *Adjuvari quippe nos, non decipi, beneficio oportet*, D. 13. 6. 17. § 3.

Further, we may observe that, although a man has a right to keep an animal which is *feræ naturæ*, and no one can interfere with him in doing so until some mischief happens, yet, as soon as the animal has caused bodily hurt to any person, then the act of keeping it becomes, as regards that person, an act for which the owner is [*393] *responsible; and there is, in truth, as judicially observed, no distinction between the case of an animal which breaks through the tameness of its nature and is fierce, and *known by the owner to be so*, and one which is *feræ naturæ*.[1] "Whosoever," says Lord Denman, C. J.,[2] "keeps an animal accustomed to attack and bite mankind, with knowledge that it so accustomed, is *primâ facie* liable in an action on the case at the suit of any person attacked and injured by the animal, without any averment of negligence or default in the securing or taking care of it. The gist of the action is the *keeping* the animal after *knowledge* of its mischievous propensities."[3] No proof of the *scienter*, however, need now be given where the complainant sues for hurt done to his *cattle*[4] or sheep by the defendant's dog.[5]

We may add that, where an accident happens entirely from a superior agency, and without default on the part of the defendant, or blame imputable to him, an action for injury resulting from such accident cannot be maintained.[6] A carrier, though an insurer, is not liable for damage arising from an inherent defect in the chattel delivered to him to be carried.[7] Nor will a railway [*394] *company be liable for an accident arising from a fire in a

[1] Jackson *v.* Smithson, 15 M. & W. 563, 565; May *v.* Burdett, 5 Q. B. 101 (58 E. C. L. R.). See also Mason *v.* Keeling, 1 Lord Raym. 606; Jenkins *v.* Turner, Id. 109, and cases *infra*.

[2] Judgm., 9 Q. B. 110, 111 (43 E. C. L. R.); Card *v.* Case, 5 C. B. 622, 633, 634 (57 E. C. L. R.); Hudson *v.* Roberts, 6 Exch. 697.

[3] See Judgm., 5 H. & N. 685; Worth *v.* Gilling, L. R. 3 C. P. 1; Cox *v.* Burbridge, 13 C. B. N. S. 430, 437 (106 E. C. L. R.). See Cook *v.* Waring, 2 H. & C. 332.

[4] See Wright *v.* Pearson, L. R. 4 Q. B. 582.

[5] Stat. 28 & 29 Vict. c. 60.

As to damage done by a dog to plaintiff's game, see Read *v.* Edwards, 17 C. B. N. S. 245 (112 E. C. L. R.).

[6] Wakeman *v.* Robinson, 1 Bing. 213, 215 (8 E. C. L. R.); Hammack *v.* White, 11 C. B. N. S. 508 (103 E. C. L. R.); Hall *v.* Fearnley, 3 Q. B. 919 (43 E. C. L. R.); Weaver *v.* Ward, Hobart 134; per Alderson, B., Skinner *v.* London, Brighton and South Coast R. C., 5 Exch. 789.

[7] Hudson *v.* Baxendale, 2 H. & N. 575.

locomotive engine, *which they have been authorized by the legislature to use*,[1] provided every due precaution be taken consistent with its use.[2]

The above instances (which might easily be extended through a much greater space than it has been thought desirable to occupy) will, it is hoped, suffice to give a general view of the manner in which the maxim, *Sic utere tuo ut alienum non lædas*, is applied in our law to restrict the enjoyment of property, and to regulate in some measure the conduct of individuals, by enforcing compensation for injuries wrongfully occasioned by a violation of the principle which it involves, a principle which is obviously based in justice, and essential to the peace, order, and well-being of the community. As deducible from the cases cited in the preceding pages, and from others to be found in our Reports, the following propositions may, it is conceived, be stated:—

1. It is, *primâ facie*, competent to any man to enjoy and deal with his own property as he chooses.

2. He must, however, so enjoy and use it as not to affect injuriously the rights of his fellow-subjects.

3. Where rights are such as, if exercised, to conflict with each other, we must consider whether the exercise of the right claimed by either party be not restrained by the existence of some duty imposed on him towards the other. *Whether such duty be [*395] or be not imposed must be determined by reference to abstract rules and principles of law.

4. A man cannot by his tortious act impose a duty on another.

5. But, lastly, a wrong-doer is not necessarily, by reason of his being such, disentitled to redress by action, as against the party who causes him damage, for sometimes the maxim holds that *Injuria non excusat injuriam*.[3]

[1] See Jones *v.* Festiniog R. C., L. R. 3 Q. B. 733.

[2] Vaughan *v.* Taff Vale R. C., 5 H. & N. 679 (recognizing R. *v.* Pease, 4 B. & Ad. 30 (24 E. C. L. R.)); cited and explained in Jones *v.* Festiniog R. C., L. R. 3 Q. B. 737; and approved in Hammersmith, &c., R. C. *v.* Brand, L. R. 4 H. L. 171, 201–2. *Secus*, if the company were guilty of negligence, Smith *v.* London and South-Western R. C., L. R. 5 C. P. 98.

[3] This maxim is also sometimes applicable where the action is founded upon contract. See (*ex. gr.*) Alston *v.* Herring, 11 Exch. 822, 830; Hilton *v.* Eckersley, 6 E. & B. 76 (88 E. C. L. R.); with which *acc.* Hornby *v.* Close, L. R. 2 Q. B. 153; Farrar *v.* Close, L. R. 4 Q. B. 602.

In connection with the above propositions the doctrines as to contributory negligence must be kept in mind, and the rule which has, at p. 268, been briefly noticed, that *Volenti non fit injuria.*

CUJUS EST SOLUM EJUS EST USQUE AD CŒLUM.

(Co. Litt. 4 a.)

He who possesses land possesses also that which is above it.

Land, in its legal signification, has an indefinite extent upwards, so that, by a conveyance of land, all buildings, growing timber, and water, erected and being thereupon, shall likewise pass.[1] So, if a man eject another from land, and afterwards build upon it, the building belongs to the owner of the ground on which it is built, [*396] according *to the principle *ædificatum solo solo cedit*,[2] which we shall presently consider.

From the maxim *Cujus est solum ejus est usque ad cœlum*, it follows, that a person has no right to erect a building on his own land which interferes with the due enjoyment of adjoining premises, and occasions damage thereto, either by overhanging them, or by the flow of water from the roof and eaves upon them, unless, indeed, a legal right so to build has been conceded by grant, or may be presumed by user, and by operation of the stat. 2 & 3 Will. 4, c. 71.

Where the declaration alleged that the defendant had erected a house upon his freehold, so as to project over the house of the plaintiffs *ad nocumentum liberi tenementi ipsorum*, but did not assign any special nuisance, the court, on demurrer, held the declaration good, inasmuch as the erection must evidently have been a nuisance productive of legal damage;[3] and, in a modern case, it was held,

[1] Co. Litt. 4 a; 9 Rep. 54; Allaway *v.* Wagstaff, 4 H. & N. 307. As to the distinction between "land" and "tenements," see per Martin, B., Electric Telegraph Co. *v.* Overseers of Salford, 11 Exch. 189; Judgm., Vauxhall Bridge Co. *v.* Sawyer, 6 Exch. 508; Fredericks, app., Howie, resp., 1 H. & C. 381.

[2] *Post*, p. 401.

[3] Baten's Case, 9 Rep. 53. See also Penruddocke's Case, 5 Rep. 100.

that the erection of a cornice projecting over the plaintiff's garden was a nuisance, from which the law would infer injury to the plaintiff, and for which, therefore, an action on the case would lie.[1]

With respect to the nature of the remedy for an injury of the kind to which we are now alluding, the general rule is, that case is the proper form of action for the consequential, and trespass for the immediate and direct injury caused by the act complained of.[2] And not *only for such injury will an action lie at suit of the occupier, but the reversioner may also sue where injury has been done to the reversion; provided such injury be of a *permanent* character,[3] or prejudicially affect the plaintiff's reversionary interest.[4] It is now well settled, that a man may be guilty of a nuisance as well in continuing as in erecting a building on the land of another.[5]

[*397]

Not only will a man be liable who erects a building either upon or so as to overhang his neighbor's land,[6] but an action will lie against him if the boughs of his trees are allowed to grow so as to overhang the adjoining land, which they had not been accustomed

[1] Fay *v.* Prentice, 1 C. B. 828 (50 E. C. L. R.); per Pollock, C. B., Solomon *v.* Vintners' Co., 4 H. & N. 600.

[2] See Reynolds *v.* Clarke, 2 Ld. Raym. 1399; Thomas *v.* Thomas, 2 Cr., M. & R. 34; 9 Rep. 54; Wells *v.* Ody, 1 M. & W. 452; Crofts *v.* Haldane, L. R. 2 Q. B. 194, 198, 199.

[3] Simpson *v.* Savage, 1 C. B. N. S. 347 (87 E. C. L. R.), where the cases are collected. See particularly Mumford *v.* Oxford, Worcester and Wolverhampton R. C., 1 H. & N. 34; Battishill *v.* Reed, 18 C. B. 696 (86 E. C. L. R.); Cox *v.* Glue, 5 C. B. 533 (57 E. C. L. R.); Tucker *v.* Newman, 11 A. & E. 40 (39 E. C. L. R.); Jackson *v.* Pesked, 1 M. & S. 234; Kidgill *v.* Moor, 9 C. B. 364 (67 E. C. L. R.); Bell *v.* Midland R. C., 10 C. B. N. S. 287 (100 E. C. L. R.).

As to the distinction between injuries to realty of a permanent and of a merely temporary kind, see also Hammersmith and City R. C. *v.* Brand, L. R. 4 H. L. 171; Ricket *v.* Metropolitan R. C., L. R. 2 H. L. 175.

Case will lie by the reversioner for a permanent injury to a chattel let out on hire: Mears *v.* London and South-Western R. C., 11 C. B. N. S. 850 (103 E. C. L. R.).

[4] Metropolitan Association *v.* Petch, 5 C. B. N. S. 504 (94 E. C. L. R.).

[5] Battishill *v.* Reed, 18 C. B. 713 (86 E. C. L. R.); citing Holmes *v.* Wilson, 10 A. & E. 503 (37 E. C. L. R.); Thompson *v.* Gibson, 7 M. & W. 456; Bowyer *v.* Cook, 4 C. B. 236 (56 E. C. L. R.).

[6] 3 Inst. 201; Vin. Abr., "*Nuisance*" (G); per Pollock, C. B., 4 H. & N. 600.

to do.[1] In a case before Lord Ellenborough, at Nisi Prius,[2] which was an action of trespass for nailing a board on the defendant's own wall, so as to overhang the plaintiff's garden, and where the [*398] maxim *Cujus est solum ejus est *usque ad cœlum* was cited in support of the form of action, his lordship observed, that he did not think it was a *trespass* to interfere with the column of air superincumbent on the close; that, if it was, it would follow, that an aëronaut was liable to an action of trepass *qu. cl. fr.* at the suit of the occupier of every field over which his balloon might happen to pass; since the question, whether or not the action was maintainable, could not depend upon the length of time for which the superincumbent air was invaded; and the Lord Chief Justice further remarked, that, if any damage arose from the object which overhung the close, the remedy was by action on the case, and not by action of trespass.[3]

It must be observed, moreover, that the maxim under consideration is not a presumption of law applicable in all cases and under all circumstances; for example, it does not apply to chambers in the inns of court;[4] for "a man may have an inheritance in an upper chamber, though the lower buildings and soil be in another."[5]

Not only has land in its legal signification an indefinite extent upwards, but in contemplation of law it extends also downwards, so that whatever is in a direct line between the surface of any land and the centre of the earth belongs to the owner of the surface; and hence the word "land," which is *nomen generalissimum*, includes not only the face of the earth, but everything under it or over it; and, therefore, if a man grants all his lands, he grants thereby all his mines, his woods, his waters, and his houses, as well as his fields [*399] and meadows.[6] Where, *however, a demise was made of premises lately in the occupation of A. (particularly de-

[1] Norris *v.* Baker, 1 Roll. Rep. 393, *ad fin.* See Brook *v.* Jenney, 2 Q. B. 265 (42 E. C. L. R.).

[2] Pickering *v.* Rudd, 4 Camp. 219; per Shadwell, V.-C. E., Saunders *v.* Smith, ed. by Crawford 20; Kenyon *v.* Hart, 6 B. & S. 249, 252 (118 E. C. L. R.).

[3] See Reynolds *v.* Clarke, 2 Ld. Raym. 1399; Fay *v.* Prentice, 1 C. B. 828 (50 E. C. L. R.).

[4] Per Maule, J., 1 C. B. 840 (50 E. C. L. R.).

[5] Co. Litt. 48 b.

[6] 2 Com. by Broom & Hadley 15, 17.

scribed), part of which was a yard, it was held, that a cellar, situate under the yard, and late in the occupation of B., did not pass by the demise; for though *primâ facie* it would do so, yet that might be regulated and explained by circumstances.[1]

The maxim, then, above cited, gives to the owner of the soil all that lies beneath its surface, and accordingly the land immediately below is his property. Whether, therefore, it be solid rock, or porous ground, or venous earth, or part soil and part water, the person who owns the surface may dig therein, and apply all that is there found to his own purposes, at his free will and pleasure;[2] although, as already stated, he may in some cases incur liability by so digging and excavating at the extremity and under the surface of his own land as to occasion damage to the house or other building of his neighbor.[3]

But, although the general rule, which obtains in the absence of any express covenant or agreement between the parties interested in land, is as above stated, and although it is a presumption of law that the owner of the freehold has a right to the mines and minerals underneath, yet this presumption may be rebutted by showing a distinct title to the surface, and to that which is beneath; for mines may form a distinct possession and different inheritance; and, indeed, it frequently happens that a person, being entitled both to the mines and to *the land above, grants away the land, excepting out of the grant the mines, which would otherwise have passed under the conveyance of the land, and also reserving to himself the power of entering upon the surface of the land which he has granted away, in order to do such acts as may be necessary for the purpose of getting the minerals excepted out of the grant, a fair compensation being made to the grantee for so entering and working the mines. In this case one person has the land above, the other has the mines below, with the power of getting the minerals; and the rule is, according to the maxim *Sic utere tuo ut alienum non lædas*, already considered, that each shall so use his own right of property as not to injure his neighbor;

[*400]

[1] Doe d. Freeland *v.* Burt, 1 T. R. 701. See Denison *v.* Holliday, 1 H. & N. 631; and the maxim *Cuicunque aliquis quid concedit concedere videtur et id sine quo res ipsa esse non potuit,—post.*

[2] Judgm., 12 M. & W. 324, 354.

[3] 1 Crabb, Real. Prop., p. 93.

and, therefore, the grantor will be entitled to such mines only as he can work, leaving a reasonable support to the surface. And here we may observe, that the bare exception of the mines and minerals, without a reservation of right of entry, would vest in the grantor the whole of the mines and minerals; but he would have no right to work or get them except by the consent of the plaintiff, or by means of access through other shafts and channels, with which the grantee's land had nothing to do, because, in the case here put, the two properties, viz., in the surface and in the subterranean products, are totally distinct.[1] So, if there be a grant of an upper room in a house, with a reservation by the grantor of a lower room, he undertaking not to do anything which will derogate [*401] from the right to occupy the *upper room; in this case, if the grantor were to remove the supports of the upper room, he would be liable in an action of covenant.[2]

Quicquid plantatur Solo Solo Cedit.

(Wentw. Off. Ex., 14th ed., 145.)

Whatever is affixed to the soil belongs thereto.

It may be stated, as a general rule of great antiquity, that whatever is affixed[3] to the soil becomes, in contemplation of law, a part of it, and is consequently subjected to the same rights of property as the soil itself. In the Institutes of the Civil Law it is laid down that if a man builds on his own land with the materials of another, the owner of the soil becomes, in law, the owner of the building also—*quia omne quod solo inœdificatur solo cedit.*[4] In this case, indeed, the property in the materials used still continued in the

[1] Harris *v.* Ryding, 5 M. & W. 60, 66, 73; Humphries *v.* Brogden, 12 Q. B. 739 (64 E. C. L. R.); Keyse *v.* Powell, 2 E. & B. 132, 144, 145 (75 E. C. L. R.), and cases cited *ante*, p. 371. See Earl of Rosse *v.* Wainman, 14 M. & W. 859; s. c., 2 Exch. 800; Micklethwait *v.* Winter, 6 Exch. 644; 1 Crabb' Real Prop. 95.

[2] 5 M. & W. 71, 76.

[3] "In several of the old books the word *fixatur* is used as synonymous with *plantatur*" in the maxim *supra*, Judgm., L. R. 3 Ex. 260.

[4] I. 2. 1. 29; D. 47. 3. 1.

original owner; and although, by a law of the XII. Tables, the object of which was to prevent the destruction of buildings, he was unable, unless the building were taken down, to reclaim the materials *in specie*, he was, nevertheless, entitled to recover double their value as compensation, by the action *de tigno juncto*.[1] On the other hand, if a person built, with his own materials, on the land of another, the house likewise belonged to the owner of the soil; for in this case, the builder was presumed intentionally to have transferred his property in the materials *to such owner.[2] In [*402] like manner, if trees were planted or seed sown in the land of another, the proprietor of the soil became proprietor also of the tree, the plant, or the seed, as soon as it had taken root.[3] And this latter proposition is fully adopted, almost in the words of the civil law, by our own law writers—Britton, Bracton, and Fleta.[4] According to the Roman law, indeed, where buildings were erected upon, or improvements made to property, by the party in possession, *bonâ fide* and without notice of any adverse title, compensation was, it seems, allowed for such buildings and improvements to the party making them, as against the rightful owner;[5] and although this principle is not recognized by our own common law, nor to its full extent by courts of equity, yet, where a man, supposing that he has an absolute title to an estate, builds upon the land with the knowledge of the rightful owner, who stands by, and suffers the erection to proceed, without giving any notice of his own claim, he will be compelled, by a court of equity, in a suit brought for recovery of the land, to make due allowance and compensation for such improvements.[6] "As to the equity arising from valuable and lasting improvements, I do not consider," remarked Lord Chancellor

[1] I. 2. 1. 29; D. 47. 3. 1. [2] I. 2. 1. 30.

[3] I. 2. 1. 31 & 32; D. 41. 1. 7. 13.

[4] Britton (by Wingate), c. 33, 180; Bracton, c. 3, ss. 4, 6; Fleta, lib. 3, c. 2, s. 12.

[5] *Sed quamvis ædificium fundo cedat, fundi tamen dominus condemnari solet ut cum duntaxat recipiat, reddito sumptu quo pretiosior factus est, aut super fundo atque ædificio pensio imponatur ex meliorationis æstimatione si maluerit:* Gothofred. *ad.* I. 2. 1. 30.

[6] 1 Story, Eq. Jurisp., 6th ed., s. 388; 2 Id., s. 1237; *ante*, p. 174. Where a sale is set aside on account of the inadequacy of the consideration, the purchaser will be allowed for lasting and valuable improvements: Sugd., V. & P., 14th ed., 287.

[*403] Clare,[1] "that a man who is conscious of a *defect in his title, and with that conviction on his mind expends a sum of money in improvements, is entitled to avail himself of it. If the person really entitled to the estate will encourage the possessor of it to expend his money in improvements, or if he will look on and suffer such expenditure without apprising the party of his intention to dispute his title, and will afterwards endeavor to avail himself of such fraud—upon the ground of fraud the jurisdiction of a court of equity will clearly attach upon the case."

Having thus touched upon the general doctrine, that what has been affixed to the freehold becomes a portion of it, we shall proceed to consider in what manner, and with what qualifications, the maxim, *Quicquid plantatur solo solo cedit*, applies with reference to—1st, trees; 2dly, emblements; 3dly, away-going crops; and 4thly, fixtures;—treating these important subjects with brevity, and merely endeavoring to give a concise outline of the law respecting each.

1. The general property in trees, being *timber*, is in the owner of the inheritance of the land upon which they grow; that in bushes and underwood, on the other hand, is in the tenant. The tenant cannot indeed, without rendering himself liable to an action on the case for waste, do anything which will change the nature of the thing demised; he cannot, for instance, stub up a wood, or destroy a park paling; neither can he destroy young plants destined to become trees, nor grub up or cut down and destroy fences; nor, in short, do any act prejudicial to the inheritance. He may, however, [*404] cut down trees *which are not timber, either by general law, or by particular local custom; and he may likewise cut down such trees as are of seasonable wood, *i. e.*, such as are usually cut as underwood, and in due course grow up again from the stumps, and produce again their ordinary and usual profit by such growth.[2]

It follows from the rule just stated, that if trees, being timber,

[1] Kenney *v.* Browne, 3 Ridgw. Par. Cas. 462, 519; cited, arg. Austin *v.* Chambers, 6 Cl. & Fin. 31. See, per Lord Brougham, C., Perrott *v.* Palmer, 3 My. & K. 640.

[2] Lord D'Arcy *v.* Askwith, Hob. 234; Judgm., Phillipps *v.* Smith, 14 M. & W. 589; per Tindal, C. J., Berriman *v.* Peacock, 9 Bing. 386, 387 (23 E. C. L. R.); Com. Dig., "*Biens*" (H.).

are blown down by the wind, the lessor shall have them, for they are part of his inheritance, and not the tenant for life or years; but, if they be dotards, without any timber in them, the tenant for life or years shall have them.[1]

So, where timber is severed by a trespasser, and by wrong, it belongs to him who has the first vested estate of inheritance, whether in fee or in tail, and he may bring trover for it.[2] And if there are intermediate contingent estates of inheritance, and the timber is cut down by combination between the tenant for life and the person who has the next vested estate of inheritance, or, if the tenant for life himself has such an estate, and fells timber, in these cases the Court of Chancery will order it to be preserved for him who has the first contingent estate of inheritance under the settlement.[3]

On the other hand, where trees not fit for timber are cut down by the lessor, the property in such trees vests in the tenant; for the lessor would have no right to them if severed by the act of God, and, therefore, can have no *right to them where they have been severed by his own wrongful act; and the same rule holds where they are severed by a stranger.[4] [*405]

A tenant, who is answerable for waste only, may cut down trees for the purpose of reparation, without committing waste, either where the damage has accrued, during the time of his being in possession, in the ordinary course of decay, or where the premises were ruinous at the time he entered; if, however, the decay happened by his default, in this case to cut down trees, in order to do the repair, would be waste;[5] and, at all events, the tenant can only justify felling such trees as are fit for the purposes of repair.[6] It is, moreover, a general rule, that waste can only be committed of the thing demised: and, therefore, if trees are excepted out of the demise, no waste can be committed of them.[7]

[1] Herlakenden's Case, 4 Rep. 62, 3d Resolution; Countess of Cumberland's Case, Moore 813.

[2] Woodf., L. & T., 9th ed., 513; Ward v. Andrews, 2 Chit. R. 636.

[3] Bewick v. Wintfield, 3 P. Wms. 368.

[4] Channon v. Patch, 5 B. & C. 897, 902 (11 E. C. L. R.); Ward v. Andrews, 2 Chit. R. 636.

[5] Woodf., L. & T., 9th ed., 514.

[6] Simmons v. Norton, 7 Bing. 640 (20 E. C. L. R.).

[7] Goodright v. Vivian, 8 East 190; Rolls v. Rock, cited, 2 Selw. N. P. 13th ed., 1244.

A tenant "without impeachment of waste" is entitled to cut down timber, which he could not otherwise do; but this clause does not extend to allow destructive or malicious waste, such as cutting down timber which serves for the shelter or ornament of the estate.[1] A tenant for life without impeachment of waste has as full power to cut down trees for his own use as if he had an estate of inheritance, and is equally entitled to the timber if severed by others, so that an action of trover for such timber will not lie against him at suit of a tenant in tail expectant on the termination of a life estate.[2]

[*406] But, if the tenant *for life cut timber so as not to leave enough for repairs, or, if he cut down trees planted for ornament or shelter to the mansion-house, or saplings not fit to be felled for timber, a court of equity will restrain him by injunction.[3] And where a tenant for life without impeachment of waste pulled down a mansion-house and rebuilt it in a more eligible situation, an act which was not complained of by the remainderman, an injunction was granted to restrain the tenant for life from destroying timber which had formed an ornament and shelter to the original mansion.[4]

Lastly, it is an inseparable incident to an estate tail, that the tenant shall not be punished for committing waste by felling timber; but this power must be exercised, if at all, during the life of the tenant in tail; for, at the instant of his death, it ceases. If, therefore, tenant in tail sells trees growing on the land, the vendee must cut them down during the life of the tenant in tail; for otherwise they will descend to the heir as part of the inheritance.[5] Tenant in tail, after a possibility of issue extinct, is not liable for waste,[6] though equity would, in this case, interfere to restrain extravagant and malicious devastation.[7]

2. The next exception to the general rule, that whatever is planted or annexed to the soil or freehold passes with it, occurs in

[1] Packington's Case, 3 Atk. 215. [2] Pyne *v.* Dor, 1 T. R. 55.

[3] Woodf., L. & T., 9th ed., 963; Drewry on Injunct. 144.

[4] Morris *v.* Morris, 16 L. J. Chanc. 201. See Duke of Leeds *v.* Earl Amherst, Id. 5; s. c., 2 Phill. 117.

[5] Woodf., L. & T., 9th ed., 514.

[6] Williams *v.* Williams, 15 Ves. jun. 427; 2 Com. by Broom & Hadley 244.

[7] 2 Bla. Com., 16th ed., 283, n. (10).

the case of emblements, which term *comprises not only corn sown, but roots planted, and other annual artificial profits of the land;[1] and these, in certain cases, are distinct from the realty, and subject to many of the incidents attending personal property. [*407]

The rule upon this subject at common law, and irrespectively of a recent statute hereinafter noticed, as already stated,[2] is, that those only are entitled to emblements who have an uncertain estate or interest in land, which is determined by the act of God, or of the law, between the period of sowing and the severance of the crop.[3] Where, however, the tenancy is determined by the tenant's own act, as by forfeiture for waste committed, or by the marriage of a *fême* copyholder or a tenant *durante viduitate*, or in other similar cases, the tenant is not entitled to emblements; for the principle on which the law gives emblements is, that the tenant may be encouraged to cultivate by being sure of receiving the fruit of his labor, notwithstanding the determination of his estate by some unforeseen and unavoidable event.[4] By this rule, however, the tenant is not entitled to all the fruits of his labor, or such right might be extended to things of a more permanent nature, such as trees, or to more crops than one, since the cultivator very often looks for a compensation for his capital and labor in the produce of successive years; but the principle is limited to this extent, that he is entitled to one crop of that species only which ordinarily repays the labor by which it is produced within the year in which that labor is bestowed, though the crop may, in extraordinary seasons, be delayed beyond that period.[5]

*If, then, a tenant for life, or *pur autre vie*, sows the land, and dies before harvest, his personal representatives shall have the emblements or profits of the crop; and if the tenant for life sows the land, and afterwards grants over his estate, and the grantee dies before the corn is severed, it shall go to the tenant [*408]

[1] Com. Dig., "*Biens*" (G. 1).

[2] *Ante*, p. 239.

[3] Co. Litt. 55 a.

[4] Com. Dig., "*Biens*" (G. 2).

[5] Judgm., Graves *v.* Weld, 5 B. & Ad. 117, 118 (27 E. C. L. R.); citing Kingsbury *v.* Collins, 4 Bing. 202 (13 E. C. L. R.). In Latham *v.* Atwood, Cro. Car. 515, hops growing from ancient roots were held to be *like* emblements, because they are "such things as grow by the manurance and industry of the owner."

for life, and not to the grantee's executor; and, if a man sows land, and lets it for life, and the lessee for life dies before the corn is severed, the revisioner, and not the lessee's executor, shall have the emblements, although, if the lessee had sown the land himself, it would have been otherwise.[1]

Further, the under-tenants or lessees of tenant for life will be entitled to emblements in cases where tenant for life shall not have them, viz., where the title estate determines by the act of the last-mentioned party; as, in the case of a woman who holds *durante viduitate*, her taking husband is her own act, and therefore deprives her of the emblements; but if she leases her estate to an under-tenant, who sows the land, and she then marries, this act shall not deprive the tenant of his emblements; for he is a stranger and could not prevent her.[2] All these cases evidently involve the application of the general principle above stated.

The rule as to emblements likewise applies where a life estate is determined by the act of law; therefore if a lease be made to husband and wife during coverture, which gives them a determinable estate for life, and the husband sows the land, and afterwards the [*409] parties are *divorced *à vinculo matrimonii*, the husband shall have the emblements; for the sentence of divorce is the act of law, and *actus legis nemini facit injuriam*.[3]

So, the parochial clergy are tenants for their own lives, and the advantages of emblements are expressly given to them by stat. 28 Hen. 8, c. 11, s. 6, together with a power to enable the parson to dispose of the corn by will; but if the estate is determined by the act of the party himself, as by resigning his living, according to the principle above stated, he will not be entitled to emblements. The lessee of the glebe of a parson who resigns is, however, in a different situation; for, his tenancy being determined by the act of another, he shall have the emblements.[4]

A tenant for years, or from year to year, is not entitled to em-

[1] Arg. Knevett *v.* Pool, Cro. Eliz. 464; Woodf., L. & T., 9th ed., 588.

[2] Co. Litt. 55 b.

[3] Oland's Case, 5 Rep. 116; 1 Roll. Abr. 726, "*Emblements*," (A.). But in this case the marriage was void *ab initio—causa præcontractus;* and therefore the supposed husband never had any estate: see Davis *v.* Eyton, 7 Bing. 159, 160 (15 E. C. L. R.).

[4] Bulwer *v.* Bulwer, 2 B. & Ald. 470, 472; Woodf., L. & T., 9th ed., 588.

blements where the duration of the tenancy depends upon a certainty; as, if tenant for years holds for a term of ten years from midsummer, and, in the last year, sows a crop of corn which is not ripe and cut before midsummer, at the end of the term his landlord shall have it; for the tenant knew the expiration of his term, and, therefore, it was his own folly to sow that of which he could never reap the profits.[1] But where the tenancy for years, or from year to year, depends upon an uncertainty, as upon the death of the lessor being himself only tenant for life, or being a husband seised in right of his wife, or if the term of years be determinable upon a life or lives, in *these and similar cases, the estate not being certainly to expire for a time foreknown, but merely by the act of God, the tenant, or his representatives, shall have the emblements in the same manner as a tenant for life would be entitled to them;[2] and, if the lessee of tenant for life be disseised, and the lessee of the disseisor sow, and then the tenant for life dies, and the remainderman enters, the latter shall not have the corn, but the lessee of the tenant for life.[3] [*410]

Where, however, a tenant for years, or from year to year, himself put an end to the tenancy, as if he does anything amounting to a forfeiture, the landlord shall have the emblements;[4] and it is a general rule that he shall take them when he enters for a condition broken, because he enters by title paramount, and is in as of his first estate.[5] Where a lease was granted on condition, that, if the lessee contracted a debt on which he should be sued to judgment, followed by execution, the lessor should re-enter as of his former estate; it was held that the lessor, having accordingly re-entered after a judgment and execution, was entitled to the emblements.[6]

Where a tenant of any farm or lands holds the same at a rack-rent, it is now provided by stat. 14 & 15 Vict. c. 25, s. 1, that instead of claiming emblements he "shall continue to hold and occupy

[1] But the lessee would be entitled to emblements, if there was a special covenant to that effect: Co. Litt. 55 a, and Mr. Hargrave's note (5).

[2] Woodf., L. & T., 9th ed., 588.

[3] Knevett *v.* Pool, Cro. Eliz. 463.

[4] Co. Litt. 55 b.

[5] Per Bosanquet, J., 7 Bing. 160 (20 E. C. L. R.); Com. Dig., "*Biens*," (G. 2); Co. Litt. 55 b.

[6] Davis *v.* Eyton, 7 Bing. 154 (20 E. C. L. R.).

such farm or lands until the expiration of the then current year of his tenancy, and shall then quit, upon the terms of his lease or holding, in the same manner as if such lease or tenancy were then [*411] *determined by effluxion of time or other lawful means during the continuance of his landlord's estate;" and the section further provides for an apportionment of the rent as between the tenant and the succeeding landlord or owner. The above Act applies to any tenancy in respect of which there is a substantial claim to emblements.[1]

It has been mentioned that emblements are subject to many of the incidents attending personal property. Thus, by stat. 11 Geo. 2, c. 19, they may be distrained for rent,[2] they are forfeitable by outlawry in a personal action, they were devisable by testament before the Statute of Wills, and at the death of the owner they vest in his executors and not in his heir.[3] So, where tenant in fee or in tail dies after the corn has been sown, but before severance, it shall go to his personal representatives and not to the heir.[4] If, however, tenant in fee sows land, and then devises the land by will and dies before severance, the devisee shall have the corn, and not the devisor's executors;[5] and although it is not easy to account for this distinction, which gives corn growing to the devisee, but denies it to the heir,[6] it is clear law that the growing crops pass to the devisee of the land unless they be expressly bequeathed by the will to some one else.[7] The remainderman for life shall [*412] also have *the emblements sown by the devisor in fee, in preference to the executor of the tenant for life;[8] and the legatee of goods, stock, and movables, is entitled to growing corn in preference both to the devisee of the land and the executor.[9]

[1] Haines v. Welch, L. R. 4 C. P. 91.

See also as to the operation of the above statute, Lord Stradbroke v. Mulcahy, 2 Ir. C. L. Rep. N. S. 406.

[2] See also stat. 56 Geo. 3, c. 50; Hutt v. Morrell, 11 Q. B. 425 (63 E. C. L. R.).

[3] 2 Com. by Broom & Hadley 282.

[4] Com. Dig., "*Biens*" (G. 2); Co. Litt. 55 b, note (2), by Mr. Hargrave.

[5] Anon., Cro. Eliz. 61; Co. Litt. 55 b, n. (2); Spencer's Case, Winch. 51.

[6] See Co. Litt. 55 b, n. (2); Gilb. Ev. 250.

[7] Cooper v. Woolfitt, 2 H. & N. 122, 127; citing Shepp. Touch. (ed. by Preston) 472.

[8] Toll. Exors. 157.

[9] Cox v. Godsalve, 6 East 604, note; West v. Moore, 8 East 339.

In the case of strict tenancy at will, if the tenant sows his land, and the landlord, before the corn is ripe, or before it is reaped, puts him out, yet the tenant shall have the emblements, since he could not possibly know when his landlord would determine his will, and therefore could make no provision against it; but it is otherwise when the tenant himself determines the will, for in this case the landlord shall have the profits of the land.[1]

Tenants under execution are entitled to emblements when, by some sudden and casual profit, arising between seed-time and harvest, the tenancy is put an end to by the judgment being satisfied.[2] Again, if A. acknowledge a statute or recognizance, and afterwards sow the land, and the conusee extend the land, the latter shall have the emblements;[3] and where judgment was given against a person, and he then sowed the land and brought a writ of error to reverse the judgment, but it was affirmed, it was held, that the recoveror should have the corn.[4]

3. An away-going crop may be defined to be the crop sown during the last year of tenancy, but not ripe until *after [*413] its expiration. The right to this is usually vested in the out-going tenant, either by the express terms of the lease or contract, or by the usage or custom of the country; but in the absence of any contract or custom, and provided the law of emblements does not apply, the landlord is entitled to crops unsevered at the determination of the tenancy, as being a portion of the realty, and by virtue of that general maxim the exceptions to which we are now considering.

The common law, it has been observed, does so little to prescribe the relative duties of landlord and tenant, that it is by no means surprising the courts should have been favorably inclined to the introduction of those regulations in the mode of cultivation which custom and usage have established in each district to be the most beneficial to all parties.[5] The rule, therefore, is, that evidence of custom is receivable, although there be a written instrument of demise, provided the incident which it is sought to import by such

[1] Litt. s. 68, with the commentary thereon; Co. Litt. 55.

[2] Woodf., L. & T., 9th ed., 589.

[3] 2 Leon. R. 54.

[4] Wicks *v.* Jordan, 2 Bulstr. 213.

[5] Judgm., Hutton *v.* Warren, 1 M. & W. 466.

evidence into the contract is consistent with the terms of such contract; but evidence of custom is inadmissible if inconsistent with the express or implied terms of the instrument; and this rule applies to tenancies as well by parol agreement as by deed or written contract of demise.[1]

In Wigglesworth *v.* Dallison,[2] which is a leading case on this subject, the tenant was allowed an away-going crop, although there [*414] was a formal lease under seal. *There the lease was entirely silent on the subject of such a right; and Lord Mansfield said that "the custom did not alter or contradict the lease, but only added something to it."

The same point subsequently came under the consideration of the Court of King's Bench in the case of Senior *v.* Armytage,[3] which was an action by a tenant against his landlord for compensation for seed and labor under the denomination of tenant right. Mr. Justice Bayley, on its appearing that there was a written agreement between the parties, nonsuited the plaintiff; but the court afterwards set aside the nonsuit, and held, that though there was a written contract between landlord and tenant, the custom of the country would still be binding, if not inconsistent with the terms of such written contract, and that, not only all common law obligations, but those imposed by custom, were in full force where the contract did not vary them; and the court seems to have held, that the custom operated, unless it could be collected from the instrument, either expressly or impliedly, that the parties did not mean to be governed by it. On the second trial, the Lord Chief Baron Thompson held, that the custom prevailed, although the written instrument contained an express stipulation, that all the manure made on the farm should be spent on it, or left at the end of the tenancy, without any compensation being paid; such a stipulation certainly not excluding by implication the tenant's right to receive a compensation for seed and labor.[4]

[1] Wigglesworth *v.* Dallison, 1 Dougl. 201; Faviel *v.* Gaskoin, 7 Exch. 273; Muncey *v.* Dennis, 1 H. & N. 216; Clarke *v.* Roystone, 13 M. & W. 752.

[2] 1 Dougl. 201; affirmed in error, Id. 207, n. (8). See Beavan *v.* Delahay, 1 H. Bla. 5; recognized Griffiths *v.* Puleston, 13 M. & W. 358, 360; Knight *v.* Bennett, 3 Bing. 361 (11 E. C. L. R.); White *v.* Sayer, Palm. R. 211.

[3] Holt N. P. C. 197 (3 E. C. L. R.).

[4] In Holding *v.* Pigott, 7 Bing. 465 (20 E. C. L. R.), it is observed, that the rights of landlord and tenant may be governed by the terms of the agree-

*The next reported case as to the admissibility of evidence of custom respecting the right to an away-going [*415] crop is Webb *v.* Plummer,[1] in which there was a lease of down lands, with a covenant to spend all the produce on the premises, and to fold a flock of sheep upon the usual part of the farm, and also, in the last year of the term, to carry out the manure on parts of the fallowed farm pointed out by the lessor, the lessor paying for fallowing land and carrying out the dung, but nothing for the dung itself, and paying for grass on the ground and threshing the corn. The claim was for a customary allowance for foldage (a mode of manuring the ground), but the court held, that, as there was an express provision for some payment, on quitting, for the things covenanted to be done, and an omission of foldage, the customary obligation to pay for the latter was excluded, the language in the lease being equivalent to a stipulation that the lessor should pay for the things mentioned and no more.

The substance of the preceding remarks is extracted from the judgment delivered in the case of Hutton *v.* Warren,[2] where it was held that a custom, by which the tenant, cultivating according to the course of good husbandry, was entitled on quitting to receive from the landlord or incoming tenant a reasonable allowance for seeds and labor bestowed on the arable land in the last year of the tenancy, and was bound to leave the manure for the landlord, if he would purchase it, was not excluded by a stipulation in the lease to consume three-fourths of the hay and straw on the farm, and spread the manure *arising therefrom, and leave such of it as should not be so spread on the land for the use of the [*416] landlord on receiving a reasonable price for it.

Where a tenant continues to hold over after the expiration of his lease, without coming to any fresh agreement with his landlord, he must be taken to hold generally under the terms of the lease,[3] on which, therefore, the admissibility of evidence of custom will depend.[4]

ment during the tenancy, and by the custom immediately afterwards. Holding *v.* Pigott was followed in Muncey *v.* Dennis, 1 H. & N. 216, 222.

[1] 2 B. & Ald. 750.

[2] 1 M. & W. 466. Proof of the custom lies on the outgoing tenant: Caldecott *v.* Smythies, 7 C. & P. 808 (32 E. C. L. R.).

[3] See further as to this, Hyatt *v.* Griffiths, 17 Q. B. 505 (79 E. C. L. R.); Thomas *v.* Packer, 1 H. & N. 669.

[4] Boraston *v.* Green, 16 East 71; Roberts *v.* Barker, 1 Cr. & M. 808; Griffiths *v.* Puleston, 13 M. & W. 358. See Kimpton *v.* Eve, 3 Ves. & B. 349.

The principle with respect to the right to take an away-going crop applies equally to the case of a tenancy from year to year as to a lease for a longer term;[1] such custom, it has been observed, is just, for he who sows ought to reap, and it is for the benefit and encouragement of agriculture. It is, indeed, against the general rule of law concerning emblements, which are not allowed to tenants who know when their term is to cease, because it is held to be their fault or folly to have sown when they knew their interest would expire before they could reap. But the custom of a particular place may rectify what otherwise would be imprudence or folly.[2] It may be observed, too, that the question as to away-going crops under a custom is quite a different matter from emblements, which are by the common law.[3]

[*417] *4. The doctrine as to fixtures is peculiarly illustrative of the legal maxim under consideration; for the general rule, as laid down in the old books, is, that "whenever a tenant has affixed anything to the demised premises during his term, he can never again sever it without the consent of his landlord."[4] "The old rule" upon this subject, observes Martin, B.,[5] "laid down in the old books, is that if the tenant or the occupier of a house or land annex anything to the freehold, neither he nor his representatives can afterwards take it away, the maxim being *Quicquid plantatur solo solo cedit.* But as society progressed, and tenants for lives or for terms of years of houses, for the more convenient or luxurious occupation of them, or for the purposes of trade, affixed valuable and expensive articles to the freehold, the injustice of denying the tenant the right to remove them at his pleasure, and deeming such things practically forfeited to the owner of the fee

[1] Onslow *v.* ——, 16 Ves. Jun. 173. See Thorpe *v.* Eyre, 1 A. & E. 926 (28 E. C. L. R.), where the custom was held not to be available in the case of a tenancy which was determined by an award. Ex parte Mandrell, 2 Mad. 315.

[2] Judgm., Wigglesworth *v.* Dallison, 1 Dougl. 201; Dalby *v.* Hirst, 1 B. & B. 224 (5 E. C. L. R.).

[3] Per Taunton, J., 1 A. & E. 933 (28 E. C. L. R.); citing Com. Dig., "*Biens*" (G. 2).

[4] Amos & Fer., on Fixtures, 2d ed., 19.

[5] 10 Exch. 507, 508, citing Minshall *v.* Lloyd, 2 M. & W. 450. See also per Wood, V.-C., Mather *v.* Fraser, 2 K. & J. 536.

simple by the mere act of annexation, became apparent to all; and there long ago sprung up a right, sanctioned and supported both by the courts of law and equity, in the temporary owner or occupier of real property, or his representative, to disannex and remove certain articles, though annexed by him to the freehold, and these articles have been denominated *fixtures*."

Questions respecting the right to what are ordinarily called fixtures principally arise between three classes of persons: 1st, between heir and executor or administrator of tenant in fee; 2dly, between the personal representative of tenant for life or in tail and *the remainderman or reversioner; 3dly, between landlord [*418] and tenant. In the first of these cases, the general rule obtains with the most rigor in favor of the inheritance, and against the right to disannex therefrom, and to consider as a personal chattel anything which has been affixed thereto;[1] in the second case, the right to fixtures is considered more favorably for the personal representatives than in the preceding; and, in the last case, the greatest latitude and indulgence have always been allowed in favor of the tenant;[2]—so that decisions, establishing the right of the personal representatives to fixtures in the first and second of the above cases, will apply, *à fortiori*, to the third.

It is here necessary to remark, that the term "fixtures" is often used indiscriminately in reference to those articles which are not by law removable when once attached to the freehold, as well as to those which are severable therefrom.[3] But, in its correct sense, the word

[1] Per Lord Ellenborough, C. J., Elwes *v.* Maw, 3 East 51; per Abbott, C. J., Colegrave *v.* Dias Santos, 2 B. & C. 78 (9 E. C. L. R.).

[2] Ibid.

[3] Per Parke, B., Minshall *v.* Lloyd, 2 M. & W. 459; Judgm., L. R. 3 Ex. 260. "There is no doubt that sometimes things annexed to land remain chattels as much after they have been annexed as they were before. The case of pictures hung on a wall for the purpose of being more conveniently seen may be mentioned by way of illustration. On the other hand things may be made so completely a part of the land, as being essential to its convenient use, that even a tenant could not remove them. An example of this class of chattel may be found in doors or windows. Lastly, things may be annexed to land for the purposes of trade, or of domestic convenience or ornament, in so permanent a manner as really to form a part of the land, and yet the tenant who has erected them is entitled to remove them during his term, or it may be within a reasonable time after its expiration." Judgm., L. R. 4 Ex. 329;

[*419] "fixtures" *includes such things only of a personal nature as have been annexed to the realty, and which may be afterwards severed or removed by the party who united them, or his personal representatives, against the will of the owner of the freehold.[1] The word "fixtures" has been described as "very modern," and is generally understood to comprehend "any article which a tenant has a power of removing."[2] The precise signification of this word, when used in an indenture of demise, may have to be determined by reference to the context.[3]

In connection with the law of distress, the true meaning of the word "fixtures" often needs consideration, things fixed to the freehold not being at common law distrainable.[4] In regard to the question, whether certain machines were to be deemed parcel of the freehold or not, it has been observed that it was really one of fact, depending on the particular circumstances of the case, and principally on two considerations: 1st, the mode and extent of annexation to the soil or fabric of the house, whether the machines could easily be removed *integrè salvè, et commodè*, or not, without injury thereto or to the fabric of the building;[5] 2dly, on the object and purpose [*420] *of the annexation, whether it was for the permanent and substantial improvement of the dwelling, in the language of the civil law *perpetui usûs causâ*,[6] or in that of the Year Book,[7]

Longbottom *v.* Berry, L. R. 5 Q. B. 123, 139; per Blackburn, J., Reg. *v.* Lee, L. R. 1 Q. B. 253.

[1] Judgm., Hallen *v.* Runder, 1 Cr., M. & R. 276; adopted, per Martin, B., 10 Exch. 508. See also the word "fixtures," defined per Lord Cranworth, C., Ex parte Barclay, 5 DeG., M. & G. 410 (where the leading cases at common law concerning fixtures are reviewed); London Loan, &c., Co. *v.* Drake, 6 C. B. N. S. 798, 808.

[2] Judgm., Wiltshear *v.* Cottrell, 1 E. & B. 690 (72 E. C. L. R.); per Parke, B., Sheen *v.* Rickie, 5 M. & W. 182; per Martin, B., 10 Exch. 507. See Horsfall *v.* Hey, 2 Exch. 778.

[3] Bishop *v.* Elliott, 11 Exch. 113; s. c., 10 Id. 496. See Burt *v.* Haslett, 18 C. B. 162 (86 E. C. L. R.); s. c., Id. 893.

[4] The law upon this subject is stated in the note to Simpson *v.* Hartrop, 1 Smith, L. C., 6th ed., 390; Swire *v.* Leach, 18 C. B. N. S. 479 (114 E. C. L. R.).

[5] If the injury be very trifling, the law will not regard it, in accordance with the maxim *De minimis non curat lex* (*ante*, p. 142); Judgm., Martin *v.* Roe, 7 E. & B. 244 (90 E. C. L. R.).

[6] See Mackeld. Civ. L. 152.

[7] 20 Hen. 7, 13.

pour un profit del inheritance, or merely for a temporary purpose, or the more complete enjoyment and use of it *as a chattel*.[1]

Where the article annexed to the land is irremovable, it is viewed in law as part of the freehold, and is subject to the rules and incidents of real property.[2]

With the above preliminary remarks we shall proceed very briefly to consider the three classes of cases specified at p. 417, viz., between heir and the personal representatives of tenant in fee; —between the personal representatives of tenant for life or in tail and the remainderman or reversioner;—between landlord and tenant; noticing also under these heads the right to fixtures as between some other parties.

In the class of cases arising between heir and executor, the rule has been thus stated: that whatever is strongly affixed to the freehold or inheritance, and cannot be severed thence without violence or damage, *quod ex ædibus non facile revellitur*, is become a member of the inheritance, and shall, therefore, pass to the heir;[3] and, in the first place, it must be observed, that a chattel *does not [*421] lose its personal nature unless fixed in or to the ground, or in or to some foundation which in itself forms part of the freehold. It is not sufficient that the article in question merely rests upon the soil, or upon such foundation;[4] unless there be annexation, no difficulty can under any circumstances occur. It is frequently, however, a matter of doubt, whether the annexation can be considered as sufficient; and in such cases the best test appears to be whether the removal can be effected without substantial injury to the freehold.[5]

[1] Judgm., Hellawell *v.* Eastwood, 6 Exch. 312, followed in Waterfall *v.* Penistone, 6 E. & B. 876, 889, 891 (88 E. C. L. R.); and Reg. *v.* Lee, L. R. 1 Q. B. 254, and distinguished in Climie *v.* Wood, L. R. 3 Ex. 257, 4 Id. 328, and Longbottom *v.* Berry, L. R. 5 Q. B. 123, where various cases concerning fixtures are collected.

[2] Per Parke, B., Minshall *v.* Lloyd, 2 M. & W. 459; recognized, Mackintosh *v.* Trotter, 3 M. & W. 186; cited in Dumergue *v.* Rumsey, 2 H. & C. 777, 790; Judgm., Wiltshear *v.* Cottrell, 1 E. & B. 674 (72 E. C. L. R.).

[3] See Shep. Touch. 469, 470; Com. Dig., "*Biens*" (B).

[4] Wiltshear *v.* Cottrell, 1 E. & B. 674 (72 E. C. L. R.); Huntley *v.* Russell, 13 Q. B. 572 (66 E. C. L. R.); Hutchinson *v.* Kay, 23 Beav. 413; Mather *v.* Frazer, 2 K. & J. 536; R. *v.* Inhabs. of Otley, 1 B. & Ad. 161, 165 (20 E. C. L. R.). See also Wood *v.* Hewett, 8 Q. B. 913 (55 E. C. L. R.); Lancaster *v.* Eve, 5 C. B. N. S. 717 (94 E. C. L. R.).

[5] Avery *v.* Cheslyn, 3 A. & E. 75 (30 E. C. L. R.); Judgm., Martin *v.* Roe, 7

The strictness of the rule under consideration was, it may be remarked, very early relaxed, as between landlord and tenant, in favor of such fixtures as are partly or wholly essential to trade or manufacture;[1] and the same relaxation has, in several modern cases, been extended to decisions of that class which we are now considering, viz., those between heir and executor. In the case of Elwes *v.* Maw, which is justly regarded as a leading authority on the subject of fixtures, Lord Ellenborough observed,[2] that, in determining whether a particular fixed instrument, machine, or even building, should be considered as removable by the executor as between him and the heir, the court in three principal cases[3] on the [*422] subject may be considered as *having decided mainly on this ground, that where the fixed instrument, engine, or utensil (and the building covering the same falls within the same principle) was an accessory to a matter of a personal nature, it should be itself considered as personalty. In two of these cases,[4] a fire-engine was considered as an accessory to the carrying on the trade of getting and vending coals—a matter of a personal nature. In Lord Dudley *v.* Lord Ward, Lord Hardwicke, says, "A colliery is not only an enjoyment of the estate, but in a part carrying on a trade;" and in Lawton *v.* Lawton he says, "One reason that weighs with me is its being a mixed case, between enjoying the profits of the land and carrying on a species of trade; and considering it in this light, it comes very near the instances in brewhouses, &c., of furnaces and coppers." Upon the same principle Lord C. B. Comyns may be considered as having decided the case of the cider-mill,[5] *i. e.*, as a mixed case, between enjoying the prof-

E. & B. 244 (90 E. C. L. R.), where the right to remove ornamental fixtures as between the executors of an incumbent and his successor is considered.

[1] Judgm., 3 East 51, 52; per Story, J., delivering the judgment in Van Ness *v.* Pacard, 2 Peters (U. S.) R. 143, 145.

[2] 3 East 38.

[3] Viz., Lawton *v.* Lawton, 3 Atk. 13, which was the case of a fire-engine to work a colliery erected by tenant for life; Lord Dudley *v.* Lord Ward, Amb. 113, which was also the case of a fire-engine; and Lawton *v.* Salmon, 1 H. Bla. 259, n., which was trover for salt pans brought by the executor against the tenant of the heir-at-law.

[4] Lawton *v.* Lawton, 3 Atk. 13; Lord Dudley *v.* Lord Ward, Amb. 113.

[5] Cited in Lawton *v.* Lawton, 3 Atk. 13; but see the observations respecting this case by Lord Hardwicke in Lawton *v.* Salmon, 1 H. Bla. 259, n.; Lord Dud-

its of the land and carrying on a species of trade, and as considering the cider-mill as properly an accessory to the trade of making cider. In the case of the salt-pans,[1] Lord Mansfield does not seem to have considered *them as accessory to the carrying on a trade, but as merely the means of enjoying the benefit of the inheritance. Upon this principle he considered them as belonging to the heir as parcel of the inheritance, for the enjoyment of which they were made, and not as belonging to the executor as the means or instrument of carrying on a trade.[2] [*423]

In a modern case before the House of Lords, it appeared that the absolute owner of land, for the purpose of better using and enjoying that land, had erected upon and affixed to the freehold certain machinery. It was held that, in the absence of any disposition by him of this machinery it would go to the heir as part of the real estate; and, further, that if the *corpus* of the machinery passed to the heir, all that belonged to such machinery, although more or less capable of being detached from it, and of being used in such detached state, must also be considered as belonging to the heir.[3]

As between devisee and executor the rule seems, in principle, to be the same as that already considered, the devisee standing in place of the heir as regards his right to fixtures; for, if a freehold house be devised, fixtures pass;[4] but if the tenant for life or in tail

ley *v.* Lord Ward, Amb. 113; and in Ex parte Quincey, 3 Atk. 477, and Bull. N. P. 34. It seems that no rule of law can be extracted from a case of the particulars of which so little is known; see per Lord Cottenham, Fisher *v.* Dixon, 12 Cl. & Fin. 329; and see as to the cider-mill case, per Wood, V.-C., Mather *v.* Fraser, 2 K. & J. 536, reviewing the prior authorities.

[1] Lawton *v.* Salmon, 1 H. Bla. 259, n.

[2] Per Lord Ellenborough, C. J., 3 East 54. See Winn *v.* Ingelby, 5 B. & Ald. 625 (7 E. C. L. R.); R. *v.* St. Dunstan, 4 B. & C. 686, 691 (10 E. C. L. R.); Harvey *v.* Harvey, Stra. 1141.

[3] Fisher *v.* Dixon, 12 Cl. & Fin. 312. In this case the exception in favor of trade was held not applicable; the judgments delivered contain, however, some remarks as to the limits of this exception, which are well worthy of consideration. See also Mather *v.* Fraser, 2 K. & J. 536, 545; Judgm., Climie *v.* Wood, L. R. 4 Ex. 330; Judgm., Longbottom *v.* Berry, L. R. 5 Q. B. 136, which latter cases also show that the decisions establishing a tenant's right to remove trade fixtures (*post*, p. 425) "do not apply as between mortgagor and mortgagee any more than between heir-at-law and executor."

[4] Per Best, J., Colegrave *v.* Dias Santos, 2 B. & C. 80 (9 E. C. L. R.).

[*424] devise fixtures, *his devise is void, he having no power to devise the realty to which they are incident. He may, however, devise such fixtures as would pass to his executor.[1]

As between the heir and devisee, it may be considered as a rule that the latter will be entitled to all articles which are affixed to the land, whether the annexation in fact took place prior or subsequent to the date of the devise, according to the maxim, *Quod ædificatur in areâ legatâ cedit legato;* and, therefore, by a devise of a house, all personal chattels which are annexed to the house, and which are essential to its enjoyment, will pass to the devisee.[2]

As between vendor and vendee, everything which forms part of the freehold passes by a sale and conveyance of the freehold itself, if there be nothing to indicate a contrary intention.[3]

Thus, in Colegrave *v.* Dias Santos,[4] the owner of a freehold house, in which there were various fixtures, sold it by auction. Nothing was said about the fixtures. A conveyance of the house was executed, and possession given to the purchaser, the fixtures still remaining in the house. It was held, that they passed by the conveyance of the freehold; and that, even if they did not, the vendor, after giving up possession, could not maintain trover for them.

[*425] The result of various recent decisions[5] is that the *old maxim *quicquid plantatur solo solo cedit* applies in all its integrity to the relation of mortgagor and mortgagee, for a mortgage being a security or pledge for a debt, it is not unreasonable if a fixture be annexed to land at the time of a mortgage, or if the mortgagor in possession afterward annexes a fixture to it, that the fixture shall be deemed an additional security for the debt—whether it be a trade fixture or a fixture of any other kind; though upon

[1] Shep. Touch. 469, 470; 4 Rep. 62.

[2] Amos & Fer., Fixtures, 2d ed., 246.

[3] Colegrave *v.* Dias Santos, 2 B. & C. 76 (9 E. C. L. R.); cited, arg. Id. 610; per Parke, B., Hitchman *v.* Walton, 4 M. & W. 416; per Patteson, J., Hare *v.* Horton, 5 B. & Ad. 730 (27 E. C. L. R.). See Steward *v.* Lombe, 1 B. & B. 506, 513 (5 E. C. L. R.); Ryall *v.* Rolle, 1 Atk. 175; Thompson *v.* Pettit, 10 Q. B. 101 (59 E. C. L. R.); Wiltshear *v.* Cottrell, 1 E. & B. 674 (72 E. C. L. R.).

[4] 2 B. & C. 76 (9 E. C. L. R.). See Manning *v.* Bailey, 2 Exch. 45.

[5] Collected in Climie *v.* Wood, L. R. 3 Ex. 257, affirmed L. R. 4 Ex. 328, with which *acc.* Longbottom *v.* Berry, L. R. 5 Q. B. 123. See Tebb *v.* Hodge, L. R. 5 C. P. 73.

the true construction of a mortgage deed trade fixtures may be removable by the mortgagor.[1] It has accordingly been established that trade fixtures which have been annexed to the freehold for the more convenient using of them, and not to improve the inheritance, and which are capable of being removed without appreciable damage to the freehold, pass under a mortgage of the freehold to the mortgagee.[2]

The effect of a mortgage then with regard to fixtures is, in brief, similar to that of a conveyance;[3] and trover will not lie against either vendee or mortgagee[4] in possession for chattels affixed to the freehold, but which *might have been removed before possession was given under the deed. [*426] Where, however, there was a mortgage of dwelling-houses, foundries, and other premises, "together with all grates, &c., in and about the said two dwelling-houses, and the brewhouses thereto belonging," it was held that, although without these words the fixtures in the foundries would have passed, yet by them the fixtures intended to pass were confined to those in the dwelling-houses and brewhouses.[5]

In case of an absolute sale of premises, where the conveyance is not general, but contains a stipulation that "the fixtures are to be taken at a valuation," those things only should in strictness be valued which would be deemed personal assets as between heir and executor, and would not pass with the inheritance.[6]

[1] Judgm., L. R. 3 Ex. 260.

[2] Climie *v.* Wood, L. R. 3 Ex. 257, affirmed in error, L. R. 4 Ex. 328; Longbottom *v.* Berry, L. R. 5 Q. B. 123; Tebb *v.* Hodge, L. R. 5 C. P. 73, in which case the prior decisions are collected.

[3] Per Parke, B., 4 M. & W. 416; Longstaff *v.* Meagoe, 2 A. & E. 167 (29 E. C. L. R.). See Trappes *v.* Harter, 2 Cr. & M. 153; cited Hellawell *v.* Eastwood, 6 Exch. 313; and in Ex parte Barclay, 5 De G., M. & G. 412; but said, per Cresswell, J., to have been overruled (Wilde *v.* Waters, 16 C. B. 647 (81 E. C. L. R.)). Trappes *v.* Harter has, however, frequently been recognized as an authority: Mather *v.* Fraser, 2 K. & J. 536. It was cited and distinguished in Walmsley *v.* Milne, 7 C. B. N. S. 133–4 (97 E. C. L. R.). See Haley *v.* Hammersley, 30 L. J. Chanc. 771; Watson *v.* Lane, 11 Exch. 769.

[4] 2 B. & C. 76 (10 E. C. L. R.); Longstaff *v.* Meagoe, 2 A. & E. 167 (29 E. C. L. R.). See Boydell *v.* M'Michael, 1 Cr., M. & R. 177; Ex parte Bentley, 2 M. D. & De G. 591.

[5] Hare *v.* Horton, 5 B. & Ald. 726 (27 E. C. L. R.) (distinguished in Mather *v.* Fraser, cited *supra*, n. 3; Haley *v.* Hammersley, and Walmsley *v.* Milne, *supra;* Metropolitan Counties Assurance Co. *v.* Brown, 26 Beav. 454.

[6] Amos & Fer., Fixtures, 2d ed., 221.

With respect to ornamental fixtures, there are some cases in which the executor has been permitted to remove even these against the heir.[1] But on the whole, as observed by a learned writer, it would seem that the law is by no means clearly settled respecting the right of the executor of tenant in fee to fixtures set up for ornament or domestic convenience.[2]

Secondly, we have already observed,[3] that the heir is more favored in law than the remainderman or reversioner, and, therefore, all cases in which an executor or administrator of the tenant in fee would be entitled to [*427] *fixtures as against the heir, will apply *à fortiori*, to support the claim of the representatives of tenant for life, or in tail, against the remainderman or reversioner. The personal representatives, therefore, in the latter case, seem clearly entitled to fixtures erected for purposes of trade, as against the party in remainder or reversion.[4]

In the third class of cases above mentioned, that, viz., between landlord and tenant, the general rule, that whatever has once been annexed to the freehold becomes a part of it, and cannot afterwards be removed, except by or with the consent of him who is entitled to the inheritance,[5] must be qualified more largely than in the preceding classes: thus, the tenant may take away during the continuance of his term, or at the end of it, although not after he has quitted possession, such fixtures as he has himself put upon the

[1] See Harvey *v.* Harvey, Stra. 1141; Squier *v.* Mayer, 2 Freem. 240; Beck *v.* Rebow, 1 P. Wms. 94.

[2] 1 Williams Executors, 6th ed., 697.

[3] *Ante*, p. 418.

[4] Lawton *v.* Lawton, 3 Atk. 13; Lord Dudley *v.* Lord Ward, Amb. 113.

[5] Co. Litt. 53 a; per Kindersley, V.-C., Gibson *v.* Hammersmith R. C., 32 L. J. Chanc. 340 *et seq.* Trover does not lie for fixtures until after severance; Dumergue *v.* Rumsey, 2 H. & C. 777, 790; Minshall *v.* Lloyd, 2 M. & W. 450; recognized, Mackintosh *v.* Trotter, 3 Id. 184–186; Roffey *v.* Henderson, 17 Q. B. 574, 586 (79 E. C. L. R.); London Loan, &c., Co. *v.* Drake, 6 C. B. N. S. 798, 811 (95 E. C. L. R.). In Wilde *v.* Waters, 16 C. B. 651 (81 E. C. L. R.), Maule, J., delivering the judgment of the court, observes, "Generally speaking, no doubt, fixtures are part of the freehold, and are not such goods and chattels as can be made the subject of an act of trover. But there are various exceptions to this rule, in respect of things which are set up for ornament or for the purpose of trade, or for other particular purposes. As to these, there are many distinctions, some of which are nice and intricate." See also Clarke *v.* Holford, 2 C. & K. 540 (47 E. C. L. R.).

demised premises, either for the purposes of trade, or for the ornament or furniture of his house;[1] but here a distinction must be observed *between erections for the purposes of trade annexed to the freehold, and those which are for purposes merely agricultural.[2] With respect to the former, the exception engrafted upon the general rule is of almost as high antiquity as the rule itself, being founded upon principles of public policy, and originating in a desire to encourage trade and manufactures. With respect to the latter class, however, it has been expressly decided that to such cases the general rule must (irrespective of the stat. 14 & 15 Vict. c. 25) be applied. [*428]

In the leading case on this subject,[3] it was held that a tenant in agriculture, who erected at his own expense, and for the necessary and convenient occupation of his farm, a beast-house, and carpenter's shop, &c., which buildings were of brick and mortar, and tiled, and let into the ground, could not legally remove the same even during his term, although by so doing he would leave the premises in the same state as when he entered; and a distinction was here taken between annexations to the freehold for the purposes of trade, and those made for the purposes of agriculture and for better enjoying the immediate profits of the land. Where, indeed,

[1] Such as stoves, grates, ornamental chimney-pieces, wainscots fastened with screws, coppers, a pump very slightly affixed to the freehold, and various other articles; per Erle, J., and Crowder, J., Bishop *v.* Elliott, 11 Exch. 115; Grimes *v.* Boweren, 6 Bing. 437 (19 E. C. L. R.); and per Tindal, C. J., Id. 439, 440; Horn *v.* Baker, 9 East 215, 238. In Buckland *v.* Butterfield, 2 B. & B. 54 (6 E. C. L. R.), which is another important decision on this subject, it was held, that a conservatory erected on a brick foundation, attached to a dwelling-house, and communicating with it by windows, and by a flue passing into the parlor chimney, becomes part of the freehold, and cannot be removed by the tenant or his assignees. See West *v.* Blakeway, 2 M. & Gr. 729 (40 E. C. L. R.); Burt *v.* Haslett, 18 C. B. 162 (86 E. C. L. R.); s. c., Id. 893.

See also Powell, app., Farmer, resp., 18 C. B. N. S. 168, 178 (114 E. C. L. R.); Powell, app., Boraston, resp., Id. 175.

[2] Per Lord Kenyon, C. J., Penton *v.* Robart, 2 East 90; Judgm., Earl of Mansfield *v.* Blackburne, 3 Bing. N. C. 438 (32 E. C. L. R.). A nurseryman may, at the end of his term, remove trees planted for the purpose of sale: Amos & Fer., Fixtures, 2d ed., 68.

[3] Elwes *v.* Maw, 3 East 38. See Smith *v.* Render, 27 L. J. Ex. 83; and cases there cited.

[*429] a superincumbent *shed is erected as a mere accessory to a personal chattel, as an engine, it may, as coming within the definition of a trade fixture, be removed; but where it is accessory to the realty it can in no case be removed.[1]

Where the tenant of a farm or land, with the consent in writing of his landlord, erects at his own cost farm-buildings, engines, or machinery, either for agricultural purposes, or for the purposes of trade and agriculture, they will now be the property of the tenant, and removable by him, subject to the provisions of the statute below cited,[2] although built in or permanently fixed to the soil, or the landlord may purchase them at his election.

It has been stated, that the right of removal, where it exists, should be exercised during the continuance of the term; for, if the tenant forbears to exercise it within that period, or during such further period as he holds the premises under a right still to consider himself as tenant, or after the expiration of the term, but whilst he remains in possession of the premises—though the precise state of the law upon this point is somewhat doubtful[3]—the tenant will be presumed to have voluntarily relinquished the claim in favor of his landlord.[4] It is also important to remark, that the legal right of the tenant to remove fixtures is capable of being either extended or controlled by the express agreement of the parties; [*430] and *the ordinary right of the tenant to disannex tenants' fixtures during the term may thus be renounced by him;[5] it is, in fact, very usual to introduce into a lease a covenant for this purpose, either specifying what fixtures shall be removable by the tenant, or stipulating that he will, at the end of the term, deliver up all fixtures annexed during its continuance to the landlord's

[1] Whitehead *v.* Bennett, 27 L. J. Ch. 474.

[2] 14 & 15 Vict. c. 25, s. 3.

[3] Judgm., Leader *v.* Homewood, 5 C. B. N. S. 553 (94 E. C. L. R.).

[4] See per Jervis, C. J., Heap *v.* Barton, 12 C. B. 280; per Patteson, J., Roffey *v.* Henderson, 17 Q. B. 586 (79 E. C. L. R.); per Parke, B., 3 M. & W. 186; Leader *v.* Homewood, 5 C. B. N. S. 546 (94 E. C. L. R.); per Williams, J., Stransfeld *v.* Mayor, &c., of Portsmouth, 4 C. B. N. S. 128 (93 E. C. L. R.); and in London Loan, &c., Co. *v.* Drake, 6 Id. 810; Amos & Fer., Fixtures 87; cited by Lord Tenterden, C. J., Lyde *v.* Russell, 1 B. & Ad. 395 (20 E. C. L. R.); Weeton *v.* Woodcock, 7 M. & W. 14, 19; Lee *v.* Risdon, 7 Taunt. 188 (2 E. C. L. R.).

[5] Dumergue *v.* Rumsey, 2 H. & C. 777.

use.[1] Where a lessee mortgaged tenant's fixtures, and afterwards surrendered his lease to the lessor, who granted a fresh lease to a third party, the mortgagees were held entitled to enter and sever the fixtures.[2]

In an action of trespass for breaking and entering the plaintiff's apartment, and for taking a certain brass plate from the outer door of the dwelling-house, the defendant pleaded, first, not guilty; and, secondly, as to removing the brass plate, that the plaintiff was not possessed thereof; no evidence was given as to whether it was or was not a fixture, nor was any question as to this point raised at the trial. The jury assessed the damages separately, for the breaking and entering, and for the removal of the door-plate; and the court held, that, after verdict, it must be assumed that the said plate was not a fixture, and that the defendant, having treated it as an independent chattel, and thereby thrown the plaintiff off his guard, could not, the verdict being against him, turn round and treat the matter differently;[3] for this would *have been "blowing hot and cold," and therefore inadmissible, as opposed to a principle already mentioned.[4] [*431]

It is also worthy of notice, that the right of property in fixtures may be modified by proof of a special usage prevailing in the particular neighborhood:[5] and it may, also, as in case of landlord and tenant, be modified by evidence of the intention of the parties; *ex. gr.*, a chattel placed by the owner upon the freehold of another, but severable from it without injury thereto, does not necessarily become part of the freehold; it is matter of evidence whether by agreement it does not remain the property of the original owner.[6]

[1] See Bishop *v.* Elliott, 11 Exch. 113; Stansfield *v.* Mayor, &c., of Portsmouth, 4 C. B. N. S. 120 (93 E. C. L. R.); Earl of Mansfield *v.* Blackburne, 3 Bing. N. C. 438 (32 E. C. L. R.); Foley *v.* Addenbrooke, 13 M. & W. 174; Sleddon *v.* Cruikshank, 16 M. & W. 71; Heap *v.* Barton, 12 C. B. 274 (74 E. C. L. R.), citing Penton *v.* Robart, 2 East 88.

[2] London Loan, &c., Co. *v.* Drake, 6 C. B. N. S. 798 (95 E. C. L. R.).

[3] Lane *v.* Dixon, 3 C. B. 776 (54 E. C. L. R.); cited Huddert *v.* Rigby, L. R. 5 Q. B. 139.

[4] *Ante*, p. 169.

[5] Vin. Abr., "*Executors*," U. 74. See Davis *v.* Jones, 2 B. & Ald. 165, 168.

[6] Wood *v.* Hewett, 8 Q. B. 913 (55 E. C. L. R.), followed in Lancaster *v.* Eve, 5 C. B. N. S. 717, 722, 727, 728 (94 E. C. L. R.), where Williams, J.,

In concluding these remarks concerning fixtures, we may observe that the uncertainty of the law on this subject results necessarily from the fact, that each case involving a question as to the right to fixtures is professedly and necessarily, in a great measure, decided according to its own particular circumstances; and a perusal of the preceding pages will sufficiently show that the maxim *Quicquid plantatur solo solo cedit* is held up by our law only to be departed from on account of the acknowledged ill effects which would ensue from too strict an application of it.

[*432] *DOMUS SUA CUIQUE EST TUTISSIMUM REFUGIUM.

(5 Rep. 92.)

Every man's house is his castle.[1]

In a leading case which well exemplifies the application of the above maxim, the facts may be shortly stated thus:—The defendant and one B. were joint tenants of a house in London. B. acknowledged a recognizance in the nature of a statute staple to the plaintiff, and, being possessed of certain goods in the said house, died, whereupon the house in which the goods remained became vested in the defendant by survivorship. Plaintiff sued out process of extent on the statutes to the sheriffs of London; and, on the sheriffs having returned the conusor dead, he had another writ to extend all the lands which B. had at the time of acknowledging the statute, or at any time after, and all the goods which he had at the day of his death. This writ plaintiff delivered to the sheriffs, and told them that divers goods belonging to B. at the time of his death were in the defendant's house; upon which the sheriffs charged the jury to make inquiry according to the said writ, and the sheriffs and jury

observes, "No doubt the maxim *Quicquid plantatur solo solo cedit* is well established; the only question is, what is meant by it? It is clear that the mere putting a chattel into the soil by another cannot alter the ownership of the chattel. To apply the maxim, there must be such a fixing to the soil as reasonably to lead to the inference that it was intended to be incorporated with the soil."

In connection with what has been said *supra*, respecting the right to fixtures as between landlord and tenant, may be consulted the cases cited *ante*, p. 425, which concern mortgagor and mortgagee.

[1] *Nemo de doma suâ extrahi debet*, D. 50. 17. 103.

came to the house aforesaid, and offered to enter in order to extend the goods, the outer door of the house being then open; whereupon the defendant, *præmissorum non ignarus*, and intending to disturb the execution, shut the door against the sheriffs and jury, whereby the plaintiff lost the benefit of his writ.[1]

In the above case, the following points, which bear upon the present subject, were resolved, and may be thus shortly stated.

*1st. That the house of every one is his castle, as well [*433] for his defence against injury and violence, as for his repose; and, consequently, although the life of man is a thing precious and favored in law, yet if thieves come to a man's house to rob or murder him, and the owner or his servants kill any of the thieves in defence of himself and his house, this is not felony. So, if any person attempt to burn or burglariously[2] to break and enter any dwelling-house in the night-time, or attempt to break open a house in the day-time with intent to rob, and be killed in the attempt, the slayer shall be acquitted and discharged, for the homicide is justifiable.[3] And in such cases, not only the owner whose person or property is thus attacked, but the servants and the members of his family, or even strangers who are present at the time, are equally justified in killing the assailant.[4]

In order, however, that a case may fall within the preceding rule, the intent to commit such a forcible and atrocious crime as above mentioned must be clearly manifested by the felon; otherwise the homicide will amount to manslaughter, at least, if not to murder.[5]

2dly. It was resolved in the principal case, that when any house is recovered by ejectment, the sheriff may break the house, in order to deliver seisin and possession thereof to the lessor of the

[1] Semayne's Case, 5 Rep. 91; cited per Tindal, C. J., Hollier *v.* Laurie, 3 C. B. 339 (54 E. C. L. R.).

[2] In determining what is a *burglarious* entry of a dwelling-house, our law has, *in favorem vitæ*, resorted to many refinements and much nicety of construction. See per Coltman, J., 6 C. B. 10 (60 E. C. L. R.).

[3] 1 Hale P. C. 481, 488. By stat. 24 & 25 Vict. c. 100, s. 7, no punishment or forfeiture shall be incurred by any person who shall kill another in his own defence.

[4] 1 Hale P. C. 481, 484, *et seq.*

[5] 1 Hale P. C. 484; R. *v.* Scully, 1 C. & P. 319 (12 E. C. L. R.).

plaintiff. The officer may, if necessary, break open doors, in order [*434] to execute a writ *of *habere facias possessionem*, if the possession be not quietly given up; or he may take the *posse comitatus* with him, if he fear violence;[1] and he may remove all persons, goods, &c., from off the premises before he gives possession.[2] After verdict and judgment in ejectment, it is in practice usual for the lessor of the plaintiff to point out to the sheriff the premises recovered, and then the sheriff gives the lessor, at his own peril, execution of what he demands.[3] By the stat. 1 & 2 Vict. c. 74, s. 1,[4] which was passed in order to facilitate the recovery of tenements held at a rent not exceeding 20*l.* a year, the officers acting under the warrant obtained in pursuance of that Act are expressly authorized to enter by force, if needful, into the premises of which possession is sought to be recovered, and to give possession of the same to the landlord or his agent; and a summary mode of obtaining possession of small tenements is also, in certain cases, available under the County Court Acts.[5]

3dly. The third exception to the general rule is, where the execution is at suit of the crown, as where a felony or misdemeanor has been committed, in which case the sheriff may break open the outer door of the defendant's dwelling-house, having first signified the cause of his coming and desired admission.[6]

[*435] *But bare suspicion touching the guilt of the party will not warrant the proceeding to this extremity, though a felony has been actually committed, unless the officer comes armed with a warrant from a magistrate grounded on such suspicion.[7]

[1] 5 Rep. 91.

[2] Upton *v.* Wells, 1 Leon. R. 145.

[3] Ad. Eject., 4th ed., 300, 301. See per Patteson, J., Doe d. Stevens *v.* Lord, 6 Dowl. 256, 266.

[4] See Delaney *v.* Fox, 1 C. B. N. S. 166 (87 E. C. L. R.).

[5] As to recovering possession of a tenement in the County Court, see Broom's C. C. Pr., 2d ed., 288, 292.

[6] Semayne's Case, 3d resolution; Finch's Law 39. See also Sherwin *v.* Swindall, 12 M. & W. 783; Launock *v.* Brown, 2 B. & Ald. 592, which was a case of arrest for a misdemeanor; Burdett *v.* Abbott, 14 East 157, 158, where the plaintiff was arrested under the speaker's warrant for a breach of privilege: Foster on Homicide 320. As to the power of arrest under the warrant of a Secretary of State, see R. *v.* Wilkes, 2 Wils. 151; Entick *v.* Carrington, Id. 275; s. c., 19 Howell, St. Tr. 1030.

[7] Foster on Homicide 320.

And a plea justifying the breaking and entering a man's house without warrant, on suspicion of felony, ought distinctly to show, not only that there was reason to believe that the suspected person was there, but also that the defendant entered for the purpose of apprehending him.[1]

4thly. In all cases where the outer door of a house is open the sheriff may enter and do execution, either of the body or goods of the occupier, at the suit of any subject of the crown, and the landlord may, in such case, likewise enter to distrain for rent, or may even open the outer door in the ordinary manner—as by lifting the latch—to levy the distress,[2] or he may, it has been held, for that purpose enter through an open window.[3] But the sheriff cannot, in order to execute a writ of *ca. sa.* or **fi. fa.* at suit of a private person, break open the outer door of a man's house even after request made, and refusal to open it.[4] [*436] "Nothing is more certain than that in the ordinary cases of the execution of civil process between subject and subject, no person is warranted in breaking open the outer door in order to execute such process; the law values the private repose and security of every man in his own house, which it considers as his castle, beyond the civil satisfaction

[1] Smith *v.* Shirley, 3 C. B. 142 (54 E. C. L. R.).

[2] Ryan *v.* Shilcock, 7 Exch. 72.

[3] Nixon *v.* Freeman, 5 H. & N. 652, as to which see per Cockburn, C. J., L. R. 2 Q. B. 502. *Secus* if the window be fastened by a hasp, Hancock *v.* Austin, 14 C. B. N. S. 634 (108 E. C. L. R.); Attack *v.* Bramwell, 3 B. & S. 520 (113 E. C. L. R.).

"The ground of holding entry through a closed but unfastened door to be lawful is that access through the door is the usual mode of access, and that the license from the occupier to any one to enter who has lawful business may therefore be implied from his leaving the door unfastened. Entry through a window is not the usual mode of entry, and, therefore, no such license can be implied from the window being left unfastened;" per Lush, J., L. R. 2 Q. B. 593.

[4] Duke of Brunswick *v.* Slowman, 8 C. B. 317 (65 E. C. L. R.); Curlewis *v.* Laurie, 12 Q. B. 640 (64 E. C. L. R.). See Percival *v.* Stamp, 9 Exch. 167.

Where the sheriff's officer put his hand into the debtor's dwelling-house and touched the debtor, who was inside the house, saying, "You are my prisoner," and thereupon broke open the outer door and seized the debtor, the arrest was held to have been legally effected: Sandon *v.* Jervis, E., B. & E. 935 (96 E. C. L. R.); discussed and explained in Nash *v.* Lucas, L. R. 2 Q. B. 590, 594.

of a creditor.[1] Nor can the outer door of a house be broken open, nor an entry be made through a window which is shut but not fastened,[2] in order to make a distress, except in the case of goods fraudulently removed, and under the provisions of the stat. 11 Geo. 2, c. 19;[3] neither can a landlord break open the outer door of a stable, though not within the curtilage, to levy an ordinary distress for rent.[4]

Where, however, the sheriff has obtained admission to a house, he may justify subsequently breaking open inner doors, if he finds that necessary, in order to execute his process.[5] Where A., therefore, let a house, except one [*437] *room, which he reserved for himself and occupied separately, and, the outer door of the house being open, a constable broke open the door of the inner room occupied by A. in order to arrest him; it was held that trespass would not lie against the constable.[6] So, where it appeared that the front door of the house was in general kept fastened, the usual entrance being through the back door, and that the sheriff, having entered by the back door while it was open in the night, broke open the door of an inner room in which A. B. was with his family, and there arrested him; the arrest was held to have been lawful.[7] In an action of trespass against a sheriff for breaking and spoiling a lock, bolt, and staple, affixed to the outer door of plaintiff's dwelling-house, the defendant pleaded that, being lawfully in a room of the dwelling-house occupied by D., as tenant to the plaintiff, he peaceably entered into the residue of the said house through the door communicating between the room and the residue, and took plaintiff's goods in execution under a *fi. fa.*; and because the outer door was shut and fastened with the lock, bolt, and staple, so that defendant could not otherwise take away the goods, and because neither plaintiff nor any other on his behalf was in the dwelling-house to whom request could be made,[8] defendant did, for

[1] Per Lord Ellenborough, C. J., Burdett *v.* Abbot, 14 East 154.

[2] Nash *v.* Lucas, L. R. 2 Q. B. 590.

[3] Williams *v.* Roberts, 7 Exch. 618. See Thomas *v.* Watkins, Id. 630.

[4] Brown *v.* Glenn, 16 Q. B. 254 (71 E. C. L. R.).

[5] Lee *v.* Gansel, Cowp. 1; Ratcliffe *v.* Burton, 3 B. & P. 223; Browning *v.* Dann, Cas. temp. Hardw. 167. See Woods *v.* Durrant, 16 M. & W. 149; Hutchison *v.* Birch, 4 Taunt. 619.

[6] Williams *v.* Spence, 5 Johns. (U. S.) R. 352.

[7] Hubbard *v.* Mace, 17 Johns. (U. S.) R. 127.

[8] See Ratcliffe *v.* Burton, 3 B. & P. 223.

the purpose aforesaid, open the outer door, and, in so doing, did break and spoil the lock, &c., doing no unnecessary damage.[1] The court held that the plea was good, although it was not shown how the defendant entered into the house, nor *who fastened the outer door; they also thought it sufficiently appeared that there was no other way of getting out than that adopted; and that, in the absence of the plaintiff, the sheriff was excused from making a demand, and was justified in breaking the lock, &c., as matter of necessity, in order to get the goods out to execute the writ. In the previous case of White *v.* Whitshire,[2] it had been held that, though the sheriff cannot break open a house in order to make execution under a *fi. fa.*, yet, if the door is open, and the bailiffs enter and are disturbed in their execution by the parties who are within the house, he may break into the house and rescue his bailiffs, and so take execution. In this case, as observed by the court in Pugh *v.* Griffith, above cited, the breaking into the house was justified, because the plaintiff himself had occasioned the necessity of it; but it does not follow that there may not be other occasions where the outer door may be broken.[3]

[*438]

The privilege which, by the fourth resolution in Semayne's Case, was held to attach to a man's house, must, however, be strictly confined thereto, and does not extend to barns or outhouses unconnected with the dwelling-house.[4] It admits also of this exception, that if the defendant escape from arrest, the sheriff may, after demand of admission and refusal, break open either his own house or that of a stranger for the purpose of retaking him.[5] Moreover, if the sheriff breaks open an outer door when he is not justified in doing so, this, it would seem, does not vitiate the execution, but merely *renders the sheriff liable to an action of trespass.[6] A sheriff's officer, in execution of a bailable writ, peaceably obtained entrance by the outer door; but before he could

[*439]

[1] Pugh *v.* Griffith, 7 A. & E. 827 (34 E. C. L. R.).

[2] Palm. R. 52; Cro. Jac. 555.

[3] Judgm., 7 A. & E. 840 (34 E. C. L. R.).

[4] Penton *v.* Browne, 1 Sid. 186; distinguished in Brown *v.* Glenn, 16 Q. B. 254, 257 (71 E. C. L. R.).

[5] Anon., 6 Mod. 105; Lloyd *v.* Sandilands, 8 Taunt. 250 (4 E. C. L. R.). See Genner *v.* Sparkes, 1 Salk. 79.

[6] See 4th resolution, in Semayne's Case, *ad finem;* 2 Bac. Abr., "*Execution*" (N.); Percival *v.* Stamp, 9 Exch. 167.

make an actual arrest, was forcibly expelled from the house, and the outer door fastened against him. The officer thereupon, having obtained assistance, broke open the outer door and made the arrest; and it was held that he was justified in so doing; for, the outer door being open in the first instance, the officer was entitled to enter the house under civil process, and, being lawfully in the house, the prosecutor was guilty of a trespass in expelling him; and that, the act of locking the outer door being unlawful, the prosecutor could confer no privilege upon himself by that unlawful act. In the above case it was further held, that a demand of re-entry by the officer was not, under the circumstances, requisite to justify him in breaking open the outer door; for "the law, in its wisdom, only requires this ceremony to be observed when it possibly may be attended with some advantage, and may render the breaking open of the outer door unnecessary."[1]

5thly. It was resolved that a man's house is not a castle for any one but himself, and shall not afford protection to a third party who flies thither, or to his goods if brought or conveyed into the house to prevent a lawful execution, and to escape the ordinary process of law. In these latter cases, therefore, the sheriff may, after request and denial, break open the door, or he may enter if the door be [*440] *open.[2] It must be observed, however, that the sheriff does so at his peril; and if it turn out that the defendant was not in the house, or had no property there, he is a trespasser.[3]

The distinction being now clearly established, that, if a sheriff enters the house of the defendant himself for the purpose of arresting him or taking his goods, he is justified, provided he has reasonable grounds for believing that the party is there or his goods; but if he enters the house of a stranger with the like object in view, he can be justified only by the event.[4]

It may not be inappropriate to add, in connection with the

[1] Aga Kurboolie Mahomed *v.* The Queen, 4 Moore P. C. Cas. 239.

[2] Semayne's Case, *supra;* per Tindal, C. J., Cook *v.* Clark, 10 Bing. 21; Com. Dig., "*Execution*" (C. 6); Penton *v.* Browne, 1 Sid. 186.

[3] Johnson *v.* Leigh, 6 Taunt. 246 (1 E. C. L. R.); Morrish *v.* Murray, *infra;* Com. Dig., "*Execution*" (C. 5).

[4] Morrish *v.* Murray, 13 M. & W. 52, 57; Cooke *v.* Birt, 5 Taunt. 765 (1 E. C. L. R.).

maxim under consideration, that although, as a general rule, where a house has been unlawfully erected on a common, a commoner, whose enjoyment of the common has been thus interrupted, may pull it down; he is, nevertheless, not justified in doing so *without previous notice or request*,[1] if there are persons actually in it at the time.[2] But, as remarked by Lord Campbell, C. J.,[3] it would be giving a most dangerous extension to the doctrine thus laid down "to hold that the owner of a house could not exercise the right of pulling it down because a trespasser was in it." And notwithstanding some conflict amongst judicial dicta upon the subject,[4] *it seems that in trespass "it is a perfectly good justification to say that the plaintiff was in possession of the land against the will of the defendant, who was owner, and that he entered upon it accordingly, even though in so doing a breach of the peace was committed."[5] The learned judge whose words have been just quoted further intimates an opinion[6] that "where a breach of the peace is committed by a freeholder who, in order to get into possession of his land, assaults a person wrongfully holding possession of it against his will, although the freeholder may be responsible to the public in the shape of an indictment for a forcible entry,[7] he is not liable to the other party."

[*441]

We may conclude these remarks with observing, that, although the law of England has so particular and tender a regard to the

[1] Davies v. Williams, 16 Q. B. 546, 556.

[2] Perry v. Fitzhowe, 8 Q. B. 757 (55 E. C. L. R.); Jones v. Jones, 1 H. & C. 1.

[3] Burling v. Read, 11 Q. B. 904, 908 (63 E. C. L. R.); Davison v. Wilson, Id. 890.

[4] See Newton v. Harland, 1 M. & Gr. 644 (39 E. C. L. R.); Pollen v. Brewer, 7 C. B. N. S. 371 (97 E. C. L. R.); per Cresswell, J., Davis v. Burrell, 10 C. B. 825 (70 E. C. L. R.); per Parke, B., and Alderson, B., 14 M. & W. 437. In Delaney v. Fox, 1 C. B. N. S. 166 (87 E. C. L. R.), the point above mentioned was also raised. See Butcher v. Butcher, 7 B. & C. 399 (14 E. C. L. R.).

[5] Per Parke, B., Harvey v. Brydges, 14 M. & W. 442; s. c., 1 Exch. 261. See per Cresswell, J., Meriton v. Coombes, 9 C. B. 789.

[6] 14 M. & W. 442; cited Judgm., Blades v. Higgs, 10 C. B. N. S. 721 (100 E. C. L. R.); s. c., 11 H. L. Cas. 621 (where the principle laid down *supra* was applied to the retaking of chattels); Pollen v. Brewer, 7 C. B. N. S. 371 (97 E. C. L. R.).

[7] See per Lord Kenyon, C. J., Taunton v. Costar, 7 T. R. 432.

immunity of a man's house, that it will not suffer it to be violated with impunity,—and although, for this reason, outward doors cannot, in general, be broken open to execute any civil process (the main exception which occurs to the rule, viz., in criminal cases, resulting from the principle that the public safety should supersede the private),—yet, in the words of an eminent lawyer,[1] "This rule, [*442] that every man's house is his castle, when *applied to arrests in legal process, hath been carried as far as the true principles of political justice will warrant—perhaps beyond what, in the scale of sound reason and good policy, they will warrant."

---

§ III.—The Transfer of Property.

The two leading maxims relative to the transfer of property are, first, that alienation is favored by the law; and, secondly, that an assignee holds property subject to the same rights and liabilities as attached to it whilst in the possession of the grantor. Besides the above very general principles, we have included in this section several minor maxims of much practical importance, connected with the same subject; and each of these, according to the plan pursued throughout this work, has been briefly illustrated by decided cases.

Alienatio Rei præfertur Juri accrescendi.

(Co. Litt. 185 a.)

Alienation is favored by the law rather than accumulation.

Alienatio is defined to be, *omnis actus per quem dominium transfertur*,[2] and it is the well-known policy of our law to favor alienation, and to discountenance every attempt to tie up property unreasonably, or, in other words, to create a perpetuity.

The reader will at once remark, that the feudal policy was directly

[1] Sir M. Foster, Discourse of Homicide, p. 319.

[2] Brisson. ad verb. "*Alienatio.*"

opposed to those more wise and liberal views *which have now long prevailed. It is, indeed, generally admitted,[1] that, under the Saxon sway, the power of alienating real property was altogether unrestricted; and that land first ceased to be alienable when the feudal system was introduced into this country, shortly after the Norman conquest; for, although the Conqueror's right to the crown of England seems to have been founded on title, and not on conquest, yet, according to the fundamental principle of that system, all land within the king's territories was held to be derived, either mediately or immediately, from him as the supreme lord, and was subjected to those burthens and restrictions which were incident to the feudal tenure. Now this tenure originated in the mutual contract between lord and vassal, whereby the latter, in consideration of the feud with which he was invested, bound himself to render certain services to the former; and as the feudatory could not, without the consent of his lord, substitute the services of another for his own,[2] so neither could the lord, without the feudatory's consent, transfer his fealty and allegiance to another.[3] It is, however, necessary to bear in mind the distinction which was recognized by the feudal laws between alienation and subinfeudation; for, although alienation, meaning thereby the transfer of the original feud, and substitution of a new for the old feudatory, was strictly prohibited, yet subinfeudation, whereby a new and inferior feud was carved out of that originally created, was practiced and permitted. Moreover, as feudatories did in fact, under color of subinfeudation, frequently dispose of their lands, this practice, which *was in its tendency opposed to the spirit of the feudal institutions, was expressly restrained by the 32d chap. of Magna Charta, which was merely in affirmance of the common law on this subject, and which allowed the tenants of common or mesne lords—though not, it seems, such as held directly of the crown—to dispose of a *reasonable part* of their lands to subfeudatories.

[*443]

[*444]

The right of subinfeudation to the extent thus expressly allowed by statute evidently prepared the way for the more extensive power of alienation which was conferred on mesne feudatories by the statute *Quia Emptores*, 18 Edw. 1, st. 1, c. 1. This statute, which effected,

[1] Wright, Tenures, 154 *et seq.*

[2] See Bradshaw *v.* Lawson, 4 T. R. 443.

[3] Wright, Tenures, 171; Mr. Butler's note, Co. Litt. 309 a (1).

indeed, a most material change in the nature of the feudal tenure, by permitting the transfer or alienation of lands in lieu of subinfeudation, after stating, by way of preamble, that, in consequence of this latter practice, the chief lords had many times lost their escheats, marriages, and wardships of lands and tenements belonging to their fees, enacted, "that from henceforth it shall be lawful to every freeman to sell at his own pleasure his lands and tenements, or part of them, so that the feoffee shall hold the same lands and tenements of the chief lord of the same fee, by such service and customs as his feoffee held before."

This statute, it will be observed, did not extend to tenants *in capite;* and although by the subsequent Act, 17 Edw. 2, c. 6, *De Prærogativâ Regis*, it was declared that no one holding of the crown by military service can, without the king's license, alien the *greater part* of his lands, so that enough shall not remain for the due performance of such service—from which it has been inferred that, prior to this enactment, tenants *in capite* possessed the same right [*445] of subinfeudation as ordinary *feudatories possessed prior to the stat. *Quia Emptores*—yet it does not appear that even after the stat. of *De Prærogativâ*, alienation of any part of lands held *in capite* ever occurred without the king's license; and, at all events, this question was set at rest by the subsequent stat. 34 Edw. 3, c. 15, which rendered valid such alienations as had been made by tenants holding under Henry 3, and preceding sovereigns, although there was a reservation of the royal prerogative as regarded alienations made during the reigns of the two first Edwards.

Having thus remarked, that, by a fiction of the feudal law, all land was held, either directly or (owing to the practice of subinfeudation) mediately of the crown, we may next observe that gifts of land were in their origin simple, without any condition or modification annexed to them; and although limited or conditional donations were gradually introduced for the purpose of restraining the right of alienation, yet, since the courts construed such limitations liberally, in order to favor that right which they were intended to restrain, the stat. of Westm. 2, 13 Edw. 1, usually called the statute *De Donis*, was passed, which enacted, "That the will of the giver, according to the form in the deed of gift, manifestly expressed, shall be from henceforth observed, so that they to whom the land was given under such condition shall have no power to alien the land so given, but that it shall remain unto the issue of them to whom it was given after their death, or shall revert unto the giver, or his heir, if issue fail." The effect, therefore, of the above statute was to prevent a tenant in tail from alienating his estate for a greater term than that of his own life; or rather, its effect was to render the grantee's estate certain and indefeasible during the life of the tenant in *tail only, upon whose death it became defeasible by his issue or the remainderman or reversioner.[1] [*446]

Prior to this Act, indeed, where land was granted to a man and the heirs of his body, the donee was held to take a conditional fee-simple, which became absolute the instant issue was born; but after the passing of the statute *De Donis*, the estate was, in contemplation of law, divided into two parts, the donee taking a new kind of particular estate, which our judges denominated a fee-tail, the ultimate fee-simple of the land expectant on the failure of issue remaining vested in the donor.

"At last," says Lord Mansfield, C. J.,[2] "the people having groaned for two hundred years under the inconveniences of so much property being unalienable; and the great men, to raise the pride of their families, and (in those turbulent times) to preserve their estates from forfeitures, preventing any alteration by the legislature," the judges adopted various modes of evading the statute *De Donis*, and of enabling tenants in tail to charge or alien their estates.[3] The first of these was founded on the idea of a recompense in value; in consequence of which it was held, that the issue in tail was bound by the warranty of his ancestor, where assets of equal value descended to him from such ancestor. In the next place, they were held, in the reign of Edw. IV, that a feigned recovery should bar the issue in tail and the remainders and reversion.[4] And, by the stat. 32 Hen. 8, c. 36, *the legislature expressly declared that a fine should be a bar to the issue in tail.[5] [*447]

[1] 1 Cruise, Dig., 4th ed., 77, 78.

[2] Taylor *v.* Horde, 1 Burr. 115.

[3] In Mary Portington's Case, 10 Rep. 35 b, it was held, in accordance with prior authorities, that tenant in tail could not be restrained by any condition or limitation from suffering a common recovery.

[4] Taltarum's Case, Yr. Bk. 12 Edw. 4, 14, 19, where the court expressly founded their argument upon the assumption that a recovery properly suffered would destroy an entail, although they decided that, under the particular circumstances of that case, the entail had not been destroyed.

[5] Except where the reversion was in the crown, 34 & 35 Hen. 8, c. 20. As

Further, under the Act for abolishing fines and recoveries, 3 & 4 Will. 4, c. 74, a tenant in tail may, by any species of deed duly enrolled, and otherwise made in conformity with the Act, absolutely dispose of the estate of which he is seised in tail in the same manner as if he were absolutely seised thereof in fee;[1] and the sale of "settled estates"[2] is, by the stat. 19 & 20 Vict. c. 120 (amended and extended by 21 & 22 Vict. c. 77),[3] much facilitated.

Having thus seen in what manner the restrictions which were, in accordance with the spirit of the feudal laws, imposed upon the alienation of land by *deed*, have been gradually relaxed, we must further observe, that the power of disposing of land by *will* was quite as much opposed to the policy of those laws; and, consequently, although land in this country was devisable until the conquest, yet it shortly afterwards ceased to be so, and, in fact, remained inalienable by will[4] until the stats. 32 Hen. 8, c. 1, and 34 & 35 Hen. 8, c. 5; the latter of which statutes is explanatory of the former, and declares that every person (except as therein mentioned) having a sole estate or interest or being seised in fee-simple of and in any manors, [*448] lands, tenements, *rents or other hereditaments in possession, reversion, remainder, or of rents or services incident to any reversion or remainder, shall have full and free liberty, power and authority to give, dispose, will, or devise to any person or persons (except bodies politic and corporate) by his last will and testament in writing, all his said manors, lands, tenements, rents, and hereditaments, or any of them, at his own free will and pleasure. It is, indeed, true, that, by the above statutes, some restriction was imposed upon the right of alienating by will lands held by military tenure; yet since such tenures were by the stat. 12 Car. 2, c. 24, converted into free and common socage tenures, we do, in fact, derive from the Acts passed in the reign of Hen. VIII the important right of disposing by will of all (except copyhold[5]) lands

to the respective effects of the stats. 4 Hen. 7, c. 24, and 32 Hen. 8. c. 36, see Mr. Hargrave's note (1), Co. Litt. 121 a.

[1] See 1 Cruise Dig., 4th ed., 83.

[2] For the statutory signification of this term, see the interpretation clause (s. 1).

[3] See also 27 & 28 Vict. c. 45, s. 3.

[4] A tenant in gavelkind, however, could devise by will prior to the Statute of Wills: Wright Tenures 207.

[5] As to which, see now 1 Vict. c. 26, s. 3; Shelf. Copyholds 52.

and tenements: a privilege which has received some important extensions by the modern stat. 1 Vict. c. 26 (amended by 15 & 16 Vict. c. 24), and which now attaches to all real and personal estate to which an individual may be entitled, either at law or in equity, at the time of his death.[1]

It remains to consider how far the right of alienation exists at common law, when viewed without reference to the arbitrary restrictions which were imposed under the feudal system, and to show in what manner this right has been recognized and favored by our courts of law, and encouraged by the legislature. And, in the first place, we must observe, that the *potestas alienandi*, or right of alienation, is a right necessarily incident, in contemplation of law, to an estate in fee-simple; it is inseparably annexed to it, and cannot, in general, be indefinitely restrained by any proviso or condition whatsoever;[2] *for, although a "fee-simple" is explained by Littleton[3] as being *hæreditas pura*, yet it is not so described [*449] as importing an estate purely allodial (for we have already seen that such an estate did not, in fact, exist in this country), but because it implies a simple inheritance clear of any condition, limitation, or restriction to any particular heirs, and descendible to the heirs general, whether male or female, lineal or collateral.[4] In illustration of the above incident of an estate in fee-simple, we find it laid down,[5] that "if a man makes a feoffment on condition that the feoffee shall not alien to any, the condition is void, because, where a man is enfeoffed of land or tenements, he has power to alien them to any person by the law; for, if such condition should be good, then the condition would oust him of the whole power which the law gives him, which would be against reason, and therefore such condition is void." A testator devised land to A. B. and his heirs forever; but in case A. B. died without heirs, then to C. D. (who was a stranger in blood to A. B.) and his heirs; and, in case A. B. offered to mortgage or suffer a fine or recovery upon the whole or any part thereof, then to the said C. D. and his heirs. It was held, that A. B. took an estate in fee, with an executory devise

[1] S. 3.

[2] 4 Cruise Dig., 4th ed., 330. And see the analogous cases, cited *post*, pp. 452, 455.

[3] S. 1.

[4] Wright Tenures 147.

[5] Mildmay's Case, 6 Rep. 42; Co. Litt. 206 b.

over, to take effect upon the happening of conditions which were void in law, and that a purchaser in fee from A. B. would have a good title against all persons claiming under the said will.[1] So, if a man, before the statute *De Donis*, had made a gift to one and the heirs of his body, after issue born he had, by the common law, [*450] **potestatem alienandi;* and, therefore, if the donor had in such a case added a condition, that after issue the donee should not alien, the condition would have been repugnant and void. And, by like reasoning, if after the statute a man had made a gift in tail, on condition that the tenant in tail should not suffer a common recovery, such condition would have been void; for, by the gift in tail, the tenant has an absolute power given to suffer a recovery, and so to bar the entail.[2] And here we may conveniently remark, that the distinction which exists between real and personal property is further illustrative of the present subject; for, with respect to the latter, it is laid down, that, where an estate tail in things personal is given to the first or any subsequent possessor, it vests in him the total property, and no remainder over shall be permitted on such a limitation; for this, if allowed, would tend to a perpetuity, as the devisee or grantee in tail of a chattel has no method of barring the entail; and, therefore, the law vests in him at once the entire dominion of goods, being analogous to the fee-simple which a tenant in tail may acquire in real estate.[3] A. B.,[4] wishing to devise his estates to each son and his issue successively in remainder, and to prevent the possibility of alienation, so as to defeat the remainder over, caused an indenture to be made to this purport: "that the lands and tenements were given to his eldest son upon such condition; that, if the eldest son alien in fee or in fee tail, &c., or if any of his sons alien, &c., that then their estate [*451] should cease and be void, and that then *the same lands and tenements immediately should remain to the second son, and to the heirs of his body begotten, *et sic ultra*, the remainder to his other sons;" and livery of seisin was made accordingly. "But," observes Littleton,[5] "it seemeth by reason, that all such remainders

[1] Ware *v.* Cann, 10 B. & C. 433 (21 E. C. L. R.).

[2] 6 Rep. 41; arg. Taylor *v.* Horde, 1 Burr. 84; Corbet's Case, 1 Rep. 83; Portington's Case, 10 Rep. 35.

[3] 2 Com. by Broom & Hadley 593, 611.

[4] Litt. s. 720; Co. Litt. 379 b (1).

[5] Litt. s. 721.

in the form aforesaid are void and of no value." And if, in the case put, the eldest son had aliened in fee, the estates would thereupon have vested in the alienee, and the parties in remainder would have been barred; that is to say, the condition which the testator attempted to annex to the estate would have been inoperative.

We may, in connection with this subject, likewise refer to Sir W. Blackstone's celebrated judgment in Perrin *v.* Blake,[1] where a distinction is drawn between those rules of law which are to be considered as the fundamental rules of the property of this kingdom,[2] and which cannot be exceeded or transgressed by any intention of a testator, however clearly or manifestly expressed, and those rules of a more arbitrary, technical, and artificial kind, which the intention of a testator may control. Amongst rules appertaining to the first of these two classes, Sir W. Blackstone mentions these:—1st, that every tenant in fee-simple or fee-tail shall have the power of alienating his estates by the several modes adapted to their respective interests; and, 2dly, that no disposition shall be allowed which, in its consequence, tends to a perpetuity.[3] Mr. Butler, moreover, remarks,[4] with reference to the case from Littleton above cited, that it "is one of the many attempts which have been [*452] *made at different times to prevent the exercise of that right of alienation which is inseparable from the estate of a tenant in tail."

Not only will our courts oppose the creation of a perpetuity by deed, but they will likewise frustrate the attempt to create it by will; and, therefore, "upon the introduction of executory devises, and the indulgence thereby allowed to testators, care was taken that the property which was the subject of them should not be tied up beyond a reasonable time, and that too great a restraint upon alienation should not be permitted.[5] The rule is accordingly well established, that, although an estate may be rendered inalienable during the existence of a life or of any number of lives in being, and twenty-one years after, or, possibly, even for nine months beyond

[1] Hargrave's Tracts, fol. 500.

[2] See also Egerton *v.* Earl Brownlow, 4 H. L. Cas. 1, *passim.*

[3] Mr. Butler's note, Co. Litt. 376 b (1).

[4] Co. Litt. 381 a, note.

[5] Judgm., Cadell *v.* Palmer, 10 Bing. 142 (25 E. C. L. R.). See Ware *v.* Cann, 10 B. & C. 433 (21 E. C. L. R.).

the twenty-one years, in case the person ultimately entitled to the estate should be an infant, *in ventre sa mère*,[1] at the time of its accruing to him, yet that all attempts to postpone the enjoyment of the fee for a longer period are void.[2]

With respect to trusts for accumulation, we may observe, that these are now regulated by stat. 39 & 40 Geo. 3, c. 98, an Act [*453] which was passsed in consequence of the *will of the late Mr. Thellusson, and subsequently to the decision establishing the validity of that will in the well-known case of Thellusson *v.* Woodford.[3] The above-mentioned statute enacts, that no person shall thenceforth, by any deed, surrender, will, codicil, or otherwise, settle or dispose of any real or personal property, so that the rents or produce thereof shall be wholly or partially accumulated for any longer term than the life of the grantor or settlor, or the term of twenty-one years from the death of the grantor, settlor, or testator, or during the minority or respective minorities of any person or persons who shall be living, or *in ventre sa mère*, at the time of the death of such grantor or testator, or during the minority or respective minorities only of any person or persons who, under the uses or trusts of the deed, surrender, will, or other assurance, directing such accumulations, would, for the time being, if of full age, be entitled to the rents or annual produce so directed to be accumulated.

It will be evident, from the preceding remarks and cases already cited, that the rule against perpetuities is observed by courts both of law and of equity.[4] In consequence, however, of the peculiar jurisdiction which courts of equity exercise, for the protection of the in-

[1] In an executory devise, the period of gestation may be reckoned both at the beginning and the end of the twenty-one years; thus, if land is devised with remainder over in case A.'s son die under the age of twenty-one, and A. dies leaving a son *in ventre sa mère*, then if the son marries in his twenty-first year, and dies leaving his widow *enceinte*, the estate vests, nevertheless, in the infant *in ventre sa mère*, and does not go over. See, per Lord Eldon, C., Thellusson *v.* Woodford, 11 Ves. jun. 149.

[2] Cadell *v.* Palmer, 10 Bing. 140. See Lord Dungannon *v.* Smith, 12 Cl. & Fin. 546, distinguished in Christie *v.* Gosling, L. R. 1 H. L. 279, 292; Spencer *v.* Duke of Marlborough, 3 Bro. P. C. 232.

[3] 4 Ves. jun. 227; s. c., 11 Id. 112, in which case Mr. Hargrave's argument respecting perpetuities is well worthy of perusal.

[4] See also, per Wilmot, C. J., Bridgeman *v.* Green, Wilmot, Opin. 61.

terests of married women, the right of alienation has, in one case, with a view to their benefit, been restricted, and that restriction thus imposed may, in fact, be regarded as an exception to the operation of the maxim in favor of alienation, which we have been considering. It is now fully established, that where property is conveyed to the *separate use of a married woman in fee, with a clause in restraint of anticipation, such clause is valid; [*454] for equity, having in this instance created a particular kind of estate, will reserve to itself the power of modifying that estate in such manner as the court may think fit, and will so regulate its enjoyment as to effect the purpose for which the estate was originally created.[1] The law upon this subject may be considered to have been finally settled by the decisions in Tullett *v.* Armstrong[2] and Scarborough *v.* Borman,[3] where Lord Cottenham, C., after an elaborate review of the cases and authorities, held that a gift to the sole and separate use of a woman, whether married or unmarried, with a clause against anticipation, was good against an after-acquired husband; and this decision has been in subsequent cases fully recognized and adopted.[4]

The reason of the rule thus established is fully stated by his lordship, in a subsequent case, in these words:—"When first, by the law of this country, property was settled to the separate use of the wife, equity considered the wife as a *fême sole*, to the extent of having a dominion over the property. But then it was found that that, though useful and operative, so far as securing to her a dominion over the property so devoted to her support, was open to this difficulty—that she, being considered as a *fême sole*, was of course at liberty to dispose of it as a *fême sole* might have disposed of it, and that, of course, exposing her to the influence of her husband, was found to destroy the object of giving her a separate property; *therefore, to meet that, a provision was adopted of prohibiting the anticipation of the income of the property, so [*455] that he had no dominion over the property till the payments actually became due."[5] To the above exposition of the doctrine of

[1] See, per Lord Lyndhurst, C., Baggett *v.* Meux, 1 Phill. 627; s. c., 1 Coll. 138.

[2] 4 My. & Cr. 377, 390. See Wright *v.* Wright, 2 Johns. & Hem. 647, 652.

[3] 4 My. & Cr. 378.

[4] Baggett *v.* Meux, *supra.*

[5] Per Lord Cottenham, Rennie *v.* Ritchie, 12 Cl. & Fin. 234.

courts of equity we must add that, by various sections of the stat. 20 & 21 Vict. c. 85, for amending the law relating to divorce and matrimonial causes, a *fême covert* will, for her protection, be considered as a *fême sole* with respect to her acquired property, and for the purpose of suing and contracting.[1]

Conformable to the spirit of the elementary maxim now under consideration is the stat. 20 & 21 Vict. c. 57, intituled "An Act to enable married women to dispose of reversionary interests in personal estate."

Having thus observed that our law favors the alienation of real property, or, to use the words of Lord Mansfield, that "the sense of wise men, and the general bent of the people in this country, have ever been against making land perpetually unalienable;" and having seen that "the utility of the end was thought to justify any means to attain it,"[2] it remains to add, that the same policy obtains with reference to personality; and, in support of this remark, may be adduced the well-known rule of the law merchant, that, for the encouragement of commerce, the right of survivorship, which is ordinarily incident to a joint tenancy, shall not exist amongst trading partners—*jus accrescendi inter mercatores pro beneficio commercii locum non habet*,[3]—a rule which applies to manufac- [*456] turers *as well as to merchants[4]—to trade fixtures also, which, being removable, are part of the stock in trade—and has been[5] extended to real as well as personal property: so that all property, whatever be its nature, purchased with partnership capital for the purposes of the partnership trade, continues to be partnership capital, and to have to every intent the quality of personal estate,[6] unless, indeed, a special stipulation be made

[1] See ss. 21, 25, 26.

[2] Per Lord Mansfield, C. J., 1 Burr. 115.

[3] Co. Litt. 182 a; Brownl. 99; Noy, Max., 9th ed., 79; 1 Beawes Lex Merc., 6th ed., 42.

[4] Buckley *v.* Barber, 6 Exch. 164, by comparing which case with Crossfield *v.* Such, 8 Exch. 825, and Morgan *v.* Marquis, 9 Exch. 145, the signification and operation of the maxim, as to *jus accrescendi*, will be perceived.

[5] Buckley *v.* Barber, *supra.*

[6] Per Sir J. Leach, M. R., Phillips *v.* Phillips, 1 My. & K. 663; and in Fereday *v.* Wightwick, 1 Russ. & My. 49; Townsend *v.* Devaynes, 1 Mont., Partnership, 2d ed., note, p. 96 (2 A.); per Lord Eldon, C., Selkrig *v.* Davis, 2 Dow 242; Houghton *v.* Houghton, 11 Sim. 491; Crawshay *v.* Maule, 1

between the partners to prevent the application of this equitable doctrine.[1] The rule which thus holds in cases of partnership evidently favors alienation, by rendering capital invested in trade applicable to partnership purposes, and directly available to the creditors of the firm.

We have already had occasion to observe, that there cannot be an estate tail in personality;[2] so neither can a perpetuity be created in property of this description. Indeed, where the subject-matter of a grant is a personal chattel, it is impossible so to tie up the use and enjoyment of it as to create in the donee a life estate which he may not alien. It is true, however, that this object may be attained indirectly, in a manner consistent with the *known [*457] rules of law, by annexing to the gift a forfeiture or defeasance on the happening of a particular event, or on a particular act being done; for in that case the donee takes by the limitation a certain estate, of which the event or act is the measure, and upon the happening of the event, or the doing of the act, a new and distinct estate accrues to a different individual. If, for instance, a testator be desirous to give an annuity without the power of anticipation, he can only do so by declaring that the act of alienation shall determine the interest of the legatee, and create a new interest in another."[3]

Property may also be given to a party to be enjoyed by him until he becomes bankrupt, and, if this event should happen, the property may be given over to another party. A person cannot, however, create an absolute interest in property, and, at the same time, deprive the party to whom that interest was given of those incidents and of that right of alienation which belonged, according to the elementary principles of the common law, to the ownership of the estate. Where, therefore, a testator directed his trustees to pay an annuity to his brother, until he should attempt to charge it, or some other person should claim it, and then to apply

Swanst. 521, cited Baxter *v.* Newman, 8 Scott N. R. 1035; Phillips *v.* Phillips, *supra*, was overruled as to a different point therein decided by Taylor *v.* Taylor, 3 De G., M. & G. 190.

[1] Balmain *v.* Shore, 9 Ves. jun. 500.

[2] As to heirlooms, see the maxim *Accessorium sequitur principale,—post.* As to annexing personal to real estate, the latter being devised in strict settlement, see 2 Jarm. Wills, 2d ed., 492.

[3] Per Lord Brougham, 2 My. & K. 204.

it for his support and maintenance, it was held that, on the insolvency of the annuitant, his assignees became entitled to the annuity.[1]

The distinction between a proviso or condition subsequent and a limitation, above exemplified, may be further explained in the words of Lord Eldon, who says: "There is no doubt that property may be given to a man until he shall become bankrupt. It is equally [*458] clear, generally *speaking, that, if property is given to a man for his life, the donor cannot take away the incidents to a life estate, and * * * a disposition to a man until he shall become bankrupt, and after his bankruptcy over, is quite different from an attempt to give to him for his life, with a *proviso* that he shall not sell or alien it. If that condition is so expressed as to amount to a limitation, reducing the interest short of a life estate, neither the man nor his assignees can have it beyond the period limited."[2]

The preceding remarks will suffice to establish the truth, and to show the very wide application, of the proposition, that, in our law, *alienatio rei præfertur juri accrescendi;* for, as we have seen, the power of alienation, whether by deed or by will, of which the land-owners were deprived on the introduction of the feudal system, has been in succeeding ages gradually restored to them. Both our courts of law and our legislature have discountenanced attempts to create perpetuities, either by an astute application of legal machinery, for the purpose of defeating them, or by special enactments calculated to effect the same salutary object. A perpetuity has, indeed, been pronounced to be "a thing odious in law and destructive to the commonwealth,"[3] inasmuch as its tendency is to put a stop to commerce, and to prevent the free circulation of the riches of the kingdom; and we may accordingly ascribe to the policy of our law in favoring alienation, not only those extensive innovations on the feudal system to which we have above adverted, but likewise the various measures which have from time to time [*459] been adopted, as well for simplifying the forms of conveyance as for rendering the realty liable to *debts,[4] and

[1] Younghusband *v.* Gisborne, 1 Colly. 400.

[2] Brandon *v.* Robinson, 18 Ves. 433, 434.

[3] 1 Vern. 164.

[4] The feudal restraint of alienation necessarily prevented land from being

making property in general more easily available to creditors, and therefore more directly applicable to the exigences of the trading portion of the community. The *alienatio rei* has, moreover, been effectually promoted by the negotiable character which has been established as belonging to bills of exchange, and which has been specifically annexed to promissory notes and some other mercantile instruments. And the disposition of our legislature still is to favor the assignment of choses in action, and thus to afford increased facilities for the transfer and circulation of property, which are essential to the true interests of a great commercial country.

CUJUS EST DARE EJUS EST DISPONERE.

(Wing. Max. 53.)

The bestower of a gift has a right to regulate its disposal.[1]

It will be evident, from a perusal of the preceding pages, that the above general rule must at the present day be received with very considerable qualification. It does, in fact, set forth the principle on which the old feudal system of feoffment depended: *tenor est qui legem dat feudo*[2]—it is the tenor of the feudal grant which regulates its effect and extent; and the maxim itself is, in another form, still applicable to modern grants—*modus legem dat donationi*[3]—the bargainor of an estate may, since the land moves from him, annex such conditions as *he pleases to the estate bargained, [*460] provided they are not illegal, repugnant, or impossible.[4] Moreover, it is always necessary that the grantor should expressly limit and declare the continuance and quantity of the estate which he means to confer; for, by a bare grant of lands, the grantee will take an estate for life only, a feoffment being still considered as a gift, which is not to be extended beyond the express limitation or manifest intention of the feoffor.[5] As, moreover, the owner may,

subject to the debts of the tenant; but by Stat. Westm. 2, 13 Edw. 1, st. 1, c. 18, one moiety of the land was made liable to execution. Wright Tenures 169, 170.

[1] Bell, Dict. & Dig. of Scotch Law 242.

[2] Craig, Jus Feud., 3d ed., 66.

[3] Co. Litt. 19 a.

[4] 2 Rep. 71.

[5] Wright Tenures 151, 152.

subject to certain beneficial restrictions, impose conditions at his pleasure upon the feoffee, so he may likewise, by insertion of special covenants in a conveyance or demise, reserve to himself rights of easement and other privileges in the land so conveyed or demised, and thus surrender the enjoyment of it only partially, and not absolutely, to the feoffee or tenant. "It is not," as remarked by Lord Brougham, C.,[1] "at all inconsistent with the nature of property, that certain things should be reserved to the reversioners all the while the term continues. It is only something taken out of the demise—some exception to the temporary surrender of the enjoyment: it is only that they retain more or less partially the use of what was wholly used by them before the demise, and what will again be wholly used by them when that demise is at an end."

It must not, however, therefore, be inferred that "incidents of a novel kind can be devised and attached to property at the fancy or caprice of any owner."[2] "No man," remarked Lord St. Leonards, [*461] in Egerton *v.* Earl *Brownlow,[3] "can attach any condition to his property which is against the public good," nor can he "alter the usual line of descent by a creation of his own. A man cannot give an estate in fee-simple to a person and his heirs on the part of his mother. Why? Because the law has already said how a fee-simple estate shall descend."

In the Marquis of Salisbury *v.* Gladstone,[4] the validity of a custom came under consideration—that the copyholders of inheritance of a certain manor might, without license from the lord, break the surface, and dig and get clay without limit, from and out of their copyhold tenements, for the purpose of making the same into bricks, to be sold off the manor. In giving his opinion in favor of this custom, Lord Cranworth thus expressed himself,[5] referring to the maxim under notice:—"It is true that a custom

[1] 2 My. & K. 536, 537.

[2] Per Lord Brougham, C., 2 My. & K. 535; Ackroyd *v.* Smith, 10 C. B. 164 (70 E. C. L. R.); Bailey *v.* Stephens, 12 C. B. N. S. 91 (104 E. C. L. R.); Ellis *v.* Mayor, &c., of Bridgnorth, 15 C. B. N. S. 58, 78 (109 E. C. L. R.); Tulk *v.* Moxhay, 2 Phill. 774; Hill *v.* Tupper, 2 H. & C. 121, 128; per Cresswell, J., and Watson, B., in Rowbotham *v.* Wilson, 8 E. & B. 123 (92 E. C. L. R.); s. c., 8 H. L. Cas. 348.

[3] 4 H. L. Cas. 241, 242.

[4] 9 H. L. Cas. 692.

[5] 9 H. L. Cas. 701.

to be valid must be reasonable.[1] It is not easy to define the meaning of the word 'reasonable' when applied to a custom regulating the relation between a lord and his copyholders. That relation must have had its origin in remote times by agreement between the lord, as absolute owner of the whole manor in fee-simple, and those whom he was content to allow to occupy portions of it as his tenants at will. The rights of these tenants must have depended in their origin entirely on the will of the lord; and it is hard to say how any stipulations regulating such rights can, as between the tenant and the lord, be deemed void as being unreasonable—*cujus est dare ejus est disponere.* Whatever restrictions, therefore, or conditions *the lord may have imposed, or whatever rights the tenants may have demanded, all were within the competency of the lord to grant or. of the tenants to stipulate for. And if it were possible to show that before the time of legal memory any lawful arrangement had been actually come to between the lord and his tenants as to the terms on which the latter should hold their lands, and that that arrangement had been afterwards constantly acted on, I do not see how it could ever be treated as being void because it was unreasonable. In truth, I believe that when it is said that a custom is void because it is unreasonable, nothing more is meant than that the unreasonable character of the alleged custom conclusively proves that the usage, even though it may have existed immemorially, must have resulted from accident or indulgence, and not from any right conferred in ancient times on the party setting up the custom."

[*462]

Doubtless in feudal times the maxim under our notice had special vitality and importance; it may be further illustrated by the relation of landlord and tenant which descended to us from them.

"The general principle," says Mr. Justice Ashhurst,[2] "is clear that the landlord having the *jus disponendi* may annex whatever conditions he pleases to his grant, provided they be not illegal or unreasonable." It is, for instance, reasonable that a landlord should exercise his judgment with respect to the person to whom he trusts the management of his estate; and, therefore, a covenant not to assign is legal, and ejectment will lie on breach of such a covenant.[3]

[1] See under the maxim *Optimus interpres rerum usus,—post*, Chap. X.

[2] Roe d. Hunter *v.* Galliers, 2 T. R. 137.

[3] Per Ashhurst, J., 2 T. R. 138.

[*463] In accordance with the above maxim, it is also laid *down that a college or charity is the founder's creature; that he may dispose and order it as he will, and may give it whatever shape he pleases, provided it be a legal one. And hence the founder of any lay corporation, whether civil or eleemosynary, may appoint himself, his heirs or assigns, or any other person specially named as trustees, to be the visitors; such trustees being, however, subject to the superintending power of the Court of Chancery, as possessing a general jurisdiction, in all cases of an abuse of trust, to redress grievances and suppress frauds.[1]

On this principle, likewise, an agreement by defendant to allow plaintiff, with whom he cohabited, an annuity for life, provided she should continue single, was held to be valid, for this was only an original gift, with a condition annexed; and *cujus est dare ejus est disponere.* Moreover, the grant of the annuity was not an inducement to the plaintiff to continue the cohabitation, it was rather an inducement to separate.[2]

Another remarkable illustration of the *jus disponendi* presents itself in that strict compliance with the wishes of the grantor, which was formerly[3] regarded as essential to the due execution of a power.[4]

As, moreover, the wishes and intention of a testator will, as far [*464] as possible, be complied with, and carried into *effect in a court of justice,[5] a person taking under a will may have a right of alienating the property devised in his lifetime, and yet have no power of disposing of it by any testamentary instrument. For instance, A. devised his copyhold and real estates to B., his heirs

[1] Bell, Dict. and Dig. of Scotch Law 242. See 1 Kyd on Corporations 50; 2 Id. 195; Skin. R. 481, 502.

[2] Gibson *v.* Dickie, 3 M. & S. 463, cited arg. Parker *v.* Rolls, 14 C. B. 697 (78 E. C. L. R.).

[3] By 1 Vict. c. 26, s. 10, every will executed as prescribed by that Act will be a valid execution of a power of appointment by will, although other required solemnities may not have been observed. This Act, however, does not extend to any will made before January 1, 1838.

[4] Rutland *v.* Doe d. Wythe, 12 M. & W. 357, 373, 378; s. c., 10 Cl. & Fin. 419; Doe d. Earl of Egremont *v.* Burrough, 6 Q. B. 229 (51 E. C. L. R.); Doe d. Bloomfield *v.* Eyre, 3 C. B. 557 (54 E. C. L. R.).

[5] As illustrating this well-known principle, see per Lord Brougham, Prendergast *v.* Prendergast, 3 H. L. Cas. 218, 219; *et vide post*, Chap. VIII.

and assigns, with a restriction upon alienation in these words: "In case B. shall depart this life without leaving any issue of his body lawfully begotten then living or being no such issue, and he my said son shall not have *disposed and parted with* his interest of, in, and to the aforesaid copyhold estate and premises;" and then followed a devise over to C. The court held, that the intention of the testator evidently was to give to his son absolute dominion over the estate, provided he chose to exercise that dominion in his lifetime; that the restriction imposed upon the power of alienation became effectual by the son dying seised; and that a devise of the estate in question was not a *disposing* of it within the meaning of the will.[1]

Without citing additional instances showing the application of the maxim *cujus est dare ejus est disponere*, here mentioned as introductory merely to that which concerns rights and liabilities passing by an assignment of property, we may observe, that although, in general, the law permits every man to part with his own interest, and to qualify his own grant, as it pleases himself, it nevertheless does not permit any allowance or recompense to be made, if the thing granted be not taken *as* it is granted; or, in the words of Lord Bacon's maxim—*Quod sub certâ *formâ concessum vel reservatum est non trahitur ad valorem vel compensationem*;—and, therefore, if I grant common for ten beasts for three years, and the grantee neglect for two years to use the right thus given, he shall not the third year have common for thirty beasts, for the time is certain and precise.[2] [*465]

Assignatus utitur Jure Auctoris.

(Halk. Max., p. 14.)

An assignee is clothed with the rights of his principal.[3]

It is laid down as a general and leading rule with reference to alienations and forfeitures, that *quod meum est sine facto meo vel*

[1] Doe d. Stevenson *v.* Glover, 1 C. B. 448 (50 E. C. L. R.).

[2] Bac. Max., reg. 4.

[3] "*Auctores*" *dicuntur a quibus jus in nos transiit.* Brisson. ad verb. "*Auctor.*"

defectu meo amitti vel in alium transferri non potest,[1] where *factum* may be translated "alienation," and *defectus* "forfeiture;"[2] and it seems desirable to preface our remarks as to the rights and liabilities which pass by the transfer of property, by stating this elementary and obvious principle, that where property in land or chattels has once been effectively and indefeasibly acquired, the right of property can only be lost by some act amounting to alienation or forfeiture on the part of the owner or his representatives.

[*466] An "assignee" is one who, by such act as aforesaid, *or by the operation of law, as in the event of death, possesses a thing or enjoys a benefit; the main distinction between an *assignee*[3] and a *deputy* being, that the former occupies in his own right, whereas the latter occupies in the right of another.[4]

A familiar instance of the first mode of transfer just mentioned presents itself in the assignment of a lease by deed; and of the second, in the case of the heir of an intestate who is an assignee in law of his ancestor.[5]

Further, under the term "assigns"[6] is included the assignee of an assignee *in perpetuum*,[7] provided the interest of the person originally entitled is transmitted on each successive devolution of the estate or thing assigned; for instance, the executor of A.'s executor is the assignee of A., but not so the executor of A.'s administrator, or the administrator of A.'s executor, who is in no sense the representative of A., and to whom, therefore, the unadministered residue of A.'s estate will not pass.

[1] This maxim is well illustrated by Vyner *v.* Mersey Docks, &c., Board, 14 C. B. N. S. 753 (108 E. C. L. R.).

[2] 1 Prest. Abs. Tit. 147, 318. The kindred maxims are, *Quod semel meum est amplius meum esse non potest*, Co. Litt. 49 b; *Duo non possunt in solido unam rem possidere*, Co. Litt. 368 a. See 1 Prest. Abs. Tit. 318; 2 Id. 86, 286; 2 Dods. Adm. R. 157; 2 Curt. 76.

[3] See Bromage *v.* Lloyd, 1 Exch. 32; Bishop *v.* Curtis, 18 Q. B. 878 (83 E. E. C. L. R.); Lysaght *v.* Bryant, 9 C. B. 46 (67 E. C. L. R.).

[4] Perkins' Prof. Bk. s. 100; Dyer 6.

[5] Spencer's Case, 5 Rep. 16.

[6] As to the meaning of the word "assigns" in a covenant, see Judgm., Bailey *v.* De Crespigny, L. R. 4 Q. B. 186.

See also Mitcalfe *v.* Westaway, 17 C. B. N. S. 658 (112 E. C. L. R.). An underlease of the whole term amounts to an assignment, Beardman *v.* Wilson, L. R. 4 C. P. 57.

[7] Co. Litt. 384 b.

In order to place in a clear light the general bearing and application of the maxim *assignatus utitur jure auctoris*, we propose to inquire, first, as to the quantity; and, secondly, as to the quality or nature of the interest in property which can be assigned by the owner to another party. And, 1st, it is a well-known rule, imported *into our own from the civil law, that no man can transfer a greater right or interest than he himself possesses [*467] —*Nemo plus juris ad alium transferre potest quam ipse haberet.*[1] The owner, for example, of a base or determinable fee can do no more than transfer to another his own estate, or some interest of inferior degree created out of it; and if there be two joint tenants of land, a grant or a lease by one of them will operate only on his own moiety.[2] In like manner, where the grantor originally possessed only a temporary or revocable right in the thing granted, and this right becomes extinguished by efflux of time or by revocation, the title of the assignee must, of course, cease to be valid, according to the rule *resoluto jure concedentis resolvitur jus concessum.*[3] We find it, however, laid down that the maxim above mentioned, which is one of the leading rules as to titles, or the equivalent maxim, *non dat qui non habet*, did not, prior to the stat. 8 & 9 Vict. c. 106, apply to wrongful conveyances or tortious acts;[4] for instance, before the passing of that Act, if a tenant for years made a feoffment, this feoffment vested in the feoffee a defeasible estate of freehold; for, according to the ancient doctrine, every person having possession of land, however slender, or however tortious his possession might be, was, nevertheless (unless, indeed, he were the mere bailiff of the party having title), considered to be in the seisin of the fee, so as to be able by livery to transfer it to another; and, consequently, if, in the case above supposed, the feoffee had, subsequently to the conveyance, levied a fine, such fine would, at the end of five years after the expiration *of the term, have barred the lessor.[5] But now by sec. 4 of the statute just cited,[6] [*468] a feoffment "shall not have any tortious operation."

[1] D. 50. 17. 54; Wing. Max., p. 56.
[2] 3 Prest. Abs. Tit. 25, 222.
[3] Mackeld. Civ. Law 179.
[4] 3 Prest. Abs. Tit. 25; Id. 244.
[5] The reader will find this subject elaborately considered in Mr. Butler's note (1) Co. Litt. 330 b; Machell *v.* Clarke, 2 Lord Raym. 778; 1 Cruise Dig., 4th ed., 80.
[6] See Shelford Real Prop. Stats., 6th ed., 595.

In connection with copyhold law also, an exception presents itself to the elementary rule above noticed, for the lord of a manor having only a particular interest therein as tenant for life, may grant by copy for an estate which may continue longer than his own estate in the manor, or for an estate in reversion, which may not come into possession during the existence of his own estate.[1] The special principle on which the grants of a lord *pro tempore* stand good after his estate has ceased, being that the grantee's estate is not derived out of the lord's only, but stands on the custom.[2]

Also, as between the assignor and assignee, an interest in realty may, in the following cases, be granted to, or vested in, an assignee, although greater than that which the assignor himself possessed. A jury found that the lessor had nothing in the land when he made the lease to the plaintiff, and afterwards the lessor entered and ejected him, and it was held that this lease was good as between the parties.[3] So, where a termor having previously assigned the term by way of mortgage, makes a sub-demise, such lease will be good by way of estoppel, as between the mortgagor and tenant; and if in this case the mortgagor should subsequently re-acquire the legal estate, the lease by estoppel would become a lease in interest, and the relation of landlord and tenant would [*469] *thereupon exist, as perfectly as if the lessor had been actually seised of the land at the time when the lease was made.[4]

In mercantile transactions, as well as in those unconnected with real property, the general rule undoubtedly is, that a person cannot transfer to another a right which he does not himself possess. The law does not "enable any man by a written engagement to give a floating right of action at the suit of any one into whose hands the writing may come, and who thus may acquire a right of action better than the right of him under whom he derives title."[5]

Of the rule above stated, a familiar instance is noticed by M. Pothier, who observes that, where prescription has begun to run

[1] Shelford Copyholds 20. [2] Id. ibid.

[3] Rawlyns' Case, 4 Rep. 52; cited Pollexf. 62.

[4] Sturgeon *v.* Winfield, 15 M. & W. 224, 230; Pargeter *v.* Harris, 7 Q. B. 708 (53 E. C. L. R.); Blake *v.* Foster, 8 T. R. 487; Stokes *v.* Russell, 3 T. R. 678; Webb *v.* Austin, 8 Scott N. R. 419. See arg. Weld *v.* Baxter, 11 Exch. 816.

[5] Per Lord Cranworth, C., Dixon *v.* Bovill, 3 Macq. Sc. App. Cas. 16.

against a creditor, it will continue to do so as against his heir, executors, or assigns, for the latter succeed only to the rights of their principal, and cannot stand in a better position than he did himself,—*nemo plus juris in alium transferre potest quam ipse habet.*[1] The assignee of a mortgage cannot stand in any different character, or hold any different position from that of the mortgagee himself, although the mortgagor may not have been a party to the assignment.[2] So the endorsee of an order for the delivery of goods acquires by the endorsement no better title and no higher right than the endorser had before;[3] nor could the assignee of such an order *sue upon it.[4] However, in considering hereafter [*470] maxims applicable to the law of contracts,[5] we shall have occasion to notice several cases which are directly opposed in principle to the rule now under review. Bearing upon this part of the subject we find in a recent case[6] the following remarks:—"The general rule of law is undoubted, that no one can transfer a better title than he himself possesses, *Nemo dat quod non habet.* To this there are some exceptions, one of which arises out of the rule of the law-merchant as to negotiable instruments. These being part of the currency are subject to the same rule as money; and if such an instrument be transferred in good faith for value before it is overdue, it becomes available in the hands of the holder notwithstanding fraud, which would have rendered it unavailable in the hands of a previous holder. This rule, however, is only intended to favor transfers in the ordinary and usual manner, whereby a title is acquired according to the law-merchant, and not to a transfer which is valid in equity, according to the doctrine respecting the assignment of choses in action, now indeed recognized, and in many instances enforced by courts of law; and it is therefore clear that in order to acquire the benefit of this rule the holder of the bill must, if it be payable to order, obtain an endorsement, and that he is affected by notice of a fraud received before he does so. Until

[1] 2 Pothier Oblig. 263. The maxim *supra* is also applied per Parke, B., Awde *v.* Dixon, 6 Exch. 872.

[2] Walker *v.* Jones, L. R. 1 P. C. 50, 61.

[3] Griffiths *v.* Perry, 1 E. & E. 680, 689 (102 E. C. L. R.).

[4] Dixon *v.* Bovill, 3 Macq. Sc. App. Cas. 1.

[5] Chap. IX.

[6] Whistler *v.* Forster, 14 C. B. N. S. 248, 257–8 (108 E. C. L. R.). See Deuters *v.* Townsend, 5 B. & S. 613, 616 (117 E. C. L. R.).

he does so, he is merely in the position of the assignee of an ordinary chose in action, and has no better right than his assignor. When he does so, he is affected by fraud, which he knew of before the endorsement."

[*471] *Further, by a sale in market overt, one wrongfully in possession of a chattel may convey a good title to a *bonâ fide* purchaser;[1] and, in like manner, the holder of a negotiable instrument, who could not himself recover upon it as against the rightful owner, may sometimes, as above intimated, by transferring it for value, vest a perfectly valid and unimpeachable title in the assignee. And although, according to our law as it stood before the passing of the Factor's Act (5 & 6 Vict. c. 39), a man could only transfer that which he himself possessed, the legislature by that statute intended to make an exception in the case of a person being an agent, and being as such intrusted with the possession of goods for sale.[2]

Another remarkable exception to the rule occurs in connection with the important subject of stoppage *in transitu;* for although, as between the consignor and consignee of goods, the title to the goods, and the question whether or not the property in them has passed, will depend upon the real contract entered into by the parties; yet, if the consignor and original owner endorses and delivers the bill of lading to the consignee, he thereby puts it in the power of the latter to transfer the property in the goods to a *bonâ fide* purchaser for a valuable consideration, and thus to deprive himself of any right of stoppage *in transitu* which he might have had as against the consignee prior to such transfer.[3] "The actual [*472] holder of an endorsed bill of lading," said Tindal, C. J.,[4] "may undoubtedly, by endorsement, *transfer a greater

[1] *Post.*

[2] Per Cockburn, C. J., Fuentes *v.* Montis, L. R. 4 C. P. 96.

[3] Pease *v.* Gloahec, L. R. 1 P. C. 219; per Erle, C. J., L. R. 2 C. P. 45.

[4] Jenkyns *v.* Usborne, 8 Scott N. R. 523; s. c., 7 M. & Gr. 678 (49 E. C. L. R.). See further, as to the effect of endorsing a bill of lading, 18 & 19 Vict. c. 111, s. 1. Under this section the rights and liabilities of the endorsee of the bill of lading pass from him by endorsement over to a third person: Dracachi *v.* Anglo-Egyptian Nav. Co., L. R. 3 C. P. 190; Smurthwaite *v.* Wilkins, 11 C. B. N. S. 842 (103 E. C. L. R.).

As to the effect of re-endorsing a bill of lading, see Short *v.* Simpson, L. R. 1 C. P. 248.

right than he himself has.[1] It is at variance with the general principles of law, that a man should be allowed to transfer to another a right which he himself has not; but the exception is founded on the nature of the instrument in question, which being, like a bill of exchange, a negotiable instrument, for the general convenience of commerce, has been allowed to have an effect at variance with the ordinary principles of law. But this operation of a bill of lading, being derived from its negotiable quality, appears to us to be confined to the case where the person who transfers the right is himself in possession of the bill of lading, so as to be in a situation to transfer the instrument itself, which is the symbol of the property itself."[2]

Having thus adverted to the amount or quantity of interest assignable, with reference more especially to the grantor, we must, in the next place, observe that, as a general rule, the assignee of property takes it subject to all the obligations or liabilities,[3] and clothed with all the rights which attached to it in the hands of the assignor,[4] and this is in accordance with the maxim of *the civil law, *qui in jus dominiumve alterius succedit jure ejus uti debet.*[5] We have already given one instance illustrative of this rule, viz., where an heir or executor becomes invested with the right to property against which the Statute of Limitations has begun to run. To this we shall here add only one other example, as the same general principle will necessarily again present itself to our

[*473]

[1] See also Judgm., L. R. 2 P. C. 405, where the above exception to the general rule is said to be "founded on the negotiable quality of the document. It is confined to the case where the person who transfers the right is himself in actual and authorized possession of the document, and the transferee gives value on the faith of it, without having notice of any circumstance which would render the transaction neither fair nor honest."

[2] See Judgm., Gurney *v.* Behrend, 3 E. & B. 633, 634 (77 E. C. L. R.); 1 Smith L. C., 5th ed., 739.

[3] See White *v.* Crisp, 10 Exch. 312.

[4] As to this rule in equity, see Mangles *v.* Dixon, 3 H. L. Cas. 702, cited Higgs *v.* Assam Tea Co., L. R. 4 Ex. 396; Rodger *v.* The Comptoir d'Escompte de Paris, L. R. 2 P. C. 393, 405; Dickson *v.* Swansea Vale R. C., L. R. 4 Q. B. 44, 48. If a man gives a license and then parts with the property over which the privilege is to be exercised, the license is gone: Colman *v.* Foster, 1 H. & N. 37, 40.

[5] D. 50. 17. 177. pr. For instance, fee-simple estates are subject, in the hands of the heir or devisee, to debts of all kinds contracted by the deceased.

notice in connection with the law of contracts, which has been reserved for especial consideration in a subsequent portion of this work.

Where, then, a person pays a bill of exchange on account and for the honor of a party to the bill, the person making such payment becomes holder of the bill as upon a transfer from the party for whom the payment was made; that is to say, he is put in the situation of an endorsee under such party and is clothed with all the rights and liabilities incident to that character. Thus, if A. pays the bill for the honor of B., he thereupon has a right to consider himself as an endorsee under B., and consequently, to give notice of the dishonor to him; and if B. thereupon gives a notice to the drawer, which is within time, so far as he is concerned, A. will have a right to adopt and take advantage of it as a notice given by himself;[1]—*Qui alterius jure utitur eodem jure uti debet.*[2]

Without pursuing further our inquiry respecting the *quantity* of [*474] interest in property which is capable of being *transferred, we shall, secondly, proceed to consider briefly the *quality* or nature of that interest; and we must commence our remarks upon this branch of the subject with observing, that there is an important distinction between the transfer of the right of property in a chattel and the transfer of the right of action for the same. It is, indeed, a well-known rule of law, that a chose in action, *ex. gr.*, a debt,[3] cannot in general be assigned so as to vest in the assignee a right of action upon it in his own name,[4] nor do causes of action already accrued run with the property in goods or deeds.[5] Where,

[1] Goodall *v.* Polhill, 1 C. B. 233, 242 (50 E. C. L. R.).

[2] Pothier, Tr. de Change, pt. 1, ch. 4, art. 5, s. 114.

[3] Per Martin, B., Liversidge *v.* Broadbent, 4 H. & N. 610. See Graham *v.* Gracie, 13 Q. B. 548 (66 E. C. L. R.); Thompson *v.* Bell, 3 E. & B. 236 (77 E. C. L. R.).

"Though a bond debt cannot be assigned, the parchment on which the bond is written may be assigned:" per Willes, J., Watson *v.* McLean, E., B. & E. 81 (96 E. C. L. R.), citing 2 Roll. Abr. *Graunts* (G.), pt. 2.

[4] Lampet's Case, 10 Rep. 48; Co. Litt. 232 b; per Maule, J., Howard *v.* Shepherd, 9 C. B. 319 (67 E. C. L. R.), and in Tempest *v.* Kilner, 2 C. B. 308 (52 E. C. L. R.). See, as to this rule, the remarks of Buller, J., 4 T. R. 340; and as to a plea of the equitable assignment of a debt, see Jeffs *v.* Day, L. R. 1 Q. B. 372.

[5] Per Blackburn, J., Goodman *v.* Boycott, 2 B. & S. 9, 10 (110 E. C. L. R.).

accordingly, the drawer of a ticket in a Derby lottery sold it to the plaintiff before the race, and the horse named in it was ultimately declared to be the winner, it was held that an action for money had and received would not lie by the plaintiff against the stakeholder, there being no privity of contract originally between those parties, and the assignment of a chose in action not giving to the assignee a right of action.[1] So, although an interest in a partnership, or an equitable interest in land, is a thing of value, and may be made the subject of a valid contract, yet it is not assignable at law so as to enable the assignee to sue in his own name—for example, as co-partner, or as owner *of the beneficial interest,[2] and, although it is perfectly legal,[3] and in practice very common, [*475] to assign debts—for the benefit of creditors or otherwise—yet the assignee must sue for them in the name of the assignor.[4] Even at law, however, the assignment of a debt will, in certain cases, give to the assignee a right to sue in his own name for its recovery;[5] and, in order to constitute a good *equitable* assignment, it is in general sufficient if there be an engagement by the debtor that a particular fund shall be charged with or appropriated to the payment of the debt.[6] Courts of equity will, moreover, give effect to assignments, not only of choses in action, but likewise of property, in many cases, where such assignments would not be recognized at law as valid or effectual to pass titles; they will, for instance, support assignments

[1] Jones *v.* Carter, 8 Q. B. 134 (55 E. C. L. R.). See, now, stat. 8 & 9 Vict. c. 109, which renders wagers illegal.

[2] Tempest *v.* Kilner, 2 C. B. 300, 308 (52 E. C. L. R.); per Buller, J., Master *v.* Miller, 4 T. R. 341. See Jones *v.* Robinson, 1 Exch. 454.

[3] See per Willes, J., Balfour *v.* Off. Man. of the Sea Fire and Life Ass. Co., 27 L. J. C. P. 19.

[4] Per Bayley, J., Price *v.* Seaman, 4 B. & C. 528 (10 E. C. L. R.).

[5] Per Buller, J., Tatlock *v.* Harris, 3 T. R. 180; Fairlie *v.* Denton, 8 B. & C. 395, 400 (15 E. C. L. R.); Wharton *v.* Walker, 4 B. & C. 166 (10 E. C. L. R.); Walker *v.* Rostron, 9 M. & W. 411; Griffin *v.* Weatherby, L. R. 3 Q. B. 753; with which compare Liversidge *v.* Broadbent, 4 H. & N. 603; Com. Dig., *Action upon the case upon assumpsit* (B. 1. 3). See also Ex parte Lane, De G. Bankruptcy Cas. 300; Eastern Union R. C. *v.* Cochrane, 9 Exch. 197; London, Brighton and South Coast R. C. *v.* Goodwin, 3 Exch. 320; Judgm., 1 Exch. 643. The common law rule forbidding the assignment of a chose in action does not bind the crown: see Story Eq. Jurisp., 6th ed., 405.

[6] See 2 Story Eq. Jurisp., 6th ed., 427, 428; Rodick *v.* Gandell, 1 De G., M. & G. 763.

of contingent interests, of expectancies, and of things resting in mere possibility, and they look upon the assignment of a debt as in its nature amounting to a declaration of trust, and to an agreement to permit the assignee to make use of the name of the assignor for its recovery.[1]

[*476] *Without attempting to enumerate the various rights which are assignable, either by the express act of the party, or by the operation of the law, we may observe generally, that the maxim, *assignatus utitur jure auctoris*, is subject to very many restrictions[2] besides those to which we have just alluded; for instance, although the assignee of the reversion in land is, by the common law, entitled to sue upon covenants in law,[3] and has, under the stat. 32 Hen. 8, c. 34 (which applies only to leases by deed),[4] a right to sue on express covenants contained in the lease, yet the operation of this statute is confined to such covenants as are technically said to run with the land, that is, such as require something to be done which is in some manner annexed and appurtenant to the land itself.[5] Bills of exchange,[6] promissory notes, and checks[7] upon bankers, are in general assignable. And where a bill is endorsed in blank, the holder may hand it over to a third person to sue upon it on his behalf.[8] In like manner, the legal effect of marriage is to

[1] 2 Story Eq. Jurisp., 6th ed., 406, 407.

[2] See Sandrey *v.* Michell, 3 B. & S. 405 (113 E. C. L. R.); Young *v.* Hughes, 4 H. & N. 76; M'Kune *v.* Joynson, 5 C. B. N. S. 218 (94 E. C. L. R.).

[3] See Williams *v.* Burrell, 1 C. B. 429 (50 E. C. L. R.); Coote L. & T. 314; Vyvyan *v.* Arthur, 1 B. & C. 414 (8 E. C. L. R.); Harper *v.* Burgh, 2 Lev. 206.

[4] Per Lush, J., Elliott *v.* Johnson, L. R. 2 Q. B. 122, citing Standen *v.* Christmas, 10 Q. B. 135 (59 E. C. L. R.).

[5] Spencer's Case, 5 Rep. 16, 1st resolution; Martyn *v.* Clue, 18 Q. B. 661 (83 E. C. L. R.); Martyn *v.* Williams, 1 H. & N. 817; Hooper *v.* Clark, L. R. 2 Q. B. 200; Stevens *v.* Copp, L. R. 4 Ex. 20; Thomas *v.* Hayward, Ibid. 311; Williams *v.* Hayward, 1 E. & E. 1040 (102 E. C. L. R.); Gorton *v.* Gregory, 3 B. & S. 90 (113 E. C. L. R.); Bennett *v.* Herring, 3 C. B. N. S. 370 (91 E. C. L. R.); Sharp *v.* Waterhouse, 7 E. & B. 816 (90 E. C. L. R.).

[6] See Harrop, app., Fisher, resp., 10 C. B. N. S. 196 (100 E. C. L. R.).

[7] Keene *v.* Beard, 8 C. B. N. S. 372 (98 E. C. L. R.).

[8] Law *v.* Parnell, 7 C. B. N. S. 282 (97 E. C. L. R.). See Judgm., Ingham *v.* Primrose, 7 C. B. N. S. 85 (97 E. C. L. R.).

Policies of life and marine insurance are now assignable under stats. 30 & 31 Vict. c. 144, and 31 & 32 Vict. c. 86.

vest in the husband the right of reducing *into possession [*477] the chattels real and choses in action generally of the wife, yet if he dies without having exercised this power, the above descriptions of property will survive to the wife;[1] and, as we shall hereafter see, the rule, that a vested right of action is by death transferred to the personal representatives of the deceased, is subject to some important exceptions, and must, therefore, be applied with considerable caution.[2]

The case of a pawn or pledge of a chattel should perhaps also be referred to in connection with the principle, *assignatus utitur jure auctoris*, for here the pawner retains a property in the chattel, qualified by the right vested in the pawnee; and a sale of the chattel by its owner would, therefore, transfer to the vendee that qualified right only which the vendor himself possessed.[3] To constitute a valid pledge there must, however, be a delivery of the chattel, either actual or constructive, to the pawnee.[4]

Again, the well-known distinction between *absolute* and *special* property may be adverted to generally, as showing in what manner and under what circumstances the maxim, that an assignee succeeds to the rights of his grantor, must, in a large class of cases, be understood. *Absolute* property, according to Mr. Justice Lawrence, is, where one *having the possession of chattels has also [*478] the exclusive right to enjoy them, which right can only be defeated by some act of his own. *Special* property, on the other hand, is, where he who has the possession holds them subject to the claims of other persons.[5] According, therefore, as the property in the grantor was absolute or subject to a special lien, so will be that transferred to his assignee—*qui in jus dominiumve alterius succedit*

[1] Per Parke, B., Gaters *v.* Madeley, 6 M. & W. 426, 427; Fleet *v.* Perrins, L. R. 4 Q. B. 500, and cases there cited.

[2] See the maxim, *Actio personalis moritur cum personâ*—*post*, Chap. IX.

[3] Franklin *v.* Neate, 13 M. & W. 481, cited Re Attenborough, 11 Exch. 463. As to the true nature of a pledge, see per Parke, B., Cheesman *v.* Exall, 6 Exch. 344.

As to the right of the pledgee to sell the pledge, see Halliday *v.* Holgate, L. R. 3 Ex. 299; approving Donald *v.* Suckling, L. R. 1 Q. B. 585.

[4] Per Erle, C. J., Martin *v.* Reid, 11 C. B. N. S. 734 (103 E. C. L. R.).

[5] Webb *v.* Fox, 7 T. R. 398. See per Pollock, C. B., Lancashire Wagon Co. *v.* Fitzhugh, 6 H. & N. 506.

jure ejus uti debet; and the same principle applies where a subsequent transfer of the property is made by such assignee.[1]

It will be evident, that, with regard to a legal maxim so comprehensive and so general in its application as that before us, little can be attempted beyond giving to the reader a brief and necessarily an imperfect outline of such only of the various classes of cases exemplifying its meaning and qualifications as may seem apposite to the end which has here been kept in view, that, viz., of presenting a *compendious* statement of the most practically useful and important principles connected with the transfer of property.

We shall, therefore, without occupying additional space in remarking upon the rule above illustrated, proceed at once to an enumeration of some few other kindred maxims, which are indeed of minor importance, but, nevertheless, could not properly be omitted in even the most cursory notice of the above-mentioned branch of our legal system.

[*479] *CUICUNQUE ALIQUIS QUID CONCEDIT CONCEDERE VIDETUR ET ID SINE QUO RES IPSA ESSE NON POTUIT.

(11 Rep. 52.)

Whoever grants a thing is supposed also tacitly to grant that without which the grant itself would be of no effect.

"If you grant anything, you are presumed to grant to the extent of your power that also without which the thing granted cannot be enjoyed."[2] Thus, in The Caledonian Railway Company *v.* Sprot,[3] Lord Cranworth, C., in reference to the right to support, observes, "If the owner of a house were to convey the upper story to a purchaser, reserving all below the upper story, such purchaser would, on general principles, have a right to prevent the owner of the lower stories from interfering with the walls and beams upon

[1] As to a sale or wrongful conversion by bailee for hire, see Cooper *v.* Willomatt, 1 C. B. 672 (50 E. C. L. R.); Bryant *v.* Wardell, 2 Exch. 479; Fenn *v.* Bittleston, 7 Exch. 152; Spackman *v.* Miller, 12 C. B. N. S. 659, 676 (104 E. C. L. R.).

[2] Judgm., Lord *v.* Commissioners for City of Sydney, 12 Moo. P. C. C. 499, 500.

[3] 2 Macq. Sc. App. Cas. 449, 450, 451. See Great Western R. C. *v.* Fletcher, 5 H. & N. 689.

which the upper story rests, so as to prevent them from affording proper support. The same principle applies to the case of adjacent support, so far, at all events, as to prevent a person who has granted a part of his land from so dealing with that which he retains, as to cause that which he has granted to sink or fall. How far such adjacent support must extend is a question which, in each particular case, will depend on its own special circumstances. * * * And it must further be observed, that all which a grantor can reasonably be considered to grant or warrant, is such a measure of support as is necessary for the land in its condition at the time of the grant, or in the state for the purpose of putting it into which the grant is made. Thus, if I grant a meadow to another, retaining both the minerals under it, *and also the adjoining lands, I am bound so to work my mines and to dig my adjoining lands as not to cause the meadow to sink or fall over. But if I do this, and the grantee thinks fit to build a house on the edge of the land he has acquired, he cannot complain of my workings or diggings if, by reason of the additional weight he has put on the land, they cause his house to fall. If, indeed, the grant is made expressly to enable the grantee to build his house on the land granted, then there is an implied warranty of support, subjacent and adjacent, as if the house had already existed."

[*480]

The above reasoning is in conformity with the spirit of the maxim, *supra*, p. 479. So it is laid down, that when anything is granted, all the means to attain it,[1] and all the fruits and effects of it, are granted also, and shall pass inclusive, together with the thing by the grant of the thing itself, without the words *cum pertinentiis*,[2] or any such-like words.[3] And a right of way appurtenant to land passes to the tenant by a parol demise of the land, although nothing is said about it at the time of the demise.[4]

Therefore, by the grant of a piece of ground is granted a right

[1] See Dalton's Justice 397 (ed. 1655); cited Evans *v.* Rees, 12 A. & E. 57, 58 (40 E. C. L. R.); arg. Mayor of London *v.* Reg., 13 Q. B. 37 (66 E. C. L. R.); Free Fishers of Whitstable *v.* Gann, 11 C. B. N. S. 387 (103 E. C. L. R.); s. c., 13 Id. 853, 11 H. L. Cas. 192.

[2] As to the effect of these words, see Cort *v.* Sagar, 3 H. & N. 370; Bac. Abr. *Grant* (T. 4).

[3] Shep. Touch. 89; Hobart 234; Vaugh. R. 109. See also Jinks *v.* Edwards, 11 Exch. 775, in illustration of the above maxim.

[4] Skull *v.* Glenister, 16 C. B. N. S. 81 (111 E. C. L. R.).

of way to it over the grantor's land, as incident to the grant; and, in like manner, by a reservation of the close is reserved also a [*481] right of way to it;[1] and by the *grant of trees is granted powers to enter on the land to cut them down and take them away.[2] If a man leases his land and all mines, where there are no open ones, the lessee may dig for the minerals;[3] and by the grant of fish in a man's pond is granted power to come upon the banks and fish for them.[4] On the same principle, where trees are excepted in a lease, the lessor has a power by law, as incident to the exception, to enter upon the land demised at all reasonable times in order to fell and carry away the trees; and the like law holds with regard to a demise by parol.[5] So a rector may enter into a close to carry away the tithes over the usual way, as incident [*482] to his right to the tithes.[6] And a tenant at will, *after notice to quit, or any other party who is entitled to emble-

[1] 1 Wms. Saund. 323, n; Pinnington v. Galland, 9 Exch. 1, 12; cited, per Parke, B., Richards v. Rose, Id. 220; and distinguished in White v. Bass, 7 H. & N. 729, 732; Buckby v. Coles, 5 Taunt. 311 (1 E. C. L. R.); Robertson v. Gantlett, 16 M. & W. 289.

The mode of creating and nature of a way of necessity were much considered in Pearson v. Spencer, 1 B. & S. 571 (101 E. C. L. R.).

A right of way of necessity can only arise by grant express or implied: Proctor v. Hodgson, 10 Exch. 824. See arg. Grove v. Withers, 4 Exch. 879.

The right to use a drain may pass impliedly by the grant of a house: Pyer v. Carter, 1 H. & N. 916 (which "went to the utmost extent of the law," per Martin, B., Dodd v. Burchell, 1 H. & C. 121); cited Chadwick v. Marsden, L. R. 2 Ex. 289; Ewart v. Cochrane, 4 Macq. Sc. App. Cas. 117, 122; Hall v. Lund, 1 H. & C. 676. See Polden v. Bastard, 32 L. J. Q. B. 372.

[2] Howton v. Frearson, 8 T. R. 56; Noy, Max., 9th ed., 54, 56; Plowd. Com. 16 a; Finch Law 63; Clarke v. Cogge, Cro. Jac. 170; Beaudely v. Brook, Id. 190; per Best, C. J., 2 Bing. 83 (9 E. C. L. R.). See Robertson v. Gantlett, 16 M. & W. 289.

[3] Where minerals are granted by deed, it must *primâ facie* be presumed that the minerals are to be enjoyed, and, therefore, that a power to get them must also be granted or reserved as a necessary incident: per Lord Wensleydale, Rowbotham v. Wilson, 8 H. L. Cas. 360; per Martin, B., s. c., 8 E. & B. 149 (92 E. C. L. R.).

[4] 1 Wms. Saund. 323, n. (6); Shep. Touch. 89; Co. Litt. 59 b; Liford's Case, 11 Rep. 52; Foster v. Spooner, Cro. Eliz. 18; Saunders' Case, 5 Rep. 12; Noy, Max., 9th ed., p. 56; Doe d. Rogers v. Price, 8 C. B. 894 (65 E. C. L. R.).

[5] Hewitt v. Isham, 7 Exch. 77, 79; Liford's Case, 11 Rep. 52; Ashmead v. Ranger, 1 Ld. Raym. 552.

[6] 1 Wms. Saund. 323, note (6), *ad finem*.

ments, shall have free entry, egress, and regress, to cut and carry them away.[1] The right to emblements does not, however, give a title to the exclusive occupation of the land. Therefore, it seems that, if the executors occupy till the corn or other produce be ripe, the landlord may maintain an action for the use and occupation of the land.[2] On the same principle, where a tenant is entitled to an away-going crop, he may likewise be entitled by custom to retain possession of that portion of the land on which it grows; and, in this case, the custom operates as a prolongation of the term, or rather of the legal right of possession as to such portion.[3]

So, it has been observed, that when the use of a thing is granted, everything is granted by which the grantee may have and enjoy such use; as, if a man gives me a license to lay pipes of lead in his land to convey water to my cistern, I may afterwards enter, and dig the land, in order to mend the pipes, though the soil belongs to another, and not to me.[4]

And where an Act of Parliament empowered a railway company to cross the line of another company by means of a bridge, it was held, that the first-mentioned company had, consequently, the right of placing temporary scaffolding on the land belonging to the latter, if the *so placing it were necessary for the purpose of constructing the bridge,[5] for *ubi aliquid conceditur, conceditur et id sine quo res ipsa esse non potest.* And a person lawfully exposing goods for sale in a public market has a right to occupy the soil with baskets necessary and proper for containing the goods.[6] [*483]

In a modern case, it was held, that a certain coal-shoot, water and other pipes, all which were found, by special verdict, to be

[1] Litt. s. 68; Co. Litt 56 a, 153 a, cited 1 M. & S. 660 (28 E. C. L. R.).

[2] Woodf., L. & T., 9th ed., 586.

[3] Per Bayley, J., Boraston *v.* Green, 16 East 81; Griffiths *v.* Puleston, 13 M. & W. 358; Ex parte Mandrell, 2 Madd. 315. See Strickland *v.* Maxwell, 2 Cr. & M. 539.

[4] Per Twysden, J., Pomfret *v.* Ricroft, 1 Saund. R. 323; per Wigram, V.-C., Blackesley *v.* Whieldon, 1 Hare 180; per Story, J., Charles River Bridge *v.* Warren Bridge, 11 Peters (U. S.) R. 630, cited Richmond R. C. *v.* Louisa R. C., 13 Howard (U. S.) R. 81; Judgm., Hodgson *v.* Field, 7 East 622, 623.

[5] Clarence R. C. *v.* Great North of England R. C., 13 M. & W. 706, 721; s. c., 4 Q. B. 46 (45 E. C. L. R.). See Doe *v.* Archb. of York, 14 Q. B. 81 (68 E. C. L. R.).

[6] Townend *v.* Woodruff, 5 Exch. 506.

necessary for the convenient and beneficial use and occupation of a certain messuage, did under the particular circumstances pass to the lessee as integral parts of such messuage; and it was further held, in strict accordance with the rule of law now under consideration, that the right of passing and repassing over the soil of a certain passage for the purpose of using the said coal shoot, and using, cleaning, and repairing the said pipes, likewise passed to the lessee as a necessary incident to the subject-matter actually demised, although not specially named in the lease.[1]

In a deed of conveyance of certain land, the grantor excepted and reserved out of the grant all coal-mines, together with sufficient way-leave and stay-leave to and from the said mines, and the liberty of sinking pits: the court held, that, as the coals were excepted, and a right to dig pits for getting those coals reserved, all things "depending on that right, and necessary for the obtaining it," were, according to the above rule, reserved also, and consequently, that the owner had, as incident to the *liberty to [*484] sink pits, the right to fix such machinery as would be necessary to drain the mines, and draw the coals from the pits; and, further, that a pond for the supply of the engine, and likewise the engine-house, were necessary accessories to such an engine, and were, therefore, lawfully made.[2]

Again, the power of making by-laws is, on the same principle, incident to a corporation; for, when the crown creates a corporation, it grants to it, by implication, all powers that are necessary for carrying into effect the objects for which it is created, and securing a perpetuity of succession. Now, a discretionary power somewhere to make minor regulations, usually called by-laws, in order to effect the objects of the charter, is necessary; and the reasonable exercise of this power is, therefore, impliedly granted by the crown, and is conferred by the very act of incorporation.[3]

[1] Hinchcliffe *v.* Earl of Kinnoul, 5 Bing. N. C. 1 (35 E. C. L. R.); Hall *v.* Lund, 1 H. & C. 676; see Pheysey *v.* Vicary, 16 M. & W. 484.

[2] Dand *v.* Kingscote, 6 M. & W. 174, and cases there cited; Rogers *v.* Taylor, 1 H. & N. 706, 711; citing Dand *v.* Kingscote, *supra*, and Earl of Cardigan *v.* Armitage, 2 B. & C. 197 (9 E. C. L. R.); Hodgson *v.* Field, 7 East 613.

[3] R. *v.* Westwood, 7 Bing. 20 (20 E. C. L. R.). See Chilton *v.* London and Croydon R. C., 16 M. & W. 212; Calder and Hebble Nav. Co. *v.* Pilling, 14 M. & W. 76. A by-law is "a rule made prospectively, and to be applied

So, a corporation incorporated for trading purposes has impliedly power to contract by parol for purposes necessary for the carrying on of their trade.[1]

The above maxim, however, must be understood as applying to such things only as are incident to the grant, and *directly* necessary for the enjoyment of the thing granted: therefore, if a man, as in the instance above put, grants to another the fish in his ponds, the grantee cannot cut the banks to lay the ponds dry, for he may take the *fish with nets or other engines.[2] So, if a man, upon a lease for years, reserve a way for himself through the house of the lessee to a back-house, he cannot use it but at reasonable times, and upon request.[3] A way of necessity is also limited by the necessity which created it, and when such necessity ceases, the right of way likewise ceases; therefore, if, at any subsequent period, the party formerly entitled to such way can, by passing over his own land, approach the place to which it led by as direct a course as he would have done by using the old way, the way ceases to exist as of necessity.[4] A way of necessity once created, must, however, remain the same way as long as it continues at all.[5] [*485]

On a principle similar to that which has been thus briefly considered, it is a rule, that, when the law commands a thing to be done, it authorizes the performance of whatever may be necessary for executing its command:—*Quando aliquid mandatur, mandatur et omne per quod pervenitur ad illud.*[6] Thus when a statute gives a

whenever the circumstances arise for which it is intended to provide:" Judgm., Gosling *v.* Veley, 7 Q. B. 451 (53 E. C. L. R.); Bac. Abr., *Corporations* (D).

[1] Broom's Com., 4th ed., 564.

[2] 1 Wms. Saund. 233, n. (6), *ad finem;* Lord Darcy *v.* Askwith, Hob. 234; per Parke, B., 6 M. & W. 189.

[3] Tomlin *v.* Fuller, 1 Ventr. 48. See also, Morris *v.* Edgington, 3 Taunt. 24, cited 6 M. & W. 189; Wilson *v.* Bagshaw, 5 Man. and Ry. 448; Osborn *v.* Wise, 7 C. & P. 761 (32 E. C. L. R.).

[4] Holmes *v.* Goring, 2 Bing. 76 (9 E. C. L. R.). As to which case see, per Parke, B., Proctor *v.* Hodgson, 10 Exch. 828; Judgm., 1 B. & S. 584 (101 E. C. L. R.). See Grove *v.* Withers, 4 Exch. 875.

The maxim considered in the text is also applied, per Alderson, B., Breese *v.* Owens, 6 Exch. 417.

[5] Pearson *v.* Spencer, 1 B. & S. 571, 584 (101 E. C. L. R.).

[6] 5 Rep. 116.

In accordance with the same principle an agent is sometimes held to be

[*486] *justice of the peace jurisdiction over an offence, it impliedly gives him power to apprehend any person charged with such offence.[1] So, constables, whose duty it is to see the peace kept, may, when necessary, command the assistance of others.[2] In like manner, the sheriff is authorized to take the *posse comitatûs*, or power of the county, to help him in executing a writ of execution, and every one is bound to assist him when required so to do;[3] and, by analogy, the persons named in a writ of rebellion, and charged with the execution of it, have a right, at their discretion, to require the assistance of any of the liege subjects of the crown to aid in the execution of the writ.[4]

The foregoing are simple illustrations of the last-mentioned maxim, or of the synonymous expression, *Quando lex aliquid alicui concedit, conceditur et id sine quo res ipsa esse non potest*,[5] the full import of which has been thus elaborately set forth:[6]—"Whenever anything is authorized, and especially if, as matter of duty, required to be done by law, and it is found impossible to do that thing unless something else not authorized in express terms be also done, then that something else will be supplied by necessary intendment. But if, when the maxim comes to be applied adversely to the liberties or [*487] *interests of others, it be found that no such impossibility exists,—that the power may be legally exercised without the doing that something else, or, even going a step farther, that it is

impliedly clothed with power to act in cases of necessity. See Edwards *v.* Havill, 14 C. B. 107 (78 E. C. L. R.); Beldon *v.* Campbell, 6 Exch. 886, 889; cited per Sir R. Phillimore, The Karnak, L. R. 2 A. & E. 302; s. c., L. R. 2 P. C. 505; Frost *v.* Oliver, 2 E. & B. 301 (75 E. C. L. R.), with which cases compare Organ *v.* Brodie, 10 Exch. 449; Story on Agency, 4th ed., 110, 179, 242, 299. The maxim cited *supra* has indeed a very wide applicability in connection with the law of Principal and Agent; see, *ex. gr.*, Bayley *v.* Wilkins, 7 C. B. 886 (62 E. C. L. R.). It was unsuccessfully relied on in Brady *v.* Todd, 9 C. B. N. S. 592 (99 E. C. L. R.); with which compare Miller *v.* Lawton, 15 C. B. N. S. 834 (109 E. C. L. R.).

[1] Bane *v.* Methuen, 2 Bing. 63 (9 E. C. L. R.). See R. *v.* Benn, 6 T. R. 198.

[2] Noy, Max., 9th ed., p. 55.

[3] Foljamb's Case, 5 Rep. 116; cited 4 Bing. N. C. 583 (33 E. C. L. R.); Noy, Max., 9th ed., p. 55; 1 Chit. Archb. Pr. 11th ed., 615; Judgm., Howden *v.* Standish, 6 C. B. 521 (60 E. C. L. R.).

[4] Miller *v.* Knox, 4 Bing. N. C. 574 (33 E. C. L. R.).

[5] 12 Rep. 131.

[6] Fenton *v.* Hampton, 11 Moo. P. C. C. 360.

only in some particular instances, as opposed to its general operation, that the law fails in its intention unless the enforcing power be supplied,—then in any such case the soundest rules of construction point to the exclusion of the maxim, and regard the absence of the power which it would supply by implication as a *casus omissus.*"

The mode of applying the maxim just cited may be thus exemplified:—

The Lower House of Assembly of the island of Dominica is a legislative assembly constituted under royal proclamation,[1] and empowered by various commissions given subsequently to the governor for the time being, to make, with the advice and consent of the Council, laws for the peace, welfare, and good government of the inhabitants of the colony.[2] The question not long since arose,[3] has this legislative assembly authority to commit and punish for contempts committed, and for interruptions and obstructions to the business of the said House by its members or others in its presence and during its sittings? In deciding this question adversely to the asserted right, the Judicial Committee of the Privy Council observed in substance as follows:—It must be conceded that as the common law sanctions the exercise of the prerogative by which the Assembly was created, the principle of the common law, embodied in the maxim, *quando lex aliquid concedit, concedere videtur et illud* **sine quo res ipsa esse non potest*, applies to the body so created. The question therefore is reduced to this: Is the power [*488] to punish and commit for contempts committed in its presence, one necessary to the existence of such a body as the Assembly of Dominica and the proper exercise of the functions which it is intended to execute? It is necessary to distinguish between a power to punish for a contempt, which is a judicial power, and a power to remove any obstruction offered to the deliberations or proper action of a legislative body during its sittings, which last power is necessary for self-preservation. If a member of a Colonial House of Assembly is guilty of disorderly conduct in the House whilst sitting, he may be removed, or excluded for a time, or even expelled; but there is a great difference between such powers and the judicial power of inflicting a penal sentence for the offence. The right to

[1] 21st June, A. D. 1775. [2] Clark, Col. L. 134.

[3] Doyle *v.* Falconer, 4 Moo. P. C. C. N. S. 203; S. C., L. R. 1 P. C. 328.

remove for self-security is one thing, the right to inflict punishment is another. The former is all that is warranted by the maxim above cited, but the latter is not its legitimate consequence. To establish a right to the particular privilege claimed, it must be shown to be essential to the existence of the Assembly—an incident *sine quo res ipsa esse non potest.*[1]

To take another exemplification of the foregoing maxim: By sect. 86 of the stat. 8 & 9 Vict. c. 20, power is given to a railway company within its provisions to use and employ locomotive engines. If then such locomotive engines cannot possibly be used without occasioning vibration and consequent injury to neighboring houses, [*489] *upon the principle of law that *cuicunque aliquis quid concedit, concedere videtur et id sine quo res ipsa esse non potuit*, it must be taken that power is given to cause that vibration without liability to an action. The right given to use the locomotives would otherwise be nugatory, as each time a train passed upon the line and shook the houses in the neighborhood, actions might be brought by their owners which would soon put a stop to the use of the railway.[2]

On the other hand, *quando aliquid prohibetur, prohibetur et omne per quod devenitur ad allud*[3]—whatever is prohibited by law to be done directly cannot legally be effected by an indirect and circuitous contrivance;[4]—a transaction will not be upheld which is "a mere device for carrying into effect that which the legislature has expressly said shall not be done;[5] of which maxim the following instances must suffice:—the donee of a power of appointment

[1] Judgm., 4 Moo. P. C. C. N. S. 219, 221; Kielley *v.* Carson, 4 Moo. P. C. C. 63, overruling Beaumont *v.* Barrett, 1 Id. 59.

[2] Per Lord Chelmsford, Hammersmith and City R. C. *v.* Brand, L. R. 4 H. L. 202.

[3] 2 Inst. 48.

[4] Booth *v.* The Bank of England, 7 Cl. & Fin. 509; Judgm., 12 Peters (U. S.) R. 605; Co. Litt. 223 b; Wing. Max., p. 618; per Lord Kenyon, C. J., 8 T. R. 301, 415. See Hughes *v.* Statham, 4 B. & C. 187, 193 (10 E. C. L. R.); Duke of Marlborough *v.* Lord Godolphin, cited 2 T. R. 251, 252. A court of law will not use a power which it has for the purpose of indirectly exercising a power which it has not: A.-G. *v.* Bovet, 15 M. & W. 71. "In actions for the infringement of patent rights, it is of constant recurrence that the gravamen is laid, not as a direct infringement, but as something amounting to a colorable evasion of the right secured to the party:" per Tindal, C. J., 7 Cl. & Fin. 546.

[5] Morris *v.* Blackman, 2 H. & C. 912, 918.

must exercise the power without any indirect object, and in doing so must act with good faith and sincerity, and with an entire and single view to the real purpose and object of the power, and for the purpose of accomplishing any bye or sinister object which he may *desire to effect.[1] If a tenant, under covenant not [*490] to "let, set, assign, transfer or make over" the indenture of lease, give a warrant of attorney to confess judgment to a creditor, for the express purpose of enabling such creditor to take the lease in execution under the judgment, this is in fraud of the covenant, and the landlord, under a clause of re-entry in the lease for breach of the condition, may recover the premises in ejectment from a purchaser under the sheriff's sale. In this case, the tenant could not by any assignment, under-lease, or mortgage, have conveyed his interest to a creditor, and, consequently, he cannot convey it by an attempt of this kind. If the lease had been taken by the creditor under an adverse judgment, the tenant not consenting, it would not have been a forfeiture; but in the above case, the tenant concurred throughout, and the whole transaction was performed for the very purpose of enabling the tenant to convey his term to the creditor.[2]

But, although the above is, no doubt, the general rule, and is evidently consistent with sound sense and common honesty, yet there are cases, as was recently observed with reference to the *modus operandi* of a court of equity, in which that court will effect, by an indirect course, that which it could not do directly. For instance, the court will not by any direct order compel a person who has improperly erected a wall which is a nuisance to another, *to pull it down; but the court can make an order re- [*491] quiring him not to continue the nuisance, and this order will necessarily have the effect of compelling him to pull down the wall.[3]

[1] Duke of Portland *v.* Topham, 11 H. L. Cas. 32, 54.

[2] Doe d. Mitchinson *v.* Carter, 8 T. R. 300; s. c., Id. 57; Croft *v.* Lumley, 6 H. L. Cas. 739–40; 5 E. & B. 648, 682, 688 (85 E. C. L. R.); per Martin, B., Price *v.* Worwood, 4 H. & N. 513. In Hill *v.* Cowdery, 1 H. & N. 360, 365, Bramwell, B., citing Croft *v.* Lumley, observes, that the doctrine there laid down is, that "when a person covenants that he will not do an act, he does not break his covenant if he does an act which indirectly brings about the result provided against."

[3] Per Lord Lyndhurst, C., Hills *v.* Croll, 1 Cooper Pract. Cas. 86; Colman *v.* Morris, 18 Ves. jun. 437; Kerr on Injunctions 230.

Accessorium non ducit sed sequitur suum Principale.

(Co. Litt. 152 a.)

The incident shall pass by the grant of the principal, but not the principal by the grant of the incident.[1]

Upon the maxim *Res accessoria sequitur rem principalem*,[2] depended the important doctrine of *accessio*[3] in the Roman law, *accessio* being that particular mode of acquisition of property whereby the proprietor of the principal thing became, *ipso jure*, proprietor also of all belonging to the principal as accessory to it. Two extensive classes of cases were accordingly comprised within the operation of the above-mentioned principle: 1st, that in which [*492] the proprietor of a thing acquired a right of *property in the organic products of the same, as in the young of animals, the fruit and produce of trees, the alluvion or deposit on land, and in some other descriptions of property originating under analogous circumstances. The second class of cases above alluded to comprised those in which one thing becomes so closely connected with and attached to another that their separation cannot be effected at all, or at all events not without injury to one or other of them; and in such cases the owner of the principal thing was held to become proprietor also of the accessory connected therewith.[4]

The above maxim, *Accessorium non ducit sed sequitur suum prin-*

[1] Co. Litt. 152 a, 151 b; per Vaughan, B., Harding *v.* Pollock, 6 Bing. 63 (19 E. C. L. R.).

[2] "A principal thing (*res principalis*) is a thing which can subsist by itself, and does not exist for the sake of any other thing. All that belongs to a principal thing, or is in connection with it, is called an accessory thing (*res accessoria*)." Mackeld. Civ. Law 155. See *ex. gr.* Ashworth, app., Heyworth, resp., L. R. 4 Q. B. 316, 319.

[3] "*Accessio* is the general name given" in the Roman law "to every accessory thing, whether corporeal or incorporeal, that has been added to a principal thing from without, and has been connected with it, whether by the powers of nature or by the will of man, so that in virtue of this connection it is regarded as part and parcel of the thing. The *appurtenances* to a thing are to be noticed as a peculiar kind of accession; they are things connected with another thing, with the view of serving for its perpetual use." Mackeld. Rom. Law 155, 156.

[4] See Mackeld. Civ. Law 279, 281; I. 2. 1, *De Rerum Divisione;* Brisson. ad verb. "*Accessorium.*"

cipale, is, then, derived from the Roman law, and signifies that the accessory right follows the principal;[1] it may be illustrated by the remarks appended to the rule immediately preceding,[2] as also by the following examples:—

An easement to take water from a river to fill a canal ceases when the canal no longer exists.[3] The owner of land has, *primâ facie*, a right to the title-deeds, as something annexed to his estate in the land, and it is accordingly laid down, that, if a man seised in fee conveys land to another and his heirs, without warranty, all the title-deeds belong to the purchaser, as incident to the land,[4] though not granted by express words.[5] In like manner, [*493] *heirlooms are such goods and chattels as go by special custom to the heir along with the inheritance, and not to the executor or administrator of the last owner of the estate; they are due to the heir by custom, and not by the common law, and he shall accordingly have an action for them. There are also some other things in the nature of heirlooms which likewise descend with the particular title or dignity to which they are appurtenant.[6]

Again, rent is incident to the reversion, and, therefore, by a general grant of the reversion, the rent will pass; though, by the grant of the rent generally, the reversion will not pass, for *Accessorium non ducit sed sequitur suum principale:* however, by the introduction of special words, the reversion may be granted away, and the rent reserved.[7] So, an advowson appendant to a manor is so entirely and intimately connected with it, as to pass by the grant of the manor *cum pertinentiis*, without being expressly mentioned or referred to; and, therefore, if a tenant in tail of a manor with an advowson appendant suffered a recovery, it was not necessary for him to make any express mention of his intention to include the advowson in the recovery; for any dealing with the manor, which is

[1] Bell, Dict. and Dig. of Scotch Law, p. 7. See also Co. Litt. 389 a.

[2] See also Chanel *v.* Robotham, Yelv. 68; Wood *v.* Bell, 5 E. & B. 772 (85 E. C. L. R.).

[3] National Guaranteed Manure Co. *v.* Donald, 4 H. & N. 8.

[4] See per Tindal, C. J., Tinniswood *v.* Pattison, 3 C. B. 248 (54 E. C. L. R.), *et vide* Id. n. (*b*).

[5] Lord Buckhurst's Case, 1 Rep. 1; Goode *v.* Burton, 1 Exch. 189, 193, *et seq.*; Allwood *v.* Heywood, 32 L. J. Ex. 153.

[6] See 1 Crabb Real Prop. 11, 12.

[7] 2 Com. by Broom & Hadley 339; Litt. s. 229; Co. Litt. 143 a.

the principal, operates on the advowson, which is the accessory, whether expressly named or not. It is, however, to be observed, that, although the conveyance of the manor *primâ facie* draws after it the advowson also, yet it is always competent for the owner to sever the advowson from the manor, either by conveying the advowson away from the manor, or by conveying the manor without the advowson;[1] and hence there is a *marked distinction between the preceding cases and those in which the incident is held to be inseparably connected with the principal, so that it cannot be severed therefrom. Thus, it is laid down that estovers, or wood granted to be used as fuel in a particular house, shall go to him that hath the house; and that, inasmuch as a court baron is incident to a manor, the manor cannot be granted and the court reserved.[2] In some cases, also, that which is parcel or of the essence of a thing passes by the grant of the thing itself, although at the time of the grant it were actually severed from it; by the grant, therefore, of a mill, the mill-stone will pass, although severed from the mill.[3]

[*494]

Again, common of pasture *appendant* is the privilege belonging to the owners or occupiers of arable land holden of a manor, to put upon the wastes of the manor their horses, cattle, or sheep; it is appendant to the particular farm, and passes with it, as incident to the grant.[4] But divers things which, though continually enjoyed with other things, are only appendant thereto, do not pass by a grant of those things; as, if a man has a warren in his land, and grants or demises the land, by this the warren does not pass, unless, indeed, he grants or demises the land *cum pertinentiis*, or with all the profits, privileges, &c., thereunto belonging, in which case the warren might, perhaps, pass.[5]

[1] Judgm., Moseley *v.* Motteux, 10 M. & W. 544; Bac. Abr., "*Grants*" (I. 4).

[2] Finch's Law 15.

[3] Shep. Touch. 90. See Wyld *v.* Pickford, 8 M. & W. 443. As to what shall be deemed to pass as appendant, appurtenant, or incident, see Bac. Abr., "*Grants*" (I. 4). Smith *v.* Ridgway, 4 H. & C. 37, 577; Langley *v.* Hammond, L. R. 3 Ex. 161.

[4] Shep. Touch. 89, 240; Bac. Abr., "*Grants*" (I. 4); Co. Litt., by Thomas, vol. i., p. 227.

[5] Shep. Touch. 89; 1 Crabb Real Prop. 488. See Pennell *v.* Mill, 3 C. B. 625 (54 E. C. L. R.); Graham *v.* Ewart, 1 H. & N. 550; s. c., 11 Exch. 320;

*Another well-known application of the maxim under consideration is to covenants running with the land, which pass therewith, and on which the assignee of the lessee, or the heir or devisee of the covenantor, is in many cases liable, according to the kindred maxim of law, *transit terra cum onere*;[1] a maxim, the principle of which holds not merely with reference to covenants, but likewise with reference to such customs as are annexed to land —for instance, it is laid down that the custom of gavelkind, being a custom by reason of the land, runs therewith, and is not affected by a fine or recovery had of the land; but "otherwise it is of lands in ancient demesne partible among the males, for there the custom runneth not with the land simply, but by reason of the ancient demesne; and, therefore, because the nature of the land is changed, by the fine or recovery, from ancient demesne to land at the common law, the custom of parting it among the males is also gone."[2] [*495]

With reference to titles, moreover, one of the leading rules is *cessante statu primitivo cessa derivativus*[3]—the derived estate ceases on the determination of the original estate; and the exceptions to this rule have been said to create some of the many difficulties which present themselves in the investigation of titles.[4] The rule itself may be illustrated by the ordinary case of a demise *for years by a tenant for life, or by any person having a particular or defeasible estate, which, unless confirmed by the remainderman or reversioner, will determine on the death of the lessor; and the same principle applies whenever the original estate determines according to the express terms or nature of its limitation, or is defeated by a condition in consequence of the act of the party, as by the marriage of a tenant *durante viduitate*, or by the resignation of the parson who has leased the glebe lands or tithes belonging to the living.[5] [*496]

cited in Jeffryes *v.* Evans, 19 C. B. N. S. 266 (115 E. C. L. R.); Earl of Lonsdale *v.* Rigg, 11 Exch. 654; s. c., 1 H. & N. 923.

[1] Co. Litt. 231 a. [2] Finch's Law 15, 16. [3] 8 Rep. 34.

[4] 1 Prest. Abs. Tit. 245.

The maxim *supra* "applies only when the original estate determines by limitation or is defeated by a condition. It does not apply when the owner of the estate does any act which amounts to an alienation or transfer, though such alienation or transfer produces an extinguishment of the original estate." Shep. Touch., by Preston, 286. See London, &c., Loan Co. *v.* Drake, 6 C. B. N. S. 798, 810 (95 E. C. L. R.).

[5] 1 Prest. Abs. Tit. 197, 317, 358, 359.

The law relative to contracts and mercantile transactions likewise presents many examples of the rule that the accessory follows and cannot exist without its principal; thus, where framed pictures are sent by a carrier, the frames, as well as the pictures, are within the Carriers' Act (11 Geo. 4 & 1 Will. 4, c. 68, s. 1).[1] Again, the obligation of the surety is accessory to that of the principal, and is extinguished by the release or discharge of the latter, for *quum principalis causa non consistit ne ea quidem quæ sequuntur locum habent*,[2] and *quæ accessionum locum obtinent extinguuntur cùm principales res peremptæ fuerint*.[3] The converse, however, of the case just instanced does not hold, and the reason is that *accessorium non trahit principale*.[4] As it would be tedious to enumerate cases illustrative of maxims so evidently true and so widely applicable as the above, we shall merely add that, as a general rule, and except under special circumstances—as where the County Court [*497] Acts *operate to deprive of costs—costs follow the verdict. So, likewise, interest of money is accessory to the principal, and must, in legal language, "follow its nature;"[5] and, therefore, if the plaintiff in any action is barred from recovering the principal, he must be equally barred from recovering the interest.[6] And, "If by a will the whole of the personal estate, or the residue of the personal estate, be the subject of an executory bequest, the income of such personal estate follows the principal as an accessory, and must, during the period which the law allows for accumulation, be accumulated and added to the principal."[7]

Freight[8] is also said to be "the mother of wages," so that where

[1] Henderson v. London and North-Western R. C., L. R. 5 Ex. 90; distinguishing Treadwin v. Great Eastern R. C., L. R. 3 C. P. 308.

[2] D. 50. 17. 129, § 1; 1 Pothier Oblig. 413.

[3] 2 Pothier Oblig. 202.

[4] 1 Pothier Oblig. 477; 2 Id. 147, 202.

[5] 3 Inst. 139; Finch's Law 23.

[6] Judgm., Clarke v. Alexander, 8 Scott N. R. 165. See per Lord Ellenborough, C. J., 3 M. & S. 10; 2 Pothier Oblig. 479. "The giving of interest is not by way of a penalty, but is merely doing the plaintiff full justice, by having his debt with all the advantages properly belonging to it. It is in truth a compensation for delay." Judgm., 16 M. & W. 144.

See Hollis v. Palmer, 2 Bing. N. C. 713 (87 E. C. L. R.); Florence v. Drayson, 1 C. B. N. S. 584 (29 E. C. L. R.); Florence v. Jennings, 2 Id. 454.

[7] Per Lord Westbury, C., Bective v. Hodgson, 10 H. L. Cas. 665.

[8] Defined per Platt, B., Gibson v. Sturge, 10 Exch. 637.

freight is not earned wages were not, as a general rule, recoverable at common law.[1]

Lastly, in criminal law it is also true that *accessorius sequitur naturam sui principalis;*[2] and, therefore, an accessory cannot be guilty of a higher crime than his principal, being only punished as a partaker of his guilt.[3]

---

*LICET DISPOSITIO DE INTERESSE FUTURO SIT INUTILIS TAMEN FIERI POTEST DECLARATIO PRÆCEDENS QUÆ SORTIATUR EFFECTUM INTERVENIENTE NOVO ACTU. [*498]

(Bac. Mac., reg. 14.)

Although the grant of a future interest is invalid, yet a declaration precedent may be made which will take effect on the intervention of some new act.

"The law," says Lord Bacon, "doth not allow of grants except there be a foundation of an interest in the grantor; for the law that will not accept of grants of titles, or of things in action which are imperfect interests, much less will it allow a man to grant or encumber that which is no interest at all, but merely future. But of declarations precedent, before any interest vested, the law doth allow, but with this difference, so that there be some new act or conveyance to give life and vigor to the declaration precedent."[4]

With respect to the first part of the above rule, viz., that a disposition of after-acquired property is altogether inoperative, it was observed in a recent case,[5] that Lord Bacon assumes this as a proposition of law which is to be considered as beyond dispute, and accordingly we find the same general rule laid down by all the older writers of authority. "It is," says Perkins,[6] "a common

[1] Smith, M. L., 5th ed., 430; Hawkins *v.* Twizell, 5 E. & B. 883 (85 E. C. L. R.).

"The effect of a mortgage of a ship, under a contract for earning freight, is to transfer the freight to the mortgagee." Per Martin, B., Rusden *v.* Pope, L. R. 3 Ex. 276.

[2] 3 Inst. 139.

[3] 4 Com. by Broom & Hadley 35. See stat. 24 & 25 Vict. c. 94.

[4] Bac. Max., reg. 14.

[5] Judgm., 1 C. B. 386.

[6] Tit. "*Grants*," s. 65. See also Vin. Abr., "*Grants*" (H. 6); Noy, Max., 9th ed., 162; Com. Dig., "*Grant*" (D).

learning in the law, that a man cannot grant or charge that which he hath not." And again, it is said, that if a man grants unto me all the wool of his sheep, meaning thereby the wool of sheep which [*499] the grantor at *that time has, the grant is good;[1] but a man cannot grant all the wool which shall grow upon his sheep that he shall buy hereafter, for then he hath it neither actually nor potentially.[2] So, it has been held that a man cannot by deed or bargain and sale pass the property in goods which are not in existence,[3] or, at all events, which are not belonging to the grantor at the time of executing the deed;[4] "the law," indeed, "has long been settled, that a person cannot by deed, however solemn, assign that which is not in him;"[5] and, in accordance with this principle, where a bill of sale purported to be an absolute assignment of furniture and farming stock, "and other things, which are now, or which at any time *during the continuance of this security* shall be in, and about, and belonging to the dwelling-house," the Court of Queen's Bench held, that such deed could not operate as an assignment of the goods thereafter to be brought upon the premises, and not specified therein.[6]

[*500] *It will be observed, however, that, according to the distinction just stated, a grant of the future produce of prop-

[1] Perkins, tit. "*Grants*," s. 90.

[2] Grantham *v.* Hawley, Hob. 132. See Shep. Touch., by Preston, 241.

In Webster *v.* Power, L. R. 2 P. C. 69, a mortgage of a certain number of branded sheep and herds of cattle, on a run in the colony of New South Wales, with the issue, increase, and produce thereof, was held limited to the issue and increase of the specific sheep, and not to include sheep afterwards brought upon the run, though in substitution of those specified in the original mortgage.

[3] "If a chattel is sold, and at the time of the sale *the chattel does not exist*, the contract is not binding upon the purchaser:" per Martin, B., Strickland *v.* Turner, 7 Exch. 215; citing Barr *v.* Gibson, 3 M. & W. 390; Couturier *v.* Hastie, 8 Exch. 40; s. c., 9 Exch. 102; 5 H. L. Cas. 673; Risbourg *v.* Bruckner, 3 C. B. N. S. 812 (91 E. C. L. R.).

[4] Lunn *v.* Thornton, 1 C. B. 379 (which was founded on the maxim *Nemo dat qui non habet*, per Willes, J., Chidell *v.* Galsworthy, 6 C. B. N. S. 478 (95 E. C. L. R.). See Tapfield *v.* Hillman, 6 Scott N. R. 967; Price *v.* Groom, 2 Exch. 542, 547; and cases cited *post*.

[5] Per Pollock, C. B., Belding *v.* Read, 3 H. & C. 961.

[6] Gale *v.* Burnell, 7 Q. B. 850 (53 E. C. L. R.) (affirming the principle laid down in Lunn *v.* Thornton, 1 C. B. 379 (50 E. C. L. R.)); per Williams, J., Baker *v.* Gray, 17 C. B. 481 (84 E. C. L. R.); *post*.

erty actually in the possession of the grantor at the time of the grant is valid. "He that hath it (land) may grant all fruits that may arise upon it after, and the property shall pass as soon as the fruits are extant;"[1] and this proposition was fully recognized in a recent case, where a tenant for years of a farm, being indebted to his landlord, assigned to him, by deed, all his household goods, &c., and also all his "tenant right and interest yet to come and unexpired" in and to the farm and premises; and it was held that, under this assignment, the tenant's interest in crops grown in future years of the term passed to the landlord.[2]

It remains, then, to consider the second part of Lord Bacon's rule above stated, viz., that a declaration, *if followed by some act or conveyance*, may be effectual in transferring property not actually in possession of the party at the time of making such declaration. For instance, a power contained in an indenture to seize future crops, if unexecuted, would be of no avail against an execution levied, as giving no legal or equitable title to any specific crops; yet, if the power be subsequently executed by the grantee taking possession of the then growing crops, the seizure will be good as against an execution afterwards levied;[3] for the act done by the *grantor is sufficient to give effect to the antecedent declaration, within the scope and meaning of Lord Bacon's maxim. [*501]

Further, in commenting on the rule before us, Lord Bacon thus exemplifies the qualification with which it is to be received: "If," he says,[4] "there be a feoffment by a disseisee, and a letter of attorney to enter and make livery of seisin, and afterwards livery of

[1] Grantham *v.* Hawley, Hobart 132.

[2] Petch *v.* Tutin, 15 M. & W. 110; recognizing and following Grantham *v.* Hawley, Hobart 132.

[3] Congreve *v.* Evetts, 10 Exch. 298. *Acc.* Hope *v.* Hayley, 5 E. & B. 830 (85 E. C. L. R.); Chidell *v.* Galsworthy, 6 C. B. N. S. 471 (95 E. C. L. R.); Belding *v.* Read, 3 H. & C. 955, 963, 965, distinguishing Holroyd *v.* Marshall, 10 H. L. Cas. 191, cited *post.* See Baker *v.* Gray, 17 C. B. 462 (84 E. C. L. R.); Reeve *v.* Whitmore, 33 L. J. Chanc. 63; s. c., 32 Id. 497.

In connection with the subject above touched upon, the stat. 17 & 18 Vict. c. 36, intituled "An Act for preventing Frauds upon Creditors by secret Bills of Sale of personal Chattels" (amended by 29 & 30 Vict. c. 96), should be consulted.

[4] Max., reg. 14.

seisin is made accordingly, this is a good feoffment, although the feoffor had a right only at the time of making the feoffment; the reason assigned being that a deed of feoffment is but matter of declaration and evidence, and there is a new act, that is to say, the livery subsequent, which gives effect and validity to the prior conveyance." In like manner, "if I grant unto J. S. authority by my deed to demise for years the land whereof I am now seised, or hereafter shall be seised, and after I purchase lands, and J. S., my attorney, doth demise them, this is a good demise, because the demise of my attorney is a new act, and all one with a demise by myself;" and "Where by deed indented a man represents himself as the owner of an estate, and affects to convey it for valuable consideration, having at the time no possession or interest in the estate, and where nothing therefore can pass, whatever be the nature of the conveyance, there if by any means he afterwards acquire an interest in the estate, he is estopped, in respect of the solemnity of the instrument, from saying, as against the other party to the indenture, contrary to his averment in that indenture, that he had not such interest at the time of its execution."[1]

[*502] *In a modern case, also, we read that "At law an assignment of a thing which has no existence actual or potential at the time of the execution of the deed is altogether void.[2] But where future property is assigned, and after it comes into existence possession is either delivered by the assignor or is allowed by him to be taken by the assignee, in either case there would be the *novus actus interveniens* of the maxim of Lord Bacon, and the property would pass."[3]

The effect and operation of agreements relating to future property is, indeed, different at law and in equity. At law property non-existing but to be acquired at a future time is not assignable; in equity it is so. At law, although a power is given in the deed of assignment to take possession of after-acquired property, no interest is transferred, even as between the parties themselves, unless possession is actually taken; in equity the moment the property comes into existence the agreement operates upon it.[4]

[1] Per Sir John Leach, V.-C., Bensley *v.* Burdon, 2 Sim. & St. 526.

[2] Citing Robinson *v.* Macdonnell, 5 M. & S. 228.

[3] Per Lord Chelmsford, Holroyd *v.* Marshall, 10 H. L. Cas. 216.

[4] Per Lord Chelmsford, 10 H. L. Cas. 220; Brown *v.* Bateman, L. R. 2 C. P. 272.

We may conclude accordingly that, although, subject to the restrictions above stated, a grant of goods which are not in existence, or do not belong to the grantor at the time of executing the deed, is void, yet the grantor may ratify his grant by some act done by him with that view, after he has acquired the property in the goods, or by some act indicating his intention that they should pass under the deed already executed.[1]

From the instances above given, it sufficiently appears in what manner "there must be some new act or conveyance *to [*503] give life and vigor to the declaration precedent,"[2] as laid down by Lord Bacon—there must be some new act, to be done by the grantor in furtherance of the original disposition, and for the avowed object and with the view of carrying it into effect.

But although a conveyance of future property is thus, in many cases, inoperative and void, yet, by will, property to which the testator has become entitled subsequently to its execution will, undoubtedly, pass;[3] a will, however, is an instrument of a peculiar nature, being ambulatory and revocable during the life of the testator, and speaking only at his death, unless an intention to the contrary is clearly manifested,[4] according to the maxims, *Ambulatoria enim est voluntas defuncti usque ad vitæ supremum exitum*,[5]

[1] Lunn *v.* Thornton, *ante*, p. 499; 1 Fonb. Eq. 216.

[2] Bac. Max., reg. 14.

[3] 1 Vict. c. 26, s. 3. See per Lord Mansfield, C. J., 1 Cowp. 305, 306; Norris *v.* Norris, 2 Coll. 719; Jepson *v.* Key, 2 H. & C. 873. In Doe d. Cross *v.* Cross, 8 Q. B. 714 (55 E. C. L. R.), a point arose as to whether an instrument operated as a gift *inter vivos* or by way of devise. In regard to gifts *inter vivos*, see Bourne *v.* Fosbrooke, 18 C. B. N. S. 515 (114 E. C. L. R.); Shower *v.* Pilck, 4 Exch. 478; Flory *v.* Denny, 7 Exch. 581; cited per Williams, J., Maugham *v.* Sharpe, 17 C. B. N. S. 464 (112 E. C. L. R.); per Parke, B., Oulds *v.* Harrison, 10 Exch. 575; Milnes *v.* Dawson, 5 Exch. 950.

[4] 1 Vict. c. 26, s. 24; O'Toole *v.* Browne, 3 E. & B. 572 (77 E. C. L. R.); per Sir J. Leach, M. R., Gittings *v.* M'Dermott, 2 My. & K. 73. See per Lord Brougham, C., 1 My. & K. 485.

[5] D. 34. 4. 4; 4 Rep. 61. "Delivery" of a will implies "something whereby the party acknowledges that the instrument is a complete act containing his final mind—that it is no longer ambulatory;" per Parke, B., Curteis *v.* Kenrick, 3 M. & W. 471; *et vide* per Lord Abinger, C. B., Id. 472; Vincent *v.* Bishop of Sodor and Man, 8 C. B. 905, 933 (65 E. C. L. R.).

As bearing on the finality of a testamentary instrument, see Doe d. Strickland *v.* Strickland, 8 C. B. 724 (65 E. C. L. R.); Plenty *v.* West, 6 C. B. 201 (60 E. C. L. R.); Andrew *v.* Motley, 12 C. B. N. S. 514 (104 E. C. L. R.).

and *Omne testamentum morte consummatum est.*[1] It is, indeed, the ambulatory and revocable quality of a will just adverted to, which [*504] makes the *present effect of such an instrument different from that of a disposition by deed postponing the possession or enjoyment, or even the vesting of an estate, until the death of the disposing party, although in both these cases the effect upon the usufructuary enjoyment is precisely the same; for instance, if a man by deed limit lands to the use of himself for life, with remainder to the use of A. in fee; the effect, with reference to the enjoyment, is the same as if he should by his will make an immediate devise of such lands to A. in fee; and yet in the former case, A., immediately on the execution of the deed, becomes entitled to a remainder in fee, though it is not to take effect in possession until the decease of the settlor; whereas, in the latter, he would take no interest whatever until the decease of the testator should have called the instrument into operation.[2]

Upon the whole, then, the case of a devise by will of after-acquired property does not seem to offer any exception to the maxim laid down by Lord Bacon, which appears to be strictly correct when explained and qualified in accordance with his own suggestions, and with subsequent authorities and decisions, to some of which we have adverted.

[1] Co. Litt. 322 b.

[2] 1 Jarman on Wills, 3d ed., 12.

*CHAPTER VII. [*505]

Rules Relating to Marriage and Descent.

It has been thought convenient to insert a selection of rules relating to Marriage and Descent immediately after those which concern the legal rights and liabilities attaching to property in general. For additional information on the subjects treated of in this chapter, the authorities and references below given may with advantage be consulted.[1]

Consensus, non Concubitus, facit Matrimonium.

(Co. Litt. 33 a.)

It is the consent of the parties, not their concubinage, which constitutes a valid marriage.[2]

Marriage is constituted by the *conjunctio animorum*, *or [*506] *present* consent of the parties, expressed under such circumstances as by law required, so that, though they should, after consent so given, by death or disagreement or any other cause, happen not to consummate the marriage *conjunctione corporum*, they are, nevertheless, entitled to all the legal rights consequent thereon.[3]

[1] 2 Com. by Broom & Hadley, vol. 1, chap. 15, which treats of Husband and Wife; the important judgments delivered in Reg. *v.* Millis, 10 Cl. & Fin. 534; Beamish *v.* Beamish, 9 H. L. Cas. 274; Brook *v.* Brook, Id. 193; Dolphin *v.* Robins, 7 H. L. Cas. 390; Shaw *v.* Gould, L. R. 3 H. L. 55, 79; Fenton *v.* Livingston, 3 Macq. Sc. App. Cas. 497; Yelverton *v.* Longworth, 4 Id. 743; Reg. *v.* Inhabs. of Brighton, 1 B. & S. 447 (101 E. C. L. R.); Hall *v.* Wright, E., B. & E. 746 (96 E. C. L. R.), which contain learned researches respecting the nature and requisites of the marriage contract: Cruise Dig., 4th ed., vol. 3, tit. 29, chaps. 1, 2, 3, which treat of Descent and Consanguinity; and the elaborate judgment of Kindersley, V.-C., respecting the operation of the stat. 3 & 4 Will. 4, c. 106, in re Don's Estate, 4 Drew. 194.

[2] As to this maxim, see per Lord Campbell, C., 9 H. L. Cas. 335; as to its applicability in relation to the Scotch law of marriage, see Yelverton *v.* Longworth, 4 Macq. Sc. App. Cas. 743, 856, 861.

[3] See Bell, Dict. & Dig. of Scotch Law, p. 217. See Field's Marriage Annulling Bill, 2 H. L. Cas. 48.

The above maxim has been adopted from the civil law[1] by the common lawyers, who, indeed, have borrowed (especially in ancient times) almost all their notions of the legitimacy of marriage from the canon and civil laws;[2] and by the latter, as well as by the earlier ecclesiastical law, marriage was a mere *consensual* contract, only differing from other contracts of this class in being indissoluble even by the consent of the contracting parties. It was always deemed to be "a contract executed without any part performance;" so that the maxim was undisputed and peremptory, *Consensus, non concubitus, facit nuptias vel matrimonium.*[3]

[*507] By the law of England,[4] also, marriage is considered *in the light of a contract, and therefore the ordinary principles which attach to contracts in general are, with some exceptions, applied to it. The principle expressed in the above maxim, and which alone we propose to consider, is, that, in order to render a marriage valid, the parties must be willing to contract. The weight of authority, indeed, seems to show that, even prior to the Marriage Act (26 Geo. 2, c. 33), a present and perfect consent, that is, a consent expressed *per verba de præsenti*, was sufficient to render a contract of marriage indissoluble between the parties themselves, and to afford to either of them, by application to the spiritual court, the power of compelling the solemnization of an actual marriage; but that such contract never constituted a full and complete marriage in itself, unless made in the presence and with the intervention of a minister in holy orders.[5]

[1] *Nuptias non concubitus sed consensus facit*, D. 50. 17. 30.

[2] 1 Com. by Broom & Hadley 524; Co. Litt. 33 a. See 2 Voet Com. Pandect. lib. 23, tit. 2.

[3] Per Lord Brougham, in Reg. *v.* Millis, 10 Cl. & Fin. 719. See also Lord Stowell's celebrated judgment in Dalrymple *v.* Dalrymple (by Dodson), p. 10 (a), where many authorities respecting this maxim are collected. See also the remarks upon this case, 10 Cl. & Fin. 679; and, per Cresswell, J., Brook *v.* Brook, 27 L. J. Chanc. 401; s. c., 9 H. L. Cas. 193. Field's Marriage Annulling Bill, *supra*, well illustrates the maxim cited in the text.

[4] The following authorities may be referred to, as explanatory of the law of Scotland respecting marriages *per verba de præsenti*: Yelverton *v.* Longworth, 4 Macq. Sc. App. Cas. 743; Dalrymple *v.* Dalrymple, 2 Hagg. Cons. R. 54; Hamilton *v.* Hamilton, 9 Cl. & Fin. 327; Stewart *v.* Menzies, 8 Id. 309; Bell *v.* Graham, 13 Moo. P. P. C. 242; Shelf. on Marriage and Div. 91.

[5] Per Tindal, C. J., delivering the opinion of the judges in Reg. *v.* Millis, 10

In Reg. *v.* Millis,[1] the facts were these :—A. and B. entered into a present contract of marriage *per verba de præsenti* in Ireland, in the house and in the presence of a placed and regular Presbyterian minister. A. was a member of the Established Church; B. was either a *member of the Established Church, or a Protestant dissenter. A religious ceremony of marriage was performed on the occasion by the said minister between the parties according to the usual form of the Presbyterian Church in Ireland. A. and B., after the contract and ceremony, cohabited and lived together for two years as man and wife. A. afterwards, and whilst B. was living, married C. in England. It was held, that A. was not indictable for bigamy.

[*508]

Where, prior to the stat. 7 & 8 Vict. c. 81, a clergyman of the Church of England, being in holy orders, performed a ceremony of marriage between himself and a certain woman, by reading the form of solemnization of matrimony as set forth in the Book of Common Prayer, without witnesses, other than one who happened to see what was passing from an adjoining yard: the marriage having been consummated, was held, by the House of Lords, conformably to the *ratio decidendi* in Reg. *v.* Millis, to have been invalid.[2]

In Yelverton *v.* Longworth,[3] a marriage celebrated in Ireland by a Roman Catholic priest between a Roman Catholic lady and a gentleman of a Protestant family who had been brought up a Protestant, and who at the ceremony declared himself a "Protestant Catholic," was held per Lords Wensleydale and Chelmsford to be void under the Irish Act, 19 Geo. 2, c. 13, s. 1.

Cl. & Fin. 655; Catherwood *v.* Caslon, 13 M. & W. 261; Beamish *v.* Beamish, 9 H. L. Cas. 274.

There is a strong legal presumption in favor of marriage: Piers *v.* Piers, 2 H. L. Cas. 331; Reg. *v.* Manwaring, Dearsl. & B. 132. In Shelden *v.* Patrick, L. R. 1 Sc. App. Cas. 470, the presumption of a marriage prior to the birth of children arising from cohabitation and acknowledgment was held to be completely rebutted by evidence of the strongest kind.

[1] 10 Cl. & Fin. 534 (as to which case, see the observations of Lord Campbell, C., 9 H. L. Cas. 338–9; of Dr. Lushington, Catterall *v.* Catterall, 1 Robertson 582; per Willes, J., Reg. *v.* Manwaring, Dearsl. & B. 139); Beamish *v.* Beamish, 9 H. L. Cas. 274. See 7 & 8 Vict. c. 81, s. 83; 5 & 6 Vict. c. 113; 19 & 20 Vict. c. 119.

[2] Beamish *v.* Beamish, 9 H. L. Cas. 274.

[3] 4 Macq. Sc. App. Cas. 743, 746, 862, 893.

In Reg. *v.* Millis, above abstracted, are to be found the following remarks apposite to the principal maxim under our notice, and deserving of perusal:—

"It will appear, no doubt," says Tindal, C. J., delivering the [*509] opinion of the judges in the case just cited, "upon *referring to the different authorities, that at various periods of our history there have been decisions as to the nature and description of the religious ceremonies necessary for the completion of a perfect marriage, which cannot be reconciled together; but there will be found no authority to contravene the general position, that, at all times, by the common law of England, it was essential to the constitution of a full and complete marriage, that there must be some religious solemnity; that both modes of obligation should exist together, the civil and religious; that, besides the civil contract, that is, the contract *per verba de præsenti*, which has always remained the same, there has at all times been also *a religious ceremony*, which has not always remained the same, but has varied from time to time, according to the variation of the laws of the Church; with respect to which ceremony, it is to be observed, that, whatever at any time has been held by the law of the Church to be a sufficient religious ceremony of marriage, the same has at all times satisfied the common law of England in that respect." Where, for instance, the Church has held, as it often has done, down to the time of passing the Marriage Act, that a marriage celebrated by a minister in holy orders, but not in a church, or by such minister in a church, but without publication of banns, and without license, is irregular, and renders the parties liable to ecclesiastical censures, but is sufficient, nevertheless, to constitute the religious part of the obligation, and that the marriage is valid notwithstanding such irregularity; the law of the land has followed the spiritual court in that respect, and held such marriage to be valid. "But it will not be found in any period of our history, either that the Church of England has held the religious celebration sufficient to constitute [*510] a valid marriage, unless it *was performed in the presence of an ordained minister, or that the common law has held a marriage complete without such celebration."[1]

In support of the position thus laid down, the learned Chief Justice, whose words we have above quoted, refers to the state

[1] 10 Cl. & Fin. 655, 656.

of the law relative to the validity of marriages of Quakers and Jews, both prior and subsequent to the Marriage Act. Since the passing of this Act, he observes, it has generally been supposed that the exception contained therein, as to the marriages of Quakers and Jews, amounted to a tacit acknowledgment by the legislature, that a marriage solemnized with the religious ceremonies which they were respectively known to adopt ought to be considered sufficient; but before the passing of that Act, when the question was left perfectly open, we find no case in which it has been held that a marriage between Quakers was a legal marriage, on the ground that it was a marriage by a contract *per verba de præsenti*, but, on the contrary, the inference is strong that it was never considered legal. As to the case of the Jews, he subsequently proceeds to remark: it is well known, that, in early times, they stood in a very peculiar and excepted condition. For many centuries they were treated not as natural-born subjects, but as foreigners, and scarcely recognized as participating in the civil rights of other subjects of the crown. The ceremony of marriage by their own peculiar forms might, therefore, be regarded as constituting a legal marriage, without affording any argument as to the nature of a contract of marriage, *per verba de præsenti*, between other subjects.[1]

The preceding remarks, with reference to the requisites *at common law of the marriage contract,[2] must, of course, [*511] be understood as subject to restriction by the various enactments which have from time to time been passed by the legislature with reference to this subject. Without entering at length into their provisions, we may observe that the stat. 6 & 7 Will. 4, c. 85, recognizes marriage as essentially a civil contract; and by the 20th section enacts, that marriages may be solemnized in places registered for the purpose in the presence of a registrar and two witnesses, and, subject to certain provisoes, according to such form and ceremony as the parties may see fit to adopt. By the 21st section it is further provided, that persons who shall object to marry under the provisions of the Act in any registered building may, after due notice and certificate issued, contract and solemnize marriage at the office of the superintendent registrar in the manner therein pointed out.[3]

[1] 10 Cl. & Fin. 671, 673.
[2] See Shelf. Marriage, Index, " Statutes."
[3] See also 19 & 20 Vict. c. 119.

Having thus observed that marriage is a contract entered into by consent of the parties, and with certain forms, either of a purely civil or of a religious nature, prescribed and sanctioned by the law, it is important further to remark the difference which exists between a contract of marriage *per verba de præsenti* and a contract *per verba de futuro;* for the latter does not, under any circumstances, constitute a marriage by our law; it only gives a right of action for damages in case of its violation, though mutual consent will relieve the parties from their engagement;[1] and this, like most [*512] other contracts, is *voidable, unless the party making the promise be of the full age required by law, viz., twenty-one; so that, if there are mutual promises to marry between two persons, one of whom has attained the age of twenty-one, and the other of whom is within that age, the first is so far bound by the contract as to be liable to an action, if it be broken;[2] but the latter may avoid it, if he pleases;[3] and this distinction is founded on the well-known principle, that, where a contract may be to the benefit of an infant, or to his prejudice, the law so far protects him as to give him an opportunity of reconsidering it when he comes of age, and it is good or voidable at his election.[4]

Not only moreover is want of age sufficient to avoid a contract of marriage to take place *in futuro*, but, in some cases, it renders void, or rather voidable, the actual ceremony, by reason of the presumed imbecility of judgment in the parties contracting, and their consequent inability to consent. Therefore, if a boy under fourteen, or a girl under twelve years of age, marries, this marriage is only inchoate and imperfect; and, when either of them comes to full age, that party may disagree, and declare the marriage void, without any divorce or sentence in the spiritual court; and this is founded on the civil law; whereas the canon law pays greater regard to the constitution than the age of the parties, and, if they are *habiles ad matrimonium*, the marriage is good, whatever be

[1] Per Lord Lyndhurst, C., 10 Cl. & Fin. 837. As to a plea of exoneration and the evidence necessary to support it, see particularly King *v.* Gillett, 7 M. & W. 55, 59. See also the cases cited *ante*, pp. 250, 284.

[2] Per Lord Ellenborough, C. J., Warwick *v.* Bruce, 2 M. & S. 209 (28 E. C. L. R.); s. c., affirmed in error, 6 Taunt. 118 (1 E. C. L. R.); Holt *v.* Ward, 2 Stra. 937.

[3] Judgm., 2 Stra. 939.

[4] Id.

their respective ages; and in our law the marriage will be good to this extent, that, if at the age of consent they agree to continue together, they need not be married again. If, moreover, the husband be of years of discretion, *and the wife under twelve, [*513] when she comes to years of discretion he may disagree as well as she, for in contracts the obligation must be mutual; both must be bound, or neither; and so it is, *vice versâ*, when the wife is of years of discretion, and the husband under.[1]

Again, by the common law, if the parties themselves were of the age of consent, the concurrence of no other party was necessary in order to make the marriage valid, and this was agreeable to the canon law. Where, however, one of the contracting parties is under age, the law is now regulated by the stat. 4 Geo. 4, c. 76, which enacts (sec. 8), that, from and after the 1st of November, 1823, no parson shall be punishable by ecclesiastical censures for solemnizing a marriage without the consent of parents or guardians between persons, both or one of whom shall be under twenty-one, after banns published, unless such parson shall have notice of the dissent of such parents or guardians. And if such parents or guardians shall openly declare their dissent at the time of publication, such publication shall be void. And by sec. 14, where either of the parties (not being a widower or widow) shall be under the age of twenty-one, it is required[2] that one of the parties shall personally swear that the consent of those persons whose consent is necessary has been obtained. By sec. 16, the father, if living, of any party under twenty-one, not being a widow or widower, or, if the father be dead, the guardian of the person of the party so under age, and if no guardian, then the mother, if unmarried, and, if married, the guardian appointed by the Court of Chancery, shall have authority to give consent *to the marriage of such [*514] party; and by sec. 17, if the father shall be *non compos*, or the guardian or mother shall be *non compos*, or in parts beyond seas, or shall unreasonably withhold consent, application may be made to the Court of Chancery, by petition, in a summary way; and if the marriage shall appear to be proper, it shall be so declared. It has, moreover, been held, that the language of the 17th

[1] 1 Com. by Broom & Hadley 526, 527.

[2] See also 6 & 7 Will. 4, c. 85, s. 12; 19 & 20 Vict. c. 119, ss. 2, 17, 18.

section only goes to require consent, and the marriage is not absolutely void if solemnized without it.[1]

Further, by 6 & 7 Will. 4, c. 85[2] (amended by 1 Vict. c. 22, 3 & 4 Vict. c. 72, and 19 & 20 Vict. c. 119), the like consent is required to any marriage in England solemnized by license, as would have been required by law in a case of marriage solemnized by license immediately before the passing of the Act; and every person whose consent to a marriage by license is required by law, is thereby authorized to forbid the issue of the superintendent registrar's certificate, whether the marriage is intended to be with license or without.

Lastly, in connection with this branch of the subject, viz., as to the consent of other than the contracting parties to the marriage, we may observe that, by the Royal Marriage Act (12 Geo. 3, c. 11), no descendant of the body of King George II. (other than the issue of princesses married into foreign families) is capable of contracting matrimony without the previous consent of the sovereign, signified under the great seal, and any marriage contracted without such consent is void; provided, that such of the said descendants as are above the age of twenty-five may, after a twelvemonth's [*515] notice *given to the Privy Council, contract and solemnize marriage without the consent of the crown, unless both Houses of Parliament shall, before the expiration of the said year, expressly declare their disapprobation of such intended marriage. In order to bring a marriage within the prohibition of this statute, it is not necessary that it should have been contracted within the realm of England; but the statute extends to prohibit and to annul marriages wherever the same be contracted or solemnized, either within the realm of England or without.[3]

The rule that *consensus facit matrimonium* is also applicable to cases in which either party, at the date of the marriage, is laboring under mental incapacity; for, without a competent share of reason, neither this nor any other express contract can be valid, for consent

[1] R. *v.* Birmingham, 8 B. & C. 35 (15 E. C. L. R.).

[2] Sec. 10.

[3] The Sussex Peerage, 11 Cl. & Fin. 85; and see the opinion of Cresswell, J., in Brook *v.* Brook, 27 L. J. Chanc. 401; s. c., 9 H. L. Cas. 193; in connection with which case, see also Reg. *v.* Chadwick, 11 Q. B. 173 (63 E. C. L. R.).

is absolutely requisite to matrimony, and persons *non compotes mentis* are incapable of consenting to anything.[1]

HÆRES LEGITIMUS EST QUEM NUPTIÆ DEMONSTRANT.

(Co. Litt. 7 b.)

The common law takes him only to be a son whom the marriage proves to be so.[2]

The word "heir,"[3] in legal understanding, signifies him to whom lands, tenements, or hereditaments, by the act of God and right of blood, descend, of some estate of *inheritance, for *Deus solus hæredem facere potest non homo*, and he only is heir who is *ex justis nuptiis procreatus*.[4] It is, then, a rule or maxim of our law, with respect to the descent of land in England from father to son, that the son must be "*hæres legitimus*"—thus in a recent case the facts were these:— [*516]

An English marriage took place between two English persons, who never lived together, the husband committed adultery, and some years afterwards consented to go to Scotland to found jurisdiction against himself. He did so, and the Scotch court pronounced a decree of divorce *à vinculo matrimonii*. Held, that a Scotch marriage duly celebrated between the divorced wife and an Englishman (who was thenceforth domiciled in Scotland) did not give to their children the character of "lawfully begotten," so as to enable them to succeed to property in England—the Scotch divorce not having dissolved the English marriage.[5]

Again, in order that land in England may descend from father to

[1] 1 Com. by Broom & Hadley 527; 15 Geo. 2, c. 30; Judgm., 1 Hagg. Cons. R. 417.

[2] Mirror of Justices, p. 70; Fleta, lib. 6, c. 1.

[3] As to the popular and technical meaning of the word "ancestor," see, per Kindersley, V.-C., in re Don's Estate, 27 L. J. Chanc. 104, 105; s. c., 4 Drew. 194.

[4] Co. Litt. 7 b; cited 5 B. & C. 440, 454. The rule respecting property in the young of animals is in accordance with the Roman law, *partus sequitur ventrem:* I. 2. 1. 19; D. 6. 1. 5, § 2; per Byles, J., 6 C. B. N. S. 852 (95 E. C. L. R.).

[5] Shaw *v.* Gould, L. R. 3 H. L. 55. See Birt *v.* Boutinez, L. R. 1 P. & D. 487.

son, the son must have been born after actual marriage between his father and mother; and this is a rule *juris positivi*, as indeed are all the laws which regulate succession to real property, this particular rule having been framed for the direct purpose of excluding, in the descent of land in England, the application of the rule of the civil and canon law, *pater est quem nuptiæ demonstrant*,[1] by which the subsequent marriage between the father and mother was held to [*517] make the son *born before marriage legitimate; and this rule of descent, being a rule of positive law, annexed to the land itself, cannot be broken in upon or disturbed by the law of the country where the claimant was born. Therefore, in the case of Doe d. Birtwhistle *v.* Vardill,[2] it was held, that a person born in Scotland of parents domiciled there, but not married till after his birth, though legitimate by the law of Scotland,[3] could not take real estate in England as heir, the father having died intestate. And in re Don's Estate, Kindersley, V.-C., held that the father of an *ante natus* born in Scotland, and legitimated by the subsequent marriage of his parents, could not, under the statute 3 & 4 Will. 4, c. 106, succeed to real estate whereof the son had died seised in England.[4]

The rule of descent just referred to is, then, one of a positive, inflexible nature, applying to and inherent in the land itself, which is the subject of descent,—of the same nature and character as that rule which prohibited the descent of land to any but those who were of the whole blood to the last taker,—or like the custom of gavelkind or borough English, which causes the land to descend in the one case to all the sons together, in the other to the younger son alone.[5]

If, moreover, the parent be incapable of inheriting land himself, he has no heritable blood in him which he can transmit to his child, according to the maxim and old acknowledged rule of

[1] D. 2. 4. 5.

[2] 2 Cl. & Fin. 571; s. c., 1 Scott N. R. 828; 6 Bing. N. C. 385 (37 E. C. L. R.); 5 B. & C. 438 (11 E. C. L. R.); explained per Lord Brougham, Fenton *v.* Livingstone, 3 Macq. Sc. App. Cas. 432; per Lord Cranworth, Id. 544. See also Shedden *v.* Patrick, L. R. 1 Sc. App. Cas. 470.

[3] See Countess of Dalhousie *v.* M'Dowall, 7 Cl. & Fin. 817; Munro *v.* Munro, Id. 842; Birtwhistle *v.* Vardill, Id. 895.

[4] 4 Drew. 194.

[5] 1 Scott N. R. 838.

descent, *qui doit inheriter al père* *doit inheriter al fitz,— he who would have been heir to the father shall be heir to [*518] the son; and therefore, if, in the case first above put, Doe d. Birtwhistle *v.* Vardill, the son had died, leaving a child, before the intestate, such child could not, according to the English law, have inherited under the circumstances;[1] and if in re Don's Estate there had been a son *post natus*, such son could not have inherited to his *ante natus* brother.

Formerly also the rule was that attainder so entirely corrupted the blood of the person attainted that not only could no person inherit from him, but no person could inherit through him: so that if there were grandfather, father, and son—three generations, and the father was attainted and the grandfather died seised of lands in fee, the attainted father being dead in the meantime, the grandson could not have inherited to the grandfather.[2] Now, however, it is enacted by stat. 3 & 4 Will. 4, c. 106, s. 10, that when the person from whom the descent of any land is to be traced shall have had any relation who, having been attainted, shall have died before such descent shall have taken place, then such attainder shall not prevent any person from inheriting such land who would have been capable of inheriting the same by tracing his descent through such relation if he had not been attainted, unless such land shall have escheated in consequence of such attainder before the first day of January, 1834. This Act, however, by sec. 11, shall not extend to any descent which shall take place on the death of any person dying before that day.

*There is likewise another rule of law immediately connected with, and similar in principle to, the preceding, [*519] which may be here properly mentioned; it is as follows:—*Qui ex damnato coitu nascuntur inter liberos non computentur*[3]—neither a bastard[4] nor any person not born in lawful wedlock can be, in the legal sense of the term, an heir;[5] for a bastard is reckoned by the

[1] 1 Scott N. R. 842.

[2] Per Kindersley, V.-C., 27 L. J. Chanc. 102, 103; s. c., 4 Drew. 194. See further as to the former law upon the subject above adverted to, Kynnaird *v.* Leslie, L. R. 1 C. P. 389.

[3] Co. Litt. 8 a.

[4] "The strictly technical sense of the term 'bastard' is one who is not born in lawful wedlock:" per Kindersley, V.-C., 27 L. J. Chanc. 102.

[5] Glanville, lib. 7, c. 13; Shaw *v.* Gould, *ante*, p. 516.

law to be *nullius filius*, and, being thus the son of nobody, he has no inheritable blood in him,[1] and, consequently, cannot take land by succession; and, if there be no other claimant than such illegitimate child (a circumstance which, however, can rarely happen), the land shall escheat to the lord. Moreover, as a bastard cannot be heir himself, so neither can he have any heirs but those of his own body; for, as all collateral kindred consists in being derived from the same common ancestor, and, as a bastard has no legal ancestors, he can have no collateral kindred, and, consequently, can have no legal heirs, but such as claim by a lineal descent from himself; and, therefore, if a bastard purchases land, and dies seised thereof without issue and intestate, the land shall escheat to the lord of the fee.[2]

Under the stat. 3 & 4 Will. 4, c. 106, s. 2, descent is now to be traced from the purchaser, and under this section a son claiming by descent from an illegitimate father who was the purchaser could not have transmitted the estate by descent, upon failure of his own issue, to his [*520] *heir *ex parte maternâ*. But this has been remedied by the stat. 22 & 23 Vict. c. 35, and in such a case, instead of escheating the land will descend, the descent being traced from the person last entitled to it as if he had purchased it.

In Clarke *v.* Wright,[3] a question arose involving an inquiry respecting the applicability of the maxim last cited, viz., whether a limitation of real estate in an antenuptial settlement to an illegitimate child of the woman, the settlor, was void by the stat. 27 Eliz. c. 4, as against a person claiming under a mortgage executed by the settlor and her husband subsequently to the marriage. The Court of Exchequer Chamber, affirming the judgment of the Court of Exchequer, held that the limitation was valid.

It may be proper to add one remark, although not strictly connected with the maxim which has given rise to the preceding observations, viz., that there is a manifest distinction between the right of succession to real property in this country being dependent on the law of England respecting legitimacy, and the fact of a marriage contracted according to the *lex loci* being con-

[1] See the argument, Stevenson's Heirs *v.* Sullivant, 5 Wheaton (U. S.) R. 226, 227; Id. 262, note.

[2] 2 Com. by Broom & Hadley 398; Co. Litt. 3 b; Finch Law 117, 118.

[3] 6 H. & N. 849; s. c., 5 Id. 401.

sidered as valid by our tribunals: for, after an examination of the cases below referred to, there could be no doubt but that marriage, which is a personal contract, when entered into according to the rites of the country, the *lex loci*, where the parties are domiciled and the marriage celebrated, would be considered and treated as a perfect and complete marriage throughout the whole of Christendom.[1] It does not, however, therefore follow, that, with the *adoption of the marriage contract, the foreign law adopts also *all* the conclusions and consequences which hold good [*521] in the country where the marriage was celebrated;[2] as, for instance, its retrospective operation in legitimatizing the *ante natus*. Hence, although the right of inheritance does not follow the law of the domicile of the parties, but that of the country where the land lies, yet, with respect to personal property, which has no locality, and is of an ambulatory nature, it is part of the law of England that this description of property should be distributed according to the *jus domicilii*.[3] "It is a clear proposition," observed Lord Loughborough, "not only of the law of England, but of every country in the world where law has the semblance of science, that personal property has no locality. The meaning of that is, not that personal property has no visible locality, but that it is subject to that law which governs the person of the owner, both with respect to the disposition of it, and with respect to the transmission of it,

[1] Dalrymple *v.* Dalrymple, 2 Hagg. Cons. R. 54; Shaw *v.* Gould, L. R. 3 H. L. 55; per Abbott, C. J., Lacon *v.* Higgins, 3 Stark. 183 (3 E. C. L. R.); Kent *v.* Burgess, 11 Sim. 361; Catherwood *v.* Caslon, 13 M. & W. 261; Reg. *v.* Millis, and Re Don's Estate, *ante*, pp. 505, 507; Connelly *v.* Connelly, 7 Moore P. C. C. 438.

By stat. 4 Geo. 4, c. 91, marriages performed by a minister of the Church of England in the chapel of any British embassy or factory, or in the ambassador's house, or by an authorized person within the British lines, are declared to be valid. See Lloyd *v.* Petitjean, 2 Curt. 251.

The marriage of an officer celebrated by a chaplain of the British army within the lines of the army when serving abroad is valid under the 9 Geo. 4, c. 91, although such an army is not serving in a country in a state of actual hostility, and though no authority for the marriage was previously obtained from the officer's superior in command: The Waldegrave Peerage, 4 Cl. & Fin. 649.

[2] 1 Scott N. R. 839.

[3] Per Abbott, C. J., 5 B. C. 451, 452 (11 E. C. L. R.); per Holroyd and Bayley, JJ., Id. 454.

either by succession, or by the act of the party; it follows the law of the person. The owner in any country may dispose of his personal property. If he dies, it is not the law of the country in [*522] which *the property is, but the law of the country of which he was a subject, that will regulate the succession."[1] *Mobilia sequunter personam*,[2] is the maxim of our own as of the Roman law. The personal estate of a testator accompanies him wherever he may reside and become domiciled, so that he acquires the right of disposing of and dealing with it, according to the law of his domicile.[3]

NEMO EST HÆRES VIVENTIS.

(Co. Litt. 22 b.)

No one can be heir during the life of his ancestor.

By law, no inheritance can vest, nor can any person be the actual complete heir of another till the ancestor is dead; before the happening of this event, he is called the heir apparent or heir presumptive,[4] and his claim, which can only be to an estate remaining in the ancestor at the time of his death, and of which he has made no testamentary disposition, may be defeated by the superior title or an alienee in the ancestor's lifetime, or of a devisee under his will. Therefore, if an estate be made to A. for life, remainder to the heirs of B.; now, if A. dies before B., the remainder is at an end; for, during B.'s life, he has no heir; but if B. dies first, the re- [*523] mainder then *immediately vests in his heir, who will be entitled to the land on the death of A.[5]

[1] Sill *v.* Worswick, 1 H. Bla. 690; per Lord Wensleydale, Fenton *v.* Livingstone, 3 Macq. Sc. App. Cas. 547; per Lord Brougham, Bane *v.* Whitehaven and Furnace Junction R. C., 3 H. L. Cas. 19; Doglioni *v.* Crispin, L. R. 1 H. L. 301.

[2] Story Conf. of Laws, 3d ed., 638, 639.

[3] Doglioni *v.* Crispin, L. R. 1 H. L. 301; Bremer *v.* Freeman, 10 Moo. P. C. C. 306; Hodgson *v.* De Beauchesne, 15 Id. 285; Crookenden *v.* Fuller, 29 L. J., P. M. & A. 1; s. c., 1 Swab. & Tr. 441; Anderson *v.* Lanerville, 9 Id. 325.

[4] 2 Bla. Com., by Stewart 231; Co. Litt. 8 a.

[5] Per Patteson, J., Doe d. Winter *v.* Perratt, 7 Scott N. R. 23, 24; s. c., 9 Cl. & Fin. 606; per Littledale, J., 5 B. & C. 59; 2 Com. by Broom & Hadley 211.

So it has been said that "a will takes effect only on the testator's death; during his life it is subject to his control, and, until it was consummated by his death, no one had, in a legal view, any interest in it—*Nemo est hæres viventis*."[1]

The general rule being that the law recognizes no one as heir until the death of his ancestor, it follows that, though a party may be heir apparent or heir presumptive, yet he is not very heir, living the ancestor; and therefore, where an estate is limited to one as a purchaser under the denomination of heir, heir of the body, heir male, or the like, the party cannot take as a purchaser unless, by the death of the ancestor, he has, at the time when the estate is to vest, become very heir. But this rule has been relaxed in many instances, and an exception engrafted on it that, if there be sufficient on the will to show that by the word "heir" the testator meant heir apparent, it shall be so construed; and in such a case the popular sense shall prevail against the technical.[2] In other words, the authorities appear to establish this proposition, that, *primâ facie*, the word "heir" is to be taken in its strict legal sense, but that, if there be a plain demonstration in the will that the testator used it in a different sense, such different sense may be assigned to it. What will amount to such plain *demonstration must in each case depend on the language used [*524] and the circumstances under which it was used, and is not a question to be determined by reference to reported cases, but by a careful consideration of that language and those circumstances in the particular case under discussion.[3]

Hence, if a devise be made to A. for life, remainder to the heirs of the body of B. so long as B. shall live, an estate *pur autre vie* being given, and the ancestor being *cestui que vie*, the rule of law would plainly be excluded. So a devise to A. for life, remainder to the right heirs of B. now living, vests the remainder in B.'s heir apparent or presumptive; and a devise to A. for life, remainder to the right heir of B., he paying to B. an annuity upon coming into

[1] Per Spencer, J., Mann *v.* Pearson, 2 Johnson (U. S.) R. 36.

[2] Doe d. Winter *v.* Perratt, 10 Bing. 207, 208, 229 (25 E. C. L. R.). See s. c., 7 Scott N. R. 45 *et seq.*; Egerton *v.* Earl Brownlow, 4 H. L. Cas. 103, 137; 1 Fearne Cont. Rem., 10th ed., 210; and see further, as to the rule, *supra*, Id., Index, tit. *Maxims*.

[3] Per Patteson, J., 7 Scott N. R. 26.

possession, would clearly vest the remainder in B.'s heir apparent.[1] In like manner the familiar expressions "heir to the throne," "heir to a title or estate," "heir apparent," "heir presumptive," prove that the existence of a parent is quite consistent with the popular idea of heirship in the child. In all such cases the legal maxim has no place, nor can it have in any in which the person speaking knows of the existence of the parent, and intends that the devise to the child shall take effect during the life of the parent. It would appear that the question proper to be asked in each such case would be, "Did the testator use the word 'heir' in the strict legal sense, or in any other sense?" and if the answer should be that he used the term not in the legal and technical but in some popular sense, the sense thus ascertained should be carried out.[2]

[*525] *Respecting the subject here touched upon, detailed information must be sought for in treatises more technical than this.

Non Jus sed Seisina facit Stipitem.

(Fleta, lib. vi. c. 14.)

It is not the right, but the seisin, which makes a person the stock from which the inheritance must descend.[3]

No person, according to the law as it existed prior to the stat. 3 & 4 Will. 4, c. 106, could be properly such an ancestor as that an inheritance of lands or tenements could be derived from him unless he had had actual seisin of such lands, either by his own entry or by the possession of his own or his ancestor's lessee for years, or by receiving rent from a lessee of the freehold, or unless he had had what was equivalent to corporeal seisin in hereditaments that were incorporeal, such as the receipt of rent, a presentation to the church in case of an advowson, and the like. But he could not be accounted an ancestor who had had only a bare right or title to enter or be otherwise seised; for the law required this notoriety of possession as evidence that the ancestor had that property in him-

[1] Per Lord Brougham, 7 Scott N. R. 46, 50.

[2] Per Lord Cottenham, 7 Scott N. R. 60, 61; s. c., 5 B. & C. 48 (11 E. C. L. R.).

[3] Noy, Max., 9th ed., p. 72, n. (b).

self which was to be transmitted to his heir. The seisin, therefore, of any person, thus understood, made him the root or stock from which all future inheritance by right of blood was to be derived; and this was expressed by the maxim, *Seisina facit stipitem.*[1]

The rule of law, therefore, with respect to the descent [*526] *of land, where such descent took place prior to the 1st of January, 1834, was, and still is,[2] that the heir had not *plenum dominium*, or full and complete ownership, till he had made an actual corporeal entry into the land; for, if he died before entry made, his heir would not have been entitled to take the possession, but the heir of the person who was last actually seised. It was not, therefore, a mere right to enter, but the actual entry, that made a man complete owner, so as to transmit the inheritance to his own heirs.[3]

It may, then, be stated briefly, as the clear result of all the authorities, that, wherever a party succeeded to an inheritance by descent, he must have obtained an actual seisin or possession, as contradistinguished from a seisin in law, in order to make himself the root or stock from which the future inheritance by right of blood must have been derived; that is, in other words, in order to make the estate transmissible to his heirs.[4]

With respect, however, to descents taking place on deaths since January 1st, 1834, the law has been entirely altered by the stat. 3 & 4 Will. 4, c. 106, of which sec. 1 enacts, that, in the construction of that Act, the expression, "person last entitled to land," shall extend to the last person who had a right thereto, whether he did or did not obtain possession or receipt of the rents and profits thereof; and sec. 2 enacts, that such person shall be deemed the purchaser.

The effect of these statutory provisions may be thus illustrated.—If A. died seised of land, and B., his heir, *died without [*527] making entry; according to the former law, the heir of A., and not of B., would have succeeded to the land,—that is, would have had the right of entry thereon; but, by the operation of the

[1] 2 Com. by Broom & Hadley 374.

[2] The stat. 3 & 4 Will. 4, c. 106, does not apply to any descent which took place prior to January 1, 1834. (See sec. 11.)

[3] 2 Com. by Broom & Hadley 374.

[4] Judgm., Doe d. Parker *v.* Thomas, 4 Scott N. R. 468.

Act, B. must now be deemed the purchaser, and would accordingly transmit the estate to his own heir.

The maxim, *Non jus sed seisina facit stipitem*, did not, however, hold in the descent of estates tail, it being only necessary, in deriving a title to an estate of this kind by descent, to deduce the pedigree from the first purchaser, and to show that the claimant is heir to him; for the issue in tail claim *per formam doni*, that is, they are as much within the view and intention of the donor, and as personally and precisely described in the gift, as any of their ancestors.[1] Likewise, if the estate which descended was of a kind in which the owner cannot acquire actual seisin of the land (as is the case with a reversion or remainder expectant upon freehold, where the actual seisin belongs to the particular tenant), the rule was, that the claimant must trace his descent from, or, as it was usually expressed, *make himself heir to*, the purchaser.[2]

HÆREDITAS NUNQUAM ASCENDIT.

(Glanville, lib. 7, c. 1.)

The right of inheritance never lineally ascends.

The above was an express rule of the feudal law, and remained an invariable maxim[3] until the recent stat. 3 & 4 Will. 4, c. 106, [*528] which effected so great a change in *the law of inheritance. The rule is thus stated and illustrated by Littleton:[4] If there be father and son, and the father has a brother, who is, therefore, uncle to the son, and the son purchase land in fee-simple, and die without issue, living his father, the uncle shall have the land as heir to the son, and not the father, although the latter is nearer in blood, because it is a maxim in law that the inheritance may lineally descend, but not ascend. Yet if the son in this case die with-

[1] Cruise Dig., 3d ed., vol. 3, p. 439 (cited arg. 7 Scott N. R. 236); Id., 4th ed., p. 386.

[2] Ratcliff's Case, 3 Rep. 42 a. See Judgm., Doe d. Andrew v. Hutton, 3 B. & P. 648.

[3] 2 Com. by Broom & Hadley 378; 3 Cruise Dig., 4th ed., 331.

[4] Sec. 3.

out issue, and his uncle enter into the land as heir to the son, and afterwards the uncle die without issue, living the father, the father shall have the land as heir to the uncle, and not as heir to the son, for he should rather come to the land by collateral descent than by lineal ascent.

It was, moreover, a necessary consequence of this rule, coupled with the maxim, *Seisina facit stipitem*, that if, in the instance above put, the uncle did not enter into the land, the father could not inherit it, because a man claiming as heir in fee simple by descent must make himself heir to him who was last seised of the actual freehold and inheritance; and if the uncle, therefore, did not enter, he would have had but a freehold in law, and no actual freehold, and the last person seised of the actual freehold was the son, to whom the father could not make himself heir.[1]

The maxim, *Hæreditas nunquam ascendit*, therefore, applied only to exclude the ancestors in a direct line, for the inheritance might ascend *indirectly*, as in the preceding example, from the son to the uncle.[2]

The above rule has, however, been altered with respect [*529] *to descents on deaths on or after the 1st of January, 1834, it being enacted by stat. 3 & 4 Will. 4, c. 106, s. 6, that every lineal ancestor shall be capable of being heir to any of his issue; and in every case where there shall be no issue of the purchaser, his nearest lineal ancestor shall be his heir in preference to any person who would have been entitled to inherit either by tracing his descent through such lineal ancestor, or in consequence of there being no descendant of such lineal ancestor, so that the father shall be preferred to a brother or sister, and a more remote lineal ancestor to any of his issue other than a nearer lineal ancestor or his issue. But by sec. 7 it is provided, that none of the maternal ancestors of the person from whom the descent is to be traced, nor any of their descendants, shall be capable of inheriting until all his paternal ancestors and their descendants shall have failed; and also that no female paternal ancestor of such person, nor any of her descendants, shall be capable of inheriting until all his male paternal ancestors and their descendants shall have failed,

[1] Co. Litt. 11 b.

[2] 2 Bla. Com., 16th ed., 212 n. (5); Bracton, lib. 2, c. 29.

and that no female maternal ancestor of such person, nor any of her descendants, shall be capable of inheriting until all his male maternal ancestors and their descendants shall have failed.

And here we may conveniently advert to a well-known maxim of our law, which is thus expressed: *Linea recta semper præfertur transversali*[1]—the right line shall always be preferred to the collateral. It is a rule of descent that the lineal descendants *in infinitum* of any person deceased shall represent their ancestor, that is, shall stand in the same place as the person himself would have done had he been living.[2]

[*530] *Hence it is, that the son or grandchild, whether son or daughter, of the eldest son succeeds before the younger son, and the son or grandchild of the eldest brother before the younger brother; and so, through all the degrees of succession, by the right of representation the right of proximity is transferred from the root to the branches, and gives them the same preference as the next and worthiest of blood.[3]

Another rule, immediately connected with the preceding, was that which related to the exclusion of the half blood, but which originally, it would seem, extended only to exclude a *frater uterinus* from inheriting land descended *à patre: frater fratri uterino non succedet in hæreditate paternâ*.[4] This rule, however, although expressed with considerable limitation in the maxim just cited, had this more extended signification—that the heir, in order to take by descent, need not be the nearest kinsman of the whole blood; but, although a distant kinsman of the whole blood, he should nevertheless be admitted to the total exclusion of a much nearer kinsman of the half blood; and, further, that the estate should escheat to the lord, rather than the half blood should inherit.[5]

It has, however, been observed by Mr. Preston, that the mere circumstance that a person was of the half blood to the person last seised would not have excluded him from taking as heir, if he were of the whole blood to those ancestors through whom the descent was to be derived by *representation;* thus, if two first cousins, D. and E., had intermarried, and had issue a son, F., and

[1] Co. Litt. 10 b; Fleta, lib. 6, c. 1. [2] 3 Cruise Dig., 4th ed., 333.

[3] Hale Hist., 6th ed., 322, 323; 3 Cruise Dig., 4th ed., 333.

[4] Fort. de Laud. Leg. Ang., by Amos, p. 15.

[5] Per Kindersley, V.-C., 27 L. J. Chanc. 102.

D. had married again and had issue, G., and F. died seised, [*531] *G. could not have taken as half brother of F., but he might as maternal cousin to him;[1] *Quando duo jura in unâ personâ concurrunt æquum est ac si essent in diversis.*[2]

The law on this subject has been, however, entirely altered and materially improved by the stat. 3 & 4 Will. 4, c. 106, s. 9, which enables the half blood to inherit next after any relation in the same degree of the whole blood and his issue, where the common ancestor is a male, and next after the common ancestor where a female, so that the brother of the half blood on the part of the father shall inherit next after the sisters of the whole blood on the part of the father and their issue, and the brother of the half blood on the part of the mother shall inherit next after the mother.

We may add that the rule excluding the half blood did not hold on the descent of the crown. Therefore, if a king had issue a son and a daughter by one venter, and a son by another venter, and died; on the death of the eldest son without issue, the younger son was entitled to the crown, to the exclusion of the daughter. For instance the crown actually did descend from King Edward VI. to Queen Mary, and from her to Queen Elizabeth, who were respectively of the half blood to each other. Nor did the rule apply to estates tail.[3]

---

*POSSESSIO FRATRIS DE FEODO SIMPLICI FACIT SOROREM ESSE HÆREDEM. [*532]

(3 Rep. 41.)

The brother's possession of an estate in fee simple makes the sister to be heir.

One consequence of the rule, *Seisina facit stipitem*, should here perhaps very briefly be noticed:—If a man, being seised of land, had issue a son and a daughter by one venter, and a younger son

[1] 2 Prest. Abs. Tit. 447.

[2] Id. 449. The maxim *supra* is exemplified by Jones *v.* Davies, 7 H. & N. 507; s. c., 5 Id. 766.

[3] 1 Com. by Broom & Hadley 228; Chit. Pre. Crown 10; Litt. ss. 14, 15; 3 Cruise Dig., 4th ed., 386. See also Hume's Hist. of England, vol. 4, pp. 242, 265.

by another venter, and the father died, and then the elder son entered and died, the daughter would have inherited the land as heir to her brother, who was the person last actually seised.[1] This rule, however, did not apply to estates tail.[2] And the doctrine of *possessio fratris* has been held not to affect the descent of a dignity by writ.[3]

We have already seen,[4] that, by the recent Inheritance Act, entry is no longer necessary in order to constitute a good ancestor; and likewise, that a sister must now trace her descent through the father, and not directly from her brother of the whole blood, and, therefore, the rule of *possessio fratris* is, by the operation of that Act, virtually abolished, and is inapplicable to any case which has occurred since the 1st January, 1834.

[*533] *PERSONA CONJUNCTA ÆQUIPARATUR INTERESSE PROPRIO.

(Bac. Max., reg. 18.)

The interest of a personal connection is sometimes regarded in law as that of the individual himself.

In the words of the civil law, *jura sanguinis nullo jure civili dirimi possunt*,[5] the law according to Lord Bacon, hath so much respect for nature and conjunction of blood, that in divers cases it compares and matches nearness of blood with consideration of profit and interest, and, in some cases, allows of it more strongly. Therefore, if a man covenant, in consideration of blood, to stand seised to the use of his brother or son, or near kinsman, an use is well raised by his covenant without transmutation of possession.[6]

[1] Noy, Max., 9th ed., p. 72. See further as to this doctrine, per Abbott, C. J., Bushby *v.* Dixon, 3 B. & C. 304 (10 E. C. L. R.).

[2] Ratcliff's Case, 3 Rep. 41; Doe d. Gregory *v.* Whichelo, 8 T. R. 211; Noy, Max., 9th ed., p. 73. See also the argument in Tolson, dem., Kaye, deft., 7 Scott N. R. 236 *et seq.*, where the authorities on the above point are cited and reviewed.

There might, however, be a *possessio fratris* of an equitable as well as of a legal estate: Buchanan *v.* Harrison, 1 Johns. & H. 662.

[3] The Hastings Peerage Case, 8 Cl. & Fin. 144.

[4] *Ante*, p. 526.

[5] D. 50. 17. 8; Bac. Max., reg. 11.

[6] Bac. Max., reg. 18.

"So if a man menace me, that he will imprison or hurt in body my father or my child, except I make unto him an obligation, I shall avoid this duress as well as if the duress had been to mine own person."[1]

The above maxim, as to *persona conjuncta*, is likewise, in some cases, applicable in determining the liability of an infant on contracts for what cannot strictly be considered as "necessaries" within the ordinary meaning of that term.[2] Thus, as observed by Lord Bacon, "if a man under the years of twenty-one contract for the nursing of his lawful child, this contract is good, and shall not be avoided by infancy, no more than if he had contracted for his own aliments or erudition." The like legal principle was, in a modern case, extended so as to render an infant widow liable upon her contract *for the funeral of her husband, who had left no property [*534] to be administered; for, as observed by Alderson, B., in delivering judgment in the case just referred to, the law permits an infant to make a valid contract of marriage, and all necessaries furnished to those with whom he becomes one person by or through the contract of marriage are, in point of law, necessaries to the infant himself. "Now, there are many authorities which lay it down that decent Christian burial is a part of a man's own rights; and we think it is no great extension of the rule to say, that it may be classed as a personal advantage, and reasonably necessary to him. His property, if he leaves any, is liable to be appropriated by his administrator to the performance of this proper ceremonial. If, then, this be so, the decent Christian burial of his wife and lawful children, who are the *personæ conjunctæ* with him, is also a personal advantage, and reasonably necessary to him; and then the rule of law applies, that he may make a binding contract for it. This seems to us to be a proper and legitimate consequence from the proposition that the law allows an infant to make a valid contract of marriage. If this be correct, then an infant husband or parent may contract for the burial of his wife or lawful children; and then the question arises, whether an infant widow is in a similar situation. It may be said that she is not, because, during the coverture, she is incapable of contracting, and, after the death of the husband, the relation of marriage has ceased. But we think

[1] Bac. Max., reg. 18.

[2] As to which see Ryder *v.* Wombwell, L. R. 4 Ex. 32.

this is not so. In the case of the husband, the contract will be made after the death of the wife or child, and so after the relation which gives validity to the contract is at an end, to some purposes. But if the husband can contract for this, it is because [*535] *a contract for the burial of those who are *personæ conjunctæ* with him by reason of the marriage is as a contract for his own personal benefit; and, if that be so, we do not see why the contract for the burial of the husband should not be the same as a contract by the widow for her own personal benefit. Her coverture is at an end, and so she may contract; and her infancy is, for the above reasons, no defence, if the contract be for her personal benefit. It may be observed, that, as the ground of our decision arises out of the infant's previous contract of marriage, it will not follow from it that an infant child or more distant relation would be responsible upon a contract for the burial of his parent or relative."[1]

The maxim under consideration does not, however, apply so as to render a parent liable on the contract of the infant child, even where such contract is for "necessaries," unless there be some evidence that the parent has either sanctioned or ratified the contract. If, says Lord Abinger, C. B.,[2] a father does any specific act from which it may reasonably be inferred that he has authorized his son to contract a debt, he may be liable in respect of the debt so contracted; but the mere moral obligation on the father to maintain his child affords no inference of a legal promise to pay his debts. "In order to bind a father in point of law for a debt incurred by his son, you must prove that he has contracted to be bound, just in [*536] *the same manner as you would prove such a contract against any other person; and it would bring the law into great uncertainty if it were permitted to juries to impose a liability in each particular case, according to their own feelings or prejudices." "It is," observed Parke, B., in the same case, "a clear

[1] Chapple *v.* Cooper, 13 M. & W. 259, 260.

[2] Mortimore *v.* Wright, 6 M. & W. 487; Shelton *v.* Springett, 11 C. B. 452 (73 E. C. L. R.). See Ambrose *v.* Kerison, 10 C. B. 776 (70 E. C. L. R.), (followed in Bradshaw *v.* Beard, 12 C. B. N. 344 (104 E. C. L. R.)); Read *v.* Legard, 6 Exch. 636, and Rice *v.* Shepherd, 12 C. B. N. S. 332 (104 E. C. L. R.); Richardson *v.* Dubois, L. R. 5 Q. B. 51 (as showing under peculiar circumstances the liability of the husband in respect of his wife); Bazeley *v.* Forder, L. R. 3 Q. B. 559.

principle of law, that a father is not under any legal obligation to pay his son's debts, except, indeed, by proceedings under the 43 Eliz.,[1] by which he may, under certain circumstances, be compelled to support his children according to his ability; but the mere moral obligation to do so cannot impose upon him any legal liability."[2]

Again, we read, "It hath been resolved by the justices that a wife cannot be produced either against or for her husband, *quia sunt duæ animæ in carna unâ*, and it might be a cause of implacable discord and dissension between the husband and the wife, and a mean of great inconvenience."[3] At common law, however, the above rule did not apply where a personal injury had been committed by the husband against the wife, or *vice versâ*.[4] And the rule in question has recently been in great part abrogated by the legislature, for by "The Evidence Amendment Act, 1853" (16 & 17 Vict. c. 83), ss. 1–3, husband and wife may give evidence for or against each other—subject to these exceptions: 1st, that the husband shall not be competent or compellable to give evidence for or against his wife, nor the wife for or against her husband, "in any criminal proceeding;" and 2dly, that *"no husband shall be compellable to disclose any communication made to him [*537] by his wife during the marriage, and no wife shall be compellable to disclose any communication made to her by her husband during the marriage." Further, "the parties to any proceeding instituted in consequence of adultery, and the husbands and wives of such parties," are now, by the stat. 32 & 33 Vict. c. 68, s. 3, "competent to give evidence in such proceeding."

In the sense then above explained, and with the restrictions above suggested, must be understood the maxim illustrated by Lord Bacon, and with which we conclude our list of rules relative to marriage and descent—*Persona conjuncta æquiparatur interesse proprio.*

[1] See Grinnell *v.* Wells, 7 M. & Gr. 1033 (49 E. C. L. R.); Ruttinger *v.* Temple, 4 B. & S. 491 (116 E. C. L. R.).

[2] For courts of law "are to decide according to the *legal obligations* of parties:" per Alderson, B., Turner *v.* Mason, 14 M. & W. 117.

[3] Co. Litt. 6 b.

[4] Lord Audley's Case, 3 How. St. Tr. 402, 413.

[*538] *CHAPTER VIII.

THE INTERPRETATION OF DEEDS AND WRITTEN INSTRUMENTS.

IN the pages immediately following, an attempt has been made to give a general view of such maxims as are of most practical utility, and are most frequently cited with reference to the mode of construing deeds and written instruments; and some remarks have been occasionally added, showing how these rules apply to the interpretation of wills and statutes. As the authorities and decided cases on the above subject are extremely numerous, and as in a work like the present it would be undesirable, and indeed impossible, to refer to any considerable portion of them, those only have been cited which exhibit and tend to elucidate most clearly the meaning, extent, and qualifications of the various maxims; and, as far as was consistent with this plan, the more modern judgments of the courts of law have been especially consulted and selected for reference, because the principles of interpretation are better understood at the present day, and, consequently, more clearly defined and more correctly applied than they formerly were. The importance of fixed and determinate rules of interpretation is manifest, and not less manifest is the importance of a knowledge of those rules. In construing deeds and testamentary instruments, the language of which, [*539] owing *to the use of inaccurate terms and expressions, frequently falls short of, or altogether misrepresents, the views and intentions of the parties, such rules are necessary in order to insure just and uniform decisions; and they are equally so where it becomes the duty of a court of law to unravel and explain those intricacies and ambiguities which occur in legislative enactments, and which result from ideas not sufficiently precise, from views too little comprehensive, or from the unavoidable and acknowledged imperfections of language.[1] In each case, where doubt or difficulty arises, peculiar principles and methods of interpretation are applied, reference being always had to the general scope and intention of the instrument, the nature of the transaction, and the legal rights and situation of the parties interested.

[1] See Lord Teignmouth's Life of Sir W. Jones 261.

The principles developed in this chapter, being applicable to the solution of many questions connected with the Law of Contracts and of Evidence, have been considered before proceeding to the subjects specified, which are briefly treated of in the concluding chapters of this work.

The rules of construction and interpretation separately considered in this chapter are the following:—1st, that an instrument shall be construed liberally and according to the intention of the parties; 2dly, that the whole context shall be considered; 3dly, that the meaning of a word may often be known from the context; 4thly, that a deed shall be taken most strongly against the grantor; 5thly, that a latent ambiguity may, but a patent ambiguity cannot, be explained by extrinsic evidence; 6thly, that where there is no ambiguity, the natural construction shall prevail; 7thly, that an instrument or expression *is sufficiently certain which can be made so; 8thly, that surplusage may be rejected; 9thly, [*540] that a false description is often immaterial; 10thly, that general words may be restrained by reference to the subject-matter; 11thly, that the special mention of one thing must be understood as excluding another; 12thly, that the expression of what is implied is inoperative; 13thly, that a clause referred to must be understood as incorporated with that referring to it; 14thly, that relative words refer to the next antecedent; 15thly, that that mode of exposition is best which is founded on a reference to contemporaneous facts and circumstances; 16thly, that he who too minutely regards the form of expression takes but a superficial and, therefore, probably an erroneous view of the meaning of an instrument.

BENIGNÆ FACIENDÆ SUNT INTERPRETATIONES PROPTER SIMPLICITATEM LAICORUM UT RES MAGIS VALEAT QUAM PEREAT; ET VERBA INTENTIONI, NON E CONTRA, DEBENT INSERVIRE.

(Co. Litt. 36 a.)

A liberal construction should be put upon written instruments, so as to uphold them, if possible, and carry into effect the intention of the parties.

The two rules of most general application in construing a written instrument are—1st, that it shall, if possible, be so interpreted *ut res magis valeat quam pereat*,[1] and 2dly, that such a meaning shall [*541] be given to it as may *carry out and effectuate to the fullest extent the intention of the parties. These maxims are, indeed, in some cases restricted by the operation of technical rules, which, for the sake of uniformity, ascribe definite meanings to particular expressions; and, in other cases, they receive certain qualifications when applied to particular instruments, such qualifications being imposed for wise and beneficial purposes; notwithstanding, however, these exceptions and qualifications, the above maxims are undoubtedly the most important and comprehensive which can be used for determining the true construction of written instruments.

It is then laid down repeatedly by the old reporters and legal writers, that, in construing a deed, every part of it must be made, if possible, to take effect, and every word must be made to operate in some shape or other.[2] The construction, likewise, must be such as will preserve rather than destroy;[3] it must be reasonable, and agreeable to common understanding;[4] it must also be favorable, and as near the minds and apparent intents of the parties as the [*542] rules of law will admit,[5] and, as *observed by Lord Hale, the judges ought to be curious and subtle to invent reasons

[1] See per Erle, C. J., Cheney *v.* Courtois, 13 C. B. N. S. 640 (106 E. C. L. R.); Broom *v.* Batchelor, 1 H. & N. 255; cited in Heffer *v.* Meadows, L. R. 4 C. P. 600; Steele *v.* Hoe, 14 Q. B. 431, 445 (68 E. C. L. R.); Ford *v.* Beech, 11 Q. B. 852, 866, 868, 870 (63 E. C. L. R.); Oldershaw *v.* King, 2 H. & N. 517; s. c., Id. 399; Stratton *v.* Pettit, 16 C. B. 420 (81 E. C. L. R.); Mare *v.* Charles, 5 E. & B. 978 (85 E. C. L. R.); approved in Penrose *v.* Martyr, E., B. & E. 503 (96 E. C. L. R.).

"All contracts should, if possible, be construed *ut res magis valeat quam pereat*:" per Byles, J., Vestry of Shoreditch *v.* Hughes, 17 C. B. N. S. 162 (112 E. C. L. R.).

The maxim *supra* was applied in Reg. *v.* Inhabitants of Broadhempston, 1 E. & E. 154, 163 (102 E. C. L. R.); Pugh *v.* Stringfield, 4 C. B. N. S. 364, 370 (93 E. C. L. R.). See Blackwell *v.* England, 8 E. & B. 541, 549 (92 E. C. L. R.).

"If a plea admits of two constructions, one of which gives a sensible effect to the whole, and the other makes a portion of it idle and insensible, the court is bound to adopt the former construction:" per Williams, J., Peter *v.* Daniel, 5 C. B. 579 (57 E. C. L. R.).

[2] Shep. Touch. 84; Plowd. 156.

[3] Per Lord Brougham, C., Langston *v.* Langston, 2 Cl. & Fin. 243; cited arg. Baker *v.* Tucker, 3 H. L. Cas. 116.

[4] 1 Bulst. 175; Hob. 304.

[5] 1 Anderson 60; Jenk. Cent. 260.

and means to make acts effectual according to the just intent of the parties;[1] they will not, therefore, cavil about the propriety of words when the intent of the parties appears, but will rather apply the words to fulfill the intent, than destroy the intent by reason of the insufficiency of the words.[2]

It may, indeed, chance that, on executing an agreement under seal, the parties thereto failed to contemplate the happening of some particular event, or the existence of some particular state of facts at a period subsequent thereto;[3] and all the court can do in such a case, is to ascertain the meaning of the words actually used; and, in construing the deed, they will adopt the established rule of construction, "to read the words in their ordinary and grammatical sense, and to give them effect, unless such a construction would lead to some absurdity or inconvenience, or would be plainly repugnant to the intention of the parties to be collected from other parts of the deed."[4] For "the golden rule of construction," to which we shall presently revert,[5] "is that words are to be construed according to their natural meaning, unless such a construction would either render them senseless or would be opposed to the general scope and intent of the instrument, or unless there be some very cogent reason of convenience in favor of a different interpretation."[6]

Deeds, then, shall be so construed as to operate according to the intention of the parties, if by law they may; *and if they cannot in one form, they shall operate in that which by law will effectuate the intention: *Quando res non valet ut ago, valeat quantum valere potest.*[7] For, in these later times, the judges have gone further than formerly, and have had more consideration for the substance, to wit, the passing of the estate according to the

[*543]

[1] Crossing v. Scudamore, 2 Lev. 9; per Lord Hobart, Hob. R. 277, cited Welles R. 682; Moseley v. Motteux, 10 M. & W. 533.

[2] 1 Plowd. 159, 160, 162.

[3] See Judgm., Lloyd v. Guibert, L. R. 1 Q. B. 120.

[4] Per Parke, B., Bland v. Crowley, 6 Exch. 529.

[5] *Post*, p. 569.

[6] Per Bramwell, B., Fowell v. Tranter, 3 H. & C. 461.

[7] Per Lord Mansfield, C. J., Goodtitle v. Bailey, Cowp. 600; cited Roe d. Earl of Berkeley v. Archbishop of York, 6 East 105; 1 Ventr. 216. See also the instances of the above rule mentioned in Gibson v. Minet, 1 H. Bla. 614, 620.

intent of the parties, than the shadow, to wit, the manner of passing it.[1] For instance, a deed intended for a release, if it cannot operate as such, may amount to a grant of the reversion, an attornment, or a surrender, and *è converso*.[2] And the court, acting on the principle *interpretatio chartarum benigne facienda est ut res magis valeat quam pereat*, has held an instrument which was, in fact, a release made by a joint tenant of a copyhold, but, having been executed before admittance, could not operate as such, to be equivalent to a disclaimer.[3]

So, if a man makes a feoffment in fee, with a letter of attorney to give livery, and no livery is given, but there is, in the same deed, a covenant to stand seised to the uses of the feoffment, provided there be a consideration sufficient to raise the uses of the covenant, this will amount to a covenant to stand seised.[4] And, where A., in consideration of natural love and of 100*l*., by deeds of lease and [*544] *release, granted, released, and confirmed certain premises, after his own death, to his brother B., in tail, remainder to C., the son of another brother of A., in fee; and he covenanted and granted that the premises should, after his death, be held by B. and the heirs of his body, or by C. and his heirs according to the true intent of the deed; it was held, that, although the deed could not operate as a release, because it attempted to convey a freehold *in futuro*, yet it was good as a covenant to stand seised.[5] So, a deed of bargain and sale, void for want of enrollment, will operate as a grant of the reversion.[6] So, if the king's

[1] Osman *v.* Sheaf, 3 Lev. 370; cited Doe d. Lewis *v.* Davies, 2 M. & W. 516; per Willes, C. J., Smith *v.* Packhurst, 3 Atk. 136; cited Marquis of Cholmondeley *v.* Lord Clinton, 2 B. & Ald. 637; Tarleton *v.* Staniforth, 5 T. R. 695; per Maule, J., Borradaile *v.* Hunter, 5 Scott N. R. 431, 432; 2 Wms. Saund. 96 a, n. (1); 3 Prest. Abstr. Tit. 21, 22; 1 Id. 313.

[2] Shep. Touch. 82, 83; Co. Litt. 49 b; cited 5 B. & C. 106 (11 E. C. L. R.).

[3] Lord Wellesley *v.* Withers, 4 E. & B. 750; cited and explained in Bence *v.* Gilpin, L. R. 3 Ex. 82.

[4] Shep. Touch. 82, 83.

[5] Roe *v.* Trammarr, Willes R. 682. See the cases collected 2 Wms. Saund. 96 a, n. (1); 1 Prest. Abstr. Tit. 313; 1 Rep. 76; Perry *v.* Watts, 4 Scott N. R. 366; Doe d. Daniell *v.* Woodroffe, cited *ante*, p. 214.

"The general rule, also, is that a covenant not to sue when it does not affect other parties, and is so intended, may be pleaded as a release:" per Byles, J., Ray *v.* Jones, 19 C. B. N. S. 423 (115 E. C. L. R.).

[6] 2 Smith L. C., 6th ed., 474; Haggerston *v.* Hanbury, 5 B. & C. 101 (11 E. C. L. R.); Adams *v.* Steer, Cro. Jac. 210.

charter will bear a double construction, one of which will carry the grant into effect, the other which will make it inoperative, the former is to be adopted.[1] And generally, "if words have a double intendment, and the one standeth with law, and the other is against law, they are to be taken in the sense which is agreeable to law."[2]

In accordance with the same principle of construction, where divers persons join in a deed, and some are able to make such deed, and some are not able, this shall be said to be his deed alone that is able;[3] and if a deed be made to one that is incapable and another that is capable, *it shall enure only to the latter.[4] So, if mortgagor and mortgagee join in a lease, this enures as the lease of the mortgagee, and the confirmation of the mortgagor.[5] And if there be a joint lease by tenant for life and remainderman, such lease operates during the life of the tenant as his demise, confirmed by the remainderman, and afterwards as the demise of such last-mentioned party.[6]

[*545]

The preceding examples may suffice to show that where a deed cannot operate in the precise manner or to the full extent intended by the parties, it shall, nevertheless, be made as far as possible to effectuate their intention. Acting, moreover on a kindred principle, the court will endeavor to affix such a meaning to words of obscure and doubtful import occurring in a deed, as may best carry out the plain and manifest intention of the parties, as collected from the four corners of the instrument,—with these qualifications, however, that the intent of the parties shall never be carried into effect contrary to the rules of law, and that, as a general rule, the court will not introduce into a deed words which are not to be found there,[7] nor strike out of a deed words which are there, in order to

1 Per Tindal, C. J., Rutter *v.* Chapman, 8 M. & W. 102.

2 Shep. Touch. 80, adopted per Martin, B., Fussell *v.* Daniel, 10 Exch. 597; Co. Litt. 42 a, 183; Noy, Max., 9th ed., 211.

3 Shep. Touch. 81; Finch Law 60.

4 Shep. Touch. 82.

5 Doe d. Barney *v.* Adams, 2 Cr. & J. 232; per Lord Lyndhurst, C. B., Smith *v.* Pocklington, 1 Cr. & J. 446.

6 Treport's Case, 6 Rep. 15.

7 *Vide*, per Willes, C. J., Parkhurst *v.* Smith, Willes 332; cited and applied, per Alexander, C., B., Colemore *v.* Tyndall, 2 Yo. & J. 618; per Lord Brougham, C., Langston *v.* Langston, 2 Cl. & Fin. 243; Pannell *v.* Mill, 3 C. B. 625, 637 (54 E. C. L. R.).

make the sense different.[1] The following important illustrations of the above propositions may advantageously be noticed, and many others of equal practical importance will, doubtless, suggest themselves to the reader.

[*546] *In cases prior to and excluded from the operation of the recent stats. 7 & 8 Vict. c. 76, s. 4,[2] and 8 & 9 Vict. c. 106, s. 3,[3] the question whether a particular instrument should be construed as a lease or as an agreement for a lease must be answered by considering the intention of the parties, as collected from the instrument itself; and any words which suffice to explain the intent of the parties, that the one should divest himself of the possession, and the other come into it for such a determinate time, whether they run in the form of a license, covenant or agreement, will of themselves be held, in construction of law, to amount to a lease for years as effectually as if the most proper and pertinent words had been made use of for that purpose.[4] "The rule," observes Parke, B., "which is laid down in all the cases, is, that you must look at the whole of the instrument to judge of the intention of the parties, as declared by the words of it, for the purpose of seeing whether it is an agreement or a lease."[5]

The rules applicable and the case decided with reference to the construction of covenants will also be found to furnish strong and abundant instances of the anxiety [*547] *which our courts evince to effectuate the *real intention*[6] of the parties to a deed or

[1] White *v.* Burnby, 16 L. J., Q. B. 156; *secus* as to mere surplusage, *post.*

[2] See Burton *v.* Reevell, 16 M. & W. 307; Bond *v.* Rosling, 1 B. & S. 371 (101 E. C. L. R.).

[3] See Rollason *v.* Leon, 7 H. & N. 73.

[4] Bac. Abr. "*Leases*" (K.); and 2 Shep. Touch., by Preston, 272; cited, Judgm., Doe d. Parsley *v.* Day, 2 Q. B. 152 *et seq.* (42 E. C. L. R.); Alderman *v.* Neate, 4 M. & W. 704.

[5] Gore *v.* Lloyd, 12 M. & W. 478; Doe d. Morgan *v.* Powell, 8 Scott N. R. 687; Doe d. Wood *v.* Clarke, 7 Q. B. 211 (53 E. C. L. R.); per Wightman, J., Jones *v.* Reynolds, 1 Q. B. 517 (41 E. C. L. R.); Chapman *v.* Towner, 6 M. & W. 100; per Mansfield, C. J., Morgan *v.* Bissell, 3 Taunt. 72 (cited, per Jervis, C. J., Stratton *v.* Pettit, 16 C. B. 436 (81 E. C. L. R.), doubted and distinguished in Rollason *v.* Leon, 7 H. & N. 73, 77, 78; Curling *v.* Mills, 7 Scott N. R. 709, 725; Tarte *v.* Darby, 15 M. & W. 601. See Drury *v.* Macnamara, 5 E. & B. 612 (85 E. C. L. R.).

[6] Such intention may however be frustrated by the operation of a positive and technical rule of law. "A technical rule is one which is established by authority and precedent, which does not depend upon reasoning or argument,

agreement;[1] for it is not necessary, in order to charge a party with a covenant, that there should be express words of covenant or agreement, but it is enough if the intention of the parties to create a covenant be apparent.[2] Where, therefore, words of recital[3] or reference manifest a clear intention that the parties shall do certain acts, the courts will, from these words, infer a covenant to do such acts, and will sustain actions of covenant for their non-performance as effectually as if the instruments had contained express covenants to perform them.[4] In brief, "no particular form of words is necessary to form a covenant; but wherever the court can collect from the instrument an engagement on the one side to do or not to do something, it amounts to a covenant, whether it is in the recital or in any other part of the instrument."[5]

*In like manner where the language of a covenant is such that the covenant may be construed either as joint or as several, it shall be taken, at common law, to be joint or several, according to the interest of the covenantees. Where, however, the covenant is in its terms expressly and positively joint, it must be construed as a joint covenant, in compliance with the declared intention of the parties.[6] [*548]

but is a fixed established rule to be acted upon, and only discussed as regards its application—in truth is the law." Such a rule is that where a deed is made *inter partes*, no one who is not expressed to be a party can sue upon a covenant contained in it: Chesterfield, &c., Colliery Co. *v.* Hawkins, 3 H. & C. 677, 691, cited in Gurrin *v.* Kopera, Id. 699.

[1] See Doe d. Rogers *v.* Price, 8 C. B. 894 (65 E. C. L. R.).

[2] Per Tindal, C. J., Courtney *v.* Taylor, 7 Scott N. R. 765; Wood *v.* The Copperminers' Co., 7 C. B. 906 (62 E. C. L. R.); per Parke, B., Rigby *v.* Great Western R. C., 14 M. & W. 815; and in James *v.* Cochrane, 7 Exch. 177; s. c., 8 Id. 556; Farrall *v.* Hilditch, 5 C. B. N. S. 840 (94 E. C. L. R.). See Bealey *v.* Stuart, 7 H. & N. 753, 759.

[3] See Lay *v.* Mottram, 19 C. B. N. S. 479 (115 E. C. L. R.).

[4] Judgm., Aspdin *v.* Austin, 5 Q. B. 683 (48 E. C. L. R.); cited Dunn *v.* Sayles, Id. 692; and in Churchward *v.* Reg., L. R. 1 Q. B. 191, 208, and Rust *v.* Nottidge, 1 E. & B. 104 (72 E. C. L. R.); Williams *v.* Burrell, 1 C. B. 429 (50 E. C. L. R.), where the distinction between express covenants and covenants in law is pointed out. Per Crompton, J., 2 B. & S. 516 (110 E. C. L. R.).

[5] Per Parke, B., Great Northern R. C. *v.* Harrison, 12 C. B. 609 (74 E. C. L. R.); Judgm., Rashleigh *v.* South-Eastern R. C., 10 C. B. 632 (70 E. C. L. R.), as to which case see Knight *v.* Gravesend and Milton Waterworks Co., 2 H. & N. 10, 11.

[6] Judgm., Bradburne *v.* Botfield, 14 M. & W. 564, 572; Haddon *v.* Ayres,

In like manner, the rule has been established by a long series of decisions in modern times, that the question, whether covenants are to be held dependent or independent of each other, is to be determined by the intention or meaning of the parties as it appears on the instrument, and by the application of common sense to each particular case; to the intention, when once discovered, all technical forms of expression must give way.[1] Where, therefore, a question [*549] arose whether certain covenants *in marriage articles were dependent or not, Lord Cottenham, C., observed, "If the provisions are clearly expressed, and there is nothing to enable the court to put upon them a construction different from that which the words import, no doubt the words must prevail; but if the provisions and expressions be contradictory, and if there be grounds appearing upon the face of the instrument, affording proof of the real intention of the parties, then that intention will prevail against the obvious and ordinary meaning of the words. If the parties have themselves furnished a key to the meaning of the words used, it is not material by what expression they convey their intention."[2]

1 E. & E. 118 (102 E. C. L. R.); Pugh v. Stringfield, 3 C. B. N. S. 2 (91 E. C. L. R.); per Maule, J., Beer v. Beer, 12 C. B. 78 (74 E. C. L. R.), citing Wetherell v. Langston, 1 Exch. 634; Hopkinson v. Lee, 6 Q. B. 964 (51 E. C. L. R.); Foley v. Addenbrooke, 4 Q. B. 207 (45 E. C. L. R.); followed in Thompson v. Hakewill, 19 C. B. N. S. 713, 728 (115 E. C. L. R.); Sorsbie v. Park, 12 M. & W. 146; Mills v. Ladbroke, 7 Scott N. R. 1005, 1023; per Parke, B., Wootton v. Steffenoni, 12 M. & W. 134; Harrold v. Whitaker, 11 Q. B. 147, 163 (63 E. C. L. R.); Wakefield v. Brown, 9 Q. B. 209 (58 E. C. L. R.), followed in Magnay v. Edwards, 13 C. B. 479 (76 E. C. L. R.).

[1] Judgm., Stavers v. Curling, 3 Bing. N. C. 368 (32 E. C. L. R.); Baylis v. Le Gros, 4 C. B. N. S. 537 (93 E. C. L. R.); London Gas Light Co. v. Vestry of Chelsea, 8 C. B. N. S. 215 (98 E. C. L. R.); Sibthorp v. Brunel, 3 Exch. 826, 828; Hemans v. Picciotto, 1 C. B. N. S. 646 (87 E. C. L. R.). See Mackintosh v. Midland Counties R. C., 14 M. & W. 548.

The answer to the question, what is or what is not a condition precedent, depends not on merely technical words, but on the plain intention of the parties to be deduced from the whole instrument: Roberts v. Brett, 11 H. L. Cas. 337, 354.

[2] Per Lord Cottenham, C., Lloyd v. Lloyd, 2 My. & Cr. 202. In the notes to Pordage v. Cole, 1 Wms. Saund. 319, are specified various cases in which the court has done great violence to the strict letter of covenants, for the purpose of carrying into effect what was considered to be the real intention of the parties.

See Marsden v. Moore, 4 H. & N. 504, where Pordage v. Cole is cited and distinguished.

The construction of covenants, it has also been truly said, is the same in equity as at law. "But, though the construction is the same, it is most certain the performance may differ in the one court from what it is in the other. At law a covenant must be strictly and literally performed according to the true intent and meaning of the parties, so far as circumstances will admit; but if, by unavoidable accident,—if by fraud, by surprise or ignorance, not willful, parties may have been prevented from executing it literally,—a court of equity will interfere, and, upon compensation being made, the party having done everything in his power and being prevented by the means I have alluded to, will give relief."[1]

The same sense, we may in the next place observe, *is to [*550] be put upon the words of a contract in an instrument under seal as would be put upon the same words in any instrument not under seal: that is to say, the same intention must be collected from the same words, whether the particular contract in which they occur be special or not.[2]

In the case, then, of a contract or agreement, whether by deed or parol, the courts are bound so to construe it, *ut res magis valeat quam pereat*, that it may be made to operate rather than be inefficient; and, in order to effect this, the words used shall have a reasonable intendment and construction.[3] Words of art, for instance, which, in the understanding of conveyancers, have a peculiar technical meaning, shall not be scanned and construed with a conveyancer's acuteness, if, by so doing, one part of the instrument is made inconsistent with another, and the whole is incongruous and unintelligible; but the court will understand the words used in their popular sense, and will interpret the language of the parties *secundum subjectam materiem*, referring particular expressions to the particular subject-matter of the agreement, so that full and complete force may be given to the whole.[4]

[1] Per Sir R. P. Arden, M. R., 3 Ves. jun. 692.

[2] Per Lord Ellenborough, C. J., 13 East 74.

[3] Com. Dig., "*Pleader*" (C. 25); Bac. Works, vol. 4, p. 25; Noy, Max., 9th ed., p. 50.

[4] Hallewell *v.* Morrell, 1 Scott N. R. 309; per cur. Hill *v.* Grange, Plowd. 164, 170; cited arg. 2 Q. B. 509 (42 E. C. L. R.); per Willes, C. J., Willes R. 332; Heseltine *v.* Siggers, 1 Exch. 856.

As to construing an award, see Law *v.* Blackburrow, 14 C. B. 77 (78 E. C. L. R.); Mays *v.* Cannell, 15 C. B. 107 (80 E. C. L. R.), and cases there cited.

Whether, for example, a particular clause in a charter-party shall be held to be a condition, upon the non-performance of which [*551] by the one party, the other is at *liberty to abandon the contract, and consider it at an end,—or whether it amounts to an agreement only, the breach whereof is to be recompensed by an action for damages,—must depend, in each particular case, upon the intention of the parties, to be collected from the terms of the agreement itself, and from the subject matter to which it relates; it cannot depend on any formal arrangement of the words, but on the reason and sense of the thing, as it is to be collected from the whole contract.[1] In such a case, therefore, the rule applies, *In conventionibus contrahentium voluntas potius quam verba spectari placuit*[2]—in contracts and agreements the intention of the parties, rather than the words actually used by them, should be considered.[3]

Subject, however, to the preceding remarks, courts both of law and of equity will apply the ordinary rules of construction in interpreting instruments, and will construe words according to their strict and primary acceptation, unless from the immediate context or from the intention of the parties apparent on the face of the instrument, the words appear to have been used in a different sense, or unless, in their strict sense, they are incapable of being carried into effect. It must, moreover, be observed that the meaning of a particular word may be shown by parol evidence to be different in some [*552] specified place, trade or *business from its proper and ordinary acceptation;[4] various cases illustrating this remark will be hereafter cited.

With respect to patents, it was long since observed by Lord

[1] Judgm., Glaholm *v.* Hays, 2 Scott N. R. 482; recognized in Ollive *v.* Booker, 1 Exch. 416, 423; Behn *v.* Burness, 32 L. J., Q. B. 204; s. c., 1 B. & S. 877 (101 E. C. L. R.); Seeger *v.* Duthie, 8 C. B. N. S. 45 (98 E. C. L. R.); Oliver *v.* Fielden, 4 Exch. 135, 138; and Crookewit *v.* Fletcher, 1 H. & N. 911; Gattorno *v.* Adams, 12 C. B. N. S. 560 (104 E. C. L. R.); per Lord Ellenborough, C. J., Ritchie *v.* Atkinson, 10 East 306; Judgm., Furze *v.* Sharwood, 2 Q. B. 415 (42 E. C. L. R.). See White *v.* Beeton, 7 H. & N. 42.

[2] 17 Johns. (U. S.) R. 150, and cases there cited.

[3] Dimech *v.* Corlett, 12 Moo. P. C. C. 199, 228, citing Glaholm *v.* Hays, *supra.*

[4] See per Pollock, C. B., Mallan *v.* May, 13 M. & W. 511; Lewis *v.* Marshall, 8 Scott N. R. 477, 494; per Parke, B., Clift *v.* Schwabe, 3 C. B. 469, 470 (54 E. C. L. R.); per Lord Cranworth, C., 6 H. L. Cas. 78; *post*, Chap. X.

Eldon, that they are to be considered as bargains between the inventor and the public, to be judged of on the principles of good faith, by making a fair disclosure of the invention, and to be construed as other bargains.[1] Moreover, although formerly there seems to have been very much a practice, with both judges and juries, to destroy the patent right even of beneficial patents, by exercising great astuteness in taking objections as to the title of the patent, and more particularly as to the specification, in consequence of which many valuable patent rights have been destroyed; yet, more recently, the courts have not been so strict in taking objections to the specifications, but have rather endeavored to deal fairly both with the patentee and the public, willing to give to the patentee, on his part, the reward of a valuable patent, but taking care to secure to the public, on the other hand, the benefit of that proviso (*i. e.*, the proviso requiring a specification) which is introduced into the patent for their advantage, so that the right to the patent may be fairly and properly expressed in the specification.[2] In construing *a specification accordingly, the whole instrument must be taken together, and a fair and reasonable interpretation is to be given to the words used in it;[3] the words of the specification being construed according to their ordinary and proper meaning, unless there be something in the context to give them a different meaning, or unless the facts properly in evidence, and with reference to which the patent must be construed, should show that a different interpretation ought to be made.[4]

[*553]

The following remarks of Lord Ellenborough, C. J., with refer-

[1] Per Alderson, B., Neilson *v.* Harford, Webs. Pat. Cas. 341; Norman on Patents 78, 79.

The mode of construing a patent as between the patentee and the crown is stated *post.*

[2] Per Parke, B., Neilson's Patent, Webs. Pat. Cas. 310; per Alderson, B., Morgan *v.* Seward, Id. 173, who observes: "It is the duty of a party who takes out a patent to specify what his invention really is; and although it is the bounden duty of a jury to protect him in the fair exercise of his patent right, it is of great importance to the public, and by law it is absolutely necessary, that the patentee should state in his specification, not only the nature of his invention, but how that invention may be carried into effect.

[3] Beard *v.* Egerton, 8 C. B. 165 (65 E. C. L. R.).

[4] Judgm., Elliott *v.* Turner (in error), 2 C. B. 446, 461 (52 E. C. L. R.). As to construing a specification which contains terms of art, see Betts *v.* Menzies, 10 H. L. Cas. 117.

ence to a policy of insurance, here also occur to mind as generally applicable. "The same rule of construction," says that learned judge, "which applies to all other instruments, applies equally to this instrument of a policy of insurance, viz., that it is to be construed according to its sense and meaning, as collected, in the first place, from the terms used in it, which terms are themselves to be understood in their plain, ordinary and popular sense, unless they have generally, in respect to the subject-matter,—as by the known usage of trade, or the like,—acquired a peculiar sense distinct from the popular sense of the same words, or unless the context evidently points out that they must, in the particular instance, and in order to effectuate the immediate intention of the parties to that contract, be understood in some other special and peculiar sense."[1] And again, "the *contract of insurance," it has been said, [*554] "though a mercantile instrument, is to be construed according to the same rules as all other written contracts, namely, the intention of the parties, which is to be gathered from the words of the instrument, interpreted together with the surrounding circumstances. If the words of the instrument are clear in themselves, the instrument must be construed accordingly, but if they are susceptible of more meanings than one, then the judge must inform himself by the aid of the jury and the surrounding circumstances which bear on the contract."[2]

In construing a will, it has been said, that the intention of the testator is the polar star by which the court should be guided, provided no rule of law is thereby infringed.[3] "It is the duty of those who have to expound a will, if they can, *ex fumo dare lucem*."[4] In other words, the first thing for consideration always

[1] Robertson *v.* French, 4 East 135, 136; cited, per Lord Tenterden, C. J., Hunter *v.* Leathley, 10 B. & C. 871 (21 E. C. L. R.).

[2] Per Erle, C. J., Carr *v.* Montefiore, 5 B. & S. 428 (117 E. C. L. R.); citing Robertson *v.* French, *supra.*

[3] Per Lord Kenyon, C. J., Watson *v.* Foxon, 2 East 42; per Willes, C. J., Doe *v.* Underdown, Willes R. 296; per Buller, J., Smith *v.* Coffin, 2 H. Bla. 450; cases cited, arg. Ley *v.* Ley, 3 Scott N. R. 168; Doe d. Amlot *v.* Davies, 4 M. & W. 599, 607; Doe d. Tremewen *v.* Permewen, 11 A. & E. 131 (39 E. C. L. R.); per Parke, B., Grover *v.* Burningham, 5 Exch. 191; Martin *v.* Lee, 14 Moo. P. C. C. 142.

[4] Per V.-C. E., De Beauvoir *v.* De Beauvoir, 15 L. J. Chanc. 308; S. C., 15 Sim. 163; 3 H. L. Cas. 524.

is, what was the testator's intention at the time he made the will; and then the law carries that intention into effect as nearly as it can according to certain settled technical rules.[1]

*"Touching the general rules to be observed for the true construction of wills," says Dodderidge, J.,—"*in testamentis plenius testatoris intentionem scrutamur.* But yet this is to be observed with these two limitations: 1st, his intent ought to be agreeable to the rules of law; 2dly, his intent ought to be collected out of the words of the will. As to this it may be demanded, how shall this be known? To this it may thus be answered: first, to search out what was the scope of his will; secondly, to make such a construction, so that all the words of the will may stand; for to add anything to the words of the will, or in the construction made to relinquish and leave out any of the words, is *maledicta glossa.* But every string ought to give its sound."[2] [*555]

In a modern case, involving important interests,[3] the following were laid down as the leading and fundamental rules for construing a will. In the first place, the intention of the testator ought to be the only guide of the court to the interpretation of his will; yet it must be his intention as collected from the words employed by himself in his will.[4] No surmise or conjecture of any object which

[1] Judgm., Doe d. Scott *v.* Roach, 5 M. & S. 490; Hodgson *v.* Ambrose, Dougl. 341; Festing *v.* Allen, 12 M. & W. 279; Alexander *v.* Alexander, 16 C. B. 59 (81 E. C. L. R.); Doe d. Bills *v.* Hopkinson, 5 Q. B. 223 (48 E. C. L. R.); Doe d. Stevenson *v.* Glover, 1 C. B 459 (50 E. C. L. R.).

"The general rule in interpreting a will and codicil is that the whole of the will takes effect, except in so far as it is inconsistent with the codicil." Judgm., Robertson *v.* Powell, 2 H. & C. 766–7; citing Doe d. Hearle *v.* Hicks, 1 Cl. & F. 20; Judgm., Richardson *v.* Power, 19 C. B. N. S. 799 (115 E. C. L. R.).

[2] Per Dodderidge, J., Blamford *v.* Blamford, 3 Buls. 103. See Parker *v.* Tootal, 11 H. L. Cas. 143.

[3] Earl of Scarborough *v.* Doe d. Savile, 3 A. & E. 897 (30 E. C. L. R.).

[4] In Doe d. Sams *v.* Garlick, 14 M. & W. 701, Parke, B., observes, that difficulties have arisen from confounding the testator's *intention* with his *meaning*. "*Intention* may mean what the testator intended to have done, whereas the only question in the construction of wills is on the *meaning of the words.*" In Grover *v.* Burningham, 5 Exch. 194, Rolfe, B., also observes, "We are to ascertain by construing the will *non quod voluit sed quod dixit*, or rather we are to ascertain *quod voluit* by interpreting *quod dixit.*" And see, per Lord Wensleydale, Grey *v.* Pearson, 6 H. L. Cas. 106; and in Slingsby *v.* Grainger, 7 H. L. Cas. 284.

the testator may be supposed to have had in view can be allowed to [*556] have any weight in the construction of *his will, unless such object can be collected from the plain language of the will itself. If, for instance, there be a question as to the meaning of a proviso in a will, and its application to a given state of facts, the court will consider whether the testator has, by the proviso, declared an intention with sufficient clearness to reach the particular case which has actually happened, and whether he has employed such machinery in his will as is capable of carrying such declared intention into effect.[1]

In the second place, it is a necessary rule in the investigation of the intention of a testator, not only that regard should be paid to the words of the will, in order to determine the operation and effect of the devise, but that the legal consequences which may follow from the nature and qualities of the estate, when once collected from the words of the will itself, should be altogether disregarded;[2] for example, in determining whether the intention of the testator was, in any particular case, to give the devisee an estate tail, or for life only, it is not a sound or legitimate mode of reasoning to import into the consideration of the question, that, if the estate is held to be an estate tail, the devisee will have the power of defeating the intention of the testator altogether; for the court will not assume that the testator was ignorant of the legal consequence and effect of the disposition which he has himself made;[3] and a person ought to direct his meaning according to the law, and not seek to [*557] mould *the law according to his meaning; for, if a man were assured, that, whatever words he made use of, his meaning only would be considered, he would be very careless about the choice of his words, and the attempt to explain his meaning in each particular case would give rise to infinite confusion and uncertainty.[4]

[1] Judgm., Earl of Scarborough *v.* Doe d. Savile, 3 A. & E. 962, 963 (30 E. C. L. R.); cited 8 M. & W. 200.

[2] At the same time the circumstance, that the language if strictly construed will lead to a consequence inconsistent with the presumable intention, is not to be left out of view, especially if other considerations lead to the same result: Judgm., Quicke *v.* Leach, 13 M. & W. 228.

[3] 3 A. & E. 963, 964 (30 E. C. L. R.); per Parke, B., Morrice *v.* Langham, 8 M. & W. 207.

[4] Plowd. 162.

Hence, although it is the duty of the court to ascertain and carry into effect the intention of the party, yet there are, in many cases, fixed and settled rules by which that intention is determined; and to such rules the wisest judges have thought proper to adhere, in opposition to their own private opinions as to the probable intention of the party in any particular case.[1]

The object, indeed, of all such technical rules is to create certainty, and to prevent litigation, by enabling those who are conversant with these subjects to give correct advice, which would evidently be impossible, if the law were uncertain and liable to fluctuation in each particular case.[2]

In accordance with the remarks above offered, Parke, B., in an important case respecting the application of the rule against perpetuities, thus expressed himself:—"We must first ascertain the intention of the testator, or more properly the meaning of his words, in the clause under consideration, and then endeavor to give effect to them so far as the rules of law will permit. Our first duty is to construe the will, and this we must do exactly in the same way as if the rule against perpetuity had never been established, or were repealed when the will was made, not varying the construction in order to avoid the effect of *that rule, but interpreting the words of the testator wholly without reference to it."[3] [*558]

The rule in Shelley's Case[4]—by which, where an estate of freehold is limited to a person, and the same instrument contains a limitation, either mediate or immediate, to his heirs or the heirs of his body, the word "heirs" is construed as a word of limitation[5]—will occur to the reader as a familiar instance of an arbitrary and technical rule of construction, the authority of which is acknowledged by the courts, even where its application may tend to defeat the intention of the testator.

In like manner, it is a rule which has through a long series of cases been uniformly acted upon, although now by a recent statute

[1] See per Alexander, C. B., 6 Bing. 478; Judgm., 2 Phill. 68.

[2] Per Pollock, C. B., Doe d. Sams v. Garlick, 14 M. & W. 707.

[3] Per Parke, B., Lord Dungannon v. Smith, 12 Cl. & Fin. 599; distinguished in Christie v. Gosling, L. R. 1 H. L. 279.

[4] As to which, see 2 Com. by Broom & Hadley 330.

[5] 2 Jarm. Wills, 2d ed., 273. See Harrison v. Harrison, 8 Scott N. R. 862, 873; Cole v. Goble, 13 C. B. 445 (76 E. C. L. R.); Jordan v. Adams, 6 C. B. N. S. 748 (95 E. C. L. R.).

rendered inapplicable in the case of wills,[1] that a power of appointment over realty shall not be considered as executed, unless the instrument which is relied upon as an execution of the power contain a reference thereto, or to the property which was the subject of the power, or unless the provision made by the person entrusted with the power would have been ineffectual, and would have had nothing to operate upon unless it were considered as an execution of such power.[2]

[*559] *So, in construing a power to lease contained in a will, the court have said, it "becomes necessary to look to the language of the testator in the creation of the power itself, and to ascertain his intention by considering the true meaning of the language which he has used, giving to it its natural signification according to the ordinary rules of interpretation; giving effect, if possible, to every part of the clause; and if any part of it be ambiguous, interpreting it by reference to the context, to the general intent of the will, and, if necessary, to the surrounding circumstances."[3]

So, in the case of personalty, the rule under the law as it formerly existed was, that a general bequest does not exercise a power, unless, indeed, an intention so to do can be collected from the entire instrument; and in a case before Sir W. Grant, M. R., to which this rule was applied,[4] and which, notwithstanding the recent statutory alteration of the law, may be mentioned as apposite to our present subject, it appeared that a person had power to appoint 100*l.* by her will, and possessed nothing but a few articles of furniture of her own to answer the bequest; and the learned judge

[1] The rule does not apply to any will made or republished since the stat. 1 Vict. c. 26 came into operation. See sect. 27, which provides that real and personal property over which the testator has a power of appointment shall pass by a general devise or bequest, unless a contrary intention shall appear.

[2] Denn d. Nowell *v.* Roake, 6 Bing. 475; s. c., 4 Bligh. N. S. 1; Doe d. Caldecott *v.* Johnson, 8 Scott N. R. 761; Logan *v.* Bell, Id. 872; Hughes *v.* Turner, 3 My. & K. 666.

[3] Judgm., Jegon *v.* Vivian, L. R. 2 C. P. 427; s. c., affirmed, L. R. 3 H. L. 285.

"Facts extrinsic to the will must be ascertained for the court in the usual manner, either by admission of the parties or by a jury. When they have been ascertained the operation of construction is to be performed by the court:" Judgm., Webber *v.* Stanley, 16 C. B. N. S. 752 (111 E. C. L. R.).

[4] Jones *v.* Tucker, 2 Mer. 533.

observed, "In my own private opinion I think the intention was to give the 100*l.*, which the testatrix had a power to dispose of, but I do not conceive that I can judicially declare it to have been executed."

"If," says Lord Cottenham, in a more recent case, "there be any ambiguity, then it is the duty of the *court to put that construction upon the words which seems best to carry the intention into effect; but if there be no ambiguity, however unfortunate it may be that the intention of the testator should fail, there is no right in any court of justice to say those words shall not have their plain and unambiguous meaning."[1] [*560]

Not only are there fixed and established rules by which the courts will, in certain cases, be guided in determining the legal effect and operation of a testamentary instrument, but there are likewise certain technical expressions, of which the established legal interpretation is different from the meaning which in ordinary language would be attributed to them; and, consequently, a will in which such expressions occur may, in some cases, be made to operate in a manner different from that intended by the testator;[2] the duty of the court being to give effect to *all* the words of the will, if that can be done without violating any part of it, and also to construe technical words in their proper sense, where they can be so understood consistently with the context.[3]

[1] Earl of Hardwicke *v.* Douglas, 7 Cl. & Fin. 815; per Lord Kenyon, C. J., Denn *v.* Bagshawe, 6 T. R. 512; per Lord Alvanley, Poole *v.* Poole, 3 B. & P. 627–629.

[2] See 2 Powell on Devises, by Jarman, 3d ed., 564, *et seq.*; Doe d. Blesard *v.* Simpson, 3 Scott N. R. 774; cited, per Byles, J., Richards *v.* Davies, 13 C. B. N. S. 87 (106 E. C. L. R.), and distinguished in Hardcastle *v.* Dennison, 10 C. B. N. S. 606 (100 E. C. L. R.).

[3] Judgm., Doe d. Cape *v.* Walker, 2 Scott N. R. 334; Towns *v.* Wentworth, 11 Moo. P. C. C. 526, 543; per Martin, B., Biddulph *v.* Lees, E., B. & E. 317 (96 E. C. L. R.); per Alderson, B., Lees *v.* Mosley, 1 Yo. & Coll. 589; cited arg. Greenwood *v.* Rothwell, 6 Scott N. R. 672. See also arg. Festing *v.* Allen, 12 M. & W. 286; Jack *v.* M'Intyre, 12 Cl. & Fin. 158; Jenkins *v.* Hughes, 8 H. L. Cas. 571.

Where the testator appears to have been very illiterate, "the rules of grammar and the usual meaning of technical language may be disregarded in construing his will:" per Lord Campbell, C., Hall *v.* Warren, 9 H. L. Cas. 427.

Generally as to the duty of the court in construing a will containing technical words, see, further, per Lord Westbury, C., Young *v.* Robertson, 4

[*561] *The following observations of V.-C. Knight Bruce, although having reference to the particular circumstances of the case immediately under his consideration, show clearly the general principles which guide the court in assigning a meaning to technical expressions, and it may be almost unnecessary to remark that such principles are recognized and acted upon by courts of common law as well as of equity.

"Both reason and authority, I apprehend," says the learned judge, "support the proposition that the defendants are entitled to ask the court to read and consider the whole of the instrument in which the clause stands; and in reading and considering it, to bear in mind the state of the testator's family, as at the time when he made the codicil he knew it to be; and if the result of so reading and considering the whole document with that recollection is to convince the court, from its contents, that the testator intended to use the words in their ordinary and popular sense, and not in their legal and technical sense, as distinguishable from their ordinary and popular sense, to give effect to that conviction by deciding accordingly."[1]

The following instances may serve to illustrate the above remarks:[2]—If a testator leaves his property to be divided amongst his "children," which is a word bearing a strict technical meaning in law, the court would at [*562] *once construe "children" as meaning children born in wedlock; and if there were any such children to whom that term could be applied, the bequest would be limited to them, although it might also appear that the testator had other children born out of wedlock; and no evidence would be admissible to show that he intended that his property should be equally distributed amongst all his children, whether legitimate or illegitimate. But if, upon the evidence, it should appear that the testator never was married, so that it was impossible to apply the language of his will in its strict and primary sense, and if it

Macq. Sc. App. Cas. 325; distinguished in Richardson *v.* Power, 19 C. B. N. S. 798 (115 E. C. L. R.); Ralston *v.* Hamilton, 4 Macq. Sc. App. Cas. 397; Jenkins *v.* Hughes, 8 H. L. Cas. 571.

[1] Per Knight Bruce, V.-C., Early *v.* Benbow, 2 Coll. 353.

[2] As to the meaning of the word "unmarried," see Clarke *v.* Colls, 9 H. L. Cas. 601,—of the words "eldest male lineal descendant," Thellusson *v.* Lord Rendlesham, 7 H. L. Cas. 429.

further appeared that he had illegitimate children whom he had always treated as his children, such evidence, and any other that would tend to prove that these were the intended objects of his bounty, might be used for the purpose of construing the bequest according to the less strict and technical meaning of the term "children," so as to give effect to the bequest of the testator, which would otherwise be wholly inoperative.[1]

In like manner, where a bequest is made to the "children" or "issue" of A. B., the whole context of the will must be considered, in endeavoring to ascertain the proper effect to be attributed to the word "children" or "issue." It may be, that the word "children" must be enlarged and construed to mean "issue" generally, or the word "issue" restricted so as to mean "children," and each case must depend on the peculiar expressions used, and the structure of the sentences.[2] When, however, *the context is doubtful, the court, so far as it can, will prefer that construction which will most benefit the testator's family generally, on the supposition that such a construction must most nearly correspond with his intention.[3] [*563]

Again, the general rule of construction which had prior to the recent Wills Act been established by a long course of decided cases, was, that the words "dying without leaving issue,"[4] unless they were qualified and controlled by other words in the context, must, when applied to realty, be taken to refer to an indefinite failure of issue; and that any executory devise over, which was made to depend on the general failure of issue, was void, on the

[1] Per Erskine, J., Shore *v.* Wilson, 5 Scott N. R. 990. See Sir James Wigram's Treatise on Extr. Evid., 3d ed., 43, 58.

[2] Also, where in a devise there is a gift over on general failure of "issue," the word "issue" must, *primâ facie*, be understood to mean "heirs of the body," unless from the context it clearly appear that the testator intended to give it a different meaning: Roddy *v.* Fitzgerald, 6 H. L. Cas. 823. See Bradley *v.* Cartwright, L. R. 2 C. P. 511; Eastwood *v.* Avison, L. R. 4 Ex. 141; per Lord Chelmsford, C., Williams *v.* Lewis, 6 H. L. Cas. 1021.

[3] Per Lord Langdale, M. R., Farrant *v.* Nichols, 9 Beav. 329, 330; Slater *v.* Dangerfield, 15 M. & W. 263; Richards *v.* Davies, 13 C. B. N. S. 69 (106 E. C. L. R.).

[4] But now, by stat. 7 Will. 4 & 1 Vict. c. 26, s. 29, the words "die without issue," or "die without leaving issue," shall be construed to mean a want or failure of issue in the lifetime, or at the time of the death of the testator, unless a contrary intention shall appear by the will.

ground of its being too remote. The point to be considered, therefore, in determining whether or not the above words must bear their proper and technical meaning, whenever the point arises with reference to a will unaffected by the recent statute, is, whether the testator has or has not shown, upon the face of the will, an intention that those words should receive a more limited and qualified construction.[1]

[*564] Further, it has been placed beyond doubt by a great *variety of decisions, that the word "estate"[2] in a will is in itself sufficient to pass the fee-simple; but the court will nevertheless examine the context and other parts of the will to ascertain if anything be there introduced to qualify its import; and the material question, if the late Act does not apply, is, whether the word is to be understood as describing the quantity of interest of the testator in the property devised, or the local situation of the property only, or whether the meaning is left in too great uncertainty to defeat the claim of the heir-at-law, which cannot be done without express words or necessary implication.[3]

Lastly, in determining whether an estate tail or a life estate only passes under the words of a given testamentary instrument made before the 1st of January, 1838,[4] the same general rule of interpreta-

[1] Judgm., Walker *v.* Petchell, 1 C. B. 661 (50 E. C. L. R.); Bamford *v.* Lord, 14 C. B. 708 (78 E. C. L. R.); Biss *v.* Smith, 2 H. & N. 105, 113. See Eden *v.* Wilson, 4 H. L. Cas. 257; Darley *v.* Martin, 13 C. B. 683 (76 E. C. L. R.).

[2] "Estate," in Latin, *status*, "indicates the condition of the owner with regard to his property:" 2 Com. by Broom & Hadley 206.

[3] Doe d. Lean *v.* Lean, 1 Q. B. 229, 239, 240 (41 E. C. L. R.), and cases cited; arg. Hoare *v.* Byng, 10 Cl. & Fin. 528; Lloyd *v.* Jackson, L. R. 2 Q. B. 269; Manning *v.* Taylor, 4 H. & C. 382; Doe d. Tofield *v.* Tofield, 11 East 246; Smith *v.* Smith, 11 C. B. N. S. 121 (103 E. C. L. R.); Doe d. Burton *v.* White, 2 Exch. 797; s. c., 1 Id. 526; Burton *v.* White, 7 Exch. 720; Doe d. Atkinson *v.* Fawcett, 3 C. B. 274 (54 E. C. L. R.); Butt *v.* Thomas, 11 Exch. 235; Key *v.* Key, 4 De G., M. & G. 73; Vaugh. R. 262. In Doe d. Haw *v.* Earles, 15 M. & W. 450, the maxim above considered was applied in determining the construction of a will, per Platt, B., *diss.* The reader is also referred to 2 Jarm. on Wills, 3d ed., 255, *et seq.*; Sanderson *v.* Dobson, 1 Exch. 141; s. c., 7 C. B. 81 (62 E. C. L. R.); Doe d. Roberts *v.* Williams, 1 Exch. 414; and note 2, *infra*.

As to the doctrine of "implication" and examples of it, see per Lord Westbury, C., Parker *v.* Tootal, 11 H. L. Cas. 161.

[4] By stat. 7 Will 4 & 1 Vict. c. 26, a devise of real estate without words of

tion above considered is applicable, and has thus been forcibly stated and illustrated by Lord Brougham, who observes—"I take the *principle of construction as consonant to reason and [*565] established by authority to be this—that where by plain words, in themselves liable to no doubt, an estate tail is given, you are not to allow such estate to be altered and cut down to a life estate, unless there are other words which plainly show the testator to have used the former as words of purchase, contrary to their natural or ordinary sense, or unless in the rest of the provisions there be some plain indication of a general intent inconsistent with an estate tail being given by the words in question, and which general intent can only be fulfilled by sacrificing the particular provisions, and regarding the expressions as words of purchase. Thus, if there is a gift first to A. and the heirs of his body, and then, in continuation, the testator, referring to what he had said, plainly tells us that he used the words 'heirs of the body' to denote A.'s first and other sons, then, clearly, the first taker would only take a life estate. So, again, if a limitation is made afterwards, and is clearly the main object of the will, which never can take effect unless an estate for life be given instead of an estate tail: here, again, the first words become qualified, and bend to the general intent of the testator, and are no longer regarded as words of limitation, which, if standing by themselves, they would have been."[1]

To the general maxims of construction applicable to wills, viz., *Benignè faciendæ sunt interpretationes et verba intentioni debent inservire*, the doctrine of cy-près is referable.[2] According to this doctrine, which proceeds upon the principle of carrying into effect as far and as *nearly as possible the intention of the tes- [*566] tator, if there be a general and also a particular intention apparent on the will, and the particular intention cannot take effect, the words shall be so construed as to give effect to the general intention.[3] The doctrine of cy-près, though fully recognized at law,

limitation shall, in the absence of a contrary intention, be construed to pass the whole estate or interest of which the testator had power to dispose by will.

[1] Fetherston *v.* Fetherston, 3 Cl. & Fin. 75, 76; per Lord Brougham, C., Thornhill *v.* Hall, 2 Cl. & Fin. 36.

[2] See per Lord St. Leonards, East *v.* Twyford, 4 H. L. Cas. 556.

[3] Per Buller, J., Robinson *v.* Hardcastle, 2 T. R. 254; Shep. Touch. 87. The rule as to cy-près is stated, per Lord St. Leonards, C., Monypenny *v.*

is, however, carried into more efficient practical operation by courts of equity, as in the case of a condition precedent annexed to a legacy, with which a literal compliance becomes impossible from unavoidable circumstances, and without any default of the legatee; or where a bequest is made for charitable purposes, with which a literal compliance becomes inexpedient or impracticable: in such cases a court of equity will apply the doctrine of cy-près, and will endeavor substantially, and as nearly as possible, to carry into effect the intention of the testator.[1]

The remarks above made, and authorities referred to, will serve to give a general view of the mode of applying to the interpretation of wills those very comprehensive maxims which we have been endeavoring to illustrate and explain, and which are, indeed, comprised in the well-known saying,—*Ultima voluntas testatoris est perimplenda secundum veram intentionem suam.*[2]

[*567] We shall, therefore, sum up this part of our subject *with observing, that the only safe course to pursue in construing a will is to look carefully for the intention of the testator, as it is to be derived from the words employed by him within the whole of the will, regardless alike of any general surmise or conjecture from without the will, as of any legal consequences annexed to the estate itself, when such estate is discovered within the will;[3] bearing in mind, however, that where technical rules have become established, such rules must be followed, although opposed to the testator's presumable and probable intention—that where technical expressions occur they must receive their legal meaning, unless, from a perusal of the entire instrument, it be evident that the testator employed them in their popular signification —that words which have no technical meaning shall be understood in their usual and ordinary sense, if the context do not manifestly

Dering, 2 De G., M. & G. 173. See per Lord Kenyon, C. J., Brudenell *v.* Elwes, 1 East 451.

[1] 1 Story Eq. Jurisp., 6th ed., 319; 2 Id. 596, where this doctrine is considered; 1 Jarm. Wills, 3d ed., 233; Ironmongers' Co. *v.* A.-G., 10 Cl. & Fin. 908; Miles *v.* Farmer, 19 Ves. 483. The entire doctrine of equity with regard to trusts, and especially such as are raised in a will by precatory words, will at once occur to the reader as fraught with illustrations of the maxims commented on in the text.

[2] Co. Litt. 322 b.

[3] Judgm., 3 A. & E. 964 (30 E. C. L. R.).

point to any other[1]—and, lastly, that where the particular intention of the testator cannot literally be performed, effect will, in many cases, be given to the general intention, in order that his wishes may be carried out as nearly as possible, and *ut res magis valeat quàm pereat.*

It may not be uninteresting further to remark, that the rules laid down in the Roman law upon the subject under consideration, are almost identical with those above stated, as recognized by our own jurists at the present day. Where, for instance, ambiguous expressions occurred, the rule was, that the intention of him who used them should especially be regarded,—*In ambiguis orationibus maximè sententia spectanda est ejus *qui eas protulisset,*[2] a rule [*568] which we learn was confined to the interpretation of wills wherein one person only speaks, and was not applicable to agreements generally, in which the intention of both the contracting parties was necessarily to be considered;[3] and, accordingly, in another passage in the Digest, we find the same rule so expressly qualified and restricted—*Cum in testamento ambigue aut etiam perperam scriptum est benigne interpretari et secundum id quod credibile est cogitatum credendum est*[4]—where an ambiguous or even an erroneous expression occurs in a will, it should be construed liberally, and in accordance with the testator's probable meaning. In like manner we find it stated, that a departure from the literal meaning of the words used is not justifiable, unless it be clear that the testator himself intended something different therefrom:—*Non aliter a significatione verborum recedi oportet quàm cum manifestum est aliud sensisse testatorem;*[5] and, lastly, we find the general principle of interpretation to which we have already adverted thus concisely worded—*In testamentis plenius voluntates testantium interpretantur*[6]—that is to say, a will shall receive a more liberal construction than its strict meaning, if alone considered, would permit.[7]

[1] The question as to what will pass under the word "portrait" in a will is elaborately discussed, Duke of Leeds *v.* Earl Amherst, 9 Jur. 359; s. c., 13 Sim. 459.

[2] D. 50. 17. 96.

[3] Wood Inst. 107.

[4] D. 34. 5. 24; *vide* Brisson. ad verb. "*Perperam;*" Pothier ad Pand. (ed. 1819), vol. 3, p. 46, where examples of this rule are collected.

[5] D. 32. 69. pr. applied per Knight Bruce, L. J., 2 De G., M. & G. 313.

[6] D. 50. 17. 12.

[7] Cujac. *ad. loc.*, cited 3 Pothier ad Pand. 46.

The construction of a statute, like the operation of a devise, depends upon the apparent intention of the maker, to be collected [*569] either from the particular provision *or the general context, though not from any general inferences drawn merely from the nature of the objects dealt with by the statute.[1] Acts of Parliament and wills ought to be alike construed according to the intention of the parties who made them;[2] and the preceding remarks as to the construction of deeds and testamentary instruments will, therefore, in general hold good with reference to the construction of statutes, the great object being to discover the true intention of the legislature; and where that intention can be indubitably ascertained, the courts are bound to give it effect, whatever may be their opinion of its wisdom or policy;[3] "acting upon the rule as to giving effect to all the words of the statute, a rule universally applicable to all writings, and which ought not to be departed from, except upon very clear and strong grounds."[4]

"The general rule," as observed by Byles, J.,[5] "for the construction of Acts of Parliament is, that the words are to be read in [*570] their popular, natural, and ordinary *sense, giving them a meaning to their full extent and capacity, unless there is reason upon their face to believe that they were not intended to bear that construction, because of some inconvenience which could not have been absent from the mind of the framers of the Act, which must arise from the giving them such large sense."

[1] Fordyce *v.* Bridges, 1 H. L. Cas. 1. Where a *casus omissus* occurred in a statute, the doctrine of cy-près was applied, Smith *v.* Wedderburne, 16 M. & W. 104. See Salkeld *v.* Johnson, 2 C. B. 757 (52 E. C. L. R.).

[2] It is said that a will is to be favorably construed, because the testator is *inops consilii:* "This," observed Lord Tenterden, "we cannot say of the legislature, but we may say that it is *magnas inter opes inops.*" 9 B. & C. 752, 753 (17 E. C. L. R.).

See the remarks of Wood, V.-C., as to the determining whether a mandatory enactment is to be considered directory only, or obligatory with an implied nullification for disobedience: Liverpool Borough Bank *v.* Turner, 29 L. J. Chanc. 827; s. c., 30 Id. 379, approved in Ward *v.* Beck, 13 C. B. N. S. 675–6 (106 E. C. L. R.).

[3] See the analogous remarks of Lord Brougham, with reference more particularly to the common law, in Reg. *v.* Millis, 10 Cl. & Fin. 749; also, per Vaughan, J., 9 A. & E. 980 (36 E. C. L. R.); Judgm., Fellowes *v.* Clay, 4 Q. B. 349 (45 E. C. L. R.); per Alexander, C. B., 2 Yo. & J. 215.

[4] Judgm., 8 Exch. 860.

[5] Birks, app., Allison, resp., 13 C. B. N. S. 23 (106 E. C. L. R.).

And again—"In construing an Act of Parliament, when the intention of the legislature is not clear, we must adhere to the natural import of the words; but when it is clear what the legislature intended, we are bound to give effect to it notwithstanding some apparent deficiency in the language used."[1]

Hence, although the general proposition be undisputed that "an affirmative statute giving a new right, does not of itself and of necessity destroy a previously existing right," it will nevertheless have such effect, "if the apparent intention of the legislature is that the two rights should not exist together."[2]

A remedial statute, therefore, shall be liberally construed, so as to include cases which are within the mischief which the statute was intended to remedy;[3] whilst, on the other hand, where the intention of the legislature is doubtful, the inclination of the court will always be against that construction which imposes a burthen,[4] *tax,[5] or duty[6] on the subject. It has been designated as a "great rule" in the construction of fiscal laws, "that they [*571]

[1] Per Pollock, C. B., Huxham *v.* Wheeler, 3 H. & C. 80.

[2] Per Lord Cranworth, C., O'Flaherty *v.* M'Dowell, 6 H. L. Cas. 157. See Ex parte Warrington, 3 De G., M. & G. 159.

[3] See Twyne's Case, 3 Rep. 80.

[4] Per Lord Brougham, Stockton and Darlington R. C. *v.* Barrett, 11 Cl. & Fin. 607; per Parke, B., Ryder *v.* Mills, 3 Exch. 869, and in Wroughton *v.* Turtle, 11 M. & W. 567. "All Acts which restrain the common law ought themselves to be restrained by exposition:" Ash *v.* Abdy, 3 Swanst. 664. Mere permissive words shall not abridge a common law right, *ante*, p. 34. Ex parte Clayton, 1 Russ. & My. 372; per Erle, C. J., Caswell, app., Cook, resp., 11 C. B. N. S. 652 (103 E. C. L. R.).

[5] Per Parke, B., Re Mickletbwait, 11 Exch 456 (cited arg. 2 H. & N. 373), and in A.-G. *v.* Bradbury, 7 Exch. 116, citing Denn *v.* Diamond, 4 B. & C. 243 (10 E. C. L. R.); Mayor of London *v.* Parkinson, 10 C. B. 228 (70 E. C. L. R.); Judgm., Vauxhall Bridge Co. *v.* Sawyer, 6 Exch. 509.

[6] Judgm., Marquis of Chandos *v.* Commissioners of Inland Revenue, 6 Exch. 479; per Wilde, C. J., 5 C. B. 135 (57 E. C. L. R.). See, per Bramwell, B., Foley *v.* Fletcher, 3 H. & N. 781, 782.

"Acts of Parliament," however, "imposing stamp duties ought to be construed according to the plain and ordinary meaning of the words used:" Judgm., Lord Foley *v.* Commissioners of Inland Revenue, L. R. 3 Ex. 268.

If a statute imposing a toll contain also exemptions from it in favor of the crown and of the public, any clause so exempting from toll is "to have a fair, reasonable, and not strict construction:" per Byles, J., Toomer *v.* Reeves, L. R. 3 C. P. 66.

are not to be extended by any labored construction, but that you must adhere to the strict rule of interpretation; and if a person who is subjected to a duty in a particular character or by virtue of a particular description no longer fills that character or answers that description, the duty no longer attaches upon him, and cannot be levied."[1] A penalty, moreover, must be imposed by clear words.[2] The words of a penal statute[3] shall be restrained for the benefit of him against whom the penalty is inflicted.

[*572] *"The principle," remarked Lord Abinger, C. B., "adopted by Lord Tenterden,[4] that a penal law ought to be construed strictly, is not only a sound one, but the only one consistent with our free institutions. The interpretation of statutes has always in modern times been highly favorable to the personal liberty of the subject, and I hope will always remain so."[5]

This rule, however, which is founded on the tenderness of the law for the rights of individuals, and on the plain principle that the power of punishment is vested in the legislature and not in the judicial department, must not be so applied as to narrow the words of the statute to the exclusion of cases which those words in their ordinary acceptation, or in that sense in which the legislature has obviously used them, would comprehend.[6]

[1] Per Lord Westbury, C., Dickson *v.* Reg., 11 H. L. Cas. 184.

[2] Per Alderson, B., Woolley *v.* Kay, 1 H. & N. 309; Judgm., Ryder *v.* Mills, 3 Exch. 869, *et seq.*; Coe *v.* Lawrence, 1 E. & B. 516, 520 (72 E. C. L. R.); Archer *v.* James, 2 B. & S. 61, 103 (110 E. C. L. R.).

[3] In A.-G. *v.* Sillem, 2 H. & C. 431, the method of construing a penal statute was much considered, and there (Id. 530) Bramwell, B., says, "The law that governs this case is a written law, an Act of Parliament, which we must apply according to the true meaning of the *words* used in it. We must not extend it to anything not within the natural meaning of those words, but within the mischief or supposed mischief intended to be prevented, nor must we refuse to apply it to what is within that natural meaning, because not, or supposed not to be within the mischief." See also per Pollock, C. B., Id. 509.

"I suppose 'within the equity' means the same thing as 'within the mischief' of the statute:" per Byles, J., Shuttleworth *v.* Le Fleming, 19 C. B. N. S. 703 (115 E. C. L. R.).

[4] See Proctor *v.* Mainwaring, 3 B. & Ald. 145 (5 E. C. L. R.).

[5] Per Lord Abinger, C. B., Henderson *v.* Sherborn, 2 M. & W. 236; Judgm., Fletcher *v.* Calthrop, 6 Q. B. 887 (51 E. C. L. R.); cited and adopted Murray *v.* Reg., 7 Q. B. 707 (53 E. C. L. R.).

[6] See Judgm., United States *v.* Wiltberger, 5 Wheaton (U. S.) R. 95; per Pollock, C. B., 3 H. & N. 812.

We may add, in connection with this part of the subject, that although the enacting words of a statute are not necessarily to be limited or controlled by the words of the preamble, but in many instances go beyond it, yet, on a sound construction of every Act of Parliament, the words in the enacting part must be confined to that which is the plain object and general intention of the legislature in passing the Act; and the preamble affords a good clue to discover what that object was.[1] "The only rule," it *has been said, "for the construction of Acts of Parliament is, [*573] that they should be construed according to the intent of the Parliament which passed the Act. If the words of the statute are in themselves precise and unambiguous, then no more can be necessary than to expound the words in their natural and ordinary sense. The words themselves alone do, in such case, best declare the intention of the lawgiver. But if any doubt arises from the terms employed by the legislature, it has always been held a safe means of collecting the intention to call in aid the ground and cause of making the statute, and to have recourse to the preamble, which, according to Chief Justice Dyer,[2] is a 'key to open the minds of the makers of the Act, and the mischiefs which they intended to redress.'"[3]

[1] Per Lord Tenterden, C. J., Halton *v.* Cave, 1 B. & Ad. 538 (20 E. C. L. R.); Judgm., Salkeld *v.* Johnson, 2 Exch. 283, and cases there cited; per Kelly, C. B., Winn *v.* Mossman, L. R. 4 Ex. 300; Carr *v.* Royal Exchange Ass. Co., 1 B. & S. 956 (101 E. C. L. R.); per Maule, J., Edwards *v.* Hodges, 15 C. B. 484 (80 E. C. L. R.), citing, per Lord Cowper, C., Copeman *v.* Gallant, 1 P. Wms. 314; per Coleridge, J., Pocock *v.* Pickering, 18 Q. B. 797, 798 (83 E. C. L. R.); Co. Litt. 79 a; per Buller, J., Crespigny *v.* Wittenoom, 4 T. R. 793; arg. Skinner *v.* Lambert, 5 Scott N. R. 206; and cases cited in Whitmore *v.* Robertson, 8 M. & W. 472; Stockton and Darlington R. C. *v.* Barrett, 11 Cl. & Fin. 590; arg. Sterry *v.* Clifton, 9 C. B. 110 (67 E. C. L. R.).

[2] Plowd. 369.

[3] Per Tindal, C. J., delivering the opinion of the judges in the Sussex Peerage, 11 Cl. & Fin. 143.

See further as to the office of the preamble, per Buller, J., R. *v.* Robinson, 2 East P. C. 1113, cited R. *v.* Johnson, 29 St. Tr. 303.

The *title* of a statute "is certainly no part of the law, and in strictness ought not to be taken into consideration at all:" Judgm., Salkeld *v.* Johnson, 2 Exch. 283, and cases there cited. See 8 H. L. Cas. 603 (h); per Willes, J., Claydon *v.* Green, L. R. 3 C. P. 522.

The heading of a portion of a statute may be referred to to determine the

The "golden rule" by which judges are to be guided in the construction of Acts of Parliament has been [*574] *frequently thus stated,[1] that they ought "to look at the precise words of the statute and construe them in their ordinary sense only, if such construction would not lead to any absurdity or manifest injustice; but if it would, then they ought so to vary and modify the words used as to avoid that which it certainly could not have been the intention of the legislature should be done." The "golden rule," however, thus worded, must certainly be applied with much caution. "If," remarked the late Chief Justice Jervis,[2] "the precise words used are plain and unambiguous in our judgment, we are bound to construe them in their ordinary sense, even though it do lead, in our view of the case, to an absurdity or manifest injustice. Words may be modified or varied, where their import is doubtful or obscure. But we assume the functions of legislators when we depart from the ordinary meaning of the precise words used, merely because we see, or fancy we see, an absurdity or manifest injustice from an adherence to their literal meaning."

The "golden rule" may, however, safely be understood as requiring that "the words of an Act of Parliament, or other written instrument,[3] be read in their natural and ordinary sense, giving

sense of any doubtful expression in a section ranged under it: Hammersmith and City R. C. *v.* Brand, L. R. 4 H. L. 171, 203 (but see per Lord Cairns, Id. 217); Eastern Counties R. C. *v.* Marriage, 9 H. L. Cas. 32.

The marginal note to a section of a statute in the copy printed by the queen's printer forms no part of the statute itself, and does not bind as explaining or construing the section: Claydon *v.* Green, L. R. 3 C. P. 511, 522.

[1] Per Jervis, C. J., Abbey *v.* Dale, 11 C. B. 390 (73 E. C. L. R.); in Castrique *v.* Page, 13 C. B. 463, 464 (76 E. C. L. R.); and in Mattison *v.* Hart, 14 C. B. 385 (78 E. C. L. R.); Judgm., Macdougal *v.* Paterson, 11 C. B. 769 (73 E. C. L. R.); per Maule, J., Gether *v.* Capper, 15 C. B. 706 (80 E. C. L. R.); s. c., 18 Id., 866; per Parke, B., Perry *v.* Skinner, 2 M. & W. 476; Eastern Union R. C. *v.* Cochrane, 9 Exch. 204; and in Hollingworth *v.* Palmer, 4 Exch. 281, 282; and Heslop *v.* Baker, 6 Exch. 75; per Burton, J., Warburton *v.* Loveland d. Ivie, 1 Huds. & Brooke 648; per Pollock, C. B., A.-G. *v.* Hallett, 2 H. & N. 375; and in Re Hammersmith Rent-Charge, 4 Exch. 100, and see, per Parke, B., Id. 107; per Byles, J., 4 C. B. N. S. 410 (93 E. C. L. R.).

[2] 11 C. B. 391 (73 E. C. L. R.); per Pollock, C. B., 9 Exch. 465. See Woodward *v.* Watts, 2 E. & B. 457 (75 E. C. L. R.).

[3] *Ante*, p. 542.

them a meaning to their full extent *and capacity; unless there is strong reason upon the face of it to show that the [*575] words were not intended to bear that construction, because of some inconvenience which could not have been absent from the mind of the framers of the Act or the instrument, which must arise from the giving them such large sense. Where that argument applies, the rule of construction may be restricted."[1]

"Words," remarks Parke, B., in Miller *v.* Solomons,[2] "which are plain enough in their ordinary sense, may, when they would involve any absurdity or inconsistency, or repugnance to the clear intention of the legislature, to be collected from the whole of the Act or Acts *in pari materiâ* to be construed with it, or other legitimate grounds of interpretation, be modified or altered, so as to avoid that absurdity, inconvenience, or repugnance, but no further; for then we may predicate that the words never could have been used by the framers of the law in such a sense."

It may then safely be stated as an established rule of construction, that an Act of Parliament should be read according to the ordinary and grammatical sense of the words,[3] unless, being so read, it would be absurd or inconsistent with the declared intention of the legislature, *to be collected from the rest of the Act,[4] [*576] or unless a uniform series of decisions has already established a particular construction,[5] or unless terms of art are used,

[1] Per Maule, J., Arnold *v.* Ridge, 13 C. B. 763 (76 E. C. L. R.); *acc.* per Byles, J., cited *ante*, p. 569.

[2] 7 Exch. 546; s. c. (in error), 8 Id. 778, where the rules of construction applicable to statutes were much considered. See also, per Pollock, C. B., Waugh *v.* Middleton, 8 Exch. 356, 357.

[3] "It is a good rule, in the construction of Acts of Parliament, that the judges are not to make the law what they may think reasonable, but to expound it according to the common sense of its words:" per Cresswell, J., Biffin *v.* Yorke, 6 Scott N. R. 235. See also, Judgm., R. *v.* Hall, 1 B. & C. 123 (8 E. C. L. R.); cited 2 C. B. 66 (52 E. C. L. R.); and in The Lion, L. R. 2 P. C. 530; Stracey *v.* Nelson, 12 M. & W. 541; United States *v.* Fisher, 2 Cranch (U. S.) R. 286; cited 7 Wheaton (U. S.) R. 169.

[4] Judgm., Smith *v.* Bell, 10 M. & W. 389; Turner *v.* Sheffield R. C., Id. 434; Judgm., Steward *v.* Greaves, 10 M. & W. 719; per Alderson, B., A.-G. *v.* Lockwood, 9 M. & W. 398; Judgm., Hyde *v.* Johnson, 2 Bing. N. C. 780 (29 E. C. L. R.).

[5] Per Parke, B., Doe d. Ellis *v.* Owens, 10 M. & W. 521; per Lord Brougham, C., The Earl of Waterford's Peerage, 6 Cl. & Fin. 172.

which have a fixed technical signification: as, for instance, the expression "heirs of the body," which conveys to lawyers a precise idea, as comprising in a legal sense only certain lineal descendants; and this expression shall, therefore, be construed according to its known meaning.[1]

It is also a rule of the civil law adopted by Lord Bacon, which was evidently dictated by common sense, and is in accordance with the spirit of the maxim which we have been considering, that, where obscurities, ambiguities, or faults of expression render the meaning of an enactment doubtful, that interpretation shall be preferred which is most consonant to equity, especially where it is in conformity with the general design of the legislature. *In ambiguâ voce legis ea potius accipienda est significatio quæ vitio caret, præsertim cum etiam voluntas legis ex hoc colligi possit.*[2]

[*577] *Ex antecedentibus et consequentibus fit optima Interpretatio.

(2 Inst. 173.)

A passage will be best interpreted by reference to that which precedes and follows it.

It is a true and important rule of construction, that the sense and meaning of the parties to any particular instrument should be collected *ex antecedentibus et consequentibus;* that is to say, every part of it should be brought into action, in order to collect from the whole one uniform and consistent sense, if that may be done;[3] or in other words, the construction must be made upon the entire instrument, and not merely upon disjointed parts of it;[4] the whole context must be considered, in endeavoring to collect the intention of the

[1] 2 Dwarr. Stats. 702; Poole *v.* Poole, 3 B. & P. 620.

[2] D. 1. 3. 19; Bac. Max., reg. 3.

[3] Per Lord Ellenborough, C. J., Barton *v.* Fitzgerald, 15 East 541; Shep. Touch. 87; per Hobart, C. J., Winch. 93. See Micklethwait *v.* Micklethwait, 4 C. B. N. S. 790, 862 (93 E. C. L. R.).

[4] Lord North *v.* Bishop of Ely, cited, 1 Bulst. 101; and Judgm., Doe d. Meyrick *v.* Meyrick, 2 Cr. & J. 230; Maitland *v.* Mackinnon, 1 H. & C. 607.

parties, although the immediate object of inquiry be the meaning of an isolated clause.[1] In short, the law will judge of a deed, or other instrument, consisting of divers parts or clauses, by looking at the whole; and will give to each part its proper office, so as to ascertain and carry out the intention of the parties.[2]

Thus, in the case of a bond, without a condition, the latter may be read and taken into consideration, in order to correct and explain the obligatory part of the instrument.[3] So, in construing an agreement in the form of *a bond in which a surety becomes liable for the due fulfillment of an agent's duties therein [*578] particularly enumerated, a general clause in the obligatory part of the bond must be interpreted strictly, and controlled by reference to the prior clauses specifying the extent of the agency.[4] On the same principle, the recital in a deed or agreement may be looked at in order to ascertain the meaning of the parties, and is often highly important for that purpose;[5] and the general words of a subsequent distinct clause or stipulation may often be explained or qualified by the matter recited.[6] Where, indeed, "the words in the operative part of a deed of conveyance are clear and unambiguous, they cannot be controlled by the recitals or other parts of the deed." But where, on the other hand, "those words are of doubtful meaning, the recitals and other parts of the deed may be used as a test to discover the intention of the parties, and to fix the true meaning of those words."[7] So, covenants are to be construed according to the obvious intention of the parties, as collected from

[1] Coles *v.* Hulme, 8 B. & C. 568 (15 E. C. L. R.); Hobart 275; cited Gale *v.* Reed, 8 East 79.

[2] See Hobart 275; Doe d. Marquis of Bute *v.* Guest, 15 M. & W. 160.

[3] Coles *v.* Hulme, 8 B. & C. 568 (15 E. C. L. R.); and cases cited, Id. 574, n. (*a*).

[4] Napier *v.* Bruce, 8 Cl. & Fin. 470.

[5] Shep. Touch. 76; The Marquis Cholmondeley *v.* Lord Clinton, 2 B. & Ald. 625; s. c., 4 Bligh 1.

[6] Payler *v.* Homersham, 4 M. & S. 423; cited in Harrison *v.* Blackburn, 17 C. B. N. S. 691 (112 E. C. L. R.); Simons *v.* Johnson, 3 B. & Ad. 180 (23 E. C. L. R.); Boyes *v.* Bluck, 13 C. B. 652 (76 E. C. L. R.); Solly *v.* Forbes, 2 B. & B. 38 (6 E. C. L. R.); Charleton *v.* Spencer, 3 Q. B. 693 (43 E. C. L. R.); Sampson *v.* Easterby, 9 B. & C. 505 (17 E. C. L. R.); s. c. (affirmed in error), 1 Cr. & J. 105; Price *v.* Barker, 4 E. & B. 760, 777 (82 E. C. L. R.); Henderson *v.* Stobart, 5 Exch. 99.

[7] Judgm., Walsh *v.* Trevanion, 15 Q. B. 751.

the whole context of the instrument containing them, and according to the reasonable sense of the words; and, in conformity with the rule above laid down, a covenant in large and general terms has [*579] frequently been narrowed and restrained,[1] where *there has appeared something to connect it with a restrictive covenant, or where there have been words in the covenant itself amounting to a qualification;[2] and it has, indeed, been said, in accordance with the above rule, that, "however general the words of a covenant may be, if standing alone, yet, if from other covenants in the same deed it is plainly and irresistibly to be inferred that the party could not have intended to use the words in the general sense which they import, the court will limit the operation of the general words."[3]

We have also already observed, that covenants are to be construed as independent or restrictive of each other, according to the apparent intention of the parties, upon an attentive consideration of the whole deed: every particular case, therefore, must depend upon the precise words used in the instrument before the court, and the distinctions will be found to be nice and difficult.[4]

It is, moreover, as a general proposition, immaterial in what part of a deed any particular covenant is inserted;[5] for the construction of a deed does not depend on the order of the covenants, or upon the precise terms of them; but regard must be had to the object, and the whole scope of the instrument.[6] For instance, in the indenture of lease of a colliery, two lessees covenanted "jointly [*580] and severally in manner following;" and then *followed a number of covenants as to working the colliery; after which was a covenant, that the moneys appearing to be due should be accounted for, and paid by the lessees, their executors, &c., not

[1] Per Lord Ellenborough, C. J., Iggulden *v.* May, 7 East 241; Plowd. 329; Cage *v.* Paxton, 1 Leon. 116; Broughton *v.* Conway, Moor 58; Gale *v.* Reed, 8 East 89; Sicklemore *v.* Thisleton, 6 M. & S. 9, cited, Jowett *v.* Spencer, 15 M. & W. 662; Hesse *v.* Stevenson, 3 B. & P. 365. See Doe *v.* Godwin, 4 M. & S. 265.

[2] Judgm., Smith *v.* Compton, 3 B. & Ad. 200 (23 E. C. L. R.).

[3] Judgm., Hesse *v.* Stevenson, 3 B. & P. 574. See the maxim as to *verba generalia—post.*

[4] 1 Wms. Saund., 6th ed., 60, n. (*l*); *ante*, p. 548.

[5] Per Buller, J., 5 T. R. 526; 1 Wms. Saund. 60, n. (*l*).

[6] Per Wilde, C. J., Richards *v.* Bluck, 6 C. B. 441 (60 E. C. L. R.).

saying, "and each of them;" it was held, that the general words at the beginning of the covenants by the lessees extended to all the subsequent covenants throughout the deed on the part of the lessees, there not being anything in the nature of the subject to restrain the operation of those words in the former part only of the lease.[1]

Again, words may be transposed, if it be necessary to do so in order to give effect to the evident intent of the parties;[2] as, if a lease for years be made in February, rendering a yearly rent payable at Michaelmas-day and Lady-day during the term, the law will make a transposition of the feasts, and read it thus, "at Lady-day and Michaelmas-day," in order that the rent may be paid yearly during the term. And so it is in the case of an annuity.[3] And, although courts of law have no power to alter the words, or to insert words which are not in the deed, yet they may and ought to construe the words in a manner most agreeable to the meaning of the grantor, and may reject any words that are merely insensible.[4] Likewise, if there be two clauses or parts of a deed[5] repugnant the one to the other, the former shall be received, and the latter rejected, unless there be some special reason to the contrary;[6] for instance, in a grant, if words of *restriction are added which are repugnant to the grant, the restrictive words must be rejected.[7] [*581]

It seems, however, to be a true rule, that this rejection of repugnant matter can be made in those cases only where there is a full and intelligible contract left to operate after the repugnant matter is excluded; otherwise, the whole contract, or such parts of it as are defective, will be pronounced void for uncertainty.[8] And as

[1] Duke of Northumberland *v.* Errington, 5 T. R. 522; Copland *v.* Laporte, 3 A. & E. 517 (30 E. C. L. R.).

[2] Parkhurst *v.* Smith, Willes R. 332; s. c., 3 Atk. 135.

[3] Co. Litt. 217 b.

[4] Per Willes, C. J., 3 Atk. 136; s. c., Willes R. 232; Savile 71.

[5] *Secus* of a will, see p. 554, n. 3.

[6] Shep. Touch. 88; Hardr. 94; Walker *v.* Giles, 6 C. B. 662 (60 E. C. L. R.), cited In re Royal Liver Friendly Society, L. R. 5 Ex. 80.

[7] Hobart 172; Mills *v.* Wright, 1 Freem. 247.

[8] 2 Anderson R. 103. In Doe d. Wyndham *v.* Carew, 2 Q. B. 317 (42 E. C. L. R.), a proviso in a lease was held to be insensible. In Youde *v.* Jones, 13 M. & W. 534, an exception introduced into a deed of appointment under a

already observed, "if a deed can operate two ways, one consistent with the intent, and the other repugnant to it, the courts will be ever astute so to construe it, as to give effect to the intent," and the construction must be made on the entire deed.[1]

A marriage settlement recited that it was the intention of the parties to settle a rent-charge or annuity of 1000*l.* per annum on the intended wife, in case she should survive her husband. In the body of the deed the words used were, 1000*l.* sterling lawful money of Ireland." It was held that the words "of Ireland" must be excluded, for the expression could have no meaning unless some of the words were rejected, and it is a rule of law, that, if the first words used would give a meaning, the latter words must be excluded.[2] So, we read that, if one makes a lease for ten years "at the will of the lessor," this is a *good lease for ten years certain, and the last words are void for the repugnancy.[3] And without multiplying examples to a like effect, the result of the authorities seems to be that "when a court of law can clearly collect from the language within the four corners of a deed or instrument in writing the real intention of the parties, they are bound to give effect to it by supplying anything necessarily to be inferred from the terms used, and by rejecting as superfluous whatever is repugnant to the intention so discerned."[4]

[*582]

The principle above stated applies to wills as well as to other instruments, for all the parts of a will are to be construed in relation to each other, and so as, if possible, to form one consistent whole.[5] Speaking with reference to the mode of construing a will, Lord

power was held to be repugnant and void. See also Furnivall *v.* Coombes, 6 Scott N. R. 522; cited in Kelner *v.* Baxter, L. R. 2 C. P. 186; White *v.* Hancock, 2 C. B. 830 (52 E. C. L. R.). In Scott *v.* Avery, 8 Exch. 487; s. c., 5 H. L. Cas. 811, various authorities having reference to repugnant stipulations in contracts are cited.

[1] Per Turner, V.-C., Squire *v.* Ford, 8 Hare 57.

[2] Cope *v.* Cope, 15 Sim. 118.

[3] Bac. Ab., tit. *Leases and Terms for Years*, L. 3, cited and distinguished in Morton *v.* Woods, L. R. 4 Q B. 305.

[4] Per Kelly, C. B., Gwyn *v.* Neath Canal Co., L. R. 3 Ex. 215, where the functions of a court of equity in reforming an instrument are also considered.

[5] Per Lord Eldon, C., Gittins *v.* Steele, 1 Swanst. 28; per Lord Brougham, C., Foley *v.* Parry, 2 My. & K. 138.

Wensleydale thus expressed himself:[1] "Our duty is to ascertain not what the testator may be supposed to have intended, but the meaning of the words he has used, and these we must construe according to their ordinary and grammatical sense, unless some obvious absurdity, or some repugnance or inconsistency with the declared intentions of the writer, to be collected from the whole instrument, followed from it, or, it may be added, some inconsistency with the subject on which the will is meant to operate, and then the sense might be modified so as to avoid those consequences, but no farther."

*Where, however, two clauses or gifts in a will are irreconcilable, so that they cannot possibly stand together, the [*583] clause or gift which is posterior in position shall prevail, the subsequent words being considered to denote a subsequent intention: *Cum duo inter se pugnantia reperiuntur in testamento ultimum ratum est.*[2] It is well settled that where there are two repugnant clauses in a will, the last shall prevail, as being most indicative of the intent,[3] and this results from the general rule of construction; for, unless the principle were recognized of adopting one and rejecting the other of two repugnant clauses, both would be necessarily void, each having the effect of neutralizing and frustrating the other.[4] Therefore, if a testator, in one part of his will, gives to a person an estate of inheritance in land, or an absolute interest in personalty, and in subsequent passages unequivocally shows that he means the devisee or legatee to take a life-interest only, the prior gift is restricted accordingly.[5]

The maxim last mentioned must, however, in its application, be restricted by, and made subservient to, that general principle, which requires that the testator's intention shall, if possible, be ascertained and carried into effect.

"I think it may be taken as clearly established," observed Coleridge, J.,[6] "that this rule must not be acted on so as to clash with

[1] Slingsby *v.* Grainger, 7 H. L. Cas. 284; Abbott *v.* Middleton, Id. 114; Grey *v.* Pearson, 6 H. L. Cas. 106; Baker *v.* Baker, Id. 630; Bullock *v.* Downes, 9 H. L. Cas. 24.

[2] Co. Litt. 112 b.

[3] 16 Johns. (U. S.) R. 546.

[4] 1 Jarm. Wills, 3d ed., 442. Also, words and passages in a will, which cannot be reconciled with the general context, may be rejected: Id. 449.

[5] Id. 442. See also Doe d. Murch *v.* Marchant, 7 Scott N. R. 644.

[6] Morrall *v.* Sutton, 1 Phill. 545, 546. See Greenwood *v.* Sutcliffe, 14 C. B.

another paramount rule, which is, that, before all things, we must look for the [*584] *intention of the testator as we find it expressed or clearly implied in the general tenor of the will; and when we have found that on evidence satisfactory in kind and degree, to that we must sacrifice the inconsistent clause or words, whether standing first or last, indifferently: and this rests upon good reason; for although, when there are repugnant dispositions, and nothing leads clearly to a preference of one, or rejection of the other, convenience is strongly in favor of some rule, however arbitrary; yet the foundation of this rule, as of every other established for the interpretation of wills, obviously is, that it was supposed to be the safest guide, under the circumstances, to the last intention of the testator."

And, in the same case, Parke, B., stated the principal rules applicable to the interpretation of wills to be, "that technical words are *primâ facie* to be understood in their strict technical sense; that the clause is, if possible, to receive a construction which will give to every expression in it some effect, so that none may be rejected; that all the parts of the will are to be construed so as to form a consistent whole; that of two modes of construction, that is to be preferred which would prevent an intestacy; and that where two provisions of a will are totally irreconcilable, so that they cannot possibly stand together, *and there is nothing in the context or general scope of the will which leads to a different conclusion*, the last shall be considered as indicating a subsequent intention, and prevail."[1]

"There are," said Sir J. Leach, "two principles of construction, upon which it appears to me that a court [*585] *may come to a conclusion without the necessity, which, if possible, is always to be avoided, of declaring the will void for uncertainty. First, if the general intention of the testator can be collected upon the whole will, particular terms used which are inconsistent with that intention may be rejected as introduced by mistake or ignorance on the part of the testator as to the force of the words used.

226, 235 (*a*) (78 E. C. L. R.); Plenty *v.* West, 6 C. B. 201, 219 (60 E. C. L. R.).

[1] The two learned judges, whose remarks are cited in the text, differed in the case referred to, but merely as to the *application* of the rule in question.

Secondly, where the latter part of the will is inconsistent with a prior part, the latter part of the will must prevail."[1]

Lastly, it is an established rule, in construing a statute, that the intention of the lawgiver and the meaning of the law are to be ascertained by viewing the whole and every part of the Act. One part of a statute must be so construed by another that the whole may, if possible, stand;[2] and that, if it can be prevented, no clause, sentence, or word shall be superfluous, void or insignificant; and it is a sound general principle, in the exposition of statutes, that less regard is to be paid to the words used than to the policy which dictated the Act; as, if land be vested in the king and his heirs by Act of Parliament, saving the right of A., and A. has at that time a lease of it for three years, in this case A. shall hold it for his term of three years, and afterwards it shall *go to the king; for this interpretation furnishes matter for every clause to work and operate upon.[3] [*586]

Also, if any section be intricate, obscure or doubtful, the proper mode of discovering its true meaning is by comparing it with the other sections, and finding out the sense of one clause by the words or obvious intent of another.[4] This, as Sir E. Coke observes, is the most natural and genuine method of expounding a statute;[5] and it is, therefore, a true principle, that *verba posteriora propter certitudinem addita ad priora quæ certitudine indigent sunt referenda*[6]—refer-

[1] Sherratt *v.* Bentley, 2 My. & K. 157. And see, also, per Lord Brougham, C., Id. 165.

As to construing a will and codicil, *ante*, p. 554, n. 3.

[2] Thus, in Fitzgerald's Case, L. R. 5 Ex. 33, Pigott, B., referring to stat. 15 & 16 Vict. c. 57, says, "We must deal with the Act in the ordinary way, that is, put on it a reasonable construction; and if the words are ambiguous, we must interpret it *ut res magis valeat quàm pereat;*" *ante*, p. 540.

Where the proviso of an Act of Parliament is directly repugnant to the purview, the proviso shall stand and be a repeal of the purview, as it speaks the last intention of the makers: A.-G. *v.* Chelsea Waterworks Co., Fitzgib. 195.

[3] 1 Com. by Broom & Hadley 96, 97; Bac. Abr., "*Statute*" (I. 2); arg. Hine *v.* Reynolds, 2 Scott N. R. 419.

[4] Stowell *v.* Lord Zouch, Plowd. 365; Doe d. Bywater *v.* Brandling, 7 B. & C. 643 (14 E. C. L. R.).

[5] Co. Litt. 381 a.

[6] Wing. Max., p. 167; 8 Rep. 236. See 4 Leon R. 248.

ence should be made to a subsequent section in order to explain a previous clause of which the meaning is doubtful.

We may add, too, that, "Where an Act of Parliament has received a judicial construction, putting a certain meaning on its words, and the legislature in a subsequent Act *in pari materiâ* uses the same words, there is a presumption that the legislature used those words intending to express the meaning which it knew had been put upon the same words before; and unless there is something to rebut that presumption, the Act should be so construed, even if the words were such that they might originally have been construed otherwise."[1]

"It is, in my opinion," observed Mr. Justice Coleridge, in a modern case,[2] "so important for the court, in construing modern [*587] statutes, to act upon the principle of *giving full effect to their language, and of declining to mould that language in order to meet either an alleged inconvenience or an alleged equity, upon doubtful evidence of intention, that nothing will induce me to withdraw a case from the operation of a section which is within its words, but clear and unambiguous evidence that so to do is to fulfill the general intent of the statute, and also, that to adhere to the literal interpretation is to decide inconsistently with other and overruling provisions of the same statute. When the evidence amounts to this, the court may properly act upon it; for the object of all rules of construction being to ascertain the meaning of the language used, and it being unreasonable to impute to the legislature inconsistent intents upon the same general subject-matter, what it has clearly said in one part must be the best evidence of what it has intended to say in the other; and if the clear language be in accordance with the plain policy and purview of the whole statute, there is the strongest reason for believing that the interpretation of a particular part inconsistently with that is a wrong interpretation. The court must apply, in such a case, the same rules which it would use in construing the limitations of a deed; it must look to the whole context, and endeavor to give effect to all the provisions, enlarging or restraining if need be, for that purpose, the literal interpretation of any particular part."

[1] 11 H. L. Cas. 480–1.

[2] R. *v.* The Poor Law Commissioners (St. Pancras), 6 A. & E. 7 (33 E. C. L. R.). See also per Parke, B., Perry *v.* Skinner, 2 M. & W. 476.

*NOSCITUR A SOCIIS. [*588]

(3 T. R. 87.)

The meaning of a word may be ascertained by reference to the meaning of words associated with it.[1]

It is a rule laid down by Lord Bacon, that *copulatio verborum indicat acceptationem in eodem sensu*[2]—the coupling of words together shows that they are to be understood in the same sense. And, where the meaning of any particular word is doubtful or obscure, or where the particular expression when taken singly is inoperative, the intention of the party who has made use of it may frequently be ascertained and carried into effect by looking at the adjoining words, or at expressions occurring in other parts of the same instrument, for *quæ non valeant singula juncta juvant*[3]—words which are ineffective when taken singly operate when taken conjointly; one provision of a deed or other instrument must be construed by the bearing it will have upon another.[4]

It is not proposed to give many examples of the application of the maxim *Noscitur à sociis*, nor to enter at length into a consideration of the very numerous cases which might be cited to illustrate it: it may, in truth, be said to be comprised in those principles which universally obtain, that courts of law and equity will, in construing a *written instrument, endeavor to discover and give effect to the intention of the party, and with a view to [*589] so doing, will examine carefully every portion of the instrument. The maxim is, moreover, applicable, like other rules of grammar, whenever a construction has to be put upon a will, statute or agreement; and although difficulty very frequently arises in applying it,

[1] This, it has been observed, in reference to King *v.* Melling, 1 Vent. 225, was a rule adopted by Lord Hale, and was no pedantic or inconsiderate expression when falling from him, but was intended to convey, in short terms, the grounds upon which he formed his judgments. See 3 T. R. 87; 1 B. & C. 644 (8 E. C. L. R.); arg. 13 East 531. See also Bishop *v.* Elliott, 11 Exch. 113; s. c., 10 Id. 496, 519, which offers an apt illustration of the maxim *supra;* Burt *v.* Haslett, 18 C. B. 162 (86 E. C. L. R.); s. c., Id. 893.

[2] Bac. Works, vol. 4, p. 26.

[3] 2 Bulstr. 132.

[4] Arg. Galley *v.* Barrington, 2 Bing. 391 (9 E. C. L. R.); per Lord Kenyon, C. J., 4 T. R. 227.

yet this results from the particular words used, and from the particular facts existing in each individual case; so that one decision, as to the inference of a person's meaning or intention, can be considered as an express authority to guide a subsequent decision only where the circumstances are similar, and the words are identical or nearly so.

The following instance of the application of the maxim, *Noscitur à sociis*, to a mercantile instrument may be mentioned on account of its importance, and will suffice to show in what manner the principle which it expresses has been made available for the benefit of commerce. The general words inserted in a maritime policy of insurance after the enumeration of particular perils are as follow:—"and of all perils, losses, and misfortunes, that have or shall come to the hurt, detriment, or damage of the said goods and merchandises, and ship, &c., or any part thereof." These words, it has been observed, must be considered as introduced into the policy in furtherance of the objects of marine insurance, and may have the effect of extending a reasonable indemnity to many cases not distinctly covered by the special words: they are entitled to be considered as material and operative words, and to have the due effect assigned to them in the construction of this instrument; and this will be done by allowing them to comprehend and cover other cases of marine damage of the like kind with those which are [*590] *specially enumerated, and occasioned by similar causes; that is to say, the meaning of the general words may be ascertained by referring to the preceding special words.[1]

That the exposition of every will must be founded on the whole instrument, and be made *ex antecedentibus et consequentibus*, is, observes Lord Ellenborough, one of the most prominent canons of testamentary construction; and therefore, in this department of legal investigation, the maxim *Noscitur à sociis* is necessarily of

[1] See Judgm., Cullen *v.* Butler, 5 M. & S. 465; cited in Davidson *v.* Burnand, L. R. 4 C. P. 117, 120 (19 E. C. L. R.); Lozano *v.* Janson, 2 E. & E. 160 (105 E. C. L. R.); Phillips *v.* Barber, 5 B. & Ald. 161 (7 E. C. L. R.); Devaux *v.* J'Anson, 5 B. & C. 519 (11 E. C. L. R.). In Borradaile *v.* Hunter, 5 M. & Gr. 639, 667, this maxim is applied by Tindal, C. J. (*diss.* from the rest of the court), to explain a proviso in a policy of life insurance. In Clift *v.* Schwabe, 3 C. B. 437 (54 E. C. L. R.), the same maxim was likewise applied in similar circumstances; see Dormay *v.* Borradaile, 5 C. B. 380 (57 E. C. L. R.).

very frequent practical application: yet where between the parts there is no connection by grammatical construction, or by some reference, express or implied, and where there is nothing in the will declarative of some common purpose, from which it may be inferred that the testator meant a similar disposition by such different parts, though he may have varied his phrase or expressed himself imperfectly, the court cannot go into one part of a will to determine the meaning of another, perfect in itself, and without ambiguity, and not militating with any other provision respecting the same subject-matter, notwithstanding that a more probable disposition for the testator to have made may be collected from such assisted construction. For instance, if a man should devise generally his lands, after payment of his debts and legacies, his trust[1] estates *would not pass; for, in such case, *Noscitur à sociis* what the land is which the testator intended to pass by such devise: it is clear he could only mean lands which he could subject to the payment of his debts and legacies. But, from a testator having given to persons standing in a certain degree of relationship to him a fee-simple in certain land, no conclusion which can be relied on can be drawn, that his intention was to give to other persons standing in the same rank of proximity the same interest in another part of the same land; and where, moreover, the words of the two devises are different, the more natural conclusion is, that, as the testator's expressions are varied, they were altered because his intention in both cases was not the same.[2]

[*591]

In addition to the preceding remarks, a few instances may here conveniently be referred to, illustrating the distinction between the *conjunctive* and the *disjunctive*, which it is so essential to observe in construing a testamentary instrument.

A leasehold estate for a long term was devised after the death of A., to B. for life, remainder to his child or children by any woman

[1] Roe d. Reade *v.* Reade, 8 T. R. 118; 1 Jarman on Wills, 2d ed., 596.

[2] Judgm., Right *v.* Compton, 9 East 272, 273; 11 East 223; Hay *v.* Earl of Coventry, 3 T. R. 83; per Coltman, J., Knight *v.* Selby, 3 Scott N. R. 409, 417; arg. 1 M. & S. 333 (28 E. C. L. R.). See Sanderson *v.* Dobson, cited *ante*, p. 564; and per Byles, J., Jegon *v.* Vivian, L. R. 1 C. P. 24; s. c., 2 Id. 422, L. R. 3 H. L. 289; Doe d. Haw *v.* Earles, 15 M. & W. 450. See, also, Vandeleur *v.* Vandeleur, 3 Cl. & Fin. 98, where the maxim is differently applied.

whom he should marry, and his or their executors, &c., forever, upon condition, that, in case the said B. should die, "an infant, unmarried, and without issue," the premises should go over to his father and his three other children, share and share alike, and their heirs, executors, &c.:—Held, that the devise over [*592] *depended upon one contingency, viz., B.'s dying an infant, attended with two qualifications, viz., his dying without leaving a wife surviving him, or dying childless; and that the devise over could only take effect in case B. died in his minority, leaving neither wife nor child; and it was observed by Lord Ellenborough, in delivering judgment, that, if the condition had been, "if he dies an infant, *or* unmarried, *or* without issue," that is to say, in the disjunctive throughout, the rule would have applied, *in disjunctivis sufficit alteram partem esse veram;*[1] and, consequently, that if B. had died in his infancy, leaving children, the estate would have gone over to B.'s father and his children, to the prejudice of B.'s own issue.[2] According to the same rule of grammar, also, where a condition inserted in a deed consists of two parts in the conjunctive, both must be performed, but otherwise where the condition is in the disjunctive; and where a condition or limitation is both in the conjunctive and disjunctive, the latter shall be taken to refer to the whole; as, if a lease be made to husband and wife for the term of twenty-one years, "if the husband *and* wife, *or* any child between them shall so long live," and the wife dies without issue, the lease shall, nevertheless, continue during the life of the husband, because the above condition shall be construed throughout in the disjunctive.[3]

In the construction of statutes, likewise, the rule *Noscitur à* [*593] *sociis* is very frequently applied, the meaning *of a word, and, consequently, the intention of the legislature, being ascertained by reference to the context, and by considering whether the word in question and the surrounding words are, in fact, *ejus-*

[1] Co. Litt. 225 a; 10 Rep. 58; Wing. Max., p. 13; D. 50. 17. 110, § 3.

[2] Doe d. Everett *v.* Cooke, 7 East 272; Johnson *v.* Simcock, 7 H. & N. 344; s. c., 6 Id. 6. As to changing the copulative into the disjunctive, see 1 Jarman on Wills, 3d ed., 471, *et seq.*; Mortimer *v.* Hartley, 6 Exch. 47; s. c., 6 C. B. 819 (60 L. C. L. R.); 3 De G. & S. 316.

[3] Co. Litt. 225 a; Shep. Touch. 138, 139. See, also, Burgess *v.* Bracher, 2 Lord Raym. 1366.

dem generis, and referable to the same subject-matter.[1] Especially must it be remembered that "the sages of the law have been used to collect the sense and meaning of the law by comparing one part with another and by viewing all the parts together as one whole, and not of one part only by itself—*nemo enim aliquam partem rectè intelligere possit antequam totum iterum atque iterum perlegerit.*"[2]

As it is, however, needless to cite additional cases for the purpose of illustration, or with a view to explaining the significance of the rule in question, we shall conclude these remarks with observing, that the three rules or canons of construction with which we have commenced this chapter are intimately connected together,—that they should, perhaps, in strictness, rather have been considered under one head than treated separately,—and that they must always be kept in view collectively when the practitioner applies himself to the interpretation of a doubtful instrument.

---

*VERBA CHARTARUM FORTIUS*ACCIPIUNTUR CONTRA PROFERENTUM. [*594]

(Co. Litt. 36 a.)

The words of an instrument shall be taken most strongly against the party employing them.

"The prevailing rule is, that the words of a contract must be construed most strongly against the contractor,"[3] a rule "which, however, ought to be applied only where other rules of construction fail."[4]

[1] Per Coleridge, J., Cooper *v.* Harding, 7 Q. B. 941 (53 E. C. L. R.); Judgm., Stephens *v.* Taprell, 2 Curt. 465; per Channell, B., Pearson *v.* Hull Local Board of Health, 3 H. & C. 944.

The maxim *supra* was applied to construe a statute in Hardy *v.* Tingey, 5 Exch. 294, 298—to ascertain the meaning of libellous words in Wakeley *v.* Cooke, 4 Exch. 511, 519.

[2] Arg. 7 Howard (U. S.) R. 637, citing Lincoln College Case, 3 Rep. 596.

[3] Per Channell, B., Bastifell *v.* Lloyd, 1 H. & C. 395.

[4] Judgm., Lindus *v.* Melrose, 3 H. & N. 182; approved in Alexander *v.* Sizer, L. R. 4 Ex. 102, 106.

Accordingly, the words in a deed are to be construed most strongly *contra proferentum*—regard being had, however, to the apparent intention of the parties, as collected from the whole context of the instrument;[1] for, as observed by Sir W. Blackstone, the principle of self-preservation will make men sufficiently careful not to prejudice their own interest by the too extensive meaning of their words, and hereby all manner of deceit in any grant is avoided; for men would always affect ambiguous and intricate expressions, provided they were afterwards at liberty to put their own construction upon them.[2] Moreover, the adoption of this rule puts an end to many questions and doubts which would otherwise arise as to the meaning and intention of the parties, which, in the absence of it, might be differently construed by different [*595] *judges; and it tends to quiet possession, by taking acts and conveyances executed beneficially for the grantees and possessors.[3]

We may remark, also, that the general rule above stated has been held to apply still more strongly to a deed-poll[4] than to an indenture, because in the former case the words are those of the grantor only.[5] But though a deed-poll is to be construed against the grantor, the court will not add words to it, nor give it a meaning contradictory to its language.[6]

If, then, a tenant in fee simple grants to any one an estate for life generally, this shall be construed to mean an estate for the life of the grantee, because an estate for a man's own life is higher than for the life of another;[7] and a grant is, in the absence of any clear indication of the intention of the parties, to be construed

[1] Per Lord Kenyon, C. J., Barrett *v.* Duke of Bedford, 8 T. R. 605; per Lord Eldon, C. J., 2 B. & P. 22; per Bayley, J., 15 East 546; per Park, J., 1 B. & B. 335 (5 E. C. L. R.); Miller *v.* Mainwaring, Cro. Car. 400; 3 Ves. jun. 48; Co. Litt. 183 a; Noy, Max., 9th ed., p. 48.

[2] 2 Bla. Com., 21st ed., 380. See Saunderson *v.* Piper, 5 Bing. N. C. 425 (35 E. C. L. R.); Reynolds *v.* Barford, 8 Scott N. R. 238, 239; per Pollock, C. B., and Parke, B., Ashworth *v.* Mounsey, 9 Exch. 186, 187; Rodger *v.* The Comptoir d'Escompte de Paris, L. R. 2 P. C. 393.

[3] Bac. Max., reg. 3, which treats of the general rule.

[4] See stats. 8 & 9 Vict. c. 106, s. 5; 7 & 8 Vict. c. 76, s. 11.

[5] Plowd. 134; Shep. Touch., by Preston, 88, n. (81).

[6] Per Williams, J., Doe d. Myatt *v.* St. Helens R. C., 2 Q. B. 373 (43 E. C. L. R.).

[7] Co. Litt. 42 a; Plowd. 156; Finch's Law 63; Shep. Touch. 88.

most strongly against the grantor,[1] and "as favorably as possible for the grantee."[2]

But if tenant for life leases to another for life, without specifying for whose life, this shall be taken to be a lease for the lessor's own life; for this is the greatest estate which it is in his power to grant.[3] And, as a general rule, it appears clear, that, if a doubt arise as to the construction of a lease between the lessor and lessee, the lease must be construed most beneficially for the latter.[4]

*In like manner, if two tenants in common grant a rent of 10*s*., this is several, and the grantee shall have 10*s*. [*596] from each; but if they make a lease, and reserve 10*s*., they shall have only 10*s*. between them.[5] So, it is a true canon of construction, that where there is any reasonable degree of doubt as to the meaning of an exception in a lease, the words of the exception, being the words of the lessor, are to be taken most favorably for the lessee, and against the lessor;[6] and where a deed may enure to divers purposes, he to whom the deed is made shall have election which way to take it, and he shall take it in that way which shall be most to his advantage.[7] But it seems that the instrument should, in such a case, if pleaded, be stated according to its legal effect, in that way in which it is intended to have it operate.[8] The general rule, however, being that "in pleading (except in deducing title) a deed may be set out either in its terms, leaving the court to construe it according to the legal effect of those terms, or the party may take the responsibility of stating it according to the legal effect which it is contended to have."[9]

According to the principle above laid down, it was held, that leasehold lands passed by the conveyance of the freehold, "and all

[1] Per Willes, J., Williams *v.* James, L. R. 2 C. P. 581; *secus* as to a grant from the crown, *post*, p. 607.

[2] Per Wilde, C. J., Re Stroud, 8 C. B. 529 (65 E. C. L. R.).

[3] Finch's Law 55, 56. See also Id. 60.

[4] Dunn *v.* Spurrier, 3 B. & P. 399, 403, where various authorities are cited. See also Judgm., 1 Cr. & M. 657.

[5] 5 Rep. 7; Plowd. 140; Co. Litt. 197 a, 267 b.

[6] Per Bayley, J., Bullen *v.* Denning, 5 B. & C. 847 (11 E. C. L. R.).

[7] Shep. Touch. 83; cited, 8 Bing. 106 (21 E. C. L. R.).

[8] 2 Smith L. C., 6th ed., 479, and cases there cited.

[9] Judgm., Lord Newborough *v.* Schröder, 7 C. B. 397 (62 E. C. L. R.); Price *v.* Williams, 1 M. & W. 6, 14.

lands or meadows to the said messuage or mill belonging, or used, occupied, and enjoyed, or deemed, taken or accepted as part thereof." "This," said Lord Loughborough, C. J., "being a case arising on a deed, [*597] *is to be distinguished from cases of a like nature which have arisen on wills. In general, where there is a question on the construction of a will, neither party has done anything to preclude himself from the favor of the court. But, in the present instance, the legal maxim applies, that *a deed shall be construed most strongly against the grantor.*[1]

The rule of law, moreover, that a man's own act shall be taken most strongly against himself, not only obtains in grants, but extends, in principle, to other engagements and undertakings.[2]

Thus, the return to a writ of *fi. fa.* shall, if the meaning be doubtful, be construed against the sheriff; nor, if sued for a false return, shall he be allowed to defend himself by putting a construction on his own return which would make it bad, when it admits of another construction which will make it good.[3]

In like manner, with respect to contracts not under seal, the generally received doctrine of law undoubtedly is, that the party who makes any instrument should take care so to express the amount of his own liability, as that he may not be bound further than it was his intention that he should be bound; and, on the other hand, that the party who receives the instrument, and parts with his goods on the faith of it, should rather have a construction [*598] *put upon it in his favor, because the words of the instrument are not his, but those of the other party.[4] This principle applies to a condition in a policy of insurance which "being the language of the

[1] Doe d. Davies *v.* Williams, 1 H. Bla. 25, 27.

[2] 1 H. Bla. 586.

A release in deed, being the act of the party, shall be taken most strongly against himself: Co. Litt. 264 b; cited Judgm., Lord *v.* Beech, 11 Q. B. 869 (63 E. C. L. R.).

"Although the words of a covenant are to be construed according to the intent of the parties, yet they are to be taken most strongly against the party who stipulates:" per Holroyd, J., Webb *v.* Plummer, 2 B. & Ald. 752. See West London R. C. *v.* London and North-Western R. C., 11 C. B. 254, 309, 339 (73 E. C. L. R.).

[3] See Reynolds *v.* Barford, 7 M. & Gr. 449, 456 (49 E. C. L. R.).

[4] Per Alderson, B., Mayer *v.* Isaac, 6 M. & W. 612; commenting on the observations of Bayley, B., in Nicholson *v.* Paget, 1 Cr. & M. 48. See Alder *v.* Boyle, 4 C. B. 635 (56 E. C. L. R.).

company must, if there be any ambiguity in it, be taken most strongly against them."[1]

If the party giving a guarantee leaves anything ambiguous in his expressions, it has been said that such ambiguity must be taken most strongly against himself;[2] though it would rather seem that the document in question is to be construed according to the intention of the parties to it as expressed by the language which they have employed, understood fairly in the sense in which it is used, the intention being, if needful, ascertained by looking to the relative position of the parties at the time when the instrument was written.[3]

If a carrier gives two different notices, limiting his responsibility in case of loss, he will be bound by that which is least beneficial to himself.[4] In like manner, where a party made a contract of sale as agent for A., and, on the face of such agreement, stated, that he made the purchase, paid the deposit, and agreed to comply with the conditions *of sale, for A., and in the mere character of agent, it was held that this act of the contracting party [*599] must be taken *fortissimè contra proferentem;* and that he could not, therefore, sue as principal on the agreement, without notice to the defendant before action brought, that he was the party really interested.[5] So, if an instrument be couched in terms so ambiguous as to make it doubtful whether it be a bill of exchange or promissory note, the holder may, as against the party who made the instrument, treat it as either.[6]

[1] Per Cockburn, C. J., Notman *v.* Anchor Ass. Co., 4 C. B. N. S. 481 (93 E. C. L. R.); Fitton *v.* Accidental Death Insur. Co., 17 C. B. N. S. 134, 135 (112 E. C. L. R.); Fowkes *v.* Manchester and London Life Ass. Co., 32 L. J. Q. B. 153, 157, 159; per Lord St. Leonards, Anderson *v.* Fitzgerald, 4 H. L. Cas. 484; per Blackburn, J., Braunstein *v.* Accidental Death Insur. Co., 1 B. & S. 799 (101 E. C. L. R.).

[2] Hargreave *v.* Smee, 6 Bing. 244, 248; Stephens *v.* Pell, 2 Cr. & M. 710. See Cumpston *v.* Haigh, 2 Bing. N. C. 449, 454 (29 E. C. L. R.).

[3] Per Bovill, C. J., Coles *v.* Pack, L. R. 5 C. P. 70; Wood *v.* Priestner, L. R. 2 Ex. 66, 282.

[4] Munn *v.* Baker, 2 Stark. N. P. C. 255 (2 E. C. L. R.). See Phillips *v.* Edwards, 3 H. & N. 813, 820.

[5] Bickerton *v.* Burrell, 5 M. & S. 383, 386, as to which case, see Rayner *v.* Grote, 15 M. & W. 359. See also Boulton *v.* Jones, 2 H. & N. 564, and cases there cited; Carr *v.* Jackson, 7 Exch. 382.

[6] Edis *v.* Bury, 6 B. & C. 433 (13 E. C. L. R.); Black *v.* Bell, 1 M. & Rob.

In the Roman law, the rule under consideration for the construction of contracts may be said, in substance, to have existed, although its meaning differed considerably from that which attaches to it in our own: the rule there was, *Fere secundum promissorem interpretamur*,[1] where *promissor*, in fact, signified the person who contracted the obligation,[2] that is, who replied to the *stipulatio* proposed by the other contracting party. In case of doubt, then, the clause in the contract thus offered and accepted was interpreted against the *stipulator*, and in favor of the *promissor; in stipulationibus cùm quœritur quid actum sit verba contra stipulatorem interpretanda sunt;*[3] and the reason given for this mode of construction is *quia stipulatori liberum fuit verba late concipere:*[4] the [*600] person stipulating should *take care fully to express that which he proposes shall be done for his own benefit. But, as remarked by Mr. Chancellor Kent, the true principle appears to be "to give the contract the sense in which the person making the promise believed the other party to have accepted it, if he in fact did so understand and accept it;"[5] though this remark must necessarily be understood as applicable only where an ambiguity exists after applying those various and stringent rules of interpretation by which the meaning of a passage must, in very many cases, be determined. When dealing with a *mercantile* instrument, moreover, "the courts are not restrained to such nicety of construction as is the case with regard to conveyances, pleadings, and the like;" and in reference to a charter-party, it has been observed,[6] that "generally speaking, where there are several ways in which the contract might be performed, that mode is adopted which is the least profitable to the plaintiff and the least burthensome to the defendant." Further, in reference to the same instrument, it has been remarked

149; Lloyd *v.* Oliver, 18 Q. B. 471 (83 E. C. L. R.); Forbes *v.* Marshall, 11 Exch. 166.

In M'Call *v.* Taylor, 19 C. B. N. S. 301 (115 E. C. L. R.), the instrument in question was held to be neither a bill of exchange nor a promissory note.

[1] D. 45. 1. 99. pr.

[2] Brisson. *ad verb.* "*Promissor*," "*Stipulatio;*" 1 Pothier, by Evans, 58.

[3] D. 45. 1. 38, § 18.

[4] D. 45. 1. 99. pr.; D. 2. 14. 39.

[5] 2 Kent Com., 7th ed., 721; 20 Conn. (U. S.) R. 281; Paley Moral Phil., 4th ed., 125, 127; 1 Duer Insur. 159, 160.

[6] Per Maule, J., Cockburn *v.* Alexander, 6 C. B. 814 (60 E. C. L. R.), and in Gether *v.* Capper, 15 C. B. 707 (80 E. C. L. R.); s. c., 18 Id. 866.

that the merchant "is in most cases the party best acquainted with the trade for which the ship is taken up, and with the difficulties which may impede the performance by him of his contract; words, therefore, in a charter-party relaxing in his favor a clause by which an allowance to him of time for a specified object is in the interest of the ship precisely limited, must be read as inserted on his requirement, and construed at the least with this degree of strictness against him, that they shall not have put upon them an addition to their *obvious meaning;" though where that meaning is ambiguous it must be gathered from the surrounding circumstances to which the charter-party was intended to apply.[1] [*601]

Further, where in pleading two different meanings present themselves, that construction shall be adopted which is most unfavorable to the party pleading:[2] *ambiguum placitum interpretari debet contra proferentem;*[3] for every man is presumed to make the best of his own case,[4] and it is incumbent on him to make his meaning clear.[5] Though it is also a general rule that "every pleading, if it be fairly susceptible of such a construction, must, as against the party pleading, be taken to have been pleaded agreeably to the rules of pleading; and it is not open to him to contend that he has ill pleaded. It would be opening a wide door to fraud and trickery if this were otherwise."[6] Nor does the maxim just cited apply to the pleading of matters which are peculiarly within the knowledge of the opposite party.[7]

It has indeed frequently been laid down that ambiguity is cured by pleading over; and that at subsequent stages of the cause, that

[1] Judgm., Hudson *v.* Ede, L. R. 2 Q. B. 578.

[2] Steph. Plead., 6th ed., 310; Bac. Max., reg. 3. "It is a maxim in the construction of pleadings that everything shall be taken most strongly against the pleader:" per Coleridge, J., Howard *v.* Gosset, 10 Q. B. 383 (59 E. C. L. R.); per Buller, J., Doveston *v.* Payne, 2 H. Bla. 531; per Parke, B., Dendy *v.* Powell, 3 M. & W. 444.

[3] If a plaintiff feels embarrassed by the mode in which a plea is framed, he may apply to a judge at chambers to rectify it. See, for instance, Brooks *v.* Jennings, L. R. 1 C. P. 476, 480.

[4] Co. Litt. 303 b; Hobart 242; Finch's Law 64.

[5] Per Pollock, C. B., Goldham *v.* Edwards, 18 C. B. 399 (86 E. C. L. R.).

[6] Per Wilde, C. J., Moore *v.* Forster, 5 C. B. 224.

[7] Judgm., Murphy *v.* Glass, L. R. 2 P. C. 419, citing Hobson *v.* Middleton, 6 B. & C. 302 (13 E. C. L. R.).

[*602] construction of the ambiguous expression *must be adopted which is most favorable to the party by whom it was used.[1] "If," said Maule, J., "the language of the declaration is ambiguous, and the defendant pleads over, it must, if capable of such a construction, be taken in a sense that will require an answer."[2] And, as remarked by Lord Truro,[3] "it is a clear rule of law that if a declaration contains allegations capable of being understood in two senses, and if understood in one sense it will sustain the action, and in another it will not; after verdict, it must be construed in the sense which will sustain the action." It has, however, been observed that "there is no distinction in the mode of construing a plea, whether it comes before the court upon a motion for judgment *non obstante veredicto*, or upon a demurrer."[4] In either case the plea is to receive a fair and reasonable construction; and we may add, that, in construing a plea, it ought to be read like any other composition, and that no violent or forced construction ought to be made beyond the ordinary and fair meaning of the words employed, either to support or to invalidate it.[5]

It has also been laid down as a rule in equity pleading, that "The presumption is always against the pleader, because the plaintiff is presumed to state his case in the most favorable way for [*603] himself; and, therefore, if he has *left anything material to his case in doubt, it is assumed to be in favor of the other party;"[6] though the rule that an ambiguous pleading is to be construed *contra proferentem* is subject to an exception already

[1] Fletcher *v.* Pogson, 3 B. & C. 192, 194 (10 E. C. L. R.); Lord Huntingtower *v.* Gardner, 1 B. & C. 297 (8 E. C. L. R.); 10 C. B. 182 (70 E. C. L. R.) (*a*); per Parke, B., Norman *v.* Thompson, 4 Exch. 750; Smith *v.* Keating, 6 C. B. 152 (60 E. C. L. R.); per Williams, J., 5 C. B. 271 (57 E. C. L. R.); per Jervis, C. J., 13 Id. 551.

[2] Boydell *v.* Harkness, 3 C. B. 171, 172 (54 E. C. L. R.); citing Hobson *v.* Middleton, 6 B. & C. 302 (13 E. C. L. R.); Judgm., Bevins *v.* Hulme, 15 M. & W. 97.

[3] Emmens *v.* Elderton, 13 C. B. 542 (76 E. C. L. R.).

[4] Per Pollock, C. B., Goldham *v.* Edwards, 18 C. B. 399 (86 E. C. L. R.); arg. Goldham *v.* Edwards, 17 C. B. 143 (84 E. C. L. R.).

[5] Judgm., Hughes *v.* Done, 1 Q. B. 640 (41 E. C. L. R.); and cases cited *supra*.

[6] Per Lord Cottenham, C., Columbine *v.* Chichester, 2 Phill. 28; and in A.-G. *v.* Mayor of Norwich, 2 My. & Cr. 422, 423; Vernon *v.* Vernon, Id. 145; Bowes *v.* Fernie, 2 My. & Cr. 632.

noticed, and does not apply to the pleading of matters which are peculiarly within the knowledge of the other party.[1]

It must further be observed, that the general rule in question, being one of some strictness and rigor, is the last to be resorted to, and is never to be relied upon but when all other rules of exposition fail.[2] In some cases, indeed, it is possible that any construction which the court may adopt will be contrary to the real meaning of the parties; and, if parties make use of such uncertain terms in their contracts, the safest way is to go by the grammatical construction, and if the sense of the words be *in equilibrio*, then the strict rule of law must be applied.[3]

Moreover, the principle of taking words *fortius contra proferentem* does not seem to hold when a harsh construction would work a wrong to a third person, it being a maxim that *Constructio legis non facit injuriam*.[4] Therefore, if tenant in tail make a lease for life generally, this shall be taken to mean a lease for the life of the lessor,[5] for this stands well with the law; and not for *the life of the lessee, which it is beyond the power of a tenant in tail to grant.[6] [*604]

Acts of Parliament are not, in general, within the reason of the rule under consideration, because they are not the words of *parties*, but of the legislature; neither does this rule apply to wills.[7] Where, however, an Act of Parliament is passed for the benefit of a canal, railway, or other company, it has been observed, that this, like many other cases, is a bargain between a company of adventurers and the public, the terms of which are expressed and set forth in the Act, and the rule of construction[8] in all such cases is

[1] Judgm., Murphy *v.* Glass, L. R. 2 P. C. 419.

[2] Bac. Max., reg. 3; 1 Duer Insur. 210.

[3] Per Bayley, J., Love *v.* Pares, 13 East 86.

[4] Co. Litt. 183 a; Shep. Touch. 88; Judgm., Rodger *v.* The Comptoir d'Escompte de Paris, L. R. 2 P. C. 406.

[5] Per Bayley, J., Smith *v.* Doe d. Earl of Jersey, 2 B. & B. 551 (6 E. C. L. R.); Finch Law 60.

[6] 2 Com. by Broom & Hadley 507.

[7] 2 Dwarr. Stats. 688; Bac. Max., reg. 3.

[8] The rule that a private Act of Parliament "is to be construed as a contract or a conveyance, is a mere rule of construction;" per Byles, J., 6 C. B. N. S. 218-9 (95 E. C. L. R.). As to the recitals in a private Act, see The Shrewsbury Peerage, 7 H. L. Cas. 1.

now fully established to be, that any ambiguity in the terms of the contract must operate against the adventurers, and in favor of the public, the former being entitled to claim nothing which is not *clearly* given to them by the Act.[1] Where, therefore, by such an Act of Parliament, rates are imposed upon the public and for the benefit of the company, [*605] *such rates must be considered as a tax upon the subject; and it is a sound general rule, that a tax shall not be considered to be imposed (or at least not for the benefit of a subject) without a plain declaration of the intent of the legislature to impose it.[2]

In a well-known case, which is usually cited as an authority with reference to the construction of Acts for the formation of companies with a view to carrying works of a public nature into execution, the law was thus laid down by Lord Eldon:—"When I look upon these Acts of Parliament, I regard them all in the light of contracts made by the legislature on behalf of every person interested in anything to be done under them; and I have no hesitation in asserting, that, unless that principle is applied in construing statutes of this description, they become instruments of greater oppression than anything in the whole system of administration under our constitution. Such Acts of Parliament have now become extremely numerous, and from their number and operation they so much affect individuals, that I apprehend those who come for them to Parliament do in effect undertake that they shall do and submit to whatever the legislature empowers and compels them to do, and

[1] Per Lord Tenterden, C. J., Stourbridge Canal Co. *v.* Wheeley, 2 B. & Ad. 793 (22 E. C. L. R.); recognized Priestley *v.* Foulds, 2 Scott N. R. 228; per Coltman, J., Id. 226; cited arg. Id. 738; Judgm., Gildart *v.* Gladstone, 11 East 685; recognized, Barrett *v.* Stockton and Darlington R. C., 2 Scott N. R. 370; s. c., affirmed in error, 3 Scott N. R. 803; and in the House of Lords, 8 Scott N. R. 641; cited Ribble Navigation Co. *v.* Hargreaves, 17 C. B. 385, 402 (84 E. C. L. R.); per Maule, J., Portsmouth Floating Bridge Co. *v.* Nance, 6 Scott N. R. 831; Blakemore *v.* Glamorganshire Canal Nav., 1 My. & K. 165 (as to the remarks of Lord Eldon in which case, see per Alderson, B., Lee *v.* Milner, 2 Yo. & C. 618; per Lord Chelmsford, C., Ware *v.* Regent's Canal Co., 28 L. J. Chanc. 157; per Erle, C. J., Baxendale *v.* Great Western R. C., 16 C. B. N. S. 137 (111 E. C. L. R.)); arg. Thicknesse *v.* Lancaster Canal Co., 4 M. & W. 482; *ante*, p. 5, *et seq.*

[2] Judgm., Kingston-upon-Hull Dock Co. *v.* Browne, 2 B. & Ad. 58, 59 (22 E. C. L. R.); Grantham Canal Nav. Co. *v.* Hall (in error), 14 M. & W. 880; *ante*, pp. 570, 571.

that they shall do nothing else; that they shall do and shall forbear all that they are thereby required to do and to forbear, as well with reference to the interests of the public as with reference to the interests of individuals."[1] Acts of Parliament, such as here referred to,[2] have been *called "Parliamentary bargains made with each of the landowners. Perhaps more correctly they [*606] ought to be treated as conditional powers given by Parliament to take the land of the different proprietors through whose estates the works are to proceed. Each landowner, therefore, has a right to have the powers strictly and literally carried into effect as regards his own lands, and has a right also to require that no variation shall be made to his prejudice in the carrying into effect the bargain between the undertakers and any one else."[3]

So, with respect to Railway Acts, it has been repeatedly laid down, that the language of these Acts of Parliament is to be treated as the language of the promoters of them; they ask the legislature to confer great privileges upon them, and profess to give the public certain advantages in return. Acts passed under such circumstances should be construed strictly against the parties obtaining them, but liberally in favor of the public.[4] "The statute," says Alderson, B.,[5] speaking of a railway company's Act, "gives this company power to take a man's land without any conveyance at all; for if they cannot find out who can make a conveyance to them, or if he refuses to convey, or if he fail to make out a title, they may pay their money into Chancery, and the land is at once vested in them by a parliamentary title. But in order to enable them to exercise this power, they must *follow the words of the Act strictly*." And it is clear that the words of a *statute will not be strained beyond their reasonable import to impose [*607] a burthen upon, or to restrict the operation of, a public company.[6]

[1] Blakemore *v.* Glamorganshire Canal Nav., 1 My. & K. 162; cited Judgm., 1 E. & B. 868, 869 (72 E. C. L. R.).

[2] See also *supra* 603, n. 8; 604, n. 1.

[3] Per Alderson, B., Lee *v.* Milner, 2 Yo. & C. 611, 618; adopted Judgm., York and North Midland R. C. *v.* Reg., 1 E. & B. 869 (72 E. C. L. R.).

[4] Judgm., Parker *v.* Great Western R. C., 7 Scott N. R. 870.

[5] Doe d. Hutchinson *v.* Manchester, Bury and Rosendale R. C., 14 M. & W. 694; Webb *v.* Manchester and Leeds R. C., 1 Railw. Cas. 576, 599; per Lord Langdale, M. R., Gray *v.* Liverpool and Bury R. C., 4 Id. 240.

[6] Smith *v.* Bell, 2 Railw. Cas. 877; Parrett Nav. Co. *v.* Robins, 3 Id. 383; with which *acc.* Cracknell *v.* Mayor, &c., of Thetford, L. R. 4 C. P. 634, 637.

It will, of course, be borne in mind that the general principle of construing an Act of Parliament of the kind above alluded to *contra proferentem*, can only be applied where a doubt presents itself as to the meaning of the legislature; for such an Act, and every part of it, must be read according to the ordinary and grammatical sense of the words used, and with reference to those established rules of construction which we have already stated.

Lastly with reference to the maxim *fortius contra proferentem*, —where a question arises on the construction of a grant from the crown, the rule under consideration is reversed; for such grant is construed most strictly against the grantee, and most beneficially for the crown, so that nothing will pass to the grantee but by clear and express words;[1] the method of construction just stated seeming, as judicially remarked,[2] "to exclude the application of either of these two phrases,[3] *expressum facit cessare tacitum*, or *expressio unius est exclusio alterius*. That which the crown has not granted by express, clear and unambiguous terms, the subject has no right to claim under a grant or charter."[4]

[1] Arg. R. *v.* Mayor, &c., of London, 1 Cr., M. & R. 12, 15, and cases there cited; Chit. Pre. of the Crown 391; Finch's Law 101.

[2] Per Pollock, C. B., Eastern Archipelago Co. *v.* Reg., 2 E. & B. 906, 907 (75 E. C. L. R.); s. c., Id. 310.

[3] *Post*, p. 651.

[4] "It is established on the best authority, that in construing grants from the crown, a different rule of construction prevails from that by which grants from one subject to another are to be construed. In a grant from one subject to another, every intendment is to be made against the grantor, and in favor of the grantee, in order to give full effect to the grant; but in grants from the crown an opposite rule of construction prevails. Nothing passes except that which is expressed, or which is matter of necessary and unavoidable intendment, in order to give effect to the plain and undoubted intention of the grant. And in no species of grant does this rule of construction more especially obtain than in grants which emanate from, and operate in derogation of, the prerogative of the crown:" *ex. gr.* where a monopoly is granted. Judgm., Feather *v.* Reg., 6 B. & S. 283–4 (118 E. C. L. R.); citing, per Lord Stowell, The Rebekah, 1 Rob. 227, 230.

*AMBIGUITAS VERBORUM LATENS VERIFICATIONE SUPPLETUR; NAM QUOD EX FACTO ORITUR AMBIGUUM VERIFICATIONE FACTI TOLLITUR. [*608]

(Bac. Max., reg. 23.)

Latent ambiguity may be supplied by evidence; for an ambiguity which arises by proof of an extrinsic fact may, in the same manner, be removed.

Two kinds of ambiguity occur in written instruments: the one is called *ambiguitas latens*,[1] *i. e.*, where the writing appears on the face of it certain and free from ambiguity, but the ambiguity is introduced by evidence of something extrinsic, or by some collateral matter out of the instrument: the other species is called *ambiguitas patens*, *i. e.*, an ambiguity apparent on the face of the instrument itself.[2]

Ambiguitas patens, says Lord Bacon, cannot be holpen by averment, and the reason is, because the law will not couple and mingle matter of specialty, which is of the *higher account, [*609] with matter of averment, which is of the lower account in law, for that were to make all deeds hollow, and subject to averment; and so, in effect, to make that pass without deed which the law appoints shall not pass but by deed;[3] and this rule, as above stated and explained, applies not only to deeds, but to written contracts in general;[4] and especially, as will be seen by the examples immediately following, to wills.

[1] Of which see an example, Raffles *v.* Wichelhaus, 2 H. & C. 906.

[2] Bac. Max., reg. 23. The remarks respecting ambiguity here offered should be taken in connection with those appended to the five maxims which successively follow. The subject of latent and patent ambiguities, and likewise of misdescription, has been very briefly treated in the text, since ample information thereupon may be obtained by reference to the masterly treatise of Sir James Wigram, upon the "Admission of Extrinsic Evidence in Aid of the Interpretation of Wills."

[3] Bac. Max., reg. 23; Doe d. Tyrrell *v.* Lyford, 4 M. & S. 550; Lord Cholmondeley *v.* Lord Clinton, 2 Mer. 343; Judgm., Doe d. Gord *v.* Needs, 2 M. & W. 139; S. P., Stead *v.* Berrier, Sir T. Raym. 411.

[4] See Hollier *v.* Eyre, 9 Cl. & Fin. 1.

"A contract," observes Pollock, C. B., in Nichol *v.* Godts, 10 Exch. 194, "must be read according to what is written by the parties, for it is a well-known principle of law, that a written contract cannot be altered by parol. If A. and B. make a contract in writing, evidence is not admissible to show that A. meant something different from what is stated in the contract itself,

On this principle, a devise to "one of the sons of J. S." (who has several sons) cannot be explained by parol proof;[1] and if there be a blank in the will for the devisee's name, parol evidence cannot be admitted to show what person's name the testator intended to insert;[2] it being an important rule, that, in expounding a will, the court is to ascertain, not what the testator actually intended as contradistinguished from what his words express, but what is the meaning of the words he has used.[3]

[*610] *If, as observed by Sir James Wigram, the Statute of Frauds merely had required that a nuncupative will should not be set up in opposition to a written will, parol evidence might, in many cases, be admissible to explain the intention of the testator, where the person or thing intended by him is not adequately described in the will; but if the true meaning of that statute be, that the writing which it requires shall itself express the intention of the testator, it is difficult to understand how the statute can be satisfied by a writing merely, if the description it contains have nothing *in common with* that of the person intended to take under it, or not enough to determine his identity. To define that which is indefinite is to make a material addition to the will.[4] In accordance with these observations, where a testator devised his real estates "first to K., then to ——, then to L., then to M., &c.," and the will referred to a card as showing the parties designated by the letters in the will, which card, however, was not shown to have been in existence at the time of the execution of the will, it was held clearly inadmissible in evidence; the court observing, that this was a case of a patent ambiguity; and that, according to all the authorities on

and that B. at the time assented to it. If that sort of evidence were admitted, every written document would be at the mercy of witnesses who might be called to swear anything." See Besant *v.* Cross, 10 C. B. 895 (70 E. C. L. R.); Martin *v.* Pycroft, 2 De G., M. & G. 785; *post*, Chap. X.

[1] Strode *v.* Russell, 2 Vern. 624; Cheyney's Case, 5 Rep. 68. See Castledon *v.* Turner, 3 Atk. 257; Harris *v.* Bishop of Lincoln, 2 P. Wms. 136, 137; per Tindal, C. J., Doe d. Winter *v.* Perratt, 7 Scott N. R. 36. See also, per Littledale, J., and Parke, J., in Shortrede *v.* Cheek, 1 A. & E. 57 (28 E. C. L. R.).

[2] Baylis *v.* A.-G., 2 Atk. 239; Hunt *v.* Hort, 3 Bro. C. C. 311; cited, 8 Bing. 254 (21 E. C. L. R.).

[3] Per Parke, J., Doe d. Gwillim *v.* Gwillim, 5 B. & Ad. 129 (27 E. C. L. R.).

[4] See Wigram, Extrin. Evid., 3d ed., 120, 121.

the subject, parol evidence to explain the meaning of the will could not legally be admitted.[1]

If, then, as further observed in the treatise already cited, a testator's words, aided by the light derived from the circumstances with reference to which they were used, do not express the intention ascribed to him, evidence to prove the sense in which he intended to use them is, *as a general proposition, inadmissible; in other words, the judgment of a court in expounding a will must be simply declaratory of what is in the will;[2] and to make a construction of a will where the intent of the testator cannot be known has been designated as *intentio cæca et sicca*.[3] [*611]

The devise, therefore, in cases falling within the scope of the above observation, will, since the will is *insensible* and not really *expressive of any intention*, be void for uncertainty.[4]

The rule as to patent ambiguities which we have just been considering is by no means confined in its operation to the interpretation of wills; for instance, where a bill of exchange was expressed in figures to be drawn for 245*l*., and in words for two hundred pounds, value received, with a stamp applicable to the higher amount, evidence to show that the words "and forty-five" had been omitted by mistake was held inadmissible;[5] for, the doubt being on the face of the instrument, extrinsic evidence could not be received to explain it. The instrument, however, was held to be a good bill for the smaller amount, it being a rule laid down by commercial writers, that, where a difference appears between the figures and the words of a bill, it is safer to attend to the words.[6] But, although a patent ambiguity cannot be explained by extrinsic evidence, it may, in some cases, be helped by *construction, or a careful comparison of other portions of the instrument with that particular part in which the ambiguity arises; and in others, it may be helped by a right of election vested in the grantee [*612]

[1] Clayton *v.* Lord Nugent, 13 M. & W. 200.

[2] Wigram, Extrin. Evid., 3d ed., 87th and following pages, in which many instances of the application of this rule are given. And refer to Goblet *v.* Beechey, Id. p. 185; s. c., 3 Sim. 24.

[3] Per Rolle, C. J., Taylor *v.* Web, Styles 319.

[4] In the Mayor, &c., of Gloucester *v.* Osborn, 1 H. L. Cas. 272, legacies were held to have failed for uncertainty of purpose.

[5] Saunderson *v.* Piper, 5 Bing. N. C. 425 (15 E. C. L. R.).

[6] Id. 431, 434.

or devisee,[1] the power being given to him of rendering certain that which was before altogether uncertain and undetermined. For instance, where a general grant is made of ten acres of ground adjoining or surrounding a particular house, part of a larger quantity of ground, the choice of such ten acres is in the grantee, and a devise to the like effect is to be considered as a grant;[2] and if I grant ten acres of wood where I have one hundred, the grantee may elect which ten he will take; for, in such a case, the law presumes the grantor to have been indifferent on the subject.[3] So, if a testator leaves a number of articles of the same kind to a legatee and dies possessed of a greater number, the legatee and not the executor has the right of selection.[4]

On the whole, then, we may observe, in the language of Lord Bacon, that all ambiguity of words within the deed, and not out of the deed, may be helped by construction, or, in some cases, by election, but never by averment, but rather shall make the deed void for uncertainty.[5]

The general rule, however, as to patent ambiguity must be received with this qualification, viz., that extrinsic evidence is unquestionably admissible for the purpose of showing that the uncertainty [*613] which appears on the face of *the instrument does not, in point of fact, exist; and that the intent of the party, though uncertainly and ambiguously expressed, may yet be ascertained, by proof of facts, to such a degree of certainty as to allow of the intent being carried into effect;[6] in cases falling within the scope of this remark, the evidence is received, not for the purpose of proving the testator's intention, but of explaining the words which he has used. Suppose, for instance, a legacy "to one of the children of A.," by her late husband B.; suppose, further, that A. had only one son by B., and that this fact was known to the testator; the necessary consequence, in such a case, of bringing the words of the will into contact with the circumstances to which they refer,

[1] See Duckmanton v. Duckmanton, 5 H. & N. 219.

[2] Hobson v. Blackburn, 1 My. & K. 571, 575.

[3] Bac. Max., reg. 23. See also, per cur., in Richardson v. Watson, 4 B. & Ad. 787 (24 E. C. L. R.); Vin. Abr., "*Grants*" (H. 5).

[4] Jacques v. Chambers, 2 Colly. 435.

[5] Bac. Max., reg. 23; per Tindal, C. J., 7 Scott N. R. 36; Wigram, Extrin. Evid., 3d ed., 83, 101.

[6] 2 Phill. Evid., 10th ed., 389.

must be to determine the identity of the person intended, it being the form of expression only, and not the intention, which is ambiguous; and evidence of facts requisite to reduce the testator's meaning to certainty would not, it should seem, in the instance above put, be excluded; though it would be quite another question if A. had more sons than one, or if her husband were living.[1]

"In the case of a patent ambiguity," remarks Sir T. Plumer, "that is, one appearing on the face of the instrument, as a general rule, a reference to matter *dehors* the instrument is forbidden. It must, if possible, be removed by construction and not by averment. But in many cases this is impracticable; where the terms used are wholly indefinite and equivocal and carry on the face of them no certain or explicit meaning, and the instrument furnishes no materials by which the ambiguity thus arising can be removed; if in such cases the court were *to reject the only mode by which the meaning could be ascertained, viz., the resort to extrinsic circumstances, the instrument must become inoperative and void. As a minor evil, therefore, common sense and the law of England (which are seldom at variance) warrant the departure from the general rule, and call in the light of extrinsic evidence."[2] [*614]

With respect to *ambiguitas latens*, the rule is, that, inasmuch as the ambiguity is raised by extrinsic evidence, so it may be removed in the same manner.[3] Therefore, if a person grant his manor of S. to A. and his heirs, and the truth is, he hath the manors both of North S. and South S., this ambiguity shall be helped by averment as to the grantor's intention.[4] So, if A. levies a fine to William, his son, and A. has two sons named William, the aver-

[1] Wigram, Ex. Evid., 3d ed., 66.

[2] Per Sir Thos. Plumer, M. R., Colpoys *v.* Colpoys, 1 Jac. R. 463, 464, where several instances are given; Collision *v.* Curling, 9 Cl. & Fin. 88.

[3] 2 Phill. Evid., 10th ed., 392; Wigram, Extrin. Evid., 3d ed., 101; per Williams, J., Way *v.* Hearn, 13 C. B. N. S. 305; Judgm., Bradley *v.* Washington Steam Packet Co., 13 Peters (U. S.) R. 97. "A latent ambiguity is raised by evidence:" per Coleridge, J., Simpson *v.* Margitson, 11 Q. B. 25 (63 E. C. L. R.).

Where parol evidence has been improperly received to explain a supposed latent ambiguity, the court *in banco* will decide upon the construction of the instrument without regard to the finding of the jury upon such evidence: Bruff *v.* Conybeare, 13 C. B. N. S. 263 (106 E. C. L. R.).

[4] Bac. Max., reg. 23; Plowd. 85 b; Miller *v.* Travers, 8 Bing. 248 (21 E. C. L. R.).

ment that it was his intention to levy the fine to the younger is good, and stands well with the words of the fine.[1] So, if one devise to his son John, when he has two sons of that name,[2] or to the eldest son of J. S., *and two persons, as in the case of [*615] a second marriage, meet that designation,[3] evidence is admissible to explain which of the two was intended. Wherever, in short, the words of the will in themselves are plain and unambiguous, but they become ambiguous by the circumstance that there are two persons, to each of whom the description applies, then parol evidence may be admitted to remove the ambiguity so created.[4]

A like rule applies also where the subject-matter of a devise or bequest is called by divers names, "as if I give lands to Christchurch in Oxford, and the name of the corporation is *Ecclesia Christi in Universitate*, Oxford, this shall be holpen by averment, because there appears no ambiguity in the words."[5]

In all cases, indeed, in which a difficulty arises in applying the words of a will to the thing which is the subject-matter of the devise, or to the person of the devisee, the difficulty or ambiguity which is introduced by the admission of extrinsic evidence may be rebutted and removed by the production of further evidence upon the same subject, calculated to explain what was the estate or subject-matter really intended to be devised, or who was the person really intended to take under the will; and this appears to be the extent of the maxim as to *ambiguitas latens*.[6] The characteristic of these cases is, that the words of the will *do* describe the object or subject *intended, and the evidence of the declarations [*616] of the testator has not the effect of varying the instrument

[1] Altham's Case, 8 Rep. 155; cited, 8 Bing. 251 (21 E. C. L. R.).

[2] Counden *v.* Clerke, Hob. 32; Fleming *v.* Fleming, 1 H. & C. 242; Jones *v.* Newman, 1 W. Bla. 60; Cheyney's Case, 5 Rep. 68; per Tindal, C. J., Doe d. Winter *v.* Perratt, 7 Scott N. R. 36.

[3] Per Erskine, J., 5 Bing. N. C. 433 (35 E. C. L. R.); Doe d. Gore *v.* Needs, 2 M. & W. 129; Richardson *v.* Watson, 4 B. & Ad. 792 (24 E. C. L. R.). And see the cases on this subject, cited, 2 Phill. Evid., 10th ed., 393, *et seq.*

[4] Per Alderson, B., 13 M. & W. 206, and in Smith *v.* Jeffryes, 15 M. & W. 561; The Duke of Dorset *v.* Lord Hawarden, 3 Curt. 80.

[5] Bac. Max., reg. 23.

[6] Judgm., Miller *v.* Travers, 8 Bing. 247, 248; per Abbott, C. J., Doe d. Westlake *v.* Westlake, 4 B. & Ald. 58 (24 E. C. L. R.); distinguished in Fleming *v.* Fleming, 1 H. & C. 242, 247.

in any way whatever; it only enables the court to reject one of the subjects or objects to which the description in the will applies, and to determine which of the two the devisor understood to be signified by the description which he used in the will.[1]

A devise was made of land to M. B., for life, remainder to "her three daughters, Mary, Elizabeth and Ann," in fee, as tenants in common. At the date of the will, M. B. had two legitimate daughters, Mary and Ann, living, and one illegitimate, named Elizabeth. Extrinsic evidence was held admissible to rebut the claim of the last-mentioned, by showing that M. B. formerly had a legitimate daughter named Elizabeth, who died some years before the date of the will, and that the testator did not know of her death, or of the birth of the illegitimate daughter.[2]

"The rule as to the reception of parol evidence to explain a will," remarked Sir J. Romilly, M. R., in Stringer *v.* Gardiner,[3] "is perfectly clear. In every case of ambiguity, whether latent or patent, parol evidence is admissible to show the state of the testator's family or property; but the cases in which parol evidence is admissible to show the person intended to be designated by the testator are those cases of latent ambiguity, mentioned by Sir J. Wigram, where there are two or more persons who answer other descriptions in the will, each of whom, standing alone, would be entitled to take."

[*617] *It is true, moreover, that parol evidence must be admissible to some extent to determine the application of *every* written instrument. It must, for instance, be received to show what it is that corresponds with the description;[4] and the admissibility of such evidence for this purpose being conceded, it is only going one step further to give parol evidence, as in the above instances, of other extrinsic facts, which determine the application of the instrument to one subject, rather than to others, to which, on the face of it, it might appear equally applicable.[5]

"Speaking philosophically," says Rolfe, B., "you must always

[1] Judgm., Doe d. Gord *v.* Needs, 2 M. & W. 140; Lord Walpole *v.* Earl of Cholmondeley, 7 T. R. 138.

[2] Doe d. Thomas *v.* Benyon, 12 A. & E. 431 (40 E. C. L. R.); Doe d. Allen *v.* Allen, Id. 451.

[3] 28 L. J. Chanc. 758.

[4] Macdonald *v.* Longbottom, 1 E. & E. 97 (102 E. C. L. R.).

[5] 2 Phill. Ev., 9th ed., 297, 329.

look beyond the instrument itself to some extent, in order to ascertain who is meant; for instance, you must look to names and places;"[1] and, "in every specific devise or bequest it is clearly competent and necessary to inquire as to the thing specifically devised or bequeathed."[2] Thus "parol evidence is always necessary to show that the party sued is the person making the contract, and bound by it."[3] So, if the word Blackacre be used in a will, there must be evidence to show that the field in question is Blackacre.[4] Where there is a devise of an estate purchased of A., or of a farm in the occupation of B., it must be shown, by extrinsic evidence, what estate it was that A. purchased, or what farm was in the occupation of B., before it can be *known what is devised.[5] So, whether parcel or not of the thing demised is always matter of evidence.[6] In these and similar cases, the instrument appears on the face of it to be perfectly intelligible, and free from ambiguity, yet extrinsic evidence must, nevertheless, be received, for the purpose of showing what the instrument refers to.[7]

[*618]

The rule as to *ambiguitas latens*, above briefly stated, may likewise be applied to mercantile instruments, with a view to ascertain the *intention*, though not to vary the *contract* of the parties.[8] And although, generally speaking, the construction of a written contract is for the court, when it is shown by extrinsic evidence that the terms of the contract are ambiguous, evidence is admissible to

[1] 13 M. & W. 207.

[2] Per Lord Cottenham, C., Shuttleworth *v.* Greaves, 4 My. & Cr. 38.

[3] Judgm., Trueman *v.* Loder, 11 A. & E. 594 (39 E. C. L. R.). See Stebbing *v.* Spicer, 8 C. B. 827.

[4] Doe d. Preedy *v.* Holtom, 4 A. & E. 82 (31 E. C. L. R.); recognized Doe d. Norton *v.* Webster, 12 A. & E. 450 (40 E. C. L. R.); cited, per Williams, J., Doe d. Hemming *v.* Willetts, 7 C. B. 715 (62 E. C. L. R.); per Bovill, C. J., Horsey *v.* Graham, L. R. 5 C. P. 14.

[5] Per Sir Wm. Grant, M. R., 1 Mer. 653.

[6] Per Buller, J., Doe d. Freeland *v.* Burt, 1 T. R. 701, 704; Paddock *v.* Fradley, 1 Cr. & J. 90; Doe d. Beach *v.* Earl of Jersey, 3 B. & C. 870 (10 E. C. L. R.); Lyle *v.* Richards, L. R. 1 H. L. 222.

[7] Per Patteson, J., and Coleridge, J., 4 A. & E. 81, 82 (31 E. C. L. R.). See Doe d. Norton *v.* Webster, 12 A. & E. 442 (40 E. C. L. R.). Evidence of co-existing circumstances admitted to explain the condition of a bond: Montefiore *v.* Lloyd, 15 C. B. N. S. 203 (109 E. C. L. R.). Evidence admitted to identify pauper with person described in indenture of apprenticeship: Reg. *v.* Wooldale, 6 Q. B. 549 (51 E. C. L. R.).

[8] Smith *v.* Jeffryes, 15 M. & W. 561.

explain the ambiguity, and to show what the parties really meant. "Where there is an election between two meanings, it is, properly, a question for the jury."[1]

Where, as we shall hereafter see, a contract is entered into with reference to a known and recognized use of particular terms employed by the contracting parties, or with reference to a known and established usage, evidence may be given to show the meaning of those terms, or the *nature of that usage, amongst persons conversant with the particular branch of commerce or business to which they relate. [*619] But cases of this latter class more properly fall within a branch of the law of evidence which we shall separately consider, viz., the applicability of usage and custom to the explanation of written instruments.[2]

Quoties in Verbis nulla est Ambiguitas, ibi nulla Expositio contra Verba fienda est.

(Wing. Max., p. 24.)

In the absence of ambiguity, no exposition shall be made which is opposed to the express words of the instrument.

It seems desirable, before proceeding with the consideration of some additional maxims relative to the subject of ambiguity in written instruments, to take this opportunity of observing that, according to the rule which stands at the head of these remarks, it is not allowable to interpret what has no need of interpretation, and that the law will not make an exposition against the express words and intent of the parties.[3] Hence, if I grant to you that you and your heirs, or the heirs of your body, shall distrain for a rent of forty shillings within my manor of S., this, by construction of law, *ut res magis valeat*, shall amount to a grant of rent out of

[1] Per Maule, J., Smith *v.* Thompson, 8 C. B. 59 (65 E. C. L. R.). As to ambiguous contracts, see also Boden *v.* French, 10 C. B. 886, 889 (70 E. C. L. R.).

[2] See the remarks on the maxim, *Optimus interpres rerum unus—post*, Chap. X.

[3] Co. Litt. 147 a; 7 Rep. 103; per Kelynge, C. J., Lanyon *v.* Carne, 2 Saunds. R. 167. See Jesse *v.* Roy, 1 Cr., M. & R. 316.

my manor of S., in fee-simple or fee-tail; for the grant would be of little force or effect if the grantee had but a bare distress and no rent. But if a rent of forty shillings be [*620] *granted out of the manor of D., with a right to distrain if such rent be in arrear in the manor of S., this will not amount to a grant of rent out of the manor of S., for the rent is granted to be issuing out of the manor of D., and the parties have expressly limited out of what land the rent shall issue, and upon what land the distress shall be taken.[1]

It may, moreover, be laid down as a general rule, applicable as well to cases in which a written instrument is required by law as to those in which it is not, that where such instrument appears on the face of it to be complete, parol evidence is inadmissible to vary or contradict the agreement, *ex. gr.*, to show that the word "and" was inserted in it by mistake:[2] in such cases the court will look to the written contract, in order to ascertain the meaning of the parties, and will not admit the introduction of parol evidence, to show that the agreement was in reality different from that which it purports to be.[3] Although, moreover, it has been said that a somewhat strained interpretation of an instrument may be admissible where an absurdity would otherwise ensue, yet if the intention of the parties is not clear and plain, but *in equilibrio*, the words shall receive their more natural and proper construction.[4]

The general rule, observes a learned judge, I take to be, that where the words of any written instrument are free from ambiguity in themselves, and where external circumstances do not create any doubt or difficulty as to the proper application of those words to claimants under the [*621] *instrument, or the subject-matter to which the instrument relates, such instrument is always to be construed according to the strict plain common meaning of the words themselves; and that, in such cases, evidence *dehors* the instrument, for the purpose of explaining it according to the surmised or alleged intention of the parties to the instrument, is utterly in-

[1] Co. Litt. 147 a.

[2] Hitchin *v.* Groom, 5 C. B. 515 (57 E. C. L. R.).

[3] Per Bayley and Holroyd, JJ., Williams *v.* Jones, 5 B. & C. 108 (11 E. C. L. R.); Spartali *v.* Benecke, 10 C. B. 212 (70 E. C. L. R.).

[4] Earl of Bath's Case, Cart. R. 108, 109, adopted 1 Fonbl. Eq., 5th ed., 445 n.

admissible.[1] The true interpretation, however, of every instrument being manifestly that which will make the instrument speak the intention of the party at the time it was made, it has always been considered as an exception from—or, perhaps, to speak more precisely, not so much an exception from as a carollary to—the general rule above stated, that, where any doubt arises upon the true sense and meaning of the words themselves, or any difficulty as to their application under the surrounding circumstances, the sense and meaning of the language may be investigated and ascertained by evidence *dehors* the instrument itself; for both reason and common sense agree that by no other means can the language of the instrument be made to speak the real mind of the party.[2] "You may," observes Coleridge, J.,[3] with reference to a guarantee under the old law,[4] "explain the meaning of the words used by any legal means. Of such legal means, one is to look at the situation of the parties. Till you have done that, it is a fallacy to say that the language *is ambiguous: that which ends in certainty is not ambiguous." [*622]

The following cases may be mentioned as falling within the scope of the preceding remarks: 1st, where the instrument is in a foreign language, in which case the jury must ascertain the meaning of the terms upon the evidence of persons skilled in the particular language;[5] 2dly, ancient words may be explained by contemporaneous usage; 3dly, if the instrument be a mercantile contract, the meaning of the terms must be ascertained by the jury according to their acceptation amongst merchants; 4thly, if the terms are technical terms of art, their meaning must, in like manner, be ascertained by the evidence of persons skilled in the art to which they refer. In such cases, the court may at once determine, upon the inspection of the instrument, that it belongs to the province of the jury to ascer-

[1] Per Tindal, C. J., Shore *v.* Wilson, 5 Scott N. R. 1037. For an instance of the application of this rule to a will, see Doe d. Oxenden *v.* Chichester, 3 Taunt. 147; s. c. (affirmed in error), 4 Dow 65; cited and explained Wigram, Extrin. Evid., 3d ed., 77.

[2] Per Tindal, C. J., 5 Scott N. R. 1037, 1038; Montefiore *v.* Lloyd, 15 C. B. N. S. 203 (109 E. C. L. R.).

[3] Bainbridge *v.* Wade, 16 Q. B. 100 (71 E. C. L. R.).

[4] See, now, stat. 19 & 20 Vict. c. 97, s. 3.

[5] As to this proposition, *ante*, p. 107.

tain the meaning of the words, and, therefore, that, in the inquiry, extrinsic evidence to some extent must be admissible.[1]

It may be scarcely necessary to observe, that the maxim under consideration applies equally to the interpretation of an Act of Parliament; the general rule being, that *a verbis legis non est recedendum.*[2] A court of law will not make any interpretation contrary to the express letter of the statute; for nothing can so well explain the meaning of the makers of the Act as their own direct words, since *index animi sermo,* and *maledicta expositio quæ corrumpit textum;*[3] it would be dangerous to give scope for [*623] *making a construction in any case against the express words, where the meaning of the makers is not opposed to them, and when no inconvenience will follow from a literal interpretation.[4] "Nothing," observed Lord Denman, C. J., in a recent case,[5] "is more unfortunate than a disturbance of the plain language of the legislature, by the attempt to use equivalent terms."

Certum est quod certum reddi potest.

(Noy, Max., 9th ed., 265.)

That is sufficiently certain which can be made certain.

The above maxim, which sets forth a rule of logic as well as of law, is peculiarly applicable in construing a written instrument. For instance, although every estate for years must have a certain beginning and a certain end, "albeit there appear no certainty of years in the lease, yet, if by reference to a certainty it may be made certain, it sufficeth;"[6] and, therefore, if a man make a lease to another for so many years as J. S. shall name, this is a good lease for years; for though it is at present uncertain, yet when

[1] Per Erskine, J., 5 Scott N. R. 988; per Parke, B., Clift *v.* Schwabe, 3 C. B. 469, 470 (54 E. C. L. R.). As to the construction of a settlement in equity, see per Lord Campbell, Evans *v.* Scott, 1 H. L. Cas. 66.

[2] 5 Rep. 119; cited, Wing. Max., p. 25.

[3] 4 Rep. 35; 2 Rep. 24; 11 Rep. 33; Wing. Max., p. 26.

[4] Eldrich's Case, 5 Rep. 119; cited, arg. Gaunt *v.* Taylor, 3 Scott N. R. 709.

[5] Everard *v.* Poppleton, 5 Q. B. 184 (48 E. C. L. R.); per Coltman, J., Gadsby *v.* Barrow, 8 Scott N. R. 804.

[6] Co. Litt. 45 b.

J. S. hath named the years, it is then reduced to a certainty. So, if a parson makes a lease for more than twenty or more years, if he shall so long live, or if he shall so long continue parson, it is good, for there is a certain period fixed, beyond which it cannot last, though it may determine sooner on the death of the lessor, or his ceasing to be parson.[1]

[*624] *It is true, said Lord Kenyon, C. J., that there must be a certainty in the lease as to the commencement and duration of the term, but that certainty need not be ascertained at the time; for if, in the fluxion of time, a day will arrive which will make it certain, that is sufficient. As, if a lease be granted for twenty-one years after three lives in being, though it is uncertain at first when that term will commence, because those lives are in being, yet when they die it is reduced to a certainty, and *Id certum est quod certum reddi potest*, and such terms are frequently created for raising portions for younger children.[2]

Again, it is a rule of law, that, "no distress can be taken for any services that are not put into certainty nor can be reduced to any certainty, for *Id certum est quod certum reddi potest;*"[3] and, accordingly, where land is demised at a rent which is capable of being reduced to a certainty, the lessor will be entitled to distrain for the same.[4]

In like manner, in the case of a feoffment, the office of the premises of the deed is twofold: first, rightly to name the feoffor and the feoffee; and secondly, to comprehend the certainty of the lands or tenements to be conveyed by the feoffment; and this may be done either by express words, or by words which may by reference be reduced to a certainty, according to the principle, *Certum est quod certum reddi potest.*[5] So, a grant shall be void if it [*625] *be totally uncertain; but if the king's grant refers to

[1] 2 Com. by Broom & Hadley 279, 280; 6 Rep. 35; Co. Litt. 45 b.

[2] Goodright d. Hall *v.* Richardson, 3 T. R. 463.

[3] Co. Litt. 96 a, 142 a; Parke *v.* Harris, 1 Salk. 262.

[4] Daniel *v.* Gracie, 6 Q. B. 145 (51 E. C. L. R.). See Pollitt *v.* Forrest, 11 Q. B. 949 (63 E. C. L. R.).

[5] Co. Litt. 6 a; 4 Cruise Dig., 4th ed., 269. See also Maugham *v.* Sharpe, 17 C. B. N. S. 443, 463 (112 E. C. L. R.).

The office of the *habendum* is to limit, explain, or qualify the words in the premises; but if the words of the *habendum* are manifestly contradictory and repugnant to those in the premises, they must be disregarded: Doe d. Timmis *v.* Steele, 4 Q. B. 663 (45 E. C. L. R.).

another thing which is certain, it is sufficient; as, if he grant to a city all liberties which London has, without saying what liberties London has.[1]

An agreement in writing for the sale of a house did not by description ascertain the particular house, but it referred to the deeds as being in the possession of A. B., named in the agreement. The court held the agreement sufficiently certain, inasmuch as it appeared upon the face of the agreement that the house referred to was the house of which the deeds were in the possession of A. B., and, consequently, the house might easily be ascertained before the master, and *Id certum est quod certum reddi potest.*[2]

A testator, having devised his estates in a particular way, directed that a different disposition of them should take place "in case certain contingent property and effects in expectancy shall fall in and become vested interests to my children." The children, it appeared, were entitled to no vested interest at the date of the will; and the court, in accordance with a rule which we have already stated, refused to admit evidence offered for the purpose of showing that the testator referred to expectations from particular individuals, which had in fact subsequently been realized. The Master of the Rolls, however, observed that if at the making of the testator's will his children had been entitled to any contingent interests, evidence would have been plainly admissible to ascertain those interests; because the expression of contingency *had a definite legal [*626] meaning, and *Id certum est quod certum reddi potest;* so that the evidence would not in that case have added to the will, but would have explained it.[3]

Again, the word "certain" must, in a variety of cases, where a contract is entered into for the sale of goods, refer to an indefinite quantity at the time of the contract made, and must mean a quantity which is to be ascertained according to the above maxim.[4]

And where the law requires a particular thing to be done, but does not limit any period within which it must be done, the act required must be done within a reasonable time; and a reasonable time is capable of being ascertained by evidence, and, when

[1] Com. Dig., "*Grant*" (E. 14), (G. 5); Finch Law 49.

[2] Owen *v.* Thomas, 3 My. & K. 353.

[3] King *v.* Badeley, 3 My. & K. 417, 425.

[4] Per Lord Ellenborough, C. J., Wildmann *v.* Glossop, 1 B. & Ald. 12.

ascertained, is as fixed and certain as if specified by Act of Parliament.[1]

Where it was awarded that the costs of certain actions should be paid by the plaintiff and defendant in specified proportions, the award was held to be sufficiently certain, since it would become so upon taxation of costs by the proper officer.[2]

---

*UTILE PER INUTILE NON VITIATUR. [*627]

(3 Rep. 10.)

Surplusage does not vitiate that which in other respects is good and valid.

It is a rule of extensive application with reference to the construction of written instruments, and in the science of pleading, that matter which is mere surplusage may be rejected, and does not vitiate the instrument or pleading in which it is found—*Surplusagium non nocet*[3] is the maxim of our law.

Accordingly, where words of known signification are so placed in the context of a deed that they make it repugnant and senseless, they are to be rejected equally with words of no known significa-

[1] Per Lord Ellenborough, C. J., Palmer *v.* Moxon, 2 M. & S. 50 (28 E. C. L. R.).

[2] Cargey *v.* Aitcheson, 2 B. & C. 170 (9 E. C. L. R.). See Pedley *v.* Goddard, 7 T. R. 73; Wood *v.* Wilson, 2 Cr., M. & R. 241; Waddle *v.* Downman, 12 M. & W. 562; Smith *v.* Hartley, 10 C. B. 800, 805 (70 E. C. L. R.); Graham *v.* Darcey, 6 C. B. 539 (60 E. C. L. R.); Holdsworth *v.* Barsham, 2 B. & S. 480 (110 E. C. L. R.).

The maxim *supra* was applied to a valuation in Gordon *v.* Whitehouse, 18 C. B. 747, 753 (86 E. C. L. R.), to an indenture of apprenticeship in Reg. *v.* Wooldale, 6 Q. B. 549, 566 (51 E. C. L. R.). It may also be applicable in determining whether an action of *debt* will lie under given circumstances: see Barber *v.* Butcher, 8 Q. B. 863, 870 (55 E. C. L. R.).

[3] Branch Max., 5th ed., 216; *Non solent quæ abundant vitiare scripturas*, D. 50. 17. 94.

"Surplusage (in pleading) is something that is altogether foreign and inapplicable:" per Maule, J. Aldis *v.* Mason, 11 C. B. 139. See also as to surplusage, Shep. Touch. 236; cited, per Williams, J., Janes *v.* Whitbread, 11 C. B. 412 (73 E. C. L. R.); Maclae *v.* Sutherland, 3 E. & B. 1, 33 (72 E. C. L. R.), illustrates the maxim *supra*.

tion.[1] It is also a rule in conveyancing, that, if an estate be granted in any premises, and that grant is express and certain, the *habendum*, although repugnant to the deed, shall not vitiate it. If, however, the estate granted in the premises be not express, but arise by implication of law, then a void *habendum*, or one differing materially from the grant, may defeat it.[2]

[*628] *A cause and all matters of difference were referred to the arbitration of three persons, the award of the three, or of any two of them, to be final. The award purported on the face of it to be made by all three, but was executed by two only of the arbitrators, the third having refused to sign it when requested so to do. This award was held to be good as the award of the two, for the statement that the third party had concurred might, it was observed, be treated as mere surplusage, the substance of the averment being that two of the arbitrators had made the award.[3]

As a further instance of the application of the above rule, we may observe, that, if a valid contract should be made between A. and B., that A. should perform a journey on B.'s lawful business, and another and distinct contract should subsequently be entered into on the same day, that on a journey A. should commit a crime, the latter contract would of course be void, but it would not dissolve the prior agreement, nor exonerate the parties from their liabilities under it. To such a case, then, it has been said that the maxim would apply, *Utile per inutile non vitiatur*.[4]

The above maxim, however, applies peculiarly to pleading; in which it is a rule, that matter immaterial cannot operate to make a pleading double, and that mere surplusage does not vitiate a plea,

[1] Vaugh. R. 176. See Whittome *v.* Lamb, 12 M. & W. 813.

[2] Arg. Goodtitle *v.* Gibbs, 5 B. & C. 712, 713 (11 E. C. L. R.), and cases there cited; Shep. Touch. 112, 113; Hobart 171. See also instances of the application of this rule to an order of removal, Reg. *v.* Rotherham, 3 Q. B. 776, 782 (43 E. C. L. R.); Reg. *v.* Silkstone, 2 Q. B. 522 (42 E. C. L. R.); to an order under 2 & 3 Vict. c. 85, s. 1, Reg. *v.* Goodall, 2 Dowl. P. C. N. S. 382; Reg. *v.* Oxley, 6 Q. B. 256 (51 E. C. L. R.); to a conviction, Chaney *v.* Payne, 1 Q. B. 722 (41 E. C. L. R.); to a notice of objection under 6 & 7 Vict. c. 18, Allen, app., House, resp., 8 Scott N. R. 987; cited, arg. 2 C. B. 9 (52 E. C. L. R.); to an information, A.-G. *v.* Clerc, 12 M. & W. 640.

[3] White *v.* Sharp, 12 M. & W. 712. See also per Alderson, B., Wynne *v.* Edwards, 12 M. & W. 712; Harlow *v.* Read, 1 C. B. 733 (50 E. C. L. R.).

[4] See 18 Johns. (U. S.) R. 93, 94.

and may be rejected.[1] *And, if an affidavit of debt allege several distinct and separate causes of action for separate and distinct sums, some of which are well and others ill stated, the affidavit is not therefore bad altogether.[2] And although the issue to be tried by the jury ought to be material, single and specific, yet a party does not make an issue upon the substantial matter bad, merely because he includes in it "something of total surplusage and immateriality."[3] [*629]

Lastly, with respect to an indictment, it is laid down, that, although an averment, which is altogether superfluous, may here be rejected as surplusage;[4] yet, if an averment be part of the description of the offence, or be embodied by reference in such description, it cannot be so rejected, and its introduction may, unless an amendment be permitted, be fatal.[5]

FALSA DEMONSTRATIO NON NOCET.

(6 T. R. 676.)

Mere false description does not make an instrument inoperative.

Falsa demonstratio may be defined to be an erroneous description of a person or thing in a written instrument;[6] and the above rule

[1] Co. Litt. 303 b; Steph. Pl., 6th ed., 310, 341.

Ring *v.* Roxburgh, 2 Cr. & J. 418 (cited per Rolfe, B., Duke *v.* Forbes, 1 Exch. 356), is an instance of the rejection of surplusage in a declaration.

A *videlicet* cannot make that immaterial which is in its nature material, though the omission of it may render that material which would otherwise not be so. For instance, a *videlicet* could not make the sum in a bill of exchange immaterial, so as to cure what would otherwise be a variance: per Patteson, J., Cooper *v.* Blick, 2 Q. B. 918 (42 E. C. L. R.); Harris *v.* Phillips, 10 C. B. 650, 656 (70 E. C. L. R.); per Coltman, J., 6 Scott N. R. 892; per Tindal, C. J., 1 C. B. 164 (50 E. C. L. R.); Drew *v.* Avery, 13 M. & W. 402; Nash *v.* Brown, 6 C. B. 584 (60 E. C. L. R.); Whitaker *v.* Harrold, 11 Q. B. 163 (63 E. C. L. R.); cited per Parke, B., Graham *v.* Gibson, 4 Exch. 771; Ryalls *v.* Reg., 11 Q. B. 781 (63 E. C. L. R.).

[2] Cunliffe *v.* Maltass, 7 C. B. 695 (62 E. C. L. R.). See Hargreaves *v.* Hayes, 5 E. & B. 272 (85 E. C. L. R.).

[3] Per Tindal, C. J., Palmer *v.* Gooden, 8 M. & W. 894.

[4] See Reg. *v.* Parker, L. R. 1 C. C. 225.

[5] Dickins. Quart. Sess., 5th ed., by Mr. Serjt. Talfourd, 175.

[6] See Bell, Dict. and Dig. of Scotch Law 420; Spooner *v.* Payne, 4 C. B.

[*630] respecting it may be thus *stated and qualified: as soon as there is an adequate and sufficient definition, with convenient certainty, of what is intended to pass by the particular instrument, a subsequent erroneous addition will not vitiate it:[1] *quicquid demonstratæ rei additur satis demonstratæ frustra est.*[2] The characteristic of cases within the principal maxim being that "the description so far as it is false applies to no subject at all,[3] and so far as it is true applies to one only." "I have always understood," observes Lord Kenyon, speaking with reference to a will,[4] "that such *falsa demonstratio* should be superadded to that which was sufficiently certain before, there must *constat de personâ;* and if to that an inapt description be added, though false, it will not avoid the devise." "I agree," observes Patteson, J.,[5] "to the doctrine that *Falsa demonstratio non nocet:* but that is only where the words of the devise, exclusive of that *falsa demonstratio*, are sufficient of themselves to describe the property intended to be devised; reference being had, if necessary, to the situation of the premises, to the names by which they have been known, or to other circumstances [*631] properly *pointing to the meaning of the description in the will." And again, the maxim as to *falsa demonstratio*, says Lord Westbury,[6] "is applicable to a case where some subject matter is devised as a whole under a denomination, which is applicable to the entire land, and then the words of description that include and denote the entire subject matter are followed by words

328, 330 (56 E. C. L. R.); Robinson *v.* Marq. of Bristol, 11 C. B. 208 (73 E. C. L. R.); s. c. (in error), Id. 241.

[1] Per Parke, B., Llewellyn *v.* Earl of Jersey, 11 M. & W. 189; recognized in Barton *v.* Dawes, 10 C. B. 261, 266 (70 E. C. L. R.); Judgm., Morrell *v.* Fisher, 4 Exch. 604; recognized in Wood *v.* Rowcliffe, 6 Exch. 407, 410; Harrison *v.* Hyde, 4 H. & N. 805; Josh *v.* Josh, 5 C. B. N. S. 454 (94 E. C. L. R.); Com. Dig., "*Fait*" (E. 4).

[2] D. 33. 4. 1, § 8.

[3] Judgm., Webber *v.* Stanley, 16 C. B. N. S. 755 (111 E. C. L. R.).

[4] Thomas *v.* Thomas, 6 T. R. 676. See also Mosley *v.* Massey, 8 East 149: per Parke, J., Doe d. Smith *v.* Galloway, 5 B. & Ad. 51 (27 E. C. L. R.); followed in Dyne *v.* Nutley, 14 C. B. 122 (78 E. C. L. R.); per Littledale, J., Doe d. Ashforth *v.* Bower, 3 B. & Ad. 459 (23 E. C. L. R.); Gynes *v.* Kemsley, 1 Freem. 293; Hobart 32, 171; Greene *v.* Armstead, Id. 65; Vin. Abr., "*Devise*" (T. b), pl. 4.

[5] Doe d. Hubbard *v.* Hubbard, 15 Q. B. 241 (69 E. C. L. R.).

[6] West *v.* Lawday, 11 H. L. Cas. 384.

which are added on the principle of enumeration, but do not completely enumerate and exhaust all the particulars which are comprehended and included within the antecedent universal or generic denomination. Then the ordinary principle and rule of law which is perfectly consistent with common sense and reason is this: that the entirety which has been expressly and definitely given shall not be prejudiced by an imperfect and inaccurate enumeration of the particulars of the specific gift."[1]

The foregoing observations are, in the main, applicable not only to wills, but to other instruments;[2] so that the characteristic of cases strictly within the above rule is this, that the description, so far as it is false, applies to no subject, and, so far as it is true, it applies to one subject only; and the court, in these cases, rejects no words but those which are shown to have no application to any subject.[3]

Where accordingly a question involving the legal doctrine *now before us arises upon a will, we must inquire, [*632] is there a devise of a thing certain? If there be, the addition of an untrue circumstance will not vitiate the devise. "Another certainty put to another thing, which was of certainty enough before, is of no manner of effect, and there is a diversity where a certainty is added to a thing that is uncertain, and where to a thing certain; as if I release *all my lands* in Dale, which I have by descent on the part of my father, and I have lands in Dale on the part of my mother, but no lands by descent on the part of my father, the release is void, and so the words of certainty added to the general words have effect; but, if the release had been of Whiteacre in Dale, which I have by descent on the part of my father, and it was not so, the release would be valid, for this thing was certainly enough expressed by the first words, and the last words were superfluous and of no effect."[4] That is to say, if the thing released

[1] See also per Lefroy, C. J., Roe *v.* Lidwell, 11 Ir. C. L. R. 326, cited arg. Skull *v.* Glenister, 16 C. B. N. S. 89 (111 E. C. L. R.).

[2] London Grand Junction R. C. *v.* Freeman, 2 Scott N. R. 705, 748. See Reg. *v.* Wilcock, 7 Q. B. 317 (53 E. C. L. R.); Jack *v.* M'Intyre, 12 Cl. & Fin. 151; Omerod *v.* Chadwick, 16 M. & W. 367; followed, per Wightman, J., Reg. *v.* Stretfield, 32 L. J. M. C. 236.

[3] See Wigram, Ex. Ev., 3d ed., 142, 165; Judgm., Morrell *v.* Fisher, 4 Exch. 604; Mann *v.* Mann, 14 Johns. (U. S.) R. 1.

[4] Plowd. 191; cited and adopted Judgm., Nightingall *v.* Smith, 1 Exch. 886;

or devised has substance and certainty enough, the untrue description is of no avail.[1]

In the case of Selwood *v.* Mildmay,[2] the testator devised to his wife part of his stock in the 4*l.* per cent. annuities of the Bank of England, and it was shown by parol evidence, that, at the time he made his will, he had no stock in the 4*l.* per cent. annuities, but that he had had some, which he had sold out, and of which he had invested the produce in long annuities: it was held in this [*633] case that the bequest was, in substance, a bequest of *stock, using the words as a denomination, not as the identical *corpus* of the stock; and as none could be found to answer the description but the long annuities, it was decided that such stock should pass, rather than the will be altogether inoperative.

A testatrix, by her will, bequeathed several legacies to different individuals, of 3*l.* per cent. consols standing in her name in the Bank of England; but, at the date of her will, as well as at her death, she possessed no such stock, nor stock of any kind whatever. It was held that the ambiguity in this case being latent, evidence was admissible to show how the mistake of the testatrix arose, and to discover her intention.[3]

But where a testatrix died possessed of property in consols, reduced annuities, and bank stock, and by her will bequeathed "the whole of my fortune now standing in the funds to E. S.:" held that the bank stock did not pass.[4]

On the same principle, in the case of a lease of a portion of a park, described as being in the occupation of S., and lying within certain specified abuttals, with all houses, &c., belonging thereto, and "which are now in the occupation of S.," it was held, that a house, situated within the abuttals, but not in the occupation of S., would pass.[5] So, where an estate is devised, called A., and de-

and, per Parke, B., Morrell *v.* Fisher, 4 Exch. 599. And, as illustrating the passage above cited, compare Doe d. Hubbard *v.* Hubbard, 15 Q. B. 227 (69 E. C. L. R.), with Doe d. Compton *v.* Carpenter, 16 Id. 181 (71 E. C. L. R.).

[1] Judgm., 1 Exch. 887.

[2] 3 Ves. jun. 306.

[3] Lindgren *v.* Lindgren, 9 Beav. 358; citing Selwood *v.* Mildmay, 3 Ves. 306; Miller *v.* Travers, 8 Bing. 244; and Doe d. Hiscocks *v.* Hiscocks, 5 M. & W. 363.

[4] Slingsby *v.* Grainger, 7 H. L. Cas. 273.

[5] Doe d. Smith *v.* Galloway, 5 B. & Ad. 43 (27 E. C. L. R.); Beaumont *v.* Field, 1 B. & Ald. 247; 3 Preston Abstr. Tit. 206; Doe d. Roberts *v.* Parry, 13 M. & W. 356.

scribed as in the occupation of B., and it was found that, though there is an estate called A., yet the whole is not *in B.'s [*634] occupation;[1] or, where an estate is devised to a person whose surname or Christian name is mistaken, or whose description is imperfect or inaccurate: in these cases parol evidence is admissible to show what estate was intended to pass, and who was the devisee intended to take, provided there is sufficient indication of intention appearing on the face of the will to justify the application of the evidence.[2] Thus, a devise of all the testator's freehold houses in Aldersgate Street, where, in fact, he had no freehold, but had leasehold houses, was held to pass the latter, the word "freehold" being rejected;[3] the rule being, that, where any property described in a will is sufficiently ascertained by the description, it passes under the devise, although *all* the particulars stated in the will with reference to it may not be true.[4] In other words, *nil facit error nominis cum de corpore vel personâ constat.*[5] "It is fit, and therefore required," observes Mr. Preston,[6] "that things should be described by their proper names; but, though this be the general rule, it admits of many exceptions, for things may pass under any denomination by which they have been usually distinguished."

In a modern case,[7] where property was devised to the second son of Edward W., of L., this devise was held, *upon the con- [*635] text of the will, and upon extrinsic evidence as to the state of the W. family, and the degree of the testator's acquaintance with the different members of it, to mean a devise to the second son of Joseph W., of L., although it appeared that there was in fact a person named Edward Joseph W., the eldest son of Joseph

[1] Goodtitle *v.* Southern, 1 M. & S. 299 (28 E. C. L. R.).

[2] Judgm., Miller *v.* Travers, 8 Bing. 248 (21 E. C. L. R.); Doe d. Hiscocks *v.* Hiscocks, 5 M. & W. 363; Rishton *v.* Cobb, 5 My. & Cr. 145.

[3] Day *v.* Trig, 1 P. Wms. 286; Doe d. Dunning *v.* Cranstoun, 7 M. & W. 1. See Parker *v.* Marchant, 6 Scott N. R. 485; Goodman *v.* Edwards, 2 My. & K. 759; Hobson *v.* Blackburn, 1 My. & K. 571.

[4] Per Parke, B., Doe d. Dunning *v.* Cranstoun, 7 M. & W. 10; Newton *v.* Lucas, 1 My. & Cr. 391.

[5] See Janes *v.* Whitbread, 11 C. B. 406 (73 E. C. L. R.).

[6] 3 Prest. Abst. Tit. 206; 6 Rep. 66.

[7] Blundell *v.* Gladstone, 1 Phil. 279; s. c., nom. Lord Camoys *v.* Blundell, 1 H. L. Cas. 778.

W., who resided at L., and who usually went by the name of Edward only; and it was remarked, that, according to the general rule of law and of construction, if there had been two persons each fully and accurately answering the whole description, evidence might be received, or arguments from the language of the will, and from circumstances, might be adduced to show to which of those persons the will applied; but that where one person, and one only, fully and accurately answers the whole description, the court is bound to apply the will to that person. It was, however, further observed, that an exception would occur in applying the above rule, where it would lead to a construction of a devise manifestly contrary to what was the intention of the testator, as expressed by his will, and that the rule must be rejected as inapplicable to a case in which it would defeat instead of promoting the object for which all rules of construction have been framed.[1]

In accordance with the spirit of the maxim under consideration, where a judge's order for the admission of documents in evidence referred to a "document mentioned in a certain notice served by the defendant's attorney or agent, dated the 4th day of March, 1845," and the notice produced at the trial was dated the 1st of March, but the plaintiff's attorney stated that it was the only notice [*636] *served in the cause, the judge at the trial allowed the document to be read; and the court held that it was admissible, on the ground that, as only one notice had been served, the misdescription was merely *Falsa demonstratio quæ non nocet.*[2]

But, although an averment to take away surplusage is good, yet it is not so to increase that which is defective in the will of the testator;[3] and, as already observed,[4] there "is a diversity where a certainty is added to a thing which is uncertain, and where to a thing certain."

In a leading case on this subject,[5] testator devised all his freehold

[1] Phil. R. 285, 286.

[2] Brittleston *v.* Cooper, 14 M. & W. 399.

[3] Per Anderson, C. J., Godbolt, R. 131, recognized 8 Bing. 253 (21 E. C. L. R.); per Lord Eldon, C., 6 Ves. Jun. 397.

[4] *Ante*, p. 632. And see per Lord Ellenborough, C. J., Doe d. Harris *v.* Greathed, 8 East 103; Hob. R. 172; Doe d. Renow *v.* Ashley, 10 Q. B. 663 (59 E. C. L. R.).

[5] Miller *v.* Travers, 8 Bing. 244 (21 E. C. L. R.), and the observations on

and real estates in the county of L. and city of L. It appeared that he had no estates in the county of L.,—a small estate in the city of L., inadequate to meet the charges in the will,—and estates in the county of C., not mentioned in the will. It was held, that parol evidence was inadmissible to show the testator's intention that his real estates in the county of C. should pass by his will. For it was observed, that this would be not merely calling in the aid of extrinsic evidence to apply the intention of the testator, as it was to be collected from the will itself, to the existing state of his property: it would be calling in aid extrinsic evidence to introduce into the will an intention not apparent upon the face of it. It would not be simply removing a difficulty arising from a defective or mistaken description, it would be *making the will speak upon a subject on which it was altogether silent, and would [*637] be the same thing in effect as the filling up a blank which the testator might have left in his will: it would amount, in short, by the admission of parol evidence, to the making of a new devise for the testator, which he was supposed to have omitted.[1] If, then, with all the light which can be thrown upon the instrument by evidence as to the meaning of the description, there appears to be no person or thing answering in any respect thereto, it seems, that, to admit evidence of a different description being intended to be used by the writer, would be to admit evidence for the substitution of one person or thing for another, in violation of the rule, that an averment is not good to increase that which is defective in a written instrument;[2] and consequently the instrument, not admitting of explanation, would be void.[3]

Included in the maxim as to *falsa demonstratio*, is the rule laid down by Lord Bacon in these words: *Præsentia corporis tollit errorem nominis, et veritas nominis tollit errorem demonstrationis;*[4] and

this decision by Sir James Wigram, in the treatise already referred to, and, per Lord Brougham, Mostyn *v.* Mostyn, 5 H. L. Cas. 168.

[1] 8 Bing. 249, 250.

[2] 2 Phil. Evid., 8th ed., 715 *et seq.*

[3] Richardson *v.* Watson, 4 B. & Ad. 787, 796 (24 E. C. L. R.); Drake *v.* Drake, 8 H. L. Cas. 172. See Doe d. Spencer *v.* Pedley, 1 M. & W. 662.

[4] Bac. Max., reg. 24; 6 Rep. 66; 1 Lord Raym. 303; 6 T. R. 675; Doe *v.* Huthwaite, 3 B. & Ald. 640 (5 E. C. L. R.); per Gibbs, C. J., s. c., 8 Taunt. 313 (4 E. C. L. R.); Nicoll *v.* Chambers, 11 C. B. 996 (73 E. C. L. R.), and Hopkins *v.* Hitchcock, 14 C. B. N. S. 65, 73 (108 E. C. L. R.), where there

[*638] which is thus illustrated *by him:—"If I give a horse to J. D., when present, and say to him, 'J. S., take this,' it is a good gift notwithstanding I call him by a wrong name. So, if I say to a man, 'Here, I give you my ring with the ruby,' and deliver it, and the ring is set with a diamond, and not a ruby, yet this is a good gift. In like manner, if I grant my close, called 'Dale,' in the parish of Hurst, in the county of Southampton, and the parish extends also into the county of Berks, and the whole close of Dale lies, in fact, in the last-mentioned county, yet this false addition will not invalidate the grant.[1] Moreover, where things are particularly described, as, 'My box of ivory lying in my study, sealed up with my seal of arms,' 'My suit of arras, with the story of the Nativity and Passion;' inasmuch as of such things there can only be a detailed and circumstantial description, so the precise truth of all the recited circumstances is not required; but, in these cases, the rule is, *ex multitudine signorum colligitur identitas vera;* therefore, though my box were not sealed, and though the arras had the story of the Nativity and not of the Passion embroidered upon it, yet, if I had no other box and no other suit, the gifts would be valid, for there is certainty sufficient, and the law does not expect a precise description of such things as have no certain denomination. Where, however, the description applies accurately to some portion only of the subject-matter of the grant, but is false as to the residue, the former part only will pass; as, if I grant all my land to D., held [*639] by *J. S., which I purchased of J. N., specified in a demise to J. D., and I have land in D., to a part of which

was a misdescription of property in a contract of sale. As to the maxim *supra*, see the remarks of Lord Brougham in Lord Camoys *v.* Blundell, 1 H. L. Cas. 792, 793; Mostyn *v.* Mostyn, 5 H. L. Cas. 155; s. c., 3 De G., M. & G. 140.

In Drake *v.* Drake, 8 H. L. Cas. 179, Lord Campbell, C., observes, "There is a maxim that the name shall prevail against an error of demonstration; but then you must first show that there is an error of demonstration, and until you have shown that, the rule *Veritas nominis tollit errorem demonstrationis* does not apply. I think that there is no presumption in favor of the name more than of the demonstration."

The maxim *supra* was applied per Byles, J., Way *v.* Hearn, 13 C. B. N. S. 307 (106 E. C. L. R.).

[1] See Anstee *v.* Nelms, 1 H. & N. 225; per Byles, J., Rand *v.* Green, 9 C. B. N. S. 477 (99 E. C. L. R.).

the above description applies, and have also other lands in D., to which it is in some respects inapplicable, this grant will not pass all my land in D., but the former portion only."[1] So, if a man grant all his estate in his own occupation in the town of W., no estate can pass except what is in his own occupation and is also situate in that town.[2]

In a recent important case[3] connected with criminal procedure, the maxim *Præsentia corporis tollit errorem nominis* was judicially applied, the facts being as under:—Preparatory to a trial for murder, the name of A., a juror on the panel, was called, and B., another juror on the same panel, appeared, and by mistake answered to the name of A., and was sworn as a juror. A conviction ensued, which a majority of the Court for the Consideration of Crown Cases Reserved held ought not to be set aside, one of the learned judges thus founding his opinion upon the maxim cited:— "The mistake is not a mistake of the man, but only of his name. The very man who, having been duly summoned, and being duly qualified, looked upon the prisoner, and was corporeally presented and shown to the prisoner for challenge, was sworn and acted as a juryman. At the bottom the objection is but this, that the officer of the court, the juryman being present, called and addressed him by a wrong name. Now, it is an old and rational maxim of law, that where the party to a transaction, or the subject of a transaction, are either of *them actually and corporeally present, [*640] the calling of either by a wrong name is immaterial. *Præsentia corporis tollit errorem nominis.* Lord Bacon, in his maxims,[4] fully explains and copiously illustrates this rule of law and good sense, and shows how it applies, not only to persons, but to things. In this case, as soon as the prisoner omitted the challenge, and thereby in effect said, 'I do not object to the juryman there standing,' there arose a compact between the crown and the prisoner that the individual juryman there standing corporeally present should try the case. It matters not, therefore, that some of the accidents of that individual, such as his name, his address, his occupation, should have been mistaken. *Constat de corpore.*"

[1] Bac. Works, vol. 4, pp. 73, 75, 77, 78; Bac. Abr. "*Grants*" (H. 1); Toml. Law Dict. "*Gift;*" Noy, Max., 9th ed., p. 50.

[2] 7 Johns. (U. S.) R. 224.

[3] Reg. *v.* Mellor, 27 L. J. M. C. 121.

[4] *Ubi supra.*

The rules, it has been remarked,[1] which govern the construction of grants have been settled with the greatest wisdom and accuracy. Such effect is to be given to the instrument as will effectuate the intention of the parties, if the words which they employ will admit of it, *ut res magis valeat quam pereat.* Again, if there are certain particulars once sufficiently ascertained which designate the thing intended to be granted, the addition of a circumstance, false or mistaken, will not frustrate the grant.[2] But when the description of the estate intended to be conveyed includes several particulars, all of which are necessary to ascertain the estate to be conveyed, no estate will pass except such as will agree with the description in every particular.[3]

[*641] In Doe d. Gains *v.* Rouse,[4] Lord Bacon's maxim *above cited was felicitously applied. There the testator—having a wife Mary, to whom he was married in 1834, and who survived him—in 1840 went through the ceremony of marriage with a woman whose Christian name was Caroline, and who continued to reside with him as his wife to the time of his death, which took place in 1845. Shortly before his decease the testator by his will devised certain property to "*my dear wife Caroline*, her heirs, &c., absolutely." It was held that Caroline took under this devise the property in question. "The testator," observed Maule, J., "devises the premises in question to his dear wife Caroline. That is a devise to a person by name, and one which appears to be that of the lessor of the plaintiff. There is no competition with any one else of the same name, to whom it can be suggested that the will intended to refer. The only question is, whether the lessor of the plaintiff, not being the lawful wife of the testator, properly fills the description of his 'dear wife Caroline.' Formerly the name was held to be the important thing. This is shown by the 25th maxim of Lord Bacon, to which I have before adverted:—'*Veritas nominis tollit errorem demonstrationis.* So, if I grant land, *Episcopo nunc Londinensi, qui me erudivit in pueritiâ;* this is a good grant, although he never instructed me.' That rule has no doubt been relaxed in modern times, and has given place to another, that the

[1] Jackson *v.* Clark, 7 Johns. (U. S.) R. 223, 224; recognized 18 Id. 84.

[2] Blayne *v.* Gold, Cro. Car. 447, 473, where the rule was applied to a devise.

[3] 3 Atk. 9; Dyer 50.

[4] 5 C. B. 422 (57 E. C. L. R.).

construction of the devise is to be governed by the evident intention of the testator. There are cases in which the courts have gone some length in opposition to the actual words of the will; but always with a view to favoring the apparent or presumed intention of the testator. Here, however, the struggle against the old rule is not that the intention of the testator may be best effectuated by a *departure from it, but to get rid of a devise to the person who was really intended to take. [*642] Here is a person fitly named, and there can be no reasonable doubt that she was the person intended. It being conceded that it was the testator's intention that Caroline should have the property, and he having mentioned her by an apt description, I see no ground for holding that because the words 'my dear wife' are not strictly applicable to her, the intention of the testator should fail and the property go to some one to whom he did not mean to give it. Caroline was *de facto* the testator's wife; and she lived with him as such down to the time of his death. It is possible that the *first* marriage may not have been a valid one. At all events, if Mary was his lawful wife, all that can be said is that the testator had been guilty of bigamy. It is not the case of a description that is altogether inapplicable to the party, but of a description that is in a popular sense applicable. The competition is between one whom the testator clearly did mean, and another whom it is equally clear that he did not mean. Interpreting the language he has used in its proper and legitimate manner, and regard being had to the circumstances existing at the time of the execution of the will, there can be no doubt that the intention of the testator is best effectuated by holding that the lessor of the plaintiff is the person designated, and that apt words have been used to convey the property in question to her."

It is, lastly, a rule, which may be here noticed, that *Non accipi debent verba in demonstrationem falsam quæ competunt in limitationem veram*,[1]—if it be doubtful upon the words, whether they import a false *reference or description, or whether they be words of restraint, limiting the generality of the former [*643] name, the law will not intend error or falsehood[2]—"where words can be applied so as to operate on a subject-matter and limit the

[1] 1 Bac. Max., reg. 13.

[2] Bac. Max., reg. 13, cited 8 East 104.

other terms employed in its description," or "where there is a subject-matter to which they all apply, it is not possible to reject any of those terms as a *falsa demonstratio*."[1] If, therefore, "I have some land wherein all these demonstrations are true, and some wherein part of them are true and part false, then shall they be intended words of true limitation, to pass only those lands wherein all those circumstances are true;"[2] and, if a man pass lands, describing them by particular references, all of which references are true, the court cannot reject any one of them.[3]

Before concluding these remarks, it may be well to state shortly the rules respecting ambiguity and *falsa demonstratio*, in connection with the exposition of wills, which seem to be applicable to four classes of cases:—

1. Where the description of the thing devised, or of the devisee, is clear upon the face of the will, but, upon the death of the testator, it is found that there is more than one estate or subject-matter of devise, or more than one person whose description follows out and fills the words used in the will; in this case parol evidence is *admissible to show what thing was intended to pass, or who was intended to take.[4] [*644]

2. Where the description contained in the will of the thing intended to be devised, or of the person who is intended to take, is true in part, but not true in every particular: in which class of cases parol evidence is admissible to show what estate was intended to pass, and who was the devisee intended to take, provided there is a sufficient indication of intention appearing on the face of the will to justify the application of the evidence.[5]

3. A third class of cases may arise, in which a judge, knowing *aliundê* for whom or for what an imperfect description was intended, would discover a sufficient certainty to act upon; although, if ignorant of the intention, he would be far from finding judicial

[1] Per Willes, J., Smith *v.* Ridgway, L. R. 1 Ex. 332–3; s. c., Id. 46; Judgm., Webber *v.* Stanley, 16 C. B. N. S. 698, 752, *et seq.* (111 E. C. L. R.).

[2] Bac. Max., reg. 13, *ad finem;* cited per Parke, J., Doe d. Ashforth *v.* Bower, 3 B. & Ad. 459, 460 (23 E. C. L. R.); Doe d. Chichester *v.* Oxenden, 3 Taunt. 147; Judgm., Morrell *v.* Fisher, 4 Exch. 604; per Willes, J., Josh *v.* Josh, 5 C. B. N. S. 463 (94 E. C. L. R.).

[3] Per Le Blanc, J., Doe *v.* Lyford, 4 M. & S. 555 (30 E. C. L. R.).

[4] 8 Bing. 248 (21 E. C. L. R.).

[5] Id.

certainty in the words of the devise; and here it would seem that evidence of intention would not be admissible, the description being, *as it stands*, so imperfect as to be useless, unless aided thereby.[1]

4. It may be laid down as a true proposition, which is indeed included within that secondly above given, that, if the description of the person or thing be wholly inapplicable to the subject intended or said to be intended by it, evidence is inadmissible to prove whom or what the testator really intended to describe.[2]

Lastly, we may observe that the maxim, *Falsa demonstratio non nocet*, which we have been considering, obtained in the Roman law;[3] for we find it laid down *in the Institutes, that an error in the proper name or in the surname of the legatee should not make the legacy void, provided it could be understood from the will what person was intended to be benefited thereby. *Si quidem in nomine, cognomine, prænomine legatarii testator erraverit, cum de personâ constat, nihilominus valet legatum.*[4] So, it was a rule akin to the preceding, that *falsâ demonstratione legatum non perimi*,[5] as if the testator bequeathed his bondsman, Stichus, whom he bought of Titius, whereas Stichus had been given to him or purchased by him of some other person;[6] in such a case the misdescription would not avoid the bequest.[7] [*645]

It is evident that the maxims above cited, and others to a similar purport which occur both in the civil law and in our own reports, are, in fact, deducible from those very general principles with the consideration of which we commenced this chapter—*Benignè faciendæ sunt interpretationes, et verba intentioni non e contrà debent inservire.*[8]

[1] See this subject considered, Wigram Extrin. Ev., 3d ed., 166, 167.

[2] Wigram Extrin. Ev., 3d ed., 163.

[3] See Phillimore Roman Law 35.

[4] I. 2. 20. 29; compare D. 30. 1. 4; also 2 Domat, Bk. 2, tit. 1, s. 6, § 10, 19; Id. s. 8, § 11.

[5] I. 2. 20. 30. See Whitfield *v.* Clemment, 1 Mer. 402.

[6] I. 2. 20. 30.

[7] Id.; Wood Inst., 3d ed., 165.

[8] It may probably be unnecessary to remind the reader that the cases decided with reference to the rule of construction considered in the preceding pages are exceedingly numerous, and that such only have been noticed as seemed peculiarly adapted to the purposes of illustration. A similar remark is equally applicable to the other maxims commented on in this chapter.

[*646] *VERBA GENERALIA RESTRINGUNTUR AD HABILITATEM REI VEL PERSONAM.

(Bac. Max., reg. 10.)

General words may be aptly restrained according to the subject-matter or persons to which they relate.[1]

"It is a rule," observes Lord Bacon,[2] "that the king's grant shall not be taken or construed to a special intent. It is not so with the grants of a common person, for they shall be extended as well to a foreign intent as to a common intent, but yet with this exception, that they shall never be taken to an impertinent or repugnant intent; for all words, whether they be in deeds or statutes, or otherwise, if they be general, and not express and precise, shall be restrained unto the fitness of the matter and the person."[3]

Thus, if I grant common "in all my lands" in D., if I have in D. both open grounds and several, it shall not be stretched to common in my several grounds, much less in my garden or orchard. So, if I grant to J. S. an annuity of 10*l.* a year, "*pro concilio, impenso et* [*647] **impendendo*" (for past and future council), if J. S. be a physician, this shall be understood of his advice in physic, and, if he be a lawyer, of his counsel in legal matters.[4] And in accordance with the same principle a right of common of

[1] Per Willes, J., Moore *v.* Rawlins, 6 C. B. N. S. 320 (95 E. C. L. R.); citing Payler *v.* Homersham, 4 M. & S. 423 (30 E. C. L. R.); and in Chorlton *v.* Lings, L. R. 4 C. P. 387.

General words may be controlled by the recital in an instrument. See Bank of British North America *v.* Cuvillier, 14 Moo. P. C. C. 187, and cases there cited.

[2] Bac. Max., reg. 10; 6 Rep. 62.

[3] The maxim *supra* was accordingly applied to restrain the words of a general covenant by a railway company to "efficiently work" a line demised to them—the covenant being construed "with a reference to the subject-matter and the character of the defendants:" West London R. C. *v.* London and North-Western R. C., 11 C. B. 254, 356 (73 E. C. L. R.).

The maxim was applied to a policy of insurance: arg. Baines *v.* Holland, 10 Exch. 805.

Though a release be general in its terms, its operation will, at law, in conformity with the doctrine recognized in courts of equity, be limited to matters contemplated by the parties at the time of its execution: Lyall *v.* Edwards, 6 H. & N. 337.

[4] Bac. Works, vol. 4, p. 46. See Com. Dig., "*Condition*" (K. 4).

turbary claimed by prescription and user has been held to be restrained to those parts of the *locus in quo* in which it could be used.[1]

In accordance, likewise, with the above maxim, the subject-matter of an agreement is to be considered in construing the terms of it, and they are to be understood in the sense most agreeable to the nature of the agreement.[2] If a deed relates to a particular subject only, general words in it shall be confined to that subject, otherwise they must be taken in their general sense.[3] The words of the condition of a bond "cannot be taken at large, but must be tied up to the particular matters of the recital,"[4] unless, indeed, the condition itself is manifestly designed to be extended beyond the recital;[5] and, further, it is a rule, that what is generally spoken shall be generally understood, *generalia verba sunt generaliter intelligenda*,[6] unless it be qualified by some special subsequent words, as it may be;[7] *ex. gr.*, the *operative words of a bill of sale may be restricted by what follows.[8] [*648]

In construing the words of any instrument, then, it is proper to

[1] Peardon *v.* Underhill, 16 Q. B. 120 (71 E. C. L. R.).

[2] 1 T. R. 703.

[3] Thorpe *v.* Thorpe, 1 Lord Raym. 235; s. c., Id. 662.

[4] Per Eyre, J., Gilb. Cas. 240. See Seller *v.* Jones, 16 M. & W. 112, 118; Stoughton *v.* Day, Aleyn 10; Lord Arlington *v.* Merrick, 2 Saund. 414; as to which, see Mayor of Berwick *v.* Oswald, 3 E. & B. 653 (77 E. C. L. R.); s. c., 5 H. L. Cas. 856; Kitson *v.* Julian, 4 E. & B. 854, 858 (82 E. C. L. R.); Napier *v.* Bruce, 8 Cl. & Fin. 470; North-Western R. C. *v.* Whinray, 10 Exch. 77.

[5] Sansom *v.* Bell, 2 Camp. 39; Com. Dig., "*Parols*" (A. 19); Evans *v.* Earle, 10 Exch. 1.

[6] 3 Inst. 76.

[7] Shep. Touch. 88; Co. Litt. 42 a; Com. Dig., "*Parols*" (A. 7).

[8] Wood *v.* Rowcliffe, 6 Exch. 407.

See also with reference to a release, the authorities cited, *ante*, p. 544, n. 5, p. 646, n. 3.

Where the words in the operative part of a deed of conveyance are of doubtful meaning, the recitals and other parts of the deed may be used as a test to discover the intention of the parties, and to fix the true meaning of those words: Judgm., Welsh *v.* Trevanion, 15 Q. B. 751 (69 E. C. L. R.). See also Young *v.* Raincock, 7 C. B. 310 (62 E. C. L. R.); *post*, p. 652, n. 3.

As to the mode of construing a deed containing restrictive covenants, see, per Dallas, C. J., Nind *v.* Marshall, 1 B. & B. 348, 349 (5 E. C. L. R.); cited arg. Crossfield *v.* Morrison, 7 C. B. 302 (62 E. C. L. R.).

consider, 1st, what is their meaning in the largest sense which, according to the common use of language, belongs to them;[1] and, if it should appear that that sense is larger than the sense in which they must be understood in the instrument in question, then, 2dly, what is the object for which they are used. They ought not to be extended beyond their ordinary sense in order to comprehend a case within their object, for that would be to give effect to an intention not expressed; nor can they be so restricted as to exclude a case both within their object and within their ordinary sense, without violating the fundamental rule, which requires that effect should be given to such intention of the parties as they have used fit words to express.[2] Thus, in a settlement, the preamble usually recites what it is which the grantor intends to do, and this, like the preamble to an Act of Parliament, is the key to what comes afterwards. It is very common, moreover, to put in a sweeping clause, the use and object of which are to *guard against any accidental omission; but in such cases it is meant to refer to estates or things of the same nature and description with those which have been already mentioned, and such general words are not allowed to extend further than was clearly intended by the parties.[3]

[*649]

So, in construing a will, a court of justice is not by conjecture to take out of the effect of general words property which those words are always considered as comprehending; the best rule of construction being that which takes the words to comprehend a subject which falls within their usual sense, unless there is something like declaration plain to the contrary.[4] Thus, it is a certain rule, that reversions are held to be included in the general words of a devise, unless a manifest intention to the contrary appears on the face of the will.[5]

Again, it is a well-known rule that a devise of an indefinite estate by will prior to the first of January, 1838, without words of

[1] 3 Inst. 76.

[2] Per Maule, J., Borradaile *v.* Hunter, 5 Scott N. R. 431, 432. See in illustration of these remarks, Moseley *v.* Motteux, 10 M. & W. 533.

[3] Per Lord Mansfield, C. J., Moore *v.* Magrath, 1 Cowp. 12; Shep. Touch., by Atherley, 79, n.

[4] Per Lord Eldon, C., Church *v.* Mundy, 15 Ves. 396; adopted per Tindal, C. J., Doe d. Howell *v.* Thomas, 1 Scott N. R. 371.

[5] 1 Scott N. R. 371.

limitation, is *primâ facie* a devise for life only; but this rule will give way to a different intention, if such can be collected from the instrument, and the estate may be accordingly enlarged.[1] So, words which would *primâ facie* give an estate tail may be cut down to a life estate, if it plainly appear that they were used as words of purchase only, or if the other provisions *of the will show [*650] a general intent inconsistent with the particular gift.[2]

The doctrine, however, that the general intent must overrule the particular intent, observes Lord Denman, C. J., has, when applied to the construction of wills, been much and justly objected to of late, as being, as a general proposition, incorrect and vague, and likely to lead in its application to erroneous results. In its origin it was merely descriptive of the operation of the rule in Shelley's Case;[3] and it has since been laid down in other cases where technical words of limitation have been used, and other words, showing the intention of the testator that the objects of his bounty should take in a different way from that which the law allows, have been rejected; but in the latter cases the more correct mode of stating the rule of construction is, that technical words, or words of known legal import, must have their legal effect, even though the testator uses inconsistent words, unless those inconsistent words are of such a nature as to make it perfectly clear that the testator did not mean to use the technical words in their proper sense.[4] The doctrine of general and particular intent, thus explained, should be applied to all wills,"[5] in conjunction with the rule already considered, viz., that every part of that which the testator meant by the words he has used should be carried into effect as far as the law

[1] Doe d. Sams *v.* Garlick, 14 M. & W. 698; Doe d. Atkinson *v.* Fawcett, 3 C. B. 274 (54 E. C. L. R.); Lewis *v.* Puxley, 16 M. & W. 733. See stat. 1 Vict. c. 26, s. 28.

In Hogan *v.* Jackson, 1 Cowp. 299, s. c., affirmed 3 Bro. P. C., 2d ed., 388, the effect of general words in a will was much considered.

[2] Fetherston *v.* Fetherston, 3 Cl. & Fin. 75, 76; *ante*, pp. 555 *et seq.*

[3] *Ante*, p. 558. See d. Cannon *v.* Rucastle, 8 C. B. 876 (65 E. C. L. R.).

[4] See Judgm., Toller *v.* Wright, 15 Q. B. 954 (69 E. C. L. R.), and cases there cited.

[5] Judgm., Doe d. Gallini *v.* Gallini, 5 B. & Ad. 621, 640 (27 E. C. L. R.); Jesson *v.* Wright, 2 Bligh 57; Roddy *v.* Fitzgerald, 6 H. L. Cas. 823; Jordan *v.* Adams, 9 C. B. N. S. 483 (99 E. C. L. R.); Jenkins *v.* Hughes, 8 H. L. Cas. 571.

[*651] will permit, but no further; and that no part should be *rejected, except what the law makes it necessary to reject.[1]

Lastly, it is said to be a good rule of construction, that, "where an Act of Parliament begins with words which describe things or persons of an inferior degree and concludes with general words, the general words shall not be extended to any thing or person of a higher degree,"[2] that is to say, "where a particular class [of persons or things] is spoken of, and general words follow, the class first mentioned is to be taken as the most comprehensive, and the general words treated as referring to matters *ejusdem generis* with such class,"[3] the effect of general words when they follow particular words being thus restricted.[4]

EXPRESSIO UNIUS EST EXCLUSIO ALTERIUS.

(Co. Litt. 210 a.)

The express mention of one thing implies the exclusion of another.

The above rule, or, as it is otherwise worded, *expressum facit cessare tacitum*,[5] enunciates one of the first principles applicable to [*652] the construction of written instruments;[6] *for instance, it seems plainly to exclude any increase of an estate by implication, where there is an estate expressly limited by will.[7] So an

[1] Judgm., 5 B. & Ad. 641 (27 E. C. L. R.).

[2] Archb. of Canterbury's Case, 2 Rep. 46 a, cited, arg. Casher *v.* Holmes, 2 B. & Ad. 594 (22 E. C. L. R.); and in Governors of Bedford Infirmary *v.* Commissioners of Bedford, 7 Exch. 772.

[3] Per Pollock, C. B., Lyndon *v.* Stanbridge, 2 H. & N. 51; per Lord Campbell, C. J., Reg. *v.* Edmundson, 2 E. & E. 83 (102 E. C. L. R.); Gibbs *v.* Lawrence, 30 L. J. Chanc. 170.

"Where a general enactment is followed by a special enactment on the same subject, the latter enactment overrides and controls the earlier one:" per Erle, C. J., 14 C. B. N. S. 433 (108 E. C. L. R.).

The rule stated in the text applies also to deeds and agreements. See, for instance, Agar *v.* Athenæum Life Ass. Soc., 3 C. B. N. S. 725 (91 E. C. L. R.).

[4] See Reg. *v.* Cleworth, 4 B. & S. 927, 934 (116 E. C. L. R.).

[5] Co. Litt. 210 a, 183 b.

[6] See per Lord Denman, C. J., 5 Bing. N. C. 185 (35 E. C. L. R.).

[7] Per Crompton, J., Roddy *v.* Fitzgerald, 6 H. L. Cas. 856.

implied covenant is to be controlled within the limits of an express covenant.[1] Where a lease contains an express covenant on the part of the tenant to repair, there can be no implied contract to repair arising from the relation of landlord and tenant.[2] So, although the word "demise" in a lease implies a covenant for title and a covenant for quiet enjoyment, yet both branches of such implied covenant are restrained by an express covenant for quiet enjoyment.[3] And, where parties have entered into *written engagements with express stipulations, it is manifestly not desirable to extend them by implications; the presumption is, that having expressed *some*, they have expressed *all* the conditions by which they intend to be bound under that instrument.[4] And it is an ordinary rule that "if authority is given expressly, though by affirm-

[*653]

[1] Nokes' Case, 4 Rep. 80; s. c., Cro. Eliz. 674; Merrill *v.* Frame, 4 Taunt. 329; Gainsford *v.* Griffith, 1 Saund. R. 58; Vaugh. R. 126; Deering *v.* Farrington, 1 Ld. Raym. 14, 19; Matthew *v.* Blackmore, 1 H. & N. 762. See Bower *v.* Hodges, 13 C. B. 765 (76 E. C. L. R.); Rashleigh *v.* South-Eastern R. C., 10 C. B. 612 (70 E. C. L. R.).

[2] Standen *v.* Christmas, 10 Q. B. 135, 141 (59 E. C. L. R.); as to which see, per Bramwell, B., Churchward *v.* Ford, 2 H. & K. 450; *et vide* Gott *v.* Gandy, 2 E. & B. 847 (75 E. C. L. R.).

"The authorities cited in the text-books establish these rules, that where there is a *general* covenant to repair and keep and leave in repair, the inference is that the lessee undertakes to repair newly erected buildings. On the other hand, where the covenant is to repair, and keep and leave in repair the *demised buildings*, no such liability arises:" per Channell, B., Cornish *v.* Cleiff, 3 H. & C. 452–3.

[3] Line *v.* Stephenson, 5 Bing. N. C. 183 (35 E. C. L. R.); Merrill *v.* Frame, 4 Taunt. 329; per Lord St. Leonards, Monypenny *v.* Monypenny, 9 H. L. Cas. 139. See Messent *v.* Reynolds, 3 C. B. 194 (54 E. C. L. R.). By stat. 8 & 9 Vict. c. 106, s. 4, it is enacted that the word "give" or "grant" in a deed executed after the 1st of October, 1845, shall not imply any covenant in law in respect of any hereditament, except by force of some Act of Parliament. A covenant for quiet enjoyment, however, is also implied by the word "demise" in a lease for years; and this implication is not taken away by either of the recent stats. (7 & 8 Vict. c. 76, and 8 & 9 Vict. c. 106).

By agreeing to let a lessor impliedly promises that he has a good title to let: Stranks *v.* St. John, L. R. 2 C. P. 376.

[4] Judgm., Aspdin *v.* Austin, 5 Q. B. 683, 684 (48 E. C. L. R.); Dunn *v.* Sayles, Id. 685; Emmens *v.* Elderton, 4 H. L. Cas. 624; M'Guire *v.* Scully, Beatt. 370.

As to Aspdin *v.* Austin, *supra*, see per Crompton, J., Worthington *v.* Ludlow, 2 B. & S. 516 (110 E. C. L. R.).

ative words, upon a defined condition, the expression of that condition excludes the doing of the act authorized, under other circumstances than those so defined: *expressio unius est exclusio alterius*."[1]

It will, however, be proper to observe, before proceeding to give instances in illustration of the maxim *expressio unius est exclusio alterius*, that a great caution[2] is requisite in dealing with it, for, as Lord Campbell, C., observed in Saunders *v.* Evans,[3] it is not of universal application, but depends upon the intention of the party as discoverable upon the face of the instrument or of the transaction; thus, where *general words* are used in a written instrument, it is necessary, in the first instance, to determine whether those general words are intended to include other matters besides such as are specifically mentioned, or to be referable exclusively to them, in which latter case only can the above maxim be properly applied.[4] [*654] Where, moreover, an expression, which is **primâ facie* a word of qualification, is introduced, the true sense and meaning of the word can only be ascertained by an examination of the entire instrument, reference being had to those ordinary rules of construction to which we have heretofore adverted.[5]

In illustration of the maxim above proposed for consideration, the following cases may be mentioned:—In an action of covenant on a charter party, whereby the defendant covenanted to pay so much freight for "goods delivered at A.," it was held, that freight could not be recovered *pro rata itineris*, the ship having been wrecked at B. before her arrival at A., although the defendant accepted his goods at B.; for, the action being on the original agreement, the defendant had a right to say in answer to it, *non hæc in fœdera veni.*[6] In order to recover freight *pro rata itineris*,

[1] Per Willes, J., North Stafford Steel, &c., Co. *v.* Ward, L. R. 3 Ex. 177.

[2] To show the caution necessary in applying the above rule may be cited Price *v.* The Great Western R. C., 16 M. & W. 244; Attwood *v.* Small, 6 Cl. & Fin. 482, and see the remarks, *post*, p. 667.

[3] 8 H. L. Cas. 729; *et vide*, per Dr. Lushington, The Amalia, 32 L. J., P., M. & A. 194.

[4] See Petch *v.* Tutin, 15 M. & W. 110.

[5] In Doe d. Lloyd *v.* Ingleby, 15 M. & W. 465, 472, the maxim was applied by Parke, B., *diss.*, to a proviso for re-entry in a lease, and this case will serve to illustrate the above remark.

[6] Cook *v.* Jennings, 7 T. R. 381. See Vlierboom *v.* Chapman, 13 M. & W. 230. In Fowkes *v.* Manchester and London Life Ass. Co., 3 B. & S. 917, 930

the owner must, in such a case, proceed on the new agreement implied by law from the merchant's behavior.[1]

Again, on a mortgage of dwelling-houses, foundries, and other premises, "together with all grates, boilers, bells, and other fixtures in and about the said two dwelling-houses and the brew-houses thereunto belonging;" it was held, that although, without these words, the fixtures in the foundries would have passed, yet, by them, the fixtures intended to pass were confined to those in the *dwelling-houses and brew-houses.[2] So, where in an instrument there are general words first, and an express exception afterwards, the ordinary principle of law has been said to apply—*expressio unius exclusio alterius.*[3] [*655]

The case of Doe d. Spilsbury *v.* Burdett[4] furnishes a good illustration of the above maxim. In that case lands were limited to such uses as S. should appoint by her last will and testament in writing, to be by her signed, sealed, and published, in the presence of and attested by three or more credible witnesses. S. (prior to the stats. 7 Will. 4 & 1 Vict. c. 26)[5] signed and sealed ani nstru-

(113 E. C. L. R.), the principal maxim, *supra*, was applied to a policy of insurance. See 8 E. & B. 301 (92 E. C. L. R.).

[1] Per Lawrence, J., 7 T. R. 385; Mitchell *v.* Darthez, 2 Bing. N. C. 555, 571 (29 E. C. L. R.).

[2] Hare *v.* Horton, 5 B. & Ad. 715 (27 E. C. L. R.); cited Mather *v.* Frazer, 2 K. & J. 536. See Ringer *v.* Cann, 3 M. & W. 343; Cooper *v.* Walker, 4 B. & C. 36, 49 (10 E. C. L. R.).

[3] Spry *v.* Flood, 2 Curt. 365.

[4] 7 Scott N. R. 66, 79, 101, 104; s. c., 9 A. & E. 936 (36 E. C. L. R.); 4 A. & E. 1 (31 E. C. L. R.). The decision of the House of Lords in the above case went upon the principle, *expressio unius exclusio alterius* (per Sir H. Jenner Fust, Barnes *v.* Vincent, 9 Jur. 261; s. c. (reversed in error), 5 Moore P. C. C. 201), and the opinions delivered in it by the judges will also be found to illustrate the importance of adhering to precedents, *ante*, p. 149; the argument *ab inconvenienti*, p. 184, and the general principle of construing an instrument *ut res magis valeat quam pereat*, p. 540; Doe d. Spilsbury *v.* Burdett, is commented on per Wigram, V.-C., Vincent *v.* Bishop of Sodor and Man, 8 C. B. 929 (65 E. C. L. R.); and was followed and affirmed in Newton *v.* Ricketts, 9 H. L. Cas. 262, 269. See, also, Johns *v.* Dickinson, 8 C. B. 934 (65 E. C. L. R.); Roberts *v.* Phillips, 4 E. & B. 450, 453 (82 E. C. L. R.).

[5] Sec. 9 enacts, that every will shall be in writing, and signed by the testator in the presence of two witnesses at one time; and sec. 10, that appointments by will shall be executed like other wills, and shall be valid, although other required solemnities are not observed. *Ante*, p. 558.

ment, containing an appointment, commencing thus: "I, S., do publish and declare this to be my last will and testament;" and concluding, "I declare this only to be my last will and testament; in witness whereof I have to this my last will and testament set my hand and seal, this 12th of December, 1789." And then followed [*656] *the attestation, thus: "Witness C. B., E. B., A. B." It was decided by the House of Lords that the power was well executed; and this case was distinguished from several,[1] in which the attestation clause, in terms, stated the performance of one or more of the required formalities, but was silent as to the others, and in which, consequently, the power was held to have been badly exercised, on the ground, that legal reasoning would necessarily infer the non-performance of such others in the presence of the witnesses, but that a general attestation clause imported an attesting of *all* the requisites.

The operation of the principle under consideration is, moreover, the same, whether the contract be under seal or by parol. For instance, in order to prevent a debt being barred by the Statute of Limitations, a conditional promise to pay "as soon as I can," or "as soon as convenient," is not sufficient, unless proof be given of the defendant's ability to perform the condition; and the reason is, that upon a general acknowledgment, where nothing is said to prevent it, a general promise to pay may and ought to be implied; but where the party guards his acknowledgment, and accompanies it with an express declaration to prevent any such implication, then the rule, *expressum facit cessare tacitum*, applies.[2] In like manner, when the drawer of a bill, when applied to for payment, does not state that he has received no notice of dishonor, but instead of [*657] doing so, sets up some other *matter in excuse of non-payment, from this conduct the jury may infer an admission that the valid ground of defence does not in fact exist.[3]

[1] See particularly Wright *v.* Wakeford, 17 Ves. jun. 454; s. c., 4 Taunt. 213; commented on per Wigram, V.-C., 8 C. B. 929 *et seq.* (65 E. C. L. R.); Doe d. Mansfield *v.* Peach, 2 M. & S. 576; Doe d. Hotchkins *v.* Pearse, 2 Marsh. 102; s. c., 6 Taunt. 402 (1 E. L. C. R.). See per Patteson, J., 7 Scott N. R. 120, 121; per Tindal, C. J., Id. 126.

[2] Judgm., Tanner *v.* Smart, 6 B. & C. 609 (13 E. C. L. R.); Edmunds *v.* Downes, 2 Cr. & M. 459. See Irving *v.* Veitch, 3 M. & W. 90, 112; Broom's Com., 4th ed., 185.

[3] Campbell *v.* Webster, 2 C. B. 258, 266 (52 E. C. L. R.).

The above cases will sufficiently show the practical application and utility of the maxim or principle of construction, *expressum facit cessare tacitum;* and several of them will likewise serve to illustrate the general rule, which will be considered more in detail hereafter,[1] viz., that parol evidence is, except in certain cases, wholly inadmissible to show terms upon which a written instrument is silent; or, in other words, that, where there is an express contract between parties, none can be implied.[2] The court will not, "by inference, insert in a contract implied provisions with respect to a subject which the contract has expressly provided for. If a man sell a horse and warrant it to be sound, the vendor knowing at the time that the purchaser wants it for the purpose of carrying a lady, and the horse though sound proves to be unfit for that particular purpose, this would be no breach of the warranty. So, with respect to any other kind of warranty: the maxim *expressum facit cessare tacitum* applies to such cases. If this were not so, it would be *necessary for the parties to every agreement to provide in terms that they are to be understood not to be bound by anything which is not expressly set down,—which would be manifestly inconvenient."[3] [*658]

The following cases may here properly be noticed in further illustration of the maxim before us:—where the rent of a house was specified in a written agreement to be 26*l.* a year, and the landlord, in an action for use and occupation, proposed to show, by parol evidence, that the tenant had also agreed to pay the ground-rent, the court refused to admit the evidence.[4]

[1] See the maxim, *Nihil tam conveniens est naturali æquitati quam unumquodque dissolvi eodem ligamine quo ligatum est—post,* Chap. IX., and the maxim, *Optimus interpres rerum usus—post,* Chap. X.

[2] Per Bayley, J., Grimman *v.* Legge, 8 B. & C. 326 (15 E. C. L. R.); Moorsom *v.* Kymer, 2 M. & S. 316, 320 (28 E. C. L. R.); Cook *v.* Jennings, 7 T. R. 383, 385; per Lord Kenyon, C. J., Id. 137; Cowley *v.* Dunlop, Id. 568; Cutter *v.* Powell, 6 T. R. 320; s. c., 2 Smith L. C., 6th ed., 1 (with which compare Taylor *v.* Laird, 1 H. & N. 266; Button *v.* Thompson, L. R. 4 C. P. 330); per Buller, J., Toussaint *v.* Martinnant, 2 T. R. 105; per Parke, B., Bradbury *v.* Anderton, 1 Cr., M. & R. 190; Mitchell *v.* Darthez, 2 Bing. N. C. 555 (29 E. C. L. R.); Lawrence *v.* Sydebotham, 6 East 45, 52; per Blackburn, J., Fowkes *v.* Manchester and London Life Ass. Co., 3 B. & S. 930 (113 E. C. L. R.).

[3] Per Maule, J., Dickson *v.* Zizinia, 10 C. B. 610, 611 (70 E. C. L. R.).

[4] Preston *v.* Merceau, 2 W. Bla. 1249; Rich *v.* Jackson, 4 Bro. C. C. 515.

By an agreement between plaintiff and defendant for the purchase by the former of the manor of S., it was agreed that, on the completion of the purchase, the purchaser should be entitled to the "rents and profits of such parts of the estate as were let" from the 24th day of June, 1843: it was held, that the plaintiff was not, by virtue of this agreement, entitled to recover from the defendant the amount of a fine received by the latter on the admittance of a tenant of certain copyhold premises, part of the said manor, this admittance, after being postponed from time to time, having taken place on the 1st of July, 1843, and the fine having been paid in the December following; for the condition above mentioned was held applicable to such parts of the estate only as might be "let" in the ordinary sense of that word, and *expressio unius est exclusio* [*659] *alterius;* the lands in question *not having been let, it could not be said that the plaintiff was entitled to the sum of money sought to be recovered, the agreement binding the vendor to pay over the *rents* only, and not extending to the casual profits.[1]

On the same principle, where the conditions of sale of growing timber did not state anything as to *quantity*, parol evidence, that the auctioneer at the time of sale warranted a certain quantity, was held inadmissible.[2] And here we may observe that, as a general rule, whatever particular *quality* a party warrants, he shall be bound to make good to the letter of the warranty, whether such quality be otherwise material or not; and it is only necessary for the buyer to show that the article sold is not according to the warranty. Where, however, an article is sold by description merely, and the buyer afterwards discovers a *latent* defect, in this case *expressum facit cessare tacitum;* he must, therefore, go further, and show that the description was false within the knowledge of the seller. Thus, where a warranty of a horse was in these terms—"Received of B. 10*l.* for a gray four-year-old colt, warranted sound"—it was held, that the warranty was confined to soundness; and that, without proving fraud, it was no ground of

See Sweetland *v.* Smith, 1 Cr. & M. 585, 596; Doe d. Rogers *v.* Pullen, 2 Bing. N. C. 749, 753 (29 E. C. L. R.), where the maxim considered in the text is applied by Tindal, C. J., to the case of a tenancy between mortgagor and mortgagee.

[1] Earl of Hardwicke *v.* Lord Sandys, 12 M. & W. 761.

[2] Powell *v.* Edmunds, 12 East 6.

action, that the colt was only three years old.[1] So, upon a sale of hops by sample, with a warranty that the bulk of the commodity answered the sample, although a fair merchantable price was given, it was held, that the seller was not responsible for a latent defect (which existed both in the sample and the bulk) unknown to him, but arising from the fraud of the *grower from whom he [*660] purchased.[2] In this case, the general warranty, implied by law, that the goods were merchantable, was excluded by the express warranty of the vendor.

This distinction must, however, be taken, that, where the warranty is one which the law implies,[3] it is clearly admissible in evidence, notwithstanding there is a written contract, if such contract be entirely silent on the subject. For instance, the defendant sold to the plaintiff a barge, and there was a contract in writing between the parties; but it was held, that a warranty was *implied* by law that the barge was *reasonably fit* for use, and that evidence was admissible to show that, in consequence of the defective construction of the barge, certain cement, which the plaintiff was conveying therein, was damaged, and that the plaintiff incurred expense in rendering her fit for the purpose of his trade—a purpose to which the defendant knew, at the time of the contract, that she was intended to be applied.[4] And where defendant undertook to supply the plaintiffs with troop stores, "guaranteed to pass survey of the East India Company's officers," this express guarantee was held not to exclude the warranty implied by law, that the stores should be reasonably fit for the purpose for which they were intended.[5] And where goods are to be supplied according to sample, the sell-

[1] Budd *v.* Fairmaner, 8 Bing. 48, 52 (21 E. C. L. R.). See per Parke, B., Mondel *v.* Steel, 8 M. & W. 865; and the cases cited under the maxim *caveat emptor—post*, Chap. IX.

[2] Parkinson *v.* Lee, 2 East 314, recognized, 8 Bing. 52 (21 E. C. L. R.). See, also, Laing *v.* Fidgeon, 6 Taunt. 108 (1 E. C. L. R.); Chanter *v.* Hopkins, 4 M. & W. 399; recognized, Pacific Steam Nav. Co. *v.* Lewis, 16 M. & W. 783; and in Prideaux *v.* Bunnett, 1 C. B. N. S. 613, 617 (87 E. C. L. R.).

[3] As to implied warranties and undertakings, see under the maxim *caveat emptor—post*, p. 768.

[4] Shepherd *v.* Pybus, 4 Scott N. R. 434; Gardiner *v.* Gray, 4 Camp. 144

[5] Bigge *v.* Parkinson, 7 H. & N. 955.

[*661] ing by sample excludes the implied warranty that *the goods shall be of merchantable quality only with respect to such matters as could be judged of by the sample.[1]

A marked distinction will at once be noticed between cases falling within the class just noticed and those in which it has been held, that, where a warranty or contract of sale has reference to a certain specified chattel, the purchaser will be liable for the price agreed upon, on proof that the particular chattel specified has been duly sent according to the order, and will not be permitted to engraft any additional terms upon the contract. If, for instance, a "two-color printing-machine," being a known and ascertained article, has been ordered by the defendant, he cannot excuse himself from liability to pay for it, by showing that the article in question does not answer his purpose, because the sole undertaking in this case on the part of the vendor was to supply the particular article ordered, and that undertaking has been performed by him. If, on the other hand, the article ordered by the defendant were not a known and ascertained article—as if he had merely ordered, and plaintiff had agreed to supply, a machine for printing two colors—the defendant would not be liable unless the instrument were reasonably fit for the purpose for which it was ordered.[2] As we shall, in the ensuing chapter, have occasion to revert to the subject of implied warranty, we may for the present content ourselves with the single instance just given as sufficiently showing the distinction to which allusion has above been made.

[*662] *But although the maxim, *Expressio unius est exclusio alterius*, ordinarily operates to exclude evidence offered with the view of annexing incidents to written contracts[3] in matters

[1] Mody *v.* Gregson, L. R. 4 Ex. 49.

[2] Ollivant *v.* Bayley, 5 Q. B. 288 (48 E. C. L. R.); Prideaux *v.* Bunnett, 1 C. B. N. S. 613 (87 E. C. L. R.); Parsons *v.* Sexton, 4 C. B. 899 (56 E. C. L. R.); Mallan *v.* Radloff, 17 C. B. N. S. 588 (112 E. C. L. R.); and cases cited, *post*, Chap. IX., under the maxim *Caveat emptor*.

[3] See Cutter *v.* Powell, 6 T. R. 320; Pettitt *v.* Mitchell, 5 Scott N. R. 721; Moon *v.* Witney Union, 3 Bing. N. C. 814, 818 (32 E. C. L. R.); cited and distinguished in Moffat *v.* Laurie, 15 C. B. 583, 592 (80 E. C. L. R.); and in Scrivener *v.* Pask, 18 C. B. N. S. 785, 797 (114 E. C. L. R.); Reg. *v.* Stoke-upon-Trent, 5 Q. B. 303 (48 E. C. L. R.). It is a general rule that, upon a mercantile instrument, evidence of usage may be given in explanation of an ambiguous expression: Bowman *v.* Horsey, 2 M. & Ry. 85. Generally as to

with respect to which they are silent, yet it has long been settled, that, in commercial transactions, extrinsic evidence of custom and usage is admissible for this purpose.[1] The same rule has, moreover, been applied to contracts in other transactions of life, especially to those between landlord and tenant,[2] in which known usages have been established and prevailed; and this has been done upon the principle of presuming that in such transactions the parties did not mean to express in writing the whole of the contract by which they intended to be bound, but a contract with reference to those known usages.[3] Whether such a relaxation of the strictness of the common law was wisely applied where formal instruments have been entered into, and particularly leases under seal, may, it has been observed, well be doubted; but this relaxation has been established by such authority, and the relations of landlord and tenant have been so long regulated upon the supposition that all customary obligations, not altered by the contract, are to [*663] *remain in force, that it is too late to pursue a contrary course, since it would be productive of much inconvenience if the practice were now to be disturbed.[4] As an instance of the admissibility of evidence respecting any special custom, may be mentioned the ordinary case in which an agreement to farm according to the custom of the country is held to apply to a tenancy where the contract to hold as a tenant is in writing, but is altogether silent as to the terms or mode of farming.[5]

Every demise, indeed, between landlord and tenant in respect of matters as to which the parties are silent, may be fairly open to explanation by the general usage and custom of the country, or of the district where the land lies; for all persons, under such circumstances, are supposed to be cognizant of the custom, and to contract with a tacit reference to it.[6]

the admissibility of evidence of usage to explain mercantile instruments, see Broom's Com., 4th ed., Book II., Chap. IV.

[1] Syers *v.* Jonas, 2 Exch. 111, 117; cited per Willes, J., Azémar *v.* Casella, L. R. 2 C. P. 439; and cases collected under the maxim *optimus interpres rerum usus*—*post*, Chap. X.

[2] *Ante*, pp. 412 *et seq.*

[3] Per Parke, B., Smith *v.* Wilson, 3 B. & Ad. 728 (23 E. C. L. R.).

[4] Judgm., Hutton *v.* Warren, 1 M. & W. 475, 478; Wigglesworth *v.* Dallison, cited *ante*, p. 413, is the leading case upon the subject above noticed.

[5] Judgm., 4 Scott N. R. 446.

[6] Per Story, J., 2 Peters (U. S.) R. 148.

It is, however, a settled rule, that, although in certain cases evidence of custom or usage is admissible to annex incidents to a written contract, it can in no case be given in contravention thereof;[1] and the principle of varying written contracts by the custom of trade has been in many cases, of which some few are cited *infra*, distinctly repudiated.[2]

[*664] *A statute, it has been said,[3] is to be so construed, if possible, as to give sense and meaning to every part; and the maxim was never more applicable than when applied to the interpretation of a statute, that *expressio unius est exclusio alterius*.[4] The sages of the law, according to Plowden, have ever been guided

[1] Yeats *v.* Pym, 6 Taunt. 446; Clarke *v.* Roystone, 13 M. & W. 752; Suse *v.* Pompe, 8 C. B. N. S. 538 (98 E. C. L. R.). See Palmer *v.* Blackburn, 1 Bing. 61 (8 E. C. L. R.).

[2] Spartali *v.* Benecke, 10 C. B. 212, 223 (70 E. C. L. R.); Dickenson *v.* Jardine, L. R. 3 C. P. 639; Johnstone *v.* Usborne, 11 A. & E. 549, 557 (39 E. C. L. R.); Trueman *v.* Loder, Id. 589 (as to which case see Dale *v.* Humfrey, E., B. & E. 1004 (96 E. C. L. R.); s. c., 7 E. & B. 266, 277 (90 E. C. L. R.); Browne *v.* Byrne, 3 E. & B. 703 (77 E. C. L. R.)); Jones *v.* Littledale, 6 A. & E. 486 (33 E. C. L. R.); Magee *v.* Atkinson, 2 M. & W. 440. See Graves *v.* Legg, 2 H. & N. 210; s. c., 11 Exch. 642, 9 Id. 709; Pym *v.* Campbell, 6 E. & B. 370 (88 E. C. L. R.); cited in Rogers *v.* Hadley, 2 H. & C. 249; Stewart *v.* Aberdein, 4 M. & W. 211. The law applicable to this subject will be stated more at length when we have to consider the mode of dissolving contracts, and the application of evidence to their interpretation.

[3] Per cur., 9 Johns. (U. S.) R. 349.

[4] See Gregory *v.* Des Anges, 3 Bing. N. C. 85, 87 (32 E. C. L. R.); Atkinson *v.* Fell, 5 M. & S. 240; Cates *v.* Knight, 3 T. R. 442, 444; cited arg. Albon *v.* Pyke, 5 Scott N. R. 245; R. *v.* North Nibley, 5 T. R. 21; per Tindal, C. J., Newton *v.* Holford (in error), 6 Q. B. 926 (51 E. C. L. R.); A.-G. *v.* Sillem, 10 H. L. Cas. 704. The maxim, *supra*, is applied to a statute in Reg. *v.* Caledonian R. C., 16 C. B. 31 (81 E. C. L. R.), and in Edinburgh and Glasgow R. C. *v.* Magistrates of Linlithgow, 3 Macq. Sc. App. Cas. 717, 730. Watkins *v.* Great Northern R. C., 16 Q. B. 961 (71 E. C. L. R.), also proceeded on the above maxim; per Lord Campbell, C., Caledonian R. C. *v.* Colt, 3 Macq. Sc. App. Cas. 839. See Lawrence *v.* Great Northern R. C., 16 Q. B. 643, 653 (71 E. C. L. R.).

In Bostock *v.* North Staffordshire R. C., 4 E. & B. 832 (82 E. C. L. R.), Lord Campbell says, with reference to certain statutes granting powers to a navigation and a railway company, "In construing instruments so loosely drawn as these local Acts, we can hardly apply such maxims as that, '*the expression of one thing is the exclusion of another*,' or that *the* '*exception proves the rule*.'"

in the construction of statutes by the intention of the legislature, which they have always taken according to the necessity of the matter, and according to that which is consonant to reason and sound discretion.[1]

Thus, it sometimes happens that in a statute, the language of which may fairly comprehend many different cases, some only are expressly mentioned by way of example merely, and not as excluding others of a similar nature. So, where the words used by the legislature are *general*, and the statute is only declaratory of the common *law, it shall extend to other persons and things besides those actually named, and, consequently, in such cases, the ordinary rule of construction cannot properly apply. [*665] Sometimes, on the contrary, the expressions used are restrictive, and intended to exclude all things which are not enumerated. Where, for example, certain specific things are taxed, or subjected to any charge, it seems probable that it was intended to exclude everything else even of a similar nature, and *à fortiori*, all things different in *genus* and description from those which are enumerated. So, it is agreed that mines in general are not ratable to the poor within the stat. 43 Eliz. c. 2, and that the mention in that statute of coal-mines is not by way of example, but in exclusion of all other mines.[2]

By stat. 2 Will. 4, c. 45, s. 27,[3] the right of voting in boroughs is given to every person who occupies, either as owner or tenant, "any house, warehouse, counting-house, shop, or other building, being, either separately or jointly with any land" within such city or borough, occupied therewith by him under the same landlord, of the clear yearly value of not less than 10*l.*; it was held, that, under this section, two distinct buildings cannot be joined together in order to constitute a borough qualification. "The rule, *expressio unius est exclusio alterius*," observed Tindal, C. J., "is, I think, applicable here. I cannot see why the legislature should have provided for the joint occupation of a building and land, and not for

[1] Plowd. 205 b.

[2] See arg. R. *v.* Woodland, 2 East 166; and in R. *v.* Bell, 7 T. R. 600; R. *v.* Cunningham, 5 East 478; per Lord Mansfield, C. J., Governor of Company for Smelting Lead *v.* Richardson, 3 Burr. 1344; Steer Par. L., 3d ed., 486, 487.

[3] In connection with which see, now, stat. 30 & 31 Vict. c. 102, s. 3.

[*666] that of two *different buildings, if it had been intended that the latter should confer the franchise."[1]

Lastly, where a general Act of Parliament confers immunities which expressly exempt certain persons from the effect and operation of its provisions, it excludes all exemptions to which the subject might have been before entitled at common law; for the introduction of the exemption is necessarily exclusive of all other independent extrinsic exceptions.[2]

The following remarks of an eminent legal authority, showing the importance of the maxim considered in these preceding pages, when regarded as a rule of evidence rather than of construction, are submitted as well deserving attention:—

"It is a sound rule of evidence, that you cannot alter or substantially vary the effect of a written contract by parol proof. This excellent rule is intended to guard against fraud and perjuries; and it cannot be too steadily supported by courts of justice. *Expressum facit cessare tacitum—vox emissa volat—litera scripta manet*, are law axioms in support of the rule; and law axioms are nothing more than the conclusions of common sense, which have been formed and approved by the wisdom of ages. This rule prevails equally in a court of equity and a court of law; for, generally speaking, the rules of evidence are the same in both courts. If the words of a contract be intelligible, says Lord Chancellor Thurlow,[3] there is no instance where parol proof has been admitted to give them a different sense. 'Where there is a deed in writing,' [*667] *he observes in another place,[4] 'it will admit of no contract which is not part of the deed.' You can introduce nothing on parol proof that adds to or deducts from the writing. If, however, an agreement is by *fraud* or *mistake* made to speak a different language from what was intended, then, in those cases, parol proof is admissible to show the fraud or mistake. These are cases excepted from the general rule."[5]

We do not propose to dwell at length upon the maxim, *Expressum facit cessare tacitum;* a cursory glance even at the con-

[1] Dewhurst, app., Fielden, resp., 8 Scott N. R. 1013, 1017.

[2] Dwarr. Stats., 2d ed., 605; R. *v.* Cunningham, 5 East 478; 3 T. R. 442.

[3] Shelburne *v.* Inchiquin, 1 Bro. C. C. 341.

[4] Lord Irnham *v.* Child, 1 Bro. C. C. 93.

[5] Per Kent, C. J., 1 Johns. (U. S.) R. 571, 572.

tents of the preceding pages will show it to be of important and extensive practical application, both in the construction of written instruments and verbal contracts, as also in determining the inferences which may fairly be drawn from expressions used or declarations made with regard to particular circumstances. It is, indeed, a principle of logic and of common sense, and not merely a technical rule of construction, and might, therefore, be illustrated by decided cases, having reference probably to every branch of the legal science. It, moreover, has an important bearing upon the doctrine of our law as to implied undertakings and obligations. If A. covenants or engages by contract to buy an estate of B. at a given price, although that contract may be silent as to any obligation on the part of B. to sell; yet, as A. cannot buy without B. selling, the law will imply a corresponding obligation on the part of B. to sell.[1] So, if a man engages to work and render services which necessitate great outlay of money, time, and trouble, and he is only to be paid by the measure of the work he has performed, the contract *necessarily presupposes and implies on the part of the person who engages him, an obligation to supply the work. [*668] So where there is an engagement to manufacture some article, a corresponding obligation on the other party is implied to take it, for otherwise it would be impossible that the party bestowing his services could claim any remuneration.[2]

Many instances similar to the foregoing might be put,[3] where the act to be done by the party binding himself can only be done upon something of a corresponding character being done by the opposite party, and where a corresponding obligation to do the things necessary for the completion of the contract would be implied. In any case, where a contract is thus silent, the court or jury who are called upon to imply an obligation on the other side, which does not appear in the terms of the contract, must take care that they do not make the contract speak where it was intentionally silent;

[1] Pordage v. Cole, 1 Wms. Saund. 319 l.

[2] Per Cockburn, C. J., Churchward v. Reg., L. R. 1 Q. B. 195.

[3] There is an implied covenant by a grantor that he shall not derogate from his grant, *ante*, p. 282, Gerard v. Lewis, L. R. 2 C. P. 305.

The doctrine as to implied undertakings was much considered in Francis v. Cockrell, L. R. 5 Q. B. 184; Readhead v. Midland R. C., L. R. 4 Q. B. 379; Ford v. Cotesworth, L. R. 4 Q. B. 127; Stirling v. Maitland, 5 B. & S. 840 (117 E. C. L. R.); Harmer v. Cornelius, 5 C. B. N. S. 236 (94 E. C. L. R.).

and, above all, that they do not make it speak entirely contrary to what, as may be gathered from the whole terms and tenor of the contract, was the intention of the parties.[1]

The maxim above commented on is, however, as recently remarked,[2] "by no means of universal conclusive application. For example: it is a familiar doctrine that though where a statute [*669] makes unlawful that which was *lawful before, and appoints a specific remedy, that remedy must be pursued, and no other; yet where an offence was antecedently punishable by a common law proceeding, as by indictment, and a statute prescribes a particular remedy in case of disobedience, that such particular remedy is *cumulative*, and proceedings may be had either at common law or under the statute." And where a charter incorporating a trading company declared in case "the defendants should fail to enter into and execute a deed of settlement, and deposit it as directed, or in case they should not comply with any other of the directions and conditions contained in the letters patent, that it should be lawful for the crown, *by any writing under the great seal or under the sign manual*, to revoke and make void the charter, either absolutely or under such terms and conditions as the queen thought fit," it was held that the intention of the proviso was to give a remedy in addition to that by way of *scire facias*, and that the maxim *Expressum facit cessare tacitum* was consequently inapplicable.[3]

EXPRESSIO EORUM QUÆ TACITE INSUNT NIHIL OPERATUR.

(2 Inst. 365.)

The expression of what is tacitly implied is inoperative.

"The expression of a clause which the law implies works [*670] nothing."[4] For instance, if land be let to two *persons for the term of their lives, this creates a joint tenancy;

[1] Per Cockburn, C. J., L. R. 1 Q. B. 195–6.

[2] Per Williams, J., 2 E. & B. 879 (75 E. C. L. R.).

[3] Eastern Archipelago Co. *v.* Reg., 2 E. & B. 856 (75 E. C. L. R.); s. c., 1 E. & B. 310 (72 E. C. L. R.).

[4] 4 Rep. 73; 5 Rep. 11; Wing. Max., p. 235; Finch's Law 24; D. 50. 17. 81. In Hobart R. 170, it is said that this rule "is to be understood having respect to itself only, and not having relation to other clauses." The rule

and if the words "and the survivor of them" are added, they will be mere surplusage, because, by law, the term would go to the survivor.[1] So, upon a lease reserving rent payable quarterly, with a proviso that, if the rent were in arrears twenty-one days next after the day of payment being lawfully demanded, the lessor might re-enter, it was held that, five years' rent being in arrear, and no sufficient distress on the premises, the lessor might re-enter without a demand, and the above maxim was held to apply; for, previous to the stat. 4 Geo. 2, c. 28, a demand was necessary as a consequence of law, whether the lease contained the words "lawfully demanded" or not. Then the statute says, that "in all cases where half a year's rent shall be in arrear, and the landlord has a right of entry," the remedy shall apply, provided there be no sufficient distress; that is, the statute has dispensed with the demand which was required at the common law, whether expressly provided for by the stipulation of the parties or not.[2] In like manner, if there be a devise of "all and singular my effects," followed by the words "of what nature or kind soever," the latter words are comprehended in the word "all," and only show that the testator meant to use "effects" in its largest natural sense: this devise, therefore, will not pass real property, unless it can *be collected from the will itself that such was the testator's intention.[3] [*671]

Again, every interest which is limited to commence and is capable of commencing on the regular determination of the prior particular estate, at whatever time the particular estate may determine, is, in point of law, a vested estate; and the universal criterion for distinguishing a contingent interest from a vested estate is, that a contingent interest cannot take effect immediately, even though the

supra is applied in Wroughton *v.* Turtle, 11 M. & W. 569, 570; and in Lawrence *v.* Boston, 7 Exch. 28, 35, in reference to the operation of the Stamp Acts. See also Ogden *v.* Graham, 1 B. & S. 773 (101 E. C. L. R.).

[1] Co. Litt. 191 a, cited, arg. 4 B. & Ald. 306 (6 E. C. L. R.); 2 Prest. Abst. Tit. 63. See also per Lord Langdale, M. R., Seifferth *v.* Badham, 9 Beav. 374. The maxim *supra* is applied, per Martin, B., in Scott *v.* Avery, 5 H. L. Cas. 829.

[2] Doe d. Scholefield *v.* Alexander, 2 M. & S. 525; Doe d. Earl of Shrewsbury *v.* Wilson, 5 B. & Ald. 364, 384 (7 E. C. L. R.).

[3] See Doe *v.* Dring, 2 M. & S. 448, 459; Doe d. Scruton *v.* Snaith, 8 Bing. 146, 154 (21 E. C. L. R.).

former estate were determined, while a vested estate may take effect immediately, whenever the particular estate shall determine. Hence it often happens, that a limitation expressed in words of contingency is in law treated as a vested estate, according to the rule *Expressio eorum quæ tacite insunt nihil operatur*. If, for instance, a limitation be made to the use of A. for life, and, if A. shall die in the lifetime of B., to the use of B. for life, this limitation gives to B. a *vested* estate, because the words expressive of a contingency are necessarily implied by the law as being in a limitation to A. for life and then to B.; and without those words a vested interest would clearly be given.[1]

In accordance with the same principle, where a person makes a tender, he always means that the amount tendered, though less than the plaintiff's demand, is all that he is entitled to in respect of it. Where, therefore, the person making the tender said to plaintiff, "I am come with the amount of your bill," upon which plaintiff refused the money, saying, "I shall not take that, it is not my bill," and nothing more passed, the tender [*672] *was held sufficient; and in answer to the argument, that a tender made in such terms would give to its acceptance the effect of an admission, and was consequently bad, it was observed, that the plaintiff could not preclude himself from recovering more by accepting an offer of part, accompanied by expressions which are implied in every tender.[2]

The above instances, taken in connection with the remarks appended to the maxim, *Expressio unius est exclusio alterius*, will serve to show that an expression, which merely embodies that which would in its absence have been by law implied, is altogether inoperative; such an expression, when occurring in a written instrument, is denominated by Lord Bacon *clausula inutilis;* and, according to him, *clausula vel dispositio inutilis per præsumptionem vel causam remotam ex post facto non fulcitur ;* a rule which he thus explains, —*clausula vel dispositio inutilis* is "when the act or the words do work or express no more than the law by intendment would have supplied;" and such a clause or disposition is not supported by any subsequent matter "which may induce an operation of those idle words or acts."[3]

[1] See per Willes, C. J., 3 Atk. 138 ; 1 Prest. Abst. Tit. 108, 109.

[2] Henwood *v.* Oliver, 1 Q. B. 409, 411 (41 E. C. L. R.) ; recognized in Bowen *v.* Owen, 11 Q. B. 130, 135 (63 E. C. L. R.).

[3] Bac. Max., reg. 21.

*VERBA RELATA HOC MAXIME OPERANTUR PER REFERENTIAM UT IN EIS INESSE VIDENTUR. [*673]

(Co. Litt. 159 a.)

Words to which reference is made in an instrument have the same effect and operation as if they were inserted in the clause referring to them.[1]

It is important to bear in mind, when reading any particular portion of a deed or written instrument, that regard must be paid not only to the language of the clause in question, but to that also of any other clause or covenant which may by reference be incorporated with it; and, since the application of this rule, so simple in its terms, is occasionally attended with difficulty,[2] it has been thought desirable in this place briefly to examine it.[3]

Where, by articles under seal, the defendant bound himself under a penalty to deliver to the plaintiff by a certain day "the whole of his mechanical pieces as per schedule annexed;" the schedule was held to form part of the deed, for the deed without it would be insensible and inoperative.[4] And if a contract of sale refer to *an inventory, the entire contents thereof will become incorporated with the contract.[5] [*674]

In like manner, if a contract, or an Act of Parliament, refer to a plan, such plan will form a part of the contract or Act, for the purpose for which the reference is made.[6] And a deed of conveyance,

[1] The rule is that, "by referring in a document signed by the party to another document, the person so signing in effect signs a document containing the terms of the one referred to:" per Crompton, J., Fitzmaurice v. Bayley, 9 H. L. Cas. 99, where the question arose on the 4th section of the Statute of Frauds.

[2] See Reg. v. Registrar of Middlesex, 15 Q. B. 976 (69 E. C. L. R.); Fishmongers' Co. v. Dimsdale, 12 C. B. 557 (74 E. C. L. R.); Betts v. Walker, 14 Q. B. 363 (68 E. C. L. R.); Stewart v. Anglo-Californian Gold-mining Co., 18 Q. B. 736 (83 E. C. L. R.).

[3] Boydell v. Drummond, 11 East 141, 153, 156, 157 (distinguished in Crane v. Powell, L. R. 4 C. P. 123, 129), and Wilkinson v. Evans, L. R. 1 C. P. 407, may be consulted in connection with the above maxim. See also Ridgway v. Wharton, 6 H. L. Cas. 238; cited Judgm., Barker v. Allen, 5 H. & N. 72; Sillem v. Thornton, 3 E. & B. 868, 880 (77 E. C. L. R.).

[4] Weeks v. Maillardet, 14 East 568, 574; cited and distinguished, Dyer v. Green, 1 Exch. 71; and in Daines v. Heath, 3 C. B. 938, 945 (54 E. C. L. R.).

[5] Taylor v. Bullen, 5 Exch. 779. See Wood v. Rowcliffe, 6 Exch. 407.

[6] North British R. C. v. Tod, 12 Cl. & Fin. 722, 731; Reg. v. Regent's Canal Co., 28 L. J. Chanc. 153. See Galway v. Baker, 5 Cl. & Fin. 157; Brain v.

made under the authority of an Act of Parliament, and in the form prescribed thereby, must be read as if the sections of the Act applicable to the subject-matter of the grant and its incidents were inserted in it.[1]

In a modern case, a deed recited a contract for the sale of certain lands, by a description corresponding with that subsequently contained in the deed, and then proceeded to convey them, with a reference for that description to three schedules. The portion of the particular schedule relating to the piece of land in question stated, in one column, the number which this piece was marked on a certain plan, and, in another column, under the heading "description of premises," it was stated to be "a small piece, marked on the plan;" and by applying the maxim, *Verba illata inesse videntur*, the Court of Exchequer considered on the above state of facts, that it was the same thing as if the map or plan referred to in the schedule had been actually inserted in the deed, since it was, by operation of the above principle, incorporated with it.[2]

[*675] *Where a question arose respecting the sufficiency of an affidavit, Heath, J., observed, "The court generally requires, and it is a proper rule, that the affidavit shall be intituled in the cause, that it may be sufficiently certain in what cause it is to admit of an indictment for perjury; but this affidavit refers to the annexed plea, and the annexed plea is in the cause, *Verba relata inesse videntur;* therefore it amounts to the same thing as if the affidavit were intituled; and the plaintiff could prosecute for perjury on this affidavit."[3]

So, with reference to an indictment, it has been observed, that "there are many authorities to show that one count thereof may refer to another, and that under such circumstances the maxim applies, *Verba relata inesse videntur*."[4]

Harris, 10 Exch. 908; Reg. *v.* Caledonian R. C., 16 Q. B. 197 (71 E. C. L. R.).

[1] Elliot *v.* North-Eastern R. C., 10 H. L. Cas. 333, 353.

[2] Llewellyn *v.* Earl of Jersey, 11 M. & W. 183, 188; Lyle *v.* Richards, L. R. 1 H. L. 222; Barton *v.* Dawes, 10 C. B. 261, 263, 266 (70 E. C. L. R.). See also as to the admissibility of parol evidence to identify a plan referred to in an agreement for a lease, Hodges *v.* Horsfall, 1 Russ. & My. 116.

[3] Per Heath, J., Prince *v.* Nicholson, 5 Taunt. 337 (1 E. C. L. R.). See in connection with the maxim above noticed, Duke of Brunswick *v.* Slowman, 8 C. B. 617.

[4] Judgm., Reg. *v.* Waverton, 17 Q. B. 570.

The above rule is also applied to the interpretation of wills,[1] although the courts will not construe a will with the same critical precision which would be prescribed to a grammarian; for instance, where the words "the said estates," occurring in a will, seemed in strictness to refer to certain freehold land, messuages, and tenements, before devised, on which construction the devisee would only have taken an estate for life, according to the strict rule which existed prior to the stat. 1 Vict. c. 26; yet it was observed by Lord Ellenborough, that, in cases of this *sort, unless the testator uses expressions of absolute restriction, it may in general be taken for granted that he intends to dispose of the whole interest; and, in furtherance of this intention, courts of justice have laid hold of the word "estate" as passing a fee, wherever it is not so connected with mere local description as to be cut down to a more restrained signification.[2] [*676]

Another important application of the maxim before us occurs where reference is made in a will to an extrinsic document, in order to elucidate or explain the testator's intention, in which case such document will be received as part of the will, from the fact of its adoption thereby, provided it be clearly identified as the instrument to which the will points.[3] But parol evidence is inadmissible to show an intention to connect two instruments together, where there is no reference to a foreign instrument, or where the description of it is insufficient.[4] A further illustration, moreover, of the general principle presents itself, where a question arises as to whether the execution of a will is intended to apply to the several papers in

[1] See Doe d. Earl of Cholmondeley *v.* Maxey, 12 East 589; Wheatley *v.* Thomas, Sir T. Raym. 54.

The maxim may apply where a power of appointment by will is exercised. See, for instance, Re Baker, 7 H. & N. 109.

[2] Roe d. Allport *v.* Bacon, 4 M. & S. 366, 368. See stat. 1 Vict. c. 26, ss. 26, 28. In Doe d. Woodall *v.* Woodall, 3 C. B. 349 (54 E. C. L. R.), the question was as to the meaning of the words "in manner aforesaid" occurring in a will. And see the cases on this subject, cited 1 Jarman on Wills, 3d ed., 710 (q).

[3] Molineux *v.* Molineux, Cro. Jac. 144; Dickinson *v.* Stidolph, 11 C. B. N. S. 341 (103 E. C. L. R.); 1 Jarman on Wills, 3d ed., 83. As to incorporating in the probate of wills of personalty papers referred to thereby, but not *per se* testamentary, see Sheldon *v.* Sheldon, 1 Robert 81; Allen *v.* Maddock, 11 Moo. P. C. C. 427.

[4] See Clayton *v.* Lord Nugent, 13 M. & W. 200.

which the will is contained, or is confided to that with which it is more immediately associated, and whether an attested codicil communicates the efficacy of its attestation to an unattested will or prior codicil, so as to render effectual any devise or bequest [*677] *which may be contained in such prior unattested instrument.[1]

Without adducing further instances of the application of the maxim, *Verba illatai nesse videntur*, it will be proper to notice a difficulty which sometimes arises where an *exoeption*[2] or *proviso*[3] either occurs in or is by reference imported into a general clause in a written instrument; the difficulty[4] being in determining whether the party who relies upon the general clause should aver that the particular case does not fall within the exceptive proviso, or whether it should be left to the party who relies upon that provision to avail himself of it.

Now the rule usually laid down upon this subject is, that where matter is introduced by way of *exception* into a general clause, the plaintiff must show that the particular case does not fall within such exception, whereas a *proviso* need not be noticed by the plaintiff, but must be pleaded by the opposite party.[5] "The difference is, [*678] *where an exception is incorporated in the body of the clause, he who pleads the cause ought also to plead the exception; but when there is a clause for the benefit of the

[1] 1 Jarman on Wills, 3d ed., 107 *et seq.*; Allen *v.* Maddock, 11 Moo. P. C. C. 427; In the goods of Gill, L. R. 2 P. & D. 6.

[2] Logically speaking, an *exception* ought to be of that which would otherwise be included in the category from which it is excepted, but there are a great many examples to the contrary: per Lord Campbell, Gurley *v.* Gurley, 8 Cl. & Fin. 764.

[3] The office of a *proviso* in an Act of Parliament is either to except something from the enacting clause, or to qualify or restrain its generality, or to exclude some possible ground of misinterpretation of it as extending to cases not intended by the legislature to be brought within its purview: per Story, J., delivering judgment, 15 Peters (U. S.) R. 445.

[4] An analogous difficulty may also arise with reference to the repeal or modification of a prior by a subsequent statute (see Bowyer *v.* Cook, 4 C. B. 236 (56 E. C. L. R.)); and, with reference to the restriction of general by special words, see Howell *v.* Richards, 11 East 633; *ante*, p. 646.

[5] Spieres *v.* Parker, 1 T. R. 141; R. *v.* Jukes, 8 T. R. 542; per Lord Mansfield, C. J., R. *v.* Jarvis, cited 1 East 646, note; Stevens *v.* Stevens, 5 Exch. 306.

pleader, and afterwards follows a proviso which is against him, he shall plead the clause, and leave it to the adversary to show the proviso."[1]

Hence, if an Act of Parliament or a private instrument contain in it, first, a general clause, and afterwards a separate and distinct clause, which has the effect of taking out of the general clause something which would otherwise be included in it, a party relying upon the general clause in pleading may set out that clause only, without noticing the separate and distinct clause which operates as an exception. If, on the other hand, the exception itself be incorporated in the general clause, then the party relying upon the general clause must, in pleading, state it with the exception, and if he state it as containing an absolute unconditional stipulation, without noticing the exception, it will be a variance.[2]

In accordance with the first of the above rules, where one section of a penal statute creates an offence, and a subsequent section specifies certain exceptions thereto, the exceptions need not be negatived by the party prosecuting.[3] So, where the exception is created by a distinct subsequent Act of Parliament, as well as where *it occurs in a subsequent section of the same Act, the above remark applies;[4] and this rule has likewise been held [*679] applicable where an exception was introduced by way of proviso in a subsequent part of a section of a statute which imposed a penalty, and on a former part of which section the plaintiff suing for the penalty relied.[5] "There is," remarked Alderson, B., in the case referred to, "a manifest distinction between a proviso and an exception. If an exception occurs in the description of the offence

[1] Per Treby, C. J., 1 Lord Raym. 120; cited 7 T. R. 31; Russell *v.* Ledsam, 14 M. & W. 574. See Crow *v.* Falk, 8 Q. B. 467 (55 E. C. L. R.).

[2] Vavasour *v.* Ormrod, 6 B. & C. 430 (13 E. C. L. R.); cited arg. Tucker *v.* Webster, 10 M. & W. 373; per Lord Abinger, C. B., Grand Junction R. C. *v.* White, 8 M. & W. 221; Thibault *v.* Gibson, 12 M. & W. 94; cited per Lord Denman, C. J., Palk *v.* Force, 12 Q. B. 672 (64 E. C. L. R.). See Roe *v.* Bacon, 4 M. & S. 366, 368; Paddock *v.* Forrester, 3 Scott N. R. 715; 1 Wms. Saunds. 262 b (1); R. *v.* Jukes, 8 T. R. 542.

[3] Van Boven's Case, 9 Q. B. 669 (58 E. C. L. R.). See 15 M. & W. 318.

[4] See, per Lord Abinger, C. B., Thibault *v.* Gibson, 12 M. & W. 94.

[5] Simpson *v.* Ready, 12 M. & W. 736 (as to which case see, per Alderson, B., Mayor of Salford *v.* Ackers, 16 M. & W. 92); per Parke, B., Thibault *v.* Gibson, 12 M. & W. 96.

in the statute, the exception must be negatived, or the party will not be brought within the description. But, if the exception comes by way of proviso, and does not alter the offence, but merely states what persons are to take advantage of it, then the defence must be specially pleaded, or may be given in evidence under the general issue, according to circumstances."[1]

The latter of the two rules above mentioned may be thus illustrated:—Where an exception was introduced into the reservation of rent in a demise, not in express terms, but by reference only to some subsequent matter in the instrument, viz., by the words, "except as hereinafter mentioned," and the plaintiff in his declaration stated the reservation without the exception, referring to a subsequent proviso, this was held, according to the above rule, to be a variance.[2]

[*680] *AD PROXIMUM ANTECEDENS FIAT RELATIO, NISI IMPEDIATUR SENTENTIA.

(Noy, Max., 9th ed., p. 4.)

Relative words refer to the next antecedent, unless by such a construction the meaning of the sentence would be impaired.

Relative words must ordinarily be referred to the next antecedent, where the intent upon the whole deed or instrument does not appear to the contrary,[3] and where the matter itself doth not hinder it.[4] The "last antecedent" being the last word which can be made an antecedent so as to have a meaning.[5]

[1] Per Alderson, B., Simpson *v.* Ready, 12 M. & W. 740; s. c., 11 Id. 344; per Lord Mansfield, C. J., Spieres *v.* Parker, 1 T. R. 144, and in R. *v.* Jarvis, 1 East 644 (d); Bousfield *v.* Wilson, 16 M. & W. 185. See Tennant, app., Cumberland, resp., 1 E. & E. 401 (102 E. C. L. R.).

[2] Vavasour *v.* Ormrod, 6 B. & C. 430 (13 E. C. L. R.), and cited cases *supra*, p. 678, n. 2.

[3] Com. Dig. "*Parols*" (A. 14, 15); Jenk. Cent. 180; Dyer 46 b; Wing. Max., p. 19. See Bryant *v.* Wardell, 2 Exch. 479; Piatt *v.* Ashley, 1 Exch. 257; Electric Telegraph Co. *v.* Brett, 10 C. B. 838 (70 E. C. L. R.); Reg. *v.* Brown, 17 Q. B. 833 (79 E. C. L. R.), with which compare In re Jones, 7 Exch. 586; Eastern Counties R. C. *v.* Marriage, 9 H. L. Cas. 32; s. c., 2 H. N. 625; cited per Channell, B., Tetley *v.* Wanless, L. R. 2 Ex. 29, s. c., Id. 275; and in Latham *v.* Lafone, Id. 123; Bristol and Exeter R. C. *v.* Garton, 8 H. L. Cas. 477.

[4] Finch Law 8.

[5] Per Tindal, C. J., 1 A. & E. 445 (28 E. C. L. R.). See Esdaile *v.* Mac-

But, although the above general proposition is true in strict grammatical construction, yet there are numerous examples in the best writers to show that the context may often require a deviation from this rule, and that the relative may be connected with nouns which go before the last antecedent, and either take from it or give to it some qualification.[1]

*For instance, an order of magistrates was directed to the parish of W., in the county of R., and also to the parish of M., in the county of L., and the words "county of R." were then written in the margin, and the magistrates were, in a subsequent part of the order, described as justices of the peace for the county aforesaid; it was held, that it thereby sufficiently appeared that they were justices for the county of R.[2] [*681]

The above rule of grammar is, of course, applicable to wills as well as to other written instruments; for instance:—A testator devised the whole of his *property* situated in P., and also his farm called S., to his adopted child M. He left to his nephew, W., all his other lands, situated in H. and M.; and the will contained this subsequent clause: "And should M. have lawful issue, *the said property* to be equally divided between her lawful issue." It was held, that these words, "the said property," did not comprise the lands in H. and M. devised to the nephew, although it was argued that they must, according to the true grammatical construction of the will, either comprise *all* the property before spoken of, or must refer to the next antecedent.[3]

lean, 15 M. & W. 277; Williams *v.* Newton, 14 M. & W. 747; Peake *v.* Screech, 7 Q. B. 603 (53 E. C. L. R.); Reg. *v.* Inhabs. of St. Margaret, Westminster, Id. 569; Ledsam *v.* Russell (in error), 16 M. & W. 633; s. c., 1 H. L. Cas. 687.

[1] Judgm., Staniland *v.* Hopkins, 9 M. & W. 192; in which case a difficulty arose as to the proper mode of construing a statute. See also, A.-G. *v.* Shillibeer, 3 Exch. 71; Beer, app., Santer, resp., 10 C. B. N. S. 435 (100 E. C. L. R.); Beckh *v.* Page, 7 Id. 861; Earl of Kintore *v.* Lord Inverury, 4 Macq. Sc. App. Cas. 520.

[2] R. *v.* St. Mary's, Leicester, 1 B. & Ald. 327; Reg. *v.* Inhabs. of Casterton, 6 Q. B. 507 (51 E. C. L. R.); Baring *v.* Christie, 5 East 398; R. *v.* Chilverscoton, 8 T. R. 178.

[3] Peppercorn *v.* Peacock, 3 Scott N. R. 651; Hall *v.* Warren, 9 H. L. Cas. 420. See also Doe d. Gore *v.* Langton, 2 B. & Ad. 680, 691 (22 E. C. L. R.); Cheyney's Case, 5 Rep. 68; and the cases collected in R. *v.* Richards, 1 M. & Rob. 177; Owen *v.* Smith, 2 H. Bla. 594 Galley *v.* Barrington, 2 Bing.

[*682] *CONTEMPORANEA EXPOSITIO EST OPTIMA ET FORTISSIMA IN LEGE.

(2 Inst. 11.)

The best and surest mode of expounding an instrument is by referring to the time when, and circumstances under which, it was made.[1]

There is no better way of interpreting ancient words, or of construing ancient grants, deeds, and charters, than by usage;[2] and the uniform course of modern authorities fully establishes the rule, that, however general the words of an ancient grant may be, it is to be construed by evidence of the manner in which the thing granted has always been possessed and used; for so the parties thereto must be supposed to have intended.[3] Thus, if it be doubtful on the face of an instrument whether a present demise or future letting was meant, the intention of the parties may be elucidated by the conduct they have pursued;[4] and where the words of the instrument are ambiguous, the court will call in aid acts done under it as a clue to the intention.[5] "Contemporaneous usage," observed Lord Cottenham, C., in Drummond *v.* The Attorney-General,[6] "is a strong ground for the [*683] *interpretation of doubtful words or expressions, but time affords no sanction to established breaches of trust."

Upon the same principle, also, depends the great authority which, in construing a statute, is attributed to the construction put

387 (9 E. C. L. R.); Doe d. Beech *v.* Nall, 6 Exch. 102; Peacock *v.* Stockford, 3 De G., M. & G. 73, 79.

[1] The courts, however, have frequently repudiated the idea of being influenced in their interpretation of a statute by knowledge of what occurred in Parliament during the passing of the bill: see, for instance, per Pollock, C. B., 7 Exch. 617; per Alderson, B., 5 Exch. 667.

[2] Per Lord Hardwicke, C., A.-G. *v.* Parker, 3 Atk. 576; and 2 Inst. 282; cited 4 T. R. 819; per Parke, B., Clift *v.* Schwabe, 3 C. B. 469 (54 E. C. L. R.); and in Jewison *v.* Dyson, 9 M. & W. 556; R. *v.* Mashiter, 6 A. & E. 153 (33 E. C. L. R.); R. *v.* Davie, Id. 374; Senhouse *v.* Earle, Amb. 288; Co. Litt. 8 b; Lockwood *v.* Wood, 6 Q. B. 31 (51 E. C. L. R.); per Lord Eldon, C., A.-G. *v.* Forster, 10 Ves. jun. 338; Reg. *v.* Dulwich College, 17 Q. B. 600 (79 E. C. L. R.).

[3] Weld *v.* Hornby, 7 East 199; R. *v.* Osbourne, 4 East 327.

[4] Chapman *v.* Bluck, 4 Bing. N. C. 187, 195 (33 E. C. L. R.).

[5] Per Tindal, C. J., Doe d. Pearson *v.* Ries, 8 Bing. 181 (21 E. C. L. R.).

[6] 2 H. L. Cas. 861; *et vide*, per Lord Campbell, Id. 863.

upon it by judges who lived at the time when the statute was made, or soon after, as being best able to determine the intention of the legislature, not only by the ordinary rules of construction, but especially from knowing the circumstances to which it had relation;[1] and where the words of an Act are obscure or doubtful, and where the sense of the legislature cannot, with certainty, be collected by interpreting the language of the statute according to reason and grammatical correctness, considerable stress is laid upon the light in which it was received and held by the contemporary members of the profession. "Great regard," says Sir E. Coke, "ought, in construing a statute, to be paid to the construction which the sages of the law, who lived about the time or soon after it was made, put upon it; because they were best able to judge of the intention of the makers at the time when the law was made."[2] And, "it is by no means an inconvenient mode of construing statutes to presume that the legislature was aware of the state of the law at the time they passed."[3]

*Conformably to what has been above said, stress was laid by several of the judges delivering their opinions in the Fermoy Peerage Case,[4] upon the usage observed in the creation of Irish Peerages, since the passage of the Act of Union. And in Salkeld *v.* Johnson,[5] the Court of Exchequer, referring to the stat. 2 & 3 Will. 4, c. 100, intituled "An Act for shortening the time required in claims of *modus decimandi*, or exemption from or discharge of tithes," observe, that they propose to construe it "according to the legal rules for the interpretation of statutes, principally by the words of the statute itself, which we are to read in their [*684]

[1] 2 Phill. Evid., 9th ed., 347; Bank of England *v.* Anderson, 3 Bing. N. C. 666 (11 E. C. L. R.). See the resolutions in Heydon's Case, 3 Rep. 7, cited *ante*, p. 83; as to which *vide* per Pollock, C. B., A.-G. *v.* Sillem, *ante*, p. 571; Lord Camden's judgment in Entick *v.* Carrington, 19 How. St. Trials 1043, *et seq.*; per Coleridge, J., Reg. *v.* Archb. of Canterbury, 11 Q. B. 595, 596 (63 E. C. L. R.); per Crompton, J., Sharpley *v.* Overseers of Mablethorpe, 3 E. & B. 917 (77 E. C. L. R.); per Byles, J., 6 C. B. N. S. 213 (95 E. C. L. R.).

[2] Cited Dwarr. Stats., 2d ed., 562, 703; 2 Inst. 11, 136, 181; per Holt, C. J., Comb. R. 210; Corporation of Newcastle *v.* A.-G., 12 Cl. & Fin. 419.

[3] Per Pollock, C. B., Jones *v.* Brown, 2 Exch. 332.

[4] 5 H. L. Cas. 747, 785.

[5] 2 Exch. 273.

ordinary sense, and only modify or alter so far as it may be necessary to avoid some manifest absurdity or incongruity, but no further.[1] It is proper also to consider the state of the law which it proposes or purports to alter, the mischiefs which existed and which it was intended to remedy, and the nature of the remedy provided, and to look at the statutes *in pari materia*,[2] as a means of explaining this statute." These are the proper modes of ascertaining the intention of the legislature.

Usage, however, it has been observed,[3] can be binding and operative upon parties only as it is the interpreter of a doubtful law; for, as against a plain statutory law, no usage is of any avail.[4] Where, [*685] indeed, the statute, *speaking on some points, is silent as to others, usage may well supply the defect, especially if it is not inconsistent with the statutory directions, where any are given; and in like manner, where the statute uses a language of doubtful import, the acting under it for a long course of years may well give an interpretation to that obscure meaning, and reduce that uncertainty to a fixed rule; in such a case the maxim hereafter illustrated is applicable,—*Optimus legis interpres consuetudo*.[5]

[1] *Ante*, pp. 573 *et seq.*

[2] See Ex parte Copeland, 2 De G., M. & G. 914.

[3] Per Lord Brougham, Magistrates of Dunbar *v.* Duchess of Roxburghe, 3 Cl. & Fin. 354; cited arg. 13 M. & W. 411.

[4] Hence, speaking with reference to the above maxim, Pollock, C. B., in Pochin *v.* Duncombe, 1 H. & N. 856, 857, observes, "The rule amounts to no more than this, that if the Act be susceptible of the interpretation which has been put upon it by long usage, the courts will not disturb that construction:" citing The Fermoy Peerage Case, 5 H. L. Cas. 716; and see the remarks of the same learned judge in Gwyn *v.* Hardwicke, 1 H. & N. 53; per Lord Campbell, C. J., Gorham *v.* Bishop of Exeter, 15 Q. B. 73, 74 (69 E. C. L. R.).

[5] *Post*, Chap. X., where the admissibility of usage to explain an instrument is considered, and additional authorities are cited.

QUI HÆRET IN LITERA HÆRET IN CORTICE.

(Co. Litt. 283 b.)

He who considers merely the letter of an instrument goes but skin-deep into its meaning.

The law of England respects the effect and substance of the matter, and not every nicety of form or circumstance.[1] The reason and spirit of cases make law, and not the letter of particular precedents.[2] Hence it is, as we have already seen, a general and comprehensive rule connected with the interpretation of deeds and written instruments, that, where the intention is clear, too minute a stress should not be laid on the strict and precise signification of words.[3] For instance, by the grant of a remainder, a reversion may pass, and *e converso*;[4] and if a lessee covenants to leave all the timber which was *growing on the land when he took it, the covenant will be broken if, at the end of the term, he cuts it down, but leaves it there; for this would be defeating the intent of the covenant, although a literal performance of it.[5] [*686]

In accordance with this principle, it is a further rule, that *mala grammatica non vitiat chartam*[6]—the grammatical construction is not always, in judgment of law, to be followed; and neither false English nor bad Latin will make void a deed when the meaning of the party is apparent.[7] Thus, the word "and" has, as already intimated, in many cases, been read "or," and *vice versa*, when this change was rendered necessary by the context.[8] Where, however, a proviso in a lease was altogether ungrammatical and insensible,

[1] Co. Litt. 283; Wing. Max., p. 19. See per Coltman, J., 2 Scott N. R. 300.

[2] Per Lord Mansfield, C. J., 3 Burr. 1364.

[3] *Ante*, p. 542, 548.

[4] Hobart 27.

[5] Woodf., L. & T., 9th ed., 513.

[6] 9 Rep. 48; 6 Rep. 40; Wing. Max., p. 18; Vin. Abr., "*Grammar*" (A.); Lofft 441.

"It may as properly be said in Scotch as in English law that *falsa grammatica non vitiat chartam*:" per Lord Chelmsford, Gollan *v.* Gollan, 4 Macq. Sc. App. Cas. 591.

[7] Co. Litt. 223 b; Osborn's Case, 10 Rep. 133; 2 Show. 334. See Reg. *v.* Inhabs. of Wooldale, 6 Q. B. 565 (51 E. C. L. R.).

[8] *Ante*, p. 592; Chapman *v.* Dalton, Plowd. 289; Harris *v.* Davis, 1 Coll. 416.

the court declared that they did not consider themselves bound to find out a meaning for it.[1]

In interpreting an Act of Parliament, likewise, it is not, in general, a true line of construction to decide according to the strict letter of the Act; but the courts will rather (subject to the remarks already made upon this matter[2]) consider what is its fair meaning,[3] and will expound it *differently from the letter, in order to preserve the intent.[4] The meaning of particular words, indeed, in statutes, as well as in other instruments, is to be found, not so much in a strictly etymological propriety of language, nor even in popular use, as is in the subject or occasion on which they are used, and the object that is intended to be attained.[5] "Such is the imperfection of human language," remarked Sir W. Jones, "that few written laws are free from ambiguity, and it rarely happens that many minds are united in the same interpretation of them;" and hence it is that fixed rules of interpretation, which the wisdom of ages has sanctioned and established, become necessary for our guidance whensoever the sense of the words used is in any way ambiguous or doubtful. In the preceding pages we have endeavored to place before the reader such of those rules and maxims as seemed most valuable for the purpose here indicated; such, indeed, as seemed best adapted, in the language of the eminent jurist already quoted, to "serve as stars whereby the practitioner may steer his course in the construction of all public and private writings."[6]

[*687]

[1] Doe d. Wyndham *v.* Carew, 2 Q. B. 317 (42 E. C. L. R.); Berdoe *v.* Spittle, 1 Exch. 175. See Moverly *v.* Lee, 2 Ld. Raym. 1223, 1224.

[2] *Ante*, p. 573, *et seq.*

[3] Per Lord Kenyon, C. J., 7 T. R. 196; Fowler *v.* Padget, Id. 509; 11 Rep. 73; Litt., s. 67, with Sir E. Coke's Commentary thereon, cited 3 Bing. N. C. 525 (32 E. C. L. R.); Co. Litt. 381 b. See Vincent *v.* Slaymaker, 12 East 372; arg. Bignold *v.* Springfield, 7 Cl. & Fin. 109, and cases there cited.

[4] 3 Rep. 27. According to the Roman law, *semper in obscuris quod minimum est sequimur*, D. 50. 17. 9, which is a safe maxim for guidance in our own; see per Maule, J., Williams *v.* Crosling, 3 C. B. 962 (54 E. C. L. R.).

[5] Judgm., R. *v.* Hall, 1 B. & C. 123 (8 E. C. L. R.); cited 2 C. B. 66.

[6] Life of Sir Wm. Jones, by Lord Teignmouth (ed. 1804), p. 262.

*CHAPTER IX. [*688]

The Law of Contracts.

A very cursory glance at the contents of the preceding pages will show that we have not unfrequently had occasion to refer to the Law of Contracts, in illustration of maxims heretofore submitted to the reader. Many, indeed, of our leading principles of law have necessarily a direct and important bearing upon the law merchant, and must, therefore, be constantly borne in mind when the attention is directed to that subject. The following pages have been devoted to a review of such maxims as are peculiarly, though by no means exclusively, applicable to contracts; and an attempt has been made, by the arrangement adopted, to show, as far as practicable, the connection which exists between them, and the relation in which they stand to each other. The first of these maxims sets forth the general principle, that parties may, by express agreement *inter se*, and subject to certain restrictions, acquire rights or incur liabilities which the law would not otherwise have conceded to or imposed upon them. The maxims subsequently considered show that a man may renounce a privilege or right which the law has conferred upon him; that one who enjoys the benefit must likewise bear the inconvenience or loss resulting from his contract; that, where the right or where the delinquency on each side is equal *in degree, the title of the party in actual possession shall prevail. Having thus stated the preliminary rules applicable to the conduct and position of the contracting parties, we have proceeded to examine the nature of the consideration essential to a valid contract—the liabilities attaching respectively to vendor and purchaser—the various modes of payment and receipt of money—and the effect of contracting, or, in general, of doing any act through the intervention of a third party as agent, together with the legal consequences which flow from the subsequent ratification of a prior act. Lastly, we have stated in what manner a contract may be revoked or dissolved, and how a vested right of action may be affected by the Statute of Limitations, or by the negligence or death of the party possessing it. It [*689] will be evident, from the above brief outline of the principles set forth in this chapter, that some of them apply to actions of tort, as well as to those founded in contract; and when such has been the case, the remarks and illustrations appended have not been in any way confined to actions of the latter description. The general object, however, has been to exhibit the most important elementary rules relative to *contracts*, and to show in what manner the law may, through their medium, be applied to regulate and adjust the infinitely varied and complicated transactions of a mercantile community.

MODUS ET CONVENTIO VINCUNT LEGEM.

(2 Rep. 73.)

The form of agreement and the convention of parties overrule the law.

[*690] The above may be regarded as the most elementary *principle of law relative to contracts,[1] and may be thus stated in a somewhat more comprehensive form: The conditions annexed to a grant or devise, the covenants inserted in a conveyance or lease, and the agreements, whether written or verbal, entered into between parties, have, when duly executed and perfected, and subjected to certain restrictions, the force of law over those who are parties to such instruments or agreements.[2] "Parties to contracts," remarks Erle, J., in a recent case,[3] "are to be allowed to regulate their rights and liabilities themselves," and "the court will only give effect to the intention of the parties as it is expressed by the contract."[4]

[1] In illustration of it, see Walsh *v.* Secretary of State for India, 10 H. L. Cas. 367; Savin *v.* Hoylake R. C., L. R. 1 Ex. 9.

[2] A "contract" is defined to be "*Une convention par laquelle les deux parties, ou seulement l'une des deux, promettent et s'engagent envers l'autre à lui donner quelque chose ou à faire ou á ne pas faire quelque chose:*" Pothier Oblig., pt. 1, chap. 1, art. 1, s. 1. *Omne jus aut consensus fecit, aut necessitas constituit, aut firmavit consuetudo:* D. 1. 3. 40. "It is the essence of a contract that there should be a concurrence of intention between the parties as to the terms. It is an agreement because they agree upon the terms, upon the subject-matter, the consideration, and the promise:" L. R. 4 Ex. 381.

[3] Gott *v.* Gandy, 23 L. J. Q. B. 1, 3; s. c., 2 E. & B. 847 (75 E. C. L. R.); per Erle, J., 4 H. & N. 343.

[4] Judgm., Stadhard *v.* Lee, 3 B. & S. 372 (113 E. C. L. R.); per Bramwell,

Where, for instance, a man seised of a reversion expectant on an estate for life grants an *interesse termini* to A. for ninety-nine years, if he shall so long live, to commence after the death of the tenant for life, reserving a heriot on the death of A., and A. dies in the lifetime of the tenant for life, the lessor is entitled to the heriot reserved on the death of A., although he never enjoyed the estate, by reason of the express contract between the *parties.[1] [*691] In like manner, where the tenant of a house covenanted in his lease to pay a reasonable share and proportion of the expenses of supporting, repairing, and amending all party-walls, &c., and to pay all taxes, duties, assessments, and impositions, parliamentary and parochial,—"it being the intention of the parties that the landlord should receive the clear yearly rent of 60*l.* in net money, without any deduction whatever,"—and during the lease the proprietor of the adjoining house built a party-wall between his own house and the house demised, under the provisions of the stat. 14 Geo. 3, c. 78: it was held, that the tenant, and not the landlord, was bound to pay the moiety of the expense of the party-wall; "for," observed Lord Kenyon, "the covenants in the lease render it unnecessary to consider which of the parties would have been liable under the Act of Parliament; *Modus et conventio vincunt legem*."[2] So, a tenancy at will is a kind of holding not favored nor readily implied by the law. If, however, an agreement be made to let premises so long as both parties like, and a compensation accruing *de die in diem*, and not referable to a year or any aliquot part of a year, be thereby reserved, such an agreement does not create a holding from year to year, but a tenancy at will strictly so called; for two persons may agree to make a tenancy at will, according to the maxim, *Modus et conventio vincunt legem*.[3]

So in Rowbotham *v.* Wilson,[4] Martin, B., observes, "I think the owner of land may grant the surface, subject *to the [*692] quality or incident that he shall be at liberty to work the

B., Rogers *v.* Hadley, 2 H. & C. 249; per Erle, C. J., Martin *v.* Reid, 11 C. B. N. S. 735 (103 E. C. L. R.).

[1] Per Kelynge, C. J., Lanyon *v.* Carne, 2 Saund. R. 167. See Doe d. Douglas *v.* Lock, 2 A. & E. 705 (29 E. C. L. R.); Winch. R. 48.

[2] Barrett *v.* Duke of Bedford, 8 T. R. 602, 605.

[3] Richardson *v.* Langridge, 4 Taunt. 128; recognized Doe d. Hull *v.* Wood, 14 M. & W. 687. See Doe d. Dixie *v.* Davies, 7 Exch. 89.

[4] 8 E. & B. 150 (92 E. C. L. R.); s. c., 8 H. L. Cas. 348.

mines underneath, and not be responsible for any subsidence of the surface. If the law of itself, under certain circumstances, protects from the consequences of an act, I think a man may contract for such protection in a case where the law of itself would not apply, *Modus et conventio vincunt legem.*"

In an action on the case for not carrying away tithe corn, the plaintiff alleged, that it was "lawfully and in due manner" set out: it was held, that this allegation was satisfied by proof that the tithe was set out according to an agreement between the parties, although the mode thereby agreed to varied from that prescribed by the common law, the tithe having been set out in shocks, and not in sheaves, as the law directs.[1]

The same comprehensive principle applies, also, to agreements having immediate reference to mercantile transactions: thus, the stipulations contained in articles of partnership may be enforced, and must be acted on as far as they go, their terms being explained, and their deficiencies supplied, by reference to the general principles of law. Although, therefore, a new partner cannot at law be introduced without the consent of every individual member of the firm, yet the executors of a deceased partner will be allowed to occupy his place, if there be an express stipulation to that effect in the agreement of partnership. Again, the lien which a factor has upon the goods of his principal[2] arises from a tacit agreement between the parties, which the law implies; but, where there is an [*693] express stipulation to the contrary, it puts an *end to the general rule of law.[3] The general lien of a banker, also, is part of the law merchant, and will be upheld by courts of justice, unless there be some agreement between the banker and the depositor, either express or implied, inconsistent with such right.[4] So, it has been remarked that, in the ordinary case of a sale of chattels, time is not of the *essence* of the contract, *unless* it be made so by

[1] Facey *v.* Hurdom, 3 B. & C. 213 (10 E. C. L. R.). See Halliwell *v.* Trappes, 1 Taunt. 55.

[2] See Dixon *v.* Stansfeld, 10 C. B. 398 (70 E. C. L. R.).

[3] Per Lord Kenyon, C. J., Walker *v.* Birch, 6 T. R. 262.

As to the general lien of a wharfinger at common law, see Dresser *v.* Bosanquet, 4 B. & S. 460, 486 (116 E. C. L. R.).

[4] Brandão *v.* Barnett, 12 Cl. & Fin. 787; s. c., 3 C. B. 519 (54 E. C. L. R.).

As to the lien of a shipowner on the cargo for freight, see How *v.* Kirchner, 11 Moo. P. C. C. 21; Kirchner *v.* Venus, 12 Id. 361.

express agreement, and this may be effected with facility by introducing conditional words into the bargain; the sale of a specific chattel on credit, therefore, although that credit may be limited to a definite period, transfers the property in the goods to the vendee, giving the vendor a right of action for the price and a lien upon the goods if they remain in his possession till that price be paid.[1]

The doctrine relative to specific performance may here simply be mentioned, as showing that courts of equity fully acknowledge the efficacy of contracts, where *bonâ fide* entered into in accordance with those formalities, if any, required by the statute law. Equity, indeed, from its peculiar jurisdiction, has power for enforcing the fulfillment of contracts which a court of law does not possess;[2] and in exercising this power, it obviously acts upon the *principle that express stipulations prescribe the law *quoad* the contracting parties. [*694] For instance, money was devised to be laid out in land to the use of B. in tail, remainder to the use of C. in fee. B., having no issue, agreed with C. to divide the money; but before the agreement was executed B. died, whereupon C., becoming, as he supposed, entitled to the whole fund, refused to complete the agreement. The court, however, upon bill filed by B.'s personal representatives, decreed a specific performance,[3]—acting thereby in strict accordance with the above maxim, *Modus et conventio vincunt legem.*[4]

Without venturing further into the wide field which is here opening upon us, we may add that it does sometimes happen, notwithstanding an express agreement between parties, that peculiar circumstances present themselves which afford grounds for the interference of a court of equity, in order that the contract entered into may be so modified as to meet the justice of the case. For instance, where an attorney, whilst he lay ill, received the sum of 120 guineas by way of premium or apprentice fee with a clerk

[1] Martindale *v.* Smith, 1 Q. B. 395 (41 E. C. L. R.); cited in Page *v.* Eduljee, L. R. 1 P. C. 145. In Spartali *v.* Benecke, 10 C. B. 216 (70 E. C. L. R.), Wilde, C. J., observes, "If a vendor agrees to sell for a deferred payment, the property passes, and the vendee is entitled to call for a present delivery without payment." See also per Blackburn, J., Calcutta and Burmah Steam Nav. Co. *v.* De Mattos, 32 L. J. Q. B. 328.

[2] See Benson *v.* Paull, 6 E. & B. 273 (88 E. C. L. R.).

[3] Carter *v.* Carter, Cas. temp. Talb. 271.

[4] See also Frank *v.* Frank, 1 Chanc. Cas. 84.

who was placed with him, and died three weeks afterwards, the court decreed a return of 100 guineas, although the articles provided that, if the attorney should die within the year, 60*l.* only should be returned.[1] With respect to this case, Lord Kenyon, indeed, observed[2] that in it the jurisdiction of a court of equity had been carried "as far as could be;" but the decision seems, [695*] from the facts stated in the pleadings,[3] *to be supportable upon a plain ground of equity, viz., that of mutual mistake, misrepresentation, or unconscientious advantage,[4] and, consequently, not really opposed to the spirit of the maxim, *Modus et conventio vincunt legem.*

The rule under consideration, however, is subject to restriction and limitation, and does not apply where the express provisions of any law are violated by the contract, nor, in general, where the interests of the public or of third parties would be injuriously affected by its fulfillment:—*Pacta, quæ contra leges constitutionesque vel contra bonos mores fiunt, nullam vim haberre, indubitati juris est;*[5] and *privatorum conventio juri publico non derogat.*[6] "If the thing stipulated for is in itself contrary to law, the paction by which the execution of the illegal act is stipulated must be held as intrinsically null, *pactis privatorum juri publico non derogatur.* It is impossible to compel one who is unwilling to disobey the law to contravene it. He is entitled to plead freedom from a contract into which he should never have entered, and to be protected in maintaining an obedience to the law which the law would of itself have interposed to enforce had the act come otherwise within its cognizance."[7]

Not only is the consent or private agreement of individuals ineffectual in rendering valid any direct contravention of the law, but it will fail altogether to make just, sufficient or effectual that which [*696] is unjust or deficient *in respect to any matter which the law declares to be indispensable and not circumstantial

[1] Newton *v.* Rowse, 1 Vern., 3d ed., 460. See Re Thompson, 1 Exch. 864.

[2] Hale *v.* Webb, 2 Bro. Chan. Rep. 80.

[3] See 1 Vern., 3d ed., 460 (2).

[4] 1 Story Eq. Jurisp., 6th ed., 537, *et vide* Id., 9th ed., 452–3.

[5] C. 2. 3. 6.

[6] D. 50. 17. 45, § 1; D. 2. 14. 38; 9 Rep. 141.

[7] Per Dr. Lushington, arguendo Phillips *v.* Innes, 4 Cl. & Fin. 241; arg. Swan *v.* Blair, 3 Cl. & Fin. 621.

merely.[1] Therefore an agreement by a married woman, that she will not avail herself of her coverture as a ground of defence to an action on a personal obligation which she has incurred, would not be valid or effective in support of the plaintiff's claim and by way of answer to a plea of coverture; for a married woman is under a total disability, and her contract is absolutely void, unless where it can be viewed as a contract on behalf of the husband through her agency.[2]

So, with reference to a provision in a foreign policy of insurance against all perils of the sea, "*nullis exceptis*," it was observed, that, although there was an express exclusion of any exception by the terms of the policy, yet the reason of the thing engrafts an implied exception even upon words so general as the above; as, for example, in the case of damage occasioned by the fault of the assured; it being a general rule that the insurers shall not be liable when the loss or damage happens by the fault or fraudulent conduct of the assured, from which rule it is not allowed to derogate by any pact to the contrary; for *nullâ pactione effici potest ut dolus præstetur*—I cannot effectually contract with any one that he shall charge himself with the faults which I shall commit;[3] a man cannot validly contract that he shall be irresponsible for fraud. Neither will the law permit a person who enters into a binding contract to *say, by a subsequent clause, that he will not be liable to be sued for a breach of it.[4] [*697]

It is equally clear that an agreement entered into between two persons cannot, in general, affect the rights of a third party, who is altogether a stranger to it; thus, if it be agreed between A. and B. that B. shall discharge a particular debt due from A. to C., such an agreement can in no way prejudice C.'s right to sue A. for its recovery; *debitorum pactionibus creditorum petitio nec tolli nec minui potest;*[5] and, according to the rule of the Roman law—*privatis pactionibus non dubium est non lædi jus cæterorum.*[6]

[1] Bell, Dict. and Dig. of Scotch Law 694.

[2] See Liverpool Adelphi Loan Ass. *v.* Fairhurst, 9 Exch. 422; Wright *v.* Leonard, 11 C. B. N. S. 258 (103 E. C. L. R.); Cannam *v.* Farmer, 3 Exch. 698; Bartlett *v.* Wells, 1 B. & S. 836 (101 E. C. L. R.).

[3] Judgm., 5 M. & S. 466; D. 2. 14. 27. 3.

[4] Per Martin, B., Kelsall *v.* Tyler, 11 Exch. 534.

[5] 1 Pothier Oblig. 108, 109.

[6] D. 2. 15. 3, pr.

In the above and similar cases, then, as well as in some others relative to the disposition of property, which have been noticed in the preceding chapter,[1] another maxim emphatically applies: *Fortior et potentior est dispositio legis quàm hominis*[2]—the law in some cases overrides the will of the individual, and renders ineffective and futile his expressed intention or contract.[3]

For instance, "surrender" is the term applied in law to "an act done by or to the owner of a particular estate, [*698] *the validity of which he is estopped from disputing, and which could not have been done if the particular estate continued to exist;" as in the case of a lessee taking a second lease from the lessor, or a tenant for life accepting a feoffment from the party in remainder, or a lessee accepting a rent charge from his lessor. In such case the surrender is not the result of *intention;* for, if there was no intention to surrender the particular estate, or even if there was an express intention to keep it unsurrendered, the surrender would be the act of the law, and would prevail in spite of the intention of the parties:[4] *Fortior et potentior est dispositio legis quàm hominis.*[5]

[1] See also per Lord Kenyon, C. J., Doe d. Mitchinson *v.* Carter, 8 T. R. 61; s. c., Id. 300; arg. 15 East 178.

[2] Co. Litt. 234 a, cited 15 East 178. The maxim *supra* is illustrated, per Williams, J., Hybart *v.* Parker, 4 C. B. N. S. 213, 214 (93 E. C. L. R.).

[3] For instance, a man cannot, by his own acts or words, render that irrevocable, which, in its own nature, and according to established rules of law, is revocable, as in the case of a will. So, "the rule which prohibits the assignment of a right to sue on a covenant is not one which can be dispensed with by the agreement of the parties, and it applies to covenants expressed to be with assignees, as well as to others:" Judgm., 1 Exch. 645. And see Judgm., Hibblewhite *v.* M'Morine, 6 M. & W. 216; Broom's Com., 4th ed., 439.

[4] Lyon *v.* Reed, 13 M. & W. 285, 306; commented on, Nickells *v.* Atherstone, 10 Q. B. 944 (59 E. C. L. R.). As to a surrender by operation of law, see also Davison *v.* Gent, 1 H. & N. 744; Doe d. Hull *v.* Wood, 14 M. & W. 682; Morrison *v.* Chadwick, 7 C. B. 266 (62 E. C. L. R.); Tanner *v.* Hartley, 9 C. B. 634 (67 E. C. L. R.); Judgm., Doe d. Biddulph *v.* Poole, 11 Q. B. 716 (63 E. C. L. R.); Phené *v.* Popplewell, 12 C. B. N. S. 334 (104 E. C. L. R.).

[5] Similarly applied in 8 Johns. (U. S.) R. 401; Co. Litt. 338 a. It may possibly happen, too, that the direction of a particular legal tribunal will have to be disregarded by a judge, as opposed to the common law; see per Coleridge, J., 15 Q. B. 192 (69 E. C. L. R.). And see other instances, in connection with illegal contracts, *post*. *Et vide* per Lord Truro, C., Ellcock

Subject to the above, however, and similar exceptions, the general rule of the civil law holds equally in our own: *Pacta conventa quæ neque contra leges neque dolo malo inita sunt omnimodo observanda sunt*[1]—compacts which are not illegal, and do not originate in fraud, must in all respects be observed.

---

*QUILIBET POTEST RENUNCIARE JURI PRO SE INTRODUCTO. [*699]

(Wing. Max. 483.)

Any one may, at his pleasure, renounce the benefit of a stipulation or other right introduced entirely in his own favor.[2]

According to the well-known principle expressed in the above maxim, any person may decline to avail himself of a defence which would be at law a valid and sufficient answer to the plaintiff's demand, as of infancy, or the Statute of Limitations;[3] and not only may he, in either of the two latter cases, waive his right to insist upon the specific defence, but he may even ratify and renew his liability, and by his own act or acknowledgment render himself clearly responsible, if this be done in such a manner as by law required.[4] So, a man may not merely relinquish a particular line of defence, but he may also renounce a claim which might have been substantiated, or release a debt which might have been recovered by ordinary legal process; or he may, by his express contract or stipula-

v. Mapp, 3 H. L. Cas, 507; per Parke, B., Hallett *v.* Dowdall, 18 Q. B. 87 (83 E. C. L. R.).

[1] C. 2. 3. 29.

[2] Bell, Dict. and Dig. of Scotch Law 545; 1 Inst. 99 a; 2 Inst. 183; 10 Rep. 101.

The words *pro se* "have been introduced into the above maxim to show that no man can renounce a right which his duty to the public, which the claims of society forbid the renunciation of:" per Lord Westbury, C., Hunt *v.* Hunt, 31 L. J. Chanc. 175.

[3] See Tanner *v.* Smart, 6 B. & C. 603 (13 E. C. L. R.); per Parke, B., Hart *v.* Prendergast, 14 M. & W. 743.

[4] See per Bayley, J., 2 M. & S. 25 (28 E. C. L. R.); per Abbott, C. J., 5 B. & Ald. 686 (7 E. C. L. R.). Graham *v.* Ingleby, 1 Exch. 651, 656, shows that a plaintiff may waive the benefit of the stat. 4 Ann. c. 16, s. 11, which requires that a plea in abatement should be verified by affidavit.

tion, exclude some more extensive right, which the law would otherwise have impliedly conferred. In all these cases, the rule holds, *Omnes licentiam habere his, quæ pro se indulta sunt, renunciare*[1]—every man may [*700] *renounce a benefit or waive a privilege which the law has conferred upon him.[2] For instance, whoever contracts for the purchase of an estate in fee simple, without any exception or stipulation to vary the general right, is entitled to call for a conveyance of the fee, and to have a good title to the legal estate made out. But, upon the principle under consideration, a man may, by express stipulation, or by contract, or even by consent testified by acquiescence or otherwise, bind himself to accept a title merely equitable, or a title subject to some encumbrance; and whatever defect there may be, which is covered by this stipulation, must be disregarded by the conveyancer to whom the abstract of title is submitted, as not affording a valid ground of objection.[3]

According to the same principle, if a man, being tenant for life, has a power to lease for twenty-one years for his own benefit, he may renounce a part of the right so given, and grant a lease for any number of years short of the twenty-one, *i. e.*, he may either exercise his right to the utmost extent of the power, or he may stop short of that; and then every part of which he abridged himself would be for the benefit of the next in remainder; he would throw back into the inheritance that portion which he did not choose to absorb for his own use.[4]

Again, the right to estovers is incident to the estate of every tenant for life or years (though not to the estate of [*701] *a strict tenant at will), unless he be restrained by special covenant to the contrary, which is usually the case; so that here

[1] C. 1. 3. 51; C. 2. 3. 29; *Invito beneficium non datur*, D. 50. 17. 69.

See, as illustrating the maxim cited in the text, Markham *v.* Stanford, 14 C. B. N. S. 376, 383 (108 E. C. L. R.); distinguished in Morten *v.* Marshall, 2 H. & C. 305.

[2] Per Erle, C. J., Rumsey *v.* North-Eastern R. C., 14 C. B. N. S. 649 (108 E. C. L. R.); Caledonian R. C. *v.* Lockhart, 3 Macq. Sc. App. Cas. 808, 822; per Martin, B., 8 E & B. 151 (92 E. C. L. R.); per Pollock, C. B., and Bramwell, B., 2 H. & C. 308, 309. See Enohin *v.* Wylie, 10 H. L. Cas. 1, 15.

[3] 3 Prest. Abs. Tit. 221.

[4] Per Lord Ellenborough, C. J., Isherwood *v.* Oldknow, 3 M. & S. 392. See also Co. Litt. 223 b.

the above maxim, or that relating to *modus et conventio*, may be applied.[1]

Another familiar instance of the application of the same principle occurs in connection with the law of bills of exchange. The general rule is, that, in order to charge the drawer or endorser of a bill, payment must be demanded of the acceptor in the first instance on the day when the bill becomes due; and, in case of refusal or default, due notice of such demand and refusal or default must be given to the drawer within a reasonable time afterwards; the reason being, that the acceptor of a bill is presumed to have in his hands effects of the drawer for the purpose of discharging the bill; and, therefore, notice to the drawer is requisite, in order that he may withdraw his effects as speedily as possible from the hands of the acceptor. Until these previous steps have been taken, the drawer cannot be resorted to on non-payment of the bill; and the want of notice to a drawer, who has effects in the hands of the acceptor, after dishonor of the bill, is considered as tantamount to payment by him. So, where a bill has been endorsed, and the holder intends to sue any of the endorsers, it is incumbent on him first to demand payment from the acceptor on the day when the bill becomes due, and, in case of refusal, to give due notice thereof within a reasonable time to the endorser; the reason being, that the endorser is in the nature of a surety only, and his undertaking to pay the bill is not an absolute but a conditional undertaking, that is, in the event of a demand made on the acceptor (who is primarily liable) at *the time when the bill becomes due, and refusal on his part, or neglect to pay.[2] As, however, the rule [*702] requiring notice was introduced for the benefit of the party to whom such notice must be given, it may, in accordance with the above maxim, be waived by that party.[3] But though a party may thus waive the consequences of laches in respect to himself, he cannot do so in respect of antecedent parties; for that would be in

[1] Co. Litt. 41 b.

[2] Where the drawer has in the drawee's hands no effects, or effects insufficient for payment of the draft (Carew *v.* Duckworth, L. R. 4 Ex. 313), he is not in general entitled to notice: Bickerdike *v.* Bollman, 1 T. R. 405; Carter *v.* Flower, 16 M. & W. 743; Bailey *v.* Porter, 14 M. & W. 44; Thomas *v.* Fenton, 16 L. J. Q. B. 362.

[3] See Steele *v.* Harmer, 14 M. & W. 831; Mills *v.* Gibson, 16 L. J. C. P. 249; Burgh *v.* Legge, 5 M. & W. 418; Allen *v.* Edmundson, 2 Exch. 719.

violation of another legal principle presently to be mentioned, which limits the application of the maxim now under consideration to those cases in which no injury is inflicted, by the renunciation of a legal right, upon a third party.

Again, persons sharing in the profits of an adventure may, by express agreement, exclude the relation of partnership from arising as between themselves, though they cannot thereby affect the rights of third persons; and a private regulation between the members of a trading company to limit the personal liability of individuals, or to regulate the contracts which each partner may enter into on behalf of the firm, although valid as between themselves, will be wholly nugatory *quoad* strangers.[1] The rights of partners *inter se* have, indeed, been created and upheld by the law of their own convenience, and may, therefore, by express stipulation, be renounced. Thus, it is a rule, that all property bought with the cash [*703] *and for the purposes of a trading partnership concern must, in equity, be looked upon as personal; and that a partner's share and interest therein will, on his death, pass to his personal representatives; but partners may stipulate between themselves, that freehold lands purchased by them shall not be subject to the application of this equitable doctrine, but shall follow the ordinary rules respecting property of that description; and, in such a case, the rule of equity yields to the ordinary course of law, coupled with the express intention of the parties.[2]

It will be seen from some of the preceding instances, that the rule which enables a man to renounce a right which he might otherwise have enforced must be applied with this qualification, that, in general, a private compact or agreement cannot be permitted to derogate from the rights of third parties,[3] or, in other words, although a party may renounce a right or benefit *pro se introductum*, he cannot renounce that which has been introduced for the benefit of another party; thus, the rule that a child within the age of nurture cannot be separated from the mother by order of removal,

[1] See further, as to partnership liability, *post*, under the maxim *qui facit per alium facit per se*.

[2] *Ante*, p. 692.

[3] 7 Rep. 23. See Brinsdon *v.* Allard, 2 E. & E. 19 (102 E. C. L. R.); Slater *v.* Mayor, &c., of Sunderland, 33 L. J. Q. B. 37

has been established for the benefit and protection of the child, and therefore cannot be dispensed with by the mother's consent.[1]

One case may, however, be mentioned to which the rule applies, without the qualification—that, *viz.*, of a release by one of several joint creditors, which, in the absence of fraud and collusion, will operate as a release of the claims of the other creditors, and may be pleaded accordingly. On the other hand, the debtee's discharge *of one joint or joint and several debtor is a discharge of all;[2] and a release of the principal debtor will discharge the sureties, unless, indeed, there be an express reservation of remedies as against them.[3] [*704]

It is also a well-known principle of law, that, where a creditor gives time to the principal debtor,[4] there being a surety to secure payment of the debt, and does so without consent of or communication with the surety, he discharges the surety from liability, as he thereby places himself in *a new situation*,[5] and exposes him to a risk and contingency to which he would not otherwise be liable;[6] *and this seems to afford a further illustration of the [*705]

[1] Reg. *v.* Birmingham, 5 Q. B. 210 (48 E. C. L. R.). See Reg. *v.* Combs, 5 E. & B. 892 (85 E. C. L. R.).

[2] Nicholson *v.* Revill, 4 A. & E. 675, 683 (31 E. C. L. R.), recognizing Cheetham *v.* Ward, 1 B. & P. 630, and cited in Kearsley *v.* Cole, *infra*, and Thompson *v.* Lack, 3 C. B. 540 (54 E. C. L. R.); Co. Litt. 232 a; Judgm., Price *v.* Barker, 4 E. & B. 777 (82 E. C. L. R.); Clayton *v.* Kynaston, 2 Salk. 573; 2 Roll. Abr. 410, D. 1; 412, G., pl. 4.

[3] Kearsley *v.* Cole, 16 M. & W. 128; Thompson *v.* Lack, 3 C. B. 540 (54 E. C. L. R.); Judgm., Price *v.* Barker, 4 E. & B. 779 (82 E. C. L. R.); Owen *v.* Homan, 4 H. L. Cas. 997, 1037.

[4] "The general rule of law where a person is surety for the debt of another is this—that though the creditor may be entitled, after a certain period, to make a demand and enforce payment of the debt, he is not bound to do so; and provided he does not preclude himself from proceeding against the principal, he may abstain from enforcing any right which he possesses. If the creditor has voluntarily placed himself in such a position that he cannot sue the principal, he thereby discharges the surety. But mere delay on the part of the creditor, unaccompanied by any valid contract with the principal, will not discharge the surety:" per Pollock, C. B., Price *v.* Kirkham, 3 H. & C. 441.

[5] See Harrison *v.* Seymour, L. R. 1 C. P. 518; Union Bank of Manchester *v.* Beech, 3 H. & C. 672; Skillett *v.* Fletcher, L. R. 2 C. P. 469, and cases there cited.

[6] Per Lord Lyndhurst, Oakley *v.* Pasheller, 4 Cl. & Finn. 233. See further

remark already offered, that a renunciation of a right cannot in general[1] be made to the injury of a third party.

Where, however, a husband, whose wife was entitled to a fund in court, signed a memorandum after marriage, agreeing to secure half her property on herself, it was held, that it was competent for the wife to waive this agreement, and that any benefit which her children might have taken under it was defeated by her waiver.[2]

Lastly, it is clear that the maxim, *Quilibet potest renunciare juri pro se introducto*, is inapplicable where an express statutory direction enjoins compliance with the forms which it prescribes; for instance, a testator cannot dispense with the observance of those formalities which are essential to the validity of a testamentary instrument; for the provisions of the Statute of Frauds, or of the modern Wills Act, were introduced with a view to the public benefit, not that of the individual, and, therefore, must be regarded as positive ordinances of the legislature, binding upon all.[3] Nor can an individual waive a matter in which the public have an interest.[4]

[*706] *Qui sentit Commodum sentire debet et Onus.

(2 Inst. 489.)

He who derives the advantage ought to sustain the burthen.

The above rule[5] applies as well in the case where an implied covenant runs with the land, as where the present owner or occu-

as to the rule above stated, per Lord Brougham, Mactaggart *v.* Watson, 3 Cl. & Fin. 541; per Lord Eldon, C., Samuell *v.* Howorth, 3 Mer. 278, adopted per Lord Cottenham, C., Creighton *v.* Rankin, 7 Cl. & Fin. 346; Manley *v.* Boycott, 2 E. & B. 46 (75 E. C. L. R.); Pooley *v.* Harradine, 7 E. & B. 431 (90 E. C. L. R.); Lawrence *v.* Walmsley, 12 C. B. N. S. 799, 808 (104 E. C. L. R.); see Bonar *v.* Macdonald, 3 H. L. Cas. 226; General Steam Nav. Co. *v.* Rolt, 6 C. B. N. S. 550 (95 E. C. L. R.); Way *v.* Hearn, 11 C. B. N. S. 774 (103 E. C. L. R.); 13 Id. 292; Frazer *v.* Jordan, 8 E. & B. 303 (92 E. C. L. R.); Taylor *v.* Burgess, 5 H. & N. 1; Bailey *v.* Edwards, 4 B. & S. 761 (116 E. C. L. R.).

[1] See Langley *v.* Headland, 19 C. B. N. S. 42 (105 E. C. L. R.).

[2] Fenner *v.* Taylor, 2 Russ. & My. 190; Macq. H. & W. 85.

[3] See, per Wilson, J., Habergham *v.* Vincent, 2 Ves. jun. 227; cited Countess of Zichy Ferraris *v.* Marquis of Hertford, 3 Curt. 493, 498; s. c., affirmed 4 Moore P. C. C. 339.

[4] Per Alderson, B., Graham *v.* Ingleby, 1 Exch. 657; *ante*, p. 699, n. 2.

[5] In exemplification whereof see Hayward *v.* Duff, 12 C. B. N. S. 364 (104 E. C. L. R.).

pier of land is bound by the express covenant of a prior occupant; whenever, indeed, the ancient maxim, *Transit terra cum onere*, holds true.[1] The burthen of repairs has, we may observe, always been thrown as much as possible, by the spirit of the common law, upon the occupier or tenant, not only in accordance with the principle contained in the above maxim, but also because it would be contrary to all justice, that the expense of accumulated dilapidation should, at the end of the period of tenancy, fall upon the landlord, when a small outlay of money on the part of the tenant in the first instance would have prevented any such expense becoming necessary; to which we may add, that, generally, the tenant alone has the opportunity of observing, from time to time, when repairs become necessary. In one of the leading cases on this subject, the facts were, that a man demised a house by indenture for years, and the lessee, for him and his executors, covenanted with the lessor to repair the house at all times necessary; the lessee afterwards assigned it over to another party, who suffered it to decay; it was adjudged that covenant lay at suit of the lessor against the assignee, although the lessee had not covenanted for him and his assigns; for the covenant to repair, which extends to the support of the thing demised, *is *quodammodo* appurtenant to it, and goes with it; and, inasmuch as the lessee had taken upon himself to bear the charges of the reparations, the yearly rent was the less, which was to the benefit of the assignee, and *Qui sentit commodum sentire debet et onus.*[2]

[*707]

The following case may also serve to illustrate the same principle: —A company was empowered under a local Act to make the river Medway navigable, to take tolls, and "to amend or alter such bridges or highways as might hinder the passage or navigation, leaving them or others as convenient, in their room." The company, in prosecuting the work, destroyed a ford across the river, in the common highway, by deepening its bed, and built a bridge over the river at the same place. It was held, on an indictment brought against the company forty years afterwards, that they were bound

[1] Co. Litt. 231 a. See Moule *v.* Garrett, L. R. 5 Ex. 13, and cases there cited.

[2] Dean and Chapter of Windsor's Case, 5 Rep. 25; cited per Tindal, C. J., Tremeere *v.* Morison, 1 Bing. N. C. 98 (27 E. C. L. R.); which case is followed in Sleap *v.* Newman, 12 C. B. N. S. 116, 124 (104 E. C. L. R.).

to keep the bridge in repair, as under a continuing condition to preserve a new passage in lieu of the old one which they had destroyed for their own benefit.[1] So, the undertakers of the Aire and Calder Navigation, who were empowered by Act of Parliament to make certain drains in lieu of those previously existing, were held bound to cleanse the drains substituted by them in pursuance of the Act, the power to make such substitution having been conferred on them for their own benefit.[2] In the two preceding cases, as well as in others of a like character, the maxim under consideration is directly applicable.[3]

[*708] *So, it has been designated a principle of "universal application" that "where a contract has been entered into by one man as agent for another, the person on whose behalf it has been made cannot take the benefit of it without bearing its burthen. The contract must be performed in its integrity."[4]

A further important illustration of the rule occurs where a party adopts a contract which was entered into without his authority, in which case he must adopt it altogether. He cannot ratify that part which is beneficial to himself, and reject the remainder; he must take the benefit to be derived from the transaction *cum onere*.[5] Where, therefore, the owner of goods who was undisclosed at the time of the contract for their sale, subsequently interferes and sues upon the contract, justice requires that, if the defendant has credited and acquired a set-off against the agent before the principal interposed, the latter should be bound by the set-off, in the same way that the agent would have been had he been the plaintiff on the record; and that the defendant should be placed in the same situation at the time of the disclosure of the real principal, as if the agent had been in truth the principal.[6]

An innkeeper was requested by his guest to allow him the use of

[1] R. *v.* Inhabs. of Kent, 13 East 220.

[2] Priestley *v.* Foulds, 2 Scott N. R. 205.

[3] Per Tindal, C. J., 2 Scott N. R. 225; Nicholl *v.* Allen, 1 B. & S. 916, 934 (101 E. C. L. R.).

[4] Per Lord Cranworth and Lord Kingsdown, Bristow *v.* Whitmore, 9 H. L. Cas. 391, 404, 418 (where there was a difference of opinion as to the application of the principal maxim, see per Lord Wensleydale, Id. 406); cited in The Feronia, L. R. 2 A. & E. 75, 77, 85 (29 E. C. L. R.).

[5] Per Lord Ellenborough, C. J., 7 East 166.

[6] See the cases cited Broom's Com., 4th ed., 539.

a private room for the purpose of showing his goods in; and to this request the innkeeper acceded, at the same time telling the guest that there was a key, and that he might lock the door, which, however, the guest *neglected to do: it was held, that the jury were justified in concluding that plaintiff received the favor [*709] *cum onere*, that is, that he accepted the chamber to show his goods in upon condition of taking the goods under his own care, and that by so taking them under his own care the innkeeper was exonerated from responsibility.[1] The liability of an innkeeper, under ordinary circumstances, in respect of goods brought to his inn, has been materially restricted by the recent stat. 26 & 27 Vict. c. 41.

Again, it is a very general and comprehensive rule, to which we have already adverted, and which likewise falls within the scope of the maxim now under consideration, that the assignee of a chose in action takes it subject to all the equities to which it was liable in the hands of the assignor; and the reason and justice of this rule, it has been observed, are obvious, since the holder of property can only alienate or transfer to another that beneficial interest in it which he himself possesses.[2] If, moreover, a person accepts anything which he knows to be subject to a duty or charge, it is rational to conclude that he means to take such duty or charge upon himself, and the law may very well imply a promise to perform what he has so taken upon himself.[3]

The above maxim may also be applied in support and explanation of that principle of the law of estoppel, in *accordance with which the record of a verdict, followed by a [*710] judgment in a suit of *inter partes*, will estop, not only the original parties, but likewise those claiming under them. A man will be bound by that which would have bound those under whom he claims *quoad* the subject-matter of the claim; for, *Qui sentit commodum sentire debet et onus*: and no man can, except in certain cases,

[1] Burgess *v.* Clements, 4 M. & S. 306, 313; Richmond *v.* Smith, 8 B. & C. 9 (30 E. C. L. R.); Dawson *v.* Chamney, 5 Q. B. 164, 169 (48 E. C. L. R.); Calye's Case, 8 Rep. 32, is the leading case as to the liability of innkeepers. See also in connection therewith, Armistead *v.* Wilde, 17 Q. B. 261 (79 E. C. L. R.); Cashill *v.* Wright, 6 E. & B. 891 (88 E. C. L. R.); Dansey *v.* Richardson, 3 E. & B. 144 (77 E. C. L. R.); Day *v.* Bather, 2 H. & C. 14.

[2] 1 Johns. (U. S.) R. 552, 553; 11 Id. 80; Brandon *v.* Brandon, 25 L. J. Chanc. 896; *ante*, p. 467.

[3] Abbott Shipp., 5th ed., 286; cited Lucas *v.* Nockells, 1 Cl. & Fin. 457.

which are regulated by the statute law and the law merchant, transfer to another a better right than he himself possesses,[1] the grantee shall not be in a better condition than he who made the grant;[2] and, therefore, privies in blood, law, and estate shall be bound by, and take advantage of, estoppels.[3]

In administering equity the maxim *Qui sentit commodum sentire debet et onus* may properly be said to merge in the yet more comprehensive rule, *equality is equity*—upon the consideration of which it is not within the scope of our present plan to enter. The following instances of the application in equity of the maxim more immediately under our notice must suffice. The legatee of a house held by the testator on lease at a reserved rent, higher than it could be let for after his death, cannot reject the gift of the lease and retain an annuity under the will, but must take the benefit *cum onere*.[4] A testator gives a specific bequest to A., and directs that in consideration of the bequest, A. shall pay his debts, and makes A. his residuary legatee and executor; the payment of the debts is, in this case, a condition annexed to the specific bequest, and if A. accept the bequest, he is *bound to pay the debts, though they should far exceed the amount of the property bequeathed to him.[5]

[*711]

We may observe also, that the Scotch doctrine of "approbate and reprobate" is strictly analogous to that of election in our own law, and may, consequently, be properly referred to the maxim now under consideration. The principle on which this doctrine depends is, that a person shall not be allowed at once to benefit by and to repudiate an instrument, but that, if he chooses to take the benefit which it confers, he shall likewise discharge the obligation or bear the *onus* which it imposes. "It is," as was remarked in an important case upon this subject, "equally settled in the law of Scotland as of England, that no person can accept and reject the same instrument. If a testator give his estate to A., and give A.'s estate to B., courts of equity hold it to be against conscience that A. should take the estate bequeathed to him, and at the same time refuse to give effect to the implied condition contained in the will of the

[1] *Ante*, pp. 467, 470.

[2] Mallory's Case, 5 Rep. 113.

[3] Co. Litt. 352 a; Outram *v.* Morewood, 3 East 346.

[4] Talbot *v.* Earl of Radnor, 3 My. & K. 252.

[5] Messenger *v.* Andrews, 4 Russ. 478.

testator. The court will not permit him to take that which cannot be his but by virtue of the disposition of the will, and at the same time to keep what, by the same will, is given or intended to be given to another person. It is contrary to the established principles of equity that he should enjoy the benefit, while he rejects the condition of the gift."[1] Where, therefore, an express condition is annexed to a bequest, the legatee cannot accept and reject, approbate and reprobate the will containing it. If, for example, the testator possessing a landed estate of small value, and a large personal estate, bequeaths by his will the personal estate to the heir, who was not otherwise *entitled to it, upon condition [*712] that he shall give the land to another, the heir must either comply with the condition, or forego the benefit intended for him.[2] We may add, that the above rule as expressed by the maxim—*Quod approbo non reprobo*—likewise holds where the condition is implied merely, provided there be clear evidence of an intention to make the bequest conditional; and in this case, likewise, the heir will be required to perform the condition or to renounce the benefit[3] —*Qui sentit commodum sentire debet et onus.*

The converse of the above maxim also holds, and is occasionally cited and applied; for instance, inasmuch as the principal is bound by the acts of his authorized agent, so he may take advantage of them,[4] *Qui sentit onus sentire debet et commodum.*[5]

In like manner, it has been observed,[6] that wherever a grant is made for a valuable consideration, which involves public duties and charges, the grant shall be construed so as to make the indemnity co-extensive with the burthen—*Qui sentit onus sentire debet et commodum.* In the case, for instance, of a ferry, there is a public charge and duty. The owner must keep the ferry in good repair, upon the peril of an indictment. He must keep sufficient accommodation for all travellers, at all reasonable times. He must content himself with a reasonable toll—such is the *jus publicum.*[7]

[1] Kerr *v.* Wauchope, 1 Bligh 21.

[2] Shaw on Obligations, s. 184.

[3] Id., s. 187.

[4] Seignior *v.* Wolmer, Godb. 360; Judgm., Higgins *v.* Senior, 8 M. & W. 844.

[5] 1 Rep. 99.

[6] Per Story, J., 11 Peters (U. S.) R. 630, 631.

[7] Paine *v.* Patrick, 3 Mod. 289, 294.

In return, the law will exclude all injurious competition, and deem every new ferry a nuisance, which subtracts from him [*713] *the ordinary custom and toll.[1] The franchise is, therefore, construed to extend beyond the local limits, and to be exclusive within a reasonable distance, this being indispensable to the fair enjoyment of the right of toll; and the same principle applies equally to the grant of a bridge, for the duties attaching to the grantee are, in this case also, *publici juris*, and pontage and passage are but different names for exclusive toll for transport.[2]

Although, moreover, the maxim *Qui sentit commodum sentire debet et onus*, to which we have above mainly adverted, applies to throw the burthen of partnership debts upon the partnership estate,[3] which is alone liable to them in the first instance, yet the converse of this maxim holds with regard to the partnership creditor.[4]

IN ÆQUALI JURE MELIOR EST CONDITIO POSSIDENTIS.

(Plowd. 296.)

Where the right is equal, the claim of the party in actual possession shall prevail.

The general rule is, that possession constitutes a sufficient title against every person not having a better title. "He that hath possession of lands, though it be by *disseisin*, hath a right against all men but against him that hath right;"[5] for, "till some act be

[1] Com. Dig., *Pischary* (B).

[2] Charles River Bridge *v.* Warren Bridge, 11 Peters (U. S.) R. 630, 631.

[3] "Perhaps the maxim that 'he who partakes the advantage ought to bear the loss' * * is only the consequence, not the cause, why a man is made liable as a partner:" per Blackburn, J., Bullen *v.* Sharp, L. R. 1 C. P. 111.

[4] The maxim *Qui sentit onus sentire debet et commodum* is applied also in equity. See, for example, Pitt *v.* Pitt, 1 T. & R. 180; Coote Mortg., 3d ed., 517 (*d*); Francis Max. 5.

[5] Doct. & Stud. 9. "I take it to be a sound and uncontroverted maxim of law, that every plaintiff or demandant in a court of justice must recover upon the strength of his own title, and not because of the weakness of that of his adversary; that is, he shall not recover without showing a *right*, although the adverse party may be unable to show any. It is enough for the latter that he is in possession of the thing demanded until the right owner calls for it. This is a maxim of common justice as well as of law:" per Parker, C. J., Goodwin *v.* Hubbard, 15 Mass. (U. S.) R. 204.

done by the *rightful owner to divest this possession and assert his title, such actual possession is *primâ facie* evidence of a legal title in the possessor, so that, speaking generally, the burthen of proof of title is thrown upon any one who claims to oust him: this possessory title, moreover, may, by length of time and negligence of him who had the right, by degrees ripen into a perfect and indefeasible title."[1] [*714]

Hence it is a familiar rule, that, in ejectment, the party controverting my title must recover by his own strength, and not by my weakness;[2] and that, "when you will recover anything from me, it is not enough for you to destroy my title, but you must prove your own better than mine; for without a better right, *Melior est conditio possidentis.*"[3]

So mere possession will support a trespass *qu. cl. fr.*, against any one who cannot show a better title.[4] And to the like effect are the rules of the civil law—*Non possessori incumbit necessitas probandi possessiones ad se pertinere*,[5] and *in pari causâ possessor potior haberi debet.*[6]

*In like manner it is a rule laid down in the Digest, that the condition of the defendant shall be favored rather than that of the plaintiff, *favorabiliores rei potius quam actores habentur*,[7] a maxim which admits of very simple illustration in the ordinary practice of our own courts: for, if, on moving in arrest of judgment, it shall appear from the whole record that the plaintiff had no cause of action, the court will never give judgment for him, for *Melior est conditio defendentis.*[8] [*715]

So, if a loss must fall upon one of two innocent persons, both

[1] 2 Com. by Broom & Hadley 368.

[2] Hobart 103, 104; Jenk. Cent. 118; per Lee, C. J., Martin *v.* Strachan, 5 T. R. 110 n. See Feret *v.* Hill, 15 C. B. 207 (80 E. C. L. R.) (cited and explained per Maule, J., Canham *v.* Barry, Id. 611); Davison *v.* Gent, 1 H. & N. 744.

[3] Vaughan R., 58, 60; Hobart 103. See Asher *v.* Whillock, L. R. 1 Q. B. 1.

[4] Every *v.* Smith, 26 L. J. Ex. 344; Jones *v.* Chapman, 2 Exch. 803, and cases there cited.

[5] C. 4. 19. 2.

[6] D. 50. 17. 128, § 1.

[7] D. 50. 17. 125. As to which maxim, *vide* arg. 8 Wheaton (U. S.) R. 195, 196.

[8] See Hobart 199.

parties being free from blame, and justice being thus *in equilibrio*, the application of the same principle will turn the scale.[1]

"We may lay it down," says Ashhurst, J.,[2] "as a broad, general principle, that wherever one of two innocent persons must suffer by the acts of a third, he who has enabled such third person to occasion the loss must sustain it."

The application of the principle above stated must, however, be made with great caution; for instance, it frequently happens, that where money has been paid and received, without fault on either side, it may, notwithstanding the above maxim, be recovered back, either as paid under a mistake of fact,[3] or on the ground of a failure [*716] of consideration,[4] or in consequence of the *express or implied terms of the contract. Thus, in Cox *v.* Prentice, the defendant received from his principal abroad a bar of silver, and took it to the plaintiffs, who melted it, and sent a piece to an assayer to be assayed at defendant's expense. They subsequently purchased the bar, paying for a certain number of ounces of silver, which by the assay it was calculated to contain, and which was afterwards discovered to exceed the true number: it was held, that the plaintiffs, having offered to return the bar of silver, were entitled to recover the difference in value between the supposed weight and true weight as money had and received to their use, for this was a case of mutual innocence and equal error,—the mistake having been occasioned by the assay-master, who was properly to be considered as the agent for both parties.[5]

It is seldom the case, however, that the scale of justice *is* exactly *in equilibrio;* it usually happens, that some degree of laches,[6] negligence, or want of caution, causes it to preponderate in favor

[1] Per Bayley, J., East India Co. *v.* Tritton, 3 B. & C. 289 (10 E. C. L. R.); arg. 3 Bing. 408 (11 E. C. L. R.). See Simmons *v.* Taylor, C. B. N. S. 528 (89 E. C. L. R.); Holland *v.* Russell, 32 L. J. Q. B. 297, which illustrates the maxim *supra* with reference to the law of marine insurance.

[2] 2 T. R. 70.

[3] *Ante*, p. 258; Shand *v.* Grant, 15 C. B. N. S. 324 (109 E. C. L. R.).

[4] See Jones *v.* Ryde, 5 Taunt. 488, 495 (1 E. C. L. R.); Devaux *v.* Connolly, 8 C. B. 640 (65 E. C. L. R.).

[5] Cox *v.* Prentice, 3 M. & S. 344; cited 8 C. B. 658–9 (65 E. C. L. R.). See Freeman *v.* Jeffries, L. R. 4 Ex. 189.

[6] This test was applied per Tindal, C. J., Keele *v.* Wheeler, 8 Scott N. R. 333. And see the maxim *Caveat emptor—post.*

either of the plaintiff or defendant. In illustration of which remark, we may refer to the doctrine which formerly existed with reference to bills of exchange and promissory notes, when received, not fraudulently, but under circumstances indicating negligence in the holder. For instance, the defendants, who were bankers in a small town, gave notes of their own to a stranger, of whom they asked no questions, in exchange for a 500*l.* Bank of England note:—and it was held, that the plaintiffs, from whom the 500*l.* note had been stolen, and who had duly advertised their *loss, might recover the note from the defendant; and it was observed, that, if, even if the loss of the note had *not* been duly advertised, yet, if it had been received under circumstances inducing a belief that the receiver knew that the holder had become possessed of it dishonestly, the true owner would be entitled to recover its value from the receiver, the negligence of the owner being no excuse for the dishonesty of the receiver; but it was further remarked, that cases might occur in which the negligence of the one party would be an excuse for the negligence of the other, and might authorize the receiver to defend himself according to the above maxim.[1] [*717]

The rule, however, upon this subject, as above intimated, has, by several more recent decisions, been materially altered, and now is, that where a party has given consideration for a bill or note, gross negligence alone will not be sufficient to disentitle him to recover upon it; "gross negligence," it has been observed, "may be evidence of *mala fides*, but is not the same thing."[2]

And in a recent case,[3] the law bearing on the subject before us is thus stated—that "a person who takes a negotiable instrument *bonâ fide* for value has undoubtedly a good title, and is not affected by the want of title of the party from whom he takes it. His having the means of knowing that the security has been lost or stolen, and neglecting to avail himself thereof, may amount to negligence; and Lord Tenterden at one time thought negligence was an answer to the action. But *the doctrine of Gill *v.* Cubitt[4] [*718]

[1] Snow *v.* Peacock, 3 Bing. 406 (11 E. C. L. R.); commented on, Foster *v.* Pearson, 1 C. M. & R. 855.

[2] Goodman *v.* Harvey, 4 A. & E. 876 (31 E. C. L. R.); Uther *v.* Rich, 10 A. & E. 790 (37 E. C. L. R.).

[3] Raphael *v.* Bank of England, 17 C. B. 161, 171 (84 E. C. L. R.).

[4] 3 B. & C. 466 (10 E. C. L. R.).

is not now approved of." A stolen note could not be said to be taken *bonâ fide* by one who had notice or knowledge of the theft, or who, having a suspicion thereof in his mind, and the means of knowledge in his power, willfully disregarded them.[1]

"The object of the law merchant," it has been judicially observed,[2] "as to bills and notes made or become payable to bearer, is to secure their circulation as money; therefore, honest acquisition confers title. To this despotic but necessary principle, the ordinary rules of the common law are made to bend. The misapplication of a genuine signature written across a slip of stamped paper (which transaction being a forgery would, in ordinary cases, convey no title) may give a good title to any sum fraudulently inscribed within the limits of the stamp. * * * Negligence in the maker of an instrument payable to bearer makes no difference in his liability to an honest holder for value; the instrument may be lost by the maker without his negligence, or stolen from him; still he must pay. The negligence of the holder, on the other hand, makes no difference in his title. However gross the holder's negligence, if it stop short of fraud, he has a title." Thus, in the case of a bill of exchange or promissory note, "the law respects the nature and uses of the instrument more than its own ordinary rules."

[*719] Likewise, in the Court of Chancery, where two persons *having an equal equity have been equally innocent and equally diligent, the rule generally applicable is, *Melior est conditio possidentis* or *defendentis*. Thus, equity constantly refuses to interfere, either for relief or discovery, against a *bonâ fide* purchaser of the legal estate for a valuable consideration, and without notice of the adverse title, provided he chooses to avail himself of the defence at the proper time and in the proper mode.[3]

Not only *in æquali jure*, but likewise *in pari delicto*, is it true that *Potior est conditio possidentis;* where each party is equally in fault, the law favors him who is actually in possession,[4]—a well-

[1] Per Willes, J., 17 C. B. 174 (84 E. C. L. R.), citing May *v.* Chapman, 16 M. & W. 355. See, also, in connection with the above subject, Berry *v.* Alderman, 13 C. B. 674 (76 E. C. L. R.); Mather *v.* Lord Maidstone, 18 C. B. 273 (86 E. C. L. R.), cited Hall *v.* Featherstone, 3 H. & N. 288.

[2] Per Byles, J., 2 H. & C. 184–5, and in Foster *v.* Mackinnon, L. R. 4 C. P. 712.

[3] See Sugden V. & P., 14th ed., 741, 742.

[4] The rule as to *par delictum* was much considered in Atkinson *v.* Denby, cited *ante*, p. 273, n. 2.

known rule, which is, in fact, included in that more comprehensive maxim to which the present remarks are appended.

"If," said Buller, J., "a party come into a court of justice to enforce an illegal contract, two answers may be given to his demand: the one, that he must draw justice from a pure fountain, and the other, that *Potior est conditio possidentis*."[1] Agreeably to this rule, where money is paid by one of two parties to such a contract to the other, in a case where both may be considered as *particeps criminis*, an action will not lie after the contract is executed to recover the money. If A. agree to give B. money for doing an illegal act, B. cannot, although he do the act, recover the money by an action; yet, if the money be paid, A. cannot recover [*720] *it back.[2] So the premium paid on an illegal insurance, to cover a trading with an enemy, cannot be recovered back, though the underwriter cannot be compelled to make good the loss.[3] In the above and similar cases the party actually in possession has the advantage—*Cum par delictum est duorum semper oneratur petitor et melior habetur possessoris causa.*[4]

Prior to the recent stat. 8 & 9 Vict. c. 109, the maxim as to *par delictum* was frequently applied in determining the right to recover back money deposited with a stakeholder to abide the result of a wager between two parties; and although, by the 18th section of that Act, all wagers are now rendered absolutely void, and the money deposited under the circumstances stated cannot after the event has been decided be recovered back,[5] yet some of the decisions

[1] Munt *v.* Stokes, 4 T. R. 564; 2 Inst. 391. See Fitzroy *v.* Gwillim, 1 T. R. 153; observed upon by Tindal, C. J., 7 Bing. 98 (20 E. C. L. R.); arg. 10 B. & C. 684 (21 E. C. L. R.); 2 A. & E. 13 (29 E. C. L. R.); per Lord Mansfield, C. J., 2 Burr. 926. See also Gordon *v.* Howden, 12 Cl. & Fin. 241, note and cases there cited.

[2] Webb *v.* Bishop, cited 1 Selw. N. P., 10th ed., 92 n. (42); Browning *v.* Morris, Cowp. 792; per Park, J., Richardson *v.* Mellish, 2 Bing. 250 (9 E. C. L. R.).

[3] Vandyck *v.* Hewitt, 1 East 96; Lowry *v.* Bourdieu, Dougl. 468; Andree *v.* Fletcher, 3 R. R. 266; Lubbock *v.* Potts, 7 East 449; Palyart *v.* Leckie, 6 M. & S. 290; Cowie *v.* Barber, 4 M. & S. 16. See Edgar *v.* Fowler, 3 East 222; Thistlewood *v.* Cracraft, 1 M. & S. 500.

[4] D. 50. 17. 154.

[5] The statute "prohibits the recovery of money which has been *won* in such a transaction, or has been deposited to abide the event of a wager, but it does not apply to the case where a party seeks to recover his stake upon a

alluded to, as well as others not affected by the statute, may properly be cited in support of the proposition, that if an illegal contract be executory, and if the plaintiff dissent from or disavow the contract before its completion, he may, on disaffirmance thereof, recover back money whilst *in transitu* to the *other contracting [*721] party, there being in this case a *locus pœnitentiæ*, and the *delictum* being incomplete.[1]

Where, however, money has been actually paid over in pursuance of an illegal contract, it cannot, subject to the remarks hereafter made, be recovered back, for the court will not assist such a transaction in any way.[2] So, where property has been placed by one party in the hands of another for illegal purposes, as for smuggling, if the latter refuses to account for the proceeds, and fraudulently or unjustly withholds them, the party aggrieved must abide by his loss, for *In pari delicto melior est conditio possidentis;* which, it has been said, is a maxim of public policy, equally respected in courts of law and courts of equity.[3]

In a case recently decided,[4] the facts were as under:—The plaintiff deposited with the defendant the half of a 50*l.* bank note, by way of pledge to secure the payment of money due from the plaintiff to the defendant, such debt having been contracted for wine and suppers supplied to the plaintiff by the defendant, in a brothel kept by her, to be there consumed in a debauch. An action brought to recover the half note so deposited failed on application of the principal maxim, which, observed the court, "is as thoroughly settled as any proposition of law can be. It is a maxim of law, established, not for the benefit of plaintiffs or defendants, but is

repudiation of the wagering contract:" per Parke, B., 10 Exch. 738; Batty *v.* Marriott, 5 C. B. 818 (57 E. C. L. R.); cited in Coombes *v.* Dibble, L. R. 1 Ex. 248, 251, or where the event has not in fact been decided, Sadler *v.* Smith, L. R. 5 Q. B. 40.

See stat. 16 & 17 Vict. c. 119, s. 5.

[1] Martin *v.* Hewson, 10 Exch. 737; Varney *v.* Hickman, 5 C. B. 271 (57 E. C. L. R.).

[2] Per Lord Ellenborough, C. J., Edgar *v.* Fowler, 3 East 225; Ex parte Bell, 1 M. & S. 751, cited, Judgm., M'Callan *v.* Mortimer, 9 M. & W. 642; Goodall *v.* Lowndes, 6 Q. B. 464 (51 E. C. L. R.). See Keir *v.* Leman (in error), 6 Q. B. 308 (51 E. C. L. R.); per Gibbs, C. J., 8 Taunt. 497 (4 E. C. L. R.).

[3] 1 Story Eq. Jurisp., 6th ed., p. 69.

[4] Taylor *v.* Chester, L. R. 4 Q. B. 309.

founded on *the principles of public policy, which will not [*722] assist a plaintiff who has paid over money or handed over property in pursuance of an illegal or immoral contract, to recover it back."[1]

As well from the case just abstracted,[2] as from prior authorities, it seems that the true test for determining whether or not the objection that plaintiff and defendant were *in pari delicto* can be sustained, is by considering whether the plaintiff can make out his case otherwise than through the medium and by the aid of the illegal transaction to which he was himself a party. For instance, A. laid an illegal wager with B., in which C. agreed with A. to take a share; B. lost the wager, and A., in expectation that B. would pay the amount on a certain day, advanced to C. his share of the winnings. B. died insolvent before the day, and the bet was never paid; it was held that A. could not recover from C. the sum thus advanced. "The plaintiff," observed Gibbs, C. J., "says the payment was on a condition which has failed, but that condition was that B., who was concerned with the plaintiff and defendant in this illegal transaction, should make good his part by paying the whole bet to the plaintiff, and it is impossible to prove the failure of this condition without going into the illegal contract, in which all the parties were equally concerned. We think, therefore, that the plaintiff's claim is so mixed with the illegal transaction, in which he and the defendant, and B., were jointly engaged, that it cannot be established without going into proof of that transaction, and, therefore, cannot be enforced in a court of law."[3] So, in a modern case, *it was held, that one of two parties to an agreement [*723] to suppress a prosecution for felony cannot maintain an action against the other for an injury arising out of the transaction in which they had thus been illegally engaged; and this case was decided on the short ground, that the plaintiff could not establish his claim, as stated upon the record, without relying upon the illegal agreement originally entered into between himself and the defendant.[4]

[1] Citing per Lord Ellenborough, C. J., Edgar *v.* Fowler, 3 East 225.

[2] See Judgm., L. R. 4 Q. B. 314.

[3] Simpson *v.* Bloss, 7 Taunt. 246, 250 (2 E. C. L. R.) (recognized and followed in Fivaz *v.* Nicholls, 2 C. B. 501, 513 (52 E. C. L. R.); with which compare Johnson *v.* Lansley, 12 C. B. 468.

[4] Fivaz *v.* Nicholls, *supra*. See also Williams *v.* Bayley, L. R. 1 H. L. 200.

Thus far we have considered the effect of *par delictum* as between the immediate parties to the illegal transaction; we must add that the maxim respecting it does not seem to apply where an action is brought by one of such parties for the recovery of money received by a third party in respect of the illegal contract. Where, for instance, A. received money to the use of B. on an illegal contract between B. and C., it was held, that A. could not set up the illegality of the contract as a defence in an action brought by B. for money had and received.[1] It seems, however, clear that if A. enter into an illegal agreement with B., and money is received by the latter party in pursuance thereof, inasmuch as A. could not sue for its recovery, so, neither could those who may subsequently have succeeded to A.'s rights maintain an action for the same.[2]

It is, in the next place, material to observe, that the maxim which [*724] we are considering does not apply unless **both* the litigating parties are *in delicto*—it cannot be insisted upon as a defence, either by or against an innocent party.[3] Where, for instance, there were two plaintiffs in an action for money had and received, and the defendant set up a receipt, which had been fraudulently obtained by him, with the privity of one of the plaintiffs, the court observed, that the maxim now under consideration was inapplicable; for, one of the plaintiffs not being *in delicto*, the defendant ought not, as against him, to be allowed to set up his own fraud.[4] Where, also, money was paid by an underwriter to a broker for the use of the assured on an illegal contract of insurance, it was held, that the assured might recover the money from the broker, on the ground that the broker could not insist on the illegality of the contract as

[1] Tenant *v.* Elliott, 1 B. & P. 3; Farmer *v.* Russell, Id. 296; Bousfield *v.* Wilson, 15 M. & W. 185; and see particularly Nicholson *v.* Gooch, 5 E. & B. 999 (85 E. C. L. R.).

[2] See Belcher *v.* Sambourne, 6 Q. B. 414 (51 E. C. L. R.); cited Ellis *v.* Russell, 10 Q. B. 952, 956 (59 E. C. L. R.).

[3] Williams *v.* Hedley, 8 East 378. An express statutory provision may enable one party to an illegal contract to sue the other, although both parties to it had knowledge of the facts constituting the illegality. See Lewis *v.* Bright, 4 E. & B. 917 (82 E. C. L. R.).

[4] Skaife *v.* Jackson, 3 B. & C. 421 (10 E. C. L. R.); Farrar *v.* Hutchinson, 9 A. & E. 641 (36 E. C. L. R.); which cases are cited and explained per Parke, B., Wallace *v.* Kelsall, 7 M. & W. 273. See Tregoning *v.* Attenborough, 7 Bing. 97 (20 E. C. L. R.).

a defence, the obligation on him arising out of the fact that the money was received by him to the use of the plaintiff, which created a promise in law to pay.[1]

Again, where defendant entered into a composition-deed, together with the other creditors of plaintiff, under an agreement that plaintiff should give defendant his promissory notes for the remainder of the debt, which were accordingly given, and the amount thereof ultimately paid by plaintiff, it was held, that he might [*725] *recover such amount from defendant in an action for money paid and money had and received; for, as observed by Lord Ellenborough, this was not a case of *par delictum;* it was oppression on one side and submission on the other; it can never be predicated as *par delictum*, when one holds the rod and the other bows to it.[2]

The decision of the Court of Error in Fisher *v.* Bridges[3] is important with reference to the subject above adverted to. There, to a declaration in covenant for the payment of a certain sum of money, the defendant pleaded that, before the making of the deed declared upon, it was unlawfully agreed between the plaintiff and defendant that the former should sell and the latter purchase of him a conveyance of land for a term of years, in consideration of a sum of money to be paid by the defendant to the plaintiff, "to the intent and in order and for the purpose, as the plaintiff at the time of the making the said agreement well knew," that the land should be sold by lottery, contrary to the form of the statutes in such case made and provided: that afterwards, "in pursuance of the said illegal agreement," the land was assigned for the term, and a part of the purchase-money remaining unpaid, the defendant, to secure the payment thereof, made the deed and covenant in the declaration mentioned. Upon these pleadings, the Court of Queen's Bench held, that the contract in question appeared to have been made

[1] Tenant *v.* Elliott, 1 B. & P. 3; Rosewarne *v.* Billing, 33 L. J. C. P. 55; Smith *v.* Linds, 5 C. B. N. S. 587 (94 E. C. L. R.). See M'Gregor *v.* Lowe, Ry. & M. 57 (21 E. C. L. R.), and cases cited in note 1, *supra.*

[2] Smith *v.* Cuff, 6 M. & S. 160, and Smith *v.* Bromley, 2 Dougl. 696, n.; which are recognized in Atkinson *v.* Denby, 7 H. & N. 934, 936; Higgins *v.* Pitt, 4 Exch. 312; Mallalieu *v.* Hodgson, 16 Q. B. 689 (71 E. C. L. R.).

[3] 3 E. & B. 642 (77 E. C. L. R.) (reversing judgment in s. c., 2 E. & B. 118 (75 E. C. L. R.)), followed in Geere *v.* Mare, 2 H. & C. 339. See A.-G. *v.* Hollingworth, 2 H. & N. 416; O'Connor *v.* Bradshaw, 5 Exch. 882.

[*726] *after the illegal transaction between the plaintiff and defendant had terminated; that it formed no part of such transaction, and was consequently unaffected by it. The judgment thus given was, however, reversed in error upon reasoning of the following kind, which seems conclusive:—the original agreement was clearly tainted with illegality, inasmuch as all lotteries are prohibited by the stat. 10 & 11 Will. 3, c. 17, s. 1; and by the 12 Geo. 2, c. 28, s. 4, all sales of houses, lands, &c., by lottery are declared to be void to all intents and purposes. The agreement being illegal, then, no action could have been brought to recover the purchase-money of the land which was the subject-matter thereof; and the covenant accordingly, being connected with an illegal agreement, could not be enforced.[1] And, further, even if the plea above abstracted were not to be understood as alleging that the covenant declared upon was given in pursuance of an illegal agreement, it would, remarked the Court of Exchequer Chamber, still show a good defence to the action, for "the covenant was given for the payment of the purchase-money. It springs from and is the creature of that illegal agreement; and if the law would not enforce the illegal contract, so neither will it allow parties to enforce a security for purchase-money which, by the original bargain, was tainted with illegality."

The decisions come to in Fisher *v.* Bridges,[2] and Simpson *v.* Bloss, already cited,[3] establish conclusively this rule, that when a demand connected with an illegal transaction can be sued on without the necessity of having recourse to the illegal transaction, the plaintiff [*727] *may maintain an action; but, wherever it is necessary to resort to the illegal transaction to make out a case, the plaintiff will fail to enforce his claim in a court of law.[4]

But although, in the cases latterly considered, the maxim, *In pari delicto potior est conditio possidentis*, forcibly applies, the doctrine expressed thereby must needs be accepted with qualification. For instance, where an instrument between two parties has been entered into for a purpose which may be considered fraudulent as

[1] Paxton *v.* Popham, 9 East 408; The Gas Light Co. *v.* Turner, 6 Bing. N. C. 324 (37 E. C. L. R.); 5 Id. 666 (35 E. C. L. R.).

[2] Followed in Geere *v.* Mare, 2 H. & C. 339.

[3] *Ante*, p. 722.

[4] See per Watson, B., A.-G. *v.* Hollingsworth, 2 H. & N. 423.

against some third person, it may yet be binding, according to the true construction of its language as between themselves.[1] Likewise, by statute an instrument may be avoided for certain purposes, and yet remain valid and effectual *quoad alia;* a conveyance fraudulently and collusively made for the mere purpose of conferring a vote, and with an understanding that it should not operate beneficially to the grantee, although it fail by virtue of the stats. 7 & 8 Will. 3, c. 25, s. 7, and 10 Ann. c. 23, s. 1, to give the right of voting, will, nevertheless, as between the parties to it, pass the interest.[2] In any such case the intention of the legislature, and the mischief to be repressed, must carefully be ascertained; and we should remember, that "the policy of the law always is not to make contracts void to a greater extent than the mischief to be remedied renders necessary."[3]

*To the above maxim respecting *par delictum* may properly be referred the general rule, that an action for contribution cannot be maintained by one of several joint wrongdoers against another, although the one who claims contribution may have been compelled to pay the entire damages recovered as compensation for the tortious act.[4] It has, however, been laid down, that this rule does not extend to cases of indemnity, where one man employs another to do acts, not unlawful in themselves, for the purpose of asserting a right.[5] Moreover, the rule as to non-contribution between wrongdoers must be further qualified in this manner, [*728]

[1] Shaw *v.* Jeffery, 13 Moo. P. C. C. 432, 454–5.

[2] Philpotts *v.* Philpotts, 10 C. B. 85 (70 E. C. L. R.); Doe d. Roberts *v.* Roberts, 2 B. & Ald. 367; Bessey *v.* Windham, 6 Q. B. 166 (51 E. C. L. R.). See Marshall, app., Brown, resp., 7 M. & Gr. 188 (49 E. C. L. R.); Doe d. Williams *v.* Lloyd, 5 Bing. N. C. 741 (35 E. C. L. R.), in connection with which see Philpott *v.* St. George's Hospital, 6 H. L. Cas. 338; Callaghan *v.* Callaghan, 8 Cl. & Fin. 374; Bowes *v.* Foster, 2 H. & N. 779; Doe d. Richards *v.* Lewis, 11 C. B. 1035 (73 E. C. L. R.); White *v.* Morris, Id. 1015.

[3] Per Maule, J., 10 C. B. 99, 100 (70 E. C. L. R.). And see per Lord Cranworth, C., Ex parte Neilson, 3 De G., M. & G. 566; Young *v.* Billiter, 8 H. L. Cas. 682.

[4] Merryweather *v.* Nixan, 8 T. R. 186. See per Lord Lyndhurst, C. B., Colburn *v.* Patmore, 1 C., M. & R. 83; Farebrother *v.* Ansley, 1 Camp. 342; cited Shackell *v.* Rosier, 2 Bing. N. C. 647 (29 E. C. L. R.). See also Campbell *v.* Campbell, 7 Cl. & Fin. 166; Blackett *v.* Weir, 5 B. & C. 387 (11 E. C. L. R.).

[5] Per Lord Kenyon, C. J., 8 T. R. 186; cited, 8 Bing. 72 (21 E. C. L. R.).

that where one party induces another to do an act which is not legally supportable, and yet is not clearly in itself a breach of law, the party so inducing shall be answerable to the other for the consequences.[1]

In equity, as at law, the general rule undoubtedly is, that relief will not be granted where both parties are *in pari delicto*, unless in cases where public policy requires the interference of the court.[2] Before proceeding, however, to apply the maxim, it is very necessary to ascertain whether, under the given circumstances, the delinquency attaching to each of the principal parties is really equal in degree. Equity, for instance, has refused to treat as *in pari delicto* [*729] the parties to a private *agreement entered into between father and son, which was illegal, as being a fraud upon the post-office; and in this case Sir W. Grant, after observing that the question was, whether the general rule, *In pari delicto melior est conditio possidentis*, should prevail, and the court should refuse relief,—both parties to the agreement, which was impeached by the bill, having been guilty of a violation of the law,—remarked that "Courts both of law and equity have held, that two parties may concur in an illegal act without being deemed to be in all respects *in pari delicto*;" and his honor thought, under the circumstances before him, that the *par delictum* between the parties had not been in fact established, the agreement being substantially the mere act of the father.[3]

Ex Dolo malo non oritur Actio.

(Cowp. 343.)

A right of action cannot arise out of fraud.

It has been thought convenient to place the above maxim in immediate proximity to that which precedes it, because these two important rules of law are intimately related to each other, and the

[1] Per Lord Denman, C. J., Betts *v.* Gibbins, 2 A. & E. 75 (29 E. C. L. R.).

[2] Reynell *v.* Sprye, 1 De G., M. & G. 660; 1 Story, Eq. Jurisp., 9th ed., 284.

[3] Osborne *v.* Williams, 18 Ves. 379; see arg. Clough *v.* Ratcliffe, 16 L. J. Chanc. 477; s. c., 1 De G. & S. 164; 1 Story Eq. Jurisp., 9th ed., 286.

cases which have already been cited in illustration of the rule as to *par delictum* may be referred to generally as establishing and justifying the position, that an action cannot be maintained which is founded in fraud, or which springs *ex turpi causâ*. The connection which exists between these maxims may, indeed, be satisfactorily shown by *reference to a case already cited. In [*730] Fivaz *v.* Nicholls,[1] an action was brought for an alleged conspiracy between B., the defendant, and a third party, C., to obtain payment of a bill of exchange accepted by the plaintiff in consideration that B. would abstain from prosecuting C. for embezzlement;[2] and it was held that the action would not lie, inasmuch as it sprung out of an illegal transaction, in which both plaintiff and defendant had been engaged, and of which proof was essential in order to establish the plaintiff's claim as stated upon the record. In this case, therefore, the maxim, *Ex dolo malo non oritur actio*, was evidently applicable; and not less so with regard either to the original corrupt agreement, or to the subsequent alleged conspiracy, was the general principle of law, *In pari delicto potior est conditio defendentis*.[3] To the class of cases also which establish that contribution cannot be enforced amongst wrong-doers, and that a person who has committed an act declared by the law to be criminal, will not be permitted to recover compensation from one who has knowingly participated with him in the commission of the crime,[4] a similar remark seems equally to apply. Bearing in mind, then, this connection between the two kindred maxims aforesaid, we shall in the ensuing pages proceed to consider briefly the important and very comprehensive principle, *Ex dolo malo*, or, more generally, *Ex turpi causâ, non oritur actio*.[5]

*In the first place, then, we may observe, that the word [*731] *dolus*, when used in its more comprehensive sense, was un-

[1] 2 C. B. 501, 512, 515 (52 E. C. L. R.).

[2] See the cases cited *post*, p. 733.

[3] See, also, Stevens *v.* Gourley, 7 C. B. N. S. 99, 108.

[4] Per Lord Lyndhurst, Colburn *v.* Patmore, 1 Cr., M. & R. 83; per Maule, J., 2 C. B. 509 (52 E. C. L. R.).

[5] The principle embodied in the above maxim is widely applicable; *ex. gr.*, an order under the stat. 20 & 21 Vict. c. 85, s. 21, protecting the after-acquired property of a married woman deserted by her husband, is confined to property of which she may be possessed, or "which she may acquire by her own *lawful* industry." See Mason *v.* Mitchell, 3 H. & C. 528.

derstood by the Roman jurists to include "every intentional misrepresentation of the truth made to induce another to perform an act which he would not else have undertaken;"[1] and a marked distinction accordingly existed in the civil law between *dolus bonus* and *dolus malus:* the former signifying that degree of artifice or dexterity which a person might lawfully employ to advance his own interest, in self-defence against an enemy, or for some other justifiable purpose;[2] and the latter, including every kind of craft, guile, or machination, intentionally employed for the purpose of deception, cheating, or circumvention.[3] As to the latter species of *dolus* (with which alone we are now concerned), it was a general and fundamental rule, that *dolo malo pactum se non servaturum;*[4] and, in our own law, it is a familiar principle, that no valid contract can arise out of a fraud; and that any action brought upon a supposed contract, which is shown to have arisen from fraud, may be successfully resisted.[5]

[*732] *It is, moreover, a general proposition, that an agreement to do an unlawful act cannot be supported at law—that no right of action can spring out of an illegal contract;[6] and

[1] Mackeld. Civ. Law 165.

[2] Ibid.; Bell, Dict. and Dig. of Scotch Law 319; D. 4. 3. 3; Brisson. *ad verb.* "*Dolus;*" Tayl. Civ. Law, 4th ed., 118.

[3] D. 4. 3. 1, § 2; Id. 50. 17. 79; Id. 2. 14. 7, § 9.

[4] D. 2. 14. 7, § 9.

[5] Per Patteson, J., 1 A. & E. 42 (28 E. C. L. R.); per Holroyd, J., 4 B. & Ald. 34 (6 E. C. L. R.); per Lord Mansfield, C. J., 4 Burr. 2300; Evans *v.* Edmonds, 13 C. B. 777 (76 E. C. L. R.); Canham *v.* Barry, 15 C. B. 597 (80 E. C. L. R.); with which compare Ferret *v.* Hill, Id. 207; Reynell *v.* Sprye, 1 De G., M. & G. 660; Curson *v.* Belworthy, 3 H. L. Cas. 742. The effect of fraud in nullifying a contract, the right to rescind a contract of sale on the ground of fraud, and the distinction between *legal* and *moral* fraud, are discussed under the maxim, *Caveat emptor*, *post*, p. 768, *et seq.* See Earl of Bristol *v.* Wilsmore, 1 B. & C. 514 (8 E. C. L. R.); Green *v.* Beaverstock, 14 C. B. N. S. 204 (108 E. C. L. R.); Clarke *v.* Dickson, E., B. & E. 148 (96 E. C. L. R.); Horsfall *v.* Thomas, 1 H. & C. 90.

As to the meaning of the word "fraud," compare per Lord Romilly, diss., Spackman *v.* Evans, L. R. 3 H. L. 239; per Lord Cairns, Reese River Silver Mining Company *v.* Smith, L. R. 4 H. L. 79, 80; Kennedy *v.* Panama, &c., Mail Co., L. R. 2 Q. B. 588; Lee *v.* Jones, 17 C. B. N. S. 482 (112 E. C. L. R.).

[6] Per Lord Abinger, C. B., 4 M. & W. 657; per Ashhurst, J., 8 T. R. 93. See Jones *v.* Waite, 5 Scott N. R. 951; s. c., 5 Bing. N. C. 341 (35 E. C. L.

this rule, which applies not only where the contract is expressly illegal, but whenever it is opposed to public policy, or founded on an immoral consideration,[1] is expressed by the well-known maxim, *Ex turpi causâ non oritur actio*,[2] and is in accordance with the doctrine of the civil law, *Pacta quæ turpem causam continent non sunt observanda*,[3] "wherever the consideration which is the ground of the promise, or the promise which is the consequence or effect of the consideration, is unlawful, the whole contract is void."[4] A court of law will not, then, lend its aid to enforce the performance of a contract which appears to have been entered into by both the contracting parties for the express purpose of carrying into effect that which is prohibited by the law of the land; and this objection to the validity of a contract must, from authority and reason, be allowed in all cases to prevail. No legal distinction can be supported between the application of this objection *to parol contracts [*733] and to contracts under seal; it would be inconsistent with reason and principle to hold, that, by the mere ceremony of putting a seal to an instrument, that is, by the voluntary act of the parties themselves, a contract, which was void in itself, as being in violation of the law of the land, should be deemed valid, and an action maintainable thereon in a court of justice.[5]

In Collins *v.* Blantern,[6] which is a leading case to show that illegality may well be pleaded as a defence to an action on a bond, the bond was alleged to have been given to the obligee as an indemnity

R.), and 1 Bing. N. C. 656 (27 E. C. L. R.); Ritchie *v.* Smith, 6 C. B. 462 (60 E. C. L. R.); Cundell *v.* Dawson, 4 C. B. 376 (56 E. C. L. R.); Sargent *v.* Wedlake, 11 C. B. 732 (73 E. C. L. R.).

[1] Allen *v.* Rescous, 2 Lev. 174; Walker *v.* Perkins, 3 Burr. 1568; Wetherell *v.* Jones, 3 B. & Ad. 225, 226 (23 E. C. L. R.); Edgerton *v.* Earl Brownlow, 4 H. L. Cas. 1.

[2] Judgm., Bank of United States *v.* Owens, 2 Peters (U. S.) R. 539.

[3] D. 2. 14. 27, § 4.

[4] 1 Bulstr. 38; Hobart 72; Dyer 356.

[5] Judgm., 5 Bing. N. C. 675 (35 E. C. L. R.).

[6] 2 Wils. 341; Williams *v.* Bayley, L. R. 1 H. L. 200. See Ward *v.* Lloyd, 7 Scott N. R. 499; Ex parte Critchley, 15 L. J. Q. B. 124; Keir *v.* Leeman, 6 Q. B. 308 (51 E. C. L. R.); s. c. (in error), 9 Q. B. 371 (58 E. C. L. R.) (where the compromise of a misdemeanor was held to be illegal); Masters *v.* Ibberson, 8 C. B. 100 (65 E. C. L. R.); Reg. *v.* Hardey, 14 Q. B. 529 (68 E. C. L. R.); Reg. *v.* Blakemore, Id. 544; Reg. *v.* Alleyne, 4 E. & B. 186 (82 E. C. L. R.).

for a note entered into by him for the purpose of inducing the prosecutor of an indictment for perjury to withhold his evidence; for the plaintiff, it was contended that the bond was good and lawful, the condition being singly for the payment of a sum of money, and that no averment should be admitted that the bond was given upon an unlawful consideration not appearing upon the face of it; but it was held, that the bond was void *ab initio*, and that the facts might be specially pleaded; and it was observed by Wilmot, C. J., delivering the judgment of the court, that "the manner of the transaction was to gild over and conceal the truth; and whenever courts of law see such attempts made to conceal such wicked deeds, they will brush away the cobweb varnish and show the transactions in their true light." And again, "this is a contract to tempt a [*734] man *to transgress the law, to do that which is injurious to the community: it is void by the common law; and the reason why the common law says such contracts are void is for the public good: *you shall not stipulate for iniquity*. All writers upon our law agree in this—no polluted hand shall touch the pure fountains of justice."[1]

It is, obviously, to the interest of the public that "the suppression of a prosecution should not be made matter of private bargain;" and it was accordingly held in a recent case,[2] that a promissory note given in consideration of the payee's forbearing to prosecute against the maker a charge of obtaining money by false pretences was illegal, and could not be enforced.

As a general rule, then, a contract or an agreement cannot be made the subject of an action if it be impeachable on the ground of dishonesty, or as being opposed to public policy,—if it be either *contra bonos mores*, or forbidden by the law.[3] In answer to an ac-

[1] See, also, Prole *v.* Wiggins, 3 Bing. N. C. 230 (32 E. C. L. R.); Paxton *v.* Popham, 9 East 408; Pole *v.* Harrobin, Id. 417 n.; Gas Light and Coke Co. *v.* Turner, 5 Bing. N. C. 666 (35 E. C. L. R.); s. c., 6 Id. 324; Cuthbert *v.* Haley, 8 T. R. 390.

[2] Clubb *v.* Hutson, 18 C. B. N. S. 414, 417 (114 E. C. L. R.), following Keir *v.* Leeman, 9 Q. B. 371 (58 E. C. L. R.).

[3] Per Lord Kenyon, C. J., 6 T. R. 16; Stevens *v.* Gourley, 7 C. B. N. S. 99 (97 E. C. L. R.); Cunard *v.* Hyde, 2 E. & E. 1 (105 E. C. L. R.). See per Holroyd, J., 2 B. & Ald. 103; per Martin, B., Horton *v.* Westminster Improvement Commissioners, 7 Exch. 791.

As to contracts void on the ground of maintenance or champerty, see Earle

tion founded on such an agreement, the maxim may be urged, *Ex maleficio non oritur contractus*[1]—a contract cannot arise out of *an act radically vicious and illegal: those who come into a court of justice to seek redress must come with clean hands, and must disclose a transaction warranted by law;[2] and, "it is quite clear, that a court of justice can give no assistance to the enforcement of contracts which the law of the land has interdicted."[3] [*735]

It does not fall within the plan of this work to enumerate, much less to consider at length, the different grounds on which a contract may be invalidated for illegality.[4] We shall merely cite some few cases in illustration of the above remarks. In strict accordance with them, it has been held, that no action could be maintained on a bond given to a person in consideration of his doing, and inducing others to do, something contrary to the terms of letters patent; and that the obligee was equally incapable of recovering, whether he knew or did not know the terms of the letters patent—the ignorance, if in fact it existed, resulting from his own fault.[5] "The question," said Lord Tenterden, in the case here alluded to, "comes to this: can a man have the benefit of a bond *by the condition of which he undertakes to violate the law? [*736]

v. Hopwood, 9 C. B. N. S. 566 (99 E. C. L. R.); Simpson *v.* Lamb, 7 C. B. N. S. 84 (97 E. C. L. R.); Sprye *v.* Porter, Id. 58; Anderson *v.* Radcliffe, E., B. & E. 806 (96 E. C. L. R.); Grell *v.* Levy, 16 C. B. N. S. 73.

[1] Judgm., 1 T. R. 734; Parsons *v.* Thompson, 1 H. Bla. 322; 8 Wheaton (U. S.) R. 152. See Nicholson *v.* Gooch, 5 E. & B. 999, 1015 (85 E. C. L. R.), which forcibly illustrates the above maxim.

[2] Per Lord Kenyon, C. J., Petrie *v.* Hannay, 3 T. R. 422.

[3] Per Lord Eldon, C., 2 Rose 351.

[4] The following cases may, however, be mentioned with reference to this subject, in addition to those already cited: Simpson *v.* Lord Howden, 9 Cl. & Fin. 61; cited per Lord Campbell, C. J., Hall *v.* Dyson, 17 Q. B. 791 (79 E. C. L. R.), (as to which see Hills *v.* Mitson, 8 Exch. 751); and per Lord St. Leonards, C., Hawkes *v.* Eastern Counties R. C., 1 De G., M. & G. 753; s. c., affirmed 5 H. L. Cas. 331; Preston *v.* Liverpool, Manchester, &c., R. C., 5 H. L. Cas. 605; Jones *v.* Waite, 9 Cl. & Fin. 101; Mittelholzer *v.* Fullarton, 6 Q. B. 989, 1022 (51 E. C. L. R.); Santos *v.* Illidge, 8 C. B. N. S. 861 (95 E. C. L. R.); s. c. 6 Id. 841 (98 E. C. L. R.); Bousfield *v.* Wilson, 16 M. & W. 185. In the great case of Atwood *v.* Small, 6 Cl. & Fin. 232, the effect of fraud on a contract of sale was much considered; but this case properly falls under the maxim *Caveat emptor*, to which, therefore, the reader is referred.

[5] Duvergier *v.* Fellowes, 1 Cl. & Fin. 39.

It seems to me that it would not be according to the principles of the law of England, which is the law of reason and justice, to allow a man to maintain an action under such circumstances; it would be to hold out an encouragement to any man to induce others to become dupes, and to pay their money for that from which they could derive no advantage."

In *scire facias* against the defendant as member of a certain steam-packet company, the plea stated that the original action was for a demand in respect of which neither the defendant in the *sci. fa.*, the packet company, nor the defendant in the original action (the public officer of the company), was by law liable, as plaintiff at the commencement of the action well knew; and that, such registered officer and the plaintiff well knowing the premises, the said officer fraudulently and deceitfully, and by connivance with plaintiff, suffered the judgment in order to charge the defendant in *sci. fa.* The court held the plea to be good, and further observed, that fraud *no doubt vitiates everything;*[1] and that, upon being satisfied of such fraud, they possessed power to vacate, and would vacate, their own judgment.[2]

To take another illustration of the maxim before us, wholly different from the preceding:—"There is no [*737] *doubt," it has been observed,[3] "that where a right of action has accrued parties cannot by contract say that there shall not be jurisdiction to enforce damages in respect of that right of action." But the general policy of the law does not prevent parties "from entering into such a contract, as that no breach shall occur until after a ref-

[1] See, for instance, Foster *v.* Mackinnon, L. R. 4 C. P. 704, 711.

A copyright may be defeated on the ground of fraud; Wright *v.* Tallis, 1 C. B. 893 (50 E. C. L. R.).

In the Carron Co. *v.* Hunter, L. R. 1 Sc. App. Cas. 362, a bequest of shares was held not to be nullified by a fraudulent concealment of their real value.

[2] Phillipson *v.* Earl of Egremont, 6 Q. B. 587, 605 (51 E. C. L. R.); Dodgson *v.* Scott, 2 Exch. 457, and cases cited *ante*, p. 731. *Et vide* per Pollock, C. B., Rogers *v.* Hadley, 32 L. J. Ex. 248.

[3] Per Lord Cranworth, C., Scott *v.* Avery, 5 H. L. Cas. 847, affirming s. c., 8 Exch. 487; Tredwen *v.* Holman, 1 H. & C. 72; Scott *v.* Corporation of Liverpool, 28 L. J. Chanc. 230, 235, 236; s. c., 27 Id. 641; Giles *v.* Spencer, 3 C. B. N. S. 244, 249 (91 E. C. L. R.). See Lowndes *v.* Earl of Stamford, 18 Q. B. 425 (83 E. C. L. R.); Hemans *v.* Picciotto, 1 C. B. N. S. 646 (87 E. C. L. R.); Wallis *v.* Hirsch, Id. 316; Clarke *v.* Westrope, 18 C. B. 765 (86 E. C. L. R.).

erence has been made to arbitration." And again, "If I covenant with A. to do particular acts, and it is also covenanted between us that any question that may arise as to the breach of the covenants shall be referred to arbitration, that latter covenant does not prevent the covenantee from bringing an action. A right of action has accrued, and it would be against the policy of the law to give effect to an agreement that such a right should not be enforced through the medium of the ordinary tribunals.[1] But if I covenant with A. that if I do or omit to do a certain act, then I will pay to him such a sum as B. shall award as the amount of damage sustained by him, then, until B. has made his award, and I have omitted to pay the sum awarded, my covenant has not been broken, and no right of action has arisen. The policy of the law does not prevent parties from so contracting."[2]

The distinction above set forth may be thus exemplified: [*738] *if the contract in question be a policy of insurance against fire, and is in such terms that a reference to a third person or to a board of directors is a condition precedent to the right of the assured, in case of loss, to maintain an action, then he is not entitled to maintain it until that condition is complied with; but if, on the other hand, the contract is to pay for the loss, with a subsequent contract to refer the question to arbitration, contained in a distinct clause collateral to the other, then that contract for reference shall not oust the jurisdiction of the courts, or deprive the party of his action.[3]

Further, it is an indisputable proposition, that as against an innocent party, "no man shall set up his own iniquity as a defence any more than as a cause of action."[4] Where, however, a contract or deed is made for an illegal purpose, a defendant against whom it is sought to be enforced may show the turpitude of both himself and the plaintiff, and a court of justice will decline its aid to

[1] See Horton *v.* Sayers, 4 H. & N. 643, 649, 651.

[2] Per Lord Cranworth, C., 5 H. L. Cas. 848; Judgm., 8 Exch. 502; per Williams, J., Northampton Gas-Light Co. *v.* Parnell, 15 C. B. 651 (80 E. C. L. R.); Roper *v.* Lendon, 1 E. & E. 825, 831 (102 E. C. L. R.); Braunstein *v.* Accidental Death Insur. Co., 1 B. & S. 782 (101 E. C. L. R.).

[3] Elliott *v.* Royal Exch. Ass. Co., L. R. 2 Ex. 237, 243.

[4] Per Lord Mansfield, C. J., Montefiori *v.* Montefiori, 1 W. Bla. 364; cited, per Abbott, C. J., 2 B. & Ald. 368. It is a maxim, that *Jus ex injuriâ non oritur*; see arg. 4 Bing. 639 (13 E. C. L. R.).

enforce a contract thus wrongfully entered into. For instance, money cannot be recovered which has been paid *ex turpi causâ quum dantist œque et accipientis turpitudo versatur.*[1] An unlawful agreement, it has been said, can convey no rights in any court to either party; and will not be enforced at law or in equity in favor of one against the other of two persons equally culpable.[2] A person who contributes to the performance of an illegal act by supplying [*739] a thing with *the knowledge that it is to be used for that purpose is precluded from recovering the price of the thing so supplied. "Nor can any distinction be made between an illegal and an immoral purpose; the rule which is applicable to the matter is, *ex turpi causâ non oritur actio*, and whether it is an immoral or an illegal purpose in which the plaintiff has participated it comes equally within the terms of that maxim, and the effect is the same; no cause of action can arise out of either the one or the other." [3]

The principle on which the rule above laid down depends is, as stated by Chief Justice Wilmot, the public good. "The objection," says Lord Mansfield,[4] "that a contract is immoral or illegal as between plaintiff and defendant, sounds at all times very ill in the mouth of the defendant. It is not for his sake, however, that the objection is ever allowed, but it is founded in general principles of policy, which the defendant has the advantage of, contrary to the real justice as between him and the plaintiff—by accident, if I may so say. The principle of public policy is this: *ex dolo malo non oritur actio*. No court will lend its aid to a man who founds his cause of action upon an immoral or an illegal act. If, from the plaintiff's own stating or otherwise, the cause of action appear to arise *ex turpi causâ* or the transgression of a positive law of this country, there the court says he has no right to be assisted. It is

107 E. 64.

[1] 1 Pothier, Traité de Vente, 186.

[2] Per Lord Brougham, C., Armstrong *v.* Armstrong, 3 My. & K. 64.

[3] Pearce *v.* Brooks, L. R. 1 Ex. 213, 218; Cowan *v.* Milbourn, L. R. 2 Ex. 230.

[4] Holman *v.* Johnson, Cowp. 343; and Lightfoot *v.* Tenant, 1 B. & P. 554; which cases are cited in Hobbs *v.* Henning, 17 C. B. N. S. 819 (112 E. C. L. R.), as showing "the distinction between a mere mental purpose that an unlawful act should be done, and a participation in the unlawful transaction itself." Jackson *v.* Duchaire, 3 T. R. 551, 553; cited Spencer *v.* Handley, 5 Scott N. R. 558.

upon that ground the court goes, not for the sake of the defendant, but because they *will not lend their aid to such a plaintiff. So, if the plaintiff and defendant were to change sides, and [*740] the defendant were to bring his action against the plaintiff, the latter would then have the advantage of it, for where both are equally in fault, *Potior est conditio defendentis*."[1]

It may here be proper to observe, that, although a court will not assist in giving effect to a contract which is "expressly or by implication forbidden by the statute or common law," or which is "contrary to justice, morality, and sound policy;" yet where the consideration and the matter to be performed are both legal, a plaintiff will not be precluded from recovering by an infringement of the law in the performance of something to be done on his part; such infringement not having been contemplated by the contracting parties.[2]

In determining, moreover, the effect of a penal statute[3] upon the validity of a contract entered into by one who has failed in some respects to comply with its provisions, it is necessary to consider whether the object of the statute was merely to inflict a penalty on the offending party for the benefit of the revenue, or whether the legislature intended to prohibit the contract itself for the protection of the public. In the former case, an action may lie upon the contract; but in the latter case the *maxim under consideration will apply, and even if the contract be prohibited for [*741] revenue purposes only, it will be altogether illegal and void, and no action will be maintainable upon it.[4]

[1] See also arg. 15 Peters (U. S.) R. 471; per Tindal, C. J., 2 C. B. 512 (52 E. C. L. R.).

[2] Wetherell *v.* Jones, 3 B. & Ad. 225, 226 (23 E. C. L. R.). See Redmond *v.* Smith, 8 Scott N. R. 250.

[3] With reference to a breach of the revenue laws Lord Stowell observes, "It is sufficient if there is a contravention of the law—if there is a *fraus in legem*. Whether that may have arisen from mistaken apprehension, from carelessness, or from any other cause, it is not material to inquire. In these cases it is not necessary to prove actual and personal fraud." The Reward, 2 Dods. Adm. R. 271.

[4] D'Allex *v.* Jones (Exch.), 2 Jur. N. S. 979; Taylor *v.* Crowland Gas & Coke Co., 10 Exch. 293, 296; Bailey *v.* Harris, 12 Q. B. 905 (64 E. C. L. R.); Smith *v.* Mawhood, 14 M. & W. 452; Cope *v.* Rowlands, 2 M. & W. 149; Cundell *v.* Dawson, 4 C. B. 376 (56 E. C. L. R.); Pidgeon *v.* Burslem, 3 Exch. 465; Oulds *v.* Harrison, 10 Exch. 572; Jessopp *v.* Lutwyche, Id. 614; Rose-

It must be observed, however, that a contract, although illegal and void as to part, will not necessarily be void *in toto*. Thus, if there be a bond, with condition to do several things, some of which are agreeable to law and some against the common law, the bond shall be good as to the former, and void as to the latter only;[1] and this rule is generally true with respect to a contract void and illegal in part as against public policy, and yet good as to the residue. Where, for instance, the defendant covenanted that he would not, during his life, carry on the trade of a perfumer "within the cities of London and Westminster, *or* within the distance of 600 miles from the same respectively," the court held that the covenant was divisible, and was good so far as it related to the cities of London and Westminster, though void as to the residue."[2]

[*742] *It seems, then, upon the whole, a true proposition, that, if any part of a contract is valid, it will avail *pro tanto* although another part of it may be prohibited by statute, provided the statute does not expressly or by necessary implication render the whole void, and provided also that the sound part can be separated from the unsound. Where, however, a particular proceeding, though not in itself illegal, is inseparably connected with another which is so, in such a manner that both form parcels of one transaction—*ex. gr.*, of one trading adventure—such transaction becomes altogether illegal, because bottomed in and originating out of that which was in itself illegal; and in this wide and comprehensive sense must therefore be understood the rule, *Ex pacto illicito non oritur actio.*[3]

warne *v.* Billing, 33 L. J. C. P. 55, 56; Johnson *v.* Hudson, 11 East 180. See per Holt, C. J., Bartlett *v.* Viner, Carth. 252; cited Judgm., De Begnis *v.* Armistead, 10 Bing. 110 (25 E. C. L. R.); and in Fergusson *v.* Norman, 5 Bing. N. C. 85 (35 E. C. L. R.). See another instance illustrating the text, per Parke, B., Bodger *v.* Arch, 10 Exch. 337; cited Amos *v.* Smith, 1 H. & C. 241. And see Jones *v.* Giles, 10 Exch. 119, 144; s. c., affirmed in error, 11 Exch. 393; Ritchie *v.* Smith, 6 C. B. 462 (60 E. C. L. R.).

[1] Chesman *v.* Nainby, 2 Ld. Raym. 1456, 1459; Pigot's Case, 11 Rep. 27.

[2] Price *v.* Green (in error), 16 M. & W. 346; s. c., 13 Id. 695; following Mallan *v.* May, 11 M. & W. 653, and Chesman *v.* Nainby, *supra*. See, further, as to contracts in restraint of trade, Broom's Com., 4th ed., 365 *et seq.*; Farrer *v.* Close, L. R. 4 Q. B. 602; Reg. *v.* Stainer, L. R. 1 C. C. 230.

[3] See Stewart *v.* Gibson, 7 Cl. & Fin. 729.

"The general rule is that where you cannot sever the illegal from the legal

An agreement between the plaintiff and defendant recited that the plaintiff had for a long time carried on business as a law-stationer, and also had been a sub-distributor of stamps and collector of assessed taxes, and it then stated, "that, in consideration of 300*l.*, payable by installments, the plaintiff agreed to sell, and the defendant agreed to purchase, the business of a law-stationer, theretofore carried on by the plaintiff; and it was thereby further agreed between them that the plaintiff should not after the 1st of March then next carry on the business of a law-stationer, *or collect any of the assessed *taxes*, &c., but that he, the plaintiff, would use [*743] his utmost endeavors to introduce the defendant to the said business and offices, &c.: the court held, that this agreement was for the sale of an office within the 5 & 6 Edw. 6, c. 16, that it formed one entire contract, though embracing several distinct acts, and that the declaration was consequently bad.[1]

We may add, that where a party to a contract, which might be impugned on the ground of fraud, knowing of the fraud, nevertheless elects to treat the transaction as a binding contract, he thereby loses his right of rescinding it; for fraud only gives a right to avoid or rescind a contract.[2] Thus if a party be induced to purchase an article by fraudulent misrepresentations of the seller respecting it, and, after discovering the fraud, continne to deal with the article as his own, he cannot recover back the money paid from the seller; nor does there seem any authority for saying that a party must, in such a case, know all the incidents of a fraud before he deprives himself of the right of rescinding; the proper and safe course is to repudiate the whole transaction at the time of discovering the fraud.[3] "Where an agreement has been procured

part of a covenant, the contract is altogether void; but where you can sever them, whether the illegality be created by statute or by the common law, you may reject the bad part and retain the good." Per Willes, J., Pickering *v.* Ilfracombe R. C., L. R. 3 C. P. 250.

[1] Hopkins *v.* Prescott, 4 C. B. 578 (56 E. C. L. R.), and cases there cited. See Sterry *v.* Clifton, 9 C. B. 110 (67 E. C. L. R.).

[2] Judgm., Stevenson *v.* Newnham, 13 C. B. 302, 303 (76 E. C. L. R.); per Parke, B., 2 Exch. 541; Reese River Silver Mining Co. *v.* Smith, L. R. 4 H. L. 64; Oakes *v.* Turquand, L. R. 2 H. L. 325.

[3] Campbell *v.* Fleming, 1 A. & E. 40 (28 E. C. L. R.); Clarke *v.* Dickson, E., B. & E. 148 (96 E. C. L. R.); Horsfall *v.* Thomas, 1 H. & C. 90; White *v.* Garden, 10 C. B. 919 (70 E. C. L. R.); cited Billiter *v.* Young, 6 E. & B. 25

[*744] by fraud," observes Maule, J., "the party *defrauded may at his election treat it as void, but he must make his election within a reasonable time. The party guilty of the fraud has no such election."

Lastly, when the act which is the subject of the contract may, according to the circumstances, be lawful or unlawful, it will not be presumed that the contract was to do the unlawful act; the contrary is the proper inference.[2] Thus, where an act is required to be done by a person, the omission of which would make him guilty of a criminal neglect of duty, the law presumes that he has duly performed it, and throws the burden of proving the negative on the party who may be interested in doing so.[3] And the presumption of law is clearly against fraud.[4]

Having in the preceding pages directed attention to some leading points connected with the *illegality* of the consideration for a promise or agreement, and having selected from very many cases some only which seemed peculiarly adapted to throw light upon the maxim, *Ex dolo malo non oritur actio*, we may further pray in aid of the above very cursory remarks respecting it, the observations [*745] already made upon the yet more general principle, that *a man shall not be permitted to take advantage of *his own*

(88 E. C. L. R.); Harnor *v.* Groves, 15 C. B. 667 (80 E. C. L. R.). See Kingsford *v.* Merry, 1 H. & N. 503; s. c., 11 Exch. 577; Higgons *v.* Burton, 26 L. J. Ex. 342.

[1] East Anglian R. C. *v.* Eastern Counties R. C., 11 C. B. 803 (73 E. C. L. R.); citing Campbell *v.* Fleming, *supra.* Judgm., Bwlch-y-Plwm Lead Mining Co. *v.* Baynes, L. R. 2 Ex. 326; Oakes *v.* Turquand, L. R. 2 H. L. 325. In Pilbrow *v.* Pilbrow's Atmospheric R. C., 5 C. B. 453 (57 E. C. L. R.), Maule, J., observes, "It is not true that a *deed* that is obtained by fraud is therefore void. The rule is that the party defrauded may, at his election, treat it as void."

[2] Lewis *v.* Davison, 4 M. & W. 654; 1 B. & Ald. 463; Judgm., Garrard *v.* Hardey, 6 Scott N. R. 477. See, per Parke, B., Jackson *v.* Cobbin, 8 M. & W. 797; Harrison *v.* Heathorn, 6 Scott N. R. 735; 10 Rep. 56; C. 2. 21. 6.

[3] Williams *v.* East India Co., 3 East 192; cited, per Lord Ellenborough, C. J., 2 M. & S. 561.

[4] See, per Parke, B., 8 Exch. 400; per Lord Kenyon, C. J., R. *v.* Fillongley, 2 T. R. 711; adopted per Patteson, J., Reg. *v.* St. Marylebone, 16 Q. B. 305 (71 E. C. L. R.). Duke *v.* Forbes, 1 Exch. 356, 368, shows that illegality will not be presumed. And see the maxim *Omnia præsumuntur ritè esse acta*—*post*, Chap. X.

wrong,[1] and shall at once proceed to offer some remarks as to the rule that a consideration is needed to support a *promise, and as to the sufficiency and essential requisites thereof.

Ex nudo Pacto non oritur Actio.

(Noy, Max. 24.)

No cause of action arises from a bare promise.

Nudum pactum may be defined, in the words of Ulpian, to be where *nulla subest causa propter conventionem*,[2] *i. e.*, where there is no consideration for the promise or undertaking of one of the contracting parties; and it is a fundamental principle in our system of law, that from such a promise or undertaking no cause of action can arise. "A consideration of some sort or other is so necessary to the forming of a contract, that a *nudum pactum*, or agreement to do or pay something on one side, without any compensation on the other, will not at law support an action; and a man cannot be compelled to perform it."[3] A valid and sufficient consideration or recompense for making, or motive or inducement to make, the promise upon which a party is sought to be charged, is of the very essence of a simple contract. There must be, in the language of Pothier, *une cause d'où naisse l'obligation*,[4] and without this no action can be maintained upon it. Accordingly, if one man promises to *give another 100*l.*, there is no consideration moving from the promisee, and therefore there is nothing binding on the promisor.[5] A gratuitous promise or undertaking may indeed form the subject of a moral obligation, and may be binding in honor, but it does not create a legal responsibility.[6] Nor will a

[*746]

[1] *Ante*, p. 279.

[2] D. 2. 14. 7, § 4; Plowd. 309, n.; Vin. Abr., "*Nudum Pactum*" (A). See 1 Powell Contr. 330 *et seq.* As to the doctrine of *nudum pactum* in the civil law, see Pillans *v.* Van Mierop, 3 Burr. 1670 *et seq.*; 1 Fonbl. Eq., 5th ed., 335 (a).

[3] 3 Com. by Broom & Hadley 159; Noy, Max., 9th ed., p. 348. See McManus *v.* Bark, L. R. 5 Ex. 65.

[4] 1 Pothier Oblig. 5.

[5] 3 Com. by Broom & Hadley 159; Vin. Abr., "*Contract*" (K).

[6] Judgm., 1 H. Bla. 327. See Balfe *v.* West, 13 C. B. 466 (76 E. C. L. R.); Elsee *v.* Gatward, 5 T. R. 143, 149.

mere voluntary courtesy or service uphold an *assumpsit*, unless moved by a previous request.[1] In these and similar cases the rule is *nuda pactio obligationem non parit.*[2]

Where indeed a promise is made under seal, the solemnity of that mode of delivery is held to import, at law, that there was a sufficient consideration for the promise, so that the plaintiff is not in this case required to prove such consideration; nor can the deed be impeached by merely showing that it was made without consideration, unless proof be given that it originated in fraud.[3] Neither [*747] is a consideration necessary for the *validity of a conveyance operating at common law; but unless a case is expressly limited thereby, or it appears to be the intention of the grantor to part with the estate without a consideration, the use will result in his favor. If, however, such should not appear to be the intention of the grantor, and yet an express limitation of the use should prevent the estate from resulting at law, there would still be in equity a resulting trust in his favor. Even in the case of a deed, moreover, it is necessary to observe the distinction between a *good* and a *valuable* consideration; the former is such as that of blood, or of natural love and affection, as when a man grants an estate to a near relative, being influenced by motives of generosity, prudence, and natural duty. Deeds made upon this consideration are looked upon by the law as merely *voluntary*, and although good as between the parties, are frequently set aside in favor of creditors and *bonâ fide* purchasers.[4] On the other hand a valuable consideration is

[1] Lampleigh *v.* Brathwait, Hob. 105; per Park, J., Reason *v.* Wirdnam, 1 C. & P. 434; Bartholomew *v.* Jackson, 20 Johns. (U. S.) R. 28. Physicians at common law have no title to remuneration, unless an express agreement or actual contract be shown: Veitch *v.* Russell, 3 Q. B. 928 (43 E. C. L. R.).

But *secus*, where a physician, registered under stat. 21 & 22 Vict. c. 90, attends a patient professionally, and is not by any by-law of the College of Physicians prohibited from suing: Gibbon *v.* Budd, 2 H. & C. 92. See De la Rosa *v.* Prieto, 16 C. B. N. S. 578 (111 E. C. L. R.).

"The relation of counsel and client renders the parties mutually incapable of making *any* contract of hiring and service concerning the advocacy in litigation:" Judgm., Kennedy *v.* Broun, 13 C. B. N. S. 727 (106 E. C. L. R.); where the cases are collected. See Broun *v.* Kennedy, 33 L. J. Chanc. 71.

[2] D. 2. 14. 7, § 4; C. 4. 65. 27; Brisson. ad verb. "*Nudus.*"

[3] 2 Bla. Com., 16th ed., 446, n. (4). Per Parke, B., Wallis *v.* Day, 2 M. & W. 277.

[4] 2 Com. by Broom & Hadley 479, 480, 3 Id. 158; per Lord Tenterden, C. J.,

such as money, marriage, or the like; and this is esteemed by the law as an equivalent given for the grant.[1]

When, therefore, a question arises between one who has paid a valuable consideration for an estate, and one who has given nothing, it is a just presumption of law, that such voluntary conveyance, founded only on considerations of affection and regard, if coupled with a subsequent sale, was meant to defraud those who should afterwards become purchasers for a valuable consideration, it being, upon the whole, more fit that a voluntary grantee [*748] *should be disappointed, than that a fair purchaser should be defrauded.[2]

A *consideration* for a simple contract has been defined thus:—"any act of the plaintiff from which the defendant derives a benefit or advantage, or any labor, detriment, or inconvenience sustained by the plaintiff, however small the benefit or inconvenience may be, is a sufficient consideration, if such act is performed, or such inconvenience suffered, by the plaintiff with the consent, either express or implied, of the defendant."[3] And again, "consideration means something which is of some value to the eye of the law moving from the plaintiff. It may be some benefit to the defendant or some detriment to the plaintiff, but at all events, it must be moving from the plaintiff.[4] For instance, the compromise of a claim may

Gully *v.* Bishop of Exeter, 10 B. & C. 606 (21 E. C. L. R.). See Bac. Max., reg. 18.

[1] 2 Com. by Broom & Hadley 480, 3 Id. 158; 10 B. & C. 606 (21 E. C. L. R.).

[2] Judgm., Doe d. Otley *v.* Manning, 9 East 66. See 2 Q. B. 860 (42 E. C. L. R.).

[3] 1 Selw. N. B., 10th ed., 41; Judgm., 2 E. & B. 487–8 (75 E. C. L. R.); per Parke, B., Moss *v.* Hall, 5 Exch. 49; Bracewell *v.* Williams, L. R. 2 C. P. 196; Crowther *v.* Farrer, 15 Q. B. 677, 680 (69 E. C. L. R.); Hulse *v.* Hulse, 17 C. B. 711 (84 E. C. L. R.). See also Nash *v.* Armstrong, 10 C. B. N. S. 259 (100 E. C. L. R.); Shadwell *v.* Shadwell, 9 C. B. N. S. 159 (99 E. C. L. R.); Davis *v.* Nisbett, 10 C. B. N. S. 752 (100 E. C. L. R.); Surtees *v.* Lister, 7 H. & N. 1; Scotson *v.* Pegg, 6 H. & N. 295; Westlake *v.* Adams, 5 C. B. N. S. 248 (94 E. C. L. R.); Hartley *v.* Ponsonby, 7 E. & B. 872 (90 E. C. L. R.).

[4] Per Patteson, J., Thomas *v.* Thomas, 2 Q. B. 859 (42 E. C. L. R.); Price *v.* Easton, 4 B. & Ad. 433 (24 E. C. L. R.); Tweddle *v.* Atkinson, 1 B. & S. 393 (101 E. C. L. R.); Edwards *v.* Baugh, 11 M. & W. 641; Bridgman *v.* Dean, 7 Exch. 199; Wade *v.* Simeon, 2 C. B. 548 (52 E. C. L. R.); Llewellyn *v.* Llewellyn, 15 L. J. Q. B. 4; Crow *v.* Rogers, 1 Stra. 592; Lilly *v.* Hays, 5

be a good consideration for a promise, although litigation may not have actually commenced.[1] So [*749] *where plaintiff stipulated to discharge A. from a portion of the debt to himself, and to permit B. to stand in his place as to that portion, defendant stipulating, in return, that B. should give plaintiff a promissory note; the consideration moving from plaintiff, and being an undertaking detrimental to him, was held sufficient to sustain the promise by defendant.[2] Where, however, A. being indebted to plaintiff in a certain amount, and B. being indebted to A. in another amount, the defendant, in consideration of being permitted by A. to sue B. in his name, promised to pay A.'s debt to the plaintiff, and A. gave such permission, whereupon defendant recovered from B., judgment was arrested, on the ground that plaintiff was a mere stranger to the consideration for the promise made by defendant, having done nothing of trouble to himself or of benefit to the defendant.[3]

So, where in an action of *assumpsit* the consideration for the defendant's promise was stated to be the release and conveyance by the plaintiff of his interest in certain premises, at the defendant's request, but the declaration did not show that the plaintiff had any interest in the premises except a lien upon them, which was expressly reserved by him, the declaration was held bad, as disclosing no legal consideration for the alleged promise.[4]

[*750] *In debt for money had and received, &c., the defendant pleaded the execution and delivery to the plaintiff of a deed

A. & E. 548 (31 E. C. L. R.); approved in Noble *v.* National Discount Co., 5 H. & N. 225, 228; Galloway *v.* Jackson, 3 Scott N. R. 753, 763; Thornton *v.* Jenyns, 1 Scott N. R. 52; Jackson *v.* Cobbin, 8 M. & W. 790; Cowper *v.* Green, 7 M. & W. 633; 1 Roll. Abr. 23, pl. 29; Fisher *v.* Waltham, 4 Q. B. 889 (45 E. C. L. R.); Wilson *v.* Wilson, 1 H. L. Cas. 538.

[1] Cook *v.* Wright, 1 B. & S. 559 (101 E. C. L. R.). See also as to the sufficiency of a consideration, Hart *v.* Miles, 4 C. B. N. S. 371 (93 E. C. L. R.), and cases *infra*.

[2] Peate *v.* Dicken, 1 Cr., M. & R. 422; Tipper *v.* Bicknell, 3 Bing. N. C. 710 (32 E. C. L. R.); Harper *v.* Williams, 4 Q. B. 219 (45 E. C. L. R.).

[3] Bourne *v.* Mason, 1 Ventr. 6; Liversidge *v.* Broadbent, 4 H. & N. 603, 610, and Tweddle *v.* Atkinson, 1 B. & S. 393 (101 E. C. L. R.), also illustrate the maxim *supra*.

[4] Kaye *v.* Dutton, 7 M. & Gr. 807 (49 E. C. L. R.); recognizing Edwards *v.* Baugh, 11 M. & W. 641; Lyth *v.* Ault, 7 Exch. 669; Strickland *v.* Turner, Id. 208; Fremlin *v.* Hamilton, 8 Exch. 308; see Cooper *v.* Parker, 14 C. B. 118 (78 E. C. L. R.); Millward *v.* Littlewood, 5 Exch. 775; Wild *v.* Harris, 7 C. B. 999 (62 E. C. L. R.); Holmes *v.* Penney, 9 Exch. 584, 589.

securing to the plaintiff a certain annuity, and acceptance of the same by the plaintiff in full satisfaction and discharge of the debt; replication, that no memorial of the annuity deed had been enrolled pursuant to the statute; that, the annuity being in arrear, the plaintiff brought an action to recover the amount of the arrears; that defendant pleaded in bar the non-enrollment of the memorial; and that plaintiff thereupon elected and agreed that the indenture should be null and void, and discontinued the action. The replication was held to be a good answer to the plea, since it showed that the accord and satisfaction thereby set up had been rendered nugatory and unavailing by the defendant's own act.[1]

It will be evident from the cases just cited, and from the additional authorities presently referred to, that, in defining *nudum pactum* to be, *ubi nulla subest causa propter conventionem*, the word *causa* must be taken to mean a consideration, which confers that which the law regards as a benefit on the party; it must not be confounded with a *motive* which induces or disposes a person to enter into a contract;[2] nor will it suffice, if colorable merely and illusory.[3]

An agreement was entered into between plaintiff, who was the widow, and defendant and S. T., who were the executors of J. T., by which, after reciting that J. T. had *verbally expressed [*751] his desire that plaintiff should have a certain house, &c., during her life, and reciting also, that defendant and S. T. were desirous that such intention should be carried into effect: it was witnessed that, "in consideration of such desire, and of the premises," the executors would convey the house, &c., to the plaintiff for her life; "provided nevertheless, and it is hereby further agreed and declared," that the plaintiff should, during her possession, pay to the executors 1*l.* yearly towards the ground-rent, payable in respect of the said house and adjoining premises, and should keep the said house, &c., in repair, it was held, that the agreement so to pay, and to keep the premises in repair, was a consideration for the agreement by the defendant and S. T., and that respect for the wishes of the testator formed no part of the legal consideration for

[1] Turner *v.* Browne, 3 C. B. 157 (54 E. C. L. R.).

[2] Per Lord Denman, C. J., and Patteson, J., 2 Q. B. 859 (42 E. C. L. R.); Id. 861 (*a*).

[3] White *v.* Bluett, 23 L. J. Exch. 36. See Gough *v.* Findon, 7 Exch. 48; Frazer *v.* Hatton, 2 C. B. N. S. 512 (89 E. C. L. R.); Gorgier *v.* Morris, 7 C. B. N. S. 588 (97 E. C. L. R.).

their agreement, and need not be stated in the declaration.[1] This case, therefore, is illustrative of the position, that the motive which actuates a man is quite distinct from, and forms no part of, the legal consideration for his promise, and serves likewise to illustrate the remark of Pothier, who says, *La cause de l'engagement que contracte l'une des parties est ce que l'autre. des parties lui donne ou s'engage de lui donner ou le risque dont elle se charge.*[2]

[*752] After some conflict in the decisions and dicta[3] *respecting the sufficiency of a mere moral obligation, it is now established that such a consideration will not, subject to the remarks hereafter made, support a subsequent express promise. "Mere moral feeling," says Lord Denman, C. J., in a modern case, "is not enough to affect the legal rights of parties;[4] nor can a subsequent express promise convert into a debt that which of itself was not a legal debt;[5] and although the mere fact of giving a promise creates a moral obligation to perform it, yet the enforcement of such promises by law, however plausibly justified by the desire to effect all conscientious engagements, might be attended with mischievous consequences to society; one of which would be the frequent preference of voluntary undertakings to claims for just debts. Suits would thereby be multiplied, and voluntary undertakings would also be multiplied, to the prejudice of real creditors.[6]

[1] Thomas *v.* Thomas, 2 Q. B. 851 (42 E. C. L. R.); possibly such an agreement as the above would be held to be a mere voluntary conveyance as against a subsequent purchaser for value: per Patteson, J., Id. 860. See also, per Coleridge, J., Id. 861.

[2] 1 Pothier Oblig. 52.

[3] See Judgm., Littlefield *v.* Shee, 2 B. & Ad. 813; Judgm., Monkman *v.* Shepherdson, 11 A. & E. 415, 416 (39 E. C. L. R.); and in Eastwood *v.* Kenyon, Id. 450; Meyer *v.* Haworth, 8 A. & E. 467 (35 E. C. L. R.). See also Lee *v.* Muggeridge, 5 Taunt. 36 (1 E. C. L. R.); the doctrine laid down in which case is qualified, 2 B. & Ad. 812; 11 A. & E. 450 (39 E. C. L. R.); per Pollock, C. B., 1 H. & C. 716; 2 Wms. Saund., 5th ed., 137 c. note (*b*).

[4] Beaumont *v.* Reeve, 8 Q. B. 483 (55 E. C. L. R.); cited and recognized Fisher *v.* Bridges, 3 E. & B. 642 (77 E. C. L. R.); s. c., 2 Id. 118 (75 E. C. L. R.); Eastwood *v.* Kenyon, 11 A. & E. 438 (39 E. C. L. R.); Wennall *v.* Adney, 3 B. & P. 247, 249 (*a*). In Jennings *v.* Brown, 9 M. & W. 501, Parke, B., observes, in reference to Binnington *v.* Wallis (4 B. & Ald. 650 (6 E. C. L. R.)), that the giving up the annuity was "a mere moral consideration, which is nothing."

[5] Per Tindal, C. J., Kaye *v.* Dutton, 7 M. & Gr. 811–12 (49 E. C. L. R.).

[6] Judgm., 11 A. & E. 450, 451 (39 E. C. L. R.). See Roberts *v.* Smith, 4 H. & N. 315.

A good and sufficient consideration is, then, essential to the validity of a simple contract, whether such contract be written or verbal. The law of England, indeed, does not recognize any other distinction than that between agreements by specialty and those by parol. If agreements are merely written, and not specialties, they are parol agreements, and a consideration must be proved. The law, it has been observed,[1] "supplies no means *nor affords any remedy to compel the performance of an agreement [*753] made without sufficient consideration. Such agreement is *nudum pactum ex quo non oritur actio;* and whatsoever may be the sense of this maxim in the civil law, it is in the last-mentioned sense only that it is to be understood in our law."

A promise, therefore, by A. (the father) to pay for goods previously supplied to B. (his illegitimate child) without his (A.'s) sanction or request would not be binding;[2] though where the father of an illegitimate child promised the mother that if she would abstain from affiliating the child, he would pay a weekly sum for its maintenance, an action was held to lie for a breach of this undertaking.[3] And a husband has been held liable for the necessary expense of the interment of his wife to a mere volunteer.[4]

As regards bills of exchange and promissory notes the rule is, that either of these instruments is presumed to be made upon, and *primâ facie* imports, consideration.[5] And the words "value received" express only what the law will imply from the nature of the instrument, and the relation of the parties apparent upon it,[6] and then the maxim *Expressio eorum quæ tacitè insunt nihil operatur*, is applicable.[7] In an action upon a bill or note

[1] Per Skynner, C. B., Rann *v.* Hughes, 7 T. R. 350, n. (a). See, per Lord Kenyon, C. J., 3 T. R. 421; Judgm., Bank of Ireland *v.* Archer, 11 M. & W. 389.

[2] Shelton *v.* Springett, 11 C. B. 452 (73 E. C. L. R.); Mortimore *v.* Wright, 6 M. & W. 482. See Ruttinger *v.* Temple, 4 B. & S. 491 (116 E. C. L. R.).

[3] Linnegar *v.* Hodd, 5 C. B. 437 (57 E. C. L. R.); Smith *v.* Roche, 6 C. B. N. S. 223 (95 E. C. L. R.), and cases there cited.

[4] Ambrose *v.* Kerrison, 10 C. B. 776 (70 E. C. L. R.), recognizing Jenkins *v.* Tucker, 1 H. Bla. 91; *ante*, p. 535 n. 2.

[5] Per Martin, B., 1 H. & C. 710; Watson *v.* Russell, 3 B. & S. 34 (113 E. C. L. R.)

[6] Hatch *v.* Trayes, 11 A. & E. 702 (39 E. C. L. R.); per Lord Ellenborough, C. J., Grant *v.* Da Costa, 3 M. & S. 352 (30 E. C. L. R.).

[7] *Ante*, p. 669.

[*754] *between the immediate parties thereto, the consideration may be inquired into; and if it be proved that the plaintiff gave and the defendant received no value, the action will fail.[1] Where, observes Cresswell, J.,[2] there is a promise to pay a certain sum, all being supposed to be due, "each part of the money expressed to be due is the consideration for each part of the promise; and the consideration as to any part failing, the promise is *pro tanto nudum pactum.*"

In actions not between immediate parties to a bill or note, the established rule is, that some suspicion must be passed upon the plaintiff's title before he can be compelled to prove what consideration he has given for it. If, for instance, a promissory note were proved to have been obtained by fraud, or affected by illegality, such proof affords a presumption that the person guilty of the illegality would dispose of it, and would place it in the hands of another person to sue upon it, and consequently casts upon the plaintiff the burden of showing that he was a *bonâ fide* endorsee for value.[3]

As it appears needless to cite additional cases in support or illustration of a maxim so comprehensive and so well established as that now under review, we may [*755] *proceed to observe, that, not only must the consideration for a promise be sufficient in the contemplation of law, but it must, as already intimated, *move from the plaintiff*, that is to say there must be a legal *privity* between the parties to the contract alleged.[4] Where, therefore, B.,

[1] Southall *v.* Rigg, and Forman *v.* Wright, 11 C. B. 481, 492 (73 E. C. L. R.); Crofts *v.* Beale, 11 C. B. 172; Kearns *v.* Durell, 6 Id. 596 (60 E. C. L. R); and cases cited *infra.*

[2] 11 C. B. 494; see Warwick *v.* Nairn, 10 Exch. 762.

[3] Per Parke, B., Bailey *v.* Bidwell, 13 M. & W. 73; Boden *v.* Wright, 12 C. B. 445 (74 E. C. L. R.); Smith *v.* Braine, 16 Q. B. 244, 250–1 (71 E. C. L. R.); Harvey *v.* Towers, 6 Exch. 656; Mather *v.* Lord Maidstone, 1 C. B. N. S. 273 (87 E. C. L. R.); s. c., 18 C. B. 273 (86 E. C. L. R.); Hall *v.* Featherstone, 3 H. & N. 284; Berry *v.* Alderman, 14 C. B. 95 (78 E. C. L. R.); Dobie *v.* Larkan, 10 Exch. 776. The proposition stated in the text is more fully set forth per Lord Campbell, C. J., Fitch *v.* Jones, 5 E. & B. 238 (85 E. C. L. R.). See also Munroe *v.* Bordier, 8 C. B. 862 (65 E. C. L. R.); Judgm., May *v.* Seyler, 2 Exch. 566; Robinson *v.* Reynolds (in error), 2 Q. B. 196 (42 E. C. L. R.).

[4] See Playford *v.* United Kingdom Telegraph Co., L. R. 4 Q. B. 706; Becher *v.* Great Eastern R. C., L. R. 5 Q. B. 241; Jennings *v.* Great Northern

the country attorney of A., sent a sum of money to the defendants, who were his London agents, to be paid to C. on account of A., and the defendants promised B. to pay the money according to his direction, but afterwards, being applied to by C., refused to pay it, claiming a balance due to themselves from B. on a general account between them, it was held that an action for money had and received would not lie against the defendants at the suit of A.[1] "The general rule," observed Lord Denman, C. J., "undoubtedly is, that there is no *privity* between the agent in town and the client in the country; and the former cannot maintain an action against the latter for his fees, nor the latter against the former for negligence."

A. employs B., an attorney, to do an act for the benefit of C., A. having to pay B., and there being no intercourse of any sort between B. and C. If, through the gross negligence or ignorance of B. in transacting the business, *C. loses the benefit intended for him by A., C. cannot maintain an action against B. to recover damages for the loss sustained. If the law were otherwise, a disappointed legatee might sue the solicitor employed by a testator to make a will in favor of a stranger, whom the solicitor never saw or before heard of, if the will were void for not being properly signed and attested.[2] [*756]

Having thus briefly shown the nature of the *consideration* and of the *privity* which are necessary to a valid contract, we may proceed to specify the important distinctions which exist between considerations *executed*, *concurrent*, *continuing*, and *executory;* and, in the

R. C., L. R. 1 Q. B. 7; Alton *v.* Midland R. C., 19 C. B. N. S. 213 (115 E. C. L. R.); Watson *v.* Russell, 5 B. & S. 968 (117 E. C. L. R.); s. c., 3 Id. 34 (113 E. C. L. R.).

[1] Cobb *v.* Becke, 6 Q. B. 930 (51 E. C. L. R.); Robbins *v.* Fennell, 11 Q. B. 248 (63 E. C. L. R.); Bluck *v.* Siddaway, 15 L. J. Q. B. 359; Hooper *v.* Treffry, 1 Exch. 17. See Litt *v.* Martindale, 18 C. B. 314 (86 E. C. L. R.), where there seems to have been very slight (if any) evidence of privity; Johnson *v.* Royal Mail Steam Packet Co., L. R. 3 C. P. 38; Moore *v.* Bushell, 27 L. J. Exch. 3; Gerhard *v.* Bates, 2 E. & B. 476 (75 E. C. L. R.); Brewer *v.* Jones, 10 Exch. 655; Barkworth *v.* Ellerman, 6 H. & N. 605; Painter *v.* Abel, 2 H. & C. 113; Collins *v.* Brook, 5 H. & N. 700; s. c., 4 Id. 270.

[2] Per Lord Campbell, C., Robertson *v.* Fleming, 4 Macq. Sc. App. Cas. 177.

As to privity in connection with the relation of attorney and client, see Fish *v.* Kelly, 17 C. B. N. S. 194 (112 E. C. L. R.); Helps *v.* Clayton, Id. 553.

first place, we may observe that a bygone, or completely executed, consideration, unless supported by an antecedent request, either express or implied, will not suffice in law to sustain a subsequent promise. If, for example, a man disburse money about the affairs of another, without request, and then the latter promise that, in consideration that the former had disbursed the money for him, he will pay him 20*l.*, this is not a good consideration, because it is executed;[1] but if, in such a case, there were a previous request to pay the money, then the subsequent promise would not be a bare or naked one, but would couple itself with the precedent request, and with the merits of the party which were procured by that request, and would, therefore, be founded upon a good consideration.[2]

[*757] *A declaration in *assumpsit* stated that in consideration of the plaintiff's *agreeing* to stay proceedings in an action against B., the defendant promised to pay the amount upon a certain event; at the trial, the following agreement was proved: "In consideration of the plaintiff's *having agreed* to stay proceedings against B., &c.;" it was held that the contract was an executory contract, and a continuing agreement to stay proceedings, and that there was therefore no variance.[3]

But although in general a past consideration will not support a promise at law, there are, nevertheless, cases in which a past or executed consideration will be supported by an *implied* antecedent request. Where, for instance, the party sought to be charged has derived benefit from that which is alleged to be the consideration for his promise, the acceptance and enjoyment of this benefit will, in legal contemplation, be deemed sufficient to support the averment of defendant's promise and request, because from such subsequent enjoyment the law will imply a previous request; thus, if a man pays money, or buys goods for me, without my knowledge or request, and afterwards I agree to the payment, or receive the goods; my conduct, as showing a ratification of the contract, will

[1] Per Tindal, C. J., Thornton *v.* Jenyns, 1 Scott N. R. 74, citing Hunt *v.* Bate, Dyer 272, and 1 Roll. Abr. 11. See particularly Roscorla *v.* Thomas, 3 Q. B. 234 (43 E. C. L. R.).

[2] Lampleigh *v.* Brathwait, Hob. R. 106; per Parke, J., Reason *v.* Wirdman, 1 C. & P. 434; 1 Wms. Saund. 264 (1).

[3] Tanner *v.* Moore, 9 Q. B. 9 (58 E. C. L. R.).

have a retrospective operation, and will be held tantamount to a previous request, according to a maxim which will be hereafter considered, *Omnis ratihabitio retrotrahitur et mandato priori æquiparatur.*[1]

In Paynter *v.* Williams,[2] the facts were these:—A *pauper, whose settlement was in the parish of A., resided [*758] in the parish of B., and whilst there received relief from the parish of A., which relief was afterwards discontinued, the overseers objecting to pay any more unless the pauper removed into his own parish. The pauper was subsequently taken ill, and attended by the plaintiff, an apothecary, who, after continuing to attend him for nine weeks, sent a letter to the overseers of A., upon the receipt of which they directed the allowance to be renewed, and it was accordingly continued to the time of the pauper's decease: it was held, that the overseers of A. were liable to pay so much of the apothecary's bill as was incurred after the letter was received, for they knew of the plaintiff's attendance, which knowledge amounted, under the circumstances of the case, to an acceptance, retainer, or adoption of the plaintiff's services, and created a legal liability.[3]

The law will also imply an antecedent request where the consideration consists in this—that the plaintiff has been compelled to do that to which the defendant was legally compellable—on which principle depends the right of a surety, who has been damnified, to recover an indemnity from his principal,[4] or contribution from a co-surety or joint contractor.[5]

Where, moreover, the consideration is past, it appears *to be unnecessary to *allege a request*, if the act stated as [*759] the consideration cannot, from its nature, have been a gratuitous

[1] See also 1 Wms. Saund. 264 (1); Simpson *v.* Eggington, 10 Exch. 845: Streeter *v.* Horlock, 1 Bing. 34 (8 E. C. L. R.).

[2] 1 Cr. & M. 810.

[3] 1 Cr. & M. 819, 820; Wing *v.* Mill, 1 B. & Ald. 104; Atkins *v.* Banwell, 2 East 505.

[4] Toussaint *v.* Martinnant, 2 T. R. 100; Done *v.* Walley, 2 Exch. 198.

[5] Per Lord Kenyon, C. J., 8 T. R. 186; Batard *v.* Hawes, 3 E. & B. 287, 296 (77 E. C. L. R.); Earl of Mounteashell *v.* Barber, 14 C. B. 53 (78 E. C. L. R.); Holmes *v.* Williamson, 6 M. & S. 158; Kemp *v.* Finden, 13 M. & W. 421; Edger *v.* Knapp, 6 Scott N. R. 707; Davies *v.* Humphreys, 6 M. & W. 153, 168; Browne *v.* Lee, 6 B. & C. 689 (13 E. C. L. R.); Cowell *v.* Edwards, 2 B. & P. 268. See Reynolds *v.* Wheeler, 10 C. B. N. S. 561 (100 E. C. L. R.).

kindness, but imports a consideration *per se*.[1] Thus, in a recent case, which was an action of assumpsit for money lent, it was held unnecessary to allege that the money was lent at the defendant's request; for there cannot be a claim for money lent unless there be a loan, and a loan implies an obligation to pay.[2] In the case of money paid, however, the above doctrine will not apply, because a gratuitous payment would not create a legal obligation; and "no man can be a debtor for money paid unless it was paid at his request."[3]

In assumpsit for work and labor done by the plaintiff for the defendant, in consideration whereof the latter promised to pay, after judgment by default and error brought, it was objected, that this was a past consideration, and, not being laid to be done at the defendant's request, it could be no consideration to raise an assumpsit; and the court said, they took the rule of law to be, that a past consideration is not sufficient to support a subsequent promise, unless there was a request of the party, either express or implied, at the time of performing the consideration, and the judgment was accordingly reversed.[4]

[*760] *A distinction will be noted between cases like the above, and those in which it has been held that an express promise may effectually revive a precedent good consideration, which might have been enforced at law, through the medium of an implied promise, had it not been suspended by some positive rule of law, as in the case of infancy, or of a debt barred by the Statute of Limitations, "which is still a good consideration for a promise in writing to pay."[5]

"The cases," says Lord Denman, C. J.,[6] "in which it has been

[1] See 1 M. & Gr. 265 note (39 E. C. L. R.); cited per Parke, B., 12 M. & W. 759.

[2] Victors *v.* Davies, 12 M. & W. 758; per Pollock, C. B., 1 H. & C. 716; M'Gregor *v.* Graves, 3 Exch. 34.

[3] Per Parke, B., 12 M. & W. 760; Brittain *v.* Lloyd, 14 M. & W. 762, cited in Lewis *v.* Campbell, 8 C. B. 541, 547 (65 E. C. L. R.); and per Parke, B., Hutchinson *v.* Sydney, 10 Exch. 439. See the Forms 15 & 16 Vict. c. 76, Sched. (B.) Nos. 3, 4.

[4] Hayes *v.* Warren, 2 Stra. 933, cited 1 Wms. Saund. 264 (1). See, in further illustration of the subject above touched upon, Dietrichsen *v.* Giubelei, 14 M. & W. 845; per Parke, B., King *v.* Sears, 2 Cr., M. & R. 53; Emmens *v.* Elderton, 4 H. L. Cas. 624.

[5] La Touche *v.* La Touche, 3 H. & C. 576, 588.

[6] Roscorla *v.* Thomas, 3 Q. B. 237 (43 E. C. L. R.); Judgm., 1 C. B. 870 (41 E. C. L. R.).

held, that, under certain circumstances, a consideration insufficient to raise an implied promise will nevertheless support an express one, will be found collected and reviewed in the note to Wennall *v.* Adney,[1] and in the case of Eastwood *v.* Kenyon.[2] They are cases of *voidable* contracts subsequently ratified, of debts barred by operation of law subsequently revived, and of equitable and moral obligations, which, but for some rule of law, would of themselves have been sufficient to raise an implied promise."

The principle of the rule stated as above by Lord Denman, and previously laid down by Lord Mansfield,[3] has been thus more recently explained,[4] "that where the consideration was originally beneficial to the party promising, yet if he be protected from liability by some provision of the statute or common law meant for his advantage, he may renounce the benefit of that law; and *if he promises to pay the debt, which is only what an honest man ought to do, he is then bound by the law to perform it." Debts, for instance, barred by the Statute of Limitations, "are unquestionably a sufficient consideration for every promise absolute or unqualified, qualified or conditional, to pay them.[5] Promises to pay a debt simply, or by installments, or when the party is able, are all equally supported by the past consideration, and, when the debts have become payable *instanter*, may be given in evidence" in support of the ordinary indebitatus counts. "So when the debt is not already barred by the statute, a promise to pay the creditor will revive it and make it a new debt, and a promise to an executor to pay a debt due to a testator creates a new debt to him. But it does not follow that though a promise revives the debt in such cases, any of those debts will be a sufficient consideration to support a promise to do a collateral thing, as to supply goods or perform work and labor.[6] In such case it is but an accord unexecuted, and no action will lie for not executing it."[7]

[1] 3 B. & P. 249.

[2] 11 A. & E. 438 (39 E. C. L. R.).

[3] Hawkes *v.* Sanders, Cowp. 290; Atkins *v.* Hill, Id. 288.

[4] Judgm., Earle *v.* Oliver, 2 Exch. 90.

[5] See Lee *v.* Wilmot, L. R. 1 Ex. 364; Bush *v.* Martin, 2 H. & C. 311.

[6] Citing Reeves *v.* Hearne, 1 M. & W. 323.

[7] Judgm., 2 Exch. 90; per Parke, B., Smith *v.* Thorne, 18 Q. B. 139 (83 E. C. L. R.).

With reference to the above class of cases, we must remark that the distinction is very material between a *void* and a *voidable* contract. For instance, in the case of infancy, the original contract is in many cases voidable only, not absolutely void, so that the liability of the contracting party may be ratified or renewed without any fresh consideration;[1] whereas the contract of a married [*762] *woman is absolutely void;[2] and, therefore, if the record states that goods were supplied to a married woman, who, after her husband's death, promised to pay, this is not sufficient, because the debt was never owing from her.[3]

Recent cases may be adverted to as showing that a contract, which could not originally have been made the ground of an action, may be converted, by a subsequent express promise, into a cause of action which the law will recognize as valid. A verbal agreement was entered into between the plaintiff and defendants respecting the transfer of an interest in land. The transfer was effected, and nothing remained to be done but to pay the consideration; it was held, that the agreement not being in writing, as required by the Statute of Frauds, could not be enforced by action, but that, the transferee, after the transfer, having admitted to the transferor that he owed him the stipulated price, the amount might be recovered upon the count upon an account stated in the declaration.[4] Also bills of exchange given after the repeal of the usury law, by 17 & 18 Vict. c. 90, in renewal of bills given while that law was in force to secure payment of money lent at usurious interest, have been held valid, the receipt of the money being a sufficient consideration to support a new promise to pay it. In the case referred to, this [*763] qualified proposition was sanctioned by the majority *of the court: "That a man by express promise may render him-

[1] Per Patteson, J., 8 A. & E. 470 (35 E. C. L. R.). See the note (a) to Wennall *v.* Adney, 3 B. & P. 249.

[2] See Neve *v.* Hollands, 18 Q. B. 262 (83 E. C. L. R.).

[3] Meyer *v.* Haworth, 8 A. & E. 467, 469 (35 E. C. L. R.). In Traver *v.* ——, 1 Sid. 57, a woman, after her husband's death, promised the plaintiff, a creditor, that, if he would prove that her husband had owed him 20*l.*, she would pay the money. This was held a good consideration, "because it was a trouble and charge to the creditor to prove his debt." See Cope *v.* Albinson, 8 Exch. 185.

[4] Cocking *v.* Ward, 1 C. B. 858, 870 (50 E. C. L. R.). See Lemere *v.* Elliott, 6 H. & N. 656; Smart *v.* Harding, 15 C. B. 652, 659 (80 E. C. L. R.); Green *v.* Saddington, 7 E. & B. 503 (90 E. C. L. R.).

self liable to pay back money which he has received as a loan, though some positive rule of law or statute intervened at the time to prevent the transaction from constituting a legal debt."[1]

We must, in the next place, observe that the subsequent promise, like the antecedent request, may, in many cases, be implied. For instance, the very name of a loan imports that it was the understanding and intention of both parties that the money should be repaid;[2] a promise to pay interest will be implied by law from the forbearance of money at the defendant's request;[3] and from money being found due on accounts stated, the law implies a promise to pay it;[4] but where the consideration has been executed, and a promise would, under the circumstances, be implied by law, it is clearly established that no express promise made in respect of that prior consideration, differing from that which by law would be implied, can be enforced;[5] for, were it otherwise, there would be two coexisting promises on one consideration.[6] It has, however, been said that the cases establishing this proposition may have proceeded on another principle, viz., that the consideration was exhausted by the promise implied by law from the very execution of it, and that, consequently, any promise made afterwards must be *nudum pactum*, there remaining no consideration to support it.[7] "But the case may perhaps be *different where there is a consideration from which no promise would be implied by law, that is, [*764] where the party suing has sustained a detriment to himself or conferred a benefit on the defendant, *at his request*, under circumstances which would not raise any implied promise. In such cases it appears to have been held, in some instances, that the act done at the request of the party charged is a sufficient consideration to render binding a promise afterwards made by him in respect of the act so done."[8]

But however this may be, it is, as previously stated, quite clear,

[1] Flight *v.* Reed, 1 H. & C. 703, 716.
[2] Per Pollock, C. B., 1 H. & C. 716.
[3] Nordenstrom *v.* Pitt, 13 M. & W. 723.
[4] Per Crompton, J., Fagg *v.* Nudd, 3 E. & B. 652 (77 E. C. L. R.).
[5] Judgm., Kaye *v.* Dutton, 7 M. & Gr. 815 (49 E. C. L. R.), and cases there cited.
[6] Per Maule, B., Hopkins *v.* Logan, 5 M. & W. 249.
[7] See Deacon *v.* Gridley, 15 C. B. 295 (80 E. C. L. R.).
[8] Judgm., 7 M. & Gr. 816 (49 E. C. L. R.).

that, where the consideration is past, the promise alleged, even if express, must be identical with that which would have been implied by law from the particular transaction; in other words, "a past and executed consideration will support no other promise than such as may be implied by law;"[1] thus, in assumpsit, the declaration stated, that, in consideration that plaintiff, at the request of defendant, *had bought* a horse of defendant at a certain price, defendant promised that the horse was *free from vice*, but deceived the plaintiff in this, to wit, that the said horse was vicious. On motion in arrest of judgment, this declaration was held bad; for the executed consideration, though laid with a request, neither raised by implication of law the promise charged in the declaration, nor would support such promise if express; the court in this case observing, that the only promise which would result from the consideration, as stated, and be co-extensive with it, would be to deliver the horse upon request.[2]

[*765] *In an action against the public officer of an insurance and loan company, the second count of the declaration stated, that it was agreed between the company and the plaintiff, that from the 1st of January then next, the plaintiff, as the attorney of the said company, should receive a salary of 100*l.* per annum, in lieu of rendering an annual bill of costs for general business; and in consideration that the plaintiff had promised to fulfill the agreement on his part, the company promised to fulfill the same on their part, *and to retain and employ the plaintiff as such attorney*;[3] the verdict being in favor of the plaintiff, the judgment was afterwards arrested by the Court of Common Pleas, upon this ground, that there was no sufficient consideration to sustain that part of the count above referred to, which alleged a promise to retain and employ the plaintiff, the court holding that the language of the agreement, as stated, imported an obligation to furnish actual employment to the plaintiff in his profession of an attorney, and that inasmuch as the consideration set forth was in the past,

[1] Per Parke, B., Atkinson *v.* Stevens, 7 Exch. 572; Judgm., Earle *v.* Oliver, 2 Exch. 89; Lattimore *v.* Garrard, 1 Exch. 809, 811.

[2] Roscorla *v.* Thomas, 3 Q. B. 234, 237 (43 E. C. L. R.).

[3] Emmens *v.* Elderton, 4 H. L. Cas. 624; s. c., 13 C. B. 495 (76 E. C. L. R.); 6 Id. 160 (60 E. C. L. R.); 4 Id. 479 (56 E. C. L. R.); cited Payne *v.* New South Wales, &c., Steam Nav. Co., 10 Exch. 283, 290.

that the plaintiff *had* promised to perform his part of the agreement, such consideration being a past or executed promise was exhausted by the like promise of the company to perform the agreement, and did not enure as a consideration for the additional part of the promise alleged to retain and employ the plaintiff in the sense before mentioned, as also to perform the agreement. The view thus taken, however, was pronounced erroneous by the Court of Exchequer Chamber, and afterwards by the House of Lords, who held that the averment as to retaining and *employing the plaintiff was not to be understood as importing a contract beyond the strict legal effect of the agreement, whence it followed that the mutual promises to perform such agreement laid in the count of the declaration objected to, were a sufficient legal consideration to sustain the defendant's promise.[1] [*766]

A *concurrent* consideration is where the act of the plaintiff and the promise of the defendant take place at the same time; and here the law does not, as in the case of a bygone transaction, require that, in order to make the promise binding, the plaintiff should have acted at the request of the defendant;[2] as, where it appeared from the whole declaration taken together, that, at the same moment, by a simultaneous act, a promise was made, that, on the plaintiff's accepting bills drawn by one of the parties then present, the defendants should deliver certain deeds to the plaintiff when the bills were paid, it was held, that a good consideration was disclosed for the defendant's promise.[3] So, where the promise of the plaintiff and that of the defendant are simultaneous, the one may be a good and sufficient consideration for the other;[4] as where two parties, upon the same occasion, and at the same time, mutually promise to perform a certain agreement not then actually entered into, the consideration moving from the one party is sufficient to support the promise by the other.[5]

[1] Emmens *v.* Elderton, *supra.*

[2] Per Tindal, C. J., 3 Bing. N. C. 715 (32 E. C. L. R.).

[3] Tipper *v.* Bicknell, Id. 710; West *v.* Jackson, 16 Q. B. 280 (71 E. C. L. R.).

[4] As to *mutuality* in contracts, see Broom's Com., 4th ed., 305 *et seq.*; Bealey *v.* Stewart, 31 L. J. Ex. 281; Westhead *v.* Sproson, 6 H. & N. 728; Whittle, app., Frankland, resp., 2 B. & S. 49 (110 E. C. L. R.).

[5] Thornton *v.* Jenyns, 1 M. & Gr. 166 (39 E. C. L. R.). See King *v.* Gillett, 7 M. & W. 55; Harrison *v.* Cage, 1 Ld. Raym. 386; cited Smith *v.* Woodfine, 1 C. B. N. S. 667 (87 E. C. L. R.).

[*767] *Again, where, by one and the same instrument, a sum of money is agreed to be paid by one of the contracting parties, and a conveyance of an estate to be at the same time executed by the other, the payment of the money and the execution of the conveyance may very properly be considered concurrent acts; and, in this case, no action can be maintained by the vendor to recover the money until he executes or offers to execute a conveyance.[1] It may, indeed, be stated, generally, that neither party can sue on such an entire contract without showing a performance of, or an offer, or, at least, a readiness and willingness to perform, his part of the agreement, or a wrongful discharge or prevention of such performance by the other party; in which latter case the party guilty of the wrongful act shall not, in accordance with a maxim already considered, be allowed to take advantage of it, and thereby to relieve himself from liability for breach of contract.[2]

In addition to cases in which the consideration is concurrent, or is altogether past and executed, others occur wherein the consideration is *continuing* at the time of making the promise; thus, it has been held, that the mere relation of landlord and tenant is a sufficient consideration for the tenant's promise to manage a farm in a husbandlike manner.[3]

[*768] *Lastly, "whenever the consideration of a promise is *executory*, there must," it has been said,[4] "*ex necessitate rei*, have been a request on the part of the person promising; for if A. promise to remunerate B., in consideration that B. will perform something specified, that amounts to a request to B. to perform the act for which he is to be remunerated." Here the consideration constitutes a condition precedent to be performed by B. before his right of action accrues; but whether or not, in any given case, one *promise* be the consideration of another, or whether the *performance*, and not the

[1] Per Lord Tenterden, C. J., Spiller *v.* Westlake, 2 B. & Ad. 157 (22 E. C. L. R.); Bankart *v.* Bowers, L. R. 1 C. P. 484.

[2] *Ante*, p. 279 *et seq.* "If a party does all he can to perform the act which he has stipulated to do, but is prevented by the wrongful act of the other party, he is in the same situation as if the performance had been perfected:" per Holroyd, J., Studdy *v.* Saunders, 5 B. & C. 637 (11 E. C. L. R.); see also Caines *v.* Smith, 15 M. & W. 189.

[3] Powley *v.* Walker, 5 T. R. 373; recognized Beale *v.* Sanders, 3 Bing. N. C. 850 (32 E. C. L. R.); Massey *v.* Goodall, 17 Q. B. 310 (79 E. C. L. R.).

[4] Smith L. C., 6th ed., 142.

mere promise, be the consideration, must be gathered from, and depends entirely upon, the words and nature of the agreement, and the intention of the contracting parties.[1]

Caveat Emptor.

(Hob. 99.)

Let a purchaser beware.

It seems clear, that, according to the civil law, a warranty of title was, as a general rule, implied on the part of the vendor of land, so that in case of eviction an action for damages lay against him at the suit of the vendee, *sive tota res evincatur, sive pars, habet regressum emptor in venditorem;*[2] and again, *non dubitatur, etsi specialiter venditor evictionem non promiserit, re evictâ, ex empto competere actionem.*[3] With us, however, the above proposition does not hold, and it is laid down, that, "if a man buys lands whereunto another hath title, which the buyer knoweth not, yet ignorance shall not excuse *him."[4] By the civil law, as observed by Sir E. Coke, every man is bound to warrant the thing that he sells or conveys, albeit there be no express warranty; but the common law binds him not, *unless there be a warranty*, either in deed[5] or in law; for *Caveat emptor*,[6] *qui ignorare non debuit quod jus alienum emit*[7]—let a purchaser, who ought not to be ignorant of the amount and nature of the interest which he is about to buy, exercise proper caution.

[*769]

The following examples may suffice to show generally the mode in which the maxim *Caveat emptor* has been applied in practice to the sale of realty; and, since it would be incompatible with the plan of this volume to enter at any length into an examination of the very numerous cases which have been decided at law and in

[1] Thorpe *v.* Thorpe, 1 Ld. Raym. 662; s. c., 1 Salk. 111, is a leading case upon this subject.

[2] D. 21. 2. 1.

[3] C. 8. 45. 6.

[4] Doct. and Stud, bk. 2, ch. 47.

[5] See Worthington *v.* Warrington, 5 C. B. 635 (57 E. C. L. R.).

[6] Co. Litt. 102 a. "I have always understood that in purchases of land the rule is *Caveat emptor:*" per Lawrence, J., Gwithin *v.* Stone, 3 Taunt. 439.

[7] Hobart 99.

equity with respect to the operation of the above rule, we must content ourselves with referring below to works of high authority in which this important subject will be found minutely treated.[1]

Where, on the sale of an estate, certain woods were falsely represented as actually producing 250*l.* per annum, on an average of the fifteen preceding years, but it appeared that the manner of making the calculation was explained at the sale, that a paper was exhibited, showing that the woods had not been equally cut, and that the purchaser likewise sent down his own surveyors, who [*770] thought that the woods had been cut in an improper *manner, Lord Thurlow refused to give the purchaser relief by ordering an allowance to be made, and held that the maxim, *Caveat emptor*, applied; but he observed, that if the representation were made generally, and it were distinctly proved that the fact stated, though literally true, yet was made out by racking the woods beyond the course of husbandry, that would be a fraud in the representation, which might be relieved against; and he further remarked, that the maxim *Caveat emptor* does not apply "where there is a positive representation essentially material to the subject in question, and which, at the same time, is false in fact," provided proper diligence be used by the purchaser in the course of the transaction.[2]

By agreement for the purchase of a piece of land, entered into between the defendants, who were the assignees of B., and the plaintiff, it was stipulated on behalf of the defendants that they should not be obliged to make any warranty of title, the plaintiff having agreed to accept a conveyance of such right or title as might be the defendants'; with all faults and defects, if any. Before any conveyance was executed, the plaintiff asked the defendants whether any rent had ever been paid for the land, and they replied that none had been paid by the bankrupt, nor by any person under whom he claimed, whereas, in fact, rent had been paid by the person who had sold the land to the bankrupt. The plaintiff, having been evicted, sued the defendant for recovery of his purchase-money, and the judge having left to the jury the question whether the non-communication of the fact of payment of rent was fraudulent or not, a verdict was found for the defendants. This verdict the court in

[1] Sugd., V. & P., 14th ed., 328, *et seq.*; 1 Story Ex. Jurisp., 9th ed., Chap. VI.

[2] Lowndes *v.* Lane, 2 Cox 363.

banc *refused to set aside, and Bayley, J., observed, "I make no distinction between an active and a passive com- [*771] munication; if a seller fraudulently conceal that which he ought to communicate, it will render the contract null and void. But the authorities establish that the concealment must be fraudulent."[1] The case just cited is a direct authority in support of the rule of law laid down by Lord St. Leonards that—"If, at the time of the contract, the vendor himself was not aware of any defect in the estate, it seems that the purchaser must take the estate with all its faults, and cannot claim any compensation for them."[2]

Where, however, a particular description of the estate is given, which turns out to be false, and the purchaser cannot be proved to have had a distinct knowledge of its actual state and condition, he will be entitled to compensation, although a court of equity will compel him to perform his contract. The rule of *Caveat emptor*, indeed, has no application where the defect is a *latent* one, and of such a nature that the purchaser cannot by the greatest attention discover it, and if, moreover, the vendor be cognizant of it, and do not acquaint the purchaser with the fact of its existence; for in this case the contract would not be considered binding at law, and equity would not enforce a specific performance.[3] It appears, however, to be settled, that if the subject-matter of the contract of sale be agreed to be taken "with all faults," the insertion of this condition will *excuse the vendor from stating those within his knowledge, although he will not be justified in using any [*772] artifice to conceal them from the purchaser. And even if the purchaser might, by the exercise of proper precaution, have discovered the defect, equity will not assist the vendor in case he has *industriously* concealed it.[4] So, from Attwood *v.* Small, the principle is clearly deducible, that if a purchaser, choosing to judge for himself, does not effectually avail himself of the knowledge or means of knowledge accessible to him or his agents, he cannot afterwards be permitted to say that he was deceived and misled by the vendor's

[1] Early *v.* Garrett, 9 B. & C. 928, 932 (17 E. C. L. R.); Duke of Norfolk *v.* Worthy, 1 Camp. 337; White *v.* Cuddon, 8 Cl. & Fin. 766; Turner *v.* Harvey, 1 Jac. 169, 178; Phillips *v.* Duke of Bucks, 1 Vern. 227.

[2] Sudg. V. & P., 14th ed., 1.

[3] Ibid. 333. See also 1 Story, Eq. Jurisp., 6th ed., 247.

[4] Sugd. V. & P., 14th ed., 335.

misrepresentations; for the rule in such a case is *Caveat emptor*, and the knowledge of his agents is as binding on him as his own knowledge. It is his own folly and laches not to use the means of knowledge within his reach, and he may properly impute any loss or injury in such a case to his own negligence and indiscretion.[1]

Where the defects are *patent*, and such as might have been discovered by a vigilant man, or where the contract was entered into with full knowledge of them, equity will not afford relief; for, in the former case, the rule is, *Vigilantibus non dormientibus jura subveniunt*, and in the latter, *Scientia utrinque par pares contrahentes facit*—the law will not assist an improvident purchaser, nor will it interpose where both the contracting parties were [*773] *equally well informed as to the actual condition of the subject-matter of the contract.[2]

It will appear from the foregoing brief observations that the maxim *Caveat emptor* applies, with certain specific restrictions and qualifications, both to the *title* and *quality* of the land sold. We may further remark, that, as to the title, it applies equally, whether the vendor is in or out of possession, for he cannot hold the lands without *some* title; and the buyer is bound to see it, and to inspect the title-deeds, at his peril. He does not use common prudence if he relies on any other security.[3] The ordinary course, indeed, which is adopted on the sale of real estates is this: the seller submits his title to the inspection of the purchaser, who exercises his own or such other judgment as he confides in, on the goodness of the title; and if it should turn out to be defective, the purchaser has no remedy, unless he take special covenant or warranty, provided there be no fraud practiced on him to induce him to purchase.[4]

[1] Attwood *v.* Small, 6 Cl. & Fin. 232, 233; see Wilde *v.* Gibson, 1 H. L. Cas. 605; commented on, Sudg. V. & P., 14th ed., 328–330. Equity will not "interpose in favor of a man who willfully was ignorant of that which he ought to have known,—a man who, without exercising that diligence which the law would expect of a reasonable and careful person, committed a mistake, in consequence of which alone the proceedings in court have arisen:" per Lord Campbell, Duke of Beaufort *v.* Neeld, 12 Cl. & Fin. 248, 286.

[2] See Sugd. V. & P., 14th ed., 1.

[3] 3 T. R. 56, 65; Roswell *v.* Vaughan, Cro. Jac. 196; per Holt, C. J., 1 Salk. 211.

[4] Per Lawrence, J., 2 East 323; Judgm., Stephens *v.* De Medina, 4 Q. B. 428 (45 E. C. L. R.); per Erle, C. J., Thackeray *v.* Wood, 6 B. & S. 773 (118 E. C. L. R.); per Martin, B., Id. 775.

Thus, if a regular conveyance is made, containing the usual covenants for securing the buyer against the acts of the seller and his ancestors only, and his title is actually conveyed to the buyer, the rule of *Caveat emptor* applies against the latter, so that he must, at his peril, perfect all that is requisite to his assurance; and, as he might protect his purchase by proper covenants, none can be added.[1] An administrator found, among the *papers of [*774] his intestate, a mortgage deed, purporting to convey premises to him, and without arrears of interest. Not knowing it to be a forgery, he assigned it, covenanting, not for good title in the mortgagor, but only that nothing had been done by himself or the deceased mortgagee to encumber the property; and, as this precluded all presumption of any further security, the assignee was held bound to look to the goodness of the title, and failed to recover the purchase money.[2] The case of an ordinary mortgage, however, differs from that of a conveyance, because the mortgagor covenants that, at all events, he has a good title.[3]

In cases respecting the demise of land, any question as to the conditions of the demise must, in the absence of fraud, be determined by considering both the express contract and likewise the warranty, which may, according to circumstances, either arise by implication of law or be inferred from the conduct of the parties. Bearing upon this part of our subject, the following cases may be mentioned: In Sutton *v.* Temple,[4] A. agreed, in writing, to take eatage (that is, the use of the herbage to be eaten by cattle) of twenty-four acres of land from B. for seven months, at a rent of 40*l.*, and stocked the land with beasts, several of which died a few days afterwards from the effects of a poisonous substance, which had accidentally been spread over the field without B.'s knowledge. It was held by the Court of Exchequer, that A., nevertheless, continued liable for the whole rent, and was not entitled to throw up the land. In this case *it was not suggested that the [*775] plaintiff B. had the least knowledge of that which caused

[1] See note (*h*); Judgm., Johnson *v.* Johnson, 3 B. & P. 170; arg. 3 East 446; 4 Rep. 25; 5 Rep. 84.

[2] Bree *v.* Holbech, Dougl. 655; cited 6 T. R. 606; per Gibbs, C. J., 1 Marsh. R. 163 (4 E. C. L. R.); Thackeray *v.* Wood, 6 B. & S. 766 (118 E. C. L. R.).

[3] Per Lord Kenyon, C. J., Cripps *v.* Reade, 6 T. R. 607.

[4] 12 M. & W. 52.

the injury when the land was let; but it was contended, that under the above circumstances, there was an implied warranty on the part of the plaintiff that the eatage was wholesome food for cattle; the rule of law was, however, stated to be, that, if a person contract for the use and occupation of land for a specific time, and at a specific rent, he will be bound by his bargain, even though he take it for a particular purpose, and that purpose be not attained. The word "demise," it was observed, certainly does not carry with it any such implied undertaking as that above mentioned; the law merely annexes to it a condition that the party demising has a good title to a premises, and that the lessee shall not be evicted during the term.[1]

In the subsequent case of Hart *v.* Windsor,[2] the court also held it to be clear, upon the old authorities, that there is no implied warranty on a lease of a house or of land that it is, or shall be, reasonably fit for habitation or cultivation; and still less is there a condition implied by law on the demise of real property only, that it is fit for the purpose for which it is let. "The principles of the common law do not warrant such a position; and though, in the case of a dwelling-house taken for habitation, there is no apparent injustice in inferring a contract of this nature, the same rule must [*776] *apply to land taken for other purposes,—for building upon, or for cultivation,—and there would be no limit to the inconvenience which would ensue. It is much better to leave the parties in every case to protect their interests themselves by proper stipulations; and, if they really mean a lease to be void by reason of any unfitness in the subject for the purpose intended, they should express that meaning.[3] A distinction is, moreover, to be

[1] 12 M. & W. 62, 64. In Kintrea *v.* Perston, 1 H. & N. 357, it was held that upon a contract for the sale of an agreement for a lease, it is not an implied condition that the lessor has power to grant the lease. See Jinks *v.* Edwards, 11 Exch. 775. A covenant for quiet enjoyment during the term is implied by law from a demise by parol, but not a covenant for good title. Bandy *v.* Cartwright, 8 Exch. 913; followed in Hall *v.* London Brewery Co., 2 B. & S. 742 (110 E. C. L. R.).

[2] 12 M. & W. 68.

[3] Judgm., 12 M. & W. 86, 87, 88. This was an action of debt for rent due under an agreement to let a house and garden-ground with certain fixtures; and the plea alleged that the house was infested with bugs, and was consequently unfit for habitation, and that the defendant accordingly quitted before any part of the rent became due.

drawn between the preceding cases and Smith *v.* Marrable,[1] where it was held, that in letting a ready-furnished house, there is an implied condition or obligation that the house is in a fit state to be inhabited, so that a tenant may quit without notice if the premises are unfit for habitation.

We may add, that the principle laid down in Hart *v.* Windsor, above cited, viz., that there is no implied warranty on the demise of a house, that it is, or shall be, reasonably fit for habitation, was fully confirmed and acted upon in Surplice *v.* Farnsworth,[2] where it was held, that assumpsit for use and occupation would lie against a tenant who held under a parol agreement, by which the landlord was to do the necessary repairs, and who quitted, because the premises, owing to the landlord's default, were in an untenantable state, although there had not been and could not be any actual beneficial *occupation during the period for which the rent was claimed. [*777]

We shall, in the next place, consider how far the maxim *Caveat emptor* applies in the case of a sale of goods and chattels, first, in regard to the *quality* of the goods, and secondly, in regard to the *title* to them. Now, with respect to the *quality*, the following general rule was laid down by Tindal, C. J.: "If a man purchase goods of a tradesman, without, in any way, relying upon the skill and judgment of the vendor, the latter is not responsible for their turning out contrary to his expectations; but, if the tradesman be informed at the time the order is given of the purpose for which the article is wanted, the buyer relying upon the seller's judgment, the latter impliedly warrants that the thing furnished shall be reasonably fit and proper for the purpose for which it is required."[3] Accordingly, where an agreement is for a specific chattel in its *then state*, there is no implied warranty of its fitness or merchantable quality;[4] but if a person is employed to *make* a specific chattel,

[1] 11 M. & W. 5. As to this case, see 12 M. & W. 60, 87; and per Coltman, J., 7 M. & Gr. 585 (49 E. C. L. R.).

[2] 7 M. & Gr. 576 (49 E. C. L. R.); recognizing Izon *v.* Gorton, 5 Bing. N. C. 501 (35 E. C. L. R.). See Keates *v.* Earl of Cadogan, 10 C. B. 591 (70 E. C. L. R.), cited, *post.*

[3] Brown *v.* Edgington, 2 Scott N. R. 504; recognized per Parke, B., 12 M. & W. 64; Jones *v.* Bright, 5 Bing. 533 (15 E. C. L. R.); recognized 4 M. & W. 406; per Abbott, C. J., Gray *v.* Cox, 4 B. & C. 108, 115 (10 E. C. L. R.); Wright *v.* Crooks, 1 Scott N. R. 685.

[4] Parkinson *v.* Lee, 2 East 314; recognized 8 Bing. 52 (21 E. C. L. R.), and

there the law implies a contract on his part that it shall be fit for the purpose for which it is ordinarily used.[1] And upon a sale not by sample, and without warranty, of merchandise, which the buyer has no opportunity of inspecting, a condition that the [*778] *article shall fairly and reasonably answer the description in the contract is implied.[2]

Where the defendant, a broker, bought for the plaintiff certain scrip certificates in a projected railway company, which turned out to be spurious, but which were, in fact, the only certificates which passed current in the market, in an action brought to recover the price paid for them from the defendant, the proper question for the jury was held to be, whether the plaintiff had or had not obtained for his money that particular thing which he desired to purchase.[3] It has been held, however, that the vendor of the bill of exchange impliedly warrants that it is of the kind and description which on the face of it it purports to be.[4]

12 M. & W. 64; Chanter *v.* Hopkins, 4 M. & W. 399; Laing *v.* Fidgeon, 6 Taunt. 108 (1 E. C. L. R.); Power *v.* Barham, 4 A. & E. 473 (31 E. C. L. R.); and cases cited *ante*, p. 659, *et seq.*

[1] Shepherd *v.* Pybus, 3 M. & Gr. 868 (42 E. C. L. R.); Camac *v.* Warriner, 1 C. B. 356 (50 E. C. L. R.); Street *v.* Blay, 2 B. & Ad. 456; Kennedy *v.* Panama, &c., Mail Co., L. R. 2 Q. B. 587, 588 (42 E. C. L. R.); Keele *v.* Wheeler, 7 M. & Gr. 663 (42 E. C. L. R.).

[2] Miles *v.* Schilizzi, 17 C. B. 619 (84 E. C. L. R.). See Bull *v.* Robinson, 10 Exch. 342, 345.

The law relating to the subject discussed *supra* may therefore be summed up thus:—Where a buyer buys a specific chattel, the maxim *Caveat emptor* applies; but where the buyer orders goods *to be supplied*, and trusts to the judgment of the seller to select goods which shall be applicable to the purpose for which they are ordered, there is an implied warranty that they shall be reasonably fit for that purpose. Judgm., Bigge *v.* Parkinson, 7 H. & N. 961; Judgm., Emmerton *v.* Mathews, Id. 593.

[3] Lamert *v.* Heath, 15 M. & W. 486 (in connection with which case see Westropp *v.* Solomon, 8 C. B. 345 (65 E. C. L. R.)); Hall *v.* Condor, 2 C. B. N. S. 22, 40, 42 (89 E. C. L. R.); Smith *v.* Neale, Id. 67, 89; Smith *v.* Scott, 6 C. B. N. S. 771, 780, 782 (95 E. C. L. R.); Hopkins *v.* Hitchcock, 14 C. B. N. S. 65 (118 E. C. L. R.); Josling *v.* Kingsford, 13 C. B. N. S. 447 (106 E. C. L. R.); Lawes *v.* Purser, 6 E. & B. 930 (88 E. C. L. R.). See Mitchell *v.* Newhall, 15 M. & W. 308; Chanter *v.* Dewhurst, 12 M. & W. 823; Taylor *v.* Stray, 2 C. B. N. S. 175 (89 E. C. L. R.), cited in Cropper *v.* Crook, L. R. 3 C. P. 198, and Whitehead *v.* Izod, L. R. 2 C. P. 238.

[4] Gompertz *v.* Bartlett, 2 E. & B. 849 (75 E. C. L. R.) (recognizing Jones *v.* Ryde, 5 Taunt. 488 (1 E. C. L. R.), and Young *v.* Cole, 3 Bing. N. C. 724

The circumstances under which the maxim *Caveat emptor* does or does not apply in regard to the quality of goods sold were recently much considered in Jones *v.* *Just,[1] and the cases bearing upon the subject were there classified as under:— [*779]

1st.—Where goods are *in esse* and may be inspected by the buyer, and there is no fraud on the part of the seller, the maxim *Caveat emptor* applies, even though the defect which exists in them is latent and not discoverable on examination, at least where the seller is neither the grower nor the manufacturer.[2] The buyer in such a case has the opportunity of exercising his judgment upon the matter; and if the result of the inspection be unsatisfactory, or if he distrusts his own judgment, he may if he chooses require a warranty. In such a case it is not an implied term of the contract of sale that the goods are of any particular quality or are merchantable.

2dly.—Where there is a sale of a definite existing chattel, specifically described, the actual condition of which is capable of being ascertained by either party, there is no implied warranty.[3]

3dly.—Where a known described and definite article is ordered of a manufacturer, although it is stated to be required by the purchaser for a particular purpose, still if the known, described, and defined thing be actually supplied, there is no warranty that it shall answer the particular purpose intended by the buyer.[4]

*4thly.—Where a manufacturer or a dealer contracts to supply an article which he manufactures or produces, or in which he deals, to be applied to a particular purpose, so that the [*780]

(32 E. C. L. R.)); Pooley *v.* Brown, 11 C. B. N. S. 566 (103 E. C. L. R.); Gurney *v.* Womersley, 4 E. & B. 133 (82 E. C. L. R.).

[1] L. R. 3 Q. B. 197.

[2] Parkinson *v.* Lee, 2 East 314, cited Judgm., Mody *v.* Gregson, L. R. 4 Ex. 54.

[3] Barr *v.* Gibson, 3 M. & W. 390.

[4] Chanter *v.* Hopkins, 4 M. & W. 399; Ollivant *v.* Bayley, 5 Q. B. 288 (48 E. C. L. R.). See Mallan *v.* Radloff, 17 C. B. N. S. 588 (112 E. C. L. R.).

The distinction must be noticed between a contract to supply goods answering a particular description, and a contract to sell specific goods with a warranty that they are similar to sample; in the former case the buyer may reject the goods if they do not answer the description, in the latter case he cannot do so. Azémar *v.* Casella, L. R. 2 C. P. 677; Heyworth *v.* Hutchinson, L. R. 2 Q. B. 447, 451, 452.

buyer necessarily trusts to the judgment or skill of the manufacturer or dealer, there is in that case an implied term or warranty that it shall be reasonably fit for the purpose to which it is to be applied.[1] In such a case the buyer trusts to the manufacturer or dealer, and relies upon his judgment.

5thly.—Where a manufacturer undertakes to supply goods manufactured by himself, or in which he deals, but which the vendee has not had the opportunity of inspecting, it is an implied term in the contract that he shall supply a merchantable article.[2]

6thly.—If, therefore, it must be taken as established that on the sale of goods by a manufacturer or dealer to be applied to a particular purpose, it is a term in the contract that they shall reasonably answer that purpose, and on the sale of an article by a manufacturer to a vendee who has not had the opportunity of inspecting it during the manufacture that it shall be reasonably fit for use, or shall be merchantable, as the case may be, it seems to follow that a similar term is to be implied on a sale by a merchant to a merchant or dealer who has had no opportunity of inspection;[3] and in the judgment from which the foregoing remarks have been extracted the proposition is thus stated, that "in every contract to supply goods [*781] of a *specified description which the buyer has had no opportunity to inspect, the goods must not only in fact answer the specific description, but must also be salable or merchantable under that description;"[4] and the maxim *Caveat emptor* consequently does not apply.

It will be collected, from what has been before said, that the vendor of a chattel may in all cases expressly limit his responsibility in respect of the quality of the thing sold, or, in other words, he may, by express stipulation, exclude that contract which the law would otherwise have implied; and, referring the reader to the

[1] Brown *v.* Edgington, 2 M. & Gr. 279 (40 E. C. L. R.); and Jones *v.* Bright, 5 Bing. 533 (15 E. C. L. R.); as to which cases see per Lush, J., Readhead *v.* Midland R. C., L. R. 2 Q. B. 418, 419, 428 (42 E. C. L. R.); s. c., 4 Id. 379 (distinguished in Francis *v.* Cockrell, L. R. 5 Q. B. 184); Macfarlane *v.* Taylor, L. R. 1 Sc. App. Cas. 245.

[2] Laing *v.* Fidgeon, 4 Camp. 169; 6 Taunt. 108 (1 E. C. L. R.); Shepherd *v.* Pybus, 3 M. & Gr. 868 (42 E. C. L. R.).

[3] Bigge *v.* Parkinson, 7 H. & N. 955.

[4] Judgm., Jones *v.* Just, L. R. 3 Q. B. 205; approved in Judgm., Mody *v.* Gregson, L. R. 4 Ex. 52.

remarks heretofore made and authorities cited as to this point,[1] we may observe, that a warranty will not necessarily be implied by law from a simple commendation of the quality of goods by the vendor; for in this case the rule of the civil law—*Simplex commendatio non obligat*[2]—has been adopted by our own, and such *simplex commendatio* will, in most cases, be regarded merely as an invitation to custom, since every vendor will naturally affirm that his own wares are good,[3] unless it appear on the evidence, or from the words used, that the affirmation at the time of sale was intended to be a warranty, or that such must be its necessary meaning:[4] it is, therefore, laid down, that in a *purchase without warranty, a man's eyes, taste, and senses must be his protection;[5] [*782] and that where the subject of the affirmation is mere matter of opinion,[6] and the vendee may himself institute inquiries into the truth of the assertion, the affirmation must be considered a "nude assertion," and it is the vendee's fault from his own laches that he is deceived.[7] Either party may, therefore, be innocently silent as to grounds open to both to exercise their judgment upon; and

[1] *Ante*, p. 659; Sharp *v.* The Great Western R. C., 9 M. & W. 7.

[2] D. 4. 3. 37; per Byles, J., 17 C. B. N. S. 597 (112 E. C. L. R.).

[3] See per Sir Jas. Mansfield, C. J., Vernon *v.* Keys, 4 Taunt. 488, 493; arg. West *v.* Jackson, 16 Q. B. 282, 283 (71 E. C. L. R.); Chandelor *v.* Lopus, Cro. Jac. 4. A. bought a wagon at sight of B., which B. affirmed to be worth much more than its real value. Held that no action would lie against B. for the false affirmation, there being no express warranty nor any evidence of fraud: Davis *v.* Meeker, 5 Johns. (U. S.) R. 354.

[4] Per Buller, J., 3 T. R. 57; Allen *v.* Lake, 18 Q. B. 560 (83 E. C. L. R.); Jones *v.* Clark, 27 L. J. Ex. 165; Vernede *v.* Weber, 1 H. & N. 311; Simond *v.* Braddon, 2 C. B. N. S. 321 (89 E. L. C. R.); Shepherd *v.* Kain, 5 B. & Ald. 240 (7 E. C. L. R.); Freeman *v.* Baker, 5 B. & Ad. 797 (27 E. C. L. R.); Budd *v.* Fairmaner, 8 Bing. 52 (21 E. C. L. R.); Coverley *v.* Burrell, 5 B. & Ald. 257 (7 E. C. L. R.).

[5] Fitz. Nat. Brev. 94; 1 Roll. Abr. 96.

[6] See Power *v.* Barham, 4 A. & E. 473 (31 E. C. L. R.); Jendwine *v.* Slade, 2 Esp. N. P. C. 572.

[7] Per Grose, J., 3 T. R. 54, 55; Bayley *v.* Merrel, Cro. Jac. 386; s. c., 3 Bulstr. 94; cited and distinguished in Brass *v.* Maitland, 6 E. & B. 470 (88 E. C. L. R.); Risney *v.* Selby, 1 Salk. 211; s. c., 2 Ld. Raym. 1118; recognized Dobell *v.* Stevens, 3 B. & C. 625 (10 E. C. L. R.); per Tindal, C. J., Shrewsbury *v.* Blount, 2 Scott N. R. 594. See Price *v.* Macauley, 2 De G., M. & G. 339.

in this case, *Aliud est celare, aliud tacere*—silence is by no means equivalent to concealment.[1]

Where, moreover, goods have been sold to a party who subsequently repudiates them, on the ground that he was laboring under some misconception as to their quality, two questions will have substantially to be submitted to the jury: first, what was the bargain actually made between the parties? and, secondly, did the vendor, by his fraud, or by any preponderance of laches on his part, mislead [*783] the purchaser as to the subject-matter of the *sale? If fraud be negatived, but it is found that the contract declared upon was not that in fact made according to the real understanding between the parties, the defendant will not, *primâ facie*, be fixed with the character of *emptor*, and the maxim, *Caveat emptor*, will not therefore apply; and in this case, both parties being innocent, the question will simply be, whose conduct has exhibited the greater laches, since on him should fall the loss.[2]

Where the vendor affirms that the thing sold has not a defect, which is a visible one, and obvious to the senses, the rule, *Caveat emptor*, is without doubt applicable—*Ea quæ commendandi causâ in venditionibus dicuntur, si palam appareant, venditorem non obligant.*[3] It is, indeed, laid down by the older authorities, that defects, apparent at the time of a bargain, are not included in a warranty,[4] however general, because they can form no subject of deceit or fraud; and, originally, the mode of proceeding for breach

[1] Per Lord Mansfield, C. J., 3 Burr. 1910; cited per Best, C. J., 3 Bing. 77 (11 E. C. L. R.); arg. Jones *v.* Bowden, 4 Taunt. 851. See Laidlaw *v.* Organ, 2 Wheaton (U. S.) R. 178; arg. 9 Id. 631, 632; per Abbott, C. J., Bowring *v.* Stevens, 2 C. & P. 341 (12 E. C. L. R.).

As to what will constitute fraudulent concealment in the view of a court of equity, see Central R. C. of Venezuela *v.* Kisch, L. R. 2 H. L. 99. By such court the maxim, *Qui vult decipi decipiatur*, is recognized: see Rynell *v.* Sprye, 1 De G., M. & G. 687, 710.

[2] Keele *v.* Wheeler, 7 M. & Gr. 665 (49 E. C. L. R.). See Gregson *v.* Ruck, 4 Q. B. 437 (45 E. C. L. R.); where specified work is contracted for but not completed, that party whose default occasioned the non-completion will fail in an action by the contractor for not being permitted to proceed with the work: Pontifex *v.* Wilkinson, 2 C. B. 349 (52 E. C. L. R.); s. c., 1 C. B. 75 (50 E. C. L. R.).

[3] D. 18. 1. 43. pr.

[4] See as to warranty, Bartholomew *v.* Bushnell, 20 Conn. (U. S.) R. 271, *post.*

of warranty was by an action of deceit, grounded on a supposed fraud; and it may be presumed, that there can be no deceit where a defect is so manifest that both parties discuss it at the time of the bargain. A party, therefore, who should buy a horse, *knowing* it to be blind in both eyes, could not sue on a general warranty of soundness.[1] However, if, without *such knowledge on the part of the purchaser, a horse is warranted sound, which, [*784] in reality, wants the sight of an eye, though this seems to be the object of one's senses, yet, as the discernment of such defects is frequently matter of skill, it has been held, that an action lies to recover damages for this imposition.[2]

We have already, in noticing the maxim as to *dolus malus*,[3] had occasion to observe generally the effect of *fraud* in vitiating every kind of contract, and, certainly, the remarks then made apply with peculiar force to the contract of sale; for not only may such contract, before its completion, be repudiated on the ground of fraud, but if the price of the goods sold has been actually paid, an action on the case will lie at suit of the purchaser to recover damages from the vendor. "If," it has been said in a case already cited,[4] "two parties enter into a contract, and if one of them, for the purpose of inducing the other to contract with him, shall state that which is not true in point of fact, *which he knew at the time he stated it not to be true*, and if, upon that statement of what is not true, and what is known by the party making it to be false, this contract is entered into by the other party, then, generally speaking, and unless there is more than that in the case, there will be at law an action open to the party entering into such contract, an action of damages grounded upon the deceit; and there will be a relief in equity to the same party to escape from the contract which he has so been inveigled into making by the false representation of the other contracting party."

[1] Per Tindal, C. J., Margetson *v.* Wright, 7 Bing. 605 (20 E. C. L. R.). See Liddard *v.* Kain, 2 Bing. 183 (9 E. C. L. R.); Holliday *v.* Morgan, 1 E. & E. 1 (102 E. C. L. R.).

[2] Butterfeilds *v.* Burroughs, 1 Salk. 211; Holliday *v.* Morgan, 1 E. & E. 1 (102 E. C. L. R).

[3] *Ante*, p. 729.

[4] Attwood *v.* Small, 6 Cl. & Fin. 444; per Lord Chelmsford, C., Central R. C. of Venezuela *v.* Kisch, L. R. 2 H. L. 121.

[*785] *"Fraud gives a cause of action if it leads to any sort of damage; it avoids contracts only where it is the ground of the contract, and where, unless it had been employed, the contract never would have been made."[1]

In the common law reports, accordingly, many cases are to be found, of which Pasley *v.* Freeman[2] is usually cited as the leading decision, which sufficiently establish that a false affirmation made by the defendant, with intent to defraud the plaintiff, whereby the plaintiff receives damage, will lay the ground of an action upon the case in the nature of deceit; and this proposition may, in fact, be considered as included in one yet more general, viz., that where there is fraud or breach of duty, and damage, the result of such fraud or breach of duty is not from an act remote and consequential, but one contemplated by the defendant at the time as one of its results, the party guilty of that fraud or negligence is responsible to the party injured.[3] Therefore, where A. sold a gun, with a fraudulent warranty to B. for the use of C., to whom such warranty was either directly or indirectly communicated, and who was injured by the bursting of the gun; it was held, that A. was liable to B. on the warranty, by reason of the privity of contract, and to C. for the injury resulting from the false representation.[4] And a chemist [*786] *compounding an article sold for a particular purpose, and knowing of the purpose for which it is bought, will be

[1] Per Lord Wensleydale, Smith *v.* Kay, 7 H. L. Cas. 775–76; citing Small *v.* Attwood, 6 Cl. & F. 232.

"Contemporaneous fraudulent statements avoid the contract:" per Byles, J., Hotson *v.* Browne, 9 C. B. N. S. 445 (99 E. C. L. R.).

[2] 3 T. R. 51; Com. Dig., "*Action upon the Case for a Deceit*" (A. 1); Moens *v.* Heyworth, 10 M. & W. 147; Murray *v.* Mann, 2 Exch. 538. See Pontifex *v.* Bignold, 3 Scott N. R. 390.

[3] Judgm., Langridge *v.* Levy, 2 M. & W. 532; s. c. (affirmed in error), 4 M. & W. 337; George *v.* Skivington, L. R. 5 Ex. 1; Pilmore *v.* Hood, 5 Bing. N. C. 97 (35 E. C. L. R.); Taylor *v.* Ashton, 11 M. & W. 401. See Mummery *v.* Paul, 1 C. B. 316 (50 E. C. L. R.).

[4] Langridge *v.* Levy, 2 M. & W. 519, 529, 532; s. c., 4 Id. 337 (explained per Maule, J., Howard *v.* Shepherd, 9 C. B. 312 (67 E. C. L. R.); and per Willes, J., Collis *v.* Seldon, L. R. 3 C. P. 498, and approved in Alton *v.* Midland R. C., 19 C. B. N. S. 239, 245 (115 E. C. L. R.)); Eastwood *v.* Bain, 3 H. & N. 738; Farrant *v.* Barnes, 11 C. B. N. S. 553 (103 E. C. L. R.); Winterbottom *v.* Wright, 10 M. & W. 109; Priestley *v.* Fowler, 3 M. & W. 1; Blakemore *v.* Bristol and Exeter R. C., 8 E. & B. 1035 (92 E. C. L. R.), and cases cited *post*.

liable to an action on the case for unskillfulness and negligence in the manufacture of it, causing damage to the person using it, and for whose use the chemist knew that it was meant.[1]

In order, however, to entitle a person to recover for damage sustained in consequence of misrepresentation, it must appear that the communication, or false affirmation, which occasioned the damage, was made *willfully*. Where a party, who is applied to for his opinion, gives an honest, although mistaken, one, it is all that can be expected: it is not enough to show that the representation is false, and that it turned out to be altogether unfounded, if the party making it acted upon a fair and reasonably well-grounded belief that it was true.[2]

It must, however, be observed, that there may be a fraudulent representation sufficient to avoid a contract, or to form the ground of an action, without actual active declaration from the party contracting: there may be a sort of tacit acquiescence in a representation fraudulent within the party's knowledge, or in the communication of a falsehood by a third person, originally flowing from himself.[3] *In cases belonging to this class, a maxim applies, which is well known and admitted to be correct in [*787] many of the ordinary occurrences of life—*Qui tacet consentire videtur*[4]—silence implies consent;[5] and such consent may be inferred from the party's subsequent conduct.[6] For instance, defendant, being about to sell a public-house, falsely represented to B., who

[1] George *v.* Skivington, L. R. 5 Ex. 1.

[2] Haycraft *v.* Creasy, 2 East 92; cited, Adamson *v.* Jarvis, 4 Bing. 73, 74 (13 E. C. L. R.); Shrewsbury *v.* Blount, 2 Scott N. R. 588; per Parke, B., 11 M. & W. 413. In connection with this subject, see also Longmeid *v.* Holliday, 6 Exch. 761, 766; cited in Francis *v.* Cockrell, L. R. 5 Q. B. 194; Gerhard *v.* Bates, 2 E. & B. 476 (75 E. C. L. R.).

[3] See per Coltman, J., 5 Bing. N. C. 109 (35 E. C. L. R.); Wright *v.* Crookes, 1 Scott N. R. 685.

[4] Jenk. Cent. 32. See in illustration of this maxim, Morrish *v.* Murrey, 13 M. & W. 52; Lucy *v.* Mouflet, 5 H. & N. 229; Cooper *v.* Law, 6 C. B. N. S. 502, 508 (95 E. C. L. R.); Morgan *v.* Evans, 3 Cl. & Fin. 205; Marq. of Salisbury *v.* Great Northern R. C., 5 C. B. N. S. 174 (94 E. C. L. R.).

[5] For instance, "where there is a duty to speak, and the party does not, an assent may be inferred from his silence:" per Bramwell, B., 4 H. & N. 798.

[6] Jenk. Cent. 32, 68, 226; Hunsden *v.* Cheney, 2 Vern. 150, offers an illustration of this maxim. See also 2 Inst. 305; Richardson *v.* Dunn, 2 Q. B. 218 (42 E. C. L. R.); Wright *v.* Crookes, 1 Scott N. R. 685.

had agreed to purchase, that the receipts were 180*l.* per month, and B., to the knowledge of defendant, communicated this representation to plaintiff, who became the purchaser instead of B.; it was held, that an action lay against defendant at suit of the plaintiff, who had sustained damage in consequence of having acted on the representation.[1]

There is, however, no implied duty cast on the owner of a house being in a ruinous and unsafe condition to inform a proposed tenant that it is unfit for habitation, nor will an action of deceit lie against him for omitting to disclose the fact.[2]

Before proceeding further, it may be proper to distinguish between a warranty and a representation. A warranty forms a part [*788] of the contract, but a representation *may be altogether collateral to the contract, and not incorporated with it.[3] If, indeed, the representation be of a fact, without which the other party would not have entered into the contract at all,[4] or at least on the same terms, it may, if untrue, avoid the contract, or give a right to sue for damages on the ground of fraud. For instance, in the case of an action by the purchaser of a public-house, who has been induced to buy or to give a greater price for the good-will of the house, by a representation of the extent of its business, if that representation turns out to be false, it has never been doubted that the contract may be avoided, and that the buyer may recover back

[1] Pilmore *v.* Hood, 5 Bing. N. C. 97 (35 E. C. L. R.). See Dobell *v.* Stevens, 3 B. & C. 623 (10 E. C. L. R.).

[2] Keates *v.* Earl of Cadogan, 10 C. B. 591 (70 E. C. L. R.); distinguishing Hill *v.* Gray, 1 Stark. N. P. C. 434 (2 E. C. L. R.), as containing the element of "aggressive deceit."

[3] Hence the main question in the cause may be, What was the real contract between the parties? See for instance Foster *v.* Smith, 1 H. & N. 156. And if verbal stipulations are afterwards embodied in a written contract, the parties will of course be bound by *that* alone, subject to be interpreted by the usages of trade: Harnor *v.* Groves, 15 C. B. 667, 674 (80 E. C. L. R.). As illustrating the difference between a warranty and a description, collateral representation or mere expression of an opinion or intention, see Cranston *v.* Marshall, 5 Exch. 395; Taylor *v.* Bullen, Id. 779; Hopkins *v.* Tanqueray, 15 C. B. 130 (80 E. C. L. R.); with which compare Percival *v.* Oldacre, 18 C. B. N. S. 398 (114 E. C. L. R.); Stuckley *v.* Baily, 1 H. & C. 405; Benham *v.* United Guarantee, &c., Co., 7 Exch. 744; Barker *v.* Windle, 6 E. & B. 675 (88 E. C. L. R.); Gorrissen *v.* Perrin, 2 C. B. N. S. 681 (89 E. C. L. R.), and cases there cited.

[4] Bannerman *v.* White, 10 C. B. N. S. 844 (100 E. C. L. R.).

his money as had and received to his use.[1] It must be borne in mind, however, that "the intention of the parties governs in the making and in the construction of all contracts. If the parties so intend, the sale may be absolute, with a warranty superadded; or the sale may be conditional, to be null if the warranty is broken."[2]

*It is further material to observe, with reference to the distinction between an action upon the case for a false representation and one purely *ex contractu* upon a warranty, that, to support the former, three circumstances must combine:—1st, it must appear that the representation was contrary to the fact; 2dly, that the party making it knew it to be contrary to the fact; and, 3dly, that it was the false representation which gave rise to the contracting of the other party.[3] [*789]

In the latter case above specified, viz., that of an action *ex contractu* for breach of warranty, it is not necessary that all those three circumstances should concur in order to ground an action for damages at law or a claim for relief in a court of equity; for where a warranty is given by which the party undertakes that the article sold shall in point of fact be such as it is described, no question can be raised upon the *scienter*, upon the fraud or willful misrepresentation.[4]

Conformably to what has been above said, it was observed in reference to a life policy, by Lord Cranworth, C.,[5] that "there is a great distinction between that which amounts to what is called a warranty and that which is merely a representation inducing a party to enter into a contract. Thus, if a person effecting a policy of insurance says, 'I warrant such and such things which are here stated,' and that is part of the contract, then, whether they are

[1] See, per Lord Abinger, C. B., 6 M. & W. 378; per Parke, B., Id. 373; Pickering *v.* Dowson, 4 Taunt. 779, 786, cited Kain *v.* Old, 2 B. & C. 634 (9 E. C. L. R.); Mummery *v.* Paul, 1 C. B. 316 (50 E. C. L. R.); Pilmore *v.* Hood, 5 Bing. N. C. 97 (35 E. C. L. R.).

[2] Judgm., 10 C. B. N. S. 860 (100 E. C. L. R.); Judgm., Behn *v.* Burness, 32 L. J. Q. B. 206; Russell *v.* Nicolopulo, 8 C. B. N. S. 362 (98 E. C. L. R.).

[3] Per Lord Brougham, Attwood *v.* Small, 6 Cl. & Fin. 444, 445; Milne *v.* Marwood, 15 C. B. 778 (80 E. C. L. R.); Behn *v.* Kemble, 7 C. B. N. S. 260 (97 E. C. L. R.).

[4] 6 Cl. & Fin. 444, 445.

[5] Anderson *v.* Fitzgerald, 4 H. L. Cas. 503–4; Wheelton *v.* Hardisty, 8 E. & B. 185, 232; Jones *v.* Provincial Insur. Co., 3 C. B. N. S. 65 (91 E. C. L. R.).

material or not is quite unimportant: the party must adhere to his [*790] warranty whether material *or immaterial. But if the party makes no warranty at all, but simply makes a certain statement, if that statement has been made *bonâ fide*, unless it is material it does not signify whether it is false or not false. Indeed, whether made *bonâ fide* or not, if it is not material the untruth is quite unimportant. * * * If there is no fraud in a representation of that sort, it is perfectly clear that it cannot affect the contract; and even if material, but there is no fraud in it, and it forms no part of the contract, it cannot vitiate the right of the party to recover." In applying the principle thus set forth, reference must of course be made to the wording of the policy and the declaration of the assured upon which it may be founded.[1]

With respect to an action upon the case for false representation, although fraud and an intent to deceive the plaintiff are imputed in the declaration to the defendant, and although it is expressly laid down that "fraud and falsehood must concur to sustain this action,"[2] yet the law will *infer* an improper motive if what the defendant says *is false within his own knowledge* and is the occasion of damage to the plaintiff.[3] In Polhill *v.* Walter[4] a bill was presented for acceptance at the *office of the drawee, who was [*791] absent. A., who lived in the same house with the drawee, being assured by one of the payees that the bill was perfectly regular, was induced to write on the bill an acceptance, as by the procuration of the drawee, believing that the acceptance would be sanctioned and the bill paid by the latter. The bill was dishonored when due, and the endorsee having, on proof of the above facts, been non-

[1] Fowkes *v.* Manchester and London Life, &c., Assur. Co., 32 L. J. Q. B. 153; Judgm., 3 C. B. N. S. 85 (91 E. C. L. R.).

[2] Per Gibbs, C. J., Ashlin *v.* White, Holt N. P. C. 387 (3 E. C. L. R.).

[3] Per Tindal, C. J., Foster *v.* Charles, 6 Bing. 483 (19 E. C. L. R.); s. c., 7 Bing. 105 (20 E. C. L. R.); Murray *v.* Mann, 2 Exch. 538; Gerhard *v.* Bates, 2 E. & B. 476, 491 (75 E. C. L. R.); Tatton *v.* Wade, 18 C. B. 371 (114 E. C. L. R.); Thom *v.* Bigland, 8 Exch. 725; Randell *v.* Trimen, 18 C. B. 786 (86 E. C. L. R.); per Lord Campbell, C. J., Wilde *v.* Gibson, 1 H. L. Cas. 633; see Crawshay *v.* Thompson, 5 Scott N. R. 562; Rodgers *v.* Nowill, 5 C. B. 109 (57 E. C. L. R.), and cases cited *ante*, p. 786.

[4] 3 B. & Ad. 114 (23 E. C. L. R.), cited Smout *v.* Ilbery, 10 M. & W. 10, and 5 Scott N. R. 596, 599; and per Parke, B., 2 Exch. 541; Eastwood *v.* Bain, 3 H. & N. 738.

suited in an action against the drawee, sued A. for falsely, fraudulently, and deceitfully representing that he was authorized to accept by procuration; the jury, on the trial, negatived all fraud in fact, yet the defendant was held to be liable, because he had made a representation untrue to his own knowledge; and the plaintiff, acting upon the faith of that representation, and giving credit to the acceptance which, in the ordinary course of business, was its natural and necessary result, had in consequence thereof sustained damage. It was observed in this case, that the defendant must be taken to have *intended* that *all* persons should give credit to the acceptance to whom the bill might be offered in the course of circulation, and that the plaintiff was one of those persons.

The case just cited will suffice to show that there may be legal fraud, without proof of any morally fraudulent *motive* for the particular act from which it is inferred; and we may observe, generally, that it is fraud in law if a party makes representations which he knows to be false, and from which injury ensues, although the motive from which the representations proceeded may not have been bad; and that the person making them will nevertheless be responsible for the consequences.[1] Fraud *may, moreover, consist as well in the *suppressio veri*—the suppression of what is true, [*792] as in the *suggestio falsi*—the representation or suggestion of what is false,[2] of which one familiar instance presents itself in the case of a sea policy of insurance, which is made upon an implied contract between the parties, that everything material known to the assured shall be disclosed by him, and which instrument will be invalidated if any material fact be withheld. "When a policy of insurance," as observed by Lord Abinger,[3] "is said to be a contract *uberrimæ*

[1] Per Tindal, C. J., 7 Bing. 107 (20 E. C. L. R.); cited Judgm., Rawlings *v.* Bell, 1 C. B. 959, 990 (50 E. C. L. R.).

[2] Per Chambre, J., Tapp *v.* Lee, 3 B. & P. 351; cited 6 Bing. 403 (19 E. C. L. R.).

[3] 6 M. & W. 379; Carter *v.* Boehm, 3 Burr. 1905; Harrower *v.* Hutchinson, L. R. 4 Q. B. 523, 536, and cases there cited. Lindenau *v.* Desborough, 8 B. & C. 586 (15 E. C. L. R.); Carr *v.* Montefiore, 5 B. & S. 408 (117 E. C. L. R.). A fact known to the underwriter need not be mentioned by the assured, for *Scientia utrinque par pares contrahentes facit:* 3 Burr. 1910; Bates *v.* Hewitt, L. R. 2 Q. B. 609. See Mackintosh *v.* Marshall, 11 M. & W. 116; Stokes *v.* Cox, 1 H. & N. 533; s. c., Id. 320, and cases there cited.

Wheelton *v.* Hardisty, 8 E. & B. 285, 232 (92 E. C. L. R.), is important as regards the effect of fraud upon a life policy; *et vide ante*, p. 789.

fidei, this only means that the good faith which is the basis of all contracts is more especially required in that species of contract in which one of the parties is necessarily less acquainted with the details of the subject of the contract than the other. Now, nothing is more certain, than that the concealment or misrepresentation, whether by principal or agent, by design or by mistake, of a material fact, however innocently made, avoids the contract on the ground of a legal fraud."[1] The rule, however, here stated does not extend to guarantees—the concealment which will vitiate such an instrument must be fraudulent.[2]

[*793] *The necessity of showing "*moral fraud*," and of proving the *scienter* in an action on the case for misrepresentation, has been much discussed.

In Cornfoot *v.* Fowke,[3] the plaintiff declared in *assumpsit* for the non-performance of an agreement to take a ready-furnished house. The defendant pleaded that he had been induced to enter into the contract by the fraud and covin of the plaintiff; and on this plea issue was joined. It appeared on the trial, that the plaintiff, being the owner of the house in question, employed an agent to let it, and the defendant, being in treaty with such agent for hiring, asked him if there was "anything objectionable about the house," upon which the agent replied, "nothing whatever." On the day after signing the agreement, the defendant discovered that the adjoining house was a brothel, and on that ground declined to fulfill the contract. It further appeared that the plaintiff was fully aware of the existence of the brothel, but that the agent was not. It was held by the majority of the Court of Exchequer (*dissentiente* Lord Abinger, C. B.), that it was not sufficient to support the plea that the representation turned out to be untrue, but that, for that purpose, it ought to have been proved to have been *fraudulently* made; whereas, the principal, though he knew the fact, was not cognizant of the representation being made, and never directed the agent to

[1] *Acc.*, Anderson *v.* Thornton, 8 Exch. 425; Russell *v.* Thornton, 6 H. & N. 140; s. c., 4 Id. 788; Holland *v.* Russell, 4 B. & S. 14 (116 E. C. L. R).

[2] North British Insur. Co. *v.* Lloyd, 10 Exch. 523.

[3] 6 M. & W. 358. Compare with Cornfoot *v.* Fowke, *supra*, the judgment in Smout *v.* Ilbery, 10 M. & W. 1; and Collen *v.* Wright, 7 E. & B. 301 (90 E. C. L. R.); s. c., 8 Id. 647 (92 E. C. L. R.); Spedding *v.* Nevell, L. R. 4 C. P. 212. See also Wilde *v.* Gibson, 1 H. L. Cas. 605.

make it. The agent, though he made a misrepresentation, yet did not know it to be one at the time he made it, but gave his answer *bonâ fide. It is obvious that the decision in this case, which has been much canvassed,[1] in no degree conflicts [*794] with the proposition which seems consistent with reason and authority,[2] that "if an agent is guilty of fraud in transacting his principal's business, the principal is responsible"[3]—that "the fraud of the agent who makes the contract is the fraud of the principal."[4] And, "with respect to the question whether a principal is answerable for the act of his agent in the course of his master's business, and for his master's benefit, no sensible distinction," it has been observed,[5] "can be drawn between the case of fraud and the case of any other wrong. The general rule is, that the master is answerable for every such wrong of the servant or agent as is committed in the course of the service, and for the master's benefit, though no express command or privity of the master can be proved."

In Fuller *v.* Wilson, which was an action on the case for a fraudulent misrepresentation of the value of a house, the facts were as follows:—The defendant, being the owner of a house in the city, employed her attorney to put it in a course of being sold by auction; he described it to the auctioneer as being free from rates and taxes, and it was bought by the plaintiff on that representation, *for 600*l.* It was, in fact, subject to rates and taxes, amounting to about 16*l.* on a rent of 100*l.*, and would have [*795] been sold for no more than 470*l.* if that representation had not been made. The plaintiff brought his action for this difference of price. It appeared that the defendant had, in fact, made no representation at all, and that her attorney, who made the representation, did not know it to be false. The action was, nevertheless, held to

[1] In Wheelton *v.* Hardisty, 8 E. & B. 270 (92 E. C. L. R.), Lord Campbell, C. J., intimates that "the voice of Westminster Hall was rather in favor of the dissentient Chief Baron."

[2] In Udell *v.* Atherton, 7 H. & N. 172 (where the authorities are collected), the judges of the Court of Exchequer were equally divided in opinion as to the mode of applying the proposition *supra*, to the facts before them. See Judgm., Barwick *v.* English Joint Stock Bank, L. R. 2 Ex. 265.

[3] Per Parke, B., Murray *v.* Mann, 2 Exch. 540, and in Cornfoot *v.* Fowke, 6 M. & W. 373.

[4] Judgm., Wheelton *v.* Hardisty, 8 E. & B. 260 (92 E. C. L. R.).

[5] Judgm., Barwick *v.* English Joint Stock Bank, L. R. 2 Ex. 265.

be maintainable, on this express ground, that, whether there was moral fraud or not, if the purchaser was actually deceived in his bargain, the law would relieve him from it; that the principal and his agent were, for this purpose, completely identified; and that the question to be considered was, not what was passing in the mind of either, but whether the purchaser was, in fact, deceived by them, or either of them.[1]

It seems, however, clear that the principle on which the judgment given by the Court of Queen's Bench in the above case was founded is at variance with that which must now be considered as established: for, in the subsequent [*796] *case of Collins *v.* Evans,[2] it is expressly laid down that "a mere representation, untrue in fact, but honestly made," will not suffice to form the groundwork of an action on the case for misrepresentation; and in Ormrod *v.* Huth,[3] where the question as to "moral fraud" was much discussed, case for a false and fraudulent representation respecting the quality of goods sold by sample was held not maintainable without showing that such representation was false to the knowledge of the seller, or that he acted fraudulently or against good faith in making it. "The rule," said Tindal, C. J., delivering judgment, "which is to be derived from all the cases, appears

[1] Fuller *v.* Wilson, 3 Q. B. 58 (43 E. C. L. R.). The facts of this case were afterwards turned into a special verdict; and on the facts *so stated* the judgment of the Court of Queen's Bench was reversed in the Exchequer Chamber; s. c., 3 Q. B. 68 and 1009 (43 E. C. L. R.). The court of error did not, however, enter into the principle on which the decision below was founded, nor into the question discussed in Cornfoot *v.* Fowke, *supra.* See also Humphrys *v.* Pratt, 5 Bligh N. S. 154, which may be supported on another ground, as pointed out by Tindal, C. J., 5 Q. B. 829 (48 E. C. L. R.); Railton *v.* Matthews, 10 Cl. & Fin. 934; cited North British Insur. Co. *v.* Lloyd, 10 Exch. 529, 533. As to statements by an agent under a misconception of facts, see particularly Smout *v.* Ilbery, 10 M. & W. 1; Collen *v.* Wright, 7 E. & B. 301 (90 E. C. L. R.); s. c., 8 Id. 647 (92 E. C. L. R.); Spedding *v.* Nevell, L. R. 4 C. P. 212.

Adverting to Cornfoot *v.* Fowke, and Fuller *v.* Wilson, *supra*, Wilde, B., observes: "The artificial identification of the agent and principal by bringing the words of the one side by side with the knowledge of the other, induced the apparent logical consequence of fraud. On the other hand, the real innocence of both agent and principal repelled the notion of a constructive fraud in either:" Udell *v.* Atherton, 7 H. & N. 184.

[2] In error, 5 Q. B. 820 (48 E. C. L. R.), reversing judgm. in s. c., Id. 804.

[3] 14 M. & W. 651.

to us to be, that where, upon the sale of goods, the purchaser is satisfied, without requiring a warranty (which is a matter for his own consideration), he cannot recover upon a mere representation of the quality by the seller, unless he can show that the representation was bottomed in fraud. If, indeed, the representation was false to the knowledge of the party making it, this would in general be conclusive evidence of fraud; but if the representation was honestly made, and believed at the time to be true by the party making it, though not true in point of fact, we think this does not amount to fraud in law, but that the rule of *Caveat emptor* applies and the representation itself does not furnish a ground of action."

Further, the correctness of the principle laid down in Collins *v.* Evans, above cited, was recognized by the Court of Queen's Bench in Barley *v.* Walford,[1] which shows, that, if A. knowingly utter a falsehood to B., with *intent to defraud B., and with a [*797] view to his own profit, and B., giving credit to the falsehood, is injured thereby, he may maintain an action against A. for the false representation ; though, as there observed by Lord Denman, C. J., "if every untrue statement which produces damage to another would found an action at law, a man might sue his neighbor for any mode of communicating erroneous information, such (for example) as having a conspicuous clock too slow, since plaintiff might be thereby prevented from attending to some duty or acquiring some benefit."

So, in another case, bearing on the law of principal and agent, Parke, B., observed, that, to make out fraud, some willful misrepresentation must be shown, and that a mere untruth innocently told is not sufficient.[2]

Nor does it seem at variance with the proposition just stated to affirm—in accordance with some high authorities—that if a man having the means of knowledge in regard to a certain fact, but neglecting to avail himself of them, undertakes to publish as true

[1] 9 Q. B. 197, 207, 208 (58 E. C. L. R.).

[2] Atkinson *v.* Pocock, 12 Jur. 60; s. c., 1 Exch. 796; referring to Chandelor *v.* Lopus, Cro. Jac. 4, and Cornfoot *v.* Fowke, 6 M. & W. 358. "It seems to us that a statement false in fact, but not false to the knowledge of the party making it, as in Polhill *v.* Walter, nor made with any intention to deceive, will not support an action, unless from the nature of the dealing between the parties a contract to indemnify can be implied:" Judgm., Rawlings *v.* Bell, 1 C. B. 959, 960 (50 E. C. L. R.).

that which he does not know to be true, he will be responsible if it should turn out to be false.[1] "If," says Maule, J.,[2] "a man, having no knowledge whatever on the subject, takes upon himself to represent a certain state of facts to exist, he does so at his peril; and if it be done either with a view *to secure some benefit to himself, or to deceive a third person, he is in law guilty of a fraud; for he takes upon himself to warrant his own belief of the truth of that which he so asserts. Although the person making the representation may have no knowledge of its falsehood, the representation may still have been fraudulently made." And again —"I apprehend it to be the rule of law," says Lord Cairns,[3] "that if persons take upon themselves to make assertions as to which they are ignorant, whether they are true or untrue, they must, in a civil point of view, be held as responsible as if they had asserted that which they knew to be untrue." In the case here put, an element or admixture of moral fraud is quite apparent.

[*798]

It seems established law that victuallers, brewers, and other common dealers in victuals, who, in the ordinary course of their trade, sell provisions unfit to be the food of man, are civilly liable to the vendee, without proof of fraud on their part, and in the absence of any express warranty of the soundness of the thing sold; though such liability would not attach to a private person, not following any of the above trades, who sells an unwholesome article for food.[4] And a salesman offering for sale a carcass with a defect of which he is not only ignorant but has not any means of knowledge (the defect being latent) does not as a matter of law impliedly warrant that the carcass is fit for human food, and is not bound to refund the price should it turn out not to be so.[5] It has been held, also, that a person affirming himself to have authority to act as agent, who has it not, *may be liable, *ex contractu*, in respect of damage thereby caused to another.[6] But the case last cited in no degree affects the discussion as to moral fraud.

[*799]

[1] See, per Cresswell, J., Jarrett *v.* Kennedy, 6 C. B. 322 (60 E. C. L. R.); per Lord Mansfield, C. J., Pawson *v.* Watson, Cowp. 785.

[2] Evans *v.* Edmunds, 13 C. B. 786 (76 E. C. L. R.).

[3] Reese River Silver Mining Co. *v.* Smith, L. R. 4 H. L. 79, 80.

[4] Burnby *v.* Bollett, 16 M. & W. 644, and authorities there cited.

[5] Emmerton *v.* Mathews, 7 H. & N. 586; cited Judgm., Jones *v.* Just, L. R. 3 Q. B. 202. See 23 & 24 Vict. c. 84.

[6] Collen *v.* Wright, 7 E. & B. 301 (90 E. C. L. R.); s. c., 8 E. & B. 647 (92

The remarks immediately preceding may suffice to indicate some of the more important qualifications of the rule *Caveat emptor*, as applied to the quality and description of goods sold. It is now proposed to consider briefly how far this maxim holds with reference to the title of the vendor to goods which form the subject-matter of a sale or contract. According to the civil law, it is clear that a warranty of title was implied on every sale of a chattel;[1] and this doctrine of the civil law seems to have been partially adopted by the American courts of judicature.[2] It is, however, now established that there is "by the law of England no warranty of title in the actual contract of sale, any more than there is of quality. The rule of *Caveat emptor* applies to both; but if the vendor knew that he had no title, and concealed that fact, he was always held responsible to the purchaser as for a fraud, in the same way that he is if he knew of the defective quality."[3] But although such is the general rule of *our law, the circumstances attending the sale of a chattel may necessarily import a warranty of title. [*800] Thus, if articles are bought in a shop professedly carried on for the sale of goods, the shop-keeper would, doubtless, be considered as warranting "that those who purchase will have a good title to keep the goods purchased. In such a case the vendor sells 'as his own,' and that is what is equivalent as a warranty of title."[4]

As between vendor and purchaser, indeed, the result of the older authorities seems to be, that, where a person sells goods to which in fact he has no title, he will not be responsible to the purchaser if the latter be subsequently disturbed in his possession by the true

E. C. L. R.); Spedding *v.* Nevell, L. R. 4 C. P. 212; Simons *v.* Patchett, 7 E. & B. 568 (90 E. C. L. R.); Randell *v.* Trimen, 18 C. B. 786 (86 E. C. L. R.). See Wilson *v.* Miers, 10 C. B. N. S. 348 (100 E. C. L. R.).

[1] D. 21. 2. 1. Voet ad Pand., 6th ed., vol. i., p. 922. "By the civil law vendors were bound to warrant both the title and estate against all defects, whether they were or were not cognizant of them." 1 Sugd. V. & P., 11th ed., p. 2; this doctrine was however qualified as there stated.

[2] Kent Com., 7th ed., vol. 2, pp. 608, 609. See Defreeze *v.* Trumper, 1 Johns. (U. S.) R. 274; Rew *v.* Barber, 3 Cowen (U. S.) R. 272.

[3] Judgm., Morley *v.* Attenborough, 3 Exch. 510; cited per Pollock, C. B., Bandy *v.* Cartwright, 8 Exch. 916; and commented on per Lord Campbell, C. J., Sims *v.* Marryatt, 17 Q. B. 290, 291 (79 E. C. L. R.); per Bovill, C. J., Bagueley *v.* Hawley, L. R. 2 C. P. 625, 628; Chapman *v.* Speller, 14 Q. B. 621 (68 E. C. L. R.); per Martin, B., Aiken *v.* Short, 1 H. & N. 213.

[4] Judgm., 3 Exch. 513; Eichholz *v.* Bannister, 17 C. B. N. S. 708 (112 E. C. L. R.).

owner, unless there be either a warranty or a fraudulent misrepresentation as to the property in the goods by the vendor.[1] This doctrine has, however, been much restricted in its practical operation by holding that a simple assertion of title is equivalent to a warranty,[2] and generally that any representation may be tantamount thereto, if the party making it appear from the circumstances under which it was made *to have had an intention to warrant, or to have meant that the representation should be understood as a warranty.[3] [*801]

Upon the whole, then, we may safely conclude, that with regard to the sale of ascertained chattels, "there is not any implied warranty of either *title* or *quality*,[4] unless there are some circumstances beyond the mere fact of a sale, from which it may be implied."[5]

[1] See Peto *v.* Blades, 5 Taunt. 657 (1 E. C. L. R.); Jones *v.* Bowden, 4 Taunt. 847; Sprigwell *v.* Allen, Aleyn R. 91; and Paget *v.* Wilkinson, cited 2 East 448, n. (*a*). In Early *v.* Garrett, 9 B. & C. 932, Littledale, J., observes, "It has been held, that where a man sells a horse as his own (Sprigwell *v.* Allen, *supra*), when in truth it is the horse of another, the purchaser cannot maintain an action against the seller, unless he can show that the seller knew it to be the horse of the other at the time of the sale; the *scienter* or fraud, being the gist of the action, *where* there is no warranty; for there the party takes upon himself the knowledge of the title to the horse, and of his qualities." See Robinson *v.* Anderton, Peake N. P. C. 94; Street *v.* Blay, 2 B. & Ad. 456; cited Dawson *v.* Collis, 10 C. B. 527, 532 (70 E. C. L. R.); and in Kennedy *v.* Panama, &c., Mail Co., L. R. 2 Q. B. 587.

[2] See Collen *v.* Wright, 7 E. & B. 301 (90 E. C. L. R.); s. c., 8 Id. 647 (92 E. C. L. R.), and cases cited *ante*, p. 799, n. 6, which proceeded on a similar principle.

[3] Crosse *v.* Gardner, Carth. 90; Medina *v.* Stoughton, 1 Salk. 210; cited, per Patteson, J., 17 Q. B. 293 (79 E. C. L. R.). See Bartholomew *v.* Bushnell, 20 Conn. (U. S.) R. 271; Furnis *v.* Leicester, Cro. Jac. 474; Judgm., Adamson *v.* Jarvis, 4 Bing. 73 (13 E. C. L. R.). See, per Buller, J., 3 T. R. 57, 58; Sanders *v.* Powell, 1 Lev. 129. As to an express warranty, see per Lord Ellenborough, C. J., Williamson *v.* Allison, 2 East 451, which was an action on the case for breach of warranty of goods; Gresham *v.* Postan, 2 C. P. 540 (12 E. C. L. R.); Denison *v.* Ralphson, 1 Ventr. 365.

[4] In support of this proposition as regards *quality*, see the cases *ante*, pp. 779, *et seq.* In Hill *v.* Balls, 2 H. & N. 304, Martin, B., remarks, "In my view of the law, where there is no warranty, the rule *Caveat emptor* applies to sales, and except there be deceit, either by a fraudulent concealment or fraudulent misrepresentation, no action for unsoundness lies by the vendee against the vendor upon the sale of a horse or other animal."

[5] Judgm., Hall *v.* Conder, 2 C. B. N. S. 40 (89 E. C. L. R.); recognizing Morley *v.* Attenborough, 3 Exch. 500.

With respect, also, "to *executory* contracts of purchase and sale, *where the subject is unascertained*, and is afterwards to be conveyed, it would probably be implied that both parties meant that a good title to that subject should be transferred, in the same manner as it would be implied, under similar circumstances, that a merchantable article was to be supplied. Unless goods, which the party could enjoy as his own, and make full use of, were delivered, the contract would not be performed. The purchaser could not be bound to accept if he discovered the defect of title before delivery; and if he did, and the goods were recovered from him, he would not be bound to pay, or, *having paid, he would be entitled to recover [*802] back the price as on a consideration which had failed."[1]

We may add to the above brief *resumé* of the law in regard to the application of the maxim *Caveat emptor* on a sale of goods, that it has been laid down as a general proposition, that, "if goods be sold by a person who is not the owner, and the owner be found out and be paid for those goods, the person who sold them under pretended authority has no right to call upon the defendant to pay him also."[2] In an action, however, by an auctioneer for the price of a horse, sold by him in that capacity and delivered to the purchaser, it was held to be no answer to plead that the horse was sold by the plaintiff, as an auctioneer, agent, and trustee for A., and that after the sale, and before suit brought, defendant paid to A. the purchase-money.[3]

We have already had to observe, that, as a general rule, no man can acquire a title to chattels from a person who has himself no title to them except only by a *bonâ fide* sale in market overt.[4]

[1] Judgm., 3 Exch. 509–10; per Lord Campbell, C. J., Sims *v.* Marryatt, 17 Q. B. 291 (79 E. C. L. R.).

As to implied warranty of title to a thing pledged, see Cheeseman *v.* Exall, 6 Exch. 341.

On a contract for the sale of goods in the possession of a third person, the vendor impliedly undertakes that they shall be delivered, on application, within a reasonable time: Buddell *v.* Green, 27 L. J. Ex. 33.

[2] Judgm., Allen *v.* Hopkins, 13 M. & W. 102; citing Dickinson *v.* Naul, 4 B. & Ad. 638 (24 E. C. L. R.). See Walker *v.* Mellor, 11 Q. B. 478 (63 E. C. L. R.).

[3] Robinson *v.* Rutter, 4 E. & B. 954 (82 E. C. L. R.).

[4] Peer *v.* Humphrey, 2 A. & E. 495 (29 E. C. L. R.); per Abbott, C. J., Dyer *v.* Pearson, 3 B. & C. 42 (10 E. C. L. R.); *post*, p. 804.

The second vendee of a chattel cannot, in general, stand in a better situation than his vendor.[1] For instance, if a master intrusts his servant with the care of plate or other valuables, and the servant [*803] *sells them, still, unless they are sold in market overt, the master may recover them from the purchaser.[2] And we find it laid down that "the owner of property wrongfully taken has a right to follow it, and, subject to a change by sale in market overt, treat it as his own, and adopt any act done to it."[3] It has been said, indeed, that if the real owner of goods suffer another to have possession of his property, or of those documents which are the *indicia* of property, and thus enable him to hold himself out to the world as having not the possession only but the property, then, perhaps, a sale by such a person would bind the true owner.[4] Though it seems that the proposition here stated ought to be limited to cases where the person who had possession of the goods was one who, from the nature of his employment, might be taken *primâ facie* to have the right to sell.[5] And where a transfer of goods was obtained under a delivery order without authority and by false pretences, it was held that mere possession of the goods, with no further *indicia* of title than the delivery order, would not suffice to entitle a *bonâ fide* pawnee of the person fraudulently obtaining possession of the goods from the true owner, to resist the claim of the latter in an action of trover.[6]

[*804] Moreover, where parties contract with a known agent *or factor intrusted with goods for their purchase, even with notice of being such agent, and pay for the same in pursuance of

[1] Per Littledale, J., Dixon *v.* Yates, 5 B. & Ad. 339 (27 E. C. L. R.); *ante*, p. 470, *et seq.*

[2] Per Abbott, C. J., Baring *v.* Corrie, 2 B. & Ald. 143; per Holroyd, J., Id. 149; Cro. Jac. 197.

[3] Per Pollock, C. B., Neate *v.* Harding, 5 Exch. 350; citing Taylor *v.* Plumer, 3 M. & S. 562 (30 E. C. L. R.).

[4] Per Abbott, C. J., 3 B. & C. 42 (10 E. C. L. R.); per Bayley, J., 6 M. & S. 23, 24; per Best, C. J., 3 Bing. 145 (11 E. C. L. R.). See also Gordon *v.* Ellis, 8 Scott N. R. 290.

[5] Per Martin, B., Higgins *v.* Burton, 26 L. J. Ex. 343, 344; citing Chitt. Contr. 6th ed., 344.

[6] Kingsford *v.* Merry, 1 H. & N. 503; s. c., 11 Exch. 577, as to which case see per Bramwell, B., Higgons *v.* Burton, 26 L. J. Ex. 334; per Willes, J., Fuentes *v.* Montis, L. R. 3 C. P. 282, 283.

the contract, it is enacted that such contract and payment shall be binding upon and good against the real owner, if made in the ordinary course of business, and without notice that the agent is not authorized to sell;[1] and the like protection has been extended to *bonâ fide* advances upon goods and merchandise in the hands of an agent when made under similar circumstances.[2] It has been held, that, in order to bring a case within the protection of the second section of the stat. 6 Geo. 4, c. 94, there must be not only a possession by the factor of the document upon which the advance is made, but an actual intrusting of him with such document by the owner of the goods, or a possession under such circumstances as that an actual intrusting may be inferred therefrom.[3]

A sale of goods, even by a party who has himself only the possession, and not the property, as a thief or a finder, will be valid against the rightful owner, provided it be made in market overt during the usual market hours, unless such goods were the property of the king,[4] or unless the buyer knew that the property was not in the seller, or there was any other fraud in the transaction.[5]

[*805] *Market overt, we may observe, is defined to be a fair or market held at stated intervals in particular places, by virtue of a charter or prescription;[6] it has been characterized as "an open, public, and legally constituted market."[7] In the city of London, however, the custom is, that every shop is, except on Sunday, market overt in regard to the goods usually and publicly sold therein;[8] and a sale within the city of London, in an open

[1] 6 Geo. 4, c. 94, ss. 2, 4.

[2] 5 & 6 Vict. c. 39, ss. 1, 3. See Baines *v.* Swainson, 4 B. & S. 270 (116 E. C. L. R.); Fuentes *v.* Montis, L. R. 4 C. P. 93.

[3] Hatfield *v.* Phillips, 14 M. & W. 665; s. c., 12 Cl. & Fin. 343.

[4] Chitt. Pre. Cr. 195, 285. The doctrine of our law as to the effect of a sale in market overt is stated per Cockburn, C. J., Crane *v.* London Dock Co., 5 B. & S. 313, 318 (117 E. C. L. R.), where a sale by sample was held not entitled to the privileges of a sale in market overt.

[5] 2 Com. by Broom & Hadley 172; 2 Inst. 713; Hilton *v.* Swan, 5 Bing. N. C. 413 (35 E. C. L. R.).

[6] Jacob, Law Dict., tit. "*Market;*" 2 Inst. 713. Case of Market Overt, 5 Rep. 84.

[7] Per Jervis, C. J., 18 C. B. 601 (86 E. C. L. R.).

[8] Jacob, Law Dict., tit. "*Market;*" Harris *v.* Shaw, Cas. temp. Hardw. 349; and authorities cited *supra.*

shop, of goods usually dealt in there, is a sale in market overt, though the premises are described in evidence as a warehouse, and are not sufficiently open to the street for a person on the outside to see what passes within.[1] By stat. 1 Jac. 1, c. 21, it is enacted, that the sale of any goods wrongfully taken to any pawnbroker in London, or within two miles thereof, shall not alter the property; for this, being usually a clandestine trade, is therefore made an exception to the general rule.[2]

With respect to stolen goods, the stat. 24 & 25 Vict. c. 96, s. 100,[3] enacts, that, if any person, guilty of any such [*806] *felony or misdemeanor as therein mentioned, in stealing, taking, obtaining, extorting, embezzling, or converting or disposing of, or in knowingly receiving any chattel, money, valuable security, or other property whatsoever, shall be indicted by or on behalf of the owner, his executor, or administrator, and convicted, in such case, the property shall be restored to the owner or his representative, and the court shall have power to award writs of restitution, or to order restitution in a summary manner.[4] But this statute would not extend to charge a person who purchased the goods in market overt after the felony, and had disposed of them again before the conviction.[5] Where, however, a purchase of stolen property was

[1] Lyons v. De Pass, 11 A. & E. 326 (39 E. C. L. R.). But a sale by public auction at a horse repository out of the city of London is not a sale in market overt: Lee v. Bayes, 18 C. B. 599 (86 E. C. L. R.).

[2] See also stat. 39 & 40 Geo. 3, c. 99, ss. 12, 13. A metropolitan police magistrate may order goods unlawfully pawned to be delivered up to their owner: 2 & 3 Vict. c. 72, s. 28.

[3] This section likewise contains a proviso that restitution shall not be awarded in the case of any valuable security which shall have been *bonâ fide* paid or discharged by the party liable to the payment thereof, or in that of a negotiable instrument taken by transfer or delivery for a just and valuable consideration, without notice or cause to suspect that the same had been stolen.

The above section does not apply to the case where a trustee, banker, or agent intrusted with the possession of goods, or documents of title to goods, is prosecuted for any misdemeanor under the Act.

[4] The order of restitution under the corresponding enactment previously in force (7 & 8 Geo. 4, c. 29, s. 57) was held to be "cumulative to the ordinary remedy by action," and "not a condition precedent to such remedy:" Scattergood v. Sylvester, 15 Q. B. 506, 511 (69 E. C. L. R.). See also 30 & 31 Vict. c. 35, s. 9.

[5] Horwood v. Smith, 2 T. R. 750.

made *bonâ fide*, but *not* in market overt, and the plaintiff gave notice to the defendant, who subsequently sold the goods in market overt, after which the plaintiff prosecuted the felon to conviction, the plaintiff was held entitled to recover from the defendant the value of the property in trover.[1] It is, however, now well established that the obligation which the law imposes on a plaintiff to prosecute the party who has stolen his goods before proceeding for their recovery, does not apply where the action is against a third party, innocent of the felony.[2]

[*807] *One rather peculiar case may here properly be mentioned, which is not only illustrative of the general legal doctrines regulating the rights of purchasers, but likewise of another principle,[3] which we have already considered in connection with criminal law, viz., where a man buys a chattel which, unknown to himself and to the vendor, contains valuable property. In a modern case,[4] on this subject, a person purchased, at a public auction, a bureau, in a secret drawer of which he afterwards discovered a purse containing money, which he appropriated to his own use. It appeared that, at the time of the sale, no person knew that the bureau contained anything whatever. The court held, that, although there was a delivery of the bureau, and a lawful property in it thereby vested in the purchaser, yet that there was no delivery so as to give him a lawful possession of the purse and money, for the vendor had no intention to deliver it, nor the vendee to receive it; both were ignorant of its existence; and when the purchaser discovered that there was a secret drawer containing the purse and money, it was a simple case of finding,[5] and then the law applicable to all cases of finding would apply to this. It was further observed,

[1] Peer *v.* Humphrey, 2 A. & E. 495 (29 E. C. L. R.). See also Parker *v.* Patrick, 5 T. R. 175, which was decided under stat. 21 Hen. 8, c. 11, repealed by 7 & 8 Geo. 4, c. 27, s. 1. As to the statutes respecting stolen horses (2 P. & M. c. 7, and 31 Eliz. c. 12), see 2 Bla. Com., 21st ed., 450; Oliphant's Law of Horses, 2d ed., p. 45.

[2] Lee *v.* Bayes, 18 C. B. 599, 602 (86 E. C. L. R.); following White *v.* Spettigue, 13 M. & W. 603, and overruling a dictum of Littledale, J., in Peer *v.* Humphrey, *supra.*

[3] *Actus non facit reum nisi mens sit rea*—*ante*, p. 306.

[4] Merry *v.* Green, 7 M. & W. 623.

[5] See Armory *v.* Delamirie, 1 Stra. 504; Bridges *v.* Hawkesworth, 21 L. J. Q. B. 75 (which is important with reference to the above subject); Buckley *v.* Gross, 32 L. J. Q. B. 129.

that the old rule,[1] that "if one lose his goods, and another find them, though he convert them, *animo furandi*, to his own use, it is no larceny," has undergone, in more recent times, some limitations.[2] [*808] One is, that *if the finder knows who the owner of the lost chattel is, or if, from any mark upon it, or the circumstances under which it is found, the owner could be reasonably ascertained, then the taking of the chattel, with a guilty intent, and the subsequent fraudulent conversion to the taker's own use, may constitute a larceny. To this class of decisions the case under consideration was held to belong, *unless* the plaintiff had reason to believe that he bought the contents of the bureau, if any, and consequently had a *colorable* right to the property in question.

Lastly, we may observe, that negotiable instruments form the most important exception to the rule, that a valid sale cannot be made except in market overt of property to which the vendor has no right. In the leading case on this subject, it was decided, that property in a bank-note passes, like that in cash, by delivery, and that a party taking it *bonâ fide*,[3] and for value, is entitled to retain it as against a former owner from whom it has been stolen.[4] It is, however, a general rule, that no title can be obtained through a forgery, and hence a party from whom a promissory note was stolen, and whose endorsement on it was subsequently forged, was held entitled to recover the amount of the note from an innocent [*809] holder for value.[5] And if a person obtains in good faith *change for a check which turns out to be worthless, the loss must fall on him.[6] It should further be observed, that every

[1] 3 Inst. 108.

[2] See this rule with its qualifications considered at length: Broom's Com., 4th ed., 955 *et seq.*

[3] See Hilton *v.* Swan, 5 Bing. N. C. 413 (35 E. C. L. R.), and the next note.

[4] Miller *v.* Race, 1 Burr. 452. The reader is referred for full information on this subject, and also on that of *bona fides* in the holder, to the note appended to the above case, Smith L. C., 6th ed., vol. 1, p. 477; Judgm., Guardians of Lichfield Union *v.* Greene, 1 H. & N. 884, 889; *ante*, p. 470.

[5] Johnson *v.* Windle, 3 Bing. N. C. 225, 229 (32 E. C. L. R.); Gurney *v.* Womersley, 4 E. & B. 133 (82 E. C. L. R.); Robarts *v.* Tucker, 16 Q. B. 560 (71 E. C. L. R.) (distinguished in Woods *v.* Thiedemann, 1 H. & C. 478, 491, 495); Simmons *v.* Taylor, 2 C. B. N. S. 528 (89 E. C. L. R.).

[6] Per Lord Campbell, C. J., Timmins *v.* Gibbins, 18 Q. B. 726 (83 E. C. L. R.); Woodland *v.* Fear, 7 E. & B. 519, 521 (90 E. C. L. R.).

Where a banker pays a forged check or letter of credit, the banker must,

negotiable instrument, being in its nature precisely analogous to a bank-note payable to bearer, is subject to the same rule of law;—whoever is the holder of such an instrument has power to give title to any person honestly acquiring it.[1]

In the preceding remarks upon the maxim *Caveat emptor*, we have confined our attention to those classes of cases to which alone it appears to be strictly applicable, and in connection with which reference to it is, in practice, most frequently made. This maxim may, indeed, be said to have some application under circumstances altogether dissimilar from those presenting themselves in the various decisions above alluded to; where, for instance, a question arises as to what amounts to an acceptance of goods; or as to the performance of conditions precedent to the vesting of the property, or to the right of action; or, where some specified act has to be done by the vendor, in order to perfect the transfer of the things sold; or wherever the right and title to property are disputed as between the original owner and the assignee or bailee of some subsequent holder; the principle set forth by the maxim *Caveat emptor* may, perhaps, be thought in some measure applicable. A consideration of the topics just specified, however, although necessary in a treatise upon contracts generally, would evidently have been out of place in the present volume, and irrelevant to its immediate *design. We have not, therefore, extended our inquiries beyond the subject of warranty on the sale or demise of [*810] property, and have examined those decisions only which seemed calculated to throw light upon the question, whether or not the vendee has a remedy against the vendor for a defect either in the title to or quality of the subject-matter of the sale.

in general, bear the loss: British Linen Co. *v.* Caledonian Insur. Co., 4 Macq. Sc. App. Cas. 107; Young *v.* Grote, 4 Bing. 253 (13 E. C. L. R.).

[1] Per Abbott, C. J., Gorgier *v.* Mieville, 3 B. & C. 47 (10 E. C. L. R.).

QUICQUID SOLVITUR, SOLVITUR SECUNDUM MODUM SOLVENTIS—QUICQUID RECIPITUR, RECIPITUR SECUNDUM MODUM RECIPIENTIS.

(Halk. M., p. 149.)

Money paid is to be applied according to the intention of the party paying it: and money received, according to that of the recipient.[1]

"According to the law of England, the debtor may, in the first instance, appropriate the payment—*solvitur in modum solventis;* if he omit to do so, the creditor may make the appropriation[2]—*recipitur in modum recipientis;* but if neither make any appropriation, the law appropriates the payment to the earlier debt;"[3] "where a creditor receives without objection what is offered by [*811] *his debtor, *solvitur in modum solventis*, it must be implied that the debtor paid it in satisfaction;"[4] where "the party to whom the money is offered does not agree to apply it according to the expressed will of the party offering it, he must refuse and stand upon the rights which the law gives him."[5] And again—"Wherever there is an intention expressed by the payer that the money is paid upon a particular account, and the payee receives it under a different intention, it is the duty of the latter to give the former an opportunity to retract." Such "was the rule

[1] For more detailed information than can here be offered in regard to this maxim the reader is referred to a learned article by Mr. N. Lindley, in the Law Mag. for Aug. 1855, p. 21.

[2] "Where a claim consists of several items, the party making the tender has a right of appropriation; but if he omits to make any appropriation, the right to appropriate is transferred to the other party;" per Wilde, C. J., Hardingham *v.* Allen, 5 C. B. 797 (57 E. C. L. R.); and in Wood *v.* The Copper Miners' Co., 7 Id. 935 (62 E. C. L. R.).

[3] Per Tindal, C. J., Mills *v.* Fowkes, 5 Bing. N. C. 461 (35 E. C. L. R.); per Bayley, J., 2 B. & C. 72 (9 E. C. L. R.); per Sir L. Shadwell, V.-C. E., Greenwood *v.* Taylor, 14 Sim. 522; Toulmin *v.* Copland, 2 Cl. & Fin. 681. See James *v.* Child, 2 Cr. & J. 678; Newmarch *v.* Clay, 14 East 239; Id. 243 (*c*).

[4] Per Tindal, C. J., Webb *v.* Weatherby, 1 Bing. N. C. 505 (27 E. C. L. R.); Croft *v.* Lumley,. 6 H. L. Cas. 672, 694, 697, 714, 722, where the mode of applying the maxim *supra* was much discussed.

[5] Judgm., Croft *v.* Lumley, 5 E. & B. 680 (85 E. C. L. R.); s. c., 6 H. L. Cas. 672, 706. As to evidence of assent to an appropriation, see Beale *v.* Caddick, 2 H. & N. 326.

of the civil law—*Dum in re agendâ hoc fiat: ut vel creditori liberum sit non accipere vel debitori non dare, si alio nomine exsolutum quis eorum velit; cœterum postea non permittitur.* What is intended must be said at the time."[1]

Thus succinctly, in the above proposition, has the law relative to the principal maxim been explained, and, in accordance with this explanation, it has been held, that, where the defendant, being indebted to the plaintiff for goods supplied to his wife *dum sola*, and to himself after the marriage, made a payment without any specific appropriation, the plaintiff might apply the money in discharge of the debt contracted by the wife *dum sola;*[2] that where part of a debt was barred by the Statute of Limitations, a payment of money made generally might be applied in liquidation of that part;[3] *and that a creditor receiving money without any specific appropriation by the debtor, shall be permitted in a court [*812] of law to apply it to the discharge of a prior and purely equitable debt.[4] Moreover, it has been held that the creditor is not bound to state at the time when a payment is made, to what debt he will apply it, but that he may make such application at any period before the matter comes under the consideration of a jury.[5]

A case further illustrating the practical operation of the doctrine respecting the appropriation of payments may here be presented from a modern judgment:[6]—Suppose a contract, under seal, whereby a builder contracts to build a house, and the owner of the land covenants to pay 1000*l.* as the price of the work, and also to

[1] Per Byles, J., Kitchin *v.* Hawkins, L. R. 2 C. P. 31.

[2] Goddard *v.* Cox, 2 Stra. 1194.

[3] Mills *v.* Fowkes, 5 Bing. N. C. 455 (35 E. C. L. R.); Williams *v.* Griffiths, 5 M. & W. 300. See Baildon *v.* Walton, 1 Exch. 617. In Walker *v.* Butler, 6 E. & B. 510 (88 E. C. L. R.), Erle, J., observes, "I do not by any means assent to the doctrine that where there are two debts existing, and a payment is made not specifically appropriated to either, there is necessarily no sufficient evidence of a payment on account of either of those debts to take it out of the Statute of Limitations. It must depend on the special circumstances of each case. In general there would be evidence to go to the jury of a payment on account of both debts."

[4] Bosanquet *v.* Wray, 6 Taunt. 597 (1 E. C. L. R.). In Goddard *v.* Hodges, 1 Cr. & M. 33, it was held that a general payment must be applied to a prior legal, and not to a subsequent equitable, demand.

[5] Philpott *v.* Jones, 2 A. & E. 41 (29 E. C. L. R.).

[6] Judgm., 3 Exch. 306, 307.

pay for any extra work authorized *in writing* by the architect. During the progress of the work the architect authorizes extra work to the amount of 500*l.*, which the builder completes in a proper manner and to the satisfaction of the owner of the land, but *without any authority in writing*. Suppose, further, that the owner of the land pays the builder from time to time 1200*l.* on account generally, and that more than six years after the whole had been [*813] completed, the builder brings an action of *covenant against the owner for non-payment of the balance, and the owner pleads payment. Under such circumstances, the owner of the land might be taken to have entered into a new parol contract to pay for the extras, independently of his liability under the deed. There would, in the case here put, be two debts due from the owner of the land, one a debt arising by deed, the other a debt on simple contract, and the doctrine as to the application of indefinite payments would apply. The creditor being entitled to say to his debtor, "I have applied 500*l.*, part of the 1200*l.*, in discharge of the simple contract debt, which would otherwise be barred by the Statute of Limitations; what I seek to recover is the balance of the original contract sum of 1000*l.*" This doctrine, however, never has been held "to authorize a creditor receiving money on account, to apply it towards the satisfaction of what does not, nor ever did, constitute any legal or equitable demand against the party making payments."

But although it is true that, where there are distinct accounts and a general payment, and no appropriation made at the time of such payment by the debtor, the creditor may apply it to which account he pleases; yet, where the accounts are treated by the parties as one entire account, this rule does not apply.[1] For instance, in the case of a banking account, where all the sums paid in form one blended fund, the parts of which have no longer any distinct existence, there is no room for any other appropriation than that which arises from the order in which the receipts and payments take [*814] place, *and are carried into the account. Presumably, it is the sum first paid in that is first drawn out. It is the first item on the debit side of the account that is discharged or reduced by the first item on the credit side. The appropriation

[1] Per Bayley, J., Bodenham *v.* Purchas, 2 B. & Ald. 45. See Labouchere *v.* Tupper, 11 Moo. P. C. C. 198.

is made by the very act of setting the two items against each other. Upon that principle all accounts current are settled, and particularly cash accounts.[1] In like manner, where one of several partners dies, and the partnership is in debt, and the surviving partners continue their dealings with a particular creditor, and the latter joins the transactions of the old and the new firm in one entire account, then the payments made from time to time by the surviving partners must be applied to the old debt. In that case it is to be presumed that all the parties have consented that it should be considered as one entire account, and that the death of one of the partners has produced no alteration whatever.[2] It must be borne in mind, notwithstanding the preceding remarks, that, although the payment of money on account generally, without making a specific appropriation of it, would, in many cases, go to discharge the first part of an account, yet that rule *cannot be taken to be conclusive—it is evidence of an appropriation only; and other evidence may be adduced, as of a particular mode of dealing, or of an express stipulation between the parties, which may vary the application of the rule.[3] [*815]

Where a person has two demands, one recognized by law, the other arising on a matter forbidden by law, and an unappropriated payment is made to him, the law will afterwards appropriate it to the demand which it acknowledges, and not to the demand which it prohibits.[4]

[1] Per Sir Wm. Grant, M. R., Clayton's Case, 1 Mer. 608; cited per Erle, C. J., 8 C. B. N. S. 786 (98 E. C. L. R.); Pennell v. Deffell, 4 De G., M. & G. 372; per Lord Lyndhurst, C., Pemberton v. Oakes, 4 Russ. 169; Bodenham v. Purchas, 2 B. & Ald. 39; arg. Labouchere v. Tupper, 11 Moo. P. C. C. 212; Judgm., Henniker v. Wigg, 4 Q. B. 794 (45 E. C. L. R.). As to Clayton's Case, *supra*, see also the remarks in the Law Mag. (Aug. 1855), p. 36.

Ordinarily, "where two parties settle an account of moneys due to each side, cross items allowed in such account may be treated as payments:" Judgm., Roberts v. Shaw, 4 B. & S. 56 (116 E. C. L. R.).

[2] Per Bayley, J., Simpson v. Ingham, 2 B. & C. 72 (9 E. C. L. R.); Smith v. Wigley, 3 Mo. & Sc. 174 (30 E. C. L. R.).

As to evidence of adoption of the liabilities of an old firm by the new copartnership, see Rolfe v. Flower, L. R. 1 P. C. 27.

[3] Judgm., Wilson v. Hirst, 4 B. & Ad. 767 (24 E. C. L. R.); Henniker v. Wigg, 4 Q. B. 792 (45 E. C. L. R.). See Ex parte Johnson, 3 De G., M. & G. 218.

[4] Judgm., Wright v. Laing, 3 B. & C. 171 (10 E. C. L. R.). Payment into

Again, where a person bought two parcels of goods of a broker, the property of different persons, and paid *generally* to the broker a sum larger than the amount of either demand, but less than the two together, and afterwards the broker stopped payment; it was held that such payment ought to be equitably apportioned as between the several owners of the goods sold, who were only respectively entitled to recover the difference from the buyer.[1]

The following remarks made in a modern case will serve to show some additional important limitations of the maxim under consideration:—"If, in the course of dealing between A. and B., various debts are from time to time incurred, and payments made by B. to A., and no acknowledgment is made by A., nor inquiry by B. [*816] *how the payments are appropriated, the law will presume that the priority of debt will draw after it priority of payment and satisfaction, on the ground that the oldest debt is entitled to be first satisfied. That doctrine is recognized in Devaynes *v.* Noble,[2] but the principle was never applied to cases where the obligations were *alio jure*, nor to other cases, as, for instance, where, in dealings between B. and C., the latter directs B. to receive moneys due to him, the law will not presume an appropriation of these moneys to the payment of a debt due to A. and B. in the absence of any specific directions."[3]

Where a bill of exchange or promissory note has been given by a debtor to his creditor, it is not unfrequently a matter of some difficulty to determine whether the giving of such instrument should be considered as payment, and as operating to extinguish the original debt; or whether it should be regarded merely as security for its payment, and as postponing the period of payment until the bill or note becomes due. Upon this subject, which is one of great practical importance, the correct rule is thus laid down by Lord Langdale, M. R.:—"The debt," says his lordship, "may be con-

court is an admission of, and will be applied to, a legal demand only; Ribbans *v.* Crickett, 1 B. & P. 264. See Philpott *v.* Jones, 2 A. & E. 41 (29 E. C. L. R.). Where there has been a running cash and bill account between a bankrupt and a banking company, "the court will appropriate the early payments to the early items of the account, and to the legal and not the illegal part of the demand:" Ex parte Randleson, 2 D. & C. 534, 540.

[1] Favenc *v.* Bennett, 11 East 36.

[2] 1 Meriv. 608.

[3] Per Lord Brougham, C., Nottidge *v.* Prichard, 2 Cl. & Fin. 393.

sidered as actually paid if the creditor, at the time of receiving the note, has agreed to take it in payment of the debt, and to take upon himself the risk of the note being paid; or if, from the conduct of the creditor, or the special circumstances of the case, such a payment is legally to be implied. But in the absence of any special circumstances, throwing the risk of the note upon the creditor, his receiving the note in lieu of present payment of the debt is no more *than giving extended credit, postponing the demand for immediate payment, or giving time for payment on a [*817] future day, in consideration of receiving this species of security. Whilst the time runs, payment cannot legally be enforced, but the debt continues till payment is actually made; and if payment be not made when the time has run out, payment of the debt may be enforced as if the note had not been given. If payment be made at or before the expiration of the extended time allowed, it is then for the first time that the debt is paid."[1]

QUI PER ALIUM FACIT PER SEIPSUM FACERE VIDETUR.

(Co. Litt. 258 a.)

He who does an act through the medium of another party is in law considered as doing it himself.

The above maxim enunciates the general doctrine on which the law relative to the rights and liabilities of principal and agent depends. It can, however, in this volume be but briefly and cursorily considered.

Where a contract is entered into with A., *as agent for* B., it is deemed, in contemplation of law, to have been entered into with B., and the principal is, in most cases, the proper party to sue[2] or be

[1] Sayer *v.* Wagstaff, 5 Beav. 415; recognized, In re Harries, 13 M. & W. 3; per Lord Kenyon, C. J., Stedman *v.* Gooch, 1 Esp. 5; cited 6 Scott N. R. 945. See also as to what may amount to or constitute payment, Turney *v.* Dodwell, 3 E. & B. 136 (77 E. C. L. R.); Thomas *v.* Cross, 7 Exch. 728, 732; Underwood *v.* Nicholls, 17 C. B. 239 (84 E. C. L. R.); Pollard *v.* Ogden, 2 E. & B. 459 (75 E. C. L. R.); per Erle, C. J., Martin *v.* Reid, 11 C. B. N. S. 735 (103 E. C. L. R.); Wright *v.* Hickling, L. R. 2 C. P. 199.

[2] To entitle a person to sue upon a contract, it must be shown that he himself made it, or that the contract was made on his behalf by an agent au-

[*818] sued for a breach of *such contract,—the agent being viewed simply as the medium through which it was effected:[1] *Qui facit per alium facit per se.* For instance, the defendant was employed by its owner to sell a certain farm, and entered into a written agreement to sell the farm to the plaintiff for 2700*l.*, without naming the seller. 100*l.* deposit in part of the purchase-money was paid by the plaintiff to the defendant; two days afterwards the former signed a contract for sale by S. (the owner), to himself, whereby he agreed to pay on its execution 100*l.* as a deposit, for which S. undertook to pay interest till the completion of the purchase. For want of a title in S. the contract was subsequently rescinded; but the defendant, before he had notice of the rescission, paid S. 50*l.*, retaining the other 50*l.*, though without the consent of S., under an agreement with S. to give him (the defendant) one half of any sum he might get for the farm over 2600*l.* The court held, that the plaintiff could not recover in an action against the defendant any part of the 100*l.* paid as above stated.[2]

The following instances, which are of ordinary occurrence and practical importance, may be mentioned as illustrative of the rule, which, for certain purposes, identifies the agent with the principal:—Payment to an authorized agent,[3] as an auctioneer, in the regular [*819] *course of his employment,[4] is payment to his principal.[5] Thus:—M. employed R. & Co., bankers in Edinburgh, to

thorized to act for him at the time, or whose act has been subsequently ratified and adopted by him: Watson *v.* Swann, 11 C. B. N. S. 756 (103 E. C. L. R.).

[1] Thus, in Depperman *v.* Hubersty, 17 Q. B. 766 (79 E. C. L. R.), Coleridge, J., observes: "Here an avowed agent of a principal sues another avowed agent of the same principal; and the action must fail for want of privity of contract between the two parties to the suit." See Lee *v.* Everest, 2 H. & N. 285, 291; Cooms *v.* Bristol and Exeter R. C., 3 H. & N. 1.

[2] Hurley *v.* Baker, 16 M. & W. 26.

[3] Bostock *v.* Hume, 8 Scott N. R. 590.

[4] See Mews *v.* Carr, 1 H. & N. 484.

[5] Sykes *v.* Giles, 5 M. & W. 645; approved in Williams *v.* Evans, L. R. 1 Q. B. 352 (which shows that an auctioneer has no authority to receive payment by a bill of exchange).

"The general rule of law is, that where a creditor's agent is bound to pay the whole amount over to the principal, he must receive it in cash from the debtor; and that a person who pays such agent, and who wishes to be safe,

obtain for him payment of a bill drawn on a person resident at Calcutta. R. & Co. accepted the employment, and wrote, promising to credit M. with the money when received. R. & Co. transmitted the bill, in the usual course of business, to C. & Co., of London, and by them it was forwarded to India, where it was duly paid. R. & Co. wrote to M., announcing the fact of its payment, but never actually credited him in their books with the amount; the house in India having failed, it was held that R. & Co. were the agents of M., to obtain payment of the bill; that payment having been actually made, they became *ipso facto* liable to him for the amount received, and that he could not be called on to suffer any loss occasioned by the conduct of the sub-agents, as between whom and himself no privity existed. "To solve the question in this case," said Lord Cottenham, "it is not necessary to go deeper than to refer to the maxim, *Qui facit per alium facit per se.* R. & Co. agreed for consideration to apply for payment of the bill, they necessarily employed agents for that purpose who received the amount, their receipt was in *law a receipt by them, and subjected them to all the consequences. The appellant with whom they so agreed cannot have anything to do with the conduct of those whom they so employed, or with the state of the account between different parties engaged in this agency."[1]

[*820]

The above case shows that the receipt of money by an authorized agent will charge the principal,[2] and, in like manner, a tender made to an authorized agent will in law be regarded as made to the principal;—thus, where the evidence showed that the plaintiff directed his clerk not to receive certain money from his debtor if it should be offered to him, that the money was offered to the clerk, and that he, in pursuance of his master's orders, refused to receive it; upon the principle *Qui facit per alium facit per se*, the tender to the servant was held to be a good tender to the master.[3] Payment also by an agent as such is equivalent to payment by the

must see that the mode of payment does enable the agent to perform this his duty." Per Bovill, C. J., Bridges *v.* Garrett, L. R. 4 C. P. 587–8, and cases there cited.

See Catterall *v.* Hindle, L. R. 2 C. P. 368; Stephens *v.* Badcock, 3 B. & Ad. 354 (23 E. C. L. R.); cited arg. Whyte *v.* Rose, 3 Q. B. 498 (43 E. C. L. R.); Parrott *v.* Anderson, 7 Exch. 93.

[1] Mackersy *v.* Ramsays, 9 Cl. & Fin. 818, 850.

[2] See also Thompson *v.* Bell, 10 Exch. 10.

[3] Moffat *v.* Parsons, 5 Taunt. 307 (1 E. C. L. R.).

principal. Where, for example, a covenant was "to pay or cause to be paid," it was held, that the breach was sufficiently assigned by stating that the defendant had not paid, without saying, "or caused to be paid;" for, had the defendant caused to be paid, he had paid, and, in such a case, the payment might be pleaded in discharge.[1] So payment to an agent, if made in the ordinary course of business, will operate as payment to the principal.[2] On the same principle, the delivery of goods to a carrier's servant is a delivery of them to the carrier;[3] and the [*821] *delivery of a check to the agent of A. is a delivery to A.[4] Railway companies, moreover, are not to be placed in a different condition from all other carriers. They will be bound in the course of their business as carriers by the contract of the agent whom they put forward as having the management of that branch of their business. So that, where it appeared from the evidence, that certain goods were undoubtedly received by a railway company, for transmission on some contract or other, and that the only person spoken to respecting such transmission was the party stationed to receive and weigh the goods; it was held, that this party must have an implied authority to contract for sending the goods, and that the company were consequently bound by that contract.[5] It has been held, that the station-master of a railway company has not, though the general manager of the company has,[6] implied authority to bind the company by a contract for surgical attendance on an injured passenger.[7]

[1] Gyse *v.* Ellis, 1 Stra. 228.

[2] See Williams *v.* Deacon, 4 Exch. 397; Kaye *v.* Brett, 5 Exch. 269; Parrott *v.* Anderson, 7 Exch. 93; Underwood *v.* Nicholls, 17 C. B. 239 (84 E. C. L. R.).

[3] Dawes *v.* Peck, 8 T. R. 330; Brown *v.* Hodgson, 2 Camp. 36; per Lord Ellenborough, C. J., Griffin *v.* Langfield, 3 Camp. 254; Fragano *v.* Long, 4 B. & C. 219 (10 E. C. L. R.); Great Western R. C. *v.* Goodman, 12 C. B. 313 (74 E. C. L. R.). Moreover, a delivery to the carrier is in law (except under special circumstances) a delivery to the consignee; see the above cases; Dunlop *v.* Lambert, 6 Cl. & Fin. 600, and in cases cited 3 Com. by Broom & Hadley 161–3. But an acceptance by the carrier is not an acceptance by the consignee: per Parke, B., Johnson *v.* Dodgson, 2 M. & W. 656.

[4] Samuel *v.* Green, 10 Q. B. 262 (59 E. C. L. R.).

[5] Pickford *v.* Grand Junction R. C., 12 M. & W. 766; Heald *v.* Carey, 11 C. B. 977 (73 E. C. L. R.).

[6] Walker *v.* Great Western R. C., L. R. 2 Ex. 228.

[7] Cox *v.* Midland Counties R. C., 3 Exch. 268. See Poulton *v.* London and South-Western R. C., L. R. 2 Q. B. 534.

Where an agent for the sale of goods contracts in his own name, and *as a principal*, the general rule is, that an action may be supported, either in the name of the party by whom the contract was made, and privy to it, or *of the party on whose behalf and [*822] for whose benefit it was made.[1] Even where the agent is a factor, receiving a *del credere* commission, the principal may, at any period after the contract of sale has been concluded, demand payment of the sum agreed on to himself, unless such payment had previously been made to the factor, in due course, and according to the terms of the contract.[2] The following rules, respecting the liability of parties on a contract for the purchase of goods, are likewise illustrative of the doctrine under consideration, and are here briefly stated on account of their general importance and applicability:—1st, an agent, contracting as principal, is liable in that character; and, if the real principal be known to the vendor at the time of the contract being entered into by the agent, dealing in his own name, and credit be given to such agent, the latter only can be sued on the contract.[3] 2dly, if the principal be unknown at the time of contracting, whether the agent represent himself as such or not, the vendor may, within a reasonable time after discovering the principal, debit either at his election.[4] *But, 3dly, if a person act as agent without authority, [*823] he is personally and solely liable; and if he exceed his

[1] Per Bayley, J., Sargent *v.* Morris, 3 B. & Ald. 280 (5 E. C. L. R.); Sims *v.* Bond, 5 B. & Ad. 393 (27 E. C. L. R.); Duke of Norfolk *v.* Worthy, 1 Camp. 337; Cothay *v.* Fennell, 10 B. & C. 672 (21 E. C. L. R.); Bastable *v.* Poole, 1 Cr., M. & R. 413; per Lord Abinger, C. B., 5 M. & W. 650; Garrett *v.* Handley, 4 B. & C. 656 (56 E. C. L. R.); distinguished in Agacio *v.* Forbes, 14 Moo. P. C. C. 160, 170, 171; see Ramazotti *v.* Bowring, 7 C. B. N. S. 851 (97 E. C. L. R.); Ferrand *v.* Bischoffsheim, 4 Id. 710; Higgins *v.* Senior, 8 M. & W. 844.

[2] Hornby *v.* Lacy, 6 M. & S. 172; Morris *v.* Cleasby, 4 M. & S. 566, 574; Sadler *v.* Leigh, 4 Camp. 195; Grove *v.* Dubois, 1 T. R. 112; Scrimshire *v.* Alderton, 2 Stra. 1182.

[3] Paterson *v.* Gandasequi, 15 East 62; Addison *v.* Gandasequi, 4 Taunt. 574; Franklin *v.* Lamond, 4 C. B. 637 (56 E. C. L. R.). See Smith *v.* Sleap, 12 M. & W. 585, 588.

[4] Thomson *v.* Davenport, 9 B. & C. 78 (17 E. C. L. R.); cited, per Martin, B., Barber *v.* Pott, 4 H. & N. 767; Smethurst *v.* Mitchell, 1 E. & E. 622, 631 (102 E. C. L. R.); Heald *v.* Kenworthy, 10 Exch. 734; Risbourg *v.* Bruckner, 3 C. B. N. S. 812 (91 E. C. L. R.); per Park, J., Robinson *v.* Gleadow, 2

authority, the principal is not bound by acts done beyond the scope of his legitimate authority.[1] If A. employs B. to work for C., without warrant from C., A. is liable to pay for the work done;[2] nor would it in this case make any difference if B. believed A. to be in truth the agent of C.; for, in order to charge the last-mentioned party, the plaintiff must prove a contract with him, either express or implied, and with him in the character of a principal, directly, or through the intervention of an agent.[3]

The question, how far an agent is personally liable, who, having in fact no authority, professes to bind his principal, has on various occasions been discussed. There is no doubt, it was observed in a recent judgment,[4] that, in the case of a fraudulent misrepresentation [*824] *of his authority, with an intention to deceive, the agent would be personally responsible;[5] but independently of this, which is perfectly free from doubt, there seem to be still two other classes of cases, in which an agent, who without actual

Bing. N. C. 161, 162 (29 E. C. L. R.); Paterson *v.* Gandasequi, 15 East 62; Wilson *v.* Hart, 7 Taunt. 295 (2 E. C. L. R.); Higgins *v.* Senior, 8 M. & W. 384; Humfrey *v.* Dale, 7 E. & B. 266 (90 E. C. L. R.); s. c., E., B. & E. 1004 (96 E. C. L. R.).

[1] Woodin *v.* Burford, 2 Cr. & M. 391; Wilson *v.* Barthrop, 2 M. & W. 863; Fenn *v.* Harrison, 3 T. R. 757; Polhill *v.* Walter, 3 B. & Ad. 114 (23 E. C. L. R.); per Lord Abinger, C. B., Acey *v.* Fernie, 7 M. & W. 154; Davidson *v.* Stanley, 3 Scott N. R. 49; Harper *v.* Williams, 4 Q. B. 219 (45 E. C. L. R.). See Downman *v.* Williams, 7 Q. B. 103 (53 E. C. L. R.), (where the question was as to the construction of a written undertaking); Cooke *v.* Wilson, 1 C. B. N. S. 153 (87 E. C. L. R.); Gillett *v.* Offor, 18 C. B. 905 (86 E. C. L. R.); Green *v.* Kopke, Id. 549; Parker *v.* Winlow, 7 E. & B. 942, 949 (90 E. C. L. R.); Wake *v.* Harrop, 1 H. & C. 202; s. c., 6 H. & N. 768; Oglesby *v.* Yglesias, E., B. & E. 930 (96 E. C. L. R.); Williamson *v.* Barton, 7 H. & N. 899.

[2] Per Lord Holt, C. J., Ashton *v.* Sherman, Holt R. 309 (3 E. C. L. R.); cited 2 M. & W. 218.

[3] Thomas *v.* Edward, 2 M. & W. 215.

[4] Smout *v.* Ilbery, 10 M. & W. 1, 9. In this case, which was an action of debt, a man, who had been in the habit of dealing with the plaintiff for meat supplied to his house, went abroad, leaving his wife and family resident in this country, and died abroad:—Held, that the wife was not liable for goods supplied to her after his death, but before information of his death had been received.

[5] "All persons directly concerned in the commission of a fraud are to be treated as principals. No party can be permitted to excuse himself on the ground that he acted as the agent or as the servant of another:" per Lord Westbury, C., Cullen *v.* Thomson's Trustees, 4 Macq. Sc. App. Cas. 432–3.

authority, makes a contract in the name of his principal, is personally liable, even where no proof of such fraudulent intention can be given. First, where he has no authority, and knows it, but nevertheless, makes the contract, as having such authority; in which case, on the plainest principles of justice, he is liable; for he induces the other party to enter into the contract on what amounts to a misrepresentation of a fact peculiarly within his own knowledge; and it is but just, that he who does so should be considered as holding himself out as one having competent authority to contract, and as guaranteeing the consequences arising from any want of such authority. There is also a second class in which the courts have held, that, where a party making the contract as agent, *bonâ fide* believes that such authority is vested in him, but has, in fact, no such authority, he is still personally liable. In these cases the agent is not indeed actuated by any fraudulent motives, nor has he made any statement which he knows to be untrue; but still, his liability depends on the same principles as before. It is a wrong, differing only in degree, but not in its essence, from the former case, to state as true, what the individual making such statement does not know to be true, even though he does not know it to be false, but believes, without *sufficient grounds, that the statement will ultimately turn out to be correct,[1] and, if [*825] that wrong produces injury to a third person, who is wholly ignorant of the grounds on which such belief of the supposed agent is founded, and who has relied on the correctness of his assertion, it is equally just that he who makes such assertion shall be personally liable for its consequences. The true principle derivable from the cases is, that there must be some wrong or omission of right on the part of the agent, in order to make him personally liable on a contract made in the name of his principal; in all of them, it will be found that the agent has either been guilty of some fraud, has made some statement which he knew to be false, or has stated as true what he did not know to be true, omitting at the same time to give such information to the other contracting party as would enable him, equally with himself, to judge as to the authority under which he proposed to act. Polhill *v.* Walter,[2] which has been noticed in another page of this work, is an instance

[1] As to this proposition, *ante*, p. 797.

[2] 3 B. & Ad. 114 (23 E. C. L. R.); *ante*, p. 790.

of the first of the two classes of decisions just alluded to; and cases in which the agent never had any authority to contract at all, but believed that he had, as where he acted on a forged warrant of attorney, which he thought to be genuine, and the like, are instances of the second class.[1] To the various states of facts just put, we may add that if a person contracts *as agent* with another, he will in law be held to impliedly undertake and promise that he is what he represents himself to be, so that for any direct damage arising to the other party from a breach of such promise, he will, [*826] *without proof of any fraudulent representation, be responsible.[2]

In further illustration of the rule before us, reference may be made to the contract of insurance, which has been said[3] to be a contract *uberrimæ fidei*,[4] the principles which govern it being those of an enlightened and moral policy. The underwriter must be presumed to act upon the belief that the party procuring insurance is not, at the time, in possession of any facts material to the risk which he does not disclose, and that no known loss has occurred which, by reasonable diligence, might have been communicated to him. If a party, having secret information of a loss, procures insurance without disclosing it, this is a manifest fraud which avoids the policy. If, knowing that his agent is about to procure insurance, he withholds the same information for the purpose of misleading the underwriter, it is no less a fraud, for, under such circumstances, the maxim applies, *Qui facit per alium facit per se.* His own knowledge in such a case infects the act of his agent in the same manner and to the same extent that the knowledge of the agent himself would do. And even if there be no intentional fraud, still the underwriter has a right to a disclosure of all material facts which it was in the power of the party to communicate by ordinary means, and the omission is fatal to the insurance. The true principle

[1] Judgm., 10 M. & W. 10.

[2] Collen *v.* Wright (65 E. C. L. R.), 7 E. & B. 301 (90 E. C. L. R.); s. c., 8 Id. 647 (with which compare Randell *v.* Trimen, 18 C. B. 786 (86 E. C. L. R.)); Spedding *v.* Nevell, L. R. 4 C. P. 212; Simons *v.* Patchett, 7 E. & B. 568 (90 E. C. L. R.).

[3] Per Story, J., delivering judgment in M'Lanahan *v.* The Universal Insurance Co., 1 Peters (U. S.) R. 185; per Yates, J., Hodgson *v.* Richardson, 1 W. Bla. 465.

[4] *Ante*, p. 792.

deducible from the authorities on this subject is, that where a party orders insurance, and afterwards *receives intelligence ma- [*827] terial to the risk, or has knowledge of a loss, he ought to communicate it to the agent as soon as with due and reasonable diligence it can be communicated, for the purpose of countermanding the order, or laying the circumstances before the underwriter. If he omits so to do, and by due and reasonable diligence the information might have been communicated, so as to have countermanded the insurance, the policy is void.

On the maxim, *Qui facit per alium facit per se*, depends also the liability of a co-partnership on a contract entered into by an individual member of the firm; for he is considered as the accredited agent of the rest, and will consequently bind the firm by his act or assurance made with reference to business transacted by it,[1] within the scope of his authority,[2] and in the absence of collusion between himself and the other contracting party.[3]

The decision in Marsh *v.* Keating[4] is important with reference to the question of the responsibility incurred by one partner for the act of his co-partner, by reason of the implied agency between parties thus situated, and affords a direct and forcible illustration of the maxim, *Qui facit per alium facit per se:* in the case referred to the facts were, that F., a partner in a banking *firm, [*828] caused stock belonging to a customer to be sold out under a forged power of attorney; the proceeds were paid to the account of the bank at the house of the bank's agents, and were appropriated by F. to his own purposes. F. was afterwards executed for other forgeries. It appeared from the special verdict, that F.'s partners were ignorant of the fraud, but might, with common diligence, have known it; and it was held by the House of Lords, in

[1] Per Abbott, C. J., Sandilands *v.* Marsh, 2 B. & Ald. 678; per Lord Wensleydale, Ernest *v.* Nicholls, 6 H. L. Cas. 417, 418; and in Cox *v.* Hickman, 8 H. L. Cas. 268, 304, 312; Waugh *v.* Carver, 2 H. Bla. 235; Judgm., 1 My. & K. 76; Bullen *v.* Sharp, L. R. 1 C. P. 86.

The stat. 28 & 29 Vict. c. 86 has materially limited partnership liability at common law.

[2] Forster *v.* Mackreth, L. R. 2 Ex. 163; Ellston *v.* Deacon, L. R. 2 C. P. 20.

[3] Per Bayley, J., Vere *v.* Ashby, 10 B. & C. 296 (21 E. C. L. R.); Wintle *v.* Crowther, 1 Cr. & J. 316; Bond *v.* Gibson, 1 Camp. 185; Lewis *v.* Reilly, 1 Q. B. 349 (41 E. C. L. R.).

[4] 2 Cl. & F. 250.

conformity with the unanimous opinion of the judges, that the customer could maintain an action against the partners for money had and received. The general proposition, it was observed, was not disputed, that if the goods of A. are wrongfully taken and sold, the owner may bring trover against the wrong-doer, or may elect to consider him as his agent—may adopt the sale and maintain an action for the price; and this general rule was held applicable to fix the innocent partners with liability under the circumstances disclosed upon the special verdict. In another more recent case,[1] the plaintiffs in equity, who were the executors and trustees of a testator, in the year 1829 employed A. and B., a firm of solicitors, to procure investments for the assets of their testator. A. wrote to the plaintiffs, naming one S. as a proposed mortgagor for a sum of 4500*l.*, on the security of freehold property, whereupon the plaintiffs forwarded to A. a check for 4500*l.*, to be so invested, and this check was paid into the bank to the partnership account. The necessary mortgage deeds were prepared, but S. afterwards declined to complete the transaction. In April, 1830, A., however, wrote to the plaintiffs, giving a list of the securities upon [*829] which he alleged that the *testator's assets were invested, and amongst others stated, "S.'s mortgage 4500*l.*, 3d October, 1829." In 1834, A. and B. dissolved partnership, and the plaintiffs continued to employ A. as their solicitor, who regularly paid interest on the 4500*l.*, down to 1841. A. became bankrupt in 1844, and the plaintiffs then first discovered that the mortgage to S. had never been effected; on bill by the plaintiffs against B. to recover the sum paid over as above stated, it was held that the fraudulent representation of A. must be taken to be the act of the firm—that the relief was properly in equity, and that the defendant was civilly liable for the fraud of his co-partner.

Without attempting to enter at length upon the subject of partnership liabilities, incurred through the act of an individual member of the firm, we may observe, that wherever a contract is alleged to have been entered into through the medium of a third person, whether a co-partner or not, the real and substantial question is, with whom was the contract made? and in answering this question the jury will have to consider whether the party through

[1] Blair *v.* Bromley, 5 Hare 542; s. c., 2 Phill. 354.

whose instrumentality the contract is alleged to have been made, had in fact authority to make it. "It would," moreover, "be very dangerous to hold," as matter of law, "that a person who allows an agent to act as a principal in carrying on a business, and invests him with an apparent authority to enter into contracts incidental to it, could limit that authority by a secret reservation."[1]

Assumpsit for work and labor, in writing certain literary articles, was brought against the defendants, *whose names appeared [*830] as proprietors of a newspaper in the declaration filed under 6 & 7 Will. 4, c. 76; they had in fact ceased to be so before the contract was entered into, at which time L. was the sole proprietor; the jury found that the contract was made by L. on his own behalf, without any authority from the defendants; and also, that the plaintiff, when he supplied the articles in question, did not know the defendants to be proprietors; it was held, that, although the declaration above mentioned was, under the provisions of the stat. (s. 8), conclusive evidence of the fact that the defendants were proprietors, yet the real question was with whom the contract had been made, and that upon the finding of the jury the defendants were not liable.[2]

In like manner, in the case of an action brought at suit of a creditor against a member of the managing or provisional committee of a railway or other company, the question of liability ordinarily resolves itself into the consideration, whether the defendant did or did not authorize the particular contract for which he is sought to be made responsible; in Barnett *v.* Lambert[3] the defendant, in answer to an application from the secretary of a railway company, consented, by letter, that his name should be placed on the list of its provisional committee. His name was accordingly published in the newspapers as a provisional committee-man, and it appeared that on one occasion he attended and acted as chairman

[1] Per Mellor, J., Edmunds *v.* Bushell, L. R. 1 C. P. 97, 100.

As to the authority of an agent see Howard *v.* Sheward, L. R. 2 C. P. 148; Baines *v.* Ewing, L. R. 1 Ex. 320.

[2] Holcroft *v.* Hoggins, 2 C. B. 488 (52 E. C. L. R.).

[3] 15 M. & W. 489, where Todd *v.* Emly, 8 M. & W. 505; Flemyng *v.* Hector, 2 M. & W. 172; and Tredwen *v.* Bourne, 6 M. & W. 461, were cited per cur. As to the liability of a partner on a contract *prior* to his joining the concern, see Beale *v.* Mouls, 10 Q. B. 976 (59 E. C. L. R.).

[*831] at a meeting of the committee. It was held, that the *defendant was liable for the price of stationery supplied by the plaintiff on the order of the secretary, and used by the committee after the date of his letter to the secretary,—the question for decision being one of fact, and matter of inference for the jury, to be drawn from the defendant's conduct, as showing that he had constituted the secretary his agent to pledge his credit for all such things as were necessary for the working of the committee, and to enable it to go on. "Where," observed Alderson, B., "a subscription has been made, and there is a fund, it is not so; because if you give money to a person to buy certain things with, the natural inference is, that you do not mean him to pledge your credit for them."[1]

In Reynell *v.* Lewis and Wylde *v.* Hopkins,[2] decided shortly after Barnett *v.* Lambert, *supra*, the Court of Exchequer took occasion to lay down the principles applicable to cases falling within the particular class under consideration; and it may probably be better to give the substance of this judgment at some length, as it affords throughout important practical illustrations of that maxim, "which," in the words of Tindal, C. J.,[3] "is of almost universal application,"—*Qui facit per alium facit per se.*

"The question," observed the court, "in all cases in which the plaintiff seeks to fix the defendant with liability upon a contract, express or implied, is, whether such contract was made by the defendant, by himself or his agent, with the plaintiff or his agent, [*832] and this is a question *of fact for the decision of the jury upon the evidence before them. The plaintiff, on whom the burthen of proof lies in all these cases, must, in order to recover against the defendant, show that he (the defendant) contracted expressly or impliedly; expressly, by making a contract with the plaintiff; impliedly, by giving an order to him under such circumstances as show that it was not to be gratuitously executed; and, if the contract was not made by the defendant personally, it must be proved that it was made by an agent of the defendant properly authorized,[4] and that it was made as his con-

[1] Higgins *v.* Hopkins, 3 Exch. 163; Burnside *v.* Dayrell, Id. 224.

[2] 15 M. & W. 517; Collingwood *v.* Berkeley, 15 C. B. N. S. 145 (109 E. C. L. R.); Cross *v.* Williams, 7 H. & N. 675; Barker *v.* Stead, 16 L. J. C. P. 160.

[3] 8 Scott N. R. 830.

[4] See Cooke *v.* Tonkin, 9 Q. B. 936 (58 E. C. L. R.).

tract. In these cases of actions against provincial committee-men of railways, it often happens that the contract is made by a third person, and the point to be decided is, whether that third person was an agent for the defendant for the purpose of making it, and made the contract as such.[1] The agency may be constituted by an express limited authority to make such a contract, or a larger authority to make all falling within the class or description to which it belongs, or a general authority to make any; or it may be proved by showing that such a relation existed between the parties as by law would create the authority, as, for instance, that of partners, by which relation, when complete, one becomes by law the agent of the other for all purposes necessary for carrying on their particular partnership, whether general or special, or usually belonging to it; or the relation of husband and wife, in which the law, under certain circumstances, considers the husband to make his wife an agent. In all these cases, if the agent in making *the contract acts on that authority, the principal is bound by the contract, and the agent's contract is his contract, [*833] but not otherwise. This agency may be created by the immediate act of the party, that is, by really giving the authority to the agent, or representing to him that he is to have it, or by constituting that relation to which the law attaches agency; or it may be created by the representation of the defendant to the plaintiff that the party making the contract is the agent of the defendant, or that such relation exists as to constitute him such; and if the plaintiff really makes the contract on the faith of the defendant's representation, the defendant is bound,—he is estopped from disputing the truth of it with respect to that contract; and the representation of an authority is, *quoad hoc*, precisely the same as a real authority given by the defendant to the supposed agent. This representation may be made directly to the plaintiff, or made publicly, so that it may be inferred to have reached him; and may be made by words and conduct. Upon none of these propositions is there, we apprehend, the slightest doubt, and the proper decision of all these questions depends upon the proper application of these principles to the facts

[1] See Riley *v.* Packington, L. R. 2 C. P. 536; Maddick *v.* Marshall, 17 C. B. N. S. 829 (112 E. C. L. R.); s. c., 16 Id. 387; Burbridge *v.* Morris, 3 H. & C. 664.

of each case, and the jury are to apply the rule with due assistance from the judge." In the course of the judgment from which we have already made so long an extract, the court further observed, that an agreement to be a provisional committee-man is merely an agreement for carrying into effect the preliminary arrangements for petitioning Parliament for a bill, and thus promoting the scheme, but constitutes no agreement to share in profit or loss, which is the characteristic of a partnership, although if the provisional committee-man subsequently acts he will be responsible for his acts. They likewise remarked, that [*834] *where the list of the provisional committee has appeared in a prospectus, published with the defendant's consent, knowledge, or sanction, the context of such prospectus must be examined, to see whether or not it contains any statement affecting his liability, as, for instance, the names of a managing committee, in which case it will be a question whether the meaning be that the acting committee shall take the whole management of the concern, to the exclusion of the provisional committee, or that the provisional committee-men have appointed the acting committee, or the majority of it, on their behalf and as their agents.[1] In this latter case, moreover, it must further be considered whether the managing and delegated body is authorized to pledge the credit of the provisional committee, or is merely empowered to apply the funds subscribed to the liquidation of expenses incurred in the formation and carrying out of the concern.[2]

The preceding remarks have reference merely, as will have been noticed, to the right of a creditor of a company or projected company with which the defendant has become connected; in an action at suit of an allottee for recovery of his deposit, the main questions for consideration usually are, 1st, whether there has been such a failure of consideration as will entitle the plaintiff to treat the

[1] See Judgm., 15 M. & W. 530, 531; Wilson *v.* Viscount Curzon, Id. 532; Williams *v.* Pigott, 2 Exch. 201.

[2] Dawson *v.* Morrison, 16 L. J. C. P. 240; Rennie *v.* Clarke, 5 Exch. 292. See also as to the liability of a provisional committee-man, Patrick *v.* Reynolds, 1 C. B. N. S. 727 (87 E. C. L. R.); or member of a committee of visitors, Moffatt *v.* Dickson, 13 C. B. 543 (76 E. C. L. R.); Kendall *v.* King, 17 Id. 483, 508. As to the authority of a resident agent, or the directors of a mining company, to borrow money on the credit of the company, see Ricketts *v.* Bennett, 4 C. B. 686 (56 E. C. L. R.), and cases there cited; Burmester *v.* Norris, 6 Exch. 796.

supposed contract as a nullity, according to the maxim, *Ex *nudo pacto non oritur actio;* and, 2dly, whether there has been such a degree of fraud or misrepresentation, such [*835] *dolus dans locum contractui*, as will nullify the contract into which the allottee has been induced to enter.[1] And from decided cases we may deduce, on the one hand, that the money deposited by a subscriber to a railway or other similar undertaking may (in the absence of special circumstances) be recovered back, 1st, where no deed has been signed and the scheme has proved altogether abortive, and has been definitely abandoned, or 2dly, where the usual deed *has* been signed, provided the money were paid and the deed executed under a misrepresentation of facts within the knowledge of or sanctioned or adopted by the defendant;[2] and, on the other hand, that the entire deposit[3] cannot be recovered where there has been no fraud, and the subscription contract has been executed, inasmuch as the provisions ordinarily inserted in such deed will afford a good defence to the action.[4]

We do not propose to dwell at much length upon the maxim now before us, in further illustration of which, however, some few additional cases may be mentioned.[5]

*The authority of the master of a ship is very large, and extends to all acts that are usual and necessary for the use [*836] and enjoyment of the ship; it is, nevertheless, subject to several well-known limitations. He may make contracts for the hire of the ship, but cannot vary that which the owner has made. He may take up money in foreign ports, and under certain circumstances at

[1] Walstab *v.* Spottiswoode, 15 M. & W. 501; Wontner *v.* Shairp, 4 C. B. 404 (56 E. C. L. R.); Willey *v.* Parratt, 3 Exch. 211; Garwood *v.* Ede, 1 Exch. 264; Hutton *v.* Thompson, 3 H. L. Cas. 161; Johnson *v.* Goslett, 3 C. B. N. S. 569.

[2] Per Parke, B., Vane *v.* Cobbold (Exch.), 12 Jur. 61; s. c., 1 Exch. 798; Atkinson *v.* Pocock, 12 Jur. 60; s. c., 1 Exch. 796; and cases *supra.*

[3] The letter of allotment may likewise empower the directors to apply the deposits in discharge of necessary expenses: Jones *v.* Harrison, 2 Exch. 52.

[4] Watts *v.* Salter, 10 C. B. 477 (70 E. C. L. R.).

[5] The authority of a counsel to bind his client by a compromise was much considered in Swinfen *v.* Swinfen, 1 C. B. N. S. 364 (87 E. C. L. R.); s. c., 18 C. B. 485 (86 E. C. L. R.); 24 Beav. 549; Swinfen *v.* Lord Chelmsford, 5 H. & N. 890; Strauss *v.* Francis, L. R. 1 Q. B. 379. As to the power of a solicitor to bind his client by a reference, see Fray *v.* Voules, 1 E. & E. 839 (102 E. C. L. R.); Chown *v.* Parrott, 14 C. B. N. S. 74 (108 E. C. L. R.).

home,[1] for necessary disbursements and for repairs, and bind the owners for repayment; but his authority is limited by the necessity of the case, and he cannot make them responsible for money not actually necessary for those purposes, although he may pretend that it is. He may make contracts to carry goods on freight, but cannot bind his owners by a contract to carry freight free. With regard also to goods put on board the ship, the master may sign a bill of lading, and acknowledge thereby the nature, quality and condition of the goods; his authority, however, to give bills of lading being limited to such goods as have been put on board.[2]

Further, the liability of the husband for necessaries supplied to the wife results from her authority being implied by law to act as her husband's agent, and to contract on his behalf for this specific purpose;[3] but the *implied authority of the wife thus to [*837] bind her husband is put an end to by her adultery.[4]

To the general principle under consideration may also be referred the numerous decisions which establish that the sheriff is liable for an illegal or fraudulent act committed by his bailiff, even if he were not personally cognizant of the transaction;[5] and such

[1] See Edwards *v.* Havill, 14 C. B. 107; 19 & 20 Vict. c. 97, s. 8.

[2] Grant *v.* Norway, 10 C. B. 665, 687 (70 E. C. L. R.); Hubbersty *v.* Ward, 8 Exch. 330; Jessel *v.* Bath, L. R. 2 Ex. 267; Valieri *v.* Boland, L. R. 1 C. P. 382; Barker *v.* Higley, 15 C. B. N. S. 27 (109 E. C. L. R.). See, further, as to the authority of the master, or ship's husband, to pledge the owner's credit, The Great Eastern, L. R. 2 A. & E. 88; The Karnak, L. R. 2 P. C. 505.

[3] Manby *v.* Scott, 1 Lev. 4; s. c., 1 Sid. 109; Montague *v.* Benedict, 3 B. & C. 631 (10 E. C. L. R.); Seaton *v.* Benedict, 5 Bing. 28 (15 E. C. L. R.) (which are leading cases on the subject of the husband's liability); Johnston *v.* Sumner, 3 H. & N. 261; Richardson *v.* Dubois, L. R. 5 Q. B. 51; Wilson *v.* Ford, L. R. 3 Ex. 63; Bazeley *v.* Forder, L. R. 3 Q. B. 559; Needham *v.* Bremner, L. R. 1 C. P. 583; Helps *v.* Clayton, 17 C. B. N. S. 553 (112 E. C. L. R.); Jolly *v.* Rees, 15 C. B. N. S. 628 (109 E. C. L. R.); Smout *v.* Ilbery, 10 M. & W. 1.

[4] Cooper *v.* Lloyd, 6 C. B. N. S. 519 (95 E. C. L. R.), and cases there cited.

[5] Per Ashhurst, J., Woodgate *v.* Knatchbull, 2 T. R. 154; Gregory *v.* Cotterell, 5 E. & B. 571 (85 E. C. L. R.); Raphael *v.* Goodman, 8 A. & E. 565 (35 E. C. L. R.); Sturmy *v.* Smith, 11 East 25; Price *v.* Peek, 1 Bing. N. C. 380 (27 E. C. L. R.); Crowder *v.* Long, 8 B. & C. 602 (15 E. C. L. R.); Smart *v.* Hutton, 8 A. & E. 568, n. (35 E. C. L. R.). See Peshall *v.* Layton, 2 T. R. 712; Thomas *v.* Pearse, 5 Price 578; Jarmain *v.* Hooper, 7 Scott N. R. 663.

decisions are peculiarly illustrative of this principle, because there is a distinction to be noticed between the ordinary cases and those in which the illegal act is done under such circumstances as constitute the person committing it the special bailiff of the party at whose suit process is executed; as, where the attorney of the plaintiff in a cause requested of the sheriff a particular officer, delivered the warrant to that officer, took him in his carriage to the scene of action, and there encouraged an illegal arrest; it was held, that the sheriff was not liable for subsequent escape.[1] Nor will the sheriff be liable if the wrong complained of be neither expressly sanctioned by him, nor impliedly committed by his authority; as, where the bailiff derived his authority, not from the sheriff, but from the plaintiff, at whose instigation he acted;[2] and it is not competent to *one whose act produces the misconduct of the bailiff to say, that the act of the officer done in breach of his duty to the sheriff, and which he has himself induced, is the act of the sheriff.[3] [*838]

One additional exemplification of our principal maxim must suffice: A contractor for supplying forage for the use of her majesty's forces is exempted by the stat. 3 Geo. 4, c. 126, s. 32, from the payment of toll in respect of any wagon conveying such forage to a government store, and a person hired by such contractor to convey it to the place of delivery will have a like privilege of exemption in accordance with the principle *Qui facit per alium facit per se.*[4]

But, notwithstanding the almost universal applicability of the legal maxim under consideration, cases may occur in which, by reason of the express provisions of the statute law, it will not apply; for instance, it was formerly held that, under the stat. 9

[1] Doe *v.* Trye, 5 Bing. N. C. 573 (35 E. C. L. R.); Ford *v.* Leche, 6 A. & E. 699 (33 E. C. L. R.); Wright *v.* Child, L. R. 1 Ex. 358; Alderson *v.* Davenport, 13 M. & W. 42; per Buller, J., De Moranda *v.* Dunkin, 4 T. R. 121; Botten *v.* Tomlinson, 16 L. J. C. P. 138.

[2] Cook *v.* Palmer, 6 B. & C. 39 (13 E. C. L. R.); Crowder *v.* Long, 8 B. & C. 598 (15 E. C. L. R.); Tompkinson *v.* Russell, 9 Price 287; Bowden *v.* Waithman, 5 Moore 183; Stuart *v.* Whittaker, R. & M. 310; Higgins *v.* M'Adam, 3 Y. & J. 1.

[3] Per Bayley, J., 8 B. & C. 603, 604 (15 E. C. L. R.).

[4] London and South-Western R. C., app., Reeves, resp., L. R. 1 C. P. 580, 582.

Geo. 4, c. 14, s. 1, an acknowledgment signed by an agent of the debtor would not revive a debt barred by the Statute of Limitations.[1] But the law upon this point has been altered by the stat. 19 & 20 Vict. c. 97, s. 13.

It has also been stated as a general rule, that a bill of discovery, in aid of a defence to an action at law, cannot be sustained against a person who is not a party to the record, although charged in the bill to be solely interested in the subject of the action; and this [*839] rule will be applied *even where the plaintiff in the original action sues as agent for the party from whom this discovery is sought, notwithstanding the maxim, *Qui facit per alium facit per se*, might at first sight appear applicable.[2]

Before terminating our remarks as to the legal consequences which flow from the relation of principal and agent in transactions founded upon contract, it becomes necessary to consider briefly a kindred principle of law, which limits the operation of the maxim *Qui facit per alium facit per se*, and will, therefore, most properly be noticed in immediate connection with it: the principle to which we allude is this, that *a delegated authority cannot be redelegated—Delegata potestas non potest delegari;*[3] or, as it is otherwise expressed, *Vicarius non habet vicarium*[4]—one agent cannot lawfully nominate or appoint another to perform the subject-matter of his agency.[5] Hence, a notice to quit, given by an agent of an agent, is not sufficient, without a recognition by the principal. To render such a notice valid, there must be either an authority to give, or a recognition of it.[6] So, a principal employs a broker from the opinion which he entertains of his personal skill and integrity; and the broker has no right, without notice, to turn his principal over to

[1] Hyde *v.* Johnson, 2 Bing. N. C. 776 (29 E. C. L. R.). See also Toms, app., Cuming, resp., 8 Scott N. R. 910; Cuming, app., Toms, resp., Id. 827; Davies, app., Hopkins, resp., 3 C. B. N. S. 376 (91 E. C. L. R.).

[2] Queen of Portugal *v.* Glyn, 7 Cl. & Fin. 466.

[3] 2 Inst. 597; arg. Fector *v.* Beacon, 5 Bing. N. C. 310 (35 E. C. L. R.).

[4] Branch Max., 5th ed., 38.

[5] See per Lord Denman, C. J., Cobb *v.* Becke, 6 Q. B. 936 (51 E. C. L. R.); Combes' Case, 9 Rep. 75. See Reg. *v.* Newmarket R. C., 15 Q. B. 702 (69 E. C. L. R.); Reg. *v.* Dulwich College, 17 Q. B. 600, 615 (79 E. C. L. R.), where Lord Campbell, C. J., incidentally observes that "the Crown cannot enable a man to appoint magistrates."

[6] Doe d. Rhodes *v.* Robinson, 3 Bing. N. C. 667, 679 (32 E. C. L. R.).

another of whom he knows nothing; and, therefore, a broker cannot, without authority from his principal, transfer consignments made to him, in his character of *broker, to another broker [*840] for sale.[1] On the same principle, where an Act of Parliament for building a bridge required, that, when any notice was to be given by the trustees appointed and acting under it, such notice should be in writing or in print, signed by three or more of the trustees; it was held, that a notice, signed with the names of the clerks to the trustees, but signed, in fact, not by such clerks, but by a clerk employed by them, was insufficient, as being an attempt to substitute for a deputy his deputy.[2]

It may, likewise, be well to observe, that delegated jurisdiction, as contradistinguished from proper jurisdiction, is that which is communicated by a judge to some other person, who acts in his name, and is called a deputy; and this jurisdiction is, in law, held to be that of the judge who appoints the substitute, or deputy, and not of the latter party; and in this case the maxim holds, *Delegatus non potest delegare*—the person to whom any office or duty is delegated,—for example, an arbitrator,—cannot lawfully devolve the duty on another, unless he be expressly authorized so to do.[3] Nor can an individual, clothed with judicial functions, delegate the discharge of *these functions, to another, unless, as in the [*841] case of a county court judge, he be expressly empowered to do so under specified circumstances.[4] For the ordinary rule is that although a *ministerial* officer may appoint a deputy, a *judicial* officer cannot.[5]

[1] Cockran *v.* Irlam, 2 M. & S. 301, n. (*a*); Solly *v.* Rathbone, Id. 298; Catlin *v.* Bell, 4 Camp. 183; Schmaling *v.* Tomlinson, 6 Taunt. 147 (1 E. C. L. R.); Coles *v.* Trecothick, 9 Ves. 251; Henderson *v.* Barnwall, 1 Yo. & J. 387.

[2] Miles *v.* Bough, 3 Q. B. 845 (43 E. C. L. R.); cited arg. Allan, app., Waterhouse, resp., 8 Scott N. R. 68, 76.

[3] See Bell Dict. and Dig. of Scotch Law 280, 281, 292; Whitmore *v.* Smith, 7 H. & N. 509; cited in Thorburn *v.* Barnes, L. R. 2 C. P. 384, 404; Little *v.* Newton, 2 Scott N. R. 509; Reg. *v.* Jones, 10 A. & E. 576 (37 E. C. L. R.); Hughes *v.* Jones, 1 B. & Ad. 388 (20 E. C. L. R.); Wilson *v.* Thorpe, 6 M. & W. 721; argument, 5 Bing. N. C. 310 (35 E. C. L. R.); White *v.* Sharp, 12 M. & W. 712; Rutter *v.* Chapman, 8 M. & W. 1. See The Case of the Masters' Clerks, 1 Phill. 650. *Et vide* Reg. *v.* Perkin, 7 Q. B. 165 (53 E. C. L. R.); Smeeton *v.* Collier, 1 Exch. 457; Sharp *v.* Nowell, 6 C. B. 253 (60 E. C. L. R.); 17 & 18 Vict. c. 125, s. 14.

[4] See Broom, Pr. C. C., 2d ed., 9.

[5] See per Parke, B., Walsh *v.* Southworth, 6 Exch. 150, 156; which illus-

A magistrate, as observed by Lord Camden, can have no assistant nor deputy to execute any part of his employment. The right is personal to himself, and a trust that he can no more delegate to another, than a justice of the peace can transfer his commission to his clerk.[1]

Although, however, a deputy cannot, according to the above rule, transfer his entire powers to another, yet a deputy possessing general powers may, in many cases, constitute another person his servant or bailiff, for the purpose of doing some particular act; provided, of course, that such act be within the scope of his own legitimate authority.

For instance, the steward of a manor, with power to make a deputy, made B. his deputy, and B., by writing under his hand and seal, made C. his deputy, to the intent that he might take a surrender of G., of copyhold lands. It was held, that the surrender taken by C. was a good surrender;[2] and Lord Holt, insisting upon the distinction above pointed out, compared the case before him to that of an undersheriff, who has power to make bailiffs and to send process all over the kingdom, and that only by virtue of his deputation.[3]

[*842] *S.'s wife was in the habit of managing his business, and *inter alia* of drawing, accepting, and endorsing bills in his name. On one occasion a promissory note was endorsed by S.'s daughter, in his name, in the presence and by the direction of her mother, who then delivered it to the plaintiff. Upon an issue as to the endorsement of the said note by S., the question was held to be one of fact, whether or not the evidence showed an authority given by the husband to the wife to endorse in the way mentioned. The maxim, *Delegatus non potest delegare*, observed Maule, J., "has no application at all here;" and again, "there was evidence that the wife had the general management of her husband's business. And when he authorized her to draw, accept, and endorse bills, in his name, that they may fairly be extended to authorizing her to

trates the former part of the rule stated *supra*. See Baker *v.* Cave, 1 H. & N. 674.

[1] Entick *v.* Carrington, 19 Howell St. Trials 1063.

[2] Parker *v.* Kett, 1 Ld. Raym. 658, cited in Bridges *v.* Garrett, L. R. 4 C. P. 591.

[3] 1 Ld. Raym. 659; Leak *v.* Howell, Cro. Eliz. 533.

select some person, *pro hâc vice*, to write the name of her husband for her.[1]

The rule as to delegated functions must, moreover, be understood with this necessary qualification, that, in the particular case, no power to re-delegate such functions has been given.[2] Such an authority to employ a deputy may be either *express* or *implied* by the recognized usage of trade; as in the case of an architect or builder, who employs a surveyor to make out the quantities of the building proposed to be erected; in which case the maxim of the civil law applies, *In contractis tacitè insunt quæ sunt moris et consuetudinis*[3]—terms which are in accordance with and warranted by custom and usage may, in some cases, be tacitly imported into contracts.

---

*Respondeat Superior. [*843]

(4 Inst. 114.)

Let the principal be held responsible.

The above maxim is, in principle, almost identical with that immediately preceding, but is more usually and appropriately applied with reference to actions *ex delicto*, than to such as are founded in contract. Where, for instance, an agent commits a tortious act, under the direction or with the assent of his principal, each is liable at suit of the party injured: the agent is liable, because the authority of the principal cannot justify his wrongful act; and the person who directs the act to be done is likewise liable, according to the maxim, *Respondeat superior*.[4] "If the servant

[1] Lord *v.* Hall, 8 C. B. 627 (65 E. C. L. R.). See Lindus *v.* Bradwell, 5 C. B. 583 (57 E. C. L. R.); Smith *v.* Marsack, 6 C. B. 486 (60 E. C. L. R.).

[2] See 2 Prest. Abs. Tit. 276.

[3] 3 Bing. N. C. 814, 818 (32 E. C. L. R.).

[4] 4 Inst. 114; Sands *v.* Child, 3 Lev. 352; Jones *v.* Hart, 1 Ld. Raym. 738; Britton *v.* Cole, 1 Salk. 408; Gauntlett *v.* King, 3 C. B. N. S. 59 (91 E. C. L. R.); per Littledale, J., Laugher *v.* Pointer, 5 B. & C. 559 (11 E. C. L. R.); Perkins *v.* Smith, 1 Wils. 338; cited 1 Bing. N. C. 418 (27 E. C. L. R.); Stephens *v.* Elwall, 4 M. & S. 259; Com. Dig., "*Trespass*" (C. 1). See Collett *v.* Foster, 2 H. & N. 356; Bennett *v.* Bayes, 5 H. & N. 391.

A person who deals with the goods of a testator, as agent of the executor, cannot be treated as executor *de son tort*, whether the will has been proved or not: Sykes *v.* Sykes, L. R. 5 C. P. 113.

commits a trespass by the command or encouragement of his master, the master shall be guilty of it, though the servant is not thereby excused, for he is only to obey his master in matters that are honest and lawful;"[1] and "all persons directly concerned in the commission of fraud are to be treated as principals."[2]

[*844] *A railway company may be liable in trover for a conversion by their agent.[3] The rule, indeed, so far as regards the method of applying the maxim before us, being the same between a private individual and a railway company as it is where the same matter is in dispute between two private individuals.[4]

In the case of domestic servants, and such agents as are selected by the master, and appointed to perform any particular work, although, possibly, not in his immediate employ or under his direct or personal superintendence, the maxim, *Respondeat superior*, is also very often applicable.

"Upon the principle that *Qui facit per alium facit per se*," it was said, in a leading case upon this subject, "the master is responsible for the acts of his servant, and that person is undoubtedly liable who stood in the relation of master to the wrong-doer—he who had selected him as his servant, from the knowledge of, or belief in, his skill and care, and who could remove him for misconduct, and whose orders he was bound to receive and obey, and whether such servant has been appointed by the master directly, or intermediately through the intervention of an agent authorized by him to appoint servants for him, can make no difference."[5]

Where, for instance, a man is the owner of a ship, he himself

[1] 1 Com. by Broom & Hadley 518; *et vide* per Platt, B., Stevens *v.* Midland Counties R. C., 10 Exch. 356; Eastern Counties R. C. *v.* Broom, 6 Exch. 314.

[2] *Ante*, p. 824, n. (*b*).

Scrivener *v.* Pask, L. R. 1 C. P. 715, 719, shows that to charge a principal for the misrepresentation of his agent, three things must be proved: (1) the agency; (2) that the agent was guilty of fraud or misrepresentation; and (3) that the principal knew of and sanctioned it.

Also the intentional concealment of a material fact from the underwriter by the agent of the ship-owner, though unknown to the last-mentioned party, will vitiate the policy: Proudfoot *v.* Montefiore, L. R. 2 Q. B. 511.

[3] Taff Vale R. C. *v.* Giles, 2 E. & B. 822 (75 E. C. L. R.). See Poulton *v.* London and South-Western R. C., L. R. 2 Q. B. 534.

[4] Roe *v.* Birkenhead, Lancashire and Cheshire R. C., 7 Exch. 36, 40.

[5] Quarman *v.* Burnett, 6 M. & W. 509; cited L. R. 1 H. L. 114; Tobin *v.* Reg., 16 C. B. N. S. 350 (111 E. C. L. R.).

appoints the master, and desires the master to *appoint and select the crew: the crew thus become appointed by the [*845] owner, and are his servants for the management and government of the ship, and if any damage happens through their default, it is the same as if it happened through the immediate default of the owner himself.[1] By a policy of insurance, however, the assured makes no warranty to the underwriters that the master and crew shall do their duty during the voyage; and their negligence or misconduct is no defence to an action on the policy, where the loss has been immediately occasioned by the perils insured against; nor can any distinction be made in this respect between the omission by the master and crew to do an act which ought to be done, and the doing an act which ought not to be done, in the course of the navigation.[2] In the case just supposed, however, if the ship be chartered for the particular voyage, or for a definite period, it is always a question of fact under whose direction and control the vessel was at the time of the occurrence complained of; and this question must be solved by ascertaining whose are the crew, and by considering whether the reasonable interpretation of the charter-party is, that the owners meant to keep the control of the vessel in their own hands, or to make the freighter the responsible owner *pro tempore;*[3] and a state of facts *might perhaps occur in which the charterer would be answerable as well as the [*846] owner.[4]

[1] Per Littledale, J., 5 B. & C. 554 (11 E. C. L. R.); Martin *v.* Temperley, 4 Q. B. 298 (45 E. C. L. R.); Dunford *v.* Trattles, 12 M. & W. 529; Bland *v.* Ross, 14 Moo. P. C. C. 210.

[2] Judgm., Dixon *v.* Sadler, 5 M. & W. 414; cited in The Duero, L. R. 2 A. & E. 393; Biccard *v.* Shepherd, 14 Moo. P. C. C. 471.

[3] Fenton *v.* City of Dublin Steam Packet Co., 8 A. & E. 835 (35 E. C. L. R.); Dalyell *v.* Tyrer, E., B. & E. 899 (96 E. C. L. R.); Fletcher *v.* Braddick, 2 N. R. 182; recognized, 5 B. & C. 556 (11 E. C. L. R.); Newberry *v.* Colvin, 7 Bing. 190 (20 E. C. L. R.); cited Judgm., Shuster *v.* M'Kellar, 7 E. & B. 724 (90 E. C. L. R.); Trinity House *v.* Clark, 4 M. & S. 288.

[4] Per Lord Denman, C. J., and Patteson, J., 8 A. & E. 842, 843 (35 E. C. L. R.).

As to the owner's liability in trover for the act of the master, see Ewbank *v.* Nutting, 7 C. B. 797 (62 E. C. L. R.).

As to the liability of the master for damage done to goods in the loading thereof, see Blaikie *v.* Stembridge, 6 C. B. N. S. 694 (95 E. C. L. R.), (distinguished in Sack *v.* Ford, 13 C. B. N. S. 90 (106 E. C. L. R.)); Sandeman *v.* Scurr, L. R. 2 Q. B. 86.

"The principle upon which a master is in general liable to answer for accidents resulting from the negligence or unskillfulness of his servant, is, that the act of his servant is in truth his own act.[1] If the master is himself driving his carriage, and from want of skill causes injury to a passer-by, he is of course responsible for that want of skill. If, instead of driving the carriage with his own hands, he employs his servant to drive it, the servant is but an instrument set in motion by the master. It was the master's will that the servant should drive, and whatever the servant does in order to give effect to his master's will may be treated by others as the act of the master, *Qui facit per alium facit per se*."[2] The general rule being that "a master is responsible for all acts done by his servant in the course of his employment, though without particular directions;"[3] even whilst engaged in private business of [*847] his own, provided he be at the time *engaged generally on that of his master.[4] The tests applicable for determining the liability of the master being—is the servant "*in the employ* of his master at the time of committing the grievance?"[5]—was he authorized by his master to do the act complained of?[6] "The master," observes Maule, J.,[7] "is liable even though the servant in the performance of his duty is guilty of a deviation or a failure to perform it in the strictest and most convenient manner. But where

[1] So in Lumley *v.* Gye, 22 L. J. Q. B. 478; s. c., 2 E. & B. 216 (75 E. C. L. R.), Coleridge, J., observes, "The maxims *Qui facit per alium facit per se*, and *Respondeat superior*, are unquestionable; but where they apply, the wrongful act is properly charged to be the act of him who has procured it to be done; he is sued as a principal trespasser, and the damage, if proved, flows directly and immediately from his act, though it was the hand of another—and he a free agent—that was employed."

[2] Judgm., Hutchinson *v.* York, Newcastle *v.* Berwick R. C., 5 Exch. 350. See Sharrod *v.* The London and North-Western R. C., 4 Exch. 580, 585; citing Gregory *v.* Piper, 9 B. & C. 591.

[3] Per Lord Holt, C. J., Tuberville *v.* Stampe, 1 Lord Raym. 266; Seymour *v.* Greenwood, 7 H. & N. 355, 357, 358; s. c., 6 Id. 359.

[4] Patton *v.* Rea, 2 C. B. N. S. 606 (89 E. C. L. R.); Mitchell *v.* Crassweller, 13 C. B. 237 (76 E. C. L. R.); Storey *v.* Ashton, L. R. 4 Q. B. 476; Judgm., Tobin *v.* Reg., 16 C. B. N. S. 350–352 (111 E. C. L. R.).

The same principle applies to fix a corporation aggregate with liability: Green *v.* London General Omnibus Co., 7 C. B. N. S. 290 (97 E. C. L. R.).

[5] Per Jervis, C. J., 13 C. B. 246; Storey *v.* Ashton, *supra*.

[6] Gordon *v.* Rolt, 8 Exch. 365.

[7] 13 C. B. 247 (106 E. C. L. R.).

the servant, instead of doing that which he is employed to do, does something which he is not employed to do at all, the master cannot be said to do it by his servant, and therefore is not responsible for the negligence of the servant in doing it."

A master may also be civilly responsible for the fraud of his servant acting in the course of his employment.[1] And "where a corporation is formed for the purpose of carrying on a trading or other speculation for profit, such as forming a railway, these objects can only be accomplished through the agency of individuals; and there can be no doubt that if the agents employed conduct themselves fraudulently, so that if they had been acting for private employers, the persons for whom they were acting would have been affected by their fraud, the same principles must prevail where the principal under whom the agent acts is a corporation."[2]

*If A. employs B. to do an illegal act, or an act necessarily to be done in an unlawful way, A. will be responsible [*848] to C., who sustains damage consequential on the act thus done, there being here the *injuria et damnum*, which suffice to constitute a cause of action.[3]

If, however, the act in question might be done without injury, public or private, the maxim *Respondeat superior* will apply only where the relation of master and servant *pro hâc vice* is established, as between the actual wrongdoer and the defendant.[4]

The principle of *Respondeat superior* does not, moreover, apply where an injury is committed by a servant willfully, whilst neither employed in his master's service, nor acting within the scope of his authority;[5] as if a servant, authorized merely to distrain cattle

[1] Barwick *v.* English Joint Stock Bank, L. R. 2 Ex. 259.

[2] Per Lord Cranworth, C., Ranger *v.* Great Western R. C., 5 H. L. Cas. 86, 87.

[3] Ellis *v.* Sheffield Gas Consumers' Co., 2 E. & B. 767 (75 E. C. L. R.), and Hole *v.* Sittingbourne and Sheerness R. C., 6 H. & N. 488; cited in Pickard *v.* Smith, 10 C. B. N. S. 470 (100 E. C. L. R.). See Gray *v.* Pullen, 5 B. & S. 970 (117 E. C. L. R.); Peachey *v.* Rowland, 13 C. B. 187 (117 E. C. L. R.); Sadler *v.* Henlock, 4 E. & B. 570 (76 E. C. L. R.); Gayford *v.* Nicholls, 9 Exch. 702; Newton *v.* Ellis, 5 E. & B. 115 (85 E. C. L. R.); Ward *v.* Lee, 7 E. & B. 426.

[4] Id.

[5] See Storey *v.* Ashton, L. R. 4 Q. B. 476; Whatman *v.* Pearson, L. R. 3 C. P. 422; Williams *v.* Jones, 3 H. & C. 602; Limpus *v.* London General Omnibus

damage-feasant, drives cattle from the highway into his master's close, and there distrains them.[1] Neither does the rule apply where the relation of principal and agent has terminated before the commission of the act complained of. Thus, the sheriff is not [*849] liable in trover for a conversion *by his bailiff of goods seized under process of attachment issuing out of the county court after the bailiff has had notice of a *supersedeas*. The ground of the sheriff's liability for the acts of his bailiff is, that he is casting upon another a duty which the law imposes upon him, and, consequently, that he is acting by a servant; but the effect of the *supersedeas* is to render the writ inoperative from the moment it was delivered to the sheriff, and not the writ only, but the warrant also; and the consequence is, that, though the sheriff was responsible for everything that was done up to the time of the *supersedeas*, yet that which was done afterwards was done in defiance of his authority, and to hold him liable for this would be holding him to be a wrongdoer for the act of his servant after his authority had been determined.[2]

The liability of the master for the tort of the servant when acting under his implied authority results, then, as above stated, from the fact, that servants are hired and selected by the master to do the business required of them, and their acts consequently stand on the same footing as his own;[3] as in the case of coach proprietors, who are answerable for an injury sustained by a passenger through the driver's misconduct.[4] A difficulty, however, often

Co., 1 H. & C. 534; per cur., Croft *v.* Alison, 4 B. & Ald. 590 (6 E. C. L. R.); Lyons *v.* Martin, 8 A. & E. 512 (35 E. C. L. R.); M'Manus *v.* Crickett, 1 East 106; Lamb *v.* Palk, 9 C. & P. 629 (38 E. C. L. R.); Gordon *v.* Rolt, 4 Exch. 365; A.-G. *v.* Siddon, 1 Cr. & J. 220; Joel *v.* Morison, 6 C. & P. 501 (25 E. C. L. R.); per Lord Kenyon, C. J., 8 T. R. 533; per Ashhurst, J., Fenn *v.* Harrison, 3 T. R. 760; Gregory *v.* Piper, 9 B. & C. 591 (17 E. C. L. R.); Huzzey *v.* Field, 2 C. M. & R. 432.

[1] Lyons *v.* Martin, 8 A. & E. 512 (35 E. C. L. R.).

[2] Brown *v.* Copley, 8 Scott N. R. 350. The ground and extent of the sheriff's liability are explained, per Jervis, C. J., Gregory *v.* Cotterell, 5 E. & B. 584 (85 E. C. L. R.); per Maule, J., Smith *v.* Pritchard, 8 C. B. 588 (65 E. C. L. R.); Woods *v.* Finnis, 7 Exch. 363; Hooper *v.* Lane, 6 H. L. Cas. 443.

[3] Per Littledale, J., Laugher *v.* Pointer, 5 B. & C. 553, 554 (11 E. C. L. R.).

[4] White *v.* Boulton, Peake N. P. C. 81; Jackson *v.* Tollett, 2 Stark. N. P. C. 37 (3 E. C. L. R.). See the cases 2 Selw. N. P. 12th ed., 446, 1119.

arises in applying this general and fundamental rule to particular facts, and in determining between what parties the relationship of master and servant *actually subsists;[1] for although that [*850] party will usually be liable with whom the act complained of ultimately originates, yet the applicability of this test fails in one case; for where he who does the injury (either in person or by his servant) exercises an independent employment, the party employing him is clearly not liable;[2] as in the instance of a butcher who employs a drover, whose deputy does the mischief by his careless driving;[3] or of a builder who contracts to make certain alterations in a club-house, together with the necessary gas-fittings, and who employs a gas-fitter for the latter purpose under a sub-contract, through the negligence of whom, or of whose servants, the plaintiff sustains an injury:[4] in these cases the relation of master and servant does not subsist between the principal and the person who occasions the injury, and the former is, therefore, not liable for the misconduct of the latter,[5] unless he has adopted or sanctioned the particular act by which the injury in respect whereof compensation is sought has been occasioned, or there be evidence to show that he has interfered with or had control over the work in the performance of which the damage has been caused;[6] or unless the act which *occasions the injury is one which the contractor was em- [*851] ployed to do; or unless the injury is occasioned by neglect of the contracter to perform a duty incumbent on his employer, but

[1] As between pilot and owner of ship, *post*, p. 864; captain of ship and inferior officer, Nicholson *v.* Mouncey, 15 East 384, and cases there cited; postmaster-general and clerk, Lane *v.* Cotton, 1 Salk. 17; s. c., 15 Mod. 472; per Lord Ellenborough, C. J., 15 East 392; Whitfield *v.* Lord Despencer, Cowp. 754; cited per Lord Wensleydale, L. R. 1 H. L. 111, 124.

[2] Per Williams, J., and Coleridge, J., 12 A. & E. 742 (40 E. C. L. R.); Gary *v.* Pullen, 5 B. & S. 970 (117 E. C. L. R.).

[3] Milligan *v.* Wedge, 12 A. & E. 737 (40 E. C. L. R.).

[4] Rapson *v.* Cubitt, 9 M. & W. 710. See Wilson *v.* Peto, 6 Moore 47; Witte *v.* Hague, 2 D. & R. 33.

[5] See Judgm., Quarman *v.* Burnett, 6 M. & W. 509, 510; per Parke, B., 9 M. & W. 713. See also the remarks on Bush *v.* Steinman (1 B. & P. 404), and Sly *v.* Edgley (6 Esp. N. P. C. 6), in 5 B. & C. 559, 560; and per Le Blanc, J., Harris *v.* Baker, 4 M. & S. 29.

[6] Burgess *v.* Gray, 1 C. B. 578 (50 E. C. L. R.) (distinguishing Bush *v.* Steinman, 1 B. & P. 404), and cases cited *post*.

with the performance of which he was intrusted,[1] or to select a competent subordinate.[2]

"The liability," remarks Rolfe, B., delivering the judgment of the court in Reedie *v.* The London and North-Western Railway Company,[3] "of any one other than the party actually guilty of any wrongful act, proceeds on the maxim, *Qui facit per alium facit per se;* the party employing has the selection of the party employed; and it is reasonable that he who has made choice of an unskillful or careless person to execute his orders, should be responsible for any injury resulting from the want of skill or care of the person employed; but neither the principle of the rule nor the rule itself can apply to a case where the party sought to be charged does not stand in the character of employer to the party by whose negligent act the injury has been occasioned."

It is, however, obviously not essential "that the relation of principal and agent in the sense of one commanding and the other obeying should subsist in order to make one responsible for the [*852] tortious act of another: it is *enough if it be shown to have been by his procurement and with his assent. The cases where the liability of one for the wrongful act of another has turned upon the relation of principal and agent are quite consistent with the party's liability, irrespective of any such relation: as if I agree with a builder to build me a house, according to a certain plan, he would be an independent contractor, and I should not be liable to strangers for any wrongful act unnecessarily done by him in the performance of his work, but clearly I should be jointly liable with him for a trespass on the land if it turned out that I had no right to build upon it."[4]

[1] Pickard *v.* Smith, 10 C. B. N. S. 470, 480 (100 E. C. L. R.) (with which compare Welfare *v.* London and Brighton R. C., L. R. 4 Q. B. 693); Ellis *v.* Sheffield Gas Co., 2 E. & B. 767 (75 E. C. L. R.); Blake *v.* Thirst, 32 L. J. Ex. 188; s. c., 2 H. & C. 20.

[2] See Brown *v.* Accrington Cotton Co., 3 H. & C. 511; Murphy *v.* Caralli, Id. 462.

[3] 4 Exch. 244, 255; followed in Butler *v.* Hunter, 7 H. & N. 826, 834; per Cresswell, J., Overton *v.* Freeman, 11 C. B. 873 (73 E. C. L. R.); and per Maule, J., Peachey *v.* Rowland, 13 C. B. 187 (76 E. C. L. R.); Sadler *v.* Henlock, 4 E. & B. 570 (82 E. C. L. R.); Cuthbertson *v.* Parsons, 12 C. B. 304 (74 E. C. L. R.); Gayford *v.* Nicholls, 9 Exch. 702; Grote *v.* Chester and Holyhead R. C., 2 Exch. 251. See Mills *v.* Holton, 2 H. & N. 14.

[4] Per Willes, J., Upton *v.* Townend, 17 C. B. 71 (84 E. C. L. R.).

A railroad company entered into a contract with A. to construct a portion of their line. A. contracted with B., who resided in the country, to erect a bridge on the line. B. had in his employment C., who acted as his general servant, and as a surveyor, and had the management of B.'s business in London, for which he received an annual salary. B. entered into a contract with C., by which C. agreed for 40*l.* to erect a scaffold, which had become necessary in the building of the bridge; but it was agreed that B. should find the requisite materials and lamps, and other lights. The scaffold was erected upon the footway by C.'s workmen; a portion of it improperly projected, and owing to that and the want of sufficient light, D. fell over it at night, and was injured. After the accident, B. caused other lights to be placed near the spot, to prevent a recurrence of similar accidents. Held, that an action was not maintainable by D. against B. for the injury thus occasioned.[1]

*Where the owner of a carriage hires horses of a stable- [*853] keeper, who provides a driver, through whose negligence an injury is done, the driver must be considered as the servant of the stable-keeper or job-master, against whom, consequently, the remedy must be taken; unless there be special circumstances showing an assent, either express or implied, to the tortious act, of the party hiring the horses, or showing that such party had control over the servant, and was, in fact, *dominus pro tempore*.[2]

The maxim, *Respondeat superior*, does not, moreover, apply to make the master responsible to a servant who sustains bodily hurt whilst discharging the duties incidental to his employment, such

[1] Knight *v.* Fox, 5 Exch. 721 (distinguishing Burgess *v.* Gray, 1 C. B. 578 (50 E. C. L. R.)); Steel *v.* South-Eastern R. C., 16 C. B. 550 (81 E. C. L. R.).

[2] The following cases may be referred to on this subject, which can only be briefly noticed in the text:—M'Laughlin *v.* Pryor, 4 Scott N. R. 655; s. c., 1 Car. & M. 354; Quarman *v.* Burnett, 6 M. & W. 499; the judgments of Abbott, C. J., and Littledale, J., in Laugher *v.* Pointer, 5 B. & C. 547 (11 E. C. L. R.); Dalyell *v.* Tyrer, E., B. & E. 898 (96 E. C. L. R.); Hart *v.* Crowley, 12 A. & E. 378 (40 E. C. L. R.); Taverner *v.* Little, 5 Bing. N. C. 678 (35 E. C. L. R.); Croft *v.* Alison, 4 B. & Ald. 590 (6 E. C. L. R.); Judgm., Seymour *v.* Greenwood, 7 H. & N. 358; s. c., 6 Id. 359; Smith *v.* Lawrence, 2 Man. & Ry. 1; Sammell *v.* Wright, 5 Esp. N. P. C. 263; Scott *v.* Scott, 2 Stark. N. P. C. 438 (3 E. C. L. R.); Brady *v.* Giles, 1 M. & Rob. 494; per Patteson, J., 8 A. & E. 839 (35 E. C. L. R.).

hurt having been caused by his own carelessness or negligence,[1] or through a defect in machinery,[2] or a deficiency of hands,[3] of which the injured party must necessarily have been cognizant,[4] or occasioned by the negligence of a fellow-servant, provided the master has been reasonably cautious in selecting as his associates persons [*854] possessed of ordinary *skill and care.[5] If A. and B. are fellow-servants of C., and by the unskillfulness of A., B. is injured while they are jointly engaged in the same service, B. will, under ordinary circumstances, have no claim against C., for A. and B. "have both engaged in a common service, the duties of which impose a certain risk on each of them; and, in case of negligence on the part of the other, the party injured knows that the negligence is that of his fellow-servant and not of his master. He knew when he engaged in the service that he was exposed to the risk of injury, not only from his own want of skill or care, but also from the want of it on the part of his fellow-servant; and he must be supposed to have contracted on the terms, that as between himself and his master he would run this risk."[6] And the principle here

[1] Dynen *v.* Leach, 26 L. J. Ex. 221; Senior *v.* Ward, 1 E. & E. 385 (102 E. C. L. R.).

[2] Dynen *v.* Leach, *supra;* Priestley *v.* Fowler, 3 M. & W. 1. See Winterbottom *v.* Wright, 10 M. & W. 109; Mellors *v.* Shaw, 1 B. & S. 437, 446.

[3] Skipp *v.* Eastern Counties R. C., 9 Exch. 223; Seymour *v.* Maddox, 16 Q. B. 326 (71 E. C. L. R.).

[4] See Assop *v.* Yates, 2 H. & N. 768, which likewise illustrates the maxim *In jure non remota causa sed proxima spectatur—ante,* p. 216.

[5] Hutchinson *v.* York, Newcastle and Berwick R. C., 5 Exch. 343; Wigmore *v.* Jay, Id. 354; Tarrant *v.* Webb, 18 C. B. 797, 804 (86 E. C. L. R.); Ormond *v.* Holland, E., B. & E. 102 (96 E. C. L. R.); Priestley *v.* Fowler, 3 M. & W. 1, which has often been recognized (see, for instance, Waller *v.* South-Eastern R. C., 32 L. J. Ex. 205, 209; s. c., 2 H. & C. 112; per Keating, J., Searle *v.* Lindsay, 11 C. B. N. S. 439 (103 E. C. L. R.)); Southcote *v.* Stanley, 1 H. & N. 247, 250.

[6] Judgm., 5 Exch. 351; Tunney *v.* Midland R. C., L. R. 1 C. P. 291.

"The rule has been settled by a series of cases beginning with Priestley *v.* Fowler (5 Exch. 343), and ending with Morgan *v.* Vale of Neath R. C. (L. R. 1 Q. B. 149), that a servant when he engages to serve a master undertakes as between himself and his master, to run all the ordinary risks of the service, including the risk of negligence upon the part of a fellow-servant when he is acting in the discharge of his duty as servant of him who is the common master of both:" per Erle, C. J., L. R. 1 C. P. 296. See also Murphy *v.* Smith, 19 C. B. N. S. 361 (115 E. C. L. R.); Gallagher *v.* Piper, 16 C. B. N. S. 669 (111 E. C. L. R.).

stated may be applied where the work on which the one servant is employed is very dissimilar from that on which the other is employed,[1] or to the case where the servant of a sub-contractor *receives a bodily hurt, through the negligence of a servant of the principal.[2] [*855]

In The Bartonshill Coal Company v. Reid,[3] which came before the House of Lords on appeal from the Court of Session in Scotland, the question for decision was whether, if in the working of a mine one of the servants employed is killed or injured by the negligence of another servant employed in some common work, that other servant having been a competent workman and properly employed to discharge the duties intrusted to him, the common employers of both are responsible to the servant who is injured, or to his representatives for the loss occasioned by the negligence of the other.

In answering the above question in the negative, Lord Cranworth thus remarks upon the doctrine of our law respecting the liability of a master to a stranger or to his own servant for bodily hurt sustained through negligence:—"Where," he says, "an injury is occasioned by any one by the negligence of another, if the person injured seeks to charge with its consequences any person other than him who actually caused the damage, it lies on the person injured to show that the circumstances were such as to make some other person responsible. In general, it is sufficient for this purpose to show that the person whose neglect caused the injury was at the time when it was occasioned acting not on his own account but in the course of his employment as a servant in the business of a master, and that the damage resulted from the servant so employed not having conducted his master's business *with due care. In such a case, the maxim *Respondeat superior* prevails, and the master is responsible. [*856]

"Thus, if a servant driving his master's carriage along the highway carelessly runs over a bystander, or if a gamekeeper employed to kill game carelessly fires at a hare, so as to shoot a person pass-

[1] Morgan v. Vale of Neath R. C., L. R. 1 Q. B. 149, distinguished in Warburton v. Great Western R. C., L. R. 2 Ex. 30, 33; Wilson v. Merry, L. R. 1 Sc. App. Cas. 326, 338; Feltham v. England, L. R. 2 Q. B. 33.

[2] Wiggett v. Fox, 11 Exch. 832.

[3] 3 Macq. Sc. App. Cas. 266; Weems v. Mathieson, 4 Id. 215.

ing on the ground, or if a workman employed by a builder in building a house negligently throws a stone or brick from a scaffold and so hurts a passer by; in all these cases (and instances might be multiplied indefinitely)[1] the person injured has a right to treat the wrongful or careless act as the act of the master: *Qui facit per alium facit per se.*[2] If the master himself had driven his carriage improperly, or fired carelessly, or negligently thrown the stone or brick, he would have been directly responsible, and the law does not permit him to escape liability because the act complained [*857] *of was not done with his own hand. He is considered as bound to guarantee third persons against all hurt arising from the carelessness of himself or of those acting under his orders in the course of his business. Third persons cannot, or at all events may not, know whether the particular injury complained of was the act of the master or the act of his servant. A person sustaining injury in any of the modes I have suggested has a right to say, I was no party to your carriage being driven along the road, to your shooting near the public highway, or to your being engaged in building a house. If you chose to do, or cause to be done, any of these acts, it is to you, and not to your servants, I must look for

[1] So in Barwick *v.* English Joint Stock Bank, L. R. 2 Ex. 265–6, the court observe, "The general rule is that the master is answerable for every such wrong of the servant or agent as is committed in the course of the service and for the master's benefit, though no express command or privity of the master be proved. That principle is acted upon every day in running-down cases. It has been applied also to direct trespass to goods, as in the case of holding the owners of ships liable for the act of masters abroad improperly selling the cargo (Ewbank *v.* Nutting, 7 C. B. 797 (62 E. C. L. R.)). It has been held applicable to actions of false imprisonment in cases where officers of railway companies intrusted with the execution of by-laws relating to imprisonment, and intending to act in the course of their duty, improperly imprison persons who are supposed to come within the terms of the by-laws (Goff *v.* Great Northern R. C., 3 E. & E. 672 (107 E. C. L. R.)). It has been acted upon where persons employed by the owners of boats, to navigate them and to take fares, have committed an infringement of a ferry, or such like wrong (Huzzey *v.* Field, 2 C., M. & R. 440). In all these cases it may be said that the master has not authorized the act. It is true he has not authorized the particular act, but he has put the agent in his place to do that class of acts, and he must be answerable for the manner in which the agent has conducted himself in doing the business which it was the act of the master to place him in."

[2] *Ante*, p. 817.

redress if mischief happens to me as their consequence. A large portion of the ordinary acts of life are attended with some risk to third persons, and no one has a right to involve others in risks without their consent. This consideration is alone sufficient to justify the wisdom of the rule which makes the person by whom or by whose orders these risks are incurred responsible to third persons for any ill consequences resulting from want of due skill or caution."[1]

"But," continues Lord Cranworth, "do the same principles apply to the case of a workman injured by the want of care of a fellow-workman engaged together in the same work? I think not. When the workman contracts to do work of any particular sort, he knows, or ought to know, to what risk he is exposing himself; he knows, if such be the nature of the risk, that want of care on the part of a fellow-workman may be injurious or fatal to him, and that against such want of care his *employer cannot by possibility protect him. If such want of care should occur, [*858] and evil is the result, he cannot say that he does not know whether the master or the servant was to blame. He knows that the blame was wholly that of the servant. He cannot say the master need not have engaged in the work at all, for he was a party to its being undertaken.

"Principle, therefore, seems to me opposed to the doctrine, that the responsibility of a master for the ill consequences of his servant's carelessness is applicable to the demand made by a fellow-workman in respect of evil resulting from the carelessness of a fellow-workman when engaged in a common work."[2]

In the consideration of any case falling within the class above adverted to, viz., where bodily hurt is caused to one servant by his

[1] *Acc.*, per Lord Chelmsford, C., Bartonshill Coal Co. *v.* McGuire, 3 Macq. Sc. App. Cas. 306.

[2] 3 Macq. H. L. Cas. 282–4. (The learned lord whose words are above cited then proceeds to comment *seriatim* on the following cases: Priestley *v.* Fowler, 3 M. & W. 1; Hutchinson *v.* York, Newcastle and Berwick R. C., 5 Exch. 349; Wigmore *v.* Jay, Id. 354; Skipp *v.* Eastern Counties R. C., 9 Exch. 223; Couch *v.* Steel, 3 E. & B. 402 (77 E. C. L. R.);—also on the Scotch appeal cases—Paterson *v.* Wallace, 1 Macq. Sc. App. Cas. 748; Bryden *v.* Stewart, 2 Id. 30.) Bartonshill Coal Co. *v.* McGuire, 3 Macq. Sc. App. Cas. 300; Hall *v.* Johnson, 3 H. & C. 589; Senior *v.* Ward, 1 E. & E. 385, 391 (102 E. C. L. R.); Riley *v.* Baxendale, 6 H. & N. 445.

fellow-servant, it is necessary, as remarked by Lord Chelmsford, C., in The Bartonshill Coal Company *v.* McGuire,[1] to ascertain whether the servants were fellow-laborers in the same work when the catastrophe occurred, "because although a servant may be taken to have engaged to encounter all risks which are incident to the service which he undertakes, yet he cannot be expected to anticipate those which may happen to him on occasions foreign to his employment. Where servants, therefore, are engaged in different [*859] departments of duty, *an injury committed by one servant upon the other by carelessness or negligence in the course of his peculiar work is not within the exception, and the master's liability attaches in that case in the same manner as if the injured servant stood in no such relation to him. There may be some nicety and difficulty in particular cases in deciding whether a common employment exists, but, in general, by keeping in view what the servant must have known or expected to have been involved in the service which he undertakes, a satisfactory conclusion may be arrived at."[2]

The doctrine asserted by the House of Lords in The Bartonshill Coal Company *v.* Reid has been frequently applied, *ex. gr.*, in Clarke *v.* Holmes,[3] in which case Cockburn, C. J., observes, that "where a servant is employed on machinery from the use of which danger may arise, it is the duty of the master to take due care and to use all reasonable means to guard against and prevent any defects from which increased and unnecessary danger may occur. No doubt when a servant enters on an employment from its nature necessarily hazardous, he accepts the service subject to the risks incidental to it; or if he thinks proper to accept an employment on machinery defective from its construction, or from the want of proper repair, and with knowledge of the facts enters on the service, the master cannot be held liable for injury to the servant within the scope of the danger which both the contracting parties contemplated as incidental to the employment." But the

[1] 3 Macq. Sc. App. Cas. 307–8.

[2] Waller *v.* South-Eastern R. C., 32 L. J. Ex. 205, 209; s. c., 2 H. & C. 102; Abraham *v.* Reynolds, 5 H. & N. 143; Vose *v.* Lancashire and Yorkshire R. C., 2 H. & N. 728.

[3] 7 H. & N. 937, 943–4; s. c., 6 Id. 349.

danger contemplated *on entering into the contract must [*860] not be aggravated by any omission on the part of the master to keep the machinery in the condition in which, from the terms of the contract or the nature of the employment, the servant had a right to expect that it would be kept.[1] "A master," as remarked on another occasion,[2] "is by law bound to provide proper and efficient machinery and reasonably competent workmen," but is not responsible for damage caused to his servant through a defect in such machinery due to the negligence of a fellow-servant.[3]

The rule laid down by Lord Cranworth in The Bartonshill Coal Company *v.* Reid,[4] also holds where the individual injured was at the time of sustaining the injury voluntarily assisting the defendant's servants in their work.[5] But the cases above cited do not, of course, apply to exonerate a master who has been guilty of personal negligence from liability to his servant in respect of damage thence resulting.[6]

This part of our subject may accordingly be summed up in the words of a learned lord,[7] who says that the master is not, and cannot be, liable to his servant unless there be negligence on the part of the master in that which he, the master, has contracted or undertaken with his servant to do. The master has not contracted or *undertaken to execute in person the work connected [*861] with his business. But the master, in the event of his not personally superintending and directing the work, is to select proper and competent persons to do so, and to furnish them with adequate materials and resources for the work.

In Blakemore *v.* The Bristol and Exeter Railway Company,[8]

[1] Per Cockburn, C. J., 7 H. & N. 944; Weems *v.* Mathieson, 4 Macq. Sc. App. Cas. 215.

[2] Per Keating, J., 11 C. B. N. S. 439 (103 E. C. L. R.).

[3] Searle *v.* Lindsay, 11 C. B. N. S. 429 (103 E. C. L. R.).

[4] *Ante*, p. 855.

[5] Degg *v.* Midland R. C., 1 H. & N. 773; affirmed in Potter *v.* Falkner, 1 B. & S. 800, 806 (101 E. C. L. R.).

[6] Roberts *v.* Smith, 2 H. & N. 213; Ormond *v.* Holland, E., B. & E. 102 (96 E. C. L. R.); Tarrant *v.* Webb, 18 C. B. 797, 804 (86 E. C. L. R.); Mellors *v.* Shaw, 1 B. & S. 437 (101 E. C. L. R.).

[7] Lord Cairns, C., Wilson *v.* Merry, L. R. 1 Sc. App. Cas. 332.

[8] 8 E. & B. 1035 (92 E. C. L. R.) (followed in MacCarthy *v.* Young, 6 H. & N. 329, 336), in connection with which see Langridge *v.* Levy, 2 M. & W. 519; s. c., 4 Id. 337; Longmeid *v.* Holliday, 6 Exch. 761.

the plaintiff sued under Lord Campbell's Act, as administratrix of her husband, whose death had been caused by the defective condition of a chain used in the raising and removing of goods from the trucks of the defendants' company, on arriving at the terminus of their transit. The onus of removing these goods lay, by virtue of the conditions under which they were carried, on the consignee, and the peculiar feature of the case was this—that the deceased, though not in the employ of the consignee, was asked by one of the consignee's servants to assist in the removal of the goods, which had to be raised by a crane from the trucks of the company, with a view to their being deposited in the carts and wagons of the consignee. During this process the chain gave way, and the deceased being struck by the crane sustained a mortal hurt. Upon these facts the action at suit of the administratrix of the deceased was held not to be sustainable, and the case was distinguished from Langridge *v.* Levy,[1] on the ground of absence of fraud, and because the duty of providing a safe engine for the transfer and removal of goods could under the circumstances only arise from the contract [*862] in law between the company and *consignee, to which contract the deceased was in no way privy.

It has been held that the owner of realty is not responsible for a nuisance committed thereon by the occupying tenant, unless, indeed, he has been a party to the creation of the nuisance after the demise, or has demised land with the nuisance existing.[2] The question moreover was on a recent occasion raised, but not decided, "whether, in any case, the owner of real property, such as land or houses, may be responsible for nuisances occasioned by the mode in which his property is used by others, not standing in the relation of servants to him, or part of his family;" and the court observed that "it may be that in some cases he is so responsible. But then his liability must be founded on the principle that he has not taken due care to prevent the doing of acts which it was his duty to prevent, whether done by his servants or others. If, for instance, a person occupying a house or a field should permit another to carry on there a noxious trade, so as to be a nuisance to his neighbors, it may be that he would be responsible, though the acts

[1] 2 M. & W. 519; s. c., 4 Id. 337.

[2] Rich *v.* Basterfield, 4 C. B. 783 (56 E. C. L. R.); cited in Brown *v.* Bussell, L. R. 3 Q. B. 261.

complained of were neither his acts nor the acts of his servants; he would have violated the rule of law *Sic utere tuo ut alienum non lædas*."[1] And to the foregoing observations the court add that "in none of the more modern cases has the alleged distinction between *real and *personal* property," in regard to the civil liability of its owner, "been admitted."[2] [*863]

With respect to public functionaries having authority, such as judges civil or ecclesiastical, or magistrates, these parties are, in general, protected from the consequences of an illegal and wrongful act done by an officer or other person employed in an inferior ministerial capacity, provided that the principal himself acted in the discharge of his duty, and within the scope of his jurisdiction and of the authority delegated to him. The principle, however, on which a private person or a company is liable for damage caused by the neglect of servants has been held applicable to a corporation which has been intrusted by statute to perform certain works, and to receive tolls for the use of such works, although those tolls, unlike the tolls received by the private person or the company, are not applied to the use of the corporation, but are devoted to the maintenance of the works, and in case of any surplus existing, to a proportionate diminution of the tolls.[3]

"The law requires that the execution of public works by a public body shall be conducted with a reasonable degree of care and skill; and if they, or those who are employed by them, are guilty of negligence in the performance of the works intrusted to them, they are responsible to the party injured."[4]

[1] Judgm., Reedie *v.* London and North-Western R. C., 4 Exch. 256 (citing Rich *v.* Basterfield, *supra*, and Bush *v.* Steinman, 1 B. & P. 404); Gandy *v.* Jubber, 5 B. & S. 78 (117 E. C. L. R.), explained in Bartlett *v.* Baker, 3 H. & C. 160; Saxby *v.* Manchester, Sheffield, &c., R. C., L. R. 4 C. P. 198; Gayford *v.* Nicholls, 9 Exch. 702; Pickard *v.* Smith, 10 C. B. N. S. 470, 479 (100 E. C. L. R.); Bishop *v.* Trustees of Bedford Charity, 1 E. & E. 697, 714 (102 E. C. L. R.).

[2] Citing Milligan *v.* Wedge, 12 A. & E. 737 (40 E. C. L. R.), and recognizing Allen *v.* Hayward, 7 Q. B. 960 (53 E. C. L. R.).

[3] Mersey Docks Trustees *v.* Gibbs; Same *v.* Penhallow, L. R. 1 H. L. 93, where the cases are reviewed.

[4] Clothier *v.* Webster, 12 C. B. N. S. 790, 796 (104 E. C. L. R.). See Brownlow *v.* Metropolitan Board of Works, 16 C. B. N. S. 546 (111 E. C. L. R.); Gibson *v.* Mayor, &c., of Preston, L. R. 5 Q. B. 518; Parsons *v.* St. Mathew, Bethnal Green, L. R. 3 C. P. 56; Hyams *v.* Webster, L. R. 4 Q. B. 138.

[*864] In an ordinary case, moreover, where such commissioners *in execution of their office enter into a contract for the performance of work, it seems clear that the person who contracts to do the work "is not to be considered as a servant, but a person carrying on an independent business, such as the commissioners were fully justified in employing to perform works which they could not execute for themselves, and who was known to all the world as performing them."[1] And the person thus employed may himself, by virtue of an express statutory clause, be protected or absolved from liability to a suit whilst acting under the direction of the commissioners.[2] And a shipowner is not responsible at common law[3] for injuries occasioned by the unskillful navigation of his vessel whilst under the control of a pilot whom the owner was compelled to take on board, and in whose selection he had no voice.[4]

It is clear, also, that a servant of the crown, contracting in his official capacity, is not personally liable on the contracts so entered into: in such cases, therefore, the rule of *Respondeat superior* does not apply, such exceptions to it resulting from motives of public policy; for no prudent person would accept a public situation at the hazard of exposing himself to a multiplicity of suits by parties thinking themselves aggrieved.[5]

[*865] *Lastly, the maxim *Respondeat superior* does not apply in the case of the sovereign; for, as we have before seen, the sovereign is not liable for personal negligence;[6] and, therefore, the principle, *Qui facit per alium facit per se*—which is applied to render the master answerable for the negligence of his servant, because this has arisen from his own negligence or imprudence in selecting or retaining a careless servant—is not applicable to the sovereign, in whom negligence or misconduct cannot be implied, and

[1] Judgm., Allen v. Hayward, 7 Q. B. 975 (53 E. C. L. R.); citing Quarman v. Burnett, 6 M. & W. 499; Milligan v. Wedge, 12 A. & E. 737 (40 E. C. L. R.); and Rapson v. Cubitt, 9 M. & W. 710.

[2] Ward v. Lee, 7 E. & B. 426; Newton v. Ellis, 5 E. & B. 115.

[3] See also stat. 17 & 18 Vict. c. 104, s. 388; Gen. Steam Nav. Co. v. British and Colonial Steam Nav. Co., L. R. 4 Ex. 238; The Lion, L. R. 2 P. C. 525.

[4] The Halley, L. R. 2 P. C. 193, 201, 202.

See The Thetis, L. R. 2 A. & E. 365 (29 E. C. L. R.).

[5] Per Dallas, C. J., Gidley v. Lord Palmerston, 3 B. & B. 286, 287; per Ashhurst, J., Macbeath v. Haldimand, 1 T. R. 181, 182.

[6] *Ante*, p. 52.

for which, if it occurs in fact, the law affords no remedy. Accordingly, in a modern case, already alluded to, it was observed by Lord Lyndhurst, that instances have occurred of damage occasioned by the negligent management of ships of war, in which it has been held, that, where an act is done by one of the crew without the participation of the commander, the latter is not responsible; but that, if the principle contended for in the case then before the court were correct, the negligence of a seaman in the service of the crown would, in such a case, render the crown liable to make good the damage; a proposition which certainly could not be maintained.[1]

[1] Viscount Canterbury *v.* A.-G., 1 Phill. 306; Feather *v.* Reg., 6 B. & S. 294, *et seq.*; Tobin *v.* Reg., 16 C. B. N. S. 310 (111 E. C. L. R.); Reg. *v.* Prince, L. R. 1 C. C. 150. See Hodgkinson *v.* Fernie, 2 C. B. N. S. 415 (89 E. C. L. R.).

It seems almost superfluous to observe, that the above remarks upon the maxim *Respondeat superior* are to some considerable extent applicable in criminal law. On the one hand, a party employing an innocent agent is liable for an offence committed through this medium; on the other, if the agent had a guilty knowledge he will be responsible as well as his employer. See Bac. Max., reg. 16. Though "it is a rule of criminal law that a person cannot be criminally liable for acting as the agent of another without any knowledge that he was acting wrongly:" per Crompton, J., Hearne *v.* Garton, 2 E. & E. 76 (105 E. C. L. R.).

In Coleman *v.* Riches, 16 C. B. 118 (81 E. C. L. R.), Jervis, C. J., specifies various cases in which criminal responsibility will be entailed on a master for the acts of his servants in the ordinary course of their employment.

"There are," moreover, "many acts of a servant for which, though criminal, the master is civilly responsible by action:" per Jervis, C. J., Dunkley *v.* Farris, 11 C. B. 458 (73 E. C. L. R.); Palmer *v.* Evans, 2 C. B. N. S. 151 (89 E. C. L. R.); Roberts, app., Preston, resp., 9 C. B. N. S. 208 (99 E. C. L. R.).

Upon the above subject Lord Wensleydale thus observes:—"I take it to be a clear proposition of law, that if a man employs an agent for a perfectly legal purpose, and that agent does an illegal act, that act does not affect the principal unless a great deal more is shown: unless it is shown that the principal directed the agent so to act, or really meant he should so act, or afterwards ratified the illegal act, or that he appointed one to be his general agent to do both legal and illegal acts:" Cooper *v.* Slade, 6 H. L. Cas. 793; and see Parkes *v.* Prescott, L. R. 4 Ex. 169.

Also, in Wilson *v.* Rankin, 6 B. & S. 216, the Court of Queen's Bench thus remark:—"It is a well-established distinction, that while a man is civilly responsible for the acts of his agent when acting within the established limits of his authority, he will not be criminally responsible for such acts unless express authority be shown, or the authority is necessarily to be implied from the nature of the employment, as in the case of a bookseller held liable for

[*866] *A subject sustaining a legal wrong at the hands of a minister of the crown is not, however, without a remedy, for "as the sovereign cannot authorize wrong to be done, the authority of the crown would afford no defence to an action brought for an illegal act committed by an officer of the crown."[1]

Lastly, assuming that an act which would *primâ facie* be a trespass is done by order of the government, the party who commits the trespass is clearly exempted from liability, and whether the injury "is an act of state without remedy, except by appeal to the justice of the state which inflicts it, or by application of the individual suffering to the government of his country to insist upon [*867] *compensation from the government of this—in either view, the wrong is no longer actionable."[2]

Omnis Ratihabitio retrotrahitur et Mandato priori Æquiparatur.

(Co. Litt. 207 a.)

A subsequent ratification has a retrospective effect, and is equivalent to a prior command.

It is a rule of very wide application, and one which we find repeatedly laid down in the Roman law, that *ratihabitio mandato comparatur*,[3] where *ratihabitio* is defined to be "the act of assenting to what has been done by another in my name."[4] "No maxim," remarks Mr. Justice Story, "is better settled in reason and law than the maxim, *Omnis ratihabitio retrotrahitur et mandato priori æquiparatur*,[5] at all events, where it does not prejudice the rights

the sale by his shopman of a libellous publication. Under ordinary circumstances the authority of the agent is limited to that which is lawful. If in seeking to carry out the purpose of his employment he oversteps the law, he outruns his authority, and his principal will not be bound by what he does." See also Reg. *v.* Stephens, L. R. 1 Q. B. 702.

[1] Judgm., Feather *v.* Reg., 6 B. & S. 296 (118 E. C. L. R.).

[2] *Vide* per Parke, B., Buron *v.* Denman, 2 Exch. 189; explained in Feather *v.* Reg., 6 B. & S. 296 (118 E. C. L. R.).

[3] D. 46. 3. 12, § 4; D. 50. 17. 60; D. 3. 5. 6, § 9; D. 43. 16. 1, § 14.

[4] Brisson. ad verb. "*Ratihabitio.*"

[5] Co. Litt. 207 a; 258 a; Wing. Max. 485. Many instances of the application of this maxim are given in 18 Vin. Abr., p. 156, tit. "*Ratihabitio.*" See

of strangers. And the civil law does not, it is believed, differ from the common law on this subject."[1]

It is, then, true as a general rule, of which instances have occurred in the preceding pages, and with respect to *which [*868] we shall merely make a few additional observations in this place,[2] that a subsequent ratification and adoption of what has been already done has a retrospective effect, and is equivalent to a previous command. For instance, if the goods of A. are wrongfully taken and sold, the owner may either bring trover against the wrong-doer, or may elect to consider him as his agent, may adopt the sale, and maintain an action for the price.[3] So, if a principal ratifies the purchase by his agent of a chattel which the vendor had no right to sell, the principal is guilty of a conversion, although at the time of the ratification he had no knowledge that the sale was unlawful.[4] So, if the agent of a vendor misrepresent the subject-matter of the sale to the vendee, it will be proper for the jury to infer from the vendor's subsequent conduct,—as, *ex. gr.*, from his not having repudiated a warranty, when apprised of it,—that he was privy to, or impliedly assented to, the misrepresentation of the

Ward *v.* Broomhead, 7 Exch. 726; Sievewright *v.* Archibald, 17 Q. B. 103 (79 E. C. L. R.); cited per Erle, C. J., Heyworth *v.* Knight, 17 C. B. N. S. 308 (112 E. C. L. R.). (See also Parton *v.* Crofts, 16 C. B. N. S. 11 (111 E. C. L. R.); Doe d. Gutteridge *v.* Sowerby, 7 C. B. N. S. 599, 626 (97 E. C. L. R.).)

[1] Per Story, J., delivering judgment, Fleckner *v.* United States Bank, 8 Wheaton (U. S.) R. 363. As to the ratification of a promise by an infant under stat. 9 Geo. 4, c. 14, s. 5, see Mawson *v.* Blane, 10 Exch. 206; Rowe *v.* Hopwood, L. R. 4 Q. B. 1.

[2] The operation of the maxim as to *ratihabitio* with reference to the law of principal and agent, is considered at length in Story on Agency, 7th ed., pp. 283 *et seq.*

See Mitcheson *v.* Nicol, 7 Exch. 929; Simpson *v.* Egginton, 10 Exch. 845 (which forcibly illustrates the maxim, *supra*, and in connection with which, see per Maule, J., Tassell *v.* Cooper, 9 C. B. 532 (67 E. C. L. R.); Kemp *v.* Balls, Id. 607); Earl of Mountcashell *v.* Barber, 14 C. B. 53 (78 E. C. L. R.); Maclae *v.* Sutherland, 3 E. & B. 1 (77 E. C. L. R.); Fagan *v.* Harrison, 8 C. B. 388 (65 E. C. L. R.); Fitzmaurice *v.* Bayley, 9 H. L. Cas. 78.

[3] *Ante*, p. 296; Smith *v.* Hodson, 4 T. R. 211; Rodgers *v.* Maw, 15 M. & W. 448; England *v.* Marsden, L. R. 1 C. P. 529. See Saunderson *v.* Griffiths, 5 B. & C. 909 (11 E. C. L. R.); Underhill *v.* Wilson, 6 Bing. 697 (19 E. C. L. R.); Kynaston *v.* Crouch, 14 M. & W. 266.

[4] Hilbery *v.* Hatton, 2 H. & C. 822.

agent.[1] Again, the title of an administrator relates back to the time of the death of the intestate, so as to entitle the personal representative to sue for the price of goods sold by one who intended [*869] to act as agent for the person, whoever he might *happen to be, who legally represented the intestate's estate,—the sale having been ratified by the plaintiff after he became administrator; for, when one means or professes to act as agent for another, a subsequent ratification by that other is equivalent to a prior command; and it is no objection, that the intended principal was unknown at the time to the person who intended to be the agent.[2] H., the managing owner of a ship, directed an insurance-broker to effect an insurance on the entire ship, upon an adventure in which all the part-owners were jointly interested; the amount of the entire premium was carried to the ship's account in H.'s books, which were open to the inspection of all the part-owners, who saw the account, and never objected to it. It did not, however, appear that the insurance-broker knew the names of all the part-owners, or whether or not they had given authority to H. to insure. It was observed that the maxim as to *ratihabitio* well applied to such a case; and it was held, that the jury were warranted in inferring a joint authority to insure, and that the part-owners were jointly liable for the premium to the insurance-broker, although he had debited H. alone, and divided with him the profits of commission, upon effecting the insurance.[3] It is, indeed, true that "no one can sue upon a contract unless it has been made by him, or has been made by an agent professing to act for him, and whose act has been ratified by him;" and although persons who could not be named or [*870] ascertained *at the time when a policy of insurance was effected are allowed to come in and take the benefit of the insurance, yet they must be persons who were contemplated when the policy was made.[4]

Again—"if an arbitrator omits to enlarge the time limited for

[1] Wright *v.* Crookes, 1 Scott N. R. 685.

[2] Foster *v.* Bates, 12 M. & W. 226; Hull *v.* Pickersgill, 1 B. & B. 282 (5 E. C. L. R.); cited per Parke, B., Heslop *v.* Baker, 8 Exch. 417. See also Tharpe *v.* Stallwood, 6 Scott N. R. 715; Campanari *v.* Woodburn, 15 C. B. 400 (80 E. C. L. R.); Crosthwaite *v.* Gardner, 18 Q. B. 640 (83 E. C. L. R.).

[3] Robinson *v.* Gleadow, 2 Bing. N. C. 156, 161 (29 E. C. L. R.). See Prince *v.* Clark, 1 B. & C. 186 (8 E. C. L. R.); Clark *v.* Perrier, 2 Freem. 48.

[4] Watson *v.* Swann, 11 C. B. N. S. 756, 769 (103 E. C. L. R.).

making his award, but continues to act as if he had enlarged it, even to making his award, although in fact he has no authority, yet he is a person *animo agendi*, and if the parties afterwards choose to ratify his act by agreeing that the time shall be enlarged or otherwise, though the act was not enforceable, yet if ratified it would be just as binding as if done with original authority."[1]

Without unnecessarily multiplying instances to the same effect as the preceding, it may be sufficient to state the general proposition that the subsequent assent by the principal to his agent's conduct not only exonerates the latter from the consequences of a departure from his orders, but likewise renders the principal liable on contracts made in violation of such orders, or even where there has been no previous retainer or employment; and this assent may be inferred from the conduct of the principal.[2] The subsequent sanction is considered the same thing, in effect, as assent at the time; the difference being that, where the authority is given beforehand, the party *giving it must trust to his agent; if it be given [*871] subsequently to the contract, the party knows that all has been done according to his wishes.[3] "That an act done for another by a person not assuming to act for himself, but for such other person, though without any precedent authority whatever, becomes the act of the principal if subsequently ratified by him, is the known and well-established rule of law. In that case the principal is bound by the act, whether it be for his detriment or advantage, and whether it be founded on a tort or a contract, to the same extent as by, and with all the consequences which follow from, the same act done by his previous authority."[4]

It is, however, a doctrine of equity, applicable also, it would

[1] Per Blackburn, J., Lord *v.* Lee, L. R. 3 Q. B. 404, 408.

[2] Smith Merc. Law, 5th ed., 124, 138, and cases there cited; Judgm., Wilson *v.* Tumman, 6 M. & Gr. 242 (46 E. C. L. R.). See Hasleham *v.* Young, 5 Q. B. 833 (48 E. C. L. R.). The maxim is applied to a notice to quit given by the agent and subsequently recognized by the lessors, who were joint tenants: per Abbott, C. J., Goodtitle *v.* Woodward, 3 B. & Ald. 686, 692 (5 E. C. L. R.). See Wright *v.* Cuthell, 5 East 491. As to a policy of insurance, per Buller, J., Wolff *v.* Horncastle, 1 B. & P. 323; arg. 13 East 280; as to a past consideration, *ante*, p. 756.

[3] Per Best, C. J., Maclean *v.* Dunn, 4 Bing. 727 (13 E. C. L. R.).

[4] Wilson *v.* Tumman, 6 M. & Gr. 242 (46 E. C. L. R.); Ancona *v.* Marks, 7 H. & N. 686, 695–6.

seem, in a court of law, that there can be no ratification of an invalid transaction where the person performing the supposed act of ratification has been kept by the conduct of the party in whose favor it is made unaware of its validity, and where he has not at the time of the supposed ratification the means of forming an independent judgment.[1]

"The doctrine *Omnis ratihabitio retrotrahitur, et mandato æquiparatur* is one," remark the Court of Exchequer in a modern case,[2] "intelligible in principle, and easy in its application when applied to cases of contract. If A., unauthorized by me, makes a contract on my behalf with B., which I afterwards recognize and adopt, there is no difficulty in dealing with it, as having been originally [*872] *made by my authority. B. entered into the contract on the understanding that he was dealing with me, and when I afterwards agreed to admit that such was the case, B. is precisely in the condition in which he meant to be; or if he did not believe A. to be acting for me, his condition is not altered by my adoption of the agency, for he may sue A. as principal at his option, and has the same equities against me, if I sue, which he would have had against A." The ratification of a contract must, however, be made by an existing person, on whose behalf the contract might have been made at the time.[3]

"In cases of tort," as further observed by the court in a case just now cited,[4] "there is more difficulty. If A., professing to act by my authority, does that which *primâ facie* amounts to a trespass, and I afterwards assent to and adopt his act, there he is treated as having from the beginning acted by my authority, and I become a trespasser unless I can justify the act, which is to be deemed as having been done by my previous sanction. So far there is no difficulty in applying the doctrine of ratification even in cases of tort. The party ratifying becomes, as it were, a trespasser by estoppel; he cannot complain that he is deemed to have authorized that which he admits himself to have authorized.

[1] Savery *v.* King, 5 H. L. Cas. 627, 664.

[2] Bird *v.* Brown, 4 Exch. 798, 799; per Lord Wensleydale, Ridgway *v.* Wharton, 6 H. L. Cas. 296.

[3] Kelner *v.* Baxter, L. R. 2 C. P. 174, 185–6; with which *acc.* Scott *v.* Lord Ebury, Id. 255, 264, 267.

[4] Bird *v.* Brown, *supra*, n. 2.

"But the authorities go much further, and show that, in some cases, where an act, which if unauthorized would amount to a trespass, has been done in the name and on behalf of another, but without previous authority, the subsequent ratification may enable the party on whose *behalf the act was done to take advantage of it, and to treat it as having been done by his direction. [*873] But this doctrine must be taken with the qualification that the act of ratification must take place at a time and under circumstances when the ratifying party might himself have lawfully done the act which he ratifies."[1]

In accordance with the foregoing remarks it has been held, that a railway company may be liable for an assault ratified by them, if the act complained of could be said to have been done for the use or benefit of the company: *ex. gr.*, the assault and imprisonment of a party liable to the company for not having paid his fare is an act of a servant of the company which manifestly might have been for their benefit; it might therefore be ratified by them.[2]

By the common law, says Sir E. Coke,[3] "he that receiveth a trespasser, and agreeth to a trespass after it be done, is no trespasser *unless the trespass was done to his use or for his benefit*, and then his agreement subsequent amounteth to a commandment; for, in that case, *Omnis ratihabitio retrotrahitur et mandato æquiparatur.*" The question of liability by ratification depends accordingly upon this consideration—whether the act was originally intended to be done to the use or for the benefit of the party who is afterwards said to have ratified it.[4] A person, therefore, who knowingly receives *from another a chattel which the latter has wrongfully seized, and afterwards on demand refuses [*874] to give it back to the owner, does not thereby become a joint trespasser, unless the chattel was seized for his use.[5] In a well-known

[1] *Acc.* per Bovill, C. J., Ainsworth *v.* Creeke, L. R. 4 C. P. 486; cited in Medwin *v.* Streeter, Id. 496.

[2] Judgm., Eastern Counties R. C. *v.* Broom, 6 Exch. 326, 327; Roe *v.* Birkenhead, Lancashire and Cheshire R. C., 7 Exch. 36.

[3] 4 Inst. 317; cited per Parke, J., 4 B. & Ad. 616; per Willes, J., Stacey, app., Whitehurst, resp., 18 C. B. N. S. 356 (114 E. C. L. R.); arg. Nicoll *v.* Glennie, 1 M. & S. 590; 6 Scott N. R. 897. See another application of the maxim to a tort, per Lord Ellenborough, C. J., 9 East 281.

[4] Judgm., 6 Exch. 327; James *v.* Isaacs, 12 C. B. 791 (74 E. C. L. R.).

[5] Wilson *v.* Barker, 4 B. & Ad. 614 (24 E. C. L. R.).

case, it was held, that, where goods are wrongfully seized by the sheriff under a *valid* writ of *fi. fa.*, the execution-creditor does not, by a *subsequent* ratification only, become liable in trespass for the original seizure; and the rule stated at page 871 was laid down by Tindal, C. J., delivering the judgment of the court.[1] Trespass does not lie against an attorney who improperly caused an attachment to be issued out of Chancery under which the plaintiff was arrested and detained until discharged by an order of the Lords Justices; nor would trespass under such circumstances lie as against the attorney's client, who, though not ordering the plaintiff's arrest, knew of it and did not interfere. Where an execution is set aside on the ground of an erroneous judgment, the plaintiff or his attorney is no more liable than is the sheriff who executes the process.[2]

A landlord authorized bailiffs to distrain for rent due to him from the tenant of a farm, directing them not to take anything except on the demised premises. The bailiffs distrained cattle of another person (supposing them to be the tenant's) beyond the boundary of the farm: the cattle were sold, and the landlord received the proceeds. It was held, that the landlord was not liable in trover for the value of the cattle, *unless* it were found [*875] *by the jury that he ratified the act of the bailiffs with knowledge of the irregularity, or that he chose, without inquiry, to take the risk upon himself, and to adopt the whole of their acts.[3]

Generally speaking, the subsequent ratification of an act done *as agent* is equal to a prior authority. This proposition, however, is *not* universally true. In the case of a tenant from year to year, who has by law a right to a half-year's notice to quit, if such notice be given by an agent without the authority of the landlord, the tenant is not bound by it.[4] Where, moreover, a person commits a tortious act,—as, if he seize goods, claiming property in them him-

[1] Wilson *v.* Tumman, 6 M. & Gr. 242 (46 E. C. L. R.); followed in Woollen *v.* Wright, 1 H. & C. 554; per Bramwell, B., Withers *v.* Parker, 4 H. & N. 534; Walker *v.* Hunter, 2 C. B. 324 (52 E. C. L. R.). See Trent *v.* Hunt, 9 Exch. 14.

[2] Williams *v.* Smith, 14 C. B. N. S. 596 (108 E. C. L. R.).

[3] Lewis *v.* Read, 13 M. & W. 834; Freeman *v.* Rosher, 13 Q. B. 780, 789 (66 E. C. L. R.); per Blackburn, J., Lord *v.* Lee, L. R. 3 Q. B. 408; Haseler *v.* Lemoyne, 5 C. B. N. S. 530 (94 E. C. L. R.); Collett *v.* Foster, 2 H. & N. 356, 361.

[4] Judgm., 2 Exch. 188.

self,—the subsequent agreement of another party will not amount to a ratification of his authority at the time.[1] So, if two out of three executors contract with another person on their own account, *and as agents* for the third executor, such last-mentioned party may adopt the contract, and all three may sue upon it, although it was made with the two only; but if the contract was with the two *on their own account only*, they could not; for to such a case, according to the distinction above mentioned, the maxim which we have been illustrating does not apply.[2]

Such being the law as between private individuals, the question arose in Buron *v.* Denman,[3] whether it applies likewise where the crown ratifies the act of one of its *officers, and the majority of the judges, presiding at the trial at bar in that case, held clearly that it does so; Parke, B., however, suggesting a distinction between the effect of a ratification by the sovereign and that by a private person; for if an individual ratifies an act done on his behalf, the nature of the act remains unchanged; it is still a mere trespass, and the party injured has his option to sue either the actual wrong-doer or him who ratifies the tort: whereas, "if the crown ratifies an act, the character of the act becomes altered; for the ratification does not give the party injured the double option of bringing his action against the agent who committed the trespass, or the principal who ratified it; but a remedy against the crown only."[4]

[*876]

To one who has glanced, however cursorily, over the preceding pages, it must be evident that the three maxims latterly considered, viz., *Qui facit per alium facit per se*—*Respondeat superior*—and *Omnis ratihabitio retrotrahitur et mandato priori æquiparatur*—will often simultaneously claim attention from the practitioner, where a state of facts involving the relation of principal and agent is placed before him. It may well therefore be imagined, that the effort

[1] Judgm., 6 Scott N. R. 904.

[2] Heath *v.* Chilton, 12 M. & W. 632, 638. As to contracts by executors and administrators, see further, Broom's Com., 4th ed., 611, *et seq.*

[3] 2 Exch. 167; recognized in Sec. of State of India *v.* Sahaba, 13 Moo. P. C. C. 86.

[4] *Ante*, pp. 52, 866. See Reg. *v.* Dring, Dearsl. & B. 329, as to the effect of an adoption by the husband of his wife's receipt of stolen goods.

would be vain to separate from each other and systematically classify reported cases illustrating the maxims specified. Little has consequently been here attempted in dealing with these elementary principles beyond offering to the reader a selection of decisions, arranged under the respective heads to which they [*877] seemed specially appropriate, fitted for impressing on *his mind the meaning and leading qualifications of the legal principles above commented on.

NIHIL TAM CONVENIENS EST NATURALI ÆQUITATI QUAM UNUMQUODQUE DISSOLVI EO LIGAMINE QUO LIGATUM EST.

(2 Inst. 360.)

Nothing is so consonant to natural equity as that every contract should be dissolved by the same means which rendered it binding.

Every contract or agreement ought to be dissolved by matter of as high a nature as that which first made it obligatory.[1] And again, "it would be inconvenient that matters in writing, made by advice and consideration, and which finally import the certain truth of the agreement of the parties, should be controlled by averment of the parties, to be proved by the uncertain testimony of slippery memory."[2] Hence it is laid down, that, "an obligation is not made void but by a release; for *Naturale est quidlibet dissolvi eo modo quo ligatur:* a record by a record; a deed by a deed; and a parol promise or agreement is dissolved by parol; and an Act of Parliament by an Act of Parliament. This reason and this rule of law are always of force in the common law."[3]

In the first place, with respect to statutes of the realm, we may remark that these, being created by an exercise of the highest authority which the constitution of this country acknowledges, cannot be dispensed with, altered, [*878] *amended, suspended, or repealed, but by the same authority by which they were made—*Jura eodem modo destituuntur quo constituunter.*[4] It was,

[1] Jenk. Cent. 166; Id. 74.

[2] Countess of Rutland's Case, 5 Rep. 26.

[3] Jenk. Cent. 70.

[4] Dwarr. Stats. 2d ed., 529; Bell Dict. and Dig. of Scotch Law 636. In

indeed, a maxim of the civilians that, as laws might be established by long and continued custom, so they could likewise be abrogated by desuetude, or be annulled by contrary usage,—*ea vero quæ ipsa sibi quæque civitas constituit sæpe mutari solent vel tacito consensu populi vel aliâ postea legè latâ.*[1] The law of England, however, as above stated, follows a different and much safer maxim, viz., that every statute continues in force till repealed by a subsequent Act of the legislature.[2]

We propose, in the next place, to consider the three following species of obligations: viz., by record, by specialty, and by simple contract; as to the first of which it will suffice to say, that an obligation by record may clearly be discharged by a release under seal;[3] and that a judgment or decree of the House of Lords can, due regard being had to constitutional principles, only be reversed or corrected by Act of Parliament.[4]

*In the case of a specialty, no rule of our common law [*879] is better established than that such a contract can, before breach, only be discharged by an instrument of equal force;[5] that a subsequent parol, that is to say, written or verbal agreement, not under seal, dispensing with or varying the time or mode of per-

Sydney's Discourse concerning Government, p. 15, we find the following passage:—"*Cujus est instituere ejus est abrogare.* We say, in general, he that institutes may also abrogate, most especially when the institution is not only by but for himself. If the multitude, therefore, do institute, the multitude may abrogate; and they themselves, or those who succeed in the same right, can only be fit judges of the performance of the ends of the institution."

[1] I. 1. 2. 11; Irving Civ. Law, 4th ed., 123.

[2] The case of Ashford *v.* Thornton, 1 B. & Ald. 405, affords a remarkable instance of the revival of an obsolete law. See also, per Patteson, J., Reg. *v.* Archbishop of Canterbury, 11 Q. B. 627 (63 E. C. L. R.).

[3] Per Parke, B., Barker *v.* St. Quintin, 12 M. & W. 453 (cited in Ex parte Games, 3 H. & C. 299); Litt. s. 507, and the commentary thereon; Shep. Touch., by Preston, 322; Farmer *v.* Mottram, 7 Scott N. R. 408.

[4] Tommey *v.* White, 3 H. L. Cas. 49; per Lord Campbell, C. J., 1 E. & B. 804 (72 E. C. L. R.); *ante*, p. 333, n. 4. See Frith *v.* Wollaston, 7 Exch. 194. A local custom may, of course, be abrogated by statute, see (*ex. gr.*) Truscott *v.* Merchant Tailors' Co., 11 Exch. 855; Cooper *v.* Hubbuck, 12 C. B. N. S. 456 (104 E. C. L. R.).

[5] Per Bosanquet, J., 3 Scott N. R. 216. But in certain cases an equitable plea may be available that performance has been dispensed with by an instrument not under seal; see, per Pollock, C. B., 1 H. & N. 458.

formance of an act covenanted to be done, cannot be pleaded in bar to an action, on an instrument under seal, for non-performance of the act in the manner thereby prescribed;[1]—in short, that the terms of a deed cannot be contradicted or varied by parol; that a parol license cannot be set up in opposition to a deed.[2]

For instance, a defeasance, not under seal, cannot be pleaded to an action on a bond, being a specialty;[3] nor to an action on a bond conditioned to perform an award, can a parol agreement between the parties to waive and abandon the award be set up successfully in defence.[4] It has, however, been already observed, and must be here repeated, that if the performance of the condition be [*880] *rendered impossible by, or the breach result from, an act of the obligee, undoubtedly he can maintain no action on the bond.[5] The following case[6] will, it is conceived, show clearly the application of the general rule of law under consideration:—An action of covenant was brought by the surviving executor of the lessor against the lessee, the breach being, *inter alia*, the pulling down and removing a greenhouse which had been erected during the term, in contravention of the lessee's covenant to yield up the premises at the expiration of the term, together with all "erections and improvements" which, during the term, should be erected, made, or set up, in or upon the premises. The defendant pleaded, by way of answer to this breach, an agreement by parol between the lessor and one H., to whom the defendant's term in the premises came by assignment, whereby the lessor promised and agreed, that, if H. would erect a greenhouse upon the demised premises, he (H.) should be at liberty to pull down and remove such green-

[1] Heard *v.* Wadham, 1 East 619; Gwynne *v.* Davy, 2 Scott N. R. 29; cited, per Cockburn, C. J., L. R. 3 Q. B. 127; Roe *v.* Harrison, 2 T. R. 425; Blake's Case, 6 Rep. 43; Peytoe's Case, 9 Rep. 77; Kaye *v.* Waghorn, 1 Taunt. 428; Jenk. Cent. 66; Cocks *v.* Nash, 9 Bing. 341 (23 E. C. L. R.); Harden *v.* Clifton, 1 Q. B. 522 (41 E. C. L. R.); Rippinghall *v.* Lloyd, 5 B. & Ad. 742 (27 E. C. L. R.), is particularly worthy of perusal in connection with the above subject.

[2] Per Lush, J., Albert *v.* Grosvenor Investment Co., L. R. 3 Q. B. 128.

[3] Blemerhasset *v.* Pierson, 3 Lev. 234.

[4] Braddick *v.* Thompson, 8 East 344.

[5] Per Tindal, C. J., 2 M. & Gr. 750, 751 (40 E. C. L. R.); *ante*, p. 283.

[6] West *v.* Blakeway, 2 M. & Gr. 729 (40 E. C. L. R.); Harris *v.* Goodwyn, 2 M. & Gr. 405; cited Judgm., Cort *v.* Ambergate, &c., R. C., 17 Q. B. 146 (79 E. C. L. R.).

house at the expiration of the term, provided no injury was thereby done to the premises. This plea was found by the jury to be true in fact, but it was held bad, on motion to enter judgment for the plaintiff *non obstante veredicto*, as presenting no legal answer to the action. "I agree," observed Tindal, C. J., "that, if it amounted to an assertion that the lessor himself, by active interference, prevented the lessee from performing the covenant, the plea would have been an answer[1]—not, however, on the footing of an agreement *or dispensation, but on the ground that the breach of covenant complained of would, in that case, have [*881] been the act of the lessor, and not of the lessee; but that which is here set up is nothing more than a parol license or permission.[2] Now, I apprehend, no rule of law is better established than this: that a covenant under seal can only be discharged by an instrument of equal force and validity—*Quodque dissolvitur eodem ligamine quo ligatur.*" And his lordship further here remarked, that the argument derived from conditions that are waived,[3] or rendered impossible of performance, seemed not necessarily to be applicable to the case of covenants under seal; that, in the former case, the obligation is under seal, but "the condition is of a thing resting on evidence only. It may be compared to matter *in pais*;"[4] whereas, in the latter, the whole obligation is under the seal of the party, and, therefore, his discharge can only be effected by an instrument of the like nature and validity with that upon which he is sued.[5] So it has more recently been held, that a covenant to pay a sum certain after notice given could not, before breach, be discharged by delivery to the covenantee of goods and chattels by the covenantor—this being matter purely *in pais*.[6]

[1] See Cort *v.* Ambergate, &c., R. C., 17 Q. B. 127, 146 (79 E. C. L. R.); *ante*, p. 282.

[2] See Cocks *v.* Nash, 9 Bing. 341 (23 E. C. L. R.); Judgm., Doe d. Muston *v.* Gladwin, 6 Q. B. 962 (51 E. C. L. R.).

[3] See 2 M. & Gr. 751 (40 E. C. L. R.). A parol license could not be pleaded as such in discharge of a covenant: see Rawlinson *v.* Clarke, 14 M. & W. 187, 191, 192; Thames Haven Dock and R. C. *v.* Brymer, 5 Exch. 696; s. c., 2 Exch. 549; Mutual Guarantee Co. *v.* Froane, 7 H. & N. 5, 14; Thames Iron Works Co. *v.* Royal Mail Steam Packet Co., 13 C. B. N. S. 358, 376 (106 E. C. L. R.).

[4] See Peytoe's Case, 9 Rep. 79 b.

[5] See Harris *v.* Goodwyn, 2 Scott N. R. 459; Gwynne *v.* Davy, Id. 29.

[6] Spence *v.* Healey, 8 Exch. 668, and cases there cited Id. 669, (*b*).

[*882] In The Mayor, &c., of Berwick *v.* Oswald,[1] the *defendant was sued in covenant upon a bond which he had entered into as surety for the due performance of his duty by one M., who had been elected to fill the office of treasurer of the town of Berwick. The breaches assigned were, that the said M. had not paid over, nor truly accounted for, certain moneys to the plaintiffs. In answer to this declaration the defendant pleaded, *inter alia*, that, after the making of the bond in question, and before any of the breaches of covenant alleged, the said M., and others as his sureties, executed and delivered to the plaintiffs, and the plaintiffs accepted and received from them, another bond "in full satisfaction and discharge of" that declared upon, and of all covenants, &c., contained therein. The bond thus alleged to have been given in lieu of that declared upon was similar to it, save that the defendant was not named therein as a surety. The court held, that the plea thus put on the record was clearly bad, because an accord and satisfaction cannot be pleaded to an action upon a deed before breach,[2] and there was nothing in the second deed which could operate as a release of that previously executed.

Again, where there has been a breach of a contract under seal, and the damages are unliquidated, accord with satisfaction of the damages resulting from such breach may be a good plea to an [*883] action on the specialty; for this *defence is by no means equivalent to setting up a parol contract in contravention of a prior contract by deed, the action being founded, not merely on the deed and the subsequent wrong, which wrong is the cause of action and for which damages are recoverable.[3] "Nothing," however, "can discharge a covenant to pay on a certain day,

[1] 1 E. & B. 295 (72 E. C. L. R.); s. c., 3 Id. 653; 5 H. L. Cas. 856; Blake's Case, 6 Rep. 44; Snow *v.* Franklin, 1 Lutw. 358; Kaye *v.* Waghorn, 1 Taunt. 428.

[2] In covenant for non-payment of rent, the defendant pleaded accord with satisfaction of the covenant *before* any breach:—Held bad, on demurrer: Snow *v.* Franklin, Lutw. 358. See Kaye *v.* Waghorn, 1 Taunt. 428; Drake *v.* Mitchell, 3 East 251; Scholey *v.* Mearns, 7 East 147; Rogers *v.* Payne, cited 1 Selw. N. P., 10th ed., 511. As to the plea of accord and satisfaction in debt on bond before the day of payment, see Id. 541;—in an action for libel, Boosey *v.* Wood, 3 H. & C. 484; and as to the plea of *solvit post diem* in an action, see Broom's Com., 4th ed., 177.

[3] Blake's Case, 6 Rep. 43.

but actual payment or tender on that day."[1] "Accord and satisfaction is no bar to an action for a debt certain covenanted to be paid."[2] In other words, where the damages are liquidated, the rule laid down per curiam in Blake's Case does not apply. Where, indeed, a covenant is entered into by A. to pay to B. a sum of money in gross on a day certain, it is incumbent on the covenantor, when the day specified arrives, to seek out the person to be paid, and pay or tender him the money, for A. has contracted so to do.[3]

In Smith *v.* Trowsdale,[4] the declaration, after stating that a submission to arbitration *under seal* had been entered into between the plaintiff and the defendants, and that an award had been made thereupon, set forth as the gist of the action the non-payment of money due under the award. The plea to this declaration set up a new agreement *after the breach* of duty arising out of the award, whereby, in consideration of the defendants' paying a smaller sum at an earlier time, the parties mutually stipulated that this new agreement, and the performance of it by the defendants, should be accepted by the plaintiff in satisfaction of all that was to be done under the award, *and of all damages sustained by reason of the breach of it. The court were of opinion [*884] that this plea was substantially a plea of accord and satisfaction, and that there was no necessity for showing that the agreement which it set up was under seal, the action not being brought directly on the deed of submission, but for the breach of duty in not performing the award. "The deed," remarked Wightman, J., "is only stated by way of inducement, to show that the arbitrator had authority to bind the parties. The declaration need not have alleged that the submission was by deed."

The preceding remarks may, therefore, be summed up thus:—That, in order to relieve a party liable on a specialty, there must either be an agreement under seal to that express effect, or an accord and satisfaction after breach, the damages being unliquidated.[5]

[1] Per Parke, B., Poole *v.* Tumbridge, 2 M. & W. 223, 226.

[2] Judgm., Massey *v.* Johnson, 1 Exch. 253.

[3] Judgm., Haldane *v.* Johnson, 8 Exch. 696.

[4] 3 E. & B. 83 (77 E. C. L. R.), with which compare Braddick *v.* Thompson, 8 East 344.

[5] See per Tindal, C. J., Harris *v.* Goodwyn, 2 Scott N. R. 466; s. c., 2 M. & Gr. 405 (40 E. C. L. R.).

The extent of applicability of the maxim, *Unumquodque dissolvitur eodem ligamine quo ligatur*, to simple contracts, may be thus concisely indicated: "It is," says Parke, B., in Foster *v.* Dawber,[1] "competent for both parties to an *executory* contract, by mutual agreement, without any satisfaction, to discharge the obligation of that contract.[2] But an *executed* contract cannot be discharged, except by release under seal, or by performance of the obligation, as by payment, where the obligation is to be performed by [*885] payment," [3] or by accord and *satisfaction. A promissory note or a bill of exchange, however, appears to stand on a different footing, and the obligation on such an instrument may, even after breach, be discharged by the assent or waiver of the holder.[4]

With respect, then, to simple contracts, which are neither within the operation of the Statute of Frauds, nor under the control of any Act of Parliament, the rule is, that such contracts may, before breach, be dissolved by parol; the term *parol* being understood as applicable indifferently to written and verbal contracts. By the general rules of the common law, and independently of any statutory enactment, if there be a contract which has been reduced into writing, and which is meant in itself to constitute an entire agreement, *verbal* evidence is not allowed to be given of what passed between the parties, either before the written instrument was made, or during the time that it was in a state of preparation, so as to add to, or subtract from, or in any manner to vary or qualify, the [*886] written contract;[5] but, after the instrument has *been reduced into writing, it is competent to the parties, at any

[1] 6 Exch. 839, 851.

[2] See De Bernardy *v.* Harding, 8 Exch. 822.

[3] Goldham *v.* Edwards, 17 C. B. 141 (84 E. C. L. R.). "It is a general rule of law, that a simple contract may *before* breach be waived or discharged without a deed and without consideration; but *after* breach there can be no discharge, except by deed or upon sufficient consideration." Byles on Bills, 7th ed., p. 168, adopted per Bramwell, B., Dobson *v.* Espie, 2 H. & N. 79, 83 (which shows that "leave and license" cannot be pleaded to a declaration for breach of contract). Clay *v.* Turley, 27 L. J. Ex. 2.

[4] Cook *v.* Lister, 13 C. B. N. S. 543, 593 (106 E. C. L. R.); Judgm., Foster *v.* Dawber, 6 Exch. 851. See Harmer *v.* Steele, 4 Exch. 1, where the waiver set up was before breach.

[5] See Eden *v.* Blake, 13 M. & W. 614 (which presents a good illustration of this rule); Abrey *v.* Crux, L. R. 5 C. P. 37; Laurie *v.* Scholefield, L. R. 4 C.

time before breach of it, by a new contract, not in writing, either altogether to waive, dissolve, or annul the former agreement, or in any manner to add to, or subtract from, or vary, or qualify the terms of it, and thus to make it a new contract, which is to be proved partly by the written agreement, and partly by the subsequent verbal terms engrafted upon what will be thus left of the written agreement.[1] It should be observed, that the first part of the above rule is confined and must be restricted in its application to a contemporaneous *verbal* agreement. It has been expressly decided, that, in an action on a bill or note, a contemporaneous agreement, *in writing*, may be set up to vary the contract evidenced by such instrument.[2] A *verbal* agreement, also, may be set up in suspension—though not in defeasance—of a written contract.[3]

In King *v.* Gillett[4] (which may be cited as an instance to show

P. 622; per Willes, J., Heffield *v.* Meadows, L. R. 4 C. P. 599; Lockett *v.* Nicklin, 2 Exch. 93; Shelton *v.* Livius, 2 Cr. & J. 411; Martin *v.* Pycroft, 2 De G., M. & G. 785; Adams *v.* Wordley, 1 M. & W. 374, 380; recognized in Flight *v.* Gray, 3 C. B. N. S. 320, 322 (91 E. C. L. R.); Hughes *v.* Statham, 4 B. & C. 187; Hoare *v.* Graham, 3 Camp. 57; cited, per Tindal, C. J., 5 Scott N. R. 254; Henson *v.* Coope, 3 Scott N. R. 48; Reay *v.* Richardson, 2 Cr., M. & R. 422; per Bayley, J., Lewis *v.* Jones, 4 B. & C. 512 (10 E. C. L. R.); per Lord Abinger, C. B., Allen *v.* Pink, 4 M. & W. 140, 144; Knapp *v.* Harden, 1 Gale 47; Soares *v.* Glyn, 8 Q. B. 24 (55 E. C. L. R.); Manley *v.* Boycot, 2 E. & B. 46 (75 E. C. L. R.).

See Maplas *v.* London and South-Western R. C., L. R. 1 C. P. 336.

A mistake in the original written contract may sometimes be set up by way of equitable defence: see Steele *v.* Haddock, 10 Exch. 643; Reis *v.* Scottish Equitable Life Ass. Soc., 2 H. & N. 19; Wake *v.* Harrop, 6 H. & N. 768.

But an equitable defence to an action is admissible only where it sets up matter in respect of which a court of equity would have granted relief unconditionally: Flight *v.* Gray, *supra.*

[1] Judgm., Goss *v.* Lord Nugent, 5 B. & Ad. 64, 65 (27 E. C. L. R.); Hargreaves *v.* Parsons, 13 M. & W. 561. Taylor *v.* Hilary, 1 Cr., M. & R. 741, and Giles *v.* Spencer, 3 C. B. N. S. 244 (91 E. C. L. R.), present instances of substituted agreements. See also Patmore *v.* Colburn, Id. 65; Douglas *v.* Watson, 17 C. B. 685 (84 E. C. L. R.).

[2] Brown *v.* Langley, 5 Scott N. R. 249; per Gibbs, J., Bowerbank *v.* Monteiro, 4 Taunt. 846; Young *v.* Austen, L. R. 4 C. P. 553, 557. See Strong *v.* Foster, 17 C. B. 201 (84 E. C. L. R.); Halhead *v.* Young, 6 E. & B. 312 (88 E. C. L. R.); Pooley *v.* Harradine, 7 E. & B. 431 (90 E. C. L. R.); cited in Ewin *v.* Lancaster, 6 B. & S. 576 (118 E. C. L. R.).

[3] Wallis *v.* Littell, 11 C. B. N. S. 369 (103 E. C. L. R.).

[4] 7 M. & W. 55; Davis *v.* Bomford, 6 H. & N. 245.

[*887] that a contract to marry, founded on *mutual promises, is not within the 4th section of the Statute of Frauds), the Court of Exchequer held, that to a declaration on such a contract, it is a good plea that, after the promise, and before any breach thereof, the plaintiff absolved, exonerated, and discharged the defendant from his promise and the performance of the same; and we have here more particularly mentioned this case, because it seems to afford an exact illustration of the rule now under consideration, and which we find laid down in the Digest in these words: *Nihil tam naturale est quam eo genere quidque dissolvere quo colligatum est; ideo verborum obligatio verbis tollitur, nudi consensûs obligatio contrario consensu dissolvitur.*[1] So, in Langden *v.* Stokes,[2] which was recognized and followed by the court in deciding the above case, and which was an action of assumpsit, the defendant pleaded that, before any breach, the plaintiff on &c. *exoneravit eum* of the alleged promise, and, on demurrer, the plea was held good, on the ground that, as this was a promise by words, it might be discharged by words before breach. In order, however, to sustain such a plea as that just mentioned, if issue be taken thereon, the defendant, it has been observed, must prove "a proposition to exonerate on the part of the plaintiff, acceded to by himself, and this in effect will be a rescinding of the contract previously made."[3]

[*888] *Where a contract is required to be in writing by the statute law, it clearly cannot be varied by any subsequent verbal agreement between the parties; for, if this were permitted, the intention of the legislature would be altogether defeated.[4] A

[1] D. 50. 17. 35. [2] Cro. Car. 383.

[3] Judgm., 7 M. & W. 59. In Wood *v.* Leadbitter, 13 M. & W. 838, it was held that a parol license to enter and remain for some time on the land of another, even though money were paid for it, is revocable at any time, and without paying back the money. In this case the law respecting the revocation of a license was much considered. See also Roffey *v.* Henderson, 17 Q. B. 586 (79 E. C. L. R.); Adams *v.* Andrews, 15 Q. B. 284 (69 E. C. L. R.); Taplin *v.* Florence, 10 C. B. 744 (70 E. C. L. R.).

As to the proper mode of pleading a contemporaneous or subsequent agreement, varying that entered into between the parties, see per Parke, B., Heath *v.* Durant, 12 M. & W. 440, which was an action of assumpsit on a policy of insurance.

[4] With reference to the Statute of Frauds, see Goss *v.* Lord Nugent, 5 B. & Ad. 58 (27 E. C. L. R.); Caton *v.* Caton, L. R. 2 H. L. 127; per Maule, J.,

contract, for instance, falling within the operation of the 4th section of the Statute of Frauds cannot be waived and abandoned in part; for the object of the statute[1] was to exclude all oral evidence as to contracts for the sale of land; and, therefore, any contract sought to be enforced must be proved by writing only; and if such a contract could be verbally waived in part, the new contract between the parties would have to be proved partly by the former written agreement, and partly by the new verbal agreement.[2] And this reasoning applies also to a contract for the sale of goods falling within the operation of the 17th section of the same statute. Such a contract cannot be varied or altered by a subsequent verbal agreement. Where, therefore, a contract for the bargain and sale of goods is made, stating a time for the delivery of them, an agreement to substitute another day for that purpose must, in order to be valid, be in writing.[3]

*A. entered into the service of B., as clerk, under a written agreement, which specified the salary to be payable [*889] "at the following rates, viz., for the first year, 70*l.*; for the second, 90*l.*; for the third, 110*l.*; for the fourth, 130*l.*; and 150*l.* for the fifth and following years that you may remain in my employment:" it was held, that this agreement was one required by the Statute of Frauds to be in writing, and that, there being a precise stipulation for yearly payments, evidence was inadmissible to show, that, at or after the date of the agreement, it was *verbally* agreed between the parties, that the salary should be paid quarterly. "This appears to me," said Tindal, C. J., "to be a contract within the Statute of

Pontifex *v.* Wilkinson, 2 C. B. 361 (52 E. C. L. R.); per Alderson, B., Eden *v.* Blake, 13 M. & W. 616; Stowell *v.* Robinson, 3 Bing. N. C. 928, 938 (32 E. C. L. R.).

[1] See Wain *v.* Warlters, 5 East 10; Morely *v.* Boothby, 3 Bing. 112 (11 E. C. L. R.).

[2] Judgm., Goss *v.* Lord Nugent, 5 B. & Ad. 66 (27 E. C. L. R.); recognized, Marshall *v.* Lynn, 6 M. & W. 117; Earl of Falmouth *v.* Thomas, 1 Cr. & M. 89; which cases are recognized, Harvey *v.* Grabham, 5 A. & E. 74 (31 E. C. L. R.); Judgm., Morley *v.* Boothby, 3 Bing. 112 (11 E. C. L. R.); per Lord Denman, C. J., Clancy *v.* Piggott, 2 A. & E. 480 (29 E. C. L. R.).

[3] Noble *v.* Ward, L. R. 2 Ex. 135; Marshall *v.* Lynn, 6 M. & W. 109 (cited arg. Hargreaves *v.* Parsons, 13 M. & W. 568); Stead *v.* Dawber, 10 A. & E. 57 (37 E. C. L. R.); Moore *v.* Campbell, 10 Exch. 323, 332. See Ingram *v.* Lea, 2 Camp. 521.

Frauds; it was not to be performed within a year.[1] . . . The question, therefore, is, whether we can supply an alleged defect in the contract by parol evidence of a contemporaneous or subsequent agreement for the payment of the salary quarterly. I think that would be a direct violation of the statute."[2]

But although a contract, which is required to be in writing, cannot be *varied* by a subsequent verbal agreement, it seems that neither the 4th nor the 17th section of the Statute of Frauds can apply to prevent a verbal *waiver* or *abandonment* of a contract within its operation from being set up as a good defence to an action upon the contract. Under the former of these sections, indeed, the remedy by action is taken away in certain specified cases if there be no written agreement, and under the *latter [*890] the particular contract is invalidated; but it does not appear that a verbal rescission of the contract would be void as within the language of either section, nor that the policy of the statute would lead to such a conclusion.[3] A verbal alteration of a contract required by statute to be in writing, being invalid, does not effect an implied rescission of the original contract.[4]

We may further observe, in connection with the maxim under consideration, that payment of a portion of a liquidated and ascertained demand cannot be in law a satisfaction of the whole; for here the contract between the parties consists in reality of two

[1] See Smith *v.* Neale, 2 C. B. N. S. 67 (89 E. C. L. R.); confirmed in Reuss *v.* Picksley, L. R. 1 Ex. 342.

[2] Giraud *v.* Richmond, 2 C. B. 834, 840 (52 E. C. L. R.); recognizing Goss *v.* Lord Nugent, *supra.*

[3] See Judgm., Goss *v.* Lord Nugent, 5 B. & Ad. 65, 66 (27 E. C. L. R.); cited, Harvey *v.* Grabham, 5 A. & E. 74 (31 E. C. L. R.); Stead *v.* Dawber, 10 A. & E. 65 (37 E. C. L. R.); Judgm., Noble *v.* Ward, L. R. 2 Ex. 137, 138. See Moore *v.* Campbell, *supra.* To an action for breach of a parol contract, accord and satisfaction is a good plea, because damages only are recoverable; see Selw. N. P., 10th ed., 118; per cur., Taylor *v.* Hilary, 1 C., M. & R. 743; Griffiths *v.* Owen, 13 M. & W. 58; Carter *v.* Wormald, 1 Exch. 81; Bainbridge *v.* Lax, 16 L. J. Q. B. 85. As to what will constitute or support a plea of accord and satisfaction, see Hall *v.* Flockton, 16 Q. B. 1039 (71 E. C. L. R.); s. c., 14 Id. 380; Williams *v.* London Commercial Exchange Co., 10 Exch. 569; Gabriel *v.* Dresser, 15 C. B. 622 (80 E. C. L. R.); Perry *v.* Attwood, 6 E. & B. 691 (88 E. C. L. R.), and cases there cited.

[4] Noble *v.* Ward, L. R. 2 Ex. 135. See Ogle *v.* Earl Vane, L. R. 3 Q. B. 272.

parts, viz., payment, and an agreement to give up the residue; which latter agreement is void, as being made without consideration.[1] The above rule does not, however, apply if the claim is *bonâ fide* disputable; nor, if there has been an acceptance of a chattel or of a negotiable security in satisfaction of the debt, will the court examine whether that satisfaction were a reasonable one, but it will merely inquire *whether the parties actually came to such an agreement. A man, therefore, may give in satisfaction of a debt of 100*l.* a horse of the value of 5*l.*, but not 5*l.*; and a sum of money payable at a *different time* may be a good satisfaction of a larger sum payable at a future day.[2] Moreover, although the obligor of a bond cannot, at the day appointed, pay a less sum in satisfaction of the whole, yet if the obligee then receive a part and give his acquittance under seal for the whole, this will be a good discharge, according to the maxim, *Eodem ligamine quo ligatum est dissolvitur.*[3]

[*891]

Lastly, the maxim which has been here considered has been held to apply in some cases which do not fall within the law of contracts: thus, a donative is a benefice merely given and collated by the patron to a man, without either presentation to, or institution by, the ordinary, or introduction by his order. In this case, the resignation of the donative by the incumbent must be made to the patron; for a donative begins only by the erection and foundation of the donor, and he has the sole visitation and correction, the ordinary having nothing to do therewith; and, as the incumbent comes in by the patron, so he may restore to him that which he conferred, for *Unumquodque eodem modo quo colligatum est dissolvitur.*[4]

[1] Sibree *v.* Tripp, 15 M. & W. 23; qualifying the decision in Cumber *v.* Wane, 1 Stra. 426.

See per Parke, B., Curlewis *v.* Clark, 3 Exch. 377, and in Evans *v.* Powis, 1 Exch. 606; Pinnel's Case, 5 Rep. 117; Jones *v.* Sawkins, 5 C. B. 142 (94 E. C. L. R.); Grimsley *v.* Parker, 3 Exch. 610; Hall *v.* Conder, 2 C. B. N. S. 22 (89 E. C. L. R.).

[2] 15 M. & W. 34, 38; Cooper *v.* Parker, 14 C. B. 118 (78 E. C. L. R.).

[3] Co. Litt. 212 b; per Parke, B., 15 M. & W. 34.

[4] Per Littledale, J., Rennell *v.* Bishop of Lincoln, 7 B. & C. 160 (14 E. C. L. R.); s. c., 8 Bing. 490 (21 E. C. L. R.); citing Fairchild *v.* Gaire, Yelv. 60; s. c., Cro. Jac. 65; 3 Burn Eccles. Law, 9th ed., 541.

[*892] *VIGILANTIBUS, NON DORMIENTIBUS, JURA SUBVENIUNT.

(2 Inst. 690.)

The laws assist those who are vigilant, not those who sleep over their rights.[1]

We have already, under the maxim *Caveat emptor*,[2] considered cases illustrative of the proposition that courts of justice require and expect that each party to a contract or bargain shall exercise a due degree of vigilance and caution; we shall now, therefore, confine our attention to the important subject of the limitation of actions, which will serve to exemplify that general policy of our law, in pursuance of which "the using of legal diligence is always favored, and shall never turn to the disadvantage of the creditor;"[3] merely prefacing that this principle is well known[4] and of very extensive applicability, and might be illustrated by reference to very many reported cases.[5] Thus, where the right to claim compensation is given by Act of Parliament—*ex. gr.*, an enclosure Act—which also directs that the claim shall be made within a certain [*893] *specified time, this right will be forfeited by an omission to assert it within the given time, and in such a case the maxim under consideration has been held forcibly to apply;[6] and the rule before us is obviously applicable whenever a party debars himself of a legal right or remedy by his own negligence or laches.[7]

[1] See Wing. Max., p. 672; Hobart R. 347; cited, *ante*, p. 772.

[2] *Ante*, p. 768. See, also, the maxim, *Prior tempore, potior jure*,—*ante*, p. 345.

[3] Per Heath, J., Cox *v.* Morgan, 2 B. & P. 412.

[4] In 2 B. & P. 412, Heath, J., observes, that this is one of the maxims which we learn on our earliest attendance in Westminster Hall. It is applied in courts of equity as well as in courts of law; see per Lord Cranworth, in Leather Cloth Co. *v.* American Leather Cloth Co., 11 H. L. Cas. 535; Spackman *v.* Evans, L. R. 3 H. L. 220; Downes *v.* Ship, Id. 343; McDonnel *v.* White, 11 H. L. Cas. 570; and cases cited, *ante*, p. 743.

[5] The principle applies to construing statutes which (*ex. gr.*) should not be so interpreted as to deprive a creditor of a right actually existing and vested in him, "unless they be clear and direct upon the point:" Judgm., Bottomley *v.* Hayward, 7 H. & N. 569, 570.

The maxim applies also where there has been undue delay in instituting a suit for divorce on the ground of adultery: 20 & 21 Vict. c. 85, s. 31; and cases cited in Inderwick, Div. Acts, p. 27. See also Castleden *v.* Castleden, 4 Macq. Sc. App. Cas. 159.

[6] Doe d. Watson *v.* Jefferson, 2 Bing. 118, 125 (9 E. C. L. R.).

[7] See, for instance, Camidge *v.* Allenby, 6 B. & C. 373 (with which com-

Relative to the doctrine of limitation of actions,[1] Mr. Justice Story has observed, "It has often been matter of regret in modern times that, in the construction of the Statute of Limitations (21 Jac. 1, c. 16), the decisions had not proceeded upon principles better adapted to carry into effect the real objects of the statute; that, instead of being viewed in an unfavorable light as an unjust and discreditable defence, it had not received such support as would have made it what it was intended to be, emphatically a statute of repose. It is a wise and beneficial law, not designed merely to raise a presumption of payment of a just debt from lapse of time, but to afford security against stale demands after the true state of the transaction may have been forgotten, or be incapable of explanation by reason of the death or removal of witnesses."[2] So in the ancient possessory actions, "there was a time of limitation settled, beyond which no man should avail himself of the possession of himself or his ancestors, or take advantage of the wrongful possession of *his adversary; for if he were negligent for a long and unreasonable time, the law refused afterwards to lend him any assistance to recover the possession merely; both to punish his neglect, *nam leges vigilantibus, non dormientibus, subveniunt*, and also because it was presumed that the supposed wrong-doer had in such a length of time procured a legal title, otherwise he would sooner have been sued."[3] . . . And further, Sir W. P. Wood, V.-C., remarks, in Manby *v.* Bewicke,[4] that, "the legislature has in this, as in every civilized country that has ever existed, thought fit to prescribe certain limitations of time, after which persons may suppose themselves to be in peaceable possession of their property

[*894]

pare Timmins *v.* Gibbins, 18 Q. B. 722 (83 E. C. L. R.)); Guardians of Lichfield Union *v.* Greene, 1 H. & N. 884. The maxim *supra* was applied, per Coltman, J., in Onions, app., Bowdler, resp., 5 C. B. 74 (57 E. C. L. R.), where a mistake occurred in the overseers' list of persons qualified to vote for a borough.

[1] Which may also be referred to the maxim, *Interest reipublicæ ut sit finis litium*—*ante*, pp. 331, 343.

[2] Bell *v.* Morrison, 1 Peters (U. S.) R. 360.

[3] 3 Com. by Broom & Hadley 270, 271. As to the doctrine of Prescription in the Roman law, see Mackeld. Civ. Law 290. *Usucapio constituta est ut aliquis litium finis esset;* D. 41. 10. 5; Wood, Civ. Law, 3d ed., 123.

[4] 3 K. & J. 352; Trustees of Dundee Harbor *v.* Dougall, 1 Macq. Sc. App. Cas. 317.

and capable of transmitting the estates of which they are in possession, without any apprehension of the title being impugned by litigation in respect of transactions which occurred at a distant period, when evidence in support of their own title may be most difficult to obtain."

Such being the policy on which our Statutes of Limitation are founded, reference will briefly be made to the more important clauses of them—some few cases being cited *in notis* explanatory of their meaning.[1] Under stat. 21 Jac. 1, c. 16, s. 1, the plaintiff in ejectment must have proved either actual possession or a [*895] *right of entry within twenty years, or have accounted for the want of it; for, by force of that statute, an uninterrupted adverse[2] possession for that period operated as a complete bar, except in those cases of disability which fell within section 2, viz., infancy, coverture, unsoundness of mind, imprisonment, and absence beyond seas, in which cases the party who was suffering under the disability at the time when the right of entry first accrued was allowed to bring his action at any time within ten years after its removal; and now, by stat. 3 & 4 Will. 4, c. 27, s. 2, no person shall make an entry or distress, or bring an action to recover any land or rent, but within twenty years next after the time at which the right to make such entry or distress, or to bring such action, shall have first accrued[3] to some person through whom he claims; or, if such right shall not have accrued to any person through whom he claims, then within twenty years next after the time at which the right to make such entry or distress, or to bring such action, shall have first accrued to the person making or

[1] In Wilson *v.* Braddyll, 9 Exch. 718, 720, Pollock, C. B., observes, "Parties are entitled by agreement to make a covenant, which shall operate as a release; but they cannot enter into a covenant to the effect that a matter shall be pleadable in bar which in point of law is no bar." Nor could two parties agree that the Statute of Limitations should not be pleaded to a debt. Id.

[2] Respecting the doctrine of adverse possession before the stat. 3 & 4 Will. 4, c. 27, see Taylor d. Atkyns *v.* Horde, 1 Burr. 60. And as to the same doctrine since that statute, see Nepean *v.* Doe (in error), 2 M. & W. 894; and also the note to these cases, 2 Smith L. C., 6th ed., 611 *et seq.* The latter case decides that the doctrine of *non-adverse* possession is done away with by the above Act.

[3] Section 3 declares when the right shall be deemed first to have accrued.

bringing the same.[1] By section 16 of the same Act it is provided that persons under disability of infancy, lunacy or coverture, or beyond seas, and their representatives, shall be allowed ten years from the termination of their disability or death; provided,[2] nevertheless, that no action shall *be brought beyond forty years after the right of action accrued. [*896]

Again, by stat. 3 & 4 Will. 4, c. 42, s. 3, it is enacted that all actions of debt for rent upon an indenture of demise, all actions of covenant[3] or debt upon any bond or other specialty, and all actions of debt or *sci. fa.* upon any recognizance, and also all actions of debt upon any award where the submission is not by specialty, or for any fine due in respect of any copyhold estate, or for an escape, or for money levied on any *fi. fa.*, and all actions for penalties, damages, or sums of money given to the party grieved by any statute then or thereafter to be in force, that shall be sued or brought at any time after the end of the then session of Parliament, shall be commenced and sued within the time and limitation following, that is to say,—the said actions of debt for rent upon an indenture of demise, or covenant or debt upon any bond or *other specialty*,[4] or actions of debt or *sci. fa.* upon recognizance, within ten years after the end of the then session of Parliament, or within twenty years after the cause of such actions or suits, but not after; the said actions by the party grieved, one year[5] after the end of the then session, or within two years after the cause of such actions or suits, but not after; and the said other actions, within three years after the *end of the then session, or within six years after the cause of such actions or suits, but not after.[6] It is, [*897]

[1] See as to the operation of the above section Manning *v.* Phelps, 10 Exch. 59, and cases there cited.

[2] Sec. 17.

[3] See Dixon *v.* Holroyd, 7 E. & B. 903 (90 E. C. L. R.).

[4] An action of debt by a railway company for calls under the 8 & 9 Vict. c. 16, and the Companies Special Act, must be brought within *twenty* years of the accruing of the cause of action: Cork and Bandon R. C. *v.* Goode, 13 C. B. 826 (76 E. C. L. R.); s. c., Id. 618. See Shepherd *v.* Hills, 11 Exch. 55, 65, 67 (where the action was likewise held to be founded on a statute); Tobacco-Pipe Makers *v.* Loder, 16 Q. B. 765 (71 E. C. L. R.); Jones *v.* Pope, 1 Wms. Saund. 38.

[5] See stat. 31 Eliz. c. 5, s. 5; Dyer *v.* Best, 4 H. & C. 189.

[6] See Sturgis *v.* Darell, 4 H. & N. 622.

however, further provided that nothing in this Act shall extend to any action given by any statute where the time for bringing such action is or shall be by any statute specially limited.

By section 4 of the same statute it is further enacted that if any person entitled to any such action or suit as above mentioned shall, at the time of such cause of action accruing, be within the age of twenty-one years, *feme covert*, *non compos mentis* [or beyond the seas[1]], then such person shall be at liberty to bring the same, provided it be commenced within the specified time after coming to or being of full age, discovert, of sound memory [or returned from beyond the seas[2]]; and a provision is inserted in the same section which applies to the case of a defendant similarly circumstanced.[3]

The doctrine of limitation in the case of simple contracts is founded upon a presumption of payment or release arising from length of time, as it is not common for a creditor to wait so long without enforcing payment of what is due; and as presumptions are founded upon the ordinary course of things, *ex eo quod plerumque fit*, the laws have formed the presumption that the debt, if not recovered within the time prescribed, has been acquitted or released. Besides, a debtor ought not to be obliged to take care forever of the acquittances which prove a demand to be satisfied; and it is proper to limit a time beyond which he shall not be under [*898] the necessity *of producing them. This doctrine has also been established as a punishment for the negligence of the creditor. The law having allowed him a time within which to institute his action, the claim ought not to be received or enforced when he has suffered that time to elapse.[4]

For the above reasons it was enacted by stat. 21 Jac. 1, c. 16, s. 3,[5] that all actions of account and of assumpsit (other than such accounts as concern the trade of merchandise between merchant

[1] See 19 & 20 Vict. c. 97, s. 10, cited *post*, p. 899.

[2] Id.

[3] See Forbes *v.* Smith, 11 Exch. 161.

[4] 1 Pothier by Evans 451.

[5] "This statute," observes Pollock, C. B., in Gulliver *v.* Gulliver, 1 H. & N. 176, "applies in terms to actions at law only, though by analogy courts of equity have adopted the provision; but the 85th section of the Com. Law Proc. Act, 1854, cannot alter the effect of the Statute of Limitations in courts of law." See Harris *v.* Quine, L. R. 4 Q. B. 653.

and merchant, their factors or servants), and all actions of debt grounded upon any lending or contract without specialty, and all actions of debt or arrearages of rent,[1] shall be commenced and sued within six years next after the cause of such action or suit, and not after.[2] And now by stat. 19 & 20 Vict. c. 97, s. 9, it is further provided that, "All actions of account or for not accounting, and suits for such accounts as concern the trade of merchandise between merchant and merchant, their factors or servants, shall be commenced and sued within six years *after the cause of such actions or suits, or, when such cause has already arisen, then within six years after the passing of this Act; and no claim in respect of a matter which arose more than six years before the commencement of such action or suit shall be enforceable by action or suit by reason only of some other matter of claim comprised in the same account having arisen within six years next before the commencement of such action or suit." [*899]

The 7th section of the statute of James, above cited, contains also a proviso, similar to those already mentioned, with respect to infants, married women, *non compotes mentis* [and persons imprisoned or beyond the seas],[3] viz., that an action may be commenced in the above cases within six years after the particular disability shall have ceased. The action of debt for not setting out tithes is not within the above statute; but, by 53 Geo. 3, c. 127, s. 5, no action shall be brought for the recovery of any penalty for not setting out tithes, unless such action be brought within six years from the time when such tithes became due.

With respect to certain of the statutory disabilities above specified, it has been recently enacted that "no person or persons who

[1] See 3 & 4 Will. 4, c. 27, s. 42; 19 & 20 Vict. c. 97, ss. 10, 11.

[2] See Hartland *v.* Jukes, 1 H. & C. 667. No time less than six years is unreasonable, as between drawer and holder of a check, for its presentment, unless loss is occasioned by the delay: Laws *v.* Rand, 3 C. B. N. S. 442 (91 E. C. L. R.). See also as to payment by check, Hopkins *v.* Ware, L. R. 4 Ex. 268.

Inasmuch as a debt which accrued more than six years before action brought may have been renewed within that period (*ante*, p. 656), a plea of the Statute of Limitations ought to allege that the debt did not accrue within the six years. See Bush *v.* Martin, 2 H. & C. 311; *et vide* Everett *v.* Robertson, 1 E. & E. 16 (102 E. C. L. R.).

[3] See 19 & 20 Vict. c. 97, s. 10.

shall be entitled to any action or suit, with respect to which the period of limitation within which the same shall be brought is fixed," by the 21 Jac. 1, c. 16, s. 3; 4 Ann. c. 16, s. 17; 53 Geo. 3, c. 127, s. 5; 3 & 4 Will. 4, c. 27, ss. 40, 41, 42; and 3 & 4 Will. 4, c. 42, s. 3, "shall be entitled to any time within which to commence and sue such action or suit beyond the period so fixed [*900] for the same by the enactments aforesaid, *by reason only of such person, or some one or more of such persons, being at the time of such cause of action or suit accrued beyond the seas, or in the cases in which by virtue of any of the aforesaid enactments imprisonment is now a disability, by reason of such person or some one or more of such persons being imprisoned at the time of such cause of action or suit accrued."[1]

Also by the next ensuing section of the Act just cited[2] it is further enacted that, "where such cause of action or suit with respect to which the period of limitation is fixed by the enactments aforesaid, or any of them, lies against two or more joint debtors, the person or persons who shall be entitled to the same shall not be entitled to any time within which to commence and sue any such action or suit against any one or more of such joint debtors who shall not be beyond the seas at the time such cause of action or suit accrued, by reason only that some other one or more of such joint debtors was or were at the time such cause of action accrued beyond the seas; and such person or persons, so entitled as aforesaid, shall not be barred from commencing and suing any action or suit against the joint debtor or joint debtors who was or were beyond seas at the time the cause of action or suit accrued after his or their return from beyond seas, by reason only that judgment was already recovered against any one or more of such joint debtors who was not or were not beyond seas at the time aforesaid."

[*901] *The 14th section also provides in reference to the 21 Jac. 1, c. 16, s. 3, and 3 & 4 Will. 4, c. 42, s. 3, that

[1] 19 & 20 Vict. c. 97, s. 10. In Cornill *v.* Hudson, 8 E. & B. 429 (92 E. C. L. R.), Lord Campbell, C. J., observes, that the above 10th section of the Act prevents any action being commenced after the period has elapsed within which the right to bring the action is limited by statute irrespective of the circumstances that the plaintiff has been abroad or in prison. See Townsend *v.* Deacon, 3 Exch. 706.

[2] 19 & 20 Vict. c. 97, s. 11.

"when there shall be two or more co-contractors or co-debtors, whether bound or liable jointly only, or jointly and severally, or executors or administrators of any contractor, no such co-contractor or co-debtor, executor or administrator shall lose the benefit of the said enactments or any of them so as to be chargeable in respect or by reason only of payment of any principal, interest, or other money, by any other or others of such co-contractors or co-debtors, executors or administrators." This section of the recent statute for amending the laws affecting trade and commerce has been held not to be retrospective in its operation.[1]

With respect to actions *ex delicto*, the period of limitation[2] in trespass *qu. cl. fr.*, or for taking goods or cattle, as also in trover, detinue, replevin, and case (except for slander), is six years; in trespass for assault, battery, or false imprisonment,[3] it is four years; and in case for slander, two years. Where defendant caused damage to the plaintiff's ancient house by working coal mines near to it, the act having been done more than six years before the commencement of the action, but the damage having occurred within that period, the Statute of Limitations was held to be no answer to the action.[4] And to a plea *of the Statute of Limitations [*902] in an action of trespass for taking coal from under the plaintiff's land, a replication that the trespasses were fraudulently concealed from the plaintiff till within the six years was not allowed.[5]

Lastly, in connection with this part of the subject, it may be observed, that "no judgment in any cause shall be reversed or avoided for any error or defect therein, unless error be commenced or brought and prosecuted with effect within six years after such judg-

[1] Jackson *v.* Woolley, 8 E. & B. 778, 784 (92 E. C. L. R.); Flood *v.* Patterson, 30 L. J. Chanc. 487. As to the effect of part payment, generally, in connection with the statute of James, see Chitt. Contr., 8th ed., pp. 763 *et seq.*

[2] 21 Jac. 1, c. 16, s. 3.

[3] See Coventry *v.* Apsley, Salk. 420.

[4] Backhouse *v.* Bonomi, 9 H. L. Cas. 503; s. c., E., B. & E. 623, 646 (96 E. C. L. R.). See Smith *v.* Thackerah, L. R. 1 C. P. 564; Whitehouse *v.* Fellows, 10 C. B. N. S. 765, 785 (100 E. C. L. R.); Violett *v.* Sympson, 8 E. & B. 344 (92 E. C. L. R.). As to an action for libel, see Duke of Brunswick *v.* Harmer, 14 Q. B. 185 (68 E. C. L. R.).

[5] Hunter *v.* Gibbons, 1 H. & N. 459; Imperial Gas Light and Coke Co. *v.* London Gas Light Co., 10 Exch. 39.

ment signed or entered of record."[1] But if any person entitled to bring error be, "at the time of such title accrued, within the age of twenty-one years, *feme covert*, *non compos mentis*, or beyond the seas, then such person shall be at liberty to bring error as aforesaid, so as such person commences or brings and prosecutes the same with effect, within six years after coming to or being of full age, discovert, of sound memory, or shall return from beyond the seas; and if the opposite party shall, at the time of the judgment signed or entered of record, be beyond the seas, then error may be brought, provided the proceedings be commenced and prosecuted with effect within six years after the return of such party from beyond seas."[2]

It is not intended, nor would it be consistent with the plan of this work, to consider in detail, either from what period limitation runs, or the mode in which a claim may be taken out of the operation of the statute, or, when barred by any statute, may be revived by a subsequent promise or acknowledgment. These subjects will be found minutely treated of in works devoted to an exposition of the law of real property, and of contracts and *mercantile [*903] transactions. There is, however, one maxim which naturally suggests itself in this place, and which is illustrated by those provisions in the different statutes of limitations, which, in the case of infancy and coverture, and others similar, suspend their operation until the removal of such disability. The maxim alluded to is expressed thus: *Contra non valentem agere nulla currit præscriptio*—prescription does not run against a party who is unable to act. For instance, in the case of a debt due, it only begins to run from the time when the creditor has the right to institute his suit, because no delay can be imputed to him before that time.[3] Where, therefore, a debt is suspended by a condition; as, if the contract be to pay money at a future period, or upon the happening of a certain event, as, "when J. S. is married," the six years are to be dated, in the first instance, from the arrival of the specified period; in the

[1] 15 & 16 Vict. c. 76, s. 146. [2] Id. s. 147.

[3] 1 Pothier by Evans 451; Hemp *v.* Garland, 4 Q. B. 519, 524 (45 E. C. L. R.); Flood *v.* Patterson, 30 L. J. Chanc. 486; Huggins *v.* Coates, 5 Q. B. 432 (48 E. C. L. R.); Holmes *v.* Kerrison, 2 Taunt. 323; Cowper *v.* Godmond, 9 Bing. 748 (23 E. C. L. R.). See, also, Davies *v.* Humphreys, 6 M. & W. 153; Bell Dict. and Dig. of Scotch Law 223.

Where a loan is made by check the Statute of Limitations runs from the date of payment of the check: Garden *v.* Bruce, L. R. 3 C. P. 300.

second, from the time when the event occurred.[1] Where, however, the breach of contract, which, in assumpsit, is the gist of the action,[2] occurred more than six years before the commencement of the proceedings, the statute will afford a good defence, although the plaintiff did not discover the injury resulting from the breach, till within the six *years.[3] So, in trover, the six years run from the conversion, though it was not discovered at the time.[4] [*904]

Where, however, the statute has once begun to run, no subsequent disability interrupts it;[5] such, for instance, as the death of the defendant, and the non-appointment of an executor by reason of litigation as to the right to probate.[6]

ACTIO PERSONALIS MORITUR CUM PERSONA.

(Noy, Max. 14.)

A personal right of action dies with the person.

The legal meaning and application of this maxim will, perhaps, most clearly be shown by stating concisely the various actions

[1] 1 Pothier by Evans 451; Shutford *v.* Borough, Godb. 437; Fenton *v.* Emblers, 1 W. Bla. 353.

[2] "The rule is firmly established that in assumpsit the *breach of contract* is the cause of action, and that the statute runs from the time of the breach, even where there is fraud on the part of the defendant:" per Lord Campbell, East India Co. *v.* Paul, 7 Moo. P. C. C. 111.

[3] Short *v.* M'Carthy, 3 B. & Ald. 626 (5 E. C. L. R.); Brown *v.* Howard, 2 B. & B. 73 (6 E. C. L. R.); Howell *v.* Young, 5 B. & C. 259 (11 E. C. L. R.); Bree *v.* Holbech, 2 Dougl. 654; Smith *v.* Fox, 6 Hare 386.

[4] Granger *v.* George, 5 B. & C. 149 (11 E. C. L. R.). See Philpott *v.* Kelley, 3 A. & E. 106 (30 E. C. L. R.).

[5] Baird *v.* Fortune, 4 Macq. Sc. App Cas. 127, 139.

[6] Rhodes *v.* Smethurst, 4 M. & W. 42; s. c., 6 M. & W. 351; approved in Penny *v.* Brice, 18 C. B. N. S. 396, 397 (114 E. C. L. R.) (which decided that it is not competent to an executor to maintain an action for a debt which accrued to his testator and for which he might have sued more than six years before the issuing of the writ); cited and followed Judgm., Homfray *v.* Scroope, 13 Q. B. 513 (66 E. C. L. R.); Freake *v.* Cranefeldt, 3 My. & Cr. 499.

The 4th sect. of stat. 21 Jac. 1, c. 16, applies to the limitations of actions after judgment or outlawry reversed; as to what cases are within the equity of this clause of the Act, see Curlewis *v.* Lord Mornington, 7 E. & B. 283 (distinguished Rhodes *v.* Smethurst, *supra*), Judgm., Sturgis *v.* Darell, 4 H. & N. 629.

which may be maintained by and against executors and administrators, as well as those rights of actions which die with the person,—to which alone the above rule may be considered in strictness to apply.

The personal representatives are, as a general rule, entitled to [*905] sue on all covenants broken in the lifetime of *the covenantee; as for rent then due, or for breach of covenant for quiet enjoyment,[1] or to discharge the land from encumbrances.[2] A distinction must, however, be remarked between a covenant running with the land and one purely collateral. In the former case, where the formal breach has been in the ancestor's lifetime, but the substantial damage has taken place since his death, the real and not the personal representative is the proper plaintiff; whereas, in the case of a covenant not running with the land, and intended not to be limited to the life of the covenantee, as a covenant not to fell trees, excepted from the demise, the personal representative is alone entitled to sue.[3] In a recent case, it was held, that the executor of a tenant for life may recover for a breach of a covenant to repair committed by the lessee of the testator in his lifetime, without averring a damage to his personal estate; and, in this case, the rule was stated to be, that unless the particular covenant be one for breach whereof, in the lifetime of the lessor, the *heir alone* can sue, the executor may sue, unless it be a mere personal contract, to which the rules applies, that *Actio personalis moritur cum personâ.*[4]

[*906] The personal representative, moreover, may sue, not *only for the recovery of all debts due to the deceased by specialty

[1] Lucy *v.* Levington, 2 Lev. 26. By 13 Edw. 1, st. 1, c. 23, executors shall have a writ of account. In the stat. 31 Edw. 3, st. 1, c. 11, originated the office of administrator.

[2] Smith *v.* Simonds, Comb. 64.

[3] Raymond *v.* Fitch, 2 C., M. & R. 598, 599; per Williams, J., and Parke, B., Beckman *v.* Drâke, 2 H. L. Cas. 596, 624; per Parke, J., Carr *v.* Roberts, 5 B. & Ad. 84 (27 E. C. L. R.); Kingdom *v.* Nottle, 1 M. & S. 355; 4 M. & S. 53; King *v.* Jones, 5 Taunt. 518 (1 E. C. L. R.); s. c. (in error), 4 M. & S. 188.

[4] Ricketts *v.* Weaver, 12 M. & W. 718, recognizing Raymond *v.* Fitch, *supra.* As to a covenant respecting a chattel, see per Parke, J., Doe d. Rogers *v.* Rogers, 2 Nev. & Man. 555; in an indenture of apprenticeship, Baxter *v.* Burfield, 2 Stra. 1266; Cooper, app., Simmons, resp., 7 H. & N. 707.

or otherwise, but on all contracts with him, whether broken in his lifetime or subsequently to his death, of which the breach occasions an injury to the personal estate,[1] and which are neither limited to the lifetime of the deceased, nor, as in the instance of a submission to arbitration containing no special clause to the contrary, revoked by his death.[2] An administrator, moreover, may sue for the price of goods sold and delivered between the death of the intestate and the taking out letters of administration,[3] but he cannot sue in his representative character upon contracts made after the death of the intestate in the course of carrying on the intestate's business.[4]

An action, however, is not maintainable by an executor or administrator for a breach of promise of marriage made to the deceased, where no special damage is alleged;[5] and, generally, with respect to injuries affecting the life or health of the deceased,—such, for instance, as arise out of the unskillfulness of a medical practitioner, or the negligence of an attorney, or a coach-proprietor,—the maxim as to *actio personalis* is applicable, unless some damage done to the personal estate of the deceased be stated on *the record.[6] But, where the breach of a contract relating to the person occasions a damage, not to the person [*907] only, but also to the personal estate; as, for example, if in the case of negligent carriage or cure there was consequential damage —if the testator had expended his money, or had lost the profits of a business or the wages of labor for a time; or if there were a joint contract to carry both the person and the goods, and both were injured; it seems a true proposition, that, in these cases, the

[1] Judgm., 2 C., M. & R. 596, 597; per Tindal, C. J., Orme *v.* Broughton, 10 Bing. 537 (25 E. C. L. R.); Stubbs *v.* Holywell R. C., L. R. 2 Ex. 311; 1 Wms. Saund. 112, n. (1); Edwards *v.* Grace, 2 M. & W. 190; Webb *v.* Cowdell, 14 M. & W. 820.

[2] Cooper *v.* Johnson, 2 B. & Ald. 394; per Bayley, J., Rhodes *v.* Haigh, 2 B. & C. 346, 347 (9 E. C. L. R.); M'Dougal *v.* Robertson, 4 Bing. 435 (13 E. C. L. R.); Tyler *v.* Jones, 3 B. & C. 144 (10 E. C. L. R.); Clarke *v.* Crofts, 4 Bing. 143 (13 E. C. L. R.); Knights *v.* Quarles, 2 B. & B. 102 (6 E. C. L. R.), which was an action against an attorney for negligence in investigating a title.

[3] Foster *v.* Bates, 12 M. & W. 226.

[4] Bolingbroke *v.* Kerr, L. R. 1 Ex. 222.

[5] Chamberlain *v.* Williamson, 2 M. & S. 408.

[6] Judgm., 2 M. & S. 415, 416; Beckham *v.* Drake, 2 H. L. Cas. 579, 596, 624. See Knights *v.* Quarles, 2 B. & B. 104.

executor might sue for the breach of contract, and recover damages to the extent of the injury to the personal estate.[1]

The personal representatives, on the other hand, are liable, as far as they have assets, on all the covenants and contracts of the deceased broken in his lifetime,[2] and likewise on such as are broken after his death, for the due performance of which his skill or taste was not required,[3] and which were not to be performed by the deceased in person.[4] "The executors," observes Parke, B.,[5] "are in truth contained in the person of the testator, with respect to all [*908] his contracts, except indeed *in the case of a *personal* contract, that is, a contract depending on personal skill, in which is always implied the condition that the person is not prevented by the act of God from completing the work. That condition is peculiar to personal contracts." The distinction must, moreover, be noticed between a mere authority and a contract, the former being revoked by death, whereas the latter is not determined thereby, except as above mentioned.[6]

Further, the personal representatives are liable on a covenant by deceased for their performance of a particular act, as for payment of a sum of money;[7] for building a house left unfinished by the deceased;[8] or on his contract for the performance of work by the plaintiff, before the completion of which he died, but which was

[1] Judgm., 8 M. & W. 854, 855.

[2] *Semble.* "Where a relation exists between two parties which involves the performance of certain duties by one of them, and the payment of reward to him by the other, the law will apply, or the jury may infer a promise by each party to do what is to be done by him;" and for breach of such a promise by deceased, his executors might sue: Morgan *v.* Ravey, 6 H. & N. 265, 276.

[3] Per Parke, B., Siboni *v.* Kirkman, 1 M. & W. 423; per Patteson, J., Wentworth *v.* Cock, 10 A. & E. 445, 446 (37 E. C. L. R.); Hopwood *v.* Whaley, 6 C. B. 744 (60 E. C. L. R.); Bac. Abr. "*Executors and Administrators*" (P. 1); Com. Dig. "*Administration*" (B. 14).

[4] Hyde *v.* Dean of Windsor, Cro. Eliz. 552, 553; per cur., Marshall *v.* Broadhurst, 1 Cr. & J. 406.

[5] Wills *v.* Murray, 4 Exch. 866. See Tasker *v.* Shepherd, 6 H. & N. 575.

[6] Bradbury *v.* Morgan, 1 H. & C. 249.

[7] Ex parte Tindal, 8 Bing. 404, 405 (21 E. C. L. R.), and cases there cited; Powell *v.* Graham, 7 Taunt. 580 (2 E. C. L. R.).

[8] Quick *v.* Ludborrow, 3 Bulstr. 30; recognized, 1 M. & W. 423. See per cur., 1 Cr. & J. 405, 406; per Lord Abinger, C. B., 3 M. & W. 353, 354.

subsequently completed.[1] And the same principle was held to apply where an intestate had entered into an agreement to receive from plaintiffs a certain quantity of slate monthly for a certain period, a portion of which, when tendered after his death, but before the expiration of the stipulated period, his administrator refused to accept.[2]

The action of *debt* on simple contract, except for rent,[3] did not, however, formerly lie against the personal representative for a debt contracted by the deceased,[4] unless the undertaking to pay originated *with the representative;[5] and the reason of this was, [*909] that executors or administrators, when charged for the debt of the deceased, were not admitted to wage their law, and consequently were deprived of a legal defence which the deceased himself might have made use of; but this reason did not apply to assumpsit, which, therefore, might always have been brought.[6] Now, however, by stat. 3 & 4 Will. 4, c. 42, s. 13, wager of law is abolished; and by sec. 14 it is enacted, that an action of debt on simple contract shall not be maintainable in any court of common law against an executor or administrator.

It is, however, to actions in form *ex delicto* that the rule *Actio personalis moritur cum personâ* is peculiarly applicable; indeed, it has been observed that this maxim is not applied in the old authorities to causes of action on contracts, but to those in tort which are founded on malfeasance or misfeasance to the person or property of another; which latter are annexed to the person, and die with the person, except where the remedy is given to the personal representative by the statute law;[7] it being a general rule that an action founded in tort, and in form *ex delicto*, was considered as *actio personalis*, and within the above maxim.[8] But, by stat. 4

[1] Corner *v.* Shew, 3 M. & W. 350, 352. See per Alderson, B., Prior *v.* Hembrow, 8 M. & W. 889, 890.

[2] Wentworth *v.* Cock, 10 A. & E. 42 (37 E. C. L. R.).

[3] Narwood *v.* Read, Plowd. 180. [4] Barry *v.* Robinson, 1 N. R. 293.

[5] Riddell *v.* Sutton, 5 Bing. 206 (15 E. C. L. R.).

[6] 3 Bla. Com., 16th ed., 347, and n. (12). In Perkinson *v.* Gilford, Cro. Car. 539, debt was held to lie against the executors of a sheriff who had levied under a *fi. fa.*, and died without paying over the money. As to a set-off by an executor sued as such, see Mardall *v.* Thellusson, 6 E. & B. 976 (88 E. C. L. R.); s. c., 18 Q. B. 857 (83 E. C. L. R.).

[7] Per Lord Abinger, C. B., 2 C., M. & R. 597.

[8] Wheatley *v.* Lane, 1 Wms. Saund. 216, n. (1).

Edw. 3, c. 7, reciting, that, in times past, executors had not had actions for a trespass done to their testators,—as of the goods and chattels of the said testators carried away in their lifetime,—it is [*910] enacted, that the executors, in such *cases, shall have an action against the trespassers, in like manner as they whose executors they are should have had if they were living.[1] This Act has always been expounded liberally;[2] and, by virtue of it, executors may maintain ejectment, *quare impedit*, trover, or replevin, the conversion or taking having been in the testator's lifetime.[3] Case also lies by an executor against a sheriff for a false return to a *fi. fa.* made in the lifetime of testator,[4] or for an escape on final process.[5]

And here we may remind the reader that the right of an executor to the personal estate of the testator is derived from the will, and the property in the personal goods and chattels of the testator is vested in him immediately upon the testator's death, and he is deemed to be in legal possession of them from that time, though before probate granted.[6] The title of an administrator, however, is derived from the letters of administration, though it has relation back, for many purposes, to the date of the death; for instance, trespass has been held maintainable by an administrator for an act [*911] done between the death and the *grant of the letters of administration.[7] Detinue, however, will not lie by an

[1] An administrator is within the equity of this statute (Smith *v.* Colgay, Cro. Eliz. 384); and by stat. 25 Edw. 3, st. 5, c. 5, a similar remedy is extended to the executors of executors.

[2] See per Lord Ellenborough, C. J., Wilson *v.* Knubley, 7 East 134, 135; 1 Wms. Saund. 216, n. (1); Emerson *v.* Emerson, 1 Ventr. 187.

[3] 1 Wms. on Executors, 6th ed., 738 *et seq.*; Bro. Abr. "*Executors*," 45; Doe d. Shore *v.* Porter, 3 T. R. 13; Rutland *v.* Rutland, Cro. Eliz. 377; Com. Dig. "*Administration*" (B. 13); 1 Wms. Saund. 217 n. See Doe d. Stace *v.* Wheeler, 15 M. & W. 623.

[4] Williams *v.* Gray, 1 Ld. Raym. 40; Com. Dig. "*Administration*" (B. 13).

[5] Per Holt, C. J., Berwick *v.* Andrews, 2 Lord Raym. 973. See Palgrave *v.* Windham, 1 Stra. 212; Le Mason *v.* Dixon, Sir W. Jones 173.

[6] Judgm., Pemberton *v.* Chapman, 7 E. & B. 217 (90 E. C. L. R.); citing Smith *v.* Milles, 1 T. R. 480.

[7] Tharpe *v.* Stallwood, 5 M. & Gr. 760 (44 E. C. L. R.); recognized Foster *v.* Bates, 12 M. & W. 226. See Welchman *v.* Sturgis, 13 Q. B. 552 (66 E. C. L. R.). In Bodger *v.* Arch, 10 Exch. 333, the doctrine of relation was also held applicable, under peculiar circumstances, so as to prevent the operation of the Statute of Limitations. See per Parke, B., Id. 339, 340.

administrator for goods of the intestate, which the defendant has re-delivered prior to the grant of administration.[1]

In regard to the doctrine of relation just mentioned, we may add, in the words of a very learned judge, that "an act done by one who afterwards becomes administrator, to the *prejudice* of the estate, is not made good by the subsequent administration. It is only in those cases where the act is for the *benefit* of the estate, that the relation back exists, by virtue of which relation the administrator is enabled to recover against such persons as have interfered with the estate, and thereby prevent it from being prejudiced and despoiled."[2]

Previously to the stat. 3 & 4 Will. 4, c. 42, no remedy was provided for injuries to the real estate of any person deceased committed in his lifetime;[3] but section 2 of that statute enacts, that an action of trespass, or trespass on the case, as the case may be, shall be maintainable by the executors or administrators of any person deceased, for any injury to the real estate of such person committed in his lifetime, for which an action might have been maintained by such person, so as such injury shall have been committed within six calendar months before the death of such deceased person, and provided such action shall be brought within one year after the death of such person; and the *damages, when recovered, shall be part of the personal estate of such person.[4] [*912]

Notwithstanding, however, the statutory exceptions above noticed to the general rule which was recognized by the common law, this rule still applies where a tort is committed to a man's person, feelings, or reputation, as for assault, libel, slander, or seduction of his daughter: in such cases, no action lies at suit of the executors or administrators, for they represent not so much the person as the personal estate of the testator or intestate, of which they are in law the assignees.[5]

Again, prior to the 9 & 10 Vict. c. 93 (amended by 27 & 28 Vict. c. 95), an action was not maintainable against a person who,

[1] Crossfield *v.* Such, 8 Exch. 825.

[2] Per Parke, B., Morgan *v.* Thomas, 8 Exch. 307.

[3] 1 Wms. Saund. 217, n.

[4] See Adam *v.* Inhabs. of Bristol, 2 A. & E. 389, 402 (29 E. C. L. R.); 1 Wms. on Executors, 6th ed., 748.

[5] 3 Bla. Com., 16th ed., 302, n. (9); Com. Dig. "*Administration*" (B. 13).

by his wrongful act, occasioned the death of another; but by sec. 1 of that statute it is enacted, that "whensoever the death of a person shall be caused by wrongful act, neglect, or default, and the act, neglect, or default is such as would (if death had not ensued) have entitled the party injured to maintain an action, and recover damages in respect thereof,[1] then and in every such case the person who would have been liable if death had not ensued, shall be liable to an action for damages, notwithstanding the death of the person [*913] injured, and although the death shall have been caused *under such circumstances as amount in law to felony." By sec. 2, it is further enacted, that "every such action shall be for the benefit of the wife, husband, parent,[2] and child,[3] of the person whose death shall have been so caused, and shall be brought by and in the name of the executor or administrator of the person deceased; or if there be no executor or administrator of the deceased, or such action as aforesaid be not brought within six calendar months after his death, then it may be brought in the name or names of all or any of the persons for whose benefit the personal representatives of the deceased would have sued.[4] In every such action the jury may give such damages as they may think proportioned to the injury resulting from such death to the parties respectively for whom and for whose benefit such action shall be brought; and the amount so recovered, after deducting the costs not recovered from the defendant, shall be divided amongst the before-mentioned parties, in such shares as the jury by their verdict shall find and direct." And, by sec. 3, the action for damages must be brought within twelve calendar months after the death of such deceased person. It will be observed, that this statute only applies where death ensues from the particular wrongful act, and does not, there-

[1] These words have reference, "not to the nature of the loss or injury sustained, but to the circumstances under which the bodily injury arose, and the nature of the wrongful act, neglect, or default complained of:" thus, if the deceased had by his own negligence materially contributed to the accident whereby he lost his life, inasmuch as he, if living, could not have maintained an action for damages, although there had been negligence on the part of the defendant, an action would not lie under the statute: Pym *v.* Great Northern R. C., 2 B. & S. 759, 767 (110 E. C. L. R.).

[2] S. 5.

[3] Id.; see Dickinson *v.* North-Eastern R. C., 2 H. & C. 735.

[4] 27 & 28 Vict. c. 95, s. 1; see also s. 2; Read *v.* Great Eastern R. C., L. R. 3 Q. B. 555; *et vide* stat. 31 & 32 Vict. c. 119, ss. 25, 26.

fore, affect the class of cases above mentioned, viz., where a tort is committed to the person which does not occasion death.[1]

By the statute 3 & 4 Will. 4, c. 42, s..2, already mentioned, trespass and case will also lie against personal *representatives [*914] for any wrong committed by any person deceased, in his lifetime, to another in respect of his property, real or personal, so as such injury shall have been committed within six calendar months before such person's death, and so as such action shall be brought within six months after the executors or administrators shall have taken upon themselves the administration of the estate and effects of such person.[2] Prior to this Act, the remedy for a tort to the property of another, real or personal, by an action in form *ex delicto*,—such as trespass, trover, or case for waste, for diverting a watercourse, or obstructing lights,—could not have been enforced against the personal representatives of the tort-feasor;[3] and, even now, no action can be maintained against them under that statute for a personal tort committed by him.[4] Cases, however, do occur where an action founded in tort may be brought in assumpsit, and such an action will, it seems,[5] independently of the above Act, lie against the executor.[6] For instance, the executors of an innkeeper have been held answerable for the value of articles lost *by [*915] the plaintiff whilst staying in the inn kept by the deceased.[7]

[1] See, further, as to the operation of the above statute, Broom's Com., 4th ed., 715, *et seq.*

[2] With reference to this statute, see Richmond *v.* Nicholson, 8 Scott 134; Powell *v.* Rees, 7 A. & E. 426 (34 E. C. L. R.).

[3] 1 Wms. Saund. 216, n. (1). See Bacon *v.* Smith, 1 Q. B. 348 (41 E. C. L. R.). Where chattels, wrongfully in the possession of testator, continued *in specie* in the hands of his executor, replevin or detinue would have been maintainable to recover the specific goods: Bro. Abr., "*Detinue*," pl. 19; Le Mason *v.* Dixon, Sir W. Jones 173, 174. See Crossfield *v.* Such, 8 Exch. 825.

[4] 1 Wms. Saund. 216, n. (1); Com. Dig., "*Administration*" (B. 15); 2 Inst. 382; Ireland *v.* Champneys, 4 Taunt. 884. By stats. 30 Car. 2, st. 1, c. 7, and 4 & 5 Will. & M., c. 24, s. 12, the representatives of an executor or administrator who has committed waste are rendered liable: see 2 Wms. on Executors, 5th ed., 1567; Huntley *v.* Russell, 13 Q. B. 572 (66 E. C. L. R.).

As to the liability of the executor of an executor for a *devastavit* by the latter, see Coward *v.* Gregory, L. R. 2 C. P. 153.

[5] *Ante*, p. 907, n. 2.

[6] Per Lord Mansfield, C. J., Hambly *v.* Trott, 1 Cowp. 373; recognized, 4 B. & Ad. 829 (24 E. C. L. R.).

[7] Morgan *v.* Ravey, 6 H. & N. 265. See stat. 26 & 27 Vict. c. 41.

In a recent case, where the question arose, whether the reigning sovereign was liable to make compensation for a wrong done by the servants and during the reign of his predecessor, Lord Lyndhurst, C., observed, that if the case had been between subject and subject, an action could not have been supported, upon the principle that *Actio personalis moritur cum personâ;* and, although it was contended that a different rule prevails where the sovereign is a party, that some authority should be adduced for such a distinction.[1]

For a tort committed to the person, it is clear, then, that at common law no action can be maintained against the personal representatives of the tort-feasor, nor does the stat. 9 & 10 Vict. c. 93, as amended by 27 & 28 Vict. c. 95, supply any remedy against the *executors* or *administrators* of the party who, by his "wrongful act, neglect, or default," has caused the death of another; for the first section of this Act renders that person liable to an action for damages, "who would have been liable if death had not ensued," in which case, as already stated, the personal representatives of the tort-feasor would *not* have been liable.

It may be observed, in concluding this subject, that cases occur, *ex. gr.*, respecting the right of action by or against a *feme covert*[2] surviving her husband, for an injury to her person or property, or for her tortious act committed before or during coverture, which are exceedingly similar in principle and analogous to those which [*916] *have been here cited and commented on. It cannot, however, be said with propriety that the maxim above illustrated is *strictly* applicable to such cases; and it has, therefore, been thought better to confine our attention to those in which the right of action or liability either survives the death of the party, or, in the words of the maxim, *moritur cum personâ.*[3]

[1] Visc. Canterbury *v.* A.-G., 1 Phill. 322.

[2] See per Erle, C. J., Capel *v.* Powell, 17 C. B. N. S. 747 (112 E. C. L. R.).

[3] As to actions by and against the executors of a parson in respect of waste and dilapidations, see Ross *v.* Adcock, L. R. 3 C. P. 655; Bunbury *v.* Hewson, 3 Exch. 558; Warren *v.* Lugger, Id. 579; Bryan *v.* Clay, 1 E. & B. 38 (72 E. C. L. R.); Martin *v.* Roe, 7 E. & B. 237 (90 E. C. L. R.); Wise *v.* Metcalfe, 10 B. & C. 299 (21 E. C. L. R.). In Bird *v.* Relph, 4 B. & Ad. 830 (24 E. C. L. R.), Patteson, J., observes, that "the action against the executor of a parson for dilapidations is an anomalous action, and appears like an exception to the general rule that '*Actio personalis moritur cum personâ.*'" See also Gleaves *v.* Parfitt, 7 C. B. N. S. 838 (97 E. C. L. R.).

*CHAPTER X. [*917]

Maxims Applicable to the Law of Evidence.

We have, in a previous chapter, investigated certain rules of the law of evidence which relate peculiarly to the interpretation of written instruments; it is proposed, in these concluding pages, to state some few additional rules of evidence. Very little, however, has been here attempted beyond a statement and brief illustration of them; because, on reflection, it appeared desirable at once to refer the reader to treatises of acknowledged authority on the subject, from which, after patient consideration of the more important cases there indicated, a clear perception of the extensive applicability of the following maxims can alone be derived.

Optimus Interpres Rerum Usus.

(2 Inst. 282.)

Usage is the best interpreter of things.

Custom, *consuetudo*, is a law not written, established by long usage and the consent of our ancestors;[1] and hence it is said that usage, *usus*, is the legal evidence of custom.[2] Moreover, where a law is established by an implied consent, it is either common law or custom; if *universal, it is *common law;*[3] if particular [*918] to this or that place, then it is *custom.* When any practice was, in its origin, found to be convenient and beneficial, it was naturally repeated, continued from age to age, and grew into a law,

[1] Jacob, Law Dict., tit. "*Custom.*"

[2] Per Bayley, J., 10 B. & C. 440 (21 E. C. L. R.).

[3] "In point of fact, the common law of England, *lex non scripta*, is nothing but custom:" Judgm., Nunn *v.* Varty, 3 Curt. 363. But the claim of any particular place to be exempt from the obligation imposed by the common law may also be properly called a custom. Id.

either local or national.[1] A custom, therefore, or customary law, may be defined to be an usage which has obtained the force of law, and is, in truth, the binding law within a particular district, or at a particular place, of the persons and things which it concerns:[2] *Consuetudo loci est observanda.*[3]

There are, however, several requisites to the validity of a custom, which can here be but briefly specified.

First, it must be *certain*, or capable of being reduced to a certainty.[4] Therefore, a custom that lands shall descend to the most worthy of the owner's blood is void; for how shall this worth be determined? but a custom to descend to the next male of the blood, exclusive of females, is certain, and therefore good. And a custom [*919] to *pay a year's improved value for a fine on a copyhold estate is good; for, although the value is a thing uncertain, yet it may at any time be ascertained.[5]

Secondly, the custom must be *reasonable* in itself;[6] it is not, however, unreasonable merely because it is contrary to a particular maxim or rule of the common law, for *Consuetudo ex certâ causâ rationabili usitata privat communem legem*[7]—custom, when grounded on a certain and reasonable cause, supersedes the common law;[8] in proof of which may be instanced the customs of gavelkind and borough English,[9] which are directly contrary to the law of de-

[1] 3 Salk. 112. *Ex non scripto jus venit quod usus comprobavit; nam diuturni mores consensu utentium comprobati legem imitantur:* I. 2. 9. *Consuetudinis jus esse putatur id quod voluntate omnium sine lege vetustas comprobavit*—Cic. de Invent. ii. 22.

[2] Le Case de Tanistry, Davys R. 31, 32; cited Judgm., 9 A. & E. 421 (36 E. C. L. R.); and in Rogers *v.* Brenton, 10 Q. B. 26, 63 (59 E. C. L. R.).

[3] 6 Rep. 67; 10 Rep. 139. See Busher, app., Thompson, resp., 4 C. B. 48 (56 E. C. L. R.).

[4] *Ante*, p. 623; Bluett *v.* Tregonning, 3 A. & E. 554, 575 (30 E. C. L. R.), (where the custom alleged was designated, per Williams, J., as "uncertain, indefinite and absurd"); Constable *v.* Nicholson, 14 C. B. N. S. 230 (108 E. C. L. R.); A.-G. *v.* Mathias, 27 L. J. Chanc. 761; Padwick *v.* Knight, 7 Exch. 854; Wilson *v.* Willes, 7 East 121; Broadbent *v.* Wilkes, Willes 360; s. c. (in error), 1 Wils. 63 (which also shows that a custom must be *reasonable*); with this case compare Rogers *v.* Taylor, 1 H. & N. 706; Carlyon *v.* Lovering, Id. 784.

[5] 1 Com. by Broom & Hadley 71; 1 Roll. Abr. 565; Davys R. 33.

[6] Co. Litt. 113 a; Tyson *v.* Smith (in error), 9 A. & E. 406, 421 (36 E. C. L. R.).

[7] Litt. s. 169; Co. Litt. 33 b. [8] Ib. See Judgm., 5 Bing. 293.

[9] See Muggleton *v.* Barnett, 2 H. & N. 653; s. c., 1 Id. 282. The law takes

scent; or, again, the custom of Kent, which is contrary to the law of escheat.[1] Referring to a peculiar custom respecting the descent of copyhold land in a manor, Cockburn, C. J., observes in a recent case,[2] that such "local customs are remnants of the older English tenures, which, though generally superseded by the feudal tenures introduced after the dominion of the Normans had become firmly established, yet remained in many places, probably in manors which instead of passing into the possession of Norman lords remained in the hands of the English proprietors. These customs, therefore, are not merely the result of accident or caprice, but were originally founded on some general principle or rule of descent."

[*920] *Further, a custom is not necessarily unreasonable because it is prejudicial to the interests of a private man, if it be for the benefit of the commonwealth; as the custom to turn the plough upon the headland of another, which is upheld in favor of husbandry; or to dry nets on the land of another, which is likewise upheld in favor of fishing and for the benefit of navigation.[3] So, a custom, the exercise of which causes interruption to a highway for a beneficial purpose and during a limited time, may be reasonable.[4] And a custom that the tenant shall have the way-going crop after the expiration of his term,[5] or that a tenant, who is bound to use a farm in a good and tenantable manner and ac-

notice of the custom of borough English, and the nature of this custom need not, therefore, be specially set forth in pleading. (Judgm., Doe d. Hamilton *v.* Clift, 12 A. & E. 579 (40 E. C. L. R.).) The same remark applies to the custom of gavelkind. (Co. Litt. 175 b.)

[1] See 2 Com. by Broom & Hadley 170.

[2] Muggleton *v.* Barnett, 2 H. & N. 681; s. c., 1 Id. 282; *ante*, p. 461.

[3] Judgm., Tyson *v.* Smith (in error), 9 A. & E. 421 (36 E. C. L. R.); Co. Litt. 33 b. See Lord Falmouth *v.* George, 5 Bing. 286, 293 (15 E. C. L. R.). A custom for all the inhabitants of B., as such, to enter the close of the plaintiff and take fish there without limit would be bad: Lloyd *v.* Jones, 6 C. B. 81, 89 (60 E. C. L. R.); citing Gateward's Case, 6 Rep. 60 b; A.-G. *v.* Mathias, 27 L. J. Chanc. 761. See Mounsey *v.* Ismay, 1 H. & C. 729; 3 Id. 486.

A custom for the inhabitants of a parish to exercise and train horses at all seasonable times of the year in a place beyond the limits of the parish, is bad: Sowerby *v.* Coleman, L. R. 2 Ex. 96.

[4] Elwood *v.* Bullock, 6 Q. B. 383 (51 E. C. L. R.).

[5] Wigglesworth *v.* Dallison, Dougl. 201; s. c., 1 Smith L. C., 6th ed., 539, and note thereto.

cording to the rules of good husbandry, shall be at liberty on quitting the farm to charge his landlord with a portion of the expense of draining land which needs drainage according to the rules of good husbandry, though the drainage is done without the landlord's knowledge or consent,[1] is not unreasonable.[2] But, on the other [*921] *hand, a custom which is contrary to the public good, or injurious or prejudicial to the many, and beneficial only to some particular person, is repugnant to the law of reason, for it could not have had a reasonable commencement. For example, a custom set up in a manor on the part of the lord, that the commoner cannot turn in his cattle until the lord has put in his own, is clearly bad, for it is injurious to the multitude, and beneficial only to the lord.[3] So, a custom, that the lord of the manor shall have 3*l.* for every pound-breach of any stranger,[4] or that the lord of the manor may detain a distress taken upon his demesnes until fine be made for the damage at the lord's will, is bad.[5] In these and similar cases,[6] the customs themselves are held to be void, on the ground of their having had no reasonable commencement,—as being founded in wrong and usurpation, and not on the voluntary consent of the people to whom they relate;[7] for it is a true principle, that no custom can prevail against right, reason, or the law of nature. The will of the people is the foundation of that custom which subsequently becomes binding on them; but, if it be grounded, not upon reason, but error, it is not the will of the people,[8]

[1] Mousley *v.* Ludlam, 21 L. J. Q. B. 64; Dalby *v.* Hirst, 1 B. & B. 224.

In Cuthbert *v.* Cumming, 10 Exch. 809; s. c., 11 Exch. 405, a question arose as to the reasonableness of an alleged usage of trade. See Grissell *v.* Bristowe, L. R. 4 C. P. 36; Cropper *v.* Cook, L. R. 3 C. P. 194; Baines *v.* Ewing, L. R. 1 Ex. 320.

[2] The Marquis of Salisbury *v.* Gladstone, 9 H. L. Cas. 692 (cited *ante*, p. 461, and followed in Blewett, app., Jenkins, resp., 12 C. B. N. S. 16 (104 E. C. L. R.)), is important with reference to the reasonableness of a custom; *et vide* Phillips *v.* Ball, 6 C. B. N. S. 811 (95 E. C. L. R.).

[3] Year Bk., 2 H. 4, fol. 24, B. pl. 20; 1 Com. by Broom & Hadley 70.

[4] See the references, 9 A. & E. 422, n. (*a*) (36 E. C. L. R.).

[5] *Ante*, p. 158.

[6] Douglas, app., Dysart, resp., 10 C. B. N. S. 688 (100 E. C. L. R.). See Phillips *v.* Ball, 6 C. B. N. S. 811 (95 E. C. L. R.).

[7] Judgm., 9 A. & E. 422 (36 E. C. L. R.).

[8] See Taylor Civ. Law, 3d ed., 245, 246; Noy, Max., 9th ed., p. 59, n. (*a*); Id. 60.

and to such a custom the established maxim of law applies, *Malus usus est abolendus*[1]—an evil or invalid custom ought to be abolished.

*Thirdly, the custom must have existed from time immemorial;[2] so that, if any one can show its commencement, it is no good custom.[3] [*922]

Fourthly, the custom must have continued without any interruption; for any interruption would cause a temporary cessation of the custom, and the revival would give it a new beginning, which must necessarily be within time of memory, and consequently the custom will be void. But this must be understood with regard to an interruption of the *right;* for an interruption of the possession only, for ten or twenty years, will not destroy the custom. As, if the inhabitants of a parish have a customary right of watering their cattle at a certain pool, the custom is not destroyed though they do not use it for ten years; it only becomes more difficult to prove; but, *if the right be in any way discontinued for a single day, the custom is quite at an end.[4] [*923]

[1] Litt. s. 212; 4 Inst. 274, Hilton *v.* Earl Granville, 5 Q. B. 701 (48 E. C. L. R.) (which is an important case with reference to the reasonableness of a manorial custom or prescriptive right), commented on, but followed in Blackett *v.* Bradley, 1 B. & S. 940, 954 (101 E. C. L. R.). See also Rogers *v.* Taylor, 1 H. & N. 706; Clayton *v.* Corby, 5 Q. B. 415 (48 E. C. L. R.) (where a prescriptive right to dig clay was held unreasonable); cited, per Lord Denman, C. J., 12 Q. B. 845 (64 E. C. L. R.); Gibbs *v.* Flight, 3 C. B. 581 (54 E. C. L. R.); Bailey *v.* Stephens, 12 C. B. N. S. 91 (104 E. C. L. R.); Constable *v.* Nicholson, 14 C. B. N. S. 230, 241 (108 E. C. L. R.). In Lewis *v.* Lane, 2 My. & K. 449, a custom inconsistent with the doctrine of resulting trusts was held to be unreasonable.

"The superior courts have at all times investigated the customs under which justice has been administered by local jurisdiction; and, unless they are found consonant to reason and in harmony with the principles of law, they have always been rejected as illegal:" Judgm., Cox *v.* Mayor of London, 1 H. & C. 358; s. c., L. R. 2 H. L. 239.

[2] See as to the proofs whence immemorial usage, or the legal origin of a toll, may be presumed, Holford, app., George, resp., L. R. 3 Q. B. 639, 649, 650; Bryant *v.* Foot, Id. 497; Lawrence *v.* Hitch, Id. 521; Shepherd *v.* Payne, 16 C. B. N. S. 132 (111 E. C. L. R.); Foreman *v.* Free Fishers of Whitstable, L. R. 4 H. L. 266, and cases there cited.

[3] 1 Com. by Broom & Hadley 68. The above requisite of a good custom is, however, qualified by the Prescription Act, 2 & 3 Will. 4, c. 71.

[4] 1 Com. by Broom & Hadley 69.

Fifthly, the custom must have been *peaceably enjoyed* and *acquiesced in*, not subject to contention and dispute. For, as customs owe their origin to common consent, their being immemorially disputed, either at law or otherwise, is a proof that such consent was wanting.[1]

Sixthly, a custom, though established by consent, must, when established, be *compulsory*, "and not left to the option of every man whether he will use it or no. Therefore a custom that all the inhabitants shall be rated towards the maintenance of a bridge will be good; but a custom that every man is to contribute thereto at his own pleasure is idle and absurd, and indeed no custom at all."[2]

Seventhly, customs existing in the same place "must be *consistent with each other;* one custom cannot be set up in opposition to another. For if both are really customs, then both are of equal antiquity, and both established by mutual consent: which to say of contradictory customs is absurd."[3]

Eighthly, customs in derogation of the common law, or of the general rights of property, must be strictly construed.[4]

Where, then, continued custom, characterized as above mentioned, has acquired the force of an express law,[5] reference must of course be made to such custom in *order to determine the rights [*924] and liabilities of parties, arising out of transactions which are affected by it; for *Optimus interpres rerum usus*. This maxim is, however, likewise applicable to many cases, and under many circumstances, which are quite independent of customary law in the sense in which that term has been here used, and which are regulated by mercantile usage and the peculiar rules recognized by merchants.

The law merchant, it has been observed, forms a branch of the law of England, and those customs which have been universally and notoriously prevalent amongst merchants, and have been found by experience to be of public use, have been adopted as a part of it, upon a principle of convenience, and for the benefit of trade and

[1] 1 Com. by Broom & Hadley 69.

[2] Id. 73.

[3] Id.

[4] Id.; Judgm., 10 Q. B. 57 (59 E. C. L. R.); per Bayley, J., 2 B. & C. 839 (9 E. C. L. R.). See as to the above rule, per Cockburn, C. J., 2 H. & N. 680, 681.

[5] See Judgm., 9 A. & E. 425, 426 (36 E. C. L. R.).

commerce; and, when so adopted, it is unnecessary to plead and prove them.[1]

In cases, also, relating to mercantile contracts, courts of law will, in order to ascertain the usage and understanding of merchants, examine and hear witnesses conversant with those subjects; for merchants have a style peculiar to themselves, which, though short, yet is understood by them, and of which usage and custom are the legitimate interpreters.[2] And this principle is not *confined to mercantile contracts or instruments, although it [*925] has been more frequently applied to them than to others;[3] but it may be stated generally, that where the words used by parties have, by the known usage of trade, by any local custom, or amongst particular classes, acquired a peculiar sense, distinct from the popular sense of the same words, their meaning may be ascertained by reference to that usage or custom.[4] And the question in such cases usually is, whether there was a recognized practice and usage with reference to the transaction out of which the written contract between the parties arose, and to which it related, which gave a particular sense to the words employed in it, so that the parties might

[1] Judgm., 7 Scott N. R. 327; *ante*, p. 919, n. 9. See Brandao *v.* Barnett, 12 Cl. & F. 787; s. c., 3 C. B. 519 (54 E. C. L. R.); Bellamy *v.* Majoribanks, 7 Exch. 389; Jones *v.* Peppercorne, 28 L. J. Chanc. 158.

As to the mode of proving mercantile usages, see Mackenzie *v.* Dunlop, 3 Macq. Sc. App. Cas. 22.

[2] 3 Stark. Ev. 1033 (Id. 4th ed., 701); cited 3 B. & Ad. 733 (23 E. C. L. R.); per Lord Hardwicke, C., 1 Ves. sen. 459. See Startup *v.* Macdonald, 7 Scott N. R. 269 (where the question was respecting the reasonableness of the time at which a tender of goods was made, in the absence of any usage of trade on the subject); Coddington *v.* Paleologo, L. R. 2 Ex. 193, 197.

Evidence of former transactions between the same parties is receivable for the purpose of explaining the meaning of the terms used in their written contract: Bourne *v.* Gatliff, 11 Cl. & Fin. 45.

See, further, Johnson *v.* Usborne, 11 A. & E. 549 (39 E. C. L. R.); Stewart *v.* Aberdein, 4 M. & W. 211, as to which case, see 1 Arnould Mar. Insur., 2d ed., p. 154 (*a*).

[3] Per Parke, J., Smith *v.* Wilson, 3 B. & Ad. 733 (23 E. C. L. R.), which case has been repeatedly recognized, and where evidence was held admissible to show that, by the custom of the country where a lease was made, the word *thousand*, as applied to rabbits, denoted *twelve hundred*. Spicer *v.* Cooper, 1 Q. B. 424 (41 E. C. L. R.), is also in point.

[4] Judgm., Robertson *v.* French, 4 East 135. See Carter *v.* Crick, 4 H. & N. 412.

be supposed to have used such words in that particular sense. "The character and description of evidence admissible for that purpose" being "the fact of a general usage and practice prevailing in that particular trade or business, not the judgment and opinion of the witnesses, for the contract may be safely and correctly interpreted by reference to the fact of usage, as it may be presumed such fact is known to the contracting parties, and that they contract in conformity thereto; but the judgment or opinion of the witnesses called affords no safe guide for interpretation, as such judgment or opinion is confined to their own knowledge."[1]

[*926] *The following examples must here suffice in illustration of the subject just adverted to,[2] and in the margin will be found references to a few cases, showing the operation of the well-known rule, that evidence of usage—mercantile or otherwise—cannot be admitted to vary a written contract.[3]

In an action for the breach of a contract for the sale by the defendants to the plaintiffs of a quantity of gambier, evidence was held admissible to show that by the usage of the trade, a "bale" of gambier was understood to mean a package of a particular description, and, consequently, that the contract would not be duly

[1] Judgm., Lewis *v.* Marshall, 8 Scott N. R. 493; Russian Steam Nav. Co. *v.* Silva, 13 C. B. N. S. 610 (106 E. C. L. R.).

As to mercantile words see also Peek *v.* North Staffordshire R. C., 10 H. L. Cas. 543.

[2] See further from this subject, Broom's Com., 4th ed., Bk. II. Chap. 4, and cases cited, *infra*.

[3] In the under-mentioned cases, evidence of custom or usage was held inadmissible for construing a mercantile instrument: Dickenson *v.* Jardine, L. R. 3 C. P. 639; Hall *v.* Janson, 4 E. & B. 500 (82 E. C. L. R.); Cockburn *v.* Alexander, 6 C. B. 791 (60 E. C. L. R.); Spartali *v.* Benecke, 10 C. B. 212 (70 E. C. L. R.); distinguished in Godts *v.* Rose, 17 C. B. 229, 234 (84 E. C. L. R.), and in Field *v.* Lelean, 6 H. & N. 617; Courturier *v.* Hastie, 8 Exch. 40; s. c., 9 Exch. 102; Re Stroud, 8 C. B. 502 (65 E. C. L. R.). See Miller *v.* Tetherington, 6 H. & N. 278; s. c., 7 Id. 954; Symonds *v.* Lloyd, 6 C. B. N. S. 691 (95 E. C. L. R.); Foster *v.* Mentor Life Ass. Co., 3 E. & B. 48 (77 E. C. L. R.).

• Parol evidence may be admitted to show that a person whose name appears at the head of an invoice as vendor was not in fact a contracting party: Holding *v.* Elliott, 5 H. & N. 117, or to show that there never was any contract between the parties, Rogers *v.* Hadley, 2 H. & C. 227; Kempson *v.* Boyle, 3 Id. 763; Hurst *v.* Great Western R. C., 19 C. B. N. S. 310 (115 E. C. L. R.).

performed by making tender of packages of a totally different size and description.[1]

*Where evidence of an established local usage—as on the stock exchange of a particular town[2]—is admitted to [*927] add to or to affect the construction of a written contract, it is admitted on the ground that the contracting parties are both cognizant of the usage, and must be presumed to have made their agreement with reference to it. But no such presumption arises where one of the parties is ignorant of it.[3]

In Dale *v.* Humfrey[4] the facts were as under:—the action was for the price of linseed oil, alleged to have been bargained and sold by the plaintiff to the defendants, and not accepted by them. The plaintiff had employed Messrs. T. & M., brokers, to sell for him the oil in question; and the defendants, also brokers, were employed by S. to purchase oil for him; the defendants accordingly, dealing with the plaintiff's brokers, delivered to them a bought note in these terms, "Sold this day for Messrs. T. & M., to our principals, ten tons of linseed oil," &c. (signed by the defendants); the sold note, signed by the plaintiff's brokers, stated the oil to have been sold to the defendants. The bought note was delivered to the

[1] Gorrissen *v.* Perrin, 2 C. B. N. S. 681 (89 E. C. L. R.). See Devaux *v.* Conolly, 6 C. B. 640 (65 E. C. L. R.).

In the following cases evidence of mercantile usage has been admitted to explain words or phrases occurring in written contracts:—"month," Simpson *v.* Margitson, 11 Q. B. 27 (63 E. C. L. R.); "net proceeds," Caine *v.* Horsfall, 1 Exch. 519; "wet," as applied to palm oil, Warde *v.* Stuart, 1 C. B. N. S. 88 (87 E. C. L. R.); "in regular turns of loading," Leidemann *v.* Schultz, 14 C. B. 38 (78 E. C. L. R.) (with which compare Hudson *v.* Clementson, 18 C. B. 213 (86 E. C. L. R.)). See Boden *v.* French, 10 C. B. 866 (70 E. C. L. R.); Moore *v.* Campbell, 10 Exch. 323; Metzner *v.* Bolton, 9 Exch. 518; Sotilichos *v.* Kemp, 3 Exch. 105.

[2] Bayliffe *v.* Butterworth, 1 Exch. 425; Pollock *v.* Stables, 12 Q. B. 765 (64 E. C. L. R.); Bayley *v.* Wilkins, 7 C. B. 886 (62 E. C. L. R.); Taylor *v.* Stray, 2 C. B. N. S. 174 (89 E. C. L. R.); Cropper *v.* Cook, L. R. 3 C. P. 194, 198; Viscount Torrington *v.* Lowe, L. R. 4 C. P. 26; Grissell *v.* Bristowe, Id. 36; Maxted *v.* Paine, L. R. 4 Ex. 81, 203; Davis *v.* Haycock, L. R. 4 Ex. 373; Kidston *v.* Empire Mar. Ins. Co., L. R. 1 C. P. 535, L. R. 2 C. P. 357; Chapman *v.* Shepherd, L. R. 2 C. P. 228.

[3] Kirchner *v.* Venus, 12 Moo. P. C. C. 361, 399; Sweeting *v.* Pearce, 9 C. B. N. S. 534 (99 E. C. L. R.); s. c., 7 Id. 449 (97 E. C. L. R.). See Buckle *v.* Knopp, L. R. 2 Ex. 125, 333.

[4] E., B. & E. 1004 (96 E. C. L. R.); s. c., 7 E. & B. 266 (90 E. C. L. R.).

plaintiff's brokers by the defendants, without disclosing the name of their principal, who afterwards became insolvent, and [*928] *did not accept the oil. In order to charge the defendants, proof was given at the trial of a custom in the trade that, when a broker purchased without disclosing the name of his principal, he was liable to be looked to as purchaser; the evidence thus given was held by the Court of Queen's Bench to have been admissible, and the action was held maintainable against defendants.

"In a certain sense," remarked Lord Campbell, C. J., delivering judgment in the above case,[1] "every material incident which is added to a written contract varies it, makes it different from what it appeared to be, and so far is inconsistent with it. If by the side of the written contract without, you write the same contract with, the added incident, the two would seem to import different obligations and be different contracts. To take a familiar instance by way of illustration: on the face of a bill of exchange at three months after date, the acceptor would be taken to bind himself to the payment precisely at the end of the three months; but by the custom he is only bound to do so at the end of the days of grace, which vary, according to the country in which the bill is made payable, from three up to fifteen. The truth is that the principle on which the evidence is admissible is that the parties have not set down on paper the whole of their contract in all its terms, but those only which were necessary to be determined in the particular case by specific agreement, and which of course might vary infinitely, leaving to implication and tacit understanding all those general and unvarying incidents which a uniform usage would annex, and according to which they must in reason be [*929] *understood to contract, unless they expressly exclude them. To fall within the exception, therefore, of repugnancy, the incident must be such as, if expressed in the written contract, would make it insensible or inconsistent;"[2] and again, "It is the business of courts reasonably so to shape their rules of evidence as to make them suitable to the habits of mankind, and such as are not likely to exclude the actual facts of the dealings between parties when they are

[1] 7 E. & B. 274, 275 (90 E. C. L. R.); Judgm., Field *v.* Lelean, 6 H. & N. 627. See also the cases cited *ante*, p. 926.

[2] See also Judgm., Brown *v.* Byrne, 3 E. & B. 715 (77 E. C. L. R.), where the prior cases are reviewed.

to determine on the controversies which grow out of them. It cannot be doubted, in the present case, that in fact this contract was made with the usage understood to be a term in it: to exclude the usage is to exclude a material term of the contract, and must lead to an unjust decision."[1]

Besides cases such as have been just considered, there is another extensive class of decisions referred to in a former chapter,[2] in which evidence of usage is admitted to explain and construe ancient grants or charters, or to support claims not incompatible therewith.[3] Nor is there any difference in this respect between a private deed and the king's charter:[4] in either case, evidence of *usage [*930] may be given to expound the instrument, provided such usage is not inconsistent with, or repugnant to, its express terms.[5] So, the immemorial existence of certain rights or exemptions, as a modus or a claim to the payment of tolls, may be inferred from uninterrupted modern usage.[6]

[1] 7 E. & B. 278, 279 (90 E. C. L. R.). In the following cases evidence of usage has also been admitted to interpret or annex incidents to written contracts: Syers *v.* Jonas, 2 Exch. 111; cited Harnor *v.* Grooves, 15 C. B. 667, 674; and, per Alderson, B., Phillipps *v.* Briard, 1 H. & N. 25, who observes that "evidence of custom is admissible to annex incidents to written contracts, that is, *something which is tacitly in the contract itself.*" In this case, Pollock, C. B, observes that Brown *v.* Byrne, *supra*, "went a long way." See, however, Judgm., Hall *v.* Janson, 4 E. & B. 510 (82 E. C. L. R.); Judgm., 7 E. & B. 279 (90 E. C L. R.). Brown *v.* Byrne was followed in Lucas *v.* Bristow, E., B. & E. 907, 913 (96 E. C. L. R.).

[2] *Ante*, p. 682.

[3] Bradley *v.* Pilots of Newcastle, 2 E. & B. 427 (75 E. C. L. R.); Duke of Beaufort *v.* Mayor of Swansea, 3 Exch. 413, 425; and cases cited, *ante*, p. 922, n. 2.

[4] "All charters or grants of the crown may be repealed or revoked when they are contrary to law, or uncertain or injurious to the rights and interests of third persons, and the appropriate process for the purpose is by writ of *scire facias*." Judgm., Reg. *v.* Hughes, L. R. 1 P. C. 87.

[5] Per Lord Kenyon, C. J., Withnell *v.* Gartham, 6 T. R. 398; R. *v.* Salway, 9 B. & C. 424, 435 (17 E. C. L. R.); Stammers *v.* Dixon, 7 East 200; per Lord Brougham, C., A.-G. *v.* Brazen Nose Coll., 2 Cl. & Fin. 317; per Tindal, C. J., 8 Scott N. R. 813.

[6] See per Parke, B., Jenkins *v.* Harvey, 1 Cr., M. & R. 894; per Richardson, J., Chod *v.* Tilsed, 2 B. & B. 409 (6 E. C. L. R.); Foreman *v.* Free Fishers of Whitstable, L. R. 4 H. L. 266, and cases there cited; Earl of Egremont *v.* Saul, 6 A. & E. 924 (33 E. C. L. R.); Brune *v.* Thompson, 4 Q. B. 543 (45 E. C. L. R.).

Generally, as regards a deed (as well as a will),[1] the state of the subject to which it relates at the time of execution may be inquired into; and where a deed is ancient, so that the state of the subject-matter at its date cannot be proved by direct evidence, modern usage and enjoyment for a number of years are admissible as evidence raising a presumption that the same course was adopted from an earlier period, and so to prove contemporaneous usage and enjoyment at the date of the deed. Such a deed may, therefore, be construed by evidence of the manner in which the subject to which it refers has been possessed or used—*Optimus interpres rerum usus.*[2]

[*931] Lastly, evidence of usage is likewise admissible to aid *in interpreting Acts of Parliament, the language of which is doubtful; for *jus et norma loquendi* are governed by usage. The meaning of things spoken or written must be such as it has constantly been received to be by common acceptation,[3] and that exposition shall be preferred which, in the words of Sir E. Coke,[4] "is approved by constant and continual use and experience:" *Optima enim est legis interpres consuetudo.*[5]

We shall conclude these very brief remarks upon the maxim *Optimus interpres rerum usus* in the words of Mr. Justice Story, who observes, "The truth and appropriate office of a usage or custom is, to interpret the otherwise indeterminate intentions of parties, and to ascertain the nature and extent of their contracts, arising, not from express stipulations, but from mere implications and presumptions, and acts of a doubtful and equivocal character. It may also be admitted to ascertain the true meaning of a particular word or of particular words in a given instrument, when the word or words have various senses, some common, some qualified, and some technical, according to the subject-matter to which they

[1] *Ante*, p. 613.

[2] Per Lord Wensleydale, Waterpark *v.* Furnell, 7 H. L. Cas. 684; citing Weld *v.* Hornby, 7 East 199; Duke of Beaufort *v.* Swansea, 3 Exch. 413; A.-G. *v.* Parker, 1 Ves. 43; 3 Atk. 576; per Lord St. Leonards, A.-G. *v.* Drummond, 1 Dru. & W. 368. See the maxim as to *contemporanea expositio* —*ante*, p. 682. As to construing the rubrics and canons see Martin *v.* Mackonochie, L. R. 2 A. & E. 195.

[3] Vaughan R. 169; per Crowder, J., The Fermoy Peerage, 5 H. L. Cas. 747; arg. R. *v.* Bellringer, 4 T. R. 819.

[4] 2 Inst. 18.

[5] D. 1. 3. 37; per Lord Brougham, 3 Cl. & Fin. 354.

are applied. But I apprehend that it can never be proper to resort to any usage or custom to control or vary the positive stipulations in a written contract, and, *à fortiori*, not in order to contradict them. An express contract of the parties is always admissible to supersede, or vary, or control a usage or custom; for the latter may always be waived at the will of the parties. But a written and express contract cannot be controlled, or varied, or contradicted by a usage *or custom; for that would not only be to admit [*932] parol evidence to control, vary, or contradict written contracts: but it would be to allow mere presumptions and implications, properly arising in the absence of any positive expressions of intention, to control, vary, or contradict the most formal and deliberate declarations of the parties."[1]

CUILIBET IN SUA ARTE PERITO EST CREDENDUM.

(Co. Litt. 125 a.)

Credence should be given to one skilled in his peculiar profession.

Almost all the injuries, it has been observed, which one individual may receive from another, and which lay the foundation of numberless actions, involve in them questions peculiar to the trades and conditions of the parties; and, in these cases, the jury must, according to the above maxim, attend to the witnesses, and decide according to their number, professional skill and means of knowledge. Thus, in an action against a surgeon for ignorance, the question may turn on a nice point of surgery. In an action on a policy of life insurance, physicians must be examined. So, for injuries to a mill worked by running water, and occasioned by the erection of another mill higher up the stream, mill-wrights and engineers must be called as witnesses. In like manner, many questions respecting navigation arise which must necessarily be decided by a jury, as in the ordinary case of deviation on a policy of marine insurance, of seaworthiness, or where one ship runs down another at sea in consequence of bad steering.[2]

[1] The Schooner Reeside, 2 Sumner (U. S.) R. 567.

[2] Johnstone *v.* Sutton (in error), 1 T. R. 538, 539.

[*933] *Respecting matters, then, of science, trade,[1] and others of the same description, persons of skill may not only speak as to facts, but are even allowed to give their opinions in evidence,[2] which is contrary to the general rule, that the opinion of a witness is not evidence. Thus the opinion of medical men is evidence as to the state of a patient whom they have seen; and even in cases where they have not themselves seen the patient, but have heard the symptoms and particulars of his state detailed by other witnesses at the trial, their opinions on the nature of such symptoms have been admitted.[3] In prosecutions for murder, they have, therefore, been allowed to state their opinion, whether the wounds described by witnesses were likely to be the cause of death.[4]

With respect to the admissibility in evidence of the opinion of a medical man as to the state of mind of a prisoner when on his trial for an alleged offence, the following question was recently proposed to the judges by the House of Lords:[5] "Can a medical man, conversant with the disease of insanity, who never saw the prisoner previously to the trial, but who was present during the whole trial and the examination of all the witnesses, be asked his opinion as to the state of the prisoner's mind at the time of the commission of the alleged crime, or his opinion whether the prisoner was conscious, at the time of doing the act, that he was acting [*934] *contrary to law, or whether he was laboring under any, and what, delusion at the time?" To the question thus proposed, the majority of the judges returned the following answer, which removes much of the difficulty which formerly existed with reference to this, the most important practical application of the maxim under review, and must be considered as laying down the rule upon the subject: "We think the medical man, under the circumstances supposed, cannot, in strictness, be asked his opinion in the terms above stated, because each of those questions involves the determi-

[1] The importance attached to the *lex mercatoria*, or custom of merchants, and the implied warranty by a skilled laborer, artisan, or artist, that he is reasonably competent to the task he undertakes, may be referred to the maxim *supra*.

[2] 1 Stark. Ev., 3d ed., 173, 175; Stark. Ev., 4th ed., 96, 273.

[3] 1 Phil. Ev., 10th ed., 521.

[4] Id. ibid.

[5] M'Naghten's Case, 10 Cl. & F. 211, 212.

nation of the truth of the facts deposed to, which it is for the jury to decide, and the questions are mere questions upon a matter of science, in which case such evidence is admissible. But where the facts admitted are not disputed, and the question becomes substantially one of science only, it may be convenient to allow the question to be put in that general form, though the same cannot be insisted on as a matter of right."

Further, on the principle expressed by the maxim, *Cuilibet in suâ arte perito est credendum*, ship-builders have been allowed to state their opinions as to the seaworthiness of a ship from examining a survey which had been taken by others, and at the taking of which they were not present; and the opinion of an artist is evidence as to the genuineness of a picture.[1] But, although [*935] *witnesses conversant with a particular trade may be allowed to speak on a prevalent practice in that trade, and although scientific persons may give their opinions on matters of science, it has been expressly decided that witnesses are not receivable to state their views on matters of legal or moral obligation, nor on the manner on which others would probably have been influenced if particular parties had acted in one way rather than another.[2] For instance, in an action on a policy of insurance, where a broker stated, on cross-examination, that in his opinion certain letters ought to have been disclosed, and that, if they had, the policy would not have been underwritten: this was held to be mere opinion, and not evidence.[3] And, in like manner, it seems, notwithstanding some

[1] Phil. Ev., 10th ed., 522. So evidence as to the genuineness of handwriting given by a witness possessing the requisite experience and skill is admissible, although little or no weight has, by many judges, been thought to be due to testimony of this description. 2 Phil. Ev., 10th ed., 308; Doe d. Mudd *v.* Suckermore, 5 A. & E. 703 (31 E. C. L. R.); Doe d. Jenkins *v.* Davies, 10 Q. B. 314 (59 E. C. L. R.). See Brooks *v.* Tichbourne, 5 Exch. 929, 931; Newton *v.* Rickets, 9 H. L. Cas. 262.

And now by stat. 17 & 18 Vict. c. 125, s. 27, it is enacted that "comparison of a disputed writing with any writing *proved to the satisfaction of the judge to be genuine* shall be permitted to be made by witnesses; and such writings, and the evidence of witnesses respecting the same, may be submitted to the court and jury as evidence of the genuineness, or otherwise, of the writing in dispute."

[2] Judgm., 5 B. & Ad. 846 (27 E. C. L. R.). See also Greville *v.* Chapman, 5 Q. B. 731.

[3] Carter *v.* Boehm, 3 Burr. 1905, 1913, 1914; Campbell *v.* Rickards, 5 B. & Ad. 840 (27 E. C. L. R.); with which compare Rickards *v.* Murdock, 10 B. &

conflicting decisions, that the opinions of underwriters as to the materiality of facts, and the effect they would have had upon the amount of premium, would not, in general, be admissible in evidence; it being the province of the jury, and not of any witness, to decide what facts ought to be communicated.[1] Where, however, the fixing the fair price and value upon a contract to insure is a matter of skill and judgment, and must be effected according to certain [*936] *general rules and principles of calculation applied to the particular circumstances of each individual case, it seems to be matter of evidence to show whether the fact suppressed would have been noticed as a term in the particular calculation. In some instances, moreover, the materiality of the fact withheld would be a question of pure science; in others, it is very possible that mere common sense, although sufficient to comprehend that the disclosure was material, would not be so to understand to what extent the risk was increased by that fact; and, in intermediate cases, it seems difficult in principle wholly to exclude evidence of the nature alluded to, although its importance may vary exceedingly according to circumstances.[2] Thus, it has been said[3] that the time of sailing may be very material to the risk. How far it is so must essentially depend upon the nature and length of the voyage, the season of the year, the prevalence of the winds, the conformation of the coasts, the usages of trade as to navigation and touching and staying at port, the objects of the enterprise, and other circumstances political and otherwise, which may retard or advance the general progress of the voyage. The material ingredients of all such inquiries are mixed up with nautical skill, information, and experience, and are to be ascertained in part upon the testimony of maritime persons, and are in no case judicially cognizable as matter of law. The ultimate fact itself, which is the test of materiality, that is, whether the risk be increased so as to enhance the premium, is, in many [*937] cases, an inquiry dependent upon the judgment of underwriters *and others who are conversant with the subject of insurance.

C. 257 (21 E. C. L. R.), and Chapman *v.* Walton, 10 Bing. 57. Upon the above subject see 1 Arnould Mar. Ins., 2d ed., pp. 189 *et seq.*

[1] Per Gibbs, C. J., Durrell *v.* Bederly, Holt N. P. C. 286 (3 E. C. L. R.).

[2] 3 Stark. Ev., 3d ed., 887, 888.

[3] Per Story, J., delivering judgment, M'Lanahan *v.* Universal Insurance Co., 1 Peters (U. S.) R. 188.

The Sussex Peerage Case will be found to offer a good illustration of the above maxim as it applies to the *legal* knowledge of a party whose evidence it is proposed to take. In order to prove the law prevailing at Rome on the subject of marriage, a Roman Catholic bishop was there tendered as a witness, and was subjected to examination as to the nature and extent of the duties of his office in its bearing on the subject of marriage, with the view of ascertaining whether he had such a peculiar knowledge of the law relative to marriage as would render him competent to give evidence respecting it. It appeared from this examination that the witness had resided more than twenty years at Rome, and had studied the ecclesiastical law prevailing there on the above subject; that a knowledge of this law was necessary in order to the due discharge of an important part of the duties of his office; that the decision of matrimonial cases, so far as they might be affected by the ecclesiastical and canon law, fell within the jurisdiction of Roman Catholic bishops; and, further, that the tribunals at Rome would respect and act upon his decision or judgment in any particular case if it was unappealed from. It was held that the witness came within the definition of *peritus*, and was admissible accordingly.[1] In a more recent case it has been held that the mercantile custom or usage of a foreign country *bearing on any particular [*938] subject may be proved by one who, though not a lawyer by profession, nor having filled any official appointment as judge, advocate, or solicitor, can satisfy the court that he had special and peculiar means of acquiring knowledge respecting it.[2]

Lastly, although, in accordance with the principal maxim, a skilled witness may be examined as to mercantile usage, or as to

[1] The Sussex Peerage, 11 Cl. & Fin. 85. See also Di Sora *v.* Phillipps, 10 H. L. Cas. 624; per Lord Langdale, M. R., in Earl Nelson *v.* Lord Bridport, 8 Beav. 527; Baron de Bode *v.* Reg., 8 Q. B. 208, 246, 250, *et seq.* (55 E. C. L. R.); The Perth Peerage, 2 H. L. Cas. 865, 874. "A long course of practice sanctioned by professional men is often the best expositor of the law;" per Lord Eldon, C., Chandler *v.* Chandler, 1 Jac. 232.

[2] Vander Donckt *v.* Thellusson, 8 C. B. 812 (65 E. C. L. R.). See Reg. *v.* Povey, 22 L. J. Q. B. 19; s. c., Dearsl. C. C. 32. In Bristow *v.* Sequeville, 5 Exch. 275, a witness was held inadmissible to prove the law of a foreign country, whose knowledge of it had been acquired solely by studying it at a university there situate.

the meaning of a term of art, he cannot be asked to construe[1] a written document, for *Ad quæstionem legis respondent judices.*[2]

OMNIA PRÆSUMUNTUR CONTRA SPOLIATOREM.

(Branch, Max., 5th ed., p. 80.)

Every presumption is made against a wrong-doer.

The following case will serve forcibly to illustrate the above maxim. An account of personal estate having been decreed in equity, the defendant charged the plaintiff with a debt as due to the estate. It was proved that the defendant had wrongfully opened a bundle of papers relating to the account, which had been sealed up and left in his hands. It further appeared that he had altered and displaced the papers, and that it could not be known what papers might have been abstracted. The court, upon proof of these facts, disallowed the defendant's whole demand against the [*939] plaintiff, although the Lord Chancellor *declared himself satisfied, as indeed the defendant swore, that all the papers entrusted to the defendant had been produced; the ground of this decision being that *in odium spoliatoris omnia præsumuntur.*[3]

Again, "if a man, by his own tortious act, withhold the evidence by which the nature of his case would be manifested, every presumption to his disadvantage will be adopted."[4] Where a party has the means in his power of rebutting and explaining the evidence adduced against him, if it does not tend to the truth, the omission to do so furnishes a strong inference against him.[5] Thus, where a person who has wrongfully converted property will not produce

[1] Kirkland *v.* Nisbet, 3 Macq. Sc. App. Cas. 766.

[2] *Ante*, p. 102.

[3] Wardour *v.* Berisford, 1 Vern. 452; s. c., Francis, M., p. 8. Sanson *v.* Rumsey, 2 Vern. 561, affords another illustration of the maxim. See also Dalston *v.* Coatsworth, 1 P. Wms. 731; cited, per Sir S. Romilly, S.-G., arg. Lord Melville's Trial, 29 St. Tr. 1194; Gartside *v.* Ratcliff, 1 Chanc. Cas. 292.

[4] 1 Smith L. C., 6th ed., 323; 1 Vern. 19. The maxim likewise applies to the spoliation of ships' papers: The Hunter, 1 Dods. Adm. R. 480, 486; The Emilie, 18 Jur. 703, 705.

[5] 3 Stark. Ev., 3d ed., 937.

it, it shall be presumed, as against him, to be of the best description.[1] On the other hand, if goods are sold without any express stipulation as to the price, and the vendor prove the delivery of the goods but give no evidence to fix their value, they are presumed to be worth the lowest price for which goods of that description usually sell; but if the vendee himself be shown to have suppressed the means of ascertaining the truth, then a contrary *presumption arises, and the goods are taken to be of the very best description.[2] [*940]

According to the same principle, if a man withhold an agreement under which he is chargeable, after notice to produce it, it is presumed, as against him, to have been properly stamped, until the contrary appear.[3] Where a public officer, such as a sheriff, produces an instrument the execution of which he is bound to procure, as against him it is presumed to have been duly executed.[4] Moreover, if a person is proved to have defaced or destroyed any written instrument, a presumption arises that, if the truth had appeared, it would have been against his interest, and that his conduct is attributable to his knowledge of this circumstance; and accordingly slight evidence of the contents of the instrument will usually, in such a case, be sufficient.[5] A testator made a will, by which he devised certain premises to A., and afterwards made another will, which was lost, and which the jury found, by special verdict, to have been different from the former will, though they did not find in what particular the difference consisted: the court

[1] Armory *v.* Delamirie, 1 Stra. 504 (followed in Mortimer *v.* Cradock, 12 L. J. C. P. 166, and applied by Lord Cairns, Hammersmith and City R. C. *v.* Brand, L. R. 4 H. L. 224, and by Sir S. Romilly, S.-G., arg. Lord Melville's Trial, 29 St. Tr. 1193–4). But "a person who refuses to allow his solicitor to violate the confidence of the professional relation" cannot be regarded in the same odious light as was the jeweller in the above case: per Lord Chelmsford, Wentworth *v.* Lloyd, 10 H. L. Cas. 591.

[2] Clunnes *v.* Pezzey, 1 Camp. 8; followed Lawton *v.* Sweeney (Exch.), 8 Jur. 964. See Hayden *v.* Hayward, 1 Camp. 180.

[3] Crisp *v.* Anderson, 1 Stark. N. P. C. 35 (2 E. C. L. R.).

[4] Scott *v.* Waithman, 3 Stark. N. P. C. 168; Plumer *v.* Brisco, 11 Q. B. 52 (63 E. C. L. R.); Barnes *v.* Lucas, 1 Ry. & M. 264 (21 E. C. L. R.).

[5] 1 Phil. Ev., 10th ed., 477, 478, where various cases are cited exemplifying the maxim in the text; Annesley *v.* Earl of Anglesey, 17 Howell St. Tr. 1430; 1 Stark. Ev., 3d ed., 409; Roe d. Haldane *v.* Harvey, 4 Burr. 2484; Lord Trimlestown *v.* Kemmis, 9 Cl. & F. 775.

decided that the devisee under the first will was entitled to the estate; but Lord Mansfield observed that, in case the devisee under the first will had destroyed the second, it would have been a good ground for the jury to find a revocation.[1]

[*941] *With reference to the class of cases last mentioned, viz., where a deed or other instrument, which ought to be in the possession of a litigant party, is not produced, the general rule is that the law excludes such evidence of facts as, from the nature of the thing, supposes still better evidence in the party's possession or power. And this rule is founded on a sort of presumption that there is something in the evidence withheld which makes against the party producing it.[2] Twyman *v.* Knowles[3] may be referred to in connection with this part of the subject. That was an action of trespass *qu. cl. fr.*, at the trial of which the plaintiff relied upon his bare possession of the *locus in quo*, although it appeared that he had taken the said premises under an agreement in writing which was not produced: the judge directed the jury that, having proved that he was in possession of the close at the time when the trespass was committed, the plaintiff must have a verdict;[4] but that to entitle himself to more than nominal damages, he should have shown the duration of his term. And this direction was upheld by the court *in banco*, Maule, J., observing that the plaintiff had the means of showing the quantum of his interest, and that "the non-production of the lease raised a presumption that the production of it would do the plaintiff no good."

If indeed the evidence alleged to be withheld is shown to be unattainable, the presumption *contra spoliatorem* ceases, and the inferior evidence is admissible. [*942] If, therefore, *a deed be in the possession of the adverse party, and not produced, or if it be lost and destroyed, no matter whether by the adverse party or not, secondary evidence is clearly admissible; and if the deed be in the possession of a third person, who is not by law compellable

[1] Harwood *v.* Goodright, Cowp. 86.

[2] As illustrating the nature and force of this presumption, see Lumley *v.* Wagner, 1 De G., M. & G. 604, 633, 634.

[3] 13 C. B. 222 (76 E. C. L. R.).

[4] It is a well-known rule that "a person in possession is held to have a good title against everybody except the legal owner of the estate." See, *ex. gr.*, Daintry *v.* Brocklehurst, 3 Exch. 207, 210; *ante*, p. 713.

to produce it, and he refuses to do so, the result is the same, for the object is then unattainable by the party offering the secondary evidence.[1]

The fabrication of evidence, we may further remark, is calculated to raise a presumption against the party who has recourse to such a practice, even stronger than when evidence has been suppressed or withheld.

A considerable degree of caution should, nevertheless, be applied in cases of this latter description, more especially in criminal proceedings,[2] for experience shows that a weak but innocent man will sometimes, when appearances are against him, have recourse to falsehood and deception, for the purpose of manifesting his innocence and ensuring his safety.[3]

OMNIA PRÆSUMUNTUR RITE ET SOLENNITER ESSE ACTA.

(Co. Litt. 6 b. 332.)

All acts are presumed to have been rightly and regularly done.

Ex diuturnitate temporis omnia præsumuntur ritè et solenniter esse acta.[4] "Antiquity of time fortifieth *all titles and supposeth the best beginning the law can give them."[5] And [*943] again, "it is a maxim of the law of England to give effect to everything which appears to have been established for a considerable course of time, and to presume that what has been done was done of right and not of wrong."[6] This maxim applies as well

[1] Judgm., Doe d. Gilbert *v.* Ross, 7 M. & W. 121; Marston *v.* Downes, 1 A. & E. 31 (28 E. C. L. R.); Cooke *v.* Tanswell, 8 Taunt. 450 (4 E. C. L. R.).

[2] As to the maxim in such cases, see, per Mounteney, B., 17 Howell St. Tr. 1430; Norden's Case, Fost. C. L. 129.

[3] 1 Stark. Ev., 3d ed., 564, 565.

[4] Jenk. Cent. 185; Roberts *v.* Bethell, 12 C. B. 778 (74 E. C. L. R.), seems to offer an illustration of the presumption *omnia solenniter esse acta.* See Potez *v.* Glossop, 3 Exch. 191; observed upon, per Lord Wensleydale, Buller *v.* Mountgarrett, 7 H. L. Cas. 647; Morgan *v.* Whitmore, 6 Exch. 716.

[5] Hob. 257; Ellis *v.* Mayor of Bridgnorth, 15 C. B. N. S. 52 (109 E. C. L. R.).

[6] Per Pollock, C. B., 2 H. & N. 623; and in Price *v.* Worwood, 4 H. & N. 514, where the same learned judge observes, "The law will presume a state of things to continue which is lawful in every respect; but, if the continuance is unlawful, it cannot be presumed.

where matters are in contest between private persons as to matters public in their nature.[1]

For instance: a lease contained a covenant on the part of the lessee that he would not, without the consent of the lessor, use, exercise, or carry on in the demised premises, any trade or business whatsoever, nor convert the demised dwelling-houses into a shop, nor suffer the same to be used for any other purpose than dwelling-houses. One of the dwelling-houses was converted into a public-house and grocery shop, and the lessor, with full knowledge thereof, for more than twenty years received the rent. The plaintiff, having purchased from the lessor the reversion of the premises in question, brought an action of ejectment for breach of the covenant above specified. Held, that user of the premises in their altered state for more than twenty years, with the knowledge of the lessor, was evidence from which a jury might presume a license.[2] Where, indeed, [*944] a private right is in question, the *presumption *omnia ritè esse acta* may, as already stated, under various and wholly dissimilar states of facts arise *ex diuturnitate temporis.* Thus, the enrollment of a deed may be presumed; where there has been a conveyance by lease and release, the existence of the lease may be presumed on the production of the release; and livery of seisin, the surrender of a copyhold estate, or a reconveyance from the mortgagee to the mortgagor, may be presumed.[3]

Again, where acts are of an official nature, or require the concurrence of official persons, a presumption arises in favor of their due

[1] See, per Pollock, C. B., Reed *v.* Lamb, 6 H. & N. 85, 86; per Crompton, J., Dawson *v.* Surveyor of Highways for Willoughby, 5 B. & S. 924 (117 E. C. L. R.).

[2] Gibson *v.* Doeg, 2 H. & N. 615.

[3] Per Watson, B., 2 H. & N. 777; and cases cited, Doe d. Robertson *v.* Gardiner, 12 C. B. 319 (74 E. C. L. R.). So a lease will be presumed, in the absence of evidence to the contrary, on production of the counterpart: Hughes *v.* Clark, 10 C. B. 905 (70 E. C. L. R.). Upon a sale of leasehold property, without any condition protecting the vendor against the production of deeds, the vendor is bound to produce the lease which is the root of his title, although the lease is more than sixty years old: Frend *v.* Buckley, L. R. 5 Q. B. 213. In Avery *v.* Bowden (in error), 6 E. & B. 973 (88 E. C. L. R.), Pollock, C. B., observes, that "where the maxim of *Omnia ritè acta præsumuntur* applies, there indeed, if the event ought properly to have taken place on *Tuesday*, evidence that it did take place on *Tuesday* or *Wednesday* is strong evidence that it took place on the *Tuesday*.

execution. In these cases the ordinary rule is, *Omnia præsumuntur ritè et solenniter esse acta donee probetur in contrarium*[1]—everything *is presumed to be rightly and duly performed until the contrary is shown.[2] The following may be mentioned [*945] as general presumptions of law illustrating this maxim:—That a man, acting in a public capacity, was properly appointed and is duly authorized so to do;[3] that in the absence of proof to the contrary, credit should be given to public officers who have acted *primâ facie* within the limits of their authority, for having done so with honesty and discretion;[4] that the records of a court of justice have been correctly made,[5] according to the rule, *Res judicata pro veritate accipitur;*[6] that judges and jurors do nothing causelessly and mali-

[1] Co. Litt. 232; Van Omeron *v.* Dowick, 2 Camp. 44; Doe d. Phillips *v.* Evans, 1 Cr. & M. 461; Powell *v.* Sonnett, 3 Bing. 381 (17 E. C. L. R.), offers a good instance of the application of this maxim. Presumption as to signature, Taylor *v.* Cook, 8 Price 653. The court will not presume any fact so as to vitiate an order of removal: per Lord Denman, C. J., R. *v.* Stockton, 5 B. & Ad. 550 (27 E. C. L. R.). See Reg. *v.* St. Paul, Covent Garden, 7 Q. B. 232 (53 E. C. L. R.); Reg. *v.* Justices of Warwickshire, 6 Q. B. 750 (51 E. C. L. R.); Reg. *v.* St. Mary Magdalen, 2 E. & B. 809 (75 E. C. L. R.). As to an order of affiliation, see Watson *v.* Little, 5 H. & N. 472, 478. As to an award, see, per Parke, B., 12 M. & W. 251; as to presuming an indenture of apprenticeship, Reg. *v.* Inhabs. of Fordingbridge, E., B. & E. 678 (96 E. C. L. R.); Reg. *v.* Inhabs. of Broadhampton, 1 E. & E. 154, 162, 163 (102 E. C. L. R.).

Quære whether the maxim applies to the performance of a *moral* duty, see per Willes, J., Fitzgerald *v.* Dressler, 7 C. B. N. S. 399 (97 E. C. L. R.).

[2] See per Story, J., delivering judgment, Bank of the United States *v.* Dandridge, 12 Wheaton (U. S.) R. 69, 70 (where the above maxim is illustrated and explained); Davies *v.* Pratt, 17 C. B. 183 (84 E. C. L. R.).

[3] Per Lord Ellenborough, C. J., R. *v.* Verselet, 3 Camp. 432; Monke *v.* Butler, 1 Roll. R. 83; M'Gahey *v.* Alston, 2 M. & W. 206; Faulkner *v.* Johnson, 11 M. & W. 581; Doe d. Hopley *v.* Young, 8 Q. B. 63 (55 E. C. L. R.); Reg. *v.* Essex, Dearsl. & B. 369; M'Mahon *v.* Lennard, 6 H. L. Cas. 970. See the above maxim applied, per Erle, C. J., Bremner *v.* Hull, L. R. 1 C. P. 759.

[4] Judgm., Earl of Derby *v.* Bury Improvement Commissioners, L. R. 4 Ex. 226.

[5] Reed *v.* Jackson, 1 East 355.

[6] D. 50. 17. 207; Co. Litt. 103 a; Judgm., Magrath *v.* Hardy, 4 Bing. N. C. 796 (33 E. C. L. R.); per Alderson, B., Hopkins *v.* Francis, 13 M. & W. 670; Irwin *v.* Gray, L. R. 2 H. L. 20; Smith *v.* Sydney, L. R. 5 Q. B. 203.

A family Bible is in the nature of a record, and being produced from the proper custody, is itself evidence of pedigrees entered in it: Hubbard *v.* Lees, L. R. 1 Ex. 255, 258.

ciously;[1] that the decisions of a court of competent jurisdiction are well founded, and their judgments regular;[2] and that facts without [*946] proof of which the *verdict could not have been found, were proved at the trial.[3]

Where the judgment of a court of competent jurisdiction is brought under review, Lord Wensleydale[4] thus indicates the degree of weight attributable to it—"I take it to be perfectly clear," remarks his lordship, "that when a court of error is considering a former decision on appeal, that decision is not to be overturned unless the court of error is perfectly satisfied that the decision is wrong. *Primâ facie* it is to be considered a right decision, and is not to be deprived of its effect unless it is clearly proved to the satisfaction of the judge that this decision is wrong; but he must consider the whole circumstances together, and if he still feels satisfied upon the whole of the case that the decision is wrong, he ought undoubtedly to overturn it; it is only to be considered as *primâ facie* right. The *onus probandi* lies on the opposite party to show that it is wrong, and, if he satisfies the conscience of the judge that it is wrong, it ought to be reversed."[5]

Besides the cases below cited,[6] which strikingly illustrate the presumption of law under our notice, the following may be adduced:—

[1] Sutton *v.* Johnstone, 1 T. R. 503. See Lumley *v.* Gye, 3 E. & B. 114 (77 E. C. L. R.).

[2] Per Bayley, J., Lyttleton *v.* Cross, 3 B. & C. 327 (10 E. C. L. R.); Reg. *v.* Brenan, 16 L. J. Q. B. 289. See Lee *v.* Johnstone, L. R. 1 Sc. App. Cas. 426; Morris *v.* Ogden, L. R. 4 C. P. 687, 699.

[3] Per Buller, J., Spieres *v.* Parker, 1 T. R. 145, 146. If the return to a mandamus be certain on the face of it, that is sufficient, and the court cannot intend facts inconsistent with it, for the purpose of making it bad. Per Buller, J., R. *v.* Lyme Regis, 1 Dougl. 159. See R. *v.* Nottingham Waterworks Co., 6 A. & E. 355 (33 E. C. L. R.).

[4] Mayor, &c., of Beverley *v.* A.-G., 6 H. L. Cas. 332, 333.

[5] *Et vide* per Lord Chelmsford, *ante*, p. 168.

[6] See, as to presuming an Act of Parliament in support of an ancient usage, Judgm., Reg. *v.* Chapter of Exeter, 12 A. & E. 532 (40 E. C. L. R.)—the passing of a by-law by a corporation from usage, Reg. *v.* Powell, 3 E. & B. 377 (77 E. C. L. R.); in favor of acts of commissioners having authority by statute, Horton *v.* Westminster Improvement Commissioners, 7 Exch. 780; Reg. *v.* St. Michael's, Southampton, 6 E. & B. 807 (88 E. C. L. R.); an order of justices for stopping up a road, Williams *v.* Eyton, 2 H. & N. 771, 777; s. c., 4 Id. 357. See, also, Woodbridge Union *v.* Guardians of Colneis, 13 Q. B. 269 (66 E. C. L. R.).

*It is a well-established rule that the law will presume in favor of honesty and against fraud;[1] it will moreover strongly presume against the commission of a criminal act, *ex. gr.*, that a witness has perjured himself.[2] [*947]

The law will also presume strongly in favor of the validity of a marriage, especially where a great length of time has elapsed since its celebration[3]—indeed the legal presumption as to marriage and legitimacy is only to be rebutted by "strong, distinct, satisfactory and conclusive" evidence.[4]

Where the claimant of an ancient barony, which has been long in abeyance, proves that his ancestor sat as a peer in Parliament, and no patent or charter of creation can be discovered, it is now the established rule to hold that the barony was created by writ of summons and sitting, although the original writ of summons or enrollment of it is not produced.[5] In the Hastings Peerage, it was proved that A. B. was summoned by special writ to Parliament in the 49th Hen. 3, but there was no proof that he ever sat, there being no rolls or journals of that *period. A. B.'s son and heir, C. D., sat in the Parliament of 18 Edw. 1, but there was no proof that he was summoned to that Parliament, there being no writs of summons or enrollments of them extant from 49 Hen. 3 to 23 Edw. 1. It further appeared that C. D. was summoned to the Parliament of 23 Edw. 1, and to several subsequent Parliaments, but there was no proof that he sat in any of them. Held, that it might be well presumed that C. D. sat in the Parliament of the [*948]

[1] Middleton *v.* Barned, 4 Exch. 241; per Parke, B., Id. 243; and in Shaw, app., Beck, resp., 8 Exch. 400; Doe d. Tatum *v.* Catomore, 16 Q. B. 745, 747 (71 E. C. L. R.), with which compare Doe d. Shallcross *v.* Palmer, Id. 747. See Trott *v.* Trott, 29 L. J., P., M. & A. 156.

[2] Per Lord Brougham, McGregor *v.* Topham, 3 H. L. Cas. 147, 148; per Turner, L. J., 4 DeG., M. & G. 153.

[3] Piers *v.* Piers, 2 H. L. Cas. 331; Sichel *v.* Lambert, 15 C. B. N. S. 781, 787, 788 (80 E. C. L. R.). And see Reg. *v.* Manwaring, Dearsl. & B. 132, 144; *ante*, p. 507, n. 5.

[4] Per Lord Brougham, 2 H. L. Cas. 373; citing, per Lord Lyndhurst, Morris *v.* Davies, 5 Cl. & F. 265. See Lapsley *v.* Grierson, 1 H. L. Cas. 498; The Saye and Sele Peerage, Id. 507; per Erle, J., Walton *v.* Gavin, 16 Q. B. 58 (71 E. C. L. R.); Harrison *v.* Mayor of Southampton, 4 De G., M. & G. 137, 153.

[5] The Braye Peerage, 6 Cl. & Fin. 757; The Vaux Peerage, 5 Cl. & Fin. 526.

18th Edw. 1, in pursuance of a summons, on the principle that *Omnia præsumuntur legitime facto donec probetur in contrarium.*[1]

As regards the acts of private individuals, the presumption *omnia ritè esse acta* forcibly applies where they are of a formal character, as writings under seal.[2] Likewise, upon proof of title, everything which is collateral to the title will be intended, without proof; for, although the law requires exactness in the derivation of a title, yet where that has been proved, all collateral circumstances will be presumed in favor of right;[3] and, wherever the possession of a party is rightful, the general rule of presumption is applied to invest that possession with a legal title.[4] No greater obligation, it has, indeed, been [*949] *said,[5] lies upon a court of justice than that of supporting long continued enjoyment by every legal means, and by every reasonable presumption; this "doctrine of presumption goes on the footing of validity, and upholds validity by supposing that everything was present which that validity required." *Omnia præsumuntur ritè fuisse acta* is the principle to be observed.

In reference also to a claim by the rector of a parish to certain fees, founded on prescription, it has been judicially observed that "the true principle of the law applicable to this question is that where a fee has been received for a great length of time, the right to which could have had a legal origin, it may and ought to be assumed that it was received as of right during the whole period of

[1] The Hastings Peerage, 8 Cl. & Fin. 144.

[2] See arg. and Judgm. in Ricard *v.* Williams, 7 Wheaton (U. S.) R. 59; Strother *v.* Lucas, 12 Peters (U. S.) R. 452; S. P., 2 Id. 760; 2 Exch. 549; D'Arcy *v.* Tamar, &c., R. C., 4 H. & C. 463, 467, 468.

As to presumption that a foreign bill of exchange was duly stamped at the time of its indorsement to plaintiff, Bradlaugh *v.* De Rin, L. R. 3 C. P. 286.

As to presumption of evidence of probate, see Doe d. Woodhouse *v.* Powell, 8 Q. B. 576 (55 E. C. L. R.).

As to presumption that a will was duly executed, Lloyd *v.* Roberts, 12 Moo. P. C. C. 158, 165; Trott *v.* Trott, 29 L. J., P., M. & A. 156.

[3] 3 Stark. Ev., 3d ed., 936; 2 Wms. Saund., 5th ed., 42., n. (7).

[4] Per Lord Ellenborough, C. J., 8 East 263. See Simpson, app., Wilkinson, resp., 8 Scott N. R. 814; Doe d. Dand *v.* Thompson, 7 Q. B. 897 (53 E. C. L. R.).

[5] Per Lord Westbury, Lee *v.* Johnstone, L. R. 1 Sc. App. Cas. 435.

legal memory, that is, from the reign of Richard I. to the present time, unless the contrary is proved."[1]

On the same principle it is a general rule that, where a person is required to do an act, the not doing of which would make him guilty of a criminal neglect of duty, it shall be intended that he has duly performed it unless the contrary be shown—*stabit præsumptio donec probetur in contrarium*;[2] negative evidence rebuts this presumption, that all has been duly performed.[3] Thus, on an indictment for the non-repair of a road, the presumption, that an award, in relief of the defendants, was duly made according to the directions of an inclosure *Act, may be rebutted by proof of repairs subsequently done to the road by the defendants; for, if the fact had been in accordance with such presumption, they ought not to have continued to repair.[4] [*950]

It is, however, important to observe, in addition to the above general remarks, that, in inferior courts and proceedings by magistrates, the maxim, *Omnia præsumuntur ritè esse acta*, does not apply *to give jurisdiction*.[5]

Thus, the Lord Mayor's Court in London is an inferior court. When therefore process had issued out of that court against C. as a garnishee, and he declared in prohibition, a plea which set up the custom of foreign attachment, but did not allege, and the fact did not warrant, any such allegation, that the original debt or the debt alleged to be due from the garnishee to the defendant arose within the city, or that any one of the parties to the suit was a citizen or was resident within the city, was held insufficient to show the existence of jurisdiction.[6]

[1] Bryant *v.* Foot, L. R. 3 Q. B. 565; Lawrence *v.* Hitch, Id. 521.

[2] Wing. Max. 712; Hob. R. 297; per Sir W. Scott, 1 Dods. Adm. R. 266; Davenport *v.* Mason, 15 Mass. (U. S.) R., 2d ed., 87. "It seems reasonable that presumption which is not founded on the basis of certainty should yield to evidence, which is the test of truth." Id.

[3] Per Lord Ellenborough, C. J., R. *v.* Haslingfield, 2 M. & S. 561; recognizing Williams *v.* East India Co., 3 East 192.

[4] R. *v.* Haslingfield, 2 M. & S. 558; Manning *v.* Eastern Counties R. C., 12 M. & W. 237; Doe d. Nanney *v.* Gore, 2 M. & W. 321; Heysham *v.* Forster, 5 Man. & Ry. 277.

[5] Per Holroyd, J., 7 B. & C. 790 (14 E. C. L. R.). See Reg. *v.* Inhabs. of Gate Fulford, Dearsl. & B. 74.

[6] The Mayor, &c., of London *v.* Cox, L. R. 2 H. L. 239.

Again, where the examination of a soldier, taken before two magistrates, was tendered in evidence to prove his settlement, but it did not appear by the examination itself, or by other proof, that the soldier, at the time when he was examined, was quartered in the place where the justices had jurisdiction, it was held not to be admissible.[1] So, in the case of an order by magistrates, their jurisdiction must appear on the face of such order; otherwise, it is a [*951] nullity, and not merely voidable.[2] *Where an examination before removing justices left it doubtful whether the examination had been taken by a single justice or by two, the court stated that they would look at the document as lawyers, and would give it the benefit of the legal presumption in its favor; and it was observed, that the maxim, *Omnia præsumuntur ritè esse acta*, applied in this case with particular effect, since the fault, if there really had been one, was an irregular assumption of power by a single justice, as well as a fraud of the two, in pretending that to have been done by two, which was, in fact, done only by one.[3]

In a case before the House of Lords some remarks were made in reference to this subject, which may be here advantageously inserted:—It cannot be doubted, that where an inferior court (a court of limited jurisdiction, either in point of place or of subject-matter) assumes to proceed, its judgment must set forth such facts as show that it has jurisdiction, and must show also in what respect it has jurisdiction. But it is another thing to contend that it must set forth all the facts or particulars out of which its jurisdiction arises. Thus, if a power of commitment or other power is given to justices of a county, their conviction or order must set forth that they are two such justices of such county, in order that it may be certainly known whether they constitute the tribunal upon which the statute they assume to act under has conferred the authority to make that order or pronounce that conviction. But, although it is necessary that the jurisdiction of the inferior court should [*952] appear, *yet there is no particular form in which it should be made to appear. The court above, which has to ex-

[1] R. *v.* All Saints, Southampton, 7 B. & C. 785 (14 E. C. L. R.).

[2] Per Bayley, J., 7 B. & C. 790 (14 E. C. L. R.); R. *v.* Hulcott, 6 T. R. 583; R. *v.* Helling, 1 Stra. 8; R. *v.* Chilverscoton, 6 T. R. 178; R. *v.* Holm, 11 East 381; Reg. *v.* Totness, 11 Q. B. 80 (63 E. C. L. R.).

[3] Reg. *v.* Silkstone, 2 Q. B. 520 (42 E. C. L. R.), and cases cited, Id. p. 729, note (*p*).

amine, and may control, the inferior court, must be enabled, somehow or other, to see that there is jurisduction such as will support the proceeding; but in what way it shall so see it is not material, provided it does so see it.[1] The rule, therefore, may be stated to be, that, where it appears upon the face of the proceedings that the inferior court has jurisdiction, it will be intended that the proceedings are regular;[2] but that, unless it so appears,—that is, if it appear affirmatively that the inferior court has no jurisdiction, or if it be left in doubt whether it has jurisdiction or not,—no such intendment will be made.[3] "The old rule for jurisdiction is, that nothing shall be intended to be out of the jurisdiction of the *superior* court but that which specially appears to be so; nothing is intended to be within the jurisdiction of an *inferior* court but that which is expressly alleged."[4] And again, "it is necessary for a party, who relies upon the decision of an inferior tribunal, to show that the proceedings were within the jurisdiction of the court."[5]

*In the great case of Gosset *v.* Howard,[6] the Court of Exchequer Chamber held, that the warrant of the speaker of the House of Commons must be construed by the rules applied in determining as to the validity of the warrants and writs issuing from a *superior* court; and they remarked that, with respect [*953]

[1] Per Lord Brougham, Taylor *v.* Clemson, 11 Cl. & Fin. 610, affirming the judgment of the Exchequer Chamber in s. c., 2 Q. B. 978 (42 E. C. L. R.). In this case, and in The Mayor, &c., of London *v.* Cox, L. R. 2 H. L. 239, many authorities as to the necessity of showing jurisdiction are collected and reviewed.

[2] A presumption in favor of regularity in official practice is often made. See (*ex. gr.*) Barnes *v.* Keane, 15 Q. B. 75, 82 (69 E. C. L. R.); Re Warne, 15 C. B. 767, 769 (80 E. C. L. R.); Baker *v.* Care, 1 H. & N. 674; Cheney *v.* Courtois, 13 C. B. N. S. 634 (106 E. C. L. R.); Robinson *v.* Collingwood, 17 C. B. N. S. 777 (112 E. C. L. R.).

[3] Per Tindal, C. J., Dempster *v.* Purnell, 4 Scott N. R. 39 (citing Moravia *v.* Sloper, Willes 30, and Titley *v.* Foxall, Id. 688); per Erle, J., Barnes *v.* Keane, 15 Q. B. 84 (69 E. C. L. R.).

[4] Arg. Peacock *v.* Bell, 1 Wms. Saund. 73; adopted Gosset *v.* Howard, 10 Q. B. 453 (59 E. C. L. R.); and in The Mayor, &c., of London *v.* Cox, L. R. 2 H. L. 259. See also further in connection with the text, Id. 261, *et seq.*

[5] Per Alderson, B., Stanton *v.* Styles, 5 Exch. 583; *acc.* The Mayor, &c., of London *v.* Cox, *ubi supra.*

[6] 10 Q. B. 411 (59 E. C. L. R.), where the cases with respect to the validity of warrants were cited in argument.

to writs so issued, it must be presumed that they are duly issued, that they have issued in a case in which the court had jurisdiction, unless the contrary appear on the face of them, and that they are valid of themselves, without any allegation other than that of their issue, and a protection to all officers and others in their aid acting under them. Many of the writs issued by superior courts do, indeed, upon the face of them, recite the cause of their issuing, and show their legality—writs of execution, for instance. Others, however, do not, and, though unquestionably valid, are framed in a form which, if they had proceeded from magistrates or persons having a special jurisdiction unknown to the common law, would have been clearly insufficient, and would have rendered them altogether void. With respect to the speaker's warrant, the court held themselves bound to construe it with at least as much respect as would be shown to a writ out of any of the courts of Westminster; observing, in the language of Mr. Justice Powys,[1] that "the House of Commons is a great court, and all things done by them are intended to have been *ritè acta*."[2]

[*954] *RES INTER ALIOS ACTA ALTERI NOCERE NON DEBET.

(Wing. Max., p. 327.)

A transaction between two parties ought not to operate to the disadvantage of a third.[3]

Of maxims relating to the law of evidence, the above may certainly be considered as one of the most important and most practically useful; its effect is to prevent a litigant party from being concluded, or even affected, by the evidence, acts, conduct, or declarations of strangers.[4] On a principle of good faith and

[1] Reg. *v.* Paty, 2 Lord Raym. 1105, 1108.

[2] Judgm., Gosset *v.* Howard, 10 Q. B. 457 (59 E. C. L. R.).

[3] *Res inter alios judicatæ neque emolumentum afferre his qui judicio non interfuerunt neque prejudicium solent irrogare.*—Cod. 7. 56. 2.

[4] The maxim as to *res inter alios acta* was much considered in Meddowcroft *v.* Huguenin, 3 Curt. R. 303 (where the issue of a marriage which had been pronounced null and void by the Consistorial Court, attempted unsuccessfully to impeach that sentence in the Prerogative Court). s. c., 4 Moore P. C. C. 386; cited *ante*, p. 342, n. 3. See Reg. *v.* Fontaine Moreau, 11 Q. B. 1028 (63 E. C. L. R.), and cases *infra*.

mutual convenience, a man's own acts are binding upon himself, and are, as well as his conduct and declarations, evidence against him; yet it would not only be highly inconvenient, but also manifestly unjust, that a man shall be bound by the acts of mere unauthorized strangers; and if a party ought not to be bound by the acts of strangers, so neither ought their acts or conduct to be used as evidence against him.[1]

The above rule, then, operates to exclude all the acts, declarations, or conduct of others as evidence to bind a party, either directly or by inference; so that, in general, no declaration, written entry, or affidavit made by a *stranger, is evidence [*955] against a man; nor can a person be affected, still less concluded, by any evidence,[2] decree, or judgment to which he was not actually, or in consideration of law, privy.[3] From an important case,[4] immediately connected with this subject, the following remarks are extracted: It is certainly true, as a general principle,

[1] 1 Stark. Evid., 3d ed., 58, 59, from which valuable work many of the remarks appended to the above maxim have been extracted. See Armstrong *v.* Normandy, 5 Exch. 409; Reg. *v.* Ambergate, &c., R. C., 1 E. & B. 372, 381 (72 E. C. L. R.); Salmon *v.* Webb, 3 H. L. Cas. 510.

[2] See Humphreys *v.* Pensam, 1 My. & Cr. 580.

[3] "It cannot be doubted that a man's assertions or admissions, whether made in the course of a judicial proceeding or otherwise, and, in the former case, whether he was himself a party to such proceeding or not, may be given in evidence against him in any suit or action in which the fact so asserted or admitted becomes material to the issue to be determined. And in principle there can be no difference whether the assertion or admission be made by the party himself, who is and ought to be affected by it, or by some one employed, directed, or invited by him to make the particular statement on his behalf. In like manner a man who brings forward another for the purpose of asserting or proving some fact on his behalf, whether in a court of justice or elsewhere, must be taken himself to assert the fact which he thus seeks to establish:" per Cockburn, C. J., Richards *v.* Morgan, 4 B. & S. 661 (116 E. C. L. R.).

[4] See the opinion of the judges in the Duchess of Kingston's Case, 11 Howell St. Tr. 261. See, also, Needham *v.* Bremner, L. R. 1 C. P. 583; Natal Land, &c., Co. *v.* Good, L. R. 2 P. C. 121; Davies, demand., Lowndes, ten., 7 Scott N. R. 141; Doe d. Bacon *v.* Brydges, Id. 333; Lord Trimlestown *v.* Kemmis, 9 Cl. & Fin. 781, cited Boileau *v.* Rutlin, 2 Exch. 665, 667. The general rule stated in the text has, however, been departed from in certain cases; for instance, in questions relating to manorial rights, public rights of way, immemorial custom, disputed boundary, disputed modus, and pedigrees.

that a transaction between two parties in judicial proceedings ought not to be binding upon a third party, for it would be unjust to bind any person who could not be admitted to make a defence, or to examine witnesses, or to appeal from a judgment which he might think erroneous; and, therefore, the depositions of witnesses in another cause[1] in proof of a fact, the verdict of a jury finding the [*956] fact, and the *judgment of the court upon facts found, although evidence against the parties and all claiming under them, are not, in general, to be used to the prejudice of strangers.[2]

As between the parties to the original suit, it will be merely necessary to observe, that the judgment of a court of concurrent jurisdiction directly upon the point is as a plea, a bar, or as evidence, conclusive, between *the same parties* upon the same matter directly in question in another court.[3] But, where the judgment of a court of competent jurisdiction has been pronounced *in rem*, and has actually operated upon the *status* of a particular thing, it may happen that some other court, proceeding likewise *in rem*, may pronounce a contrary judgment on the same subject-matter, in which case it must be looked upon as arrogating to itself and exercising the functions of a court of appeal, and it is only in this point of view that its decision can be considered as warrantable. It must be further observed, that in no case can a judgment be evidence of any matter which came collaterally in question, though within the jurisdiction of the court, nor of any matter incidentally cognizable, nor of any matter to be inferred by argument from the judgment; and the above rule applies not only to the parties to the judgment, but likewise to the privies thereto.[4]

As regards third persons, it is peculiarly necessary to notice the distinction between judgments strictly *inter partes* and those *in rem*; a judgment *inter partes* being, in general, conclusive between the original parties only [*957] *and their privies;[5] whereas a judgment *in rem* renders the thing adjudicated upon, *ipso*

[1] See, for instance, Morgan *v.* Nicholl, L. R. 2 C. P. 117.

[2] See, also, Judgm., King *v.* Norman, 4 C. B. 898 (56 E. C. L. R.).

[3] *Ante*, p. 334.

[4] Duchess of Kingston's Case, *ubi supra*, and note thereto, 2 Smith L. C. 6th ed., 679 *et seq.*; Doe d. Lord Downe *v.* Thompson, 9 Q. B. 1037 (58 E. C. L. R.).

[5] See, for instance, Lady Wenman *v.* Mackenzie, 5 E. & B. 447 (85 E. C. L. R.).

facto, such as it is thereby declared to be, and is, therefore, of effect as between all persons whatever.[1] Thus, a grant of probate or of administration is in the nature of a decree *in rem*, and actually invests the executor or administrator with the character which it declares to belong to him; and such grant of probate or administration is accordingly (if genuine, unrevoked, and granted by a court of competent jurisdiction) conclusive as against all the world.[2] So, the sentence of a foreign Court of Admiralty, duly constituted and of competent jurisdiction, decreeing a ship to be lawful prize, is conclusive as to that which is in it, and as to the existence of the ground on which it professes to proceed, against all persons, until reversed by a regular court of appeal; all the world, it has been said, are parties to such a sentence.[3] And, generally, where any statute or law, decree or judgment, is of a public nature, or operates *in rem*, the rule as to *res inter alios acta* does not apply, for to such proceedings all are privy.[4]

*It is likewise requisite to notice the distinction which exists between the case in which a verdict or judgment *inter partes* is offered in evidence, with a view to establish the mere fact that such a verdict was given, or such a judgment pronounced, and that in which it is offered as a means of proving some fact which is either expressly found by the verdict, or upon the supposed existence of which the judgment can alone be supported. In the latter case, as above stated, the evidence will not, in general, be admissible to conclude a third party; whereas, in the former, the judgment itself is invariably not only admissible as the proper legal evidence to prove the fact, but is usually conclusive evidence for [*958]

[1] But a verdict of guilty and judgment thereon on an indictment for obstructing a public highway cannot be pleaded as an estoppel in an action afterwards brought by the party convicted against a third person for using the way: Petrie *v.* Nuttall, 11 Exch. 569.

[2] See, per Buller, J., Allen *v.* Dundas, 3 T. R. 129; Prosser *v.* Wagner, 1 C. B. N. S. 289 (87 E. C. L. R.).

[3] Per Lord Mansfield, C. J., Bernardi *v.* Motteux, Dougl. 581; Hughes *v.* Cornelius, 2 Show. 232; per Lord Ellenborough, C. J., Bolton *v.* Gladstone, 5 East 160; 2 Park. Mar. Insur., 8th ed., 718; Kindersley *v.* Chase, cited Id. 743. As to the weight due to, and efficacy of a foreign judgment, see 2 Smith L. C., 6th ed., pp. 725, *et seq.*

[4] 1 Stark. Evid., 3d ed., 61, 62; Pim *v.* Currell, 6 M. & W. 234.

See Cammell *v.* Sewell, 5 H. & N. 728; s. c., 3 Id. 617, which was finally decided, however, by reference to the *lex loci contractûs*.

that purpose, since it must be presumed that the court has made a faithful record of its own proceedings. Moreover, the mere fact that such a judgment was given can never be considered as *res inter alios acta,* being a thing done by public authority; neither can the legal consequences of such a judgment be ever so considered, for, when the law gives to a judgment a particular operation, that operation is properly shown and demonstrated by means of the judgment, which is no more *res inter alios* than the law which gives it force.[1]

Having thus noticed that the general rule as to *res inter alios acta* is not applicable, first, where a judgment is *in rem*, and, secondly, where it is offered as evidence merely to show that such a judgment was, in fact, given, we may proceed to observe briefly on several extensive classes of cases, in which, likewise, this rule has no application.

[*959] *Thus, where the acts or declarations of others have any legal operation material to the subject of inquiry, they must necessarily be admissible in evidence, and the legal consequences resulting from their admission can no more be regarded as *res inter alios acta* than the law itself. For instance, where a question arises as to the right to a personal chattel, evidence is admissible even against an owner who proves that he never sold the chattel, of a subsequent sale of the chattel in market overt; for, although he was no party to the transaction, which took place entirely between others, yet, as such a sale has a legal operation on the question at issue, the fact is no more *res inter alios* than the law which gives effect to such a sale. So, in actions against the sheriff, it very frequently happens that the law depends wholly on transactions to which the sheriff is personally an entire stranger; as, where the question is as to the right of ownership in particular property seized under an execution; and in these cases all transactions and acts between others are admissible in evidence, which, in point of law, are material to decide the right of property.[2]

In an action of assumpsit for making and fixing iron railings to certain houses belonging to the defendant, the defence was, that the

[1] 1 Stark. Evid., 3d ed., 252; King *v.* Norman, 4 C. B. 884 (56 E. C. L. R.); Thomas *v.* Russell, 9 Exch. 764; Drout *v.* Taylor, 16 C. B. 671 (81 E. C. L. R.); Boileau *v.* Rutlin, 2 Exch. 665.

[2] 1 Stark. Evid., 3d ed., 61.

credit was given to A., by whom they were built under a contract, and not to the defendant. A., who had become a bankrupt since the railing was furnished, was called as a witness for the defendant, and having stated that the order was given by him, he was asked what was the state of the account between himself and the defendant in reference to the building of the houses at the time of his bankruptcy. To this question *A.'s reply was, that the defendant had overpaid him by 350*l.* On the part of the [*960] plaintiff it was insisted that the state of the account between A. and the defendant was not admissible in evidence; that it was *res inter alios acta;* and that the inquiry was calculated improperly to influence the jury. It was held, however, by the court in banc, that the evidence was properly received; and Erle, J., remarked, that in an action for goods sold and delivered, a common form of defence is, that the defendant is liable to pay another person, and that in such cases the jury usually come to the conclusion that the defendant in reality wants to keep the goods without paying for them; that the evidence in question went to show the *bona fides* of the defence by proving payment to such third person; and that it was not, therefore, open to the objection of being *res inter alios acta.*[1]

An exception similar to the preceding occurs where the conduct or declaration of another operates, not by way of admission or mere statement, but as evidence which the law admits, as being, under the particular circumstances, not only free from objection, but conducive to the ends of justice. Thus, if A. makes a private memorandum of a fact in which B. has an interest, this memorandum, generally speaking, would not be evidence against B.: it would fall within the description of *res inter alios acta;* but, if it were a memorandum of a fact peculiarly within the knowledge of A., and made in the usual course of business, and especially if A. by that entry charged himself, it would be admissible in evidence after the death of A.;—not that it operates against B. by way of admission of the fact; for, if so, it would be admissible whether A. *were living or dead; but because, under the circumstances above stated, the law considers the entry to be a proper [*961] medium for communicating the original fact to the jury, the testimony of A. himself being unattainable.[2]

[1] Gerish *v.* Chartier, 1 C. B. 13, 17 (50 E. C. L. R.).

[2] 1 Stark. Evid., 3d ed., 62.

It has long been an established principle of evidence, that, if a party who has knowledge of a fact make an entry of it, whereby he charges himself or discharges another upon whom he would otherwise have had a claim, such entry is admissible after his death in evidence of the fact, because it is against his own interest;[1] or, as it has been said, an entry by a man against his own interest is evidence against all the world:[2] and, in order to render an entry such as the above admissible, it is only necessary to prove the handwriting and death of the party who made it.[3]

In the leading case on this subject, it was held, that an entry made by a man-midwife, who had delivered a woman of a child, of his having done so on a certain day, referring to his ledger, in which he had made a charge for his attendance, which was marked as "paid," was evidence upon an issue as to the age of such child at the time of his afterwards suffering a recovery.[4] Here, it [*962] *will be remarked, the entry was admitted, because the party, by making it, discharged another, upon whom he

[1] See per Bayley, J., Doe d. Reece *v.* Robson, 15 East 34.

[2] Per Bayley, B., Gleadow *v.* Atkin, 1 Cr. & M. 423, adverting to Middleton *v.* Melton, 10 B. & C. 317 (21 E. C. L. R.). In Doe d. Sweetland *v.* Webber, 1 A. & E. 740 (28 E. C. L. R.), Lord Denman, C. J., observes, "Mere want of interest, not coupled with other circumstances, has never, as far as I know, been held a ground for admitting declarations as evidence." And *a multo fortiori* a declaration of a deceased person obviously for his interest could not be received: see Judgm., Plant *v.* Taylor, 7 H. & N. 238.

[3] Per Parke, J., 3 B. & Ad. 889.

[4] Higham *v.* Ridgway, 10 East 109 (distinguished in Doe d. Kinglake *v.* Beviss, 7 C. B. 456, 496, 509, 512 (62 E. C. L. R.); and in Smith *v.* Blakey, L. R. 2 Q. B. 326); Bradley *v.* James, 13 C. B. 822, 925 (76 E. C. L. R.); Percival *v.* Nanson, 7 Exch. 1; Edie *v.* Kingsford, 14 C. B. 759 (78 E. C. L. R.); Doe d. Earl of Ashburnham *v.* Michael, 17 Q. B. 276 (79 E. C. L. R.).

In Higham *v.* Ridgway, it should be observed, there was evidence to show that the work for which the charge was made was actually done. (See Doe d. Gallop *v.* Vowles, 1 M. & Rob. 261.) Moreover it will not be a valid objection to the admissibility of an entry, that it purports to charge the deceased, and afterwards to discharge him; for such an objection would go to the very root of this sort of evidence. (Per Lord Tenterden, C. J., Rowe *v.* Benton, 3 Man. & Ry. 267.) In The Sussex Peerage, 11 Cl. & Fin. 112, Lord Brougham remarks that, "The law in Higham *v.* Ridgway has been carried far enough, although not too far." It is applied in Reg. *v.* Overseers of Birmingham, 1 B. & S. 763 (101 E. C. L. R.), (where a declaration was against the *proprietary* interest of the party making it), with which *acc.* Reg. *v.* Exeter, L. R. 4 Q. B. 341, 345.

would otherwise have had a claim. In another case, which was an action of trover by the assignees of a bankrupt, two entries made by an attorney's clerk, in a daybook kept for the purpose of minuting his transactions, were held admissible, by the first of which the clerk acknowledged the receipt of 100*l.* from his employer for the purpose of making a tender, and in the second of which he stated the fact of tender and refusal; for if an action had been brought by the official assignee of the bankrupt against the clerk for money had and received, the plaintiff could have proved by the first entry that the defendant had received the 100*l.*; and, by the second, he could have shown that the object for which the money was placed in defendant's hands had not been attained. Consequently, the declaration might be considered as the entry of a fact within the knowledge of the deceased, which rendered him subject to a pecuniary demand.[1] And, generally, it may be observed, that the rule as to *res inter alios acta* does not apply to exclude entries made by receivers, stewards, and other agents *charging themselves with the receipt of money; such entries being admissible after their decease, to prove the fact of their receipt of such money.[2]

[*963]

Nor does this rule operate in other cases to exclude the admission in evidence of declarations against the interest of the deceased. For instance, an occupier proved to be in possession of a piece of land, is *primâ facie* presumed to be owner in fee, and his declaration is receivable in evidence, when it shows that he was only tenant for life or years.[3] So, in an issue between A. and B., whether C. died possessed of certain property, her declaration, that she had assigned it to A., was held admissible.[4] But it is clear, that a person who has parted with his interest in property cannot be allowed to divest the right of another claiming under him by any statement which he may choose to make;[5] and, therefore, the declarations of a person who had conveyed away his interest in an

[1] Marks *v.* Lahèe, 8 Bing. N. C. 408 (21 E. C. L. R.).

[2] Per Parke, J., Middleton *v.* Melton, 10 B. & C. 327 (21 E. C. L. R.).

[3] Judgm., Crease *v.* Barrett, 1 C., M. & R. 931; per Mansfield, C. J., Peaceable *v.* Watson, 4 Taunt. 16; Davies *v.* Pearce, 2 T. R. 53; Lord Trimlestown *v.* Kemmis, 9 Cl. & Fin. 780.

[4] Ivat *v.* Finch, 1 Taunt. 141.

[5] Per Lord Denman, C. J., 1 A. & E. 740 (28 E. C. L. R.).

estate by executing a settlement, and had subsequently mortgaged the same estate, were, after the death of the mortgagor, held inadmissible, on behalf of the mortgagee, to show that money had actually been advanced upon the mortgage.[1]

An entry will also be admissible in evidence, if made at the time of the transaction to which it relates, in the usual course and routine of business, by a person (since *deceased) who had no [*964] interest to misstate what had occurred. The case[2] usually referred to as establishing the above rule, was an action brought by the plaintiff, who was a brewer, against the Earl of Torrington, for beer sold and delivered; and the evidence given to charge the defendant showed, that the usual way of the plaintiff's dealing was, that the draymen came every night to the clerk of the brewhouse, and gave him an account of the beer they had delivered out, which he set down in a book kept for that purpose, to which the draymen signed their names; and that the drayman was dead whose name appeared signed to an entry stating the delivery of the beer in question. This was held to be good evidence of a delivery.

In another important case on this subject, at the trial of an action of ejectment, it was proved to be the usual course of practice in an attorney's office for the clerks to serve notices to quit on tenants, and to indorse on duplicates of such notices the fact and time of service; that, on one occasion, the attorney himself prepared a notice to serve on a tenant, took it out with him, together with two others, prepared at the same time, and returned to his office in the evening, having indorsed on the duplicate of each notice a memorandum of his having delivered it to the tenant; and two of the notices were proved to have been delivered by him on that occasion. The indorsements so made were held admissible, after the attorney's death, to prove the service of the third notice.[3]

[1] Doe d. Sweetland *v.* Webber, 1 A. & E. 733 (28 E. C. L. R.). As to declarations against interest, see also The Sussex Peerage, 11 Cl. & Fin. 85; Smith *v.* Blakey, L. R. 2 Q. B. 326; per Lord Denman, C. J., Davis *v.* Lloyd, 1 Car. & K. 276 (47 E. C. L. R.).

[2] Price *v.* Earl of Torrington, 1 Salk. 285; cited arg. Malcomson *v.* O'Dea, 10 H. L. Cas. 605; and in Smith *v.* Blakey, L. R. 2 Q. B. 329, 333.

[3] Doe d. Patteshall *v.* Turford, 3 B. & Ad. 890 (23 E. C. L. R.); cited, per Sir J. Romilly, M. R., Bright *v.* Legerton, 29 L. J. Chanc. 852, 854; Stapylton *v.* Clough, 2 E. & B. 933 (75 E. C. L. R.); Eastern Union R. C. *v.* Symonds, 5 Exch. 237; Doe d. Padwick *v.* Wittcomb, 4 H. L. Cas. 425; s. c.,

[*965] *It is necessary, however, that the particular entry be contemporaneous with the circumstances to which it relates; that it be made in the course of performing some duty, or discharging some office; and that it be respecting facts necessary to the performance of such duty; for, if the entry contain a statement of other circumstances, however naturally they may be thought to find a place in the narrative, it will not be legal proof of those circumstances.[1]

In like manner, the declarations of deceased persons, and evidence of reputation in matters of public prescription, pedigree, and character, are admissible; not because strangers have any power to conclude a party by what they may choose wantonly to assert upon the subject in question; but because the law considers such evidence to be sufficiently deserving of credit, as a means of communicating the real fact, to be offered to a jury. So, where declarations accompany an act, they must either be regarded as part of the *res gestæ*, or as the best and most proximate evidence of the nature and quality of the act; their connection with which either sanctions them as direct evidence, or constitutes them indirect evidence from which the real motive of the actor may be duly estimated.[2]

[*966] Thus, an action was brought by a man on a policy of *insurance on the life of his wife; and the question arose as to the admissibility of declarations made by the wife, when lying in bed, apparently ill, as to the bad state of her health, at the period of getting the regular surgical certificate, and down to that time. These declarations were made to the witness, who was produced at the trial to relate the wife's own account of the cause of her being found in bed by witness at an unseasonable hour, and with the appearance of being ill, and were held admissible, on the same ground that inquiries of patients, by medical men, with the answers to them, are evidence of the state of health of the patient

6 Exch. 601. See Doe d. Padwick *v.* Skinner, 3 Exch. 84; Reg. *v.* St. Mary, Warwick, 1 E. & B. 816, 820, 825 (72 E. C. L. R.); Reg. *v.* Inhabs. of Worth, 4 Q. B. 132 (45 E. C. L. R.). See also Poole *v.* Dicas, 1 Bing. N. C. 649 (27 E. C. L. R.).

[1] Chambers *v.* Bernasconi (in error), 1 C., M. & R. 347; per Blackburn, J., Smith *v.* Blakey, L. R. 2 Q. B. 332; per Parke, J., 3 B. & Ad. 897, 898 (23 E. C. L. R.); per Pollock, C. B., Milne *v.* Leister, 7 H. & N. 795.

[2] See Ford *v.* Elliott, 4 Exch. 78; per Pollock, C. B., Milne *v.* Leister, 7 H. & N. 796.

at the time; and it was further observed, that this was not only good evidence, but the best evidence which the nature of the case afforded.[1]

So, where a bankrupt has done an equivocal act, his declarations accompanying the act have been held admissible to explain his intentions; and, in order to render them so, it is not requisite that such declarations were made at the precise time of the act in question.[2]

So, in cases of treason and conspiracy, it is an established rule, that, where several persons are proved to have combined together for the same illegal purpose, any act done by one of the party in pursuance of the plan originally concerted, and with reference to the common object, is, in the contemplation of law, the act of the whole party;[3] though, where a question arises as to the admissibility of documentary evidence, for the purpose of *implicating a party, and showing his acquiescence in such illegal purpose and common object, it will always be necessary to consider, whether the rule *scribere est agere* applies,[4] or whether the evidence in question is merely the narrative of some third party of a particular occurrence, and therefore in its nature hearsay, and not original evidence.

[*967]

The substance of the preceding remarks, showing the more important limitations of the general rule, *Res inter alios acta alteri nocere non debet*, may be thus stated in the words of a learned judge:—One great principle in the law of evidence is, that all such facts as have not been admitted by the party against whom they are offered, or some one under whom he claims, ought to be proved under the sanction of an oath (or its statutory equivalent), either on the trial of the issue, or some other issue involving the same question, between the same parties, or those to whom they are privy. To this rule certain exceptions have been recognized, some from very early times, on the ground of necessity or convenience;

[1] Averson *v.* Lord Kinnaird, 6 East 188; 1 Phill. Evid., 10th ed., 149.

[2] Bateman *v.* Bailey, 5 T. R. 512. Per Tindal, C. J., Ridley *v.* Gyde, 9 Bing. 352 (23 E. C. L. R.); Rawson *v.* Haigh, 2 Bing. 99 (9 E. C. L. R.). See Smith *v.* Cramer, 1 Bing. N. C. 585 (27 E. C. L. R.).

[3] Per Bayley, J., Watson's Case, 32 Howell St. Tr. 7; Reg. *v.* Blake, 6 Q. B. 126 (51 E. C. L. R.).

[4] *Ante*, p. 312.

such as the proof of the quality and intention of acts by declarations accompanying them, of pedigrees and of public rights by the statement of deceased persons presumably well acquainted with the subject, as inhabitants of the district, in the one case, or relations, within certain limits, in the other; and another exception occurs, where proof of possession is allowed to be given by the entries of deceased stewards or receivers charging themselves, or proof of facts of a public nature by public documents.[1]

---

*NEMO TENETUR SEIPSUM ACCUSARE. [*968]

(Wing. Max. 486.)

No man can be compelled to criminate himself.[2]

The general policy of our law[3] is in accordance with the rule above stated. A justice of the peace, therefore, before receiving the statement of the accused, is required, under the stat. 11 & 12 Vict. c. 42, s. 18, to administer to him the caution therein specifically set forth. A witness also is, in general,[4] privileged from answering not merely where his answer will criminate him directly, but where it may have a tendency to criminate him.[5] "The proposition is clear," remarked Lord Eldon in Ex parte Symes,[6] "that no man can be compelled to answer what has any tendency to criminate him,"—which proposition is, it seems, to be thus qual-

[1] Per Parke, B., 7 A. & E. 384, 385 (34 E. C. L. R.). For additional information as to the maxim respecting *res inter alios acta*, the reader is referred to 1 Tayl. Evid., 5th ed., pp. 334, *et seq.*

[2] A man is *competent* to prove his own crime, though not *compellable:* per Alderson, B., Udal *v.* Walton, 14 M. & W. 256.

[3] As to the Scotch law on the above point, see Longworth *v.* Yelverton, L. R. 1 Sc. App. Cas. 218.

[4] See cases cited *infra.*

[5] Fisher *v.* Ronalds, 12 C. B. 762 (74 E. C. L. R.); per Pollock, C. B., Adams *v.* Lloyd, 3 H. & N. 362; R. *v.* Garbett, 1 Den. C. C. 236. The cases supporting this proposition are collected in Rosc. Law of Evidence in Crim. Cas., 4th ed., pp. 162, *et seq.* See Ex parte Fernandez, 10 C. B. N. S. 3 (100 E. C. L. R.); Re Fernandez, 6 H. & N. 717; Bradlaugh *v.* Evans, 11 C. B. N. S. 377 (103 E. C. L. R.).

[6] 11 Ves. 525.

ified, that the danger to be apprehended by the witness must be "real and appreciable with reference to the ordinary operation of law in the ordinary course of things, not a danger of an imaginary and unsubstantial character having reference to some extraordinary and barely possible contingency, so improbable that no reasonable man would suffer it to influence his conduct," for such a possibility should not be suffered to obstruct the administration of justice.[1]

[*969] *And, although a party to a cause, who has been subpœnaed as a witness, cannot object to be sworn on the ground that any relevant questions would tend to criminate him,[2] he may, when such objectionable questions are put, claim his privilege.[3] Further, an individual charged with the commission of a criminal act cannot, conformably to the course of justice in our tribunals, be interrogated by the court, with a view to eliciting the truth, nor is he a competent witness in the case.[4]

Where, however, the reason for the privilege of the witness or

[1] Reg. *v.* Boyes, 1 B. & S. 311, 330 (101 E. C. L. R.). See Re Mexican and South American Co., 28 L. J. Chanc. 631.

[2] Boyle *v.* Wiseman, 10 Exch. 647.

[3] The objection that interrogatories delivered under 17 & 18 Vict. c. 125, s. 51, tend to criminate the party sought to be interrogated must come from himself when sworn: Osborn *v.* London Dock Co., 10 Exch. 698, followed in Chester *v.* Wortley, 17 C. B. 410, 426 (84 E. C. L. R.); and in Bartlett *v.* Lewis, 12 C. B. N. S. 249.

As to interrogatories tending to criminate, see Edmunds *v.* Greenwood, L. R. 4 C. P. 70; Villeboisnet *v.* Tobin, Id. 184.

As to compelling a person to produce documents, the production of which might subject him to penalties, see Pritchett *v.* Smart, 7 C. B. 625 (62 E. C. L. R.), citing Bullock *v.* Richardson, 11 Ves. 373.

Whether or not a witness is compellable to answer questions having a tendency to *disgrace* him, is ably discussed by Mr. Best in his Principles of the Law of Evidence, 2d ed., pp. 163, *et seq.*, to which the reader is referred. See 17 & 18 Vict. c. 125, s. 25.

In a criminal suit against a clergyman under the stat. 3 & 4 Vict. c. 86, the defendant has been held to be competent to give evidence: Bishop of Norwich *v.* Pearse, L. R. 2 A. & E. 281.

[4] See A.-G. *v.* Radloff, 10 Exch. 84; Cattell *v.* Ireson, E., B. & E. 91 (96 E. C. L. R.), in connection with the 14 & 15 Vict. c. 99, s. 3. See also Parker *v.* Green, 2 B. & S. 299.

As to the evidence of a witness implicated in any proceeding "instituted in consequence of adultery," see Hebblethwaite *v.* Hebblethwaite, L. R. 2 P. & D. 29; 32 & 33 Vict. c. 68, s. 3, cited *ante*, p. 537.

party interrogated ceases, the privilege will cease also;[1] as if the prosecution to which the witness might be exposed or his liability to a penalty or forfeiture *is barred by lapse of time, or if the offence has been pardoned or the penalty or forfeiture waived.[2] [*970]

The rule *Nemo tenetur seipsum accusare*, which has been designated[3] "a maxim of our law as settled, as important and as wise as almost any other in it," is, however, sometimes trenched upon, and the privilege which it confers is in special cases abrogated.[4] And the legislature will sometimes on grounds of policy extend indemnity—partial or entire—to a witness whose privilege is taken away[5] or not insisted on; thus by the 24 & 25 Vict. c. 96 ("An Act to consolidate and amend the statute law of England and Ireland relating to larceny and other similar offences") it is enacted (s. 85), that nothing in any of the preceding ten sections of that Act contained, which relate to frauds by agents, bankers and factors, "shall enable or entitle any person to refuse to make a full and complete discovery by answer to any bill in equity, or to answer any question or interrogatory in any civil proceeding in any court or upon the hearing of any matter in bankruptcy or insolvency; and no person shall be liable to be convicted of any of the misdemeanors in any of the said sections mentioned by any evidence whatever in respect of any act done by him, if he shall at any time previously to his being charged with such offence have *first disclosed such act on oath in consequence of any compulsory process of any court of law or equity in any action, suit or proceeding which shall have been *bonâ fide* instituted by any party aggrieved, or if [*971]

[1] Wigr. on Discovery, 2d ed., p. 83, where the equity cases upon the point *supra* are collected.

[2] See Ex parte Fernandez, and Reg. *v.* Boyes, *ante*, 967, n. 5, and 968, n. 1.

[3] Per Coleridge, J., Dearsl. & B. 61.

[4] It was held by a majority of the Court of Criminal Appeal, that the examination of a bankrupt taken under the repealed statute 12 & 13 Vict. c. 106 (s. 117) may, although tending to criminate, afterwards be used as evidence against him on a criminal proceeding: Reg. *v.* Scott, Dearsl. & B. 47; Reg. *v.* Cross, Id. 68; Reg. *v.* Skeen, Bell C. C. 97; Reg. *v.* Robinson, L. R. 1 C. C. 80, 85, 87, 90.

[5] For instance, under the 15 & 16 Vict. c. 57 (an Act to provide for more effectual inquiry into the existence of corrupt practices at elections for members to serve in Parliament), ss. 9, 10, 11.

he shall have first disclosed the same in any compulsory examination or deposition before any court upon the hearing of any matter in bankruptcy or insolvency."[1] Also by sec. 86 it is further enacted that nothing in any of the eleven preceding sections of the Act "nor any proceeding, conviction, or judgment to be had or taken thereon against any person under any of the said sections, shall prevent, lessen, or impeach any remedy at law, or in equity, which any party aggrieved by any offence against any of the said sections might have had if this Act had not been passed; but no conviction of any such offender shall be received in evidence in any action at law or suit in equity against him, and nothing in the said sections contained shall affect or prejudice any agreement entered into or security given by any trustee having for its object the restoration or repayment of any trust property misappropriated."

The disclosure of any such illegal act as above referred to, in order to be available as a protection, must have been made *bonâ fide*, and must not have been a mere voluntary statement, made for the express purpose of screening the person making it from the penal consequences of his act.[2]

Lastly, in Reg. *v.* Gillyard,[3] the facts were as under:—a maltster, suspected of having violated the excise laws, [*972] *obtained a conviction against his servant for the purpose, as was suspected and charged, of relieving himself from penalties in respect of the same transaction by force of the stat. 7 & 8 Geo. 4, c. 52, s. 46. In support of a rule *nisi* to quash the conviction thus had the affidavits stated circumstances, showing that the conviction in question had been collusively obtained, and *no affidavit was made in opposition to the rule.* On behalf of the maltster it was urged that he ought not (regard being had to the maxim now under consideration) to have been called upon to defend himself by affidavit on a charge which was virtually of a criminal nature.[4] But the conviction nevertheless was quashed as being "a fraud and mockery, the result of conspiracy and subornation of perjury,"

[1] See, also, 24 & 25 Vict. c. 95, s. 29, which has reference to the stealing or fraudulent destruction of testamentary instruments.

[2] See Reg. *v.* Strahan, 7 Cox. C. C. 85; which was decided under the repealed statute, 7 & 8 Geo. 4, c. 29, s. 52.

[3] 12 Q. B. 527 (64 E. C. L. R.).

[4] Citing Stephens *v.* Hill, 10 M. & W. 28.

Coleridge, J., remarking that, "where the court observes such dishonest practices it will interfere, although judgment has been given," and that "no honest man ought to think it beneath him or a hardship upon him to answer upon affidavit a charge of dishonesty made upon affidavit against him. If a man, when such a serious accusation is preferred against him, will not deny it, he must not complain if the case is taken *pro confesso*."

HAVING thus briefly touched upon some few rules relating chiefly to the admissibility of evidence, and having considerably exceeded the limits originally prescribed to myself, I now feel compelled reluctantly to take leave of the reader, trusting that, however slight or disproportionate this attempt to illustrate our legal maxims may appear, when compared with the extent and importance *of the subject, I have yet, in the language of Lord Bacon, applied myself, not to that which might seem most for the ostentation of mine own wit or knowledge, but to that which might yield most use and profit to the student; and have afforded some materials for acquiring an insight into those conclusions of reason—those *legum leges*—essential to the true understanding and proper application of the law—whereof, though some may strongly savor of human refinement and ingenuity, the greater portion claim from us instinctively, as it were, recognition—and why? they have been "written with the finger of Almighty God upon the heart of man."[1] [*973]

[1] See Calvin's Case, 7 Rep. 126.

INDEX.

The pages referred to are those between brackets [ ].

STATUTES CITED—*continued.*

STATUTES CITED—*continued.*

CPSIA information can be obtained at www.ICGtesting.com
Printed in the USA
LVOW11s2034201114

414822LV00001B/205/P